TO JANET HENRY

Friends, like antiques, if well chosen become more valued and loved through the years. When they are gone the memory remains to remind us of the joys of another day. Janet Henry was a friend who gave advice, a listening ear, humor, and a lot of great times.

Dear Reader,

Twenty years of prices! Looking back over the changes in the antiques market makes it clear that both collecting and collectors have changed. We have read millions of prices and used thousands of pictures in *Kovels' Antiques & Collectibles Price List*. Prices listed here include a random selection of pieces offered for sale *this* year. We report on the everyday antiques like pressed glass and oak furniture, the exotic Tiffany and Lalique, and the uncommon skorps and roemers. The smallest item is probably a bookmark, the largest a 12-foot soda fountain.

The book is changed slightly each year. Categories are arranged, added, or omitted to make it easier for you to find your antiques. The book remains about 800 pages long because it is written to go with you to the sales. We try to have a balanced format, not too much glass, pottery, or collectibles, not too many items that sell for over $5,000. The prices are *from* the North American market *for* the North American market. No European sales are reported.

Old *Kovels'* price books should be saved for reference, tax, and appraisal information. The index, written by a special computer program, is so complete it amazes us. Use it often. An internal alphabetical index is also included. For example, there is a category for "celluloid." Most items will be found there, but if there is a toy made of celluloid, it will be listed under "toy" and also indexed under "celluloid."

All pictures and prices are new every year, except pictures that are pattern examples shown in Depression Glass and Pressed Glass. All objects on the cover are priced. They are not museum pieces but are items recently offered for sale.

The hints are set in easy-to-notice special type. Leaf through the book and learn how to wash porcelains, store textiles, guard against theft, and much more.

Every year a new type of collectible makes news. Sporting equipment for non-team sports, from decoys to fishing reels and marbles, set the records in 1986. A preening pintail duck carved by A. E. Crowell in 1915 sold for $319,000 in July; a model 925 Kosmic trout fly reel, about 1890, sold the same month for $2,970. Other records included a wooden frog fishing lure by Lou Rhead at $645, a minnow lure for $605, a rare end-of-day marble for $750, and a painting of a golfer in knickers for $32,000.

Those who collect out of the mainstream also were willing to pay high prices. An animation cel from "Snow White" brought $30,800, an Elizabethan man's cap topped out at $11,000, and a Campbell's Soup can sign, made of tin and shaped like a flag, attracted $11,000 from a hungry bidder. The smallest collectible to set a record was a mechanical bank trade card that sold for $1,400; while a hefty Mr. Peanut floor scale weighed in at $6,000. A mahogany cookie board made about 1800 sold for $11,000, a long-face 29-inch Jumeau doll found a loving owner at $45,000, the Schoenhut Teddy Roosevelt set went to a new home for $11,000, while the bandwagon from a Humpty-Dumpty Schoenhut circus moved at $13,000, $1,000 more than the price for a 33-piece set of Britain's Boer War Army Service soldiers.

American furniture continued to set records. The highest auction price ever paid for any piece of furniture was $2,750,000 for the 1770 Cadwalader Chippendale carved mahogany wing armchair. All styles seem popular. A carved oak wainscot armchair, c.1675, auctioned for $528,000; a Victorian Herter table brought $40,700; a Frank Lloyd Wright chair sold at $198,000; a Louisiana armoire for $43,450; a Shaker trestle table for $42,000; and a 1907 Stickley Mission knock-down even arm settle for $36,300.

American pottery also set records. A Pewabic green matte vase brought $4,950; a Newcomb pottery vase with iris blossoms $4,700; an S.E.G. decorated pitcher with Viking ships $4,900; a Rookwood plaque showing a windmill $5,720; a Rookwood silver overlay vase by Matt Daly $8,800; a Teco green matte jar $4,675; and an Overbeck vase $4,675. An 1860 stoneware butter churn decorated with a cobalt rooster set a record at $31,900.

Folk art is still fashionable. "Dapper Dan," a life-size figure made about 1880, auctioned at $258,500, a Looff carousel greyhound was $59,400; a full-bodied train weather vane brought $203,000; a swordsman whirligig sold for $42,900; and a painted checkerboard gameboard for $4,675. Other decorative art records included a blown glass lily pad pitcher for $19,000; a pressed glass blue lacy Sandwich compote for $17,000; a Baltimore album quilt for $176,000; a sampler dated 1788 for $192,500; a silver pear-shape teapot by Peter van Dyck for $93,500; a toleware tray for $5,500; and an 1824 hearth rug for $25,300.

Perhaps the wildest record-setting collectible of the year was the

TWENTIETH EDITION

KOVELS'
ANTIQUES &
COLLECTIBLES
PRICE LIST

For the 1988 Market

Ralph and Terry Kovel

Illustrated

Crown Publishers, Inc.
New York

Books by Ralph and Terry Kovel

Dictionary of Marks—Pottery and Porcelain
Kovels' New Dictionary of Marks
A Directory of American Silver, Pewter and Silver Plate
American Country Furniture 1780—1875
Kovels' Antiques & Collectibles Price List
Kovels' Bottle Price List
The Kovel's Collector's Guide to American Art Pottery
Kovels' Organizer for Collectors
The Kovels' Price Guide for Collector Plates, Figurines,
    Paperweights, and Other Limited Editions
The Kovels' Illustrated Price Guide to Royal Doulton
The Kovels' Illustrated Price Guide to Depression Glass and
    American Dinnerware
Kovels' Know Your Antiques
Kovels' Know Your Collectibles
The Kovels' Book of Antique Labels
The Kovels' Collectors' Source Book
Kovels' Advertising Collectibles Price List
Kovels' Guide to Selling Your Antiques & Collectibles

Copyright © 1987 by Ralph Kovel and Terry Kovel

Published by Crown Publishers,Inc., 225 Park Avenue South, New York,
New York 10003, and represented in Canada by
the Canadian MANDA Group

CROWN is a trademark of Crown Publishers, Inc.

Manufactured in the United States of America

Library of Congress Catalog Card Number: 83-643618

ISBN 0-517-56579-X

10   9   8   7   6   5   4   3   2   1

First Edition

original art for the cover of the first *Mad Magazine*, sold at auction for $15,500.

Record prices are often reported in newspapers and on TV because they are so surprising to the non-collector. Those who follow the antiques market know dozens of records are set each year as collectors find new interests, and the changing values of money, silver, and stocks influence prices.

The prices in this book are reports of the general antiques market, not the record-setting examples. Each year every price in the book is new. We do *not* estimate or "update" prices. The most expensive item listed is $14,000; least expensive is $.50. Prices are the actual asking price, although the buyer may have negotiated to a lower figure. No price is an estimate. *We do not ask dealers and writers to estimate prices.* Experience has shown that a collector of one type of antique is prejudiced in favor of that item; and prices are usually high or low, but rarely a true report. If a price range is given, it is because at least two identical items were offered for sale at different places. The computer records the prices and prints the high and low figures. Price ranges are found only in categories like "pressed glass," where identical items can be identified. Some prices in *Kovels' Antiques & Collectibles Price List* may seem high and some may seem low because of regional variations. But each price is one you could have paid for the object.

If you are selling your collection, do *not* expect to get retail value unless you are a dealer. Wholesale prices for antiques are from 20 to 50 percent less than retail. Remember, the antiques dealer must make a profit or go out of business.

HOW TO USE THIS BOOK

There are a few rules for using this book. Each listing is arranged in the following manner: CATEGORY (such as pressed glass or furniture), OBJECT (such as vase), DESCRIPTION (as much information as possible about size, age, color, and pattern). Some types of glass are exceptions to this rule. These are listed CATEGORY, PATTERN, OBJECT, DESCRIPTION. All items are presumed to be in good condition, undamaged, unless otherwise noted.

Several special categories were formed to make a more sensible listing possible. "Kitchen" and "tool" include special equipment. The casual collector might not know the proper name for an "adze" or "trephine," so we have created special categories. The index can help you locate items.

Several idiosyncrasies of style appear because the book is printed by computer. Everything is listed according to the computer alphabetizing system. This means words such as "mt." are alphabetized as "M-T," not as "M-O-U-N-T." All numerals are before all letters, thus 2 comes before Z. A quick glance will make this clear, as it is consistent throughout the book.

We made several editorial decisions. A bowl is a "bowl" and not a dish unless it is a special dish, such as a pickle dish. A butter dish is a "butter." A salt dish is called a "salt" to differentiate it from a saltshaker. It is always "sugar and creamer," never "creamer and sugar." Where one dimension is given, it is the height, or if the object is round, the dimension is the diameter. Height of a picture is listed before width. Glass is clear unless a color is indicated.

Every entry is listed alphabetically. The problem of language remains. Some antiques terms, like "Sheffield" or "snow baby," have two meanings. Be sure to read the paragraph headings to know the meaning used. All category headings are based on the language of the average person at an average show, and we use terms like "mud figures" even if not technically correct.

This book does not include price listings of fine art paintings, books, comic books, stamps, coins, and other special categories.

All pictures in *Kovels' Antiques & Collectibles Price List* are listed with the prices asked by the seller. "Illus" (illustrated on the page) and "cover" (shown on the cover) are part of the description if a picture is shown.

There have been misinformed comments about how this book is written. We *do* use the computer. It alphabetizes, ranges prices, sets type, and does other time-consuming jobs. Because of the computer, the book can be produced quickly. The last entries are added in June; the book is available in October. This is six months faster than would be possible any other way. But it is human help that finds prices and checks accuracy. We read everything at least twice, sometimes more. We edit from 100,000 entries to the 45,000 entries found here. We correct spelling, remove incorrect data, write category headings, and decide on new categories. We sometimes make errors.

Prices are reports of sales from all parts of the United States or Canada (translated to U.S. dollars) between June 1986 and June 1987. A few prices are from auctions, but most are from shops and shows. Every price is checked for accuracy, but we are not responsible for errors.

It is unprofessional for an appraiser to set a value for an unseen item. Because of this we cannot answer your letters asking for specific price information. But please write if you have any requests for categories to be included in future editions.

When you see us at the shows, stop and say hello. Don't be surprised if we ask for your suggestions for the next edition of *Kovels' Antiques & Collectibles Price List.* Or you can write us at P.O. Box 22200, Beachwood, Ohio 44122.

Ralph & Terry Kovel
Senior Members, American Society of Appraisers
June 1987

ACKNOWLEDGMENTS

Some of the antiques photographed for the cover belong to Gwynby Antiques of Cleveland, Ohio. They sell fine English and American antiques at shows in all parts of the country. We thank Eleanor Wilkins and Dr. James B. Sauers for being so helpful. The cover picture is by Ed Nano, our favorite antiques photographer. Special thanks should also go to others who helped us with pictures and deeds. Anne Young (Christie's), Gene Harris, Inc., Marissa Longo (Phillips), David Rago, Ginger Sawyer (Robert Skinner, Inc.), Magda Gregorian (Sotheby's), Rachel Davis (Wolf's Gallery), and Woody Auction Company. Lee Markley has once again made suggestions for the Carnival glass problems.

The color pictures in this special report were furnished by Biltmore House and Garden, Margaret Woodbury Strong Museum, and Smithsonian Institution. The carousel horse is from the Eleanor and Mabel Van Alstyne collection of American Folk Art, Smithsonian Institution.

To the others in the antiques trade who knowingly or unknowingly contributed prices or pictures to this book, we say "Thank You!" We cannot do it without you. Some of you are: Mitchell Abraham, Adair & Hartley, Adams House, William Adorjan, Neal Alford, American Antiques, American Eagle Antiques, Anderson Mulkins Antiques, Anglo American Antiques, Annis Antique Mall, Antique & Colonial Lighting, Antique Gallery, Antique Lady, Antique Lantern, Antique Week, Antiques & Interiors, Antiques & Stuff, Antiques & Things, Antiques by Mah Jong, Antiques by Wallace, Antiques from Frank & Caryl, Antiques Oriental Arts, Antiques Par Ronay, Antiques Ltd., Anton Galleries, Betty Apt, W. Graham Arader III, Arman Absentee Auctions, Art Deco Collectibles, Art Investments, Art Trading Ltd., Asherhouse Antiques, Marion Ashmore, Attenson Antiques, Audrey's Odditiques, B-J Collectibles, Barbara Babcock, Babcock Gifts, Al & Judy Bagon, Barbara Bako, Jack & Bonita Baldwin, R.J. Barron, Twyla Barron, Barzizza Estate Sales, Monty Baus, Shirley Beaver, Beehive, Ed & Kay Berg, Bill Bertoia, Maxine Berv, Bettiques, Betty's Doll Haven, Beverly's Antiques, Bickford Antiques, John Bilane, Birchland Antiques, Michael Birdsall, Bischoff Galleries, Eloise Bishop, Richard Blair, Blake's Antiques, David Blevens, Blue Onion Antiques, Bonnie's Antiques, Dee Boston, Richard A. Bourne Co. Inc., Gene & Marie Boyd, Nancy Brant, Brass Connection, Allan Brink, Britannia, Brookwood Antiques, Paul Brown, Brown & Cotten, Brown-Trump Antiques, Ilona Brownell, Robert Brunswick, Bryant Antiques, Buchanan Shoppe, Buckley's Antiques, Jean Burns, Butterfield & Butterfield, Charles Calderone, Calkins Antiques, Callie's Antiques, Glen Campbell, Cascade Valley Farms, Caskey & Lees, Lavonia Chait, Judith Charbonneau, Leon Chase, Phil Chasen, Chicago Old Telephone Co., Peter Chillingworth, Churchills Antiques, Trudy and Howard Clapper, Classic Antiques, Cobweb Corner Antiques, Ed Coggins, Mrs. Marion Cohen, Marvin Cohen Auctions, Collector's Gallery, Colony Shop, Common Market, Conover Antiques, Consignments, Joan Coulter, Country Cricket, Country House & Fringe Benefits, Cox Street Antiques, Crandalls Antiques, Crawford & Delo, Cricket House, Robert Crump, Gary & Marianne Cunard, Curiosities, Todd Czerwinski, Dianna Dalton, Daze, Decadence Manor, Joan Deibel, Don & Jill DeSapri, Jeff Dickeson, Marian Dieter, Craig Dinner, Jeannine Dobbs, L.R. Les Docks, Dorian House, Betty Dorow, William Doyle Galleries Inc., Richard & Eileen Dubrow, Gail Dunn, Early's Antiques & Auction Co., East End Galleries, Eaton's, Economy Furniture & Antique Center, Robert C. Eldred Co. Inc., Elegant Pleasures, Joan & Gage Ellis, Elm Antiques, Larry Engle, English Country Antiques, Jack Ericson, European Antique Importers, Jane Evans, Joseph O. Ewing,

Arlene P. Fagan, Faith Enterprises Inc., Fantasy Illustrated, Ferrini Galleries, Robert J. Flagor, Jane Fletcher Antiques, Flo-Blue Shop, Flying Cranes Antiques, Forescore & More, Thomas Forshee Antiques, J.S. Fortas, Frances Jenkins, David Franklin Ltd., Fred's Antiques, Thomas French, Rae Friedman, From the Cutter's Wheel, Janet Frowine, Pam Roy Fruge, Kyle & Doris Fuller, Gaab's Antiquarian Prints, Don & Barbara Garber, Garth's Auctions Inc., Gatsby Ltd., Gerda's Antiques, J. Getz, Joan Giles, Gilham Antiques, Shirley Glotzbach, Gold Nugget Antiques, Morton Goldberg Auction Galleries, Marc Goodman, Gordon's Antiques, Gourmet Antiques, June Greenwald, Grosse Pointe Antiques, Grunewald Antiques, Guernsey's, Sharlee Guster, Gypsy's, Marilyn Haley, Barbara Hall, Hammer Antiques, Harbach & Culver, Harwood Arms, Mabel Hawk, Hawksmoor House Antiques, Hebe's Antiques, Stan & Peggy Hecker, Tom Heisey, Heller's Antiques, Heritage Collectors' Society, Heritage House Antiques, Charles Hilliard, Hillside House Antiques, Leslie Hindman Auctioneers, Charles Hodges, Lee Hoekje, Sharon Hoffman, Homewood's Haviland, Ellie Hoover, Billie Hoskins, Spencer House, House of Hein, House of Yesteryear, Idlewild House, Inglett-Watson-Forster, Helen & Frank Ireland, Isom-Wichers Antiques, Ivory Tower Antiques, J & M Antiques, Jac-Karl Antiques, Nicole Jans, Loretta Januska, Jay Cue Antiques, D. Johnson Antiques, Barbara Johnston, Robert Jordan, Joy's Antique Jewelry, June's Antiques, Richard Karam, Keeping Room, Mark Keily, Silber Keller, Michael Kellogg, Kendra's Antiques, Ruth Keneda Antiques, Kerns-Wood Ltd., Lawrence King, Olin King, Kinnett's Antiques, Kirschen Fine Art, Charles Kleinman, Gus Knapp, Pat Knepp, Bob Koenig, Ann & Jim Kopp, David Kozloff, Dave Kreuzenstein, Ted Kromer, The Krugs, Alice Kwartler, Patricia Lamb, Richard Lampert, Jane Langol, Bob Laroski, Nancy Lawson, Le Cheval Blanc, Dorothy Lerner, Les Temps Passes, Denise Letourneau, Mimi & Steve Levine, Sol Lewanda, Carol Lewis, Linen Press, Little's Antiques, Lloyd's of Mentor Antiques, Marilyn Loch, Lost Nations, Lost Time Antiques, Lotus Gallery, Carl Loucks, Lu Ree Antiques, Debbie Lund, Lyon's Den, Jack MacRichie, Mad Hatter Antiques, Madison Avenue Antiques, Sheilagh Malo, Manion's, Marian Antiques, Mariwynne Shop, Jan Marks, Marshy Hope Nautical, Tim & Barb Martien, Martines' Antiques, Matthews & Shank, Sally McAdoo, McClellan's Antiques, Tony McCormack, McCullough's Antiques, Ann McDonald, Charlotte McGuire, McIlwain Antiques, James McIntire, McKinley & Hill Antiques, Mark Meaders, H.L. Melick, Memory Lane Antiques, Ruth Might, Mike's Antique Mall, Alden Miller, Joan Miller, Richard Miller, Milwaukee Auction Gallery, Brian Mitchell, Sandra Mitchell, Nellie Momchilov, Ray & Kathy Mongenas, Bill Monthie, Mary Ellen Morrissey, Stephen H. Morse, Moser's Collectables, Mostly Majolica, Ed Mowka, Cookie Mullen, Walt Nagorski, Neale & Schlotfeldt, Elva Needles, New-Strom Antiques, Ruth Newberry, Ney-Londes, Robert Nichols, Odell's Antiques, Old Town Hill Antiques, Richard W. Oliver, James Olney, Jackie Olson, Oneida Gallery, Richard Opfer Auctioneering Inc., Marion Paltz, Gene Parker, Pascoe & Co., Barbara Paterson, C.O. Patterson, Walter Paul, Peacock Roost, Pennypacker Auction Center, Perdue & Podner, Phyllis Petruska, Pine Cone Antiques, Pine Pony Antiques, Terry & Paulette Piper, Judy Posner, Pottery Place, Kay Previte, Proctor Galleries, Inc., Gary & Judy Lee Promey, Sam & Judy Feller Publick House Antiques, Jon Quisenberry, R & L Collectibles, The Ragman, Ralph's Antiques & Collectibles, Lloyd Ralston, Randall Antiques, RC Antiques, Marian Redmond, Regal Eagle, Regency II, Renaissance Antiques, Renee's Antique Shoppe, Jack & Berta Reynolds, Reynolds' Antiques, Rings & Things, Riverside Antiques, Robertsons Antiques, Robin Bellamy Antiques, Dorothy Robinson, Gloria Robinson, Vincent Rocco, Carol Roether, John Rogers, Rombert's Antiques, Walter & Rosalie Roscha, Rose-N-Sons, Rosemarie Antiques, Nancy Roth, J.L. Roush, Ryan's Antiques, Sadagurskys, Salt Box Antiques, Salt Lady Antiques, Saltbox House Antiques, Michael Sanderson, Miles Sandler, Jan Schmidt, Carol Schulman, Anthony Scornavacco, Jean Scott, Sebree Galleries, Second Hand Rose, Seekers Antiques, L.H. Selman, Shafer's Antiques, Shaver-Ramsey Oriental Galleries, Shop of Tut-Uncommon, Sign of the Dove, Silver Plus, J. Simon, Betty Parker Simpson, Sister's Antiques, Bill Smith, Elizabeth Lisy Smith, Robert Smith Jr., Al & Barb Snitcher, Cloanne Snyder, Something Different, Virginia South, Bill & Polly Spaulding, William Spencer, Springer Antiques, Sprott Antiques, Daniel Stein, Charles Stephens, Sterling Age, Philip Stewart, Ellen Stirn, Eve Stone & Son, Stone Balloon Antiques, Dick Stroll, Stutzman Antiques, Suitsus II, Gene Switzer, Bernese Sylak, Dick Taylor, Jean Taylor, Judy Taylor, Teachers' Room Antiques, Team Antiques, Teasel Top Antiques, Mayann Theohar, Theriault's, Helen & Dick Thompson, Three Behrs, Time Again Antiques, Time for Antiques, Timepiece Antiques & Estate Jewelry, Toby House, Robert Todd, Gladys Tomes, Town & Country Antiques, Traub of London, Don Treadway, Treasures of Imperial Russia, Tulver Antiques, Two Morrows, Ethel Vallos, Ruth Van Kuren, Victor's Antiques, Victorian Belle, Victorian Galleries, Norm & Cathy Vigue, Vintage Connection, Wacky Wicker, H. Alan Wainwright, Carol Walker, Don & Ruth Walker, Vi Walker, Alex Walker, Wanna Buy A Duck, Barbara Warner, Richard & Susan Webb, Wedgwood Antiques, Annette Weintraub, White Dolphin, Whitman-Crafford Antiques, Sally Wiesenberger, Betty Williams, John & Ellen Williams, Don Williams Antiques, Betty Willis Antiques, Willow House Antiques, Windsor Antiques, Richard W. Withington Inc., Bill & Jane Woodring, Lynn & Michael Worden, Years Ago Antiques, Yesterday's Toys, Larry & Gitana Young, Young Collectors, Al Zaika, Charles & Audrey Zeder.

MORE ANTIQUE PRICE NEWS

Each year *Kovels' Antiques & Collectibles Price List* is completely rewritten. Every entry is new because of the changing antiques market. Many collectors need more current information about prices, trends, and sales. We have been writing a newsletter *Kovels' on Antiques and Collectibles* for the collector and investor for thirteen years. Information is included about what to buy, sell, how to refinish, reviews of price books, marks, fakes, and more. It is a 12-page, picture-filled newsletter about antiques that interest the collector and dealer. For more information about *Kovels' on Antiques and Collectibles*, send a stamped, self-addressed envelope to Kovels, P.O. Box 22200-K, Beachwood, Ohio 44122.

In the fall of 1987 we will be appearing on Public Broadcasting Television in a thirteen-week series about collecting. The show includes news, prices, and information. Watch "Kovels on Collecting" and see the best in antiques.

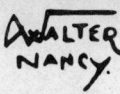

Almaric Walter made pate–de–verre glass under contract at the Daum glassworks from 1908 to 1914. He started his own firm in Nancy, France, in 1919. Pieces made before 1914 are signed "Daum, Nancy" with a cross. After 1919 the signature is "A. Walter Nancy."

A.WALTER, Ashtray, Triangular, Blue, Yellow Butterfly, Pate–De–Verre 875.00
Bookends, Satyr, Pate–De–Verre, Descomps, C.1930, 6 1/2 In. 6500.00
Box, Yellow Sides, Rim of Roses, Pate–De–Verre, C.1918, 3 In. 150.00
Figurine, Kneeling Nude Woman, Green and Rose, C.1920, 8 1/2 In. 3300.00
Pendant, Insect, Silk Cord, Pate–De–Verre, 1 1/2 In. 750.00
Vase, Scarab, Trumpet Shape, Pate–De–Verre, C.1920, 6 1/2 In. 3575.00

ABC plates, or children's alphabet plates, were most popular from 1780 to 1860, but are still being made. The letters on the plate were meant as teaching aids for children learning to read. The plates were made of pottery, porcelain, metal, or glass.

ABC, Bowl, Little Jack Horner, Nursery Rhyme Characters, 1920s. 40.00
Cup, Kewpie 45.00
Dish, Child's, Feeding, Henny Penny Verse 38.00
Dish, Mary Had A Little Lamb, Deep 38.00
Plate, Aesop's Fables, Dog In The Manger 85.00
Plate, Alphabet Maxim, Farmer, Workers On Hay Wagon, Staffordshire 85.00
Plate, Alphabet Sides, Dog & Dog House, 7 In. 45.00
Plate, Alphabet, Bead Design Center, Glass, 5 In. 30.00
Plate, Aluminum, Dated 1915 .... 15.00
Plate, Applied Alphabet, Sterling Silver, Gorham 160.00
Plate, Barnyard Fowl, Gold Trim, Germany, 7 In. 27.00
Plate, Beatrix Potter Type Rabbits, Along Stream, China, S.M.Dupont 39.00
Plate, Boy & Girl With Hoop, Tin, 3 In. ....85.00 To 125.00
Plate, Bulldog, Glass 45.00
Plate, Cat In Shoe, Milk Glass 55.00
Plate, Centennial Exhibition, 1776–1876, Eagle, Pressed Glass, 7 In. 47.50
Plate, Chickens In Center, Clear Glass, 6 In. 45.00
Plate, Children, Umbrella 48.00
Plate, Chinonca Watching Departure of Cavalcade, Gray Green 50.00
Plate, Clock Face, Amethyst Glass, Scalloped Border 65.00
Plate, Clock, Numbers, Months, Green 28.00
Plate, Crusoe Finding The Footprints, 8 In. 40.00
Plate, Crusoe Rescues Friday, Staffordshire, Signed .... 75.00 To 85.00
Plate, Dish, Child's, Feeding, Baby Shape In Bunting, Germany 165.00
Plate, Dog In Grass, Stippled Center, Alphabet On Rim, 6 In. 65.00
Plate, Donkey, Green Transfer, 6 In. 65.00
Plate, Ducks 30.00
Plate, Elephant, Glass 48.00
Plate, Fishing Elephant, Pink, Staffordshire ....38.00 To 50.00
Plate, Frosted Santa Claus, 6 1/16 In. 50.00
Plate, Girls Gardening, Blue & White, Staffordshire 40.00
Plate, Hide & Seek, Alphabet Border, C.1845, 5 1/2 In. 75.00
Plate, Kitten, Ohio Art 15.00
Plate, Mary Had Little Lamb, Dancing Bears Edge, Clear, 6 In. 95.00
Plate, Merchant Selling Clothes, Sign To Let, Staffordshire, 4 1/2 In. 125.00
Plate, Milk Glass 50.00
Plate, Panda, Glass 45.00
Plate, Piper Followed By Pigs, Black Transfer 35.00
Plate, Rabbit In Meadow, Glass, 6 In. 45.00
Plate, Roosevelt Bears, Dutch Children Border 50.00
Plate, Rooster, Numbers 50.00
Plate, Seal Hunt, Staffordshire 70.00
Plate, Stork, Carnival Glass, Marigold ....50.00 To 65.00
Plate, Teaching Their Dog To Be Polite, Staffordshire, 5 1/2 In. 40.00
Plate, Tom Thumb, Thompson, 6 1/2 In. 33.00
Plate, Umbrella Kids 35.00
Plate, Village Blacksmith, Alphabet Border, C.1845, 6 In. 75.00

Adams, Vase, Jasperware, Venus Bound, Blue,
White, C.1785, 3 Piece

Protect your home and antiques from theft. Use a timer on your lights at all times, even when you are at home. This will set a pattern of certain lights going on and off each day. When you are away, the house will appear to have normal activity. If possible, when you are away, park a car near the front of the house. The car will block your driveway so a burglar cannot load up through your garage. Have someone keep your trash cans filled. This will help to make the house look occupied. Keep the grass mowed. Stop your mail and paper deliveries.

Plate, Washington & Stars, Tin	85.00
Plate, Who Killed Cock Robin, Tin	35.00 To 60.00

Abingdon Pottery was established in 1934 by Raymond E. Bidwell as the Abingdon Sanitary Manufacturing Company. The company made art pottery and other wares. Sixteen varieties of cookie jars are known. The factory ceased production of art pottery in 1950.

ABINGDON, Bookends, Dolphin	36.00
Bookends, Dolphin, White	45.00
Bookends, Horsehead, Black	75.00
Bookends, Horsehead, White	65.00
Candleholder, Standing Shell, Gold Trim, 4 In., Pair	25.00
Console Set, Rose, Double Candleholders, 3 Piece	22.00
Cookie Jar, Clock	38.00
Cookie Jar, Daisy	20.00 To 23.00
Cookie Jar, Jack–In–The–Box	32.00
Cookie Jar, Little Miss Muffet	95.00
Cookie Jar, Money Bag	35.00
Cookie Jar, Mother Goose	200.00
Cookie Jar, Pineapple	45.00
Cookie Jar, Pumpkin	100.00

Cookie Jar, Train .... 38.00 To 50.00
Cornucopia, Blue 12.00
Figurine, Blue Heron 19.00
Flowerpot, Cattails .... 10.00 To 12.00
Flowerpot, Floral 14.00
Flowerpot, Morning Glory 10.00
Inkwell, First State & Savings, Abingdon, Ill. 59.50
Planter, Mexican Boy .... 30.00 To 37.00
Planter, Pooch, Green 10.00
Salt & Pepper, Blue Daisy 8.00
Sugar & Creamer, Tea Room, Green, Tray 42.00
Urn, Gold Design, 10 In. 40.00
Vase, Blue Star, 7 1/2 In. 14.50
Vase, Clam Shell, Pink, White Flowers, 7 In. 10.00
Vase, Pink, 11 In. 20.00
Vase, Pink, Handles, 9 3/4 In. 16.00
Vase, Tulip Each Side, Glossy Cream & Yellow, 6 2/8 In. 18.00
Wall Pocket, Light Green, 8 3/4 In. 18.00
Wall Pocket, Lily, Pink 14.00
Wall Pocket, Little Red Riding Hood 165.00
Wall Pocket, Sunflower, Red 30.00

Adams china was made by William Adams and Sons of Staffordshire, England. The firm was founded in 1769 and is still working. All types of tablewares and useful wares have been made through the years. Other pieces of Adams will be found listed under Flow Blue.

ADAMS, Cup & Saucer, Calyx Ware, Hand Painted 15.00
Plate, Calyx Ware, Hand Painted, 10 In. 10.00
Plate, Dr.Syntax Tied To Tree By Highwaymen, 8 In. 75.00
Vase, Jasperware, Venus Bound, Blue, White, C.1785, 3 Piece ....*Illus* 1430.00

The old country store with the crackers in a barrel and a potbellied stove is a symbol of an earlier, less hectic time. The advertisements, containers, and products sold in these stores are now all collectibles. We have tried to list items in the logical places, so large store fixtures will be found under the Architectural category, enameled tin dishes under Graniteware, etc. Listed here are many of the advertising items. Other similar pieces may be found under the product name such as Planters Peanuts.

ADVERTISING, Ashtray & Match Holder, American Seating Co., Embossed Desk 25.00
Ashtray & Match Holder, Diamond Match Co., Amber 14.00
Ashtray, Ames Heating Pumps, Metal, Figural, Heating Pump 10.00
Ashtray, B.F.Goodrich, Tire Shape, 100 Anniversary 16.00
Ashtray, Chrysler Motor, Century of Progress, Copper, 3 In. 15.00
Ashtray, Diamond Match Co., Clear 12.00
Ashtray, Dobbs Hat, Black Glass 22.00
Ashtray, Firestone Tire, Golden Gate Exposition, 1939 .... 18.00
Ashtray, Firestone, Century of Progress, 1934 .... 30.00
Ashtray, Goodrich Silvertown, Tire, Green Glass 10.00
Ashtray, Griswold, Pan Shape 9.50
Ashtray, Guinness, Copper 15.00
Ashtray, Harker Promotional, Black Factory Transfer, White 10.00
Ashtray, Heineken Beer, 50th Anniversary 6.00
Ashtray, Highlander Beer, Glass 3.00
Ashtray, John Deere, Brass, 4 3/4 In. 150.00
Ashtray, Kelly Tire 6.00
Ashtray, Mack Truck, Dog, Chrome 15.00
Ashtray, Mission Orange, Bottle Stands In Middle, Glass, 3 In. 135.00
Ashtray, Mohawk, Rubber Tire 6.00
Ashtray, Monarch, Metal, Dated 1905, 3 1/2 X 6 In. 22.00
Ashtray, Mountain States Telegraph, Telephone, Porcelain 50.00
Ashtray, Red Cab, Phone Number, Blue Glass, 25 Cent 15.00
Ashtray, Roxo Ice Cream, Brass 38.00

Ashtray, Steelworker, Figural, P & H Special, Iron 55.00
Ashtray, Stromberg Carlson, Brass 15.00
Ashtray, Sullivan's Cigars, Red, Porcelain 23.00
Ashtray, Sunkist, Splatter Glass, Signed, 15 In. 24.00
Ashtray, Tin Box, Chesterfield 25.00
Ashtray, TWA, Prop Over, Chrome 95.00
Bag, Shopping, Moxie 9.00
Bag, Union Workman, Says Free Sample Not To Be Sold, Paper 2.00
Bag, Wing Milling Co., 10 Lb. 30.00
Bag, Wing Milling Co., 100 Lb. 25.00
Bandana, Carhartt, World's Largest Overall Mfg., 1901, 24 In. 20.00
Banner, Atlantic Oil, Baying Wolf Picture, 3 X 5 Ft. 175.00
Banner, Mobile Oil, Calling All Cars, C.1930, 6 Ft. 78.00
Banner, Prince Albert Tobacco, Men, Pocket Tin, 42 X 94 In. 80.00
Banner, Prince Albert, Canvas, Hanging, 1943, 8 Ft. 115.00
Banner, Quickmeal Stove, Canvas, Framed, 18 In.X 6 Ft. 450.00
Banner, Sir Walter Raleigh Tobacco, Man With Pipe, Cloth 50.00
Banner, Sprite Boy, Family Size Too!, 1955, 20 X 36 In. 7.50
Beater Jar, Wesson Oil, Stoneware 65.00
Bench, Star Shoes 275.00
Bill Holder, Johnson's Hats, Black Man 20.00
Bill Hook, South Bend Malleable Steel Range 20.00
Bill Spike, National Cash Register 22.00
Billboard, Armour's Star, Cloth, 9 X 20 Ft. 165.00
Bin, Beech–Nut Gum, Little Girl, 1916, 15 X 6 In. 225.00
Bin, Dillworth's Coffee, Tin 125.00
Bin, Duke's Mixture Tobacco 450.00
Bin, Honest Scrap Tobacco, Tin, Dog & Cat, Counter 695.00
Bin, Jersey Coffee, Wooden 450.00
Bin, Murad Turkish Cigarettes 17.50
Bin, Sweet Cuba Tobacco, Lift Lid, Female Portrait, Green 80.00
Bin, Sweet Cuba Tobacco, Yellow, Small 155.00
Blotter, DuPont Explosives 12.00
Blotter, Edison Mazda, Parrish, 1924 .... 25.00
Blotter, Frog Prince, C.M.Burd, 1920s, 4 X 5 1/2 In. 3.50
Blotter, Kentucky Dew Whiskey, Louisville, 3 X 5 In. 4.50
Blotter, Morton Salt 1.00
Blotter, Mutual Life Insurance of New York, 1893, 4 X 9 In. 3.50
Blotter, National Cash Register 10.00
Blotter, Porcelain, Victor Dealer 35.00
Blotter, Red Goose 10.00
Blotter, Sonora, Color, Postcard Size 20.00
Blotter, Texaco Motor Oil, Mount Joy, Pa. 5.00
ADVERTISING, BOOK, see Paper, Box
Booklet, Shaker Salt Doll, Diamond Crystal Salt, 1911 .... 275.00
Booklet, Teddy Bear Bread, 1908 .... 20.00
Bookmark, Leather, Compliments of Lydia E.Pinkham, Green Ink 13.25
Boots, Goodyear, Embossed Glove Logo, Salesman Sample 25.00
ADVERTISING, BOTTLE, see Bottle
Bottle Stopper, Moxie, Metal 5.00
Bowl, Campbell Soup, Alphabet 8.00
Bowl, Cream of Wheat Premium 135.00
Bowl, Diamond Salt, Clear Glass, 7 1/2 In. 15.00
Bowl, Keen's Chophouse, NYC, Gold Advertising, Hall 54.00
Bowl, Wheaties, Breakfast of Champions 10.00
ADVERTISING, BOX, see also Box
Box, Beichs Candy, Victorian Woman, Tin, Dated 1906 .... 16.00
Box, Birthday Candles, Fairy, Fairies With Wands, 1930s, 3 Doz. 5.00
Box, Bossie's Best Brand Butter, Jersey Cows, 1 Lb. 2.50
Box, Butterfinger 5 Cent Candy Bar, Curtiss Candy Co. 25.00
Box, Caldwell's Syrup Pepsin, Mid–1920s, 20 X 8 In. 50.00
Box, Candy, Chocolate Maid, Redwood, Chocolate Shop, 9 X 5 In. 22.50
Box, Cigar, Diamond Joe 5 Cent War Size 4.50
Box, Cigar, Flor De Lorente, Wooden, 50 Cigars, 1917 .... 30.00

Box, Cigar, Havana's Say-So, Tin 22.00
Box, Cigar, La Palina, Wooden, 50 Senators In Foil, 1918 .... 40.00
Box, Cigar, Telonette, Cardboard, 10 Cigars, Unopened, 1919 .... 20.00
Box, Cigarette, Afternoon Egyptian, Blue & Gold 12.00
Box, Cigarette, Mogul Egyptian, Litho, Unopened 20.00
Box, Cigarette, Reyno, White & Gold 12.00
Box, Domes of Silence, 1920s Woman, Putting Castors On Chair 5.00
Box, Dupont Dynamite, Wooden 12.50
Box, Firestone, Blue Tin, 12 X 3 1/2 X 2 3/4 In. 30.00
Box, Gold Dust, Twins, Unopened, 8 Oz. 15.00
Box, Gunpowder Tea, No.10, Hinged Lid, Paper Covered Wood 40.00
Box, Hat, Stetson, Doll Size Felt Hat 14.00
Box, Holleb's Brownie Toasted Corn Flakes 25.00
Box, Keen's Mustard 49.50
Box, Kentucky Sour Mash Whiskey, Wooden 20.00
Box, La Reclama Habana Cigars, Wooden, Metal Clasp & Hinges 15.00
Box, Log Cabin Brownies, Palmer Cox Brownies, Cardboard 125.00
Box, Mother Hubbard, Energy Flour, Salesman's Sample 24.00
Box, N.B.C. Cookies, Brass Front 85.00
Box, Nabisco Premium Crackers, Tin, 14 Oz. 8.00
Box, Pan-A-Min Poultry Feed, Chickens, Unopened, 1900s 15.00
Box, Quaker Oats, Quaker Picture 20.00
Box, Recipe, Gold Medal Flour, Oak 22.50
Box, Reliable Seed, Store, Sioux City, Ia., Display 65.00
Box, Ross' Seed, 25 In. 187.00
Box, Sherman's Haddon Hall, Coffee, Cardboard, Tin, 1900s, 1 Lb. 22.00
Box, Shredded Wheat, 1911 .... 35.00
Box, Silver Star Oleo, Coated, Shipped Flat, 1920 .... 3.50
Box, Texaco Cup Grease, Wooden, Logo 22.50
Box, William's Root Beer Extract, Wooden, 5 X 10 X 7 In. 125.00
Bracelet, Charm, Borden, Elsie 10.00
Bread Tray, Farber & Shlevin, 12 1/2 In. 20.00
Brush, Mirrored, Andy Gump, Buick, Box 40.00
Bucket, Luzianne Coffee, Bail Handle, Lid, 3 Lb. 75.00
Bumper Sticker, Moxie, 1970s 7.00
Button, A & P Greeting, Holly & Red Bow, 1930s, 1 3/4 In. 6.00
Button, Bond Bread 22.00
Button, Buy American, Mid-Depression, 1930s, 7/8 In. 8.00
Button, Chevrolet, Watch The Leader, 1933, 3/4 In. 7.50
Button, Chrysler, Traveling Men's Day, Texas Centennial, 1936 .... 9.00
Button, Goodyear, Liberty Head, 1 1/8 In. 12.00
Button, Heinz Pickles, 1930s 10.00
Button, Ritz Crackers, 1936, 1 In. 5.00
Cabinet, Diamond Dyes, Kids With Balloons 550.00
Cabinet, Diamond Dyes, Mansion 465.00
Cabinet, Diamond Dyes, Witches, Maypole 750.00
Cabinet, Dr.Lesseurs, Veterinary, Tin Front 775.00
Cabinet, Humphrey's Remedies, Lion Trademark, 19th Century 250.00
Cabinet, Munyon's Pharmacy, Hanging, Oak 450.00
Cabinet, Perfection Dye, Tin Insert Front, Victorian 395.00
Cabinet, Putnam Dyes, Horseback Rider, Tin, Large 125.00
Cabinet, Spool, Clark's O.N.T., Etched Glass, 6 Drawers 1025.00
Cabinet, Spool, Merrick, 4 Wide Drawers, 2 Small Drawers 335.00
Cabinet, Spool, Richardson Thread, 14 Drawers 265.00
Can, Eveready Prestone Antifreeze, Dated 1929, 1 Gal. 13.50
Can, Kerosene, Uncle Sam's Best, Tin, 1 Gal. 12.00
Can, Syrup, Hires, 1 Gal. 38.00
Candy Dish, Schraffts Chocolates, Pressed Glass 50.00
      ADVERTISING, CANISTER, see Advertising, Tin
Carrier, 7-Up, Wooden 38.00
Case, Counter, Gilt Edge Confectionery 1 Side, Heides Other 100.00
Case, Display, Boye Sewing Supplies 425.00
Case, Display, Boye Sewing Thread, Tin 425.00
Case, Display, Cigar, M.& O., Slant Front 75.00

Case, Display, Gillette Razors, Top, Wooden, 17 X 13 In. 28.00
Case, Display, Knife, Remington, Counter 125.00
Case, Display, Lisle Elastic, Triangular, Oak, 10 X 16 In. 165.00
Case, Display, Wooden Diamond Dye, Glass Top, 1 Drawer 55.00
Case, Knife, Remington, Large 250.00
Chair, Folding, Wooden, Piedmont Tobacco, 2 Sided Granite Back 115.00
Chair, Sargent Floor, Furniture Enamel 155.00

ADVERTISING, CHANGE RECEIVER, see also Advertising, Tip Tray

Change Receiver, Baby Ruth Gum, Glass, With Tin Display Rack 85.00
Change Receiver, Cuticura, Glass 30.00
Charm, RCA Victor, Nipper, Celluloid, Brass Top, 1 In. 8.00
Chop Sticks, TWA, Red Letters, Chinese Characters, Package 20.00
Cigar Box Opener, Duke of Parma, Worn Chrome 12.00
Cigar Box, Rudolph Valentino, Pop-Up Rudy Lid, Cardboard 20.00
Cigar Cutter, Charles Denby Cigars, Cast Iron, Etched Glass 120.00
Cigar Cutter, King Alfred 10 Cent Cigar, Cast Iron, 1901 .... 575.00
Cigar Cutter, Tirado 375.00
Cigarette Rolling Machine, Bugler Tobacco, Box, 1920 .... 49.00
Clicker, Banjo, Metal, Banjo Shape, Black & Brown, 1 3/4 In. 8.00
Clicker, Casino De Paree Theater Restaurant, NYC, Wooden 20.00
Clicker, Red Goose Shoes, Tin 6.00
Clipboard, Sunoco Oil 26.00
Coaster, Blatz, Taste That Golden Flavor, 1955, 4 In. 50.00
Coaster, Cab Ale, Red & Black, Carriage, Horse, 4 1/4 In. 2.00
Coaster, Dick's Beer, 4 In. 18.00

ADVERTISING, COFFEE GRINDER, see Coffee Grinder

Coffeepot, Sanka, Individual 5.00
Cooler, Maxwell House Iced Tea, Push Spigot 175.00
Counter, Store, 16 Ft. 300.00
Crate Opener, Beech-Nut Gum, Iron, Ship Oldest Stock First 60.00
Creamer, All Star Dairy 8.00
Creamer, Elsie The Cow, 5 In. 25.00
Creamer, Lone Oak Farms, Glass, Individual 7.00
Creamer, Post Cereals Embossed In Bottom 8.00
Crock, Apple Butter, Heinz 325.00
Crock, Bosell's Cottage Cheese, Blue Lettering, 8 Lb. 38.50
Crock, Coors Malted Milk 130.00
Crock, Koehler & Kimricks, Cheese, St.Paul, 1886, 6 X 6 In. 125.00
Crock, Soda Fountain, Johnston, Cold Fudge 175.00
Cup, Armour's Vigoral, Pink Carnations, China 25.00
Cup, Baby, Gerber, Green, Embossed Baby 15.00
Cup, Coffee, Walgreen's, China, Scalloped Rim, 1940s 10.00
Cup, Lion Coffee, Pink Roses, China, 1 1/4 In. 12.00
Cup, Measuring, Quoddy's Digestive Tablets 14.00
Cup, Punch Peanut Butter, Tin 35.00
Cup, Roma Spaghetti, China, Girl Serving Pasta Picture, 1930s 10.00
Cup, Skippy, Silver Plate, Box 75.00
Dish, Auto, Royal Crown 8.00
Dish, Child's, Ralston Purina, 1925 .... 35.00
Dish, John Deere, Metal, Sample 28.00
Dish, Schrafft's Candy, Glass 10.00
Dispenser, Alka Seltzer, Chrome, Blue 85.00
Dispenser, Bromo Seltzer, Cobalt Blue 200.00
Dispenser, Buckey Root Beer, Tree Stump, 4 Elf Handle Mugs 350.00
Dispenser, Buckeye Syrup, Vase Shape 1000.00
Dispenser, Grape Juice, Clear Glass, Gold Paint 385.00
Dispenser, Green River, Syrup, Nickel Plated Brass 95.00
Dispenser, Hires Root Beer, Hourglass Shape 285.00
Dispenser, Horlick's Malted Milk 75.00
Dispenser, Liberty Root Beer 400.00
Dispenser, Little Boy Blue, Liquid Bluing, Tin, Wall 65.00
Dispenser, Match Holder, Diamond Matches, 1 Cent, 8 In.Diam. 90.00
Dispenser, Muscadine Punch, Syrup, 1915 .... 75.00
Dispenser, Needle, Boye 45.00

Dispenser, OCB, Roll Your Own Cigarette Paper	50.00
Dispenser, Orange Julep Syrup	900.00
Dispenser, Rochester Root Beer	275.00
Dispenser, Wards, Orange, Lemon & Lime, Set of 3	1900.00
Dispenser, Welch's Pure Tomato Juice, Frosted Glass, 15 In.	175.00
Display, Tetley Tea, Counter, Cardboard, 3–D, Teacups	25.00
Door Plate, Ex–Lax, Plastic, Box Picture	28.00
Door Plate, Kirk's Flake Soap, Red, White, Black, 4 X 8 In.	88.00
Door Push, Crescent Flour, Litho Tin	45.00
Door Push, Domino Cigarettes, Ballerina, 1940s, 14 X 4 In.	60.00
Door Push, Dr.Caldwell's Syrup Pepsin, Porcelain, Black	48.50
Door Push, Ex–Lax, Porcelain, Pair	50.00
Door Push, Fleischmann's Yeast, Porcelain	100.00
Door Push, Holsum Bread, Pictures Parrot, Porcelain	95.00
Door Push, Mail Pouch Tobacco, Porcelain, Pair	40.00
Door Push, Pabst Beer	20.00
Door Push, Sunbeam Bread	47.50
Door Push, Vick's, Porcelain, 2 Bottles, Blue & White, Red	85.00
Figure, Bert & Harry, Piels Beer, Metal, Dated 1953	100.00
Figure, Bulldog, Lying Down, Hanley's Ale, Papier–Mache, 17 In.	200.00
Figure, Dog, Nipper, 3 Ft.	450.00
Figure, Old Crow, Plastic, 10 In	22.50
Figure, Red Goose, Chalkware, 5 In.	50.00
Figure, Ty Cobb, Charter Whiskey, 32 In.	200.00
Flashlight, Schlitz Beer, Bottle Shape	27.50
Glass, Bromo Seltzer, Cobalt Blue	52.00
Glass, Falstaff, Emblem In Middle	1.50
Glass, Tulip, Barbarossa Beer, Stem	35.00
Globe, Schlitz Beer, Lights	35.00
Hanger, Blue Ribbon Peaches, 33 X 47 In	37.50
Holder, Watta Pop Suckers, Dog	65.00
Holder, Watta Pop Suckers, Panda Bear	225.00
Humidor, Hadden Hall Cigar, Light–Up, Reverse Glass	50.00
Humidor, La Palina Cigars, Embossed Quality Cigar Since 1896	20.00
Jar, Armour Star Products, Barrel Shape, Bale & Lid, Large	20.00
Jar, Beater, Wesson Oil	60.00
Jar, Carnation Malted Milk, Milk Glass, Lid	75.00
Jar, Eugene Bize & Frick, Bear Salve, Black Glass, 4 1/2 In.	205.00
Jar, Horlick's Malted Milk, Original Lid, Aqua, 1/2 Gal.	45.00
Jar, Kiss–Me Gum, Label, 2 Children, 2 Neck Labels	375.00
Jar, Lance Peanut Butter	70.00
Jar, Minters Log Cabin Fudge, 1 Cent, Knob Lid, 6 X 8 In.	35.00
Jar, Monarch Coffee, Glass Lid, 1 Lb.	14.00
Jar, Monarch Peanut Butter, Glass	65.00
Jar, Old Judge Coffee, Glass, 5 Lb.	25.00
Jar, Tom's Peanut Jar, Glass, 1956	30.00
Jug, Roycroft Honey, 5 In.	12.00
Key Holder, Gulf Pride Motor, Oil Can Shape, Embossed Leather	15.00
Keychain, Bull Durham Tobacco, Figural, Gold Plate	35.00
Knife, Checkerboard, Ralston	20.00
Knife, Flynn Dairy & Ice Cream	8.50
Knife, Northrup King Seeds, Kutmaster, Utica, Pocket	8.50
Label, Acme Cubana, Gold On Yellow, 6 1/2 X 8 1/2 In.	.50
Label, American Maid, Pear, 8 X 11 In.	.50
Label, Anne Arundel Pride Tomatoes, Mules, 4 X 11 In.	10.00
Label, Blue Goose, Orange Ground, Los Angeles	2.00
Label, Boy Blue, Apples, Boy Blowing Horn, Blue Ground	1.00
Label, Canadian Apples, 3 Big Apples	1.00
Label, Champ Sweet Potato, Football Player	3.75
Label, Cigar, Hand Made, Home Made, Union Made, 1890, 6 X 9 In.	7.50
Label, Coleman Cracker Co., Barrel, White Paint, 28 1/2 In.	85.00
Label, DeLuxe, Orange, Black Butler Serving Dining Couple	235.00
Label, Dixie Boy, Black Child Eating Orange, 9 In.	1.00
Label, Garrigues' Worm Confections, In 3 Languages, 1870s	4.00

Label, Indian Belle, Indian Couple, Grapefruit, 1915 .... 55.00
Label, Jackie Boy, Little Boy In Naval Clothes, Apple, 1925 .... 12.00
Label, Jewelo, Man & Woman In Field, 6 1/2 X 8 1/2 In. .... .50
Label, Juice King, Smiling Orange, Dressed As King 12.00
Label, Little Fairies Baking Powder, For Can, 1920s 1.00
Label, Marvel Corn, For Can, 1930s, 4 1/2 X 10 In. .... .50
Label, Navajo, Indian Brave, Riverside, Orange 5.00
Label, New Cuba, Cigar Box, Cuban Flag, Gomez, Garcia Portraits 20.00
Label, Our Pick, Rooster & Basket of Fruit, Pear 5.50
Label, Porto Rico, Cigar Box, Spanish Lady, Harbor Scene 75.00
Label, Ramona Memories, Senorita, San Fernando, Orange 2.00
Label, Santa, Cigar, 1887, 4 X 4 In. 7.00
Label, Santa, Lemon 2.50
Label, Sierra Vista, Orange Grove, 1920 .... 10.00
Label, Smiling Clown With A Big Red Nose 28.00
Label, Sonny, Boy Filling Red Wagon, Oranges, Florida 55.00
Label, Statue of Liberty, 9 X 11 In. 1.00
Label, Tom Cat, Cat Sitting On A Red Pillow, 1930 .... 42.00
Label, Zodiac Coffee & Chicory, Circular Zodiac Calendar 2.00
Lamp, Revolving, Budweiser, Clydesdale Horses 3000.00
      ADVERTISING, LUNCH BOX, see Lunch Box
Match Box, Alligator, Monon Route, Railroad Promotional 75.00
Match Box, Diamond Match Co., Tin, 8 1/2 X 5 1/4 In. 22.50
Match Holder, Crystal Spring Brewing Co. 135.00
Match Holder, Dr Pepper 35.00
Match Safe, Sulzbergers Majestic Ham, Hanging, Tin 65.00

Pocket mirrors range in size from 1 1/2 to 5 inches in diameter.
Most of these mirrors were given away as advertising promotions.

Mirror, American Line, Pocket 15.00
Mirror, Anchor Storage Co., Celluloid, Pocket 22.00
Mirror, Angelus Marshmallows, Brunette Cherub, Pocket 40.00
Mirror, Atkinson's Perfume, Bottle, Pocket 55.00
Mirror, Baby Ruth Sundae, Pocket, Oval 20.00
Mirror, Beauty Skin, Lady, Pocket 25.00
Mirror, Bell's Roasted Coffee, Pocket 28.00
Mirror, Berry Bros.Varnishes, Kids, Dog, Wagon, Oval, Pocket 175.00
Mirror, Boot & Shoe Worker's Union, Pocket 22.00
Mirror, Brotherhood Overalls, Semi-Nude In Overalls, Pocket 145.00
Mirror, Calox Tooth Powder, Pocket, 2 3/4 In. 15.00
Mirror, Cascarets, Angel Sitting On Pot, Pocket 35.00
Mirror, Ceresota Flour, Boy Cutting Bread, Pocket 75.00
Mirror, Cox Stove Co., Iron Stove Picture, Brass, Round, 2 In. 10.00
Mirror, Duffy's Malt Whiskey, Large Face, Pocket 35.00
Mirror, Dwight's Soda, Pictures Cow, Pocket 35.00
Mirror, Expansion Flour, Pocket 28.00
Mirror, Garland Stoves & Ranges, Pocket .... 14.50 To 20.00
Mirror, Haines The Shoe Wizard, Pocket 25.00
Mirror, Holeproof Hosiery, Pocket 15.00
Mirror, Horlick's Milk, Girl & Cow, Pocket 45.00
Mirror, Internat'L Shirt & Collar Co., Man On Camel, Pocket 120.00
Mirror, Johnson Hat Co., Negro Wearing Top Hat, Pocket 95.00
Mirror, Kaufman Bros.Pipes, Pocket 15.00
Mirror, Labor Union, Worker & Factory, Pocket 150.00
Mirror, Mennen's Talcum Powder, Pocket 50.00
Mirror, Monarch Typewriter, Pocket 28.00
Mirror, Monument Square Bowling Alley, Portland, Me., Pocket 16.50
Mirror, Morton Salt, Pocket 26.00
Mirror, Mother's Bread, Boy In Sailor Suit, Pocket 235.00
Mirror, Nature's Remedy, Blue, Pocket 40.00
Mirror, Ponds Extract, With Dog, Pocket, Celluloid 15.00
Mirror, Red Feather Harness & Collar, Indian Profile, Pocket 40.00
Mirror, Red Goose Shoes, Stand & Handle, 20 1/2 X 14 1/2 In. 125.00
Mirror, Robin Hood Flour, Celluloid, Pocket 20.00

Mirror, Schaeffer Pianos, Pocket	35.00
Mirror, Union Standard Shoes, Pocket	22.00
Mirror, Universal Theaters Concession Co., Pocket, Handle	25.00
Mirror, White Cat Union Suits, Pocket, Oval	28.00
Mirror, William Gable Co., Altoona, Pa., Building, Pocket	25.00
Muffin Tin, Kellogg's All–Bran	10.00
Mug, A & W Root Beer, Logo, Small	40.00
Mug, Anheuser–Busch, Clydesdale Picture, 6 1/2 In.	25.00
Mug, Armour's Vigoral, Silesia	17.50
Mug, Budweiser, Green, Ceramic	22.00
Mug, Cudahy Rexoma	19.50
Mug, Heineken, Blue & White Scene, Delft	15.00
Mug, Hires, Stoneware	65.00
Mug, Leisey Beer	20.00
Mug, Magnus Root Beer	15.00
Mug, Maxwell House Coffee	10.00
Mug, Moxie	35.00
Mug, Ovaltine, Olympic, Shake–Up, 1964	12.50
Mug, Ovaltine, Uncle Wiggley	24.50
Mug, Rochester Root Beer	10.00
Mug, Schlitz Beer, Girl On Globe	65.00
Mug, Twin Kiss Root Beer	5.00
Napkin, Moxie, Paper, Bottle Picture, Large, 1920s	10.00
Needle Case, Boye	85.00
Notebook, Cloth, Rock Island Plow Co., Pictures, 1900	10.00
Notebook, Hamilton Watch, Celluloid, Engine, Factory Picture	20.00
Notepad, I.W.Harper, Black, Gold Letters, 1904 Calendar, Maps	14.50
Nutmeg Grater, Libby's	95.00
Pail, After Glow Coffee, 4 Lb.	35.00
Pail, Armour's Veribest Peanut Butter, Mother Goose, 1 Lb.	67.50
Pail, Blue Bird Coffee, 5 Lb.	85.00
Pail, Frontenac Peanut Butter, Ganoon Grocery Co., Michigan	75.00
Pail, Jackie Coogan Peanut Butter, Green	90.00
Pail, Lovell & Coval Peanut Butter, Peter Rabbit	125.00
Pail, Miners & Puddler Tobacco, 1 Lb.	50.00
Pail, Monarch Peanut Butter, Teenie Weenie, Lid, 1 Lb.	98.00
Pail, Monarch Teenie–Weenie Peanut Butter, 2 Lb.	85.00
Pail, Nigger Hair Tobacco	145.00
Pail, Plow Boy Tobacco	60.00
Pail, Queen of Hearts, Candy, Tin	75.00
Pail, Santa Claus, Merry Christmas, Candy, 1900	145.00
Pail, Seven–Up, Hand Of Cards	85.00
Pail, Shedd's Peanut Butter, 5 Lb.	15.00
Pail, Toyland Peanut Butter	75.00
Pail, White Seal, Seal On Iceberg, Lid, Lard, Bail Handle	20.00
Pail, Wishbone Coffee, 4 Lb.	30.00 To 36.00
Pail, Yankee Peanut Butter	42.00
Paper Doll, Durham Tobacco Company, Blackwell, Copy.1895	375.00
Paper Doll, Hood's Sarsaparilla	25.00
Pen, Arm & Hammer Soda, Black Celluloid Case, Glass	25.00
Pen, Sheaffer, Holsum Bread, Loaf On Black Lucite, Desk	45.00
Pencil Box, Red Goose Shoes	20.00
Pencil Box, Skippy	35.00
Pencil Sharpener, Baker's Chocolate, Figural Girl	12.00
Pencil Sharpener, Radio Shape, 1930s	22.00
Pencil, Oxydol For Every Soap Purpose, Celluloid Mammy	45.00
Plate, Bakers Cocoa, Tin, 6 In.	55.00
Plate, Bread, Pioneer White Wings Flour, 90th Anniversary	50.00
Plate, Crawford Stoves & Ranges	95.00
Plate, How About Buying Me, Crosley Auto.Dishwasher, 10 In.	15.00
Plate, Reddy Kilowatt, The Little Electric Man, 9 In., Pair	20.00
Plate, Waltham Clock Co., Wedgwood, 1904	75.00
Push Plate, Dr.Caldwell's Pepsin Syrup	30.00
Puzzle, Goodrich Tires	35.00

Puzzle, Heinz 57 Varieties, Jigsaw, 4 Children Picture 8.00
Puzzle, Hood's Sarsaparilla, Auto Race 35.00
Puzzle, Tip-Top Town U.S.A., Envelope, 8 1/2 X 7 1/2 In. 15.00
Rack, Alfred J.Brown Seed Co., Grand Rapids, Wooden 260.00
Ring, American Airlines, 1940s 20.00
Ring, Poll Parrot 35.00
Rolling Pin, G.E.Schultz, Bradford, Iowa, Crockery 185.00
Sack, Bread Flour Donated By People of America, Cloth 7.00
Sack, Occident Flour, Russel–Miller Milling, Minn., 98 Lbs. 500.00
Salt & Pepper, Esso, Gas Pump Shape, Box, Miniature 20.00
Salt & Pepper, Millie & Willie, F & F Co. 15.00
Salt & Pepper, Mogen David 10.00
Salt & Pepper, Morton Salt, Black, 1931 .... 25.00
Salt & Pepper, Nipper, Lenox .... 22.00 To 40.00
Salt & Pepper, Schlitz Beer 3.00
ADVERTISING, SCALE, see also Scale
Scale, Wrigley Gum, Brass Pan & Face, Decals 185.00
Scarf, R.C.A., Embroidered 200.00
Scissors, Star Brand Shoes Are Better 25.00
Scraper, Pabst Blue Ribbon Beer 15.00
Scraper, Virginia Dare 35.00
Settee, Red Goose Shoes, 3 Seat, Atlantic Shoes For Men 995.00
Shot Glass, Berliner Magen Bitters 28.00
Shot Glass, Petzold's German Bitters 55.00
Shot Glass, RCA, Red Logo In Relief, Aluminum 15.00
Shot Glass, Red Star Kentucky Bourbon, Etched 15.00
Showcase, Hanging, Kryptok Decal, Eye Glasses, Glass Front 195.00
Sign, A–1 Pilsner Beer, Porcelain, Oval, 3 Ft.X 18 In. 35.00
Sign, A.H.Seals, Undertaker, Wooden, Stenciled, 12 1/2 X 25 In. 75.00
Sign, Alaska Fur Co., Wood, 1890s, 54 X 55 In. 3500.00
Sign, American Gasoline, Glass Gas Pump, Red, White, 10 X 4 In. 20.00
Sign, American Lady Shoes, Framed, 5 1/2 X 8 In. 10.00
Sign, Arm & Hammer Brand Soda, Cardboard, 15 X 12 1/2 In. 20.00
Sign, Bakers Vanilla, Children, Milk, Porcelain, 34 X 36 In. 475.00
Sign, Ballantine Beer, Cavalier, Tin, 1908, 22 X 34 In. 2200.00
Sign, Bauer Whiskey, Cowboy, Indian, Paperboard, 24 X 33 In. 550.00
Sign, Belle of Anderson Mash, Reverse On Glass, 32 X 41 In. 1275.00
Sign, Blackhawk Brewing Co., Chief Blackhawk, 21 X 24 In. 95.00
Sign, Borden's, Embossed Elsie, Lettering, Tin, 24 X 44 In. 200.00
Sign, Boston Tea Store, Horizontal, 17 In. 192.50
Sign, Brown's Jumbo Bread, Elephant, Die Cut, 15 In. 125.00
Sign, Brown's Jumbo Bread, Tin, Die Cut, 1930s, 13 X 15 In. 140.00
Sign, Budweiser, Porcelain, Neon, Preprohibition, 8 Ft. 250.00
Sign, Canada Dry, Porcelain, 1950s, 25 X 8 In. 25.00
Sign, Cherry Blossom Beverage, Tin, 13 X 19 In. 25.00
Sign, Chesterfield Cigarettes, Tin, 12 1/2 X 17 In. 22.00
Sign, Chicago Varnish Co., Indian, Wood, 11 X 18 In. 125.00
Sign, Climax Tobacco, White, Blue, Porcelain, 15 X 15 In. 45.00
Sign, Concord Cigar, Girl, Red Dress, Paper–Board, 27 X 21 In. 450.00
Sign, Curity First Aid, Tin, Rolled Ends, C.1930, 9 X 24 In. 35.00
Sign, DeLaval Cream Separator, Tin Litho, 1908, 6 X 3 In. 110.00
Sign, Donald Duck Bread, Pictures, 20 X 40 In. 135.00
Sign, Dr Pepper, Cardboard, 16 X 24 In. 10.00
Sign, Dr.Daniel's Loose Catnip, Cardboard, 11 X 15 In. 65.00
Sign, Dr.Daniel's, Blue, Raised White Letters, 28 X 17 In. 95.00
Sign, Dupont, Gun Powder, Hunting Dogs, Tin, 22 X 28 In. 650.00
Sign, Durr's Quality Foods, Tin, Frame, 1920s, 20 X 27 In. 195.00
Sign, Early Times Whiskey, Distillery, Plaster, 27 X 23 In. 275.00
Sign, Eigenbrot Brewery's Schiller Beer, Tin, 9 X 13 In. 68.00
Sign, Elgin Watch, Boy Holding Watch, Wood, 1910, 15 X 23 In. 255.00
Sign, Endicott–Johnson Shoes, Tin, Embossed, 13 1/2 X 39 In. 22.00
Sign, Esso, Plastic, 42 X 30 In. 45.00
Sign, Evinrude Outboard Motors, Fishermen, 20 X 9 In. 130.00
Sign, Falstaff Beer, Tin, Round, 30 In. 95.00

Sign, Fatima Cigarettes, Harem Girl, Tin, 1900, 15 X 21 In.	255.00
Sign, Fleishmann's Yeast, Blue, Red, White, 1930s, 4 X 5 In.	35.00
Sign, Ford Authorized Service Station, Porcelain, 27 X 60 In.	135.00
Sign, Garland Stove, Porcelain, 2 Sides, 24 X 24 In.	325.00
Sign, Genuine Ford Parts, Enameled, Oval, 16 X 24 In.	140.00
Sign, Grand Council Cigars, Framed, Paper–Board, 17 X 14 In.	250.00
Sign, Grubbs–Kemker Candy & Cracker, Paper, 14 X 16 1/2 In.	245.00
Sign, Gus' Topper Beer, Tin, 23 X 17 In.	65.00
Sign, Hamms Beer, Eagle, Porcelain, Round, 1910, 10 In.	225.00
Sign, Handy Pack Dyes, Cherubs, Paperboard, 15 X 19 In.	135.00
Sign, Heileman's, Steel, 3 X 2 Ft.	19.00
Sign, Helmar Cigarettes, Old West Girl, Framed, 28 X 22 In.	650.00
Sign, Hood Tire, Man With Flag, Tin, 12 X 24 In.	75.00
Sign, Hoster's Brewery, Inebriated Monk, Tin, 1900, 26 X 24 In.	595.00
Sign, Houk Hubcaps, Soldier, Battle, Litho, Canvas, 23 X 33 In.	650.00
Sign, Hunter Cigars, Fox Hunter, Horse, Tin, 1915, 19 X 27 In.	250.00
Sign, Illinois Watch Co., Gold Leaf Frame, 10 X 7 In.	225.00
Sign, Jap Rose Soap, Children, Paperboard, 1910, 28 X 39 In.	285.00
Sign, Keen Kutter Tools, Tin, 10 X 28 In.	55.00
Sign, Kellogg Girl, Cardboard, 1910, 25 X 34 1/2 In.	135.00
Sign, Kools, Embossed Tin, 1940s, 27 X 11 In.	20.00
Sign, Kyanize Paints, Varnished, Porcelain, 11 X 19 In.	35.00
Sign, Lone Ranger, Merita Bread, Embossed, Tin, 24 X 36 In.	475.00
Sign, Ma's Old Fashion Root Beer, Tin, 19 X 27 In.	50.00
Sign, Mack Truck Service, Porcelain, 26 X 30 In.	95.00
Sign, Mail Pouch Tobacco, Cardboard, Counter, 14 X 21 In.	45.00
Sign, Marigold Ice Cream, Flanged, Steel, 24 X 12 In.	28.00
Sign, Marvel Cigarettes, Metal, 2 Packs, 1940s, 3 X 18 In.	30.00
Sign, Mazda Lamps, Cardboard, Diecut, 1920s, 22 X 26 In., 5 Pc.	100.00
Sign, Metzger's Mild, Die Cut Porcelain, Milk Bottle, 3 Ft.	575.00
Sign, Miller High Life Brew, Girl On Moon, Tin, 11 X 17 In.	125.00
Sign, Miller Tire, Porcelain, 22 X 72 In.	110.00
Sign, Minneapolis Moline Tractors, Metal, 13 X 19 In.	45.00
Sign, Mohawk Authorized Retreading, Indian, Tin, 18 X 72 In.	25.00
Sign, Moore & Yesbera Dry Goods, 2 Sides, Tin, 43 X 48 In.	110.00
Sign, Mound City Horseshoe Paint, Tin, 28 In.	50.00
Sign, Muriel Cigars, Cardboard, Printer's Proof, 18 X 14 In.	39.00
Sign, Nash Authorized Service, Porcelain, 42 X 42 In.	125.00
Sign, National Tires, Tin, 17 X 53 In.	20.00
Sign, Nehi, Embossed Tin, 28 X 11 In.	45.00
Sign, New Hampshire Fire Insurance Co., Auto, Tin, 24 X 20 In.	475.00
Sign, O.F.C.Whiskey, Hunters, Paperboard, 1890, 22 X 31 In.	350.00
Sign, Oh Boy Gum, Boy, With Gum, Tin, 1930s, 15 X 17 In.	75.00
Sign, Old Dutch Beer, Reverse On Glass, 1930s, Round, 12 In.	95.00
Sign, Old Gold Cigarettes, Glass, 7 1/2 X 14 In.	150.00
Sign, Old Overholt Whiskey, Dog, Farmer, Tin, 26 X 35 In.	595.00
Sign, Oshkosh B'Gosh Work Clothes, Tin, 5 Color, 9 X 13 In.	40.00
Sign, Pabst Blue Ribbon Beer, Couples Drinking, 8 X 12 In.	20.00
Sign, Paul Jones Whiskey, Farmer Pouring Drink, 28 X 22 In.	950.00
Sign, Pawn Broker, 3 Gilded Copper Balls, Iron, 53 In.	325.00
Sign, Pears Soap, Comical Baby, Cardboard, Glass, 23 X 18 In.	125.00
Sign, Pepsi–Cola, Embossed Cardboard, 1940s, 16 X 10 In.	85.00
Sign, Pfeiffer's Beer, Kentucky Derby Winners, 18 X 14 In.	200.00
Sign, Policeman, Double–Sided, School Zone, 7–Up, 5 Ft.	300.00
Sign, Railway Express, Porcelain, Green, 4 X 56 In.	125.00
Sign, Ram's Head Ale, Light Up Glass, 13 X 22 In.	100.00
Sign, Red Cross Cotton, Blacks, Paperboard, 1894, 24 X 33 In.	235.00
Sign, Red Goose Shoes, Sulphur Lick, Yellow, Tin, 13 X 19 In.	65.00
Sign, Red Jacket Tobacco, Baseball, Cardboard, 11 X 28 In.	145.00
Sign, Red Rose Farm Feeds, Cattle Crossing, Tin, 18 X 24 In.	60.00
Sign, Royal Crown Cola, Embossed Tin, 1940s, 28 X 12 In.	40.00
Sign, Salzburger Beer, Lobster, Beer, Flowers, Metal, 24 In.	550.00
Sign, Satin Skin Powder, Girl With Fan & Cream, 28 X 42 In.	38.50
Sign, Sedgwick Rye, Blacks, Paperboard, 1925, 15 X 22 In.	195.00

Sign, Sieberling Tires, Triangular, Porcelain, 16 X 30 In. 35.00
Sign, Standard Oil Co., Red Crown, Porcelain, 12 X 15 In. 30.00
Sign, Tennessee Brewing Co., 51 Splits, Tin, 20 X 28 In. 40.00
Sign, Texaco, Porcelain Both Sides, 85 1/2 X 53 1/2 In. 150.00
Sign, Tom's Toasted Peanuts, 5 Cents, Tin, 4 1/2 In. 10.00
Sign, True Fruit, Self–Framed, Tin, 2 X 3 Ft. 385.00
Sign, Twenty Grand Cigarettes, Cardboard, 19 X 25 1/2 In. 38.00
Sign, Two–In–One Shoe Polishes, Tin, 6 1/2 X 28 In. 15.00
Sign, Uneeda Baker, Slicker Boy, Paper, 11 1/2 X 6 In. 14.00
Sign, Union Mills Flour, Litho Tin, Baby, C.1905, 15 X 19 In. 95.00
Sign, Voight Flour, Doll, Red, White & Blue, 1920s, 20 X 16 In. 12.00
Sign, Watchmaker's, Pocket Watch, Wooden, 2 Sided, 31 In. 1150.00
Sign, Waterman's Ideal Fountain Pen, Porcelain, 8 X 30 In. 175.00
Sign, Welch Penn Oil, Tin, 1940s, 24 X 9 In. 20.00
Sign, Whiz Motor Products, Cans Attached, Tin, 38 X 48 In. 650.00
Sign, Winchester, Antler Gun Rack, Tin, 1913, 30 X 36 In. 1650.00
Sign, Zu Zu, National Biscuit Co., C.1920, 25 X 19 In. 150.00
Soap, Pearline, Procter & Gamble Product, Unopened 18.00
Spatula, Rettberg's Scrapple, Dated 1914 .... 15.00
Spoon, Dose, Rexall Drugs, Sterling Silver 16.00
Spoon, Ice Cream Soda, Liggett's, Signature, Pair 59.00
Spoon, Rolex, Silver Plate 7.00
Spoon, Towle's Log Cabin Syrup, Tin 16.00
Spoon, Wilcox & Co., Five O'Clock Tea, Silver Plate, Set of 8 .... 140.00
Spoon, Wooden, Kellogg's 8.00
Stand, Clark's Teaberry Gum, Vaseline Glass 55.00
Stickpin, Anchor Buggy Co., Anchor Shape 15.00
Stickpin, Doe–Wah–Jack, Indian Head, Brass 16.00
Stickpin, International Harvest Co., Brass, Logo, 1900s 5.00
Stickpin, Sharples, Celluloid, Oval, Early 1900s, 1 In. 15.00
Stickpin, Toledo Scale 10.00
Stickpin, Ware–Ever Aluminum 10.00
String Holder, Handy Box French Shoe Blacking, Iron, 1883 .... 335.00
String Holder, Midas Flour, Tin 3000.00
String Holder, Olo Soap Powder, Tin, Woman Washing Dishes 275.00
String Holder, Red Goose Shoes 1200.00
ADVERTISING, THERMOMETER, see Thermometer
Tie Clasp, 7–Up, Bottle Shape, Gold 15.00
Tie Clasp, Texaco, 20 Year Service, 14K Gold 20.00
Tie Tac, Mack Bulldog 10.00
Tie Tac, White Sewing Machines 15.00

> The English language is sometimes confusing. Tin cans or canisters
> were first used commercially in the United States in 1819 and were
> called "tins." Today the word "tin" is used by most collectors to
> describe many types of containers, including food tins, biscuit boxes,
> roly poly tobacco containers, gunpowder cans, talcum powder
> sprinkle–top cans, cigarette flat–fifty tins, and more. Beer cans are
> listed in their own section. Things made of undecorated tin are
> listed under Tinware.

Tin, Abbotts Ice Cream, Amish Girl, Round, 6 X 5 In. 20.00
Tin, Admiration Coffee, Round, 1 Lb. 35.00
Tin, Archer Oil, Indian, Full, 1 Qt. 45.00
Tin, Baby's Bottle Tobacco, British, Round, 4 In. 15.00
Tin, Bagdad Tobacco, Bagdad On Top, Upright, Pocket ....50.00 To 100.00
Tin, Baking Powder, Gold Label, 7 In. 16.00
Tin, Banquet Gunpowder Tea, Green, Red, Emblem On Lid, Round 16.00
Tin, Battleship Coffee, 3 Lb. 35.00
Tin, Beverly Club Steel Cut Coffee, 1 Lb. 10.00
Tin, Big Ben Tobacco, Horse, Pocket 35.00
Tin, Biscuit Box, Uneeda, Pastoral Scenes, 7 1/2 X 11 1/2 In. 190.00
Tin, Biscuit, Great Animal Show, Wheels 85.00
Tin, Blanke's Coffee Saratoga Trunk, Red, Gold, 5 X 7 In. 44.00
Tin, Blanke's Tea, Grant's Cabin, 2 X 3 X 5 In. 80.00

Tin, Bon Ami, Chick, Lady Washing Windows, Unopened, 2 1/2 In. 20.00
Tin, Bond Street Tobacco, Pocket, 4 X 2 In. 22.00
Tin, Borden's Meadow Brand Malted Milk, 5 Lb. 18.50
Tin, Bordens Malted Milk, 10 Lb. .... 18.50 To 26.50
Tin, Bouquet Coffee, Litho On Tin, Screw Cap, 1 Lb. 30.00
Tin, Bowl of Roses Tobacco, Pocket, 3 X 2 In. 175.00
Tin, Brier Plug, Canada, Round, 5 X 4 In. 15.00
Tin, Briggs, Pocket, 4 X 2 In. 15.00
Tin, Buckingham Tobacco, Sample, 1 X 1 In. 60.00
Tin, Bugler Cigarettes, Pocket, 2 X 2 In. 15.00
Tin, Bulldog Tobacco, Pocket, 4 X 3 In. 195.00
Tin, But–A–Kiss, 24 In. 85.00
Tin, Camel Coffee, With Measuring Spoon, 1920s, L Lb. 34.00
Tin, Campbell Coffee, 4 Lb. 45.00
Tin, Campfire Marshmallows, 5 Lb. 20.00
Tin, Caswell Coffee, Poppies, 3 Lb. 38.00
Tin, Central Union Tobacco, Pocket, 4 X 3 In. 225.00
Tin, Champ Prophylactics, Ted Williams Picture, 1 Dozen 50.00
Tin, Chase & Sanborn Seal Brand Coffee, 1902, Pat., 3 Lb. 10.00
Tin, Chesterfield, Flat Fifty 8.50
Tin, Colgates Baby Talc, Child Holding Can, 6 In. 65.00
Tin, Cottolene Shortening, 8 Lb. 30.00
Tin, Culture Tobacco, Pocket, 4 X 2 In. .... 60.00 To 110.00
Tin, Dan Patch, 4 X 6 In. 30.00
Tin, Dial Tobacco, Turn To A Real Smoke, Pocket, 4 X 2 In. 40.00
Tin, Dill's Best Sliced Cut Plug, Box, 6 X 3 X 1 In. 35.00
Tin, Dill's Best Smoking Tobacco, Pocket, 4 X 2 In. 10.00
Tin, Donniford, Pocket, 4 X 2 In. 85.00
Tin, Douce O'Deur Talc, Round, 4 In. 6.00
Tin, Dr.Koch's Ginger, 1/2 Lb. 20.00
Tin, Dref's Gout & Rheumatism Cure, Counter, 2 In. 7.00
Tin, Du Maurier Cigarettes, Flat, Pocket 10.00
Tin, DuPont Gunpowder, Ships, Oval, 5 X 3 In. 75.00
Tin, Edgeworth Tobacco, 4 1/2 X 3 1/4 In. 17.50
Tin, Edgeworth Tobacco, Pocket, Sample 55.00
Tin, El Verso Cigar, 10 Cent Size, Flat, 4 X 2 X 1 In. 15.00
Tin, Elgin Watch Co., Main Springs, 5 X 2 X 1/2 In. 20.00
Tin, Empress Coffee, 5 Lb. 18.00
Tin, Eve Tobacco, Pocket, 4 X 2 In. 250.00
Tin, Eveready Antifreeze, Pictures Auto, Dated 1929, 1/2 Gal. 18.50
Tin, Ex–Lax, Sample 17.50
Tin, Forest & Stream Tobacco, 2 Men In Canoe, Pocket, 4 X 2 In. 500.00
Tin, Forest & Stream Tobacco, Canister, 2 Fishermen, 3 X 2 In. 45.00
Tin, Forest & Stream Tobacco, Ducks, Gold, Pocket, 4 X 2 In. 50.00
Tin, Fougera Mustard Plaster, Red & Black Graphics, 4 In. 15.00
Tin, Four Roses Tobacco, Silver, Pocket, 4 X 2 In. 125.00
Tin, Fuller Furniture Polish, Sample 18.00
Tin, Gail & Ax, Navy, Canister, 1 Lb. 225.00
Tin, Goldshield Coffee, Seattle, Wash., 20 Lb. 38.50
Tin, Grain Tobacco, Upright, Slide Top, 3 X 3 In. 35.00
Tin, Grandma Tea, A.& P., 1 Lb. 75.00
Tin, Granger Tobacco, Canister, 5 X 3 In. 15.00
Tin, Granulated 54 Tobacco, Pocket, 4 X 2 In. 60.00
Tin, Gravely Tobacco, 3 X 5 In. 35.00
Tin, Hand Made Tobacco, Upright, Pocket, 4 X 2 In. 100.00
Tin, Hardy's Pure Lard, Pig Dressed, Carrying Umbrella, 4 Lb. 26.00
Tin, Hi–Plane Tobacco, 1 Engine, Pocket.4 X 2 In. 50.00
Tin, Hi–Plane Tobacco, 4 Engines, Pocket, 4 X 2 In. 250.00
Tin, Hills Bros.Coffee, 1922, 2 Lb. 25.00
Tin, Hindoo Tobacco, Hindoo On Top, Pocket, 3 X 2 In. 795.00
Tin, Holtzman's Pretzel, 12 In. 15.00
Tin, Honey Moon Tobacco, Pictures Man, Moon, Pocket, 4 X 2 In. 85.00
Tin, Huntley & Palmer, Bell 135.00
Tin, Huntley & Palmer, Book 75.00

Tin, Huntley & Palmer, King Tut Urn 145.00
Tin, Huntley & Palmer, Lantern 145.00
Tin, Huntley & Palmer, Marble Column, Beige 85.00
Tin, Huntley & Palmer, World Globe 185.00
Tin, Hurley Burley, Canister, Humidor Top, 6 In. 18.00
Tin, Jap Rose Talc, 6 In. 25.00
Tin, John Ruskin Cigars, Upright, 6 X 2 X 2 In. 75.00
Tin, John Sexton Teas, Coffees & Spices, 5 Lb. 50.00
Tin, Jumbo Popcorn, 10 Lb. 75.00
Tin, Justice Cocoa, Miss Liberty, Wm.Baker, Syracuse, 4 In. 24.00
Tin, Kaffee Hag, Copyright 1925, 1 Lb. 25.00
Tin, Kennedy's, Biscuit, 9 In. 38.00
Tin, Kentucky Club, Pocket, 4 X 2 In. 15.00
Tin, King Midas Flour, Girl Standup, 3 1/4 In. 30.00
Tin, Lady Hellen Coffee, Beautiful Woman, C.1923, 1 Lb. 20.00
Tin, Lady Hellen Coffee, Pictures Beautiful Lady, C.1923, 1 Lb. 20.00
Tin, Lipton Tea, Indian Woman, 10 X 7 X 4 In. 65.00
Tin, Log Cabin Syrup, 5 Lb. 45.00
Tin, Log Cabin, Red, 12 Oz. 30.00
Tin, Loose Wiles Biscuit Co., Hiawatha, Bail Handle, 3 X 9 In. 150.00
Tin, Lucky Strike Cut Plug, Flat, Pocket, 4 X 3 In. 30.00
Tin, Lucky Strike, 1 Lb. 165.00
Tin, Lucky Strike, 4 1/2 X 2 3/4 X 3/4 In. 18.00
Tin, Luziane Coffee, 1961, 1 Lb. 25.00
Tin, Mammy's Favorite Coffee, Round, 8 In. 190.00
Tin, Maryland Club Tobacco, Orange, Pocket, 3 X 3 In. 200.00
Tin, Maxwell House Tea, 1/2 Lb. 12.00
Tin, Mayo Cut Plug, Top Handle, 7 X 5 X 3 In. 20.00
Tin, Mayo's, Pocket, Flat, 4 X 2 In. 55.00
Tin, Mazawattee Tea, Old Folks At Home, 8 X 5 3/4 In. 25.00
Tin, Mazon & SS Pierce Coffee, 1 Lb. 20.00
Tin, McCormick Tea, 5 In. 7.00
Tin, Meritt Powder, Sample 6.00
Tin, Model Tobacco, White, Orange Canister, 5 X 3 In. 55.00
Tin, Mohican Coffee, Indian, 1 Lb. 75.00
Tin, Monarch Light of Asia Tea, Lady, 5 X 3 X 3 In. 55.00
Tin, Monarch Teenie Weenie Coffee, 1 Lb. 75.00
Tin, Montgomery Ward's Oriental Tea, 4 Sides, Canister, 5 Lb. 125.00
Tin, Nash's Coffee, 3 Lb. 45.00
Tin, Ojibwa Fine Cut Tobacco, Indian On Front, 2 X 6 In. 50.00
Tin, Old Bond Cigars, Oval, 6 X 5 X 2 In. 35.00
Tin, Old Colony Tobacco, Silver, Pocket 75.00
Tin, Old Gold Cigarettes, King Size 12.00
Tin, Opaline Oil, 1920s Racecar, 1 Gal. 135.00
Tin, Orcico Cigars, Square, 6 X 6 X 4 In. 185.00
Tin, Oriental Tea, Canister, 5 Lb. 115.00
Tin, Parma Coffee, Paper Label, 1 Lb. 42.50
Tin, Peachy Tobacco, Pocket, 3 X 2 In. .... 50.00 To 75.00
Tin, Peanut Butter, No.2 .... 45.00
Tin, Peanuts, Bunnies, Canister, 10 Lb. 320.00
Tin, Penzoil Oil, 1940s Airplane, 1 Qt. 18.00
Tin, Pep Boys Oil, Cartoon Cowboys On Bonco, 2 Gal. 55.00
Tin, Perfect Brand Coffee, Round, Litho, 6 X 3 In. 30.00
Tin, Peter Pan Peanut Butter, Pictures of Pan, 25 Lb. 95.00
Tin, Philip Morris, Pocket, 4 X 2 X 1 In. 12.00
Tin, Picobac Tobacco, Large Leaf, Tin, Box, 4 X 2 X 1 In. 50.00
Tin, Player's Navy Cut, 6 1/2 X 3 X 1 1/2 In. 40.00
Tin, Prince Albert, Christmas, Santa Claus, Canister, 5 In. 20.00
Tin, Prince Albert, Paper Tag, Dated 1910, Canister, 6 X 5 In. 15.00
Tin, Puritan Tobacco, Pocket, Dark Gray, 4 X 2 In. 195.00
Tin, Ramon's Liver Ailment, Contents, 3 In. 4.00
Tin, Rawleigh's Good Health Cocoa, Litho, 1 Lb. 15.00
Tin, Red Jacket Tobacco, Pocket, 4 X 2 In. .... 15.00 To 18.00
Tin, Red Moon Tea, Japan, Hinged Cover, 15 X 18 In. 35.00

Tin, Regal Tobacco, Pocket, 4 X 2 In.	300.00
Tin, Requa's Charcoal Tablets, Top, 3 X 2 1/2 X 1 1/2 In.	3.50
Tin, Revelation Tobacco, Upright, 3 X 2 In.	10.00
Tin, Rex, Pocket, 4 X 2 In.	95.00
Tin, Roly Poly, Dutchman, Mayo	350.00
Tin, Roly Poly, Mammy, Dixie Queen	375.00
Tin, Roly Poly, Satsified Customer, Mayo	450.00
Tin, Roosa–Ratliff Mutton Tallow, Sample	10.00
Tin, Runkel Cocoa, 1/2 Lb.	45.00
Tin, San Blas Coconut, Green Monkeys, 5 In.	125.00
Tin, Shedd's Peanut Butter, Elves, Animals, 5 Lb.	17.50
Tin, Sheik Prophylactic, Sheik Riding Horse, 1931, 1 3/4 In.	25.00
Tin, Sir Walter Raleigh Smoking Tobacco, Canister, 6 In.	38.00
Tin, Sir Walter Raleigh Tobacco, Christmas, Box, 5 X 4 X 3 In.	35.00
Tin, Sir Walter Raleigh Tobacco, Pocket, 4 X 2 In.	10.00
Tin, St.Julien Tobacco, Pocket, 4 X 2 In.	2.00
Tin, St.Leger Little Cigars, Flat, Red, 3 X 3 1/4 In.	10.00
Tin, Stag, Pocket, Small Oval, 2 X 4 In.	30.00
Tin, Stillboma Oriental Polish, Deer, Square, 5 X 1 1/2 In.	15.00
Tin, Sultana Peanut Butter, 4 X 3 In.	25.00
Tin, Sunset Trail Cigars, Red, Box, 6 X 3 X 3 In.	250.00
Tin, Sunshine Biscuit, Deep Hinged Lid, 12 X 11 X 3 In.	35.00
Tin, Swee–Touch–NE, Red & Gold Trunk, 6 In.	25.00
Tin, Sweet Burley Tobacco, 2 X 8 In.	25.00
Tin, Sweet Burley Tobacco, Yellow, Canister, 14 X 8 In.	145.00
Tin, Sweet Cuba Dark, 5 Lb.	45.00
Tin, Sweet Cuba Tobacco, Gold Seals, Gold & Brown, 14 X 8 In.	60.00
Tin, Sweet Cuba, Red, Yellow, White, Canister, 6 In.	65.00
Tin, Sweet Mist Tobacco, Blue, 2 X 8 In.	150.00
Tin, Sweet Tips, Pocket, Oval Paper Label, 4 In.	35.00
Tin, Tetley Tea, Elephant On Lid, 2 X 1 In.	15.00
Tin, Tiger Chewing Tobacco, 6 X 4 In.	35.00
Tin, Tiger Tobacco, Red, 14 X 8 In.	175.00
Tin, Trout–Line, Oval, 3 X 3 In.	135.00
Tin, Tuxedo Tobacco, Upright, Sample	135.00
Tin, Tuxedo, Vacuum, Man Smoking Pipe, Canister, 3 X 4 1/2 In.	35.00
Tin, Twin Oaks Tobacco, Pocket, 4 X 2 In.	55.00
Tin, U.S.Marine Tobacco, Upright, Pocket, 4 X 3 In.	195.00
Tin, Uncle Ben's Rice 40th Anniversary, 1943–1983, 7 1/2 In.	18.00
Tin, Union Leader Cut Plug, 3 In.	27.00
Tin, Union Leader Cut Plug, 8 In.	16.00
Tin, Union Leader, 6 X 4 In.	35.00
Tin, Union Leader, Tobacco, Eagle, Canister, 1 Lb.	85.00
Tin, Union Leader, Uncle Sam, White Ground, Pocket, 6 X 3 In.	75.00
Tin, Vanko Cigars, Horse, Oval.6 X 6 X 4 In.	75.00
Tin, Velvet, Pipe & Cigarette, Flat Lid, Pocket, 4 X 2 In.	12.00
Tin, Venice Palace Candy, Italy, 9 X 7 X 1 In.	15.00
Tin, War Eagle Cigars, Red, Canister, 6 X 4 In.	25.00
Tin, Wedding Breakfast Coffee, 1 Lb.	55.00
Tin, Whip Tobacco, Pocket, 4 X 2 In.	500.00
Tin, White House Tea, Round, 2 1/2 In.	35.00
Tin, White Star Line Cigarette, 3 X 4 1/4 X 5 In.	30.00
Tin, Willoughby Taylor Pipe Mixture, Pocket, 4 X 2 In.	45.00
Tin, Yale Mixture, 1908, Sample	15.00
Tin, Yankee Boy Tobacco, Brunette Boy, Pocket, 3 X 2 In.	325.00

A tip tray is a decorated metal tray less than 5 inches in diameter.
It was placed on the table or counter to hold either the bill or the
coins that were left as a tip. A change receiver could be made of
glass, plastic or metal. It was kept on the counter near the cash
register and held the money passed back and forth by the cashier.

Tip Tray, American Steamship Lines	75.00
Tip Tray, Arnold's Bread, Tin	35.00

Tip Tray, Blatz, Ball Players, 1956	22.00
Tip Tray, Booth Bros.Bottlers, Dutch Girls	38.00
Tip Tray, Booth Shoe Co.	55.00
Tip Tray, Bromo Seltzer	35.00
Tip Tray, Buffalo Brewing, Bottle Shape	350.00
Tip Tray, Butts' Sporting Goods, Dog, Ducks, C.1890	40.00
Tip Tray, Cape Brewery & IC Co., Drummers With Bottle	95.00
Tip Tray, Che–On–Tea, Victorian Girl, Green Dress	85.00
Tip Tray, Clover Brand Shoes Always Just Correct, Black Boy	85.00
Tip Tray, Columbus Brewing Co., Christopher Columbus	115.00
Tip Tray, DeLaval, Woman, Separator	35.00
Tip Tray, Doubleware Work Clothes	27.00
Tip Tray, Erie Brewery, Logo	95.00
Tip Tray, Fairy Soap	40.00 To 80.00
Tip Tray, Franklin Insurance, 4 In.	14.00
Tip Tray, Gallagher & Burton Whiskey	45.00
Tip Tray, Garland Stoves	50.00
Tip Tray, German American Brewery, Factory, Pre–Prohibition	250.00
Tip Tray, Globe Wernicke Bookcases	30.00
Tip Tray, Goebel Beer, European Man	75.00
Tip Tray, Highland Evaporated Cream	38.00
Tip Tray, Hupfel Brewing Co.	45.00
Tip Tray, Hyroler Whiskey	38.00
Tip Tray, Indianapolis Brewery, Bottle	75.00
Tip Tray, Koppitz–Melchers Brewing Co., Detroit	65.00
Tip Tray, Larkin Cleanser	12.00
Tip Tray, Lehnerts Brewery, Dog With Cigar	125.00
Tip Tray, Los Angeles Brewing, Pictures Factory	125.00
Tip Tray, Monticello Whiskey	45.00
Tip Tray, Moxie, Purple Flowers & Lady	175.00
Tip Tray, Oakville Co., Waterbury, Conn., Hand, Safety Pin	60.00
Tip Tray, Oertel Brewery, Women, Dove	85.00
Tip Tray, Parsley Salmon	45.00
Tip Tray, Pfeiffer Brewery, Bottle	95.00
Tip Tray, Phil Schneider Brewery, Old Couple	125.00
Tip Tray, Phoenix Brewery, Eagle	95.00
Tip Tray, Phos–Ferrone, Beautiful Woman	95.00
Tip Tray, Pittsburgh Brewing Co., Tech Beer, 3 Men	150.00
Tip Tray, President Suspenders, Girl Portrait	30.00
Tip Tray, Prudential Life Insurance	16.00
Tip Tray, Quick Meal Ranges, Picture of Chick, Oval	68.00
Tip Tray, Red Cross Stove	45.00
Tip Tray, Red Raven Splits, World's Fair, 1904	65.00
Tip Tray, Resinol, Girl With Roses	30.00
Tip Tray, Rockford Watches	60.00
Tip Tray, Round Oak Stoves	16.00
Tip Tray, S & H Green Stamps, Girl	55.00
Tip Tray, Schaefer	15.00
Tip Tray, Slade's Peanut Butter	27.00
Tip Tray, Stegmaier Beer, Pictures Factory	80.00
Tip Tray, Union Made Cigars, Child Labor Theme	65.00
Tip Tray, Waterfill Bourbon	15.00
Tip Tray, Welsbach Lighting	45.00
Tip Tray, White Rock, With Nude	45.00 To 60.00
Tip Tray, Yoeman Insurance	40.00
Tip Tray, Yuengling's Brewery, Eagle	95.00
Tobacco Cutter, Brown & Williamson	65.00
Tobacco Cutter, R.J.Reynold Tobacco Co., Brown Mule	40.00
Tobacco Cutter, S.W.Venable & Co., American Machine Co.	70.00
Tobacco Cutter, Spearhead, Ornate	240.00
Tobacco Cutter, Star, Save The Tags, Iron, Pat.Jan.20, 1885	70.00
Toothbrush, Dr.West's Germ Fighter, Oversized, Bakelite	65.00
Tray, Anheuser–Busch, Oval, Cherubs, Eagle, 13 1/2 X 17 In.	1200.00
Tray, Barth Scholzen, Racine, Wis., Oval, 16 1/2 In.	95.00

Tray, Beer, Calumet Brewing Co., Cavalier Scene, 12 X 17 In. 250.00
Tray, Boston Brewery Co., Truck 475.00
Tray, Brownies, Tin Litho, Fat–Bellied, 10 1/2 X 13 1/2 In. 135.00
Tray, Budweiser Beer, 1914, Levee Scene 87.00
Tray, Budweiser, St.Louis In Early 1870s, 1914 .... 185.00
Tray, Buffalo Beer, N.Y., Table Scene 210.00
Tray, C.Pfeiffer, Detroit, Bottle & Factory 150.00
Tray, Cabello Cigar, Long–Haired Brunette, Oval, 17 In. 165.00
Tray, Canada's Best, Frontenac Factory 90.00
Tray, Cherry Prost Ice Cream 85.00
Tray, Chief Oshkosh, Pre–Prohibition 130.00
Tray, Climax Stove 255.00
Tray, Conrad Seipp Brewery, Braided Lady .... 275.00 To 350.00
Tray, Dictator Beer 125.00
Tray, Dobler Brewing, Pretty Lady 50.00
Tray, Duquesne, Prince Holding Pilsner Glass 20.00
Tray, Eat Snyders Ice Cream, White Script, Red 38.00
Tray, Edelweiss, Schoenhofen Brewing Co. 100.00
Tray, Feigenspon Brewery, Newark, 13 In. 25.00
Tray, Fish, A.J.Smith & Son, Colchester, Illinois, Tin, 16 In. 50.00
Tray, Fort Schuyler 30.00
Tray, Fox Head Beer, Picture of Fox 45.00
Tray, Frank Fehr Brewing Co., Louisville, Ky., Brass, 12 In. 100.00
Tray, Free State Beer, Pictures Innkeeper 30.00
Tray, Geo.T.Stagg Co., Bust of Stag Center, 12 In. 50.00
Tray, Golden State, Milwaukee Brewery of San Francisco 125.00
Tray, Green River Whiskey, Mule & Black Man 200.00
Tray, Hanley, Connoisseur 95.00
Tray, Henley's Peerless Ale, Gentleman 45.00
Tray, Hershey Chocolate Co., Adm.Dewey, Manilla, 10 X 14 In. 35.00
Tray, Holihan Beer, Law, Mass., Tiger & Lady 150.00
Tray, Holland Ice Cream 15.00
Tray, Iroquois Beer, Litho Indian Head, 12 In.Diam. 20.00
Tray, Jung Beer, Picture of Bertha, Milwaukee, Dated 1908 .... 75.00
Tray, Kist, Bottle & Risque Girl, Orange 45.00
Tray, Koppitz–Melchers, Detroit, Mich., Elves Making Beer 150.00
Tray, Kuntz's Car, Dayton Ohio, 1920s 115.00
Tray, Levee, Budweiser 125.00
Tray, Lion Brewery, Buffalo 325.00
Tray, Miller Beer, Girl On Moon .... 28.00 To 55.00
Tray, Narragansett Ale, Red & Gold 55.00
Tray, Neff Bros.Brewing Co., Denver, Dogs, 16 X 13 In. 95.00
Tray, Old Dutch Beer, Gentleman 60.00
Tray, Old Pepper Whiskey, Flag Motif, Oval, 17 In. 225.00
Tray, Olympia Beer, Lady In Flowing Robe 68.00
Tray, Ortliebs Beer, Round 25.00
Tray, Pabst, Medieval Figures, Beer Cellar, Oval, 19 In. 195.00
Tray, Pickwick Ale 45.00
Tray, Purity Ice Cream, 13 X 13 In. 55.00
Tray, Rainier Beer, Lady With Bear 185.00
Tray, Red Raven, Bird By Bottle, Square, 13 In. 150.00
Tray, Rheingold Beer, Men At Table 200.00
Tray, Ritz Crackers, Flapper Scene 20.00
Tray, Ritzy Rich Midwest Ice Cream 17.50
Tray, Seitz Beer, Easton Round Eagle 135.00
Tray, Simon Pure Beer, Pre–Prohibition, Wooden 125.00
Tray, Sol Superior Beer, Indian Maid 150.00
Tray, Standard Brewing Co., Hanging of 38 Indians 225.00
Tray, Stegmaier, Young Girl 150.00
Tray, Supreme Bread, Lunch With Uncle Pete 22.00
Tray, Teck Beer 10.00
    ADVERTISING, TRAY, TIP, see Advertising, Tip Tray
Tray, Utica Club Beer 18.00
Tray, Walters Brewing Co. 75.00

Clean alabaster by dusting with a solf brush. Then use turpentine or dry-cleaning fluid. Do not use water. Polish with paste furniture wax.

Clean alabaster with dry cleaning fluid. It dissolves in water.

Clean the feathers on a stuffed bird with chunks of fresh white bread. After cleaning, spray lightly with hair spray.

Tray, Welz & Zerwick Beer, Oval	250.00
Tray, Yellowstone Whiskey	125.00
Tray, Yosemite Beer, Lady On Horse	350.00
Tray, Yuengling's Beer, Lady	80.00
Tumbler, 7–Up, Dark Green, Old Trademark, 4 In.	5.00
Tumbler, Budweiser Near Beer, BEVO, Prohibition	10.00
Tumbler, General Electric, 8 Oz.	3.00
Tumbler, Grain Belt Beer	5.00
Tumbler, Heinz Tomato Juice, Man In Top Hat Picture	10.00
Whistle, Baby Ruth, Tin, Candy Bar Picture, 1930s	20.00
Whistle, Butternut	15.00
Whistle, Ex–Lax, Wooden	6.00
Whistle, Poll Parrot Shoes	8.00
Whistle, Smith's Ice Cream, Cream of Perfection, Black, Orange	23.00
Wine Cooler, Virginia Dare, Glass, Garrett Co., 8 1/2 In.	250.00
Wrapper, Baby Ruth Candy, Jackie Cooper, 1 Cent	10.00
Wrapper, Candy, Grumpy, Walt Disney Ent., 1938	40.00
Yardstick, Winchester	50.00
Yo–Yo, Sprite, Russell, Green	4.50

Agata glass was made by Joseph Locke of the New England Glass Company of Cambridge, Massachusetts, after 1885. A metallic stain was applied to New England Peachblow and the mottled design characteristic of agata appeared.

AGATA, Finger Bowl, Mottled, 5 1/2 X 2 1/2 In.	685.00
Tumbler, 3 7/8 In., Pair	800.00
Vase, Lily, Mottled, 6 In., Pair	525.00
Vase, Mottled, 7 1/2 In.	695.00

Akro agate glass was made in Clarksburg, West Virginia, from 1932 to 1951. Before that time, the firm made children's glass marbles. Most of the glass is marked with a crow flying through the letter A.

AKRO AGATE, Ashtray, Orange	10.00
Ashtray, White Leaf, Blue	10.00
Basket, White & Green, 2 Handles	27.50
Cart, Wheeled, Yellow, 4 X 6 In.	10.50
Crock, Salt, 1 Qt.	15.00
Cup, Child's, Pumpkins, Green	14.00
Dish Set, Child's, Topaz, Original Box	110.00
Dish, Scotty Dog Cover, White, Signed	30.00
Flower Pot, Green, Signed, 2 3/4 In.	7.00
Match Holder, With 4 3–In.Ashtrays, White & Green	24.00
Pail, Blue & White, Tin Lid	30.00
Plate, Child's, Deep Yellow, Octagonal, 3 1/2 In., Set of 4	11.50
Powder Jar, Colonial Lady, White	28.00 To 30.00
Powder Jar, Scotty Dog, Powder Blue	65.00

Shot Glass, Amber	
Tea Set, American Maid, Box, 7 Piece	5.00
Tea Set, Child's, Concentric Ring, Blue, Green, White, 14 Piece	75.00
Tea Set, Child's, Green & Yellow, Box, 16 Piece	85.00
Tea Set, Interior Panel, Blue & White Swirl, 13 Piece	118.00
	145.00

Alabaster is a very soft form of gypsum, a stone that resembles marble. It was often carved into vases or statues in Victorian times. There are alabaster carvings being made even today. Because the alabaster is very porous, it will dissolve if kept in water, so do not use alabaster vases for flowers.

ALABASTER, Box, Oil Painted Deco Woman, Playing Lute, Egg Shape, Covered	125.00
Figurine, Scholar, A.Frilli Firenze, Signed, 26 In.	1800.00
Powder Jar, Art Deco Lady Painted Top, 6 In.	49.00
Vase, Rose, Leaves, S–Handle, 20 In., Pair	1600.00

Alexandrite is a name with many meanings. It is a form of the mineral chrysoberyl that changes from green to red under artificial light. A man–made version of this mineral is sold in Mexico today. It changes from deep purple to aquamarine blue under artificial light. The Alexandrite listed here is glass made in the late nineteenth and twentieth centuries. Thomas Webb & Sons sold their transparent glass shaded from yellow to rose to blue under the name Alexandrite. Stevens and Williams had a cased Alexandrite of yellow, rose, and blue. A. Douglas Nash Corporation made an amethyst–colored Alexandrite. Several American glass companies of the 1920s made a glass that changed color under electric lights and these were called Alexandrite too.

ALEXANDRITE, Spooner, Expanded Diamond Interior, Sapphire Blue, Webb	645.00
Tazza, Honeycomb, Fluted, Pedestal Foot, 5 1/2 X 2 In.	795.00

Alhambra is a pattern of tableware made in Vienna, Austria, in the twentieth century. The geometric designs are in applied gold, red, and dark green. Full sets of dishes can be found in this pattern.

ALHAMBRA, Cup & Saucer, Marked, Cup, 2 3/8 In.	45.00
Plate, 8 1/2 In.	30.00
Sugar & Creamer, Covered, Marked, 4 3/4 In.	110.00

Aluminum was more expensive than gold or silver until the 1850s. Chemists learned how to refine bauxite to get aluminum. Jewelry and other small objects were made of the valuable metal until 1914 when an inexpensive smelting process was invented. The aluminum collected today dates from the 1930s through 1950s. Hand–hammered pieces are the most popular.

ALUMINUM, Basket, Embossed Daisies	15.00
Bucket, Miner's	22.00
Drip–O–Lator, Enterprise Aluminum Co., Flamingos	30.00
Juicer, Fruit, Wearever, Box	15.00
Tray, Hammered, Canterbury Arts, Handles, 7 1/2 X 17 In.	13.00
Tray, Hammered, Partial World Map, A.Armour, 13 X 9 In.	14.00
Tray, Relish, Tulip, Flowerchain Basket Handle, Rodney Kent	14.00
AMBER, see Jewelry	

Amber glass is the name of any glassware with the proper yellow–brown shading. It was a popular color just after the Civil War and many pressed glass pieces were made of amber glass. Depression glass of the 1930s–1950s was also made in shades of amber glass. All types are being reproduced.

AMBER GLASS, Banana Boat, Sterling Silver Overlay, 12 In.	66.00
Bowl, Jersey Swirl, Flat Base, 9 1/2 In.	49.00
Bowl, Rock Crystal, 12 In.	45.00
Cruet, Blown, Applied Aqua Handle, Clambroth Stopper, 8 In.	44.00
Cruet, Blown, Blue Spiral Handle, Faceted Stopper, 9 In.	88.00
Cuspidor, Lady's, Miniature	55.00

Decanter, Hinged Pewter Top, Pewter Holder, 11 1/8 In. 295.00
Decanter, Marked Rye, Silver Overlay 175.00
Dresser Set, Butterfly Design, 6 Piece 85.00
Salt & Pepper, Horseshoe 30.00
Salt, Christmas, Agitator Lid, Dana K.Alden, Pat.1887, 3 In. 70.00
Stein, Munich Maid, Enameled, Prunts At Top & Base, 14 1/2 In. 495.00
Sugar & Creamer, Covered, Fine Cut 50.00
Tumbler, Inverted Thumbprint, Enameled Flowers, 3 3/4 In. 40.00
Vase, Cut, Late 19th Century, 7 In. 85.00
Vase, Engraved Deer, Buildings & Foliage, Flashed, 5 In., Pair 70.00

     AMBERETTE, see Pressed Glass, Klondike

Amberina is a two-toned glassware made from 1883 to about 1900. It was patented by Joseph Locke of the New England Glass Company. The glass shades from red to amber.

AMBERINA, see also Baccarat; Bluerina; Plated Amberina

AMBERINA, Berry Bowl, Daisy & Button, 5 X 5 In. 85.00
Berry Bowl, Daisy & Button, 9 X 9 In. .... 100.00 To 200.00
Castor, Pickle, Inverted Thumbprint, Ribbed 395.00
Celery, Inverted Thumbprint, 3 3/4 X 6 1/2 In. 510.00
Celery, Reverse Thumbprint, Square Ruffled Edge 175.00
Creamer, Inverted Thumbprint, Amber Handle, 3 1/2 In. 165.00
Cruet, Baby Thumbprint, Clear Handle & Stopper 97.50
Cruet, Blown, Handle, Globular Stopper, 19th Century, 6 In. 143.00
Decanter, Enameled Flowers & Leaves, Amber Stopper, 9 In. 275.00
Dish, Daisy & Button, 7 In. .... 300.00 To 325.00
Dish, Ice Cream, Daisy, No.101 .... 145.00
Finger Bowl, Fluted, 5 1/2 X 2 1/2 In. 235.00
Lamp, Daisy & Button, 11 1/2 In. 175.00
Mug, Inverted Thumbprint, Smooth Amber Handle, 2 3/4 In. 50.00
Pitcher, Applied Amber Handle, 10 1/2 In. 165.00
Pitcher, Draped Pattern, Melon Ribbed, Amber Handle, 8 In. 295.00
Pitcher, Herringbone Pattern, Amber Handle, Square, 5 In. 225.00
Pitcher, Inverted Thumbprint, Reeded Handle, Scalloped Top, 9 In. 235.00
Pitcher, Melon Rib, Herringbone, Amber Handle, Square, 5 In. 250.00
Pitcher, New England, Amber Reeded Handle, Square Mouth, 8 In. 225.00
Pitcher, Quatrefoil Rim, Amber Handle, Coin Spot Body, 8 In. 225.00
Pitcher, Square Melon Rib, Herringbone, Amber Handle, 5 In. 250.00
Pitcher, Thumbprint, Scalloped, Clear Handle, 9 1/2 In. 195.00
Plate, Dessert, Daisy & Button, Set of 8 .... 1250.00
Punch Cup, Diamond-Quilted, Smooth Amber Handle, 2 3/4 In. 35.00
Punch Cup, Expanded Diamond, Smooth Amber Handle .... 85.00 To 95.00
Punch Cup, Inverted Thumbprint, Reeded Amber Handle 125.00
Salt & Pepper, Inverted Thumbprint 135.00
Salt Dip, Set of 4 .... 50.00
Saltshaker, Inverted Thumbprint, Tubular Shape, 3 5/8 In. 85.00
Sherry, Ground Pontil, New England Glass, 4 3/8 In. 235.00
Tieback, Pewter Post, Sandwich Glass, 3 1/2 In., Pair 68.00
Toothpick, Baby Thumbprint, 2 1/2 In. 75.00
Toothpick, Thumbprint, 2 In. 185.00
Toothpick, Venetian Diamond 235.00

Glassware, old or new, requires careful handling. Stand each piece upright, not touching another. Never nest pieces. Wash in moderately hot water and mild detergent. Avoid wiping gold or platinum-banded pieces while glasses are hot. Never use scouring pads or silver polish on glass. For an automatic dishwasher, be sure the water temperature is under 180 degrees.

Tumbler, Diamond Pattern, Fuchsia, New England Glass Co. 115.00
Tumbler, Diamond–Quilted, New England, Red To Amber, 3 3/4 In. 90.00
Tumbler, Expanded Diamond, Etched Scroll Design, 4 In. 195.00
Tumbler, Expanded Diamond, Fuchsia 175.00
Tumbler, Honeycomb, Rose To Olive Amber 38.00
Tumbler, Inverted Thumbprint, 3 In., 4 Piece 145.00
Vase, Amber Around Crown, 6 Amber Feet, 12 In. 750.00
Vase, Cranberry To Olive Amber, Gold Floral, 12 3/4 In., Pair 425.00
Vase, Fan, Amber Wishbone Feet, Amber Edging, 8 1/4 In. 135.00
Vase, Fluted Top, Amber Edge, Lion's Head On Feet, 12 1/2 In., Pr. 595.00
Vase, Inverted Thumbprint, Square Mouth, 2 Amber Handles, 5 In. 275.00
Vase, Lily, Fuchsia, 6 1/2 In. 145.00
Vase, Lily, Fuchsia, 9 1/4 In. 175.00
Vase, Scalloped, 11 In. 65.00
Vase, Stork, Joseph Locke 275.00
Vase, Thumbprint, Amber Handles, 5 In. 195.00
Vase, Trumpet, Blown, 7 1/2 In. 165.00
Vase, Trumpet, Ruffled Edge, Blown Circular Foot, 7 1/2 In. 185.00
Vase, Trumpet, Ruffled Edge, Circular Foot, 7 1/2 In. 185.00
Water Set, Reverse Thumbprint, Square Neck, 6 Pear Shaped Mugs 750.00
Whiskey, Diamond–Quilted, 2 5/8 In. 95.00

The American Encaustic Tiling Company was founded in Zanesville, Ohio, in 1875. The company planned to make a variety of tiles to compete with the English tiles that were selling in the United States for use in fireplaces and other architectural needs. The first glazed tiles were made in 1880, embossed tiles were added in 1881, faience tiles in the 1920s. The firm closed in 1935 and reopened in 1937 as the Shawnee Pottery.

AMERICAN ENCAUSTIC TILING CO., Plaque, Portrait of Shepherd, 17 3/4 In. 250.00
Tile, 3 Tile Figure of Woman 225.00
Tile, Mottled Blue, Square, 6 In. 20.00
Tile, Polly Put The Kettle On, 6 X 6 In. 40.00
Tile, Sailing Ship, Framed, 6 X 3 In. 85.00
Tile, Simple Simon, 6 X 6 In. 50.00
Woman, Draped, Blowing Horn, 18 X 6 In. 275.00

Amethyst glass is any of the many glasswares made in the dark purple color of the gemstone called amethyst. Included in this section are many pieces made in the nineteenth and twentieth centuries. Very dark pieces are called black amethyst and are listed under that heading.

AMETHYST GLASS, Bowl, Bigler Variant, 4 1/2 X 3 In. 175.00
Box, Enameled Flowers On Cover, Sprays On Side, 2 3/4 In. 118.00
Canoe, Daisy & Button, 8 In. 30.00
Dish, Hen On Nest Cover, 5 1/2 In. 125.00
Lamp, Masonic Designs, 3 Part Mold, 2 3/4 In. 260.00
Lemonade Set, Silver Overlay, 7 Piece 125.00
Pitcher, Wooden Pail 140.00
Powder Box, Hinged Gold & Enamel Lid, Pair 225.00
Punch Bowl Set, Gold Scroll Trim, Ladle, 18 In.Bowl, 8 Pc. 995.00
Rose Bowl, Swirl Hobnail, Dark 300.00
Salt & Pepper, Enameled Flowers, Silver Plated Holder 145.00
Sheet, Art Deco, 1/2 In.Thick, 28 X 53 In. 500.00
Sugar & Creamer, Silver Overlay 65.00
Tankard, Enameled Horse Head, Pewter Rimmed Top, C.1850 .... 135.00
Tumbler, 8 Flute Pattern, Hexagon Shape Base, 3 5/8 In. 100.00
Vase, 3–Pronged Tree Stump, Thorns, 6 In. 45.00
Vase, Carved Peonies, Buds, Leaves, Peony Finial Lid, 9 In. 375.00
Vase, Swirled Trumpet Body, Hexagonal Base, 8 In. 100.00
AMPHORA, see Teplitz
ANDIRON AND RELATED FIREPLACE ITEMS, see Fireplace

Stuffed animals or fish, rugs made of animal skins, and other similar collectibles are listed in this section. Collectors should be aware of the endangered species laws that make it illegal to buy and sell some of these items. Any eagle feathers, many types of cats, such as leopard, and many forms of tortoiseshell can be confiscated if discovered by the government.

ANIMAL TROPHY, Bear Head, Mounted 125.00
   Bearskin, Kodiak, Head, Claws, Hanging 2500.00
   Beaver, Chewing Log, Full Body 255.00
   Bobcat, Head Mount, Pelt 250.00
   Brown Bear, Full Body, 6 1/2 Ft. 1450.00
   Buffalo Head, Mounted 450.00
   Deer Head, Antlers, Large 85.00
   Frog Band, Carved Instruments, 8 1/4 In., 12 Piece 120.00
   Horns, Big Horn Sheep 20.00
   Mountain Goat Head .... 150.00 To 175.00
   Muskrat, Albino, Eastern Shore, Mounted 110.00
   Peacock, Full Body 100.00
   Texas Long Horns, 6 Ft. 150.00
   Warthog, African, Head Mount, Tusks, 13 In. 435.00
   Water Buffalo, Head & Shoulders 825.00
   Wild Boar Head, Mounted 150.00
   Wild Turkey, Mounted, Full Body 100.00

Animation cels are painted drawings on celluloid that are needed to make an animated cartoon. Hundreds of cels are made, then photographed in sequence to make a cartoon showing moving figures. The earliest examples were by the Walt Disney Studios, but even today animation art continues to be made.

ANIMATION ART, Book, Wizard of Oz, Julian Wheir 30.00
   Cel, Aristocats, 2 Male Kittens, Movie, Matted, Disney 35.00
   Cel, Barney, From Flintstones, Matted 55.00
   Cel, Bear, Jungle Book 85.00
   Cel, Beatles, Lucy In The Sky, 1968, 9 3/4 X 13 1/2 In. 1100.00
   Cel, Bugs Bunny & Friends, Warner Brothers 20.00
   Cel, Chip & Dale, Working For Peanuts, 1952, 8 In. 660.00
   Cel, Cinderella 150.00
   Cel, Der Fuehrer's Face, 1943, 7 1/2 X 9 In. 2090.00
   Cel, Donald Duck & Jiminy Cricket, Label 100.00
   Cel, Donald Duck & Jose Carioca, Three Caballeros, 1945 .... 600.00
   Cel, Donald Duck's Nephews, Framed, 1940s, 7 1/2 X 10 In. 220.00
   Cel, Lady & Tramp 290.00
   Cel, Mickey Mouse 350.00
   Cel, Mother Goose Goes Hollywood, Walt Disney, 1938, 8 In. 825.00
   Cel, Pinocchio, Jiminy Cricket Removing Hat, 1939, 9 1/2 In. 3850.00
   Cel, Pinocchio, Submerged, Seahorses, Bubbles, 1939, 7 3/4 In. 2970.00
   Cel, Pinocchio, Walt Disney Studios, C.1941 .... 3575.00
   Cel, Possum, Terrytoons, 1967 .... 25.00
   Cel, Snow White & The Seven Dwarfs, Dopey Sweeping, 9 In. 2640.00
   Cel, Snow White, Chipmunk, Pie, 1937, 8 1/2 X 7 1/2 In. 2090.00
   Cel, Tinkerbell, Cowboy Outfit, Matted, Framed, Walt Disney 65.00
   Cel, Winnie The Pooh, C.1970 .... 165.00
   Cel, Winnie The Pooh, In Rabbit Hole, Matted, Walt Disney 50.00

The Anna Pottery was started in Anna, Illinois, in 1859 by Cornwall and Wallace Kirkpatrick. They made many types of utilitarian wares, bricks, drain tiles, and gift ware. The most collectible pieces made by the pottery are the pig-shaped bottles and jugs with special inscriptions, applied animals and figures. The pottery closed in 1894.

ANNA POTTERY, Inkwell, Green Frog Sits On Brown Rock, Dated 1879 .... 600.00
   APPLE PEELER, see Kitchen, Peeler, Apple

This section includes a variety of collectibles, usually very large, that have been removed from buildings. Hardware, backbars, doors, paneling, and even old bathtubs are now wanted by collectors. Pieces of the Victorian, Art Nouveau, and Art Deco styles are in greatest demand.

ARCHITECTURAL, Altar Bar, Carved Leaf Design, Hard Maple Top, 7 Ft. 700.00
Backbar, Drugstore, Marble Top, Stained Glass, 8 1/2 Ft. 2750.00
Backbar, Showcases, Drugstore, Oak, American, 80 Ft. 5500.00
Backbar, Soda Fountain, Stained Glass, 62 In. X 9 Ft. 3500.00
Backbar, Soda, Stained Glass Panels, Cherry, Mahogany, 9 Ft. 3600.00
Bar, Corner, Home, Raised Panel Mahogany, Beveled Mirrors 6500.00
Bathtub, Child's, Lead 150.00
Bathtub, Copper, Claw Feet 595.00
Bathtub, Portable, Folding 250.00
Bin, Grain, Original Red Buttermilk Paint 165.00
Bin, Pine, Primitive, Worn Red Paint, 41 1/2 X 24 X 33 In. 95.00
Booth, Phone, Oak, Double Wall Construction, 1 Pc.Door, 1915 .... 2200.00
Cabinet, 80 Drawers On Top, 24 Drawers On Bottom, Wood 1200.00
Capital, From State House, Boston, C.1795, 33 In. 3000.00
Column, Fluted Mahogany, Carved Corinthian Capital, 50 In. 175.00
Commode, Cottage Type, Painted Wood Grain & Burl, 1870 .... 275.00
Cornice, Stenciled Basket of Fruit Design, 42 1/2 In., Pair 1700.00
Cupboard, Built-In, Red, 1 Door, From Old Ship's Church 525.00
Door Knocker, Brass, Putti, Scrolled Shield, On Board, 8 In. 350.00
Door Pull, Mercury, 1880 .... 18.00
Door, Bevel Glass Window, Mahogany, 2 Panels, 3 X 7 Ft. 1250.00
Door, Original Gray, Iron Key Box, 18th Century 75.00
Door, Oval Leaded Beveled Window, Mahogany, 3 X 7 Ft. 875.00
Door, Saloon, Carved Panels, Beveled Windows, Pair 850.00
Door, Saloon, Oak, Stained Glass 300.00
Door, Saloon, Swinging, Oak, Set of 2 .... 295.00
Door, Side Windows, Leaded Glass Panels, 7 Ft., 3 Piece 3750.00
Doorknob, Egg Shape, Brass, Patented 1880, Set 25.00
Doorknob, N.Y.C.Board of Education 15.00
Eagle, Cast Iron, From New York State Building 375.00
Eagle, Perched On Sphere, White, Cast Iron, C.1880, 24 In. 1500.00
Eagle, Pilot House, Cast Iron, American, C.1880 .... 775.00
Eagle, Standing, Metal, Concrete Base, Large 250.00
Fountain, 2 Children Cavort With Dolphin, Cast Lead, 27 In. 1000.00
Fountain, Neo–Classical, Lead, French, 41 X 30 In. 400.00
Garden Gate, Iron, Serpentine Design, Red Paint, 51 X 36 In. 175.00
Leaded Glass Dome, With Ceiling Fixture, Yellow Slag Brick 400.00
Mantel, Floral Center Panel, Ebonized Pilasters, 48 3/4 In. 110.00
Mantel, George III, Carved Pine, 4 Ft.7 In.X 6 Ft.7 In. 9000.00
Mantel, Pine, Marble Painted, New England, 1830, 51 X 62 In. 150.00
Mantel, Pine, Primitive, Southern American, 1875 .... 300.00
Newell Post, Walnut, Custom Made, Mid–1800s 325.00
Ornament, 2 Sailing Ships On Either Side of Globe, 5 Ft. 2240.00
Ornament, Roof, Chinese, Late 19th Century, 9 1/2 In. 275.00
Ornament, Schooners, Grid Hemisphere, Bronze, 34 X 65 In. 2200.00
Panel, German Head, Kingfisher, Lilies, Rushes, 19 X 8 In. 115.00
Pew, Church, Oak, 5 Ft. 250.00
Phone Booth, Glass On 3 Sides, Wooden, 1920s 325.00
Pillar, Driveway, Concrete, Ornate, Square, 3 X 2 In., Pair 250.00
Rack, 4 Shelves, National Biscuit Co., Oak, 47 X 72 In. 300.00
Shoeshine Stand, Oak, 2 Chairs 1500.00
Showcase, Oak, 1887 .... 200.00
Soda Fountain, Marble, Ice Cream Chest, 12 Ft. 2750.00
Staircase, Circular, Rails, 35 Step, Cast Iron, 1911, 27 Ft. 2250.00
Staircase, Spiral, Iron, Pierced Steps, J & A Law, 94 In. 4250.00
Stoplight, Not Working, Large, 1920 .... 400.00
Sundial, Brass, Masonic Symbolism, 1763, 8 X 8 In. 175.00
Thumb Latch, Door, Cast Iron, Complete Set 15.00

Toilet Seat, Mahogany	48.00
Trolley Fare Box, With Lighted Stand, Early 20th Century	95.00
Urn, Garden, Lead, 14 In., Pair	1320.00

Arequipa Pottery was produced from 1911 to 1918 by the patients of the Arequipa Sanitorium in Marin County Hills, California.

AREQUIPA, Bowl, Scalloped Top, Lavender, 7 X 3 In.	45.00
Vase, Blue, Incised Floral, 5 In.	300.00

ARGY–ROUSSEAU, see G.Argy–Rousseau

Arita is a port in Japan. Porcelain was made there from about 1616. Many types of decorations were used, including the popular Imari designs, which are listed under Imari in this book.

ARITA, Ginger Jar, Flowers, Blue, Red, 8 In.	500.00
Plate, Birds, Flowers, Red, Green, Blue, 10 In.	125.00
Vase, Polychrome Birds, Flowers, Mt.Fuji Ground, Signed, 9 In., Pair	175.00

Art Deco, or Art Moderne, a style started at the Paris Exposition of 1925, is characterized by linear, geometric designs. All types of furniture and decorative arts, jewelry, book bindings, and even games were designed in this style.

ART DECO, Ashtray, Bisque Nude Figure, White, Porcelain, 6 X 3 In.	65.00
Ashtray, Female Head, Flowing Hair, Frosted Glass, 8 In.	200.00
Bookend, Flamingo, Gold Paint, Iron, Pair	75.00
Bookends, Musicians, Gilded, Pair	100.00
Bowl, Ducks, Black Ground, Solian Ware, Soho, Jacobean, 13 In.	80.00
Bowl, With Nude Figurine Interior, Salmon, Poppy Trail, Romanelli	95.00
Box, Powder, Nudes, Pink Frosted, Ramses, Paris, N.Y.	65.00
Box, Silvered Metal, Floriform Handle, E.Brandt, 1925, 8 In.	1980.00
Candlestick, Eiffel Tower, Amberina, 10 1/2 In.	85.00
Chandelier, Frosted Glass, 7–Light, Multicolor, 30 X 22 In.	700.00
Clock, Mantel, Chimes Half Hour & Hour	110.00
Cocktail Set, Cobalt Blue, Sterling Overlay, 1920s, 9 Piece	375.00
Console Set, Deep Amber, 3 Piece	100.00
Dish, Pin, Embossed Clown Head On Cover, Germany, 2 1/4 In.	25.00
Dresser Set, Gold, Silver Triangles On Lid, Germany, 4 Piece	95.00
Ewer, Black, White & Gold, Waldershof, Bavarian, 13 In.	265.00
Figurine, Dancer, Nude, Egyptian, Lying On Tummy, Black, 14 In.	275.00
Figurine, Dancing Girl, Tambourine, Black Marble, Sam Lipchytz	2100.00
Figurine, Duck, Guillard, France, 9 In.	65.00
Figurine, Sitting Black Cat, Glazed, 12 In.	55.00
Flower Frog, Dancer, Hand Painted, Germany, 6 1/2 In.	29.00
Holder, Pen, Marble	85.00
Incense Burner, Nude Lady, Basket, Metal, Bronze Finish, 6 1/4 In.	10.00
Jar, Embossed Willow of Boston, Real Perfumer, Brass Lid, Large	69.00
Lamp, Nude Girl Sitting On Rock, Looking Into Light	125.00
Lunch Box, Train Oval Shape	39.00
Plate, Imperial Roman Scene, Sicar, Czechoslovakia, 10 3/4 In.	75.00
Plate, Lady's Head Profile, Pink Poppies In Hair, 8 1/2 In.	45.00
Powder Box, Flapper Head Finial, Frosted Green, Nudes Sides	34.00
Powder Jar, Green Glass, Seminude Handle, Nudes On Base, Ramses	17.50
Powder Jar, Harlequin Clown Head Finial, Vaseline Satin, 12 Feet	39.00
Shade, Lamp, Double Nude Mercury	190.00
Sugar & Creamer, Orange, Green, Lavender	25.00
Table Set, Nursery Rhyme, 4 Piece	250.00
Tete–A–Tete Set, Child's, Green Luster, Red Hearts, 7 Piece	200.00
Tete–A–Tete Set, Red Hearts, Green Ground, Blue Trim	175.00
Tray Set, Pink Flamingos On Black, 10 Piece	35.00
Vase, Disc Shape, Ballerina, Standing Beside, Ceramic	17.00
Vase, Enameled On Copper, Faceted Ovoid Form, Limoges, 12 1/4 In.	4125.00
Vase, Graduating Rings, Orange Cut To Clear, 3 In.	55.00
Vase, Orange, Tulips, Black Trim, Bulbous, Czechoslovakia, 10 In.	45.00

Art glass means any of the many forms of glassware made during the late nineteenth century or early twentieth century. These wares were expensive and production was limited. Art glass is not the typical commercial glass that was made in large quantities, and most of the art glass was produced by hand methods.

ART GLASS, see also separate headings such as Burmese; Cameo Glass; Tiffany; etc.

ART GLASS, Basket, Applied Cherries, 7 In.	225.00
Basket, Herringbone, Shaded Pink, Quatrefoil Rim, 9 1/2 In.	350.00
Basket, Maroon Swirl Striped Overlay, Applied Handle, 7 In.	165.00
Basket, Rose Bowl Shape, Opaque, Pink Applied Flowers, 8 In.	195.00
Basket, White To Apricot, 6 1/2 X 8 In.	155.00
Bottle, Aqua, Globular, 16 Rib Mold, Folded Rim, 7 1/2 In.	170.00
Bottle, Cologne, Swirl, Threaded, Stopper, 10 Sides, 1870s, 3 In.	185.00
Bowl, 3 Molded Birds, Lalique Style, 1900, 8 In.	100.00
Bowl, Amethyst, Turned Down Rim, Enameled Floral, 9 1/2 In.	135.00
Bowl, Iridescent Blue, Art Nouveau Bronze Holder, Handles, 7 In.	75.00
Bowl, Lemon To Tangerine, White Ground, Tangerine, 4 In.	135.00
Bull's Eye, Tiffany Type, Iridescent Pink & Gold, Rondel	190.00
Candleholder, Crystal Twisted Thorn Stem, 8 In.	275.00
Candleholder, Pulled Feather Gold Shades, Brass, Handle, Pair	895.00
Compote, 12 Panel, Engraved Leaf & Daisy, Bakewell, 9 1/2 In.	5200.00
Cordial Set, 6 Cut Panels, Gold Florals, Lobmyer, 5 Piece	585.00
Darner, Sock, Cased Opaque White, Red Loopings, 7 1/4 In.	525.00
Dish, Sweetmeat, Pink Overlay, Silver Plated Holder, 5 1/2 In.	95.00
Dish, White Ground, Pink, Blue & Yellow Striped, Overlay, 7 In.	125.00
Ewer, White, Tricorner, Pink & Blue Stripes, Overlay, 7 In., Pair	210.00
Flower Holder, Bridge Shape, Enameled Floral, 8 1/2 In.	75.00
Inkwell, Brass Lid, Art Nouveau Head, Iridescent Purple	225.00
Lamp Base, Green Aventurine, Miniature	50.00
Panel, Molded Pink, Swan, Pond, Framed, Hunebelle, 34 X 63 In.	4400.00
Pitcher, Emerald, Lily of The Valley, Applied Handle, 4 In.	32.00
Pitcher, Floral Design, Yellow Orange, 13 In.	1150.00
Plate, Dancing Nudes, Pink, Consolidated Glass, 7 1/2 In.	75.00
Rolling Pin, Aqua, White Looping, 14 1/2 In.	160.00
Salt & Pepper, Fish, Pink Cased	75.00
Shade, Vaseline Glass, Stalactite Flame Shape, 8 In.	125.00
Vase & Underplate, Pink, Ruffled, Enameled Flowers, 11 In.	195.00
Vase, Autumn, Enameled Design, Autumn Leaves, D.Labino, 4 In.	350.00
Vase, Blue Satin Ribbon Design, Orange Ground, Bulbous, 9 In.	130.00
Vase, Blue, Gray, Iridescent, Bulbous, Lundberg Studios, 5 In.	50.00
Vase, Cranberry To Clear, Enameled White Floral Sprays, 11 In.	85.00
Vase, Enameled Green, Floral, Iridescent, 10 1/2 In.	70.00
Vase, Floral Design, Frosted Rose Base, Blue Top, 8 1/2 In.	200.00
Vase, Green, Gold Coil Wrapped, Iridescent, Hand Blown, 9 In.	40.00
Vase, Green, Goldstone, Enameling, Narrow Top, Lobmyer, 3 1/2 In.	250.00
Vase, Molded Relief, Pink Overlay, 1870, 10 In., Pair	45.00
Vase, Orient & Flume, Gold Iridescent, Footed, Signed, 4 5/8 In.	45.00
Vase, White Opalescent, Violet Blossoms, 13 1/2 In., Pair	245.00

Art Nouveau is a style of design that was at its most popular from 1895 to 1905. Famous designers, including Rene Lalique and Emile Galle, produced furniture, glass, silver, metalwork, and buildings in the new style. Ladies with long flowing hair and elongated bodies were among the more easily recognized design elements. Copies of this style are being made today. Many modern pieces of jewelry can be found.

ART NOUVEAU, see also Furniture; various glass categories; etc.

ART NOUVEAU, Ashtray, Floor, Girl, Standing	190.00
Ashtray, Nude, 4 1/2 In.	18.00
Book Rack, Lady's Faces, Brass Finish	44.00
Firescreen, French Bronze, Dragonfly, Whiplashes, Signed	1150.00
Humidor, Lady's Head Sculpted, Flowers In Hair, Austria	165.00

Lamp, Crouching Female, Silver Leaf, Opaline Shade, 20 In.	145.00
Lemonade Set, China, Signed Sunquist, Vienna, 9 Piece	175.00
Plate, Lady's Portrait, Pair	200.00
Plate, Spaniel Portrait	65.00
Salt & Pepper, Sterling Silver, 5 In.	32.50

The first American art pottery was made in Cincinnati, Ohio, during the 1870s. The pieces were hand thrown and hand decorated. The art pottery tradition continued until the 1920s when studio potters began making the more artistic wares.

ART POTTERY, see also under factory name

ART POTTERY, Box, Cigarette, White, Circle Design, Marked, 5 1/2 X 2 In.	12.50
Figurine, Lion, Stalking, Dickota, 16 In.	220.00
Figurine, Mr.Pickwick, Bretby, 9 In.	115.00
Lamp, Pierced Copper & Slag Shade, C.1905, 14 1/2 In.	600.00
Mug, Pinched Devil Portrait, Green Glaze, Walley, 5 1/2 In.	350.00
Plaque, Moonlit Landscape, Hand-Painted, 6 X 10 In. ....*Illus*	210.00
Spoon-Warmer, Grotesque Red Toad, Bermantoft, 1885, 6 In.	145.00
Tea Set, Byrdcliffe, 4 Piece	475.00
Urn, Stand, 3 Lobed Molded Woman Busts, French, 4 Ft.8 3/4 In.	3575.00
Vase, 2 Dragon Handles, Turquoise, Burmantofts, 1880, 13 In.	215.00
Vase, Black, Rosecraft, Part Paper Label, 7 In.	20.00
Vase, Blue, Fluted, Georgia, 7 In.	20.00
Vase, Clover Edge, Raised Foot, Bennett Pottery, C.1880, 5 In.	1900.00
Vase, Covered, Seed Poppy, Blue Ground, Signed, 15 1/2 In.	240.00
Vase, Enameled Bird Design, Bretby, 9 In., Pair	95.00
Vase, Flowers, Gilt Bronze Mount, Handles, 34 In.	1320.00
Vase, Gunmetal Drip Glaze Over Gray, Walley, 6 In.	325.00
Vase, Handles, Green, Brannam Barum, 7 In.	40.00
Vase, Merrimac, Carved Back Undulating Leaves	3850.00

ARTHUR OSBORNE, see Ivorex

AURENE Aurene glass was made by Frederick Carder of New York about 1904. It is an iridescent gold or blue glass, usually marked "Aurene" or "Steuben."

AURENE, Basket, Berry Prunts Each Side, Gold, Blue, Signed, 6 X 7 1/2 In.	800.00
Bottle, Perfume, Purple & Silver Highlights, Signed, 7 3/4 In.	495.00
Bowl, Blue Globe Shape, Pink & Gold Base, Ground Pontil, 5 1/2 In.	300.00
Bowl, Gold, Marked, 7 3/4 X 3 In.	200.00
Bowl, Silver Blue, Millefiori Flowers, Green Vine, 2 In.	2300.00
Candlestick, Blue Iridescent, Signed, 4 1/2 In.	255.00
Compote, Iridescent Gold, Signed, 6 1/4 In.	425.00
Decanter, Blue, Signed, 5 7/8 In.	725.00
Goblet, Twist Stem, Signed	216.00
Perfume Atomizer, Melon Ribbed, Signed, 5 In.	250.00
Rose Bowl, Ribbed Body, Scalloped Turned-In Top Rim, 3 In.	275.00
Sherbet, Underplate, Calcite, 2 Piece	135.00
Vase, Blue Iridescent, Signed, 5 In.	475.00
Vase, Bud, Gold Iridescent, 3 Sections, Steuben, C.1920, 6 1/4 In.	375.00
Vase, Bud, Trumpet Shape, Blue, Signed, 6 In.	395.00
Vase, Flower Form, No.184, Signed, 9 3/4 In.	950.00
Vase, Pinch Bottle, Iridescent Gold, Signed, 5 1/2 In.	395.00
Vase, Ruffled & Stretched Top, Butterscotch, Signed, 5 1/2 In.	275.00
Vase, Turquoise Blue, Purple & Silver Highlights, Blue, 3 1/4 In.	975.00

AUSTRIA, see Royal Dux; Kauffmann; Porcelain

Auto parts and accessories are collectors' items today. Gas pump globes and license plates are part of this specialty. Prices are determined by age, rarity, and condition.

AUTO, Book, Chevrolet Owner's Manual, 62 Pages, 1942	20.00
Book, Chevrolet, Car & Truck, Construction, Operation, 1932	37.50
Booklet, Operation & Care National Motor Car, Script From Car	100.00
Bottle, Oil, Standard Polerine, Embossed, 150-VIS Label, 1 Qt.	35.00
Buckle, Belt, Plymouth, 1 Year Safe Driver Award, Initial CED, 1937-39	25.00

Buckle, Model T Ford, Fancy Front, Back Signed, 1913–14 .... 65.00
Cabinet, Tire Gauge Shape, Contents, Original Paint, C.1930, 2 In. 169.50
Can, Grease, Phillips, 1 Lb. 8.00
Can, Lube, Texaco, 1 Gal. 14.00
Can, Oil, Ford, Small 9.00
Can, Oil, Mobil, 5 Qt. 18.00
Can, Oil, Phillips, Maroon & Red Logo, 1 Qt. 9.00
Can, Oil, Primrose, Full, 1 Qt. 12.50
Can, Oil, Texaco, Square, 5 Gal. 35.00
Can, Oil, Utility, 1 Qt. 9.00
Card, Playing, Nash 20.00
Charm, Mercedes Logo, 14K Gold 22.00
Chime Whistle, Auto Exhaust, Brass, 15 In. 65.00
Coil, Model T Ford 2.50
Coupon Book, Auto Supply, 1930 .... 5.00
Display, Pontiac Indian, Feathered Headdress Shaped 10.00
Gas Pump Globe, Aetna, Glass Body 95.00
Gas Pump Globe, Champlin, Plastic Body 125.00
Gas Pump Globe, Coltex Service Gasoline 155.00
Gas Pump Globe, Elroco, Buy Miles Not Gallons 225.00
Gas Pump Globe, MFA 125.00
Gas Pump Globe, Mobilgas, Metal Frame, 15 In. 190.00
Gas Pump Globe, Newport Gasoline, 1 Piece 285.00
Gas Pump Globe, Paraland Gas, Oval 150.00
Gas Pump Globe, Shamrock 95.00
Gas Pump Globe, Shell 190.00
Gas Pump Globe, Skelley Keotone, Plastic 85.00
Gas Pump Globe, Skelly Premium .... 145.00 To 155.00
Gas Pump Globe, Standard Crown Gas, Blue 275.00
Gas Pump Globe, Standard Oil, Red Crown 265.00
Gas Pump Globe, Standard Oil, White Crown 175.00
Gas Pump Globe, Standard's Blue Crown, Aviation Fuel 290.00
Gas Pump Globe, Texaco, Leaded Glass 2500.00
Gas Pump Globe, Tharps Anti–Knock Gas 250.00
Gas Token, Mobil Good Luck 8.00
Gasoline Gauge, Atwater Kent 22.00
Gauge Stick, Gas, Ford 4.00
Gauge, Tire, Model T Ford 9.00
Gauge, Tire, Peerless, Dial 50.00
Goggles, Touring, Tinted, Wilson 15.00
Hanger, Folding, 1930 .... 8.50
Headlight, Model T Ford, Glass Jewels 65.00
     AUTO, HOOD ORNAMENT, see also Lalique
Hood Ornament, Art Deco, Flying Lady, Box 45.00
Hood Ornament, Bulldog, Mack, Chrome, Base 4 1/4 In. 18.00
Hood Ornament, Female With Wings 9.00
Hood Ornament, Ford Greyhound, 1933 .... 65.00
Hood Ornament, Nude, Colored Plastic Wings 50.00
Hood Ornament, Pontiac 45.00
Hood Ornament, Ram, Dodge, 1934 .... 24.95
Hood Ornament, Roland Pilain, Winged Spinx, 1930 .... 110.00
Horn, Brass, Circular Bulb No.14 Is Torn 17.50
Horn, Model A Ford, 1930 .... 14.00
Hubcap, Cadillac, 5 In. 35.00
Hubcap, Essex, Aluminum, 2 3/4 In. 18.00
Hubcap, Jeffery, Base 4 1/2 In. 35.00
Hubcap, Model T Ford 8.00
Hubcap, Nash, Aluminum 18.00
Hubcap, Sphynx, Winged, Bust, Round, Base 3 In. 45.00
Inspection Sticker, Pennsylvania, World War II 5.00
Jack, Model T Ford, 2 In.Height Extension 15.00
Keychain, Texaco, Scottie, 1936 .... 16.00
Knob, Gear Shift, Off White Glass, Brown Swirl, Metal Threaded 20.00
Knob, Gearshift, Red & White Swirl 15.00

Lamp, Edison Mazda, Original General Electric Container 35.00
Lamp, Table, Packard, 12 Auto Parts 110.00
License Attachment, Drive Safely, Mobilgas 25.00
License Plate, Alabama, 1941 .... 15.00
License Plate, Alabama, National Guard, 1973 .... 2.50
License Plate, Alaska, 1954, Truck 20.50
License Plate, Canada, North West Territories, 1977, Bear Shape 12.50
License Plate, Canada, Ontario, 1959 .... 2.50
License Plate, Colorado, 1937 .... 10.50
License Plate, Colorado, Handicap, 1974 .... 5.50
License Plate, Connecticut, 1917 .... 13.50
License Plate, Florida, 1957 .... 10.00
License Plate, Florida, 1968 .... 4.00
License Plate, Georgia, 1941, Peach Decal 60.00
License Plate, Germany, Agriculture, Green On White 5.50
License Plate, Illinois, 1945, Soybean 15.00
License Plate, Illinois, 1951 .... 3.25
License Plate, Indiana, 1938, Chauffeur's 7.50
License Plate, Iowa, 1929 .... 6.50
License Plate, Iowa, 1932 .... 5.00
License Plate, Kentucky, 1928 .... 15.50
License Plate, Maine, 1915 .... 45.00
License Plate, Massachusetts, 1915 .... 17.00
License Plate, Michigan, 1937 .... 6.00
License Plate, Minnesota, 1915 .... 20.50
License Plate, Mississippi, 1932 .... 7.50
License Plate, Montana, 1961, Prison Made 10.00
License Plate, Nebraska, 1942 .... 12.00
License Plate, Nevada, 1965 .... 4.00
License Plate, New Hampshire, 1915, Porcelain 65.00
License Plate, New Hampshire, 1917 .... 50.00
License Plate, New Jersey, 1912 .... 20.00
License Plate, New Jersey, 1915, Porcelain 60.00
License Plate, New Mexico, 1944 .... 11.00
License Plate, New York, 1922 .... 7.50
License Plate, Ohio, 1920 .... 11.50
License Plate, Pennsylvania, 1983, Pittsburgh Bicentennial 3.00
License Plate, Telephone Co., Line Repairman's 58.00
License Plate, U.S.Forces In Germany, 1959 .... 15.50
License Plate, Washington, D.C., 1967 .... 5.50
License Plate, West Virginia, 1927 .... 17.50
License Plate, Wyoming, 1942 .... 12.00
Light, Hupmobile 40.00
Luggage Rack, Model T 35.00
Manual, Owners, Maxwell, 1918 .... 35.00
Motometer, Packard, With Crossbar, 1923 .... 60.00
Ornament, Bulldog, Mack Truck 30.00
Pliers, Ford Script 18.00
Radiator Cap, 1927 Chrysler, Brass, Winged, Marked 45.00
Screwdriver, Ratchet, Ford, Truck Dept.Gift, 3 Recessed Blades 26.00
Sign, Ford Authorized Service Station, Porcelain, 27 X 60 In. 135.00
Sign, Mack Truck Service, Porcelain, 27 X 60 In. 95.00
Sign, Nash Authorized Service, Porcelain, 42 X 42 In. 125.00
Sign, Restroom Key Holder, Texaco 22.00
Speedometer, Cadillac, Brass, 1909–19 .... 450.00
Spotlight, Buick, On Arm, 1929 .... 25.00
Tester, Sparkplug, Champion, With Coil 35.00
Tin, Captain Motor Oil, Pictures Early Car, 1930, 2 Gal. 35.00
Tire Gauge, Brass, Model A 10.50
Tire Tester, Motometer 10.00
Tool Key, Mechanic's Chevrolet 125.00
Tool, Gauge Setter, Adjusting Spark Plugs, Brass, 8 Sizes, 2 1/2 In. 12.50
Turn Signal Set, Montgomery Ward, Self–Cancelling, 1935–50 Car, Box 75.00
Windshield Wiper, 8 In. 5.00

Wrench, Ford Script, 9 In. 6.50
Wrench, Ford, 6 Point Boxed End, Open Other End, No.35 .... 24.00
Wrench, Ford, Dated 1917, 5 1/4 In. 9.00
Wrench, Maxwell 8.00
Wrench, Pierce Arrow 25.00

Autumn Leaf pattern china was made for the Jewel Tea Company from 1933. Hall China Company of East Liverpool, Ohio, Crooksville China Company of Crooksville, Ohio, Harker Potteries of Chester, West Virginia, and Paden City Pottery, Paden City, West Virginia, made dishes with this design. Autumn Leaf has remained popular and was still being made by Hall China Company until 1978. Some other pieces in the Autumn Leaf pattern are still being made.

AUTUMN LEAF, Baker, Round, 8 In. 14.00
Bean Pot, Handle, Hall 375.00
Booklet, Jewel News, 2 Issues, 1930 & 1931 .... 15.00
Bowl, Vegetable, Round, Jewel Tea, 9 In. 40.00
Butter, Covered, 4 Lb. 60.00
Butter, Covered, Jewel Tea, 1/4 Lb. 110.00
Butter, Covered, Square Handle, Jewel Tea, 1/4 Lb. 345.00
Cake Carrier, Jewel Tea 18.00
Cake Plate, Footed 125.00
Cake Plate, Jewel Tea, Hall, 9 1/2 In. 8.00
Cake Safe 35.00
Candy Dish, Covered 375.00
Canister Set, Square, Hall, 4 Piece 130.00
Card, Deck, Jewel Tea 100.00
Casserole, Covered, 2 Qt. 18.00
Clock, Jewel Tea .... 335.00 To 400.00
Coffee Maker, Drip, Insert, 4 Piece 195.00
Coffeepot, Jewel Tea, Dripolator 37.50
Cookie Jar, Big Ears 95.00
Cookie Jar, Jewel Tea 115.00
Cooler, Picnic, Jewel Tea 400.00
Creamer, Jewel Tea, Flower, White, 5 In. 20.00
Cup & Saucer, Jewel Tea .... 6.50 To 15.00
Dish, Soup, Flanged, Edwards, 9 In. 23.00
Dish, Tidbit, 3 Tier 53.00
Drip Jar, Covered, Hall 10.00
Fork, Olive, Jewel Tea 30.00
Goblet, Iced Tea, Frosted, Jewel Tea 12.00
Gravy Boat, Leaf Shape, Jewel Tea, Hall 12.00
Mug, Beverage, Gold Trim 32.00
Mug, Cone, Hall 55.00
Mug, Irish Coffee, Jewel Tea .... 50.00 To 80.00
Mug, Irish Coffee, Set of 4 .... 225.00
Mustard, Covered, Underplate 40.00
Percolator, Electric, Jewel Tea 320.00
Pitcher, Ball Jug 16.00
Pitcher, Jewel Tea, 5 3/4 In. 20.00
Plate, D–Style, Ruffled, 10 In. 8.00
Plate, Jewel Tea, 9 In. .... 5.00 To 10.00
Plate, Jewel Tea, 10 In. 10.00
Platter, Jewel Tea, 13 In. 15.00
Range Set, 3 Piece 25.00
Shelf Paper, Jewel Tea, 4 Sheets, Original Wrapper 50.00
Sifter, Jewel Tea 125.00
Soup, Hall, Flat 8.00
Sugar & Creamer, Ribbed, Jewel Tea 50.00
Tablecloth, Jewel Tea, 54 X 72 In. .... 65.00 To 85.00
Teapot, Aladdin, Jewel Tea .... 28.00 To 40.00
Teapot, Aladdin, With Infuser 38.50
Teapot, Jewel Tea, Long Spout, 7 In. .... 39.50 To 60.00

Teapot, Newport, Jewel Tea	125.00
Tray, Metal, Red Trim	45.00
Tray, Tidbit, 3 Tier	55.00
Tray, Wooden Handles, 19 1/2 X 11 In.	65.00
Truck, Jewel Tea, Metal, Old, Modern Delivery Truck, 3 In., Pr.	4.00
Tumbler, Brockway, Jewel Tea, 13 Oz.	15.00
Tumbler, Frosted, 12 Oz.	10.00
Tumbler, Frosted, 5 1/2 In.	15.00
Tumbler, Frosted, 5 5/8 In.	10.00
Tumbler, Jewel Tea, 14 Oz.	12.00
Tumbler, Jewel Tea, Frosted, 5 1/2 In., Set of 8	85.00
Tumbler, Juice, Frosted, Jewel Tea, 9 Oz.	20.00
Vase, Bud	150.00
Warmer, Oval, Jewel Tea	125.00
Warmer, Round, Jewel Tea	114.00

AVON, see Bottle, Avon

Baccarat glass was made in France by La Compagnie des Cristalleries de Baccarat, located 150 miles from Paris. The factory was started in 1765. The firm went bankrupt and began operating again about 1822. Cane and millefiori paperweights were made during the 1860 to 1880 period. The firm is still working near Paris making paperweights and glasswares.

BACCARAT, Bottle, Cologne, Rose Teinte, Embossed Swirl, 6 3/4 In.	68.00
Bottle, Perfume, Atomizer, Etched Floral, Chrome Top, Signed	80.00
Bottle, Perfume, Ciro 4, 4 In.	45.00
Bottle, Perfume, Diamond Cut	70.00
Bottle, Perfume, Diamond Cut Crystal, 5 1/2 In.	65.00
Bottle, Perfume, Pinwheel Pattern, Stopper, 1935, 6 1/4 In.	45.00
Bottle, Perfume, Rose Teinte, Square, 8 In.	98.00
Bottle, Perfume, Shalimar, Carnival Glass Stopper, Box	78.00
Bowl & Garniture, Crystal	3300.00
Bowl, Swirled To Gold Trimmed Rim, Footed, Signed	45.00
Box, Jewel	125.00
Box, Ribbed, 5 1/2 In.	85.00
Candlestick, Eiffel Tower Pattern, Amberina, 10 3/4 In., Pair	225.00
Carafe, Water, Matching Tumbler, Underplate, Rose Teinte	198.00
Celery, Cranberry	65.00
Compote, Rose Teinte, Swirl Design, Signed, 4 1/2 X 3 3/4 In.	58.00
Dresser Set, Amberina Swirl, Brass Rack, Art Deco, 5 Piece	625.00
Dresser Set, Art Deco, Amberina Swirl, Brass Rack, Mirror, 5 Piece	625.00
Dresser Set, Brass Rack, Beveled Mirror, Signed, 5 Piece	625.00
Finger Bowl, Rose Teinte Swirl, Signed, 5 In.	110.00
Goblet, Wine, Cobalt Blue, Clear Round Stem, 7 3/4 In., Set of 8	495.00
Inkwell, Crystal & Gilt Bronze, Figure of Putto, 12 1/4 In.	3575.00
Jam Jar, Frosted Gold, Metal Holder, Signed, 6 1/2 In.	225.00
Jewelry Box, Brass Fittings, Button & Bow Pattern, Signed, 4 In.	120.00
Lamp, Boudoir, Pair	235.00
Lamp, Fairy, Sunburst Pattern, Rose Teinte, 5 1/2 X 4 1/2 In.	225.00
Paperweight, 1 Pansy, 1 Clear Bud, Star Cut Base, 2 1/2 In.	650.00
Paperweight, Cane of Rooster, Floral, Animal Canes	105.00
Paperweight, Lady Bug, Flowers, Opaque Green Ground, 1976, 3 In.	450.00
Paperweight, Looped Garland of Stars Around Circle, 3 In.	875.00
Paperweight, Pansy, Flower & Bud On Stems & Leaves, 2 1/2 In.	650.00
Paperweight, Sulfide, Andrew Jackson, Green	255.00
Paperweight, Sulfide, Benjamin Franklin, Brandy Color, 3 In.	550.00
Paperweight, Sulfide, Eleanor Roosevelt, Amethyst .... 115.00 To	255.00
Paperweight, Sulfide, Elizabeth & Phillip, Double Fan, 2 3/4 In.	255.00
Paperweight, Sulfide, James Monroe, Orange .... 45.00 To	255.00
Paperweight, Sulfide, Theodore Roosevelt, Amethyst	255.00
Paperweight, Thousand Petal Rose	3600.00
Pitcher, Water, Harcourt, Large	14.00
Plate, Rose Teinte Swirl, Signed, 7 In.	85.00

Art Pottery, Plaque, Moonlit Landscape,
Hand-Painted, 6 X 10 In.

Baccarat, Vase, Cut Crystal,
Ribbon Handles,
10 In.

Relish, Rose Teinte Swirl, Signed, 9 1/2 In.	95.00
Ring Tree, Swirl Design, Signed, Vaseline, 3 3/4 X 3 In.	48.00
Salt Set, Sailboat Form Holder, 6 3/4 In., 5 Piece	85.00
Toothpick, Diamond Point	47.50
Vase, Cut Crystal, Ribbon Handles, 10 In. ....*Illus*	320.00
Vase, Mounted In Bronze Dore Sphinxes, Bronze Feet	225.00
Vase, Rib & Star, Amber Insets, Signed, 14 In.	200.00

Badges have been used since before the Civil War. Collectors search for examples of all types, including law enforcement and company identification badges. Well-known prison or law enforcement badges are most desirable. Most are made of nickel or brass. Many recent reproductions have been made.

BADGE, California Hunting, 1941	10.00
Chauffeur, Illinois, 1942	10.00
Chauffeur, Indiana, 1938	6.00
Chauffeur, Missouri, 1927	15.00
Checker Cab, 1930s	25.00
Colorado Pioneer, Ribbon, 1894	10.00
Constable Horse Thief Association, Anderson, Ind., Round, With Star	38.00
Dan Patch, Pinback	50.00
Ecclesiastical Figure, Crowned, Holds A Fleur-De-Lis, Leaf & Tin	125.00
Fire Department, Honorary, Kensington	20.00
Fleur-De-Lis, Purity Symbol, Refers To Virgin Mary, 15th Century	75.00
Illinois Commerce Commission Chairman, Star Shape	35.00
Member Carpenters & Joiners Local Union No.918, Manhattan, Kans.	15.00
Messenger, WF & CO, Hat	45.00
Motorcoach Operators Union, 1930s	10.00
National Newsboy, Brass	22.50
Police, Honorary, New Mexico	27.50
Porter, Pullman, Black Man	25.00
Railway Center World Market, Brass, Pinback, 1920	18.00
Remember The Maine, Pinback	17.00
Sing-Sing Prison, Breast & Hat, 2 Piece	150.00
Spanish American War, Returning Volunteer, Dated 1899	25.00
U.A.W.Union, 1930s	14.00

    BAG, BEADED, see Purse

Metal banks have been made since 1868. There are still banks, mechanical banks, and registering banks (those which show the total money deposited on the face of the bank). Many old banks have been reproduced since the 1950s in iron or plastic.

BANK, ABC, For A Good Girl, Tin, 1890 .... 145.00
Abraham Lincoln, Bank Bottle, Cast Iron .... 20.00 To 25.00
Alice In Wonderland, Pottery, Walt Disney 18.00
Allis Chalmers 26.50
American Mission To Lepers, Original Tag 45.00
Andy Gump, Cast Iron 850.00
Andy Gump, Tin 240.00
Apple, Pottery, Pale Red, 3 In.Diam. 55.00
Aunt Jemima, China, 6 1/2 In. 20.00
Baby & Cradle, Cast Iron 250.00
Bank Building, Cast Iron 75.00
Bank Vault, Mosler, Double Door, 2 Combinations 10.00
Barrel, Savings Bank, Plastic, Metal End, Box, 2 3/4 X 1 3/4 In. 5.00
Barrel, Sunny Future Bank, New York, N.Y., 3 1/2 In. 8.00
Baseball & 3 Bats, Cast Iron, 1914 .... 430.00
Baseball, Clear Glass 25.00
Baseball, With Cap, Sox Midwest Bank Trust, Ceramic 20.00
Bat Rack, American League, Tin 10.00
Battleship Maine, White, With Green, Red & Black, Iron, 10 1/4 In. 350.00
Battleship, Oregon, Cast Iron 220.00
Bear, Black Paint, Cast Iron, 7 In. 475.00
Bear, Blue Overalls, Teddy Pushing Wheelbarrow, Porcelain, 7 In. 25.00
Bear, Standing, Cast Iron, 6 1/4 In. 65.00
Beehive, Wooden 15.00
Ben Franklin, Thrift 85.00
Billiken, Good Luck, Old Gold Paint, Cast Iron, 6 3/8 In. 65.00
Billiken, On Throne, Cast Iron .... 65.00 To 130.00
Bird, Tin, Windup, West Germany 20.00
Black Boy, 2–Faced, Black & Gold Paint, Cast Iron, 4 In. 110.00
Black Mammy, Holding Frying Pan, Cast Iron, Blue Paint, 2 Piece, 6 In. 125.00
Black, Nodder, Papier–Mache 12.00
Book, Leather, Original Box 25.00
Book, Mickey Mouse, Oilcloth Covering, Brass Fittings, 4 In. 27.50
Book, Sun Insurance, Embossed Green Leatherette 25.00
Book, Sun Life Insurance Co., Dated 7/3/23 .... 17.50
Book, Washing Machine On Front 20.00
Boscul Coffee, Liberty Bell & Waiter's Picture, Key, 1776–1926 .... 35.00
Bowling, Tin Litho, Battery Operated 50.00
Buffalo, Cast Iron .... 70.00 To 75.00
Building, Turreted, Cast Iron, 4 3/8 In. 35.00
Bumble Bee, Key, Wooden 25.00
Buster Brown & Tige, Horse, With Horseshoe, Good Luck, 4 In. 105.00
Buster Brown & Tige, Old Gold Paint, Cast Iron, 5 1/8 In. 130.00
Calumet Baby Powder, Tin, Baby Head Insert 95.00
Camel, Kneeling, Cast Iron 475.00
Camel, Standing, Cast Iron .... 40.00 To 42.00
Campbell Kids, Cast Iron 185.00
Captain Kidd 210.00
Car, 1920s Sedan, Cast Iron 60.00
Car, 1924, Banthrico 15.00
Cash Register, 3 Coin, Home Savings, Tin 35.00
Cash Register, Stevens Jr., Key 145.00
Casper The Ghost, Ceramic 35.00
Cat, Glass Eyes, China, 3 1/2 X 3 In. 65.00
Cat, On Tub 115.00
Cat, Sitting, Bow Tie, Lock On Neck, Cast Iron 40.00
Cat, Sitting, Open Front Legs, Black Paint, Red Mouth, Cast Iron, 4 In. 95.00
Cat, Sitting, Polychrome Paint, Cast Iron, 4 1/4 In. 60.00
Champion Thrift Bank, Old Red & Blue Paint, Cast Iron, 4 1/8 In. 30.00

Charlie Chaplin, Polychrome Paint, Pressed Glass, Tin Lid, 4 1/8 In. 215.00
Chest, Scroddleware, Revival Pawfoot, 5 Drawers, English, C.1830 .... 425.00
Chicken Feed, Papier–Mache 22.00
Church, Tin 32.00
Cigarette Machine Dispenser, Chrome, Coin Slot Dispenses Cigarettes 58.00
Circus, Tin, Daily Dime 17.00
City Bank, Traces of Bronze Finish, Cast Iron, 4 1/8 In. 65.00
Clown, Gilt Paint, Cast Iron 55.00
Clown, Roly Poly, Silver Colored 15.00
Coffee Grinder, Cast Iron Fittings, Wooden, 4 1/2 In. 35.00
Coffin, Metal, Japan, 1950s 65.00
Colonel Sanders, Plastic, 12 In. 17.50
Corn, Amherst Stoves, Buffalo, Cast Iron 75.00
Coronation Bank, 1911, Traces of Old Paint, Cast Iron, 6 5/8 In. 45.00
Covered Bridge, 1930s 35.00
Covered Wagon, Oregon Mutual Savings, Portland, Ore.Name Plate 25.00
Cow, Kicking, Cast Iron 275.00
Cow, Standing, Cast Iron, Gilt, 5 1/4 X 3 1/2 In. 75.00
Cradle, Sleeping Child, Bird Perched On End, Cast Iron, Rocks 70.00
Crown, Figural, On Tassled Footing, Red Paint & Gilt, England, 1953 .... 55.00
Curtis Candy, Marx, Box 35.00
Deer, Antlers, Cast Iron 35.00
Deer, Cast Aluminum 45.00
Devil, 2–Faced, Red Paint, With Black & White, Cast Iron, 4 1/4 In. 500.00
Dime Register, Eastman Kodak, Amount For Brownie Camera Purchases 50.00
Dime Register, National Cookware Co., Tin, Key ....:........ 35.00
Dime Register, Popeye .... 35.00 To 50.00
Dime Register, U.S., Blue, Cast Iron 50.00
Dime Register, Uncle Sam, 3 Coin .... 15.00 To 42.00
Dime Register, Uncle Sam, Tin, Battery Operated 25.00
Dime, Round, Celluloid 20.00
Dime, Snow White & 7 Dwarfs, Tin 95.00
Dime, Superman, Tin 130.00
Dime–A–Day, Book–Calendar, New York Life Giveaway 45.00
Dog Head, Brown Rockingham Glaze, White Clay, 2 7/8 In. 75.00
Dog Head, Sponged Black, Yellow, & Green, Clear Glaze, Pottery, 3 In. 55.00
Dog, Basset Hound, Old Gold Paint, 3 1/8 In. 775.00
Dog, Boston Bull, Sitting, Painted, Cast Iron, 4 3/8 In. 115.00
Dog, Bulldog, Canada 340.00
Dog, Bulldog, Removable Head, Padlock On Spike Collar, Ceramic 45.00
Dog, Bulldog, Seated, Old Gold Paint, Cast Iron, 4 1/4 In. 40.00
Dog, Fido, Polychrome Paint, Cast Iron, 4 7/8 In. 35.00
Dog, Labrador, Black Paint, Gold Collar, 4 5/8 In. 225.00
Dog, Newfoundland, Pack On Back 75.00
Dog, Papier–Mache, Large 15.00
Dog, Scotty, Sitting, Black Pot Metal, Painted, Vanic Mark Key, 16 In. 55.00
Dog, St.Bernard, Pack On Back, Cast Iron, 5 X 3 1/2 In. 54.00
Dog, With Backpack, Cast Iron, 4 In. .... 35.00 To 60.00
Donkey, Cast Iron 30.00
Dreadnought, Polychrome Paint, Cast Iron, 7 1/8 In. 510.00
Drum, Chein 12.50
Drum, Wartime, Tin, Red, White & Blue 15.00
Duck, Kenton 130.00
Duckling, Original Polychrome Paint, Cast Iron, 5 In. 105.00
Dutch Cleanser 65.00
Eagle Pencil Co., N.Y. 13.00
Effie Sopar, 1883, Basket of Flowers, Cabin In Woods, Clay, 5 3/4 In. 500.00
Eiffel Tower, Bronze & Gold Finish, Cast Iron, 9 In. 650.00
Elephant, Jumbo, Nickle Plated Wheels, Gold Paint, Cast Iron, 4 In. 155.00
Elephant, On Tub, Gold Paint, Cast Iron, 5 1/4 In. 155.00
Elephant, Sitting On Bench On Tub, Cast Iron 95.00
Elephant, Standing On 2 Books, Bisque 22.00
Elephant, Standing On Base, Iron, 5 1/2 In. 52.00
Elephant, Tin 75.00

Elephant, With Chariot, Gray Elephant, Red, Yellow Chariot, 7 1/4 In. 525.00
Empire State Building, Die Cast, 6 In. 20.00
Equitable Insurance Co., Book Shape 10.00
Ferry Boat, Cast Iron, Gold, With Red Trim .... 150.00 To 200.00
Flag Register, Capitol 25.00
Flag Register, Gem Eagle 25.00
Flintstones, Fred & Wilma, Ceramic 85.00
Frog, Professor Pug, Metallic Green, Gold Paint, Cast Iron, 5 In. 250.00
Frowning Face, Wall Mount, No Paint, Cast Iron, 5 3/4 In. 550.00
Gas Pump, Texaco, Plastic, 1950s 60.00
General Eisenhower, Pot Metal 30.00
George Washington, Cast Iron, 6 1/4 In. 85.00
Girl & Sheep, Polychrome Paint, Cast Iron, 4 1/2 In. 275.00
Give Billy A Penny, Silver Paint, Cast Iron, 4 3/4 In. 275.00
Give Me A Penny 175.00
Globe, Ohio Art, 3 1/4 In. 8.00
Globe, On Wire Arc 120.00
Globe, Red Paint, Gold Trim, Cast Iron, 5 1/4 In. 70.00
Goat, Oscar, Old Black Paint, Cast Iron, 7 1/2 In. 125.00
Golliwog, Polychrome Paint, Aluminum, 6 In. 165.00
Graf Zeppelin, Cast Iron, 1920s, 7 In. 65.00
Grimace, Purple Ceramic, 9 In. 12.00
Gunboat, Cast Iron 725.00
Hall Clock, Cast Iron 275.00
Happy Days, Chein, Barrel 5.00
Hat, Uncle Sam, Tin, Chein 35.00
Haunted House 50.00
Hereford Bull, Nebraska Art Co., 9 X 6 In. 15.00
Hog, Cast Iron, Old Paint, 4 In. 55.00
Hole–In–One, Golf, Metal 40.00
Honey & Bear 135.00
Horse, Black Beauty, Old Paint, Cast Iron, 4 1/4 In. 75.00
Horse, Cast Iron 50.00
Horse, Cast Iron, 4 X 4 In. 37.50
Horse, In Bathtub, Rubber Wheels, A.C.Spark Plug 150.00
Horse, My Pet, Cast Iron 35.00
Horse, On Rear Legs, Cast Iron, 1960s 40.00
Horse, Prancing, Old Gold Paint, Cast Iron, 4 1/4 In. 80.00
Horse, Rearing, Black Paint, Cast Iron, 5 1/8 In. 75.00
Horse, Rearing, Pebbled Base, Iron, 7 1/2 In. 58.00
Horse, With Flynet, Gold Paint, With Red & Black, 4 1/8 In. 400.00
Horseshoe, First National Bank, Bloomsburg, Pa. 23.00
House, Red & Yellow Paint, Wooden, 5 1/2 In. 105.00
House, White Clay Glaze, Blue Outlined Door, Windows, 3 In. 175.00
House, Wooden Base, Brass, 8 In. 220.00
Humpty–Dumpty, Cast Iron 325.00
Humpty–Dumpty, On A Wall, Cast Iron 195.00
Ice Box, GE, Cast Iron 70.00
Ideal Safe Deposit, Nickle Finish, Cast Iron, 4 1/4 In. 55.00
Independence Hall Tower 350.00
Indian Chief, Cast Iron 85.00
Indian, Hand Over Eyes, Cast Iron, 5 3/4 In. 95.00
Jack Pot Game, Slot Machine Shape, Steel, Buffalo Toy & Toolworks 25.00
Jug, Blue Wreath, Word Bank In Center, Stoneware, 4 3/4 In. 145.00
Jug, Buff Clay, Clear, Brown & Green Glaze, Shenandoah, 4 5/8 In. 700.00
Jukebox, Wurlitzer, Key 35.00
Kewpie, Tin Lid, Clear Glass, Traces of Paint, 3 1/4 In. 35.00
Kitten, Sitting, Cast Iron, White Paint, Blue Ribbon On Neck, 5 In. 65.00
Kitten, White, Pink & Black Paint, Cast Iron, 5 In. 40.00
Kitten, White, Pink Bow, Cast Iron 70.00
Laurel & Hardy, 14 In., Pair 45.00
Liberty Bell, Centennial Money Bank 1876, 4 5/8 In. 45.00
Liberty Bell, Nash's Mustard, Glass 17.50
Lion, On Tub, Gold Paint, Cast Iron, 5 1/2 In. .... 95.00 To 120.00

Lion, Pull Toy, Iron Platform, Cast Iron Wheels, 19th Century, 5 In. 250.00
Log Cabin, Cast Iron 225.00
Log Cabin, Mustard Jar, Milk Glass, Original Label & Paint 125.00
Lucky Joe, Glass 22.00
Mailbox, Cast Iron, Hubley .... 25.00 To 30.00
Mailbox, Gold Eagle, Cast Iron, 3 1/2 In. 45.00
Mailbox, Hanging, U.S., Cast Iron 50.00
Mailbox, Postal Service, Metal, Box 25.00
Mammy, Cast Iron, 5 In. 95.00
Man Squatting, Trousers Down, Papier–Mache 75.00

> Mechanical banks were first made about 1870. Any bank with moving parts is considered mechanical. The metal banks made before World War I are the most desirable. Copies and new designs of mechanical banks have been made in metal or plastic since the 1920s.

Mechanical, 2 Frogs 425.00
Mechanical, Always Did 'Spise A Mule 285.00
Mechanical, Apple, Cast Iron 1000.00
Mechanical, Artillery, Cast Iron, 1900 .... 650.00
Mechanical, Bad Accident 1400.00
Mechanical, Baseball, 3 Bars, Chrome 700.00
Mechanical, Bear Stealing Pig 675.00
Mechanical, Boy On Trapeze 400.00
Mechanical, Cabin Boy 275.00
Mechanical, Chief Big Moon, Cast Iron 1350.00
Mechanical, Clown, Advertising, Plastic 16.00
Mechanical, Coffin, Hand Takes Coin, Plastic 25.00
Mechanical, Creedmore, Polychrome Paint, Cast Iron, 10 In. .... 200.00 To 300.00
Mechanical, Darkie, In Cabin 395.00
Mechanical, Darktown, Battery 1200.00
Mechanical, Dinah, Cast Iron 450.00
Mechanical, Dog & Clown, Cast Iron 500.00
Mechanical, Eagle & Eaglets, Paint, 8 1/2 In. .... 225.00 To 400.00
Mechanical, Elephant, Aluminum, Green, Ru–Garent Co., Long Beach, CA. 95.00
Mechanical, Elephant, Chein, Tin 30.00
Mechanical, Elephant, Howdah, Cranmer .... 125.00 To 130.00
Mechanical, General Butler 1125.00
Mechanical, Guided Missile, Rubber Nose Pinnacle, Box 85.00
Mechanical, Hall's Lilliput, Cast Iron 450.00
Mechanical, Hole–In–One, Flag, Coin Before Golfer, Box 95.00
Mechanical, Horserace 1000.00
Mechanical, Hungry Hal, Eats Crumbs, Tin, Friction, Windup 10.00
Mechanical, Jolly Nigger, Eyes Roll, Ears Wiggle, Starkies 195.00
Mechanical, Jolly Nigger, Starkies, Polychrome Paint, Cast Aluminum 85.00
Mechanical, Jonah & The Whale 900.00
Mechanical, Lion Hunter 2950.00
Mechanical, Mammy, Seated, Cast Iron 2450.00
Mechanical, Monkey & Parrot, Tin .... 200.00 To 225.00
Mechanical, Moody & Sam 850.00
Mechanical, Mule, Entering Barn .... 450.00 To 750.00
Mechanical, Organ Bank, With Monkey, Dog, & Cat, Iron, Dated 1892 .... 350.00
Mechanical, Organ, Monkey, Dog, Cat, Cast Iron 265.00
Mechanical, Owl, Cast Iron 275.00
Mechanical, Owl, Glass Eyes, Polychrome Paint, Cast Iron, 7 1/2 In. 180.00
Mechanical, Owl, Turns Head .... 325.00 To 350.00
Mechanical, Paddy & Pig, Polychrome Repaint, Cast Iron, 8 In. 500.00
Mechanical, Punch & Judy, Polychrome Paint, Cast Iron, 7 3/8 In. 700.00
Mechanical, Racetrack, Cast Iron, Trace of Polychrome, String Windup 235.00
Mechanical, Santa Claus, With Chimney, Cast Iron, 5 7/8 In. 750.00
Mechanical, Spaceship, Strato, 1950s 25.00
Mechanical, Speaking Dog, Paint, Cast Iron, 7 In. .... 325.00 To 650.00
Mechanical, Stump Speaker, Cast Iron, 1900 .... 1050.00
Mechanical, Tammany Bank, Polychrome Paint, Cast Iron, 5 3/4 In. 135.00

Mechanical, Tammany Hall, Iron, Pat.Dec. 23, 1876 .... 55.00
Mechanical, Teddy & Bear, Cast Iron, 10 In. ....625.00 To 1200.00
Mechanical, Trick Dog, Cast Iron, Polychrome Paint, 8 3/4 In. 550.00
Mechanical, Trick Pony .... 485.00 To 625.00
Mechanical, Uncle Remus, Cast Iron ....75.00 To 180.00
Mechanical, William Tell, Polychrome Paint, Cast Iron, 10 1/2 In. .... 275.00 To 475.00
Mechanical, World's Fair, Gold & Silver Paint, 8 1/4 In. 175.00
Mickey Mouse, 4 Figures, Screw-On Lid, Glass 85.00
Middy, Sailor, Cast Iron 115.00
Milk Truck, Hubley, Borden's, Cast Iron 600.00
Money Bag, Cast Iron 375.00
Monkey, Chein 35.00
Monkey, Regal China, 12 In. 125.00
Mr.Peanut, Vendor, Box 60.00
Mule, Cast Iron 60.00
Mutt & Jeff, Cast Iron .... 100.00 To 130.00
Nipper, Flocked White Metal, 1920s 140.00
Our Empire Bank, Bronze Finish, Cast Iron, 6 5/8 In. 105.00
Owl, Be Wise, Save Money, Gold Paint, White & Red Trim, Iron, 5 In. 115.00
Owl, Cast Iron, Square Base ....60.00 To 145.00
Owl, Glass, 7 In. 14.00
Paddlewheel Boat 190.00
Parlor Stove, Cast Iron .... 75.00 To 80.00
Parsley Brand Salmon 45.00
Pass Around The Hat, Cast Iron 70.00
Pep Boys, Savings Bonds, Tin, 1942 .... 50.00
Pershing, Cast Iron 130.00
Pig, Bank On Republic Pig Iron, Cast Iron, 7 In. 75.00
Pig, Brown & White, McCoy 35.00
Pig, Decker's Iowana, Cast Iron .... 65.00 To 85.00
Pig, Gold Coin Coming Out Of Mouth, Porcelain, Germany 50.00
Pig, Pink, Teeter-Totter On Money Bag, Porcelain 75.00
Pig, Porky, Polychrome Paint, Cast Iron, 5 3/4 In. .... 150.00 To 200.00
Pig, Seated, Black, Cast Iron 35.00
Pig, Seated, Red Mouth, Cast Iron 60.00
Pig, Seated, Smiling, Souvenir, Niagara Falls, Pottery 30.00
Pig, Smiling, Beige & Pink Paint, Cast Iron, 2 1/2 In. 78.00
Pig, Thrifty, On Hind Legs, Cast Iron, 6 1/2 In. 60.00
Pillsbury Poppin Fresh 12.00
Pirate, Pirate & Cross Bones Embossed, Brass Lock 35.00
Polish Rooster, Cast Iron 1500.00
Porky Pig, Hull 18.50
Pottery, New Geneva, Kittie In Raised Letters, Brown Glaze, 9 1/2 In. 1650.00
Purse, Cast Iron 525.00
Rabbit, Cast Iron 50.00
Rabbit, Chalkware, Carnival, 14 In. 38.00
Rabbit, Gold Paint With Red Trim, Cast Iron, 5 1/8 In. 85.00
Rabbit, Lying Down, Cast Iron 325.00
Rabbit, On Base, Cast Iron 725.00
Rabbit, On Oval Base, 1884 Bank, Green, White Paint, 2 1/4 In. 125.00
Rabbit, Sitting, Cast Iron, 5 In. 50.00
Radio, Glass 30.00
Radio, Majestic, Cast Iron .... 47.00 To 80.00
Raggedy Ann & Andy, Plastic, Yarn Hair, Royalty 30.00
Rat, In Cage With Cat, Oak Case, Brass Trim, Lid Opens, 6 1/4 In. 300.00
Red Goose, School Shoes, Cast Iron, 3 3/4 In. ....85.00 To 160.00
Redware, Tooled Shoulder Lines, Brown Splotches, 4 3/8 In. 300.00
Refrigerator, Electrolux, Cast Metal, White 78.00
Refrigerator, General Electric, Cast Iron .... 50.00 To 60.00
Refrigerator, Servel 19.50
Rhinoceros, Black, Cast Iron 320.00
Rocketship, On World, Metal, Satellite In Nose 65.00
Rockingham, Acorn Stoves, Acorn Shape, 3 In. 40.00
Rooster, Cast Iron, White Paint, Red Trim 90.00

Rooster, Old Gold Paint, Red, Cast Iron, 4 7/8 In.	90.00
Safe, Arabian, Cast Iron	78.00
Safe, Cast Iron, Key, Dated 1896, 3 3/8 In.	45.00
Safe, Columbian Exposition	325.00
Safe, Combination, Watch Dog, Moves His Mouth, Iron, Large	110.00
Safe, Fidelity Trust, Decoupage, Henry C.Hart Mfg.Co., Iron, 8 5/8 In.	55.00
Safe, Gold Combination, Black, Dated 1887, Cast Iron	60.00
Safe, Key, Cast Iron, Dated 1896, 2 1/2 X 2 1/4 In.	45.00
Safe, Keylock, No.5, Jackson Stevens Co., Cast Iron, 4 1/8 In.	45.00
Safe, Stevens, 1897, Large	145.00
Safe, Trimmed In Orange & Gold Paint, Cast Iron, 3 1/8 In.	40.00
Safe, Young America, Key, 1890s	165.00
Santa Claus, Chalkware	70.00 To 85.00
Santa Claus, Emerging From Chimney, Red, Chalkware, 10 1/2 In.	75.00
Santa Claus, In Chair, Chalkware	20.00 To 35.00
Santa Claus, On Roof, Box	85.00
Santa Claus, Pack On Back, Oval, Tin	80.00
Santa Claus, Tree, Cast Iron, 5 1/2 In.	250.00 To 335.00
Santa Claus, Wilton, Modern	45.00
Satchel, Lock On Sliding Base, Cast Brass, 5 7/8 In.	30.00
Save Your Pennies They Make Dollars, Large Eagle, Cast Iron	150.00
Security Bank Deposit, Black Paint, Brass Dial, Cast Iron, 4 3/4 In.	40.00
Security Safe Deposit, Black Paint, Gold, Nickel Plated Dial, 5 In.	30.00
Sharecropper, Cast Iron, 5 3/8 In.	85.00
Sheep, Cast Iron	90.00
Shriner, With Fez, Tin, 1963	12.00
Silo, A Marietta Silo Saves You Money, Gray & Silver, 5 1/2 In.	550.00
Skyscraper, Cast Iron	95.00
Snoopy, Ceramic, 5 1/2 In.	15.00
Soldier, Gold Paint, Red Trim, Cast Iron, 6 In.	90.00 To 115.00
Southern Comfort, Mechanical	35.00
Spaceman, Galaxy Syrup, Bottle, Lid	25.00
Squirrel, With Nut, Cast Iron	650.00
Statue of Liberty	60.00 To 65.00
Statue of Liberty, Cast Iron, 6 In.	45.00
Stoneware, Cylindrical, Applied Leaves, Cobalt Blue Design	1950.00
Tank Savings Bank, Metal, 9 1/2 In.	185.00
Tank, Wheels, Cast Iron, 9 1/4 In.	185.00
Tank, World War I, Chalkware, 1942, Box	85.00
Teddy Roosevelt, Bust, Gold, Silver & Red Paint, Cast Iron, 5 In.	95.00
Telephone, Wall, Black Tin, With Bell	55.00
Time Around The World	225.00
Time Is Money, Cast Iron	40.00
Top Hat, Supporting Taft & Sherman, C.1907, 2 1/2 In.	140.00
Transvaal Money Box, Cast Iron	500.00
Treasure Chest, Mickey Mouse	50.00
Trolley, Main Street, With Passengers, Gold Paint, Metal, 6 3/4 In.	275.00
Truck, Delivery, Armour's Meats, Cast Iron	40.00
Turtle, Brown Mottled Glaze, Marked Arthur Wood	25.00
Two Kids, Goats, Black, Green & Silver, 4 3/8 In.	775.00
Typewriter, Peter Paul Typewriter Co., Metal	72.50
U.S.Mail, Old Green Paint, Gold, Cast Iron, 5 5/8 In.	65.00
U.S.Mail, With Eagle, Green	135.00
Uncle Sam, Roseville	65.00
Uncle Tom, Cast Iron	60.00
Windmill, Silver Plate, Marked Holland	35.00
Wisconsin Beggar Boy	195.00
Wooden, Homemade, Glass, Sloped Sides, Cream, 19th Century, 5 In.	150.00
Yellow Cab, Arcade, Cast Iron, 8 In.	650.00
Zeppelin, On Wheels, Cast Iron, 8 In.	165.00

There is much confusion about the terms Banko, Korean ware, and Sumida. We are using the terms in the way most often used by antiques dealers and collectors. Korean ware is now called "Sumida" and is listed in this book under that heading. Banko is a group of rustic Japanese wares made in the nineteenth and twentieth centuries. Some pieces are made of mosaics of colored clay, some are fanciful teapots. Redware and other materials were also used.

BANKO, Figurine, Duck, 9 1/2 X 5 In. 300.00
Tea Set, Flying Cranes, 3 Piece 165.00
Teapot, Cranes & Flowers, Scenic Ground, Ribbon Shaped Handle, 4 In. 55.00
Teapot, Flying Crane Pattern, 3 In. 125.00
Teapot, Flying Cranes, Swivel Finial, 4 1/2 In. 75.00
Teapot, Quail & Locust 85.00
Vase, Boy With Ball, 8 In. 125.00
Vase, Boy, Mottled Brown, Orange Red, 4 1/2 X 2 1/2 In. 65.00
Vase, Oriental Boy, Glossy Brown, Orange Red, 4 3/4 X 2 1/4 In. 65.00

Barbershop collectibles range from the popular red and white striped pole that used to be found in front of every shop to the small scissors and tools of the trade. Barber chairs are wanted, especially the older models with elaborate iron trim.

BARBER, Backbar, 1900 .... 1000.00
Backbar, 3 Beveled Mirrors, Marble Counter, Golden Oak 2350.00
Bar, Oak, Marble Shelf, 3 Beveled Mirrors, Lion's Heads, 1890, 15 Ft. 4900.00
Cabinet, Frosted Glass, Oak 500.00
Chair, Adjustable, Brass, Oak, 19th Century 500.00
Chair, Child's, Horse's Head, Koken 1200.00
Chair, Child's, Horse's Head, Porcelain 1095.00
Chair, Hand Carved, Operable, Refinished, C.1890 .... 1500.00
Chair, Koken, Porcelain 300.00
Clippers, Enamel Swirl Handles 15.00
Coat Rack, Oak Pole, Finial Top, Oak & Brass, C.1900 .... 1400.00
Globe, Stained Glass, 10 In. 950.00
Headrest, Barber Chair, Koch 25.00
Jar, Barbicide, Germicide & Disinfectant, Metal Insert, 9 1/2 In. 20.00
Pole, Floor Model 875.00
Pole, Koken, Art Glass 750.00
Pole, Old Repaint Red, White & Blue, Gold Finial, 77 In. 475.00
Pole, Stained Glass, 5 Panels, 6 1/2 In. 3575.00
Pole, Wall Mount, 3 Ft. 400.00
Sign, Straight Razor, Movable Parts, Copper Rivets, Case, 2 X 12 In. 195.00
Sign, Tin On Curved Wood Framework, 42 In. 175.00
Stand, Shoeshine, Leather Seat & Back, Marble Base, Brass Rests 3500.00

Barometers are used to forecast the weather. Antique barometers with elaborate wooden cases and brass trim are the most desirable. Mercury column barometers are popular with collectors. It is difficult to find someone to repair a broken example so be sure your barometer is in working condition.

BAROMETER, Aneroid, Carved Oak, 1900, 26 In. 140.00
Balloonist, Mahogany, Brass, Vernier Scale, C.1835 .... 4900.00
Banjo, & Thermometer, Mahogany Inlaid, England, J.Riboldi, 39 In. 550.00
Banjo, George III, Steel Face, L.Bernascom, 14 In. X 4 Ft. 900.00
Banjo, Mahogany Inlaid, Convex Mirror, England, C.1820, 44 In. 600.00
Banjo, Mahogany, Red Liquid Thermometer, J.Albins, 38 1/2 In. 300.00
Banjo, William IV, Inlaid Mahogany, C.1890, 38 In. 200.00
Banjo, With Thermometer, J.Pensa, C.1820, 45 In. 880.00
Cistern, George III, Mahogany, Campione, 18th Century, 36 In. 990.00
Engraved Silvered Brass Face, Brass Trim, 38 In. 160.00
Figure of Semiclad Female At Top, Carved Wood, French 150.00
Open Escapement, Brass 35.00
Pinkham & Smith Co., Copper, Velvet Lined Hinged Box, 5 In. 350.00
Veitch Aneroid, Fitted Case, 1900, 6 In. 150.00

Basalt is a special type of ceramic invented by Josiah Wedgwood in the eighteenth century. It is a fine–grained, unglazed stoneware.

BASALT, Creamer, Black, 4 In. 20.00
    Figurine, Cupid, C.1830, 8 In. 950.00
    Inkwell, Vertical Engraved, B Impressed Base, 18th Century, 2 In. 160.00
    Teapot, Glazed, Cyples, 1830 .... 110.00 To 120.00
    Teapot, Widow, Staffordshire, 1800 .... 75.00

Baskets of all types are popular with collectors. Indian, Japanese, African, Shaker, and many other kinds of baskets can be found. Of course, baskets are still being made; so the collector must learn to tell the age and style of the basket to determine the value.

BASKET, Apple, Splint, Virginia, Sunflower Design, Swing Handle 325.00
    Beet, Slatted, Bentwood Rim & Bands, Wire Bail Handle 42.00
    Buttocks, Blueberry Dyed Weavers, C.1900, 6 3/4 X 7 3/4 In. 225.00
    Buttocks, Woven Splint, Bentwood Handle, 12 X 16 In. 55.00
    Buttocks, Woven Splint, Eye of God Design, Bentwood Handle, 17 In. 110.00
    Buttocks, Woven Splint, Woven Handle, 9 1/2 X 10 1/2 X 5 1/4 In. 70.00
    Cheese Weave, Hanging, Natural, Handle, 19th Century, 5 X 6 In. 475.00
    Cheese, 21 1/2 In. 495.00
    Cheese, Splint, 23 In. 450.00
    Cheese, Woven Splint, 23 1/2 X 6 1/2 In. 425.00
    Cheese, Woven Splint, 9 1/2 In. 475.00
    Cheese, Woven Splint, Pale Blue Paint Traces, 22 1/2 In. 185.00
    Chinese, Tung Chin, 1860s 150.00
    Egg, Woven Splint, Bentwood Handle, 11 X 11 1/2 X 6 In. 80.00
    Egg, Woven Splint, Eye of God At Handle, Black Paint, 12 X 7 In. 145.00
    Egg, Woven Splint, Eye of God At Handles, Pink Paint, 12 X 7 In. 55.00
    Egg, Woven Splint, Eye of God Design, Oval, 18 X 25 In. 65.00
    Egg, Woven Splint, Natural, Blue Gray, 6 3/4 X 7 1/2 In. 85.00
    Egg, Woven Splint, Radiating Ribs & Design In Red, Blue, 14 In. 95.00
    Egg, Woven Splint, Radiating Ribs, Bentwood Handle, 19 X 13 In. 55.00
    Egg, Woven Splint, Ribs, Eye of God Handle, 9 1/2 X 10 In. 475.00
    Egg, Woven Splint, Woven Design, 9 1/4 X 10 1/2 X 5 1/4 In. 65.00
    Flower Gathering, Mahogany Straw, Oval, Handle, 10 X 11 3/4 In. 30.00
    Fruit, Circle Design, Wire, Oval, 11 X 6 3/4 In. 32.00
    Gathering, Splint, Oval, Woven Handle, 2 3/4 X 17 1/2 X 19 1/4 In. 145.00
    Half, Woven Splint, Radiating Ribs, Eye of God Design, 10 1/2 In. 135.00
    Harvest, Dark Green Paint, Raised Bottom 125.00
    Laundry, Slat Construction, Amish Style 75.00
    Laundry, Woven Splint, Rim Hand Holds, 25 X 37 1/2 X 12 1/2 In. 100.00
    Nantucket, Covered, Whale Ivory Finial, 19th Century 1800.00
    Nantucket, Cylindrical, Dated 1892 .... 605.00
    Nantucket, Cylindrical, Work, Carved Side Handles, 10 X 4 In. 400.00
    Nantucket, Lightship, Pocketbook Shape, Lined, Ivory Whale Lid, 1948 .... 550.00
    Nantucket, Oval, 1920s 660.00
    Nantucket, Oval, 19th Century, Nest of 7 .... 5900.00
    Nantucket, Round Turned Wooden Base, Handle, 10 X 11 X 6 In. 775.00
    Nantucket, Round, Small, C.1930 .... 695.00
    Nantucket, Swing Handle, C.1925, 7 1/4 In. 850.00
    Nantucket, Swing Handle, Cylindrical, 1892, 3/4 X 7 In. 550.00
    Nantucket, Swing Handle, Ferdin & Sylvaro, C.1929, 14 X 11 In. 600.00
    Nantucket, Swivel Handles, Jose Formoso Reyes, 14 X 16 In. 2550.00
    Oak Splint, Field, Kicked–In Bottom, Carved Handles, 19 In. 89.00
    Oak Splint, Swing Handle 160.00
    Picnic, Wicker, Dome Hinged Lid, C.1930, 8 1/2 X 11 1/2 X 16 In. 30.00
    Picnic, Wicker, Swing Handle, 2 Lids, 1920, 8 1/2 X 10 X 17 In. 39.00
    Purse, Mid–19th Century, 14 X 12 1/2 In. 475.00
    Rye Straw, Green Paint, 12 X 4 In. 50.00
    Rye Straw, Pennsylvania, 13 X 4 In. 60.00
    Splint Willow, Twig Handle, 9 Ribs, God's Eye Lashings 75.00
    Splint, Bentwood Rim Handles, Orange, Blue, Yellow, 9 X 5 1/4 In. 450.00
    Splint, Blue Green Paint, Handle, Late 19th Century, 11 X 14 In. 250.00

Splint, Blueberry Dyed Weavers, Handle, C.1880, 4 X 7 In. 125.00
Splint, Flower Gathering 70.00
Splint, Red, Green, Yellow, Potato Print, Flower Design, 7 X 10 In. 425.00
Splint, Ribs Radiate From Handle, Impressed, 16 X 21 X 8 In. 135.00
Storage, Wicker & Wood, Oriental, 26 In., Pair 250.00
Swing Handle, Gray Paint, Rectangular, 19th Century, 18 X 13 In. 295.00
Taghkanic, Swing Handle, Ears, 7 3/4 X 4 In. 275.00
Woven Splint & Cane, 12 3/4 X 7 In. 55.00
Woven Splint & Reed, Low Rim, 11 X 14 1/2 X 2 In. 135.00
Woven Splint, Bent Splint Rim Handles, Red, Natural, 11 X 12 In. 95.00
Woven Splint, Bentwood Handle, Oval, 11 X 17 1/2 In. 35.00
Woven Splint, Bentwood Rim Handles, 10 X 3 1/4 In. 225.00
Woven Splint, Bentwood Rim Handles, 21 X 31 X 13 1/2 In. 50.00
Woven Splint, Bentwood Rim Handles, Potato Print, 9 X 5 1/4 In. 450.00
Woven Splint, Bentwood Rim Handles, Rectangular, 12 1/2 X 19 In. 415.00
Woven Splint, Bentwood Swivel Handle, 5 1/2 X 3 3/8 In. 550.00
Woven Splint, Bentwood Swivel Handle, Round, 10 X 5 1/2 In. 400.00
Woven Splint, Blue & Green Designs, C.1880, Miniature 115.00
Woven Splint, Blue Paint, 10 X 11 1/2 In. 32.50
Woven Splint, Brown Patina, Green Paint, Ear Handles, 11 X 7 In. 85.00
Woven Splint, Carved Bentwood Rim Handles, 11 X 15 In. 175.00
Woven Splint, Carved Wooden Swivel Handle, Round, 8 1/2 In. 450.00
Woven Splint, Cover, Swivel Handle, Black Paint, 15 1/2 In. 125.00
Woven Splint, Double Bentwood Handles, Hinged Lid, Painted Design 20.00
Woven Splint, Double Lids, Hinged At Center, 10 1/2 X 5 1/2 In. 250.00
Woven Splint, Eye of God Design At Handle, 7 X 3 3/4 In. 140.00
Woven Splint, Gathering, 16 X 22 In. 45.00
Woven Splint, Laced Rim, Bentwood Handle, 17 1/2 X 28 In. 55.00
Woven Splint, Lid, Black Potato Print, 18 X 24 X 14 In. 35.00
Woven Splint, Lid, Potato Print Leaf, Flower, 7 X 10 X 6 In. 425.00
Woven Splint, Lid, Potato Print, Yellow & Green, 14 X 13 In. 300.00
Woven Splint, Lid, Water Color Floral, 13 X 20 X 9 In. 150.00
Woven Splint, Melon Rib, Eye of God, Bentwood Handle, 9 In. 145.00
Woven Splint, Melon Rib, Swivel Handle, 15 X 19 X 7 In. 75.00
Woven Splint, Natural, Faded Red, Swivel Handle, 12 X 7 In. 37.50
Woven Splint, Open Rim Handle, Green Exterior, 21 X 14 In. 45.00
Woven Splint, Radiating Ribs, Eye of God, 8 X 9 1/2 In. 95.00
Woven Splint, Radiating Ribs, Eye of God, 14 X 15 In. 65.00
Woven Splint, Radiating Ribs, Eye of God, Handles, 8 X 9 X 4 In. 175.00
Woven Splint, Radiating Ribs, Plaited Diamond At Handle, 8 In. 105.00
Woven Splint, Ribs, Eye of God, Bentwood Handle, 11 X 15 In. 65.00
Woven Splint, Rim Handles, 20 X 27 X 10 1/2 In. 45.00
Woven Splint, Ring On Bottom, Carved Handle, 11 1/2 X 7 1/4 In. 175.00
Woven Splint, Shaped Bentwood Handle, 7 X 5 In. 55.00
Woven Splint, Sliding Up & Down Lid, Bentwood Handle, 12 In. 150.00
Woven Splint, Sun Bleached Finish, Bentwood Handle, 10 X 14 In. 50.00
Woven Splint, Woven Swivel Handle, Round, 10 X 7 In. 275.00
Woven Splint, Yellow Paint, Oval, 7 X 5 1/2 In. 85.00

Ernest Batchelder made ceramic and copper items in Los Angeles,
California. He died in 1957.

BATCHELDER, Pitcher, Omar Khayyam, Black Luster, 5 In. 130.00
    Tile, Impressed Landscape 65.00

**Try the old-time recipe for cleaning copper. Mix lemon juice or
vinegar with salt and use as a metal polish.**

Batman and Robin are characters from a comic strip by Bob Kane that started in 1939. In 1966, the characters became part of a popular television series. There have been radio and movie serials that featured the pair.

BATMAN, Assembly Kit, Batman & Robin, Plastic, 1966 .... 38.00
Batmobile, Box, Corgis 125.00
Book, Comic, No. 9 .... 125.00
Book, Comic, No.23, 1944 .... 65.00
Car, Black Plastic, 1974, 13 In. 15.00
Card, Playing, 1966 .... 26.00
Clock, Alarm, Talking, 1974 .... 15.00
Coins, On Display Card, 1966 .... 8.00
Colorforms, 1976 .... 15.00
Game, Board, 1978 .... 4.00
Game, Card, Box 8.00
Game, Help Batman & Robin Capture Joker, Hassenfeld Bros. 38.00
Knife, Bat Plane Shape, Germnay 17.50
Lamp, 1977 .... 30.00
Motorcycle, With Side Car, Black Plastic, 1974 .... 22.00
Mug, Child's 4.00
Pin, On Card, 1966 .... 15.00
Poster, Chapter No.1, Full Color, With Robin, 1949, 27 X 42 In. 400.00
Puppet, Ideal, 1966, Package 21.00
Record, Batman & Robin, Cover, 33 1/3, 1966 .... 12.00
Ring, Bat, 1960s Premium 15.00
Ring, Flicker 15.00
Shaker Maker, Box 23.00
Sign, Batmobile Scale Model Kit, Blown Out, 4 X 3 Ft. 300.00
Toy, Batcopter, Controlled Space Flight, Remco, Box 125.00
Toy, Batmobile, Mechanical, Tin, Plastic, Japan, Box, 12 In. 145.00
Toy, Energized, Climbs, Remco, Box 15.00
Tumbler, Batman & Robin, Clear, Stenciled, 5 In. 8.00
Tumbler, Robin, With Emblem, Super Hero, Pepsi–Cola 4.00
Walkie–Talkie, Batcoder, Batman & Robin 75.00
Yo–Yo, Duncan, Box 8.00

Battersea enamels are enamels painted on copper and made in the Battersea district of London from about 1750 to 1756. Many similar enamels are mistakenly called "Battersea."

BATTERSEA, Box, Playing Card, Game Counter Contents, Round 660.00
Box, Rabbit Form Top, Oval 1980.00
Box, Trinket, Top Says Reward of Virtue, 1768, Round, 3/4 In. 385.00
Box, Watch Face, Round 190.00
Candlestick, 18th Century, Pair 3300.00
Mirror Holder, Woman & Tomb Scene, Bilston Type, 2 In., Pair 250.00

J.A. Bauer moved his Kentucky pottery to Los Angeles, California, in 1909. The company made art pottery after 1912 and dinnerwares after 1929.

BAUER, Bowl, Mixing, Black Ring 40.00
Bowl, Mixing, Ring, Nested, Green, Tan, Cobalt, Light Blue, 4 Piece 34.00
Bowl, Ring Pattern, Orange 10.00
Bowl, Speckled Turquoise, 13 X 3 1/2 In. 12.00
Butter, Covered, Red 80.00
Carafe, Copper Handle & Lid, Yellow 25.00
Cookie Jar, Cream, Hand Painted 85.00
Creamer, Red Ring 12.00
Crock, No.6 .... 38.00
Dish, Pickle, Burgundy, Handle 14.00
Planter, Swan, Green, 10 In. 30.00

Planter, Terra Cotta, Embossed Wreath Design, 10 In. 65.00
Teapot, Burnt Orange, Covered 45.00
Teapot, Ringware, Burgundy, Small 38.00
Tumbler, Black, 6 Oz. 30.00
Tumbler, Dark Blue, 6 Oz. 15.00
Tumbler, Light Blue, 6 Oz. 10.00
Tumbler, Red, 6 Oz. 15.00
Tumbler, Yellow, 6 Oz. 10.00
Vase, Horn of Plenty 25.00

Porcelains of all types were made in the region known as Bavaria. In the nineteenth century, the mark often included the word "Bavaria." After 1871, the words "Bavaria, Germany" were used. Listed here are pieces that include the name Bavaria in some form, but major porcelain makers such as Rosenthal are listed in their own categories.

BAVARIA, Bottle, Perfume & Powder Jar, Doll Form, 7 In.Bottle, 3 Piece 135.00
Bowl, Ice Cream & Cake Plate, Roses, Green, 12–In.Plate, 2 Piece 395.00
Chocolate Pot, Large Red Roses, White Ground, Large 60.00
Cup & Saucer, Floral, Gold Bands, Schumann, Set of 9 .... 100.00
Pitcher, White Roses, Covered, Artist Signed, Small 25.00
Plate, Bird, 7 1/2 In., Set of 4 .... 100.00
Plate, Gold Stencil Design, Cabbage Roses, 8 1/2 In. 23.00

The Beatles became a famous music group in the 1960s. They first appeared on American network television in 1964. The group disbanded in 1971. Collectors search for any items picturing the four members of the group or any recordings. Because these items are so new, the condition is very important and top prices are paid only for items in mint condition.

BEATLES, Award, Gold Album, London Town, Capitol Records, 22 X 18 1/2 In. 770.00
Book, A Spaniard In The Works, In His Own Write, Lennon, 1964, Pair 75.00
Book, Beatles Illustrated Lyrics, 1st American Edition, 1969 .... 45.00
Book, Hard Day's Night, Paperback 10.00
Book, Hard Day's Night, Souvenir, Whitman, Hard Cover 40.00
Book, The Beatles, Dust Cover, 1975 .... 18.00
Book, The Beatles, Paperback 10.00
Button, I Love The Beatles, Red, White & Blue, 1964, 3 1/2 In. 8.00
Car Mascot, Paul McCartney, Bobbing Head 75.00
Card, Get Well, Yellow Submarine, George Caricature, 4 X 9 In. 8.00
Card, Membership, Cavern Club, Autographed, 1962, 2 1/2 X 4 In. 935.00
Doll Set, Inflatable 85.00
Doll, Composition, Box, Large 395.00
Doll, George Harrison, No Guitar, Remco 50.00
Doll, George, 4 In. 45.00
Doll, Inflatable, 5 Pieces 85.00
Doll, John, 4 In. 50.00
Doll, Paul McCartney, 4 In. 40.00
Doll, Paul McCartney, Remco, 1964, 4 1/2 In. 40.00
Doll, Paul McCartney, Signed, 1964, 4 1/2 In. 35.00
Game, Flip Your Wig, 1964 .... 40.00 To 80.00
Gold Record, Hard Day's Night, Inscribed Plaque, 21 1/2 X 17 In. 8800.00
Hair Brush, Original Unopened Package 70.00
Insert, Hard Day's Night, Professionally Framed 199.00
Instrument, John Lennon's Kawlabo Electric, Vinyl Case, 1970s 7150.00
Jacket, Chinese Style, Mandarin Collar, Photographs, 1960s 2860.00
Key Chain, Guitar 23.00
Lunch Box, Yellow Submarine, Metal, Dated 1968 .... 85.00
Magazine, Pictorial, Round The World, Color Issue No.1 .... 100.00
Newspaper, Mansfield News Journal, John Lennon Slain, 1980 .... 7.50
Nodder, Paul McCartney, 8 In. 100.00
Nodder, Plastic, 5 In., Set of 4 .... 125.00
Pillow .... 60.00 To 75.00
Plate, 4 Portraits & Authographs, Washington Pottery, 1960s 30.00

Postcard, Photo, Between Brick Walls, 1964, 3 1/2 X 5 1/2 In. 6.00
Poster, Yellow Submarine 10.00
Record, A Hard Day's Night, 45 Rpm 12.50
Record, Two Virgins, Lennon & Yoko, Pictured Nude, 1968 .... 125.00
Serigraph, Depicting Yoko & John On Pie, 15 1/4 X 22 1/2 In. 440.00
Sheet Music, I Want To Hold Your Hand 15.00
Sheet Music, Yesterday 15.00
Ticket, Premiere, Help & Hard Day's Night, Pair 25.00
Tumbler, 4 Colored Pictures of Beatles, 6 1/4 In. 35.00
Wristwatch, Leather Strap, Apple Promotion, Frame, 8 1/2 X 11 In. 935.00

Plates marked "R. K. Beck" were made by Buffalo Pottery and others. R. K. Beck was an artist who specialized in wildlife paintings. Many of his designs were reproduced on decals which were applied to plates.

BECK, Plate, Dog, 9 1/4 In. 55.00
Plate, Elk Scene, Signed, 8 1/4 In. 32.50
Plate, Game, Deer, Signed, 10 1/4 In. 45.00

BEEHIVE, see Royal Vienna

Beer was sold in kegs or returnable bottles until 1934. The first patent for a can was issued to the American Can Company in September of that year; and Gotfried Kruger Brewing Company, Newark, New Jersey, was the first to use the can. The cone-top can was first made in 1935, the aluminum pop-top in 1962. Collectors should look for cans in good condition, with no dents or rust. Serious collectors prefer cans that have been opened from the bottom.

BEER CAN, ABC, Maier, Los Angeles, Flat 30.00
Acme 12.00
Altes Lager Beer, 12 Oz. ....*Illus* 15.00
Beatles 10.50
Berghoff, Ft.Wayne, Cone Top 30.00
Brown Derby, Empire, Chicago, Flat 25.00
Bub's, Winona, Mn., Cone Top 45.00
Budweiser, Cone Top 15.00
Canadian Ace Ale, Chicago, Flat 15.00
Carling's Red Cap Ale, Cleveland, Ohio, Flat 15.00
Esslinger Premium, Conetop, Red, Yellow & Blue, 1 Qt. 74.50
Falstoff, Cone Top 45.00
Frankenmuth Bock, Tab Opened 25.00
Krueger Ale, Newark 160.00
New Yorker Beer 750.00
Piels, Blue & Gold, 16 Oz. 48.00
Red Top Ale, Cone Top, Gold, Red, Black & Brown, 12 Oz. 25.00
Rock & Roll, Chuck Berry Commemorative, 6 Pack, Unopened 25.00
Schlitz, Milwaukee, Flat, 1954, 16 Oz. 12.00
Tivoli Aristocrat, Tivoli Union, Denver 110.00

Bells have been made of porcelain, china, or metal through the centuries. All types are collected. Favorites include glass bells, figural bells, school bells, and cowbells. Be careful not to buy a bell made from an old glass goblet.

BELL, 19th Century Woman, Hooped Dress & Bonnet, Brass 40.00
African Woman, Circular Earrings, Painted Black, Cast Iron, 5 3/8 In. 40.00
Art Glass, Mint Green, Matching Handle, 6 X 13 In. 375.00
Brass Frogs Design, Snakes, Handle, Africa, Large 440.00
Buckeye Bell Foundry, Name On Lip, Bronze, Mounted On Frame, 23 In. 2300.00

Let your baskets share the bathroom with you when you take a shower. The hot, moist air is good for the basket.

Billy Beer cans are not worth hundreds of dollars even though this myth appears in newspapers about every six months.

To remove a musty odor from a book, sprinkle talcum powder between the pages, then wrap the book and store it for a few months. When you open it again, brush out all the powder and the musty smell will be gone.

Buckeye Bell Foundry, Van Duzen & Tift, Bronze, 1878, 28 In.	1700.00
Bust, Chamberlain, Brass, 5 1/4 In.	60.00
Cat, Sitting Up, Cat Forms Handle, Brass, 4 3/4 In.	40.00
Centennial Bell Foundry, Bronze, 1890, 51 1/4 In.	5900.00
Church, Brass, 200 Lb.	1200.00
Church, Saddle & Wheel, 30 In.Mouth	900.00
Colonial Boy, Mechanical, Metal, Marque J.P.W.Depose, 4 In.	88.00
Cranberry Diamond–Quilted, Cream Opaque Handle, 10 1/2 In.	198.00
Cranberry Glass, Acid Leaves, Flashed Gold Edge, Clapper	30.00
Cranberry, Clear Handle, Green Glass Clapper, 11 7/8 In.	165.00
Dutch Girl, Jug In Hand, Dinner, 4 1/2 In.	110.00
Dutch Girl, With Jug, Bronze, 4 1/2 In.	125.00
El Camino Real, San Diego, Bronze, 1914	42.00
Horse, Brass, 3 In.	18.00
Lady, Hoop Skirt Forms Clapper, Braided Hair, 3 1/2 In.	42.00
Lion Masque Head Handle, Brass, 6 In.	40.00
Madam Pompadour, Brass, 6 In.	50.00
Meneely West Troy, N.Y., Original & Complete, Bronze, 20 In.	1295.00
Napoleon, Brass, 4 In.	70.00
Napoleon, Figural Handle, Scene, Battle of Waterloo, Brass, 6 1/4 In.	70.00
Queen Elizabeth, Crown, Ruffled Collar, Brass, 5 1/4 In.	60.00
Queen Hemony, Sad–Faced, Brass, 6 1/2 In.	175.00
R.A.F.Victory, Metal From German Aircraft Downed, 1939–45, 6 In.	60.00
Repousse & Figural Design, Dutch, 18th Century	1200.00
Russian Troika, Imperial Lion Finial, Brass, 12 In.	275.00
School, Cast Iron, O.S.Bell Co., Hillsboro, Ohio, 24 In.	550.00
Sheep, Brass, Arched Loop For Neck Strap, 4 X 4 In.	32.00
Sleigh, 25 Graduated, Brass	220.00
Sleigh, 32 Graduated, Leather Strap	150.00
Smiling Mammy, White & Red Polka Dot Dress, 4 1/2 In.	18.00
Strip of Metal Hames, 4 Graduated Balls, 13 1/2 In., 2 Piece	110.00
Stuckstede Bell Foundry, Relief Figures, Wooden Wheel, Bronze, 30 In.	3600.00
Table, Silver, William IV, Green Handle, S.Hayne & D.Carter, 5 1/4 In.	330.00
Welsh Lady, Spinning Wheel Clapper, Brass, 3 1/4 In.	65.00
Woman, Brass, China, 3 In.	22.50

Belle Ware was made in 1903 by Carl V. Helmschmied. In 1904 he started a corporation known as the Helmschmied Manufacturing Company. His factory closed in 1908 and he worked on his own until his death in 1934.

BELLE WARE, Saltshaker, Pink Roses, Signed, Original Lid 110.00

Belleek china is made in Ireland, other European countries, and the United States. The glaze is creamy yellow and appears wet. The first Belleek was made in 1857. All pieces listed here are Irish Belleek. The mark changed through the years. The first mark, black, dates from 1863 to 1890. The second mark, black, dates from 1891 to 1926 and includes the words "Co. Fermanagh, Ireland." The third mark, black, dates from 1926 to 1946 and has the words "Deanta in Eirinn." The fourth mark, same as the third mark but green, dates from 1946 to 1955. The fifth mark, green, dates from 1955 to 1965 and has an R in a circle added in the upper right. The sixth mark, green, dates after 1965 and the words "Co. Fermanagh" have been omitted.

BELLEEK, see also Ceramic Art Co.; Haviland; Lenox; Ott & Brewer; Willets

BELLEEK, Basket, Flowers, Painted, 1890–1921, Oval, 8 1/2 In.	1250.00
Biscuit Jar, Bamboo & Ribbon, Cover, Double Finial, 1st Black Mark	422.00
Bowl, Shell & Coral, Green Mark, 4 X 5 In.	50.00
Bowl, Shell, Tab Handle, White & Pink, 1st Black Mark, 5 X 6 In.	145.00
Bowl, Tridacna, Eggshell, 1st Black Mark, 4 1/2 In.	90.00
Box, Dresser, Bisque Sleeping Baby Top, Oval, Blue Mark, 4 1/2 In.	80.00
Bread Plate, Hawthorne Pattern, 1st Black Mark, 9 1/2 In.	372.00
Bread Plate, Tridacna, 1st Black Mark, 11 1/2 In.	165.00
Butter, Shape of House Cover, Tree Handle, Green Mark	135.00
Cake Plate, Twig Handle, 2nd Black Mark	900.00
Cake Stand, Parian Shell, Basketweave Base, 2nd Black Mark	750.00
Candlestick, Allingham, 1st Black Mark	1100.00
Coffee Set, Limpet, 3rd Black Mark, 11 Piece	550.00
Compote, Minstrel, Footed, 1881	5500.00
Creamer, Argonaut Shell, 1st Black Mark, 4 3/4 In.	325.00
Creamer, Echinus, Initial, Gold Trim, 1st Black Mark, 3 7/8 In.	175.00
Creamer, Lily, 1st Black Mark	90.00
Creamer, Scale, 1st Black Mark ....90.00 To	110.00
Creamer, Shamrock, Green Mark, 3 In.	30.00
Cup & Saucer, Cone, Green Tint	185.00
Cup & Saucer, Cone, Pink Trim, 2nd Black Mark .... 175.00 To	200.00
Cup & Saucer, Erne, Green Tint, 2nd Black Mark	195.00
Cup & Saucer, Fluted, Crimped Shape, 2nd Black Mark	105.00
Cup & Saucer, Grasses, 1st Black Mark .... 125.00 To	195.00
Cup & Saucer, Harp, Shamrock, 2nd Black Mark	65.00
Cup & Saucer, Institute, 1st Black Mark	175.00
Cup & Saucer, Limpet, 3rd Black Mark, Demitasse .... 55.00 To	68.00
Cup & Saucer, Neptune, Green Trim, 2nd Black Mark .... 77.00 To	90.00
Cup & Saucer, Pink & Gold, Limpet, Demitasse	50.00
Cup & Saucer, Ring Handle, Gold Rim Stripe, 2nd Black Mark	200.00
Cup & Saucer, Ring Handle, Pink & Gold, 2nd Black Mark	200.00
Cup & Saucer, Shamrock & Basketweave, 1st Green Mark	30.00
Cup & Saucer, Shamrock, 3rd Black Mark, Demitasse	68.00
Cup & Saucer, Shamrock, Harp Handle, 2nd Black Mark	85.00
Cup & Saucer, Thistle, 1st Black Mark	175.00
Cup & Saucer, Thorn, 1st Black Mark	100.00
Cup & Saucer, Tridacna, Blue Trim, 1st Black Mark .... 195.00 To	225.00
Cup & Saucer, Tridacna, Pink, 1st Black Mark	75.00
Cup & Saucer, Tridacna, White & Green, 1st Black Mark	145.00
Dish, Cheese, Figural, Cottage, Tree Branch Handle, 1st Green Mark	165.00
Dish, Cheese, House Shape, Yellow Luster, 1st Green Mark, 6 1/2 In.	185.00
Dish, Covered, Shell, Enameled, Black Mark, 7 In.	95.00
Dish, Leaf, Black Mark, 4 1/2 In.	50.00
Dish, Sycamore Leaf, 3rd Black Mark, 4 1/2 In.	55.00
Eggcup, Holder, 1st Black Mark	1400.00
Ewer, Aberdeen, 2nd Green Mark, 9 In.	175.00
Figurine, Boy With Basket, No.640, Green Mark, 8 1/2 In.	250.00
Figurine, Dog, Prince Charles', On Cushion	800.00

Figurine, Erin, 1st Black Mark 4500.00
Figurine, Leprechaun, Colorless, 3rd Black Mark 190.00
Figurine, Madonna, Praying, 1st Green Mark, 12 In. .... 575.00 To 600.00
Figurine, Swan, 2nd Black Mark, Large 225.00
Flower Holder, Seahorse, 1st Black Mark 800.00
Flower Pot, Applied Flowers, 2nd Black Mark, 4 1/4 X 5 In. 195.00
Font, Cherub, 3rd Black Mark 250.00
Honey Pot, Beehive, Grasses Pattern, Covered, 2nd Black Mark, 6 In. 695.00
Honey Pot, Grasses, 1st Black Mark 525.00
Jam Jar, Ribbon Pattern, 1st Black Mark, 5 1/4 In. 422.00
Pitcher, Harp, 1st Black Mark 300.00
Pitcher, Milk, Shamrock, 3rd Black Mark, 6 In. 125.00
Pitcher, Nautilus, 1st Black Mark 175.00
Pitcher, Shamrock, Basketweave, 1st Green Mark, 6 In. 125.00
Plate, Artichoke, Gold Outline, 1st Black Mark, 6 1/4 In. 85.00
Plate, Caldwell Castle, 1971 .... 90.00
Plate, Grasses, 1st Black Mark, 8 In. 80.00
Plate, Ivy, Shaded Green Leaves, Grapes, 2nd Black Mark, 5 1/2 In. 57.00
Plate, Shamrock, 3rd Black Mark, 6 1/4 In. 35.00
Plate, Tridacna, Coral Rim, 1st Black Mark, 6 In. 100.00
Pot, Applied Flowers 265.00
Salt & Pepper, Tridacna, Yellow Trim 75.00
Salt, Limpet, 3 Coral Feet, 2nd Black Mark 75.00
Salt, Open, Yellow Trim, Oval, 2nd Black Mark 75.00
Salt, Seashell, 5th Green Mark 15.00
Salt, Shamrock, Washtub Shape 45.00
Spill, Fish, 1st Black Mark 475.00
Spill, Indian Corn, 1st Black Mark .... 300.00 To 375.00
Sugar & Creamer, Cleary 95.00
Sugar & Creamer, Lotus, Green, 2nd Black Mark .... 115.00 To 135.00
Sugar & Creamer, Mask, 3rd Black Mark 160.00
Sugar & Creamer, Neptune, Green, 1st Black Mark 120.00
Sugar & Creamer, Shamrock, 1st Green Mark 75.00
Sugar & Creamer, Toy Shell, 1st Green Mark 75.00
Sugar & Creamer, Yellow Ribbon, 3rd Black Mark 95.00
Sugar, Neptune, Green, 2nd Black Mark 100.00
Sugar, Scroll, Gold Trim, White & Green, 2nd Black Mark 195.00
Tankard, Monk, Signed 240.00
Tea Kettle, Tridacna, Green Trim, 2nd Black Mark, 5 1/2 X 6 In. 375.00
Tea Set, 3rd Black Mark, 9 Piece 295.00
Tea Set, Dejeuner, Shamrock, Tray, 2nd Black Mark 1825.00
Tea Set, Limpet, 3rd Black Mark, 16 Piece 750.00
Tea Set, Tridacna, Pink Trim, 1st Black Mark, 8 Piece 1000.00
Teapot, Cone, Rust Trim & Gilt, 2nd Black Mark 495.00
Teapot, Erne, Green Tint, 2nd Black Mark 495.00
Teapot, Neptune, Yellow, 2nd Black Mark .... 280.00 To 325.00
Teapot, Shell, Green Trim, 2nd Black Mark 368.00
Teapot, Sugar & Creamer, Shamrock, Green Mark 225.00
Teapot, Tridacna, 2nd Black Mark 300.00
Teapot, Tridacna, 2nd Black Mark, Medium .... 275.00 To 325.00
Teapot, Tridacna, Green Trim, 2nd Black Mark, 5 1/2 In. 395.00
Tray, Hawthorne, 1st Black Mark 350.00
Tray, Tridacna, Green Trim, 2nd Black Mark 475.00
Vase, Ewer, Aberdeen, Applied Flowers & Leaves, 2nd B.M.6 In. 325.00
Vase, Flying Fish, Pink Trim, 2nd Black Mark, 4 3/8 In. 450.00
Vase, Mums, Interior, Cream Lined, 8 In. 250.00
Vase, Pinch Purse, 1st Black Mark 495.00
Vase, Prince Arthur, 1st Green Mark, 10 1/2 In. 245.00
Vase, Rathburn, 3rd Black Mark 210.00
Vase, Sunflower, 1st Black Mark 275.00
Vase, Sunflower, 2nd Black Mark 200.00
Vase, Trellis, Roses, 1st Black Mark, 4 In. 145.00
Vase, Yellow Roses, Light Tinted Ground, Artist, 16 In. 295.00

Bennington ware was the product of two factories working in Bennington, Vermont. Both firms were out of business by 1896. The wares include brown and yellow mottled pottery, Parian, scroddled ware, stoneware, graniteware, yellowware, and Staffordshirelike vases.

BENNINGTON, Bedpan, Figural, Bird	110.00
Bottle, Coachman, Impressed 1849 Mark, 10 1/2 In.	775.00
Candlestick, Rockingham Glaze, 9 3/8 In.	200.00
Cooler, Water, Gothic Pattern, Gray Green, 1869, 16 In.	1000.00
Creamer, Cow, Enamel Glaze	150.00
Cuspidor, Octagonal, Side Vent, 10 1/2 X 5 1/4 In.	145.00
Cuspidor, Olive Brown Enameled Glaze, 1849 Mark, 9 1/2 In.	115.00
Cuspidor, Shell Pattern, Rockingham Glaze, 8 1/2 X 3 1/2 In.	129.00
Cuspidor, Shell Pattern, Side Vent, 8 1/2 X 3 1/2 In.	110.00
Dish, Soap, Feathered Edge	225.00
Doorknob, Shank Between, Pair	2.50
Figurine, Coachman, Bottle In Hand, Mustache, C.1849, 10 In.	275.00
Flask, Book Form, Flecks of Yellow, 5 5/8 In.	225.00
Flowerpot, Attached Saucer, Embossed Cattails, 6 3/4 In.	55.00
Foot Warmer, Rockingham Glaze, 9 1/2 In.	50.00
Jar, Pecking Chicken, Handles	700.00
Jug, Bird On Branch, Gray, 1 1/2 Gal.	495.00
Mold, Turk's Head, 8 1/2 In.	75.00
Pitcher, Anchor & Rope Design Both Sides, Handle	90.00
Pitcher, Jolly Fellow, 6 1/2 In.	250.00
Pitcher, Milk, Brown & Tan, Speckled	65.00
Pitcher, Zachary Taylor, C.1850, 13 In.	4200.00 To 4620.00
Spittoon, Speckled Dark Brown, 1800s	50.00
Teapot, Mottled Brown, Rockingham Glaze, 6 In.	75.00
Teapot, Mottled Yellow, Blue, Green & Brown, 8 3/4 In.	125.00
Toby Jug, Benjamin Franklin, 1849 Mark	690.00
Vase, Enameled, Flint, 6 1/8 In.	65.00
Washbowl, Mottled Yellow, Blue & Brown, 13 3/4 In.	475.00
Water Cooler, Gothic Design	1100.00

Berlin, a German porcelain factory, was started in 1751 by Wilhelm Kaspar Wegely. In 1763, the factory was taken over by Frederick the Great and became the Royal Berlin Porcelain Manufactory. It is still in operation today. Pieces have been marked in a variety of ways.

BERLIN, Figurine, Child, Princely Costume, C.1840	225.00
Plaque, Christ, Taken Down From Cross, 3 Mourners, 9 X 6 3/8 In.	440.00
Plaque, Innocence, Bust of Maiden, White Shawl, Oval, 13 5/8 In.	4500.00
Plaque, Juliete, Stained Glass Window, Stadler, 9 1/4 X 6 3/4 In.	2300.00
Plaque, Maiden, Tresses Flowing About Shoulders, 12 3/8 In.	5300.00
Plaque, Shamrock, Classical Costume, C.1910, 9 1/4 X 6 1/4 In.	2100.00
Vase, Classical Maidens, Putti, Chocolate, Madler, 16 1/4 In., Pr.	715.00

John Beswick started making earthenware in Staffordshire, England, in 1936. The company is now part of Royal Doulton Tableware, Ltd. Figurines of animals, especially dogs and horses, Beatrix Potter animals, and other wares are still being made.

BESWICK, Figurine, Cat, Black, White Face	20.00
Figurine, Dachshund, 5 1/2 X 9 In.	45.00
Figurine, Ducks, Wings Spread, C.1890, Pair	195.00
Figurine, Hereford Cow, Brown, White, Glazed, Marked, 4 1/2 X 7 In.	85.00
Figurine, Monkey, Smoking Pipe	38.00
Figurine, Spaniel, Standing, Red, Marked, 7 X 6 In.	55.00
Pitcher, Robert Burns, Picture Front & Poem Back, 8 In.	75.00
Pitcher, Underglaze Frogs In Sea Scene	30.00
Vase, Palm Tree, Blown-Out, Purple, Gold	55.00

Betty Boop, the cartoon figure, first appeared on the screen in 1931. Her face was modeled after the famous singer Helen Kane and her body after Mae West. In 1935 a comic strip was started. Although the Betty Boop cartoons were ended by 1938, there has been a revival of interest in the Betty Boop image in the 1980s and new pieces are being made.

BETTY BOOP, Ashtray, Betty & Bimbo, Glazed, 1930s	70.00
Button, Betty In Yellow Dress & Shoes, 1930s, 1 1/2 In.	20.00
Clock, Alarm, Animated	20.00
Doll, Bisque, Ribbons To Hang, Original Dress	35.00
Doll, Jointed, Bisque	35.00
Film, Duracolor, Animated, Fits Uncle Sam's Projector	25.00
Mask, Paper, 1930s	40.00
Perfume Bottle	20.00 To 40.00
Wall Pocket, With Dog	75.00

The bicycle was invented in 1839. The first manufactured bicycle was made in 1861. Special ladies' bicycles were made after 1874. The modern safety bicycle was not produced until 1885. Collectors search for all types of bicycles and tricycles.

BICYCLE, Boneshaker, Iron	1700.00
Boy's, Schwinn, B–6 Model, Spring Shock Absorber, C.1948, 26 In.	500.00
High Wheel, Columbia, 48 In.	1700.00
High Wheel, Pony Star, Smith Machine Co., New Jersy, 1880s	4000.00
Horse, On Tricycle Wheels, Jointed Legs, Gallops, As Rider Pedals	375.00
Lady's, Black Hawk, Coaster Brake, Metal Fenders	150.00
Lady's, Monarch, Balloon Tires, Spring Fork, Front Light	125.00
Man's, Roadmaster, Balloon Tires, Rear Carrier	100.00
Pony, On Tricycle, Skin Covered, Chain Drive, French, 1870s	2800.00
Racing, Gormely & Jeffrey, Rat Trap Pedals	200.00
Schwinn, Boy's, All Original, 1940–50	1500.00
Tandem, Junior Size, Balloon Tires, Mahn, New Jersey, 1950s	250.00
Tandem, Lady's & Man's, Steers Front & Rear, Remington Arms	500.00
Tandem, Remington Arms Co., Chain Steering Drive	700.00
Tandem, Rolfast Junior, 1960s	200.00
Tricycle, Child's, High Wheel, C.1900	200.00
Tricycle, Tri–Bike, All Aluminum	400.00
Wagon, Metal, Stenciled Empire State, Iron Wheels	385.00

Bing and Grondahl is a famous Danish factory making fine porcelains from 1853 to the present. Underglaze blue decoration was started in 1886. The annual Christmas plate series was introduced in 1895. Dinnerwares, stoneware, and figurines are still being made today. The firm has used the initials B & G and a stylized castle as part of the mark since 1898.

BING & GRONDAHL, Decanter, Cherry Herring, 9 In.	75.00
Figurine, 2 Children, Reading, Arm Around Girl's Neck	110.00
Figurine, Boy, Seated, Hugging Dachshund	105.00
Figurine, Cat, No.2552, Licking Paw, Gray, White, 7 1/2 In.	110.00
Figurine, Cat, Seated, White & Gray, No.2251, 7 1/2 In.	110.00
Figurine, Children Playing, No.1568	125.00
Figurine, Children Reading, No.1567	110.00 To 125.00
Figurine, Mermaid	600.00
Figurine, Seagull, No.1808, 4 In.	50.00 To 65.00
Figurine, Youthful Boldness, No.2162	165.00
Plaque, Easter, 1929	300.00
Plate, Annual, Mother's Day, 1969	250.00
Plate, Christmas, 1915	115.00
Plate, Christmas, 1959	55.00
Plate, Christmas, 1961	45.00
Plate, Christmas, 1965	65.00
Plate, Christmas, 1969	35.00
Plate, Christmas, 1970	10.00

Birdcage, Pagoda Shape, Hammered Copper,
Stand, 74 In.

Bisque, Figurine, Man, Woman,
Baroque Clothes, Marked, 27 In., Pair

Plate, Christmas, 1971 .... 20.00

All types of old binoculars are wanted by collectors. Those made in the eighteenth and nineteenth centuries are favored by serious collectors. The small, attractive binoculars called opera glasses are listed in their own section.

BINOCULARS, Case, Occupied Japan 50.00
Marine Corps, World War II, Case, 7 X 50 Size 185.00
Periscope, Bausch & Lomb, World War I 125.00
U.S.Signal, Marked 55.00

Old birdcages are collected for use as homes for pet birds and as decorative objects of folk art. Elaborate wooden cages of the past centuries can still be found. The brass or wicker cages of the 1930s are popular with bird owners.

BIRDCAGE, Brass, Hendryx 50.00
Gilt Paint, Well Shaped Waterer, Top Loop, Tin & Wire, 8 In. 35.00
Hanging, Dome Top, Brass, 12 1/2 X 16 In. 65.00
Hendryx, Stand, Brass 125.00
Iron, Red 25.00
Musical, Pull Out Drawer, Starts Music Box, Moving Bird 30.00
Pagoda Shape, Hammered Copper, Stand, 74 In. ....*Illus* 275.00
Regency, Wire Sides, Sloping Roof, Mahogany, 19th Century, 20 In. 1100.00
Tin, Wire, Light Green, Hand Painted Fleur–De–Lis 55.00
Wire Bars, Wooden, Old Red, White & Blue Paint, 11 In. 165.00
Wire, Old Orange Paint, Small 75.00

Bisque is an unglazed baked porcelain. Finished bisque has a slightly sandy texture with a dull finish. Some of it may be decorated with various colors. Bisque gained favor during the late Victorian era when thousands of bisque figurines were made. It is still being made.

BISQUE, see also named porcelain factories
BISQUE, Casserole, Hatching Chicks Cover, Basket Bottom 165.00
Dish, Dog With Bone Cover, Basketweave Gold & White Base, 9 In. 495.00
Figurine, Bathing Beauty, Lying On Stomach, Hat, German, 5 In. 125.00
Figurine, Bear, 8 In. 150.00
Figurine, Birds On Branches, Kaiser, Artist Signed, 6 In., Pair 250.00
Figurine, Black & White Child, On Potties 55.00
Figurine, Boy, With Rifle, French, 1850, 17 In. 150.00
Figurine, Cat, Blue Eyes, Seated, Facing Left & Right, 8 In., Pair 170.00

Figurine, Civil War Soldier, Sitting On Bench, Registry No.	50.00
Figurine, Dog, Glass Eyes, Ribbon Around Neck, Tan With White, 6 In.	110.00
Figurine, Fox, Standing, Wearing Red Jacket, Blue Pants, 5 In.	40.00
Figurine, Girl, Pink Dress & Hat, 8 In.	25.00
Figurine, Jackie Coogan, 2 1/2 In.	12.00
Figurine, Leprechauns, 6 1/2 In., Pair	45.00
Figurine, Little Red Riding Hood, Japan	52.00
Figurine, Man & Woman, With Dog In Apron, German, 13 1/2 In., Pr.	365.00
Figurine, Man, Woman, Baroque Clothes, Marked, 27 In., Pair ....*Illus*	850.00
Figurine, Napoleon On Horse, Marked C.D.Kenny	16.00
Figurine, Slipper, Angel Sitting On Top, Rococo Edge, 7 X 8 In.	150.00
Figurine, Young Man, Peasant Outfit, Yoke, Buckets, German, 17 In.	200.00
Font, Holy Water, Little Girl Praying	40.00
Font, Holy Water, Wall, Cross & Angels, German	30.00
Planter, Lady, Holding Fishing Net, 8 1/4 In.	150.00

Black amethyst glass appears black until it is held to the light, then a dark purple can be seen. It has been made in many factories from 1860 to the present.

BLACK AMETHYST, Ashtray, Figural, Elephant Center	20.00
Bowl, Console, Footed, 12 In.	35.00
Cake Plate, Open Handles	35.00
Candlestick, Serpentine Edge, Square, Pair	25.00
Candy Dish, 3 Feet, Beaded Rim, 7 In.	12.00
Candy, Silver Flowers, Tricorner	20.00
Compote Set	40.00
Cookie Jar, 7 In.	35.00
Cup, Floral, Silver Overlay	8.00
Cuspidor, 6 X 8 In.	55.00
Figurine, Swan, L.E.Smith, 9 X 5 1/2 In.	30.00
Ice Bucket, Bail, Hand Painted Mountain Design	30.00
Loving Cup, Art Nouveau Scene, 7 In.	24.00
Pomade Jar, Bear	295.00
Salt & Pepper, Art Deco	25.00
Sherbet, Silver Floral Overlay	10.00
Tray, Ruffled, 14 1/2 In.	35.00
Urn, Dancing Maidens, Handles, L.E.Smith, 7 In.	27.50
Vase, Art Deco, Dark Oval Protrusions, 15 In.	165.00
Vase, Ball, 6 3/4 In.	18.00
Vase, Bud, Footed, 13 In.	30.00
Vase, Enameled, 8 In.	22.00
Vase, Loving Cup, Deco Figures In Heart Reserve, 7 1/2 In.	35.00
Vase, Nudes, Art Deco, 3 Sides, L.E.Smith, 8 1/4 In.	95.00
Vase, Scalloped, 9 In.	25.00
Vase, Triangular, Standing Nudes	95.00

Black memorabilia has become an important area of collecting since the 1970s. Any piece that pictures a black person is included in this category and objects range from sheet music to salt and pepper shakers. The best material dates from past centuries, but many recent items are of interest even if not yet expensive.

BLACK, Ashtray, 2 Black Boys, With Dice	25.00
Ashtray, Black Man Nodder, Smoking Cigar	85.00
Ashtray, Naughty Black Boy, Yelling Mammy	15.00
Ashtray, Pregnant Woman, Ah Navah Knew What Love Cud Do	42.00
Ashtray, Uncle Mose Banjo Player, Cast Iron	125.00
Bank, Black Baby Face, Composition, Alfred Parker, Pharmacist, 4 In.	110.00
Bank, Nodder, Nude Pickaninny Baby, On Alligator, Plaster	48.00
Bell, Dinner, Mammy, Pink Dress, Stirring Batter, 5 In.	10.00
Blackamoor, Cornucopia Torchere, Italian Rococo, 18th Century, Pair	6875.00
Blackamoor, Parcel Gilt, Polychromed, Head Cushion, 35 In., Pair	8800.00
Box, Cream of Wheat, Rastus Picture, Unopened, Sample, 2 X 3 In.	40.00
Box, Gold Dust, Let The Gold Dust Twins Do Your Work, 15 X 13 In.	75.00
Box, Recipe, Aunt Jemima, Red, Plastic, Embossed Face	85.00

Bracelet, Dancing Girls, Metal, Wood, Shell, Watermelon Slices Between	42.00
Caddy, Potholder, Mammy, Embossed Rubber Face, Earrings, Heads, 9 In.	75.00
Card, Lobby, Little Rascals, Farina & Stymie, Framed, 17 X 14 In.	65.00
Card, Valentine, Animated, Move Watermelon, Boys Eyes Shift, 9 X 7 In.	18.00
Chef, Cookie Jar, Pearl China	150.00
Cigar Box, New Coon, Black Caricature Lid & Label, Wooden	85.00
Clicker, Black Man Playing Harmonica, Tin Litho, 1920	35.00
Clock, Aunt Jemima, Ceramic, Red Wing	100.00
Clock, Mammy .... 75.00 To 95.00
Clothes Brush, Aunt Jemima, Green & Red	20.00
Coaster, Coon Chicken Inn	60.00
Condiment Set, Black Head, Germany, 2 In., 3 Piece	285.00
Cookie Jar, Aunt Jemima, McCoy, C.1939	75.00
Cookie Jar, Big Eyes, Pink Dress, Sears, 10 In.	85.00
Cookie Jar, Chef, Pearl China	150.00
Cookie Jar, Mammy, Mosaic Tile	250.00
Cookie Jar, Mammy, Pearl China	300.00
Cookie Jar, Mammy, Yellow Dress, Brown Polka Dots, Mosaic Tile, 12 In.	250.00
Cover, Toaster, Mammy, Yellow Gingham Dress, Dotted Swiss Apron	35.00
Dish, Coon Chicken Inn, White, Syracuse China, 5 1/2 In.	40.00
Display, 10 Little Nigger Boys, Die Cut, San Fran.Fair, 1894, 6 Pc.	100.00
Document, Slave, Abingdon, Virginia, 3 Females, 1815, 5 X 6 1/2 In.	25.00
Document, Slave, Virginia, Value of Female, Ages 18 To 50	27.50
Doll, African, Beaded Bodice, 14 In.	85.00
Doll, Aunt Jemima, Holding Bowl of Pancake Batter, 1 1/2 In.	4.00
Doll, Baby, Celluloid, Jointed, Layette, Bottle, 4 1/2 In., Pr.	85.00
Doll, Baby, Composition, 18 In.	350.00
Doll, Black Mammy, Cloth, Kerchief, Dress, Apron, Handmade	35.00
Doll, Boy, Composition, Crazed Head, Movable Arms, AGD, 11 In.	75.00
Doll, Girl, Painted Hair, 3 Pigtails, Composition, 12 In.	125.00
Doll, Hard Plastic, Original Clothes, Negro Tidy, 13 In.	10.00
Doll, Mammy, Blue Dress, White Apron, Gigantic Red Lips, Cloth, 15 In.	65.00
Doll, Mammy, Pushing Stroller, Composition, C.1930	100.00
Doll, Woman, Bead Eyes, Stuffed Cloth, Old Cloth Costume, 11 1/2 In.	200.00
Egg Timer, Figural, Chef, Porcelain, Germany	45.00
Figure, Man Playing Banjo, Polychrome Paint, Wooden, 15 1/4 In.	45.00
Figure, Man's Face, Carved, Weathered, Red, White & Black, 12 In.	100.00
Figurine, Alligator With Black Nude Baby In Mouth, Grotesque, 4 In.	110.00
Figurine, Babies, Twins, Sleeping, Blue PJ's, Pink PJ's, 4 In., Pair	25.00
Figurine, Band, Playing Instruments, Occupied Japan, 5 In., 5 Piece	150.00
Figurine, Banjo Player, Ceramic, Occupied Japan, 3 In.	17.50
Figurine, Booker T.Washington, Standing, Rubber, 1900–15	135.00
Figurine, Boy On Alligator, Straw Hat, Germany, Bisque, 4 X 3 In.	95.00
Figurine, Boy, Holding Watermelon Slice, German, 3 1/2 In.	20.00
Figurine, Mammy, Red Dress, White Apron, Metal, 1940s, 2 1/2 In.	35.00
Figurine, Musician, Green, Yellow, Orange, Blue, 4 In., Set of 6	95.00
Figurine, Porter, Blue Suit & Hat, Yellow Satchel, Papier–Mache, 4 In.	18.00
Figurine, Umpire, 1941 Lafayette Rittgers, Stern Look, Plaster, 7 In.	22.00
Figurine, Way Down South, Boy With Watermelon, Yellow Shirt, 8 In.	38.00
Game, Balls In Mouth, Schultz & Co., Zanesville, Oh., Tin, Glass, 2 In.	65.00
Game, Little Black Sambo, Box	58.00
Hat, Aunt Jemima, Breakfast Club, Paper, Eat A Better Breakfast, 1940	35.00
Holder, Notepad, Mammy, Red Shirt, White Bandanna, Plastic, 10 In.	38.00
Holder, String, Mammy Head, Blue Bandanna, Chalkware, 7 1/4 In.	75.00
Holder, Thread, Thimble, Victorian, Figural, Boy, Watermelon, Pig, 4 In.	125.00
Hot Pad Holder, Mammy, Souvenir, Beloit, Wisc.	10.00
Humidor, Black Man, In High Pointed Collar, Bisque, German	200.00
Humidor, Mammy With Turban, 5 1/4 In. ....*Illus*	110.00
Jar, Black Man, Smoking Pipe, Bisque, Covered, 5 In.	115.00
Jigger, Dancing, Jointed, Wooden, White Hat, Dancing Board, 12 In.	95.00
Knocker, Cotton Club, Cab Calloway Print, Red & Black, 7 In.	35.00
Label, Fruit, Dixie Boy, Boy Eating Grapefruit, Square, 9 In.	5.00
Lamp, Pinup, Mammy's Face, Ceramic, Beige Shade, 15 In.	175.00
Lawn Sprinkler, Black Man, Wooden	60.00

Map, Amos & Andy, Weber City, Envelope 30.00
Marionette, Topsy, Wood, Plastic, Flowered Dress, 1930s, 13 1/2 In. 110.00
Matchsafe, Chef 45.00
Memo Pad, Aunt Jemima 25.00
Menu, Old Dixie Southern Barbecue, Red, White, Black, Graphics 38.00
Mug, Grinning Man's Face, Grotesque, Handle, Ceramic, Japan, 5 In. 65.00
Napkin Holder, Coon Chicken Inn, Chalkware 115.00
Napkin, Plantation Grill, N.C., Black Chef Saying Chicken What Am 35.00
Needlecase, Figural, Girl, Embroidered, Late 19th Century, 5 In. 125.00
Noisemaker, Dancing Minstrel, Yellow, Blue, Red, Wood, 6 In. 15.00
Pad, Cream of Wheat, Unused, 3 1/2 X 5 3/4 In. 18.00
Paper Doll, Aunt Jemima Family 75.00
Paper Doll, Girl, Activated, Dennison, C.1880 .... 45.00
Pennant, Philadelphia Stars Baseball, Black League, Red Felt, 23 In. 65.00
Photograph, Children, Begging For Money, Train Station, 3 X 5 In. 15.00
Pie Bird, Black Chef .... 38.00 To 40.00
Pie Bird, Mammy 38.00
Pin, Black Woman, Art Deco, Rhinestones, Gold Trim, 1 3/4 In. 45.00
Pinback, Hassan Cigarettes, Two's Company, Man, Lady, Lover, Signed 18.00
Pinback, Lasses & Honey, From Amos N'Andy Show, Celluloid, 1 1/2 In. 23.00
Pincushion, Mammy, Box, 1940s 18.00
Pincushion, Sambo, Eating Watermelon Top, Miniature 25.00
Pipe, Blackface, Pottery, Exaggerated Features, 6 In. 45.00
Pitcher, Syrup, Aunt Jemima 27.00
Pitcher, Syrup, Mammy 15.00
Planter, Black Chef On Stove, Brown Stove, Red Trim, Ceramic, 5 1/2 In 35.00
Plaque, Umbrella Boy & Girl, Pink, White Spatterware, 7 1/2 In., Pair 45.00
Plate, Black Couple Decal, On Phone, Cupid Between 85.00
Plate, Coon Chicken Inn, 5 1/2 In. 40.00
Postcard, Black Man, With Alligator 5.00
Postcard, Mammy, 3 Children, Sack On Head, 1 Child Hitching, 1941 .... 28.00
Postcard, Picking, Weighing Cotton 8.00
Potholder, Little Girl, Red, Yellow, Green, Chalkware, 5 1/2 In. 25.00
Potholder, Mammy & Chef Face, Red Dress, White Chef, 6 In., Pair 45.00
Purse, Coconut Face, Pickaninny, With 3 Braids, Painted, Round, 5 In. 27.00
Rack, Pipe, Porter, Red Cap, Large White Teeth, Wooden, 8 1/2 X 8 In. 95.00
Record, Little Black Sambo 32.00
Rolling Pin, Mammy, Hollywood Ceramic 35.00
Sack, Cornmeal, Miss Hattie, Sho Is Fine, Hattie, Muffins, 19 X 10 In. 38.00
Salad Set, Wooden Fork & Spoon, Mammy & Chef, Funnel, Cruet 125.00
Salt & Pepper, Aunt Jemima & Mose, Celluloid, Small 12.50
Salt & Pepper, Aunt Jemima, Large 27.50
Salt & Pepper, Black Boy 38.00
Salt & Pepper, Boy On Camel, Green Shirt, White Pants, 5 In., Pair 38.00
Salt & Pepper, Boy On Cuke & Corn 32.00
Salt & Pepper, Chef Serving Watermelon, Japan, 4 In. 35.00
Salt & Pepper, Chef With Milk Can, Pink, Brown, Yellow, Blue, 6 In. 45.00
Salt & Pepper, Mammy & Chef, Cast Metal 45.00
Salt & Pepper, Mammy & Chef, Fat, White Outfits, Red Trim, 5 In. 35.00
Salt & Pepper, Salty & Peppy, Pearl China, 8 In. 75.00
Salt Shaker, Mammy, Fat, 4 In. 32.00
Shade Pull, Head, With Pop Eyes, Bakelite 22.00
Shade Pull, Mammy, Plastic, Red Dress & Bandanna, 2 1/2 In. 15.00
Shaker, Range, Mammy & Chef, Yellow Outfit, Blue Trim, Newark, 7 In. 45.00
Shaker, Range, Salty & Peppy, Red, White Chef's Hat, Wood, 4 In., Pair 25.00
Shoe Shine Cloth, Cadie Man Shining Shoes 38.00
Shot Glass, Double Shot, Red Clay, Red Lips, Pink Glow, Nose 18.00
Shot Glass, Lion Chasing Black, Says One For The Road 10.00
Soap Dish, Mammy, Figural, Cast Iron 125.00
Spice Set, Aunt Jemima, Wall Rack, 6 Piece 175.00
Spoon Rest, Uncle Mose, Embossed, White Hair, Iron, 4 1/2 X 3 In. 25.00
String Holder, Aunt Jemima 26.00
String Holder, Fredericksburg Butler, Brown 75.00
String Holder, Mammy Head 50.00

String Holder, Mammy, White Dress, Holds Bouquet, Japan, 7 In. 75.00
Sugar & Creamer, Aunt Jemima & Uncle Mose, F & F Die Works 65.00
Sugar & Creamer, Aunt Jemima, Uncle Mose 125.00
Syrup, Mammy, Red, Plastic, F & F, 5 1/2 In. 18.00
Tablecloth, Black Children, With Watermelons, Square, 51 In. 85.00
Tablecloth, Mammy & Child, Man, Singing, Cotton, 50 X 45 In. 75.00
Tea Set, Mammy's Face, Bulging Eyes & Lips, Ceramic, Metal Handle 150.00
Thermometer, Black Boy, Peeking, Pressed Wood, Brown, 1949, 5 1/2 In. 10.00
Thimble, Aunt Jemima 28.00
Toaster Cover, Black Doll 40.00
Toaster Cover, Mammy, Cloth, Stuffed Torso .... 16.00 To 19.00
Tobacco Jar, Boy, With Pipe, 4 1/2 In. 85.00
Towel Holder, Mammy, Wooden 30.00
Towel, Kitchen, Banjo Farm Scene, Boy & Girl Dancing, 15 X 28 In. 28.00
Towel, Kitchen, Mammy Preparing Pancakes, Spatula, Pitcher, Red Border 35.00
Towel, Linen, Tiny Tots Playing & Eating Watermelon 60.00
Toy, Airplane Kit, Aunt Jemima, Balsa Wood, 1930s, 14 In. 20.00
Toy, Amos & Andy, Tin Litho, New York, 1930, 11 1/2 In. ....Illus 650.00
Urn, Cigarette, Male Servant, Brass, 3 1/4 X 3 1/4 In. 125.00
Vase, Lady, Orange Dress, Yellow Turban, Ceramic, 5 1/2 In. 35.00
Vase, Lady, Sepia, Club Plantation, Yellow, Orange Dress, Ceramic, 6 In. 38.00
Vase, Lady, White Feathered Turban, Gold Earrings, Ceramic, 5 In. 38.00
View Master, Little Black Sambo, 3–D, Story Booklet 50.00
Wall Bracket, Venetian Blackamoor, Gilt Robe, 21 In., Pair 1600.00

Blown glass was formed by forcing air through a rod into molten glass. Early glass and some forms of art glass were hand blown. Other types of glass were molded or pressed.

BLOWN GLASS, Bell Jar, Amber, Applied Rim & Bulbous Handle, 15 In. 155.00
Bottle, 24 Swirled Ribs, Zanesville, Aqua, 7 1/4 In. 285.00
Bottle, Apothecary, Engraved Vintage Pattern, 12 1/8 In. 130.00
Bottle, Bar, Pillar Mold, Ribbed, Shoulder, 10 In. 50.00
Bottle, Club Shape, 16 Broken Swirl Ribs, Mantua, Aqua, 8 In. 95.00
Bottle, Club Shape, Aqua, 24 Rib Swirl, Zanesville, 7 1/2 In. 85.00
Bottle, Demijohn, Applied Collar, Nienburg Label, 27 In. 225.00
Bottle, Double Gemel, White Looping, Pewter Cap, 8 In. 25.00
Bottle, Emerald Green, 15 Vertical Ribs, 11 3/8 In. 110.00
Bottle, Flattened Globular, 25 Swirled Ribs, Aqua, 9 In. 155.00
Bottle, Globular, 18 Swirled Ribs, Pale Green, 6 7/8 In. 90.00
Bottle, Globular, 30 Swirled Ribs, Pale Green, 5 1/4 In. 225.00
Bottle, Globular, Aqua, 8 3/4 In. 60.00

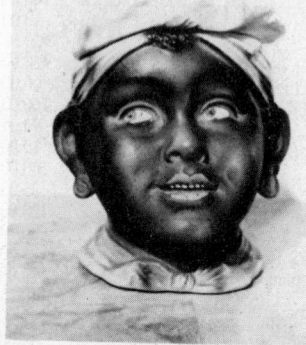

Black, Humidor, Mammy With Turban,
5 1/4 In.

Black, Toy, Amos & Andy, Tin Litho,
New York, 1930, 11 1/2 In.

Bottle, Powder Horn, Clear, Red Looping, Pittsburgh, 11 1/4 In.	250.00
Bottle, Scent, Rigaree, Coiled Tail, 3 In.	55.00
Bowl, Applied Ring Below Flared Rim, 1835–50, 3 5/8 In.	100.00
Bowl, Copper Wheel Engraved Medallion, Flared, 3 1/8 In.	145.00
Bowl, Deep Amber, Flared Rim, 3 X 7 3/4 In.	225.00
Bowl, Footed, Hollow Stem, 5 Cent 1831 Silver Piece, 4 In.	300.00
Bowl, Sapphire Blue, 16 Swirled Ribs, Flared Foot, 4 X 4 In.	135.00
Compote, Amber, White Applied Rim, 4 X 1 1/2 In.	195.00
Compote, Lily Pad, New York, C.1830	2400.00
Creamer, Blue Gray, Ribbed Mold, Collar, Folded Lip, 4 In.	235.00
Creamer, Light Green, Applied Foot, Handle, Vertical Rib, 5 In.	300.00
Creamer, Sapphire Blue, 14 Swirled Ribs, Foot & Handle, 5 In.	200.00
Cruet, Hollow Applied Handle & Stopper, Clear, 6 7/8 In.	70.00
Cuspidor, Folded Rim, Reid Bottle Co., Massillon, Oh., Amber	75.00
Decanter, 3 Applied Rings, Mushroom Stopper, Clear, 8 In.	30.00
Decanter, Chain Link Design, T.Cain, S.Boston Glass, 7 7/8 In.	315.00
Decanter, Cut Mushroom Stopper, Pouring Spout, 3 Mold, 7 In.	100.00
Decanter, Liberty, Eagle, Sunburst Stopper, Early 19th Century	425.00
Decanter, Wheel Stopper, Applied Rings, Thomas Caines, 1 Qt.	160.00
Ewer, Copper Wheel Bird Medallion, Pewter Lid, 9 1/2 In.	105.00
Flip, Base Panels, Copperwheel Engraved Rim Design, 6 In.	90.00
Flip, Copperwheel Engraved Basket of Flowers, 7 5/8 In.	250.00
Float Ball, Net Covering, 1 Green, 1 Blue, 12 In., Pair	50.00
Goblet, Baluster Stem, Paneled Bowl, Clear, 6 1/8 In.	10.00
Goblet, Cut Rayed Foot, Wafer Stem, Clear, Pittsburgh, 5 In.	30.00
Hat, Brim Turned Down On 2 Sides, Light Brown	65.00
Inkwell, 3 Mold, Olive Amber, Round, 2 1/4 In.	65.00
Jar, Bell, Clear, Base Ring, 18 1/2 In.	105.00
Jar, Preserve, Aqua, Straight Lip, 9 1/2 In.	75.00
Jigger, 12 Swirled Ribs, Amethyst, 2 7/8 In.	15.00
Mug, Applied Handle, Cobalt Rim, 2 3/4 In.	100.00
Mug, Applied Handle, Presentation, Initials E.D., 4 1/2 In.	155.00
Mug, Barrel Shape, Applied Handle, Foliage, French, 6 1/2 In.	85.00
Mug, Free–Blown, Applied Aqua Handle, 1 Pt., 5 1/4 In.	50.00
Pan, Folded Rim, Golden Amber, 17 1/2 X 3 3/4 In.	100.00
Pan, Milk, Folded Rim, Pouring Spout, Light Green, 11 5/8 In.	115.00
Pitcher, 12 Panel Base, Handle, Tooled Lip, Pittsburgh, 8 In.	250.00
Pitcher, Free–Blown, Helmet Shape, Horizontal Ribs, 8 3/8 In.	400.00
Pitcher, Lily Pad, Blue Aqua, New York, Threading, 6 1/4 In.	570.00
Pitcher, Pillar Molded, 12 Rib, 9 1/2 In.	245.00
Pitcher, Ruffled Rim, Floral Enameling, Blue	125.00
Pitcher, White Looping, Applied Handle, Pittsburgh, 8 7/8 In.	200.00
Rolling Pin, Free–Blown, Window Glass, 19th Century, 17 In.	130.00
Salt, Galleried Bowl, 12 Swirled Ribs, Clear, 2 3/4 In.	15.00
Salt, Master, 3 Mold, 12 1/8 In.	160.00
Salt, Pedestal, Flowers Engraved, 1 5/8 In.	10.00
Sugar & Creamer, Blue Applied Rim, 12 Panel Bowl, 3 5/8 In.	900.00
Sugar & Creamer, Sapphire Blue, 17 Swirled Ribs, 3 1/2 In.	420.00
Sugar, Bulbous, Gallery Rim, Domed Lid, Floral, 7 3/4 In.	800.00
Sweetmeat Jar, 2 Ribs, Dome Shaped Cover, 11 In., Pair	160.00
Tumbler, 3 Mold, 2 3/4 In.	95.00
Tumbler, Aqua, Sheared Top, Fire Polished Pontil, 19th Century	10.00
Tumbler, Barrel Shape, 3 Mold, 3 1/2 In.	200.00
Tumbler, Cobalt Blue, 3 5/8 In.	35.00
Tumbler, Light Green, Expanded Diamond, 3 5/8 In.	120.00
Tumbler, Violet Blue, 8 Panels, Pittsburgh, 3 1/4 In.	85.00
Vase, Bowl & Rim Cobalt Blue, Pittsburgh, Footed, 9 1/2 In.	1275.00
Vase, Pale Green, Tapered Body, Ribbon Side Grips, Roman, 5 In.	215.00
Vase, Pillar Mold, Baluster Stem, Pittsburgh, 10 In.	140.00
Vase, Ruby Loopings, Gauffered, Stemmed, Pittsburgh, 10 In.	950.00
Whiskey Tumbler, Arch Pattern, Cobalt Blue, C.1840, 2 1/2 In.	44.00
Wine, Double Cotton Twist, English, 5 5/8 In.	165.00
Wine, Knopped Stem, Swirled Bowl, Clear, 4 3/8 In.	55.00
Wine, Wafer Stem, Paneled Bowl, 5 3/4 In.	10.00

Witch Ball, Stand, White Looping, Scalloped Rim, Pittsburgh 225.00
    BLUE AMBERINA, see Bluerina
    BLUE GLASS, see Cobalt Blue
    BLUE ONION, see Onion

 Blue Willow pattern has been made in England since 1780. The pattern has been copied by factories in many countries, including Germany, Japan, and the United States. It is still being made. Willow was named for a pattern that pictures a bridge, birds, willow trees, and a Chinese landscape.

BLUE WILLOW, Bank, Pig, 3 Tier, 1950s, Box, Japan	20.00
Biscuit Jar, Covered, Silver Plated Rim, Lid, Bail, Minton	135.00
Bowl, Allerton, 6 1/2 In.	12.00
Bowl, Allerton, 9 In.	48.00
Bowl, Ridgway, 5 In.	18.00
Bowl, Royal China, 5 1/2 In.	2.25
Bowl, Vegetable, Allerton, 2 1/4 X 8 1/4 In.	32.00
Bowl, Vegetable, Homer Laughlin, 8 1/2 In.	24.00
Butter, Covered, 1/4 Lb.	50.00
Cake Plate, Alleron, 7 In.	15.00
Casserole, Covered, Child's	18.00
Castor Set, Child's	125.00
Chamber Pot, Mason	180.00
Chocolate Pot, Warmer, Japan	85.00
Coaster, Box	6.00
Cookie Jar, Milk Can Shape, Design On Front	11.00
Creamer, Allerton	75.00
Creamer, Booth	95.00
Cup & Saucer, Dark Blue, Japan	4.00
Ginger Jar, Mason, 8 In.	50.00
Gravy Boat, Attached Underplate, Ashworth	30.00
Gravy Tureen, Underplate, Ladle, 1950s, Box, Japan	30.00
Grill Plate	10.00
Grill Plate, Child's .... 55.00 To 75.00	
Hatpin Holder	18.00
Mustard, Covered, Attached Saucer	75.00
Pepper Mill, Chrome Fittings, 2 3/4 In.	14.50
Pitcher & Bowl, Mason	650.00
Pitcher & Bowl, Melrose, K.& Co., Oval, Pitcher, 12 In.	385.00
Pitcher, Bulbous, 9 In.	95.00
Pitcher, Juice, Dark Blue, Japan	30.00
Pitcher, Milk	50.00
Plate, Antique Willow, Gold Trim, Japan, 10 In.	10.00
Plate, Buffalo China, 9 3/4 In.	13.00
Plate, Butterfly Border, 7 1/2 In.	20.00
Plate, Dark Blue, Japan, 9 In.	5.00
Plate, Homer Laughlin, 7 1/4 In.	4.00
Plate, Maastricht, 9 1/2 In.	10.00
Plate, Old Hall, 10 In.	18.00
Plate, Royal China, 9 1/4 In.	2.50
Plate, Scalloped, Allerton, 7 In.	14.00
Plate, Wedgwood, 8 In.	12.50
Plate, Wedgwood, 10 In.	17.50
Platter, Allerton, 11 X 13 1/2 In.	65.00
Platter, Allerton, 15 1/2 In.	120.00
Platter, Barker & Sons, C.1850, 15 1/2 X 12 1/4 In.	110.00
Platter, Britannia, Mauve, 11 1/2 X 9 1/2 In.	35.00
Platter, Homer Laughlin, 9 1/2 X 12 In.	18.00
Platter, Marked Improved Willow D.& Co., 17 3/4 In.	85.00
Pot Scrubber Holder	35.00
Salt & Pepper	35.00
Saucer, Child's, 4 In.	5.00
Snack Hound	39.00
Soap Dish, Burleigh Ware	35.00

Sugar & Creamer, Homer Laughlin	31.50
Sugar & Creamer, Staffordshire	57.50
Sugar, Covered, Ridgway	55.00
Tea Set, Child's, Service For 4, 15 Piece	110.00
Teapot, Individual	35.00
Teapot, Sadler	25.00
Teapot, Strainer, C.1900	95.00
Tidbit Tray, 2 Tier, 1950s, Box, Japan	20.00
Tile, Oval, 8 In.	150.00
Tile, Round, 12 In.	50.00
Toby Jug, Willow Coat, Green Vest, Yellow Breeches, Large	145.00
Tureen, Covered, Adderly	100.00
Tureen, Johnson, Red	150.00
Tureen, Underplate, Child's, Japan	55.00

Bluerina is a type of art glass which shades from light blue to ruby. It is often called blue amberina.

BLUERINA, Vase, Amber Trim, 6 In.	135.00

The Boch Freres factory was founded in 1841 in La Louviere in eastern Belgium. The wares resemble the work of Villeroy & Boch. The factory is still in business.

BOCH FRERES, Plate, Woman's Head, 10 In.	100.00
Vase, Flowers, Sgrafitto Design, 12 In.	400.00

Osso China Company was reorganized as Edward Marshall Boehm, Inc., in 1953. The company is still working in England and New Jersey. In the early days of the factory, dishes were made, but the elaborate and lifelike bird figurines are the best known ware. Edward Marshall Boehm, the founder, died in 1961; but the firm has continued to design and produce porcelain. Today, the firm makes both limited and unlimited editions of figurines and plates.

BOEHM, Bust, Madonna, White Bisque, 6 1/2 In.	185.00
Bust, Madonna, White Glaze, Gold Trim	550.00
Figurine, Angel, Pigtails, 4 1/2 In.	400.00
Figurine, Beagle	175.00
Figurine, Bluejay	165.00
Figurine, Cedar Waxwing	165.00
Figurine, Common Tern, No.497F, Early 1900s	6500.00
Figurine, Cupid With Horn, White	250.00 To 350.00
Figurine, Deer	165.00
Figurine, Deer Mouse	150.00
Figurine, Don Quixote	120.00
Figurine, Fledging, Baby Robin, No.437J	240.00
Figurine, Fledgling, Baby Blue Jay, No.436	235.00 To 240.00
Figurine, Fledgling, Baby Bluebird, No.442	175.00 To 220.00
Figurine, Fledgling, Baby Chick, Yellow	195.00
Figurine, Fledgling, Baby Crested Flycatcher, No.458J	320.00
Figurine, Fledgling, Kingfisher, No.449	240.00
Figurine, Fledgling, Magpie, No.476	270.00 To 310.00
Figurine, Fledgling, Puffin	160.00
Figurine, Fledgling, Red Poll, No.495	220.00
Figurine, Fledgling, Western Blue Birds, No.494	350.00
Figurine, Frog On Lily Pad, 1979	160.00
Figurine, Giselle	120.00
Figurine, Goldfinch	165.00
Figurine, Lamb, On Stomach, Legs Underneath, White, 5 X 3 1/2 In.	115.00
Figurine, Meadowlark, With Dandelion & Toadstool, No.435	1495.00
Figurine, Mouse	165.00
Figurine, Nutcracker	120.00
Figurine, Orangutan	600.00
Figurine, Prothonotary Warbler, With Eggs, Fledglings, 5 1/2 In.	500.00
Figurine, Red Fox	300.00
Figurine, Rufous Hummingbird	2000.00

Figurine, Swan Lake 120.00
Figurine, Thrush 5000.00
Figurine, Tree Sparrow 375.00
Figurine, White Mouse 75.00
Figurine, Wood Thrush 5000.00
Figurine, Yellow Chick 175.00
Plate, Annual, 1970, Woodthrush, Box 225.00
Plate, Annual, 1974, Hummingbird, Box 60.00
Plate, Annual, 1975, Redstart, Box 50.00
Plate, Annual, 1976, Cardinal, Box 58.00
Plate, Annual, 1977, Robin, Box 45.00
Plate, Life's Best Wishes, Box 60.00

Bohemian glass is an ornate overlay or flashed glass made during the Victorian era. It has been reproduced in Bohemia, which is now a part of Czechoslovakia. Glass made from 1875 to 1900 is preferred by collectors.

BOHEMIAN GLASS, Bowl, Cut Vintage Design, 10 X 4 3/8 In. 50.00
Compote, Removable Epergne Center, Cut, 9 1/2 X 15 In. 125.00
Creamer, Floradora, Cranberry 70.00
Decanter Set, Ruby Cut To Clear, Deer, Birds, 3 Piece 195.00
Decanter, Blue, Overlay, Cut, 14 In., Pair .... Cover 350.00
Decanter, Deer & Castle, Ruby, Original Stopper, Dated 1888 .... 135.00
Decanter, Ship's, Ruby To Clear 275.00
Decanter, Stopper, Flamingo 75.00
Goblet, White Cut To Clear, Ruby Reserves, Engraved, 5 In. 45.00
Jardiniere, Red, Engraved Birds, Deers, Trees, 7 1/4 In. 45.00
Lantern, Victorian, Etched Glass, Cranberry Body, 12 In. 575.00
Spooner, Floradora, Cranberry 55.00
Stein, Ruby, Engraved Dog, Forest, Handle, Cover, 5 In. 300.00
Stein, Ruby, Forest Scene, Souvenir De Luchon, 4 1/2 In. 225.00
Sugar, Covered, Floradora, Cranberry 70.00
Vase, Cut & Gilt Design, Enamel Overlay, C.1880, 17 In., Pr. 1650.00
Vase, Deer, Ruby Cut To Clear, 12 1/4 In. 90.00
Vase, Enamel Overlay, Gilt Design, Lilies, 17 3/4 In., Pair 1650.00
Vase, Gilt Design, Enamel Overlay, Cranberry, 14 In., Pair 2100.00
Vase, Red, Deer, Wreath, Castle, 10 In. 225.00
Vase, Ruby Cut To Clear, Deer, 12 1/4 In. 90.00
Vase, Ruby To Clear, Deer & Castle Scene, 10 X 7 In. 115.00

Bone dishes were considered a necessary part of a table setting for the Victorian table. The crescent–shaped dish was kept at the edge of the dinner plate so the bones removed from the fish could be stored away from the uneaten food. Some bone dishes were made in more fanciful shapes and many resemble fish.

BONE DISH, Fish Shape, Blue, White 55.00
Staffordshire, Black & White Transfer 15.00

Bookends have probably been used since books became inexpensive. Early libraries kept books in cupboards, not on open shelves. By the 1870s bookends appear, especially homemade fretcarved wooden examples. Most bookends listed in this book date from the twentieth century.

BOOKENDS, Amish Man, Woman On Bench, Polychrome Paint, Cast Iron, 4 3/4 In. 30.00
Arab On Horse, Hubley 30.00
Art Deco, Dancing Girls, Iron, 1926 .... 20.00
Buccaneer, Pompano Bros.P.Hersil, 1928 .... 75.00
Bust, Abraham Lincoln, Bronzed Metal, Parson Casket Hadware Co. 48.00
Camel, Iron, Dark Finish, 5 1/8 In. 35.00
Chalkware, Celeron, N.Y., Amusement Park, Yellow 32.50
Colonial Figures, Porcelain, White, Gold Trim, 7 X 3 In. 29.00
Conestoga Wagons, Polychrome Paint, Hubley, Cast Iron, 6 5/8 In. 20.00
Copper, Art Nouveau, Initials, Floral, Hand Carved Walnut, 5 In. 27.00
Deco Lady, Holding Skirt While Dancing, Bronze 110.00

Dog, Airedale, Bronze Finish, Marked, 1929, 6 In. 18.00
Dog, Profile Figures of Terriers, Cast Iron, C.1900, 5 1/2 In. 45.00
Dutch Girls, Cast Iron 15.00
Eagles, With Star Base, Cast Iron, Unpainted, Hamilton Foundry 55.00
Egyptian Style, Masonic Emblem, Copper Finish, 6 3/4 In. 25.00
Elephant Head, Signed L.V.Aronson, Large, 1922 ..... 50.00
Football Player, Bronze Finish, 1920s 65.00
German Shepherd, Bronzed 45.00
Girl At Fountain, Cast Iron 24.00
Gleaners, Bronze Finish 27.00
Golf, Man In Knickers, Swings Club, Metal, C.1900, 5 In. 50.00
Gothic Gates, Green & Brown Paint, Cast Iron, 5 3/4 In. 15.00
Great Horned Owl, Cast Iron 50.00
Hiawatha, Dark Bronze Wash, Indian, Forest & Verse 40.00
High Top Shoes, Half Relief, Brass, 5 3/8 In. 55.00
Horse, Rearing, Hand Painted, Ceramic 140.00
Horseheads, Glass, 5 X 3/5 In. 40.00
Indian Tepee, Indian Kneeling, Bow & Arrow, Copper 295.00
Indian, On Horseback, Iron, Bronze Finish, Copyright 1927, 5 In. 15.00
Irish Setter, Brass 35.00
John & Jacqueline Kennedy, Chalkware 20.00
Leaping Foxes, Bronze 40.00
Liberty Bell, Iron 25.00
Lincoln Memorial, Bronze, B & H 40.00
Lions, Bronze, 7 3/4 In. 22.50
Monkey, Reading Book, Marble Base, J.B.Hirsh, C.1931 ..... 135.00
Monkey, Silver Bronze, Marble, Edouard M.Sandoz, C.1925, 7 In. 990.00
Musicians, Male & Female, Gilded Metal, Onyx Base, 3 1/2 X 6 In. 125.00
Nude, Cast Iron 22.00
Old Gentleman In Chair, Reading Book, Bronze, J.Rukl, 4 X 6 In. 225.00
Open Fire With Kettle, Polychrome Paint, Cast Iron, 5 7/8 In. 12.50
Owl Head, Bronze, Signed M.Carr 120.00
Owl, Glass, 1920s 18.00
Owl, White Alabaster 85.00
Owls & Trees, Painted, Bronze, Austrian 375.00
Parrot, Polychrome Paint, Cast Iron, 6 3/4 In. 85.00
Pennsylvania State Police, Brass, C.1945 ..... 60.00
Pirate, Ivory Face, Bronze, Marble Base, 5 1/2 In. 55.00
Scotty, Standing On Block, 1 Ear Up, 1 Down, Pot Metal, 6 X 7 In. 20.00
Ship, Cast Iron ..... 15.00 To 20.00
Ships, Metallic Finish, Polychrome Paint, Cast Iron, 4 In. 5.00
Ships, Polychrome Paint, Marked 2, Cast Iron, 5 7/8 In. 12.50
Squirrel, Silver, Etched & Polished, Joseph Hoffman, Signed 450.00
St.George & Dragon, Brass Finish, Marked Hubley 312, 5 5/8 In. 5.00
Stagecoach & Horses, Cast Iron, 3 In. 20.00
Teddy Roosevelt, Iron, Signed Gregory S.Allen 225.00
Thinker, Bronze Finish 15.00
Winged Nudes, Gilded Bronze, French 100.00
Wolfhounds, Art Deco, Metal, Nu–Art 65.00

 Bookmarks were originally made of parchment, cloth, or leather. Soon woven silk ribbon, thin cardboard, celluloid, wood, silver, tortoiseshell, and metals were used. Examples made before 1850 are scarce, but there are many to be found dating before 1920.

BOOKMARK, Boston Brown Flakes, Celluloid 9.00
Carnation Milk, Pan Pacific Expo., Celluloid 27.50
Clock, The Witching Hour, Celluloid 10.00
Cunningham Pianos, Celluloid ..... 6.00 To 10.00
Flag, 13 Stars, Silk 22.50
Maltene, Owl Shape, Celluloid 15.00
Pears Soap, Hand Holds Page, 7 In. 12.00
Philadelphia International Exhibit, Memorial Hall, 1876 ..... 40.00
Poole Pianos, Celluloid 12.50
Richelieu Spices, Fold Out, 1902 Calendar 13.00

Ship, Sterling Silver 32.00
Standard Sewing Machine, Little Bopeep, Gold Ground 8.00
Teddy Bear, Stove, Celluloid 20.00
Texaco, Celluloid 15.00
Velvet Candy, Monkey, Die Cut Tin 20.00
Woman Ironing, Celluloid 50.00
World's Fair, 1933, Metal 7.50

BOSTON & SANDWICH CO., see Sandwich Glass; Lutz

As soon as the commercial bottle was invented, the opener to be used with the new types of closures became a necessity. Many types of bottle openers can be found, most dating from the twentieth century. Collectors prize advertising and comic openers.

BOTTLE OPENER, 4–Eyed Man, Thick Mustache, 3 Teeth, Cast Iron 60.00
  4–Eyed Woman, Cast Iron .... 50.00 To 55.00
  Acorn Pattern, Sterling, Georg Jensen, 4 3/4 In. 65.00
  Alligator, Cast Iron, Original Paint, 6 1/4 In. 55.00
  Ashtray, Drunk Leaning On Lamppost, Cast Iron, John Wright 20.00
  Auto Jack, Cast Iron 20.00
  Baseball Cap, Black, Orange Lettering, N.Y.Mets 28.00
  Black Boy, Alligator Biting Behind, Cast Iron 110.00
  Black Man, Smiling, Wall Mount, Cast Iron 45.00
  Bottle Shape, Schlitz Beer, Wood 8.00
  Bull, Cast Iron 20.00
  Burgermeister, Wall Mount, Iron Nickle Plated, 1940s 3.00
  Chicken, Cast Iron, 3 In. 49.00
  Clown Head, Cast Iron, White Paint, 4 1/2 In. 75.00
  Cowboy, Guitar 50.00
  Crayfish, Cast Iron 40.00
  Dachshund, Brass, 4 1/2 In. 60.00
  Dancing Slipper, Manhattan Bottling, Milwaukee 12.00
  Dog, Pointer, Black & White, Iron 55.00
  Donkey, Cast Iron, Painted, 4 In. 12.00
  Dr Pepper, Drink, A Bite To Eat 11.00
  Drunk, Leaning On Palm Tree, Cast Iron 28.00
  Duck's Head, Cast Iron 45.00
  Elephant, Cast Iron, Painted, 3 1/2 In. 10.00
  Fire Hydrant, Cast Iron 20.00
  Fish 35.00
  Fisherman, Cast Iron 60.00
  Fort Pitt Beer, Metal 6.50
  Gable Tavern, Bell Shape 15.00
  Goat, Cast Iron 20.00
  Goldnugget Beer, Brass 75.00
  Hippo, Cast Iron 15.00
  Indian, Aluminum 48.00
  Jockey's Cap .... 10.00 To 15.00
  Lobster, Red Paint, Cast Iron, 4 In. 8.00
  Macaw, Long Tail, On Perch, Cast Iron 28.00
  Man, Wicked Look, Cast Iron 35.00
  Moxie, With Stopper 7.00
  Nude, Manhattan Bottling, Milwaukee 12.00
  Nude, Miss America, Chicago World's Fair 45.00
  Nude, Standing, Marked Herbert, 4 1/2 In. 24.00
  Old Crow Whiskey, Figural, Opener Springs From Bottom 10.00
  Old Snifter, Man, Top Hat, Painted, Corkscrew, 7 In. 30.00
  Parrot, On Perch, Painted, Cast Iron, Marked, 5 1/2 In. 20.00
  Pelican, Cast Iron, 3 1/4 In. 49.00
  Schlitz, Brass 28.00
  Seagull 45.00
  Shark, Aluminum, 7 In. 18.00
  Squirrel, Brass 32.00
  Stag Handle, Sterling Ferrule, Pat.1908 .... 32.00
  Trout, Original Paint, Cast Iron, 5 In. 55.00

Turtle, Corkscrew Tail, Pot Metal 25.00
Victor Beer, Metal 6.50
White Rock Ginger Ale 8.50

Bottle collecting has become a major American hobby. There are several general categories of bottles, such as historic flasks, bitters, household, and figural. For modern bottle prices and more old bottle prices, see the book "The Kovels' Bottle Price List" by Ralph and Terry Kovel.

BOTTLE, Apothecary, Deep Cobalt Blue, Ground Glass Stopper, 2 1/4 In. 65.00
Apothecary, Egyptian Style, Mushroom Ground Stopper, 12 1/2 In. 85.00
Apothecary, German Sarsaparilla Label, 8–Sided, C.1890, 10 In. 95.00
Apothecary, Tapered Shape, Mushroom Type Ground Stopper, 6 In. 20.00
Apothecary, W.N.Walton, Blue Stopper, Dated 1862, 6 1/2 In. 85.00

Avon started in 1886 as the California Perfume Company. It was not until 1929 that the name Avon was used. In 1939, it became Avon Products, Inc. Each year Avon sells figural bottles filled with cosmetic products. Ceramic, plastic, and glass bottles are made in limited editions.

Avon, 1931 Greyhound Bus Lines, After Shave, Cobalt, 7 In. 10.00
Avon, Boots & Saddle, Full, Box 10.00
Avon, Car, Cab, Checker, Box 5.00
Avon, Cement Mixer, Box 8.00
Avon, Dueling Pistol, Box 6.00
Avon, French Telephone 20.00
Avon, Pipe, Bulldog, Box 3.00
Avon, Train, Shaving Mug, Full Color Iron Horse Pictured 25.00
Baby, Hygeia, Ball, 4 Oz. 5.00
Baby, True Temp, With Thermometer 30.00
Barber, 6–Sides, Initialed, Milk Glass 40.00
Barber, Allover Gold, Tulip Design, Cobalt Blue, 7 1/2 In. 85.00
Barber, Amethyst, White Floral Design, Bulbous, 6 1/2 In. 60.00
Barber, Bay Rum, Smith Kline French, Stopper, Paper Label, 7 In. 28.00
Barber, Bristol, White & Pink Roses 40.00
Barber, Bulbous, Long Neck Pontil, Satin Pink, Enameled, 8 In. 60.00
Barber, Coinspot, Topaz, Multicolor Enamel, Square Collar, 10 In. 110.00
Barber, Cranberry Drape, 7 In. 90.00
Barber, Daisy & Fern, Opalescent Cranberry 100.00
Barber, Enameled, Amethyst, 8 1/4 In. 110.00
Barber, Opalescent Hobnails, Blue, 7 In. 135.00
Barber, Sapphire Blue, Enameled Design, 8 1/4 In. 85.00
Barber, Seaweed, Original Pewter Spout, Opalescent Cranberry 135.00
Barber, Wildroot Dandruff Remedy, Indian Maiden, Tin Cap 20.00

Beam bottles are made to hold Kentucky Straight Bourbon, made by the James B. Beam Distilling Company. The Beam series of ceramic bottles began in 1953.

Beam, Bell Ringer, Afore Ye Go 12.00
Beam, Black Mustang 85.00
Beam, Blue Hen Club 30.00

To remove a stubborn stain from the outside of a bottle, try this. Fill a bucket with soft sand. Push the bottle in and out of the sand, rotate it, and try to loosen the stain. Then wash in clean water. To remove a stain inside a bottle, put a handful of gravel in the bottle and shake vigorously.

Beam, Christmas, 1973 .... 15.00
Beam, Emmett Kelly, Signature 70.00
Beam, Falstaff, Opera 218.00
Beer, Atlantic Ale, Black Waiter's Picture, Amber 10.00
Beer, John Staton Brewing Co., Emerald Green, Blob Top 28.00
Beer, Royal Ruby, 1 Qt. 22.00
Bitters, African Stomach, Spruance, Stanley & Co., Amber, 9 1/4 In. 120.00
Bitters, American Life, Log Cabin, Golden Amber, 9 In. 850.00
Bitters, Baker's Orange Grove, Strawberry Puce, 10 In. 475.00
Bitters, Clifford & Fernald's Indian Vegetable, Aqua, 7 In. 200.00
Bitters, Dr.Harder's Wild Cherry, St.Louis, 4 1/2 In. 37.50
Bitters, Dr.Loew's, H.C.Christy Co., Cleveland, Deep Green, 9 In. 315.00
Bitters, Dr.Walkinshaw's Curative Bitters, Contents, Amber, 10 In. 225.00
Bitters, Drake's Plantation, 6 Log, Cabin, Topaz, 9 3/4 In. 290.00
Bitters, Fish, Dr.Fisch's, W.H.Ware, Amber, 11 1/2 In. 100.00
Bitters, H.E.Bucklen & Co., Chicago, Ill, Golden Amber, 9 In. 50.00
Bitters, H.H.Warner & Co., Amber, Tippecanoe, 8 3/4 In. 125.00
Bitters, JFL Capital Bitters, Pineapple, Embossed, Amber, 9 1/2 In. 1025.00
Bitters, National, Ear of Corn Shape, Amber, 12 1/2 In. 550.00
Bitters, Royal Pepsin, Amber, Embossed 70.00
Bitters, Suffolk Bitters Life Preserver, Yellow, 9 1/2 In. 395.00
Bitters, Warner's Safe Tonic Bitters, Embossed Safe, Amber, 7 In. 260.00
Bitters, Yerba Buena, Amber, 1 Pt. 25.00
Bull Dog Bluing, Pictures Bulldog, Makes Clothes White 20.00
BOTTLE, COCA-COLA, see Coca-Cola, Bottle
Cosmetic, Colgate's Quinol Hair Tonic, Clear, Contents, 6 Oz. 4.00
Cosmetic, Dr.Tebbett's Physiological Hair Regenerator, Puce 210.00
Cosmetic, Jefferson's Hair Renewer, Cobalt, 9 In. 150.00
Cosmetic, Mrs.S.A.Allen's World Hair Restorer, Yellow 160.00
Cosmetic, Professor Woods Hair Restorative, 9 In. 38.00
Cosmetic, Wildroot Dandruff Remedy, Indian Girl Picture, Tin Lid 10.00
Cure, Dewitt's Colic & Cholera Cure, Aqua, BIMAL, 5 In. 18.00
Cure, Foley's Kidney & Bladder Remedy, BIMAL, Amber, 7 1/4 In. 28.00
Cure, Warner's Safe Diabetes Cure, Amber, BIMAL 45.00
Delft, House, Heeren Canal, Set of 6 .... 70.00
Demi-John, Olive Green, Oval, Short Neck, 3 Piece Mold, 18 In. 65.00
Drug, Owl Drug Co., 8 Sides, Clear 10.00
Drug, W.H.Vickery, Pharmacist, Embossed, BIMAL 4.50
Figural, Cannon, Aqua, Portland Glass Co., C.1870, 15 In. 260.00
Figural, Cigar, Embossed With Leaf Design, Cork Mouth, Amber, 5 In. .. 18.00
Figural, Coachman, Pottery, Brown & Tan, 10 In. 500.00
Figural, Fish, Deep Amber Shaded To Yellow Amber 220.00
Figural, Fish, Screw Type Mouth, Clear, 7 In. 18.00
Figural, George Washington, Embossed, Clear, 9 1/2 In. 15.00
Figural, Grapes, Clear, French, 6 In. 25.00
Figural, Matador, Painted, Black Felt Hat, Cork Mouth, Clear, 10 In. 10.00
Figural, Pig, Olive, Black & Brown Glazed Pottery, C.1870, 6 In. 200.00
Figural, Pineapple, J.C.& Co., Amber, OP, 8 1/2 In. 475.00
Figural, Revolver, Amber 45.00
Figural, Soldier, Hessian, Clear, 7 In. 15.00
Figural, Statue of Liberty, Milk Glass, Original Stopper 265.00
Figural, Turtle, Flask, Shell Embossing, Screw Cap, Clear, 6 In. 40.00
Figural, Uncle Sam, Clear, 11 In. 35.00
Figural, Uncle Willie, Ceramic 45.00
Flask, Calabash, Sheaf & Star, Iron Pontil, Amber, 9 In. 70.00
Flask, Calabash, Union & Clasped Handle, Eagle Reverse, Aqua, 9 In. ... 55.00
Flask, Chestnut, Aqua, 18 Swirled Ribs, Midwestern, 6 3/8 In. 105.00
Flask, Eagle & Cornucopia, Aqua, 1/2 Pt. 415.00
Flask, Embalmer's, Large 25.00
Flask, McK G I-014, Washington & Eagle, Aqua, Pint 90.00
Flask, McK G I-024, Washington & Taylor, Golden Amber, Pint 625.00
Flask, McK G I-086, Lafayette & Liberty, Olive Amber, 1/2 Pint 320.00
Flask, McK G I-110, Jenny Lind & Lyre, Aqua, Quart 675.00
Flask, McK G II-041, Eagle & Tree, Aqua, Pint 80.00

Flask, McK G II–060, Eagle & Oak Tree, Golden Amber, Pint 700.00
Flask, McK G II–069, Eagle & Cornucopia, Blue Green, 1/2 Pint 150.00
Flask, McK G II–126, Double Eagle, Yellow, 1/2 Pint 120.00
Flask, McK G III–007, Cornucopia & Urn, Olive Amber, OP 35.00
Flask, McK G IV–034, Masonic & Frigate, Deep Aqua, Pint 80.00
Flask, McK G IX–001, Scroll, Sapphire Blue, Quart 675.00
Flask, McK G VIII–029, Sunburst, Deep Blue Aqua 160.00
Flask, Pink, Blue & Opaque Stripes, Lip Snap Pontil, 4 3/4 In., Pair 350.00
Flask, Pitkin, 30 Ribs, Broken Swirl, Green, 6 1/2 In. 185.00
Flask, Redware, Clear Glaze, Orange, Blue Splotches, New Eng., 8 In. 275.00
Flask, Spring Garden Glass Works, Aqua, 1/2 Pint 65.00
Flask, Whiskey, Pretzel Shape, Brown, Salt, Cork, Germany, 6 In. 25.00
Food, Chinese Soy Sauce, Dark Brown Pottery 15.00
Food, Jumbo Peanut Butter, Dated June 24 1930, Clear, Pint 4.00
Food, Mellins Food, Green, 6 In. 6.00
Food, Wan–Eta Cocoa, Boston, Brown, 7 In. 10.00
Fruit Jar, A.G.Smalley Co., Boston, Milk Glass Insert, Amber, Qt. 38.00
Fruit Jar, Atlas E–Z Seal, Clear, Pint 5.00
Fruit Jar, Atlas Strong Shoulder Mason, Miniature 25.00
Fruit Jar, Ball Ideal, Patd.July 14, 1908, Blue, Qt. 2.50
Fruit Jar, Ball Perfect Mason, Amber, 1/2 Gal. 35.00
Fruit Jar, Brockway, Sur–Grip, Clear, Pint 6.00
Fruit Jar, Dextor With A Reef, Quart 38.00
Fruit Jar, Franklin Dexter, Zinc Lid, Aqua, Qt. 32.00
Fruit Jar, Globe Tobacco Co., Detroit, Honey Amber 32.00
Fruit Jar, Lightning, Amber, 1/2 Gal. 54.00
Fruit Jar, Lightning, Amber, Lid & Bail, 1 Qt. 30.00
Fruit Jar, Lockport Mason, Quart 6.00
Fruit Jar, Mason Union, With Shield, Quart 130.00
Fruit Jar, Mason's Pat., Jar Salt, Detroit Salt Co., Aqua 15.00
Fruit Jar, Mason, Lid, Green, Dated 1858, 1/2 Gal. 16.00
Fruit Jar, Mason, Pat.Nov 30th, 1858, Zinc Cap, Aqua, Pint 325.00
Fruit, LaLorraine, Dark Green, 1 Liter 58.00
Fruit, Red Wing Mason, Black Writing, Qt. 110.00
Gin, Olive Green, Tapered Body, OP, Applied Collar, C.1810, 13 In. 230.00
Gin, Rabbit Foot Old Tom Gin, Glass Stopper, Label 25.00
Grapette, Figural, Elephant 20.00
Ink, Butlers Ink, Cincinnati, Aqua, 12 Sides, OP, 2 3/4 In. 110.00
Ink, Carter's 1897, Embossed, Aqua, 2 3/8 In. 17.00
Ink, Carter, Cobalt Blue, 6 1/8 In. 80.00
Ink, Caws Ink, New York, Embossed, Square, Bright Aqua, BIMAL 10.00
Ink, Cone, Bixby, Embossed, BIMAL, Aqua, 2 3/8 In. 12.00
Ink, Cottage, Aqua, 2 1/2 In. 130.00
Ink, Dark Olive Amber, 3–Mold, 2 1/4 In. 95.00
Ink, Harrison's Columbian Ink, Cobalt Blue, OP, 1 7/8 In. 410.00
Ink, Hohenthal Brothers & Co., Olive Green, Pour Spout, 7 1/8 In. 350.00
Ink, Ma & Pa Carter Inc., German 130.00
Ink, Master, 3 Mold, Sloping Mouth, Olive Green, 7 9/16 In. 15.00
Ink, Sanford Fountain Pen Ink, Embossd, BIMAL, Clear, 2 15/16 In. 7.00
Ink, Signet, Cobalt Blue, Quart 30.00
Ink, Teakettle, Black Amethyst, Original Cap, 2 1/4 In. 500.00
Ink, Umbrella Ink, Olive Amber, Open Pontil, Sheared Lip, 2 1/4 In. 95.00
Ink, William A Davis, Boston, Embossed, Round, Master, Aqua, 7 7/8 In. 15.00
Lucky Tiger Hair Tonic, Cork Stopper 12.00
Medicine, Ayers Cherry Pictoral, Lowell, Mass., 7 In. 30.00
Medicine, Benjamin's Blood & Liver Pills, Jamaica 6.00
Medicine, Davis Vegetable Pain Killer, OP 15.00
Medicine, Dr.Boschee's German Syrup, 7 In. 15.00
Medicine, Dr.D.C.Kellinger's Remedies, New York, Aqua, 7 1/4 In. 130.00
Medicine, Dr.Holt's Magnetic Pain Cure, 12–Sided, 5 In.Square 15.00
Medicine, Dr.J.A.Sherman's Rupture Curative Compound, Cork, Amber 20.00
Medicine, Dr.Miles Alternative Compound, Label, 8 1/2 In. 15.00
Medicine, Dr.S.Hardy's Root & Herb Tonic, Paper Label, 7 1/2 In. 5.00
Medicine, Dr.Van Wert's Balsam, Label, Aqua, Contents, 8 In. 17.00

Bottle, Milk, Palmer's Dairy,
Columbus Grove,
Oh., Dripless

Bottle, Whiskey,
I.W.Harper,
Porcelain, 15 In.

Beer Can, Altes
Lager Beer, 12 Oz.

Medicine, Eli Lilly Co., Poison Embossed, 2 Sides, Amber, 4 In.	8.00
Medicine, Hogan's Magnolia Balm, Milk Glass	18.00
Medicine, Humphrey's Marvel of Health, 5 3/4 In.	17.00
Medicine, Laudanum, Aqua, Steelman, Archer Drug, 5 In.	7.00
Medicine, Mathewson's Horse Remedy, Price 50 Cents, Aqua, 6 3/4 In.	190.00
Medicine, Moxie Nerve Food, Aqua	15.00
Medicine, Thorn's Compound Syrup of Cod Liver Oil, Aqua, 7 1/4 In.	325.00
Medicine, Warner's Safe Kidney & Liver Remedy, Yellow Amber	17.00
Medicine, Warner's Safe Tonic, Rochester, N.Y., Amber, 9 1/2 In.	180.00
Medicine, Watkin's Liniment, 8 1/2 In.	15.00
Milk, A Bottle of Milk Is A Bottle of Health, Maine Seal, Quart	5.00
Milk, Adohr, Grenade Shape, 1/2 Pint	20.00
Milk, Bayonne City Dairy, Bayonne, New Jersy, Clear, 1 Qt.	125.00
Milk, Borden's Condensed Milk Co., Embossed Eagle, Gail Borden, Qt.	85.00
Milk, Brookfield, Double Baby Face, Square, 1 Qt.	28.00
Milk, Crying Baby, Pat.June 2, L874	55.00
Milk, Curles Neck Dairy, Baby Face, Embossed	15.00
Milk, Dean Dairy, Mass Seal, 5 Cows Lined Up, Maroon, Pyro, Pint	15.00
Milk, Ditch Bros.Dairy, 1/2 Pint	8.00
Milk, Dunmyer Dairy, Baby Face, 1 Quart	20.00
Milk, Farm Dairy Quality Products, Yellow, Baby Face	17.00
Milk, Gold Spot, Green, 3 Cities, Oklahoma, Rectangular, 1/2 Gal.	50.00
Milk, Home Dairy Inc., Maine Seal, Full Cow, Round, Pint	15.00
Milk, Indian Hill Dairy, Indian Chief Picture	15.00
Milk, Isaly Dairy, Baby Face, Square, 1 Qt.	20.00
Milk, Mack Farm Dairy, Batesville, Ark., Round, Qt.	15.00
Milk, Maywood Farm Co., Maroon, Gallon	15.00
Milk, Oakhurst Dairy, Store Bottle, Round, Embossed, Quart	3.00
Milk, Old Homestead Products, Cone Shape, Crackle Glass, Quart	50.00
Milk, Palmer's Dairy, Columbus Grove, Oh., Dripless ....*Illus*	17.50
Milk, Policeman's Face, Roha's Dairy, Cop The Cream	30.00
Milk, Sheffield Farms Co., Round, Embossed, Pint	12.00
Milk, Speedwell Farms, Cow's Head Inside Belt, Acid Etched, Pint	50.00
Milk, Stewart's Dairy, Route Bottle, Round, Green Pyro, Pint	4.00
Milk, Twin Dairy Farm, Dairy Scene, Round, Orange Pyro, Pint	12.00
Milk, Virginia Dairy, Embossed In Lines	5.00
Mineral Water, James Ray, Savannah, Ga., Blob Top, Aqua, 7 1/2 In.	12.00
Mustard, Western Spice Mill, Barrel Shape, Aqua	36.00
Nurser, Acme	32.50
Nurser, Crying Baby, Dated June 2, 1874	55.00
Nurser, Embossed Teddy Bear	30.00
Nurser, Happy Baby	15.00
Nurser, Sonny Boy	17.00
Nurser, Turtle Shape, Lays Flat, Neck Up	26.00
Nursing, Words Baby Bunting, Rabbit	6.00
Oil, Edison Battery Oil	5.00

BOTTLE, PERFUME, see Perfume Bottle

Pickle, Aqua, Keg Shape, 2 Piece Mold, 4 3/4 In.	10.00
Pickle, Bunker Hill, Honey Amber	25.00
Pickle, Clear, Flower Design, 10 In.	35.00
Pickle, Gothic, Light Green, 11 3/4 In.	105.00
Pickle, Shaker Brand Pickle Jar, Olive Yellow	325.00
Poison, Coffin Poison, Diamond Design, Embossed, Blue, 4 In.	40.00
Poison, Triangle Poison, Warner Co., Skull, Crossbones, Blue, Label	8.00
Sarsaparilla, Dr.Townsend's, Albany, N.Y., Olive Amber, 9 1/2 In.	90.00
Seltzer, Statue of Liberty, Liberty Bottling Co., Working Spigot	25.00
Snuff, Blue Figural, Enameled Lid, Porcelain, Chinese, 3 In.	25.00
Snuff, Carved Agate, Cat Watching Butterfly, 2 1/4 In.	85.00
Snuff, Carved Amber, Red, Painted Gold Highlights, 3 In.	350.00
Snuff, Carved Ivory, Etched Lake & Mountain, Japanese, Writing, 3 In.	100.00
Snuff, Carved Moss Agate, Pagoda 1 Side, Green Stone Stopper	125.00
Snuff, E.Roome, Troy N.Y., Olive Amber, OP, Beveled Corners, 5 In.	110.00
Snuff, Free-Blown, Olive Green, OP, Square, Original Label, 4 3/8 In.	120.00
Snuff, Gourd Shape, Enamel On Copper, Oriental, C.1890, 2 1/4 In.	52.50
Snuff, Hand Carved Ivory, Jeweled, Carved On Obverse, 4 1/2 In.	145.00
Snuff, Inside Painted, Mountain Scenery, Serpentine Top, 3 In.	60.00
Snuff, Inside Painted, Panels of Calligraphy, Hexagonal, 3 In.	400.00
Snuff, Inside Painted, Scholars & Students, Carved Ivory Top, 3 In.	350.00
Snuff, Ivory, Carved Chinese War Lord 1 Side, Seal Other, 2 1/4 In.	85.00
Snuff, Ivory, Carved Dragons, Pearl, 2 1/4 In.	95.00
Snuff, Marble, Carved Flames, Scrolls, Mottled Green Lid, 2 3/8 In.	50.00
Snuff, Olive Amber, Applied Mouth, Rectangular, 6 1/4 In.	125.00
Snuff, Polychromed Children At Play, Chien Lung Seal, 3 1/4 In.	125.00
Snuff, Rock Crystal, Vines, Fruit, Metal Stopper, Spoon, 2 7/8 In.	125.00
Snuff, Tiger's Eye, Fish, Standing, 2 1/2 In.	38.50
Soda, Chemung Spring Water, Embossed Indian, 1/2 Gal	16.00
Soda, Empire Soda Works, Blob Top, Aqua	80.00
Soda, Pacific Bottling Works, Tacoma, Wash, Aqua, 6 7/8 In.	12.00
Soda, Sprite, Green, Hobnailed, Tin Cap, Salesman's Sample 3 In.	10.00
Stove Polish, Black Cat	35.00
Swaim's Panacea, Philadelphia, Green, Vertical Panels, 7 3/4 In.	65.00
Tippecanoe, H.H.Warner & Co., Partial Paper Label, Amber, 8 3/4 In.	55.00
Vinegar, Whitehouse Jug, With Handle & Spout, 10 In.	15.00
Vinegar, Whitehouse, With Handle, 8 In.	5.50
Whiskey, Decanter, Brooks Moose	20.00
Whiskey, Decanter, Calvert Canadian Goose	35.00
Whiskey, Demijohn, Olive Green, Free-Blown, Bubbles, 12 3/4 In.	120.00
Whiskey, Flora Temple, Harness Trot, Apricot, Handle, 8 1/2 In.	240.00
Whiskey, Hiram Walker's Royal Oak, Tax Stamp, 1936, Miniature	15.00
Whiskey, I.W.Harper, Porcelain, 15 In.	25.00
Whiskey, Meadville, Pa.Distillery, 1 Qt.	*Illus*
Whiskey, Minstrel, Pottery, Head Lifts Off, 1930-40, 12 In.	40.00
Whiskey, Mohawk, Pure Rye, Pat.Feb.11, 1868, Medium Amber, 12 3/8 In.	150.00
Whiskey, Paul Jones, Heavily Embossed, Amber	375.00
Whiskey, S.O.B.Bourbon, Peoria, Ill., Pottery, 2 Handles, 11 In.	7.00
Whiskey, Star Whiskey, W.B.Crowell Jr., N.Y., Ribbed, Amber, 8 In.	65.00
Whiskey, Wharton's, Golden Amber, Applied Handle, Spout, 10 In.	325.00
Whisky, Old Judge, San Francisco Picture, Amber, Fifth	385.00
Wine, Seal, G.B., Arm Grasping Scimitar, Olive Amber, C.1780, 9 In.	35.00
	150.00

Boxes of all kinds are collected. They were made of thin strips of inlaid wood, metal, tortoiseshell, embroidery, or other material.

BOX, see also Ivory, Box; Porcelain, Box; Shaker, Box; Tinware, Box; and various Porcelain categories

BOX, Agate, Brass Band, Azure Ripple Design, Hinged Lid, 2 1/4 In.	110.00
Alligatored Dark Brown Paint, Yellow Striping, Cherubs, Lid, 12 In.	45.00
Apple, Cherry, Scalloped, Cutout Handles, Old Finish, 10 1/2 X 12 In.	100.00
Apple, Dovetailed, Cherry, 10 X 10 X 5 3/4 In.	185.00
Ballot, Glass, Wooden Base, Round, 1884, 10 X 9 1/2 In.	175.00
Band, Wallpaper Covered, View of Providence River, C.1830, 11 X 16 In.	425.00

BOX, BATTERSEA, see Battersea, Box

Bentwood, Covered, Secured With Copper Tacks, 5 3/4 In.	115.00
Bentwood, Laced Finger Construction, Red Paint, Floral, Round, 10 In.	225.00
Bentwood, Pine, 2 Finger Construction, Laced, Handle, Lid, 1848, 20 In.	500.00
Bentwood, Traces of Gray Paint, Penciled Cream Tartar, Round, 7 In.	65.00
Bentwood, Wire Bail, Wooden Handle, Covered, Old White Paint, 11 In.	175.00
Bentwood, Wire Bail, Wooden Handle, Worn Blue Paint, 11 X 6 In.	195.00
Beveled Edge Lid & Till, Old Green Paint, 9 In.	55.00
Black Transfer Design, Greek Key Border, Yellow Paint, 17 3/4 In.	100.00
Bone, Carved Courting Scene Lid, 3 1/8 In.	40.00
Book, Pine, Lid, Bat Wing Brass End Handles, Green Paint, 18 1/4 In.	325.00
Brass Line Inlay, Inset Brass Handle, Rosewood Veneer, 12 In.	65.00
Bride's, Bentwood, Ochre, Winter Scenes, Ribbon Contents, 19 X 7 In.	600.00
Bride's, Bentwood, Polychrome Floral, Pink Ground, Oval, 16 3/4 In.	425.00
Bride's, Wooden, Blue Paint, Couple On Top, Flowers, 17 X 10 X 5 In.	138.00
Candle, Pine, Primitive, Sliding Lid, Green Paint, 12 In.	95.00
Candle, Slide Cover, Original Blue Paint, Pine, 1820, 3 1/2 X 13 In.	250.00
Cigar, Wooden, Brass Trim, 15 X 6 In.	28.00
Cigarette, Art Deco, Black, With Chrome, Cedar Lined, 3 1/2 X 2 1/2 In.	50.00
Cigarette, Malachite, Hinged Lid, 6 In.	125.00
Connestoga Wagon, Lid, Wrought Iron Strap Hinges, J.E.1833, 32 In.	175.00
Copper, Enameled Windmill, Sailboat Scene Lid, 18th Century, 4 In.	225.00
Document, Dovetailed, Original Blue Sponge Graining, 15 1/2 In.	1150.00
Document, Hinged Cover, Fan & Star Inlay, American, 6 X 7 X 12 In.	250.00
Document, Original Gold Stenciling, Crimson Overwash, 9 1/2 In.	155.00
Document, Ring Handle On Round Top, Black Tole, 4 3/4 X 8 3/4 In.	23.00
Document, Yellow & Black Smoke Grained, 15 X 9 X 6 1/2 In.	450.00
Dome Top, Floral Wallpaper Covered, Pine, 21 In.	55.00
Dome Top, Original Green Paint, Iron Lock & Hasp, 27 1/2 In.	95.00
Dome Top, Original Mustard Paint, Stylized Florals, Birds, 19 In.	300.00
Dome Top, Wallpaper Covered, Wire Hasp, Pine, 9 1/2 In.	55.00
Dough, 2-Board Top, Poplar, 22 1/2 X 44 In.	450.00
Dough, Blue Green Paint, Dovetailed, With Top, 34 In.	240.00
Dough, Turned Splayed Legs, Pine Top, Poplar, 25 X 33 3/4 X 29 In.	135.00
Egg, E.Schneider & Co., White Cross Baking Powder, Wooden, 12 In.	50.00
Enameled Coat of Arms, Gold Painted Base, English, Oval, 4 In.	225.00
English, Courting Scene On Lid, 18th Century, 2 1/2 In.	70.00
File, Shaw-Walker, Oak, 9 X 5 1/2 In.	25.00
Floral Design, Old Green Paint, Black Striping, Wire Hinges, 12 In.	85.00
Geometric Marquetry & Initials M.McD, Lid, Inside Mirror, 10 In.	75.00
Glass, Violet Blue, Footed, Allover Scarabs, Gilt Brass, France, 5 In.	225.00
Gold Ormolu, Porcelain Medallion, Lid, Artist Signed, France, 3 X 6 In.	62.00
Green & Yellow Striping, Stenciled Leaf On Lid, Iron Lock, 24 In.	200.00
Green Edge, White Striping, Putty Colored Ground, Roses, 9 In.	1300.00
Green Putty Grained, Wooden, Brass Pull, Initials, New Eng., 28 X 9 In.	425.00
Hanging, 2 Compartments, Scalloped Ends & Crest, Pine, 18 In.	500.00
Hanging, Curved Crest, Heart Cutout, Old Red Over Blue, 13 In.	300.00
Hanging, Gray Blue Paint, Crest, 2 Compass Stars, 8 X 10 3/4 In.	235.00
Hanging, Overlapping Base, Lid, Scalloped Crest, Walnut, 9 X 13 In.	160.00
Hanging, Spoon Rack, Pine, Green Paint Over Black, 12 X 6 X 26 In.	1500.00
Hat, Wallpaper Covered, Penguin Pattern, American, 1835, 16 X 12 In.	395.00
Hat, Wallpaper Covered, Pennsylvania Newspaper Lining, 14 X 18 In.	150.00
Inset Portrait of Child On Lid, Inlaid Fruitwood, 12 1/2 In.	20.00
Jewelry, Dore Bronze, Spanish Throne Chair, Seat Lifts, 3 3/4 In.	35.00
Knife, 3 Sections, Brass Handle, English, Mahogany, 14 X 17 In.	175.00
Knife, Federal, Inlaid Mahogany, Shaped Lid, C.1795, 14 X 9 X 12 In.	2420.00
Knife, Grain Painted, Deep Divided Tray, Flared Sides, 1860, 4 X 14 In.	110.00
Knife, Hepplewhite, Mahogany, Inlaid Edge, Brass Escutcheon, 15 In.	500.00
Knife, Poplar, Cutout Handle Divider, Old Red Paint, 8 X 12 In.	45.00
Knife, Serpentine, Ball & Claw Feet, Inlays, English, 14 X 12 In., Pair	1800.00
Knife, Slant Side, Pressed Sides, Center Handle, 12 X 7 1/2 In.	50.00
Knife, Turned Handle, Dovetailed, 9 1/4 X 13 1/2 In.	75.00
Lacquer, Black, Etui Cased, Mother-of-Pearl Garden Scene Lid, 5 In.	275.00
Lacquer, Black, Tooth Drawing Stencil Lid, 18th Century, 3 1/2 In.	90.00

Money, Lacquered, Gold Design, Drawer In Base, China, 16 1/4 X 6 In.	95.00
Necktie, Celluloid, Word Necktie In Script, 13 In.	25.00
Patch, Bone, Painted Woman & Flowers Scene Lid, 18th Century, 2 In.	70.00
Patch, Carved Wood, Bronze Trim, Portrait Print Lid, 4 In.Diam.	60.00
Patch, Cherub & Scroll Design, Silver, English, French Marks, 4 In.	100.00
Pencil, Flags, Eagle, Anchor, Has Key, Germany, 8 1/2 In.	15.00
Pencil, Sliding Lid, Chip Carved Diamond Design, Birch, 11 In.	85.00
Pill, Enameled Floral, Hinged Lid, 18th Century, English, 1 1/2 In.	50.00
Pin, Floral Design, Pewter Top, Victorian, Signed & Dated 1877, 2 In.	20.00
Pin, Wallpaper Covered, Blue, White & Black Design, Oval, 6 1/2 In.	315.00
Pine, Black Paint, Gold Stencil of Fruit, 10 In.	100.00
Pine, Floral Design, Red Ground, Till Removed, Dated 1722, 12 In.	95.00
Pine, Punched Tin Covered, Floral, Red & Green Paint, 28 X 18 X 17 In.	500.00
Pine, Sliding Lid, Worn Blue Sponging, White Ground, Red, 14 1/2 In.	575.00
Pipe, Oval Floral Inlay On Front Panel, Oak, English, 16 1/4 In.	200.00
Pipe, Pine, Truncated, Spire Hanger, Drawer, 7 X 4 X 21 In.	1300.00
Poplar, Alligatored Brown Flame Graining, 4 1/2 In.	175.00
Salt, Hanging, Open, With Scoop Combination, Pine, 11 1/2 In.	140.00
Salt, Hanging, Primitive, Drilled Holes Pattern In Crest, 11 In.	45.00
Salt, Poplar, Hanging, Black Paint, Yellow Stripe, 6 X 6 X 13 In.	650.00
Shoeshine, Oak, Utensils, 26 In.	28.00
Single Finger Construction On Base & Lid, Oval, Bentwood, 5 3/4 In.	135.00
Single Finger Construction, Old Blue Paint, Bentwood, Round, 7 In.	200.00
Sliding Lid, Till, Pine, Old Green Paint, 18 In.	37.50
Spice, Copper Nails, Squares, Dots, Blue Green Paint, 2 5/8 X 6 In.	375.00
Spice, Federal, Mahogany Veneer, Inlaid, Door, 1810, 12 X 10 In.	4125.00
Spice, Squares & Dots Design Cover, Blue Green Paint, 2 X 4 X 6 In.	150.00
Staple Hinges, Pine & Poplar, Brown Vinegar Graining, Yellow, 10 In.	175.00
BOX, TEA CADDY, see Tea Caddy	
Tinder, Steel, Engraved Tree & Dog In Oval Lid, With Flint, 2 In.	110.00
Tobacco, Brass, Chased Design, Oval, 18th Century, 5 1/4 In.	135.00
Tobacco, Embossed Scene of Boar Hunt, Brass, 5 3/4 In.	35.00
Tobacco, Engraved Man Giving Heart To Woman, Dutch, 4 7/8 In.	85.00
Tobacco, Wooden, Engraved Silver Plaques, Revolving Top, 3 1/2 In.	200.00
Tool, Pine, Iron Straps, Handles, Side Drawer, 11 X 35 In.	125.00
Wall, Hand Carved Eagle Front, Square Nails, Unpainted, 14 In.	108.00
Wall, Wooden, Ochre Over Green, 2 Tier, 19th Century, 12 X 4 X 11 In.	375.00
Wooden, Gilded, Paneled Sides, Scalloped Top Gallery, 29 1/2 In.	65.00
Wooden, Wallpaper Cover, Green, White, 1870 Newspaper Lined, 8 In.	75.00
Work, Hinged Scene Lid, Pine, Octagonal, Paw Feet, 1825, 5 X 12 In.	1100.00
Writing, Lady's, Marquetry Inlaid, 19th Century, 18 In.	170.00

The Boy Scout movement in the United States started in 1910. The first Jamboree was held in 1937. Collectors search for any material related to scouting, including patches, manuals, and uniforms. Girl Scouts are listed under their own heading.

BOY SCOUT, Ashtray, Troop 111 B.S.A., Harrington Park, N.J., Porcelain	35.00
Ax, Impressed Emblem On Blade, Collins, 3 X 14 In.	55.00
Ax, Official, Collins Co., Famous, Conn.	45.00
Bank, Cast Iron, Canada	365.00
Belt, Pat.'31	20.00
Book, Boy Scouts With The Red Cross, 1915	15.00
Book, Boy Scouts, Battle of Sarato, Herbert Carter, 1909	11.00
Book, Field, 1952	8.00
Book, Field, 1959	10.00
Book, Songs Scouts Sing, 1930, 95 Pages	12.50
Booklet, Merit Badge Series, 1940s, Set of 6	10.00
Calendar, 1955, Rockwell, 8 X 14 1/2 In.	15.00
Camera, Eastman Kodak, 1930	70.00
Compass, Octagon Shape, Red Plastic, Glass	10.00
Creed, Picture, Symbols, Framed, 1923, 7 1/2 X 6 1/2 In.	13.00
Flashlight, 1930s	10.00
Graduation Certificate, Cub Scout, 1957	5.00
Handbook, 1924	20.00

Boy Scout, Patch, National Jamboree,
White Felt, Pocket, 1935

Boy Scout, Sleeve Patch, Region 8,
Yellow Twill, Red Edge

Hat, Campaign, Green Felt, Star Vents, Chin Cord, Size 6 7/8	10.00
Jamboree Back Patch, National, Emblem, White Twill, 1964	8.00
Kit, First Aid, Belt Mount	18.00
Knife Hone, Original Case & Strap, 1930s	15.00
Knife, Pocket, Ulster, Medallion In Grip, 5 Different Uses	5.00
Magazine, Life, Boy Scout Jamboree, 1950	4.00
Medal, Be Prepared, Red, White, Blue Ribbon, 1940s ....*Illus*	75.00
Membership Card, Folds, Dated 1934	5.00
Merit Badge, Animal Industry, Khaki Crimped, Plastic Back	6.00
Merit Badge, Camping, Khaki Crimped, Plastic Back	5.00
Neckerchief, Alaska, First, 1917	3.00
Neckerchief, Light Green Cotton, Milwaukee Corps, 1930s, Square	10.00
Neckerchief, National Jamboree, 1957	10.00
Neckerchief, National Jamboree, Red Cotton, 1937 ....*Illus*	55.00
Neckerchief, Orange, Black Strip Edge, Universal Emblem, 1940s	5.00
Neckerchief, Silk, Jamboree, 1953	25.00
Patch, National Jamboree, White Felt, Pocket, 1935 ....*Illus*	91.00
Pin, Jamboree, Statue of Liberty, New York, 1930s	20.00
Pocket Flap, Lodge 135, Red Rolled Edge, Emblem	9.00
Pocket Flap, Maluhia Lodge 554, Red Rolled Edge ....*Illus*	15.00
Ring, Sterling Silver, Black Enameled Emblem Top, Size 8	12.00
Shirt, Explorer, National Jamboree Patch, Green Cotton, 1950	15.00
Sleeve Patch, Region 8, Yellow Twill, Red Edge ....*Illus*	10.00

Boy Scout, Medal,
Be Prepared, Red, White,
Blue Ribbon, 1940s

Boy Scout, Neckerchief,
National Jamboree,
Red Cotton, 1937

Boy Scout, Pocket Flap,
Maluhia Lodge 554,
Red Rolled Edge

T–Shirt, National Jamboree Design, White Cotton, 1950 .... 8.00
Uniform, Hat, 1920s 35.00
Wristwatch, Ingersoll, 1930s 150.00

Bradley & Hubbard Manufacturing Company made lamps and other metalwork in Meriden, Connecticut, from the 1840s. Their lamps are especially prized by collectors.

BRADLEY & HUBBARD, Andirons, Baluster Shaped Stems, Urn Shape ....
Ashtray, 2 Handles, 6 In. 150.00
Bookends, E.Young Verse, Bronze 21.00
Candlestick, Art Deco, Brass, Square 40.00
Clock, Blinking Ben, 1853 .... 17.00
Desk Set, Inkwell, Tray, Holder, Blotter, Art Deco, 5 Pc. 1550.00
Doorstop, Roman Columns, Bronze Plated, 6 X 7 In. 150.00
Inkstand, Section For Stamps, 2 Swirled Glass Wells 42.00
Lamp, Aladdin Type, Slag Glass Shade, 12 In. 115.00
Lamp, Genie, Overlay Slag Glass 450.00
Lamp, Hanging, Kerosene, Store, Brass Font, Tin Shade 450.00
Lamp, Red Metal, Hand Painted Shade, Signed, 18 In. 350.00
Lamp, Ripple Glass Shade, Flat Top, Table, Signed 175.00
Lamp, Table, 6 Caramel Panels, Acorn & Oak Leaf Base 235.00
Lamp, Table, Reverse Painted Paneled Shade, Metal Work 285.00
Letter Holder, Cherubs, Victorian, 8 X 5 In. 210.00
Letter Opener, Moose Design, Gilded Cast Iron 95.00
Mirror, Dolphins, Beveled, Brass Finish, 16 X 6 1/2 In. 85.00
Spittoon, Turtle, Cast Iron 45.00
Thermometer, Metal Stand, Regilded, 11 In. 325.00
     40.00

Brass has been used for decorative pieces and useful tablewares since ancient times. It is an alloy of copper, zinc, and other metals.

BRASS, see also Bell; Tool; Trivet; etc.
BRASS, Ashtray, Golfer, 9 In. ....
Basin, Champleve, Stylized Floral Bands, Swelled Round, 14 3/4 In. 75.00
Bed Warmer, Engraved Long Tailed Bird On Lid, Handle, 44 1/2 In. 300.00
Bed Warmer, Floral & Insect Perforated Cover, Maple Handle, 45 In. 475.00
Bed Warmer, Hinged Cover, Embossed Running Stag, Iron, Dated 1623 ...... 325.00
Bed Warmer, Perforated Cover, Stylized Fronds, Wooden Handle 325.00
Bootscraper, Iron Blades, Men Rising From Sea 175.00
Bowl, Dragons, Phoenix Bird, Mutton Jade Stones, China 325.00
Box, Tinder, With Steel & Flint, Oval, 5 1/4 In. 125.00
Bucket, Ansonia, 1868 .... 125.00
BRASS, CANDLESTICK, see Candlestick   75.00
Case, Cigar, Hinged, Dragon On Front, Silver Wash, Holds 3 Cigars ....
Cigar Cutter, Dog Shape, Paraflint Engraved Each Side, 4 X 7 In. 90.00
Clipboard, Queens Ins.Co., New York, 1891–1941, Large 230.00
Coat Rack, Victorian Style 24.00
Compote, Cornelius & Baker, 7 1/2 In. 35.00
Cup Weights, Nuremberg, 19th Century, Container, Set of 5, 2 In. 70.00
Door Knocker, Mission San Gabriel 75.00
Door Plate, Relief Gargoyle Design, Escutcheon Pendulum, 4 1/4 In. 20.00
Figurine, Boy & Dog, Marble Base, Cast, Gold Paint, 5 1/2 In. 90.00
Figurine, Buddha, China, 2 1/2 In. 25.00
Frame, Victorian, Easel, 26 Turquoise Stones Around, 1 1/2 X 2 In. 17.50
Humidor, Tobacco, Elephant Finial, Chase Brass 40.00
Incense Burner, Coal Shuttle Shaped, China, 4 In. 12.00
Inkstand, Ceramic Insert, Traces of Gilding, 10 3/4 In. 15.00
Inkstand, Cherubs & Birds, Pen Rack, 6 X 9 In. 85.00
Inkstand, Hinged Lid & Insert, 10 1/2 In. 90.00
Kettle, Hiram W.Hayden, Waterbury, Conn., Pat.Dec.16, 1861, 15 In. 90.00
Kettle, Hot Water, Copper Stand, Spherical, 18th Century, 12 1/2 In. 135.00
Kettle, Jelly, Forged Iron Handle, 21 X 12 In. 75.00
Medallion, Bust of Admiral Nelson, Dark Paint, Framed, 6 X 5 1/4 In. 70.00
Mirror, Stag, Antlers Around Mirror, 8 3/4 In. 90.00
Orrery, Spherical Wood Pedestal Frame, France, 18th Century, 18 In. 25.00
     350.00

Pail, American Brass Kettle Mfg.Spun, 13 1/4 X 9 In. 65.00
Paper Clip, Allied Brass, Turtle Shape, 4 In. 25.00
Planter, Chrysanthemum Band, Bird Ring Handles, China, 28 X 15 In. 950.00
Ruler, Foldup, 12 In. 8.00
Scissors, Wick Trimmer, Embossed Tray, 9 1/2 In. 35.00
Silent Butler, Enameled, China, 6 1/2 X 5 In. 45.00
Soap Holder, Mermaid Holding Shell Holder 25.00
Spittoon, Covered, 10 1/2 X 5 1/2 In. 15.00
Spurs, Woman's, Silver Horseshoe & Stallion, Pair 50.00
Spy Glass, D.McGregor & Co., 18th Century, 4 Ft.X 4 In. 100.00
Stand, Kettle, 9 3/4 In. 98.00
Stand, Trivet, Footed, Oblong, 8 1/2 X 6 X 5 In. 75.00
Still, Copper Drum, Iron Tripod, Handle, 19th Century, Belgium, 43 In. 200.00
Sundial, Engraved Calibrated Dial, Roman Numeral, 1658, 8 In. 125.00
Teakettle, Gooseneck Spout, Amber Glass Handle, 8 In. 75.00
Teakettle, Gooseneck Spout, Swivel Handle, Stamped 4, 7 In. 145.00
Teakettle, Wooden Finial & Handle, Fleur-De-Lis Attachment, 7 In. 400.00
Telescope, Boxwood, Daytime & Nighttime, Cox, London, 2 1/2 X 12 In. 225.00
Telescope, Leather, 3 Sections, Pigskin Case, Extends To 22 1/2 In. 115.00
Tray, Hammered, Fluted, Oval, Josef Hoffmann, C.1910, 13 1/2 In. 550.00
Trimmer, Candle, Tray, Patent Nov.24, 1852 .... 75.00
Vase, Blossom Form, Hammered, Trumpet Foot, Josef Hoffmann, 7 In. 1550.00
Watering Can, 1920s 42.50
Weight, Bell Shape, 2 3/4 In., 8 Oz. 45.00
Weight, Bird In Tree, Ashanti 95.00

BREAD PLATE, see various Pressed Glass patterns

Brides' baskets of glass were usually one-of-a-kind novelties made in American and European glass factories. They were especially popular about 1880 when the decorated basket was often given as a wedding gift. Cut glass baskets were popular after 1890. All brides' baskets lost favor about 1905.

BRIDE'S BASKET, Apple Green, Raspberry To White Interior, Silver Holder 125.00
Blue Nailsea Bowl, Ruffled, Silver Plated Holder, 7 In. 325.00
Blue Opalescent, Ruffled, Silver Plated Frame 100.00
Camphor Rim, Enamel Florals, Silver Plate Holder, Yellow 275.00
Cased Pink Satin Glass, Enameled Swan 300.00
Cut Log Bowl, 10 1/4 In. 95.00
Deep Rose To Pink To White, Silver Plated Holder, 11 In. 285.00
Fan & Loop, Scalloped, Clear Insert, 8 1/2 X 3 1/2 In. 60.00
Frame, Beaded Twist Handle, Poole Silver Co., 10 1/2 In. 58.00
Frame, Cupid & Florals, 4 Feet, Rogers–Smith 68.00
Gold Band, Enameled Flowers, Pairpoint Frame, 12 In. 325.00
Green Satin Glass, Blue Treading, Van Bergh, 11 3/4 In. 295.00
Green, Floral & Berries, Scalloped, Loetz 195.00
Painted Enamel Flowers, Stand, 6 X 12 In. 150.00
Peach Crest Bowl, Ruffled, Silver Plated Holder, 11 In. 275.00
Peachblow, Enameled, Scalloped, Webb, 11 1/4 In. 195.00
Pink and White Cased Glass, 19th Century 185.00
Pink Overlay, Enameled Flowers, Pairpoint Holder, 12 In. 325.00
Pink, Raised Floral, Holder, Webb 215.00
Red Caramel Spatter, Piecrust Rim, Silver Plated Holder 195.00
Ruffled Blue Edges, White, Silver Plated Holder 285.00
White Opalescent, Spanish Moss Inset, Small 85.00
White, Ruffled Blue Edge, Silver Plated Holder 285.00
BRIDE'S BOWL, Amber, Enameled, Silver Plate, Mt.Washington, 12 In. 450.00
Diamond–Quilted, Mother-of-Pearl, Pink, Frame, 10 1/2 In. 795.00
Knife Pleats, Cranberry Rim, Yellow Center, 11 1/2 In. 195.00
Opalescent White Swirl, Fluted, Cobalt Blue Rim 110.00
Pale To Deep Green, Enameling, Mt.Washington, 13 In. 295.00
Peachblow, Ruffled, Orange, Rose, New Martinsville, 11 In. 125.00
Pink To White, Ruffled, Plated, Applied Clear Edge, 11 In. 85.00
Ruffled Cranberry Rim, To Yellow Center, 9 In. 105.00
Ruffled, Gold Flowers, Blue, Silver Plated Stand, 14 1/4 In. 395.00

Ruffled, Molded Bead Rim, Cranberry To Yellow, 11 3/4 In. 195.00

Bristol glass was made in Bristol, England, after the 1700s. The Bristol glass most often seen today is a Victorian, lightweight opaque glass that is often blue. Some of the glass was decorated with enamels.

BRISTOL, Biscuit Jar, Enameled Flowers, Heron, Brass Fittings, 7 1/2 In. ....

Box, Cupid Scene, Blue Ground, White Outlining, Hinged, 4 3/8 In. 150.00
Box, Patch, Hinged Cover, Gold, Turquoise Blue, 1 5/8 X 1 In. 165.00
Candlestick, Gold Band Around Base, Green, 7 In., Pair 88.00
Castor Set, 3-Bottle, Silver Plated Holder, Enameled Flowers 68.00
Centerpiece, Undertray, Sapphire Blue, Footed, Gold Trim, 19 In. 110.00
Cracker Jar, Floral, Silver Plated Fittings 135.00
Cruet, Blue, Enameled Yellow Floral, 3 Petal Top, Handle, 6 1/2 In. 75.00
Decanter, Stopper, Blue, 1800s, 8 In. 75.00
Jar, Sweetmeat, Bird, Flowers, Brass Fittings, Bristol, 5 1/2 In. 75.00
Lamp, Hanging, Frame, 14 In. 45.00
Lamp, Kerosene, Gold Over White, Pair 435.00
Mantle Set, Floral, Pin Ground, Urn Covered, 11 1/2 In., 3 Piece 200.00
Mug, Opalescent, Says Forget Me Not In Gold, 19th Century, 4 In. 495.00
Rose Bowl, Turquoise, Gold Panels, Floral, Dots, Ball Feet, 5 In. 25.00
Sweetmeat Jar, Garlands of Flowers, Butterflies,, 4 1/2 In. 125.00
Urn, Covered, Boy & Girl, Lamb Medallion, Pink, 18 X 6 In. 120.00
Vase, Apricot, Green, 12 In. 595.00
Vase, Birds & Flowers, Pink Overlay, Blue Dots, Gold Trim, 15 In. 50.00
Vase, Gold Covered Black Handles, Birds, Beige, 11 3/4 In. 195.00
Vase, Opalescent Taupe, Enameled Birds, Ruffled Rim, 10 1/2 In. 165.00
Vase, Pink, With Portrait, Bottle Shape, 13 1/2 In. 30.00
Vase, Portrait, Autumnal Colors, 12 In. 90.00
Vase, Ruffled, Multicolored Birds & Flowers, 11 1/2 In. 145.00
Vase, Scenic, Italian Green, 10 1/4 In. 100.00
Vase, White, Blue Rose Spray, 10 1/2 In. 80.00
Vase, Windmill, 7 In. 26.00
　BRITANNIA, see Pewter 30.00

Bronze is an alloy of copper, tin, and other metals. It is used to make figurines, lamps, and other decorative objects.

BRONZE, Bowl, Lotus, Low Relief Petals, Spun, 5 7/8 In. ....
Brush Pot, Footed, China, C.1870 .... 75.00
Bust, Arab, On Marble Base, 9 X 7 In. 185.00
Bust, Bissell, Abraham Lincoln, 26 In. 350.00
Bust, Carmella, Girl, Flowing Hair & Band, Marble Base, 8 1/2 In. 9350.00
Bust, Codmans, Edison, Frontenac Souvenir, 1910, 4 In. 250.00
Bust, Colombo, Tricornered Hat, Brown Patina, 1885, 22 1/2 In. 195.00
Bust, Escoula, Girl, Hair Pulled & Knotted, Onyx Socle, 18 In. 1320.00
Bust, Fame De Brousse, Marie Antoinette, 26 In. 550.00
Bust, Kalish, Worker, Signed, 5 1/2 In. .... *Illus* 850.00
Bust, Villanis, Cendrillon, Girl With Handkerchief, 1892 .... 750.00
Bust, Villanis, Valkyrie, Winged Helmet, Shield, 24 In. 300.00
Bust, Wigglesworth, Woman, Hair In Kerchief, Gorham Stamp, 14 In. 2100.00
Buttonhook, Tree Branch, Figural, 10 In. 800.00
Cannon, Fires Shotgun Shells, Wooden Base, 22 In. 68.00
Cannon, Modern Carriage, Dolphin Handles, 18th Century, Set of 2 .... 225.00
Casque, 4 Knights, Dome Cover, Paw Feet, Velvet Lined, 6 X 4 In. 5000.00
Cutter, Opium, Figural, Phoenix Shape, Chinese, 19th Century 85.00
Dish, Wasp In Center, Art Nouveau, 6 In. 95.00
Door Knocker, Lion's Head, 10 In. 35.00
Figurine, A.Carrier Belleuse, Girl, Flowers, C.1850, 32 In. 165.00
Figurine, Alfred Boucher, Young Woman, Beside Fountain, 20 1/2 In. 4900.00
Figurine, Arnold, Nude, Arm Raised, Towel, C.1925, 25 1/2 In. 2100.00
Figurine, Austrian, Bedoin, Camel, Natural Quartz Formation, 10 In. 1200.00
Figurine, Bacchus, Ring Holder, Held By Snake, Domed Base, 24 In. 700.00
Figurine, Barbedienne, Orpheus & Cerberus, Lyre, 39 1/2 In. 1100.00
Figurine, Barye, Bear, Frolicking, 5 X 6 In. 5500.00
　　　　　　　　　　　　　　　　　　　　　　　　　　　　　　　　 150.00

Figurine, Barye, Panther Attacking Stag, C.1870, 14 1/2 In. 1650.00
Figurine, Barye, Stallion, Founder's Seal, Signed, 12 1/2 In. 2500.00
Figurine, Bayre, Reclining Lion, Signed, 10 3/4 In. 300.00
Figurine, Berge, Sea Urchin, Child, Arms Raised On Rounded Base 9350.00
Figurine, Bird, Green Body, Black Wings, Austrian, 4 In. ....*Illus* 125.00
Figurine, Bird, Leaning, Yellow, Brown, Austrian, 4 1/2 In. ....*Illus* 125.00
Figurine, Bonheur, Boy, With Bull 1200.00
Figurine, Boucher, Woman In Breast Plate, PAX Title, 32 In. 1750.00
Figurine, Bouret, Maiden With Harp, Marble Base, C.1890, 21 In. 660.00
Figurine, Bourgeois, Snake Charmer, Brown Patina, 25 In. 2000.00
Figurine, Boyer, Monkey On Horseback, Jockey Dressed, 5 X 8 1/8 In. 350.00
Figurine, Buddha, Seated Lotus, Hands Clasped, Gilded, 15 1/2 In. 750.00
Figurine, Burger, Lady, Art Nouveau, Throwing Ball, 5 In. 295.00
Figurine, C.F.Woerffel, Dog, Irish Setter, 19th Century, 15 In. 935.00
Figurine, Cain, Panther Feeding Cubs, Green Brown Patina, 13 In. 1200.00
Figurine, Carrier, Molieke, Man Sitting, Thinking, 24 1/2 In. 1450.00
Figurine, Cheval Turc, Stallion, Forleg Raised, 11 3/8 In. 2000.00
Figurine, Chiparus, Dancer, Aleria, Ivory, Foundry Mark, 17 In. 5000.00
Figurine, Coustou, Marley Horse, French, 18 In. 475.00
Figurine, Cumberworth, Woman With Child, Brown Patina, 21 In. 900.00
Figurine, D'Aste, Couple Among Sheep, Yellow Patina, 16 1/2 In. 1000.00
Figurine, Delaplanche, Peasant Mother & Child, 21 1/2 In. 2000.00
Figurine, Drouot, Music Teacher & Child, Brown Patina, 25 In. 1200.00
Figurine, Dubucand, Hunting Dog, Pointer, Signed, 11 In. 200.00
Figurine, Focht, Athlete, Stylized Flaming Torch, 1930, 29 1/2 In. 4125.00
Figurine, Francesco Conventi, Young Boy, C.1900, 24 1/4 In. 1200.00
Figurine, G.Ferrai, Girl, Arms Outstretched, Blindfolded, 5 1/2 In. 435.00
Figurine, Gechter, Woman, Partially Draped, Puma Cub, At Feet, 14 In. 475.00
Figurine, Germain, Woman, Standing, Greenish Patina, 1897, 39 In. 2975.00
Figurine, Gerome, Woman, Standing, Flowing Robes, 36 In. 3850.00
Figurine, Giovanni De Bologna, Hercules & Cretan Bull, 23 1/2 In. 3250.00
Figurine, Guerval, 2 Dancing Women, Partially Draped, 23 1/2 In. 1870.00
Figurine, Humphriss, Indian On Horse 900.00
Figurine, Iffland, 2 Bulls, Locking Horns, Rocky Ground, 29 In. 550.00
Figurine, Kauba, Indian, Rose Quartz Base, 14 In. 4800.00
Figurine, LaMonoca, Nude On Horse 1400.00
Figurine, Le Faguays, Woman, Message of Love, Silvered, 18 In. 935.00
Figurine, Lenordez, Horse & Dog, Angelo On Base, 16 X 20 1/8 In. 950.00
Figurine, Levy, Faneur, Young Man, Straw Hat, C.1885, 11 5/8 In. 700.00
Figurine, M.B.Mead, Dog, Reclining, 1930, 2 1/2 X 3 1/2 X 6 In. 350.00
Figurine, Mantecerde, Youth, Renaissance Outfit, 1845, 24 In. 900.00
Figurine, Mene, Fighting Stags, Pair 1100.00

Bronze, Bust, Fame De Brousse,
Marie Antoinette, 26 In.

Bronze, Figurine, Bird, Leaning, Yellow,
Brown, Austrian, 4 1/2 In.

Bronze, Figurine, Bird, Green Body,
Black Wings, Austrian, 4 In.

Bronze, Figurine,
Moreau, 2 Bacchantes,
1822–1912, 31 In.

Bronze, Figurine,
Napoleon Bonaparte, 17 In.

Figurine, Mene, Setter, 7 1/2 X 11 In.	
Figurine, Mene, Stallion, 15 1/8 In.	250.00
Figurine, Moreau, 2 Bacchantes, 1822–1912, 31 In.	1980.00
Figurine, Moreau, 2 Girls, Brown Patina, 22 In. ....*Illus*	2000.00
Figurine, Mullner, Woman & Panthers, Bronze Socle, 42 1/2 In.	1200.00
Figurine, Napoleon Bonaparte, 17 In. ....*Illus*	2100.00
Figurine, Petrier, Renaissance Lady, Hand Near Chin, 39 In.	800.00
Figurine, Preiss, Aphrodite, Polychromed, Ivory, Onyx Socle, 9 In.	4600.00
Figurine, Remington, Mountain Man, Man On Horse, 29 1/2 In.	3300.00
Figurine, Remington, Polo, 3 Horse, 1904, 20 X 22 In.	3000.00
Figurine, Sauvage, Venus De Milo, Signed, 22 1/2 In.	3500.00
Figurine, Steenackers, Gold Black Patina, C.1855, 20 In.	375.00
Figurine, Stouffer, Satyr, Mask, Roman Bronze Foundry, 7 In.	1100.00
Figurine, Troubetskoy, Elephant, Standing, Hay In Trunk, 12 In.	450.00
Figurine, Vallanis, Talisman, Signed	2300.00
Figurine, Vienna, Crested Cockatoo, Perched On Branch, 7 1/2 In.	3800.00
Figurine, Vienna, Dog, Tennis Racket In Mouth, 3 X 1 1/2 In.	300.00
Figurine, Vienna, Hockey Player, Ready To Hit Ball, Marble Base	165.00
Figurine, Woeffel, Hound, Reclining, Signed, Russia, 7 1/8 X 15 In.	245.00
Group, Benet, Two Lovers, Embracing, C.1900, 28 1/2 In.	850.00
Group, C.M.Clodion, Two Putti & Goat, C.1870, 16 1/2 In.	2300.00
Group, Fremiet, Two Racehorses With Jockeys Up, Signed, 1875, 18 In.	2200.00
Group, Susse Freres, Leda & Swan, French, C.1930, 30 1/2 In.	8500.00
Group, Woerffel, Equestrian, Cossack, Lover, Rocky Slope, 13 In.	1875.00
Incense Burner, Lion Finial, Champlave Enameled, Japan, 8 1/2 In.	2200.00
Incense Burner, Marked Ming Dynasty	115.00
Jar, Vented Lid, Relief Oriental Birds & Blossoms, 19 1/2 In.	500.00
Jardiniere, Dragons On Shoulder, Baluster, Japan, 13 1/2 In.	300.00
Jardiniere, Figural, 3 Putto, Holding Cornucopia, 1900, 4 Ft.11 In.	450.00
Lamp, Bouval, Upright Thistle Plant Form, Flower Lamp, 21 In.	1750.00
Lamp, Desk, Iridescent White Shade Signed Quezal, 16 In.	1550.00
Lamp, Empire, Maiden Playing Horns, 30 In., Pair	125.00
Locomotive Bell, Mount & Clapper, 12 In. ....*Illus*	1100.00
Mortar & Pestle, Squart Baluster, Head Handles, French, 16 In.	285.00
Mortar, Cylindrical Shape, Gargoyle Handles, Bears, 7 1/8 In.	700.00
Napkin Holder, Lions, Standing, Set of 4	350.00
Paperweight, Bunch of Grapes, Wood Base, 4 X 5 In.	100.00
Pen Wiper, Wild Bear Shape, Hand Painted, Austrian, 9 3/8 In.	55.00
Penholder, Figural, Bird	300.00
Pincushion, 2 Dore Pigs, Austria	32.00
Plaque, F.Diller, Dog, Ebonized Frame, 10 1/2 X 13 1/4 In.	35.00
	65.00

Pot, Spherical, Animal Head Spouts, Swing Handle, Germany, 6 1/4 In. 175.00
Rack, Letter, Liberty & Co., Black Marble Base, C.1900 .... 75.00
Sconce, Baroque Style, 3 Way Plaque, Ribbons, Tassels, 19 In., Pair 350.00
Tazza, Classical Goddess & Cherubs Musical Scene, Europe, 12 In. 50.00
Tazza, Figural, 3 Putti, Draped In Net & Animal Skin, Boyer, 18 In. ....*Illus* 2000.00
Urn, Classical Maidens, Upright Handles, 18 In., Pair 500.00
Urn, Covered, Louis XVI Style, Grotesque Masks, Ram's Horn Swags 1000.00
Urn, Empire, Ormolu Mounts, Ribbon Tied Wreath Mount, 13 In., Pair 2550.00
Vase, Art Nouveau, Leaf Design, Double Arms, Gorham, 8 1/2 In. 200.00
Vase, Dragons, Diaper Ground, Elephant Head Handles, China, 12 In. 100.00
Vase, Japanese, 19th Century, 7 X 9 1/2 In. 375.00
Vase, Molded Cylinders, Foo Dragons, 9 5/8 X 4 In., Pair 300.00
Vase, Pear Shape, Handles, Embossed Designs, Oriental, 14 In. 300.00
Watch Fob, Cigar Cutter, Real Habana Segars, C.1890 .... 125.00

> Brownies were first drawn in 1883 by Palmer Cox. They are characterized by large round eyes, downturned mouths, and skinny legs. Toys, books, dinnerware, and other objects were made with the Brownies as part of the design.

BROWNIES, Book, Brownies Abroad, 1899 .... 45.00
Book, Queer People, Palmer Cox Children 18.00
Book, Throughout The Union, Palmer Cox 75.00
Bottle, Soda, Palmer Cox 25.00
Butter Chip, Dancing, Gold Luster Trim, Palmer Cox, 2 3/4 In. 8.00
Cloth Panel, Printed For Stuffed Toys, Uncle Sam, Dude, Policman 225.00
Container, Crayons, Wooden, Round 45.00
Cup & Saucer, Palmer Cox 45.00
Game, Target Ball, M.H.Miller Co., Box 35.00
Humidor, Sailor of The Ship, 6 3/4 In. 330.00
Napkin Ring, Figural, Silver Plate, Cox, Engraved Florals 155.00
Package, Needles, Souvenir, 1893 Columbian Expo. 45.00
Paperweight, Metal, Palmer Cox, 5 3/4 In. 35.00
Plate, Brownies Around Border, Silver Plate, 8 1/2 In. 42.00
Plate, Lobster Chasing Brownies 55.00
Printing Blocks, Palmer Cox, Set of 10 .... 85.00
Spoon, Figural, Sterling Silver, Enameled, Palmer Cox 32.00
Thermometer, Full Figure Brownie On Base, Palmer Cox 75.00
Tin, Ointment, Brownies Both Sides, Box, 1924 .... 35.00
Toy, Jumping Jack, Papier–Mache & Wood 165.00
Toy, Push Handles, 2 Brownies Do Acrobatics, Wooden, 1915 .... 78.00

Bronze, Lamp, Empire, Maiden Playing Horns,
30 In., Pair

Bronze, Urn, Classical Maidens,
Upright Handles, 18 In., Pair

George Brush started working in 1901 in Zanesville, Ohio. He started his own pottery in 1907, but it burned to the ground and he joined McCoy in 1909. After a series of name changes, the company became The Brush Pottery in 1925. Collectors favor the figural cookie jars made by this company.

BRUSH, Cookie Jar, Baby Elephant	
Cookie Jar, Barefoot Boy	80.00
Cookie Jar, Bear, Smiling	125.00
Cookie Jar, Boy Angel, Halo	125.00
Cookie Jar, Cow, Purple	95.00
Cookie Jar, Davy Crockett	300.00
Cookie Jar, Donkey With Cart	65.00 To 80.00
Cookie Jar, Granny	35.00
Cookie Jar, Little Red Riding Hood	55.00
Cookie Jar, Pig, Formal	145.00
Cookie Jar, Pinocchio	50.00 To 80.00
Cookie Jar, Shoe	35.00
Cookie Jar, Squirrel, Happy	45.00
BRUSH MCCOY, see McCoy	50.00

Buck Rogers was the first American science fiction comic strip. It started in 1929 and continued until 1965. Buck has also appeared in comic books, movies, and, in the 1980s, in a television series. Any memorabilia connected with the character Buck Rogers is collectible.

BUCK ROGERS, Atomic Pistol, Daisy	
Badge, Solar Scout	80.00
Book, Big Little Book, Adventures Buck Rogers, Whitman, 1934	35.00
Book, Big Little Book, Friend of Space	40.00
Book, Big Little Book, On The Moons of Saturn	20.00
Book, Pop–Up, Spidership Adventures, 1935	50.00
Booklet, Sonic Ray Code	150.00
Corgi, Starfighter, Fires Rockets, Box, 1979	12.00
Doll, Mego, Box, 12 1/2 In.'	18.00
Figure Set, Britain, Complete	18.00
Game, Board, Space Ships, 1979	950.00
Game, Card	12.00
Gun, Disintegrator, 1930s	374.00
Gun, Sonic Ray, Box	75.00
Handbook, Space Patrol	25.00
Helmet	100.00
Kit, Space Ranger, Unpunched	45.00
Kite, Strato, Package, 1946	75.00
Pencil Box, 1935	24.00
Pistol, Rocket, 25th Century, Daisy	48.00
Popgun, Daisy	75.00
Poster, Onward School Supplies, 1940, 50 X 18 In.	65.00
Push–Outs, Sylvania, Space Ship, Space Gun, 6 Pages, 1952	100.00
Ring, Repeller Ray	125.00
Robot, Twiki, Mego, Box	200.00
Space Gun, Daisy	15.00
Space Ranger Kit, Complete, Compliments of Sylvania	85.00
Space Ship, Pat.March 15, 1927	185.00
Space Ship, Venus Duo–Destroyer, Marx	485.00
Strato Kite, 1946	100.00
Toy, Flying Saucer, 1930s	35.00
Toy, Rocket Ship, Tootsietoy, Box	55.00
Toy, Venus Duo–Destroyer, Tootsietoy	189.00
Watch, Pocket	65.00 To 80.00
	210.00 To 225.00

Buffalo pottery was made in Buffalo, New York, after 1902. The company was established by the Larkin Company, famous manufacturers of soap. The wares are marked with a picture of a buffalo and the date of manufacture. Deldare ware is the most famous pottery made at the factory. It is khaki-colored transfer-decorated ware.

BUFFALO POTTERY DELDARE, Bowl, Cereal, Olden Days, 6 1/2 In. 250.00
Candlestick, Village Scene, 1909, 9 1/2 In., Pair 595.00
Chop Plate, Dr.Syntax Sells Grizzle, 13 1/2 In. 875.00
Chop Plate, Fallowfield Hunt, The Start, 14 In. 495.00
Creamer, Ye Olden Days, 2 5/8 In. 165.00
Cup & Saucer, Sailor 135.00
Cup & Saucer, Ye Olden Days .... 175.00 To 190.00
Humidor, An Old Sailor .... 500.00 To 750.00
Match Holder, Village Scene 375.00
Mug, Fallowfield Hunt 400.00
Mug, The Fallowfield Hunt 190.00
Mug, Ye Lion Inn, 4 1/2 In. .... 210.00 To 250.00
Pin Tray, Ye Olden Days, 6 1/4 X 3 1/2 In. 290.00
Pitcher, Dr.Syntax, To Demand Annual Rent, 8 In. 395.00
Pitcher, English Village, Octagonal, 10 In. 435.00
Pitcher, Great Controversy, M.Sned, 12 1/2 In. 875.00
Pitcher, Manner of Telling Stories, 6 In. 400.00
Pitcher, The Great Controversy, 12 1/2 In. 725.00
Pitcher, Their Manner of Telling Stories, 6 In. 385.00
Plaque, Breakfast At Three Pigeons, 12 In. 475.00
Plaque, Dr.Syntax Sketching The Lake, 12 In. 1000.00
Plaque, Fallowfield Hunt, 12 In. 475.00
Plaque, Friday Monks Dining, 12 In. 1200.00
Plaque, Thursday Monks Fishing, 12 In. 1200.00
Plaque, Ye Lion Inn, 12 In. .... 375.00 To 475.00
Plate, Art Nouveau, Emerald, 8 1/4 In. 400.00
Plate, Fallowfield Hunt, The Start, Signed, 9 In. 150.00
Plate, Lion Inn, 14 In. .... 435.00 To 525.00
Plate, Misfortune, Tulip Hall, Emerald, 9 In. 400.00
Plate, The Death, 8 1/2 In. 125.00
Plate, The Start, 14 In. 550.00
Plate, The Start, 9 1/4 In. .... 150.00 To 190.00
Plate, Village Street, 7 1/4 In. 100.00
Plate, Ye Lion Inn, 6 1/2 In. 90.00
Plate, Ye Olden Times, 9 1/4 In. .... 125.00 To 150.00
Plate, Ye Town Crier, 8 1/4 In. .... 100.00 To 145.00
Platter, Buffalo Hunt, Dark Green, 11 X 14 In. 95.00
Powder Jar, Covered 395.00
Sugar & Creamer, Ye Olden Days .... 310.00 To 350.00
Sugar, Breaking Cover 150.00
Sugar, Village Life, 6 In. 160.00
Tankard, Fallowfield Hunt, 12 1/2 In. 900.00
Tankard, Great Controversy, 12 1/2 In. .... 445.00 To 800.00
Teapot, Ye Olden Days, Short Spout, 4 3/4 In. 175.00
Tile, Breaking Cover 65.00
Tray, Card, Dr.Syntax, Robbed of Property, 8 In. 450.00
Tray, Card, Ye Lion Inn, 8 In. 165.00
Tray, Card, Ye Olden Days, 6 1/4 X 3 1/2 In. 235.00
Tray, Dresser, Minuet 450.00
Tray, Heirlooms, Dated 1908, 14 1/2 X 10 In. 725.00
Tray, Pin, Ye Olden Days, 6 1/2 In. 175.00
BUFFALO POTTERY, Bowl, Gaudy Willow, 9 1/2 In. 100.00
Bowl, Transfer, Embossed Flowers, Gilding, 10 3/4 In. 69.00
Butter Tub, Insert, Flowers, Handles, 1915 .... 15.00
Gleaners, Beehive, Underglaze, Green, Gold Tracery, 10 In. 85.00
Pitcher, Bluebirds Flying In Formation, 6 1/2 In. 125.00
Pitcher, Cinderella .... 250.00 To 400.00

Pitcher, George Washington	450.00
Pitcher, Hounds & Stag, Signed, 1906	245.00
Pitcher, Marine Design, Sailors, Ships, Dated 1907, 9 In.	625.00
Pitcher, Robin Hood	325.00 To 375.00
Plate, Abino, 9 1/2 In.	500.00
Plate, C & O R.R., Gold Embossed, 1932, 11 In.	480.00
Plate, Christmas, 1951	50.00 To 55.00
Plate, Christmas, 1959	45.00
Plate, DeWitt Clinton, N.Y.C.	32.00
Plate, Gates Circle, Buffalo, N.Y., 7 In.	19.00
Plate, Gaudy Willow, 10 In.	85.00
Plate, Independence Hall, 7 1/2 In.	35.00
Plate, Morgan's Red Coach Tavern, 11 1/2 In.	145.00
Plate, Niagara Falls, 10 In.	50.00 To 65.00
Plate, State Capitol, Helena, Mont., 1909, 7 1/2 In.	80.00
Plate, U.S.Capitol, Green, 10 In.	33.00
Plate, W.Taft Portrait, Our Choice, 1908, 9 In.	21.00
Plate, Wanamaker, 4 In.	90.00
Platter Set, Deer, Moose, Border, R.K.Beck, 4 9–In.Plates	90.00
Platter, Buffalo Hunt, Dark Green, 11 X 14 In.	95.00
Platter, Gaudy Willow, C.1911, 10 1/2 X 8 1/2 In.	145.00
Sauce, Gaudy Willow, 5 In.	30.00
Teapot, Argyle, 1914	45.00
Teapot, Attached Tea Basket, Blue, White Argyle	125.00

Burmese glass was developed by Frederick Shirley at the Mt. Washington Glass Works in New Bedford, Massachusetts, in 1885. It is a two–toned glass, shading from peach to yellow. Some have a pattern mold design. A few Burmese pieces were decorated with pictures or applied glass flowers of colored Burmese glass.

BURMESE, see also Gunderson

BURMESE, Basket, Buttons, 6 1/4 X 6 1/4 In.	
Bowl, Waste, Crimped Rim, 2 3/4 X 5 3/4 In.	225.00
Condiment Set, Sterling Silver Holder	225.00
Fairy Lamp, Epergne, Pyramid Shade, 6 Ruffled Vase, 11 1/4 In.	450.00
Lamp, Table, Burner, Queen's Pattern, 1880s	1250.00
Mustard, Ribbed, 2 In.	2200.00
Pitcher, Pink To Yellow, Applied Yellow Handle, 5 1/4 In.	250.00
Saltshaker, Pansies, Cream Ground, Mt.Washington	150.00
Toothpick, Blue & Pink Blossoms, Swags of Green, Mt.Washington	235.00
Toothpick, Bulbous, Leaves, Enameled Blue Berries, 2 3/4 In.	465.00
Toothpick, Diamond–Quilted, Square Top, C.1887	95.00
Toothpick, Enameled Flowers, Cream Ground, Mt.Washington, 2 In.	360.00
Toothpick, Pinched Middle, Oak Leaves & Acorns, 2 3/4 In.	465.00
Toothpick, Rose Bowl Shape, Hexagonal Top	295.00
Vase, Black Dragon & Flowers, 10 In.	175.00
Vase, Bottle Shape, Fern Frond Design, 8 1/2 X 4 In.	885.00
Vase, Elongated Egg Shape, Blossoms, Foliage, Gold Enamel, 9 In.	395.00
Vase, Enameled Flower Sprays, Gourd Shape, Mt.Washington, 8 In.	785.00
Vase, Melon Ribbed, Flaring Top, Ivy Leaves, 4 1/2 X 3 3/4 In.	425.00
Vase, Ruffled, Footed, 10 1/2 X 6 In.	475.00
Vase, Thomas Hood Poem, Enameled Roses, 12 1/2 In.	550.00 To 575.00
Vase, Trumpet, Ormolu Stand, Crimped Rim, 6 3/4 In.	2250.00 To 2800.00
	200.00
BURMESE, WEBB, see Webb Burmese	

Buster Brown, the comic strip, first appeared in color in 1902. Buster and his dog Tige remained a popular comic and soon became even more famous as the emblem for a shoe company, a textile firm, and others. The strip was discontinued in 1920, but some of the advertising is still in use.

BUSTER BROWN & TIGE, Napkin Ring, Celluloid	
BUSTER BROWN, Bank, Buster Brown & Tige, Cast Iron	30.00
Book, Cartoon, Amusing Capers, 1906	140.00
Book, Paint, Cupples & Leon, 1916	35.00
	10.00

Box, Shoe, 1949 .... 20.00
Camera, Illustrated, Anthony Scovill Co., Box 290.00
Clapper, Molded Paper, Advertising 70.00
Clicker, Tin 8.00
Cup & Saucer 35.00
Dish, Cereal, Aluminum, Buster Brown & Tige 39.00
Display, Buster & Tige, Gold, Round, 17 In. 225.00
Doll, Store Display, 30 In. 95.00
Doll, Stuffed, Early 1900s 50.00
Game, School's Out, Bliss 450.00
Knife & Fork Set, Child's 24.00
Knife, Pocket, Bone Handle, Advertising 45.00
Mannequin, Boy & Girl, Yellow Hair, 32 In., Pair 160.00
Mask 10.00
Mug, With Tige 30.00
Pin, Buster Brown & Tige, 1 3/4 In. 8.00
Pitcher, ABC 95.00
Pitcher, Child's, Porcelain 36.00
Plate, 4 In. 22.00
Postcard, Buster & Tige, Leather 8.00
String Holder, Counter, Windmill Top, Iron, C.1910, 15 In. 550.00
Tile, Tea 35.00
Toy, In Cart, Pulled By Dog, Cast Iron, 1900 .... 375.00
Watch, Ansonia, Pocket 75.00
Whistle 14.00

BUTTER MOLD, see Kitchen, Mold, Butter
BUTTERMILK GLASS, see Custard Glass

Buttons have been known throughout the centuries, and there are millions of styles. Gold, silver, or precious stones were used for the best buttons but most were made of natural materials like bone or shell, or from inexpensive metals. Only a few types are listed for comparison.

BUTTON, Angel Head, Rope Edging, Sterling Silver, Dated 1904 .... 20.00
Boar Hunting, Lapel Type, French, Copper Backed, 1 1/2 In., Pair 125.00
Charles I, High Relief, Brass, 1 1/2 In. 55.00
Collar, Gold Filled, 6 On Original Card 7.00
Enameled Scenes, Hunting In England, C.1760, 1 1/2 In., 12 Piece 850.00
Enameled, Hirst Bros.Jewelers, Leeds, England, Fitted Box, 3 Piece 10.00
Flower Center, Sterling Silver, Set of 5 .... 27.50
Galleon, Sterling Silver, 7/8 In. 35.00
Hand Painted, Wild Roses, Meissen, 11/16 In. 35.00
Horse, 1900s, Set of 6 .... 4.00
Illinois Military, 1810 .... 12.50
Ivory, Art Deco, 1 1/8 In. 100.00
Jacket, Souther R.R., 4 Large, 3 Small 12.00
King Tut, Brass, Bakelite Back, 2 1/2 X 3 In. 65.00
Madame Butterfly, Relief, Brass, 1 3/16 In. 18.00
Mauve, Blue Rhinestones, Set of 4 .... 3.00
Owl Center, 1/2 In. 7.00
Police, Youngstown, Ohio, C.1920, Pair 10.00
Streetcar Uniform, Philadelphia Transit Co. 9.00
Swallow & Nest, 1 1/2 In. 15.00
Whippet's Head, Black Glass With Silver Luster, 7/8 In. 15.00

Buttonhooks have been a popular collectible in England for many years but only recently have gained the attention of American collectors. The buttonhooks were made to help fasten the many buttons of the old–fashioned high–button shoes and other items of apparel.

BUTTONHOOK, Advertising, Shoehorn & Comb, Folds, 1915 .... 10.00
Art Nouveau Handle, Sterling Silver, Shiebler 125.00
Art Nouveau, Long Haired Maiden, Calla Lilies, Sterling Silver 75.00
Chrysanthemum Repousse, Sterling Silver Handle, 8 In. 22.00

Cupid Riding Dolphin, Seahorses, Unger Bros., 8 In. ....

J.C.Penney 90.00

Lily of The Valley, Whiting, Sterling Silver, 1885 .... 18.00

Statue of Liberty 68.00

Sterling Silver, English, 2 1/2 In. 15.00

Walkover Shoes 65.00

With Snap Out Pencil, Part of Chatelaine .... 7.50 To 8.00

                                                                      85.00

Calendars made to hang on the wall or to be displayed on a desk top have been popular since the last quarter of the nineteenth century. Many were printed with advertising as part of the artwork and were given away as premiums. Calendars with gun or gunpowder or Coca-Cola advertising are most prized.

CALENDAR PAPER, 1881, Wm.Deering, Farm Machinery Picture ....

1883, Clarke's Mile-End Spool Cotton, 2 1/8 X 3 1/2 In. 25.00

1886, Hood's Sarsaparilla 7.50

1886, Sohmer Piano 25.00

1887, Higgins' Compound 20.00

1888, Schlitz Brewery, 4 Parts, 11 1/2 X 8 1/2 In. 25.00

1889, German American Ins.Co., Mermaids, 8 X 12 In. 50.00

1893, Anchor Pain Expeller, Children Pictured 25.00

1895, German Life Insurance, Agent, Fla., 4 Sheet 30.00

1896, Hanford's Celery Cure, Victorian Children 65.00

1897, Girl In Blue Bonnet, Roses, Die Cut, 12 X 17 In. 35.00

1898, John Hancock Life Insurance, Liberty Tree, Framed 100.00

1898, Shakespeare, Raphael Tuck 150.00

1900, Christy, R.H.Russell Publisher, N.Y., 18 X 12 In. 25.00

1900, Stegmaier 48.00

1903, Playing Grandma, Maud Humphrey, Framed, 17 X 21 In. 550.00

1903, Youth's Companion, Foldout, Woman 75.00

1904, Metropolitan Life, Perpetual, Celluloid 15.00

1905, Fantasy, Child, With Butterfly Wings 14.00

1905, Pabst Malt Extract, Oriental, 36 In. 28.00

1906, A.B.Rudd, Cassopolis, Mich., C.M.Russell, 5 X 9 In. 145.00

1907, Pabst Extract, Lady In Red 18.00

1908, Sweet Roses, Davidson Bros, London, 6 X 14 In. 175.00

1913, Tuscarora Fertilizer 12.00

1914, Continental Fire Insurance, First Shot, Yorktown 9.00

1914, Hood's Sarsaparilla, Woman 35.00

1916, Prudential Girl, Framed 8.00

1918, Swift's Premium, Patriotic, Artist Signed, 8 X 15 In. 35.00

1919, American Art Works, Cardboard, 5 1/2 X 10 In. 175.00

1919, Liberty Girl 8.50

1921, Pompeian Cosmetics 25.00

1924, Call of The Wild, M.M.Silva, Gen'L Merchandise 65.00

1924, Remington Ammunition, Hunter, Framed, 20 X 34 In. 8.00

1924, Yeast Foam, Yeast & Hand, 10 X 18 In. 675.00

1925, Prince, House of Arts, Framed 20.50

1925, Western Ammunition, Dogs Pictured 95.00

1926, Rexall Weather Chart 300.00

1927, Dream Girl, Rolf Armstrong, 1927, 8 X 21 3/4 In. 35.00

1927, Golden Hours, Parrish 40.00

1927, Oak Stove, Original Envelope, Sales Pamphlet 120.00

1927, Round Oak 175.00

1928, Remington 110.00

1928, Stevens 450.00

1928, Winchester 300.00

1929, Builders Supply Co., York Pa. .... 125.00 To 165.00

1929, Scotty, Die Cut 15.00

1930, Zula Kenyon, Blue Birds Bring Happiness, 24 In. 15.00

1931, DeLaval, Norman Price Illustrator 35.00

1931, Edison Mazda, Waterfall, April, Large 15.00

1931, P.R.R., Airplane, Steam Passenger Train Picture 400.00

1931, Solitude, Maxfield Parrish, Cropped, Original Frame 310.00

                                                                    145.00

1931, South Side Cafe, Aledo, Ill.	28.00
1931, Standard Auto Parts Co., Quincy, Ill.	28.00
1932, Santa Fe R.R.	55.00
1933, Gold Dust Twins	22.00
1933, Pompeian, Honeymoon In Venice	25.00
1934, Seiberling Tire, Irish Eyes, R.Armstrong, 7 X 9 In.	32.00
1935, DeLaval, Historical Scenes, 17 X 9 In.	35.00
1935, Stafford & Johnson Gas & Oil, Breckenridge, Colo.	8.00
1935, Twilight, Framed, 18 X 24 In.	95.00
1936, Black Boy, Crying	10.00
1936, Dionne Quintuplets, Photograph	16.00
1936, Poll Parrot Shoes, 10 X 17 In.	7.00
1937, L.C.Rumley, Gone Fishin', Date Pad Complete	20.00
1938, Standard Red Crown, 12 Sheets, 9 X 15 In.	14.00
1939, American Beauty Flour	12.50
1939, Friendly House, Edgar A.Guest	10.00
1939, Grocery Store Advertising	12.50
1939, Standard Oil Co., Orion, Ill., Metal Frame	15.00
1942, Dr Pepper	75.00
1942, Snow White, Morrell, 6 Pages, 16 1/2 X 31 In.	125.00
1944, Esquire, Vargas Prints, Spiral Bound, 12 X 8 1/2 In.	6.00
1944, International Harvester, Woman, Tractor, 13 X 20 In.	17.00
1944, TWA, Envelope, 14 1/2 X 23 In.	33.00
1945, Crane's Grocery & Market, Aztec, N.M.	12.00
1945, Pennsylvania R.R., Full Pad, 28 X 28 In.	40.00
1945, Rhinelander Beer	17.50
1946, Beautiful Lady Front	9.50
1946, Vargas, Bathing Suit Girl, August Page, 8 X 12 In.	16.50
1947, Earl MacPherson's Sketch Scandals, 9 X 12 In.	15.00
1948, Atlantic Ale & Beer, A Perfect Pair, 2 Leggy Girls	20.00
1948, B.& B.Four Seasons, Norman Rockwell	65.00
1948, Dr Pepper	30.00
1949, Esquire	25.00
1949, Forster & Otto Manufacturer's Representatives	3.50
1949, Gold Miners, 49ers, Hercules Powder	95.00
1949, Texaco	10.00
1950, Carson & Colorado Railroad	65.00
1950, Freeman Elliott, Pinup	15.00
1950, Movie Star, Monty Clift, Alan Ladd, Susan Hayward, Etc.	12.00
1952, Esquire, Lacks January, 4 X 5 In.	8.00
1953, Esquire	25.00
1953, Poll Parrot Shoes	10.00
1953, Royal Crown Cola, Rhonda Fleming, 11 X 24 In.	65.00
1954, Marilyn Monroe, Golden Dreams	50.00
1955, Boy Scouts, Norman Rockwell	14.00
1955, Esquire, Petty, Envelope	38.00
1955, Esquire, Vargas	38.00
1955, Girlie, Studio Sketches By Thompson, Stapled	5.00
1955, Marilyn Monroe, Golden Dreams, 12 X 19 In.	50.00
1956, Royal Crown Cola, Girl With Bottle	18.00
1956, Travelers, Currier & Ives	14.00
1957, Esquire Girl, Brule Illustrator	30.00
1961, Santa Fe R.R.	20.00
1967, Playboy, Dust Jacket	8.95
1978, Russell, Remington	5.00
1978, Star Wars, Package	30.00
Esquire, 3 1/2 X 4 1/2 In.	20.00
Perpetual, Round Brass Holder & Base	45.00

> Calendar plates were very popular in the United States from 1906 to
> 1929. Since then, plates have been made every year. A calendar and
> the name of a store, a picture of flowers, a girl, or a scene were
> featured on the plate.

CALENDAR PLATE, 1907, Santa Claus 32.00

1909, Blooming Prairie, Minn.7 1/4 In. 26.00
1909, Mansfield, Ill., 12 Months In Center 18.00
1909, Nowlin Drug Co., R.Tester, Proprietor 24.00
1910, Angels, Store Name 30.00
1910, Beautiful Lady, J.F.Turner, Augusta, Me. 32.00
1910, Cupids Ringing In New Year 34.00
1910, Holly, Berries, Chas.Washburn, Taunton, Ma. 30.00
1910, Lund, Wis., Store Name 22.00
1910, Midland, South Dakota, C.A.Joy & Co., Holly Pattern 24.00
1910, Monk Drawing Beer From Keg, 10 In. 22.00
1910, Roses 15.00
1910, The Old Swimming Hole 45.00
1911, Flowers 22.50
1911, Stamford, Nebraska, Cupids & Roses 22.00
1912, 1st Airplane 45.00
1912, Champion, Mich., Store Name 22.00
1912, Girl Sailor, American Flag 24.00
1912, H.C.Ruden, General Merchandise, Sunset Pattern 20.00
1912, Indian Maiden, Wooden Frame 35.00
1912, Owl On Book, 7 1/2 In. .... 20.00 To 25.00
1914, Liberty Bell, Philadelphia 32.50
1915, Christopher, 7 In. 20.00
1915, Owl On Book 20.00
1916, Star Union Brewing Co., Peru, Ill., Tin, 1916 .... 70.00
1920, Peace, Glenville, Minn., 9 In. 28.00
1946, Indian Chief 65.00
1954, Jubilee, Pink 9.00
1971, Wedgwood 23.00
1974, God Bless Our House 15.00

Camark Pottery started in 1924 in Camden, Arkansas. Jack Carnes founded the firm and made many types of glazes and wares. The company was bought by Mary Daniel, who still owns the firm. Production was halted in 1983.

CAMARK, Box, Cigarette, Covered, Wine, Sticker 16.50
Candlestick, Double, Iris, Paper Label, Pair 20.00
Console Set, Double Swan Frog, Double Candlesticks, 3 Piece 44.00
Jug, Brown Gloss, 5 In. 12.00
Jug, Drip Glaze, Handle, Marked, Large 30.00
Pot, Mottled Blue, Handles, 5 X 7 In. 28.00
Salt & Pepper, Alphabet Letter Shape, Ivory 5.50
Sign, Dealer's, Arkansas State Shape, 6 1/2 In. 65.00
Tumbler, Roosevelt, Chicago World's Fair, 1933 .... 30.00
Vase, Green, 2 Handles, 8 In. 11.50
Vase, Matte Yellow Crackle, Ribbed, 13 In. 70.00
Wall Pocket, Double, Sticker 28.00

Cambridge art pottery was made in Cambridge, Ohio, from about 1895 until World War I. The factory made brown glazed decorated wares with a variety of marks including an acorn, the name "Cambridge," the name "Oakwood," or the name "Terrhea."

CAMBRIDGE POTTERY, Tile, Night & Morning, Pair 350.00
Vase, Brown, Green, 7 In. 100.00

Some tea and coffee stains on dishes can be removed by rubbing them with damp baking soda.

Cambridge Glass Company was founded in 1901 in Cambridge, Ohio. The company closed in 1954, reopened briefly, and closed again in 1958. The firm made all types of glass. Their early wares included heavy pressed glass with the mark "Near Cut." Later wares included Crown Tuscan, etched stemware, clear and colored glass. The firm used a C in a triangle mark after 1920.

CAMBRIDGE, see also Depression Glass

CAMBRIDGE, Achilles, Iced Tea, 12 Oz.	30.00
Adonis, Goblet, 10 Oz.	15.00
Alexis, Tumbler, Dripping Springs Whiskey, Gold Trim, 5 Oz.	58.00
Apple Blossom, Cheese & Cracker Set, Amber, Oval	30.00
Apple Blossom, Cocktail, Pink, 3 Oz.	25.00 To 28.00
Apple Blossom, Console Set, Amber, 12 1/2 In. Bowl & Candlestick	75.00
Apple Blossom, Goblet, Yellow	30.00
Apple Blossom, Nut Cup, Footed, Signed, Set of 6	165.00
Apple Blossom, Relish, Yellow, 2 Sections, Gilt Footed Holder	58.00
Bashful Charlotte, Flower Frog, Clear, 13 In.	150.00
Bashful Charlotte, Pink, 11 In.	42.50
Bashful Charlotte, Pink, Frosted, 13 In.	220.00
Calla Lily, Candlestick, Dark Green, Pair	48.00
Calla Lily, Candlestick, Ebony	12.50
Candlelight, Bowl, 4-Toed, 12 In.	50.00
Candlelight, Compote, Etched, 5 3/8 In.	65.00
Candlelight, Relish, 2 Sections, Etched, 7 In.	38.00
Candlelight, Sugar & Creamer	32.50
Caprice, Ashtray, Triangular, 3 In.	7.00
Caprice, Ball Jug, Blue, 80 Oz.	210.00
Caprice, Bowl, Candlestick, Alpine, 12 In. Bowl, 3 Piece	115.00
Caprice, Bowl, Sauce, Underplate & Ladle, Blue, 3 Piece	45.00
Caprice, Candelabrum, Bobeche & Prisms, Crystal, Pair	165.00
Caprice, Candleholder, Triple, Blue, Pair	70.00
Caprice, Candlestick, 5-Light, Crystal, Pair	300.00
Caprice, Candlestick, Yellow, 6 In.	35.00
Caprice, Candy Bowl, Half Frosted, Half Clear, Covered, Blue	55.00
Caprice, Coaster, Blue, Set of 4	55.00
Caprice, Compote, Sterling Silver Overlay, 5 3/4 In., Pair	75.00
Caprice, Compote, Yellow	45.00
Caprice, Condiment Set, Blue, 6 Piece	255.00
Caprice, Console Set, Blue, Oval Bowl, Handles, Prisms, 3 Piece	95.00
Caprice, Creamer, Pink, Tab Handle	9.00
Caprice, Cruet, Oil, Stopper, 3 Oz.	36.00
Caprice, Cup & Saucer, Blue	22.00 To 30.00
Caprice, Goblet, Water, 10 Oz.	14.00
Caprice, Ice Bucket, Tongs, Clear	35.00
Caprice, Pitcher, Blue	130.00
Caprice, Plate, Blue, 8 In.	20.00
Caprice, Plate, Cabaret, Blue, 14 In.	87.50
Caprice, Plate, Crystal, 8 1/2 In.	11.00
Caprice, Relish, 3 Sections, Blue	85.00
Caprice, Rose Bowl, 6 In.	75.00
Caprice, Salt & Pepper	15.00
Caprice, Sherbet, Low, Blue, 6 Oz.	20.00
Caprice, Sugar & Creamer, Blue	20.00 To 28.00
Caprice, Sugar, Crystal	15.00
Caprice, Tray, Cabaret, Blue, 12 In.	49.00
Caprice, Tumbler, Footed, Blue, 12 Oz.	27.50
Caprice, Tumbler, Iced Tea, Flat, Pink, 12 Oz.	40.00
Caprice, Vase, Royal Blue, 4 In.	95.00
Caprice, Wine	20.00
Cascade, Cup & Saucer	7.00
Cascade, Goblet	14.00

Cascade, Goblet, Footed, 5 1/2 In.	8.00
Cascade, Sherbet	4.00
Cascade, Sugar & Creamer, Emerald Green	20.00
Chantilly, Basket, 2 Handles, 6 3/4 In.	20.00
Chantilly, Bowl, 4 Feet, Clear, 12 1/2 X 12 1/2 In.	35.00
Chantilly, Bowl, Gold Edge, 2 Handles, 6 In.	15.00
Chantilly, Candy Dish, Covered, 3 Sections	15.00
Chantilly, Champagne	12.00
Chantilly, Coaster, Sterling Silver Base	22.00
Chantilly, Cocktail Shaker	70.00 To 135.00
Chantilly, Compote, Sterling Base, Flared, 7 In.	60.00
Chantilly, Console Set, 11 1/2 In.Footed Bowl, 2 Candlestick	85.00
Chantilly, Cordial Set, Decanter, 12 Oz., 7 Piece	55.00
Chantilly, Creamer	10.00
Chantilly, Decanter, Sterling Base, 12 Oz.	150.00
Chantilly, Jug, Ball, Amber	26.00
Chantilly, Salt & Pepper, Sterling Silver Tops & Bases	60.00
Chantilly, Sherbet, Amber	10.00
Chesterfield, Goblet	13.00
Cleo, Candlestick, Green, 4 In.	20.00
Cleo, Compote, Green, 11 1/2 In.	65.00
Cleo, Creamer, Decagon, Amber	15.00
Cleo, Cup & Saucer, Amber	16.00
Cleo, Cup & Saucer, Green	24.00
Cleo, Goblet, Water, Green	35.00
Cleo, Ice Bucket, Green	50.00
Cleo, Ice Tub, Peachblow	52.00
Cleo, Plate, Amber, 7 3/4 In.	9.00
Cleo, Plate, Green, 8 1/4 In.	6.00
Cleo, Saucer, Amber	2.50
Cleo, Sugar & Creamer, Green	40.00
Cleo, Sugar, Amber	15.00
Colonial, Creamer, Child's	8.00
Colonial, Spooner, Child's, Cobalt Blue	22.00
Colonial, Spooner, Child's, Green	22.00
Colonial, Table Set, Child's, Green, 3 Piece	85.00
Colonial, Table Set, Cobalt Blue, Box, 4 Piece	175.00
Corinth Gyro Optic, Horn of Plenty	45.00
Cornucopia, Candlestick, 11 1/2 In.	115.00
Cornucopia, Vase, Crown Tuscan, Seashell, Footed, 9 In.	85.00
Daffodil, Bowl, 11 In.	42.50
Daisy, Cup & Saucer, Green	3.50
Decagon, Bonbon, 2 Handles	8.00
Decagon, Bowl, Willow Blue, 12 In.	15.00
Decagon, Celery, 11 In.	8.00
Decagon, Compote, Ebony, Tall, 7 In.	22.50
Decagon, Compote, Pink, 7 In.	15.00
Decagon, Creamer, Blue	6.00
Decagon, Cup, Blue	3.50
Decagon, Sugar & Creamer	14.00
Diane, Celery, 3 Sections	30.00
Diane, Cordial	30.00 To 35.00
Diane, Dish, Open Handle, 7 In.	24.50
Diane, Ice Bucket, Tongs	52.00
Diane, Plate, 14 In.	45.00
Diane, Relish, 3 Sections, 12 In.	25.00
Display Sign, Oval, Crystal	105.00
Draped Lady, Console Set, Green, Bowl, 12 3/4 In., 3 Piece	275.00
Draped Lady, Flower Frog, 13 In.	125.00
Draped Lady, Flower Frog, Amber, 13 In.	155.00
Draped Lady, Flower Frog, Green, 13 In.	300.00
Draped Lady, Flower Frog, Green, 8 1/2 In.	140.00
Draped Lady, Flower Holder, Green, 9 In.	95.00
Elaine, Bowl, Gold Design On Rim, Handle, 7 In.	17.50

Elaine, Bowl, Square, 10 7/8 In.	30.00
Elaine, Cocktail, Etched, 3 Oz.	25.00
Elaine, Compote, Jelly	20.00
Elaine, Cordial, 1 Oz.	75.00
Elaine, Sherbet	15.00
Elaine, Tumbler, Iced Tea	22.00
Everglades, Bowl, Rolled, Crystal, 13 In.	39.75
Everglades, Candlestick, 2–Light, Amber, Pair	145.00
Everglades, Candlestick, Crystal, 5 In., Pair	30.00
Everglades, Plate, 16 In.	57.50 To 65.00
Everglades, Sugar & Creamer, Blue	48.00
Everglades, Vase, Square Top, 8 In.	25.00
Feather, Decanter	25.00
Flower Frog, Girl With Goat, Marigold, 9 In.	135.00
Flying Lady, Bowl, Crown Tuscan, Gold Trim, 10 In.	165.00
Flying Lady, Flower Center, Crown Tuscan, 10 In.	125.00
Flying Nude, Centerpiece, 10 In.	250.00
Gadroon, Basket, Forest Green, 6 In.	9.00
Gadroon, Bowl, Ram's Head, 4 Feet, Amber, 11 In.	185.00
Gadroon, Relish, 4 Section	26.00
Gadroon, Sugar & Creamer, Forest Green	35.00
Gadroon, Urn, Covered, Crown Tuscan, 10 In.	85.00
Georgian, Bowl, Amber, 9 1/2 In.	10.00
Georgian, Tumbler, 9 Oz.	21.00
Georgian, Tumbler, Forest Green, 5 Oz.	8.00
Georgian, Tumbler, Smoke, 5 Oz.	16.00
Heron, Flower Frog, 9 In.	42.50
King Edward, Decanter, Sterling Silver Foot, Cut, 28 Oz.	125.00
Lady, Bookends, Frosted	190.00
Lady, Flower Frog, Peach Frosted, 9 In.	127.00
Lancelot, Tumbler, Iced Tea, Footed, Label, 12 Oz.	21.00
Marjorie, Compote, Blown, 6 1/2 In.	30.00
Marjorie, Cup, 5 Oz.	15.00
Martha Washington, Bowl, Console, Carmen, 11 In.	45.00
Martha Washington, Candleholder, Double, Pair	50.00
Martha Washington, Candy Dish, 3 Sections, Covered, Amber	32.00
Martha Washington, Plate, Carmen, 8 1/4 In., 10 Piece	240.00
Martha, Plate, Deviled Egg	27.00
Martha, Sugar & Creamer, Tray, Emerald, 3 Piece	55.00
Minerva, Nappy, Handle, 6 In.	25.00
Mt.Vernon, Cup & Saucer	10.00
Mt.Vernon, Decanter, Stopper, 40 Oz.	68.00
Mt.Vernon, Goblet, 5 3/4 In.	15.00
Mt.Vernon, Ice Bucket	32.50
Mt.Vernon, Pitcher, Ball, 80 Oz.	150.00
Mt.Vernon, Plate, 6 In.	4.50
Mt.Vernon, Relish, Forest Green, 3 Sections, 8 In.	25.00
Mt.Vernon, Stein, Amber, 14 Oz.	20.00
Mt.Vernon, Sugar & Creamer, Carmen	25.00
Mt.Vernon, Urn, Crystal	22.50
Mt.Vernon, Wine, 3 Oz.	12.50
Nautilus, Jug, Amber, 84 Oz.	45.00
Nautilus, Shaker, Royal Blue, Tilt Style, Pair	59.75
Nude Stem, Brandy, Pale Amber	150.00
Nude Stem, Bronze, Moonlight Blue	150.00
Nude Stem, Candlestick, Amethyst, Crystal Stem, Cut Prisms, Pair	750.00
Nude Stem, Candlestick, Carmen, Crystal Stem, 9 In., Pair	525.00
Nude Stem, Cigarette Box, Covered, Forest Green, Crystal Stem	450.00
Nude Stem, Claret, Dark Green	90.00
Nude Stem, Claret, Royal Blue	110.00
Nude Stem, Cocktail, Clear Bowl & Base, Ebony	80.00
Nude Stem, Cocktail, Crown Tuscan, 3 1/2 Oz.	80.00 To 98.00
Nude Stem, Cocktail, Purple Bowl	125.00
Nude Stem, Compote, Crown Tuscan, 12 X 9 In.	400.00

Nude Stem, Compote, Crown Tuscan, Marked, 7 3/4 In.	150.00
Nude Stem, Compote, Cupped, Carmen, Tall	135.00
Nude Stem, Compote, Royal Blue, Frosted Nude, Cupped	500.00
Nude Stem, Compote, Shell, Crown Tuscan	75.00 To 120.00
Nude Stem, Flower Frog, Draped, 8 1/2 In.	65.00
Nude Stem, Goblet, Carmen	95.00
Nude Stem, Goblet, Clear Stem, Amethyst Top	115.00
Nude Stem, Ivy Ball, Royal Blue	80.00
Nude Stem, Wine, Crown Tuscan	90.00
Nude Stem, Wine, Royal Blue	185.00
Portia, Cigarette Holder, With Ashtray	45.00
Portia, Cocktail Shaker, Chrome Top	100.00
Portia, Mayonnaise Set, 2 Piece	55.00
Portia, Pitcher, Water, Ice Lip, Gold Design	125.00
Portia, Sugar & Creamer, Sterling Silver Bases	35.00
Portia, Vase, Crown Tuscan, Gold, 10 In.	95.00
Portia, Wine	19.75
Pristine, Sugar & Creamer, Pink	15.00
Ram's Head, Console Set, Ivory, 3 Piece	375.00
Ribbon Candy, Cracker Jar, Covered	65.00
Rondo, Plate, 7 1/2 In.	5.00
Rose Point, Basket, 6 In.	160.00
Rose Point, Bonbon, 2 Handles, 5 In.	29.50
Rose Point, Bowl, Handles, 9 1/2 In.	55.00
Rose Point, Cake Tray, 13 In.	275.00
Rose Point, Candlestick, Calla Lily, Pair	295.00
Rose Point, Candlestick, Single Keyhole, Pair	45.00
Rose Point, Candy Dish, 3 Sections, Covered, 8 In.	95.00
Rose Point, Candy Dish, Covered, Carved, 4–Toed, 7 In.	150.00
Rose Point, Celery, 12 In.	40.00
Rose Point, Cocktail Shaker	175.00 To 200.00
Rose Point, Cocktail, Amber, Tall	45.00
Rose Point, Compote, 7 X 7 1/2 In., Pair	95.00
Rose Point, Cruet, 6 Oz.	100.00
Rose Point, Dish, Mayonnaise, 2 Sections, 8 In.	55.00
Rose Point, Dish, Nut, Individual, 2 3/4 In.	12.00
Rose Point, Goblet, Footed, 10 Oz.	26.00
Rose Point, Goblet, Iced Tea, Footed, 12 Oz.	15.00
Rose Point, Ice Bucket	165.00
Rose Point, Mayonnaise Set, Blown, 3 Piece	70.00
Rose Point, Mustard	125.00
Rose Point, Nut Cup, 4 Feet	24.00
Rose Point, Parfait, 5 Oz.	75.00
Rose Point, Pitcher, 76 Oz.	125.00 To 185.00
Rose Point, Plate, Flat, 15 In.	85.00
Rose Point, Plate, Scalloped, Handles, 13 In.	55.00
Rose Point, Relish, 2 Sections, Gold Trim, 6 In.	25.00
Rose Point, Relish, 3 Sections, 8 In.	45.00
Rose Point, Relish, 3 Sections, 12 In.	35.00
Rose Point, Relish, 5 Sections, 12 In.	45.00
Rose Point, Saltshaker	49.50
Rose Point, Sherbet, Low, Set of 4	48.00
Rose Point, Sherbet, Stem, Crystal	15.00
Rose Point, Sugar & Creamer, Individual	25.00 To 38.00
Rose Point, Tray, Center Handle, 11 In.	175.00
Rose Point, Vase, 13 1/2 In.	225.00
Rose Point, Vase, Bud, 10 1/2 In.	45.00
Rose Point, Vase, Crown Tuscan, Gold, 5 In.	95.00
Rose Point, Vase, Footed, 8 In.	45.00
Rose Point, Wine, Amethyst	70.00
Seashell, Bowl, 3 Feet, 4 In.	22.00
Seashell, Bowl, Flower Center, Crown Tuscan, 8 In.	88.00
Seashell, Candy Dish, Covered, Crown Tuscan	60.00
Seashell, Compote, Moonstone, 6 In.	20.00

Seashell, Plate, 5 In.	22.00
Seashell, Sugar & Creamer	24.00
Seashell, Vase, Royal Blue, 7 1/2 In.	150.00
September Morn, Figurine, Azurite, 10 1/2 In.	50.00
Shell, Compote, Nude Stem, Crown Tuscan	110.00
Swan, Amber, Label, 10 1/2 In.	450.00
Swan, Black, 6 1/2 In.	85.00
Swan, Black, Marked, 10 1/2 In.	145.00
Swan, Black, Marked, 3 In.	55.00
Swan, Black, Marked, 8 In.	175.00
Swan, Carmen, No.1043, 8 1/2 In.	225.00
Swan, Dianthus Pink, 10 1/2 In.	250.00
Swan, Emerald, 3 In.	35.00
Swan, Figurine, Mandarin Gold, 6 In.	89.00
Swan, Marked, Pink, 3 1/2 In.	27.50
Swan, Milk Glass, 8 1/2 In.	300.00
Swan, Punch Cup	32.00
Swan, Tail & Fins Flipped Up, Carmen	150.00
Swan, Tips of Wings Low, Marked C In Triangle, 3 1/2 In.	20.00
Swan, Wing Tips Low, Signed C In Triangle, 3 1/2 In.	25.00
Sweetheart, Goblet, 10 Oz.	38.00
Tally–Ho, Compote, Crystal, 6 1/2 In.	14.00
Tally–Ho, Compote, Forest Green, 9 In.	17.50
Tally–Ho, Decanter, Amber, Crystal Handle & Stopper, 34 Oz.	90.00
Tally–Ho, Plate, Silver Floral Design, Red, 10 1/2 In.	155.00
Tally–Ho, Punch Set, Bowl, Tray, Carmen Ladle, 8 Cups, Set	275.00
Tally–Ho, Relish, 2 Handles	9.00
Tally–Ho, Relish, 3 Sections, 2 Handles, 8 In.	68.00
Tally–Ho, Sandwich Plate, 2 Handles, Amber, 11 1/2 In.	20.00
Tally–Ho, Wine, Cobalt Blue	25.00
Thistle, Berry Bowl, Master, Green	48.00
Thistle, Creamer	22.00
Tuxedo, Goblet, Ruby	12.00
Tuxedo, Sherbet, Emerald Green	9.00
Tuxedo, Sherbet, Ruby	9.00
Virginian, Cake Plate, Original Label	57.50
Wheat, Dish, Child's, Beaded Rim, 2 1/4 In.	7.00
Wildflower, Ball Jug, Etched, 80 Oz.	135.00
Wildflower, Bonbon, Footed, 5 1/2 In.	12.00
Wildflower, Candlestick, Keyhole, 5 In.	36.00
Wildflower, Cocktail, 3 Oz.	20.00
Wildflower, Compote, 5 In.	15.00
Wildflower, Pitcher, Doulton Style	135.00
Wildflower, Plate, 14 In.	33.00
Wildflower, Relish, 2 Sections	15.00
Wildflower, Relish, 5 Sections, 12 In.	37.50
Wildflower, Salt & Pepper, Footed, Pair	30.00
Wildflower, Sugar, Gold	4.00
Wildflower, Tumbler, 12 Oz.	18.00
Wildflower, Vase, Footed, 8 In.	25.00
Wildflower, Wine	24.50

 Cameo glass was made in much the same manner as a cameo in jewelry. Parts of the top layer of glass were cut away to reveal a different colored glass beneath. The most famous cameo glass was made during the nineteenth century.

CAMEO GLASS, see also under factory names

CAMEO, Biscuit Jar, Carved White Flowers, Butterfly On Red, English, 5 In.	1750.00
Bowl, Carved Flowers, Sterling Silver Rim, Blue, English, 3 3/4 In.	550.00
Decanter, Butterfly, 3 Branches, Citron, Sterling Silver Lid, 9 In.	1750.00
Dish, Sweetmeat, Silver Plated Fittings, Ferns & Mushrooms, French	520.00

Flask, White Twig Pattern, Silver Top & Stand, English, 7 In. 950.00
Inkwell, Flowers, Hinged Silver Top, Vaseline, English, 4 1/2 In. 1395.00
Perfume Bottle, 3 Color, Lime & Rust Under Design, English, 5 In. 695.00
Perfume Bottle, Diamond–Quilted, Silver Top, English, 4 3/4 In. 950.00
Rose Bowl, 3 Color, Carved Flowers & Leaves, English, 2 1/2 In. 995.00
Rose Bowl, Leaves, Berries Cut To Blue, White Lining, English, 2 In. 995.00
Vase, Arabesque Collar, Stippled Flowers, Marked, English, 12 1/2 In. 1950.00
Vase, Blossoms and Vines, Plum, Violet, Meisenthal, 12 3/4 In. 2530.00
Vase, Brown Pine Cones Over Orange, Signed Riger, 6 X 5 In. 345.00
Vase, Bud, Green, Signed Nancy, 8 In. 300.00
Vase, Carved Christmas Rose, Butterfly At Top, Blue, English, 8 In. 1950.00
Vase, Desire Christian Meisenthal, Signed, C.1895, 13 In. ....*Illus* 2530.00
Vase, Honesdale, Cased Topaz Over Frosted Etched Design, 16 In. 495.00
Vase, Opaque Carved Flowers, Frosted Cranberry, English, 14 3/4 In. 2495.00
Vase, Opaque Carved Iris, Frosted Blue, English, 12 In. 2495.00
Vase, Pink Lilies Between Panels, Frosted, Signed Arsale, 12 In. 850.00
Vase, Red Frosted, Opaque White Flowers, English, 6 1/2 In. 1350.00
Vase, Swans On Lake, Frame of Branches, J.Michel, 8 In. 875.00
Vase, White Leaf Border, English, 2 1/8 X 3 5/8 In. 595.00
Vase, Yellow, Red Walls, Gold Highlights, Honesdale, 12 In. 450.00
    CAMPAIGN, see Political

The Campbell Kids were first used as part of an advertisement for the Campbell Soup Company in 1906. The kids were created by Grace Drayton, a popular illustrator of the day. The kids were used in magazine and newspaper ads until about 1951. They were presented again in 1966; and in 1983, they were redesigned with a slimmer, more contemporary appearance.

CAMPBELL KIDS, Block, Cutout, Alphabet Letter On Each, 5 In., 13 Piece 225.00
    Book, Have A Party, 1954 .... 13.00
    Card, Greeting, Large 8.00
    Dish, Feeding, Buffalo Pottery 75.00
    Doll, Centennial Dress, Pair 65.00
    Doll, Undressed, Composition, 12 In. 35.00
    Girl & Boy, Dressed, 17 In., Pair 150.00
    Lunch Box & Thermos, 1960s 40.00
    Mug, Plastic 12.00
    Plate, Buffalo Pottery 60.00
    Salt & Pepper, Celluloid 15.00
    Spoon, Pair 15.00

Camphor glass is a cloudy white glass that has been blown or pressed. It was made by many factories in the Midwest during the mid–nineteenth century.

CAMPHOR GLASS, Bowl, Console, Sculptured Dogwood, Purple Stain, 13 In. 45.00
    Console Set, Purple Flowers 35.00
    Dish, Brass Floral Rim, Brass Maple Leaves, 5 1/2 In. 30.00
    Dish, Hen On Nest Cover, Pink 50.00
    Goblet, Medallion, Gold, Twisted Stem, 9 Cabochon Jewels 60.00
    CANARY GLASS, see Vaseline Glass

A candlestick is designed to hold one candle; a candelabrum has more than one arm and holds many candles. The eccentricity of the English language makes the plural of candelabrum into candelabra.

CANDELABRUM, 2–Light, Geometric Base Cuts, Scrolled Arms, 14 1/4 In., Pair 450.00
    3–Light, Patinated, Gilt Bronze, Marble, C.1870, 20 In., Pair 1320.00
    3–Light, Silvered Bronze, Knight Figure, C.1845 .... 525.50
    4–Light, Continental, Scroll Branches, 19th Century, 22 In. 1045.00
    5–Light, Charles X, Cylindrical Base, Ormolu, C.1825, 26 1/4 In. 1850.00
    5–Light, Detachable Branches, Silver, Gorham, 14 1/8 In., Pair 715.00
    5–Light, Tulip Form Sconces, German Silver, 9 3/4 In. 357.00
    6–Light, Charles X, Figural, 3 Putti Support Basket, 23 1/4 In. 1900.00
    Bronze & Marble, Lion Mask Handles, 8–Light, 34 In., Pair 3025.00
    Ebonized Wood, Louis XVI, Bronze, 6–Light, 1900, 31 In., Pair 1450.00

Egyptian Revival, Gilt Bronze, 3–Light, C.1840, 17 In., Pair 2860.00
Empire Style, 6–Light, Female Figure, 6 Horn Branches, C.1890 .... 2860.00
Empire, Gilt Bronze, 5–Foliate & Mask Holders, C.1890, 27 In. 2200.00
Folk Art, Wood, Faux Green Marble, 3–Branch, 16 In. 300.00
Glass Column, Hobnail Design, 6–Light, 45 In., Pair 475.00
Louis XV, 3 Scrolled Branches, Silvered Bronze, 18 In., Pair 2640.00
Louis XVI Style, 2–Light, White Marble, 15 3/4 In., Pair 1320.00
Louis XVI, Marble Mounted, Cock Head Handles, 23 In., Pair 3575.00
On Pedestal, Woman In Draped Garment, Man Half Clad, Pair 9350.00
Regency Style, Bronze, 3–Light Globes, 5 Ft.6 In., Set of 4 .... 3850.00
Swags Flanked By Female Masks, 8–Light, 29 1/2 In., Pair 1100.00

Candlesticks were made of brass, pewter, Sandwich glass, sterling silver, plated silver, and all types of pottery and porcelain. The earliest candlesticks, dating from the sixteenth century, held the candle on a pricket (sharp pointed spike). These lost favor because in times of strife the large church candlesticks with prickets became formidable weapons, so the socket was mandated. Candlesticks changed in style through the centuries and designs range from classic to rococo to Art Nouveau to Art Deco.

CANDLESTICK, Altar, Birds, Blossoms, Bronze, Chinese, C.1820, 35 In., Pair. 8000.00
Baluster Shaft, Mid–Drip Pan, Holland, Brass, 8 3/4 In. 225.00
Bloodstone, Louis XV, Gilt Bronze Mount, 9 1/2 In., Pair 715.00
Brass, Baluster, Stem Screw Into Base, 9 5/8 In., Pair 250.00
Brass, Bulbous, Square Base, 5 3/4 In. 185.00
Brass, C.1780, 8 1/2 In., Pair .... *Cover* 75.00
Brass, Diamond Prince, Registry Mark, 11 3/4 In., Pair 230.00
Brass, Diamond Princess, Fluted, English, 11 3/4 In., Pair 220.00
Brass, English, Circular Bobeche, Square Base 522.00
Brass, Faceted Standard, Scalloped Base, English, 6 In., Pair 1200.00
Brass, Flower, China, 4 1/2 In. 13.50
Brass, French Empire Style, 11 3/4 In., Pair 70.00
Brass, Mid–Drip Pan, Middle Eastern, 16 1/4 In. 45.00
Brass, Octagonal Base, Knopped, 19th Century, 10 In., Pair 66.00
Brass, Pewter Pricket, Baroque, Dutch, Brass, 20 1/2 In., Pair 1200.00
Brass, Push–Up, Cylindrical Shaft, Samuel Blake Esq., 7 In. 110.00
Brass, Push–Up, Diamond Quilted, 11 3/4 In., Pair 90.00
Brass, Queen Anne, Bobeche, Trumpet Shaped Stem, 7 3/4 In., Pr. 200.00
Brass, Queen Anne, England, Elongated Cup, Ejector Hole, 8 In. 125.00
Brass, Queen Anne, Scalloped Base & Lip, 8 3/8 In., Pair 1650.00
Brass, Scalloped Domed Base, 10 1/2 In., Pair 750.00
Brass, Square Base, England, 19th Century, 10 In. 40.00
Bronze, Bobeche & Drip Pan, Twisted Standards, 18 In., Pair 225.00
Bronze, Louis XVI, Cloaked Maiden, Holds Nozzel, 16 1/2 In. 2200.00
Canary Glass, Hexagonal, 7 5/8 In., Pair 220.00
Caryatid, Cast Iron, 10 In., Pair 60.00
Clambroth Base, Hexagonal, Blue Socket, Sanded, 8 1/4 In., Pair 470.00
Classical Revival, Bronze, 3 Socket, Tripod, 17 1/2 In., Pair 325.00
Cut Glass, Clear Blown, 7 3/4 In., Pair 90.00
Diamond Set, Ace, King, Prince, Queen, England, 1880, 10 Piece 2700.00
Empire, Ormolu & Bronze, Wreath Border, 23 In., Pair 1200.00
Empire, Ormolu, Cross–Hatching Rosettes, Acanthus, 11 In., Pr. 1540.00
Empire, Urn Form, Ormolu & Painted Bronze, 11 1/2 In., Pair 1760.00
Empire, Vase Shaped Holder, Acanthus Cast Base, 10 In., Pair 1045.00
Gilded Brass, Marble Base, Cut Prisms, 11 1/2 In., Pair 30.00
Girandole, Turkish Woman, Marble Base, Brass, 14 In., Pair 80.00
Glass, Hexagonal Shape, 7 1/2 In. 35.00
Hog Scraper, Iron, Lift, Hanging Tab, 6 1/2 In. 85.00
Hog Scraper, Iron, Push–Up, Brass Wedding Band, 6 In. 400.00
Hog Scraper, Iron, Push–Up, Lip Hanger, Brass Band, 6 1/4 In. 145.00
Hog Scraper, Lip Hanger, Push–Up, Tin, 5 1/4 In., Pair 250.00
Hog Scraper, Push–Up, Brass Wedding Band, Iron, 8 In. 175.00
Hog Scraper, Push–Up, Iron, Ring, Marked Shaw, 6 5/8 In. 275.00
Hog Scraper, Push–Up, Lip Hanger, Cast Iron, 5 1/8 In. 75.00

Hog Scraper, Push–Up, Lip Hanger, Iron, 8 1/4 In. 275.00
Hog Scraper, Push–Up, Tin, Brass Ring, 7 3/4 In. 195.00
Hog Scraper, Tin, Brass Ring, Lip Hanger, Black, 7 1/4 In. 25.00
Hooded Cobra, Cast Iron, C.1850, 9 In. 75.00
Louis XVI, Pendant Chains, Ormolu & Marble, 10 1/2 In., Pair 775.00
Louis XVI, Urn Form, Ormolu, Patinated Bronze, 6 1/2 In., Pair 1450.00
Mahogany, Fluted, Silver Plated Socket, English, 14 In., Pair 85.00
Mid–Drip Pan, Brass, 10 3/8 In. 125.00
Oak, 4 Twisting Columns, Arts & Crafts, 16 In. 40.00
Push–Up With Brass Knob, Weighted Red Base, Tin, 9 3/4 In. 260.00
Push–Up, Saucer Base, Brass, England, C.1820, 4 3/4 In., Pair 300.00
Push–Up, Spiral, Wooden Base, 18th Century, 8 In. 225.00
Push–Up, Victorian, Brass, 9 3/4 In., Pair 130.00
Queen Anne, Brass, Removable Bobeche, 9 1/4 In., Pair 1200.00
Queen Anne, Brass, Scalloped Base, 6 7/8 In., Pair 800.00
Queen Anne, Octagonal Base, Baluster Stem, Brass, 6 7/8 In. 195.00
Queen Anne, Petal Form Cup, Ejector, Brass, 8 1/2 In. 250.00
Removable Bobeche, Brass, 19th Century, 9 In., Pair 240.00
Scalloped Foot, Balustered Stem, Drip Pan, Brass, 29 In. 35.00
Sconce, Mirror Back, Cutout Rays, 2 Brass Arms, 15 In., Pair 5000.00
Side Push–Up, Brass, 7 1/8 In. 85.00
Sterling Silver, Margaret Rose Pattern, Double, Rogers 40.00
    CANDLEWICK, see Imperial; Pressed Glass

> Candy containers have been popular since the late Victorian era. Collectors have long favored the glass containers; but now all types, including tin and papier–mache, are collected. Probably the earliest glass container sold commercially was the Liberty Bell made in 1876 for sale at the Centennial Exposition. Thousands of designs were made until the cost became too high in the 1960s. By the late 1970s, reproductions were being made and sold without the candy.

CANDY CONTAINER, Airplane, Spirit of St.Louis, Blue Glass Fuselage 225.00
Apple Shape, Doll Face, Movable Eyes & Mouth, Waxed 200.00
Auto, 2 Door Sedan 20.00
Auto, Lincoln 15.00
Auto, Model T, Victory Glass Co. 45.00
Auto, Tin Wheels, Roof 125.00
Baby Grand Piano, Painted Keyboard, 2 Piece 60.00
Baby, Naked, 3 3/4 In. 68.00
Barney Google, Metal Closure 275.00
Battleship, Pointed Prow, Guns, Tin Closure 55.00
Bean Pot, Boston Baked Beans, Brown 25.00
Birds In Nest, Cotton Batting, Bricks On Side, Japan 60.00
Boat With Sails 25.00
Bomber, Paper Prop, Candy, Cardboard Closure 30.00
Boot, Foil Cardboard, Santa's Celluloid Head, Japan,, 1935 .... 20.00
Boots, Papier–Mache & Glass 15.00
Building, Tin, West Bros., C.1914, 2 3/4 X 2 In., 4 Piece 40.00
Bull, Sitting, Spring Horns, Germany, 5 In. 75.00
Bulldog, On Haunches 30.00
Bulldog, Standing 6.00
Bunny & Cart, Yellow Wheels & Bucket, Celluloid, 4 In. 35.00
Bus, Jitney 250.00
Bus, Jitney, Tin Roof, Wheels 275.00
Camera, Lens Cap, Wooden Ball, String, Tripod Missing 125.00
Cat, Black, Papier–Mache, 8 In. 65.00
Charlie Chaplin 175.00
Cherry Tree Stump, Hatchet, Germany 60.00
Chick, Driving Car, Metal Closure 225.00
Chick, Egg, Pressed Paper, Glass Eyes, Ribbon, 5 1/2 In. 80.00
Chick, Emerging From Egg, Papier–Mache, Germany 60.00
Chick, Standing 90.00
Chick, Standing, Original Closure, Painted, 3 3/8 In. 60.00
Chicken, Papier–Mache, Red Comb, Germany, 4 1/2 In. 60.00

Chicken, Red Comb & Beak, Head On Spring, Germany, 4 In.	60.00
Christmas Bell, White Papier–Mache, 5 In.	35.00
Church, Christmas, Steeple Comes Off	55.00
Clock, Ornate Trim, Brass Closure, 4 In.	65.00
Dirigible, Los Angeles	135.00
Dog, Germany, Papier–Mache	65.00
Doll's Bottle, Nipple	10.00
Doll, Papier–Mache, C.1900	75.00
Donkey, Pulling Barrel	50.00
Dopey	75.00
Duck, On Rope Top, Basketweave Base	40.00
Duck, Polychrome Paint, Papier–Mache, Germany, 6 3/4 In.	50.00
Duck, With Bonnet, Papier–Mache	45.00
Ducks, Swimming	40.00
Dutch Windmill, Yellow Blades	65.00
Dwarf, From Snow White, Papier–Mache	26.00
Egg, Applied Bird & Nest	25.00
Egg, Easter, Papier–Mache	22.00
Egg, Flower, Lithographed Paper, German	15.00
Egg, Rabbit, Lithographed Paper, German	15.00
Electric Iron	25.00
Elephant, Papier–Mache, Gray	30.00
Fire Engine, Glass	35.00
Fire Engine, With Tin Bottom	40.00
Fire Truck, Wheels, Closure	40.00
Fish	265.00
Football, Tin, Germany	12.00
Girl's Head, Bisque, Glass Eyes, Wig	185.00
Happy Fats, On Drum	125.00
Hen On Nest, Beaded Eyes, Papier–Mache, 1924, 4 X 6 In.	85.00
Hen, J.H.Millstein, No Closure	15.00
Horn, Bears, Reading Letter, Souvenir Eaton, Ill., Tin Cap	90.00
Horse & Wagon, Glass	30.00
Hound Dog, Frosted	14.00 To 15.00
Independence Hall, Bank, Dated	150.00
Independence Hall, Dated 1776–1876	395.00
Irishman, Top Hat, Pipe, Papier–Mache, 2 In.	40.00
Irishman, Top Hat, Pipe, Papier–Mache, 4 In.	70.00
Jack–O–Lantern, Papier–Mache	35.00
Jeep, Cardboard Closure, Jeannette, Pa.	15.00
Kewpie, Glass Figure Beside Barrel, Tin Closure	120.00
Kewpie, Some Original Paint	90.00
Lantern, Clear, Red Tin Base & Lid, Jeannette, Pa.	18.00
Lantern, Closure, No.178	32.00
Lantern, Glass & Tin	25.00
Liberty Bell, Bank, Blue	75.00
Liberty Bell, Blue Glass	75.00
Liberty Bell, Original Pewter Cap, 3 1/2 In.	100.00
Locomotive	22.00 To 55.00
Mandolin, Dresden, Large	175.00
Mickey Mouse, Litho Tin	165.00
Mickey Mouse, Papier–Mache	400.00
Necco Boston Baked Beans, Brown Bean Pot	35.00
Owl, Cotton Batting, Glass Eyes, 4 In.	195.00
Owl, On Branch	50.00
Pencil, Baby Jumbo, Contents	58.00
Piano, Baby Grand, Painted Keyboard, 2 Piece	40.00
Pickle	20.00
Pistol, Full	35.00
Rabbit, Basket On Arm, 5 In.	98.00
Rabbit, Cloth Covered, Basket On Back	85.00
Rabbit, Eating Carrot, Clear	45.00
Rabbit, In Basket, Glass Eyes, Papier–Mache, 10 1/2 In.	60.00
Rabbit, On All Fours	38.00

Rabbit, Papier–Mache, 9 In.	12.00
Rabbit, Pulling Wood & Tin Cart, German	150.00
Rabbit, Sitting Up, Glass	15.00
Rabbit, With Basket, German, Pair	185.00
Radio, Wireless, With Horn, Tune In, Glass	88.00
Railroad Lantern, Paneled	15.00
Revolver, Glass, 8 In.	30.00
Rolling Pin, Glass	145.00
Roly Poly, Boy, Celluloid, Germany	30.00
Rooster Crowing, Original Paint	175.00
Rooster, Composition, Papier–Mache, Metal Legs	58.00
Santa Claus Head, Nodding Paper	55.00
Santa Claus' Boot	8.00
Santa Claus, Clear Glass, Painted, Plastic Head, 6 In.	30.00
Santa Claus, Hands In Cuffs	75.00
Santa Claus, Holding Feather Tree, Fur Beard	65.00
Santa Claus, In Chimney, Cotton	80.00
Santa Claus, In Chimney, Head First, Cardboard, 1924	65.00
Santa Claus, In Chimney, Papier–Mache	185.00
Santa Claus, On Chimney, 4 3/4 X 4 1/4 In.	25.00
Santa Claus, On Skis, Celluloid, 1940s	24.00
Santa Claus, On Sled, Basket, 2 Papier–Mache Deer, 12 In.	135.00
Santa Claus, On Sled, Papier–Mache, Robed, Germany	45.00
Santa Claus, On Sled, Reindeer Head Unscrews	395.00
Santa Claus, Outside of House, 9 In.	55.00
Santa Claus, Paneled Coat	125.00
Santa Claus, Standing By Chimney	70.00
Santa Claus, White Suit, Red Trim	48.00
Scotty	7.00 To 55.00
Shield	20.00
Ship, Glass, Tin Top & Bottom, Borgfeldt & Co.	70.00
Shoe, Lady's, High Laced, Spats, Plain Toe	20.00
Skull, Papier–Mache, Germany, 1900	80.00
Snow White & 7 Dwarfs, Tin, Walt Disney Prod.	14.00
Snowman, Papier–Mache	25.00
Spark Plug	95.00
Stork, Glass Eyes, Fuchsia Legs, Japan, 8 1/2 In.	40.00
Stork, Under Wing Opening, 8 In.	95.00
Suitcase, Clear Glass, Metal Closure	30.00
Sunbonnet Sue	40.00
Tank, 2 Guns, Paper Seal, Candy	30.00
Telephone, Candlestick, Pewter Speaker, 3 1/2 In.	60.00
Telephone, Pewter Closure, Wooden Receiver, 3 3/4 In.	85.00
Telephone, Receiver, Child's	22.00
Telephone, Wooden Receiver	35.00
Toonerville Trolley	475.00
Train	15.00 To 33.00
Trunk, Milk Glass, Bottom Closure, Gold	75.00
Turkey, Chalk Type, Metal Feet, Germany	25.00
Turkey, Composition, Lead Feet	25.00
Turkey, Papier–Mache, Rust, Large	22.50
U.S.Mailbox	25.00
Velvet Slipper, Silk Bag Insert, Dresden	145.00
Wheelbarrow, Glass	30.00
Willy's Jeep	15.00
Windmill, Glass, Red Tin Top, Teddy, Flag, 5 In.	200.00

Canes and walking sticks were used by every well–dressed man in the nineteenth century, but by World War I the style had changed. Today canes are used by few but the infirm. Collectors prize old canes made with special features such as hidden swords, whiskey flasks, or risque pictures seen through peepholes. Examples with solid gold heads or made from exotic materials such as walrus vertebrae are among the higher priced canes.

CANE, 5 Animal Heads, Natural Bark & Branches, Kentucky, 43 In.	35.00
Curly Maple, Turned Head, Pencil Post Shank, Hole In Shank, 36 In.	65.00
Glass, Bulbous Top Silver Filled, Maroon Stripes, 50 In.	160.00
Glass, Clear, Curved Handle, Twisted, 52 In.	100.00
Ivory Eagle Head, Tortoiseshell Inserts, Wooden Shaft, C.1830, 3 Ft.	650.00
Walking Stick, Animals, Snakes, Dogs, Masonic Emblem Knob, 36 In.	265.00
Walking Stick, Ball In Cage Finial, Chip Carving, 35 In.	120.00
Walking Stick, Bamboo, Pewter Top, Hunting Dog Wearing Cap	75.00
Walking Stick, Bamboo, Telescope Fishing Pole Inside	125.00
Walking Stick, Carved Bird's Head, Glass Eyes, 26 In.	25.00
Walking Stick, Carved Black Boy, Alligator, 14 In.	50.00
Walking Stick, Carved Egyptian Face	80.00
Walking Stick, Carved Gentleman With Long Hair, Frock Coat, 40 In.	275.00
Walking Stick, Century of Progress, Milk Glass, Brown Swirl Handle	95.00
Walking Stick, Duquesne Pilsner, Wood, Red Painted Letters, 36 In.	12.00
Walking Stick, Gold Filled Top, Black Paint, Initials, Dated 1890	25.00
Walking Stick, Gold Handle, Hallmarked	185.00
Walking Stick, Multicolored Swirls, Blown Glass, 45 In.	85.00
Walking Stick, Natural Growth, Coiled Snake, Handle	35.00
Walking Stick, Silver Rattlesnake Shaped Handle	35.00
Walking Stick, Totem Figures, Glass Eyes, Black, 31 3/4 In.	35.00
Walking Stick, Twisted Handle & Tip, Blown, Aqua, 47 In.	75.00
Walking Stick, Yellow Gold Head, Dated 1873	65.00

Caneware is a tan–colored, unglazed stoneware that was first developed by Josiah Wedgwood about 1770. It has been made by many companies since that time and is often used for cooking or serving utensils.

CANEWARE, Tureen, Cauliflower Finial, Leaf, Berry, Wedgwood, 5 In.	358.00

Canton china is blue–and–white ware made near Canton, China, from about 1785 to 1895. It is hand decorated with Chinese scenes.

CANTON, Bowl, Salad, 4 Rim Scallops, Raincloud Border, Genre Scene, 10 In.	500.00
Cup, Blue & White, Set of 12	200.00
Dish, Serving, Bud Finial On Domed Cover, Bridge Scene, 8 X 9 In.	225.00
Dish, Square, Raincloud Border, Bridge Scene	275.00
Plate, Bridge Scene, Raincloud Border, 19th Century, 10 In., 6 Piece	400.00
Plate, Bridge Scene, Raincloud Border, 8 3/4 In., 6 Piece	250.00
Plate, Raincloud Border, Bridge Scene, 7 In., Set of 11	225.00
Plate, Warming, Handle, Spout, Raincloud Border, Octagonal, 9 1/2 In.	600.00
Platter, Blue & White, Cut Corners, 19th Century, 15 In.	300.00
Platter, Oblong, Bridge Scene, Raincloud Border, 15 X 18 In.	125.00
Platter, Oblong, Cut Corners, Blue & White, 16 In.	350.00
Platter, Oval, Blue & White, 15 In.	225.00
Teapot, Blue & White, 5 1/4 In.	325.00
Teapot, Blue & White, 6 1/4 In.	190.00
Undertray, Dragon Design Center, Blue, Signed, 12 3/8 In.	125.00

Capo–di–Monte porcelain was first made in Naples, Italy, from 1743 to 1759. The factory moved near Madrid, Spain, and reopened in 1771 and worked to 1834. Since that time the Doccia factory of Italy acquired the molds and is using the N and crown mark. Societe Richard Ceramica is a modern–day firm often referred to as Ginori or Capo–di–Monte. This company uses the crown and N mark.

CAPO–DI–MONTE, Box, Jewel, Hunter, Bear On Cover, Gold Tracery, 5 X 3 In.	750.00
Casket, Jewelry, 18th Century Mark, 14 X 10 X 8 1/2 In.	2750.00
Compote & Dessert Plates, 19th Century, 13 Piece	800.00
Dinner Service, Putti, Musicians, Shield Mark, 41 Piece	2530.00
Figurine, Angel, Various Playful Poses, Small, 6 Piece	500.00
Figurine, Chestnut Vendor, Woman, Copper Stove, 8 X 10 In.	225.00
Figurine, Four Seasons, Mid–1700s, 13 In., 4 Piece ....*Illus*	2400.00
Frame, 8 X 10 In.	35.00
Lamp, Black, Floral, With Shade	100.00

Lamp, Girl In Chariot, With Child, 2 Swans	300.00
Lavabo, 24 In.	275.00
Napkin Ring, Enameled Roses, Signed	18.00
Plaque, Nymphs, Nudes, Round, 11 In.	75.00
Plate, Cupid Centers, Gilt Border, 9 In., Set of 6	715.00
Platter, 19 In.	150.00
Tea Set, 15 Piece	350.00
Urn, Classical Scenes, Twin Handles, 18 In.	300.00
Vase, 1875, 20 In.	275.00 To 300.00
Vase, Covered, Bird Finial, Rams' Horns, 11 3/4 In.	850.00

Captain Marvel was introduced in February 1940 in Whiz comic books. An orphan named Billy Batson met the wizard Shazam and whenever he said the magic word he was transformed into a superhero. A movie serial was released in 1940. The comic was discontinued in 1954. A second Captain Marvel appeared in 1966, a third in 1967. Only the original was transformed by shouting "Shazam."

CAPTAIN MARVEL, Bank, Dime	75.00
Cutout, Flying Captain Marvel	10.00
Decoder, Paper	250.00
Game, Sky Jump, Punch Out, Envelope, C.1940	12.00
Puzzle, Original Price 10 Cents, 1945	10.00
Toss Bag, 1940	15.00
Wristwatch, Box	225.00

Captain Midnight began as a radio show in September 1940. The first comic book appeared in July 1941. Captain Midnight was really the aviator Captain Albright, who was to defeat the Nazis. A movie serial was made in 1942 and a comic strip was published for a short time. The comic book Captain Midnight ended his career in 1948. The radio premiums are the prized collector memorabilia today.

CAPTAIN MIDNIGHT, Book, Joyce of The Secret Squadron	27.00
Card, Lobby, 11 X 14 In.	25.00
Code Book, 1942 Secret Squadron Offical	12.00
Code–O–Graph, Mirromatic	50.00
Cross, Flight Commander	105.00
Decoder Whistle, 1947	25.00
Flight Wings	35.00
Manual, 1941	110.00
Manual, Secret Squadron, 1948	50.00

Capo–Di–Monte, Figurine, Four Seasons,
Mid–1700s, 13 In., 4 Piece

Crown Milano, Ewer, Gold Flowers, Ivory,
Green Scrolling, 11 In.

Crown Milano, Pitcher, Gold & Black Floral,
Serpent Handle, 8 In.

Mug, Shake–Up, Ovaltine Premium, Red, 1957, 5 In. 50.00
Toy, Code–O–Graph 25.00
Whistle & Decoder, 1947 .... 38.00
  CARAMEL SLAG, see Chocolate Glass

    The cards listed here include advertising cards, greeting cards,
    baseball cards, playing cards, valentines, and others. Color pictures
    were rare in the nineteenth century, so companies gave away
    colorful cards with pictures of children, flowers, products, or related
    scenes that promoted the company name. These were often collected
    and stored in albums. Greeting cards are also a nineteenth–century
    idea that has remained popular. Baseball cards also date from the
    nineteenth century when they were used by tobacco companies as
    giveaways. The gum cards were started in 1933, but it was not until
    after World War II that the bubble gum cards favored today were
    produced. Today over 1,000 cards are issued each year by the gum
    companies.

  CARD, see also Postcard
CARD, Advertising, Arm & Hammer, Canvasback Bird Picture, 14 1/2 X 11 In. 35.00
 Advertising, Ayers Sarsaparilla, Child In Bonnet 2.00
 Advertising, Borden's Malted Milk, Woman With Tray, Die Cut 15.00
 Advertising, Coleman's Mustard, Bird Riding Ostrich 3.00
 Advertising, Currier & Ives, Blood Will Tell, Man, Horse, Train, 1879 .... 50.00
 Advertising, Frank Miller's Crown Dressing For Shoes, 7 In. 10.00
 Advertising, Gasser Realty Co., See Us About It, House In Background 3.00
 Advertising, Hale–Band Footwear, Boot, Man Axing Tree 3.00
 Advertising, Horlick's, Woman & Cow, Die Cut 12.00
 Advertising, Merrick Thread, Spool Shape, Child On Swing 3.00
 Advertising, National Rubber Co., Attached Metal Frog, 1890s 20.00
 Advertising, Paris Expo., Gold Medal Wood & Co., Award, 1867 .... 25.00
 Advertising, Planet Jr.Vignette, Planet Front, Plow Back, Sept.5, 1888 .... 10.00
 Advertising, Playing, Van Camp's Pork & Beans 35.00
 Advertising, Price, Antelope, Sunkist Oranges, 1920s, 11 X 9 In. 1.00
 Advertising, R.Herman & Co., New York, Daisy Hood, Patented 1886 .... 3.00
 Advertising, R.W.Bell Mfg.Co., French Villa Soap, Children On Sled 3.00
 Advertising, Shaker's Soothing Plasters 8.00
 Advertising, Union Pacific Tea Co., N.Y., Temptation Woman, 8 X 6 In. 8.00
 Advertising, Walker's Chocolates, Embossed 3.00
 Advertising, Wheeler & Wilson Sewing Machine, 3 X 5 In. 6.00
 Baseball, Bob Feller, Exhibit, Brown, Late 1940s, 3 1/2 X 5 1/2 In. 5.00
 Baseball, Fuller, Short Stop, St.Louis 45.00
 Baseball, Johnson, Center Field, Boston, Old Judge, 1880s 45.00
 Baseball, McCovey, National League 15.00
 Baseball, Otis Johnson & Russell Ford, Foldover, 2 1/4 X 5 In. 10.00
 Baseball, Thomas Clarke & H.L.Gasbar, Foldover, 2 1/4 X 5 In. 8.00
 Christmas, Floral, Silk Fringed, Opens, Prang, 1884 .... 9.00
 Christmas, Mechanical, Bird Comes Out of House, Nister, 1880s 6.00
 Christmas, Parrish, Golden Valley, Sample 15.00
 Cigarette, Airplane Picture, Wings 1.00
 Cigarette, Arms of Foreign Cities, Wills Cigarettes, 14 Piece 7.00
 Cigarette, Henry, Set of 50 .... 125.00
 Easter, Woman In Bell, Winsch, 1910 .... 4.00
 Lobby, Baby Face Nelson, Mickey Rooney, 1957 .... 10.00
 Lobby, Baby Peggy, Little Miss Hollywood 100.00
 Lobby, College Rhythm, Jack Oakie, 11 X 14 In. 20.00
 Lobby, Constance Talmadge, Scandal, Pictures, 1917, 11 X 14 In. 35.00
 Lobby, Corinne Griffith, Divorce Coupons 85.00
 Lobby, Douglas Fairbanks, In Again–Out Again, 11 X 14 In. 15.00
 Lobby, Fighting Renegade, Tim McCoy, 1930s 100.00
 Lobby, Forever & A Day, Ray Milland, 1943, 11 X 14 In. 6.00
 Lobby, Grace Darmond, Beautiful Gambler, Sepia, 1921, 11 X 14 In. 15.00
 Lobby, Hoot Gibson, Winged Horseman, Universal, 1929, 11 X 14 In. 75.00
 Lobby, Jet Attack, John Agar, 1958, 41 X 81 In. 12.00
 Lobby, King's Thief, Ann Blyth, 1955, 27 X 41 In. 9.00

Lobby, Leah Baird, Capitol, Tinted, 1919, 11 X 14 In. 15.00
Lobby, Madcap Magoo, Animated, 1955, 27 X 41 In. 18.00
Lobby, Priscilla Bonner, Outcast Souls, Tinted, 1928, 11 X 14 In. 15.00
Lobby, Sing You Sinners, Bing Crosby, 1938, 14 X 22 In. 20.00
Lobby, Sun Valley Serenade, Sonja Henie, 1941 .... 30.00
Lobby, The Dancing Masters, Laurel & Hardy, 1943, 11 X 14 In. 45.00
Lobby, The Harder They Fall, Humphrey Bogart, 1956, 11 X 14 In. 25.00
Lobby, The Lemon Drop Kid, Bob Hope, 11 X 14 In. 10.00
Lobby, The Misfits, Clark Gable, 1961, 11 X 14 In. 8.00
Lobby, The West Point Story, James Cagney, 1950, 81 X 81 In. 20.00
Lobby, Tom Mix, Canyon of Light, Tinted, 1926, 11 X 14 In. 65.00
Lobby, William S.Hart, Cradle of Courage, 1920, 11 X 14 In. 25.00
Playing, American Red Cross, Mohawk, Box 10.00
Playing, Breyer's Ice Cream, Box 18.00
Playing, Congress, Victorian Child, 1899 .... 15.00
Playing, Cuba, Souvenir, 53 Different Photos 18.00
Playing, Detroit, 250th Birthday 10.00
Playing, Hershey's, Figural, Syrup Can 15.00
Playing, Marilyn Monroe, Dated 1956 .... 8.00
Playing, Nash 15.00
Playing, Pan–American Expo 45.00
Playing, Pinochle, Alberly Coffee, Consolidated No.142 .... 50.00
Playing, Pinup, Esquire, 1947 .... 15.00
Playing, Stag Party Pack, 52 Different Naughty Cartoons, 1940s, Box 15.00
Playing, Sunshine Biscuit, Set of 8, 1932 .... 15.00
Playing, Whist, Swiss Ace Scenes, BD Frankfurt, No.174 .... 95.00
Tarot, 3 Languages, Partial Deck, Early 1800s 20.00
Valentine, All Lace, Swirly Designs At Center Oval, Signed Meek 30.00
Valentine, Black Girl, Tuck 4.50
Valentine, Boy & Girl, Verse, Motto & Butterfly, 3 7/8 X 5 5/8 In. 7.00
Valentine, Cats, In Basket, Die Cut, 2 Layer, Easel Back 8.00
Valentine, Child On Bike, Sailing Ship Behind, Layer Foldout, 8 In. 12.00
Valentine, Children Ice Skating, Drayton, Standup 8.00
Valentine, Cupids, 4 Layer Foldout, Die Cuts, 10 In. 15.00
Valentine, Cutout Design, Scalloped, New England, 1840, Round, 10 In. 400.00
Valentine, Embossed With Piercing, Oval Medallion, Late 1850s 22.50
Valentine, Folder, Lace, Flowers Spell With Love, 3 3/4 X 5 1/2 In. 5.00
Valentine, Folder, Lace, Lady, Circular Opening, 3 7/8 X 5 5/8 In. 6.00
Valentine, Girl, Pop–Up Hat On Head, Easel Back, Tuck, 5 X 6 In. 12.00
Valentine, Gray Folder, White Lace On Flowers, Girl's Head, 7 3/4 In. 9.00
Valentine, Hanging, Girl & Flowers, Die Cut & Pierced, 16 3/4 In. 13.50
Valentine, Honeycomb Heart, Foldout Carriage, 11 X 8 In. 4.00
Valentine, Jimminy Cricket, Mechanical, 1939 .... 15.00
Valentine, Lace, Applied Flowers, Sarah Glass, Feb.14, 1835 .... 62.00
Valentine, Mechanical, Black Boy, Dressed As Soldier 10.00
Valentine, Mechanical, Girl On Roller Skates, Movable, 8 1/4 In. 8.00
Valentine, Mechanical, Girl On Skis, Legs & Body Move, 7 3/4 In. 8.00
Valentine, Pink Folder, Silver & Lace Top Layer, 4 1/2 X 6 3/4 In. 6.50
Valentine, Pocket Knife Shape, Gold Trim, Forget Me Not, 3 5/8 In. 2.00
Valentine, Suffragette 28.00
Valentine, Wheel of Fortune, Foldout, 9 In. 10.00
Valentine, Windsor Couple On Horse, Applied Flowers 60.00
CARDER, see Aurene; Steuben

Carlsbad, Germany, is a mark found on china made by several factories in Germany. Most of the pieces available today were made after 1891.

CARLSBAD, Box, Hinged Cover, Hand Painted, Gold Overlay, Angels, 2 3/4 In. 235.00
Dish, Pancake, Covered 25.00
Fish Set, Platter, 23 X 7 1/2 In., 8 Piece 325.00
Plate, Oyster, Molded & Gilded Design, 8 In. 70.00
Rose Bowl, Floral Design, Gold Trim, Cream Ground, 4 3/4 In. 100.00
Vase, Floral Design, Gold Leaf Tracery, Matte Ground, 21 In. 95.00
Vase, Gold, Applied Ceramic Flowers, Signed H.Holzner, 10 1/2 In. 225.00

Carlton ware was made at the Carlton Works of Stoke–on–Trent, England, about 1890. The firm traded as Wiltshaw & Robinson until 1957. It was renamed Carlton Ware Ltd. in 1958.

CARLTON WARE, Biscuit Jar, Flowers, Tan, Cobalt Blue Trim, 9 In. 220.00
   Bowl, Enamel Design, Gold, C.1920, 3 1/2 X 4 1/2 In. 85.00
   Cup & Saucer, Enameled Gold Oriental Scene, Blue, Demitasse 60.00
   Dish, Rouge Royale, Storks & Trees, 2 Handles, Round, 7 In. 40.00
   Jam Jar, Art Deco, Orange 70.00
   Match Holder, Flow Blue Floral, Marked, 2 In. 55.00
   Relish, Lettuce Leaf 42.00
   Sugar & Creamer, Rouge Royale 28.50
   Sugar Shaker, Figural, Basket of Fruit, Marked, 5 1/4 In. 45.00
   Vase, Exotic Bird, Luster, Lid, 7 In. .... 55.00 To 65.00
   Vase, Painted Kingfisher, Yellow Luster, 10 In. 55.00

Carnival, or taffeta, glass was an inexpensive, pressed, iridescent glass made from about 1907 to about 1925. Over 1,000 different patterns are known. Carnival glass is currently being reproduced.

CARNIVAL GLASS, see also Northwood
CARNIVAL GLASS, Acanthus, Bowl, Marigold, 8 In. 35.00
   Acanthus, Chop Plate, Smokey 175.00
    ACORN BURRS & BARK, see Acorn Burrs
   Acorn Burrs, Berry Bowl, Master, Purple 140.00
   Acorn Burrs, Butter, Covered, Marigold 135.00
   Acorn Burrs, Punch Set, Purple, 7 Piece 600.00
   Acorn Burrs, Sugar & Creamer, Open, Marigold 125.00
   Acorn Burrs, Table Set, Purple, 4 Piece 475.00
   Acorn Burrs, Tumbler, Marigold, Northwood, Set of 4 .... 140.00
   Acorn Burrs, Water Set, Amethyst, 7 Piece 975.00
   Acorn Burrs, Water Set, Marigold, 7 Piece 450.00
   Acorn Burrs, Water Set, Purple, 7 Piece .... 550.00 To 595.00
   Acorn, Bowl, Purple, 7 In. 50.00
   Acorn, Bowl, Ruffled, Marigold, 7 1/2 In. 30.00
    AMARYLLIS, see Tiger Lily
    AMERICAN BEAUTY ROSES, see Wreath of Roses
   Apple Blossom Twigs, Plate, Ruffled Edge, White, 9 In. 150.00
   Apple Tree, Pitcher, Marigold 140.00
   Apple Tree, Tumbler, Marigold 40.00
   Australian Swan, Bowl, Purple, 9 1/2 In. 95.00
   Basket, Bushel, 6 Sides, White 140.00
   Basket, Bushel, Blue 90.00
   Basket, Bushel, Marigold 65.00
   Basket, Bushel, White, Northwood 150.00
    BATTENBURG LACE NO.1, see Hearts & Flowers
    BATTENBURG LACE NO.3, see Fanciful
   Beaded Cable, Rose Bowl, Amethyst .... 70.00 To 85.00
   Beaded Cable, Rose Bowl, Aqua Opalescent .... 275.00 To 345.00
   Beaded Cable, Rose Bowl, Ice Blue 1000.00
   Beaded Shell, Mug, Marigold 110.00
   Beaded Shell, Mug, White .... 1050.00 To 1100.00
   Beaded Shell, Spooner, Marigold 35.00
   Beaded Shell, Tumbler, Blue 30.00
    BEADED STAR & SNAIL, see Constellation
   Bells & Beads, Bowl, Peach, 7 In. 70.00
    BLACKBERRY B., see Blackberry Spray
   Blackberry Spray, Hat, Aqua 65.00
   Blackberry Spray, Hat, Marigold, 6 In. 32.00
   Blackberry Wreath, Bowl, Amethyst, 7 1/2 In. 40.00
   Blackberry Wreath, Bowl, Amethyst, Millersburg, 5 In. 35.00

Carnival Glass, Brooklyn Bridge, Bowl, Marigold

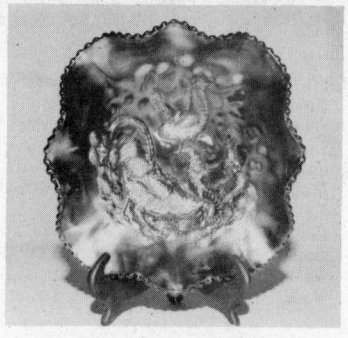

Carnival Glass, Farmyard, Bowl, Square, Purple

Blueberry, Tumbler, Marigold	35.00
Blueberry, Tumbler, White	200.00
Bouquet, Tumbler, Marigold	18.00
Bouquet, Water Set, Blue, 5 Piece	675.00
Brocaded Palms, Ice Bucket, Gold Trim, Pink	85.00
Brooklyn Bridge, Bowl, Fluted, Marigold, 8 1/2 In.	285.00
Brooklyn Bridge, Bowl, Marigold ....*Illus*	550.00
Brooklyn Bridge, Bowl, Marigold, 9 In.	245.00
Bull's Eye Beads, Vase, 10 1/2 In. .... *Cover*	35.00
BUSY CHICKENS, see Farmyard	
Butterfly & Berry, Berry Bowl, Master, Marigold	85.00
Butterfly & Berry, Bowl, Footed, Marigold, 5 In.	25.00
Butterfly & Berry, Butter, Covered, Marigold	95.00
Butterfly & Berry, Creamer, Green	95.00
Butterfly & Berry, Hatpin Holder, Blue	725.00
Butterfly & Berry, Sauce, Marigold	18.00
Butterfly & Berry, Spooner, Green	60.00
Butterfly & Berry, Sugar, Covered, Green	95.00
Butterfly & Berry, Tumbler, Blue	55.00
Butterfly & Berry, Tumbler, Purple	65.00
BUTTERFLY & CABLE, see Springtime	
Butterfly & Fern, Pitcher, Green	350.00
Butterfly & Fern, Water Set, Blue, 5 Piece	465.00
Butterfly & Fern, Water Set, Blue, 7 Piece	695.00
BUTTERFLY & GRAPE, see Butterfly & Berry	
BUTTERFLY & PLUME, see Butterfly & Fern	
BUTTERFLY & STIPPLED RAYS, see Butterfly	
Butterfly, Berry Bowl, 3 Footed, Purple, 4 5/8 In.	27.00
Buzz Saw, Cruet, Green	225.00
CABBAGE ROSE & GRAPE, see Wine & Roses	
CACTUS LEAF RAYS, see Leaf Rays	
CATTAILS & WATER LILY, see Water Lily & Cattails	
Chatelaine, Tumbler, Purple	265.00 To 275.00
CHERRIES & MUMS, see Mikado	
Cherry Chain, Bowl, Blue, 10 In.	70.00
Cherry Chain, Chop Plate, White	575.00 To 650.00
CHERRY WREATHED, see Wreathed Cherry	
Cherry, Bowl, Green, Millersburg, 10 In.	90.00

Cherry, Bowl, Ruffled, Purple, Millersburg, 10 1/2 In. 125.00
Cherry, Butter, Covered, Amethyst, Millersburg 160.00
    CHRISTMAS CACTUS, see Thistle
    CHRYSANTHEMUM WREATH, see Ten Mums
Chrysanthemum, Bowl, Footed, Blue, 11 In. 145.00
Circled Scroll, Creamer, Marigold 57.00
Circled Scroll, Pitcher, Water, Marigold 1400.00
Cleveland Ashtray, Ashtray, Memorial, Amethyst 800.00
Cobblestones, Bowl, Amethyst, Flared, 8 1/4 In. 50.00
Colonial Carnival, Candlestick, Amethyst, 10 In. 75.00
    COMET, see Ribbon Tie
Concave Diamonds, Tumbler, Vaseline 215.00
Constellation, Compote, Amethyst 65.00
    CORAL MEDALLION, see Mayan
Cosmos & Cane, Bowl, White, 9 In. 75.00
Cosmos, Bowl, Green, Millersburg, 5 1/2 In. 30.00
Courthouse, Bowl, Amethyst, Millersburg, Unlettered 875.00
Crab Claw, Water Set, Marigold, 7 Piece 75.00
Crackle, Fruit Bowl, Scalloped Rim, Marigold 60.00
Dahlia, Pitcher, White 600.00
Dahlia, Table Set, Gold Trim, White, 4 Piece 675.00
Daisy & Plume, Compote, Purple, Northwood 50.00
Daisy Block, Rowboat, Marigold 195.00
Daisy Squares, Goblet, Green 275.00
Daisy Wreath, Bowl, Blue, 9 In. 595.00
    DANDELION VARIANT, see Paneled Dandelion
Dandelion, Mug, Aqua Opalescent 475.00
Dandelion, Mug, Knight's Templer, Ice Blue, Northwood 1050.00
Dandelion, Tankard, Marigold 350.00
Dandelion, Tumbler, Ice Blue, Northwood .... 175.00 To 250.00
Diamond & Rib, Vase, Green, 10 In. 33.00
    DIAMOND BAND, see Diamond
Diamond Lace, Berry Bowl, Marigold, 8 In. 37.50
Diamond Lace, Pitcher, Water, Purple 210.00
    DIAMOND POINT & DAISY, see Cosmos & Cane
Diamond Point, Vase, Aqua Opalescent, 10 1/2 In. 385.00
Diamond Ring, Bowl, Smoky, 9 In. 15.00
Diamond, Tumbler, Amethyst, Millersburg 40.00
Diamonds, Pitcher, Aqua, Millersburg 235.00
    DOGWOOD & MARSH LILY, see Two Flowers
Dogwood Spray, Bowl, Peach, Footed, 9 In. 60.00
Double Dutch, Bowl, Footed, Marigold, 9 In. 32.00
Double Star, Pitcher, Green 350.00
Dragon & Lotus, Bowl, Footed, Marigold, 9 In. 85.00
Dragon & Lotus, Bowl, Ruffled, Amber, 9 In. .... 125.00 To 130.00
    DRAPE & TIE, see Rosalind
Drapery, Candy Dish, 3 Sides, Ice Blue 105.00
Drapery, Rose Bowl, Aqua Opalescent .... 245.00 To 295.00
Drapery, Rose Bowl, Marigold 325.00
    EGYPTIAN BAND, see Round-Up
Elk, Bell, Parkersburg, Blue, 1914 .... 650.00
    FAN & ARCH, see Persian Garden
Fanciful, Bowl, Ice Cream, Peach 250.00
Fanciful, Plate, Ruffled Edge, White, 9 In. 150.00
    FANTASY, see Question Marks
Farmyard, Bowl, Square, Purple ....*Illus* 2900.00
Fashion, Pitcher, Water, Marigold 130.00
    FEATHER & HOBSTAR, see Inverted Feather
    FEATHERED SCROLL, see Feathered Serpent
Feathered Serpent, Bowl, Green, 10 In. 75.00
    FENTON'S BUTTERFLY, see Butterfly
    FIELD ROSE, see Rambler Rose

Fieldflower, Water Set, Marigold, 6 Piece 175.00
Fine Cut & Roses, Candy Dish, Aqua Opalescent 550.00
Fine Cut & Roses, Rose Bowl, Green ....75.00 To 165.00
Fine Cut & Roses, Rose Bowl, Purple .... 50.00 To 80.00
    FINECUT & STAR, see Star & File
    FISH & FLOWERS, see Trout & Fly
    FISHERMAN'S NET, see Treebark
Fishscale & Beads, Bowl, Ruffled Edge, Peach, 7 In. 42.00
Fleur–De–Lis, Bowl, Marigold, Millersburg, 10 In. 135.00
    FLORAL & DIAMOND POINT, see Fine Cut & Roses
    FLOWERING ALMONDS, see Peacock Tail
Flowers & Beads, Plate, Peach Opalescent, 6 Sides 135.00
    FLUFFY BIRD, see Peacock
Fluffy Peacock, Water Set, Amethyst, 7 Piece ....*Illus* 450.00
Flute & Cane, Goblet, Wine, Flared, Marigold 65.00
Flute, Berry Set, Purple, 8 Piece 150.00
Folding Fan, Compote, Peach 75.00
Four Flowers, Chop Plate, Peach 425.00
Four Flowers, Plate, Peach, 6 1/2 In. 125.00
Frosted Block, Bowl, Clambroth, 7 In. 25.00
Fruits & Flowers, Bonbon, Green 300.00
Fruits & Flowers, Plate, Marigold, 7 1/2 In. 175.00
Garland, Rose Bowl, Blue 70.00
Garland, Rose Bowl, Marigold 35.00
Good Luck, Bowl, Pie Crust Rim, Green, 9 In. 245.00
Grape & Cable, Banana Boat, Ice Blue 495.00
Grape & Cable, Bonbon, Handle, Green 49.00
Grape & Cable, Bowl, Centerpiece, Footed, Purple, Northwood 360.00
Grape & Cable, Bowl, Green, 8 1/2 In. 45.00
Grape & Cable, Bowl, Ruffled, Marigold, 7 In. 25.00
Grape & Cable, Butter, Covered, Green, Northwood 150.00
Grape & Cable, Compote, Covered, Amethyst, Northwood 375.00
Grape & Cable, Cookie Jar, Marigold 200.00
Grape & Cable, Creamer, Breakfast, Green 65.00
Grape & Cable, Hat, Marigold, Northwood 20.00
Grape & Cable, Hatpin Holder, Marigold, Northwood 185.00
Grape & Cable, Hatpin Holder, Purple 225.0C
Grape & Cable, Orange Bowl, Amethyst, Northwood 190.00
Grape & Cable, Orange Bowl, Purple .... 175.00 To 285.00

Carnival Glass, Fluffy Peacock, Water Set,
Amethyst, 7 Piece

Carnival Glass, Grape & Cable, Water Set,
Amethyst, 7 Piece

Grape & Cable, Pitcher, Water, Marigold, Northwood 85.00
Grape & Cable, Plate, Footed, Marigold, 9 In. 65.00
Grape & Cable, Plate, Stippled, Blue, 9 In. 395.00
Grape & Cable, Plate, Stippled, Rose Distillery, Green, 9 In. 265.00
Grape & Cable, Powder Jar, Green 150.00
Grape & Cable, Powder Jar, Purple, Northwood .... 75.00 To 85.00
Grape & Cable, Punch Cup, Stippled, Blue 22.00
Grape & Cable, Punch Set, Purple 500.00
Grape & Cable, Sherbet, Purple, Northwood 65.00
Grape & Cable, Shot Glass, Marigold 150.00
Grape & Cable, Sweetmeat, Knob Cover, Amethyst 150.00
Grape & Cable, Sweetmeat, Purple, Northwood .... 210.00 To 250.00
Grape & Cable, Tankard, Purple, Northwood 325.00
Grape & Cable, Tobacco Jar, Purple 375.00
Grape & Cable, Tray, Dresser, Purple 185.00
Grape & Cable, Tumbler, Purple 25.00
Grape & Cable, Water Set, Amethyst, 7 Piece ....*Illus* 300.00
Grape & Cable, Water Set, Marigold, 6 Piece 235.00
Grape & Cable, Water Set, Purple, 7 Piece .... 395.00 To 425.00
Grape & Gothic Arches, Tumbler, Marigold 30.00
Grape & Gothic Arches, Water Set, Green, 7 Piece 550.00
Grape & Lattice, Tumbler, Marigold 105.00
Grape Arbor, Pitcher, Water, Marigold 350.00
Grape Arbor, Tankard, 6 Tumblers, White, Northwood ....*Illus* 1000.00
Grape Arbor, Tumbler, Ice Blue ....95.00 To 125.00
Grape Arbor, Water Set, Marigold, 7 Piece .... 335.00 To 425.00
Grape Arbor, Water Set, Purple, 7 Piece 1000.00
GRAPE DELIGHT, see Vintage
Grape Leaves, Bowl, Marigold, 8 3/4 In. 55.00
Greek Key, Water Set, Purple, 5 Piece 1400.00
Harvest Flower, Tumbler, Marigold 90.00
Heart & Vine, Bowl, Ruffled, Amethyst, 8 In. 50.00
Hearts & Flowers, Compote, Aqua Opalescent, Northwood 275.00
Heavy Grape, Chop Plate, Purple 275.00
Heavy Grape, Plate, Green, 8 In. 48.00
Heavy Iris, Tumbler, Marigold 45.00
Heavy Iris, Water Set, Purple, 5 Piece 1400.00
HERON & RUSHES, see Stork & Rushes
Heron, Mug, Purple 285.00
HOBNAIL, see also Hobnail category
Hobnail, Butter, Covered, Marigold, Millersburg 300.00
Hobnail, Creamer, Marigold, Imperial 35.00
HOBSTAR & TORCH, see Double Star
HOLLY SPRAY, see Holly Sprig
Holly Sprig, Bonbon, Amethyst, Millersburg 45.00
Holly Sprig, Bowl, Marigold, Millersburg, 8 In. .... 38.00 To 45.00
Holly, Bowl, Green, 9 In. .... 40.00 To 45.00
Holly, Bowl, Marigold, 8 In. 22.50
Holly, Plate, Blue, 9 1/2 In. .... 160.00 To 185.00
Holly, Plate, Marigold, 9 1/2 In. 95.00
HONEYCOMB COLLAR, see Fishscale & Beads
Honeycomb Rose Bowl, Rose Bowl, Peach .... 175.00 To 195.00
HORSE MEDALLIONS, see Horses' Heads
Horses' Heads, Bowl, Marigold, 8 1/2 In. 70.00
Horses' Heads, Plate, Marigold, 7 3/4 In. 100.00
Horses' Heads, Rose Bowl, Cobalt Blue 375.00
Imperial Grape, Bowl, Amber, 11 1/2 In. 40.00
Imperial Grape, Carafe, Water, Purple 129.00
Imperial Grape, Decanter, Stopper, Marigold 60.00
Imperial Grape, Goblet, Green 50.00
Imperial Grape, Punch Set, Marigold, 6 Piece 250.00
Imperial Grape, Rose Bowl, Marigold 145.00
Imperial Grape, Tumbler, Purple 55.00

Carnival Glass, Grape Arbor, Tankard,
6 Tumblers, White, Northwood

Carnival Glass, Many Fruits, Punch Bowl,
Base In Amethyst

Imperial Grape, Water Set, Purple, 7 Piece 400.00
Imperial Pansy, Dish, Pickle, Smoky, 8 1/2 In. 48.00
    INTERIOR OF CHERRIES & MUMS, see Mikado
Interior Rays, Compote, Covered, Marigold 20.00
Inverted Coin Dot, Pitcher, Water, Marigold .... 125.00 To 175.00
Inverted Feather, Cracker Jar, Covered, Green 295.00
Inverted Strawberry, Candlestick, Green, Pair 235.00
Inverted Strawberry, Powder Jar, Green 175.00
Inverted Thistle, Sugar, Covered, Purple 275.00
Iris, Goblet, Buttermilk, Green 70.00
    IRISH LACE, see Louisa
Isaac Benesch, Bowl, Amethyst 600.00
    KIMBERLY, see Concave Diamonds
Kittens, Bowl, Blue, 4 In. 190.00
Kittens, Cup & Saucer, Marigold .... 150.00 To 185.00
Kittens, Toothpick, Marigold 125.00
    LABELLE ELAINE, see Primrose
    LABELLE ROSE, see Rose Show
Lattice & Grape, Tumbler, Marigold 15.00
Lattice & Grape, Water Set, Blue, 7 Piece .... 395.00 To 435.00
    LATTICE & GRAPEVINE, see Lattice & Grape
Leaf & Beads, Bowl, Nut, Marigold 68.00
Leaf & Beads, Rose Bowl, Aqua Opalescent, Northwood 285.00
Leaf & Beads, Rose Bowl, Footed, Green, Northwood 65.00
Leaf & Little Flowers, Compote, Marigold, Millersburg 250.00
Leaf Chain, Plate, Marigold, 9 1/2 In. 90.00
Leaf Chain, Plate, White, 7 1/2 In. 250.00
    LEAF MEDALLION, see Leaf Chain
    LEAF PINWHEEL & STAR FLOWER, see Whirling Leaves
Leaf Rays, Nappy, Marigold 15.00
Lion, Bowl, Marigold, 6 In. .... 40.00 To 45.00
Little Fishes, Bowl, Ice Cream, Footed, Blue, 9 In. 160.00

To clean carnival glass, try using a mixture of 1/2 cup ammonia and 1/8 cup white vinegar.

Little Flowers, Bowl, Green, 10 In. 75.00
Little Stars, Bowl, Ruffled, Marigold, Millersburg, 7 In. 70.00
    LOOPED PETALS, see Scales
Lotus & Grape, Bonbon, Marigold, 5 3/4 In. 28.00
Louisa, Rose Bowl, Green 75.00
Lustre Rose, Pitcher, Milk, Marigold 55.00
Lustre Rose, Water Set, Marigold, 9 Piece 145.00
    MAGNOLIA & POINSETTIA, see Water Lily
Many Fruits, Punch Bowl, Base In Amethyst ....*Illus* 450.00
Many Fruits, Punch Set, White, 12 Piece 1500.00
Maple Leaf, Bowl, Bell Shape, Purple, Westmoreland 45.00
Maple Leaf, Ice Cream Set, Stemmed, Purple, 7 Piece 225.00
Maple Leaf, Tumbler, Amethyst .... 25.00 To 27.50
Mayan, Bowl, Green, 9 In. 125.00
    MELINDA, see Wishbone
Memphis, Punch Cup, Purple .... 18.00 To 20.00
Mikado, Compote, Cobalt Blue 225.00
Milady, Tumbler, Blue 70.00
    MULTI FRUIT & FLOWERS, see Many Fruits
    NESTING SWAN, see Swan, Carnival
Night Star, Bonbon, Green 285.00
    OAK LEAF & ACORN, see Acorn
Octagon, Decanter, Wine, Marigold 65.00
Octagon, Tumbler, Green 65.00
Octagon, Water Set, Marigold, 7 Piece 125.00
    OLD FASHION FLAG, see Iris
    ORANGE TREE & CABLE, see Orange Tree Orchard
Orange Tree Orchard, Tumbler, Marigold 40.00
Orange Tree Orchard, Water Set, White, 5 Piece 1025.00
Orange Tree, Bowl, Fruit, Blue 135.00
Orange Tree, Hatpin Holder, Blue 220.00
Orange Tree, Plate, Blue, 9 In. 165.00
Orange Tree, Powder Jar, Covered, Green .... 165.00 To 350.00
Orange Tree, Powder Jar, Marigold 55.00
Orange Tree, Punch Set, White, 6 Piece 550.00
Orange Tree, Rose Bowl, Marigold 40.00
Orange Tree, Water Set, Footed, Blue, 7 Piece 395.00
Oriental Poppy, Tumbler, Green .... 50.00 To 55.00
Oriental Poppy, Tumbler, Purple, 6 Piece 350.00
Oriental Poppy, Water Set, Marigold, 7 Piece 595.00
Oriental Poppy, Water Set, Purple, 7 Piece 695.00
    PANELED BACHELOR BUTTONS, see Milady
Paneled Dandelion, Pitcher, Blue 125.00
Paneled Dandelion, Tankard Set, Blue, 6 Piece 775.00
Paneled Dandelion, Tumbler, Blue 60.00
Pansy, Bowl, Marigold, 9 In. 28.50
Pansy, Creamer, Purple 30.00
Pansy, Sugar & Creamer, Green 39.00
Panther, Berry Bowl, Footed, Blue .... 50.00 To 65.00
Panther, Berry Bowl, Master, Blue 175.00
Panther, Berry Bowl, Master, Marigold 160.00
Panther, Bowl, Marigold, Footed, 5 In. 45.00
    PARROT TULIP SWIRL, see Acanthus
Peacock & Dahlia, Bowl, Ruffled, Blue, 7 1/2 In. 90.00
Peacock & Grape, Bowl, Green, 8 1/2 In. 80.00
Peacock & Grape, Bowl, Marigold, Vaseline, 9 In. 165.00
Peacock & Urn, Bowl, Amethyst, Fenton, 6 In. 45.00
Peacock & Urn, Bowl, Blue, 5 In. 55.00
Peacock & Urn, Bowl, Blue, 9 In. 75.00
Peacock & Urn, Bowl, Cobalt Blue, 9 In. 85.00
Peacock & Urn, Bowl, Fluted, Cobalt Blue, 9 In. 110.00
Peacock & Urn, Bowl, Ice Cream, Ice Blue, 10 1/2 In. 595.00
Peacock & Urn, Bowl, Purple, Millersburg, 9 1/2 In. 265.00

Peacock & Urn, Compote, Blue, Fenton 65.00
Peacock & Urn, Compote, Marigold On Vaseline 70.00
Peacock & Urn, Plate, Marigold, 9 In. 175.00
Peacock At The Fountain, Bowl, Purple, Northwood, 11 In. 275.00
Peacock At The Fountain, Butter, Covered, Purple 220.00
Peacock At The Fountain, Compote, Marigold 425.00
Peacock At The Fountain, Pitcher, Marigold 150.00
Peacock At The Fountain, Pitcher, Water, White 650.00
Peacock At The Fountain, Punch Bowl, Amethyst 310.00
Peacock At The Fountain, Punch Cup, Purple 30.00
Peacock At The Fountain, Punch Set, White, 11 Piece 2100.00
Peacock At The Fountain, Tumbler, Amethyst 35.00
     PEACOCK ON FENCE, see Peacock
Peacock Tail, Bonbon, Green, 7 In. 37.00
Peacock Tail, Bonbon, Purple, 7 In. 35.00
Peacock Tail, Bowl, Green, 7 1/2 In. 30.00
Peacock, Plate, Green, Northwood, 9 In. 245.00
Peacock, Plate, Marigold, Northwood, 9 In. 285.00
Persian Garden, Bowl, Ice Cream, Master, White, 11 In. 95.00
Persian Garden, Bowl, Marigold, 10 In. 125.00
Persian Medallion, Bonbon, Amethyst 50.00
Persian Medallion, Compote, Amethyst 125.00
Persian Medallion, Compote, Ruffled, Cobalt Blue, 6 1/2 In. 75.00
Persian Medallion, Orange Bowl, Footed, Marigold 127.00
Persian Medallion, Rose Bowl, Marigold, 4 In. 50.00
Petals & Fan, Sauce, Peach 38.00
Peter Rabbit, Bowl, Marigold, 9 In. 700.00
Pods & Posies, Plate, Peach, 6 In. 65.00
     POLKA DOT, see Inverted Coin Dot
Pond Lily, Bonbon, Blue 75.00
     POPPY SCROLL, see Poppy
Poppy Show, Plate, Blue 485.00
Poppy, Bowl, Amethyst, Northwood, 7 1/2 In. 35.00
Poppy, Candy Dish, Ruffled Rim, Marigold 20.00
Poppy, Compote, Green, Millersburg .... 345.00 To 375.00
Primrose, Bowl, Amethyst, 9 1/2 In. 80.00
Primrose, Marigold, Millersburg, 10 In. 69.00
     PRINCESS LACE, see Octagon
Puzzle, Bonbon, Stemmed, Marigold 45.00
Question Marks, Bonbon, Handle, Footed, Peach 75.00
Raindrops, Banana Boat, Dome-Footed, Purple 135.00
Raindrops, Bowl, Peach, 9 In. 45.00
Rambler Rose, Pitcher, Water, Marigold 130.00
Rambler Rose, Tumbler, Marigold .... 22.00 To 27.00
Raspberry, Pitcher, Milk, Green, Northwood 179.00
Raspberry, Pitcher, Water, Purple, Northwood .... 225.00 To 255.00
Raspberry, Tumbler, Marigold 35.00
Raspberry, Water Set, Marigold, Northwood, 7 Piece 200.00
Rays & Ribbon, Bowl, Green, Millersburg, 9 1/2 In. 55.00
Ribbon Tie, Bowl, Marigold, 8 In. 36.00
Rising Sun, Pitcher, Water, Marigold 650.00
Rosalind, Bowl, Amethyst, Millersburg, 10 In. 170.00
Rose Show, Bowl, Aqua Opalescent, 8 3/4 In. .... 325.00 To 575.00
Rose Show, Plate, Marigold, 9 In. 295.00
Rose Spray, Compote, Ruffled Top, Marigold 50.00
Round-Up, Plate, Flat, White, 9 In. 375.00
Round-Up, Plate, Ruffled, White, 8 1/2 In. 235.00
S-Repeat, Punch Cup, Purple 175.00
     SAILBOAT & WINDMILL, see Sailboats
Sailboats, Bowl, Marigold, 6 In. 45.00
Sailboats, Bowl, Red, 6 In. 500.00
Scale Band, Water Set, Marigold, 7 Piece 150.00
Scales, Bowl, Ruffled, Flat, Peach, 6 1/2 In. 40.00

Scotch Thistle, Compote, Marigold 55.00
SEA LANES, see Little Fishes
Seaweed, Bowl, Ruffled, Marigold, 9 In. 225.00
Shell & Jewel, Sugar & Creamer, Covered, Green 50.00
Singing Birds, Butter, Marigold 120.00
Singing Birds, Mug, Purple 75.00
Singing Birds, Tumbler, Green .... 30.00 To 55.00
Singing Birds, Tumbler, Purple 38.00
Singing Birds, Water Set, Green, 9 Piece 750.00
Singing Birds, Water Set, Purple, 7 Piece 650.00
Single Flower, Bowl, Peach, 9 In. .... 25.00 To 40.00
Ski Star, Banana Boat, Dome-Footed, Peach 120.00
Ski Star, Bowl, Peach, 10 1/2 In. .... 90.00 To 95.00
Soda Gold, Spittoon, Marigold 40.00
Spector's Advertising, Plate, Marigold 275.00
SPIDER WEB, see Soda Gold
SPRING FLOWERS, see Bouquet
Springtime, Creamer, Purple 95.00
Springtime, Pitcher, Water, Marigold 450.00
Stag & Holly, Bowl, Amethyst, 10 In. 60.00
Stag & Holly, Bowl, Footed, Blue, 8 In. 95.00
Stag & Holly, Bowl, Green, 11 In. 600.00
Stag & Holly, Bowl, Ice Cream, Blue, 11 In. 275.00
Stag & Holly, Bowl, Ice Cream, Footed, Purple, 8 In. 130.00
Stag & Holly, Bowl, Ice Cream, Marigold, 11 In. 95.00
Stag & Holly, Bowl, Ruffled, Footed, Blue, 10 1/2 In. 175.00
Star & File, Tumbler, Marigold 150.00
STIPPLED CLEMATIS, see Little Stars
STIPPLED DIAMOND & FLOWER, see Little Flowers
STIPPLED POSY & PODS, see Four Flowers
Stippled Rays, Bowl, Footed, Green, Northwood, 8 1/2 In. 60.00
Stippled Rays, Bowl, Marigold, Fenton, 5 In. 25.00
Stippled Rays, Bowl, Ruffled, Marigold, 9 In. 15.00
STIPPLED RIBBONS & RAYS, see Rays & Ribbon
Stork & Rushes, Basket, Marigold 85.00
Stork & Rushes, Tumbler, Aqua 130.00
STRAWBERRY, see Wild Strawberry
SUNFLOWER, see Dandelion
SUNFLOWER & WHEAT, see Fieldflower
SUNFLOWER-WHEAT-CLOVER, see Harvest Flower
Swan, Carnival, Bowl, Amethyst, Millersburg, 10 In. 250.00
Swan, Carnival, Bowl, Green, Millersburg, 10 In. 195.00
Swirl Hobnail, Rose Bowl, Embossed Green Luster, Purple 195.00
TEARDROPS, see Raindrops
Ten Mums, Bowl, Ruffled, Blue, 9 1/2 In. 120.00
Ten Mums, Tumbler, Blue 65.00
Thistle, Bowl, Amethyst, 7 1/4 In. 35.00
Thistle, Bowl, Candy Ribbon Edge, Green, 7 1/2 In. 60.00
Thistle, Bowl, Green, 9 In. 42.00
Three Fruits, Bonbon, Marigold 45.00
Three Fruits, Bowl, Aqua Opalescent, 9 1/2 In. .... 400.00 To 425.00
Three Fruits, Plate, 12 Sides, Blue, 9 1/2 In. 100.00
Tiger Lily, Pitcher, Marigold 100.00
Town Pump, Purple 450.00
Treebark, Candlestick, Marigold, 6 1/2 In., Pair 38.50
Treebark, Pitcher, Covered, Marigold, Imperial 60.00
Trout & Fly, Bowl, Amethyst, 8 3/4 In. .... 400.00 To 475.00
Trout & Fly, Bowl, Ruffled, Marigold, 8 3/4 In. 325.00
Twins, Fruit Stand, Marigold, 9 1/2 In. 80.00
TWO BAND, see Scale Band
Two Flowers, Bowl, Footed, Marigold, 10 In. 27.50
Two Flowers, Bowl, Footed, Red, 8 In. 1500.00
Two Flowers, Rose Bowl, Marigold 95.00

Victorian, Bowl, Purple, 11 1/2 In. 250.00
Vineyard, Pitcher, Marigold ....95.00 To 110.00
Vintage Banded, Pitcher, Marigold 165.00
Vintage, Bowl, Marigold, 7 In. 35.00
Vintage, Bowl, Purple, 7 1/2 In. 67.50
Vintage, Fernery, Green 30.00
Vintage, Plate, Purple, 7 In. 20.00
Waffle Block, Lamp, Marigold 200.00
Water Lily & Cattails, Pitcher, Marigold ....475.00 To 650.00
Water Lily & Cattails, Spooner, Marigold 50.00
Water Lily & Cattails, Tumbler, Marigold 45.00
Water Lily, Bonbon, Footed, Blue 45.00
Water Lily, Bowl, Marigold, Fenton, 1915, 3 1/2 X 10 In. 80.00
Whirling Leaves, Bowl, Marigold, Millersburg, 9 In. 50.00
Whirling Leaves, Bowl, Purple, 9 In. 75.00
Wide Panel, Candy Dish, Covered, Green 55.00
Wild Blackberry, Bowl, Ruffled, Marigold, 8 3/4 In. 48.00
    WILD GRAPES, see Grape Leaves
Wild Strawberry, Berry Bowl, Amethyst, 5 In. ....
Wild Strawberry, Bowl, Marigold, Northwood, 10 In. 120.00
Windflower, Plate, Marigold, 9 1/2 In. 80.00
    WINDMILL MEDALLION, see Windmill   55.00
Windmill, Pitcher, Marigold ....
Windmill, Tray, Pickle, Green, 9 In. 68.00
Windmill, Tumbler, Marigold 28.00
Wine & Roses, Water Set, Marigold, 7 Piece 15.00
Wishbone, Bowl, Footed, Marigold, 10 In. 325.00
Wishbone, Epergne, Blue 55.00
Wishbone, Pitcher, Purple 2500.00
Wishbone, Tumbler, Marigold, 6 Piece 1250.00
Wreath of Roses, Whimsey, Tricornered, Marigold 495.00
Wreathed Cherry, Banana Boat, Purple 28.50
Zig–Zag, Bowl, Tricornered, Purple, Millersburg 125.00
                                                           475.00

The first carousel or merry–go–round figures carved in the United States were made in 1867 by Gustav Dentzel. Collectors discovered the charm of the hand–carved figures in the 1970s and they were soon classed as folk art. Most desirable are the figures other than horses, such as pigs, camels, lions, or dogs. A jumper is a figure that was made to move up and down on a pole, a stander was placed in a stationary position.

CAROUSEL, Bear, Glass Eyes, Carved To Simulate Fur, Saddle, French, C.1875 .... 1450.00
Bear, Skin Saddle, Jewels, Parker, 53 In. 2000.00
Boat Ride, Wooden, 10 Cents, Coin–Operated, 3 X 6 Ft. 500.00
Camel, Tulip Flower On Saddle, 56 In. 4500.00
Cat, Fish In Mouth, Dentzel 3500.00
Chariot, Dragon, Parker, 1912, Large 4500.00
Chariot, Girl With Dog At Side, Herschell–Spillman 2000.00
Chariot, King Neptune & The Dragon, Herschell–Spillman 2000.00
Chicken, Flying, English, 62 In. 4500.00
Dog, Collar, Herschell–Spillman 3500.00
Donkey, Brass Handle, Wooden, Bayol of Angers, C.1875, 32 In. 1300.00
Dragon, Carpet Seat, Handmade 1200.00
Elephant, Pink Paint, 36 X 30 In. 9000.00
Giraffe, Flowers On Chest, 6 Ft. 2895.00
Horse, Allan Hershell, 1914 .... 2750.00
Horse, Double Seat, Parker, Wooden 3500.00
Horse, Jumper, Glass Eyes, Parker 3500.00
Horse, Jumper, Herschell, Wood & Metal, Brass Pole, C.1930, 48 In. 1200.00
Horse, Jumper, Park Paint, Stein & Goldstein 4500.00
Horse, Jumper, Peek–A–Boo Mane, Indian Face On Rear, 78 In. 5700.00
Horse, Jumping, Herschel, Park Paint 2035.00
Horse, Lifted Head, Dog On Back of Seat, Jeweled, Parker 2300.00
Horse, Middle Jumper, Park Paint, Carmel, Large 5000.00

Horse, Outside Row, Show Paint, English, C.1880	3300.00
Horse, Outside, Stein & Goldstein	7900.00
Horse, Parker, 1890	2100.00
Horse, Parker, Double Seat, Wooden, Restored, 1911	3500.00
Horse, Philadelphia Toboggan Co., 1918	600.00
Horse, Prancer, Dentzel, Metal Tail, 64 X 60 In.	4750.00
Horse, Prancer, Glass Eyes, Heyn	4000.00
Horse, Prancer, Looff, 53 X 51 In.	4250.00
Horse, Prancer, Looff, Original Park Paint, 62 X 60 In.	8500.00
Horse, Snake, Dove, Tassel Design, Showpaint, Andersons, C.1880	3850.00
Horse, Stander, Outside, Jewels, Brass Poll & Stand, Looff, 1880	8500.00
Horse, Stander, Stein & Goldstein, 40 X 48 In.	4750.00
Indian, Neil, Wood, Carved	1400.00
Jumper, Carved Rabbits & Rifle, Parker	5500.00
Jumper, Roses, Parker, C.1912	5800.00
Jumper, Wolf Head In Cantle, Parker, 1912	5000.00
Lion, Lying, Wooden, Pair	3200.00
Pig, Herschell Spillman	4500.00
Pony, Heny	1700.00
Rabbit, Bayol, C.1899	6500.00
Rooster, Herschell–Spillman	5200.00
Tiger, Heyn, 1919	4000.00

The word "carriage" has several meanings, so this section lists baby carriages, buggies for adults, horse–drawn sleighs, and even strollers. Doll–sized carriages are listed under "toy."

CARRIAGE, Baby Buggy, Canopy, Wicker, Original Leather Upholstery	650.00
Baby Buggy, Joel Ellis, Fringe On Top, C.1870	575.00
Baby Buggy, Natural Rolled Wicker, Hood	357.00
Baby Buggy, Parasol, American Stick & Ball, Wood Spokes	525.00
Baby Buggy, Wicker, Metal Spoke Wheels, Rubber Rims, American	490.00
Baby, Wicker, Unpainted, Ornate, Umbrella	500.00
Perambulator, English	325.00
Perambulator, Painted, 23 In.Rear Wooden Wheels, 37 X 51 In.	795.00
Sleigh, Grocery Delivery, Gilt Lettering, SS Pierce, Red	2000.00
Sleigh, Smoke Grained Interior, Maine, 35 X 65 In.	3000.00
Surrey, 2 Seat, Red Tufted Upholstery, Fringed Top	2000.00
Surrey, Fringe On Top, Black, Yellow Wheels	800.00
Wagon, Popcorn, Indoor, Steam Engine, Clown, Peanut Roaster	3200.00

An eye on the cash was a necessity in stores of the nineteenth century, too. The cash register was invented in 1884. John and James Ritty invented a large clocklike model that kept a record of the dollars and cents exchanged in the store. John Patterson improved the cash register with a paper roll to record the money. By the early 1900s, elaborate brass registers were made. About World War I, the fancy case was exchanged for the more modern types.

CASH REGISTER, Clay Marbles, Holes, Drawer, Bell Rings, Drawers Open, Oak	950.00
Imperial	400.00
National, 9 Drawers, Oak, 5 Ft.6 In.	3500.00
National, Candy Store, Brass	440.00
National, Model 213, Bronze Case, 21 In.	450.00
National, Model 313, Brass	825.00
National, Model 313, Rings Up To 1.95	975.00
National, Model 442, Wooden Base, Restored, 1912	1275.00
National, Model 462–C, Autographic Detail Strip, C.1916	600.00
National, Model 52 1/4, Extended Base	1200.00
National, Model 563–6f, Floor, Brass	690.00
National, Model 578–C, Double Drawer, Marble Shelf	1500.00
St.Louis, Lever, Plunger Before Keys Read Out, Oak & Metal	180.00

Castor sets holding just salt and pepper castors were used in the seventeenth century. The sugar castor, mustard pot, spice dredger, bottles for vinegar and oil, and other spice holders became popular by the eighteenth century. These sets were usually made of sterling silver. The American Victorian castor set, the type most collected today, was made of silver plated Britannia metal. Colored glass bottles were introduced after the Civil War. The sets were out of fashion by World War I. Be careful when buying sets with colored bottles; many are reproductions.

CASTOR SET, see also various Porcelain and Glass categories

CASTOR SET, 3–Bottle, Daisy & Button Pattern, Silver Plate	60.00
3–Bottle, Twisted Leaf Pattern, Shell Pattern On Holder	395.00
4–Bottle, Israel Trask, Paneled Bottles, Pewter Frame	100.00
4–Bottle, Meriden	165.00
4–Bottle, Turquoise, Milk Glass, Fenton	75.00
5–Bottle, Blue Willow, Blue Willow China Stand	112.00
5–Bottle, Button Band Pattern, Original Stoppers & Lids	135.00
5–Bottle, Etched, Wilcox Frame	80.00
5–Bottle, Gothic, Pewter Stand	125.00
5–Bottle, Horizontal Leaf Design	95.00
5–Bottle, Israel Trask, Gothic Arch Pattern, 9 1/2 In.	150.00
5–Bottle, Mahogany Case, Ivory Fittings, Silver Plated Tops	150.00
5–Bottle, Ruby Glass Cut To Clear	190.00
6–Bottle, Bellflower Bottles, Pewter Frame, 10 3/4 In.	375.00
8–Bottle, Cut Glass, Sterling Silver Tray	560.00

The pickle castor was a glass jar about six inches in height, held in a special metal holder. It became a popular dinner table accessory about 1890. The jar had a top that was usually silver or silver plate. The frame, also of a silver metal, had a handle that arched above the jar and a hook that held a pair of tongs. By 1900, the pickle castor was out of fashion. Many examples found today have reproduced glass jars in old holders.

CASTOR, PICKLE, see also various Glass categories

CASTOR, Pickle, Amber Band With Ovals, Embossed, Silver Plate	130.00
Pickle, Amber Glass, Diamond Pattern, Triple Plate Frame & Tongs	195.00
Pickle, Blue Cane Insert, Tongs, 11 In.	130.00
Pickle, Blue Glass, Bird, Flowers, Ornate Meriden Frame & Tongs	215.00
Pickle, Canary Pattern Insert, Silver Plated Frame, Tongs, Lid	185.00
Pickle, Cranberry Glass, Floral Enameled, Gold Wash Holder, Tongs	330.00
Pickle, Cupid & Venus Insert, Dog Finial On Lid	65.00
Pickle, Daisy & Button, Amber Band With Ovals	130.00

Castor, Pickle, Inverted Thumbprint, Silver Holder & Tongs; Castor, Pickle, Paneled Finecut, Blue, Silver Holder & Tongs; Castor, Pickle, Inverted Thumbprint, Cranberry, Silver Holder

Christmas, Figure, Santa Claus, Die–Cut, Mica, Germany, 16 In.

Pickle, Frosted Jar, Birds Both Sides, Silver Plated Holder, 14 In. 195.00
Pickle, Full Loops, Tongs, Silver Plate, Leaf Form 65.00
Pickle, Inverted Thumbprint, Cranberry, Daisies, Resilvered Frame 275.00
Pickle, Inverted Thumbprint, Cranberry, Silver Holder ....*Illus* 80.00
Pickle, Inverted Thumbprint, Silver Holder & Tongs ....*Illus* 110.00
Pickle, Inverted Thumbprint, Silver Plated Holder, Stork Side 395.00
Pickle, Opalescent Hobnail, Frame 225.00
Pickle, Open Heart Arches, White Satin Glass, Floral Design 245.00
Pickle, Optic Insert, Silver Plated Lid, Frame, Cranberry 148.00
Pickle, Paneled Finecut, Blue, Silver Holder & Tongs ....*Illus* 100.00
Pickle, Panels, Peaked Glass Lid, With Silver Plated Knob, Frame 265.00
Pickle, Peachblow, Enameled, Satin Cased, Egg Shape, Matching Frame 550.00
Pickle, Pink Cased Cone, Original Frame 225.00
Pickle, Raised Enameling, Cranberry, Tongs, 10 1/2 In. 180.00
Pickle, Rubena Inverted Thumbprint Insert, Flowers, 12 1/2 In. 385.00
Pickle, Spatter Glass, Cranberry, White, 6 Paneled Melon Rib, 4 In. 75.00
Pickle, Strawberry, Diamond & Fan Insert, Tongs, Meriden 85.00
Pickle, White, Crystal Nailsea, Cranberry Threading, 10 1/2 In. 300.00
CATALOG, see Paper, Catalog
CAUGHLEY, see Salopian

The firm Cauldon Limited worked in Staffordshire, Great Britain, and went through many name changes. John Ridgway made porcelain at Cauldon Place, Hanley, until 1855. The firm of John Ridgway, Bates and Co. of Cauldon Place worked from 1856 to 1859. It became Bates, Brown-Westhead, Moore and Co. from 1859 to 1862. Brown-Westhead, Moore and Co. worked from 1862 to 1904. About 1890, this firm started using the words "Cauldon" or "Cauldon ware" as part of the mark. Cauldon Ltd. worked from 1905 to 1920, Cauldon Potteries from 1920 to 1962.

CAULDON, see also Indian Tree
CAULDON, Fish Set, Blue & White, 13 Piece 600.00
  Mug, Hires Root Beer, Hourglass Shape, Boy With Mug, Set of 6 .... 195.00
  Plate Set, Different Fish, Hand Painted, Border, 11 Piece 750.00
  Plate, Hunt Scene, Brown Shades, Beige Ground 30.00
  Vase, Gilded, Teal Blue, C.1880, 7 In. 65.00

Celadon is a Chinese porcelain having a velvet-textured green-gray glaze. Japanese, Korean, and other factories also made a celadon-colored glaze.

CELADON, Creamer, Floral Pattern 18.00
  Ewer, Covered, Village & Mountain Scene, Chinese Blue, 10 3/8 In. 175.00
  Garden Seat, Barrel Form, Prunus Blossoms, Pierced, 19 In. 700.00
  Jar, Covered, Flowers, Gold Design, 6 In. 75.00
  Platter, Allover Design, Floral, Birds, Gold Rim, 19th Century, Oval 350.00
  Vase, Blue Relief Dragon, 7 In. 75.00
  Vase, Bottle, Tree of Life, 6 In. 35.00
  Vase, Flared Rim, Ovoid Body, Enameled Birds, Butterflies, 9 In. 125.00
  Vase, Relief Dragon, Blue, 7 In. 65.00
  Vase, Transparent Spray of Flowers, Bird, Green, 6 In. 400.00
  Wall Pocket, Blue Iris Design, Japan, 12 In. 59.00

Celluloid is a trademark for a plastic developed in 1868 by John W. Hyatt. Celluloid Manufacturing Company, the Celluloid Novelty Company, Celluloid Fancy Goods Company, and American Xylonite Company all used Celluloid to make jewelry, games, sewing equipment, false teeth, and piano keys. Eventually, the Hyatt Company became the American Celluloid and Chemical Manufacturing Company—the Celanese Corporation. The name "Celluloid" was often used to identify any similar plastic. Celluloid toys are listed under toys.

CELLULOID, Backcomb, Gold Paste Stones, Filigree, C.1890 .... 15.00
  Bookmark, Beich's Chocolates 25.00
  Bookmark, Denver Dry Goods 15.00

Bookmark, Dr.Reed Shoes 15.00
Bookmark, Girl On Rocking Horse 35.00
Box, Hinged Cover, Fan Shape, 8 In. 46.00
Box, Necktie 35.00
Casket, Glove, Camelback Shaped Lid, Roses, Buds, 18 X 6 In. 275.00
Comb, Green Rhinestones 25.00
Comb, Openwork, Yellow, 6 X 4 In. 25.00
Dresser Set, Amber Color, Beveled Mirror, 4 Piece 40.00
Mustache Comb, Tortoise, Silver Case 30.00
Notepad, Grabfelder Amer.Malt Whiskey, 1900 Calendar 28.50
Pen Wiper, Figural, Pig, Advertising, Ready For The Pen 20.00
Pin, Flapper Picture, Oval, 2 In. 15.00
Rattle, Bulldog 7.00
Rattle, Peter Rabbit, Pre–War Sticker, Japan, 9 In. 95.00
Stickpin, Sharples 45.00
Travel Kit, Folding Leather Case, 17 Piece 28.00

The Ceramic Art Company of Trenton, New Jersey, was established in 1889 by J. Coxon and W. Lenox and was an early producer of American Belleek porcelain. Pieces made by this company are listed here. Do not confuse this ware with the pottery made by the Ceramic Arts Studio of Madison, Wisconsin, from 1941 to 1957.

CERAMIC ART CO., Cup & Saucer, Palmer Cox Brownies, Belleek Pallette Mark 150.00
Mug, 2 Monks Sitting & Drinking Wine, Marked, 5 1/2 In. 160.00
Mug, Portrait of Man, Belleek Palette Mark, Purple 125.00
Tea Set, Ivory, Green & Gold, 1897, 7 Piece 475.00

Chalkware is really plaster of Paris decorated with watercolors. One type was molded from Staffordshire and other porcelain models and painted and sold as inexpensive decorations in the nineteenth century. Figures of plaster, made from about 1910 to 1940 for use as prizes at carnivals, are also known as chalkware.

CHALKWARE, Bank, Apple Shape, Worn Red Paint, 3 1/2 In. 125.00
Bank, Pig, Worn Black Stripes, Red Snout, Glued Leg, 14 1/2 In. 375.00
Bookends, Shape of Old Books 295.00
Box, Hen Cover, 6 In. 70.00
Deer, Original Brown Paint, 15 3/4 In. 65.00
Doll, Flapper, Carnival, 1935, 13 In. 35.00
CHALKWARE, FIGURINE, see also Kewpie
Figurine, Bird, Faded Yellow Paint, 5 3/4 In. 525.00
Figurine, Bull, White 550.00
Figurine, Bulldog, Sitting, Yellow Ringed Eyes, Carnival 20.00
Figurine, Bunny, Driving Car, Carnival, 4 1/2 In. 35.00
Figurine, Cat, Black Smoked Finish, Red, Yellow, 9 3/4 In. 700.00
Figurine, Cat, Black, Original Paint, 16 In. 1800.00
Figurine, Cocker Spaniel, Carnival 8.00
Figurine, Collie, Sitting, Carnival 55.00
Figurine, Comical Fat Man, High Hat, Polychrome Paint, 11 In. 125.00
Figurine, Deer, Reclining, White, 10 1/2 X 8 1/2 In. 225.00
Figurine, Dog, Basket In Mouth, 19th Century 235.00
Figurine, Dog, Seated, Open Front Legs, Original Design, 6 In. 125.00
Figurine, Dog, Seated, Red, Green & Black, 5 3/4 In. 100.00
Figurine, Dog, Seated, Yellow Eyes, Gray, Black, & Red Paint, 8 In. ... 105.00
Figurine, Dog, Standing, Original Red & Black Paint, 7 1/2 In. 150.00
Figurine, Dog, Wearing Hat & Scarf, Smoking Pipe, 6 In. 50.00
Figurine, Donald Duck, Carnival, 13 1/2 In. 18.50
Figurine, Dove, Polychrome Paint, Repainted, 10 3/4 In., Pair 550.00
Figurine, Dove, Solid Body & Base, Polychrome Design, 10 1/4 In. 50.00
Figurine, Flapper, Carnival, 1935, 13 In. 35.00
Figurine, Foo Dogs, Raised Design, C.1870, Pair 110.00
Figurine, Fox, Seated, Red Hunting Jacket, Carnival, 6 In. 20.00
Figurine, Goose, Red Goose Shoes, 11 1/2 In. 150.00
Figurine, Hereford Bull, Carnival 19.00
Figurine, Indian Chief, Reclining, 27 In. 75.00

Figurine, Indian Chief, Standing, Headdress, 20 In.	35.00
Figurine, Madonna & Child, Carnival, 12 In.	12.00
Figurine, Maggie & Jiggs, Carnival	45.00
Figurine, Poodle, Standing, Freestanding Front Legs, 7 1/2 In.	240.00
Figurine, Rabbit, Greenish Gold Paint, 5 In.	110.00
Figurine, Rabbit, Pink, Carnival, 2 3/4 In.	24.00
Figurine, Rabbit, Seated, Original Paint, 5 In.	230.00
Figurine, Rooster, Red, Yellow & Black Paint, 6 In.	375.00
Figurine, Shirley Temple, Sailor, Carnival	25.00
Figurine, Stag, Reclining, Large	375.00
Figurine, String Holder, Dog, Scotty, 1910	50.00
Figurine, Young Lady, Tree Stump, Le Ruisseau Hip Moreau, 18 In.	135.00
Garniture, Original Paint, 13 1/2 In., Pair	900.00
Lamp, Art Deco, Full–Length Nude, Frosted Green Conical Shade	40.00
Lamp, Wishing Well, With Boy & Dog, Carnival, Satin Glass Shade	35.00

Charlie Chaplin, the famous comic and actor, lived from 1889 to 1977. He made his first movie in 1913. He did the movie "The Tramp" in 1915. The character of the Tramp has remained famous and is in use today in a series of television commercials for computers. Dolls, candy containers, and all sorts of memorabilia picture Charlie Chaplin. Pieces are being made even today.

CHARLIE CHAPLIN, Bicycle, Tin	225.00
Book, Coloring, Comic, 1917	10.00
Button, Pinback, Figural, Painted, 2 1/2 In.	45.00
Candy Container, Borgfeldt	80.00
Card, Peep Show, 10 Scenes From Tramp, 1915, 2 1/2 X 4 In.	15.00
Case, Pencil, Tin	85.00
Cigar Band	65.00
Doll, Dressed, Louis Ambery & Son, 1920s	360.00
Figure, Wood Carving, Primitive, Black Paint, 12 1/2 In.	90.00
Game, Card, Flip Movie Backs	10.00
Ornament, Christmas Tree, Blown Glass	260.00
Pin, Figure, Plastic, 2 1/2 In.	42.00
Puppet, Cardboard, 1920s, Original Envelope	20.00
Toothpick, Plaster	35.00
Toy, Pull String, Chaplin Tips Hat, Tin, England, 4 In.	115.00

Charlie McCarthy was the ventriloquist's dummy used by Edgar Bergen from the 1930s. He was famous for his work in radio, movies, and television. The act was retired in the 1970s.

CHARLIE MCCARTHY, Book, Charlie McCarthy, Edgar Bergen, No.770, 1938	25.00
Book, Comic, In The Haunted Hideout, 1948	15.00
Book, Day With Charlie McCarthy, Edgar Bergen, Whitman	40.00
Book, Paint	20.00
Box, Pencil, Eberhard Faber, C.1938	22.50
Doll, Tuxedo, Hat, Book, Effanbee, 21 In.	185.00
Doll, Ventriloquist, Compositon Head, 25 In.	250.00
Game, Card, Rummy, 1938	20.00
Game, Radio .... 18.00 To 22.00
Money Clip, 14K Gold, 3–D Silhouette, Studio	400.00
Pencil Sharpener, Figural, Plastic, Decal, 1930s, 2 In.	25.00
Puppet, Cardboard, Chase & Sanborn Envelope	40.00
Puppet, Composition, Eyes Painted To Side, 20 In.	95.00
Puppet, Hand	55.00
Radio, White	300.00
Spoon, Figural, Silver Plate	20.00
Toy, Benzine Buggy, Tin, Marx, Box, 7 1/2 In.	485.00
Toy, Funny Car, Windup, Box	375.00
Toy, Mortimer Snerd, Mechanical, Tin, Marx, Box, 8 In.	325.00
Toy, Windup, Celluloid, Mouth Opens & Closes, 1930s	65.00

Chelsea grape pattern was made before 1840. A small bunch of grapes in a raised design, colored with purple or blue luster, is on the border of the white plate. Most of the pieces are unmarked. The pattern is sometimes called "Aynsley" or "Grandmother." Chelsea sprig is similar but has a sprig of flowers instead of the bunch of grapes.

CHELSEA GRAPE, Creamer	45.00
Cup & Saucer	25.00
Dish, Soap, Octagonal, 3 Piece	68.00
Waste Bowl	40.00
CHELSEA KERAMIC ART WORKS, see Dedham	
CHELSEA SPRIG, Bowl, 6 1/2 X 3 1/2 In.	16.00
Cup & Saucer, Ironstone	11.00
Plate, Ironstone, 7 In.	5.00

Chelsea porcelain was made in the Chelsea area of London from about 1745 to 1784. Ceramic designs were borrowed from the Meissen models of the day. Pieces were made of soft paste. The gold anchor was used as the mark but it has been copied by many other factories. Recent copies of Chelsea have been made from the original molds.

CHELSEA, Basket, Dessert, Flared, Rose & Spray Center, C.1775, 4 5/8 In.	1875.00
Figurine, Boy & Girl, Blue & White, 4 1/2 X 5 1/2 In.	200.00
Figurine, Cat, Seated, Auburn, White, Porcelain, 1 3/4 In.	105.00

Chinese export porcelain comprises all the many kinds of porcelain made in China for export to America and Europe in the eighteenth and nineteenth centuries.

CHINESE EXPORT, see also Canton; Celadon; Nanking; Rose Medallion

CHINESE EXPORT, Bowl, Barber's, Famille Verte, Oval, 1700–20, 14 1/4 In.	2200.00
Bowl, Barber's, Peony Branches, C.1750, 10 1/2 In.	605.00
Bowl, Cabbage Leaf, Insects, 1875, 12 In.	55.00
Bowl, Feathery Ground, Chinese Couple, 12 1/2 In.	1100.00
Bowl, Floral Center, Molded Gadroon Border, 5 In.	80.00
Bowl, Judgment of Paris, 1750–60, 10 1/4 In.	465.00
Bowl, Lotus, Rose To Pale Pink, Floral, C.1760, 8 In.	495.00
Bowl, Man O' War, Union Jack, Stand, C.1785, 10 1/8 In.	900.00
Bowl, Oriental Figures In Garden, Bird Panels, 11 3/8 In.	1300.00
Bowl, Sporting Scenes, Medallions, 18th Century, 6 In.	1600.00
Candleholder, Elephant Shape, Trumpet Holder, 5 1/8 In.	2300.00
Charger, Flowers, Late 18th Century, 12 In. ....*Illus*	660.00
Clock, Mantel, Famille Rose, Gilt Bronze, C.1890, 23 In.	935.00
Cream Pot, Peacock & Tree Design, C.1780, 5 1/2 In.	165.00
Creamer, Helmet, Polychromed Floral Design, 5 In.	30.00
Cup & Saucer, Teabowl, For America, Brown, 1800, Set of 12	1100.00
Dish, Hot Water, Russet Shades, 4 Figures, 10 5/8 In.	1200.00
Ewer, Armorial, Pear Shape, Grisaille, Covered, 1760, 16 In.	900.00
Ewer, Famille Verte, Helmet Shape, 1710–20, 11 1/8 In.	2250.00
Figurine, Lady, Holding Lotus Petal Urn, 11 1/4 In., Pair	7425.00
Fish Bowl, Famille Rose, Painted Scene, 19 In.	1850.00
Ginger Jar, Hand Painted, Oriental Women In Garden, 12 In.	300.00
Jar, Famille Verte, Powder Blue, Covered, C.1715, 6 3/4 In.	1650.00
Jar, Melon, Cabbage Leaf, Butterfly, 19th Century, 8 In.	70.00
Jardiniere, Red & Blue Floral, Birds, Stand, 3 In.	100.00
Lamp, Wedding, Reticulated, Floral, Blue & White, 8 1/4 In.	450.00
Mirror, Hand, Silver Gilt, Semiprecious Stones	270.00
Mug, Dragon Handle, Orange Fish Scale, Genre Scene	550.00
Pitcher, Covered, Gold Borders, Drapery, Fruit Finial, 6 In.	200.00
Plate, A La Pompadour, C.1745, 9 In.	1000.00
Plate, Bengal Tiger, 4 Panels, Red Border, 1805–15, 9 In.	1750.00
Plate, Center Landscape Scene, Flying Serpent, C.1760	200.00
Plate, Famille Rose, Bird, Spearhead Border, C.1750, 14 In.	2200.00
Plate, Famille Rose, European Boy, C.1745, 9 1/8 In., Pair	450.00

Plate, Famille Rose, Peonies, Butterflies, Birds, C.1800 .... 225.00
Plate, Grisaille Design, Cupid, Venus, 1745, 8 7/8 In., Pair 385.00
Plate, Italian Comedy, Iron Red Border, 1720–25, 9 In. 2475.00
Plate, Judgment of Paris, Shell Border, C.1750, 9 In., Pair ...~............... 1550.00
Plate, Marriage Party, Cathedral, Border, C.1740, 9 In. 450.00
Plate, Sepia Birds & Flowers, Gold & Blue, 9 1/4 In. 175.00
Plate, Young Man Center, 6 Gilt Panels, 1745, 8 1/8 In. 330.00
Platter, Armorial, Edward Arms, Motto, C.1790, 17 1/2 In. 385.00
Platter, Famille Rose, Scalloped Rim, 10 1/4 X 13 In. 175.00
Platter, Flower & Vine Design, Oval, 12 1/2 X 15 1/2 In. 325.00
Platter, Flowers In Cornucopia, Notched Rim, C.1745, 15 In. 3000.00
Platter, Imari Center, Armorial Horse, 1750, 14 In. 150.00
Platter, Silver Form, Floral Swag Rim, C.1770, 12 X 9 In. 760.00
Punch Bowl, Clipper Ships, Garlands, C.1790, 11 In. 750.00
Punch Bowl, Grisaille, Oriental Figures, C.1775, 16 1/4 In. 1980.00
Punch Bowl, Interior Genre Scenes, 14 3/4 In. ....*Illus* 2100.00
Punch Bowl, Lavender Ground, Genre Scenes, 5 X 10 In. 950.00
Sauce Boat, Water Buffalos, Scalloped, 1780–1800, Pr. 800.00
Soup Tureen, Covered, Platter, Handles, 1810, 14 In. 3850.00
Teapot, Covered, Light Tan, Bird Scene, 1664–1722, 6 In. 500.00
Teapot, Cozy, Oriental, Wire Handles, C.1850, 5 In. 150.00
Teapot, Drum Shape, Bud Finial, Ribbon Handle, 5 In. 400.00
Teapot, Knop Cover, Chrysanthemum Petals, C.1740, 3 In. 522.00
Teapot, Musician Scene, Lavender Diaper Ground, C.1800 .... 400.00
Teapot, Pewter Lid 165.00
Tureen, Lozenge Shape, Rosebud Knop Cover, 1765–75, 9 In. 1750.00
Tureen, Soup, Stand & Cover, Famille Rose, 1750–60, 15 In. 4950.00
Tureen, Undertray, Covered, Porcelain, Monogram, 10 X 13 In. 450.00
Umbrella Stand, White Flowers, C.1850, 23 X 13 In. 250.00
Urn, Pistol Handle, 1810, Russet, Gold Trim, 14 In., Pr. 7425.00
Vase, Blue Floral, Scroll Borders, Porcelain, 10 In., Pair 600.00
Vase, Famille Rose, Butterfly, Ovoid, Stand, 24 In., Pair 1500.00
Vase, Famille Rose, Chinese Figures, 1760–80, 19 1/4 In. 600.00
Vase, Mandarin, 11 1/2 In. 685.00
Vase, Trumpet, Cloisonne, Silver & Gold Birds, 10 In., Pair 1500.00
Warming Tray, Dome Cover, 18 In. 1450.00
Waste Bowl, Parrot, Blue Enameled, 1740–50, 5 1/2 In. 600.00

> Chocolate glass, sometimes mistakenly called caramel slag, was made by the Indiana Tumbler and Goblet Company of Greentown, Indiana, from 1900 to 1903.

Chinese Export, Charger, Flowers,
Late 18th Century, 12 In.

Chinese Export, Punch Bowl,
Interior Genre Scenes, 14 3/4 In.

CHOCOLATE GLASS, Berry Bowl, Cactus, Footed, Small 38.00
Bowl, Beaded Triangle, 4 1/2 In. .... 365.00 To 450.00
Bowl, Chrysanthemum Leaf, 7 In. 350.00
Bowl, Dewey, 8 In. 180.00
Butter, Cactus, Covered 190.00
Butter, Covered, Dewey, 1/4 Lb. 100.00
Butter, Covered, Fleur-De-Lis 325.00
Butter, Geneva, Covered 265.00
Butter, Leaf Bracket, Covered 95.00
Celery, Leaf Bracket 85.00
Compote, Cactus, 5 1/4 In. 195.00
Compote, Dolphin, Fish Cover, Greentown 475.00
Compote, Jelly, Geneva 85.00
Compote, Open, Teardrop & Tassel, 7 1/2 In. 55.00
Cracker Jar, Cactus .... 165.00 To 230.00
Creamer, Austrian 120.00
Creamer, Cupid, Original Lid 295.00
Creamer, Dewey, 5 In. 65.00
Creamer, Geneva .... 165.00 To 195.00
Creamer, Leaf Bracket .... 65.00 To 90.00
Cruet, Cactus, Original Stopper ....65.00 To 175.00
Cruet, Leaf Bracket, Original Stopper 145.00
Cruet, Wild Rose With Bowknot, Original Stopper 375.00
Dish, Dolphin Covered, Deep Amber Edge, 4 3/4 In. 265.00
Dish, Dolphin Lid, Beaded Top 225.00
Dish, Dolphin Lid, Smooth Top 300.00
Dish, Dolphin, Fish Cover, 7 In. .... 425.00 To 475.00
Hatpin Holder, Orange Tree 135.00
Mug, Ball & Swirl, 4 In. 650.00
Mug, Cactus 65.00
Mug, Serenade, 3 1/2 X 5 In. 170.00
Mustard, Dolphin 135.00
Nappy, Leaf Bracket 55.00
Nappy, Leaf Bracket, Triangular Handle 68.00
Pitcher, Milk, Feather 550.00
Pitcher, Running & Reclining Deer, Footed 345.00
Pitcher, Squirrel With Nut 325.00
Pitcher, Water, Ruffled Eye 495.00
Plate, Cactus, 7 1/2 In. 110.00
Salt & Pepper, Pleat Band 195.00
Sauce, Chrysanthemum Leaf, 4 In. 125.00
Sauce, Dewey, Footed 45.00
Sauce, Wild Rose & Bowknot 75.00
Saucer, Leaf Bracket, Footed, 4 5/8 X 2 In. 38.00
Spooner, Cactus 80.00
Spooner, Holly Amber 100.00
Spooner, Leaf Bracket 85.00
Spooner, Sultan 225.00
Spooner, Wild Rose With Bow Knot 115.00
Sugar, Covered, Leaf Bracket 65.00
Sugar, Covered, Sultan, Miniature 325.00
Sugar, Leaf Bracket 100.00
Syrup, Cactus, Original Cover 85.00
Syrup, Chrysanthemum Leaf 950.00
Syrup, Cord Drapery .... 135.00 To 195.00
Syrup, Shuttle .... 75.00 To 95.00
Toothpick, Cactus .... 65.00 To 75.00
Tray, Venetian, 4 X 5 In. 275.00
Tumbler, Cactus, 4 In. .... 42.00 To 55.00
Tumbler, Icicle 125.00
Tumbler, Leaf Bracket 55.00
Tumbler, Lemonade, Cactus 65.00
Tumbler, Shuttle 85.00
Tumbler, Uneeda Biscuit 95.00

CHRISTMAS PLATE, see Collector Plate

The first decorated Christmas tree in America is claimed by many states, including Pennsylvania (1747), Massachusetts (1832), Illinois (1833), Ohio (1838), and Iowa (1845). The first glass ornaments were imported from Germany about 1860. Manufacturers in the United States were making ornaments in the early 1870s. Electric lights were first used on a Christmas tree in 1882. Character light bulbs became popular in the 1920s, bubble lights in the 1940s, twinkle bulbs in the 1950s, plastic bulbs by 1955. In this book a Christmas light is a holder for a candle used on the tree. Other forms of lighting include light bulbs.

CHRISTMAS TREE, Candleholder, Colored Tin, Dated 1883, 2 1/2 In., Set of 10	45.00
Cardboard, Metal Bells On Each Branch, Germany	195.00
Feather Tree, 4 Ft.	300.00
Feather Tree, Bird Head Iron Holder, Box of Candles, 6 Ft.	1200.00
Feather Tree, Candle Holders, 6 Ft.	550.00
Feather Tree, German, 4 Ft.4 In.	850.00
Feather Tree, Green, Tin Candle Sockets, Germany, 14 In.	105.00
Feather Tree, Light Green Tips, 28 In.	225.00
Feather Tree, White, 18 In.	235.00
Fence, Green, Folding, 11 Sections, Gate, Square, 25 1/2 In.	50.00
Fence, Red, Green, Strombeck–Berker, 4 Sections, Box, 19 In.	200.00
Fence, Twig, With Gates, Germany, Square, 18 In.	45.00
Fence, Victorian, Cast Iron	250.00
Fence, Wooden, Green, Red Corner Posts, 20 In.Square, Box	72.00
Icicle, Tin, 16 Piece	10.00
Light Bulb, 3 Little Pigs, Noma, Bell Shaped Caps	85.00
Light Bulb, Apple, Japan	15.00
Light Bulb, Baby In Stocking	27.00
Light Bulb, Barney Google, Box, Set	175.00
Light Bulb, Bell, With Santa Claus Faces	12.50
Light Bulb, Betty Boop .... 33.00 To	45.00
Light Bulb, Cat With Fiddle	30.00
Light Bulb, Cross	18.00
Light Bulb, Dick Tracy, Figural, Milk Glass	65.00
Light Bulb, Dirigible	45.00
Light Bulb, Disney Silly Symphony, Noma, Box, Set of 8	450.00
Light Bulb, Doll, Milk Glass	25.00
Light Bulb, Father Christmas, 8 In.	90.00
Light Bulb, Frog	25.00
Light Bulb, Girl In Flower Bud	35.00
Light Bulb, Girl, With Muff	35.00
Light Bulb, Grape Cluster, Gold, Large	22.50
Light Bulb, Grape Cluster, Purple, Small	15.00
Light Bulb, House	12.50
Light Bulb, House, Snow Covered	25.00
Light Bulb, Ice Cream Cone	10.00
Light Bulb, Ice, G.E.	2.25
Light Bulb, Japanese Lantern	15.00
Light Bulb, Jiminy Cricket .... 28.00 To	38.00
Light Bulb, John Bull	35.00
Light Bulb, Katzenjammer Kids, King Features	90.00
Light Bulb, Kayo, Milk Glass	55.00
Light Bulb, Kewpie .... 28.00 To	30.00
Light Bulb, Kitten In Boot	30.00
Light Bulb, Lantern, Oriental, Japan	28.00
Light Bulb, Lindberg	28.00
Light Bulb, Man With Bowtie, Girl With Muff	35.00
Light Bulb, Mickey Mouse & Friends, Noma, 7 Light String	67.50
Light Bulb, Mickey Mouse & Friends, Plastic Shades, 8 Pc.	75.00
Light Bulb, Mickey Mouse, Noma, Box, 1930s	125.00
Light Bulb, Moon Mullins .... 28.00 To	45.00
Light Bulb, Mother Goose	20.00

Light Bulb, Nursery Rhyme, Noma, Original Box 55.00
Light Bulb, Orphan Annie .... 45.00 To 48.00
Light Bulb, Parakeet .... 6.00 To 25.00
Light Bulb, Parrot 25.00
Light Bulb, Pig 40.00
Light Bulb, Pinnochio 38.00
Light Bulb, Quilted, Blue Milk Glass 45.00
Light Bulb, Reindeer, Wooden Base, Papier–Mache, 1900 .... 55.00
Light Bulb, Rose 15.00
Light Bulb, Santa Claus, Celluloid 10.00
Light Bulb, Santa Claus, Face On Both Sides, 2 1/2 In. 25.00
Light Bulb, Santa Claus, Face, Bell Shape, Japan 30.00
Light Bulb, Santa Claus, Full Figure, Milk Glass 35.00
Light Bulb, Santa Claus, Roly Poly, Japan 42.50
Light Bulb, Santa Claus, With Toys, Japan 35.00
Light Bulb, Smitty, Head 45.00
Light Bulb, Snowman, Japan 22.50
Light Bulb, Star 12.00
Light Bulb, String, Colored Birds, Plastic 17.50
Light Bulb, Violin, Milk Glass 15.00
Light Bulb, Watch, Milk Glass 25.00
Light Bulb, Zeppelin, Milk Glass 40.00
Light Shade, Scrappy, Set of 8 .... 75.00
Light, Blown Glass, Diamond, Folded Rim, 3 In. 20.00
Light, Blown Glass, Ornament Shape, Silver 12.00
Light, Blown, Yellow Amber, Expanded Diamond, 3 In. 75.00
Light, Diamond–Quilted, Amethyst, Blown, 2 7/8 In. 95.00
Light, Diamond–Quilted, Emerald Green, Blown, 3 1/2 In. 80.00
Light, Expanded Diamond, Light Green, Blown, 2 7/8 In. 105.00
Ornament, 3–Masted Ship, Dresden, 4 1/2 In. 190.00
Ornament, Airship, Propellers, Silver 65.00
Ornament, Angel, Die Cut Face 100.00
Ornament, Angel, Treetop, Gold Paper, White Hair 45.00
Ornament, Angel, Treetop, Papier–Mache, 19th Century 95.00
Ornament, Angel, Wax Head, Wings & Body, Dresden 50.00
Ornament, Antique Car, Hallmark, 1977 .... 24.00
Ornament, Automobile 100.00
Ornament, Aviator, Blown Glass 15.00
Ornament, Baby In Buggy, Blown Glass 220.00
Ornament, Balloon, Die Cut, Blue, 4 In. 35.00
Ornament, Balloon, Wire Wrapped, With Die Cut Angel 35.00
Ornament, Banquet Lamp, Glass, Victorian, 5 1/2 In. 15.00
Ornament, Bear, Cotton 75.00
Ornament, Bell, With Santa Face 22.00
Ornament, Bird, Victorian, Clip–On 17.50
Ornament, Birdcage, Blown Glass 25.00
Ornament, Black Child, Leading Donkey, 3 In. 25.00
Ornament, Bonzo, Felt Over Papier–Mache, 3 1/2 In. 145.00
Ornament, Boot, Silver, Czechoslovakia 65.00
Ornament, Boy, Dutch, On Swing, Bisque, Box 85.00
Ornament, Butterfly, Composition Body, Spun Glass Wings 75.00
Ornament, Butterfly, Glass Body, Spun Glass Wings 125.00
Ornament, Candle, On Limb Clip, Frosted Glass, Victorian 20.00
Ornament, Candle, Red Flame, Silver, 6 In., 3 Piece 18.00
Ornament, Candleholder, Wooden, Goosefeather Trim, Pair 18.00
Ornament, Candyville Express, Hallmark, 1981 .... 21.50
Ornament, Cannon, Silver, Dresden, 3 1/2 In. 200.00
Ornament, Carousel, Hallmark, 1978 .... 125.00
Ornament, Cat, Black, Blown 80.00
Ornament, Cat, Dresden, 3–D 125.00
Ornament, Champagne Bottle, Silver, Dresden, 4 In. 100.00
Ornament, Child, Holding Teddy Bear, 1920s, 3 In. 150.00
Ornament, Christmas Tree, Clip–On, Victorian 26.00
Ornament, Church, Cardboard, Sand Pebble, Czechoslovakia 35.00

Ornament, Clown Head, Spike Hat, Unsilvered, Clip, 6 In. 395.00
Ornament, Clown, On Ball 65.00
Ornament, Cockatoo, In Hoop, Dresden, 3 5/8 In. 175.00
Ornament, Cornucopia, Silver Paper 30.00
Ornament, Cuckoo Clock 25.00
Ornament, Dirigible, Blown Glass 25.00
Ornament, Dog, Retriever, Dresden, 2 3/4 In. 300.00
Ornament, Dragonfly, Heart, Glass, 1920s 45.00
Ornament, Ear of Corn, Gold 75.00
Ornament, Elephant, Blown Glass 28.00
Ornament, Elf On Mushroom, Glass 40.00
Ornament, Fantasia, Box, 12 Piece 25.00
Ornament, Father Christmas, Hands Folded 60.00
Ornament, Fish, 4 In. 25.00
Ornament, Fish, Gold, Dresden, Large 145.00
Ornament, Girl, Victorian, On Swing, Bisque, Box 85.00
Ornament, Goat, Cart, Silver, Dresden, 3 3/4 In. 450.00
Ornament, Heart, 2 1/2 In. 10.00
Ornament, Horse, Blue, Blown 80.00
Ornament, Horseshoe, Jockey, Horse, Dresden, 2 In. 150.00
Ornament, House, 6 Sides, Snow On Roof 12.00
Ornament, House, Blown Glass 6.00
Ornament, Ice Cream Cone 19.00
Ornament, Jesus, Head 95.00
Ornament, Lantern, Paper, Japan, 2 1/2 In. 7.00
Ornament, Lion With Tennis Racket, Blown Glass 25.00
Ornament, Man In Moon .... 35.00 To 45.00
Ornament, Matchless Christmas, Hallmark, 1979 .... 20.00
Ornament, Mouse, Blown Glass 475.00
Ornament, Mr.Salty, Nabisco 15.00
Ornament, Mushroom, Pink, In Tinsel Basket 32.50
Ornament, Owl .... 20.00 To 25.00
Ornament, Parrot, Clip–On 65.00
Ornament, Peacock, Spun Glass Tail 25.00
Ornament, Pear, Spun Cotton, 1 1/2 In. 10.00
Ornament, Pickle, Pale Green 105.00
Ornament, Pineapple 97.50
Ornament, Pinecone, Berries, Victorian 35.00
Ornament, Pipe, Jeweled Bowl, 7 1/2 In. 125.00
Ornament, Pluto, Blown Glass 15.00
Ornament, Popeye, Holding White Star, Olive On Top, 8 In. 18.00
Ornament, Rabbit, With Lettuce, Cotton 50.00
Ornament, Reindeer, 3, German, Iron 45.00
Ornament, Revolver, Pink & Blue 125.00
Ornament, Roly Poly 45.00
Ornament, Rooster, Brown, Gold, Dresden, 3 1/8 In. 140.00
Ornament, Sailboat, Pink & Silver 20.00
Ornament, Santa Claus On Sled, Papier–Mache, 4 In. 45.00
Ornament, Santa Claus, Bendable, Paper, 1800, 2 In. 18.00
Ornament, Santa Claus, Clip–On, Large 75.00
Ornament, Santa Claus, Green Coat, With Tree, 3 In. 20.00
Ornament, Santa Claus, Metal Garland, Red Paper, 8 In. 28.00
Ornament, Santa Claus, On Pine Cone 45.00
Ornament, Ship, Blown Glass 45.00
Ornament, Snowflake, Sterling Silver, Gorham 32.50
Ornament, Snowman, Cotton Batten, 5 In. 15.00
Ornament, Snowman, Holding Broom 20.00
Ornament, Soldier, Yarn, Package, 1973 .... 18.00
Ornament, Star, 3–D Glass 40.00
Ornament, Stork, Blue Unsilvered, 1 Leg Up, Germany 50.00
Ornament, Stork, Flying 100.00
Ornament, Swan, Tail, Blown Glass 18.00
Ornament, Teapot, Blown Glass 8.00
Ornament, Teapot, Silver 35.00

Ornament, Tomato, Unsilvered Red 95.00
Ornament, Treetop, Blown Glass 7.00
Ornament, Tulip, Frosted Glass 25.00
Ornament, Umbrella, Victorian 30.00
Ornament, Watermelon Slice .... 85.00 To 90.00
Ornament, Zeppelin, Los Angeles 135.00
Stand, Green, Red Wreath, Lettering, Cast Iron, 13 In. 35.00
Stand, Musical, Eckert 450.00
Stand, Wooden, Germany 40.00
CHRISTMAS, Bank, Santa Claus, Battery Operated, HTC Co., 1960, Box 125.00
Bank, Santa Claus, Belsnickle Type, Cast Iron 300.00
Bell, Paper, Red & Green, Unfold, 14 In. 2.25
Book, Santa Claus, Fuzzy Wuzzy Picture, 1947 .... 25.00
Box, Santa, With Deer, Windup, Strauss, 12 In. 525.00
Display, Santa Claus, Cotton, Mask Face, 1940s, 26 In. 200.00
Display, Santa On Roof, Pack, Mechanical, From Marshall Fields 95.00
Figure, Father Christmas, Carrying Toys, Bisque, 4 1/4 In. 150.00
Figure, Santa Claus, Celluloid Head, Rings Bell, Windup, Japan 35.00
Figure, Santa Claus, Die Cut, Mica, Germany, 16 In. ....*Illus* 200.00
Figure, Santa Claus, In Sleigh, 1 Reindeer, Cotton Batting, 1930s 75.00
Figure, Santa Claus, Papier-Mache, 4 In. 39.00
Figure, Santa Claus, Papier-Mache, 10 1/2 In. 28.00
Figure, Santa Claus, Papier-Mache, Blue Pants, C.1900, 5 In. 100.00
Figure, Santa Claus, Papier-Mache, Red, White, 10 In. 30.00
Figure, Santa Claus, Standing, White Cotton Beard, 1930s, Large 225.00
Figurine, Santa Claus, Celluloid Face, Mesh Body, 10 In. 32.00
Figurine, Santa Claus, Red Felt, Peaked Hats, 5 In., Pair 110.00
Game, Trim-A-Tree, Santa Claus, Box 15.00
Lamp, Christmas Tree, Miniature 65.00
Mask, Santa Claus, Straw Stuffed, 24 In. 195.00
Mug, Blown-Out Santa Claus, Figural Santa Handle, Child's 28.00
Music Box, Santa Coming From Chimney, Battery Operated, Japan 35.00
Nativity Scene, Cardboard, Box, 30 In. 18.00
Plate, Merry Christmas, Blimp, 1912 .... 38.00
Plate, Roses, A Merry Christmas, Bavarian, 8 In. 20.00
Santa, Blue Trousers, Long Red Coat, Papier-Mache 115.00
Santa, In Sleigh, Pulled By Reindeer, Papier-Mache 35.00
Spoon, Santa Claus, Chimney, Fireplace, Sterling, Demitasse 48.00
Teapot, Covered, Child's, Angel, Blue 90.00
Tumbler, Santa, Holding Christmas Tree Ornament 28.00
Village Set, Fence, 8 Buildings, Cardboard 60.00

Art Deco chrome items became popular in the 1930s. Collectors are most interested in pieces made by the Chase Brass and Copper Company of Waterbury, Connecticut.

CHROME, Ashtray, Tennis Racket, Chase Brass 12.00
Bowl, Nude Holding Green Glass Bowl, Deco, Farber Bros., 7 1/2 In. 65.00
Bread Box, Roll Up Doors, Large 15.00
Cigarette Case & Lighter, Art Deco, Ronson 25.00
Cocktail Shaker, 6 Stemmed Chrome Cocktails, Tray, Handles 300.00
Cocktail Shaker, Horizontal Panels, Wood Handle, Farber Bros. 15.00
Coffee Set, Walter Von Nessen, 3 Piece 385.00
Coffee Urn, Teak Accents, Art Deco, Manning-Bowman, 15 In. 125.00
Dish, Pickle, Farberware, Oval, Amethyst Insert, Fork 18.00
Ice Cream Set, Chase, 7 Piece 47.00
Inkwell, Glass Insert, Black Glass Stand, Pen Ridge, 3 1/2 X 4 In. 35.00
Lamp, Desk, Chase 20.00
Silent Butler, Goldtone, Bakelite Handle, Marked 35.00
Toaster, Black Pulls On Side Doors 15.00
Toaster, Flip, Electric 95.00
Tray, Chase, 11 1/2 In. 15.00
Tray, Folding, 3 Tiers, Chase 15.00
Tray, Tidbit, Chase, 3 Tiers 17.00
Tumbler, Chase, 5 Piece 22.00

Carved wooden or cast iron figures were used as advertisements in front of the Victorian cigar store. The carved figures are now collected as folk art. They range in size from counter type, about three feet, to over eight feet high.

CIGAR STORE FIGURE, Indian Chief, Countertop, Plaster, C.1900	575.00
Indian Maiden, 4 Ft.	4500.00
Indian Maiden, Headdress, Tobacco In Hand, 41 1/2 In.	2800.00
Indian, Carved Wood, Painted, 6 Ft.	4500.00
Indian, Cast Iron, 19th Century, 24 In., Pair	1650.00
Indian, Painted, 6 Ft.	4500.00
Indian, Reclining, Chalkware, Word Ohio, 25 In.	250.00

Cinnabar is a vermilion or red lacquer. Some pieces are made with hundreds of thicknesses of the lacquer that is later carved.

CINNABAR, Figurine, Horse	900.00
Spoon, Snuff, Ivory	95.00

Civil War mementos are important collectors' items. Most of the pieces are military items used from 1861 to 1865.

CIVIL WAR, Bayonet, Scabbard, Springfield, Angular	60.00
Belt, Leather, Brass Buckle, Cartridge Box, Baker & McKenne	400.00
Binoculars, Lamier, Paris, Large	45.00
Bond, Military, Confederate $1000.00, Hand Signed, 1862	25.00
Buckle, Brass, Oval, Embossed U.S.	150.00
Button, Large	3.50
Button, T–E–X–A–S Between 5 Point Star, Confederate	35.00
Carbine Socket, Leather, US	15.00
Carpetbag	35.00 To 65.00
Drum, Painted, New York State Coat of Arms	600.00
Fife, Rosewood	90.00
Flag, 34 Stars, Repaired, 6 Ft.X 8 Ft.9 In.	245.00
Handcuffs, Key	125.00
Hatchet, Camp, Ft.Sanders, Wy.	4.00
Knife, Utility, Wooden Grip, Brass Rivets, 7 In.	75.00
Model, Camp Stool, Nathaniel Johnson, Hudson Street, N.Y.	125.00
Mold, Bullet, 32 Caliber	15.00
Poster, Col. David B. Birney's Zouave Regiment	13.00
Spoon, Union Soldier, Brass	4.00
Stool, Camp, Nathaniel Johnson Patent Model	80.00
Sword, Scabbard, Etched Blade	150.00
Uniform, Dress, Coat & Hat	1100.00
CKAW, see Dedham	

Clambroth glass, popular in the Victorian era, is a grayish color and is semiopaque like clambroth.

CLAMBROTH, Candlestick, Pewter Socket, Ripley, 19th Century, 11 In., Pair	200.00
Candlestick, Stareh–Blue Columnar, Boston & Sandwich, Pair	1775.00
Eggcup, Bull's–Eye Pattern, Covered, Sandwich	475.00
Lamp, Fluid, Acanthus Pattern, Jade Green	1320.00
Lamp, Stepped Base, Sanded, Tulip Font, Pewter Collar, 12 In.	375.00
Lamp, Whale Oil, Acanthus Leaf, Brass Stem, 11 In.	395.00
Loving Cup, Titonka, Iowa, 4 In.	12.50
Mug, Souvenir, Benton, Wisc.	12.00
Pickle Scoop, Hanging, Glass	17.50
Rolling Pin, Glass, Wooden Handles	45.00
Sugar, Covered, Cased Blue, Clear Foot, Pyramid Shape, 10 1/2 In.	400.00
Syrup, Paneled, Pewter Top	225.00
Toothpick, Souvenir, Manston, Wis.	18.50
Vase, Blue Flower, 10 In.	25.00

Clarice Cliff NEWPORT POTTERY ENGLAND   Clarice Cliff was a designer who began working at several English factories in the 1920s. She died in 1972.

CLARICE CLIFF, Basket, Celtic Harvest, Cream, Gold, Fruits, Flowers, 12 In.	225.00

Biscuit Jar, Bizarre, Floral Handles & Finial, 7 1/4 In.	150.00
Bowl, Cereal, Tonquin, Plum	3.00
Bowl, Fantasque, Houses, Trees, Octagonal, 8 In.	200.00 To 225.00
Bowl, Seascape & Landscape, 10 In.	150.00
Cache Pot, Fantasque, 4 In.	85.00
Candleholder, Bowl of Flowers On Post, Gold Stars, 2 In.	65.00
Chicken & 3 Eggcups, 6 In.	150.00
Cup & Saucer, Bizarre, Gay Day, Marked, Dish, 5 In.	75.00
Cup & Saucer, Geometric	40.00
Cup & Saucer, Tea Plate, Bizarre, 5 7/8 In.Plate	110.00
Cup & Saucer, Tonquin, Plum	4.00
Cup, Saucer & Plate, Bizarre, Plate 5 3/4 In.	110.00
Dish, Cheese, Covered, Fantasque	135.00 To 150.00
Flower Frog, Bizarre, Brown, Green Mottling, Gray, 4 In.	65.00
Gravy Boat & Platter, Tonquin, Miniature	40.00
Gravy Boat, Underplate, Tonquin, Small	20.00
Honey Pot, Beehive, Covered	95.00
Jam Jar, Bizarre, Apple Shape, Marked, 3 3/8 In.	110.00
Jam Jar, Celtic Harvest	125.00
Jam Jar, Gay Day	125.00
Jug, Fantasque Bizarre, Landscape, Marked, 5 3/4 In.	195.00
Match Holder, Striker, Bizarre, Nasturtium, Marked, 2 3/4 In.	135.00
Pitcher, Crocus, 8 In.	90.00 To 100.00
Pitcher, Fantasque, 7 In.	140.00 To 175.00
Plaque, Bizarre	450.00
Plate, Geometric, Square, 10 In.	95.00
Plate, Tonquin, 10 1/2 In.	15.00
Platter, Bizarre, Water Lily, Oval, 12 In.	55.00 To 65.00
Platter, Tonquin, 11 In.	30.00
Platter, Water Lily, 12 In.	50.00
Soup, Dish, Flat, Devonshire, Royal Staffordshire	3.00
Sugar & Creamer, Tonquin, Individual	23.00
Teapot, Moderne	175.00
Vase, Bizarre, Delicia, Square, 8 X 5 In.	175.00
Vase, Bizarre, Sea & Landscape, 7 In.	120.00
Vase, Blown–Out, Parrots, 8 1/2 In.	275.00
Vase, Crocus, Bizarre, Yellow Top Band, 7 3/4 In.	195.00
Vase, Fantasque, Exotic Designs, Orange Top Band, 9 1/2 In.	575.00
Vase, Parrots, 8 1/2 In.	275.00
Vase, Viscaria, 8 In.	125.00

Clewell ware was made in limited quantities by Charles Walter Clewell of Canton, Ohio, from 1902 to 1955. Pottery was covered with a thin coating of bronze, then treated to make the bronze turn different colors. Pieces covered with copper, brass, or silver were also made. Mr. Clewell's secret formula for blue patina bronze was burned when he died in 1965.

CLEWELL, Bowl, Metal Frame, 5 1/4 X 6 1/4 In.	125.00
Lamp, With Hardware, 11 In.	30.00
Vase, Bud, Patina, Marked, 8 3/4 In.	130.00
Vase, Bulbous, Ear of Corn, 10 In.	275.00
Vase, Dandelion Design, Signed, 6 In.	210.00
Vase, Flared Top, Patina, Signed, 15 1/2 In.	700.00
Vase, Slip Floral Design, Copper, Owens, 6 In.	225.00

Clews pottery was made by George Clews & Co. of Brownhill Pottery, Tunstall, England, from 1806 to 1861.

CLEWS, see also Flow Blue

CLEWS, Dish, Daisy & Button, Oriental Scene, 8 3/4 In.	125.00
Dish, Vegetable, Letter of Introduction, Errand Boy On Back, Blue	395.00
Plate, Doctor Syntax, Marked, 10 In.	150.00
Plate, Playing At Draughts, Marked, 1850, 10 In.	210.00
Plate, Valentine, Blue, 9 In.	160.00

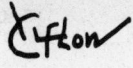

Clifton Pottery was founded by William Long in Clifton, New Jersey, in 1905. He worked there until 1908 making a line called "Crystal Patina." Clifton Pottery made art pottery. Another firm, Chesapeake Pottery, sold majolica marked "Clifton ware."

CLIFTON, Coffeepot, Bulbous Neck To Waist, Flared Base, Gold, 7 1/2 In. 145.00
    Pitcher, Indian Ware, 4 1/2 X 6 1/2 In. 45.00
    Platter, Blackberry, Marked, 10 1/2 In. 110.00
    Teapot, Crystal Patina, 7 In. .... 125.00 To 150.00
    Teapot, Lid, Matte Green, Marked 35.00
    Vase, Crystal Patina, 8 In. 170.00
    Vase, Indian, Arizona Design, 3 1/2 X 5 1/2 In. 57.00
    Vase, No.233, Indian Design, Terra–Cotta & Black, Marked, 8 X 5 In. 200.00

Clocks of all types have always been popular with collectors. The eighteenth–century tall case, or grandfather's clock, was designed to house a works with a long pendulum. In 1816, Eli Terry patented a new, smaller works for a clock; and the case became smaller. The clock could be kept on a shelf instead of on the floor. By 1840, coiled springs were used and even smaller clocks were made. Battery–powered electric clocks were made in the 1870s.

CLOCK, A.& C.Edwards, Tall Case, Fretwork Hood, Cherry, Columns, 92 In. 1000.00
    Advertising, Authorized Agent, American Airlines, Logo 40.00
    Advertising, Ballantine Beer, Lights Up 55.00
    Advertising, Blatz Beer, Stand–Up, Cast Iron 50.00
    Advertising, Borden's, Pictures Elsie 45.00
    Advertising, Budweiser Beer, Revolving Pocket Watch On Chain, Large 295.00
    Advertising, Busch Beer 25.00
    Advertising, Buster Brown Shoes, Wall, Electric, Pan Clock Co. 85.00
    Advertising, C.V.Bergen & Co.Interlaken, Walnut, 1880, 40 In. 9500.00
    Advertising, Calumet 560.00
    Advertising, Charlie The Tuna, Alarm 35.00
    Advertising, Cities Service Gas Co., Electric 45.00
    Advertising, Coca–Cola, Neon 500.00
    Advertising, Dodge–Plymouth, Neon 475.00
    Advertising, Elgin Watch, Neon 350.00
    Advertising, Eveready Safety Razor 1100.00
    Advertising, Firestone, Tire 22.50
    Advertising, Folger's Coffee, Neon 275.00
    Advertising, Goodyear, Tire Shape, Hard Rubber 45.00
    Advertising, Great Falls Beer 40.00
    Advertising, Hires Root Beer 20.00
    Advertising, Holland Beer, Delft, Key Wind 185.00
    Advertising, Kayo Chocolate Drink 85.00
    Advertising, Kelly–Springfield Tire 25.00
    Advertising, Keystone Paint, Lights Up, Celluloid 45.00
    Advertising, Kist, Telechron 110.00
    Advertising, Krueger Beer, Lighted Sign, 14 X 40 In. 65.00
    Advertising, Mapleton Milling Co., Minn., Inset Wind, 4 X 6 In. 53.00
    Advertising, Merrick's Spool Cotton, School 795.00
    Advertising, Miller Beer, Small 17.50
    Advertising, Monarch Foods 135.00
    Advertising, Morrison–Schiff Franks 40.00
    Advertising, Morton Salt, Girl On Face, Regulator, Oak, C.1913 .... 265.00
    Advertising, Old Grand Dad Whiskey 22.50
    Advertising, Olympia Beer 25.00
    Advertising, Orange Crush, Bottle Cap, Electric 125.00
    Advertising, Pabst Blue Ribbon, What'Ll You Have, Lights Up 95.00
    Advertising, Pearl Beer, Neon 350.00
    Advertising, Penn.Fire Insurance Co.1825–1925, New Haven 125.00
    Advertising, Pepsi–Cola, Neon 295.00
    Advertising, Peters Shoes, Alarm 30.00
    Advertising, Poll Parrot Shoes 575.00
    Advertising, Quaker State, Spinner, Neon 350.00

Advertising, RCA, Gold Record 175.00
Advertising, RCA, His Master's Voice, Advertising Rotates, 1950s 75.00
Advertising, Red Goose Shoes, Plastic & Metal, C.1950, 17 In. 250.00
Advertising, Reed's Tonic 2000.00
Advertising, Rexall Drug Co. 75.00
Advertising, Seagrams Whiskey, With Horses 165.00
Advertising, Sealed Power Piston Rings 12.00
Advertising, Sessions, Goodrich Tire, Non–Electric 45.00
Advertising, Snow King Baking Powder 85.00
Advertising, Stewart Warner, 1930s Refrigerator Shape, Art Deco 365.00
Advertising, Teddy Sno Crop, Bear, Tail Wags, Eyes Roll 50.00
Advertising, Three Feathers Whiskey 50.00
Advertising, Victor Red Seal Record, I Hear You Calling Me 525.00
Advertising, Victory Lozenges, Tin, Arabs, Indians & Sultans, 3 Piece 275.00
Advertising, Winston Cigarettes 22.50
Advertising, Wolf Cloth Cutters Set The Pace, Neon 275.00
Alarm, Bulldog, Cast Iron 500.00
Alarm, Camel Back, 1904 .... 25.00
Alarm, Delepine–Barrois, 1880, 6 In. 235.00
Alarm, Gilbert, Iron Case 30.00
Alarm, Lux, Chrome, Horseshoe 30.00
Alarm, Mickey Mouse, Bradley, Germany, 2 1/2 In.Face 35.00
Alarm, Snoopy, 1970 .... 15.00
Alarm, Union Leader, Blackman 245.00
Alarm, Woody Woodpecker, Animated 185.00
Albrecht Erb, 2 Train Verge Movement, Winged Cock, C.1700, 4 1/2 In. 3300.00
American Clock Co., Regulator, Battery Crystal 375.00
American Clock, Crystal Regulator 450.00
Ansonia, 2 Pillar, China, C.1910 .... 275.00
Ansonia, Bee, Original Tin Box, 1878 .... 50.00
Ansonia, Black Metal, French Style, Gold Trim, 14 In. 175.00
Ansonia, Crystal Palace, Original Dome 650.00
Ansonia, Crystal Regulator, Bow Front 275.00
Ansonia, Double Statue Swinger, Hunter & Fisherman 2900.00
Ansonia, Dresser, Royal Bonn Case, 6 1/4 In. 115.00
Ansonia, Figure of Scholar On Side, Ornate 3250.00
Ansonia, French Empire, Hunter & Fisherman, Pat.1882, 21 1/2 In. 325.00
Ansonia, Girl With Plaque, Louis XIV Style, Time & Strike 250.00
Ansonia, Hunter Model, Swinging Ball 1375.00
Ansonia, King, 8–Day, Time & Strike 250.00
Ansonia, Mantel, Art Nouveau, Cupid Top, Porcelain Dial, 13 In. 145.00
Ansonia, Mantel, Black Marble, 4 Pillars, Brass Trim, Open Escapement 145.00
Ansonia, Mantel, Black Marble, 4 Pillars, Open Escapement, Brass 125.00
Ansonia, Mantel, Cast Iron, Black Stone Blue, Brass Works, 14 In. 45.00
Ansonia, Porcelain, Open Escapement, Mauve & Pink 200.00
Ansonia, Regulator, Crystal, Cavalier 650.00
Ansonia, Swinger, Double Statue, Falconer & Fisherman 2900.00
Ansonia, Toronto, 8–Day, Oak Case 235.00
Asa Munger, Brass, 8–Day, Weight Driven, Mahogany, 1830, 22 X 39 In. 2750.00
Atkins & Porter, Weight, OG, C.1880 .... 145.00
Atlas, Wall, Dutch, Mahogany, 19 In. 100.00

If you find a clock with a complete, original paper label, add 35 percent to the value.

Austrian, Painted & Parcel Gilt, Mantel, Seated Female Atop, 23 In. 1200.00
Banjo, Federal, Mahogany, Brass Bezel, 8–Day Weight, C.1820, 32 In. 650.00
Banjo, Federal, Mahogany, Eglomise Chariot Scene, C.1825, 38 In. 1750.00
Banjo, Mahogany Case, Glass Panels, Woman, Child, Pendulum, Key, 40 In. 1350.00
Banjo, Mahogany, 8–Day, Weight Driven, New England, C.1830, 33 1/2 In. 700.00
Bayard, Mickey Mouse, Head Rocks, 1960s 225.00
Bayard, Pluto, Head Turns 80.00
Bradley, Disney Characters, Castle, Musical Alarm, 1975 .... 75.00
Briggs, Rotary, Pendulum 325.00
C.Molins, George I, Brass, Walnut, Dome Top, 18th Century, 13 In. 7700.00
Calendar, Walnut, 8–Day, Pendulum, Late 19th Century, 24 In. 200.00
Carriage, Drocourt, Repeater, Anglaise Riche, 1880, 7 In. 525.00
Carriage, France, Brass, Beveled Glass Sides, 4 3/4 In. 245.00
Carriage, Repeating, With Alarm, Paul Garnier, C.1860, 5 In. 1540.00
Cartel, Louis XVI, Parcel Gilt Bronze, Female, Clock, 37 In. 1000.00
Case, Tall, Walnut, Arched Door, C.1780, 88 In. 2000.00
Champleve, Garniture, Enameled, Onyx, Gilt Bronze, 13 In., 3 Piece 715.00
Charles X, Mother–of–Pearl Mounted, Urn Holder, Rose Holds Clock 3850.00
Chauncey Jerome, 30–Hour, Reverse Painted, St.George's Edinburgh 110.00
Chelsea, Mantel, Ship's Bell, Mahogany 285.00
Chelsea, Regulator, Walnut, Reverse Painted Door, 8–Day, 35 In. 850.00
Continental, Mantel, Mother–of–Pearl, Steel & Ormolu Mounted, 8 In. 1540.00
Daniel Pratt, Gallery, 8 Sides, Double Fusee Movement, C.1845 .... 600.00
Daniel Pratt, Gallery, Double Fusee Movement, Rosewood, C.1840 .... 695.00
Deka & March, Wall, Roman & Arabic Numerals, Mahogany, Brass, 16 In. 935.00
Desk, Welch Mfg., Brass Face, Mary, Mary Quite Contrary Scene, 6 In. 135.00
Eli Terry, Pillar & Scroll, Federal, Mahogany 1200.00
Eli Terry, Pillar & Scroll, Federal, Mahogany, 1825, 31 In. 1300.00
Eli Terry, Pillar & Scroll, Mahogany & Curly Maple, C.1835, 32 In. 1210.00
Empire Electrometer, No.48, Vestibule, C.1903 .... 685.00
Empire, Mantel, Enamel Dial, Bust of Alexander On Top, 17 /12 In. 1550.00
Ephraim Downes, Pillar & Scroll, Eglomise, C.1825, 31 In. ....*Illus* 750.00
Ezra Stone, Tall Case, Federal, Mahogany, Arched Hood, C.1800, 95 In. 9000.00
F.Kroeber, Mantel, Walnut, Adjustable Pendulum, 18 In. ....*Illus* 150.00
Figural, 3 Graces Support Sphere of Clock On Top, 37 1/2 In. 7150.00
Figural, Elephant, Clock On Top, Gilt Bronze, Sevres, C.1890, 17 In. 1870.00
Figural, Roosevelt, Man of Hour, Not Animated, Electric 85.00
Forrestville, Ogee, 8–Day 150.00
French, Art Deco, Marble, 3 Walking Elephants, 28 1/2 X 6 X 15 In. 400.00
French, Brass Ormolu, Double Bell Strike, Gilt Dial, C.1920, 19 In. 300.00
French, Carriage, Beveled Glass, Brass, 8–Day, Time & Strike, 5 In. 295.00
French, Charles X, Mantel, Lyre Form Case, Side Figures, 17 1/2 In. 880.00
French, Figural, Eagle, Holding Clock, Bronze, Onyx Plinth, 19 In. 935.00
French, Garniture, Bronze, Marble, Standing Females, 24 In., 3 Pc. 2200.00
French, Garniture, Louis XVI, 8–Branch Candelabrum, C.1860, 3 Pc. 6600.00
French, Louis XIV, Cherub At Top, Bronze Dore, C.1880, 25 1/2 In. 5000.00

Clock, Ephraim Downes,
Pillar & Scroll,
Eglomise, C.1825, 31 In.

Clock, F.Kroeber, Mantel, Walnut,
Adjustable Pendulum, 18 In.

Clock, Tall Case,
Simeon Crane, Fretwork,
Pine, C.1810, 86 In.

French, Mantel, Winged Figures Side of Pendulum, Bronze & Marble	1430.00
French, Regulator, Crystal, Bow Front, Mercury Pendulum	350.00
Garniture, Jade Green Alabaster, Art Nouveau, 4–Arm Candelabra	2500.00
General Electric, Blue Mirror	55.00
George Mitchell, Shelf, Mahogany Veneer, Mirrored Door, 35 In.	215.00
German, Angelica Kauffmann–Like Scenes, 5 7/8 X 1 5/8 In.	98.00
German, Carved Walnut, Tree Trunk & Hunter, 19th Century, 37 In.	5775.00
German, Cuckoo, Hand Carved Bird, Leaves, 2 Weights, Large	95.00
German, Cuckoo, Pear Wood, 27 In.	400.00
German, Figural, Frypan, Fork & Knife Hands	52.00
German, Westminster Chime, Mahogany, 26 In.	85.00
Gilbert, Art Nouveau, Bronzed Case, Porcelain Dial	125.00
Gilbert, Banjo, Time & Strike	175.00
Gilbert, Kitchen, Gingerbread, Time & Strike, Label	175.00
Gilbert, Mantel, Pressed Oak Case, Capital No.44, 8–Day, Alarm	125.00
Gilbert, Regulator, No.12, Jewelers, Wall, Grid Iron Pendulum, Oak	3300.00
Gilbert, School, Long Drop, Time & Calendar	335.00
Gilbert, Wall, Jeweler's, Regulator, Grid Iron Pendant	3300.00
Gold & Slate, Gray Matte Dial, Roman Numerals, Gold Hands	475.00
Gustav Becker, Free Swinger, Brass Face, Carved Oak, 4 Ft.	2750.00
Gustav Becker, Regulator, Vienna, 2 Weight, 48 In.	1100.00
Gustav Becker, Wall, C.1900	225.00
Haddon, Electric, Home Sweet Home, Animated Lady Rocking	95.00
Hamilton, Wall, Ship's Style, Sagamo, 1920s	65.00
Hamilton, Wall, Windup, 8–Day, Westminster Chimes, Oak	175.00
Hammond, Calendar, Black Bakelite Case, Art Deco	65.00
Herschede, Mantel, Westminster Chime	125.00
Herschede, Tall Case, Westminster Chimes, 5 Tubes, Mahogany, 79 In.	1650.00
Hickory, Dickory Dock, 3–D Wooden Mice Travels Up Clock, Rings Bell	995.00
Howard & Davis, No.3, Banjo, Reverse Painting, Ships At Sea, 38 In.	2050.00
Howard, Banjo, Rosewood Finish, Reverse Painted, Original Label	2000.00
Howard, Banjo, Wooden, Red Paint, Brass Movement, 3 1/2 In.	600.00
Howard, Regulator, Walnut, Gallery Top, 8–Day, Weight Driven, 40 In.	900.00
Howard, Wall, Marble Face, Brass Banjo, Wooden Case, 43 In.	600.00
Howard, Weight Driven, Watchmen's, Oak, 5 Ft. X 22 In.	1500.00
Ingersoll, Big Bad Wolf, Mouth Opens, 1934	250.00
Ingraham, Banjo, Treasure Island	450.00
Ingraham, Bugs Bunny, Arm Lifts Carrot, 1950s	325.00
Ingraham, Kitchen, Eastlake, Time & Strike	185.00
Ingraham, Roy Rogers, Roy & Trigger Move, Box, 1951	250.00
Ingraham, Store, Regulator, With Calendar	250.00
Ingraham, Time & Calendar, Oak, Store	325.00
Internationl, School, Regulator, Master, Oak, 5 Ft.	550.00
Isaac Brokaw, Tall Case, 2 Weights, Mahogany, C.1810, 8 Ft.	3630.00
Ithaca, Calendar, 8–Day, Walnut Case	1600.00
Ithaca, Double Dial Calendar, Walnut Case	975.00
Ithaca, Tall Case, C.1900, 87 In.	800.00
J.Dunning, Banjo, Mantel, 8–Day, Strike, Mahogany, C.1830, 33 1/2 In.	3000.00
J.Flickman, Bracket, Roman & Arabic Numerals, Brass Handle, 19 In.	3850.00
J.Jukes, Tall Case, Flame Veneer, Brass Works, Calendar, Mahogany	1700.00
J.Latham, George I, Ebony, Bracket, Arched Door, 18th Century	5500.00
J.Smith, Tall Case, Queen Anne, Silver Dial, Walnut, 18th Century	3750.00
Jacob Leby, Grandfather, Hepplewhite, Cherry, Calendar, 89 In.	2300.00
Jaeger Le Coultre, Atmospheric, 1960	500.00
James Wady, Tall Case, Queen Anne, Mahogany, C.1765, 7 Ft. 6 In.	9075.00
Japy Freres, Gilt Bronze, Champleve, Cherub, Chimes, 1860, 16 In.	550.00
Jefferson Golden Hour, Art Deco, Electric	185.00
Jerome & Co., Wooden Cottage, Rocket	82.00
Jerome, 8–Day, Time & Strike, Empire Column, Mahogany	175.00
Jerome, Beehive, 8–Day	185.00
Jerome, Empire, Time & Strike, 8–Day, Mahogany	175.00
Jeweler's, Regulator, Walnut, Glass Sides, Sweep Seconds	36.00
John Phillipi, Tall Case, Mahogany, C.1790	3150.00
John Taylor, Bracket, George III, Ormolu Mounted	7150.00

Clock, Mantel, Art Deco, Kneeling Women,
7 X 13 X 5 In.

Clock, Mantel, Oriental Beast,
Bronze, 21 In.

Joseph A.Wells, Gothic, Shelf, 30–Hour Time & Strike, 1845–50	3000.00
Junghans, 8–Day, Striking, C.1900	325.00
Kitchen, Wall, Green & Ivory China, 8–Day, Square, 9 In.	30.00
Lady With Fan, Fan Rocks Over Eyes, 1880s	475.00
Levi & Abel Hutchins, Tall Case, Brass Dial, Calender, 1790, 83 In.	5000.00
Liberty & Co., Art Deco, Pewter, Tudric, 9 In.	215.00
Louis Phillipe Style, Inlaid Ebony, Late 19th Century, Wall, 47 In.	400.00
Louis XVI, Carter, Enamel Dial, Scrolled Case, Urn Finial, 27 In.	1750.00
Lux, Hanging, Movable Birds	50.00
Lux, Organ Grinder With Bear, Arm Rotates, 1930s	275.00
Lux, Shoe Shine Boy, Arm Moves Up & Down, 1930	250.00
Lux, Showboat, Mississippi Steam Boat, Paddle Turns, 1950s	185.00
Lux, Spinning Wheel, Rotates, Alarm On Back, Lebanon, Tenn., 1956	95.00
Majak, Crystal Bezel Around Clock, 11 Jewels, Made In USSR	85.00
Mantel, 17th–Century Soldiers, Bell Shields, Spelter, 1870	350.00
Mantel, Art Deco, Kneeling Women, 7 X 13 X 5 In. _Illus_	120.00
Mantel, Bust of Diana, Bronze, Slate, Time & Strike, France, 21 In.	275.00
Mantel, Charles X, Chariot Wheel Clock, Bronze, Plinth, 13 X 19 In.	1050.00
Mantel, Charles X, Strike In Body of Dolphin, 14 X 21 In.	4400.00
Mantel, Double Steeple, Mahogany, Spread Eagle Painted Door, 24 In.	850.00
Mantel, Egyptian Revival, Bronze Sphinx, Basalt, C.1900, 17 In.	770.00
Mantel, Empire Parcel Gilt, Mahogany, Classical Figures, 22 In.	650.00
Mantel, Empire, Enamel Dial, Figure of Napoleon Each Side, 13 In.	990.00
Mantel, Gilbert, Black Wood, Ornate Columns, 8 Day	100.00
Mantel, Louis XV, Drum Clock, On Elephant, Bronze, French, 18 In.	6325.00
Mantel, Louis XVI, Gilt Bronze Wreath, Urns, Marble Base, 26 In.	1450.00
Mantel, Louis XVI, Neoclassical, Children Top, Bronze, Strikes, 26 In.	1760.00
Mantel, Mahogany Carved, Empire, Carved Crest, C.1825, 31 In.	1000.00
Mantel, Oriental Beast, Bronze, 21 In. _Illus_	2100.00
Mantel, Ormolu Mounted, Walnut, Floral Swag, Bracket Feet, 18 1/4 In.	700.00
Mantel, Pillar & Scroll, Mark Leavingworth, Reverse Scene Painting	2000.00
Mission, Oak, Square Face, Brass Numerals, Pendulum, Wall, 30 In.	250.00
Mueller & Sons, Topsy, Mantel, Iron	302.50
National, Time Card, Punch–In Type, Oak	575.00
New Haven, Banjo, Time & Strike, Pendulum Movement, 18 In.	225.00
New Haven, Banjo, Whitney, Time & Strike	185.00
New Haven, Figural, Ivanhoe, Porcelain Dial	350.00
New Haven, Gold Dore, White Metal Case, Cupid On Top, 12 X 7 In.	350.00
New Haven, Hand Painted, Carlsbad, Austria, Time & Strike	250.00
New Haven, Mantel, French Style, Black Iron, Ormolu Trim	85.00
New Haven, No.503, 8–Day, Strike, Walnut Case, Stenciled Glass	350.00
New Haven, Regulator, Store, Golden Oak	250.00

New Haven, School, Octagonal, 1890	295.00
New Haven, Teardrop, 8–Day, Strike, Walnut Case, 24 In.	250.00
Night, Lighted Globe, Troubadour Figure, French, C.1850	1100.00
Onyx & Champleve Enamel, Glazed Door, Shelves, C.1900, 4 Ft. 2 In.	7700.00
Parisian, 8–Day, Time & Strike, Walnut	250.00
Paul Vallette, Sterling Silver, Travel, Miniature	160.00
Peter Stretch, Tall Case, Flat Top, Walnut, 18th Century, 84 In.	9900.00
Pratt, Venetian, 8–Day, Time & Strike	165.00
Puss 'N Boots, Eyes Rotate, Blessing, 1960s	30.00
R.Whiting, Tall Case, Swan's Neck Crests, Cherry, 89 In.	2300.00
Roxbury, Tall Case, Mahogany, Strike & Time	8500.00
Royal Bayreuth, Christmas Cactus Pattern, Tapestry, Blue Mark	485.00
Sam Denton, Bracket, George I, Roman, Arabic Numerals, Walnut, 18 In.	1900.00
Sangamo, Mantel, Westminster, 1920s	150.00
Satos Clock, School, Oak, Calendar, Time, Strike, Japan	150.00
School, Short Drop, German, C.1918, Miniature	100.00
Self Winding Clock Co., Time, Western Union–Naval Observatory	1500.00
Sessions, Art Deco, Draped Nude Lady, 13 1/2 In.	110.00
Sessions, Baker & Chef, Electric	25.00
Sessions, Cathedral, Wooden Case	80.00
Sessions, School, Short Drop, Oak, C.1915	125.00
Sessions, Shelf, Black Wood, Metal Feet & Handles, 1900, 11 X 9 In.	68.00
Sessions, Tall Case, Wooden Face, Brass Finials, Cherry, 93 In.	1200.00
Seth Thomas, Banjo, Miniature, Jewelled, 8–Day, 21 In.	95.00
Seth Thomas, Banker's Double Dial Calendar	2250.00
Seth Thomas, Beehive Shape, 8–Day, 10 In.	87.50
Seth Thomas, Blue Mirror Frame, Chrome Trim, Electric, 5 X 7 In.	65.00
Seth Thomas, Carriage, Brass Trim, Nickel Plated Case, 6 1/4 In.	50.00
Seth Thomas, Cincinnati, 8–Day, Rosewood, 16 In.	265.00
Seth Thomas, Double Dial, Calendar, Dated 1878	575.00
Seth Thomas, Dresser, 4–Jewel, Wooden	25.00
Seth Thomas, Kitchen, Oak, 24 In.	195.00
Seth Thomas, Long Case, Wicker, Pendulum	6500.00
Seth Thomas, Mantel, 8–Day, Color Print of Main Hall, Expo 1876	600.00
Seth Thomas, Mantel, Black Marble, Visible Escapement	175.00
Seth Thomas, Mantel, Open Escapement, Marble, Large	250.00
Seth Thomas, Mantel, Railway, Brass, C.1910	130.00
Seth Thomas, Mantel, Tambour, Gold Dial, Roman Numerals, Mahogany	65.00
Seth Thomas, Mantle, Westminster, 8–Day	125.00
Seth Thomas, Reverse Painted Glass, Stenciled Glass Doors, 32 In.	200.00
Seth Thomas, School, Octagonal, Walnut	180.00
Seth Thomas, Semi–Humpback, Rosewood Case	65.00
Seth Thomas, Shelf, Nickel Finish, Metal Alarm, Roman Numerals, 9 In.	75.00
Seth Thomas, Ship's Bell, Art Nouveau Bronze Base, Signed Darot	325.00
Seth Thomas, Sonora, 8 Bells, Whitington & Westminster Chimes	775.00
Seth Thomas, Triple Deck, 8–Day, Time & Strike, Label	375.00
Seth Thomas, Watchman's, 30–Day, Nickel Bob & Movement, C.1900	975.00
Seth Thomas, Weight Driven, Cherry, Plymouth Hollow, 8–Day	225.00
Shaker, Wall, Projecting Cove Cornice, 30 In.	990.00
Shelf, Ansonia, Apex, 2–Vial Mercury Pendulum, Open Escapement	2900.00
Shelf, Briggs, Rotary, C.1880, 8 1/4 In.	225.00
Silver Bronze, Stepped Sides, Stylized Birds, C.1930, 8 1/4 In.	2420.00
Spilhouse, Space Astro, Lighted Type	225.00
Standard, Regulator, Oak, 5 Ft.	425.00
Standard, Regulator, Oak, With Program, 1915	600.00
Statue of Liberty, Lady's Head, Shelf, Walnut	175.00
Steeple, Mahogany, Reverse Painting, Brass Works, C.1860, 20 In.	100.00
Stewart, Case, Brass Face, Weights, Glasgow, 1840–50	4900.00
Swiss, Bracket, Musical, Painted, Rococo, Enamel Dial, 4 Ft. 3 In.	5500.00
Tall Case, Bird's–Eye Maple Door, Scrolled Crest, Wooden Works	1450.00
Tall Case, Black Lacquer, Bevel Glass Door, C.1870, 89 In.	4500.00
Tall Case, Calendar, Brass Works, Metal Face, Mahogany, 87 In.	1500.00
Tall Case, Calendar, Hepplewhite, Brass Works, Cherry, 89 1/2 In.	2300.00
Tall Case, Calendar, Moon Dial, Mahogany Veneer, Cherry, 87 1/2 In.	1600.00

Tall Case, Elliot, Westminster, Wittington Chimes, 9–Tube	8900.00
Tall Case, Federal, Cherry, Swan's Neck Crest Hood, 1790, 93 In.	4000.00
Tall Case, Hepplewhite, Cherry, Inlaid, Wooden Works, 92 1/2 In.	3750.00
Tall Case, Inlaid Mahogany, 4 Seasons, Arch, 6 Ft.11 In.	2310.00
Tall Case, J.Scott, Oak & Mahogany, C.1840	4000.00
Tall Case, New England, Glazed Door, Iron Dial, C.1790, 90 In.	3200.00
Tall Case, New Hampshire, Birch, Brass Weight, Red Paint, 93 In.	4100.00
Tall Case, Regulator, Jeweler's, Mahogany, Pinwheel Escapement	7000.00
Tall Case, Simeon Crane, Fretwork, Pine, C.1810, 86 In. ....*Illus*	5750.00
Tall Case, Stepped Corbels, Open–Sided, Mission Oak, C.1910, 74 In.	600.00
Tall Case, Walnut, Brass Weight Driven, Lancaster County, Pa., 8 Ft.	9500.00
Tall Case, Walnut, Glass Panel, Bracket Feet, Fluted Columns	3000.00
Tall Case, William & Mary, Walnut & Marquetry, G.Etherington, 84 In.	6000.00
Telegraph Synchronous, Postal, Large	80.00
Terry, 8–Day, Wooden Works	750.00
Thomas Scott, Tall Case, Admiral Lord Nelson & Fleet Scene, C.1790	2395.00
CLOCK, TIFFANY, see Tiffany, Clock	
Time Recording Co., Wall, Oak, 37 In.	375.00
Vernis Martin, Louis XV Style, In Gilt–Bronze Case, C.1900, 14 In.	1100.00
Vincenti, Mantel, Brass Ormolu, Boy On Ladder, C.1855, 16 In.	485.00
W.Anderson, Tall Case, Inlaid Mahogany, C.1800, 6 Ft.11 In.	2310.00
W.L.Gilbert, Art Pottery, Light To Dark Brown Glaze, 11 X 13 In.	475.00
W.L.Johnson, Mantel, Double Steeple, Reverse Painted Eagle, 24 In.	850.00
Wag–On–The–Wall, Brass Gears, Wooden Plates, Case & Face, 8 In.	100.00
Wag–On–The–Wall, Brass, Wooden Works, Weights, 12 X 17 In.	425.00
Waltham, Regulator, Weight Driven, Golden Oak, 42 In.	850.00
Waterbury No.70, Oak, Regulator, Large Pendulum, Roman Numerals	1155.00
Waterbury, Calendar, Time & Strike, Walnut Case	275.00
Waterbury, Castle Shape, Cast Iron Stand, Bronze Finish, 12 In.	65.00
Waterbury, Cherubs Holding Clock, Brass, Dated 1894, 8 In.	65.00
Waterbury, Eastlake Style, Belfast Model, Walnut	65.00
Waterbury, Gingerbread, 8–Day, Time & Strike, Oak	175.00
Waterbury, Kitchen, Golden Oak .... 150.00 To 250.00	
Waterbury, Oak, Gingerbread, 8–Day, Time & Strike	175.00
Waterbury, Ogee, Reverse Painting On Glass, Alarm	425.00
Waterbury, Regulator, Crystal, Open Escapement	235.00
Waterbury, School, Time, Oak, 7 In.	210.00
Waterbury, Tall Case, Detachable Base, Black Paint, Tin Face, 80 In.	200.00
Waterman, Sambo Blinking Eye, Cast Iron	900.00
Welch, Alarm, Gingerbread, Oak	150.00
Welch, Calendar, Golden Oak	450.00
Welch, Steeple, 8–Day, Time & Strike, Mahogany	195.00
Westinghouse, Porcelain On Iron, Windup, Electric Range, 1920	85.00
Westminster, Grandfather Movement, With Dial, English	150.00
Willard, Banjo, Brass Finial, 8–Day, Reverse Painted Glass, 39 In.	1600.00
Willard, Banjo, Mahogany, Reverse Painted Glass, 32 3/4 In.	2200.00
Willard, Shelf, Repainted Panels & Replaced Finial	3510.00
Williard, Lyre, Reverse Painted Naval Scene, C.1825, 39 In.	2000.00
Wood & Holley, Tall Case, Inlaid, Dated 1780	18500.00
Woody Woodpecker, Box, 1959	45.00
Yorkshire, Tall Case, Quarter–Sawn Oak, 30–Hour, Rope Driven	3250.00

Cloisonne enamel was developed during the tenth century. A glass enamel was applied between small ribbonlike pieces of metal on a metal base. Most cloisonne is Chinese or Japanese. Pieces marked "China" are twentieth–century examples.

CLOISONNE, Bowl, Design Inside & Out, Scrolls, Flowers, Brass Foot, 8 In.	225.00
Bowl, Dragon & Flaming Pearl, 8 In.	175.00
Bowl, Dragon, Covered, Stem, 1800s, 8 In.	185.00
Bowl, Infolded Rim, Foliate Designs, C.1900, 8 1/4 In.	170.00
Box, Incense, Goldstone On Lid, Sprays of Flowers, Oval, 2 In.	90.00
Box, Jewelry, Fitted Interior, 8 1/4 In.	155.00
Box, Snuff, Wall of China, Oval, 2 In.	20.00
Buckle, Belt, Symbolic Lotus Blossoms, Curved, 1 5/8 X 2 3/4 In.	45.00

Buckle, Silver To Lavender, Irises, Clouds, Leaves, 2 Parts	110.00
Bulb Bowl, Imperial Yellow Dragons, Black, Ming Mark, 12 In.	175.00
Candlestick, Floral Design, Blue Ground, Oval Base, 6 In.	65.00
Charger, 3 Butterflies, Flowers, Japanese, 12 In.	425.00
Charger, Bird, Floral, Pierced, Ormolu Mount, Japan, 12 5/8 In.	300.00
Charger, Geometric Border, Roses, Daises, Butterflies, 11 In.	335.00
Cigarette Set, Domed Hinged Box, Ashtray & Matchbox	80.00
Compote, Blue, Polychrome Borders, China, 4 3/4 X 8 In., Pair	150.00
Dish, Covered, Floral On Dark Blue Ground, 4 X 5 In.	45.00
Ewer, Wine, Duck, 1850, 13 In.	250.00
Figurine, Duck, Allover Abstract Design, Aqua, 7 In., Pair	150.00
Figurine, Rooster, Standing On Drum, Pedestal, China, 10 1/4 In.	395.00
Humidor, Foo Dog Finial, Flowers, Leaves, Teakwood Stand, 8 In.	245.00
Incense Burner, Dragon Head & Feet, 6 In.	125.00
Incense Burner, Foo Dog Finial, Allover Sunburst, 9 1/4 In.	350.00
Jar, Animal Cover, China, 19th Century, 17 3/8 In. ....*Illus*	600.00
Jar, Ball Form, Bands of Floral Designs, Japan, 4 In.	50.00
Jar, Ginger, Domed Shape, Covered, White, 4 X 4 3/4 In., Pair	145.00
Jar, Potpourri, Covered, Flowers, Butterflies, 4 1/4 In.	265.00
Jar, Powder, Gold Spattered Cover, Green Ground, 1 1/2 X 3 In.	130.00
Jar, Temple, Covered, Dragons, 19th Century, 15 In.	495.00
Jardiniere, Blue, White, Covered, Square, 12 In., Pair	375.00
Lamp, Peacocks, Yellow Ground, 7 1/4 In., Pair	300.00
Lamp, Piano, Black, Jewelled, Converted Electric, Globe, 35 In.	700.00
Lamp, Table, Ball Shade, White & Black Herons In Flight, 24 In.	1250.00
Mirror & Brush Set, Butterflies, Flowers, Goldstone, Japan, 2 Pc.	525.00
Napkin Ring, Marked China, 2 In., Pair	15.00
Plate, Phoenix Bird In Tree, 5 In.	140.00
Plate, Transparent, Silk Case, 10 In.	300.00
Rose Jar, Lozenges, Floral Sprays, Black Reserves, 4 1/2 In.	285.00
Salt & Pepper, Blue Fishscale Ground, Dragon, Japan, 2 1/2 In.	225.00
Saltshaker, Elongated Pear Shape, Copper Rim Base, 2 3/4 In.	135.00
Sword, Sheath, 1800s, 42 In.	600.00
Tea Jar, Flowers, Dark Green Ground, Inner Lid, Japan, 4 X 3 In.	489.00
Teapot, Butterflies, Panels	195.00
Teapot, Floral, Cobalt, Shield Shaped Medallions, Japan, 4 In.	235.00
Tray, 3–Toed Dragon Center, Geometric Design, 1800s, 12 In.	250.00
Tray, Dragons, Flowers, Vines, Gold Cinnabar, 12 3/8 In.	100.00
Vase, 4–Lobed, Alternating Cranes & Butterflies, Red, 6 1/4 In.	60.00
Vase, 6 Sides, Exotic Birds, Dragons, Goldstone Band, 9 1/2 In.	395.00
Vase, Bird In Cherry Tree, Blossoms, Pink Ground, 18 1/2 In.	1100.00
Vase, Birds & Flowers, Red, 11 3/4 In.	1200.00

Cloisonne, Vase, Floral, Cobalt Blue, 3 1/4 In;   Cloisonne, Jar, Animal Cover, China,
Butterfly Design, Striped Ground, 4 3/4 In.   19th Century, 17 3/8 In.

Vase, Birds & Flowers, White Branches, Green Branches, 12 In. 1200.00
Vase, Birds, Bronze, Demon Handles, Base, 19th Century, 8 In. 120.00
Vase, Butterfly Design, Striped Ground, 4 3/4 In. ....*Illus* 70.00
Vase, Chrysanthemums On Dark Green Ground, Signed, 12 5/16 In. 450.00
Vase, Chrysanthemums, Leaves, Daisies, Green Ground, 9 1/2 In. 295.00
Vase, Double Gourd, Panels of Flowers, Fruits, 9 1/2 In., Pair 360.00
Vase, Dragon, Birds, Banners, Floral Bands, Copper, Japan, 14 In. 325.00
Vase, Draped White Flowers, Black Ground, 19th Century, 4 In. 190.00
Vase, Eagles On Dogwood Branches, Blue Ground, 13 In., Pair 1250.00
Vase, Egyptian Frieze, Champleve, 1800s, 7 In. 70.00
Vase, Floral, Cobalt Blue, 3 1/4 In. ....*Illus* 40.00
Vase, Flowers, Bird, Modern Ware, Green Trim, Bulbous, 9 In. 125.00
Vase, Flowers, Spray On Back, Gray Ground, 6 1/8 In. 210.00
Vase, Foil, Irises, Blue, Red, Green, Silver, Signed Ginbari, 4 In. 175.00
Vase, Goldstone In Flowers, Phoenix Birds & Dragon, 12 In. 395.00
Vase, Goldstone, Butterflies & Flowers, 3 3/4 In. 75.00
Vase, Narrow Neck, Flared, Green Foil, Scroll Cloisons, 5 In. 95.00
Vase, Red Flowers & Woman, Japan, 5 In. 150.00
Vase, Red Stippled Ground, Roses, 7 1/2 In., Pair 70.00
Vase, Roses, Foliage, Titian Red Field, Diaper, 8 In., Pair 295.00
Vase, Rust Ground, C.1930, 5 X 9 1/2 In. 130.00
Vase, Silver Rims, Base, Vines, Red Enamel, Ruby Ground, 7 In. 135.00
Vase, Spray of Flowers, Foil, Silver Mound Top, Blue, 3 3/4 In. 400.00
Vase, Wren Perched On Flowering Tree, Japan, 8 3/8 In. 550.00

> Antique and collectible clothes of all types are listed in this section.
> Dresses, hats, shoes, underwear and more are found here. Other
> textiles are to be found in the Textile, World War I, World War II,
> Quilt, and Coverlet sections.

CLOTHING, Apron, Blue Calico 8.50
Apron, Homespun, Blue & White Checked 48.00
Baby Bunting, 1920s 18.00
Bathing Suit, Catalina, Label, 1920s 20.00
Bathrobe, White Floral Print, Voile 40.00
Bed Jacket, Quilted, Peach Rayon 10.00
Belt & Club Outfit, Policeman, 1890 .... 90.00
Beret, Red Mohair, Ice Skating, 1915 .... 30.00
Bloomers, Victorian, White Cotton 12.00
Bloomers, Woman's, White, Lace 12.00
Blouse, Ecru, Beading, 1920s 18.00
Blouse, Gibson Girl, White Embossed Net, Brussels Lace Inserts 25.00
Blouse, Irish Crochet Trim, High Neck, White, 1920s 75.00
Blouse, Middy, White Poplin, C.1910 .... 10.00
Blouse, Victorian, Woman's, Black Silk, Cap Sleeves, White Lace 45.00
Blouse, Victorian, Woman's, Brown Silk, High Collar, Capelet 40.00
Blouse, Victorian, Woman's, Ivory Lace, Embroidery, Bone Supports 30.00
Blouse, Victorian, Woman's, White Lawn, Ruffle, Voluminous Sleeves 85.00
Blouse, White Cotton, Tucks Front & Back, 3/4 Sleeves, Edwardian 48.00
Bonnet, Amish, White 40.00
Bonnet, Child's, Amish, Light Blue 25.00
Bonnet, Child's, Victorian, Green Velvet 25.00
Bonnet, Lady's, Black Straw & Net, Maroon Flowers, Lora Label 25.00
Bonnet, Victorian, Maroon Velvet, Iridescent Bird Feathers 80.00
Boots, Child's, White Canvas, Lace Up 28.00
Britches, Hiking, Man's, 1920 .... 28.00
Buckle, Shoe, Steel Beads, French, Pair 15.00
Camisole, Cut & Embroidered Yoke 25.00
Camisole, White Batiste, Pigeon–Breast Front, Size 3–10 .... 35.00
Cap, Baby, Narrow Sheer Battenburg 25.00
Cap, Bicycling, Child's, 2 Buttons Under Chin, 1930–40 .... 5.00
Cap, Christening, Baby, Pearl Buttons, Lattice Ribbon Trim 35.00
Cap, Newsboy's, 1930s, Unused 12.00
Cape, Black Beaded, Shoulder Length, C.1890 .... 20.00
Cape, Black Satin, Beaded, Ribbon, 1890s 15.00

Cape, Muskrat, 10 Tails Around Bottom, Matching Muff, C.1930	40.00
Cape, Nurse's, Wool, 1930s	25.00
Cape, Opera, Black Velvet, White Satin Lining, Full Length, Hood	95.00
Cape, Opera, Monkey Fur Collar, Georgette Lining, 1920	55.00
Cape, Victorian, Plush Velvet, Unlined, 3/4 Length	35.00
Cardigan, Black, Beaded, Pearls, 1940s	22.00
Christening Gown, Crochet Insets, Lace Trim, Slip, 1880, 34 In.	95.00
Coat, Baby's, Victorian, Cape Collar, Lace & Ribbon Trim, Long	35.00
Coat, Black Wool, Black Fur Collar & Cuffs, Cloche Hat, 1930s	15.00
Coat, Broadtail Processed Lamb, N.Y., Short, 1940s, 12–14 Size	65.00
Coat, Child's, Victorian, Brown Velvet, Buttons	30.00
Coat, Child's, White Pique, 1940s	10.00
Coat, Chinese Mandarin, Forbidden Stitch Embroidery, Blue	325.00
Coat, Christening, Yellow Embroidered Design On Skirt & Collar	35.00
Coat, Evening, Fur Trim, Pink Brocade, 1920s	75.00
Coat, Fake Leopard Fur, Girl's, Bonnet, 1920s, Size 4–6, 2 Piece	32.50
Coat, Flapper, Black Velvet, Cream Colored Fur Collar, Hat	20.00
Coat, Frock, Man's, Black	95.00
Coat, Man's, Gray Gabardine, Casablanca Style, 1940s	40.00
Coat, Mauve–Olive Mohair Blend, Lilli Ann, 1920s	65.00
Coat, Monkey Fur, Full–Length, 1930–40s, Large Size	895.00
Coat, Red Wool, Large Fox Collar, Lilli Anne, 1920s	65.00
Coat, Shearling, Chocolate Brown, Padded Shoulder, 1940s	50.00
Coat, Victorian, Child's, White Faille, White Knickers, 2 Piece	110.00
Coat, Victorian, Woman's, White Cashmere, Braid, Silk Lining	80.00
Coat, Woman's, Wool & Mouton, C.1900, Small	65.00
Collar, Arrow, Box of 10	15.00
Corset Cover, Eyelet, Drawstring Top, Buttons, 23 In.Waist	15.00
Corset Repair Kit, Deluxe, Unopened	6.50
Court Livery, Pants, Vest, Loft, English, C.1805	100.00
Cowboy Outfit, Child's, Buck Jones	85.00
Dress, Amish, Blue	32.00
Dress, Baby's, Homespun, Plaid	20.00
Dress, Ball, Gold Satin, 1890s	200.00
Dress, Batiste, White, Embroidered, 1900s	135.00
Dress, Batiste, White, Openwork Waistband, Edwardian, Size 8–10	135.00
Dress, Beaded Black On Black Net, French, 1915	130.00
Dress, Beaded, Silk Chiffon, Art Deco Design, 1920s, Size 10–12	275.00
Dress, Black & White Calico	85.00
Dress, Black Chiffon, Beaded Trim, Godets, 1930s, Size 12–14	135.00
Dress, Black Silk, Jet Beading, 1920s, Size 14	20.00
Dress, Black Wool, Beaded, Shirtwaist, Padded, 1930s, Size 12–14	55.00
Dress, Black, With Red Beading, 1920s	275.00
Dress, Bolero, Crepe, 1930s, 25 In.Waist	30.00
Dress, Bustle Back, Shirring & Ruffles, Ecru Satin, 1880s, 2 Piece	75.00
Dress, Chiffon, Beaded, 1920s	85.00
Dress, Child's, Eyelet, 1910	25.00
Dress, Child's, Kate Greenaway, White Cotton, Eyelet, Lace, Size 4	45.00
Dress, Christening, Ruffles, Tucks, C.1875	55.00
Dress, Cotton, Lace, White, Ankle Length, C.1900	50.00
Dress, Cycling, Balloon Sleeves, Plaid, 1890s, 2 Piece	125.00
Dress, Deco, Black & Red, 1930s	25.00
Dress, Edwardian, Ivory Faille, Square Neck, Tatting	25.00
Dress, Edwardian, Linen, Irish Trim	140.00
Dress, Edwardian, Pink Silk, Chiffon, Ribboned Waist, Ruffles	30.00
Dress, Embroidered, Batiste, White, 1900s	135.00
Dress, Evening, Candlelight Satin, 2–Tiered Cape, 1930s, Size 8–12	135.00
Dress, Evening, Cream & Black Lace, C.1905	1320.00
Dress, Evening, Embroidered Eyelet, Mainbocher, 1940s	137.50
Dress, Evening, Tiered Indigo Silk, Molyneux	1210.00
Dress, Filet Lace, 1920s	135.00
Dress, Floral Print, Lace Trim, Blue Silk, Victorian	150.00
Dress, Fortuny, Pleated Silk, Venetian Beads At Side, 1920s	2850.00
Dress, Georgette Crepe, Candlelight, Tucks, Lace, 1920s, Size 6–8	85.00

Dress, Graduation, White Eyelet, Victorian	35.00
Dress, Gray, Cream Lace & Satin Ribbon Trim, 1890s, 2 Piece	90.00
Dress, High Neck, Mauve Gray Silk, 1890s	95.00
Dress, Jet Beading, Gray Taffeta, Victorian, 2 Piece	95.00
Dress, Jet Beading, Silver Silk Taffeta, 1890s, 2 Piece	125.00
Dress, Lame, 1920s	80.00
Dress, Mourning, Silk Faille, 1890, Size 14	30.00 To 50.00
Dress, Net, Panels, Tiers, C.1915	35.00
Dress, Party, Brocaded Bubble Skirt, Taffeta, Blue, 1950s, Size 12	20.00
Dress, Party, Chiffon, Sequins, Blue, 1920s	20.00
Dress, Pink Chiffon, Allover Bead Work, 1920s	90.00
Dress, Pink Chiffon, Silver Beading, 1920s	85.00
Dress, Pink Wool, Lace Trim, 1890s	125.00
Dress, Prom, Organza, Pink Flowers, French, 1950s	12.50
Dress, Rhinestone Straps, Apricot Skinners Satin, 1930s	85.00
Dress, Shirt, Linen, Red Embroidered Trim, 1940s, Size 12	15.00
Dress, Silk, Pink, Beaded, Rhinestone Top, 1960	35.00
Dress, Silver Beading, Pink Chiffon, 1920s	85.00
Dress, Strapless, Black Lace Over Pink Tulle, Dior	425.00
Dress, Stripe, Brown Challis, 1860s	95.00
Dress, Taffeta, Mauve, Beaded Collar, 1930s, Size 8	45.00
Dress, Tea, Victorian, High Neck, White	68.00
Dress, Victorian, Child's, Gray Patterned Wool, Lace Collar, Cuffs	250.00
Dress, Victorian, Child's, Maroon Faille, Puffed Sleeves	400.00
Dress, Victorian, Ivory Net Over Rose Silk, Petticoat, 2 Piece	250.00
Dress, Victorian, Lace Panels & Insets, White On White	37.50
Dress, Victorian, Lady's, Black Lace, High Collar, Maroon Under	350.00
Dress, Victorian, Lady's, Gauzy Net, Leg O'Mutton Sleeves, Long	425.00
Dress, Victorian, Print, Gray, Black, Empire, Long Skirt, Size 8–10	65.00
Dress, Victorian, Silk, White, Blue Ring Pattern, Long, 2 Piece	60.00
Dress, Walking, Black Silk Faille, C.1870, 3 Piece	385.00
Dress, Walking, Teal Blue, Matching Straw Bonnet, 1900s	175.00
Dress, Wedding, High Neck, Long Sleeves, Batiste & Lace, C.1880	175.00
Dress, Wedding, Layered Skirt, Lace Inserts, Mutton Sleeves, 1890s	125.00
Dress, Wedding, Victorian, White, Pantaloons, Boning, 2 Piece	98.00
Dress, Wedding, White Batiste, Over Yellow Chintz Ruffles, 1900s	190.00
Dress, White, Cutwork Lace Top, Victorian, 2 Piece	20.00
Dress, White, Eyelet, Lace Panels, Victorian, Size 14–16	75.00
Dress, White, Lace, White Embroidery, Tucks, Long, 14–16 Size	145.00
Dress, White, Silver Beads, 1920s	95.00
Duster, Woman's, Natural Linen, Princess, Early 1900s, Size 6–8	95.00
Garters, Child's, Lord Milford, Original Card	5.00
Gown, Red Rose, Black Lace, White Sheer, 1930s	40.00
Hat, Bandeau, Black, Flowers Under Brim, Bow Back, Woman's, 1930s	15.00
Hat, Cloche, Black, 2 Flowers, Woman's, 1925–30	14.50
Hat, Derby, Man's, Black	15.00
Hat, Felt, Black, Box, 1950s	15.00
Hat, Flapper, Beaver Felt, Mr.John, Taupe & Gray	24.00
Hat, Man's, Black Felt, Moore & Sons, London, Hat Box, 1887	45.00
Hat, Woman's, Black Velvet, Large Brim, Fur & Rose Trim, 1915	50.00
Jacket & Pants, Marine, Eisenhower Type, 1940s	38.00
Jacket, Black Net & Sequin, Bow, Short, 1920s	15.00
Jacket, Combing, Small, 1880	30.00
Jacket, Dinner, White Linen, 1950s, Size 42	45.00
Jacket, Smoking, Silk Brocade, Black, Frog Closure, 1900	40.00
Jacket, Wool, 1910	25.00
Kimono, Silk & Rayon, Hand Embroidered Scenes, Florals, Chinese	30.00
Leggings, Child's, Knee High, Button, Black	17.50
Mitts, Silk, White, Lace	15.00
Muff, Black Velvet	10.00
Muff, Child's, Teddy Bear, Steiff	350.00
Nightgown, Lady's, Muslin, Hand Embroidered Yoke, 1890s	25.00
Nightgown, Victorian, Linen, Embroidered, Mother Hubbard, Size 6	65.00
Obi, Silk, Blue & Rust, On Dull Dark Cream, 148 In.	300.00

Pantaloons, White, Victorian 18.00
Pants, Tuxedo, Wide Legs, Side Stripe, 1950s 20.00
Petticoat, Hand Quilted, 1900s 75.00
Petticoat, White Batiste, Eyelet Flounce, Mid–Calf, 25 In.Waist 25.00
Petticoat, White Cotton, 16 Rows of Tucks, Full–Length 75.00
Petticoat, White, Pull Tapes For Bustle & Ruffles 75.00
Pocket, Lady's, Floral Embroidered, Linen, 18th Century, 10 In. 1870.00
Robe, Breakfast, Print, 1893, Medium Size .... 25.00 To 40.00
Robe, Fortuny, Stamped Floral Design, Bead Trim, Gauze, 1910s 2500.00
Robe, Man's, Woven Paisley, 1880 .... 68.00
Robe, Pan Velvet, Trapunto Lapels & Pocket, Royal Blue, 1940s 25.00
Rubbers, U.S.Rubber Co., Saleman's Sample 15.00
Sash, Multicolored Dragon Boats, Gold Ground, Oriental, 160 In. 175.00
Scarf, Bridal, Princess Lace, Handmade, C.1890 .... 149.00
Serape, Rio Grande, Red & Black Design, Fringe, 46 X 76 In. 55.00
Shawl, Allover Soutache Cutwork, Black Wool 75.00
Shawl, Apricot Silk, Allover Embroidered, Fringed, Victorian 57.00
Shawl, Bands of Dangling Black Beads, Black Velvet 35.00
Shawl, Paisley, 19th Century, India, 66 X 132 In. 245.00
Shawl, Paisley, Black Center, 60 X 78 In. 185.00
Shawl, Paisley, Persian, 88 X 88 In. 650.00
Shawl, Piano, Embroidered, 27 X 25 In. 35.00
Shawl, Piano, Embroidered, Brown & Pink, Silk, 53 X 58 In. 85.00
Shawl, Piano, Hand Crocheted Lace 3 Sides, 27 X 78 In. 45.00
Shawl, Piano, Hand Embroidered Birds of Paradise, Flowers 110.00
Shawl, Piano, Pictures Biplanes Circling Capitol Building 35.00
Shawl, Silk, Embroidered Flowers, Fringe, Spain, 47 X 44 In. 95.00
Shawl, Victorian, Black Lace, Scalloped Edges 60.00
Shawl, White Net, Silver Egyptian Design, 80 X 28 In. 75.00
Shawl, Wool Challis, White, Floral, 10 In.Fringe, Square, 52 In. 65.00
Shawl, Wool, Medium Blue, Cable Stitch, 58 X 20 In. 30.00
Shawl, Wool, Royal Blue, Afghan, 5 In.Fringe, 60 X 32 In. 40.00
Shawl, Wool, White, Embroidered, Silver Threads, 64 X 17 In. 50.00
Shirt, Man's, Homespun, 1890 .... 38.00
Shoes, Alligator, Sling Pumps, Red, Platform, 1940s, Size 6 .... 40.00
Shoes, Baby, White, Brown Leather Buttons 20.00
Shoes, Boy's, High Top, Kid, Red Insert Lace, Goodman, Box, Size 9 .. 35.00
Shoes, Child's, High Button, Black & White Leather 30.00
Shoes, Child's, High Button, White Leather 24.00
Shoes, Child's, High Top, Lace Up 10.00
Shoes, Flapper, Silk Brocade, Rhinestone Buckles 50.00
Shoes, High Lace, Lady's, Navy Suede, Taffeta Top, Dated 1896 ...... 40.00
Shoes, Mary Jane Style, Early 1920s 12.00
Shoes, Men's, High Button Dress, Black Leather, Suede, 1900s 45.00
Shoes, Woman's, High Lace, Brown Leather 22.00
Skirt & Shirtwaist, Bustle, 2–Tone Brown, Unused, 1870s 120.00
Skirt, Edwardian, Linen, 10–Gore 38.00
Skirt, Poodle, Beads, Flowers, Brown, 1950s, Size 12–14 .... 9.00
Skirt, Poodle, Felt, White Poodle, Jeweled Collar, 1950s, Size 10 .. 12.50
Skirt, Victorian, Ivory Satin, Ruching, Pleating, Lace Hems 150.00
Skirt, Victorian, Maroon Cotton Sateen, Wide Lace Bands 60.00
Spats, Man's, Gray, Street, Pair 10.00
Step–Ins & Bra, Mint Green Silk, Lace, 1920s, 32A, 26 In.Waist 55.00
Stockings, Long Black Cotton, Child's, Small 10.00
Stockings, Woman's, Rayon, Seamed, Pair 1.00
Suit, Boy's, Knickers, Size 14 .... 15.00
Suit, Boy's, Mustard Calico, C.1910, 2 Piece 24.00
Suit, Walking, Victorian, Woman's, Brown Velvet, Paris Label, 2 Pc. . 400.00
Suit, Woman's, Black Velvet, Red Fox Collar, 1930 .... 68.00
Swimsuit, Black & White, Matching Beach Slippers, C.1890 .... 25.00
Swimsuit, Wool Knitwear, Green & Wine, Bradley, 1920s, Unused 26.00
Teddy, Batiste, 1920s 8.00
Teddy, Crepe, Peach 15.00
Top Hat, Beaver Skin 35.50

Top Hat, Silk, Collapsible	57.50
Top Hat, Silk, Leather Case	65.00
Uniform Dress, Flying Tigers Pilot, Gen.Chenault, Insignia	400.00
Uniform.U.S.Federal, Linen, Summer Issue, Artillery, 1835	1550.00
Wedding Gown, Hand Worked, Ecru Satin, 1890, Size 3	650.00
Wedding Gown, Lace Inserts, Long Train, White, C.1905	100.00
Wrapper, Floral, Velvet Trim, 1860s	125.00

> Cluthra glass is a two–layered glass with small air pockets that form white spots. The Steuben Glass Works of Corning, New York, made it after 1903. Kimball Glass Company of Vineland, New Jersey, made Cluthra from about 1925.

CLUTHRA, see also Steuben

CLUTHRA, Vase, Blue, Ovoid Form, Steuben, 10 In.	1200.00
Vase, Cylindrical, Light Amethyst, Steuben, C.1925, 10 In. ....*Illus*	850.00
Vase, Fleur–De–Lis, White, Steuben, 8 In.	975.00
Vase, Orange & Black, Striated, Bubbles, H.Kimble, 17 1/4 In.	195.00
Vase, Ovoid Form, Amethyst, Steuben, C.1925, 8 1/4 In. ....*Illus*	850.00
Vase, White, Signed, Steuben, 8 In.	895.00
Vase, Yellow Spatter, Dark Blue Handles, 11 In.	275.00

> Coalport ware has been made by the Coalport Porcelain Works of England from 1795 to the present time. Early pieces were unmarked. About 1810–1825 the pieces were marked with the name "Coalport" in various forms. Later pieces also had the name "John Rose" in the mark. The crown mark has been used with variations since 1881.

COALPORT, Basket, Classical Portraits, White, Square, Miniature	99.00
Bowl, Indian Tree, Fluted Top, 4–Footed, 8 1/2 In.	45.00
Cauldron, Gold, Blue & Red Floral, Jeweled, Miniature	140.00
Creamer, Floral, C.1800	180.00
Cup & Saucer, Chocolate, Jeweled	400.00
Cup & Saucer, Sevres Style, Birds, Rose Pompadour Ground, C.1835	150.00
Dinner Set, Indian Tree, Coral, Scalloped, Service For 8	625.00
Figurine, Annette, 1940 Mark	100.00
Holder, Place Card, Marked, 3 Piece	22.00
Plate, Cherub & Flowers, Raised Gold Flowers, Artist, 1893, 9 In.	395.00
Plate, Dinner, Countryware, 9 In.	12.50
Teapot, Polly–Put–The–Kettle–On	250.00
Tumbler, Dawn, 8 Oz.	30.00
Urn, Lock Achray Painting, Gold Reserve, Cobalt, Cream, 11 In.	275.00
Vase, Spill, Floral, Dark Background, C.1820	295.00

Cluthra, Vase, Cylindrical,
Light Amethyst,
Steuben, C.1925, 10 In.

Cluthra, Vase, Ovoid Form,
Amethyst,
Steuben, C.1925, 8 1/4 In.

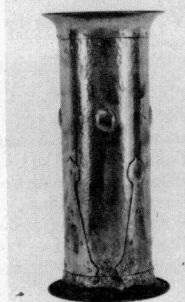

Copper, Umbrella Holder,
Gustav Stickley,
Hammered, C.1905, 27 In.

Cobalt blue glass was made using oxide of cobalt. The characteristic bright dark blue identifies it for the collector. Most cobalt glass found today was made after the Civil War.

COBALT BLUE, Bottle, 3 Mold Blown, Tam–O'–Shanter Stopper, 6 1/2 In.	375.00
Bottle, Perfume, Etched Bold Band, Faceted Brass Stopper	80.00
Bowl, Flint, 1835–50, 6 1/2 In.	55.00
Cocktail Shaker, Art Deco, 6 Tumblers	175.00
Creamer, Violet, Diamond–Quilted, Scalloped Rim, 3 3/4 In.	100.00
Cruet, Enameled Ship Design, Handle, Stopper, 6 1/2 In., Pair	121.00
Cup & Saucer, Dinner Plate, Child's, 3 Piece	12.00
Cup, Measuring, Hazel Atlas, 2 Cup	165.00
Decanter, Applied Ring Below Lip, 11 1/2 In.	370.00
Decanter, Blimp Shape, Gold, 3 Shot Glasses, Hanging, 14 In.	125.00
Decanter, Blown, Stopper, Sheared Top, Club Shape, 19th Century	180.00
Dresser Set, Enameled Flowers, Scrolls, 6 Piece	350.00
Holder, Playing Card, Souvenir, McCutchenville, Ohio	40.00
Lamp, Little Buttercup, Miniature	65.00
Mixing Bowl, 10 In.	25.00
Mug, Applied Handle, Blown, 3 1/4 In.	75.00
Mug, Chrome Nude Holder, Reticulated Oriental, 5 In.	25.00 To 45.00
Patch Box, Gold Branches, Leaves, Berries, 2 1/4 X 1 1/4 In.	88.00
Pitcher, Daiquiri, Bacardi, 5 3/4 In.	28.00
Pitcher, Water, Blown, Pedestal, 9 In.	125.00
Punch Cup, Broken Column	85.00
Salt Dip, Swan	12.50
Salt, Encased In Geometric Reticulated Sterling Silver	25.00
Salt, Lacy, 3 In.	225.00
Sherbet, Lincoln Inn	10.00
Shoe, Des Moines Public Library, Wheelock	22.00
Sugar & Creamer, Blown Glass, Gold Flowers, Mid–19th Century	350.00
Sugar & Creamer, Fernland	50.00
Sugar, Blown, Flared Lip, Applied Finial, 6 1/2 In.	95.00
Sugar, Open, Barberton High School, Grammar School, 1906	38.00
Sweetmeat, Ornate Cutout Holder, Spoon	195.00
Toothpick, Pot Shape, 3–Footed	12.50
Urn, Sterling Silver Overlay, Band On Neck & Base, 3 In.	200.00
Vase, Bud, Violin, 8 In.	28.00
Vase, Ruffled Top, 12 In.	69.00
Whiskey Taster, 6 Flute Pattern, Hexagonal Base, 2 1/4 In.	50.00
Wine, Royal Blue Bowl, Teardrop Stem, Set of 6	120.00

Coca–Cola was first served in 1886 in Atlanta, Georgia. It was advertised through signs, newspaper ads, coupons, bottles, trays, calendars, and even lamps and clocks. Collectors want anything with the word "Coca–Cola," including a few rare products like gum wrappers and cigar bands. The famous trademark was patented in 1893, the "Coke" mark in 1945. Many modern items and reproductions are being made.

COCA–COLA, Ashtray, Carnival Glass, Marigold, 1930	300.00
Ashtray, Glass, Logo, 1963	2.00
Bank, Dispenser, Miniature, Box	40.00
Banner, Santa, The Gift of Thirst, Children At Tree, 11 X 23 In.	15.00
Bat, Baseball, Enjoy Coca–Cola, Oakland A's Emblem, Rawlins	45.00
Binoculars, Folding	4.00
Blanket, Stadium, Red With White Coca–Cola Logo Both Sides	22.00
Blotter, Boy & Dog Fishing, 1932	60.00
Blotter, Child, With Bottle Cap On Head, 1953, 7 1/2 X 3 1/2 In.	12.00
Blotter, Hand Holding Bottle Aloft, 1932	75.00
Blotter, Refresh Yourself, Bottle Picture, 1916	8.50
Board, Cribbage	30.00
Book Matches, Santa With Elves, 1960s	12.50
Book, When You Entertain, 1932	12.00
Booklet, Flower Arranging Premium, 1941, 7 X 9 In.	5.00 To 8.00

Booklet, The Truth About Coca–Cola, 1912 .... 25.00 To 35.00
Bookmark, Hilda Clark 185.00
Boomerang, 1950s 7.50
Bottle Hanger, Santa & Boy At Refrigerator, 1950s 2.50
Bottle, 50th Anniversary, Gold 60.00
Bottle, Christmas, Clarksdale, Miss. 15.00
Bottle, Christmas, Dec.25, 1923, Original Contents, 6 Oz. 45.00
Bottle, Display, Coin Slot In Cap, 20 In. 120.00
Bottle, Hobbleskirt, Nov.16, 1915 .... 12.50
Bottle, Perfume, Miniature, 1930 .... 30.00
Bottle, Water, Compliments Coca–Cola Bottling Co. .... 70.00 To 75.00
Bow Tie, Clip–On, Old String–Type, Red 10.00
Bowl, Pretzel, 1935 .... 75.00
Box, 5 Cents At Soda Fountains, Wooden, Held Two 1 Gallon Jugs 125.00
Calendar, 1923, 12 X 24 In. 150.00
Calendar, 1926, Complete Pad 275.00
Calendar, 1927 .... 350.00
Calendar, 1935 .... 225.00
Calendar, 1939 .... 165.00
Cap, Beanie, 1930s 25.00
Car Key, Envelope, 1950 .... 20.00
Cards, Nature Study, Original Wrapper, Set 45.00
Cards, Playing, Box, 1944 .... 30.00 To 48.00
Cards, Playing, Stewardess, 1943, Original Box 20.00
Cards, World War II Airplanes, Pack of 20 .... 20.00 To 22.00
Case, Yellow Plastic, With 24 Plastic Bottles, C.1971 .... 10.00
Cash Register, Brass 695.00
Clock, Drink Coke, Wooden Case, Electric 120.00
Clock, Things Go Better, Lighted, 1960s 40.00
Coaster, Boy With Coke Cap For Hat, Set of 6 .... 10.00
Coin–Operated Machine, Coke, 1938 .... 695.00
Cooler, Drink Coca–Cola In Bottles, Chrome Handles, 16 X 17 In. 55.00
Cuff Links, 1923 .... 65.00
Darts, 1950s, Boxed 45.00
Dish, Pretzel, 1936 .... 65.00
Dominos, Coke Bottle On Back, Marked Hal–Sam, 28 Piece, Box 50.00
Door Knob, Glass 75.00
Door Pull, Bottle Style 100.00
Game Set, Checkers, Acey Ducey, Backgammon, Box, 1950s 65.00
Game, Cribbage Board, Wooden, 1930, 9 1/2 X 2 In. 25.00
Game, Dart Board, Instruction Booklet, 1940 .... 20.00
Game, Ring Toss, Cardboard Head of Santa, Wreath, 1960s, 10 In. 4.50
Ice Pick, Delicious & Refreshing, Box 5.00
Jar, Coke Gum, Counter, Gem, 1915 .... 170.00
Knife, Coca–Cola Bottling Co, Remington 10.00
Knife, Lady's Boot Shape, Remington, Pocket 150.00
Knife, Pocket, Bone Handle, 1908 .... 65.00 To 125.00
Knife, Pocket, Chicago World's Fair, 1933 .... 12.00 To 35.00
Knife, Pocket, Coca–Cola Logo, 2 Steel Blades, Corkscrew 25.00
Label, Coke Syrup, Guam Bottling Plant, 1970s, 4 X 8 In. .... .50
Lighter, Cigarette, Bottle Shape, 1950 .... 10.00 To 30.00
Lighter, Mini Can, 1960s 15.00
Map, Wall, United States, 1940 .... 15.00
Match Striker, Porcelain, Red, Yellow & Black 85.00
Night–Light, Courtesy of Your Coca–Cola Bottler, Red Print 3.00
Opener, Wall, Bottle Shape 7.50
Pad, Score, Bridge, Telephone Operator On Cover, Unused 7.00
Pencil Box, Complete, 10 Pieces, 1937 .... 25.00
Pencil Box, Ruler, 2 Blotters, 3 Pencils, Pen, 1930s 24.00
Pencil Sharpener, Coke Bottle, Cast Iron, 1930s 12.50
Pencil, Mechanical, Box, 1930 .... 15.00 To 25.00
Plate, Vienna Art, 1905 .... 135.00
Postcard, Truck, Color 3.50
Poster, Santa At Fireplace, 18 X 25 In. 12.50

Push Bar, Porcelain 125.00
Radio, Cooler, 1949 .... 275.00 To 375.00
Ruler, Wooden, 1930s, 12 X 7/8 In. 3.00
Sign, Bottle, Tin, 1915, 20 X 28 In. 275.00
Sign, Drink Coca–Cola, 16 In. 45.00
Sign, Figural, Policeman, School Zone, Metal 450.00
Sign, Fountain Service, Porcelain, 12 X 29 In. 45.00
Sign, Gas Today–Drink Coca–Cola While You Wait, 20 X 27 In. 135.00
Sign, Serve Coke With Meals, Paper, 1954, 15 X 29 In. 4.50
Sign, Tome Coca–Cola, La Bebida Deliciosa, 1927, 12 X 36 In. 150.00
Sign, We Sell Coca–Cola, Cardboard, 1942, 22 X 15 In. 65.00
Straws, For The Pause That Refreshes, Paper, Box of 500, 1940s 50.00
Thermometer, 1938 .... 60.00
Thermometer, 1939 .... 48.00
Thermometer, Bigger Better, Double Dot 18.00
Thermometer, Drink Coca–Cola In Bottles, Box, 1950s, 12 In. 55.00
Thermometer, Gold Bottle, Green & Black Ground, Round, 12 In. 100.00
Thimble, Aluminum, 1920 .... 27.50
Tie, String, Kit Carson 90.00
Tip Tray, 1909, Coca–Cola Girl, Flowered Hat 55.00
Tip Tray, 1910, Hamilton King 110.00
Tip Tray, 1914, Betty .... 70.00 To 95.00
Tip Tray, 1917, Elaine ....65.00 To 110.00
Toy, Fountain Dispenser, 1960s 10.00
Toy, Robot, Battery Operated, Box, 1950 ....80.00 To 105.00
Toy, Truck, Buddy L, Hand Truck 45.00
Toy, Truck, Mechanical Head & Tail Lights, Tin, Japan, Box, 12 In. 95.00
Tray, 1909, Coca–Cola, Girl With Glass 165.00
Tray, 1912, Hamilton King Girl, 11 X 15 In. 195.00
Tray, 1914, Betty, Oval 200.00
Tray, 1914, Betty, Rectangular 385.00
Tray, 1917, Elaine, Rectangular 175.00
Tray, 1922, Summer Girl 295.00
Tray, 1923, Flapper 125.00
Tray, 1925, Girl At Party 115.00
Tray, 1926, Sports Couple 100.00
Tray, 1927, Curb Service ....135.00 To 175.00
Tray, 1929, Girl With Bottle, Red Border 295.00
Tray, 1930, Bather ....90.00 To 125.00
Tray, 1930, Telephone 100.00
Tray, 1931, Rockwell ....140.00 To 395.00
Tray, 1932 .... 325.00
Tray, 1934, Weissmuller ....300.00 To 350.00
Tray, 1935, Madge Evans 85.00
Tray, 1936, Hostess 50.00
Tray, 1938, Girl In Afternoon 70.00
Tray, 1939, Springboard 60.00
Tray, 1941, Skater ....65.00 To 85.00
Tray, 1948, Redhead ....40.00 To 45.00
Tray, 1950, Girl With Menu ....20.00 To 30.00
Tray, 1957, Rooster 70.00
Tray, 1958, Picnic Basket ....20.00 To 35.00
Tray, 1961, Pansy Garden, Be Really Refreshed, 10 1/2 X 13 In. 13.00
Tray, 1961, Thanksgiving 10.00
Tray, 1977, Elaine, Oval, 10 1/2 X 13 In. 4.00
Tray, 1981, Boy Fishing, Rockwell ....4.00 To 5.00
Tray, 1982, World's Fair 5.00
Tumbler, Looks Like Can, 1976 .... 3.00
Watch Fob, Gibson Girl, Celluloid, 1910 .... 375.00
Yo–Yo, Coke 12.50

 Coffee grinders of home size were first made about 1894. They lost favor by the 1930s. Large floor-standing or counter model coffee grinders were used in the nineteenth-century country store. The renewed interest in fresh-ground coffee has produced many modern electric and hand grinders; and reproductions of the old styles are being made.

COFFEE GRINDER, Arcade No.25, Wall	65.00
Arcade, Crystal, Glass Top, Cast Iron	65.00
Arcade, Lap, Dovetailed Case, Drawer, Paper Label, Imperial	65.00
Arcade, Telephone Mill, Replaced Lid	200.00
B.Swift, Iron, Tin, Pat.1848	35.00
Charles Parker Co., Wall, Cast Iron	45.00
Chas.Parker Co., Meriden, Conn, 2 Wheel, Original Paint	530.00
Crystal, Wall	70.00
Elgin National Coffee Mill, Double Wheel, 29 In.	225.00
Elna, Painted, Square, Drawer, Crank Handle, Tin	50.00
Enterprise, Counter Top, Original Paint, Decal	250.00 To 500.00
Enterprise, Philadelphia, Store	575.00
Fairbanks-Morse, 2 Wheels, Brass Finial, 38 In.	350.00
H.M.Meier, St.Louis, Double, Tin Drawer, Oak	85.00
Imperial, Square Dovetailed Box, 5 1/2 In.	25.00
Koffee, Iron Hopper, Glass Container, Pottery	75.00
Lap, Izons & Co., Cast Iron, Brass	110.00
Logan & Strobridge, Wooden	65.00
Red Glass Jar, Marked Koffie, Crank Handle, Wall	75.00
Regal 44, Tin, Wall	35.00
Sunbeam, Attachment For Mixer, Glass	20.00
Universal, No.110, Black, Dated 1905	37.50

Coin spot is a glass pattern that was named by the collectors. It, of course, features coinlike spots as part of the glass. Colored, clear, and opalescent glass was made with the spots. Many companies used the design in the 1870-90 period. It is so popular that reproductions are still being made.

COIN SPOT, Bride's Bowl, Chartreuse, Frosted Blue Edge, Ruffled, 8 1/2 In.	750.00
Cruet, Clear Stopper, Blue	30.00
Finger Bowl, Opalescent	20.00
Hat, Ruffled Rim, White Opalescent, 3 X 4 In.	45.00
Lamp, Oil, King Melon, Aqua Opalescent	350.00
Muffineer, Cranberry	80.00
Pitcher, Blue, 10 In.	50.00
Pitcher, Water, Blue Opalescent	120.00
Salt & Pepper, Ribbed, Brass Top, Opalescent, 3 In.	35.00
Sugar Shaker, Cranberry, Fenton	40.00 To 45.00
Syrup, Blue Opalescent, Ring Neck	78.00
Syrup, Silver Plated Lid, Blue	165.00
Syrup, Squatty, White Opalescent	65.00
Syrup, Swirl	135.00
Tumbler, Christmas Snowflake Mold, Greenish Blue	60.00
Tumbler, Opalescent	16.50
Tumbler, Ribbed, Blue	55.00
Vase, Enameled Flowers, Gold Leaves, Peach, 8 1/2 In.	550.00
Vase, Ruffled Rim, Bulbous, White Opalescent, 5 X 5 1/2 In.	45.00
Vase, Ruffled Top, White Cut To Pink	42.00
Vase, Ruffled, Enameled Flowers, Gold Leaves, Peach, 8 1/2 In.	550.00
Vase, Top Hat, Vaseline, 6 In.	75.00
Water Set, Opalescent, 7 Piece	250.00

The vending machine is an ancient invention dating back to 200 B.C. when holy water was dispensed in a coin–operated vase. Smokers in seventeenth–century England could buy tobacco from a coin–operated box. It was not until after the Civil War that the technology made modern coin–operated games and vending machines plentiful. Slot machines, arcade games, and dispensers are all collected.

COIN–OPERATED MACHINE, 4 Star Chiefs, Jennings 1600.00
Automatic Phonograph, Mills 750.00
Beechnut Mints, Fruitdrops, 5 Cent, Wooden Stand 32.50
Black Beauty, Hand Load Jackpot, Mills, 50 Cents 1800.00
Boat Ride, Child's, Wooden, 10 Cent, 6 X 3 Ft. 500.00
Bronze Chief, 5 Cent, Jennings 1500.00
Buckley Kentucky Derby, Free Play, Race Horse 995.00
Chewing Gum, Baker's Chocolate 375.00
Chuck–A–Luck Cage 295.00
Collar Button, Price 460.00
Columbus Model A, Peanut, Cast Iron, 1920s 100.00
Dixie Bells, Jennings, 1st Model 1600.00
E.Z.Gumball 475.00
Elephant Snout, Raised Legs, Iron, Mills 6700.00
Foot Massage, Exhibit Supply 195.00
Futurity, Side Bender, Mills, Gold Award, 1936 .... 2150.00
Golf Ball Vendor, Jennings, 25 Cent 2950.00
Grandma Gypsy, Genco 800.00
Grip Tester, 1 Cent, C.1930 .... 200.00
Gum, Clovermint, Stick, 1923 .... 125.00
Gum, Dentyne, 5 Cent 125.00
Gum, Magic Clock 325.00
Gum, Pulver, Green 350.00
Gum, Pulver, Yellow Kid, 1930s .... 375.00 To 575.00
Gum, R.J.White, Happy Jap, Clockwork Mechanism 3700.00
Gum, Stick, Advance, Contents 175.00
Gum, Zeno, Oak 575.00
Gumball, Columbus, Model B, Columbus Stand, Lock 265.00
Gumball, E–Z, 5 Cent 340.00
Gumball, Fields, Wildcat, Counter, 1 Cent, C.1920 .... 795.00
Gumball, Master 175.00
Gumball, Mickey Mouse, Hamilton Ent., Decal, C.1938 .... 775.00
Gumball, National 200.00
Gumball, Northwestern, Model 33, Deco 185.00
Gumball, Scoopy Gum 600.00
Gumball, Zipper Skill, 1 Cent, Oak Cabinet 200.00
Indian Front, Mills, 1 Cent 1200.00
Lighter Fluid Dispenser, Gas Pump Shape, 1 Cent 375.00
Love Tester 275.00
Mason Mints, 1 Cent 80.00
Match, Cast Iron Front, Wood 250.00
Match, Columbus 175.00
Match, Griswold 175.00
Menier Chocolate Bank, Tin, Litho 600.00
Mercury, Strength Test, Table Model, 1 Cent 100.00
Mexican Baseball, Counter Top, 1 Cent 175.00
Mutoscope, Arcade, 5 Cent 245.00
Mutoscope, Digger, Oak Case 2000.00
Mutoscope, K.O.Boxers 800.00
Mutoscope, Monkey Lift 1250.00
Nut House, 1 Cent Rates Peanuts 850.00
Operator's Bell, Mills, 1910 .... 5500.00
Owl Front, Mills, 10 Cent 900.00
Peanut, Little Gem, 5 Cent, Key & Tray, 11 X 6 In. 150.00
Peanut, Magna, 1 Cent, 1934 .... 200.00
Peanut, National 275.00

Peanut, Neko	175.00
Perfume, Lion, Clockwork Mechanism, Oak, 1897	1475.00
Perfume, Vendor, Oak, 16 Original Bottles, 1900	425.00
Pinball, Avalon, 5 Cent, Pat.1936	575.00
Pinball, Jennings, Payoff	800.00
Pulver 1 Cent Gum Machine, With Yellow Kid, 1930s	375.00
Puritan, Baby Vender	400.00
Rock–Ola, Light Up	1500.00
Rockaway, Jennings	1300.00
Roman Head, Copper Award Tokens, Mills, 1 Cent	1300.00
Scale, Mills, 1 Cent, Lollipop, Iron	750.00
Scale, National, Claw Feet	850.00
Shock, Mills, Counter Model	3450.00
Slot, 4 Star Jennings Chief, 5 Cent	1050.00
Slot, Aristocrat	485.00
Slot, Bally Double Bell, 5 Cent–25 Cent	3000.00
Slot, Bally Poker Spinner	2000.00
Slot, Bally, Quarter, 1950	1800.00
Slot, Buckley Track Odds	2000.00
Slot, Callie, Doughboy	750.00
Slot, Cherry Smash, Counter Top, 5 Cent	930.00
Slot, Clawson, Dice	3250.00
Slot, Club Chief, 25 Cent	625.00
Slot, Indian Brand, 10 Cent	2650.00
Slot, Jennings Lite Up Chief, Floor Cabinets	2200.00
Slot, Jennings, Ben Hur, 1 Cent	700.00
Slot, Jennings, Century, 5 Cents, 1934	1200.00
Slot, Jennings, Chief, 4 Star, 5 Cent	1050.00
Slot, Jennings, Duchess, 5 Cent	2500.00
Slot, Jennings, Dutch Boy, Dutch Girl, 25 Cent	960.00
Slot, Jennings, Front Vendor Slot, 5 Cent	700.00
Slot, Jennings, Gooseneck, Dutch Children, 5 Cent	850.00
Slot, Jennings, Operator Bell, 5 Cent	1500.00
Slot, Jennings, Standard Chief	975.00
Slot, Jubilee, English	300.00
Slot, Keeney, Big Tent, Console	575.00
Slot, Little Duke, 1 Cent	1500.00
Slot, Mills, 4 Column Front, 25 Cent	1375.00
Slot, Mills, Aikens Extra Bell	1450.00
Slot, Mills, Black Cherry, 10 Cent	950.00
Slot, Mills, Blue Front, 5 Cent	1950.00
Slot, Mills, Bonus Horsehead, 5 Cent	1600.00
Slot, Mills, Brown Front, 5 Cent, 1938	1250.00
Slot, Mills, Bursting Cherry	1650.00
Slot, Mills, Checkboy, Pop-Up Flags, 5 Cent	4200.00
Slot, Mills, Dice, Square Badge, Restored, 25 Cent	3500.00
Slot, Mills, Ferris Wheel	2000.00
Slot, Mills, Futurity, Side Vendor, Gold Award, 1936	2150.00
Slot, Mills, Hi–Top, Silver Dollar	1875.00
Slot, Mills, Horsehead Bonus, 5 Cent	1000.00
Slot, Mills, Novelty Company Diamond Burst, 5 Cent	975.00
Slot, Mills, Operator's Bell, 1910	5500.00
Slot, Mills, Panorama Peep Show	1500.00
Slot, Mills, Poinsettia, 25 Cent	975.00
Slot, Mills, Upright Club Console, 25 Cent	2000.00
Slot, Pace, Bantam, 25 Cent	950.00
Slot, Pace, Royal Twin, 5 & 25 Cent	5200.00
Slot, Reliance, Bally, 5 Cent	3500.00
Slot, Rock–Ola, World Series, 1937	2500.00
Slot, Watling, Treasury, 5 Cent	5250.00
Slot, Williams, Music Mite	1500.00
Stamp, U.S.Postage, Uncle Sam Wants You	50.00
Target Practice, Jennings, 1 Cent	350.00
Ten Strike Bowling Machine, Evans	875.00

Trade Stimulator, Dixie Dominoes	375.00
Trade Stimulator, Ex–Ray, 5 Cent	260.00
Trade Stimulator, Horse Race, 1890	1200.00
Trade Stimulator, Tibbells, 1 Cent, Cast Iron	1900.00
U.S.Stamp Vending, 5 Cent	25.00
Vending, Cig–A–Rola, 20 Cent & 5 Cent Slot	1200.00
Vendor, Mills, Elephant Snout, Raised Legs, Iron	6700.00
Vendor, Popcorn, 10 Cent, 5 Ft.	275.00
Watling, Blue Seal, Double Jackpot, 5 Cent	1800.00
Williams, Ten Strike Bowling	600.00

Collector plates are modern plates produced in limited editions. Some will be found listed under the factory name, such as Bing & Grondahl, Royal Copenhagen, Royal Doulton, and Wedgwood. Pictures and more price information can be found in "Kovels' Price Guide for Collector Plates, Figurines, Paperweights and Other Limited Editions."

COLLECTOR PLATE, Bicentennial, Jefferson, Declaration Independence, 1973	175.00
Dali, Unicorn, Sterling Silver, 1971	100.00
DeGrazia, My First Horse	32.00
Goebel, Heavenly Angel, 1971	600.00
Gorham, Partridge In A Pear Tree, 1970	100.00
Gutman, First Step	27.00
Gutman, Pals	21.00
Holly Hobbie, Christmas, 1974, Box	12.00
Humphrey, Washday	16.00
Incolay, She Walks In Beauty, 1977	60.00
Kaiser, Swan With Cygnets, 1976	20.00
Knowles, Gone With The Wind, Bonnie & Rhett	35.00
Koutsis, Creation, Royal Cornwall, Set of 12	720.00
Olympic, 1980, Summer, Numbered, Box	20.00
Pennsbury, Yuletide, 1970	25.00
Perillo, Daniel Boone	39.00
Precious Moments, Boy, At Piano, Amazing Grace Musical	35.00
Red Skelton, Sir Freddy	65.00
Rockwell, Angel With A Black Eye, 1970	47.00

To clean a coffee grinder, grind white rice through the mill. When it appears to be clean the grinder is clean enough to use.

If you use plate hangers to display your plates, be sure they are not too tight. The clips should be covered with a soft material. The end clips may scratch or chip the plate.

To hang copper molds in your kitchen, try this method: Mount a solid brass or wooden curtain rod across the top of the hanging area. Molds can then be hung by hooks and easily moved when new ones are added.

Rockwell, Boy & His Dog, Gorham, 1971, Set of 4	260.00
Rockwell, Bringing Home The Tree, 1970	120.00
Rockwell, Toymaker, 1977	160.00
Rockwell, Under The Mistletoe, 1971	100.00
Schmid Disney, Christmas, 1973, Box	175.00
Spencer, Dear Child, Gorham	75.00
Will Rogers, Historic Run Into Oklahoma, 7 1/4 In.	35.00

Comic art, or cartoon art, is a relatively new field of collecting. Original comic strips, magazine covers, and even printed strips are collected. The first daily comic strip was printed in 1907. The paintings on celluloid used for movie cartoons are listed in this book under Animation Art.

COMIC ART, Ace Drummond, By Captain Eddie Rickenbacker, Colored, 1931	7.50
Barney Google, 1922 Sunday Comic Page, 2 Colors	20.00
Barney Google, Spark Plug, Page, Columbus Sunday Dispatch, 1926	25.00
Book, Superman No.59, 1949	35.00
Book, Tarzan, Dell No.1, 1948	125.00
Book, Wonder Woman, No.22, 1947	18.00
Bringing Up Father, Page, Columbus Sunday Dispatch, 1926	25.00
Dick Tracy, Sunday Comic Pages, 1936, 15 X 22 1/2 In.	5.00
Drawing, Animation, Two Gun Mickey	200.00
Felix, 2 Sections, Columbus Sunday Dispatch, 1927	25.00
Lone Ranger, Sunday Comic Pages, 1945, 15 X 22 1/2 In.	4.00
Mickey Mouse, Fantasia, Watercolor, Walt Disney, 1941	660.00
Page, Merely Margy, Sunday, John Held, Jr., Jan.12, 1930	330.00
Peter Arno, Cartoon, The Timid Soul, Miami Beach	3025.00
Phantom Comic Strip, '44 & '45, 65 Piece	25.00
Polly & Her Pals, Page, Columbus Sunday Dispatch, 1926	25.00
Strip, Star Trek, Spock, Kirk, U.S.S.Enterprise	125.00

Commemorative items have been made to honor members of royalty and those of great national fame. World's fairs and important historical events are also remembered with commemorative pieces.

COMMEMORATIVE, see also Coronation; World's Fair

COMMEMORATIVE, Basket, Queen Victoria, 1887	25.00
Beaker, George V, Silver Jubilee, Royal Doulton, 4 In.	60.00
Beaker, Queen Victoria, Jubilee, Sepia Portrait, Flag, 1897	35.00
Book, Coronation Souvenir Book, 1937, 160 Pages	12.00
Book, Queen Alexandra, Christmas Gift, Photographs, 1908	15.00
Box, Wooden, Queen Victoria & Family Litho, Domed Lid	25.00
Bread Tray, Queen Victoria, Jubilee, 1897	125.00
Bust, Queen Victoria, Bisque	65.00
Cup & Saucer, Edward VIII	17.50
Cup & Saucer, Queen Victoria, Jubilee, 1897	45.00
Cup & Saucer, Roosevelt & Churchill, Ironstone, Meakin	40.00
Cup Plate, Queen Victoria, Profile, 3 1/2 In.	15.00
Handkerchief, Edward VIII, Lace	25.00
Jam Jar, Crowned Head & Shoulders of Victoria Cover	165.00
Loving Mug, Queen Mother, 85th Birthday, August 4, 1985	25.00
Mug, Charles, Diana, Cupids, His Royal Highness Born 9-15-84	12.00
Mug, Edward VI, Lithophane	90.00
Mug, Edward VII Coronation, 1902, Royal Doulton	69.00
Mug, Edward VIII, Royal Doulton	110.00
Mug, George V, 1911	20.00
Mug, George VI Coronation, Royal Doulton, 1937	65.00
Mug, Marriage of Prince Charles & Lady Diana Spencer	25.00
Mug, Princess Anne's Wedding, 1973	35.00
Mug, Queen Victoria, Diamond Jubilee, Spode	165.00
Mug, Queen's Silver Wedding, Wedgwood	35.00
Pitcher, Queen Elizabeth's Coronation, 6 In.	135.00
Pitcher, Queen Victoria, 1887, 5 In.	100.00
Pitcher, Queen Victoria, 50th Anniversary, Royal Doulton	175.00
Plate, Baby, George V, Shelley	175.00

Plate, Edward VIII Coronation, 1937 .... 20.00
Plate, King George III, Pearlware, 1822 .... 350.00
Plate, King George V, Queen Mary, Silver Jubilee 16.00
Plate, President John Kennedy & Wife 12.00
Plate, Queen Louise, Austria, 8 1/2 In. .... 18.00 To 30.00
Plate, Queen Mother's 80th Birthday, Royal Doulton 45.00
Plate, Queen Victoria, Jubilee, Emblems, Dates, 1897, 9 In. 115.00
Plate, Queen Victoria, White Scalloped, 1837–1897, 8 In. 65.00
Program, Lincoln's Birthday, Silk, Reverse, 1898 .... 85.00
Saucer, Queen Victoria, Jubilee, Crown Center, Glass, 5 In. 55.00
Tape Measure & Needle Case, Queen Victoria, Stanhope 150.00
Tea Set, Panama Pacific International Expo., 1915, 5 Piece 190.00
Tea Set, Queen Victoria Jubilee, 1887, 15 Piece 1200.00
Teapot, Edward VII Coronation, Brown Pottery, 12 In. 90.00
Teapot, Edward VIII, 1937, Uncrowned 85.00
Teapot, George V, 1935, Silver Jubilee 60.00
Tin, George V & Mary, Roundtree's, 1911 .... 38.00
Tin, Queen Elizabeth, On Horseback, 1953, 9 X 5 1/2 In. 12.00
Tumbler, George VI, Glass 18.50
Vase, Prince Albert, Portrait, Grapes At Sides, 6 1/8 In. 60.00
Watch Fob, Victoria Regina, Metal, Double Faced 18.00

A woman did not powder her face in public until after World War I. By 1920 the beauty parlor, permanent waves, and cosmetics had become acceptable. A few companies sold cake face powder in a box with a mirror and a pad or puff. Soon the compact was being designed by jewelers and made of gold, silver, and precious materials. Cosmetic companies began to sell powder in attractive compacts of less valuable metal or plastic. Collectors today search for art deco designs, commemorative compacts from world's fairs or political events, and unusual examples. Many were made with companion lipsticks and other fittings.

COMPACT, Alfred Dunhill 25.00
Art Deco, Simulated Jade, Black, Gilt 75.00
Art Deco, Sterling Silver, Floral Design, 4 In. 85.00
Butterfly Wing 25.00
Celluloid, Hand Painted Flowers, With Rhinestones, Large 11.00
Century of Progress 15.00
Chicago World's Fair 15.00
Clam Shell Shape, Sterling Silver, Napier, 3 Oz. 35.00
Elgin, Art Deco, Blue Mirror Back, Sterling Silver 25.00
Embossed Stork Club Insignia, Brass 27.00
Enameled Scene of Florence, Engraved Foliage, Silver, 3 In. 95.00
Germain Monteil, Gold Tone 10.00
Gold Tone, Advertising, Friedman's Shoes, Champaign, Ill., Small .. 11.00
Mother-of-Pearl Center, Red Mariner's Wheel Outer Band 25.00
Musical, Volupte 45.00
Purse, With Chain Handle, Sterling Silver, Engraved, C.1920 .... 65.00
Rouge & Lipstick, Celluloid On Metal, Oriental Dancers, Paris 40.00
Rouge, Chrome Design, Evening In Paris 10.00
Tortoise Celluloid, Sterling Silver Catch, 5 X 3 1/2 In. 20.00

The best time to buy an antique is when you see it.

Trifari, Compact & Lipstick Combined, Stones On Top, Velvet Case 50.00
Trunk, Brass, Miniature 9.00
Turquoise Ground, Gold Basket of Roses, Enamel, 3 1/4 X 2 In. 650.00
Victorian, Mirror & Compartment, Chain, Sterling Silver, Initial 62.50

> The term "contemporary glass" refers to art glass made since 1950. Some contemporary glass factories, such as Orrefors or Baccarat, are listed under their own categories.

CONTEMPORARY GLASS, Bowl, Decorchement, Square Sides, C.1930, 3 1/4 In. 1980.00
Figurine, Fish, Venini 495.00
Vase, Decorchement, Flowers, Buds, C.1918, 4 1/2 In. 3025.00
Vase, J.Luce, Etched, Frosted, C.1930, 8 In. 3025.00

> Cookbooks are collected for various reasons. Some are wanted for the recipes, some for investment, and some as examples of advertising. Cookbooks and recipe pamphlets are included in this section.

COOKBOOK, A Friend In Need, 1924 .... 2.50
Almanac, Rawleigh, 1921 .... 12.00
Amana Recipes, 1948 .... 11.00
Antoinette Pope School, Hard Cover, 366 Pages, 1951 .... 8.00
Arm & Hammer 1896, 32 Pages 3.75
Arm & Hammer Almanac, 1921 .... 5.00
Aunt Jenny's Favorite Recipes, Spry Shortening, 1949 .... 7.00
Autumn Leaf, Jewel Tea, 1933 .... 12.00
Baker's Chocolate, Choice Recipes, Lady On Cover, 1924 .... 8.00
Betty Crocker, 1959 .... 25.00
Boston Cooking School Cookbook, 1906 .... 75.00
Cakes & Pastries, Carney, 1923 .... 18.00
Centaur Almanac, 1886, 5 X 7 In. 6.00
Ceresota, 1912 .... 12.00
Congressional Club, 1927 .... 18.00
Cook's Oracle, Boston, Munro Francis, 1822 .... 95.00
Cupid's Cookbook, Hardback, San Francisco, 1933 .... 14.00
Dr.Ward's Medical Co., 1916 .... 15.00
Electric Refrigerator Recipes, General Electric, 1929 .... 12.00
Enterprising Housekeeper, Enterprise Mfg., 1906 .... 10.00
Famous Sportsman's Recipes, DeBoth, 95 Pages, 1940 .... 11.00
Fannie Farmer, 1st Edition, 1912 .... 18.00
Fleischmann's Yeast, Litho, 1910 .... 12.00
Good Things To Eat, 1935 .... 3.00
Hoods Apothecaries Co., 1897 .... 14.50
Household Discoveries & Mrs.Curtis's Book, Leather, 1908 .... 22.00
Jell-O Girl Entertains, Rose O'Neill 20.00
Jell-O, Jack Benny & Mary Livingston, 1937 .... 15.00
Jell-O, Parrish, 1924 .... 35.00
Jewel Tea, 1927 .... 16.00
Jewel Tea, 1933 .... 16.00
Jewel Tea, 1941, American Women's 25.00
Lowney's Boston, 1912 .... 12.00
Lowney's, Hardcover, 1912 .... 9.00
Luchow's German, 1952 .... 10.00
Mentha Col, For Southern Housewives, 21 Pages, 1921, 5 X 7 In. 38.00
Mentha Col, Successful Cooking Recipes, Paper, 1921, 5 X 7 In. 38.00
New Delineator Recipes, 1930 .... 4.50
North Bros.Ice Cream Freezers, 1895 .... 10.00
Our Successful Farming, Hard Back, Loose Leaf Type, 1931 .... 16.00
Paper Bag, 1910 .... 15.00
Pillsbury, Illustrated, 1911 .... 13.00
Ralston Recipes, Woman In Shoe, 1920 .... 8.00
Rawleigh's, Almanac, Dated 1912 .... 10.00
Royal Baker & Pastry, 1911 .... 20.00
Royal Pudding Dessert, Ginger Rogers, 1940 .... 8.00
Rumford Complete, 1918 ....8.00 To 12.00

Salad, Woman's World, 1929	8.00
Shredded Wheat, The Call of The Bell, 1913	5.00
Some Good Old Maryland Recipes, Black Chef Front, 1942	15.00
Times Book of Recipes, 1949	10.00
Watkin's Co., of Winona, Minn., 1938	14.00
Watkin's, Colored Illustrations, 1925, 65 Pgs.	5.00
White House, 1890	60.00
Women's World, Wallace, 1930, 468 Pages, 7 1/2 X 10 1/2 In.	13.50

Cookie jars with brightly painted designs or amusing figural shapes became popular in the mid–1930s. Many companies made them and collectors search for cookie jars either by design or by maker's name. Listed here are examples by the less common makers. Major factories are listed under their own names in other sections of the book.

COOKIE JAR, Apple, Large	10.00
Apple, Watt	58.00
Aunt Jemima, Celluloid, F & F Mold & Die Works	135.00 To 138.00
Aunt Mary's Cookies, Blue Spongeware Banded	75.00
Baby Duck	11.00
Baby Pig, Regal China	65.00 To 85.00
Balloon Lady, Pottery Guild	55.00
Barefoot Boy	145.00 To 185.00
Barn With Animals, Regal China	60.00
Bear, Brown, Fredricksburg Art Pottery	65.00
Bear, Kraft Marshmallow	75.00
Bear, Kraft, Regal	55.00
Bear, Turnabout	20.00
Bear, Twin Winton, Calif.	27.00
Big Bird, California Originals	40.00
Black Chef, National Silver	85.00
Black Chef, Pearl China	110.00
Black Face, Mosaic, Yellow	225.00
Black Mammy, Red Dress, Brayton Laguna, 13 In.	170.00
Blackboard Girl	21.00
Boots	55.00
Bopeep	85.00
Boy & Girl Under Umbrella	18.00
Bugs Bunny, Canister	25.00
Bunny, Gray, Brush	35.00
Cat In Basket	17.00
Cat's Head, Poppytrail	40.00
Cat, Regal China	68.00
Chef, Gold, Pearl China	120.00
Chef, Ivory	25.00
Chef, Regal China	65.00
Cherry & Cable, Royal Blue, Red, Gold Trim, Westmoreland	95.00
Churn, American Bisque	15.00
Clown, Bust	20.00
Coffee Canister	200.00
Coffeepot, Bisque	22.50
Cookie Monster, Muppets	25.00
Cookie Truck, American Bisque	18.00
Cottage, Twin Winton, Calif.	33.00
Cow Jumped Over The Moon	30.00
Cow, With Cat, Brush	55.00
Davy Crockett, USA	125.00
Dog With Basket, Brush	30.00
Dogpatch Band	325.00
Donald Duck, In Sailor Suit	128.00
Dutch Boy, Spongeware	47.00
Dutch Girl, All White, 12 1/2 In.	25.00
Elephant, White	25.00

Elf, Keebler	15.00 To 42.00
Elsie The Cow, In Barrel	65.00
Engine, Brown, Twin Winton	30.00
Engine, Sierra Vista	40.00
Ernie, Muppets	25.00
Farmer Rabbit, American Bisque	35.00
Flower Girl, Florence Ceramics, 9 In.	50.00
Fred Flintstone	25.00
Geisha Scene, Child & 2 Adults	65.00
Gingerbread House, Beige, Pink	22.00
Goldilocks, Regal China	80.00 To 90.00
Gypsy Woman, Japan	30.00
Hen On Nest	20.00
Kitten On Beehive, American Bisque	20.00
Lamb, Pink Trim, Twin Winton	30.00
Lion	12.00
Little Red Riding Hood, Blue Skirt, 12 1/2 In.	95.00
Majorette	45.00
Mammy, Pearl China	195.00
Matilda, Brayton Laguna	175.00
Mickey & Minnie Mouse, Turnabout	75.00
Napkin Woman, Kreiss Co., 10 1/2 In.	35.00
Nun, Deforest of California	40.00
Old MacDonald Barn, Regal China	128.00
Oliver Hardy, Japan	30.00
Orange, With Blossoms & Leaves Lid, USA	10.00
Owl, Green, In Cap & Gown	15.00
Owl, Woodsy	45.00
Panda & Baby	25.00
Peek–A–Boo, Regal China	350.00
Peek–A–Boo, Vantellingen	300.00
Peter Pan, Brush	175.00
Peter, Peter Pumpkin Eater, Brush	125.00
Pig, Boy, Terrence Ceramics	35.00
Pig, Formal, Brush	50.00
Pluto, Turnabout	45.00
Poodle, Pink, Bisque, American	30.00
Potbelly Stove, Treasure Craft	18.50
Puppy In Basket	14.00
Puppy, Brayton	65.00
Puppy, On Lid, Red Pottery, Gonder	45.00
Puss N' Boots	35.00
Quaker Oats	65.00 To 75.00
Rabbit In Hat, American Bisque	30.00
Rabbit With Patches, Americn Bisque	35.00
Raggedy Andy, Poppy Trail	25.00
Raggedy Ann, Japan	22.00
Romper Room	35.00
Sailor	30.00
Santa Claus Head	45.00 To 55.00
Sheriff, Hole In Hat	32.00
Smokey The Bear, Twin Winton	25.00
Snappy Cookie Boy, Deforrest Calif.	25.00
Snow Bear	22.50
Spaceship, American Bisque	45.00
Strawberry	18.00
Teddy Bear Turnabout	20.00
Tigger, From Winnie The Pooh, 12 1/2 In.	65.00
Toby Cookies, Regal	300.00
Train, American Bisque	35.00
Treehouse, Keebler	35.00 To 65.00
Tuggy Tugboat	40.00
Umbrella Kid, American Bisque	30.00
White Bunny Chef, Brush, 13 In.	65.00

World War II Soldier, Khaki Clothes	60.00
Yarn Doll, American Bisque	25.00
Yogi Bear, Better Than Average Cookies	55.00

COORS U.S.A.   Coors ware was made by a pottery in Golden, Colorado, owned by the Coors Beverage Company. It was produced from the turn of the century until the pottery was destroyed by fire in the 1930s. The name "Coors" is marked on the back.

COORS, Ashtray, Colorado State Fair, 1936	8.00
Bank, Wall, Clown, Green Glaze, Empire Savings, Colo., 4 X 3 In.	33.00
Cookie Jar, Green	25.00
Honey Pot, Rosebud, Footed	27.50
Mortar & Pestle	26.50
Mug, Yellow, 1934	14.00
Pitcher, Gold Trim, Pink	110.00
Platter, Oval, Green, 11 1/2 In.	12.00
Vase, Art Deco, Ring Handle, Yellow, 5 In.	34.00
Vase, Bulbous, Narrow Neck, Flared Rim, Aqua Interior, 6 In.	14.00
Vase, Peach, 12 In.	25.00
Vase, State Fair, 1939, 9 In.	35.00
Vase, Tan, Turquoise, 6 In.	45.00
Vase, Turquoise Interior, Grecian Shape, White Matte, 12 In.	45.00
Vase, Turquoise, 5 In.	20.00
Vase, World's Fair, 1939, 9 In.	35.00
Vase, Yellow Matte, 5 1/2 In.	10.00

COPELAND SPODE ENGLAND   Josiah Spode established a pottery at Stoke-on-Trent, England, in 1770. In 1833, the firm was purchased by William Copeland and Thomas Garrett and the firm mark was changed. In 1847, Copeland became the sole owner and the mark changed again. W. T. Copeland & Sons continued until a 1976 merger when it became Royal Worcester Spode. Pieces are listed in this book under the name that appears in the mark. Copeland Spode, Copeland, and Royal Worcester have separate listings.

COPELAND SPODE, Bowl, Italian, 9 1/2 In.	60.00
Butter Chip, Rosebud Chintz, Set of 4	12.00
Chop Plate, Tower, Scalloped Border, 10 1/2 In.	22.00
Compote, Gold, Turquoise Dots, Florals, Open Rim, 9 1/2 In.	200.00
Cup & Saucer, Rosebud Chintz	25.00
Dish, Serving, Center Handle, Gold Edge, C.1906, 15 1/2 In.	75.00
Pitcher, Cameos of Pioneers, Indian, Chicago Fire, 9 In.	180.00
Pitcher, Raised Classical Figures, Dark Blue, 4 In.	95.00
Pitcher, Tower, 4 In.	25.00
Pitcher, Water, Willow, Covered, 1847–67, 8 1/2 X 8 In.	150.00
Punch Bowl, Blue Tower	140.00
Teapot, Billingsley Rose	75.00
Teapot, Salt Glaze, 5 1/4 In.	30.00
Tobacco Jar, Organ Grinder, Monkey, Musical, Bisque	110.00
COPELAND, Dish, Serving, Brown Transfer, Garrett, 13 In.	45.00
Jug, Enameled, Parian	350.00
Plate, Blue Willow, C.1885, 9 In.	26.00
Plate, Fox Pouncing On Pheasant, Sporting Scene, Wileman Mark	35.00
Plate, Red Breasted Bird, Holly & Berries, Marked, 9 1/2 In.	95.00
Soup, Dish, Blue Willow, C.1885, 7 3/4 In.	26.00
Tea Set, Classic Ruin Scenes, Acorn & Oak Leaf, 1855–65, 4 Piece	185.00

COPPER LUSTER, see Luster, Copper

 Utilitarian items, such as teakettles and cooking pans, have been handcrafted from copper in America since the days of the early colonists. Copper became a popular metal with the Arts and Crafts makers of the early 1900s and decorative pieces such as bookends and desk sets were made. Other pieces of copper may be found in the Bradley & Hubbard, Roycroft, and Kitchen categories.

COPPER, Andirons, Rooster Face	75.00

Ashtray, Poker, Benedict Studios, 6 1/2 In. 65.00
Bed Warmer, Hinged Circular Lid, Incised Vase, Flowers, 42 In. 385.00
Bed Warmer, Punched Bird Design 325.00
Blotter, Desk, Hammered, Gustav Stickley, C.1905, 25 X 15 In. 375.00
Boiler, Turned Wooden Side Handles, Oval 44.00
Bucket, Bale, Pouring Lip, N.Y.City, Marked 5 Gal. 185.00
Candlestick, Handle, Benedict Studios, 5 In., Pair 90.00
Candlestick, Handwrought, Kari Kipp, Pair 500.00
Chafing Dish, Shreve 600.00
Coffeepot, Brass Hinge, Gooseneck, Wooden Handle & Knob, 8 1/4 In. 48.00
Desk Set, Hammered, Tray, Chamberstick, Arts & Craft, Signed, 4 Piece 125.00
Dessert Set, Jarvie, Incised Signature, 20th Century, 13 Piece 325.00
Dish, Lead Flower Handle, Nekrassoff 65.00
Figurine, Eagle, Wings Spread 4400.00
Humidor, Pewter Bands, Apollo Studios, 7 1/2 In. 65.00
Jardiniere, Rolled Rim, Bulbous, Loop Handles, 8 X 16 In. 200.00
Measure, Graduated, Largest Marked 1 Gal., Set of 8 .... 300.00
Measure, Signed J.Benson, N.Y., Dated 1840, 6 To 11 1/2 In., 4 Piece 1430.00
    COPPER, MOLD, see also Kitchen, Mold
Mold, Deer Shape, Gelatin 8.00
Mold, Turk's Head, Swirl Design, Worn Tin Wash Lined, 10 In. 50.00
Pan, Tinned, Dovetailed, Curved Copper Handle, 6 1/2 In. 5.00
Pitcher, Hammered, Iron Handle, Arts & Crafts, 15 In. 100.00
Pitcher, Handmade, Sanford Ring, Cartersville, Ga., 6 1/2 In. 45.00
Pitcher, Measure, Hay Stack, Swing Handle, C.1880, 1 Gal. 65.00
Plaque, 4 Stylized Spades, G.Stickley, C.1905, 15 In. 400.00
Pot, 3 Legged, 9 X 7 In. 27.50
Pot, Footed, Iron Bail, Dovetailed, 4 X 6 In. 65.00
Sconce, Candle, Arts & Crafts 13.00
Skimmer, Hand Forged Handle 37.50
Teakettle, 10 X 7 1/2 In. 88.00
Teakettle, Brass Handle, J.M.Schwarz & Julje, 1856, 8 1/2 In. 130.00
Teakettle, Brass Stand, Alcohol Burner, English, 12 3/4 X 8 In. 165.00
Teakettle, Brass Trim, Lion Head Mark, S.O.F.A.B.E.X. 55.00
Teakettle, Child's, 2 1/4 In. 45.00
Teakettle, Dovetailed, Gooseneck Spout, Rolled Lid 250.00
Teakettle, Dovetailed, Oval, 4 X 6 In. 110.00
Teakettle, Gooseneck, Acorn Finial, Hollow Handle, Marked London 100.00
Teakettle, Gooseneck, C.Reed, Maysville, Ohio 235.00
Tray, Hammered, Gustav Stickley, Loop Handles, C.1905, 16 1/4 In. 250.00
Umbrella Holder, Gustav Stickley, Hammered, C.1905, 27 In. ....*Illus* 700.00
Urn, Hot Water, Baluster Form, Gadroon, Ivory Handles, Best, 17 In. 175.00
Vase, Cylinder, Hammered, Karl Kipp 770.00
Vase, Hammered, Gustav Stickley, No.26, C.1905, 10 1/2 In. 550.00
Vegetable, Covered, Hot Water Base, Insert, Marked Buffalo, 10 In. 85.00
Warming Pan, Brass Cover, Stylized Floral, Wood Handle, 42 In. 150.00

    Coralene glass was made by firing many small colored beads on the
    outside of glassware. It was made in many patterns in the United
    States and Europe in the 1880s. Reproductions are made today.

CORALENE, Bride's Bowl, No Basket, Blue Interior, White, Yellow Seaweed 700.00
    CORALENE, JAPANESE, see Japanese Coralene
Tumbler, Beads Form Flower, Enameled, Pontil Flashed 19.00
Tumbler, Rigaree Encircled Base, Pale Green, 4 3/4 In. 325.00
Vase, Flowers & Leaves, 3 Handles, Marked, 5 In. 185.00
Vase, Frosted White, Pink, Green, Deep Blue, Signed, 8 1/2 In. 225.00
Vase, Gold, Black Designs, Opaque Green, Signed, 12 In. 210.00
Vase, Multicolored Flowers, Leaves, Ribbed, Purple Ground, 8 In. 165.00
Vase, Panels, Outlined In Gold, Floral Center Panel, 7 In. 115.00
Vase, Scenes All Around, Pastel Colors, Marked, 7 In. 195.00
Vase, Seaweed, Gold Trim, Cranberry, 5 1/4 In. 225.00

The Cordey China Company was founded in 1942 by Boleslaw Cybis in Trenton, New Jersey. The firm produced gift shop items. Production stopped in 1950 and Cybis Porcelains was founded.

CORDEY, Box, Flower, Footed	55.00
Bust, Colonial Man & Woman, 12 In., Pair	225.00
Bust, Female, No.5014, 5 3/4 In.	55.00
Bust, Woman In Bonnet, No.5013–47	60.00
Bust, Woman, Ringlets, Lace Bodice, Floral On Lady & Base, 14 In.	210.00
Cat, Seated, Fluffy, Pink Collar, White	155.00
Figurine, Ballerina, Flowers & Lace On Costume, 11 1/2 In.	250.00
Figurine, Bambi Lamb, No.6025	95.00
Figurine, Bust, Madame DuBarry, Ringlets, Lace, Flowers, No.5084	185.00
Figurine, Cat, Seated, White	140.00
Figurine, Girl, In Riding Clothes, 17 In.	95.00
Figurine, Girl, No.5027–182	62.50
Figurine, Girl, Riding Habit, 15 In.	95.00
Figurine, Godey Lady, Ruffles, Pleats, Lace, 13 1/2 In.	130.00
Figurine, Grape Harvester, Man, No.305	90.00
Figurine, Man, No.4072, Gray Ringlet Pompadour, 13 1/2 In.	120.00
Figurine, Marcelle, 3/4 Lady, Seated, Lace Shawl, Ringlets, 10 In.	155.00
Figurine, Woman, No.4073, Bustle, Lace & Roses, Ringlets, 13 1/2 In.	120.00
Figurine, Woman, Shades of Green, No.304, 16 In.	80.00
Lamp, Madame & Monsieur, 2 Tier Base, Drum Shade, Pair	190.00
Lamp, Madame, Lace, Bustle, Streamers, 11 1/2 In.	85.00
Lamp, Woman, Full Length Figure, 14 In.	175.00
Plaque, Woman's Face, No.902	135.00
Vase, Portrait, Handles, 6 1/4 In.	200.00

There has been a need for a corkscrew since the first bottle was sealed with a cork, probably in the seventeenth century. Today collectors search for the early, unusual patented examples or the figural corkscrews of recent years.

CORKSCREW, Boar's Tusk	35.00
Bottle Shape, Brass Label, Anheuser–Busch, Brass, 1898, 3 In.	17.50
Bottle Shape, Peebles Old Cabinet Whiskey, Cincinnati, Ohio	25.00
Buccas, Legs of Steel, Marked Wolfenbuttel, C.1840	175.00
Crocodile, Carved	145.00
Figural, Lady, Celluloid, German	350.00
Folding Lady's Leg, Morgan Distilling Co., Kansas City	185.00
Horn, Sterling Ends, Embossed Flowers, Bottle Opener, 6 In.	110.00
Huntsman, Molded, 19th Century	30.00
John Gund Brewery, Wooden Handle	38.00
Kammer Whiskey, Baltimore Bullet, Dated 1903	23.00
Legs, Stoll & Co.Beer, Brass	175.00
Old Man, High Top Hat, Carrying Umbrella, Steel, C.1910, 6 In.	75.00
Pabst, Wood, Iron	17.00
Parrot, Bottle Opener, Chrome	30.00
Welch Grape Juice, Wood & Metal	25.00

Coronation cups have been made since the 1800s. Pottery or glass with a picture of the monarch and date have been souvenirs for many coronations. The pieces that mention King Edward VIII, the king who was never crowned, are not rare; and collectors should be sure to check values before buying.

CORONATION, see also Commemorative

CORONATION, Beaker, George V, Flags, Garlands, Portraits, 3 3/4 In.	55.00
Beaker, George VI & Queen Elizabeth, 1937, Green & Sand, Minton	200.00
Box, Edward VII, Queensware, Blue, Wedgwood, Round, 5 1/4 X 2 In.	50.00
Box, Elizabeth, Queensware, Wedgwood, Round, 5 In.	75.00
Cake Plate, 1937	25.00
Cup & Saucer, Edward VII & Queen Alexandra	55.00
Dish, Edward VII, Portraits, Cipher, 6 1/2 In.	23.00
Goblet, Edward VIII, Date, Quadruple Air Bubble Stem	65.00

Knife, Pocket, Queen Elizabeth II	35.00
Map, Processional Route, Woman's Journal, May 12, 1937	10.00
Paper Doll, Queen Elizabeth	20.00
Pitcher, King George VI & Queen Elizabeth, Aynsley, 4 In.	35.00
Plate, Edward & Alexandra, Portraits, Doulton, 1901, 9 In.	60.00
Plate, George VI, Beaded Wording, Pressed Glass, 10 In.	25.00
Plate, George, Elizabeth, Princesses' Portrait, 1937	32.00
Shaving Mug, Scuttle, George VI	50.00
Spoon, Tea Caddy, Edward VIII, Enameled Medallion On Handle	20.00
Teapot, Light Blue, Wedgwood, 1953	175.00
Textile, Woven Silk, Edward VII & Alexandra, 4 X 2 1/2 In.	325.00

Cosmos is a pressed milk glass pattern with colored flowers made from 1894 to 1915 by the Consolidated Lamp and Glass Company. Tablewares and lamps were made. A few pieces were also made of clear glass with painted decorations.

COSMOS, Butter, Covered	195.00 To 225.00
Butter, Pink Band, Covered	175.00 To 250.00
Condiment Set, Original Holder	350.00
Lamp, Clear, Miniature	175.00
Lamp, Floral Panels, Variant, Miniature	95.00
Lamp, Gone With The Wind, Miniature	145.00
Lamp, Miniature	65.00
Lamp, Oil	175.00
Pitcher, Pink Band, 5 In.	195.00
Pitcher, Water, Pink Band, 8 3/4 In.	225.00 To 245.00
Powder Jar, Covered	65.00
Salt & Pepper, Pink Band, 3 1/2 In.	195.00
Saltshaker, Pink Band	38.00
Table Set, Pink Band, 4 Piece	700.00

Linen or wool coverlets were made during the nineteenth century. Most of the coverlets date from 1800 to 1850. Four types were made: the double woven, jacquard, summer and winter, and overshot. Later coverlets were made of a variety of materials. Quilts are listed in this book in their own section.

COVERLET, Double Weave, Red, Blue & White, 2 Piece, 72 X 82 In.	95.00
Floral, 4 Colors, Signed & Dated 1841, 70 X 89 In., 2 Piece	695.00
Jacquard, 4 Eagles, 16 Point Star Center, White, 74 X 76 In.	200.00
Jacquard, 4 Rose Medallions, Birds, 82 X 94 In.	350.00
Jacquard, Blue & Ecru, C.1860, 85 X 64 1/2 In.	200.00
Jacquard, Blue & White Floral, Dated 1844, 73 X 89 In.	200.00
Jacquard, Blue & White, Inscription., S.Harris, 1827, 74 X 95 In.	475.00
Jacquard, Blue & White, Liberty, Washington Corners, 69 X 80 In.	325.00
Jacquard, Catherine J.Van Vleet, Lion Corners, 1843, 84 X 93 In.	425.00
Jacquard, Domed Building, Inscribed Memorial Hall, 80 X 82 In.	200.00
Jacquard, Double Weave, Blue & White Floral, 1844, 73 X 89 In.	200.00
Jacquard, Eagle Corners, Signed G.Rottman, 72 X 81 In.	525.00
Jacquard, Floral Design, Signed Corners, Dated 1848, 78 X 92 In.	375.00
Jacquard, Floral Medallions, C.Lochman, 1838, 82 X 102 In.	195.00
Jacquard, Floral, Basket of Flowers Border, M. Eversole 1876	125.00
Jacquard, Floral, Bird Border, S. Meily, Ohio, 1844, 71 X 76 In.	355.00
Jacquard, Floral, Green, Red, White & Gold, 82 X 86 In.	175.00
Jacquard, Floral, Samuel Meily, Ohio, 1848, 72 X 88 In., 2 Piece	150.00
Jacquard, Geometric Floral Design, Fringe, 73 X 84 In.	215.00
Jacquard, Hexagonal Tiles, Tulips, P.Maus, 1847, 98 X 74 In.	550.00
Jacquard, Red, Green, Blue & White, Signed & Dated, 86 X 94 In.	400.00
Jacquard, Roses, Rows of Leaves, Fringe, C.1850, 87 X 84 In.	395.00
Jacquard, Signed E.More 1839, Wool, 80 X 81 In.	600.00
Jacquard, Signed William Fleck, Findlay, Ohio, 1861, 72 X 90 In.	475.00
Jacquard, Single Weave, Floral, Center Medallion, 84 X 90 In.	350.00
Linsey–Woolsey, Calamanco, Dark Blue, 18th Century, 88 In.	2400.00
Overshot, Allover Design, 64 X 88 In.	165.00
Overshot, Blue & Red, Pennsylvania, 1844, Stripes, Red, Blue, Fringe	425.00

Cowan, Bookends, Elephant,
Lobster Red Glaze, 7 1/2 In.

Cowan, Flower Frog, Stork, 12 In.

Cowan, Flowerpot, Saucer, Orange, Red,
6 1/2 In.

Overshot, Floral Stripes, Susan Stoner 1844, 92 X 80 In.	425.00
Overshot, Green & White Wool, 96 X 60 In.	75.00
Plaid, Blue, Green & Red, 70 X 76 In., 2 Piece	75.00
Single Weave, Blue & White, 74 X 91 In.	100.00
Snowflake, Pine Tree Border, 76 X 80 In.	300.00
Trapunto, Whig Rose Variant, Oak Leaf Border, 9 Squares, 78 In.	200.00
White Popcorn, Full Size, 1939	75.00
White–On–White, 94 X 90 In.	40.00
Woven, 3 Panel, Blue & White, 90 X 108 In.	210.00

Guy Cowan made pottery in Rocky River, Ohio, a suburb of Cleveland, from 1913 to 1931. The Cowan Pottery made art pottery and wares for florists. A stylized mark with the word "Cowan" was used on most pieces. A commercial, mass–produced line was marked "Lakeware." Collectors today search for the Art Deco pieces by Guy Cowan, Viktor Schreckengost, Waylande Gregory, or Thelma Frazier Winter.

COWAN, Ashtray, Gazelle In Bottom, Flame & Brown	60.00
Bookends, Elephant, Bronze Push	155.00
Bookends, Elephant, Lobster Red Glaze, 7 1/2 In. *Illus*	150.00
Bookends, Girl & Boy, Ivory Colored	225.00
Bowl, Centerpiece, Art Nouveau, Wavy Floral Base, 8 X 5 In.	37.50
Bowl, Centerpiece, Wavy Floral Base, 8 X 6 1/4 X 5 In.	37.50
Bowl, Console, Blue Luster, 9 X 17 In.	45.00
Bowl, Frosted Brown Inside, Green Outside, 12 In.	24.00
Bowl, Oriental Red, Numbered, 15 X 11 1/2 In.	115.00
Bowl, Painted Swirl, 2 X 10 In.	60.00
Bowl, Pink Inside, Ivory Outside, 16 In.	20.00
Candelabra, 3–Light, Scroll, Cream, 4 1/2 X 7 In.	37.50
Candleholder, Seahorse, 4 In., Pair	20.00
Candlestick, Molded Nudes, White Glaze, 12 1/2 In., Pair	300.00
Candlestick, Octagonal Base, Lustrous Ivory, 3 1/4 In., Pair	20.00
Compote, Sea Monster Base, Pink & White, 3 In.	22.00
Figurine, Elephant, Black, Small	150.00
Figurine, Nude, No.698	115.00
Flower Frog, Draped Lady, 12 In.	250.00
Flower Frog, Gazelle On Leaves, 8 1/2 In.	145.00
Flower Frog, Nude, 6 1/2 In.	115.00
Flower Frog, Stork, 12 In. *Illus*	110.00
Flowerpot, Saucer, Orange, Red, 6 1/2 In. *Illus*	90.00
Lamp, Ginger Jar Shape, Embossed Leaves At Top, Matte Green, 8 In.	65.00
Lamp, Logan, Blue, Brass Fixture	65.00
Match Holder, Figural, Seahorse, Pedestal, Ivory, 6 1/2 In.	14.00
Match Holder, Ivory, 3 1/2 In.	25.00
Paperweight, Elephant, Black, 4 1/2 In.	150.00
Punch Bowl, Kazz, Turquoise, Black, Sgraffito, Schreckengost, 14 In.	8000.00

Teapot, Cream, 6 In.	85.00
Tile, Tea, Woman's Portrait	225.00
Trivet, Girl Silhouette, Dark Blue Ground, Green Border, 6 1/4 In.	200.00
Trivet, Tea, Molded Foliage, Hexagon, Ivory, 6 In.	55.00
Vase, Art Deco, Geometric Shape, Bronze, Green, 8 In.	125.00
Vase, Blue Luster, 10 In.	100.00
Vase, Brown Mottling, Orange Matte, 7 In.	50.00
Vase, Fan Shape, Seahorses At Base, Cream, 7 In.	35.00
Vase, Lakeware, 12 In.	100.00
Vase, Matte Green, Rose, 5 1/2 In.	45.00
Vase, Matte Ivory, 4 In.	30.00
Vase, Orange Luster, 5 In.	15.00
Vase, Orange Luster, Handles, 12 In.	65.00
Vase, Turquoise, Signed With Seal, 8 In.	70.00

Cracker Jack, the molasses–flavored popcorn mixture, was first made in 1896 in Chicago, Illinois. A prize was added to each box in 1912. Collectors search for the old boxes and toys and advertising materials. Many of the toys are unmarked.

CRACKER JACK, Booklet, Riddles, 32 Pages	25.00
Bookmark, Dog, Tin	7.00
Boy, With Dog, Plastic	15.00
Canister, Corn Crisp	125.00
Clock, Tin	28.00
Crate, Wooden	250.00
Daffy Dollar	10.00
Doll, Sailor Boy, In Display, Vogue, 13 In.	9.00
Funny Face, Paper	15.00
Pencil	5.00
Pin, Horse & Covered Wagon, Tin	12.00
Police Badge	15.00
Puzzle, Heart, No.13	20.00
Queer Quarter	10.00
Roulette Wheel, Spinning, Cracker Jack Man	45.00
Sailboat, Dowst Mfg.	20.00
Sign, Boy, Box, Advertising, Paper, 5 Color, 17 X 22 In.	110.00
Sign, Jack, With Dog, Porcelain, 5 X 9 In.	18.00
Spinner, Rainbow	20.00
Thermos, Plastic	10.00
Top, 4–Leaf Clover	20.00
Toy, Toonerville Trolley	275.00
Train Engine	8.00
Watch, Tin, 1 1/2 In.	18.00
Whistle, Tin	8.00 To 12.00

Crackle glass was originally made by the Venetians, but most of the ware found today dates from the 1800s. The glass was heated, cooled, and refired so that many small lines appeared inside the glass. It was made in many factories in the United States and Europe.

CRACKLE GLASS, Candlestick, Blue, Gold Flash, Pair	40.00
Liquor Set, Egg, Opens Up, Low Standard, 7 Piece	100.00
Vase, Clear, Electric Blue Applied Handles, Art Deco, 8 In.	49.00
Vase, Green, Pinched Sides, Ring Mark, 6 In.	30.00
Vase, Iridescent Blue, Frosted Panels, 14 In.	300.00

Cranberry glass is an almost transparent yellow–red glass. It resembles the color of cranberry juice. The glass has been made in Europe and America since the Civil War. It is still being made and reproductions can fool the unwary.

CRANBERRY GLASS, see also Northwood; Rubena Verde; etc.

CRANBERRY GLASS, Basket, Clear Shell Feet & Handle, Ruffled, 7 1/4 In.	150.00
Basket, Clear Twisted Applied Handle, Fluted, 6 1/4 In.	150.00
Basket, Crystal Feet, Clear Reeded Handle, Round, 7 In.	175.00

Biscuit Jar, Ribbed Body, Ruffled Crystal Panels, 8 In. 540.00
Biscuit Jar, White Craquelle Exterior, Brass, 7 In. 380.00
Bottle, Perfume, Clear To Cranberry, Cup Shape, 7 3/4 In. 300.00
Bowl Set, Fern Pattern, Ruffled, C.1894, 8 In., 7 Piece 175.00
Bowl, 3 Crystal Applied Feet & Berry Prunts, 5 In. 325.00
Bowl, Centerpiece, Gilded Iron Frame, 8 3/4 In. 95.00
Bowl, Coin Dot, Opalescent, Fenton, 10 In. 55.00
Bowl, Crystal Applied Leaves, Branches, Crimp Top, 3 In. 245.00
Box, Covered, Allover Gold, Enameled Flowers, 3 X 2 In. 35.00
Box, Enameled Colonial Girl Silhouette Cover, 4 3/8 In. 145.00
Box, Hinged Lid, Gold Flowers & Leaves, 3 1/8 X 3 In. 135.00
Box, Hinged, Enameled Colonial Girl Silhouette, 3 X 4 In. 145.00
Butter, Covered, Shell Trim At Corners, 6 X 5 1/4 In. 125.00
Castor, Pickle, Thumbprint, Daisies, Tongs 275.00
Castor, Pickle, Tongs, Raised Enameling, 10 1/2 In. 180.00
Compote, Scalloped Edge, Gold Trim, 9 X 9 1/4 In. 275.00
Compote, Sweetmeat, Covered, Honeycomb Finial, 7 1/2 In. 95.00
Cracker Jar, Inverted Thumbprint 300.00
Cruet, Clear Spun Rope Handle, Faceted Stopper, 8 In. 88.00
Cruet, Enamel Design, Clear Handle & Stopper 110.00
Cruet, Gold Trim, Faceted Finial Top, Leaves, Gold Flowers 125.00
Cruet, Hobnail, Clear Handle, Faceted Stopper, 6 1/2 In. 35.00
Cruet, Royal Ivy, Frosted 325.00
Cruet, Scrolls, Blossoms, Geometrics, Acid Etched, 7 In. 485.00
Cruet, Threaded, Brass Lid, Base, & Handle 95.00
Cruet, Thumbprint, Ribbed Handle, Clear Stopper 60.00
Cruet, Wine, Pewter Cherub Stopper, 9 In. 270.00
Cup & Saucer, Eastern Decoration, Clear Handle, Demitasse 75.00
Cup & Saucer, Lacy Gold Flowers & Leaves, Gold Trim 125.00
Decanter, Cut, Original Stopper, 16 In. 125.00
Decanter, Dot Optic 185.00
Decanter, Gold & White, Design, Clear Stopper, 11 1/2 In. 138.00
Dish, Pin, Ormolu Holder, Footed, Daisies, Flowers, 4 In. 85.00
Dish, Sweetmeat, Melon, Silver Plated Holder, 3 1/4 In. 88.00
Dresser Set, Lacy Gold Foliage, Gold Trim, 5 Piece 295.00
Epergne, Clear Stems, Crystal Leaves At Top, 16 In. 550.00
Finger Bowl, Gold Butterflies, Leaves, 4 1/8 In. 135.00
Finger Bowl, Hobnail, Polished Pontil 185.00
Finger Bowl, Inverted Thumbprint, 4 3/4 In. 85.00
Flask, Lady's, Brass Filigree, Screw Top, 5 X 1 1/4 In. 450.00
Jar, Inverted Thumbprint, Covered, Rigaree, 6 1/2 In. 125.00
Lamp Font, Hobnail, 4 X 4 1/4 In. 37.00
Lamp, Fairy, Figural, Pyramid, Double Faced Owl Head, 4 In. 195.00
Lamp, Oil, Opalescent, Coin Dot, Electrified, 8 In. 245.00
Liqueur Set, Tray, Clear Handle, Ball Stopper, 7 Piece 225.00
Peg Lamp Font, Allover Floral, 6 1/2 In. 75.00
Perfume Bottle, 10 Panels, Sterling Silver End, 5 1/4 In. 185.00
Pitcher, 3 Petal Top, Clear Handle, Ribbed, 7 1/2 In. 98.00
Pitcher, Chrysanthemum Base, Swirl, 9 1/2 In. 600.00
Pitcher, Gold Flowers, Leaves, Clear Handle & Foot, 6 In. 135.00
Pitcher, Inverted Thumbprint, Clear Handle, 5 1/2 In. 95.00
Pitcher, Optic Panels, Clear Handle, 4 1/2 In. 60.00
Pitcher, Tankard Shape, Clear Reeded Handle, 7 In. 98.00
Rose Bowl, 10 Crimp Top, Enameled Flowers, 5 X 4 In. 145.00
Rose Bowl, Egg Shape, Applied Crystal Swags, 4 3/4 In. 255.00
Rose Bowl, Pressed, Interior Melon Ribs, 3 1/2 In. 125.00
Salt & Pepper, Venetian Diamond Ring Neck 125.00
Salt, Crystal Footed, Shell Trim Center, 2 1/8 X 4 In. 60.00
Salt, Crystal Shell Trim & Feet, 2 1/8 X 3 In. 60.00
Salt, Gold Striped, Iridescent, Monot Stumpf, 1880 .... 68.00
Salt, Opaque Threading, Footed, Petal Feet, 3 X 1 1/2 In. 55.00
Salt, Scalloped Top, Crystal Shell Feet, 2 1/2 X 2 In. 40.00
Salt, Silver Plated Holder, Rigaree Center, 3 In. 95.00
Sugar & Creamer, Fluted, Crystal Petal Feet, 5 1/8 In. 125.00

Creamware, Jug, Couple Strolling, Enameled, C.1815, 8 5/8 In.

Creamware, Toby Jug, Collier, Foaming Ale, C.1775, 9 3/4 In.

Sugar Castor, Pressed, 12 Sides, Metal Top, 5 1/4 In.	150.00
Sugar Shaker, Cut Panels, 5 3/4 In.	60.00
Sugar Shaker, Opalescent Stripe, Bowling Pin Shape	75.00
Sugar Shaker, Venetian Diamond Ring Neck	125.00
Toothpick, Opalescent Stripe, Ring Neck	135.00
Tray, Dresser, Enameled Flowers, Gold, 6 1/4 X 9 1/2 In.	110.00
Tumbler, Baby Thumbprint Inverted, Enameled Floral	28.00
Tumbler, Inverted Thumbprint, Daises, Forget–Me–Nots	45.00
Tumbler, Lacy Flower Design Etched, 4 3/8 In.	30.00
Tumbler, White Enameled Lacy Work	22.50
Vase, Applied Shell Trim On Sides, Berries, 13 1/4 In.	235.00
Vase, Crystal Applied Flowers, Tricorner Top, 5 In.	175.00
Vase, Crystal Trim, Stem & Feet, Green Petals, 6 1/2 In.	125.00
Vase, Floral Panels, White Enameling, Gold Rim, 16 In.	350.00
Vase, Flowers, Leaves, Gold, Applied Tassels, 4 1/2 In.	175.00
Vase, Fluted Trumpet, Spiral Trim, Clear Foot, 8 3/8 In.	85.00
Vase, Jack–In–The–Pulpit, Flared Base, 12 3/4 In.	145.00
Vase, Jack–In–The–Pulpit, Rigaree Spirals, 9 1/2 In.	118.00
Vase, Jack–In–The–Pulpit, Spiral Trim, Footed, 9 3/8 In.	118.00
Vase, Log Shape, Crystal Applied Leaves & Feet, 2 X 7 In.	165.00
Vase, Swirl, Opalescent, Bulbous, Footed, Ruffled, 9 In.	129.00
Vase, Trumpet, Clear Edging & Foot, 12 1/8 In.	145.00
Vase, White Enameled Flowers, Leaves, Gold Leaves, 12 In.	150.00
Water Set, Blue Forget–Me–Nots, White Scrolling, 5 Piece	250.00
Water Set, Thumbprint, 7 Piece	150.00

Creamware, or queensware, was developed by Josiah Wedgwood about 1765. It is a cream-colored earthenware that has been copied by many factories.

CREAMWARE, see also Wedgwood

CREAMWARE, Bowl, Cream, Covered, Stand, Ladle, C.1780	1650.00
Candlestick, C.1790, Pair	1300.00
Jardiniere, Duck Form, Green & Brown Accents, 6 3/4 In.	275.00
Jug, Couple Strolling, Enameled, C.1815, 8 5/8 In. ....*Illus*	550.00
Orange Basket, Wedgwood, C.1775	4200.00
Sugar & Creamer, Forget–Me–Nots	135.00
Tankard Set, Dutch, 6 Different Shaped Mugs, 7 Piece	295.00
Teapot, C.1785, Miniature	525.00
Teapot, Prodigal Son, Greatbatch, C.1780	2500.00
Teapot, Red Transfer, Steamboat, Purple Luster Trim, 5 3/8 In.	125.00
Toby Jug, Collier, Foaming Ale, C.1775, 9 3/4 In. ....*Illus*	1100.00

A faience factory was established at Creil, France, in 1794. The company merged with a factory in Montereau in 1819. The firm made stoneware, mocha ware, and soft paste porcelain. The name Creil appears as part of the mark on many pieces. The Creil factory closed in 1895.

CREIL, Creamer, Woman, Child, Black Transfer 175.00
Plate, Military Scene, Black Transfer, Yellow 85.00

Crown Derby is the nickname given to the works of the Royal Crown Derby factory, which began working in England in 1859. An earlier and more famous English Derby factory existed from 1750 to 1848. The two factories were not related. Most of the porcelain found today with the Derby mark is the work of the later Derby factory.

CROWN DERBY, see also Derby; Royal Crown Derby
CROWN DERBY, Box, Cigarette, Terrier, Signed Gresley, Rectangular 195.00
Cup & Saucer, Chinese Design, C.1840 .... 130.00
Cup & Saucer, Imari Colors, Red, Cobalt, Gold, 1889, Demitasse 60.00
Cup & Saucer, Tea, Imari 110.00
Figurine, Young Girl, Victorian Dress, Holding Flowers 255.00
Jug, Floral, Green & White Ground, 2 In. 75.00
Plate, Dinner, Imari 95.00
Stirrup Cup, Hound's Head, Salmon & Iron Red Muzzle, 5 5/8 In. 605.00
Vase, Gold, Silver Allover Design, Reticulated Handles, 10 In. 325.00

Crown Milano glass was made by Frederick Shirley about 1890. It had a plain biscuit color with a satin finish. It was decorated with flowers and often had large gold scrolls.

CROWN MILANO, Biscuit Jar, Daisies, Signed Pairpoint Lid & Base 315.00
Biscuit Jar, Melon Shape, Ribbed, Raised Enameling, Signed 425.00
Biscuit Jar, Oak Branch, Leaves, Acorns, Paper Label, 9 In. 885.00
Biscuit Jar, Overall Pastel Floral & Leaf, Gilt Edging 675.00
Biscuit Jar, Sterling Silver Lid, Mums, Signed 350.00
Bottle, Cologne, Floral, Gold, Jeweled Stopper, Signed, 6 In. 210.00
Bowl, Roses, White, Metal Rim, Melon Shape, Marked, 9 In. 450.00
Box, Red Scrolls & Flowers, White Ground, Marked, 6 X 3 In. 810.00
Cracker Jar, Melon Ribbed, Blackberry Branch, Fruit 735.00
Cracker Jar, Melon Ribbed, Dresden Type Design, 8 1/2 In. 785.00
Cracker Jar, Melon Ribbed, White, Blossom Sprays, Signed, 7 In. 785.00
Cracker Jar, Molded-In Flowers & Scrolls, Silver Plated Top 485.00
Cracker Jar, Random Sprays, Tulips, Daisies, 8 1/2 In. 785.00
Cracker Jar, Ribbed, Silver Plated Lid, 8 1/2 In. 785.00
Cracker Jar, Satin Glass, Pansies, Gold Scrolling 225.00
Dish, Sweetmeat, Starfish, Signed 700.00
Ewer, Gold Flowers, Ivory, Green Scrolling, 11 In. ....*Illus* 450.00
Jar, Condiment, Gold Scrolls, Pink Roses, Silver Plated Lid 295.00
Jar, Melon Shape, Raised Enameling, Metal Top, Signed 450.00
Pitcher, Applied Handle, Signed, 7 X7 In. 300.00
Pitcher, Gold & Black Floral, Serpent Handle, 8 In. ....*Illus* 900.00
Powder Jar, Enameled Ribbons & Bouquets On Lid, 3 In. 485.00
Powder Jar, Gilt Ribboned Bouquets On Cover, Marked, 3 In. 485.00
Salt, Ribbed, Flowers & Scrolls, Footed 165.00
Spooner, Gold Flowers, Silver Plated Top 85.00
Sugar & Creamer, Lusterless, Pink Edge, Gold Trim, Violets 910.00
Sweetmeat, Pink, White, Shell, Silver Plated Holder, Signed 475.00
Syrup, Lacy Tendrils, Silver Plated Fittings 985.00
Syrup, Melon Ribbed, Tan Florals, Raised Bouquets, Signed 1250.00
Toothpick, Rust, White, Autumn Leaves, Beaded Rim, 2 1/2 In. 240.00
Vase, Cream Ground, Roses, Petals, Oval, 8 1/2 In. 450.00
Vase, Diamond-Quilted, Flower & Leaf Design, 3 1/2 In. 325.00
Vase, Enameled Dot Design, Orange Floral & Scroll, 13 In. 930.00
Vase, Enameled Free Form Geometric Pattern, Handles, 8 In. 745.00
Vase, Maiden Hair Fern, Gold Medallion, 9 In. 395.00

Vase, Square, Rounded Corners, Geometric Design, 8 In. 645.00
Vase, Thorn Handles, Pansies, Raised Gold Scrolls, 10 In. 750.00
   CROWN TUSCAN, see Cambridge

Cruets of glass or porcelain were made to hold vinegar, oil, and other condiments. They were especially popular during Victorian times but have been made in a variety of styles since the eighteenth century.

   CRUET, see also Castor Set
CRUET, Amber Glass, Blue Handle & Stopper, Ribbed, 3 Petal Top, 7 5/8 In. 65.00
  Amber Glass, Encased In Embossed Pewter, Flattened Bulbous, 8 In. 150.00
  Amber, Electric Blue, Blue Bubble Stopper & Rope Handle, 10 1/4 In. 85.00
  Beaded Medallion Pattern, Blue, Clear Stopper, 19th Century, 7 In. 55.00
  Berry, Applied Handle, Green, 19th Century, 6 In. 55.00
  Blown, Cranberry, Opalescent Fern Design, Handle, Stopper, 7 1/2 In. 65.00
  Blown, Cranberry, Opalescent Swirl Design, Handle, Stopper, 7 In. 55.00
  Blown, Emerald Green, White Enameled Floral, Footed, Handle, 8 In. 35.00
  Blown, Frosted, Clear Handle, 7 In. 55.00
  Blown, Grated Diamond & Fan, Matching Stopper, 6 In. 20.00
  Blown, Hobnail, Blue, Amber Handle, Stopper, 19th Century, 8 In. 44.00
  Chocolate Glass, 19th Century, 6 In. 77.00
  Cranberry Opalescent, Coin Dot, Smooth Handle 55.00
  Custard Glass, Floral Design, Ribbed, Clear Stopper, Blown, 6 1/2 In. 55.00
  Enameled Floral, Sapphire Blue, Amber Handle & Stopper, 7 3/4 In. 110.00
  Lime Green, Enameled Floral, Green Handle & Bubble Stopper, 8 In. 95.00
  Millefiori, Blown, Applied Clear Handle, Faceted Stopper, 7 In. 55.00
  Opalescent Cranberry, Ribbed, Clear Applied Handle, Stopper, 7 In. 99.00
  Opalescent Fern, Frosted Cranberry, Blown Glass, 7 1/2 In. 66.00
  Pink, White, Latticinio Blown Glass, Clear Handle, 8 In. 44.00
  Pressed Glass, Green, Berry Design, Applied Handle, Stopper, 5 In. 55.00
  Pressed Glass, Whimsey, Teardrop In Stopper, Applied Handle 50.00
  Royal Ivy, Rubina, Original Stopper 295.00
  Sapphire Blue, Amber Handle, Stopper, Gold Lacy Engraved, 6 5/8 In. 125.00
  Silver Overlay, Scrolled Design, 19th Century, 6 In. 110.00
  Vinegar, Blown Glass, 2 Mold, Applied Handle, 4 In.Stopper 50.00
  Virginia Pattern, Original Stopper, Tarentum Glass Co. 35.00
  Wheeling Drape, Amber, Blue 140.00

There are many marks that include the words "CT Germany." The first mark with those words was used by a company in Altwasser, Germany, in 1845. The initials stand for C. Thielsch, a partner in the firm. The Hutschenreuther firm took over the company in 1918 and continued to use the "CT."

CT GERMANY, Plate, Queen Louise, Scarf, Red Dress, 10 In. 50.00
  Vase, Scenic, Green, Blue, Gold, 10 In. 200.00

Cup plates are small glass or china plates that held the cup while a gentleman of the mid–nineteenth century drank his coffee or tea from the saucer. The most famous cup plates were made of glass at the Boston and Sandwich factory located in Sandwich, Massachusetts. There have been many new glass cup plates made in recent years for sale to the gift shops or the limited edition collectors. These are similar to the old plates but can be identified.

CUP PLATE, Corean, Mulberry, Staffordshire 35.00
  Flow Blue, Amoy, Davenport 50.00
  Fort Meigs, Sandwich Glass 50.00
  Gladstone, For The Millions, Marked 40.00
  Harp, Midwestern 80.00
  Henry Clay, Peacock Blue ....25.00 To 125.00
  Opalescent, Blue, Scalloped 50.00
  Sandwich, Lacy Opalescent 110.00
  Scalloped, Bubble Glass 27.00

Currier & Ives, Arguing The Point, 1855

Currier & Ives, First Premium Poultry,
Framed, 8 1/2 X 12 In.

Scalloped, Bull's–Eyes	165.00
Spatterware, House Scene	357.00
Spatterware, Pea Fowl	165.00
The Wedding Day & Day After	35.00
Torch Series, Midwestern	50.00
Washington & Stars	35.00

Currier & Ives made the famous American lithographs marked with their name from 1857 to 1907. The mark used on the print included the street address in New York City, and it is possible to date the year of the original issue from this information. Earlier prints were made by N. Currier and use that name from 1835 to 1847. Many reprints of the Currier or Currier & Ives prints have been made and it is the undamaged, untrimmed originals that are priced here unless otherwise noted. Many collectors also buy the insurance calendars that were based on the old prints. The words large, small, or medium folio refer to size.

CURRIER & IVES, 4 Seasons, American Homestead, 1868–69, Set of 4	1000.00
Arguing The Point, 1855 ....*Illus*	1000.00
Belle Hamlin & Justine, Hand Colored, 18 1/2 X 22 In.	90.00
Birthplace of Shakespeare, Framed, 12 1/2 X 19 In.	140.00
Camping Out, Original Frame, Large	2300.00
Champion of The Mississippi, Large	425.00
First Premium Poultry, Framed, 8 1/2 X 12 In. ....*Illus*	55.00
First Ride, Hand Colored, Frame, 12 X 15 In.	25.00
Frightened Brood, Beveled Frame, 13 X 16 1/4 In.	35.00
Fruits, Summer Varieties, Beveled Frame, 12 X 16 1/4 In.	65.00
Home In The Wilderness, Original Frame, 1870, Small	325.00
Home of Washington, Hand Colored, Frame, 19 3/4 X 25 In.	120.00
Life of A Sportsman Coming Into Camp, Framed, 1872, Small	250.00
Mamma's Pet, Hand Colored, Gilt Frame, 16 X 17 3/4 In.	105.00
Margaret, Framed, 14 1/2 X 18 1/2 In.	45.00
Memory, Anna C.Schoenberger, In German, Framed, 12 X 16 In.	40.00
Memory, Mrs.C.Sangley, Died March 2, 1844, 13 X 16 3/4 In.	225.00
Morning of Life, 11 X 15 In.	50.00
Mountain Bridge, Framed, 11 3/4 X 15 3/4 In.	45.00
Mountain Ramble, Cross Corner Frame, 11 X 15 1/4 In.	25.00
My Little White Kitties Playing Dominoes, 12 X 16 In.	85.00
New England Home, Walnut Frame, 16 X 20 In.	160.00
Night By The Campfire, Framed, C.1861, Medium	325.00
Night On The Hudson, Through At Daybreak, 18 1/2 X 24 In.	5750.00

O'Sullivan's Cascade, Matted, Framed, 17 X 19 1/2 In.	55.00
Odd Fellows, N.Currier, Framed, 12 1/4 X 16 1/4 In.	25.00
Old Farm House, Hand Tinted, Framed, C.1872, Small	500.00
Old Oaken Bucket, Hand Tinted, Framed, 1872, Small	200.00
One Flag, One Country, Zwei Lager, 12 X 15 In.	45.00
Return From The Woods, Gilt Frame, 15 3/4 X 20 1/2 In.	155.00
Return, Beveled Frame, 12 1/2 X 16 1/2 In.	13.00
Revenge, Dog Fight, Framed, 14 X 18 In.	60.00
Summer Fruits, 8 1/2 X 12 In. ......*Illus*	60.00
Summer Morning, Reprint, Framed, 11 X 17 In.	45.00
Through To The Pacific, Hand Colored, 1870, 12 X 16 In.	1200.00
Trade Card, No Ma'am I Don't Come To Shoot Birds, Hunter	50.00
Tree of Life, Mahogany Veneer Frame, 14 1/4 X 18 1/4 In.	65.00
Two Pets, Framed, 12 5/8 X 16 5/8 In.	45.00
Winter Morning, Feeding The Chickens, C.1863 ......*Illus*	4400.00
CURRIER, James Polk, Beveled Frame, Hand Colored, 13 X 16 1/2 In.	115.00
Life & Age of Man, Beveled Frame, 12 1/2 X 16 1/2 In.	145.00
Royal Mail Steamship Arabia, 23 X 30 In.	325.00

Custard glass is an opaque glass sometimes called "buttermilk glass." It was first made in the United States after 1886 at the La Belle Glass Works, Bridgeport, Ohio. It is being reproduced.

CUSTARD GLASS, see also Maize

CUSTARD GLASS, Argonaut Shell, Berry Bowl, Master, Gold, Enameled	195.00
Argonaut Shell, Butter, Covered, Northwood In Script	95.00
Argonaut Shell, Compote, Jelly	155.00
Argonaut Shell, Creamer	135.00
Argonaut Shell, Cruet, Original Stopper ......435.00 To	450.00
Argonaut Shell, Pitcher, Water, Signed	375.00
Argonaut Shell, Table Set, Gold Trim, 4 Piece	650.00
Argonaut Shell, Water Set, Northwood, 5 Piece	450.00
Beaded Circle, Berry Bowl, Northwood, Master	140.00
Beaded Circle, Spooner	80.00
Bell, Wide Band	95.00
Chrysanthemum Sprig, Berry Bowl, Blue ......125.00 To	250.00
Chrysanthemum Sprig, Berry Set, Northwood, 5 Piece	365.00
Chrysanthemum Sprig, Berry Set, Northwood, 7 Piece	550.00
Chrysanthemum Sprig, Bowl, Oval, Original Gold, 10 1/2 In.	135.00
Chrysanthemum Sprig, Butter, Covered, Marked, Blue	375.00
Chrysanthemum Sprig, Celery ......525.00 To	650.00
Chrysanthemum Sprig, Compote, Jelly ......40.00 To	70.00

Currier & Ives, Summer Fruits, 8 1/2 X 12 In.

Currier & Ives, Winter Morning,
Feeding The Chickens, C.1863

Chrysanthemum Sprig, Condiment Set	550.00
Chrysanthemum Sprig, Creamer, Northwood, Blue	235.00
Chrysanthemum Sprig, Cruet, Cream Ground, 6 1/4 In.	385.00
Chrysanthemum Sprig, Cruet, Gold, Coral, Green, 6 3/4 In.	385.00
Chrysanthemum Sprig, Cruet, Original Stopper .... 225.00 To	385.00
Chrysanthemum Sprig, Pitcher, Gold Trim, Northwood, Blue	675.00
Chrysanthemum Sprig, Pitcher, Water, Gold	360.00
Chrysanthemum Sprig, Salt & Pepper	140.00
Chrysanthemum Sprig, Saucer, Blue, Northwood, 5 In.	70.00
Chrysanthemum Sprig, Spooner, Blue .... 175.00 To	310.00
Chrysanthemum Sprig, Sugar & Creamer, Open	160.00
Chrysanthemum Sprig, Sugar, Covered, Gold Trim, Signed	375.00
Chrysanthemum Sprig, Table Set, 4 Piece	595.00
Chrysanthemum Sprig, Table Set, Northwood, Blue, 4 Piece	1695.00
Chrysanthemum Sprig, Toothpick .... 175.00 To	275.00
Chrysanthemum Sprig, Tray, Condiment, Gold Trim, Design	575.00
Chrysanthemum Sprig, Tumbler, Gold Trim	40.00
Chrysanthemum Sprig, Water Set, Gold Trim, Blue, 7 Piece	950.00
Diamond With Peg, Napkin Ring, Rose Design, Souvenir, Pair	250.00
Diamond With Peg, Toothpick, Coney Island	40.00
Diamond With Peg, Tumbler, Jefferson	35.00
Diamond With Peg, Tumbler, John Kleber	45.00
Diamond With Peg, Wine, Souvenir	40.00
Everglades, Berry Bowl, Gold Trim & Design, Small	65.00
Everglades, Berry Set, Gold Trim, Green, 7 Piece	550.00
Everglades, Spooner	135.00
Everglades, Tumbler .... 105.00 To	110.00
Fan, Creamer, Gold, Northwood	95.00
Fan, Water Set, Gold Trim, 7 Piece	650.00
Fine Cut & Roses, Rose Bowl, Nutmeg Stain .... 55.00 To	85.00
Fluted Scroll, Flower Band, Pitcher, Water, Scroll Feet	250.00
Fluted Scroll, Pitcher, Water, Flower Band, Gold Trim	250.00
Fluted Scroll, With Flower, Berry Bowl, Master	145.00
Geneva, Banana Boat	140.00
Geneva, Berry Bowl, Footed, Small, 4 Piece	120.00
Geneva, Butter, Covered, Child's	90.00
Geneva, Creamer, Gold Trim, Green	57.50
Geneva, Cruet, Original Stopper	165.00
Geneva, Saltshaker	35.00
Geneva, Spooner, Red & Green Design .... 65.00 To	75.00
Geneva, Sugar, Covered, Red & Green Design	125.00
Geneva, Sugar, Open, Green Stain	65.00
Georgia Gem, Berry Bowl, 9 In.	78.00
Georgia Gem, Butter, Covered .... 175.00 To	195.00
Georgia Gem, Creamer, Waukesha	40.00
Georgia Gem, Mug, Footed, Green, Sebasca, Me.In Gold	45.00
Georgia Gem, Pitcher, Water, Pea Green	165.00
Georgia Gem, Powder Jar, Covered, Public Library, Weare, N.H.	45.00
Georgia Gem, Sugar, Bellaire, Mich., 1903	45.00
Grape & Cable, Bowl, Fruit, Pink Stain, Northwood	800.00
Grape & Cable, Bowl, Scalloped, Nutmeg Stain, 7 1/2 In.	17.50
Grape & Cable, Fernery, Pink Stain, Northwood	2400.00
Grape & Cable, Orange Bowl, Blue Stain, Northwood....................	450.00
Grape & Cable, Plate, Tan, Basketweave, Northwood, 7 1/2 In.	47.00
Grape & Cable, Sugar & Creamer, Nutmeg Stain	95.00
Grape & Cable, Tray, Pin, Oval, Nutmeg Stain	145.00
Grape & Gothic Arches, Goblet, Nutmeg Stain	50.00
Grape & Gothic Arches, Spooner	50.00
Grape & Gothic Arches, Tumbler, Pearlized With Gold	50.00
Grape & Gothic Arches, Vase, Nutmeg Stain	55.00
Heart With Thumbprint, Tumbler, Gold Trim	55.00
Intaglio, Butter, Covered, Blue Design	165.00
Intaglio, Compote, Gold, 9 X 6 In.	375.00
Intaglio, Cruet, Blue Design	150.00

Intaglio, Cruet, Gold Trim, Green, Original Stopper 295.00
Intaglio, Spooner, Green 75.00
Intaglio, Sugar & Creamer, Green Design .... 100.00 To 150.00
Intaglio, Sugar, Covered, Gold Trim, Blue 125.00
Intaglio, Sugar, Covered, Green ....90.00 To 125.00
Intaglio, Table Set, Gold Trim, Green, 4 Piece 425.00
Intaglio, Table Set, Northwood, Green Design, 4 Piece 650.00
Inverted Fan & Feather, Berry Bowl, Green, Gold Trim 30.00
Inverted Fan & Feather, Butter, Covered .... 275.00 To 365.00
Inverted Fan & Feather, Compote, Jelly, Rose Design 255.00
Inverted Fan & Feather, Creamer, Green, Gold Trim 50.00
Inverted Fan & Feather, Pitcher, Water, Gold & Pink Trim 395.00
Inverted Fan & Feather, Punch Cup, Gold Rim 185.00
Inverted Fan & Feather, Saucer, Pink, Gold Trim, 4 In. 48.00
Inverted Fan & Feather, Spooner ....80.00 To 130.00
Inverted Fan & Feather, Sugar, Gold 65.00
Inverted Fan & Feather, Water Set, Gold Trim, 7 Piece 795.00
  IVORINA VERDE, see Winged Scroll
Jackson, Creamer 45.00
Jackson, Cruet, Clear Faceted Stopper 50.00
Jackson, Water Set, 5 Piece 435.00
  LITTLE GEM, see also Georgia Gem
Little Gem, Butter, Covered, Design 150.00
Little Gem, Cruet, Cut Faceted Stopper, 7 In. 132.00
Louis XV, Berry Bowl, Master .... 125.00 To 165.00
Louis XV, Berry Bowl, Small 40.00
Louis XV, Butter, Covered, Gold Trim 85.00
Louis XV, Pitcher 125.00
Louis XV, Sauce, Green, Gold Trim ....20.00 To 45.00
Louis XV, Spooner, Green, Gold Trim 50.00
Louis XV, Table Set, 4 Piece .... 325.00 To 348.00
Louis XV, Table Set, Green, 4 Piece 500.00
Louis XV, Tumbler 60.00
Louis XV, Tumbler, Gold Trim 45.00
  MAIZE, see Maize category
Maple Leaf With Tree of Life, Tumbler 70.00
Maple Leaf, Berry Bowl, Master 235.00
Maple Leaf, Butter, Covered .... 150.00 To 225.00
Maple Leaf, Creamer, Gold Trim, Green 115.00
Maple Leaf, Spooner ....90.00 To 95.00
Maple Leaf, Spooner, Northwood 70.00
Maple Leaf, Table Set, Gold, 4 Piece 565.00
Maple Leaf, Tumbler 55.00
Maple Leaf, Tumbler, Gold Trim 95.00
Peacock At Urn, Bowl, Ice Cream, Nutmeg Stain, 10 In. 210.00
Ribbed Drape, Cruet, Roses 175.00
Ribbed Drape, Jefferson, Ice Cream Set, Child's, 7 Piece 295.00
Ribbed Drape, Jefferson, Table Set, Rose Design, 4 Piece 375.00
Ribbed Drape, Salt & Pepper 150.00
Ribbed Drape, Spooner 60.00
Ribbed Thumbprint, Creamer, Souvenir 35.00
Ring Band, Creamer, Individual, Chicago 35.00
Ring Band, Punch Cup, Heisey 25.00
Ring Band, Tumbler, 1902 .... 65.00
Singing Bird, Mug, Nutmeg Stain 85.00
Tarentum's Victoria, Butter, Red Chrysanthemums 79.00
Tiny Thumbprint, Butter, Covered 150.00
Wild Bouquet, Creamer 165.00
Wild Bouquet, Cruet, Gold & Paint, Original Stopper 575.00
Wild Bouquet, Spooner 110.00
Winged Scroll, Berry Set, Master Bowl, 8 1/2 In., 5 Piece 225.00
Winged Scroll, Jar, Cigarette, Scalloped Rim, Heisey 175.00
Winged Scroll, Pitcher, Heisey 325.00
Winged Scroll, Spooner, Gold Trim 80.00

Cut Glass, Basket,
Notched Handle, 14 In.

Cut Glass, Goblet,
Queen's, Set of 6

Cut Glass, Punch Bowl,
Temple, 2 Piece

Winged Scroll, Syrup, Gold	285.00
Winged Scroll, Table Set, 4 Piece	350.00
Winged Scroll, Toothpick	75.00 To 95.00
Winged Scroll, Water Set, Gold Trim, 7 Piece	375.00
CUT GLASS, see also listings under factory name	
CUT GLASS, Atomizer, Harvard Pattern, Gold Washed Top, 8 In.	145.00
Basket, Bonbon, Brilliant, Applied Twisted Handle, 6 1/2 In.	175.00
Basket, Cane, Bull's–Eye, Prism & Step Cut, Handle, 11 In.	550.00
Basket, Flower Center, Monarch, J.Hoare, 3 1/2 X 3 In.	260.00
Basket, Hobstars, Fine Diamonds, Strawberries, Fans, 6 X 5 In.	255.00
Basket, Notched Handle, 14 In. ....*Illus*	1000.00
Basket, Queen's Lace Pattern, 9 3/4 X 9 1/2 In.	150.00
Basket, Songbird & Flowers, Handle, L.Straus, 21 In.	425.00
Basket, Strawberry, Diamond, Hobstars, Allover Brilliant, 14 In.	375.00
Bell, Cornflowers & Leaves, 4 1/2 In.	165.00
Bell, Fans & Squares, Strawberry Diamond, 7 In.	295.00
Bell, Hobstars, Strawberry Diamond, Fine Diamond & Fan, 6 In.	225.00
Bell, Strawberry Diamond & Fan, Dorflinger, 6 3/4 In.	550.00
Berry Bowl, Hobstars & Fans, 5 In., 8 Piece	280.00
Berry Bowl, Pinwheel & Hobstar, Strawberry, Diamond, 8 In.	75.00
Berry Bowl, Trellis, 6 In.	385.00
Berry Set, Cluster, Egginton, 7 Piece	475.00
Bottle, Catsup, Loop Handle, Monarch Pattern, Signed Hoare	750.00
Bottle, Cologne, Dorflinger, 7 1/2 X 4 1/4 In.	195.00
Bottle, Cologne, Mitered Buttons, Vesicas, Stopper, 5 In., Pair	285.00
Bottle, Perfume, Dancing Girls, Floral Dauber, 1920s	295.00
Bottle, Perfume, Intaglio Florals, 6 Sides, Stopper, 5 3/4 In.	125.00
Bottle, Perfume, Lay Down, Stopper, Sterling Silver Top	100.00
Bottle, Perfume, Thumbprint, Embossed Caps, Stopper, Case, 7 In.	275.00
Bottle, Russian Cut, 8 1/4 In.	175.00
Bottle, Water, Notched Prisms & Ellipses, Hobstar Base	95.00
Bowl, Allover Brilliant Cut, Egginton, 8 X 2 1/2 In.	250.00
Bowl, Carolyn, Hoare, 9 In.	800.00
Bowl, Crosscut Diamonds, Fans, Hobstars, 8 In.	95.00
Bowl, Encore Pattern, Strauss & Sons, 7 X 5 In.	375.00
Bowl, Fruit, Fan, Diamond, Sawtooth, 19th Century, 10 1/8 In.	175.00
Bowl, Gladys, 9 1/4 X 4 In.	250.00
Bowl, Greek Key & Laurel, Oval, 7 X 5 In.	95.00
Bowl, Hobstars, Crosshatching, 8 X 4 In.	145.00
Bowl, Ice Cream, Corinthian Pattern, 10 1/2 X 5 1/4 In.	175.00
Bowl, Maple Leaf Mark, 8 X 2 1/2 In.	180.00
Bowl, Plymouth, Pitkins & Brooks, 9 In.	350.00
Bowl, Russian, Scored Buttons, 7 1/2 X 7 In.	150.00
Bowl, Strawberry Diamond, & Fan, Higgins & Seiter, 4 3/4 In.	65.00
Bowl, Trellis Pattern, Walter Egginton, 8 In.	725.00
Box, Harvard, Hinged Cover, Round, 7 X 2 3/4 In.	475.00

Box, Hinged Russian & Hobstar Lid, Square, 5 X 4 In. 295.00
Butter Chip, Swirled Hobstar 18.00
Butter Tub, Palm, Taylor Brothers 325.00
Butter, Covered, Russian, Flowers & Leaves, 5 X 7 In. 385.00
Cake Stand, Hobstars, Fans, 8 In. 150.00
Candlestick, Panel & Diamond Point, 5 1/2 In., Pair 30.00
Candlestick, Prismatic Stem, Cane Bottom, 7 1/4 In., Pair 275.00
Candlestick, Teardrops, Prism Ball Bottom, 8 1/2 In. 475.00
Candlestick, Tuthill, Teardrop Stems, 10 In., Pair 525.00
Canoe, All Harvard, 4 3/4 X 12 In. 175.00
Canoe, Harvard Sides, Hobstar Bottom, 11 1/4 In. 175.00
Carafe, Hobstars, Pinwheels, & Diamonds 95.00
Carafe, Water, Hobstars, Notched Prisms 110.00
Celery, Clarke, 12 X 4 1/2 In. 110.00
Celery, Hobstars, 11 In. 165.00
Celery, Wedgemere, Rolled–In Sides, 11 1/2 X 4 In. 465.00
Centerpiece, Starburst Petal, Sawtooth, 13 1/2 In. 150.00
Champagne, Cane, Concave Diamonds, 32 Point Star Foot 37.50
Clock, Harvard & Cosmos, 5 1/2 In. 165.00
Compote, Air Bubble Stem, Vesicas In Strawberry, 7 1/2 In. 195.00
Compote, Cane, Hobstars & Diamond, Hobstar Base, 7 1/2 X 5 In. 140.00
Compote, Covered, Arcadia, Bergen, 9 3/4 In. 1850.00
Compote, Daisies & Foliage, 8 In. 80.00
Compote, Diamond & Fan Cut Border, Knob Stem, Sawtooth, 6 In. 170.00
Compote, Engraved, Teardrop Stem, 8 3/4 In. 215.00
Compote, Hobstars, Crosshatching, 6 X 4 1/4 In. 65.00
Compote, Hobstars, Rayed & Notched Base, 9 In. 75.00
Compote, Jelly, Prism Cut Stem, Hawkes, 9 In. 185.00
Compote, Jelly, Teardrop Stem, Scalloped Hobstar Foot, 8 X 6 In. 285.00
Compote, Teardrop Stem, Cut Base, Hobstars, 9 1/2 In. 195.00
Cracker Jar, Honeycomb, Sterling Silver Top, 5 X 6 In. 175.00
Cruet, Alhambra, Meriden, 9 1/2 In. 625.00
Cruet, Allover Brilliant, Stopper, 7 In. 75.00
Cruet, Bull's–Eye & Zipper .... 55.00 To 60.00
Cruet, Cane Cutting, Diagonal Slashes 45.00
Cruet, Hobstars, Pinwheels, Rayed Base, Notched Handle, 9 1/2 In. 68.00
Cruet, Notched Handle, Sunburst Bottom, Zipper Cuttings, 9 In. 75.00
Cruet, Strawberry, Diamond & Fan, Faceted Stopper 55.00
Decanter, Bowling Pin Shape, Harvard & Roses Pattern, 15 In. 495.00
Decanter, Double Gooseneck, Fan & Star, Stopper, 13 In. 375.00
Decanter, Harvard Cut, Panels, Controlled Bubble Stopper, 15 In. 250.00
Decanter, Strawberry Diamond, Disc Foot, 12 In. 150.00
Decanter, Swirl, Fan & Strawberry Diamond, Ball Stopper 175.00
Decanter, Wine, Blaze Stars, Lapidary Cut Stopper 168.00
Decanter, Wine, Strawberry Diamond, Lapidary Stopper, 11 In. 185.00
Dish, Cheese, Covered, Hobstars, Diamond & Fan, Sunburst 375.00
Dish, Cheese, Dome Cover, Cluster Pattern, 9 1/2 X 7 In. 595.00
Dish, Cheese, Underplate, Allover Hobstars 375.00
Dish, Heart Shape, Florence Hobstar, Cane, 9 X 8 In. 175.00
Dish, Ice Cream, Brazilian, 6 In. 85.00
Dish, Jewel, Oval, Signed Libbey, 9 X 5 3/4 In. 155.00
Ewer, Wine, Silver Plated Lid, Handle, C.1880, 11 1/2 In., Pair 750.00
Finger Bowl, Baker's Gothic, Scalloped, Clarke 85.00
Finger Bowl, Croesus, Scalloped, Hoare 150.00
Finger Bowl, Russian, Star Button, 5 1/4 X 3 In., Pair 250.00
Flask, Lady's, Serrated Ribbing, Diamond Points, Silver Cap 135.00
Flowerpot, Fans, Stars, Crosscut & Strawberry Diamonds, 5 In. 115.00
Flowerpot, Hobstars & Pineapple 900.00
Fruit Bowl, Star, Jewel & Shield, Sawtooth, 4 1/2 X 10 5/8 In. 375.00
Goblet, Queen's, Set of 6 .... *Illus* 780.00
Goblet, Strawberry, Diamond, & Fan, Higgins & Seiter, 4 1/2 In. 60.00
Goblet, Water, Croesus, J.Hoare, 6 In. 325.00
Hair Receiver, Hobstars, Fine Diamond & Fans, Silver Lid 85.00
Hair Receiver, Intaglio Flowers, Buds, Sterling Silver Cover 90.00

Humidor, Greek Key, 7 X 5 In.	1650.00
Humidor, Hobstars and Fans, 6 1/4 In.	75.00
Ice Bucket, Harvard, Tab Handles, 7 X 5 1/2 In.	595.00
Inkwell, Harvard Bottom, Sterling Silver Top, Square, 2 3/8 In.	90.00
Jar, Powder, Sterling Lid, Woman In Hammock and Mouse	185.00
Jar, Puffy, Art Nouveau Sterling Silver Lid, C.1900	175.00
Jug, Hobstars, Crosscut Hobnail, Triple Notched Handle, 8 In.	350.00
Knife Rest, Allover Notched Prisms, Hourglass Shape, 4 In.	35.00
Knife Rest, Faceted Barbell Ends, American, 6 In.	55.00
Knife Rest, Knob, Faceted, 4 In.	45.00
Lamp, Brilliant, 2–Light, 21 1/2 X 12 In.	1500.00
Lamp, Cranberry To Clear Font, Opaque White Base, 13 1/2 In.	425.00
Lamp, Harvard, Hobstars, Pointed Top, 27 In.	2750.00
Lamp, LaRabida, Straus Glass Co., 21 In.	3200.00
Lamp, Mushroom, LaRabida, 21 In.	3200.00
Lamp, Oil, Strawberry Diamond & Fan, 26 In.	2500.00
Lamp, Thistle Pattern, 15 In.	895.00
Lemonade Set, Cornflowers, Lattice Cutting, Stemware, 5 Piece	325.00
Loving Cup, Zipper Pattern, 3 Handles, 7 In.	225.00
Muffineer, Prism Cut, Beading, Notched, Silver Plated Top, 4 In.	68.00
Mustard, Ball Shape, Strawberry & Fan, Silver Plated Cover	65.00
Mustard, Lid, Underplate, Notched Prisms, Knob, Hawkes, 7 In.	135.00
Mustard, Silver Plated Hinged Lid, Ball Shape, Strawberry & Fan	58.00
Mustard, Underplate, Covered, Renais Pattern, Dorflinger	135.00
Napkin Ring, Thistle Flower, 2 1/4 In.	45.00
Nappy, Double Notched Handle, Serrated Rim, Crescent Cuttings	58.00
Nappy, Harvard, Notched Handles, 8 In.	75.00
Nappy, Hobstars, Canes, Strawberry Diamonds, Handle, 12 In.	145.00
Nappy, Pinwheel, 6 1/4 In.	45.00
Nappy, Pinwheels & Hobstar, Square	55.00
Nappy, Star of Bethlehem	65.00
Orange Bowl, Large Fans Form Scalloped Rim, Cane Pattern, 9 In.	160.00
Pitcher, 4 Rows of Strawberry Diamond Buttons, Birds, 15 In.	450.00
Pitcher, Allover Harvard Variant, Including Foot, 13 1/2 In.	1100.00
Pitcher, Champagne, Silver Cover & Handle, Signed Hoare, 10 In.	120.00
Pitcher, Harvard Panels, Intaglio Leaf Sprays, 9 1/2 In.	150.00
Pitcher, Hobstars, Urn Shaped, Fluted Neck, 9 In.	338.00
Pitcher, Pineapple, 3 In.	125.00
Pitcher, Russian, Triple–Notched Handle, 7 3/8 X 4 1/2 In.	625.00
Pitcher, Sunburst, 10 In.	350.00
Pitcher, Water, Butterflies & Floral, 11 In.	165.00
Pitcher, Water, Flying Butterfly, 1 Qt.	55.00
Pitcher, Water, Intaglio Cut Flower, Wreath, Cut Handle, 10 In.	145.00
Pitcher, Wine, Columbia, Blackmer, 12 In.	650.00
Pitcher, Wine, Elmira Cut Glass Co., Hobstar Cut Base, 12 In.	650.00
Plate, Brunswick, Hawkes, 10 In.	650.00
Plate, Claremont, Wafer Base, Dorflinger, 10 1/4 In.	75.00
Plate, Hindoo, Hoare, 7 In.	135.00
Plate, Hobstar Center, Silver Thread Edge, Libbey, 10 In.	295.00
Powder Jar, Art Nouveau, Whiplash Design, Sterling Silver Cover	75.00
Powder Jar, Butterfly & Flowers Top, Bull's–Eye Sides, 8 In.	335.00

Powder Jar, Intaglio Floral & Leaf Spray On Hinged Lid	145.00
Powder Jar, Thumbprints & Strawberry Prunts, Intaglio Floral	165.00
Puff Jar, Multi–Rayed Base, Intaglio Flowers, Hinged, 6 1/2 In.	155.00
Punch Bowl, Colonial, Dorflinger, 12 X 9 1/2 In., 2 Piece	495.00
Punch Bowl, Hobstar & Cane ....*Illus*	1350.00
Punch Bowl, Hobstars, Mitered Stars, Sawtooth, America, 14 In.	425.00
Punch Bowl, Temple, 2 Piece ....*Illus*	1000.00
Punch Cup, Pineapple & Fan, 16 Point Star Center	13.00
Relish, Pinwheel & Hobstar, 6 In.	35.00
Rose Bowl, Hobstars, Canes, 6 In.	125.00
Rose Bowl, Queen's, 9 In. ....*Illus*	1400.00
Rose Bowl, Russian, Diamonds, Buttons, 7 1/2 X 7 In.	175.00
Rose Bowl, Strawberry, Diamond & Fan, Dorflinger, 6 1/2 In.	450.00
Salt & Pepper, Deep Amethyst, Matching Tops	48.00
Salt & Pepper, Overall Star & Ray, Sterling Silver Tops	38.00
Salt, Leaf Shape, Spiral Handle, German, Late 1940s, 2 5/8 In.	15.00
Salt, Prismatic Pattern, 2 Bands Sawtooth Sides, 1 3/4 In.	6.00
Sherbet & Underplate, Kalana Lily, Dorflinger	280.00
Spooner, 6–Point Star of David	175.00
Spooner, Buzz, Diamond & Fans, 2 Handles, 4 1/2 In.	210.00
Spooner, Drape .... 125.00 To 175.00	
Spooner, Frosted Intaglio Daisies	125.00
Spooner, Hobstars, Fan, Ornate Zipper, 4 1/4 In.	125.00
Sugar & Creamer, Buzz, Fans, Hobnail, Star Foot, 6 3/4 In.	975.00
Sugar & Creamer, Covered, Ulysses, 1891	475.00
Sugar & Creamer, Hobstar, Strawberry & Double Miter	330.00
Sugar & Creamer, Hobstars, Notched Panels, Corning	60.00
Sugar Holder, Domino, Hawkes, Signed	135.00
Sugar Shaker, Allover Notching, Beaded Sterling Silver Top	130.00
Sugar Shaker, Beaded Top, Pear Shape, Notched Prisms, Stars	65.00
Sugar Shaker, Hobstars, Diamond Cuts, Cane, Sterling Top	150.00
Syrup, Hinged Lid, Serrated Prisms, Block & Thumbprint	68.00
Syrup, Strawberry, Diamond, & Fan, Sterling Silver Stopper	120.00
Syrup, Vertical Notched Prism .... 110.00 To 125.00	
Syrup, Zipper, Double Notched Handle, Silver Top	185.00
Tankard, Chocolate, Hobstars, Cut Base & Handle, 11 3/4 In.	275.00
Tazza, Greek Key, Alhambra	1200.00
Tazza, Hobstar Base, 9 1/2 In.	250.00
Tobacco Jar, Chain Hobstar, Fan, Bull's–Eye, Sterling Cover	650.00
Toothpick, Allover Hobstars, Pedestal	75.00
Toothpick, Fluted Diamonds	42.00
Toothpick, Fluted Prisms	42.00
Toothpick, Zipper Cut, 3 In.	18.00
Tray, Bread, Strawberry, 8 X 11 1/2 In.	195.00
Tray, Cane, Hobstars, Strawberry, Step Cut Tabs, 13 1/2 X 8 In.	450.00
Tray, Dresser, Russian, 11 X 6 1/4 In.	245.00
Tray, Fish Tail ....*Illus*	1100.00
Tray, Flower Center, Step Cutting At Neck, Hobstars, Fan, 10 In.	575.00
Tray, Hobstars, 8 X 12 In.	400.00
Tray, Ice Cream, Allover Hobstar, Cane, Diamonds, 14 1/2 X 8 In.	495.00
Tray, Ice Cream, Colonna, Oval, 17 1/2 X 10 In.	795.00
Tray, Leaf Shape, Hobstar Bottom, Leaf Handle, 17 X 4 In.	250.00
Tray, Sugar Cube, Engraved Bird, Floral, Foliage, 9 In.	75.00
Tub, Butter, Underplate, Covered, Russian Cut	2000.00
Tumble–Up, Flutes & Vines, Green To Clear, Rayed Base	225.00
Tumbler, Intaglio Flowers & Leaves	15.00
Tumbler, Water, Hobstars, Pair	35.00
Vase, Allover Cut, Scalloped, Toothed Rim, Egginton, 12 In.	185.00
Vase, Butterflies, Floral, Starburst, Gundy–Clopperton, 18 In.	385.00
Vase, Corset Shape, Scalloped, Overall Hobbs, Canes, 12 In.	175.00
Vase, Crestwick, Signed Egginton, 5 In.	50.00
Vase, Decanter Shape, Hobstars Allover, 14 In.	1450.00
Vase, Double Hobstar, 13 In.	75.00
Vase, Hobstar, Cane & Diamond, Baluster Form, 16 In.	800.00

Vase, Kalana Poppy, Dorflinger, 12 In.	325.00
Vase, Montrose, Dorflinger, Emerald Green, Clear, 12 In.	1650.00
Vase, Pedestal, Teardop Stem, 14 In.	225.00
Vase, Pinwheels, Sawtooth Top, Corset Shape, 8 In.	95.00
Vase, Ruby To Clear, Overlay, Eng.Glasshouse Mark, 1820, 11 In.	49.00
Vase, Step Cut, St.Louis Diamond, 12 In.	650.00
Vase, Teardrop Stem, Brilliant, Pedestal, 14 In.	225.00
Vase, Trumpet, Hobstars, Fine Diamonds, Prisms, Ladders, 16 In.	210.00
Vase, Trumpet, Hobstars, Notched Panels, Rayed Base, 16 In.	225.00
Vase, Zipper Cut, Star & Diamond Pattern, 14 In.	370.00
Water Set, Pinwheel & Sheaf, 6 Piece	290.00
Water Set, Tankard, Pinwheel & Sheaf, 6 Piece	275.00
Water Set, Tankard, Thalia, 7 Piece	280.00
Wine, Allover Cut, 5 X 3 In., 5 Piece	130.00
Wine, Cane, Concave Diamonds, 32-Point Star Foot, Set of 12	950.00
Wine, Fans, Stars, Cranberry Bowl Cut To Clear, 6 1/2 In.	55.00
Wine, Old Colony, Dorflinger	60.00

Cut velvet is a special type of art glass, made with two layers of blown glass, which shows a raised pattern. It usually had an acid finish or velvetlike texture. It was made by many glass factories during the late Victorian years.

CUT VELVET, Pitcher, Honeycomb Pattern, Blue, 8 In.	295.00

CYBIS

Boleslaw Cybis came to the United States from Poland in 1939. He started making porcelains in Long Island, New York, in 1940. He moved to Trenton, New Jersey, in 1942 to work for Cordey and started his own Cybis Porcelains in 1950. The firm is still working.

CYBIS, Box, Bicentennial, Heart Shape	80.00
Bust, Indian Boy, Full Feather Headdress	575.00
Figurine, Allegra	275.00
Figurine, American Buffalo, Standing, 3 X 5 In.	145.00
Figurine, Baby Brother	100.00
Figurine, Boy On Horse	295.00
Figurine, Buffalo	95.00 To 100.00
Figurine, Cinderella	225.00
Figurine, Egg, Bicentennial	100.00
Figurine, Eros	250.00
Figurine, Girl With Teddy Bear	250.00
Figurine, Goldilocks, Standing Behind Seated Panda Bear, 6 1/4 In.	340.00
Figurine, Gretel, 6 1/2 In.	190.00 To 230.00
Figurine, Joan & Derby, Young Horses, Standing	450.00
Figurine, Jogger	350.00 To 375.00
Figurine, Little Princess	450.00
Figurine, Madonna, Bluebird	370.00
Figurine, Mouse, Woodland Scene, Holding Acorns, 6 In.	290.00

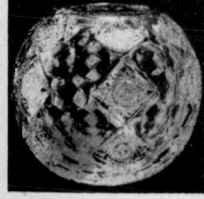

Cut Glass, Rose Bowl, Queen's, 9 In.

Cut Glass, Tray, Fish Tail

Cut Glass, Punch Bowl, Hobstar & Cane

Figurine, Sailor Monkey, 6 In.	150.00
Figurine, Squirrel	275.00
Figurine, Turtle	135.00
Figurine, Windflower, 8 In.	195.00
Figurine, Yankee Doodle Dandy	295.00 To 325.00
Vase, Egg, Eagle, Cover	150.00

There are some collectibles that are identified by the name of the country, not a factory mark. Anything marked "Czechoslovakia" is popular today. The name, first used as a mark after the country was formed in 1918, appears on glass and porcelain and other decorative items. The name is still used in some trademarks.

CZECHOSLOVAKIA, Bottle, Perfume, Flattened Round, Allover Ormolu, 2 1/4 In.	55.00
Bottle, Perfume, Topaz, 6 1/4 In.	39.50
Box, Cut Glass, Engraved, Covered, 3 X 4 In.	39.00
Candleholder, Camel, Signed Eichwold, 8 In., Pair	95.00
Canister Set, Roses, Blue Luster, 25 Piece	250.00
Canister Set, Windmill, Vinegar & Oil, 24 Piece	300.00
Cordial, Egg Shape, Coraline Design	125.00
Creamer, Cat Handle, Iridescent, Black	95.00
Creamer, Moose	28.00
Decanter, Red, White & Blue Enameled, Art Deco, Globe, 5 In.	27.00
Dish, Duck Cover, 6 1/2 X 4 In.	15.00
Dish, Lobster Cover, 5 X 3 In.	15.00
Epergne, Single Lily, White Opaline Bowl, 9 In.	80.00
Jar, Dresser, Black, Floral, Cut Glass Cover, 2 1/2 In., Pair	65.00
Lamp, Perfume, Enameled Floral, Circular Accents, 4 1/2 In.	125.00
Perfume, Steeple Stopper, 6 In.	65.00
Pitcher, Elk's Head, 3 1/4 In.	34.00
Pitcher, Rooster, Erphila, Pottery, 6 In. *Cover*	25.00
Pitcher, Vaseline Glass, Canes, Rods, 8 1/2 In.	65.00
Plate, Fish, Porcelain, Wide Gold Rim, 8 1/4 In., 3 Piece	45.00
Sugar & Creamer, Ducks	35.00
Vase, Black, Multicolored, 2 Handles, Pottery, 11 In.	85.00
Vase, Clear Glass Tree Trunk, Red Base, Glass Chain, 4 Pc.	32.00
Vase, Cobalt Blue, Bubbles Design, 6 In.	85.00
Vase, Cottage Scene, 8 In.	49.00
Vase, Emerald Green, Enameled Flowers, Victorian, 7 In.	25.00
Vase, Hand Holding Trumpet, Orange, Glass, Marked, 8 In.	27.00
Vase, Spatter & Cobalt Blue, Cased, 5 X 7 In.	50.00
Vase, White China, Double Loop Handles, 7 1/2 In.	20.00
Wall Pocket, Bird	6.00

D'Argental

D'Argental is a mark used by the St. Louis, France, glassworks. The firm made multilayered, acid-cut cameo glass in the late nineteenth and twentieth centuries. D'Argental is the French name for the city of Munzthal, home of the glassworks. Later they made enameled etched glass. Compagnie des Cristalleries de St. Louis is still working.

D'ARGENTAL, Vase, Acid Cut, Houses, White, Beige, Brown, 11 In.	950.00
Vase, Cameo, Daisies, Leaves, 8 In.	600.00
Vase, Cameo, Vines, Purple Flowers, 4 In.	300.00

Daum Nancy

Jean Daum started a glassworks in Nancy, France, in 1875. The company, now called "Cristalleries de Nancy," is still working. The "Daum Nancy" mark has been used in many variations. The name of the city and the artist are usually both included.

DAUM NANCY, Ashtray, Bird Perched On Side	175.00
Bowl, Band of Triangles, Charcoal Gray, 7 1/4 In.	825.00
Bowl, Marquetry Cameo, Amethyst, Marked, 8 X 9 1/2 In.	550.00
Box, Single Cutting Flowers, Enameled, 5 1/2 X 2 1/2 In.	625.00
Cordial Set, Gold Trim, Fleur-De-Lis Stopper, 8 Piece	425.00
Dish, Leaf Form, Loop Handle, Spring Green, Pate-De-Verre, 9 In.	1980.00
Ewer, Cut & Enameled Gold Florals, Silver Cover, 10 In.	895.00

Daum Nancy, Vase,
Silver Mounts, Gray,
Signed, C.1900, 6 1/4 In.

Daum Nancy, Vase, Cylindrical,
Yellow, Orange, Floral, 12 1/2 In.

Durand, Vase, Baluster,
Orange Feather Design, 8 1/4 In.

Lamp, 3–Arm, Acid Etched, Onion Shaped Shade, C.1900, 14 In.	2000.00
Lamp, Chandelier, Trumpet Form, Etched Glass, Iron, 4 Ft.4 In.	2750.00
Lamp, Helmet Shape Glass Shade, Wrought Iron Base, 22 1/2 In.	2475.00
Lamp, Winter Scene, Acid Etched, C.1900, 14 In.	2000.00
Pitcher, Cameo, Flowers Outlined In Gold, Frosted Handle, 3 In.	525.00
Pitcher, Orange & Yellow Mottled, Flat Sided, Marked, 7 1/2 In.	325.00
Rose Bowl, Tree Landscape, River, 3–Petal Top, Marked, 3 1/4 In.	595.00
Rose Bowl, Winter Scene, Barren Trees, Snow, Marked, 5 1/2 In.	995.00
Toothpick, Pink Flowers, Frosted	195.00
Tumbler, Autumn Colored Floral, Marked	450.00
Tumbler, Green Tree Landscape, Chartreuse Ground, 4 7/8 In.	550.00
Tumbler, Juice, Fuchsias & Leaves, Enameled, White To Purple	475.00
Tumbler, Opalescent, Cameo, Mistletoe, White Berries, 4 3/4 In.	275.00
Tumbler, Sailboats, Gold Ground, Mottled Base, Marked, 4 7/8 In.	595.00
Tumbler, Tree Landscape On Lake, Chartreuse & Blue, 4 3/4 In.	550.00
Tumbler, Yellow & Green Trees, Lake, Enameled, Marked, 5 In.	550.00
Vase, Acid Cut, Fuchsia Design, Mottled Ground, Marked, 4 In.	1160.00
Vase, Allover Geometric, Bell Form, Gray Blue, 17 In.	2475.00
Vase, Art Deco, Gold Foil, Cranberry Interior, 10 1/2 In.	1250.00
Vase, Berries, Leaves, Orange Ground, Marked, 16 In.	2150.00
Vase, Black Enameled Bird, Branch, White Ground, Marked, 8 In.	350.00
Vase, Blackbirds In Snow, Mottled, Marked, 2 1/2 In.	595.00
Vase, Cameo, Enameled Trees Scene, 4 1/4 In.	650.00
Vase, Cylindrical, Yellow, Orange, Floral, 12 1/2 In. ....*Illus*	700.00
Vase, Diamond Shape, Gold Veined, Cut Iris, Hand Polished	395.00
Vase, Double Overlay, Yellow Iris, Marked, 22 In.	1900.00
Vase, Dove Wing, Turquoise, Yellow, 7 In.	300.00
Vase, Enameled Thistle, 5 In.	230.00
Vase, Forest Fire, Cut Glass, 7 In.	1200.00
Vase, Frosted White, Green, 8 In.	325.00
Vase, Gray, Daisies, Baluster Form, C.1900, 11 3/4 In.	2200.00
Vase, Mottled Gold Ground, Barren Trees, Marked, 9 5/8 In.	1650.00
Vase, Scenic, Gold Frosted Ground, Trees, Marked, 13 3/4 In.	995.00
Vase, Silver Mounts, Gray, Signed, C.1900, 6 1/4 In.	1430.00
Vase, Snow Scene, Bulbous, Marked, 2 3/4 X 3 In.	525.00
Vase, Spider Mums, Handles, Pastel Blue Ground, 10 1/2 In.	950.00
Vase, Thistles, 4 1/2 In.	275.00
Vase, Tree Scene, Frosted Gold Ground, Stream, Marked, 13 In.	1100.00
Vase, Tricorner, Birch Trees, Mottled Ground, Marked, 3 5/8 In.	1295.00
Vase, White Trees, Green Leaves, Bullrushes In Pond, 11 In.	1250.00
Vase, White Trees, Leaves, Swans On Lake, Pedestal Foot, 11 In.	1450.00
Vase, Winter Scene, Cameo, Enameled, Signed, 4 1/2 In.	1300.00
Vase, Winter Scene, Flattened Oval, Gold, Marked, 1 5/8 In.	475.00
Vase, Winter Scene, Gold Frosted, 14 X 3 1/2 In.	995.00

DAVENPORT
LONGPORT
STAFFORDSHRE

Davenport pottery and porcelain were made at the Davenport factory in Longport, Staffordshire, England, from 1793 to 1887. Earthenwares, creamwares, porcelains, ironstone, and other ceramics were made. Most of the pieces are marked with a form of the word "Davenport."

DAVENPORT, Dinner Service, Berry & Leaf, Pink Scalloped Rims, 45 Piece	700.00
Footbath, Oriental Floral, Blue, Handles, 1850, 20 X 8 X 13 In.	175.00
Garniture Set, Gilded Handles, Female Mask Ends, 1835, 9 1/2 In.	375.00
Mug, Victoria Girls Forever, Gaudy, 4 5/8 In.	85.00
Pitcher & Bowl, Scalloped, Decagon, Ironstone	225.00
Pitcher, Luster Floral Design, Marked, 9 1/2 In.	265.00
Plate, Cyprus, 7 In.	30.00
Plate, Daffodil, Anchor Mark, C.1790, 8 1/2 In.	40.00
Plate, Tulip, Anchor Mark, C.1790, 8 1/2 In.	40.00
Relish, Vineyard, Ironstone	45.00
Sugar & Creamer, Child's, Pastoral Scene, Light Green	60.00
Vegetable, Imari Colors, 1850–70 Mark	150.00

Davy Crockett, the American frontiersman, was born in 1786 and died in 1836. He became popular again in 1954 with the introduction of a television series about his life. Coonskin caps and buckskins became popular and hundreds of different Davy Crockett items were made.

DAVY CROCKETT, Badge, Old Frontier, Cardboard	15.00
Bank, Dime	25.00
Billfold	15.00
Binoculars, Box	20.00
Bowl & Mug	5.00
Bowl, Cereal	20.00
Box, Pencil	40.00
Cap, Coonskin, Man–Made Tan Plush, 1950s, 8 1/2 X 7 In.	20.00
Clock, Pendulum, Child's, Box	45.00
Doll, Celluloid, Jointed, Suit & Cap, Japan, 4 In.	4.50
Flashlight, Signal Siren, Box	30.00
Flying Arrows, Sealed Package, 1955	12.00
Frontier Outfit, Gun, Holster, Embossed Buckle, Halco	30.00
Iron–On Patches, 1950s, Package of 5	3.00
Knife, Barlow	27.00
Knife, Frontier	10.00
Knife, Pocket, Metal, Plastic, 1950s, Opened, 3 1/2 In.	15.00
Lamp, Revolving, 1955	50.00
Neckerchief	12.00
Outfit, Pioneer, Original Box	50.00
Pencil Holder, White Textured Vinyl, 3 1/2 X 5 1/2 In.	10.00
Pez Dispenser	10.00
Pin, Hanging Ribbon, Miniature Gun	10.00
Pin, Sunbeam Bread	5.00
Poster, Disney, 27 X 41 In.	50.00
Powder Horn, Box	18.00
Rug, Picture, Shag, 32 X 19 In.	40.00
Soap Set, Figural, Box	35.00
Socks, Child's	15.00
Tie, Western, Embroidered Lettering, Blue	7.50
Towel, Linen, To Cut & Stuff, Kay–De Kut–Ups, In Plastic	5.00
Tumbler, Glass, Action Scenes, Inscriptions, 1950s, 5 In.	10.00
Wallet	9.00 To 12.00

William de Morgan made art pottery in England from the 1860s to 1907. He is best known for his luster–glazed Moorish–inspired pieces. The pottery used a variety of marks.

DE MORGAN, Plate, Luster, Red, Black, C.1885, 15 In.	6000.00
Vase, Blue Luster, 12 In.	1000.00

De Vez is a name found on special pieces of French cameo glass made by the Cristallerie de Pantin about 1890. Monsieur de Varreaux was the art director of the glassworks and he signed pieces "de Vez."

DE VEZ, Vase, Boat & Village Scene, 3 Cuttings, Signed, 16 1/8 In.	1750.00
Vase, Boat & Village Scene, Yellow Ground, Signed, 7 1/2 In.	550.00
Vase, Boats In Harbor, Village, Aqua To White, 9 1/4 In.	695.00
Vase, Cameo, Frosted White, Lavender Floral, Signed, 6 In.	295.00
Vase, Cameo, Mountains & Lake Scene, 3 Cuttings, Signed, 5 1/2 In.	650.00
Vase, Island, Mountains, Tree Branches, Pink Ground, Signed, 6 In.	495.00
Vase, Landscape, Mountains, 3 Acid Cuttings, Signed, 11 3/4 In.	695.00
Vase, Man In Gondola, Frosted Gold Ground, Signed, 6 1/8 In.	695.00
Vase, Sailboat Scene, Pink Ground, Blue To Yellow, 8 1/8 In.	695.00
Vase, Sailboats, Green Ground, Maroon To Rose, 9 5/8 In.	795.00
Vase, Scenic, Brown Frost, 5 In.	560.00
Vase, Stick, Seaweed In Purple Cameo, Signed, 8 1/2 In.	395.00
Vase, Tree Landscape, River, Mountains, Pink Ground, Signed, 5 1/4 In.	495.00

 Decoys are carved or turned wooden copies of birds or fish. The decoy was placed in the water or propped on the shore to lure flying birds to the pond for hunters. Some decoys are handmade, some are commercial products. Today there is a group of artists making modern decoys for display, not use in a pond.

DECOY, Black Duck, A.E.Crowell	3850.00
Black Duck, Cork Body, Carved Head, Glass Eyes, 14 1/2 In.	30.00
Black Duck, Glass Eyes, Branded S.F.Spear, 21 1/2 In.	400.00
Black Duck, Ken Harris	185.00
Black Duck, Mason	850.00
Black Duck, Turned Head, Anger	790.00
Black Duck, Ward Brothers, 1936	4400.00
Blue–Winged Teal, Hen, Glass Eyes, 12 In.	150.00
Bluebill Drake, Frank Coombs	460.00
Bluebill Drake, Glass Eyes, 15 3/4 In.	25.00
Bluebill Drake, Turned Head, Glass Eyes, Mason, 13 3/4 In.	60.00
Broadbill, Preening, Hollow–Carved, Albert Laing, 1811	13000.00
Canada Goose, Canvas Covered Wire & Wood Frame, 24 1/2 In.	75.00
Canada Goose, Capt.H.Jobe, 1/2 Size	100.00
Canada Goose, Cork & Wood, Canvas Covering, Repaint, 20 1/2 In.	65.00
Canada Goose, George Boyd, Seabrook, New Hampshire	2310.00
Canada Goose, Hank Walker, Mass.	575.00
Canada Goose, Paul Lacombe, Painted, 1/2 Size	115.00
Canada Goose, Primitive, Cork & Wood Body, Canvas Covering, 20 In.	25.00
Canada Goose, Swimmer, Glass Eyes, Mid–20th Century, 26 1/4 In.	370.00
Canvasback Drake, Balsa Body, Wooden Head, Branded F.C.H., 16 In.	55.00
Canvasback Drake, Chauncy Wheeler	1300.00
Canvasback Drake, Glass Eyes, 22 3/4 In.	45.00
Canvasback Drake, Harris, 1930	360.00
Canvasback Drake, R.M.Fisher	175.00
Canvasback Drake, Signed, T.A.Thomas, Roseville, Mich., 5–26–79, 8 In.	50.00
Canvasback Drake, Sleeper, J.Kelson, 1888–1968, Balsa Body, 11 In.	105.00
Canvasback Duck, Maryland Eastern Shore, C.1945	225.00
Canvasback Duck, Painted Eye, Mason, C.1915	75.00
Canvasback Hen, Mason, Premier	550.00
Cork, L.L.Bean, 1930s	35.00
Crow, Glass Eyes, Old Black Paint, Initialed WRG, 15 1/2 In.	105.00
Crow, Herters, Balsa Wood	115.00
Crow, Rubber	10.00
Crow, Silhouette, Wood, 1940s	18.00
Dowitcher, Glass Eyes, Bowman, Shot Scars	4400.00
Duck, Louis Joseph, Wooden	120.00
Eider Drake, Hissing	125.00
Geese, Stick–Up, Brant, Pair	1800.00
Goldeneye, Worn Old Paint, Chauncey Wheeler	220.00

Goose, Johnson's, Folding, Cardboard, Metal, Bag, 17 In., 12 Piece	275.00
Goose, Swimming Position, C.1900, 30 X 10 1/2 In.	195.00
Green–Winged Teal, Dodge	950.00
Green–Winged Teal, Garibaldi	550.00
Gull, Black Back, 36 In.	4840.00
Howell, Red & White Body, Tail & Fins, Painted Eyes, 8 1/2 In.	65.00
Ice Fishing, Northern, 9 In.	60.00
Mallard Drake, Cork Body, Adjustable Wooden Head, Glass Eyes, 20 In.	35.00
Mallard Drake, Glass Eyes, Original Paint, 22 1/2 In.	400.00
Mallard Drake, Hollow Body, Glass Eyes, Marked Evans, 15 1/2 In.	125.00
Mallard Drake, Hollow Body, Turned Head, Glass Eyes, S.Tyler	175.00
Mallard Drake, Papier–Mache, 1930s	22.00
Mallard Drake, Preening, Caines Brothers	15500.00
Mallard Drake, Worn Paint, Glass Eyes, Calif., 20 3/4 In.	155.00
Mallard Hen, Glass Eyes, Turned Head, W.E.B., 16 1/2 In.	55.00
Mallard Hen, Preening, Caines Brothers	3500.00
Mallard, Glass Eyes, Turned Head, Branded Hall, 17 In., Pair	70.00
Mallard, Illinois River, Williams	145.00
Mallard, Papier–Mache, Original Paint, 19 In., Pair	25.00
Mallard, Rough Sawn, Glass Eyes, 16 1/2 In., Pair	55.00
Merganser, Jester	625.00
Merganser, Tack Eyes, Mason, 16 In.	95.00
Merganser, Virginia	125.00
Monhegan Coot	125.00
Perch, Carved & Painted Tack Eyes, Carved Body, 10 In.	210.00
Perdew Crow	95.00
Pike, Green Body, Yellow Spots, White Belly, 28 In.	325.00
Pintail Drake, Hollow Body, Glass Eyes, Turned Head, Ward, 20 In.	295.00
Pintail Duck, Arness	125.00
Pintail Duck, Illinois River, Chiado	450.00
Pintail Duck, Ward Bros.	550.00
Plover, Black Bellied, Chief Cuffee, Shinnecock Reservation	550.00
Redhead Drake, Michigan, Original Paint, Glass Eyes, 13 1/2 In.	95.00
Redhead Drake, Stylized Body & Head, Tack Eyes, 15 1/2 In.	55.00
Redhead Drake, Worn Working Paint, 12 1/2 In.	75.00
Shorebird, Cobb Island, Va.	990.00
Shorebird, Glass Eyes, Iron Legs & Beak, 7 In.	135.00
Shorebird, Inserted Beak, Worn Paint, Rod, Cork Float Base, 12 In.	70.00
Shorebird, Inserted Wooden Beak, Wooden, 12 In.	375.00
Shorebird, Plover, Original Paint, Tin, Block Mounted, 6 X 10 In.	110.00
Shorebird, Stick–Up, Wooden Silhouette, Folding Head, 10 3/4 In.	250.00
Shoveler, J.R.Wells	8000.00
Snowgoose, Captain H.Jobe	185.00
Sunfish, Iron Fins, Inserted Belly Weight, 7 3/4 In.	40.00
Swan, Sam Barnes, C.1890	9000.00
Swan, Tack Eye, Gold, Original Paint, Graceful	275.00
Swan, Working, Virginia	650.00
Turtle Spearing, Faceted Brass Back, Hinged Tin Legs, 6 In.	390.00
Whistler Drake, Inset Head, Glass Eyes, Shot Scars, 14 In.	95.00

Chelsea Keramic Art Works was established in 1872 in Chelsea, Massachusetts, by members of the Robertson family. The factory closed in 1889 and was reorganized as the Chelsea Pottery U.S. in 1891. It became the Dedham Pottery of Dedham, Massachusetts, in 1895. The factory closed in 1943. It was famous for its crackleware dishes, which picture blue outlines of animals, flowers, and other natural motifs.

DEDHAM, Bowl, Bending Poppy, Cut–Edged, Stamped, 10 3/4 In.	450.00
Bowl, Duck, Stamped, 4 1/2 In.	200.00
Bowl, Rabbits, 2 In.Border, 9 X 4 In.	445.00
Bowl, Rabbits, 7 5/8 In.	285.00
Butter Chip, Buttercup Form, Chelsea Keramic Co., 3 3/4 In.	170.00
Charger, Duck, Impressed & Stamped, 12 In.	325.00
Charger, Rabbits, Early 20th Century, Stamped, 12 1/4 In.	175.00

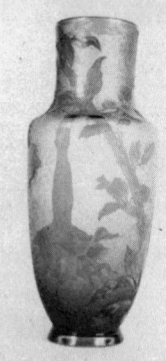 

Cameo, Vase, Yellow, Red Walls,
Gold Highlights, Honesdale, 12 In.

Delatte, Vase, Mottled Glass, Iron,
Parrot Handles, 18 In.

Coffee Cup, Snowtree	95.00
Creamer, Rabbits, 3 1/4 In.	225.00
Cup & Saucer, Rabbits	125.00 To 145.00
Cup & Saucer, Swan, Stamped, 4 In.	200.00
Flower Frog, Rabbits, Seated On Holder, 6 1/4 In.	700.00
Jam Jar, Covered, Rabbits, Stamped, 4 1/2 In.	200.00
Mug, Rabbits, Angular Handle, Stamped, 4 5/8 In.	350.00
Paperweight, Rabbits, 3 In.	500.00
Pitcher, Milk, Rabbits, Stamped, 8 1/2 In.	325.00
Plate, Butterfly, Maud Davenport, Stamped, 10 In.	275.00
Plate, Grape, Stamped, 9 3/4 In.	175.00
Plate, Large & Small Moths, Stamped, 10 In.	500.00
Plate, Lobster, Stamped, 7 3/4 In.	450.00
Plate, Moths, 6 In.	150.00
Plate, Owl, Stamped, Early 20th Century, 6 In.	650.00
Plate, Polar Bear, Stamped, Dated 1931, 8 3/4 In.	500.00
Plate, Rabbits, 6 1/8 In.	95.00
Plate, Rabbits, 8 3/8 In.	125.00
Plate, Rabbits, 10 1/2 In.	165.00
Plate, Scotty Dog, Stamped & Incised, 8 1/2 In.	1100.00
Plate, Swan, Stamped & Incised, 8 1/2 In.	325.00
Plate, Turtles, 6 1/8 In.	265.00
Plate, Turtles, 8 5/8 In.	395.00
Plate, Wild Rose, Early 20th Century, Stamped, 6 1/4 In.	1100.00
Plate, Wild Rose, Stamped, 8 1/2 In.	1000.00
Platter, Rabbits, 12 1/2 In.	220.00
Salt & Pepper, Rabbits, 2 3/4 In.	225.00
Saltshaker, Rabbits, 2 3/4 In.	135.00
Tile, Rabbits, Square, 5 1/2 In.	275.00
Tray, Bacon, Duck, Stamped, 10 In.	300.00
Tray, Crab, Waves, Signed, 9 X 5 1/4 In.	295.00
Tray, Elephant, Early 20th Century, 9 3/4 In.	325.00
Vase, Crackleware, Blue & White, Incised, Early 20th Century, 4 In.	600.00
Vase, Glossy Green, Olive Green Glaze, Marked, 7 3/4 In.	325.00
Vase, Mottled Glaze, Paper Label, C.1904, 7 1/2 In.	275.00
Vase, Oxblood Red, CKAW, 7 1/2 In.	1600.00
Vase, Panels of Daisies, Chelsea Keramic Art Works, 7 1/2 In.	450.00
Vase, Swollen Cylindrical Form, Mottled Pink, Marked, 8 3/4 In.	1200.00

Degue is a signature found acid–etched on pieces of French glass made in the early 1900s. Cameo, mold blown, and smooth glass with contrasting colored rims are the types most often found.

DEGUE, Vase, Blue Cameo Flowers, Frosted Ground, Signed, 3 1/2 In. 425.00
   Vase, Cameo Cut Flowers, Frosted Ground, Navy Blue, Signed, 3 1/2 In. 375.00
   Vase, Cameo, Sailboats Scene, Orange Mottled Ground, Signed, 5 1/2 In. 625.00
   Vase, Maroon Sailboat Scene, Orange Satin, Degue, 6 X 3 In. 450.00
   Vase, Navy Blue Cameo Flowers, Frosted, Signed, 3 1/2 In. 425.00

Delatte NANCY

Delatte glass is a French cameo glass made by Andre Delatte. It was first made in Nancy, France, in 1921. Lighting fixtures and opaque glassware in imitation of Bohemian opaline were made. There were many French cameo glass makers, so be sure to look in other appropriate sections.

DELATTE, Vase, Ear Handles, Tree Landscape, Maroon River, Signed, 9 1/4 In. 975.00
   Vase, Mottled Glass, Iron, Parrot Handles, 18 In. ....*Illus* 2200.00
   Vase, Trees, Mountains, Yellow Mottled Ground, Signed, 8 3/4 In. 1050.00
     DELAWARE, see Custard Glass; Pressed Glass
     DELDARE, see Buffalo Pottery Deldare

Delft

Delft is a tin–glazed pottery that has been made since the seventeenth century. It is decorated with blue on white or with colored decorations. Most of the pieces sold today were made after 1891, and the name "Holland" appears with the Delft factory marks.

DELFT, Bowl, Sailboats, 4 In. 20.00
   Charger, Adam & Eve, Under Tree, Serpent, 18th Century, 13 1/2 In. 700.00
   Charger, Finial Bouquet, Floral Border, Blue, White, 12 1/2 In. 200.00
   Charger, Peacock Feather Pattern, DeClauw Pottery, 1712, 13 1/2 In. 225.00
   Coffee Grinder, Wallboard 185.00
   Dish, Pin, Crossed Pipes, Windmill, 5 X 3 In. 14.00
   Figurine, Boy At The Well 25.00
   Figurine, Lion, Seated, Brown, 18th Century, 8 1/2 In., Pair ....*Illus* 900.00
   Food Warmer, Lambeth, 2 Faces In Relief, Blue, 7 In., Pair ....*Illus* 850.00
   Inkwell, Windmills, Blue & White, 1870s 65.00
   Jar, Seated Spaniel, Foot On Ball, Domed Cover, Blue & White, 25 In. 1200.00
   Jug, Blue, Scrolled Label, English, C.Anthos, 7 In. ....*Illus* 625.00
   Mug, Bristol, Leaf, Foliage, Blue, Green, Burnt Orange, 5 In. ....*Illus* 950.00
   Mug, Lambeth, Floral Design, Blue, White, C.1760, 6 1/2 In. ....*Illus* 180.00
   Plate, Blue, Ships, Wharf, Gulls, 4 1/2 In. 65.00

Delft, Figurine,
Lion, Seated, Brown, 18th
Century, 8 1/2 In., Pair

Delft, Food Warmer,
Lambeth, 2 Faces In Relief,
Blue, 7 In., Pair

Delft, Jug, Blue,
Scrolled Label, English,
C.Anthos, 7 In.

Delft, Plate, English,
Bouquet of Flowers,
Blue, Yellow, 9 In.

Delft, Mug, Lambeth,
Floral Design, Blue,
White, C.1760, 6 1/2 In.

Delft, Shoe, High Heel,
Blue, White, Floral,
C.1730, 4 X 5 1/2 In.

Delft, Mug, Bristol, Leaf,
Foliage, Blue, Green, Burnt
Orange, 5 In.

Plate, Christmas, 1917		130.00
Plate, English, Bouquet of Flowers, Blue, Yellow, 9 In. ....*Illus*		400.00
Plate, Floral Sprays, Boy & Bird On River Bank, 18th Century, 9 In.		125.00
Platter, Liverpool, Blue & White, Chamfered, Peonies, Bamboo, 19 In.		412.00
Shoe, High Heel, Blue, White, Floral, C.1730, 4 X 5 1/2 In. ....*Illus*		825.00
Tile, Adam & Eve, Manganese Purple On Tin Glaze, 6 1/8 X 6 3/8 In.		145.00
Tile, Woman & Child Waving At Planes, 1945, 5 1/2 In.		55.00
Vase, Baluster Shape, Knopped Neck, Blue, 18th Century, 8 7/8 In.		2200.00
Vase, Bird Finial Lid, Blue & White, 14 In.		85.00
Vase, Blue & White Floral, Scene of Harbor, 9 In.		85.00
Vase, Chinese Figures, Blue & White, C.1700, 25 In.		2300.00
Vase, Floral & Leaf, Blue & White, Flared, 8 Sides, C.1845, 17 In.		235.00

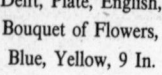 Dental cabinets, chairs, equipment, and other related items are listed here. Other objects may be found listed under Medical.

DENTAL, Bottle, Sevriton Cavity Seal, Amber, Ground Stopper, 2 In., 10 Piece		30.00
Box, Wooden, 143 Steel Tooth Forms, 3 Instruments, Dated 1910		85.00
Cabinet, 2 Tier, 3 Glass Doors, Milk Glass Lined		995.00
Cabinet, Instrument, Mahogany, 4 Drawers, Cut Glass Knobs, 1800s		275.00
Cabinet, Oak, 6 Drawers, 7 1/2 X 12 1/2 In.		145.00
Dentistry Set, Extractor, Pulling Pliers, Bleeder, Wm.B.Bailey		110.00
Dispenser, Powdered Dentifrice		15.00
Drill, Electric, Dumore		95.00
Drill, Foot Treadle, SS White		200.00
Grinder, Denture, Metal		20.00
Jar, Antiseptic Cotton, Clam Broth		25.00
Mold Guide, SS White, 150 Teeth		50.00
Postcard, Cats In Office, A.Mainzer		15.00
Postcard, Dr.Winchell's Teething Syrup, Man Holding Child		15.00
Postcard, Dr.Winslow's Teething Syrup		15.00
Postcard, Here's Something To Look Into		6.00
Postcard, Kolynos, Dentifrice, Multicolor, French		20.00
Postcard, Man With Aching Jaw, Wales, Color, 1907		12.00
Postcard, Piso's Antiseptic Tooth Powder, 1899		10.00
Postcard, Rooster With A Toothache		4.00
Poster, Dr.West Toothbrush		3.50
Potlid, American Dentifrice, Manchester, Dr.C.R.Coffin, 3 1/2 In.		75.00
Potlid, Areca Nut Tooth Paste, 2 1/2 In.		50.00
Potlid, Boot's Tooth Powder, Nottingham Chemists, 2 3/4 In.		55.00
Potlid, Sponaceous Tooth Powder, 3 1/2 In.		60.00
Tooth Color Guide, SS White		20.00
Turnkey, Wooden Handle, 18th Century		100.00

William Long of Steubenville, Ohio, founded the Lonhuda Pottery Company in 1892. In 1900 he moved to Denver, Colorado, and organized the Denver China and Pottery Company. This pottery worked until 1905 when Long moved to New Jersey and founded the Clifton Pottery. Long also worked for Weller Pottery, Roseville Pottery, and American Encaustic Tiling Company.

DENVER, Bowl, Swirls, Blue, C.1915, 6 In.		100.00
Vase, Pine Cone, 5 In.		500.00

Depression glass was an inexpensive glass manufactured in large quantities during the 1920s and early 1930s. It was made in many colors and patterns by dozens of factories in the United States. The name "Depression glass" is a modern one. For more descriptions, history, pictures, and prices of Depression glass, see the book "The Kovels' Illustrated Price Guide to Depression Glass and American Dinnerware."

DEPRESSION GLASS, ACCORDION PLEATS, see Round Robin

Adam, Ashtray, Crystal, 4 1/2 In.		7.00
Adam, Ashtray, Green, 4 1/2 In.	13.00 To	17.00
Adam, Bowl, Cereal, Green, 5 3/4 In.		32.00
Adam, Bowl, Covered, Green, 9 In.	55.00 To	60.00
Adam, Butter, Pink	50.00 To	52.50
Adam, Cake Plate, Footed, Green, 10 In.	9.00 To	13.50
Adam, Candlestick, Pink, 4 In., Pair		35.00
Adam, Candy Jar, Covered, Pink		40.00
Adam, Creamer, Green		9.50
Adam, Creamer, Pink		10.00
Adam, Plate, Green, 9 In.		11.00
Adam, Salt & Pepper, Green		75.00
Adam, Salt & Pepper, Pink		30.00
Adam, Sherbet, Pink		13.00
Adam, Sugar, Covered, Pink		24.00
Adam, Tumbler, Iced Tea, Pink, 5 1/2 In.	35.00 To	45.00
Adam, Vase, Pink, 7 1/2 In.		150.00
AMERICAN BEAUTY, see English Hobnail		
American Pioneer, Ice Bucket, Green		30.00
American Pioneer, Plate, Green, 8 In.		4.00
American Pioneer, Powder Jar, Covered, Green		75.00
American Pioneer, Tumbler, Green, 4 In.		15.00
American Sweetheart, Bowl, Pink, 6 In.	6.00 To	9.00
American Sweetheart, Console, Cobalt Blue, 18 In.		900.00
American Sweetheart, Cup & Saucer, Monax		10.00
American Sweetheart, Cup & Saucer, Pink	11.00 To	12.50
American Sweetheart, Dish, Pickle, 2 Handles, Green		18.50
American Sweetheart, Pitcher, Pink, 7 1/2 In.		290.00
American Sweetheart, Plate, Monax, 8 In.	5.50 To	6.00
American Sweetheart, Platter, Monax, 15 1/2 In.		145.00
American Sweetheart, Platter, Pink, 13 In.		18.00
American Sweetheart, Salt & Pepper, Footed, Pink		245.00
American Sweetheart, Salver, Pink		6.50
American Sweetheart, Soup, Dish, Pink		25.00
American Sweetheart, Sugar & Creamer, Monax		9.00
Anniversary, Bowl, Pink, 9 In.		18.00
APPLE BLOSSOM, see Dogwood		
Aunt Polly, Berry Bowl, Blue, 4 1/2 In.		12.00
Aunt Polly, Compote, Handles, Blue		25.00
Aunt Polly, Pitcher, Blue, 8 In.		100.00
B PATTERN, see Dogwood		
BALLERINA, see Cameo		
Bamboo Optic, Cup & Saucer, Pink		6.00
BANDED CHERRY, see Cherry Blossom		

BANDED FINE RIB, see Coronation
BANDED RAINBOW, see Ring
BANDED RIBBON, see New Century
BANDED RINGS, see Ring
BASKET, see No. 615
Beaded Block, Plate, Square, Pink, 7 3/4 In. 3.50
BEVERAGE WITH SAILBOAT, see White Ship
BIG RIB, see Manhattan
BLOCK, see Block Optic
Block Optic, Berry Bowl, Green 3.50
Block Optic, Butter, Covered, Green 37.00
Block Optic, Candy Jar, Green, 6 1/4 In. 40.00
Block Optic, Cup, Green 3.00
Block Optic, Goblet, Wine, Green, 4 1/2 In. 11.00
Block Optic, Ice Bucket, Green 25.00
Block Optic, Plate, Sandwich, Green, 10 1/2 In. 20.00
Block Optic, Plate, Sherbet, Green, 6 In. .... .75
Block Optic, Saltshaker, Footed, Green 11.00
Block Optic, Sherbet, Green, 3 1/4 In. 3.00
Block Optic, Sherbet, Green, 4 3/4 In. .... 5.00 To 7.00
Block Optic, Tumbler, Green, Flat, 14 Oz. 22.00
BOUQUET & LATTICE, see Normandie
BRIDAL BOUQUET, see No. 615
Bubble, Berry Bowl, Blue, 4 1/2 In. .... 5.00 To 6.00
Bubble, Bowl, Blue, 5 1/4 In. 6.50
Bubble, Bowl, Blue, 8 1/2 In. 8.00
Bubble, Bowl, Pink, 8 1/2 In. 13.50
Bubble, Creamer, Blue 16.00
Bubble, Cup & Saucer, Blue .... 2.00 To 4.50
Bubble, Grill Plate, Blue 8.00
Bubble, Plate, Blue, 6 3/4 In. .... 2.25 To 4.00
Bubble, Platter, Blue, 12 In. 6.00
Bubble, Saucer, Blue .... .75 To 1.50
Bubble, Sugar & Creamer, Blue 30.00
BULLSEYE, see Bubble
Burple, Berry Set, Forest Green, 5 Piece 27.00
BUTTERFLIES & ROSES, see Flower Garden with Butterflies
BUTTONS & BOWS, see Holiday
CABBAGE ROSE, see Sharon
CABBAGE ROSE WITH SINGLE ARCH, see Rosemary
Cameo, Berry Bowl, Green, 8 1/4 In. 20.00
Cameo, Bowl, Green, 5 1/2 In. 12.00
Cameo, Butter, Covered, Green 60.00
Cameo, Cake Plate, 3–Footed, Green 14.00
Cameo, Cake Plate, Flat, Green 50.00
Cameo, Candy Jar, Covered, Green, 6 1/2 In. .... 67.50 To 98.00
Cameo, Cookie Jar, Green .... 37.00 To 42.00
Cameo, Creamer, Green, 3 1/4 In. 16.50
Cameo, Cup & Saucer, Yellow 7.50
Cameo, Goblet, Wine, Green, 4 In. 55.00
Cameo, Grill Plate, Green 10.00
Cameo, Grill Plate, Yellow .... 4.00 To 5.50
Cameo, Juice Set, Green, 7 Piece 175.00
Cameo, Pitcher, Green, 6 In. .... 30.00 To 35.00
Cameo, Pitcher, Green, 8 1/2 In. .... 28.00 To 40.00
Cameo, Plate, Green, 8 In. 6.50
Cameo, Plate, Pink, 10 In. 32.00
Cameo, Plate, Yellow, 6 In. 2.00
Cameo, Salt & Pepper, Green 50.00
Cameo, Sherbet, Green, 3 1/8 In. .... 8.00 To 10.50
Cameo, Sherbet, Green, 4 3/4 In. 21.00
Cameo, Sugar & Creamer, Green, 3 1/4 In. 20.00
Cameo, Tumbler, Footed, Green, 5 3/4 In. .... 29.50 To 32.50
Cameo, Tumbler, Green, 5 In. 15.00

Cameo, Tumbler, Juice, Green, 3 3/4 In.	37.00
Cameo, Vase, Green, 8 In.	20.00
Candlewick, Cup & Saucer, Tea, Crystal	10.00
Cape Cod, Pitcher, Footed, Crystal, 5 1/2 In.	25.00
Cape Cod, Tumbler, Iced Tea, Footed, Crystal, 12 Oz.	13.00
CAPRICE, see Cambridge	
CHAIN DAISY, see Adam	
CHERRY, see Cherry Blossom	
Cherry Blossom, Berry Bowl, Pink	5.00 To 6.50
Cherry Blossom, Bowl, Green, 8 1/2 In.	16.00
Cherry Blossom, Bowl, Pink, 8 1/2 In.	10.00
Cherry Blossom, Butter, Covered, Pink	50.00
Cherry Blossom, Cake Plate, Footed, Green, 10 1/4 In.	19.00
Cherry Blossom, Cocktail Set, Pink, Box, 8 Piece	120.00
Cherry Blossom, Creamer, Pink	8.00
Cherry Blossom, Cup & Saucer, Pink	16.00 To 28.00
Cherry Blossom, Grill Plate, Pink, 9 In.	12.00
Cherry Blossom, Mug, Pink	110.00
Cherry Blossom, Pitcher, Footed, Delphite, 8 In.	75.00
Cherry Blossom, Pitcher, Pink, 8 In.	22.00
Cherry Blossom, Plate, Pink, 6 In.	3.00
Cherry Blossom, Plate, Pink, 7 In.	8.50
Cherry Blossom, Sherbet, Pink	7.50 To 10.00
Cherry Blossom, Sugar & Creamer, Green, Covered	30.00
Cherry Blossom, Sugar & Creamer, Pink	18.00
Cherry Blossom, Sugar, Child's, Pink	22.00
Cherry Blossom, Tumbler, Footed, Pink, 3 3/4 In.	11.00
Cherry Blossom, Tumbler, Footed, Pink, 4 1/2 In.	18.00
Cherry Blossom, Tumbler, Pink, 5 In.	27.50
Cherry Blossom, Tumbler, Scalloped Foot, Green, 4 1/2 In.	24.00
CHERRY–BERRY, see Strawberry	
Circle, Cup, Pink	1.25
CIRCULAR RIBS, see Circle	
CLEO, see Cambridge	
Cloverleaf, Candy Dish, Covered, Green	25.00 To 33.00
Cloverleaf, Candy Dish, Covered, Yellow	65.00
Cloverleaf, Cup & Saucer, Black	11.00
Cloverleaf, Cup, Black	7.50
Cloverleaf, Cup, Green	3.00
Cloverleaf, Plate, Black, 8 In.	9.00
Cloverleaf, Plate, Green, 8 In.	3.50

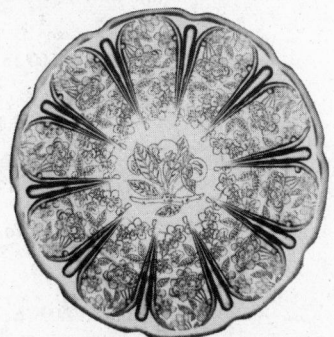

Cherry Blossom

Cubist

Cloverleaf, Salt & Pepper, Black 62.00
Cloverleaf, Salt & Pepper, Green .... 20.00 To 22.00
Cloverleaf, Tumbler, Footed, Yellow, 5 3/4 In. 19.00
Colonial, Berry Bowl, Green, 3 3/4 In. 8.00
Colonial, Bowl, Green, 9 In. 18.75
Colonial, Cup & Saucer, Green 12.50
Colonial, Goblet, Claret, Green, 5 1/4 In. 15.00
Colonial, Goblet, Cordial, Green, 3 3/4 In. 25.00
Colonial, Goblet, Gold Band, Pink, 4 In. 12.50
Colonial, Grill Plate, Green 19.50
Colonial, Pitcher, Green, Ice Lip, 7 In. 40.00
Colonial, Soup, Cream, Green .... 30.00 To 37.25
Colonial, Spooner, Pink 80.00
Colonial, Sugar, Green 8.00
Columbia, Bowl, Ruffled Edge, Crystal, 10 1/2 In. 14.90
Columbia, Butter, Crystal 11.00
Columbia, Chop Plate, Crystal .... 3.00 To 5.00
Columbia, Cup & Saucer, Crystal 6.00
Columbia, Plate, Crystal, 9 1/2 In. 2.50
Coronation, Cup & Saucer, Pink 2.50
     CUBE, see Cubist
Cubist, Bowl, Pink, 6 1/2 In. 6.00
Cubist, Butter, Covered, Pink 45.00
Cubist, Candy Jar, Covered, Pink 21.00
Cubist, Creamer, Pink 2.50
Cubist, Cup & Saucer, Green 6.00
Cubist, Pitcher, Pink, 8 3/4 In. .... 110.00 To 135.00
Cubist, Salt & Pepper, Green 20.00
Cubist, Sugar & Creamer, Pink 10.00
Cubist, Sugar, Green 2.50
     DAISY, see No. 620
     DANCING GIRL, see Cameo
     DIAMOND, see Windsor
     DIAMOND PATTERN, see Miss America
Diamond Quilted, Bowl, Green, 5 1/2 In. 3.50
Diamond Quilted, Bowl, Pink, 7 In. 3.00
Diana, Candy Jar, Covered, Pink 22.90
Diana, Cup & Saucer, Demitasse, Crystal 3.00
Dogwood, Ashtray, Yellow, 3 In. 65.00
Dogwood, Berry Bowl, Pink, 8 1/2 In. 35.00
Dogwood, Bowl, Pink, 5 1/2 In. 14.00
Dogwood, Creamer, Pink 9.00
Dogwood, Cup & Saucer, Pink 12.00
Dogwood, Grill Plate, Pink .... 9.00 To 11.50
Dogwood, Plate, Pink, 8 In. .... 2.00 To 5.00
Dogwood, Plate, Pink, 9 1/4 In. 15.00
Dogwood, Platter, Oval, Pink, 12 In. 250.00
Dogwood, Salver, 12 In. 20.00
Dogwood, Saucer, Pink 2.00
Dogwood, Sherbet, Pink .... 12.00 To 16.00
Dogwood, Sugar & Creamer, Pink .... 15.00 To 22.00
Dogwood, Tumbler, Pink, 5 In. 35.00
Doric & Pansy, Berry Bowl, Pink, 4 1/2 In. .... 5.00 To 6.50
Doric & Pansy, Bowl, Handles, Teal, 9 In. .... 18.00 To 22.00
Doric & Pansy, Plate, Pink, 6 In. 6.00
     DORIC WITH PANSY, see Doric & Pansy
Doric, Berry Set, Green, 7 Piece .... 22.00 To 35.00
Doric, Candy Dish, Cover, Green 23.00
Doric, Pitcher, Pink, 6 In. 23.00
Doric, Pitcher, Pink, 7 1/2 In. 350.00
Doric, Platter, Pink, 12 In. 10.50
Doric, Salt & Pepper, Pink 23.00
     DOUBLE SHIELD, see Mt. Pleasant

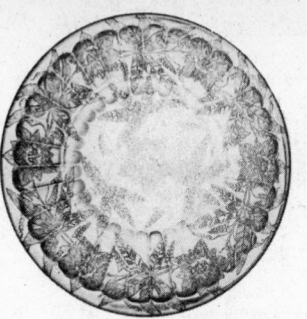  

Floral　　　　　　Florentine No. 1　　　　　　Florentine No. 2

DOUBLE SWIRL, see Swirl
DRAPE & TASSEL, see Princess
DUTCH ROSE, see Rosemary
EARLY AMERICAN ROCK CRYSTAL, see Rock Crystal
ENGLISH HOBNAIL, see also Miss America

English Hobnail, Lamp, Pink, 9 1/4 In.	75.00
English Hobnail, Saltshaker, Pink, Westmoreland	10.00
Fairfax, Salt & Pepper, Blue	60.00
Fairfax, Sauceboat, Green	25.00

FAN & FEATHER, see Adam
FINE RIB, see Homespun

Fire–King, Mug, Handle, Blue	15.00
Fire–King, Roaster, Covered, Blue, 10 In.	45.00
Floragold, Bowl, Ruffled, Iridescent, 12 In.	5.00
Floragold, Bowl, Square, Iridescent, 8 1/2 In.	13.00
Floragold, Candy Dish, Covered, Iridescent	25.00
Floragold, Creamer, Iridescent	3.00
Floragold, Cup & Saucer, Iridescent	7.00
Floragold, Platter, Cobalt Blue, 11 1/4 In.	11.00
Floragold, Salt & Pepper, Iridescent	25.00 To 30.00
Floragold, Sugar & Creamer, Covered, Iridescent	10.50 To 14.00
Floragold, Tray, Iridescent, 13 1/2 In.	23.00
Floral, Butter, Covered, Green	60.00
Floral, Candy Jar, Covered, Green	20.00
Floral, Coaster, Green	7.00
Floral, Creamer, Pink	7.75
Floral, Pitcher, Conical, Green, 8 In.	30.00
Floral, Pitcher, Footed, Pink, 8 In.	30.00
Floral, Platter, Oval, Pink, 10 3/4 In.	9.50
Floral, Relish, Divided, Green	12.50
Floral, Salt & Pepper, Pink, 4 In.	35.00
Floral, Tumbler, Footed, Green, 5 1/4 In.	25.00
Florentine No.1, Ashtray, Yellow	15.00
Florentine No.1, Berry Bowl, Pink, 5 In.	5.00
Florentine No.1, Bowl, Vegetable, Covered, Oval, Pink	15.00
Florentine No.1, Creamer, Green	10.50
Florentine No.1, Creamer, Pink	9.25
Florentine No.1, Salt & Pepper, Crystal	25.00
Florentine No.1, Sugar, Covered, Green	27.50
Florentine No.2, Ashtray, Yellow, 5 1/2 In.	27.50
Florentine No.2, Berry Bowl, Pink, 5 In.	16.00
Florentine No.2, Bowl, Vegetable, Covered, Green, 9 In.	35.00
Florentine No.2, Butter, Covered, Yellow	110.00 To 125.00
Florentine No.2, Candlestick, Yellow, Pair	40.00
Florentine No.2, Candy Dish, Covered, Pink	95.00

Florentine No.2, Cup & Saucer, Yellow 10.00
Florentine No.2, Gravy Boat, Underplate, Yellow .... 45.00 To 70.00
Florentine No.2, Pitcher, Pink, 48 Oz., 7 1/2 In. 95.00
Florentine No.2, Pitcher, Yellow, 28 Oz., 7 1/2 In. 17.00
Florentine No.2, Platter, Oval, Yellow, 11 In. 9.00
Florentine No.2, Relish, 3 Sections, Green 12.00
Florentine No.2, Salt & Pepper, Green 28.00
Florentine No.2, Salt & Pepper, Yellow 40.00
Florentine No.2, Soup, Cream, Yellow 5.50
Florentine No.2, Sugar & Creamer, Covered, Yellow 35.00
Florentine No.2, Sugar & Creamer, Green 13.00
Florentine No.2, Tumbler, Green, 4 In. 12.00
    FLOWER BASKET, see No. 615
Flower Garden With Butterflies, Tray, Dresser, Pink 33.00
    FROSTED BLOCK, see Beaded Block
Georgian, Berry Bowl, Green .... 4.25 To 5.00
Georgian, Berry Bowl, Green, 7 1/2 In. 38.50
Georgian, Butter, Covered, Green .... 65.00 To 67.50
Georgian, Cup & Saucer, Green 6.50
Georgian, Plate, Green, 8 In. 3.50
Georgian, Saucer, Green 3.00
    GLADIOLI, see Royal Lace
    HAIRPIN, see Newport
    HANGING BASKET, see No. 615
Harp, Ashtray, Pink 2.00
Harp, Cake Stand, Crystal 11.00
    HEX OPTIC, see Hexagon Optic
Hexagon Optic, Pitcher, Pink, 9 In. 25.00
    HINGE, see Patrician
Holiday, Berry Bowl, Pink, 5 1/4 In. 6.00
Holiday, Butter, Covered, Pink .... 28.00 To 32.00
Holiday, Chop Plate, Pink, 13 3/4 In. 45.00
Holiday, Creamer, Pink .... 4.00 To 4.50
Holiday, Cup & Saucer, Pink 7.00
Holiday, Pitcher, Pink, 6 3/4 In. .... 19.00 To 25.00
Holiday, Plate, Pink, 9 In. 8.50
Holiday, Soup, Dish, Pink 25.00
Holiday, Sugar & Creamer, Covered, Pink 17.50
Holiday, Tumbler, Footed, Pink, 6 In. 10.00
Holiday, Water Set, Pink, 7 Piece 95.00
Homespun, Ashtray, Pink 6.00
Homespun, Sugar, Pink 4.00
Homespun, Tumbler, Footed, Pink, 4 In. 8.00
    HONEYCOMB, see Hexagon Optic
    HORIZONTAL FINE RIB, see Manhattan

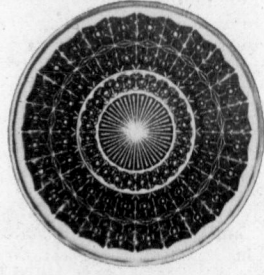

Holiday

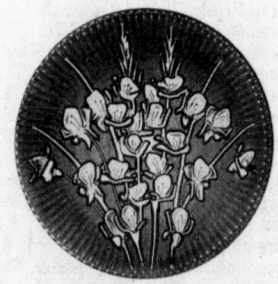

Iris, Beaded Edge

HORIZONTAL RIBBED, see Manhattan
HORIZONTAL ROUNDED BIG RIB, see Manhattan
HORIZONTAL SHARP BIG RIB, see Manhattan
HORSESHOE, see No. 612
Imperial Optic Rib, Sugar & Creamer, Amberina 20.00
IRIS & HERRINGBONE, see Iris
Iris, Bowl, Ruffled, Crystal, 11 In. 6.00
Iris, Butter, Covered, Iridescent 20.00
Iris, Creamer, Crystal 4.00
Iris, Creamer, Iridescent 6.00
Iris, Cup & Saucer, Demitasse, Iridescent 45.00
Iris, Goblet, Crystal, 8 Oz., 5 3/4 In. 12.00
Iris, Goblet, Wine, Iridescent, 4 1/2 In., 6 Piece 65.00
Iris, Pitcher, Crystal, 9 1/2 In. .... 13.00 To 14.00
Iris, Pitcher, Iridescent, 9 1/2 In. 20.00
Iris, Saucer, Iridescent 3.50
Iris, Sherbet, Green, 2 1/2 In. .... 11.00 To 12.00
Iris, Sugar & Creamer, Covered, Crystal 16.00
Iris, Tumbler, Footed, Crystal, 6 In. 8.00
Iris, Vase, Crystal, 9 In. 11.00
JADITE, see also Jane–Ray
Jadite, Pan, Drip, Refrigerator, Large 12.50
JANE–RAY, see also Jadite
Jane–Ray, Sugar & Creamer 4.50
Jubilee, Cup, Yellow 10.00
Jubilee, Goblet, Yellow, 6 In. 22.00
KNIFE & FORK, see Colonial
LACE EDGE, see also Coronation
Lace Edge, Bowl, Pink, 6 1/2 In. 10.00
Lace Edge, Butter, Covered, Pink 30.00
Lace Edge, Compote, Pink, 7 In. 10.00
Lace Edge, Platter, 5 Sections, Pink 12.00
Lace Edge, Sugar & Creamer, Pink 20.00
Lace Edge, Vase, Pink, 7 In. 175.00
LACY DAISY, see No. 618
Laurel, Berry Bowl, Powder Blue, 9 In. 15.00
Laurel, Creamer, Child's, Ivory 15.00
Laurel, Plate, Ivory, 6 In. 2.00
LILY MEDALLION, see American Sweetheart
LINCOLN DRAPE, see Princess
Lincoln Inn, Bowl, Finger, Liner, Red 35.00
Lincoln Inn, Goblet, Water, Red 25.00
Lincoln Inn, Goblet, Wine, Red 18.00
LITTLE HOSTESS, see Moderntone
LOOP, see Lace Edge
LORAIN, see No. 615
LOUISA, see Floragold
LOVEBIRDS, see Georgian
LYDIA RAY, see New Century
Madrid, Ashtray, Green 60.00
Madrid, Bowl, Blue, Oval, 10 In. 25.00
Madrid, Butter, Covered, Amber 55.00
Madrid, Candlestick, Amber, Pair 12.00
Madrid, Cookie Jar, Covered, Amber 30.00
Madrid, Creamer, Amber 5.00
Madrid, Cup & Saucer, Amber .... 7.00 To 7.50
Madrid, Cup, Amber 4.50
Madrid, Grill Plate, Crystal .... 4.00 To 5.00
Madrid, Pitcher, Square, Amber, 8 In. 30.00
Madrid, Plate, Amber, 6 In. 7.00
Madrid, Plate, Blue, 7 1/2 In. 20.00
Madrid, Plate, Blue, 9 In. 18.00
Madrid, Salt & Pepper, Footed, Amber 57.50
Madrid, Soup, Cream, Amber 9.00

Madrid   Mayfair Open Rose   Miss America

Madrid, Sugar & Creamer, Blue 30.00
Madrid, Sugar & Creamer, Covered, Amber 35.00
Madrid, Sugar, Green 4.00
Madrid, Sugar, Yellow 7.00
Madrid, Tumbler, Footed, Green, 4 In. 50.00
MAGNOLIA, see Dogwood
Manhattan, Ashtray, Crystal 3.00
Manhattan, Berry Bowl, Handle, Pink 4.00
Manhattan, Relish Insert, Ruby 17.00
Manhattan, Sugar, Pink .... 3.00 To 4.00
MANY WINDOWS, see Roulette
Mayfair Federal, Bowl, Oval, Amber, 10 In. 13.50
Mayfair Federal, Creamer, Pink 9.00
Mayfair Open Rose, Bowl, Scalloped, Green, 12 In. 22.00
Mayfair Open Rose, Butter, Covered, Blue 180.00
Mayfair Open Rose, Cake Plate, Blue 40.00
Mayfair Open Rose, Candy Dish, Covered, Pink 30.00
Mayfair Open Rose, Celery, Divided, Pink, 10 In. 75.00
Mayfair Open Rose, Cookie Jar, Covered, Pink .... 25.00 To 27.00
Mayfair Open Rose, Cup, Blue 29.00
Mayfair Open Rose, Decanter, Stopper, Pink .... 75.00 To 90.00
Mayfair Open Rose, Goblet, Cocktail, Pink, 4 In. .... 55.00 To 65.00
Mayfair Open Rose, Grill Plate, Blue 27.00
Mayfair Open Rose, Juice Set, Pink, 7 Piece 200.00
Mayfair Open Rose, Pitcher, Pink, 8 1/2 In. 44.00
Mayfair Open Rose, Plate, Handle, Blue, 12 In. 40.00
Mayfair Open Rose, Plate, Pink, 5 3/4 In. .... 6.00 To 10.00
Mayfair Open Rose, Relish, 4 Sections, Blue 28.50
Mayfair Open Rose, Salt & Pepper, Pink .... 30.00 To 48.00
Mayfair Open Rose, Sherbet, Footed, Blue, 4 3/4 In. 57.50
Mayfair Open Rose, Sugar & Creamer, Blue 125.00
Mayfair Open Rose, Sugar, Pink 12.50
Mayfair Open Rose, Tumbler, Footed, Blue, 6 1/2 In. 130.00
Mayfair Open Rose, Tumbler, Pink, 3 1/2 In. 25.00
Mayfair Open Rose, Tumbler, Pink, 5 1/4 In. 24.00
MEADOW FLOWER, see No. 618
MEANDERING VINE, see Madrid
MISS AMERICA, see also English Hobnail
Miss America, Bowl, Oval, Pink, 10 In. 14.00
Miss America, Butter, Covered, Pink 325.00
Miss America, Cake Plate, Footed, Pink, 12 In. 30.00
Miss America, Candy Jar, Covered, Pink .... 78.00 To 98.00
Miss America, Coaster, Pink .... 10.00 To 20.00
Miss America, Cup & Saucer, Pink 12.00
Miss America, Goblet, Wine, Crystal, 3 3/4 In. 16.00

Miss America, Grill Plate, Crystal	4.00
Miss America, Grill Plate, Pink	12.50
Miss America, Pitcher, Pink, 8 1/2 In.	80.00 To 90.00
Miss America, Plate, Pink, 10 In.	18.00
Miss America, Relish, 4 Sections, Pink	10.50 To 11.00
Miss America, Salt & Pepper, Pink	30.00 To 40.00
Miss America, Sherbet, Pink	11.50
Miss America, Tumbler, Green, 4 1/2 In.	12.00
Miss America, Tumbler, Pink, 4 In.	52.50
Miss America, Tumbler, Pink, 5 3/4 In.	47.50
MODERNE ART, see Tea Room	
Moderntone, Ashtray, Cobalt Blue	125.00
Moderntone, Creamer, Cobalt Blue	5.00 To 7.50
Moderntone, Cup & Saucer, Cobalt Blue	6.50 To 7.50
Moderntone, Salt & Pepper, Amethyst	35.00
Moderntone, Salt & Pepper, Cobalt Blue	22.50 To 27.00
Moderntone, Sherbet, Cobalt Blue	7.50
Moderntone, Soup, Cream, Cobalt Blue	9.00
Moderntone, Sugar & Creamer, Cobalt Blue	12.50 To 14.00
Moderntone, Sugar, Cobalt Blue	5.00
Moderntone, Tumbler, Cobalt Blue, 9 Oz.	12.00
Moderntone, Whiskey, Cobalt Blue	18.00
Moondrops, Bowl, Green, 11 1/2 In.	22.50
Moondrops, Creamer, Red, 3 3/4 In.	13.25
Moondrops, Sugar, Red, 2 3/4 In.	10.50
Moondrops, Vase, Amethyst, 9 1/4 In.	150.00
Moonstone, Bonbon, Heart, Crystal	5.00
Moonstone, Bowl, Crystal, 9 1/2 In.	10.00 To 12.50
Moonstone, Plate, Crystal, 10 In.	15.00
Moonstone, Powder Box, Green	12.50
Moonstone, Sugar & Creamer, Crystal	8.00
Mt.Pleasant, Bonbon, Handles, Amethyst	16.50
Mt.Pleasant, Bowl, Footed, Amethyst, 7 In.	17.00
Mt.Pleasant, Candleholder, Double, Amethyst, Pair	30.00
Mt.Pleasant, Candleholder, Double, Black, Pair	20.00
Mt.Pleasant, Sandwich Server, Center Handle, Amethyst	28.00
Mt.Pleasant, Sherbet, Footed, Cobalt Blue	12.50
Mt.Pleasant, Sugar & Creamer, Amethyst	25.00
New Century, Creamer, Green	3.00
New Century, Salt & Pepper, Green	20.00 To 25.00
New Century, Tumbler, Amethyst, 5 1/4 In.	9.00
Newport, Creamer, Cobalt Blue	8.00
Newport, Cup & Saucer, Amethyst	6.00
Newport, Salt & Pepper, Cobalt Blue	32.50
Newport, Soup, Cream, Amethyst	6.00 To 9.00
Newport, Sugar & Creamer, Amethyst	13.00

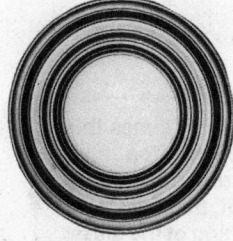  

Moderntone   Mt. Pleasant   No. 612

Normandie

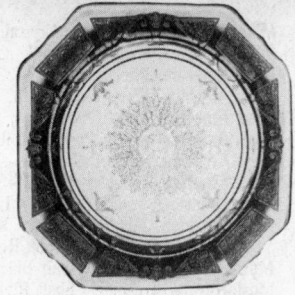

Princess

No.610, Bowl, Pink, 8 1/2 In. 17.50
No.610, Pitcher, Yellow 395.00
No.610, Relish, 4 Sections, Yellow 50.00
No.610, Tumbler, Footed, Yellow, 8 Oz. 32.00
No.612, Creamer, Green 10.00
No.612, Cup & Saucer, Green 85.00
No.612, Pitcher, Green, 8 1/2 In. 155.00
No.612, Sherbet, Yellow 10.00
No.612, Tumbler, Footed, Green, 9 Oz. .... 10.00 To 10.50
No.612, Tumbler, Green, 4 3/4 In. 45.00
No.615, Bowl, Yellow, 8 In. 145.00
No.615, Creamer, Yellow 12.75
No.615, Cup, Yellow 10.00
No.615, Relish, 4 Sections, Yellow, 8 In. 17.00
No.618, Cup & Saucer, Crystal 7.50
No.618, Plate, Dinner, Crystal, 9 1/4 In. 7.00
No.618, Sherbet, Crystal 13.00
No.618, Soup, Cream, Crystal 15.00
No.620, Bowl, Vegetable, Oval, Amber, 10 In. 11.25
Normandie, Bowl, Amber, 6 1/2 In. 7.00
Normandie, Cup, Amber 3.00
Normandie, Saucer, Pink 3.00
Normandie, Sherbet, Amber 3.00
Normandie, Sugar & Creamer, Amber 7.00
Old Cafe, Pitcher, Pink, 80 Oz. 60.00

      OLD FLORENTINE, see Florentine No.1
      OPALESCENT HOBNAIL, see Moonstone
      OPEN LACE, see Lace Edge
      OPEN ROSE, see Mayfair Open Rose
      OPEN SCALLOP, see Lace Edge
      OPTIC RIB, see Imperial Optic Rib
      ORIENTAL POPPY, see Florentine No. 2
      OVIDE, see New Century

Having trouble with stain in a glass bottle or vase? Sometimes this type of stain can be removed. Fill the bottle with water, drop in an Alka-Seltzer, and let it soak for about 24 hours. Then rub the ring with a brush or a cloth. If the deposit is a chemical deposit, this treatment should remove it. If the ring is actually caused by etching of the glass, it cannot be removed unless the bottle is polished.

Oyster & Pearl, Bowl, Handle, Crystal, 5 1/2 In. 5.00
Oyster & Pearl, Plate, Pink, 13 1/2 In. 11.00
Oyster & Pearl, Relish, Pink 4.00
  PANELED ASTER, see Madrid
  PANELED CHERRY BLOSSOM, see Cherry Blossom
  PANSY & DORIC, see Doric & Pansy
  PARROT, see Sylvan
Patrician, Bowl, Amber, 5 In. 6.50
Patrician, Bowl, Amber, 8 1/2 In. 20.00
Patrician, Butter, Covered, Green .... 74.00 To 85.00
Patrician, Butter, Covered, Pink 125.00
Patrician, Cookie Jar, Covered, Amber 45.00
Patrician, Creamer, Green 7.00
Patrician, Cup & Saucer, Amber 10.00
Patrician, Dish, Jelly, Amber 15.00
Patrician, Plate, Amber, 10 1/2 In. 5.00
Patrician, Plate, Yellow, 10 1/2 In. 12.00
Patrician, Salt & Pepper, Amber .... 30.00 To 35.00
Patrician, Sherbet, Amber 5.00
Patrician, Soup, Cream, Green 11.00
Patrician, Sugar & Creamer, Amber 11.00
Patrician, Tumbler, Amber, 4 1/2 In. .... 14.00 To 18.00
Patrician, Tumbler, Amber, 5 1/2 In. 25.00
Pear Optic, Saucer, Green 1.00
  PETAL SWIRL, see Swirl
  PINEAPPLE & FLORAL, see No. 618
  PINWHEEL, see Sierra
  POINSETTIA, see Floral
  POPPY NO. 1, see Florentine No. 1
  POPPY NO. 2, see Florentine No. 2
  PRIMUS, see Madrid
Princess, Bowl, Green, 5 In. 15.00
Princess, Bowl, Hat Shape, Green 25.00
Princess, Bowl, Octagonal, Green, 9 In. 24.00
Princess, Butter, Covered, Pink 50.00
Princess, Cake Plate, Green .... 13.00 To 15.25
Princess, Candy Dish, Covered, Green .... 25.00 To 28.00
Princess, Coaster, Green 20.00
Princess, Cookie Jar, Covered, Pink 30.00
Princess, Creamer, Green 16.25
Princess, Cup & Saucer, Topaz 5.00
Princess, Grill Plate, Green, 9 In. .... 6.50 To 10.25
Princess, Juice Set, Green, 7 Piece 150.00
Princess, Pitcher, Green, 8 In. 35.00
Princess, Plate, Green, 8 In. 8.50
Princess, Plate, Green, 9 In. 15.00
Princess, Salt & Pepper, Green 37.50
Princess, Sherbet, Yellow 20.00
Princess, Tumbler, Footed, Green, 5 1/4 In. 20.00
Princess, Tumbler, Pink, 5 1/4 In. 15.00
  PRISMATIC LINE, see Queen Mary
  PROVINCIAL, see Bubble
  PYRAMID, see No. 610
Queen Mary, Bowl, Handle, Pink, 4 In. 4.00
Queen Mary, Creamer, Pink 5.50
Queen Mary, Tumbler, Pink, 3 1/2 In. 4.00
  RASPBERRY BAND, see Laurel
  REX, see No. 610
  RIBBED, see Manhattan
Ribbon, Bowl, Green, 8 In. 7.00
Ribbon, Tumbler, Green, 5 1/2 In. 5.00
Ring, Pitcher, Green, 8 1/2 In. 12.00
Ring, Tumbler, Footed, Crystal, 6 1/2 In. 4.00
Rock Crystal, Cup, Crystal 8.00

Rock Crystal, Plate, Red, 8 1/2 In. 12.00
Rock Crystal, Tumbler, Red, 9 Oz. 35.00
  ROSE LACE, see Royal Lace
  ROSEMARY, see also Mayfair Federal
Rosemary, Bowl, Amber, 6 In. 10.00
Rosemary, Bowl, Oval, Green, 10 In. 25.00
Rosemary, Cup & Saucer, Green 18.00
Rosemary, Soup, Cream, Amber 10.00
Roulette, Pitcher, Pink 22.00
Roulette, Saucer, Crystal 1.50
Roulette, Sherbet, Crystal 2.50
Roulette, Tumbler, Pink, 3 1/4 In. 3.00
Roulette, Tumbler, Pink, 5 1/2 In. 9.00
Round Robin, Sugar & Creamer, Iridescent 8.00
Royal Lace, Bowl, 3-Footed, Ruffled Edge, Pink, 10 In. 20.00
Royal Lace, Bowl, Oval, Cobalt Blue, 11 In. 45.00
Royal Lace, Butter, Covered, Pink 75.00
Royal Lace, Cookie Jar, Covered, Cobalt Blue 225.00
Royal Lace, Cookie Jar, Covered, Green .... 45.00 To 65.50
Royal Lace, Creamer, Cobalt Blue 32.00
Royal Lace, Pitcher, Green, 8 1/2 In. .... 85.00 To 110.00
Royal Lace, Plate, Cobalt Blue, 10 In. .... 15.00 To 32.00
Royal Lace, Platter, Green, 13 In. 27.50
Royal Lace, Salt & Pepper, Cobalt Blue .... 135.00 To 195.00
Royal Lace, Salt & Pepper, Pink 40.00
Royal Lace, Sherbet, Green 8.50
Royal Lace, Sugar, Cobalt Blue 25.00
Royal Lace, Tumbler, Cobalt Blue, 4 1/8 In. 19.50
Royal Ruby, Bowl, 8 1/2 In. 11.00
Royal Ruby, Cup & Saucer 5.00
Royal Ruby, Punch Set, 7 Piece 50.00
Royal Ruby, Tumbler, 3 1/2 Oz. 6.00
Royal Ruby, Water Set, 7 Piece .... 37.50 To 45.00
  RUSSIAN, see Holiday
  SAIL BOAT, see White Ship
  SAILING SHIP, see White Ship
Sandwich Anchor Hocking, Pitcher, Crystal, 6 In. 36.00
  SAWTOOTH, see English Hobnail
  SAXON, see Coronation
  SHAMROCK, see Cloverleaf
Sharon, Bowl, Green, 10 1/2 In. 15.50
Sharon, Bowl, Pink, 6 In. 9.50
Sharon, Butter, Covered, Amber 19.00
Sharon, Butter, Covered, Pink .... 25.00 To 45.00
Sharon, Cake Plate, Footed, Pink 23.00

Sharon   Royal Lace   Swirl

Sharon, Candy Jar, Covered, Amber 35.00
Sharon, Candy Jar, Covered, Pink .... 27.50 To 35.00
Sharon, Creamer, Pink 11.00
Sharon, Cup & Saucer, Amber .... 10.00 To 11.50
Sharon, Cup, Pink 8.00
Sharon, Pitcher, Ice Lip, Amber 67.00
Sharon, Pitcher, Ice Lip, Pink. 98.00
Sharon, Plate, Pink, 9 1/2 In. 11.00
Sharon, Platter, Amber 8.50
Sharon, Salt & Pepper, Amber .... 25.00 To 32.50
Sharon, Sherbet, Amber 6.00
Sharon, Sherbet, Pink 10.00
Sharon, Sugar, Covered, Pink 21.00
Sierra, Bowl, Pink, 8 1/2 In. 10.50
Sierra, Butter, Covered, Green .... 40.00 To 45.00
Sierra, Butter, Covered, Pink 45.00
Sierra, Creamer, Pink 10.00
Sierra, Cup & Saucer, Green 12.00
Sierra, Cup, Pink 4.50
Sierra, Sugar, Covered, Green 25.00
  SMOCKING, see Windsor
  SNOWFLAKE, see Doric
  SPOKE, see Patrician
Strawberry, Bowl, Green, 7 1/2 In. 12.00
Strawberry, Pitcher, Green 115.00
Sunflower, Cake Plate, Green 7.00
Swirl, Bowl, Ultramarine, 5 1/4 In. 7.00
Swirl, Candy Dish, Covered, Green 18.00
Swirl, Creamer, Ultramarine .... 6.00 To 7.00
Swirl, Salt & Pepper, Ultramarine 21.00
Swirl, Tumbler, Ultramarine, 4 In. 11.00
  SWIRLED SHARP RIB, see Diana
Sylvan, Salt & Pepper, Green 180.00
  TASSELL, see Princess
Tea Room, Ice Bucket, Pink 25.00
Tea Room, Pitcher, Green 93.00
Tea Room, Pitcher, Pink .... 90.00 To 95.00
Tea Room, Relish, Divided, Green 15.00
Tea Room, Salt & Pepper, Pink 40.00
Tea Room, Tumbler, Footed, Green, 12 Oz. 30.00
Thistle, Cup & Saucer, Pink 20.00
  THREE PARROT, see Sylvan
Trojan, Parfait, Yellow 42.50
Trojan, Sugar & Creamer, Yellow 30.00
  VERTICAL RIBBED, see Queen Mary
Victory, Sandwich Server, Handle, Pink 20.00
  WAFFLE, see Waterford
Waterford, Goblet, Crystal, 5 1/4 In. 7.00
Waterford, Pitcher, Tilt, Pink, 80 Oz. 70.00
Waterford, Sherbet, Pink 5.00
Waterford, Tumbler, Crystal, 3 1/2 In. 14.00
  WEDDING BAND, see Moderntone
  WHITE SAIL, see White Ship
White Ship, Tumbler, 3 3/8 In. 5.25
White Ship, Tumbler, 4 5/8 In. 8.00
  WILD ROSE, see Dogwood
  WILDFLOWER, see No. 618
  WILDROSE WITH APPLE BLOSSOM, see Flower Garden with Butterflies
  WINDSOR DIAMOND, see Windsor
Windsor, Ashtray, Crystal 30.00
Windsor, Ashtray, Green 25.00
Windsor, Butter, Covered, Pink 20.00
Windsor, Cake Plate, Pink 15.00

Windsor, Creamer, Pink	4.00 To 6.50
Windsor, Pitcher, Crystal, 4 1/2 In.	13.00
Windsor, Pitcher, Crystal, 6 3/4 In.	7.00
Windsor, Pitcher, Green, 6 3/4 In.	53.00
Windsor, Plate, Pink, 9 In.	7.00
Windsor, Salt & Pepper, Pink	22.00 To 26.00
Windsor, Sherbet, Green	11.50
Windsor, Sugar & Creamer, Covered, Pink	17.00
Windsor, Tumbler, Green, 3 1/4 In.	25.00
Windsor, Tumbler, Pink, 4 In.	5.00

WINGED MEDALLION, see Madrid

Derby porcelain was made in Derby, England, from 1756 to the present. The factory changed names and marks several times. Chelsea Derby (1770–1784), Crown Derby (1784–1811), and the modern Royal Crown Derby are some of the most famous periods of the factory.

DERBY, see also Chelsea; Crown Derby; Royal Crown Derby

DERBY, Figurine, Richard III, C.1775, 10 5/8 In.	1210.00
Figurine, Richard III, Dark Hair, C.1815, 11 3/8 In.	605.00
Figurine, Tithing Group, Late 18th Century	750.00
Group, John Wilkes, C.1772–75, 12 In.	495.00
Group, Nude Man, On Donkey, 2 Women, Animal, Duesbury, 8 1/2 X 9 In.	850.00
Plate, Central Rose, Gadroon, Scalloped Border, 1830, Set of 14	300.00

The DeVilbiss Company has made atomizers of all types since 1888 but no longer makes the perfume bottle tops so popular with collectors. These were made from 1920 to 1968. The glass bottle may be by any of many manufacturers even if the atomizer says DeVilbiss.

DEVILBISS, Atomizer, Bulbous, Gold Crackle Glass, 2 1/2 In.	23.50
Atomizer, Pineapple Shape, Gilded Bottom, Blue	75.00
Atomizer, Pressed Flower Pattern, Blue Opalescent	45.00
Atomizer, Pressed Glass Bottle, 24K Gold Plated Floral, 4 In.	38.00
Bottle, Atomizer, Crackle Glass, Gold Washed Top, Label, 4 In.	45.00
Bottle, Cologne, Atomizer, 24K Gold Plate Trim, Flowers, Label	32.50
Bottle, Perfume, Atomizer, Art Deco, Bell Shape, Borders, Marked	22.00
Bottle, Perfume, Ball Shape, Gold Crackle Glass, 4 In.	65.00
Dresser Set, 3–Sided Cologne Bottle, Geometric Designs, 4 Piece	125.00
Perfume Bottle Atomizer, Ball Shape, Crackle Glass, 3 1/2 In.	65.00
Perfume Bottle Atomizer, Black Teardrops, 7 In.	65.00
Perfume Bottle Atomizer, Etched Florals, Amber, 8 In.	55.00

The comic strip "Dick Tracy" started in 1931. He was the hero of movies from 1937 to 1947, starred in a radio series in the 1940s and a television series in the 1950s. Memorabilia from all these activities is collected.

DICK TRACY, Badge, Secret Service Patrol Sergeant	35.00
Book, Big Little Book, Hotel Murders	12.00
Book, Big Little Book, Phantom Ship	24.00
Book, Comic, Popped Wheat, Famous Artists Syndicate, 1940	10.00
Book, Dick Tracy Gets His Man, 1938, Tiny	12.00
Book, Secret Code, 1938	35.00
Bottle, Soaky	6.00
Bowl, Cereal	30.00
Camera, Box	40.00
Camera, With Box	30.00
Cap Gun	20.00 To 25.00
Card Game, 1937	12.00
Card, Christmas, Dick, Junior, Tess & Sparkle, 1940s	20.00
Card, Lobby, Dick Tracy, 1945, 41 X 81 In.	50.00
Game, Card, 1937	12.00
Game, Crime Stopper, Box	40.00
Game, Dartboard, Cardboard	37.50

Game, Target, Box 100.00
Knife, Crime Stopper 48.00
Lunch Box, Thermos 25.00
Magnifying Glass, Badge & Whistle, Box 35.00
Postcard, Coca–Cola, Dated 1942 .... 42.00
Puppet, Hand 26.00
Puzzle, Crime Does Not Pay Club, Jaymar, Box 35.00
Radio, 2–Way, Official, Remco, Box 43.00
Radio, 2–Way, Wrist, 1961 Chicago Tribune, Box 40.00
Ring, Secret Compartment, Original Advertising 250.00
Salt & Pepper, Junior 45.00
Squad Car No.1, Marx, Dated 1949, 11 In. 75.00
Squad Car, Marx 45.00
Suspenders, Box .... 22.00 To 30.00
Toy, Car, Friction, Green, Marx, 7 In. 60.00
Toy, Marx, Friction, Green, 7 In. 60.00
Toy, Siren Squad Car, Tin, Battery Operated, Marx, Box, 11 In. 195.00
Toy, Squad Car, Plastic, Siren, Marx, Box, 1940s, 10 In. 95.00
Viewer, Film, Original Package 15.00
Watch, 1940s, Box 195.00

DICKENS WARE, see Royal Doulton; Weller

The Dionne quintuplets were born in Canada on May 28, 1934. The publicity about their birth and their special status as wards of the Canadian government made them famous throughout the world. Visitors could watch the girls play, reporters interviewed the girls and the staff, and thousands of special dolls and souvenirs were made picturing the quints at different ages. Emilie died in 1954, Marie in 1970. Yvonne, Annette, and Cecile still live in Canada.

DIONNE QUINTUPLETS, Blotter, 1935 & 1936, Pair 15.00
Book, 3 Year, Pictures 18.00
Booklet, Paper Doll, 1936, Uncut, Set of 5 .... 400.00
Booklet, We're Two Years Old, Whitman, 1936 .... 23.00
Bowl, Cereal, Marie In Bowl, 1935, 5 1/2 In. 20.00
Calendar, 1937 .... 30.00
Calendar, Queens of The Kitchen, 1946 .... 18.00
Doll, White Dress, 11 In. 160.00
Fan, 1 Quint, Playing In Sand, 1936 .... 22.50
Feeding Dish, Stainless Steel 40.00
Mirror, As Babies 25.00
Plate, Annette, Cecille & Yvonne, As Babies, 7 In. 24.00
Postcard, Quints & Dr.Dafoe 15.00
Print, Quaker Oats, 1935, 7 X 9 In., Set of 5 .... 44.00
Scrapbook, Clippings, Kansas City Star, Set of 3 .... 30.00
Scrapbook, Uncut Paper Dolls, 10 Books 250.00
Spoon, Annette 15.00

Walt Disney and his company introduced many comic characters to the world. Collectors search for examples of the work of the Disney Studios and the many commercial products modeled after his characters. These collectibles are called "Disneyana."

DISNEYANA, Airplane, Mickey Mouse, Rubber, 1940 .... 10.00
Ashtray, 3 Pigs, Glazed 55.00
Ashtray, Thumper, Goebel 125.00
Ball, 1950s, Box 18.00
Bank, Bambi, 7 3/4 In. 21.00
Bank, Cinderella, 6 3/4 In. 22.00
Bank, Dime Register, Donald, 1938 .... 150.00
Bank, Mickey Mouse Club House, 1957 .... 27.50
Bank, Mickey Mouse, Alarm Clock, Time To Save, 5 1/2 In. 38.00
Bank, Mickey Mouse, Brass, Book Shape, 1930s, 3 X 4 1/2 In. 50.00
Bank, Mickey Mouse, Enesco, 5 1/2 In. 35.00
Bank, Mickey Mouse, Plastic, Mickey, Red, With Baton, 1950s, 7 In. ... 25.00
Bank, Mickey Mouse, Playpal Plastic, 11 In. 18.00

Bank, Micky The Magician, Mechanical, Walt Disney, Box	25.00
Bank, Pinocchio, Hard Plastic	15.00
Bank, Post Office, Mickey Mouse, Tin	45.00
Book, Coloring, Mickey Mouse, Unused, Dean & Son Ltd., 1931	95.00
Book, Donald Duck, 1st Linen Book, 1935	50.00
Book, Fantasia, Dance of The Hours, 34 Pages, Hardcover, 1940	35.00
Book, Mickey Mouse & His Friends, Linen	90.00
Book, Mickey Mouse The Miracle Maker, 1948	18.00
Book, Mickey's Dog Pluto, Whitman, Cardboard Covers, 1937	20.00
Bowl, Beetleware, Post Cereal Co.Premium, Plastic	17.00
Box, Music, Tin, 7 Paper Rolls	150.00
Bucket, Candy, Donald Duck, 1949	35.00
Camera, Bugs Bunny	12.00
Camera, Donald Duck	10.00 To 15.00
Candy Container, Donald Duck, Papier–Mache, Western Germany	30.00
Card, Dopey, Holding Flower, 1938, 7 X 9 In.	48.00
Card, Lacing, Box	18.00
Card, Mickey's Christmas Carol, 1983, 5 X 7 In.	3.00
Card, Playing, Mickey Mouse, Russell Mfg.Co., 1946	15.00
Card, Playing, Snow White, Box, Miniature	18.00
DISNEYANA, CEL, see Animation Art	
Certificate, Membership, Mickey Mouse Club	75.00
Chair, Folding, Child's, Mickey Mouse, Canvas, Wooden Handles	110.00
Clock Radio, Mickey Mouse, G.E.	65.00
Clock, Alarm, Mickey Mouse, U.S.Time, Celluloid Case	150.00
Clock, Alarm, Mickey Mouse, W.D.P.Bradley, Germany	125.00
Cookie Cutter, Mickey Mouse, Tin	20.00
Cookie Jar, Turnabout, Mickey & Minnie Mouse	50.00
Costume, Cinderella, Unused, Box	30.00
Costume, Mickey Mouse, Box, 1934	200.00
Crayons, Donald Duck, Tin Litho Box	25.00
Creamer, Mickey Mouse, Tin	36.00
Cup & Saucer, Mickey & Minnie Mouse, Child's, Tin	30.00
Dish Set, Pinocchio, Metal, Ohio Art, 15 Piece	40.00
Dish, Feeding, Mickey Mouse, Sections	45.00
Display Rack, Donald Duck, Tin, Wire, 48 X 17 X 21 In.	200.00
Doll, Cloth, Mickey Mouse, Paper Tag, 11 In.	125.00
Doll, Donald Duck, Solid Rubber, 8 In.	20.00
Doll, Dopey, Composition Face, Cloth Body, 12 In.	65.00
Doll, Mickey & Minnie Mouse, Steiff, Tag, 1930s, 11 In., Pair	1000.00
Doll, Mickey Mouse, Jointed, Columbia, 13 In.	45.00
Doll, Mickey Mouse, Solid Rubber, 12 In.	20.00
Doll, Mickey Mouse, Wooden, Leather Ears, Jointed, Sticker, 3 In.	125.00
Doll, Mouseketeer Girl, Sun Rubber, 12 In.	38.00
Doll, Pinocchio, Composition Head, Wooden Body, Ideal, 10 1/4 In.	75.00
Doll, Snow White & 7 Dwarfs, Marx	15.00
Doorstop, Donald Duck	165.00
Figurine, 3 Little Pigs, Musical Instruments, Bisque, 4 In.	45.00
Figurine, Chihuahua, Lady & Tramp, Miniature	75.00
Figurine, Dalmation, Ceramic, 4 1/2 In.	10.00
Figurine, Donald Duck, American Pottery, 6 1/2 In.	200.00
Figurine, Donald Duck, Celluloid, Long Bill, 3 In.	50.00
Figurine, Donald Duck, On Diving Board, Bisque	40.00
Figurine, Donald Duck, Reclining, American Pottery	125.00
Figurine, Dumbo, American Pottery, Small	125.00
Figurine, Ferdinand The Bull, Porcelain, Walt Disney, 3 In.	15.00
Figurine, Jose Carioca, American Pottery, 6 In.	200.00
Figurine, Lady, Hagen Renaker, Miniature	75.00
Figurine, Mickey & Minnie, Bisque, Origianl Paint, 1930s, 3 In.	85.00
Figurine, Mickey Mouse, Rubber, Head, Arms, Legs Turn, Dakin, 7 In.	52.00
Figurine, Mickey Mouse, Soap, Ideal Tag, 1932	90.00
Figurine, Pinocchio, Blue Shorts, Yellow Gloves, Red Tie, 3 In.	18.00
Figurine, Snow White & 7 Dwarfs, Bisque, W.Disney, 1938, 8 Piece	60.00
Footstool, Mickey Mouse Club	22.00

Game, Disney Adventure Land, 1956	35.00
Game, Donald Duck, Wrist Twist, Skill	5.00
Game, Frontierland, Board, Parker Bros., 1955	25.00
Game, Mickey Mouse Club, 1955, Box	22.00
Game, Parade, 1930s	70.00
Game, Peter Rabbit	10.00
Game, Pinocchio Race, Chad Valley, 1940	50.00
Game, Target, Mickey Mouse, Box, 1930s	59.00
Glass, Disney On Parade	9.00
Glass, Horace Horsecollar	12.00
Glass, Snow White & 7 Dwarfs, 1930s, Set of 7	65.00
Globe, Rand McNally, Colorful Characters	45.00
Guitar, Mickey Mouse Mouseketeer	25.00
Handkerchief, Donald Duck	12.00
Handkerchief, Mickey Mouse, Unused, 1940s	8.00
Hat, Minnie Mouse, Mouseketeers, Unused	12.00
Hot Plate, Mickey Mouse, Iron, 3 Legs, 1928, 7 In.	200.00
Kitchen Set, Snow White, Sink, Stove, Refrigerator, Wolverine, Box	130.00
Lamp, Donald Duck, Playing Drum	35.00
Lamp, Dopey, Plaster of Paris, No Shade, La Mode Studios, 1938	85.00
Lamp, Mickey Mouse, Dated 1936, Green	75.00
Magic Slate, Donald Duck, Dated 1959	13.00
Make–Up Kit, Stage, Mickey Mouse Club, Package	22.00
Map, Mickey & Donald Treasure Island, 1939, 19 X 26 In.	35.00
Marionette, Minnie Mouse, Wood, Pottery, Original Dress, 10 In.	28.00
Mask, Party, Doc	12.00
Mask, Pinocchio, Gillette Razor Blades, Disney, 1939	6.00
Medical Kit, Mickey Mouse, 1950s, Box	20.00
Mirror, Mickey Mouse, Pocket	20.00
Movie Projector, Mickey Mouse	145.00
Mug, Pluto & Mickey, Patriot China	45.00
Music Box Night–Light, Bambi	35.00
Night–Light, Mickey Mouse, Dated 1938	110.00
Nodder, Porky Pig	10.00
Paint Box, Donald Duck, Tin Box	12.00
Paper Doll, Snow White & 7 Dwarfs, Whitman, Box	110.00
Pencil Box, Pinocchio, Contents	63.00
Pencil Sharpener, Mickey Mouse, Standing, Rubber Face	50.00
Pencil Sharpener, Snow White, Celluloid	34.00
Perfume Bottle, Figural, Dwarf, From Snow White & Seven Dwarfs	35.00
Picture, Reverse Glass, 3 Little Pigs, Reliance	30.00
Pin, Dopey, Ice Capades, 2 3/4 In.	23.00
Pincushion, Mickey Mouse, Ceramic, Early 1930s	25.00
Pincushion, Tinkerbell	20.00
Pitcher, Donald Duck, Figural, 6 In.	25.00
Pitcher, Musical, 3 Little Pigs, Wadeheath, 1934, 10 In.	450.00
Pitcher, Snow White, Music Box Base, 1938, 7 1/2 In.	240.00
Planter, Bugs Bunny	10.00 To 30.00
Planter, Dopey, Yellow, Blue, Rose, Black, 6 3/4 In.	38.00
Planter, Pluto	15.00
Planter, Snow White	30.00
Planter, Thumper	25.00
Plate, 3 Little Pigs, Divided, Patriot China, 8 In.	60.00
Plate, Dinner, Fantasia, 10 1/2 In.	42.00
Plate, Minnie Mouse, Patriot China, 7 In.	25.00
Poster, Donald Duck & Horace, Goofy, 1943, 12 1/2 X 19 In.	20.00
Poster, Donald Duck Cola, Cardboard, 10 X 8 In.	30.00
Poster, Donald Duck Cola, Cardboard, 26 X 20 In.	40.00
Program, Fantasia	55.00
Puppet, Donald Duck, Hand, Vinyl Head, Pink Flannel, 11 In.	5.00
Puppet, Dopey, Composition Head, Cloth Body, Walt Disney, 6 In.	30.00
Puppet, Hand, Jiminy Cricket	6.00
Puppet, Hand, Pluto	5.00
Puppet, Mickey Mouse, Push–Up, Gabriel	2.00

Puppet, Minnie Mouse, Plastic Head, Painted, Dotted Dress 10.00
Puppet, Pluto, Wooden Hand Base, String Operated, 1934 .... 25.00
Puppet, String, Mickey Mouse, Checked Red Shirt, Pants, Shoes 25.00
Purse, Snow White & 7 Dwarfs, Cloth 35.00
Puzzle, Jigsaw, 3 Little Pigs, Box, 300 Piece, 14 X 22 In. 10.00
Puzzle, Jigsaw, Mickey Mouse & Friends, 1940s, 14 X 22 In. 30.00
Refrigerator, Snow White, Tin, Child Size 55.00
Rug, Bambi, 57 X 45 In. 75.00
Rug, Chip 'N Dale, Teeter Tottering, Thumper, 1955, 4 X 5 Ft. 250.00
Rug, Donald Carrying Chip'N Dale, In Buckets, 37 X 21 In. 125.00
Rug, Mickey & Minnie Mouse, Wool, Label, 27 X 44 In. 50.00
Rug, Mickey & Rabbit Seesaw, 1930s 85.00
Salt & Pepper, Alice In Wonderland, China, Walt Disney 45.00
Salt & Pepper, Donald Duck, Sitting, American Bisque Co. 65.00
Salt & Pepper, Dumbo 15.00
Salt & Pepper, Ludwig Von Drake 25.00
Salt & Pepper, Pinocchio, 5 In. 68.00
Salt & Pepper, Pinocchio, Blue Shorts, Yellow Gloves, Tie, 3 In. 55.00
Salt Shaker, Mushroom, Fantasia 35.00
Saucer, Donald Duck, 1930s 22.50
Scarf, Head, Mickey Mouse 15.00
Sheet Music, Whistle While You Work, Snow White 10.00
Sheet Music, Who's Afraid of The Big Bad Wolf, 1933 .... 40.00
Sign, Donald Duck Beverages, 28 X 20 In. 400.00
Sign, Donald Duck Cola, Tin, 60 X 34 In. 800.00
Soap, Mickey Mouse Figure, Ideal Films Tag, 1932 .... 100.00
Soap, Snow White & 7 Dwarfs, Lightfoot Schultz, Box, 1939 .... 210.00
Spoon, Mickey Mouse, Branford 15.00
Stool, Folding, Mickey Mouse, Canvas Top 45.00
Straws, Box, Mickey Mouse 10.00
Sweater, Child's, Mickey Mouse, 1930s 35.00
Swim Goggles, Donald Duck, Auburn Rubber Co., Package, 1950s 14.00
Tablecloth, Paper, Mickey Mouse Club, 56 X 86 In., Unused 30.00
Tea Set, Cinderella, Tin, Ohio Art 40.00
Tea Set, Donald Duck, Tray, Teapot, 2 Cups, 2 Saucers, Ohio Art 138.00
Tea Set, Mickey Mouse, Box, 1930s, 21 Piece 140.00
Tea Set, Mickey Mouse, Tin, Marked W.D.P., Box 47.50
Toothbrush Holder, 3 Little Pigs, Bisque .... 25.00 To 40.00
Toothbrush Holder, Mickey & Minnie Mouse, Donald Duck 120.00
Toothbrush, Child's, Donald Duck, Walt Disney Enterprises 15.00
Top, Disney Characters, Musical Instruments, Chein, 1950s 18.00
Toy, Beach Buggy, Donald, Matchbox 5.00
Toy, Car, Donald Duck & Pluto, Rubber .... 35.00 To 55.00
Toy, Car, Pull, Donald Duck, Kohner 28.50
Toy, Donald Duck, Fisher Price, No.500 .... 48.00
Toy, Donald Duck, On Skis, Windup, Linemar, 6 In. 260.00
Toy, Donald Duck, Rubber, Bendey W.D., 8 1/2 In. 20.00
Toy, Donald Duck, Straight Shooter, Plastic, Marco, Box, 7 In. 135.00
Toy, Donald Duck, Windup, Metal, Felt Clothes, Schuco, 1937, 5 In. 850.00
Toy, Donald Duck, Windup, Papier–Mache, 11 In. 650.00
Toy, Donald Duck, Windup, Tin, Celluloid Head, Japan, 1950s 20.00
Toy, Dopey, Windup, Tin, Rocking, Marx, 1938, Walt Disney, 8 In. 150.00
Toy, Ferdinand The Bull, Composition, Walt Disney, 1930s 175.00
Toy, Ferris Wheel, Mickey Mouse, Chein 145.00
Toy, Fire Engine, Mickey Mouse & Donald Duck, Sun Rubber 48.00
Toy, Goofy On Surfboard, Rubber Band Driven 5.00
Toy, Gumball Machine, Mickey Mouse, Plastic, With Gumballs 15.00
Toy, Jeep, Donald Duck, Matchbox 5.00
Toy, Jiminy Cricket, Wooden, Ideal, 8 In. 375.00
Toy, Kaleidoscope, Disney Characters At Play, Mickey's Face 25.00
Toy, Mickey & Minnie, Trapeze, Windup, Borgfeldt, 1934, Large 665.00
Toy, Mickey Mouse Acrobat, Mechanical, Tin, Linemar, Box, 8 In. 375.00
Toy, Mickey Mouse Express, Marx 465.00
Toy, Mickey Mouse Krazy Kar, Battery Operated 50.00

Toy, Mickey Mouse Sparkler, Tin, Press Plunger, German, 5 1/2 In. 350.00
Toy, Mickey Mouse Trapeze, Wooden, Walt Disney, 8 1/2 In. 50.00
Toy, Mickey Mouse, In Airplane, Rubber 60.00
Toy, Mickey Mouse, Rubber, Bendey W.D., 12 In. 20.00
Toy, Mickey Mouse, With Xylophone, Tin, Linemar, Box, 6 1/2 In. 550.00
Toy, Pinnochio Roadshow, Matchbox 6.00
Toy, Pluto Pop–Up Kritter, On Poodle, Wooden Jointed 75.00
Toy, Pluto, Drum Major, Windup, Linemar 170.00
Toy, Pluto, Jointed, 14 In. 15.00
Toy, Pluto, Pop–Up Kritter, Fisher Price 15.00
Toy, Pluto, Windup, Hard Plastic, Key, Metal Tail Spins 20.00
Toy, Pull, Donald Duck, Convertible, Plastic 6.00
Toy, Squeeze, 7 Dwarfs, Vinyl, 1940–50, Set of 7 .... 200.00
Toy, Stove, Refrigerator, Sink, Snow White, Wolverine, Tin 75.00
Toy, Tool Chest, Mickey Mouse 150.00
Tumbler Set, Cinderella, Illustrations, 7 In. 30.00
Tumbler, Donald Duck, Glass, Blue Picture, 4 1/2 In. 20.00
Tumbler, Snow White & 7 Dwarfs, 8 Piece 75.00
Tumbler, Snow White, Dairy Premium, 1940s, 5 In. 15.00
Viewer, Mickey Mouse, Original Box 55.00
Wallet, Disneyland, Croyden, Original Card, 1956, 6 Piece 60.00
Washtub & Washboard, Mickey Mouse, Metal, Box, 1930s 120.00
Watch Fob, Mickey Mouse 20.00
Watch, Mickey Mouse, Ingersoll, Oblong 225.00
Watch, Mickey Mouse, Pocket 464.00
Wristwatch, Cinderella 20.00
Wristwatch, Daisy Duck, Box, 1948 .... 110.00
Wristwatch, Goofy, Runs Backward, Box 195.00
Wristwatch, Mickey Mouse, Electric, Box, 1968 .... 175.00
Wristwatch, Mickey Mouse, Timex, England, 1940 .... 150.00
Wristwatch, Mickey's 50th Birthday, Box 100.00
Wristwatch, Snow White 36.00
Wristwatch, Snow White, U.S.Time 45.00
    DOCTOR, see Medical; Dental

Doll entries are listed by marks printed or incised on the doll, if possible. If there are no marks, the doll is listed by the name of the subject or country.

DOLL, A.B.G. 1361, Character Girl, Ball–Jointed, Sleep Eyes, Braids, 25 In. 495.00
A.B.G., Brown Stationary Eyes, Ball–Jointed, Dressed, 27 In. 350.00
A.B.G., Character Baby, 27 In. 750.00
A.M. 990, Baby, Life Size, 27 In. 775.00
A.M. 990, Character Baby, Composition, Sleep Eyes, Open Mouth, 11 In. 200.00
A.M., Bisque Head, Straw–Stuffed, Muslin Body, Stationary Eyes, 17 In. 125.00
A.M., Bisque, Sleep Eyes, Jointed Kid Body, 22 In. 265.00
A.M., Googly, All Original, Bisque, 6 1/2 In. 950.00
A.M., Googly, Bisque Head, Compositon Body, Dimples, 6 In. 245.00
A.M., Rosebud Bisque, Celluloid Hands, Kid Body, 19 In. 150.00
A.M., Sleep Eyes, Open Mouth, Dimples, Original Eyes & Wig, 18 In. 265.00
A.M.210, Bisque Head, Composition Body, Googly Eyes, 7 3/4 In. 255.00
A.M.254, Bisque Socket Head, Molded Hair, Papier–Mache Body, 7 In. 300.00
A.M.323, Googly, Bisque, Toddler Body, All Original, 13 In. 1650.00
A.M.323, Googly, Blue Sleep Eyes, Composition Body, Dressed, 7 1/2 In. 575.00
A.M.329, Character Baby, Original Wig & Clothes, 11 In. 245.00
A.M.341, Dream Baby, Cloth Body, Crier, Sleep Eyes, Dressed, 14 In. 350.00
A.M.345, Kiddie Joy, Cloth Body, Celluloid Hands, 20 In. 500.00
A.M.351, Baby, Black, Sleep Eyes, Composition, Christening Gown, 13 In. 795.00
A.M.351–8, Rock–A–Bye Baby, Bisque Head, Cloth Body, Dressed, 15 In. 475.00
A.M.353, Baby, Oriental, Sleep Eyes, Composition, Clothes, 11 In. 895.00
A.M.353, Oriental, 19 1/2 In. 1850.00
A.M.362, Baby, Black, Bisque, Molded Hair, Brown Sleep Eyes, 10 In. 225.00
A.M.370, Kid Body, White Dress, Lace Stockings, Shoes, 1908, 22 In. 275.00
A.M.370, Porcelain, Leather Body, Original, 17 1/2 In. 245.00
A.M.385, Molded Head, Legs, Arms, Stuffed Body, 18 In. 2500.00

A.M.390, Bisque Head, Composition Body, Sleep Eyes, 9 In. ....*Illus* 110.00
A.M.390, Bisque Socket Head, Set Eyes, 4 Teeth, 16 In. 150.00
A.M.518, Character Baby, Bisque Head, Composition, Clothes, Box, 17 In. 650.00
A.M.560, Bisque Head, Glass Eyes, Open Mouth, Teeth, Dressed, 23 In. 340.00
A.M.971, Toddler Body, 2 Upper Teeth, Dress & Bonnet, 14 In. 450.00
A.M.996, Character Toddler, Brown Sleep Eyes, Blond Wig, 21 In. 575.00
Acme, Mama, Composition & Cloth, 24 In. 125.00
Adolf Wislizenus, Pierced Ears, 22 In. 275.00
Advertising, Allied Van Lines, Girl, Cloth, Jumper, 1970s, 17 In. 9.00
Advertising, Aunt Jemima, Cut–Out Rag, Unstuffed, Frame, Instructions 100.00
Advertising, Aunt Jemima, Plastic, 4 Piece 125.00
Advertising, Baby Ruth, Cloth, 1927 .... 38.00
Advertising, Bob's Big Boy, 8 In. ....6.00 To 10.00
Advertising, Burger King, Accessories, 17 In. 20.00
Advertising, Buster Brown & His Dog Tige 35.00
Advertising, Ceresota Flour, Original Paint, 15 In. 150.00
Advertising, Chiquita Banana, Cloth .... 14.00 To 16.00
Advertising, Coca–Cola, Buddy Lee, Composition, 1950 .... 350.00
Advertising, Cream of Wheat Chef, Cloth, 1930, 20 In. 135.00
Advertising, Cream of Wheat Chef, Cloth, Uncut, 1930, 20 In. 125.00
Advertising, Cream of Wheat, Black Waiter, Bowl, Stuffed, 1950s, 17 In. 35.00
Advertising, Cream of Wheat, Rastus, Cloth, Uncut .... 125.00 To 135.00
Advertising, Dan River, Buttons, Cloth, Painted Face, Braids, 17 In. 125.00
Advertising, Dutch Boy Paint, Cloth Body, Composition Hands, 3 Ft. 225.00
Advertising, Eskimo Pie, Cloth 6.00
Advertising, Jack Frost Sugar 10.00
Advertising, Jolly Green Giant, Cloth ....5.00 To 23.00
Advertising, Little Bopeep, Kellogg's Nursery Rhyme, Uncut, 1928 .... 25.00
Advertising, Little Bopeep, Kellogg's, Dated 1928 .... 90.00
Advertising, Miss Curity 22.50
Advertising, Mr.Peanut, Rag, Sealed In Original Package 20.00
Advertising, My Name Is Miss Korn Krisp, Cloth, Stuffed, 1900s, 26 In. 90.00
Advertising, Nabisco Pretzel 12.00
Advertising, Pillsbury, 7 In. 6.00
Advertising, Ralston Purina, Scarecrow, 1965, 25 In. 22.50
Advertising, Ronald McDonald, Striped Suit, Orange Tie, 1972, 17 In. 9.00
Advertising, Scarecrow Sam, Brach Candy Co., Cloth, 1970s, 16 In. 8.50
Advertising, Swiss Miss 22.00
Advertising, Tom The Piper's Son, Kellogg's, Cloth, 1928 .... 85.00
    DOLL, ALEXANDER, see Doll, Madame Alexander
Alt, Beck & Gottschalck, Bisque Head, Composition, Gown, Stole, 23 In. 850.00
Amberg, Baby Montgomery, Bisque, Dimples, Jointed Body, 20 In. 2750.00
Amberg, Baby, Sleep Eyes, Cloth Body, Celluloid Hands, Dressed, 16 In. 850.00
Amberg, Vanta Baby Boy, Sleep Eyes, 2 Upper Teeth, 1927, 27 In. 1500.00
American Character, Chuckles, All Original, 23 In. 185.00
American Character, Eloise, Mask Face, Cloth, 21 In. 105.00
American Character, Sweet Sue, Jointed, Bridal Gown, 30 In. 120.00
American Character, Toni, Kit's Kapers Dress, 10 In. 24.00
American Schoolboy, Kid Body, Bisque Forearms, Sailor Outfit, 20 In. 395.00
American Schoolboy, Stationary Eyes, Molded Hair, Wool Suit, 9 In. 250.00
Amish, Baby, Cloth, Faceless, Purple Dress, Apron, Bonnet, Cape, 16 In. 30.00
Amish, Straw–Stuffed, Long Black Stockings, Cape, 28 In. 425.00
Anne Shirley, Composition, All Original, 27 In. 275.00
    DOLL, ARMAND MARSEILLE, see Doll, A. M.
Arnold Print Works, Little Red Riding Hood, Cloth, 1892, Uncut, 17 In. 185.00
Arnold Schwarzenegger, 7 In. 10.00
Au–Nain Bleu, Composition, Movable Limbs, Breton Dressed, 8 In. 65.00
B.S.W., Character Baby, Flirty, Bisque, 30 In. 1500.00
Baby Brother Tenderlove, Anatomically Correct Boy, Box, 1975 .... 20.00
Baby Floria, Sleep Eyes, Molded Painted Hair, Dressed, 17 In. 975.00
Baby Happifats, Comp.Head & Hands, 12 In. 325.00
Baby Phyllis, Bisque Head, Incised, 12 In. 265.00
Baby, Black, Composition, Flirty Sleep Eyes, Coat & Bonnet, 17 In. 85.00
Baby, Black, Leather–Jointed, Dressed, 11 1/2 In. 500.00

Baby, Breather, Molded Hair, Moving Tongue, Jointed, 18 1/2 In. 650.00
Babyland, Rag, Old Clothing, 15 In. 300.00
Bahr & Proschild 6207, Character Baby, Open Mouth, 14 In. 300.00
    DOLL, BARBIE, see Doll, Mattel, Barbie
Barney Google, King Features Syndicate 28.00
Bartenstein, Two Faces, Sleeping, Crying, Signed, Old Clothes 1675.00
Beany, Talking, Pull Cord, Clothes, Working, 17 In. 33.00
Bed, Boy & Girl, Oilcloth Faces, Satin & Net Clothes, 1930s, Pair 25.00
Bed, Composition Head, Mohair Wig, Original Dress & Bonnet, 25 In. 50.00
Belton, Bisque Head, Blonde Wig, Closed Mouth, Dressed, 4 1/2 In. 75.00
Belton, Bisque Head, Composition Body, Painted Socks, Shoes, 7 1/2 In. 475.00
Belton, Bisque, C.1875, 12 In. 1050.00
Belton, French, Closed Mouth, Ecru Satin Dress, Hat, 12 1/2 In. 850.00
Belton, Threaded Blue Paperweight Eyes, Wig, Old Clothes, 16 In. 2650.00
Belton, Threaded Paperweight Eyes, Bisque, Toddler Body, 10 1/2 In. 950.00
    DOLL, BERGMANN, see also Doll, S & H; Doll, Simon & Halbig
Bergmann, Sleep Eyes, 4 Teeth, Brown Human Hair, Dressed, 26 In. 495.00
Betsy McCall, Ballerina, 22 In. 95.00
Betsy McCall, Blue Sleep Eyes, Pink Chemise, Jointed, Box, 1958, 8 In. 110.00
Betsy McCall, Girl Scout, 2 Outfits, Dress Form, Case, 8 In. 85.00
Betsy McCall, Wedding Gown, 8 In. 65.00
Betsy Wetsy, 12 In. 20.00
Betty Boop, Cloth, Sealed Bag, 17 In. 15.00
Betty Boop, Hot Pink Dress, Fur Trimmed Coat, 20 In. 60.00
Betty Boop, Vinyl Roly Poly, Blowup, Package, 1940s, 16 In. 27.50
Billiken, Two Faces, Celluloid, Japan, 4 1/2 In. 25.00
Bisque Shoulder Head, Cloth Body, Leather Arms, Dressed, 18 In. 800.00
Bisque, Baby, Black, Pigtails, Diaper, Movable Arms & Legs, 5 In. 75.00
Bisque, Baby, Flannel Gown, 2 In. 30.00
Bisque, Black, Glass Eyes, Composition Straight Wrist, 14 In. 1000.00
Bisque, Blue Eyes, Blond, Closed Mouth, German, C.1885, 4 In. 150.00
Bisque, Boy, Painted Blue Snowsuit, Stationary, Japan, 4 1/2 In. 20.00
Bisque, Bride, Painted, Stationary, 5 1/2 In. 18.00
Bisque, Dollhouse, 1910, 3 In. 225.00
Bisque, French Type, Kid Lined Body, Blue Glass Eyes, Blond, 5 In. 200.00
Bisque, French Wrestler, Bisque, Painted Socks, Boots, C.1885, 9 In. 1000.00
Bisque, Indian, German, 9 In. 60.00
Bisque, Jointed Composition Toddler Body, Coat, Box, 1933, 14 In. 300.00
Bisque, Jointed, Blond Painted Hair & Shoes, Dress, Germany, 5 1/2 In. 125.00
Bisque, Molded Hair, Painted Face, Costume, German, C.1885, 7 In. 250.00
Bisque, Painted Face, Blond Braid, In Trunk, France, C.1885, 3 In. 200.00
Bisque, Papier–Mache Body, Composition Arms, R.A.7/0, 1909, 11 In. 98.00
Bisque, Uncle Walt, Smitty, Skeezix, Herby, Marked, Box, Set of 4 .... 40.00
Black, Cloth Body, Composition Head, 9 1/2 In. 160.00
Black, Cloth, Sewn Hair, Face, Red Shoes, 19th Century, 14 In. 295.00
Black, Mechanical, Papier–Mache, 9 In. 75.00
Bonanza Set, Ben Cartwright, Little Joe & Hoss, Set of 3 .... 75.00
Bonnie Babe, Muslin Body, Composition Hands, Large 975.00
Boulogne–Sur–Mer, Clay Shoulder Head Lady, Straw Body, 1912, 11 In. 25.00
Boy, Papier–Mache, Glass Eyes, Red Tam, Matching Pants, 10 1/2 In. 150.00
Bru Jne 8, Bisque Head, Open–Close Mouth, Jointed Composition, 19 In. 2050.00
Bru Jne 8, Bisque Shoulder Head, Glass Eyes, Kid Body, Dressed, 21 In. 5000.00
Bru Jne, Black, Signed Shoes & Underwear, 17 In. 18500.00
Bru Jne, Pierced Ears, Kid, Wood Jointed Body, Bisque Arms, 22 In. 7150.00
Bru Jne, Swivel Head, Jointed Kid Body, Bisque Lower Arms, 18 In. 7975.00
Bruno Schmidt, Walker, Kiss Throwing, 25 In. 425.00
Bubbles, Composition, 15 In. 70.00
Bucherer, Mutt, Comic, Steel Ball, Jointed, 1921, 8 In. 195.00
Buddy Lee, Original Iowa Hawks Football Uniform, Leather Helmet 250.00
Buffy & Mrs.Beasley, 6 In. 150.00
Bunny Head, Porcelain, With Kewpie Face, 15 In. 50.00
Bunny, Composition Head, Stuffed Plush Bunny Body, 14 In. 22.00
Bye–Lo, Advertising, Christening Outfit, Cloth Body, 20 In. 1200.00
Bye–Lo, Baby, Bisque Head, Cloth Body, Celluloid Hands, 12 In. 295.00

Bye–Lo, Baby, Bisque, Brown Eyes, Red Stamp, 14 In.	695.00
Bye–Lo, Baby, Bisque, Molded Hair, Jointed Hips & Shoulders, 6 In.	290.00
Bye–Lo, Bisque, Swivel Neck, Sleep Eyes, 5 In.	600.00
Bye–Lo, Molded Painted Hair, Celluloid Hands, Cloth Body, 18 In.	575.00
Bye–Lo, Stamped Body, Celluloid Hands, Blue Sleep Eyes, 15 1/2 In.	650.00
C.P., Baby, Sleep Eyes, Composition, Christening Gown, 25 In.	895.00
C.P., Open Mouth, Dressed, Bangs, High Button Shoes, 38 In.	1625.00
Cameo, Bandy, For General Electric, Maxfield Parrish	750.00
Cameo, Flower Girl, 12 In.	42.50
Cameo, Ring Bearer, 12 In.	42.50
Cameo, Skootles, Composition, 1925, 16 In.	225.00
Carl Bergner, Three Faces, Jointed, Composition, 14 In.	1195.00
Carnival, Girl, On Brush, Lacy Skirt, Dotted Dress, Japan, 3 1/2 In.	38.00
Celluloid, Baby, Jointed Arms, Irwin U.S.A., 4 1/4 In.	30.00
Celluloid, Jointed, Sleep Eyes, 2 1/2 In.	35.00
Celluloid, Movable Arms & Legs, Marked Edi Germany, 6 1/2 In.	35.00
Century Doll Co., Chuckles, Composition, 17 In.	135.00
Century, Mama, Composition, 1924, 24 In.	300.00
Chad Valley, Blue Glass Eyes, Felt, 12 In.	100.00
Chase, Boy, Brown Eyes, 16 In.	450.00
Chase, Character, Signed, 21 In.	1800.00
Chase, Lady, Cloth, 15 In.	910.00
Chase, Sateen Body, Elbow & Knee Joints, 16 In.	350.00
Cheerful Cherub, Composition Head, Cloth Body, 20 In.	85.00
China Head, 1880, 21 1/2 In. *Cover*	250.00
China Head, Blond, Pantaloons, Slip & Dress, 24 In.	395.00
China Head, Brown Eyes, Dressed As Boy, 1880s Type, 28 1/2 In.	695.00
China Head, Cloth Body, Black Painted Hair, Arms & Legs, 5 In.	50.00
China Head, Leather Hands, Black Hair, Sausage Curls, 1870, 16 In.	237.00
China Shoulder Head, Molded Curly Hair, Cloth Body, Dressed, 18 In.	90.00
Cloth, Applied Nose, Sewn Features & Fingers, Dress, Cape, Hat, 16 In.	495.00
Cloth, Art Fabric Mills, 1900, 18 In.	22.00
Cloth, Little Red Riding Hood, Printed, Uncut, 1892	165.00
Cloth, Open & Close Eyes, Mask Face, Clothes, Box, 1940s, 18 In.	65.00
Cloth, Painted Face, Replaced Clothes, 1850, Kentucky, 34 In.	1750.00
Cloth, Printed, Baby Blue Eyes, Uncut, 1909, 12 In.	95.00
Cloth, Stockinette Covered Head, Dressed, C.1900, 12 In.	70.00
Cloth, Woman, Cloth, Embroidered Face, Pantaloons, Hair, 26 In.	1500.00
Cloth, Yarn Hair, Niagara Falls Embroidered On Skirt, 1910, 2 3/4 In.	15.00
Clovia, Comic Strip, Painted Head, Sleep Eyes, Rubber Body, 11 In.	35.00
Clown, Semimechanical, Bisque, Squeeze Body, Cymbals Play, 13 1/2 In.	260.00
Cocheco Co., Baby Elephant, Printed Cloth, Uncut, 1827	65.00
Cocheco Co., Cloth, Darkie, Uncut	175.00
Crown, Pinocchio, Composition, Original Clothes, 8 1/2 In.	45.00
Denamur, Bebe, Closed Mouth, Blond Human Hair, Silk Coat, 33 In.	4000.00
Denamur, Bisque Head, Cork Pate, Paperweight Eyes, 14 In.	2310.00
Dennie Dimwit, Swing & Sway, 11 In.	75.00
Dennis The Menace, Rubber, Original Clothes, Box, Dated 1958, 13 In.	55.00
Dennis The Menace, Vinyl Head, Molded Hair, Blue Overalls, 14 In.	45.00
DeNunez, Bisque Swivel Head, Kid–Lined Body, 10 In. 200.00 To	375.00
DEP 10, Walking, Bisque Head, Cries Mama, Arm Raises, 23 1/2 In.	750.00
DEP 749, Bisque Head, Open Mouth, Glass Eyes, Teeth, Dressed, 8 1/2 In.	350.00
DEP, Black, Painted Bisque, Cloth Body, 1900 Horseshoe, 11 In.	135.00
DeWees Cochran, Barbara Ann, Red Hair, Composition, 17 In.	220.00
Doctor, Celluloid, Original Outfit, 10 In.	65.00
Dollikins, Multi–Jointed, Original Clothes, Uneeda, 11 In.	15.00
Dolly Dingle, Musical, Blue Velvet, 20 In.	95.00
Dolly Parton, Colonial Dress & Hat, Musical Base, Box, 15 In.	30.00
Dream Baby, Closed Mouth, 10 In.	295.00
Dream Baby, Original Box, Germany, 10 In.	335.00
Dressel, Cuno & Otto, Ball Jointed, 23 1/2 In.	325.00
Dresser, Toy Soldier, Brush, 4 1/4 In.	35.00
Dresser, With White Parrot On Arm, Voight, Sitzendorf, 6 In.	65.00
Dresser, Yellow Dress, Cap, Madame Pompadour & E & R Stamped, 7 In.	125.00

Eden Bebe, Bisque Head, Open Mouth, Ball–Jointed, Dressed, 21 1/2 In. 1295.00
Eden Bebe, Bisque Head, Paperweight Eyes, Silk Skirt, Jacket, 22 In. 1550.00
Eden Bebe, Bisque Head, Velvet Maroon Outfit, 18 In. 2100.00
Eden Bebe, Bisque, Composition, Mama–Papa Strings, Marked, 25 In. 550.00
Effanbee, Anchors Aweigh, Boy, By Faith Wicke, 18 In. 39.00
Effanbee, Anne Shirley, C.1940, 19 In. 125.00
Effanbee, Anne Shirley, Closed Mouth, 21 In. 195.00
Effanbee, Babe Ruth, 16 In. .... 65.00 To 85.00
Effanbee, Baby Dainty, Original Clothes, 14 In. 60.00
Effanbee, Baby Grumpy, Mennonite, 13 In. 165.00
Effanbee, Bride, 18 In. 70.00
Effanbee, Brother, Composition, 16 In. 135.00
Effanbee, Bubbles, Molded Hair, Sleep Eyes, 20 In. 80.00
Effanbee, Dolly Parton, 18 In. 82.50
Effanbee, Eleanor Roosevelt, 17 In. 75.00
Effanbee, Fluffy, Blond, Sleep Eyes, Original Clothes, 1954, 11 In. 25.00
Effanbee, Girl Scout, Fluffy, Black Rooted Hair, Box, 9 In. 35.00
Effanbee, Girl, Flirty Eyes, 20 In. 95.00
Effanbee, Groucho Marx, 17 In. 55.00
Effanbee, Honey Girl, 13 1/2 In. 95.00
Effanbee, Judy Garland, 16 In. .... 70.00 To 75.00
Effanbee, Lillian Russell, Purple Dress & Hat, Cameo Brooch, 13 In. 55.00
Effanbee, Little Lady, 18 In. 18.00
Effanbee, Lovums, Fat Baby, Pajamas, Booties, Big Blue Eyes, 17 In. 24.00
Effanbee, Mae West, 17 In. ....55.00 To 100.00
Effanbee, Patsy Ann, 19 In. 55.00
Effanbee, Patsy Lou, Tin Eyes, Bracelet, Playsuit, Hat, 26 In. 350.00
Effanbee, Patsy, Composition, Jointed, 9 In. 45.00
Effanbee, Rosemary, Compositon, 26 In. 135.00
Effanbee, Sister, Composition, 12 In. 100.00
Effanbee, Skippy, Composition, Blue Sailor Suit, White Hat, 14 1/2 In. 250.00
Effanbee, Snow White, Box, Large 110.00
Effanbee, Sweetie Pie, Composition, 19 In. ....95.00 To 110.00
Effanbee, Tommy Tucker, Wig, 18 In. 195.00
Effanbee, Young Betsy, Blond, For Carson Pirie Scott, Box, 11 In. 50.00
Elfland, Composition, Box, 18 In. 50.00
Eloise, Cloth Mask Face, Original Jumper & Blouse, 22 In. 65.00
F.G., Bebe, Gesland Body, Blond Hair, 24 In. 6500.00
F.G., Brown Paperweight Eyes, Skin, Ball–Jointed Body, 15 In. 2850.00
F.G., Fashion, Bisque Head & Shoulder, Leather Body, Dressed, 16 In. 1495.00
F.G., Fashion, Bisque, Wooden Body, Cork Pate, Blond Mohair, 17 In. 3400.00
F.G., Paperweight Eyes, Closed Mouth, Antique Wig, Clothes, 27 In. 6850.00
F.S.& Co.1295, Bisque Head, Baby Body, Jointed, Dressed, 24 In. 775.00
Fairy Princess, 1961, Uneeda, 31 In. 25.00
Fashion Lady, Turned Shoulder Head, Elaborate Clothes, 1855, 25 In. 900.00
Fashion, Bisque Head, Glass Eyes, Kid Body, India Markings, 12 1/2 In. 1500.00
Fashion, Bisque Shoulder Head, Wooden Body, Marked 4, 18 In. 1600.00
Fashion, Closed Mouth, Bisque Swivel Head, Cloth Body, Box, 20 In. 1800.00
Fashion, Kid Over Wood, Bisque Lower Arms, Clothes, French, 17 In. 4400.00
Fashion, Wooden Upper Arms, Bisque Lower, Clothes, French, 20 In. 3950.00
Floradora, 15 In. 125.00
Floradora, 27 In. 400.00
Florodora, Bisque, 17 In. 195.00
Franz Schmidt, Sleep Eyes, Baby Body, Christening Gown, 28 In. 1495.00
French Fashion, Kid Body, Paperweight Eyes, Wig, 17 In. 1995.00
French, All Bisque, Stationary Eyes, 5 1/2 In. 800.00
French, Bisque, Fashion, Swivel Head, Cork Pate, Kid Body, 17 In. 1210.00
French, Fashion Bride, Bisque, Kid Body, Old Clothing, 17 In. 1950.00
French, Fashion, Bisque Head, Leather Fingers, Dressed, 16 1/2 In. 1500.00
French, Fashion, Bisque Shoulder Head, Kid Body, Old Clothes, 12 In. 1295.00
French, Fashion, Swivel Neck, 16 In. 795.00
French, Girl, Bisque Socket Head, Kid Body, Closed Mouth, 15 In. 695.00
French, Man, Bisque Head, Fur Wig & Mustache, Metal Hands, 9 1/2 In. 450.00

Doll, A.M.390, Bisque Head,
Composition Body, Sleep Eyes, 9 In.

Doll, Fulper, Bisque Character Girl,
Brown Hair, C.1917, 17 In.

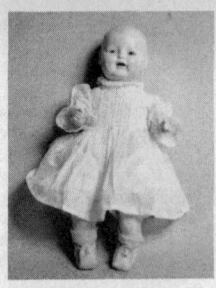

Doll, Horsman, Sleep Eyes,
Open Mouth, Composition, 15 In.

French, Pink Kid Body, Papier–Mache, 22 In.	775.00
Freudlich, Character, Wave, Composition, Molded Hat, Uniform, 15 In.	90.00
Frozen Charlie, Black, Black Features, China, 4 1/2 In.	250.00
Frozen Charlie, China, 16 In.	110.00
Frozen Charlie, Pink Luster China, Painted Bangs, Brown Eyes, 12 In.	225.00
Frozen Charlotte, Black Molded Hair, Gold Shoes, Dressed, 5 In.	45.00
DOLL, FULPER, see also Doll, Horsman	
Fulper, Baby, Sleep Eyes, Human Hair Wig, Open Mouth, Dimples, 21 In.	550.00
Fulper, Bisque Character Girl, Brown Hair, C.1917, 17 In. ....*Illus*	2000.00
Fulper, Kid Body, 19 1/2 In.	115.00
Fulper, Toddler, 17 In.	600.00
Furga Tenerella, Baby, Blond, Sleep Eyes, Box, 1970s, 14 In.	16.00
G.B.Borgfeldt, Brown Curls, Ball–Jointed Body, 25 In.	385.00
Gans & Seyforth, Ball Jointed, Composition, 24 In.	595.00
Gaultier, Bebe, Brown Paperweight Eyes, Ball–Jointed, C.1880, 21 In.	3000.00
Gaultier, Child, Bisque Socket Head, Brunette Human Hair, 28 In.	2500.00
Gaultier, Fashion Lady, Swivel Head, Bisque Shoulder, C.1870, 26 In.	4250.00
Gaultier, French Fashion, Bisque, Paperweight Eyes, Clothes, 12 In.	1295.00
Gebruder Heubach 6894, Baby, Solid Dome, Closed Mouth, 11 In.	325.00
Gebruder Heubach 8192, Child, Open Mouth, Sleep Eyes, Curly, 28 In.	1250.00
Gebruder Heubach 8192, Girl, Sleep Eyes, Ball–Jointed, 14 In.	500.00
Gebruder Heubach, Boy, Laugher, Blue Sleep Eyes, Sailor Suit, 16 In.	1000.00
Gebruder Heubach, Girl, Googly, Papier–Mache Body, 7 1/2 In.	650.00
German, 3–Faced, Crying, Sleeping, Smiling, Composition & Wood, 12 In.	880.00
German, Bisque Head, Sleep Blue Eyes, Open Mouth, Marked, 23 In.	275.00
German, Bisque Head, Toddler Body, Blue Sleep Eyes, 12 In.	450.00
German, Bisque, Closed Mouth, Blue Glass Eyes, Human Wig, 9 In.	550.00
German, Bisque, Mystery Mini, 7 1/2 In.	350.00
German, Mechanical, Bisque Head, Glass Eyes, Teeth, Cart, 11 In.	375.00
Ginger, Hand Painted Brown Hair, No Clothes, 7 1/2 In.	20.00
Ginny, Dutch Costume, Blue Sleep Eyes, Straight Legs, 1955, 8 In.	135.00
Ginny, Hard Plastic, Open Brown Eyes, Marked, 1950–53, 8 In.	65.00
Ginny, Plastic, Sleep Eyes, Walker, Tagged Coat, 1955, 8 In.	175.00
Ginny, Toni, 14 In.	55.00
Girl Scout, Composition, Handmade Uniform, 1955 Newspaper, 11 In.	80.00
Girl, Rubber, Czechoslovakia, 1930s, 8 In.	22.00
Goebel, Dolly Dingle, Box, 20 In.	250.00
Goebel, Sleep Eyes, Open Mouth, Composition, Full Bee Mark, 14 In.	235.00
Goldberger, Lady Diana & Prince Charles, Wedding Attire, 12 In., Pair	65.00
Goldilocks & 3 Bears, Topsy–Turvy, Cloth, Plush Bears, 1960s, 16 In.	48.00
Golliwog, Felt Face & Body, Fur Hair, English, 1940s, 22 In.	125.00
Googly, Bisque Head, Sleep Eyes, Right, Toddler Body, Marked, 13 In.	825.00
Googly, Bisque, Incised 543, 5 In.	875.00
Googly, Demalcol 5/0, Bisque Head, Toddler Body, Dressed, 10 1/2 In.	675.00
Gotz Weichpuppe, Girl, Cloth, Vinyl Limbs, Blond, Painted, 17 1/2 In.	38.00
Grace Putnam, Bye–Lo, 12 In.	600.00

Greiner 58, China Head, Leather Arms, Original, Old Dress, 17 In. 425.00
Greiner 72, China Head, Leather Arms, Original Body, 26 In. 465.00
Grund Mfg., Little Lulu, 15 In. 75.00
Gustav Heim, Sailor Boy, Cloth, 1920, 14 In. 475.00
H.B., Baby, Bisque, Sleep Eyes, Painted Hair, Christening Gown, 13 In. 225.00
Hahl–Kohle, Sleep Eyes, Human Hair, 23 In. 385.00
Handwerck 99, Pierced Ears, Jointed, Sleep Eyes, White Dress, 16 In. 1095.00
Handwerck 99, Socket Head, Jointed Composition, Sleep Eyes, 19 In. 450.00
Handwerck & Halbig 69, Brown Sleep Eyes, Ball–Jointed Body, 25 In. 450.00
Handwerck & Halbig, Bisque Head & Body, Sleep Eyes, Nude, 31 In. 550.00
Handwerck 109, Bisque Head, Jointed Body, Old Clothes, 16 In. 395.00
Handwerck 109, Bisque, Brown Sleep Eyes, 24 In. 550.00
Handwerck 189, Bisque, Blue Sleep Eyes, 15 In. 450.00
Handwerck, Bebe Elite, Socket Goebel Head, Clothes, Box, 23 In. 750.00
Handwerck, Bisque Head, Sleep Eyes, Composition Jointed Body, 25 In. 495.00
Handwerck, Brown Sleep Eyes, Ball–Jointed, 21 In. 350.00
Handwerck, Kid Body, Sleep Eyes, Original Wig, 18 In. 175.00
Handwerck, Set Eyes, Auburn Wig, Antique Clothing, Marked, 38 In. 2850.00
Handwerck, Sleep Eyes, Blond Mohair Wig, Antique Clothes, 24 In. 650.00
Hebee–Shebee, Bisque, Original Tagged Clothes, 8 1/2 In. 1000.00
Heidi Ott, Andrea, Brown Hair, Weighted Body, Pink Dress, 14 In. 110.00
Heidi Ott, Florina, Blond Pigtails, Blue Dress, 19 In. 140.00
Hertel, Schwab 151, Baby, Open Mouth, Sleep Eyes, Gown, 14 In. 449.00
Hertel, Schwab 152, Character Child, Sleep Eyes, Open Mouth, 20 In. 500.00
Heubach Koppelsdorf 250–5, Compositon Ball–Jointed Body, 24 In. 280.00
Heubach Koppelsdorf 251, Sleep Eyes, Open Mouth, Costume, 5 In. 95.00
Heubach Koppelsdorf 275, Sleep Eyes, Kid Body, Human Hair, 20 In. 235.00
Heubach Koppelsdorf 320, Character Doll, 28 In. 975.00
Heubach Koppelsdorf 399, Baby, Black, Bent Limb, Composition, 11 In. 210.00
Heubach Koppelsdorf 399, Black, African Boy, Bisque Head, Box, 8 In. 225.00
Heubach Koppelsdorf 444, Indian Boy, 10 In. 195.00
Heubach Koppelsdorf, Baby, Flirty, 27 In. 950.00
Heubach Koppelsdorf, Bisque Socket Head, Gibson Girl Dress, 7 In. 140.00
Heubach Koppelsdorf, Bisque, Shoulder Head, Kid Body, Wig, 12 In. 175.00
Heubach Koppelsdorf, Dressed, Box, 22 In. 750.00
Heubach Koppelsdorf, Girl, Bisque Head, Candy Container, 6 1/2 In. 195.00
Heubach, Bisque Head, Molded Hair, Open–Close Mouth, Dressed, 15 In. 795.00
Heubach, Twins, Mechanical, Squeeze, Turn Heads, Intaglio Eyes, 6 In. 325.00
Hilda, Bisque, Blue Eyes, Clothes, 20 In. 4000.00
Hobo Clown, Crochet, Stuffed, 21 In. 25.00
Horsman, Betsy McCall, All Original, 29 In. 100.00
Horsman, Blond Hair, With Hairnet, Original Red Dress, 14 In. 55.00
Horsman, Boy, Grace Drayton, 1913, 13 1/2 In., Pair 255.00
Horsman, Campbell Kid, Composition, Jointed, Romper Suit, 1948, 12 In. 250.00
Horsman, Composition, Tagged Romper, Voice Pat.B.E.Lloyd, 19 In. 115.00
Horsman, Crier, Composition Head, Arms, Legs, Blond Wig, Dressed, 23 In. 85.00
Horsman, Dimples Toddler, Redressed, 15 In. 150.00
Horsman, Ella Cinders, Composition, Original Dress, Book, 17 In. 350.00
Horsman, Mama, Nude, Composition, 16 In. 25.00
Horsman, Mary Poppins, Purple Dress, Blue Hat, 3 Outfits, Box, 12 In. 25.00
Horsman, Peggy, 25 In. 50.00
Horsman, Poor Pitiful Pearl, 12 In. 23.00
Horsman, Sleep Eyes, Open Mouth, Composition, 15 In. ....*Illus* 80.00
Housemaid Mold, Bisque, 6 1/2 In. 75.00
Hue 7247, Boy, Glass Eyes, 18 In. 2500.00
Hue 7602, Toddler, 14 1/2 In. 1150.00
Hue 7802, Toddler, Boy, 24 In. 2450.00
Hue, Coquette, 10 1/2 In. 450.00
I Love Lucy, 1950s, 27 In. 75.00
Ideal, Baby, Hard Plastic Head, Rubber Body, Sleep Eyes, Dress, 12 In. 35.00
Ideal, Black Baby, 1973, 18 In. 20.00
Ideal, Bye–Bye Baby, 25 In. 250.00
Ideal, Crier, Composition Head, Cloth Body & Legs, Tin Eyes, 16 In. 40.00
Ideal, Crissy Grow Hair, 24 In. .... 35.00 To 45.00

Ideal, Deanna Durbin, Composition, Jointed Body, Sleep Eyes, 25 In.	695.00
Ideal, Deanna Durbin, Composition, Original Wig, 1938, 21 In.	350.00
Ideal, Eloise, Cloth, Tagged Clothes, 23 In.	75.00
Ideal, Felix, Wooden, Jointed, Comic, 4 In.	125.00
Ideal, Felix, Wooden, Jointed, Comic, 7 1/2 In.	195.00
Ideal, Girl, Gro–Hair, 16 In.	18.00
Ideal, Harriet Hubbard Ayer, Original Clothes, 14 In.	85.00
Ideal, Judy Garland, Composition, 18 In.	700.00
Ideal, Magic Skin Baby Boy, Original Clothes, 25 In.	70.00
Ideal, Mary Hartline, Plastic, Majorette, Not Walking, 1950s, 16 In.	155.00
Ideal, Miss Revlon, Plastic, Nylon Ponytail, Nurse, 1956, 10 1/2 In.	85.00
Ideal, Miss Revlon, Vinyl Head, Plastic Body, Dress, Wrist Tag, 20 In.	110.00
Ideal, Mortimer Snerd, Composition, 12 In.	225.00
Ideal, Petite Patti, 16 In.	85.00
Ideal, Pinocchio, Composition Head, Wooden Body, Label, 10 In.	225.00
Ideal, Sara Stimson, Little Miss Marker, Sailor Outfit, Box, 11 In.	18.00
Ideal, Saucy Walker, 22 In.	95.00
Ideal, Saucy Walker, All Original, 23 In.	100.00
Ideal, Shirley Look–Alike, Flirty Eyes, Human Hair, C.1930, 20 In.	60.00
Ideal, Thumbelina, Black, Box, 18 In.	22.00
Ideal, Toni, 2 Outfits, Roller Skates, 14 In.	65.00
Ideal, Toni, Plastic, Brown Hair, Blue Cotton Dress, 1950s, 14 In.	175.00
Ideal, Toni, Plastic, Nylon Wig, Organdy Tagged Dress, 1950s, 19 In.	139.00
Ideal, Toni, Plastic, Red Hair, Plaid Dress, Tag, Box, 1950s, 14 In.	200.00
Ideal, Toni, Sleep Eyes, Cotton Dress, Blond Hair, 1950s, 11 In.	85.00
DOLL, INDIAN, see Indian, Doll	
Irwin, Baby, Celluloid, Jointed Arms, 4 1/4 In.	30.00
DOLL, J.D.K., see also Doll, Kestner	
J.D.K.151, Character Baby, 14 In.	450.00
J.D.K.151, Character Baby, Molded Head, Christening Gown, 18 In.	595.00
J.D.K.151, Molded Teeth, Tongue, Head, Gray Sleep Eyes, Bisque, 13 In.	375.00
J.D.K.152, Character Baby, Bisque, Bent Limb Body, 15 In.	895.00
J.D.K.211, Baby, Bisque Head, Sleep Eyes, Open Close Mouth, 18 In.	250.00
J.D.K.211, Sammy, Christening Gown, 20 In.	1575.00
J.D.K.214, Bisque Head, Jointed Body, Dressed, Little Boy Blue, 29 In.	750.00
J.D.K.226, Baby, Bisque, Original Wig, Old Clothes, 22 In.	1500.00
J.D.K.257, Toddler, 16 In.	595.00
J.D.K.260, Character Child, Bisque Head, Open Mouth, Jointed, 31 In.	1495.00
Jaymar, Indian, Wooden, Jointed, 7 In.	35.00
Jessie James, 9 1/2 In.	15.00
Jester, Stuffed, Sateen Costume, Molded Face, Painted Features, 26 In.	25.00
Joel Ellis, Wood, Metal Hands & Feet, Silk Dress, C.1873, 15 In.	900.00
Jughead, Vinyl, 9 In.	15.00
Jules Steiner, Bisque, Paperweight Eyes, Fish Teeth, 1870s, 16 In.	2100.00
Jumeau 12, Tete Bebe, Blue Paperweight Eyes, Wooden Jointed, 26 In.	2300.00
Jumeau, Bebe, Blond, Brown Paperweight Eyes, Maroon Clothes, 20 In.	4000.00
Jumeau, Bisque Head, Open Mouth, Silk Dress, Underclothes, Label, 19 In.	1195.00
Jumeau, Bisque Head, Open Mouth, Upper Teeth, Dressed, 29 1/2 In.	1795.00
Jumeau, Bisque Head, Paperweight Eyes, Jointed Body, Dressed, 26 In.	3750.00
Jumeau, Bisque Head, Paperweight Eyes, Jointed, Composition, 20 In.	3500.00
Jumeau, Bisque Head, Paperweight Eyes, Outlined Mouth, Jointed, 14 In.	1870.00
Jumeau, Bisque Head, Stationary Eyes, Jointed Wrists, Dressed, 15 In.	1950.00
Jumeau, Bisque, Blue Paperweight Eyes, Dressed, 17 In.	3900.00
Jumeau, Bisque, Long Curls, Teeth, Ball–Jointed, Blue Outfit, 24 In.	1295.00
Jumeau, Black, Paperweight Eyes, Black Wig, Jointed, Dressed, 14 In.	1200.00
Jumeau, Blond Wig, Wood & Composition Body, Silk & Lace Dress, 26 In.	3575.00
Jumeau, Brown Bisque, Paperweight Eyes, Jointed Body, 13 1/2 In.	1200.00
Jumeau, Brown Hair, Flowered Dress, 1907, 18 In.	1830.00
Jumeau, Child, Open Mouth, Feathered Brows, Lawn Dress, 1907, 32 In.	2500.00
Jumeau, Fashion, Closed Mouth, Paperweight Eyes, Silk Dress, 14 In.	1500.00
Jumeau, French, Bisque Head, Open Mouth, Upper Teeth, 18 1/2 In.	1195.00
Jumeau, Long Face, Set Eyes, Open Mouth, 1907, 24 In.	2900.00
Jumeau, Mechanical, On Box, Gold Skirt, Purse, Bisque Hands, 16 In.	3500.00
Jumeau, Open Mouth, Jointed Body, Wine Velvet Outfit, 13 1/2 In.	1250.00

Jumeau, Petite Bebe, Brown Paperweight Eyes, Socket Head, 16 In.	4250.00
Jumeau, Portrait Boy, Brown Paperweight Eyes, Brown Suit, 1880, 25 In.	5240.00
Jumeau, Portrait, Almond Eyes, Signed Body, Clothes, 15 In.	5800.00
Jumeau, Portrait, Bisque, Blue Eyes, French Clothes, Signed, 14 In.	5500.00
Jumeau, Threaded Paperweight Eyes, Dressed, Signed Body, 23 In.	5900.00
Jumeau, Walker, Open Mouth, Glass Eyes, Silk Dress, Bonnet, 21 1/2 In.	1295.00
Just Me, Bisque, Painted, 8 In.	1600.00
Jutta 1914, Baby, Bisque Head, Sleep Eyes, Composition, 18 In.	290.00
Jutta 1914, Baby, Glass Eyes, Open Mouth, Bent Limb, 14 In.	260.00
Jutta, Character Baby, Bisque Head, Sleep Eyes, Open Mouth, 27 In.	1250.00
Jutta, Character Baby, Flirty Eyes, 12 In.	395.00
Jutta, Pale Bisque, Chunky Body, 34 In.	1100.00
Jutta, Toddler, 27 In.	1395.00
K * R 13, Blue Sleep Eyes, Ball–Jointed, 26 In.	650.00
K * R 19, Bisque Head, Sleep Eyes, Open Mouth, Composition, 7 1/2 In.	220.00
K * R 26, Child, Bisque, Blue Sleep Eyes, Blond, 4 Teeth, C.1910, 10 In.	750.00
K * R 36, Baby, Bisque, Composition Body, Legs & Hands, 15 In.	390.00
K * R 53, Character, Alsatian Clothes, 19 1/2 In.	795.00
K * R 62, Bisque Head, Flirty Eyes, Jointed, Dressed, 25 In.	350.00
K * R 100, Baby, Original Body Finish, Old Clothes, 16 In.	950.00
K * R 101, Character Boy, Pouty, Composition, Marked, 15 1/2 In.	1325.00
K * R 114, Pouty Boy, Original Wig, Dressed, 14 In.	2500.00
K * R 115, Pouty Toddler Boy, Sleep Eyes, All Original, 16 In.	3500.00
K * R 115A, Original Fat Body, 22 In.	4000.00
K * R 115A, Toddler, 12 In.	2300.00
K * R 116A, Boy, Open Mouth, 20 In.	2500.00
K * R 117, Flirty Eyes, Open Mouth, Wood & Composition Body, 23 In.	715.00
K * R 121, Character Baby, 22 In.	600.00
K * R 122, Character Baby, Open Mouth, Teeth, Composition, 19 In.	650.00
K * R 124, Moritz, Flirty Eyes, 16 In.	9250.00
K * R 126, Baby, Flirty Eyes, Open Mouth, Bent Limb, Marked, 25 In.	475.00
K * R 126, Baby, Old Clothes, 20 In.	1500.00
K * R 126, Bisque Head, Flirty Eyes, Open Mouth, Jointed, 19 In.	750.00
K * R 126, Character Baby, Bisque Head, Blue Flirty Eyes, 26 In.	895.00
K * R 126, Character Baby, Flirty Eyes, Composition, Gown, 13 In.	695.00
K * R 126, Toddler, Flirty Eyes, 18 In.	750.00
K * R 126, Toddler, Wobbley Tongue, 24 In.	900.00
K * R 127, Bisque, Blue Sleep Eyes, Painted Molded Hair, 14 In.	950.00
K * R 128, Character Baby, Bisque Head, Composition Bent Limb, 24 In.	1200.00
K * R 192, All Original, 8 In.	600.00
K * R 680, Toddler, Flirty Eyes, Open Mouth, 30 In.	1850.00
K * R, Black, Molded Black Hair, Flirty Eyes, German, 12 In.	375.00
K * R, Character Baby, 25 In.	1075.00
K * R, Child, Flirty Eyes, 25 In.	750.00
K * R, Composition Body, Original Wig, 9 In.	600.00
K * R, Flossy Flirt, Original Wig, 19 In.	800.00
K * R, Girl, Flirty Eyes, Original Mohair Wig, 24 In.	450.00
K * R, Marie, 12 In.	1950.00
K * R, Oriental Baby, Bisque, 9 1/2 In.	1300.00
K * R, Peter, Character, 13 In.	2800.00
K * R, Rosemarie, Child, Composition, Box, 24 In.	110.00
K * R, Sleep Eyes, 5 Piece Body, T–Straps Painted On, 6 In.	260.00
Kachina, Albino Wolf, Painted Wood, Red Cloth, Jim Tawaki, 1932, 14 In.	175.00
Kaiser, Baby, Bisque Head, 14 In.	250.00
Kaiser, Baby, Black, 20 In.	1950.00
Kate Greenaway, Child, Holding Pink Bouquet, White, Germany, 2 1/2 In.	65.00
Kathe Kruse, Boy, Painted Hair, Cloth, Signed On Foot, 14 In.	950.00
Kathe Kruse, Child, German, Radiating Iris Eyes, 1929, 20 1/2 In.	1000.00
Kathe Kruse, Martina, 18 In.	275.00
Kathy Kruse, Fleur, 14 In.	210.00
Kathy Kruse, Nino, 18 In.	275.00
Kathy Kruse, Tina, 14 In.	210.00
DOLL, KESTNER, see also Doll, J.D.K.	
Kestner 7–145, Fixed Eyes, Heavy Brows, Kid Body, 17 1/2 In.	350.00

Kestner 129, Painted Brows, Sleep Eyes, Original Clothes, 18 In.	895.00
Kestner 142/15, Boy, Bisque, 32 In. ....*Illus*	550.00
Kestner 143, Character, Bisque Head, Pink Dress, Kid Shoes, 15 In.	750.00
Kestner 151, Bisque, Blue Eyes, Original Box, 20 In.	520.00
Kestner 152, Character Baby, 26 In.	695.00
Kestner 154, Bisque Shoulder Head, Kid Jointed Body, Dressed, 18 In.	325.00
Kestner 154, Gusset Kid Body, Sleep Eyes, Old Dress, 25 In.	395.00
Kestner 154, Kid Body, Blue Sleep Eyes, New Wig, Old Clothing, 22 In.	325.00
Kestner 154, Kid Body, Painted Brows, Maroon Middy Dress, 18 In.	325.00
Kestner 164, Boy, Mohair Wig, 28 In.	775.00
Kestner 164, Young Lady, Blond Wig, Blue Eyes, Lacy Dress, Hat, 32 In.	1000.00
Kestner 168, Bisque Head, Jointed Body, Dressed, Marked, 22 In.	425.00
Kestner 171, Daisy Mold, Blond Mohair Wig, Old Clothes, 18 1/2 In.	650.00
Kestner 171, Matte Bisque Head, Ball–Jointed, Antique Clothes, 27 In.	795.00
Kestner 184, Brown Sleep Eyes, Open Mouth, Brunette, Boots, 8 In.	400.00
Kestner 192, Ball–Jointed Body, Fur Trimmed Coat & Hat, 26 In.	550.00
Kestner 192, Walker, All Original, 6 In.	550.00
Kestner 206, Character, Closed Mouth, 18 In.	3500.00
Kestner 226, Original Wig & Clothes, 12 In.	450.00
Kestner 249, Character Child, 24 In.	950.00
Kestner 639, Paperweight Eyes, Dome Head, By Foulke, 18 1/2 In.	800.00
Kestner, Bisque Arms, Closed Mouth, Dressed, 17 In.	1250.00
Kestner, Bisque, Blue Sleep Eyes, All Original, 7 1/2 In.	2200.00
Kestner, Bisque, Paperweight Eyes, Kid Body, Original Outfit, 21 In.	900.00
Kestner, Brown Eyes, Blond, Carries White Lamb, C.1900, 5 1/2 In.	200.00
Kestner, Century Baby, Open–Close Mouth, 10 In.	550.00
Kestner, Character Baby, Bisque, Composition, Sleep Eyes, 25 In.	1150.00
Kestner, Child, Bisque, Blue Sleep Eyes, 4 Teeth, C.1910, 8 In.	350.00
Kestner, Child, Closed Mouth, Maroon Wool Dress, C.1885, 20 In.	850.00
Kestner, Closed Mouth, Spiral Eyes, Original Outfit, 23 In.	900.00
Kestner, Crown & Streamers Kid Body, Fur Brows, Wig, Dress, 18 In.	245.00
Kestner, Flapper, 8 In.	600.00
Kestner, Girl, Turned Shoulder Head, Dressed, 14 In.	700.00
Kestner, Googly, All Bisque, Sleep Eyes, Original Wig, 6 In.	1500.00
Kestner, Jointed Leather Body, Old Clothes, 26 In.	425.00
Kestner, Kid Body, Bisque Forearms, Turned Head, Mohair Wig, 21 In.	450.00
Kestner, Leather Body, Original Head & Wig, New Clothes, 21 In.	450.00
Kestner, Pouty, Mark X, 17 In.	2650.00
Kestner, Sewing, Painted Eyes, Ribbon Legs, 9 In.	200.00
Kestner, Solid Dome, Incised J.D.K., 15 In.	750.00
Kewpie Bride, Cameo, 16 In.	50.00
Kewpie, Composition, 13 In.	135.00
Kewpie, Memorial, Cameo, 27 In.	75.00
Kewpie, Vinyl, Cameo, 16 In.	75.00
Kiddie Joy, Baby, Molded Hair, Sleep Eyes, Ball–Jointed, 19 In.	325.00
Kley & Hahn 67, Baby, Christening Gown, Mohair Wig, 25 In.	875.00
Kley & Hahn 250, Socket Head, Jointed Composition, Sleep Eyes, 26 In.	525.00
Kley & Hahn 522, Baby, Bisque Head, Composition, Sleep Eyes, 12 In.	450.00
Kley & Hahn, Walker, 25 In.	595.99
Knickerbocker, Beloved Belindy, Black, Cloth, Tagged, 1965, 15 In.	85.00
Knickerbocker, Orphan Annie, Extra Party Dress, 11 In.	15.00
Knickerbocker, Raggedy Ann, Box, 36 In.	40.00
Konig & Wernicke, Character Baby, Composition, Bisque Head, 16 In.	550.00
Koppelsdorf, Bisque, Brown Eyes, Old Clothes, 14 In.	107.50
Lady, Papier–Mache, Glass Eyes, White Dress, Sparse Brown Wig, 16 In.	165.00
Lady, Wax Over Papier–Mache Body, Sleep Eyes, New Clothes, 22 In.	325.00
Le Parisien, Bisque Head, Glass Eyes, Open Mouth, Label, 22 1/2 In.	1325.00
Lenci, Boy & Girl, Hollow Felt Covered Torso, 17 1/2 In.	1500.00
Lenci, Boy, Blond Mohair Wig, 24 In.	325.00
Lenci, Corinne, Curly Brown Hair, Dress, Coat, Box, 1979, 20 In.	215.00
Lenci, Cristina, 27 In.	360.00
Lenci, Farmer Boy, 1940s, Cloth, 12 In.	200.00
Lenci, Felt, Braided Coils, Black & Royal Blue Dress, C.1925, 22 In.	825.00

Lenci, Felt, Braided Coils, Diamond Pattern Dress, Doll, 17 In.	990.00
Lenci, Felt, Curly Hair, Dress & Coat, Matching Hat, Box, C.1925, 17 In.	550.00
Lenci, Felt, Flirty Eyes, Coat, Skirt, Pocketbook, C.1930, 20 In.	2750.00
Lenci, Felt, Long Braids, Russian Costume, Boots, C.1925, 39 In.	1045.00
Lenci, Girl, Pink Organdy & Felt Costume, 17 In.	1250.00
Lenci, Lady, Flobella, Tagged, 9 In.	200.00
Lenci, Lucia, Original Dress, 14 In.	245.00
Lenci, Lucy, 18 In.	140.00
Lenci, Organdy Pink Dress, Felt Flowers, Felt Hat, Box, 1923, 18 In.	1000.00
Lenci, Pamela, All Original, 14 In.	450.00
Lenci, Samantha, 1979, 27 In.	315.00
Lenci, Scolaretta, 20 In.	260.00
Leo Moss, Composition, Original Clothes, C.1912, 19 In.	9500.00
Lil Sis, Jointed, Molded Hair, 1920s, 14 In.	55.00
Lilli, Barbie's Prototype, Germany, 1957, 7 1/4 In.	250.00
Little Genius, Molded Hair, 1 Piece Body, Christening Outfit, 8 In.	325.00
Little Red Riding Hood, Composition, Jointed, Mohair Wig, MBC, 7 In.	18.00
Lori, Baby, Open Mouth, Marked 232, 14 In.	950.00
Maberg, Baby, All Original, 16 In.	850.00
Madame Alexander, Africa, Bent Knees, 8 In.	425.00
Madame Alexander, Agatha, Turquoise, Box, 21 In. ....320.00 To 330.00
Madame Alexander, Alice In Wonderland, Tagged, All Original, 20 In.	650.00
Madame Alexander, Alice, Cloth, 1930s, 12 1/2 In.	250.00
Madame Alexander, Amy, Tagged Dress, 14 In.	150.00
Madame Alexander, Baby Jane, Sleep Eyes, Open Mouth, 6 Teeth, 15 In.	95.00
Madame Alexander, Ballerina, 16 In.	225.00
Madame Alexander, Betty Boop, Wooden, 12 In.	500.00
Madame Alexander, Bicentennial Betsy Ross, 8 In.	80.00
Madame Alexander, Big Huggums, Original Clothes, 1950s, 25 In.	130.00
Madame Alexander, Binnie Walker, 24 In.	105.00
Madame Alexander, Black Pussy Cat, 14 In.	95.00
Madame Alexander, Boy & Girl, Netherlands, Box, 8 In., Pair	125.00
Madame Alexander, Boy, Blue Suit, White Shirt, 1955, 8 In.	400.00
Madame Alexander, Bride, Blond, Bent Knee, 8 In.	125.00
Madame Alexander, Bride, Box, 14 In.	120.00
Madame Alexander, Canadian, Box, 8 In.	60.00
Madame Alexander, Cissette Ballerina, Jointed Knee, 9 1/2 In.	300.00
Madame Alexander, Cornelia Portrait, Box, 21 In.	350.00
Madame Alexander, Coronation Girl, 1950s, Pair	205.00
Madame Alexander, David Copperfield, Eyes To Side, Dressed, 16 In.	350.00
Madame Alexander, Dionne Quintuplets, Baby, 23 In.	285.00
Madame Alexander, Dionne Quintuplets, Molded Hair, Open Mouth, 12 In.	200.00
Madame Alexander, Dionne Quintuplets, Toddles, Tag, 7 1/2 In., 5 Piece	550.00
Madame Alexander, Dutch Boy & Girl, Wood Shoes, Bent Knees, 8 In., Pr.	240.00
Madame Alexander, Edith, Vinyl, 15 In.	125.00
Madame Alexander, Elsie Bride, Box, 17 In.	125.00
Madame Alexander, Forever Darling, Lucille Ball ....*Illus*	4000.00
Madame Alexander, France, 8 In.	35.00
Madame Alexander, Gone With The Wind, 14 In.	95.00
Madame Alexander, Goya, Box, 21 In.	325.00
Madame Alexander, Hansel & Gretel, 8 In., Pair	175.00
Madame Alexander, Jacqueline, White Formal, Cape, Jewelry, 21 In.	725.00
Madame Alexander, Jane Withers, Open Mouth, 21 In.	600.00
Madame Alexander, Kamkins, 19 In.	575.00
Madame Alexander, Lady Hamilton, 14 In.	85.00
Madame Alexander, Laurie, Blue Outfit, Wrist Tag, 11 In.	55.00
Madame Alexander, Leslie, Yellow Organdy Dress, Box, 1967, 17 In.	375.00
Madame Alexander, Lissy, 11 In.	75.00
Madame Alexander, Little Granny, 14 In.	90.00
Madame Alexander, Little Red Riding Hood, Box, 8 In.	75.00
Madame Alexander, Little Women, 12 In.	43.95
Madame Alexander, Lord Nelson, 11 In.	85.00
Madame Alexander, Lucinda, Aqua Dress, Umbrella, 14 In.	65.00
Madame Alexander, Madam Bea, Box, 21 In. ....375.00 To 750.00

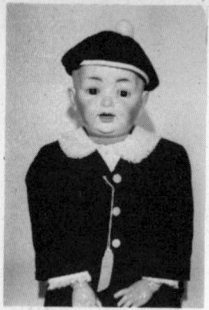

Doll, Kestner 142/15,
Boy, Bisque, 32 In.

Doll, Madame Alexander, Forever
Darling, Lucille Ball

Doll, Uncle Sam, Bisque,
Original Clothes.
Marked SI, 13 In.

Madame Alexander, Maggie Mix Up, Little Lady, Tagged, 8 In.	250.00
Madame Alexander, Manet, Box, 21 In.	325.00
Madame Alexander, Margaret O'Brien, 21 In.	295.00
Madame Alexander, Margot, Blond, Blue Eyelids, Satin Gown, 9 1/2 In.	375.00
Madame Alexander, Marie, Dionne Quintuplets, Composition, 19 In.	275.00
Madame Alexander, Mary Todd Lincoln, Box, 14 In.	225.00
Madame Alexander, McGuffey Ana, Composition, Original Dress, 16 In.	185.00
Madame Alexander, Meg, Box, 1963, 12 In.	70.00
Madame Alexander, Mexican, Box, 8 In.	60.00
Madame Alexander, Mimi, 14 In.	90.00
Madame Alexander, Monet, 21 In.	235.00
Madame Alexander, Netherlands, 8 In.	35.00
Madame Alexander, Peter Pan, 14 In.	225.00
Madame Alexander, Poor Cinderella, 14 In.	60.00
Madame Alexander, Princess Elizabeth, Composition, 24 In.	110.00
Madame Alexander, Priscilla, Colonial Girl, 8 In.	400.00
Madame Alexander, Pussy Cat, 20 In.	65.00
Madame Alexander, Queen, White Brocade Gown, Tag, C.1972, 9 1/2 In.	329.00
Madame Alexander, Scarlett & Rhett, Box, 21 In.	175.00
Madame Alexander, Scarlett O'Hara, White Organdy Dress, 14 In.	165.00
Madame Alexander, Scarlett, Velvet Outfit, Box, 21 In.	300.00 To 395.00
Madame Alexander, Sleeping Beauty, Wrist Bag, Box, 12 In.	65.00
Madame Alexander, Snow White, Box, 14 In.	95.00
Madame Alexander, Snow White, Disney Crest Colors, 14 In.	250.00 To 350.00
Madame Alexander, Southern Belle, Portrait, Box.1971, 10 1/2 In.	42.00
Madame Alexander, Southern Belle, Sleep Eyes, Original, 1941, 11 In.	325.00
Madame Alexander, Spanish Girl, Box, 8 In.	70.00
Madame Alexander, Sweet Tears, Original Clothes, 1964, 12 In.	90.00
Madame Alexander, Victoria, Baby Huggums, 14 In.	48.00
Madame Alexander, Wendy Ann, Skating Outfit, Crazed, 14 In.	75.00

If you bought a Cabbage Patch doll as an investment, it is best to keep it mint in the box. Save all papers, correspondence, and even newspaper clippings telling about the 1983 Christmas season sell-outs.

Madame Alexander, Wendy, Southern Girl, Face Tagged, 21 In.	200.00
Madame Hendren, Composition, Signed, 17 In.	95.00
Magical Burger King, Vinyl Head, Cloth Body, Tricks, Box, 20 In.	15.00
Mahatma Gandhi, Seedpod Head, In Dhoti, Ada Odenrider Signed, 3 In.	7.00
Mahr & Proschild, Character Child, Brown Eyes, Velvet Suit, 28 In.	525.00
Mama Katzenjammer, Mechanical, Mouth Opens, Cloth Dress, 1900, 11 In.	275.00
Mama, Black, Hard Plastic, Original Clothes, 30 In.	125.00
Man, Amish, Composition, Jointed, Painted Eyes, Beard, Wig, 8 1/2 In.	30.00
Mannequin, 2–Year–Old Girl, Straw Body, 1910, 35 In.	250.00
Mannequin, 6–Year–Old Boy, Straw Body, 1910, 35 In.	250.00
Mannequin, Wooden, Glass Eyes, 27 In.	250.00
Margaret O'Brien, Composition, Box, 14 In.	975.00
Marilyn Monroe, 7 Year Itch, Box, 16 1/2 In.	20.00
Marilyn Monroe, Bisque, Musical, Box, 8 1/2 In.	6.00
Marilyn Monroe, Box, 16 In.	15.00
Marilyn Monroe, Official 20th Century Fox, Box, 11 1/2 In.	10.00
Marionette, Pinocchio, Wooden & Composition, 16 In.	65.00
Marionette, Wooden Head, Clown, 14 In.	40.00
Martha Chase, Cloth, Christening Clothes, 1910, 20 In.	290.00
Martha D.Thompson, Betsy, Porcelain Shoulder Head, Original, 14 In.	270.00
Mascotte, Bebe, Closed Mouth, Brunette Human Hair, Costume, 30 In.	6250.00
Mattel, Baby Teenie Talk, 17 In.	20.00
Mattel, Ballerina Barbie, 1975, Box	30.00
Mattel, Barbie, Allen	20.00
Mattel, Barbie, Black, 1979, Box	25.00
Mattel, Barbie, Blond, Bubble Cut Hair	40.00 To 85.00
Mattel, Barbie, Blue Rhapsody Porcelain, No.1, Jointed, Dressed	280.00
Mattel, Barbie, Booklet, Gay Parisienne	30.00
Mattel, Barbie, Bubble, Blond, Nude, 1962	26.00
Mattel, Barbie, Chitty Chitty Bang Bang, All Original	195.00
Mattel, Barbie, Christie	15.00
Mattel, Barbie, Eskimo	35.00
Mattel, Barbie, Fashion Photo, Box, 1977	35.00
Mattel, Barbie, Fashion Queen	35.00
Mattel, Barbie, Gold, Necklace Charm, 1983 N.Y.Convention	125.00
Mattel, Barbie, Hispanic, Box	25.00
Mattel, Barbie, Japanese	19.00
Mattel, Barbie, Julia	20.00
Mattel, Barbie, Ken, 1st Painted Hair	35.00
Mattel, Barbie, Malibu Ken	5.00
Mattel, Barbie, Midge	30.00
Mattel, Barbie, Miss America	45.00
Mattel, Barbie, New Living	25.00
Mattel, Barbie, Nighty–Negligee, Ponytail, Box	225.00
Mattel, Barbie, Oriental, Box	25.00
Mattel, Barbie, Quick Curl, Blond, Painted Lashes, Nude, 1973	20.00
Mattel, Barbie, Redhead Ponytail, Factory Upswept Hairdo	135.00
Mattel, Barbie, Silken Flame, Brunette Ponytail, Box	550.00
Mattel, Barbie, Takara, Red Kimono	50.00
Mattel, Barbie, TNT, 1966	40.00
Mattel, Barbie, With Clothes, 1958, Japan	150.00
Mattel, Brad, Talking, Original Shirt & Trunks, 1969	22.00
Mattel, Bugs Bunny, Talks, Plush, 20 In.	7.50
Mattel, Casper The Ghost, Hard Plastic, Talking, 5 In.	6.00
Mattel, Debbie Boone, Box, 11 1/2 In.	45.00
Mattel, Doctor Doolittle, Rex Harrison Movie, Box, 6 In.	35.00
Mattel, Donnie Osmond, 1966, Box, 12 In.	9.00
Mattel, Ken, 1962	15.00
Mattel, Ken, Bent Knee	75.00
Mattel, Ken, Blond Hair, Box	50.00
Mattel, Ken, Flocked Hair, Original Swimsuit & Jacket, 1961	33.00
Mattel, Ken, Holland Outfit	45.00
Mattel, Ken, Mod Hair, Tan Suit, 1973	11.00
Mattel, Ken, No.1, 4 Outfits, In Case	75.00

Mattel, Ken, Purple Velvet Jacket, 1968	15.00
Mattel, Ken, Superstar, Blue Clothes, Diamond Ring, Box, 1976	25.00
Mattel, Marie Osmond, 1976, Box, 12 In.	15.00
Mattel, Midge, Brown Hair, Blue Eyes, Dinner At Eight Outfit, 1963	25.00
Mattel, Scooter, Skipper's Best Friend, Red Hair, 1965	20.00
Mattel, Skipper, Brunette, Suit, Box, 1964	30.00 To 38.00
Mattel, Skipper, Growing Up, Blond, Grows Breasts, 1975	15.00
Mattel, Takara Flora, Barbie's Friend	45.00
Maud, Bisque, Blue Sleep Eyes, Open Mouth, Germany, 18 In.	225.00
Maude Tousey Gangel, Sweets, Cloth, White Dress & Bonnet, 12 In.	400.00
Mego, Buck Rogers, White Clothes, 12 In.	22.00
Mego, Captain James T.Kirk, Star Trek, Box, 1979, 12 1/2 In.	11.00 To 25.00
Mego, Cher, Nude, Box, 12 In.	10.00
Mego, Hoag, Dukes of Hazzard, 8 In.	8.00
Mego, Klingon, Star Trek, 1979, 12 In.	16.00
Mego, Mr.Spock, Star Trek, Box, 1979, 12 1/2 In.	11.00 To 25.00
Melitta Wien, Hard Plastic, Blond Braids, Costume, Bee Mark, 12 In.	40.00
Mickey Mouse, Sawdust Filled, Suede Cloth, 6 In.	15.00
Mimi, Bisque, Sleep Eyes, Molded Socks & Shoes, Copyright 1920, 5 In.	575.00
Monkey, Stuffed Sock, Boy & Girl, Costume, 16 1/2 In., Pair	19.00
Moon Mullins, Wooden, Jointed, 5 1/2 In.	75.00
Morimura, Character Baby, 14 In.	210.00
Mork, Talking, Space Pack, 1979, 9 In.	8.00
Mortimer, Gray Checkered Suit, 26 In.	25.00
Mother Revlon, Gray Hair, Original Clothes, 19 In.	35.00
Mr.Magoo, Movable Legs, Green Clothes, Hat, 16 In.	175.00
Nancy Ann Storybook, Blond, Sleep Eyes, Dressed, 6 In.	18.00
Nancy Ann Storybook, Tuesday's Child, Bisque, No.181, Box, 6 In.	28.00
Nippon, Blond, With Blue Band, Bisque, Movable Arms, Painted, 5 1/2 In.	30.00
Nippon, Painted, 5 1/2 In.	135.00
Norah Wellings, Black, 11 In.	50.00
Norah Wellings, Bopeep, 22 In.	75.00
Norah Wellings, Dandy, Yellow Pants, Black Jacket, Label, 14 In.	175.00
Norah Wellings, Googly, Celluloid, 7 In.	20.00
Norah Wellings, Native, Cloth, 13 In.	45.00
Old Lady In Chair, Wax Head, String Hair, Cloth Body, Italy, 27 In.	60.00
Oriental Girl, Papier-Mache, Glass Eyes, Original Dress, Case, 19 In.	85.00
Orsini, All Bisque, Painted Blue Eyes, 5 In.	1050.00
Orsini, Mimi, Sleep Eyes, Original Wig & Clothes, Label, 4 3/4 In.	1250.00
Otta Gans, Bisque, Ball-Jointed, Crocheted Outfit, 22 In.	350.00
Otto Dressel, Kuno, Box, 21 In.	400.00
Otto-Curo, Dresser, Original Clothes, 24 In.	650.00
Otto-Curo, Original Clothes, 24 In.	850.00
Pajama, Rag, Handmade, Hangs On Wall, 34 In.	85.00
Pam, Hand Painted Hair, Red Polka Dot Dress, Socks, Shoes, 7 1/2 In.	25.00
DOLL, PAPER, see Paper Doll	
Papier-Mache Shoulder Head, Nun, In Glass Case, With Setting, 10 In.	130.00
Papier-Mache, Blue Paperweight Eyes, All Original, German, 28 In.	150.00
Papier-Mache, Cat, All Original, 7 1/2 In.	190.00
Papier-Mache, Molded Black Part Hair, Kid Body, Wooden Limbs, 7 In.	140.00
Papier-Mache, Naval Officer, Leather Joints, 22 In.	300.00
Papier-Mache, Paperweight Eyes, Cloth Body, Arms, Legs, 20 In.	125.00
Papier-Mache, Pumpkin Man, Painted, Wood & Cloth Body, Clothes, 9 In.	85.00
Papier-Mache, Straw Stuffed, Brown Glass Eyes, 24 In.	125.00
Pappy Yokum, Vinyl Head, Original Clothes, 21 In.	55.00
Parian No.5, Painted & Molded Blond, Cloth Body, Dressed, 18 1/2 In.	300.00
Parian, Cloth Body, Bisque Arms, Luster Boots, 10 In.	125.00
Parian, Lady, Cloth Body, Bisque Hands, Arms, German Costume, 15 In.	1150.00
Parian, Shoulder Head Man, Painted Molded Head, Cloth Body, 20 In.	250.00
Patsy Ann, 1936, 19 In.	225.00
Patsy, Jr., Composition, Bracelet, 11 In.	140.00
Patsyette, Original Bracelet, Undressed, 9 In.	110.00
Paul Schmidt, Composition, Jointed, Boy's Black Velvet Suit, 16 In.	250.00
Pauline, Lin Lin, Vinyl, Box, 16 In.	45.00

Pauline, Louise, Soft, Painted Features, Brown Hair, Box, 18 In. 45.00
Pedigree Delite, Plastic, Painted, Movable Arms, Model Aircraft, 7 In. 5.00
Peggy Nisbet, Princess Diana, Wedding Gown, Vinyl, Box, 15 In. 50.00
Pierotti, Lady, Poured Wax, Original Clothes, C.1900, 22 In. 1875.00
    DOLL, PINCUSHION, see Pincushion Doll
Poor Pitiful Pearl, 20 In. 65.00
Poor Pitiful Pearl, Navy Dress, Babuska, Suitcase, 1955, 17 In. 85.00
Portrait Parisienne, Bisque Shoulder, Blond Human Hair, 1875, 22 In. 2250.00
Pouty, Character, Period Clothes, Signed L.A.S.M., 1915, 15 1/2 In. 155.00
Puppet, Clarabelle, String, Red & White Suit, 15 In. 75.00
Puppet, Knight, Iron Rod, Metal Helmet, Moustache, Jointed, 34 In. 250.00
Puppet, Lion, Iron Rod, Open Mouth Baring Teeth, 14 X 24 In. 550.00
Puppet, Midshipman, Iron Rod, Metal Hat, Moustache, Jointed, 31 In. 425.00
Puppet, Sicilian Lady, Iron Rod, Carved Hair In Bun, Jointed, 27 In. 150.00
Puzzy, Boy, Composition, Jointed, Red Molded Hair, Black Shorts, 15 In. 350.00
Queen Anne, Painted, Costume, C.1750, 22 In. 5500.00
Queen Louise, Bisque Head, Jointed, Dressed, Germany, 27 In. 150.00
Queen Louise, Brown Sleep Eyes, Jointed, Composition, Dress, 29 In. 650.00
Queen Victoria, Dress, Jewelry, Scotch Shawl, 10 In. 38.50
R & B, Debuteen, Ethnic Costume, All Lace & Ribbons, Box, 21 In. 275.00
R & B, Nancy, Composition, Sleep Eyes, 4 Teeth, Original, 1940, 17 In. 125.00
R & B, Nanette, Walker, Plastic, Brunette, Sleep Eyes, 1950s, 14 In. 110.00
R & B, So Big, Cloth Body, 18 In. 95.00
R A Dep 1909, Cloth Body, Bisque, Blond, Blue Eyes, Dressed, 9 In. 110.00
R.D., Bisque Socket Head, Composition, Paperweight Eyes, 23 In. 650.00
R.D., Closed Mouth, Bisque Head, Long Curls, Print Dress, 19 In. 1795.00
Rabery & Delphieu, Child, Brown Paperweight Eyes, Wooden Body, 28 In. 2750.00
Rag, Chocolate Babyland, All Original, 15 In. 1500.00
Revalo Dep, Character Girl, Bisque Head, Molded Hair, 12 1/2 In. 260.00
Rodeo Clown, Crochet, Stuffed, 18 In. 25.00
Rohmer, Fashion, China Head, Shoulderplate & Arms, Dressed, 16 In. 4500.00
Rollinson, Cloth, Painted Features, American, C.1916, 22 In. 975.00
Rose O'Neill, Bisque, Marked, C.1919, 4 1/2 In. 145.00
Rose O'Neill, Scooties, Vinyl, Tag, 1966, 16 In. 195.00
    DOLL, S & H, see also Doll, Bergmann; Doll, Simon & Halbig
S & H 939, Straight Wrist, Open Mouth, 18 In. 550.00
S & H 949, Hat, Dress, 18 In. 1700.00
S & H 1039, Flirty Eyes, Open Mouth, Composition Body, Marked, 24 In. 575.00
S & H 1079, 19 In. 450.00
S & H 1159, Gibson Girl, 19 In. 1695.00
S & H 1169, Lady, Original Wig, 23 1/2 In. 1800.00
S & H, Bisque, Repainted Hands, Antique Clothes, 26 In. 750.00
S & H, Paperweight Eyes, Pierced Ears, All Original, 30 In. 850.00
S.& H.1385, Lady, Box, 14 In. 1500.00
S.F.B.J. 236, Bisque Head, Sleep Eyes, Open Close Mouth, 15 In. 375.00
S.F.B.J. 236, Character, Toddler Body, Bisque Head, Jointed, 23 In. 1750.00
S.F.B.J. 236, Laughing Jumeau, Toddler, Bisque, Jointed, 12 In. 1295.00
S.F.B.J. 236, Toddler Character, Bisque Head, Old Clothes, 26 In. 2000.00
S.F.B.J. 247, Toddler, 23 In. 1950.00
S.F.B.J. 251, Bisque Head, Chunky Toddler Body, Dressed, 27 In. 2200.00
S.F.B.J. 251, Toddler, Sleep Eyes, Original Lashes, 24 In. 675.00
S.F.B.J. 252, Toddler, 22 In. 2800.00
S.F.B.J. 301, All Original, Trunk, 7 In. 1250.00
S.F.B.J. 301, Bisque, Pierced Ears, Blond Wig, Underclothes, 22 In. 825.00
S.F.B.J., Bisque Head, Ball-Jointed Body, Silk Dress, 29 In. 1495.00
S.F.B.J., Bisque Head, Jointed Body, Underclothes, Shoes, 25 In. 1195.00
S.F.B.J., Bisque Head, Sleep Eyes, Jointed Wrists, Dress, 36 In. 1850.00
S.F.B.J., Jumeau Mold, Paperweight Sleep Eyes, French Body, 18 In. 2295.00
S.F.B.J., Long Blond Curls, Open Mouth, Dressed, 26 In. 1150.00
S.F.B.J., Open Mouth, Bisque, Paperweight Set Eyes, Outfit, 17 1/2 In. 650.00
S.F.B.J., Open Mouth, Jumeau Mold, Bisque Head, Sleep Eyes, 29 In. 1550.00
S.F.B.J., Open Mouth, Moving Eyes, Dressed, Wig, Size 7 .... 300.00
S.F.B.J., Papier-Mache, 8 In. 85.00
S.F.B.J., Twirp, Baby Body, 7 In. 900.00

S.F.B.J., Walker, Blows Kisses, Walking Outfit, Long Curls, 22 In. 1200.00
S.F.B.J.2238, Character Girl, Walking Body, Jewel Eyes, 15 In. 1800.00
S.F.B.M. 236, Baby, Laughing, Bisque, Antique Wig & Clothes, 15 In. 875.00
Saalfield, Little Princess Dolly, Cloth Body, 1916, Uncut, 18 In. 195.00
Saalfield, My Best Dolly, Cloth, Uncut, 1916, 22 In. .... 185.00 To 200.00
Sailor, Holland–America Ship Line, Cloth, Composition Head, 11 In. 60.00
Santa Claus, Goofy, Rubber, 1930s, 5 1/2 In. 28.50
Santa Claus, Steiff Paper Labels, 12 In. 175.00
Santa Claus, Steiff, 8 In. 90.00
Santa Claus, Straw Filled, C.1925, 25 In. 150.00
Santa Claus, Wooden, Walking Style, Clothes, 5 1/2 In. 27.50
Sasha, Girl, Red Hair, Box, 17 In. 75.00
Saucy Walker, Hard Plastic, Crier, Original Clothes, 23 In. 75.00
Sazbo The Clown, Vinyl, Black Overalls, Red Shirt, Wrist Tag, 21 In. 55.00
Schmidt 1295, Toddler Girl, Blue Sleep Eyes, Composition, 27 In. 1250.00
Schmitt, Bebe, Closed Mouth, Ball–Jointed Body, C.1880, 15 In. 5500.00
Schoenau & Hoffmeister 190, Boy, Saddle Shoes, Knicker, 25 In. 500.00
Schoenau & Hoffmeister, Bisque, Compositon Body, Marked, 20 In. 170.00
Schoenau & Hoffmeister, Black, Jointed, Composition, Bisque, 19 In. 795.00
Schoenau & Hoffmeister, Princess Elizabeth, Toddler Body, 20 In. 3000.00
Schoenhut, Boy, Carved Hair, 15 In. 1650.00
Schoenhut, Boy, Wooden, Spring Jointed, 14 In. 550.00
Schoenhut, Carved Hair, Dressed, 15 In. 1450.00
Schoenhut, Character Girl, Carved Hair, 15 In. 550.00
Schoenhut, Character, Pouty Mouth, Dressed As Boy, 15 1/2 In. 695.00
Schoenhut, Character, Wood, 2 Upper Teeth, Paper Label, 1911, 19 In. 1595.00
Schoenhut, Circus Performer, Wooden Body, Parian Head, 8 In. 625.00
Schoenhut, Clown, Wooden, Cloth Costume, 8 1/4 In. 135.00
Schoenhut, Dolly, Original Wig, 17 In. 325.00
Schoenhut, Felix, Jointed, Wood, Stickers, 5 In. 110.00
Schoenhut, Girl, Character, 18 In. 950.00
Schoenhut, Girl, Wooden, Spring Jointed, 21 In. 225.00
Schoenhut, Sleep Eyes, Wooden Head, Wood Spring Jointed Body, 22 In. 575.00
Scootles, Composition, 21 In. 650.00
Scootles, Composition, 8 In. 600.00
Shindana, Baby Nancy, Black, Vinyl, Pink Dress, Spoon & Bottle, 12 In. 55.00
Shindana, Flip Wilson–Geraldine, Cloth, Does Not Talk, Box, 16 In. 12.00
Shindana, Talking Tami, Black, Vinyl Head, Cloth Body, Dress, 15 In. 65.00
    DOLL, SHIRLEY TEMPLE, see Shirley Temple
Shoulder Head, Low Brow, China Arms, Legs, Cloth Body, Germany, 12 In. 110.00
    DOLL, SIMON & HALBIG, see also Doll, Bergmann; Doll, S & H
Simon & Halbig 156, Flirty Eyes, Straight Leg Toddler, 27 In. 950.00
Simon & Halbig 540, 22 In. 440.00
Simon & Halbig 739, Girl, Black, Brown Body, 18 In. 1100.00
Simon & Halbig 769, Bisque Head, Composition, Closed Mouth, 14 In. 2100.00
Simon & Halbig 880, All Bisque, All Original, 5 1/2 In. 450.00
Simon & Halbig 886, All Bisque, Original Wig & Clothes, 7 In. 800.00
Simon & Halbig 939, Closed Mouth, Brown Hair Coat, Bonnet, 36 In. 3000.00
Simon & Halbig 1009, Fashion Body, Kid Over Wood Upper Arms, 15 In. 550.00
Simon & Halbig 1078, Bisque, Blue Eyes, Cloth Body, Dressed, 12 In. 350.00
Simon & Halbig 1078, Completely Dressed, Box, 7 1/2 In. 975.00
Simon & Halbig 1079, Bisque Head, 4 Teeth, Antique Clothing, 33 In. 1095.00
Simon & Halbig 1079, Bisque Head, Composition, Velvet Dress, 26 In. 600.00
Simon & Halbig 1079, Open Mouth, Ball–Jointed, Dress, 29 In. 750.00
Simon & Halbig 1079, Sleep Eyes, Pierced Ears, Jointed, Dress, 33 In. 1195.00
Simon & Halbig 1080, Bride, All Original, 30 In. 850.00
Simon & Halbig 1159, Gibson Girl, Edwardian Clothes, C.1910, 19 In. 1695.00
Simon & Halbig 1249, Ball–Jointed Body, 28 In. 985.00
Simon & Halbig 1250, Kid Body, 18 In. 300.00
Simon & Halbig 1279, Taffeta Dress, Hat, 31 In. 2425.00
Simon & Halbig 1294, Character Baby, Bent Limb Body, 16 In. 995.00
Simon & Halbig 1349, Brown Bisque Head, Jointed, Composition, 13 In. 695.00
Simon & Halbig 7825, Portrait, Lady, 17 In. 4000.00
Simon & Halbig 929, Bisque Socket Head, Painted Lashes, 1885, 14 In. 1650.00

Simon & Halbig, Admiral, Bisque, Blue Eyes, Painted Mustache, 9 In.	450.00
Simon & Halbig, Brown Eyelashes, Original Clothes, Brown Wig, 32 In.	850.00
Simon & Halbig, Character, Black, Bisque Head, 27 In.	6050.00
Simon & Halbig, Character, Boy, Period Clothing, Wig & Shoes, 18 In.	7800.00
Simon & Halbig, Fashion, Blond Mohair, Muslin Body, Satin Gown, 15 In.	1300.00
Simon & Halbig, Flapper, Bisque, With Trunk & Wardrobe, 9 In.	1500.00
Simon & Halbig, Oriental, Almond Shaped Eyes, Original Dress, 14 In.	2300.00
Skeezix, Oilcloth, 14 In.	65.00
Skookum Indian, 17 In.	95.00
Skookum, Straw Filled, 6 In.	15.00
Snow Baby, Bisque Socket Head, Jointed Felt Body, Fur Parka, 12 In.	250.00
St.Nicholas, Composition, Jointed, Red Flannel Suit, Boots, 19 In.	170.00
Steiff, Caveman, Vinyl Head, Felt Body, Tooth Necklace, 7 In.	85.00
Steiff, Fireman, Felt Uniform, 17 In.	135.00
Steiff, Santa Claus, 10 In.	295.00
Steiner, A Series, Blue Paperweight Eyes, 28 In.	4300.00
Steiner, Bebe, Closed Mouth, Composition, Wooden Jointed, 1880, 25 In.	4100.00
Steiner, Bebe, Painted Lashes, Brunette Human Hair, C.1880, 23 In.	6000.00
Steiner, Bourgoin Bebe, Bisque Head, 24 In.	4620.00
Steiner, Bourgoin Bebe, Closed Mouth, Wooden Jointed, C.1880, 30 In.	5250.00
Steiner, Bourgoin, Wire Lever Sleep Eyes, Brunette, C.1885, 24 In.	5000.00
Steiner, Closed Mouth, Paperweight Eyes, French C Series, 18 In.	3900.00
Steiner, Clown, All Original, 14 In.	2900.00
Steiner, Flower Seller, Mechanical, Head & Arms Move, Dressed, 13 In.	2000.00
Steiner, Open Mouth, Colored, 12 1/2 In.	1500.00
Steiner, Paperweight Eyes, Clockwork, Says Mama, 1880, 18 In.	1795.00
Steiner, Series C, Bisque, Original Wig, Antique Clothes, 18 In.	5250.00
Steiner, Wire Eyed, Bisque, Closed Mouth, Silk Dress, Bonnet, 29 In.	5500.00
Stoneware, Blue Designed Hair & Eyes, Arms & Hands Separate, 1860s	4600.00
Straw Stuffed, Homespun Covered, Stitched Face, Fingers, 1900, 19 In.	445.00
Straw Stuffed, Wax Over Composition, Glass Eyes, Molded Shoes, 30 In.	250.00
Stroebel & Witkins, Bisque, Red Hair, 7 In.	145.00
Stuffed Cloth, Tole Head, Calico Dress, Gingham Apron, 12 In.	55.00
Sweet Rosemary, Pink Lace Gown, Jewelry, 30 In.	125.00
Sweet Sue, American Character, 19 In.	125.00
Tanagara, French Girl, 20 In.	600.00
Terri Lee, Blond Hair, 14 Piece Wardrobe, 15 In.	225.00
Terri Lee, Connie Lynn, Caracul Wig, Sleep Eyes, Pink Clothes, 19 In.	395.00
Terri Lee, Hard Plastic, Original Dress, Fur Jacket, 16 In.	175.00
Tete & Corps Bois, Wooden, Jointed, Glass Eyes, Closed Mouth, 20 In.	600.00
Tete Jumeau, Bisque Head, Jointed Composition, Glass Eyes, 13 In.	1250.00
Tete Jumeau, Blue Paperweight Eyes, Wooden Jointed, C.1880, 10 In.	3500.00
Tete Jumeau, Closed Mouth, Dressed, 1914, 27 In.	4250.00
Tete Jumeau, Closed Mouth, Paperweight Eyes, Signed Body, 22 In.	3650.00
Tete Jumeau, Deep Paperweight Eyes, 6 Teeth, Sticker, 1907, 23 In.	1995.00
Tete Jumeau, Paperweight Eyes, Bisque, Red Silk Outfit, Marked, 19 In.	3295.00
Tin Head, Jointed Cloth Body, 16 In.	45.00
Toni, Blond, Cotton Blue Dress, Marked P-91, 15 In.	50.00
Toni, Lady, 1958, 12 In.	38.00
Toodles, Rubber Body, Marked, 15 In.	30.00
Topsy-Turvy, 1 Blond Head, 1 Black Mammy Head, 7 1/2 In.	32.00
Topsy-Turvy, Cloth, Painted Features, Mid-19th Century, 16 In.	50.00
Topsy-Turvy, Litho Cloth, White Girl Side, Black Girl Other, 12 In.	275.00
Topsy-Turvy, Primitive, 14 In.	375.00
Topsy-Turvy, Rag, 15 In.	35.00
Tristar, Marilyn Monroe, 4 Different Outfits, Box, 11 1/2 In.	35.00
Tristar, Poor Pitiful Pearl, Box, 16 In.	22.00
Trudy, 3 Face, 1946, 16 In.	175.00
Trudy, 3 Face, Composition, All Original, 14 In.	125.00
U.S.Navy, Cloth, Painted, Celluloid Head, Hands & Feet, 7 In.	8.00
Uncle Sam, Bisque, Original Clothes, Marked SI, 13 In. ....*Illus*	1000.00
Uncle Sam, Papier-Mache & Cloth, C.1930, 22 In.	22.00
Unis 271, Character Boy, Ball-Jointed Body, Painted Hair, 13 In.	700.00
Unis France 301, Sleep Eyes, 4 Molded Teeth, Wrist Tag, 14 In.	395.00

Unis France, Bonnet Tied Under Chin, 16 In. 525.00
Unis France, Sleep Eyes, Jointed, Long Hair, Pink Silk Dress, 24 In. 995.00
Vichy, Mechanical, Dueler, Original Costume, Signed, 14 In. 6500.00
Vogue, Baby Dear, Painted Eyes, 1 Tuft Hair, Trunk, 18 In. 200.00
Vogue, Baby Ginny, Drinks, Wets, 11 In. 35.00
Vogue, Baby, Black Hair, Brown Eyes, Fat, 24 In. 45.00
Vogue, Crissy Grow Hair, Box, 17 In. 45.00
Vogue, Ginny, Christmas Spirit, 8 In. 225.00
Vogue, Ginny, Italian, Painted Eyes, Box, C.1977, 8 In. 45.00
Vogue, Ginny, Straight–Leg Walker, Dress, With Tag, 8 In. 95.00
Vogue, Hug–A–Bye, Original Clothes, 16 In. 12.00
Vogue, Jill, Walking, Plastic, Tagged Clothes, 10 In. 40.00
Vogue, Lil Imp, Boy, Sleep Toddler, Jointed, Vinyl, 11 In. 20.00
Vogue, Too Dear Toddler, 25 In. 375.00
Vogue, Toodles, Painted Side Glancing Eyes, Composition, 8 In. 100.00
W.Weyh, Baby, Bisque Head, Marked, 12 In. 275.00
Walker, Bisque, Costume, 12 1/2 In. 2750.00
Walters, Bisque, Blue Inset Eyes, Painted Stockings, 7 1/2 In., Pair 350.00
Walters, Lady, Bisque Shoulder Head, Muslin Body, 7 1/2 In. .... 150.00 To 450.00
Wax, Shoulder Head, Cloth Body, Glass Eyes, Wax Legs, 18 In. 850.00
Wendy Ann, Composition, 14 In. 185.00
Wernicke, German Child, Jointed, Thermoplastic, Plaid Dress, 16 In. 185.00
Whisk Broom, Mohair Wig, Painted Features, Felt Clothes, Italy, 11 In. 12.00
Wooden, Carved, Mad.Catherina, Movable Arms, On Wheels, Case, 7 In. 2925.00
Wooden, Original Paint, Worn Costume, 10 In. 95.00
World Dolls, Clark Gable, Vivien Leigh, Gone With Wind, 18 In., Pair 160.00
DONALD DUCK, see Disneyana

 Iron doorstops have been made in all types of designs. The vast
majority of the doorstops sold today are cast iron and were made
from about 1890 to 1930. Most of them are shaped like people,
animals, flowers, or ships.

DOORSTOP, Airplane, Cast Nickel Steel, Marked, 6 In. 405.00
Alligator, Allover Writing, Green, Mouth Open, 8 1/2 In. 125.00
Alligator, Fish In Mouth, Cast Iron 40.00
Alpine Child, With Basket of Flowers, Full–Bodied, Iron, 7 In. 185.00
Anne Radcliffe, First Woman Donor To Harvard 1643, Gold Paint 200.00
Aunt Jemima, Full–Bodied, Cast Iron, 9 3/4 In. 95.00
Baby Shoe, Iron, 4 In. 45.00
Basket of Flowers, Albany Foundry 135.00
Basket of Flowers, Apple Blossoms, Cast Iron 50.00
Basket of Flowers, Polychrome Paint, 10 3/4 In. 85.00
Basket of Fruit, Flatback, Original Paint, 10 1/2 In. 115.00
Bathing Beauties, Art Deco, Signed Fish, Original Paint, 11 In. 875.00
Bear, Full–Bodied, Black Paint, Cast Iron, 10 3/4 In. 225.00
Black Man, Naked To Waist, Holding Cotton Basket, 9 In. 240.00
Bobby Blake, Pink Shorts, White Shirt, Signed By Grace Drayton 350.00
Bonnie Scotland 325.00
Boot, Lady's, High, Cast Iron 50.00
Boy In Tuxedo, Cast Iron 225.00
Boy On Pillow, Oriental 75.00
Boy, Holding Teddy Bear, Albany 240.00
Buffalo, Cast Iron 80.00
Cabin In The Woods, Iron, National Foundry, 10 X 4 In. 145.00
Carpenter, Orange Shirt, Blue Pants, Hat 225.00
Cat, Angora, Bronze 95.00
Cat, Black, 8 In. 55.00
Cat, Cast Iron, Black & White Paint, Green & Yellow Eyes, 13 In. 100.00
Cat, Chalkware, Glass Eyes, C.1900, 14 In. 75.00
Cat, Dexter, Maine, Fay Scott, Cast Iron 175.00
Cat, Fireside, Blue Eyes, Blue Bow, Hubley 165.00
Cat, Full–Bodied, Gray & White Paint, Pink Trim, Hubley, 11 In. 165.00
Cat, Hunchback, Bronze & Brass, Stands, Signed Chase USA 175.00
Cat, Hunchback, Green Eyes ....55.00 To 115.00

Cat, Persian, Gray & White, Whiskers, Lashes, Blue Eyes 150.00
Cat, Persian, Sitting, Cast Iron 155.00
Cat, Raised Tail, Full–Bodied, Black Paint, Cast Iron, 10 In. 85.00
Cat, Sleeping, 13 In. 260.00
Cat, Sleeping, Bronzed 170.00
Cherub, With Grapes, Bronze, 19 In. 200.00
Child, Naked, Yawning, Full–Bodied, M.L.Corp., N.Y.C., 8 3/4 In. 105.00
Cinderella Carriage, 10 X 19 In. 135.00
Clipper Ship, Cast Iron 40.00
Coach, Driver & 2 Horses, Painted, 7 X 10 1/2 In. 95.00
Cockatoo, Pink, Green Feathers, Yellow With Black Beak, Claws 130.00
Conestoga Wagon 110.00
Cottage, Cast Iron, Bradley & Hubbard, 7 1/2 In. 75.00
Cottage, Polychrome Paint, Cast Iron, 5 In. ....70.00 To 105.00
Couple, Out On The Town, Polychrome Paint, Cast Iron, 6 In. 25.00
Covered Wagon, Gilded 75.00
Crane, Bronze 55.00
Daffodils, Original Polychrome Paint, Cast Iron, 6 3/4 In. 105.00
Daisy Bowl, Painted, Hubley, 7 In. 80.00
Dancing Couple, Polychrome Paint, Marked Fish, 8 In. 1025.00
Dog, Airedale, Sheet Steel Wedge, Polychrome, Cast Iron, 5 In. 55.00
Dog, Boston Bull, Cast Iron, Black Paint, Red Collar, 7 1/2 In. 85.00
Dog, Boston Bull, Facing Left, Cast Iron 90.00
Dog, Boston Bull, Full–Bodied, Black & White, Red Collar, 10 In. 110.00
Dog, Boston Bull, Full–Bodied, Cast Iron, Black, White, 9 In. 60.00
Dog, Boston Terrier, Paw Up, Brown & Beige 350.00
Dog, Boston Terrier, Pup, Brown & Beige 225.00
Dog, Bronze, 6 1/2 X 9 1/2 In. 45.00
Dog, Cast Iron, Original Paint, 6 3/4 In. 65.00
Dog, Cocker Spaniel, Iron, Brown & Tan Paint, 4 1/4 In. 80.00
Dog, Comic Strip, Cast Aluminum, 1927, 9 1/4 In. 20.00
Dog, Dachshund, Full–Bodied, Cast Iron, Marked, 8 3/4 In. 95.00
Dog, Dachshund, Sitting & Begging, Black, 11 1/4 In. 315.00
Dog, Dachshund, Standing, Full–Bodied, Hubley, 5 X 8 In. 375.00
Dog, Fox Terrier, Iron, Hubley, 9 1/2 X 11 In. 150.00
Dog, Fox Terrier, Wirehaired, Hubley, 7 X 6 In. 225.00
Dog, German Shepherd, Full–Bodied, Cast Iron, 9 1/2 In. 85.00
Dog, Greyhound, Green Paint, Iron, Lake City Malleable Co., 12 In. 35.00
Dog, Mutt & His Bone, Black & White, Red Mouth 245.00
Dog, Pekingese, Cast Iron 500.00
Dog, Pekingese, Cast Iron, Glass Eyes 275.00
Dog, Pekingese, Hubley, Cast Iron, 14 1/2 X 9 In. 250.00
Dog, Pointer, Full–Bodied, Black & White Paint, 8 3/4 In. 115.00
Dog, Police, Standing, Iron, Bronze Paint, 12 1/2 In. 55.00
Dog, Rin Tin Tin, Silver Toned 35.00
Dog, Scotty, 12 In. 425.00
Dog, Scotty, Begging, 15 In. 125.00
Dog, Scotty, Black, Wilton Products, Inc., 4 X 7 In. 110.00
Dog, Scotty, Cast Iron, White Paint, 5 In. 65.00
Dog, Scotty, Double, White, Cast Iron 40.00
Dog, Scotty, Original Black Paint, Cast Iron, 7 3/4 In. 65.00
Dog, Scotty, Standing, Full–Bodied, 8 X 10 In. 165.00
Dog, Sealyham 400.00
Dog, Setter, Reddish Brown 125.00
Dog, Spaniel, Full–Bodied, Black & White Repaint, Iron, 6 1/2 In. 325.00
Dog, St.Bernard, Black, Cast Iron 75.00
Dog, Terrier, Black & White, Wooden 10.00
Dog, Terrier, Pup, Sitting, Signed Hubley, 7 1/4 In. 195.00
Dog, Welch Corgi 185.00
Dog, Whippet 140.00
Dog, Wire–Haired Terrier, Black 165.00
Dog, Wolfhound, Old Green Paint, Cast Iron, 8 In. 45.00
Dog, Wooden, Brass Plated Base 75.00
Doll, Green & Brown Dress, Blue Base 105.00

Donald Duck, Signed Walt Disney Productions, 1971, 8 1/2 In. 275.00
Drum Major, Bright Blue Jacket & Hat, 13 1/2 In. 475.00
Dutch Girl, White Apron 225.00
Dwarf, Hands In Pocket, Iron, 10 1/2 X 6 In. 215.00
Elephant, By Palm Tree 225.00
Elephant, Cast Iron, Gray & Green Paint, 10 1/4 In. 125.00
Elephant, Circus, Original Paint, 4 1/2 In. 65.00
Elephant, Full-Bodied, White Metallic Paint, 11 1/2 In. 25.00
Elephant, Red With White Tusks 150.00
Fat Dowager, Black Dress & Shawl, Red Lips, Cast Iron, 5 1/2 In. 70.00
Fish, Fantail 175.00
Fisherman In Boat 225.00
Floral, Pennsylvania Dutch 335.00
Flower Pot, Hubley 250.00
Football Player, Bronze Finish, Cast Iron, 5 1/2 In. 50.00
Fox, Sleeping, Iron, Gray, 7 1/2 X 2 In. 65.00
Frog, Green Paint, Yellow & Black Eyes, Cast Iron, 3 1/2 X 5 In. 65.00
Fruits & Birds, Bronze & Copper 145.00
Geese, Hubley .... 300.00 To 375.00
Geisha 225.00
Girl, Art Deco 165.00
Girl, Curtsying, Black & White Paint, Cast Iron, 9 In. 45.00
Golfer, Club In Air, Painted, A Terrible Lie, Hubley, 10 In. 335.00
Golfer, Polychrome Paint, Cast Iron, 8 3/8 In. 305.00
Highland Light, Iron 375.00
Horse, Brown & Beige Saddle, Reins 150.00
Horse, Grazing, Black 125.00
Horse, Grazing, Saddle, Flat Back, 9 In. 85.00
Horse, Percheron, Auburn Color, Blue Bow On Tail 185.00
Horse, Standing, Black Mane & Tail, Iron, 10 1/2 X 12 In. 170.00
Horse, Trotting, Pewter, English 75.00
Horse, Western Saddle, Head Down 65.00
Horsehead, Hitching Post 325.00
House, Cape Cod, Brown Roof, Beige House 110.00
House, Log Cabin 165.00
Iris, Original Polychrome Paint, Cast Iron, 10 1/2 In. 205.00
Japanese Boy, On Pillow, Hubley 150.00
Jiggs, Folk Art, Wooden 185.00
Jill, Yellow Dress, Gold Pail, Beige Apron 350.00
Kitten, White Cat, Blue Bow, 8 In. 95.00
Kittens, Three, In Basket, Original Paint, Cast Iron, 6 3/4 In. 500.00
Knight 275.00
Lady Liberty, Liberty Cap On Pole, Iron, Black Paint, 9 3/8 In. 30.00
Lafayette, Cast Iron 350.00
Lamb, Reclining, Red Paint, Cast Iron 250.00
Landing of Columbus, Cast Iron 145.00
Lantern, Iron, Original Paint 78.00
Lighthouse With Cottage 265.00
Lilies, Cast Iron, Original Paint, 10 1/2 In. 135.00
Lion, Rampant, Cast Iron, 13 3/4 In. 105.00
Lion, Sleeping, Terra-Cotta 25.00
Lion, Standing, Cast Iron, Gilt Paint 80.00
Lizard, Painted, Green Eyes, 10 In. 135.00
Log Cabin, Cast Iron 85.00
London Royal Mail Coach, Cast Iron 65.00
Maid 225.00
Maid, Cast Iron, Repaint, 9 1/4 In. 85.00
Man In Pilgrim Clothes, With Rifle, Brass Plated, 10 3/4 In. 10.00
Man With Fiddle, Black Paint, Cast Iron, 10 In. .... 135.00 To 155.00
Man, Bust, 8 1/2 X 4 1/2 In. 350.00
Man, Top Hat, Polychrome Paint, Marked Fish, 9 1/2 In. 1025.00
Mexican, Sunbonnet Hat, Sombrero, 6 X 7 1/2 In. 235.00
Monkey, Cast Iron 75.00
Monument, Bennington 60.00

Nude Holding Flowing Robe In Back, Original Paint, 1920s 115.00
Old Sailor, Full Figure, Original Paint, 11 1/2 In. 135.00
Old Salt, Full-Bodied, Old Polychrome Paint, 11 1/4 In. 145.00
Old Salt, Polychrome Paint, Cast Iron, 8 In. 85.00
Oriental Girl, 2 Bouquets, Cast Iron, Repaint, 9 In. 225.00
Oriental Man, Gold, 9 In. 145.00
Owl, Hubley 165.00
Parrot In Ring, Polychrome Paint, Cast Iron, 7 3/4 In. 95.00
Parrot, Cast Iron, Bradley & Hubbard 175.00
Parrot, On Stump, Cast Iron 35.00
Parrot, Perched In Circle, Rectangular Base, 2 1/2 X 7 X 8 In. 85.00
Peacock, Cast Iron, Polychrome, 6 1/4 In. 45.00
Peasant Girl, Yellow Skirt, Blue Top, Petticoat 185.00
Penguin, Full-Bodied, Black & White Paint, 10 1/2 In. 250.00
Penguin, Top Hat, Full-Bodied, Original Paint, 9 3/4 In. 300.00
Peter Rabbit 350.00
Pheasants, Cast Iron, Signed Everett, 7 X 6 1/2 In. 110.00
Pink Flower, Central Bubble, Yellow Ground, Glass, 4 1/8 In. 30.00
Poppies & Snapdragons, Pink 90.00
Poppy, White 95.00
Pot of Tulips, Bronze, 10 In. 45.00
Punch & Judy, Cast Iron, Painted 375.00
Punch With Dog, Cast Iron, Traces of Old Paint, 12 In. 55.00
Queen's Coach, Worn Paint, Cast Iron, 8 3/4 In. 55.00
Rabbit, Standing On All Four Legs, Ears Up, Facing Left, 8 X 9 In. 165.00
Rabbit, Standing On Hind Legs, Ears Up, Full-Bodied, 9 In. 115.00
Ram, Black 110.00
Rooster, Full-Bodied, Repainted 215.00
Roses, In Cornucopia, Iron, Polychrome Paint, 10 In. 70.00
Royal Canadian Mounted Police, Painted, Flat Back, 6 1/2 In. 135.00
Sailor, Art Deco, Original Paint, Cast Iron, 11 1/2 In. 575.00
Santa Claus, 10 1/2 In. 250.00
Santa Claus, Cast Iron, 8 In. 135.00
Santa Claus, Glass Eyes, Cast Iron 75.00
Scotsman With Spear, Polychrome Paint, 15 1/4 In. 95.00
Scottish Highlander, Original Black Paint 195.00
Sheep 135.00
Ship, Blue, Red, Brown Boat, Beige Sails With Crosses 55.00
Ship, English Galleon, Bronze, 1928 .... 95.00
Ship, French Man of War On The High Seas, 15 1/4 In. 65.00
Ship, Sailing, Eaton, 1930 .... 45.00
Ship, Sailing, Stamped Schofield's Iron Works, Macon, Georgia 35.00
Southern Belle, Full-Bodied, Cast Iron, 6 1/2 In. 60.00
Spanish Girl, Pink & Purple 165.00
Squirrel, Sitting, Cast Iron, 7 Lbs., 6 X 7 In. 150.00
Stag, Rocks, Cast Iron, Polychrome Repaint, 12 1/2 In. 85.00
Stagecoach, Green Coach Trimmed In Red, Orange & Black, 8 X 9 In. 95.00
Stagecoach, Horse & Driver, Marked Hubley, Cast Iron, 11 1/4 In. 25.00
Sunbonnet Baby, Flat Back, Repaint, 6 In. 42.00
Sunbonnet Girl, Green Dress Bonnet 75.00
Swing Band, 6 Black Musicians, Individual, Hubley, 2 In. 450.00
Teddy Roosevelt, On Horse 175.00
Tom Sawyer, On The World 750.00
Tree Frog, Hubley, Black 70.00
Turkey, Paint, Cast Iron 875.00
Turtle, Neck Outstretched, Knobby Shell, Black, 10 In. 85.00
Two Ducks, Original Paint, Cast Iron 300.00
Victorian Lady, Cast Iron 90.00
Windmill, Repaint, 7 In. 95.00
Witch, On Broomstick, Brass 110.00
Woman, Colonial, Green Dress, Black Hat 100.00
Woman, Holding Flower Basket, Red Skirt, Blue Top 135.00
Woman, Holding Hat, Yellow Dress, Blue Flowers, Brown Hair 110.00
Woman, Tropical, Red Dress, Basket, Yellow Apron 185.00

Woodsman, Black, Cast Iron 150.00
Zinnias, Paint, Hubley No., 7 1/4 In. 85.00

   Doulton pottery and porcelain were made by Doulton and Co. of Burslem, England, after 1882. The name "Royal Doulton" appeared on their wares after 1902. Other pottery by Doulton is listed under Royal Doulton.

DOULTON, Beaker, Queen Victoria Diamond Jubilee, Stoneware, 1897, 5 In. 150.00
Biscuit Jar, Blue Flowers, Gold On White, Oval, Burslem, 9 1/4 In. 165.00
Biscuit Jar, Ferns & Plants, Beige Ground, Lambeth, 7 1/4 In. 250.00
Bowl, Hand Painted Leaves, Flowers, Burslem, C.1888, 10 In. 275.00
Charger, Lady, Child, Foliage, Flow Blue, 14 In. 325.00
Cooler, Ale, Name Impressed On Top, 5 Gal. 500.00
Cracker Jar, Chinese Pattern, Gaudy Style, Burslem, C.1860 .... 225.00
Cup & Saucer, Hand Painted Flowers, Gold Trim, Burslem, C.1888 .... 125.00
Cup & Saucer, Roses, Dated 1906, Marked, 1 5/8 In.Saucer 40.00
Dish, Ring, Owl, Perched On Dish, Blue Lining, Brown, 3 1/4 X 4 In. 325.00
Dish, Soap, Lavender Dragonfly, Green Rim, Blue Center, 4 X 6 In. 75.00
Ewer, Cobalt Blue Irises, Flowers, Butterfly, Gold Trim, Burslem 65.00
Jug, Viking Ship 60.00
Loving Cup, Deers, Dogs, Stoneware, Handles, Lambeth, 8 In. 495.00
Match Holder, Raised Flowers, Beige, Silver Rim, Lambeth, 2 1/2 In. 60.00
Mug, Viking Ship 60.00
Pitcher, Allover Brown Design, Artist E.M., Lambeth, 1880, 6 In. 110.00
Pitcher, Water, White Cows, Grazing, Hannah Barlow, 9 1/4 In. 675.00
Plate, 3 Bulls In Pasture, Flower & Bird Border, Lambeth, 11 In. 45.00
Spittoon, Green Watteau Scene 2 Sides, Burslem, 7 1/2 X 7 3/4 In. 125.00
Striker, Match, Raised Figures, Men & Dogs, Marked, 3 3/4 In. 88.00
Sugar Shaker, Country House & Church, Silver Plated Top, 7 In. 135.00
Tea Set, Lavender & Blue Flowers, Gold Scrolls, C.1895, 3 Piece 200.00
Tumbler, Deer Hunting & Drinking Scene Around, Lambeth, 5 1/2 In. 45.00
Vase, Allover Flowers, Blue Gray Ground, F.Roberts, Lambeth, 10 In. 195.00
Vase, Bird of Paradise, Titanian, 7 In. 300.00
Vase, Carrara, Salmon Flowers, Gold Trim, 7 3/5 In. 125.00
Vase, Dickens Ware, Alfred Jingle, Handles, Marked, 4 X 5 1/2 In. 88.00
Vase, Dog Chasing Rooster, Canary, Burslem, A.Eaton, 4 1/2 In. 250.00
Vase, Flow Blue, Burslem, 5 1/4 In. 80.00
Vase, Hunt Scene, Men & Lady Riding Horses, Marked, 4 3/8 In. 85.00
Vase, Isle of Man, Village Scene, Marked, 3 1/4 In. 75.00
Vase, Ivory Satin Ground, Hand Painted Flowers, Burslem 150.00
Vase, Multicolored Leaves & Fruit, Cream Ground, Burslem, 12 In. 180.00
Vase, Overall Flowers, Bulbous, Cream Ground, Burslem, 12 In. 125.00
Vase, Raised White Flowers & Vine, Tan, Burslem, EC, 10 In. 95.00
Vase, White & Blue Flowers, Gold Base, Green Flared Top, 17 In. 250.00
   DR. SYNTAX, see Adams; Staffordshire

> Moriage is a type of decoration on Japanese pottery. Raised white designs are applied to the ware. Dragonware is a form of moriage pottery. White dragons are the major raised decorations. The background color is gray and white, orange and lavender, or orange and brown. It is a twentieth–century ware.

DRAGONWARE, Cask, Whiskey, Wooden Spigot, Red Wreath Mark, 7 In. 95.00
Cookie Jar 85.00
Cup, Chocolate 15.00
Nippon, Vase, 12 In. 185.00
Pitcher, Milk, 5 1/2 In. 22.00
Plate, Divided, Gray, Handle 20.00
Plate, Salad, Set of 5 .... 30.00
Sugar, Large 15.00
Tea Set, Moriage Dragons, Jeweled Eyes, 3 Piece 125.00

Dresden china is any china made in the town of Dresden, Germany. The most famous factory in Dresden is the Meissen factory. Figurines of eighteenth–century ladies and gentlemen, animal groups, or cherubs and other mythological subjects were popular. One special type of figurine was made with skirts of porcelain–dipped lace. Do not make the mistake of thinking that all pieces marked "Dresden" are from the Meissen factory. The Meissen pieces usually have crossed swords marks, and are listed under Meissen.

DRESDEN, Bowl, Applied Flowers, Painted Flower Inside, Marked, 6 1/2 In.	115.00
Candleholder, 2 Figurines, Applied Roses, Signed, 13 In., Pair	335.00
Candlestick, Double, Applied Roses, 8 X 5 In., Pair	250.00
Clock, Ansonia, Pink Flowers	350.00
Clock, Applied Floral Trim, 10 3/4 In.	275.00
Compote, Applied Pastel Roses, Handles, Crown, Shield, 9 In.	695.00
Cup & Saucer, Flower Spray, Twig Handle, Demitasse	35.00
Cup & Saucer, Port Scenes, Iron Red, Sepia, Blue, Gold Trim	85.00
Figurine, Coach, 3 Horses, Figures, Applied Roses, Lace, 14 1/2 In.	600.00
Figurine, Colonial Gentleman, Marked, 6 In.	295.00
Figurine, Two Ballerinas, Lace Skirt, 5 1/2 In.	98.00
Figurine, West Point Cadet, 10 In.	95.00
Lamp, Three Graces	300.00
Lemonade Set, Grape Pattern, 12 In.Bowl, 8 Piece	65.00
Loving Cup, Woodland Scene, Gold Trim, 3 Handles, 6 X 7 In.	450.00
Plate, Raised Gold Design, Cupid Center, 8 1/2 In., Pair	330.00
Ramekin, Covered, Underplate, Hand Painted Flowers, Gold Trim, Pair	75.00
Salt, Master, Wheelbarrow Form, Matching Salt Spoon, Movable	118.00
Sherbet, Saucer, Hand Painted, 6 Sets	450.00
Tea Set, Rose Floral Design, Molded Head Relief, 15 Piece	850.00
Urn, Applied Porcelain Flowers, Front Portrait, Signed, 9 In.	185.00
Urn, Portrait, Applied Roses, Handles, Signed, 9 In.	180.00
Urn, Portrait, Pedestal, Applied Roses, Handles, Signed, 9 In.	180.00
Vase, Courting Scene, Cobalt Blue, Gold, Hand Painted, 8 1/2 In.	325.00
Vase, Lovers Portrait, Raised Gold Tracery, Marked, 8 In.	295.00

Duncan & Miller is a term used by collectors when referring to glass made by the George A. Duncan and Sons Company or the Duncan and Miller Glass Company. These companies worked from 1893 to 1955, when the use of the name "Duncan" was discontinued and the firm became part of the United States Glass Company. Early patterns may be listed under Pressed Glass.

DUNCAN & MILLER, Button Panel, Spooner	30.00 To 60.00
Canterbury, Bowl, Ruffled, Pink, 9 In.	20.00 To 23.00
Canterbury, Bowl, Underplate, Divided, Clear, 6 X 3 1/2 In.	25.00
Canterbury, Celery, Crystal, 11 In.	20.00
Canterbury, Cocktail, 4 1/4 In.	10.00
Canterbury, Console Set, Scalloped Bowl, Sticks 3 1/2 In.	35.00
Canterbury, Cruet, Tray, 3 Piece	45.00
Canterbury, Dish, Yellow Opalescent, 9 In.	27.50
Canterbury, Goblet, Footed, 9 Oz.	15.00
Canterbury, Mayonnaise Set, Crystal, 3 Piece	27.50
Canterbury, Mayonnaise, Sterling Silver, Marked, 3 Piece	95.00
Canterbury, Plate, 8 3/4 In., Set of 4	22.00
Canterbury, Plate, Pink, 8 In.	35.00
Canterbury, Relish, 3 Sections, Gold Overlay	25.00
Canterbury, Relish, 5 Sections, Caribbean Blue, 12 1/4 In.	45.00
Canterbury, Salad Set, 4 Piece	25.00
Canterbury, Tray, Oblong, 2 Handles, Crystal, 10 1/2 In.	18.00
Canterbury, Tray, Pickle, Crystal, 8 In.	14.00
Canterbury, Tumbler, Iced Tea, Chartreuse, 13 Oz.	10.00
Canterbury, Vase, Enameled White Leaves, Blue, 9 In.	75.00
Canterbury, Vase, Pink Opalescent, 5 In.	30.00
Caribbean, Ashtray Stack Set, Red	40.00
Caribbean, Celery, Blue	55.00

Caribbean, Compote, 4 1/4 In. 12.50
Caribbean, Decanter, Blue, 32 Oz. 50.00
Caribbean, Relish, 5 Sections, Blue, 13 In. 95.00
Caribbean, Tumbler, Turned Up, Set of 6 .... 30.00
Chanticleer, Vase, Ruffled, Blue Opalescent 75.00
Cornucopia, Blue 85.00
Diamond Ridge, Bottle, Water 55.00
Diamond Ridge, Cracker Jar, Covered, Large 95.00
Diamond Ridge, Cruet 45.00
Diamond Ridge, Pitcher, Gold Flashed At Top, 1901, 10 In. 60.00
Diamond Ridge, Syrup 95.00
Diamond Ridge, Vase, 10 In. 55.00
Diamond Ridge, Water Set, 5 Piece 150.00
Duck, Ashtray, 4 1/4 In. 7.00
Duck, Paperweight 55.00
First Love, Candlestick, 2 Lights, U Prisms, 9 X 5 In., Pr. 95.00
First Love, Dish, Ice Cream, Silver Band 12.00
First Love, Goblet, 10 Oz. 20.00
Georgian, Tumbler, Ruby, 9 Oz., 12 Piece 75.00
Granada, Goblet, Set of 8 .... 175.00
Hobnail, Candlestick, Blue, 4 In., Pair 40.00
Hobnail, Goblet, Pink 27.50
Hobnail, Mug, Amber Handle, Crystal 30.00
Hobnail, Sherbet 4.00
Hobnail, Vase, Ruffled, Blue, 4 1/2 In. 26.50
Lily of The Valley, Goblet 30.00
Mardi Gras, Cake Plate 70.00
Mardi Gras, Cordial 32.00
Mardi Gras, Jam Jar, Covered 85.00
Mardi Gras, Punch Set, Bowl 14 In., 19 Piece 350.00
Mardi Gras, Toothpick 42.00
Mardi Gras, Vase, Trumpet, 6 In. 35.00
Mardi Gras, Water Set, 7 Piece 170.00
Murano, Bowl, Crimped 35.00
Pall Mall, Swan, 7 In. .... 145.00 To 175.00
Patio, Bowl, Chartreuse, Square, & Candle Holder, 3 Pc. 65.00
Patio, Console Set, Chartreuse, Square, 3 Piece 65.00
Radiance, Cup & Saucer, Light Blue 20.00
Sandwich, Bowl, 5 In. 5.50
Sandwich, Cruet Set, Stopper, Oval Tray, 3 Piece 50.00
Sandwich, Cup & Saucer .... 10.00 To 15.00
Sandwich, Goblet, Amber 28.00
Sandwich, Goblet, Stem, 6 In. 10.00
Sandwich, Plate, 6 1/2 In. 10.00
Sandwich, Plate, 8 In. .... 10.00 To 11.00
Sandwich, Relish, 3 Sections, 10 1/2 In. 23.00
Sandwich, Sherbet, Stem, 4 1/4 In. 8.00
Sandwich, Sugar, Creamer & Tray 20.00
Sandwich, Tumbler, Iced Tea, Flat, 5 1/4 In. 9.00
Sanibel, Relish, Divided, Yellow, 9 In. 45.00
Sanibel, Tray, Blue Opalescent, 13 In. 30.00
Sanibel, Tray, Vaseline, 13 In. 30.00
Snail, Butter 125.00
Spiral Flutes, Bowl, Rimmed, Pink, 7 In. 6.00
Spiral Flutes, Pitcher, Water, Green Handle 90.00
Swag Block, Goblet, 6 Piece 300.00
Swan, Avocado Green, 7 In. 25.00
Swan, Blue, 5 1/2 In. 20.00
Swan, Bowl, 6 In. 40.00
Swan, Chartreuse, 7 In. 25.00
Swan, Crystal Neck, Red, 7 In. 28.00
Swan, Crystal, 4 1/2 In. 45.00
Swan, Crystal, 12 1/2 In. 35.00
Swan, Crystal, 8 1/2 In. 25.00

Swan, Olive Green, 10 1/2 In.	45.00
Swan, Red, 6 In.	28.00
Swan, Red, 7 In.	27.50
Swan, Red, 8 1/4 In.	55.00
Swan, Red, 10 3/4 In.	95.00
Swan, Red, Crystal Neck, 10 1/2 In.	45.00
Swan, Red, Crystal Neck, 12 In.	65.00
Swan, Sylvan, Yellow, 5 1/2 In.	45.00
Swirl, Cornucopia, Pink	65.00
Sylvan, Plate, Salad, Yellow Opalescent, 8 1/2 In.	25.00
Sylvan, Tray, Mint, Handle, 8 1/4 In.	12.50
Teardrop, Ashtray, Individual	3.00 To 5.00
Teardrop, Basket, Flower, Crimped, Cobalt Blue Handle	125.00
Teardrop, Bowl, Flower, Handles, Crystal. 12 In.	25.00
Teardrop, Candlestick, 2–Light, 7 In., Pair	55.00
Teardrop, Candlestick, Crystal, 4 In., Pair	18.00
Teardrop, Cocktail, Oyster, 3 1/2 Oz.	10.00
Teardrop, Compote, 5 X 3 1/2 In.	5.00
Teardrop, Cup	3.50 To 10.00
Teardrop, Goblet	7.00
Teardrop, Mustard, Covered	20.00
Teardrop, Relish, 3 Sections, 2 Handles, 12 In.	20.00
Teardrop, Relish, 5 Sections, 12 In.	18.00 To 24.00
Teardrop, Sherbet	3.50
Teardrop, Sugar & Creamer	12.50
Teardrop, Tumbler, Old Fashion, 7 Oz.	12.00
Tepee, Sugar Shaker	55.00
Tepee, Toothpick	32.00
Three–Face, Compote	65.00
Three–Face, Saltshaker	90.00

Durand glass was made by Victor Durand from 1879 to 1935 at several factories. Most of the iridescent Durand glass was made by Victor Durand, Jr., from 1912 to 1924 at the Durand Art Glass Works in Vineland, New Jersey.

DURAND, Atomizer, Perfume, Signed DeVilbiss, 8 In.	225.00
Bowl, Etched Floral Design, Blue, Yellow Ground, Signed, 4 X 7 In.	400.00
Goblet, Rose Pulled Feather Bowl, Yellow Stem & Base	150.00
Lamp, Boudoir, Gold Shade, Signed, 15 In.	575.00
Rose Bowl, Ruffled Rim, Blue, 3 1/2 In.	475.00
Vase, Aurene, Silver Threading, Signed, 8 3/4 In.	1150.00
Vase, Baluster, Orange Feather Design, 8 1/4 In. ....*Illus*	625.00
Vase, Blue Aurene, Ribbed, Bulbous Bottle Shape, 12 In.	600.00
Vase, Blue Iridescent, Paper Label, 16 In.	925.00
Vase, Blue Iridescent, Signed, 10 In.	650.00
Vase, Blue Lily Pad, Gold, Signed, Numbered, 6 1/2 In.	350.00
Vase, Bulbous, Flared, Blue Iridescent, Signed, 10 1/2 In.	790.00
Vase, Dark Blue Iridescent, Light Blue Design Allover, 7 In.	425.00
Vase, Feather, Gold Threading, Iridescent, C.1710, 10 1/2 In.	575.00
Vase, Feather, Iridescent Green & Brown, Signed, 7 1/2 In.	475.00
Vase, Gold Iridescent, Bulbous, 7 In.	400.00
Vase, Iridescent, Signed & Numbered, 10 1/2 In.	585.00
Vase, King Tut, Baluster, Dark Green Swirls, 8 1/2 In.	400.00
Vase, King Tut, Gold Iridescent, White, 9 In.	450.00
Vase, Metallic & Green Design, 10 1/4 In., Pair	1050.00
Vase, Random Blue Design Allover, Signed, 7 1/4 In.	425.00
Vase, Thin Neck, Gold Iridescent, 15 In.	585.00
Vase, Trumpet Lily Shape, Blue & White Pulled Feather, Gold, 7 In.	550.00
Vase, Trumpet, Aurene, Flat Circular Base, Marked, 15 In.	875.00
Wine, Peacock, Ruby, 5 1/2 In.	250.00
Wine, Topaz Bowls, Cut To Clear, Opalescent Stem, Pair	350.00

Elfinware was made from about 1918 to 1940. It is a Dresden–like porcelain that was sold in dime stores and gift shops. Many pieces were decorated with raised flowers. The small pieces are marked with the name "Elfinware" or with a crown and M mark. The words "Germany" or "Made in Germany" also appear on some pieces.

ELFINWARE, Basket, 7 In.	55.00
Bottle, Scent	15.00
Holder, Place Card, Basket of Flowers, Fan Shape, Pink Ribbon	25.00
Powder Box	15.00

Elvis Presley, the famous singer, lived from 1935 to 1977. He became famous by 1956. Elvis appeared on television, starred in twenty–seven movies, and performed in Las Vegas. Memorabilia from any of the Presley shows, his records, and even memorials made after his death are collected.

ELVIS PRESLEY, Bandana, 1956	70.00
Book, His Story, 1977	14.95
Bracelet, Charm, 1956	125.00
Button, Flasher, Plastic, 1956, 3 1/2 In.	10.00
Calendar, Pocket, RCA Victor, Cardboard, 1967, 2 X 4 In.	4.00
Card & Calendar Card, Arcade, Wallet Size, 1977	8.00
Card, Lobby, Frankie & Johnny, 1966, 22 X 28 In.	15.00
Card, Lobby, Spinout, 1966, 11 X 14 In., Set of 8	20.00
Charm Necklace	25.00
Doll, No.3, Flame Costume, World Dolls, 21 In.	75.00
Doll, No.4, American Eagle Outfit, World Dolls, 21 In.	95.00
Game, Game of Love, Teenage Publishing	475.00
Handkerchief, 1956	225.00
Hat, Tag, 1956	35.00
Knife, Pocket	6.00
Magazine, Rock & Roll, 1957	15.00
Pennant, Elvis	18.00
Record, A Touch of Gold, Volume 3, Maroon Label, 1960, 45 RPM	150.00
Record, Jailhouse Rock, 45 RPM, Elvis' Picture, 1950s	18.00
Record, King of The Whole Wide World, RCA Victor	30.00
Record, Playing For Keeps & Too Much, 45 RPM	40.00
Record, Viva Las Vegas, 1964, 45 RPM	35.00
Sheet Music, All Shook Up	13.00
Sheet Music, Heartbreak Hotel	13.00
Sheet Music, My Way	15.00
Teddy Bear, Cologne, Box	70.00
Tee Shirt	10.50

Russian, French, and English workmen of the eighteenth and nineteenth centuries made small boxes and table pieces of enamel on metal. One form of English enamel is called "Battersea" and is listed under that name.

ENAMEL, Chamberstick, Dark Blue, Turquoise, Cream, French, 6 X 2 In.	58.00
Incense Burner, Floral, Brass Cover, With Cutout Butterflies	65.00
Jug, Pewter Lid, Blue, English	85.00
Milk Container, White, 1 Gal.	38.00
Planter, 4 Panels, Putti, Pastoral Scenes, French, 10 1/2 In., Pair	1500.00
Salt, 3 Ball Feet, Czarist Russia, Marked, 1 1/2 In.	235.00
Shot Glass, 6 Color, Enameled, Marked 84, Russian, 1 7/8 In.	350.00
Spoon, Vermile Filigree, Russian, Marked, 4 In.	85.00
Tea Set, Polychromed, Venetian Red, Gilt, 6–Footed Cups, 11 Piece	185.00
Tea Strainer, Russian, Gustav Klingert	130.00
Teaspoon, Case, Russian, 12 Piece	1056.00
Tongs, Russian, Ivan Saltykov	45.00
Vase, Lady, French, Artist Signed, 3 In.	395.00
Wine, Polychrome, Stem, 6 7/8 In.	105.00

ES Germany porcelain was made at the factory of Erdmann Schlegelmilch from 1861 to 1925 in Suhl, Germany. The porcelain was sold decorated or undecorated. Other pieces were made at the factory in Saxony, Prussia, and are marked "ES Prussia." Reinhold Schlegelmilch, a brother, made the famous wares marked "RS Germany."

ES GERMANY, Bowl, Fox Hunt Scene, Dogs, Men On Horses, 9 1/2 In.	185.00
Chocolate Set, Blue, Green & Tan Fern Pattern, 9 Piece	350.00
Cup & Saucer, Fox Terrier, Hand Painted, Large	45.00
Dish, Tidbit, Center Handle, 6 1/2 In.	35.00
Ewer, Medallion of Girl Holding Conch Shell To Ear, 7 In.	75.00
Humidor, Oriental Girl	80.00
Nappy, Bluebird On Tree Limb, Handle, 4–Leaf Clover Shape	95.00
Plate, Portrait, High Hawk	70.00
Powder Jar, Hand Painted, Bluebird & Leaves, 3 1/2 X 6 In.	85.00
Vase, Butterfly & Palm Trees, White Matte, Bird Mark, 8 1/2 In.	75.00
Vase, Cobalt Blue & Gold, 7 In.	70.00
Vase, Man, 2 Victorian Ladies Scene, 2 Sides, Late 1800s, 10 In.	225.00
Vase, Portrait, Girl, Holly Wreath In Hair, Green, Handle, 10 In.	175.00
Vase, Rococo Side Handles, Yellow Ground, Gold Tracery, 16 In.	125.00
Vase, White, Yellow, Orange & Green, Hand Painted, 9 In.	69.00
ES PRUSSIA, Tankard, Fruit, Pears & Flowers On Blue, 12 1/2 In.	1000.00

All types of Eskimo artifacts are collected. Carvings of whale or walrus teeth are listed under Scrimshaw. Baskets are in the Basket category. All other types of Eskimo art are listed here.

ESKIMO, Basket, Gathering, Brown Geometric Zigzag, 8 In.	550.00
Doll, Buckskin Parka, Beading, 10 In.	150.00
Earrings, Ivory, Baleen, Cobalt Blue Russian Trade Beads	1100.00
Harpoon, Whaling, Iron	325.00
Pipe, Ivory, Walrus Tusk, Eskimo Scenes, C.1850	1500.00

ETLING FRANCE   Etling glass is very similar in design to Lalique and Phoenix glass. It was made in France for Etling, a retail shop. It dates from the 1920s and 1930s.

ETLING, Vase, Birds, 10 In.	95.00
Vase, Sea Horses, 9 In.	85.00

ФАБЕРЖЕ
КФ

Faberge was a firm of jewelers and goldsmiths founded in St. Petersburg, Russia, in 1842, by Gustav Faberge. Peter Carl Faberge, his son, was jeweler to the Russian Imperial Court from about 1870 to 1914.

FABERGE, Basket, Sweetmeat, Silver, Cut Glass, Swing Handle, 1900, 5 1/2 In.	3850.00
Beaker, Silver, Enameled, Monogram Under Coronet, C.1910, 2 7/8 In.	5500.00
Bell Push, Double, Silver, Enameled, Ribbon Swags, C.1890, 3 In.	7150.00
Bell Push, Nephrite, Silver–Gilt, Paw Feet, Aarne, C.1900, 2 1/4 In.	4070.00
Bowl, Silver, Ball & Claw Footed, 1811–1911 In Wreath, 3 3/8 In.	2530.00
Box, Cigarette, Enameled, Silver–Gilt, Foliate, Brown, C.1910, 4 In.	6050.00
Coffee & Tea Set, Silver, Bulbous, Button Finials, C.1885, 4 Piece	4675.00
Dish, Brass, Imperial Eagle, Cyrillic Inscriptions, C.1914, 4 In.	3410.00
Dish, Nephrite, Rococo Sections, Gold Chased, Perchin, C.1890, 4 In.	7150.00
Letter Opener, Nephrite, Gold, Cabochon, Holstrom, C.1900, 8 1/4 In.	7700.00

Definitions of the words differentiating the types of pottery and porcelain are difficult because there is so much overlapping of meaning. Faience is tin-glazed earthenware, especially the wares made in France, Germany, and Scandinavia. It is also correct to say that faience is the same as majolica or Delft, although usually the term refers only to the tin-glazed pottery of the three regions mentioned.

FAIENCE, Bowl, Covered, Floral, Brass Band, Signed, Restored, 7 1/2 In.	115.00
Flower Holder, Oriental Laundry Woman, 6 Colors, Calif., 6 In.	155.00
Jardiniere, Pedestal, Embossed Sunflowers, Rudolph Lorber, 40 In.	675.00

Mustard, Covered, Figural, Woman, Seated, Dated 1792 .... 145.00
Pitcher, Green, California, 8 1/2 In. 145.00
Tankard, Polychrome, Pewter Cover, Knob Finial, Holland, C.1773 .... 900.00

> Fairings are small souvenir china boxes and figurines that were sold
> at country fairs during the nineteenth century. Most were made in
> Germany. Reproductions of fairings are being made, especially of
> the famous "twelve months of marriage" series.

FAIRING, Box, Wedding Night, Man Kneeling, Woman Undressing, 4 X 3 In. 45.00
Figurine, 3 O'Clock In The Morning, 3 1/4 X 3 1/4 In. 185.00
FAMILLE ROSE, see Chinese Export

> Fans have been used for cooling since the days of the ancients. By
> the eighteenth century, the fan was an accessory for the lady of
> fashion and very elaborate and expensive fans were made. Sticks
> were made of ivory or wood, set with jewels or carved. The fans
> were made of painted silk or paper. Inexpensive paper fans printed
> with advertising were giveaways in the late nineteenth and early
> twentieth centuries.

FAN, Admiral Dewey's Picture, Oilcloth 28.00
Advertising, 666 Medicine, Baby Singing, 1920–30 .... 12.00
Advertising, 7–Up, Cardboard, Wooden Handle, Bottle & Logo Picture 12.00
Advertising, Bell Coffee, Victorian Woman, Cardboard 8.00
Advertising, Carterpillar Diesel Tractors, 1936, Pictures, Paper 11.00
Advertising, G.E., Oscillating, Art Deco, 3 Speeds 125.00
Advertising, Jamup Honey Picture, Grand Ole Opry, Cardboard, 8 X 7 In. 36.00
Advertising, Keen Kutter 15.00
Advertising, Laxative Celery Bromide, A Safe & Sure Cure 9.00
Advertising, Laxative Celery Bromide, A Safe & Sure Cure, Boy & Girl 10.00
Advertising, McCormick Spices 7.00
Advertising, Moxie, Celluloid 80.00
Advertising, Moxie, Girl & Man 45.00
Advertising, Opal Coffee 8.00
Advertising, Putnam Dye, Cardboard 5.00
Advertising, Royal Crown Cola, Buy More For The War Bonds, 1940s 25.00
Advertising, Spinner, Hambone Negro Flyer 28.00
Art Nouveau, White Silk Poppy On Black Net, Black Sequins, 13 1/2 In. 75.00
Black Ostrich Feather, Tortoise Shell Handles 48.00
Black Silk, Lavender Flowers, Victorian 22.50
Blue Silk, Sequins, Ivory Sticks, 1860 .... 45.00
Bone Sticks, White Net, Painted Flowers, 13 X 30 In. 75.00
Ceiling, Airplane .... 275.00 To 295.00
Ceiling, Emerson, Original Blades, 1920s 200.00
Chinese Palace Garden Scene, Ivory Sticks, Chinese, 12 X 22 In. 150.00
Electric, Desk, 3 Speed, Wood System, Brass 90.00
Electric, Emerson, Early 1900s 55.00
Electric, G.E., Oscillating, Brass Blade 65.00
Electric, Polar Club, Design At Base, 8 In. 20.00
Electric, Western Electric, Brass, 6 Blades 50.00
Electric, Westinghouse, 6 Brass Blades, Brass Cage, 3 Speed, Restored 110.00
Feather, Celluloid 30.00
Gold Dust Twins, St.Louis World's Fair, Color, 1904 .... 40.00
Hand Painted, Inlaid Pearlized Moon & Stars On Frame, Victorian 45.00
Hand Painted, Silk, Mother–of–Pearl Staves 27.00
Jamup & Honey, Cardboard, 8 X 7 In. 36.00
Kerosene–Fired, The Lake Breeze, Wm.J.H.Strong 2000.00
Mourning, Leather, Folding 25.00
Oriental, Pleated Paper, Hand Painted Bird, Flowers, C.1900, 34 In. 95.00
Ostrich Feather, Orange, Tortoise Shell Sticks, 20 In. 75.00
Painted Leaf, Sticks, Gilt & Silver Tracery, Mirror, Victorian 185.00
Peacock Feathers, Pierced Ivory Sticks, Chinese, C.1825 .... 125.00
Reed Woven, Victorian, Ivory Handle, Round, 8 In. 18.00
Sandalwood, Boston Peace Jubilee, Strauss Autograph, 1872, 22 In.Case 750.00
Silk Embroidered, Cock Fight, Ivory Sticks, China, Box, 12 X 20 1/2 In. 250.00

Silk, Hand Painted Maiden, Young Men, Child, Cherry Tree, 10 1/2 In. 150.00
Silver Leaves On Purple Ground, Paper On Wood Stick, 12 X 22 In. 25.00
Stuffed Bird, Ivory Handle, Fan Shape Box, 19th Century 95.00
White Ostrich Feather, Tortoiseshell, 13 In. 75.00
Zachery Taylor, Engraved Battle View On Reverse 1200.00

> Federzeichnung is the very strange German name for a pattern of
> mother-of-pearl satin glass. The pattern had irregularly shaped
> sections of brown glass covered with a pattern of gold squiggle lines.
> It was first made in the late nineteenth century.

FEDERZEICHNUNG, Vase, Brown, Gold, Mother-of-Pearl, Cream Lining, 11 In. 1695.00

> Fenton Art Glass Company, founded in Martins Ferry, Ohio, by
> Frank L. Fenton, is now located in Williamstown, West Virginia. It
> is noted for early carnival glass produced between 1907 and 1920.
> Many other types of glass were also made.

FENTON, Apple Tree, Vase, C.1933 .... 55.00
Aqua Crest, Basket 40.00
Aqua Crest, Creamer 45.00
Aqua Crest, Sugar 35.00
Aqua Crest, Vase, 9 1/2 In. 60.00
Beaded Melon, Bowl, Milk, With Emerald Crest, 7 In. 35.00
Beaded Melon, Vase, Gold Tulip, 9 In. 50.00
Beaded Melon, Vase, Green Tulip, 9 In. 45.00
Beaded Melon, Vase, Tulip, 4 In. 17.00
Blackberry, Butter, Covered, Milk Glass 75.00
Block & Star, Tumbler, 4 1/2 In., 6 Piece 50.00
Blue Ridge, Vase, Flared, 8 In. 40.00
Burmese, Bowl, Oak Leaf Design, Scalloped Edge 37.50
Burmese, Vase, Flared, Maple Leaf Design, 7 1/2 In. 25.00
Butterfly & Berry, Water Set, Marigold, 11 Piece 590.00
Cattails, Vase, Black Enamel, Crane, Jade Green, Stand, 6 1/4 In. 175.00
Coin Dot, Creamer, Lime 40.00
Coin Dot, Lamp Shade, Fluted Top, White, 10 In. 125.00
Coin Dot, Rose Jar, Moonstone Lid 125.00
Coin Dot, Vase, Cranberry Cased, 13 In., Pair 250.00
Coin Dot, Vase, Cranberry Opalescent, 7 In. 45.00
Coin Dot, Water Set, Blue, 7 Piece 185.00
Coinspot, Pitcher, 9 1/2 In. 80.00
Coinspot, Vase, Blue Opalescent, Crimped, 8 In. 95.00
Crest, Bowl, Flared, Ivory, 6 In. 25.00
Crest, Cake Plate, Footed, Emerald, 13 In. 68.00
Crest, Hat, Clear, 4 In. 9.00
Crest, Plate, Emerald, 8 1/2 In. 25.00
Crest, Plate, Rose, 6 1/2 In. 18.00
Crest, Vase, Double Crimp, Rose, 9 In. 30.00
Crest, Vase, Triangular, Aqua, 5 In. 27.00
Crest, Vase, Tulip, Cupped, Aqua, 4 1/4 In. 24.00
Daisy & Button, Candy Dish, Covered, Green 15.00
Daisy & Button, Tray, Dresser, Fan Shape 15.00
Diamond Lace, Epergne, Trumpet, Aqua Opalescent, Large 64.00
Diamond Optic, Candy Dish, Flat, Cranberry, 5 In. 85.00
Diamond Optic, Jug, Squat, Ruby Overlay, 5 1/2 In. 22.50
Diamond Optic, Tray, Sandwich, Dolphin Handle, Green, 1927 .... 25.00
Dolphin, Candlestick, Lilac, Pair 70.00
Dot Optic, Creamer, Crystal Handle, Ruby Overlay, 4 In. 35.00
Dot Optic, Vase, Tulip, Ruby Overlay, 4 1/4 X 6 1/2 In. 45.00
Figurine, Cat, Jade 25.00
Figurine, Praying Boy, Black 38.00
Figurine, Rabbit, Blue, Blown 45.00
Floral & Grape, Tumbler, Green .... 45.00 To 48.00
Flower Pot, Green Edge 22.00
Franklin, Decanter 27.50
Georgian, Salt & Pepper, Pair 7.50

Hobnail, Basket, Cranberry, 4 1/2 In.	45.00
Hobnail, Basket, Footed, Square Top, Blue, 6 1/4 In.	55.00
Hobnail, Bonbon, Cranberry Opalescent, 6 In.	18.00
Hobnail, Bonbon, Mounted On Stainless Steel Base, 15 1/2 In.	12.00
Hobnail, Bowl, Cranberry, 12 In.	45.00
Hobnail, Candle Sconce, Milk Glass	15.00
Hobnail, Candleholder, Cranberry Opalescent, Handle, 3 1/4 In.	43.50
Hobnail, Candleholder, Single, Pair	30.00
Hobnail, Creamer, Cranberry	55.00
Hobnail, Cruet, Stopper, Cranberry	40.00
Hobnail, Decanter, Blue	85.00
Hobnail, Dresser Set, Blue Opalescent, Perfume Bottles, Powder Jar	50.00
Hobnail, Fruit Bowl, Opalescent Rim, Plum, 9 In.	60.00
Hobnail, Pitcher, Water, Cranberry	200.00
Hobnail, Plate, Blue, 6 In.	12.00
Hobnail, Rose Bowl, Vaseline Opalescent, Crimped	13.50
Hobnail, Salt & Pepper, Cranberry	35.00
Hobnail, Sugar & Creamer, Small	25.00
Hobnail, Vase, 8 Point Star Top, Crimped, C.1940, 5 1/2 In.	32.00
Hobnail, Vase, Cranberry, Double Crimp, 4 1/2 In.	15.00
Hobnail, Vase, Fan, Blue, 10 X 8 1/4 In.	35.00
Hobnail, Vase, Ruffled, Cranberry, 11 In.	60.00
Hobnail, Vase, Tricorner, Cranberry, 5 1/2 In.	35.00
Hobnail, Vase, White Trim, Emerald, 4 1/4 In.	25.00
Hobnail, Water Set, Milk Glass, 6 Piece	65.00
Ivory Crest, Vase, Crimped Triangle, 10 In.	20.00
Jacqueline, Pitcher, Powder Blue, 48 Oz.	60.00
Jacqueline, Vase, Honey Amber, 6 In.	30.00
Jacqueline, Vase, Pink Opaline, 5 In.	55.00
Lamp, Cranberry, 26 In.	250.00
Lamp, Fairy, Owl, Pink Slag, 3 1/2 In.	18.00
Lamp, Opalescent Dot	125.00
Lamp, Swirl, Cranberry, Pair	145.00
Lily-of-The-Valley, Water Set, Blue, 7 Piece	4000.00
Lincoln Inn, Relish, Clear, Silver Plate Tray	30.00
Little Flowers, Bowl, Scalloped & Fluted, Blue, 10 In.	75.00
Lotus & Grape, Dish, Novelty, Custard	35.00
Ming, Console Set, 3 Piece	65.00
Peacock At Urn, Plate, Cobalt Blue, 9 In.	250.00
Polka Dot, Sugar Shaker	42.50
Prayer Rug, Bonbon, Handles	22.00
Rib Optic, Salt & Pepper, Green, Flat Lids	75.00
Rib Optic, Tumble-Up, Green	65.00
Rosaline, Vase, Bud	20.00
Rose Crest, Epergne, 4 Lily, 16 In.	250.00
Silver Crest, Banana Stand, 13 X 8 In.	35.00
Silver Crest, Basket, 10 1/2 In.	40.00
Silver Crest, Bonbon	32.00
Silver Crest, Candleholder, Cornucopia, Single	10.00
Silver Crest, Epergne, 4-Lily	145.00
Silver Crest, Hat, 4 1/2 In.	32.00
Silver Crest, Pitcher, Water	70.00
Snow Crest, Hat, Green, 10 X 7 In.	285.00
Snow Crest, Vase, Blue	60.00
Snow Crest, Vase, Emerald, 7 In.	40.00

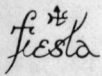

Fiesta, the colorful dinnerware, was introduced in 1936 by the Homer Laughlin China Co., redesigned in 1969, and withdrawn in 1973. The simple design was characterized by a band of concentric circles, beginning at the rim. Cups had full-circle handles until 1969, when partial-circle handles were made. Harlequin and Riviera were related wares. For more information and prices of American dinnerware, see the book "The Kovels' Illustrated Price Guide to Depression Glass and American Dinnerware."

FIESTA, Ashtray, Chartreuse 35.00
  Ashtray, Dark Blue 25.00
  Ashtray, Dark Green 40.00
  Ashtray, Red 35.00
  Ashtray, Turquoise .... 20.00 To 22.00
  Bowl, Dessert, American Sweetheart, 6 In. 29.50
  Bowl, Dessert, Red, 6 In. 21.00
  Bowl, Dessert, Turquoise 12.00
  Bowl, Fruit, Chartreuse, 5 1/2 In. 14.00
  Bowl, Fruit, Dark Green, 8 1/2 In. 26.00
  Bowl, Fruit, Dark Green, 4 3/4 In. 14.00
  Bowl, Fruit, Dark Green, 5 1/2in. 13.00
  Bowl, Fruit, Dark Green, 8 1/2 In. 23.50
  Bowl, Fruit, Green, 9 1/2 In. 45.00
  Bowl, Fruit, Rose, 4 3/4 In. 13.50
  Bowl, Fruit, Turquoise, 8 1/2 In. 15.00
  Bowl, Fruit, Yellow, 8 1/2 In. 14.25
  Bowl, Nesting, Green, 10 In. 45.00
  Bowl, Nesting, Kitchen Kraft, Nautilus, Original Carton, 3 Piece 65.00
  Bowl, Nesting, Multicolored, 7 Piece 275.00
  Bowl, Nesting, Old Ivory, 10 In. 45.00
  Bowl, Nesting, Turquoise, 8 In. 30.00
  Bowl, Nesting, Yellow, 5 In. 9.00
  Bowl, Nesting, Yellow, 6 In. 22.00
  Bowl, Salad, Footed, Old Ivory 85.00
  Bowl, Salad, Footed, Turquoise 120.00
  Bowl, Salad, Yellow, 9 1/2 In. 50.00
  Cake Plate, Green, 10 In. 175.00
  Cake Plate, Kitchen Kraft, Green 30.00
  Candleholder, Bulb, Yellow, Pair 24.00
  Candleholder, Tripod, Green, Pair 58.00
  Carafe, Cobalt Blue .... 65.00 To 75.00
  Carafe, Light Green .... 70.00 To 95.00
  Carafe, Red .... 80.00 To 95.00
  Carafe, Turquoise 65.00
  Carafe, Yellow .... 60.00 To 75.00
  Casserole, Covered, French, Medium Green .... 225.00 To 250.00
  Casserole, Covered, Kitchen Kraft, Dark Green 85.00
  Casserole, Covered, Kitchen Kraft, Red 75.00
  Casserole, Covered, Kitchen Kraft, Yellow 60.00
  Casserole, Covered, Red .... 68.00 To 75.00
  Casserole, Covered, Rose 95.00
  Casserole, Covered, Yellow .... 30.00 To 48.00
  Casserole, French, Covered, Red 100.00
  Casserole, French, Covered, Yellow .... 68.00 To 80.00
  Chop Plate, Green, 15 In. 22.00
  Chop Plate, Old Ivory, 13 In. 15.00
  Chop Plate, Red, 15 In. 25.00
  Chop Plate, Yellow, 13 In. 9.00
  Coffeepot, After Dinner, Red .... 110.00 To 125.00
  Coffeepot, Old Ivory 30.00
  Coffeepot, Turquoise .... 50.00 To 60.00
  Compote, Cobalt Blue, 12 In. 40.00
  Compote, Red, 12 In. .... 70.00 To 95.00
  Compote, Sweets, Red .... 30.00 To 45.00
  Creamer, Light Green 16.00
  Creamer, Red, Individual 75.00
  Creamer, Yellow, Individual 30.00
  Cup & Saucer, After Dinner, Red, 4 Piece 130.00
  Cup & Saucer, Chartreuse 20.00
  Cup & Saucer, Dark Green .... 22.00 To 28.00
  Cup & Saucer, Medium Green .... 20.00 To 32.00
  Cup & Saucer, Red .... 16.50 To 28.00
  Cup & Saucer, Turquoise 14.00

Cup & Saucer, Yellow .... 17.00 To 25.00
Eggcup, Cobalt Blue 22.00
Eggcup, Dark Blue 30.00
Eggcup, Dark Green 40.00
Eggcup, Gray 40.00
Eggcup, Old Ivory .... 15.00 To 23.00
Eggcup, Red .... 32.00 To 36.00
Eggcup, Turquoise 23.00
Eggcup, Yellow 23.00
Figurine, Lamb, Gold 20.00
Fork, Label, Green 35.00
Fork, Yellow 32.00
Gravy Boat, Red 18.00
Grill Plate, Dark Blue, 10 1/2 In. 20.00
Jam Jar, Kitchen Kraft, Cobalt Blue 140.00
Jam Jar, Kitchen Kraft, Green 195.00
Jam Jar, Old Ivory 80.00
Jam Jar, Yellow 115.00
Luncheon Set, Turquoise, Service For 4 .... 125.00
Mug, Chartreuse .... 40.00 To 45.00
Mug, Dark Green 20.00
Mug, Gray 45.00
Mug, Medium Green 30.00
Mug, Old Ivory, Hartford Insurance Logo 22.00
Mug, Red, Set of 4 .... 175.00
Mug, Rose 45.00
Mug, Turquoise 30.00
Mug, TWA Advertising 18.00
Mustard, Cobalt Blue 75.00
Mustard, Green, H.L.Co., Signed 100.00
Mustard, Red 95.00
Mustard, Turquoise 50.00
Pitcher, Covered, Kitchen Kraft, Large 100.00
Pitcher, Disc, Gray .... 45.00 To 80.00
Pitcher, Disc, Green .... 70.00 To 95.00
Pitcher, Disc, Red 47.50
Pitcher, Disc, Rose 75.00
Pitcher, Disc, Yellow 25.00
Pitcher, Green, 2 Pt. .... 18.00 To 35.00
Pitcher, Ice Lip, Green 35.00
Pitcher, Ice Lip, Red 65.00
Pitcher, Ice Lip, Yellow 40.00
Pitcher, Juice, Blue, 2 Gray & 2 Pink Juice Tumblers 350.00
Pitcher, Juice, Gray .... 45.00 To 85.00
Pitcher, Juice, Light Green 50.00
Pitcher, Juice, Yellow 18.00
Pitcher, Red, 2 Pt. 45.00
Pitcher, Rose, 2 Pt. 25.00
Plate, Calendar, 1955, Gold 27.50
Plate, Calendar, Old Ivory, 1954 .... 30.00
Plate, Cheese, Yellow, 15 In. 14.00
Plate, Cobalt Blue, 10 In. 11.50
Plate, Compartments, Red, 10 1/2 In. 20.00

Fiesta pottery has been reproduced since 1985, but the new pieces are made in different colors than the old ones.

Plate, Dark Blue, 10 In. 14.00
Plate, Deep, Old Ivory, 8 In. 9.00
Plate, Green, 9 In. 10.50
Plate, Kitchen Kraft, Yellow, 10 In. 24.00
Plate, Medium Green, 10 In. 17.50
Plate, Old Ivory, 7 In. 4.50
Plate, Red, 10 In. 20.00
Plate, Turquoise, 9 In. 8.00
Plate, Yellow, 10 In. ....7.00 To 12.00
Platter, Oval, Turquoise, 12 In. 12.00
Relish, Dark Blue & Yellow 65.00
Relish, Red ....40.00 To 110.00
Salt & Pepper, Kitchen Kraft, Red 50.00
Salt & Pepper, Kitchen Kraft, Yellow 55.00
Saltshaker, Yellow 5.00
Saucer, Turquoise 2.00
Saucer, Yellow 2.00
Soup, Cream, Cobalt Blue 15.00
Soup, Onion, Red 150.00
Spoon, Original Label, Red 60.00
Stack Set, Kitchen Kraft, Red Lid, Yellow, Dark Blue & Cobalt Blue 150.00
Sugar & Creamer, Figure 8 Tray, Yellow, Individual 100.00
Sugar, Covered, Gray 23.00
Sugar, Covered, Yellow ....10.00 To 14.00
Sugar, Red 20.00
Syrup, Green 55.00
Syrup, Red ....100.00 To 115.00
Syrup, Turquoise 95.00
Teapot, Chartreuse 55.00
Teapot, Nautilus, Gold Design, Light Green, Medium 38.00
Teapot, Red, Large 75.00
Teapot, Red, Medium 65.00
Teapot, Turquoise, Large 60.00
Teapot, Yellow, Medium 50.00
Tray, Individual, Figure 8 Shape, Cobalt Blue 45.00
Tumbler, Juice, Red 20.00
Tumbler, Old Ivory, 10 Oz. 20.00
Tumbler, Red, 10 Oz. ....32.00 To 35.00
Tumbler, Red, 10 Oz., Set of 4 .... 130.00
Vase, Bud, Cobalt Blue 35.00
Vase, Bud, Yellow ....22.00 To 40.00
Vase, Cobalt Blue, 10 In. 195.00
Vase, Ivory, 8 In. 165.00

Findlay, or onyx, glass was made using three layers of glass. It was manufactured by the Dalzell Gilmore Leighton Company about 1889 in Findlay, Ohio. The platinum, ruby, or black pattern was molded into the glass. The glass came in several colors, but was usually white or ruby.

FINDLAY ONYX, Celery, 12 1/2 In. 350.00
Creamer, Ruby 850.00
Spooner, Opaque White Flowers, Frosted Ruby, 4 In. 495.00
Sugar Shaker, Ivory 250.00
Sugar Shaker, Platinum ....365.00 To 395.00
Sugar, Platinum Flowers, Covered, 4 1/2 X 6 In. 485.00
Sugar, Ruby, Open 570.00
Syrup 575.00

It is said that every little boy wanted to be a fireman or a train engineer 75 years ago and the collectors today reflect this interest. All types of firefighting equipment are wanted, from fire marks to uniforms to toy fire trucks.

Firefighting, Bucket, Leather,
1824, 13 In.

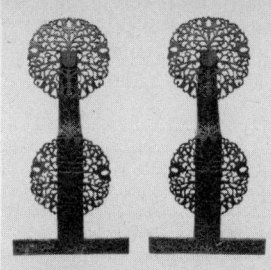

Fireplace, Andirons, Cast Iron,
Scroll, Tulip, C.1905, 22 In., Pair

Folk Art, Box, Splint, Swirl Desi
Red, Oval, 8 1/2 In.

FIREFIGHTING, Alarm Box, Gamewell, 1924	120.00
Ax, Fireman's, Hickory Handle, 35 In.	40.00
Badge, Highwood Fire Dept.Truck	35.00
Belt, 1st Vice President, V.F.A., Leather	95.00
Belt, Chicopee Falls V.F.A., Leather	90.00
Belt, Parade, Leather, Hose Type Metal Buckle	250.00
Bucket, Franklin Fire Society, Full Size	2750.00
Bucket, Leather, 11 1/4 In.	55.00
Bucket, Leather, 1824, 13 In. ....*Illus*	90.00
Bucket, Leather, Green Repaint, No.1 M.Titcomb, 1835, 12 In.	200.00
Bucket, Leather, Old Black Paint, 12 1/2 In.	65.00
Bucket, Metal, Red Paint, Word Fire, Wire Bail, C.1890	45.00
Case, Salesman's, Red Comet Extinguisher	35.00
Catalog, American La France, Clothing, Badges, 176 Pages, 1929	38.00
Certificate of Service, Silver Creek, N.Y., Framed, 1900s	65.00
Extinguisher, American La France, Brass, For Elmira, N.Y.Co.	25.00
Extinguisher, Autofyrstop Bomb, No Bracket	30.00
Extinguisher, Fire Killer	35.00
Extinguisher, Fireman Decanter, Numbered, 19th Century	60.00
Extinguisher, Gold Medal, Copper	24.00
Extinguisher, Guardene	25.00
Extinguisher, Harkness Fire Destroyer, Cobalt Blue, 6 In.	550.00
Extinguisher, Quick Aid, Brass, Wall Bracket	18.00
Extinguisher, Shur–Stop Bomb, Bracket	22.00
Extinguisher, Tin Tube, Phoenix, 15 1/2 In.	25.00
Fire Alarm Box, Gamewell, Full	65.00
Fire Alarm Register, Tape, 5 Pins, Beveled Glass, Nonpareil	650.00
Grenade, Barnum, Pat.June 26, 1869, 6 In.	500.00
Grenade, Chicago North Western R.R.	87.50
Grenade, Cobalt Blue, Raised Ribs, French, 19th Century	35.00
Grenade, Cobalt, Wax Sealer, 4 In.	350.00
Grenade, Harden, Pat.Aug.8, 1871, 6 In.	45.00
Grenade, Harden, Star, Green, Contents, 8 In.	185.00
Grenade, Hayward, Medium Amber, 6 1/4 In.	85.00
Grenade, Hayward, N.Y., Pleated, Pale Aqua, 6 In.	85.00
Grenade, Hayward, Pat.Aug.8, 1871, 6 In.	250.00
Grenade, Red Comet Firemaster, Original Box, Set of 3	70.00
Grenade, Rockford	60.00
Grenade, Shur–Stop, Metal Hanger, Clear Glass, Fluid	15.00
Grenade, Tin, Pewter	18.00
Helmet, Assistant To Chief, Leather, Cairns, 1 Letter Missing	110.00

Helmet, Fireman's, Fiberglass, Leather Shield, Size 6 7/8	35.00
Helmet, Leather, Cairns Fire Dept., Shield, Eagle	140.00
Helmet, Leather, Eagle Head Torrent, C.F.F.D.	195.00
Lantern, Dietz King, Fire Dept., Brass	170.00 To 185.00
Lantern, Dietz King, Words Fire Dept.Indented, Copper Base	65.00
Lantern, Dietz, Fire Department	125.00
Lantern, Dietz, Fitzall Nat.USA Globe, Clear Glass, 1914	95.00
License Plate, Aux Fireman, Baltimore, Md., Fire–Engine Red	35.00
Nozzle, Brass, Cord Wrapped, Tip Unscrews, 30 In.	75.00
Nozzle, Fire Hose, Bronze, Powhatan B & I Works, 30 In.	45.00
Photograph, Cabinet, Fireman, Eagle Helmet, E.Providence, 1880	18.00
Photograph, Los Angeles Fire Dept., 1929, 12 X 20 In.	75.00
Ruler, Fireman's Fund Ins., 12 In.	6.00
Sheet Music, The Midnight Fire Alarm, E.T.Paul	20.00
Sign, Hartford Fire Ins.Co., Brass, Square, 16 In.	75.00
Sign, Phoenix Fire Insurance Co., Tin, 13 X 19 In.	150.00
Sign, Republic Underwriters of Dallas, Wooden, 16 X 28 In.	125.00
Trumpet, Fire	450.00

The fireplace was used to cook and to heat the American home in past centuries. Many types of tools and equipment were used. Andirons held the logs in place, firebacks reflected the heat into the room, and tongs were used to move either fuel or food. Many types of spits and roasting jacks were made and are listed under Kitchen.

FIREPLACE, Andirons, Belted Ball Finial, Hunnenman, Boston, C.1820, 11 In.	300.00
Andirons, Brass, Ball Top, 18th Century, 14 1/2 In.	300.00
Andirons, Brass, Bell–Over–Baluster, Rhode Island	4400.00
Andirons, Brass, Iron, Acorn Arched Legs, Ball Feet, 1800, 18 In.	2420.00
Andirons, Brass, Iron, Ball & Steeple, Bailey, C.1800, 19 In.	2420.00
Andirons, Brass, Iron, Knife Blade, Urn Form, 20 In.	495.00
Andirons, Brass, Iron, Lemon Finial, Claw & Ball Feet, 19 In.	3575.00
Andirons, Brass, Iron, Steeple Top, Arched Legs, C.1805, 20 In.	990.00
Andirons, Brass, Knob Finial, Ball Feet, Tools, C.1800, 18 In.	300.00
Andirons, Brass, Ruffled Skirt, Pennsylvania, 1800s, 17 In.	275.00
Andirons, Brass, Sliding Iron Back Stops, American, 18th Century	200.00
Andirons, Bronze, Louis Potter, 20th Century	3300.00
Andirons, Cast Iron, Scroll, Tulip, C.1905, 22 In., Pair ....*Illus*	5500.00
Andirons, Gooseneck Tops, Steel Ball Finial, 22 In.	130.00
Andirons, Iron & Brass, Continental, Pierced Top, 24 In.	120.00
Andirons, Iron, Cape Cod Dolphins, Bradley & Hubbard, 14 In.	95.00
Andirons, Iron, Figural Hessian, Sliding Dovetailed Dogs	275.00
Andirons, Iron, Foliate, E.Gimson, England, C.1905, 22 In.	5500.00
Andirons, Iron, George Washington	150.00
Andirons, Iron, Gooseneck, Faceted Finial, Penny Feet, 15 1/2 In.	125.00
Andirons, Iron, Gooseneck, Iron, 18th Century, 14 In.	225.00
Andirons, Iron, Gooseneck, Iron, Faceted Finials, 14 3/4 In.	35.00
Andirons, Iron, Hessian Soldier, 20 In.	550.00
Andirons, Iron, Knife Blade, Brass Urn Finial, Iron, 21 In.	750.00
Andirons, Iron, Knife Blade, Penny Feet, Brass, 17 1/2 In.	405.00
Andirons, Iron, Owl, Glass Eyes, Perched On Branch, C.1920, 14 In.	135.00
Andirons, Iron, Twisted Shaft, Penny Feet, 18th Century, 12 In.	175.00
Bellows, Florals, Brass Tip, White Leather	25.00
Bellows, Green & Black Striping, Florals, Brass Nozzle, 16 In.	60.00
Bellows, Original Floral Design, Red Ground, Tin Nozzle, 12 In.	50.00
Bellows, Primitive, Maple, Compass Design, Brown Stain, 20 In.	235.00
Bellows, Stenciled & Freehand Fruit & Foliage, 17 1/2 In.	200.00
Bellows, Turtle Back, Brown Floral Stencil, Brass Nozzle, 18 In.	700.00
Bellows, Turtle Back, Shell Paint, Brass Nozzle, 17 In.	55.00
Bellows, Turtle Back, Stenciled Design, 17 1/4 In.	180.00
Bellows, Turtle Back, Worn Polychrome Design, Leather, 19 In.	35.00
Broiler, Fish, Iron, Tapered Spikes, Ring Handle, Arched Foot	650.00
Broiler, Iron, Back Screen Scrolls, 18th Century, 18 In.	175.00
Broom, Shaker, Geo.Salmon, Original Paper Label, 37 In.	30.00

Carrier, Hot Coals, Sheet Iron, Blacksmith Rivets, 19 In. 55.00
Chenet, Louis XV, Monkey, Conch Shell Finial, 16 In., Pair 5500.00
Chenet, Louis XV, Ormolu, Putto, Tambourine, Bagpipes, 14 In., Pair 3850.00
Coal Hod, Parlor, Inner Bucket, Claw Feet, Tole 60.00
Coal Skuttle, Brass, Helmet Shape, Dovetailed, 13 1/2 In. 30.00
Coal Skuttle, Tole, Flowers, S.Shepard, Pat.Dec.24, 1871, 24 In. 115.00
Corn Popper, Pull Loop, Tin, 30 1/2 In. 27.50
Crane, Hand-Forged Iron, 18th Century, 27 In. 150.00
Dish, Round Iron Plate, 18th Century, Deep, 8 In. 130.00
Fender, Copper, Arts & Crafts, 12 X 30 In. 50.00
Fender, Polished Brass, 6 X 18 1/2 X 10 In. 75.00
Fender, Serpentine Shape, Medallion Design, Steel, 3 1/2 Ft. 175.00
Fender, Turned Finials, Brass, 19th Century, 42 In. 190.00
Fender, Victorian, Supporting 2 Upholstered Seats, Brass 2250.00
Fender, Wire Grid, Brass Rail, 47 X 14 X 18 1/4 In. 200.00
Fire Mark, Cast Iron, Firepump Picture, U.F., Oval, 11 1/2 In. 225.00
Fireback, English Crest & Crown, Lion, Unicorn, Dated 1635, Iron 550.00
Fireback, Iron, Silhouette, Florals, 18th Century, 24 X 19 In. 650.00
Fireboard, Trees In Circle Border, Vase, Bricks, 27 5/8 X 38 In. 9500.00
Fork, Hand Forged Iron, 2 Tine, Ring Handle, 21 1/2 In. 35.00
Griddle, Forged Iron, Overhead Handle, Loop, 3-Footed, 15 In. 175.00
Griddle, Iron, Tubular Handle, Swivel Ring, For Crane, 14 1/2 In. 57.00
Gridiron, Broiler, Drip Tray, Handle, 2-Footed, 13 X 16 In. 65.00
Kettle Lifter, Hand Forged, Right-Angle Handle, 18th Century 75.00
Kettle Lifter, Hinged Bail, Wishbone Shape, 14 In. 57.00
Kettle Trammel, Sawtooth, Forged Iron, For Crane, 18th Century 95.00
Kettle, Gypsy, Iron, Footed, Side Handles, 8 X 7 In. 120.00
Ladle, Brass, Forged Iron Shaft, Wooden Handle, Ring, 16 In. 95.00
Pan, Bundt, Iron, Scalloped, Center Post, 18th Century, 10 1/2 In. 120.00
Peel, Bread, Forged Iron, Ball Finial, 18th Century, 47 In. 85.00
Peel, Iron, Ram's Head Curl Handle, 26 1/2 In. 130.00
Roaster, Apple, Tin-Footed, Half Cylinder, Strap Handle 395.00
Roaster, Iron, Brass, Carrying Handle, Penny Feet, 1833 .... 660.00
Screen, Bronze, French, Art Nouveau, Dragonfly, Signed & Numbered 1150.00
Screen, Ebonized, Inset of Silk Needlework, Trestle Feet 6412.50
Screen, French, Art Nouveau, Dragonfly, Whiplashes, Numbered 1150.00
Screen, Glass Center, Barley Twist Frame, Adjustable 195.00
Screen, Pole, George II, Floral Carved Legs, 18th Century, 51 In. 1500.00
Screen, Rosewood, Hand Needlework, Adjustable Panel 900.00
Scuttle, Coal, Copper, Helmet Shape, Handle, 19th Century 225.00
Sieve, Coal, Iron Handle, Oval Handhold, Wire Hooks, Bentwood 50.00
Skewer, Forged Iron, Twisted Shaft, Rattail Handle, 17 In. 75.00
Skewer, Iron, Twisted Shaft, Ring Handle, 18th Century, 17 In. 75.00
Skillet, Iron, Rattail Handle, 18th Century, 6 1/2 In., 1 Piece 130.00
Skimmer, Iron, Pierced Brass, Open Ring Handle, 23 In. 150.00
Spider, Handle, Cast Iron, 3 Legs 55.00
Spoon, Tasting, Hand Forged, Rattail End, Dated 1835, 15 In. 150.00
Teakettle, Iron, Ball Shape, Gooseneck, Footed, 1900s 220.00
Toaster, Iron, Swivels, Looped Wire Bracing, 32 In.Wooden Handle 150.00
Tongs, Ember, Hand Forged, Heart Shape Ram's Head, 10 1/2 In. 95.00
Tool Set, Copper On Nickel, On Rack, 15 1/2 In., 4 Piece 75.00
Trammel, Lighting, Sawtooth, Scrolled Ratchet, Old Red, 29 In. 275.00
Trivet, Hearth, Hanged Forged Iron, 3 Legs, Round, 9 1/4 X 12 In. 130.00

MF Porcelain was made in Herend, Hungary, by Moritz Fischer. The factory was founded in 1839 and continued working into the twentieth century. The wares are sometimes referred to as "Herend" porcelain.

FISCHER, Bowl, Figural Butterfly, 3 Paw Feet, Marked, 11 1/2 X 11 In. 175.00
Bowl, Figural Butterfly, Impressed Mark, 11 1/2 X 10 1/2 In. 255.00
Bowl, Figural Butterfly, Reticulated, Marked, 11 1/2 In. 295.00
Dish, Leaf Shape, 9 In. 78.00
Jug, Allover Floral, Ivory Ground, Bulbous, 6 1/2 In. 200.00

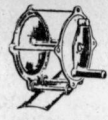

Fishing reels of brass or nickel were made in the United States by 1810. Bamboo fly rods were sold by 1860, often marked with the maker's name. Metal lures, then wooden and metal lures were made in the nineteenth century. Plastic lures were made by the 1930s. All fishing material is collected today and even equipment of the past thirty years is of interest if in good condition with original box.

FISHING, Basket, Varnished Splint, Plywood Lid, 12 1/2 In.	10.00
Box, 7 Trays, Plugs, Wooden, Abbey & Imbrie Knife, 8 X 11 1/2 In.	185.00
Box, Bait, Minnow, All Foss, Pork Rind, Tin	25.00
Box, Tole, Flies, Lures, Hooks, Sinkers	45.00
Bucket, Minnow, Metal, Racine On Cover, Handle, 2 Qt.	17.50
Cabinet, Display, Montague Rod & Reel Co., 50 Items	125.00
Calendar, Best Fishing Days, Fisherman's, 1930	38.00
Catalog, Abbey & Imbrie, No.157, New York, 1875	140.00
Catalog, Heddon, No.12, 16 Pages, 1914, 10 X 13 1/2 In.	325.00
Catalog, Heddon, No.14, Second Edition Revised, 16 Pages	400.00
Catalog, Pflueger, No.146, Order Blank, Letter, 120 Pages, 1926	45.00
Catalog, Pflueger, No.155, Original Envelope, 128 Pages, 1935	35.00
Catalog, Shakespeare, 47 Pages, C.1928, 8 X 8 1/2 In.	35.00
Catalog, South Bend, Days of Real Sport, 60 Pages, 1919	100.00
Creel, Leather, Fish Shape, Metal Head & Tail, Strap	55.00
Creel, Shaker, Sabbathday Lake, Maine	310.00
Creel, Splint, Metal Lined, Opening At Top, 10 3/4 In.	35.00
Creel, Split Willow, Iron Strap, Hinges, Back Support, 13 In.	210.00
Creel, Trout, Splint, Wooden Lid, Instruction Envelope, 10 In.	90.00
Creel, Whole Willow, 12 In.	40.00
Creel, Whole Willow, Varnished, 10 1/2 In.	25.00
Creel, Wide Splint, Hinged Wooden Top, Leather Straps & Hasp	75.00
Decoy, Carved, Spearing, George Marsguardt, Mt. Clemens, 10 In.	100.00
Decoy, Fish, Carved Wood, Red & Yellow Paint, Glass Eyes, 11 In.	25.00
Decoy, Fish, Musky, Green, Dotted Pattern, Green, Wisc., 10 In.	135.00
Decoy, Frog, Spearing, Iron Feet, Glass Eyes, 10 1/2 In.	410.00
Decoy, Perch, Carved Fins, Tail & Tack Eyes, 8 In.	50.00
Decoy, Perch, Wisconsin, Green, Tack Eyes, 8 In.	25.00
Decoy, Perch, Yellow, Oscar Peterson, 7 In.	375.00
Decoy, Perch, Yellow, Spearing, Oscar Peterson, 6 In.	412.50
Decoy, Pike, Green Body, Yellow Spots, White Belly, 28 In.	325.00
Decoy, River Chub, Fish Spearing, Tom Schroeder, 5 1/4 In.	1250.00
Decoy, Sucker, Cut–Away Belly, Red/Yellow Fin, Black Scale, 8 In.	75.00
Decoy, Trout, Oscar Peterson, Tack Eye, Wood, 7 In.	475.00
Decoy, Trout, Spearing, Oscar Peterson, 6 1/2 In.	385.00
Decoy, Turtle, Spearing, Brass Tack Back, Hinged Tin Legs, 6 In.	390.00
Desk, Fly–Tying, Made From Furniture Parts, Fishing Items	600.00
Fish, Bass, Brim, Standing, Wooden, Fishing Lure Co., 1950s, Pair	169.50
Fly Box, Coachmen, 10 Flies, Assorted Wings, Tackle & Tails	115.00
Fly Reel, Presentation, Col.T.J.Hoyt, From J.R.R., 1874, 2 1/2 In.	798.00
Fly Reel, Trout, Regulator Screw & Spool, Hardy Bhougle, 3 In.	200.00
Fly Reel, Trout, The Kosmic Reel, Case, C.1890	2970.00
Fly Rod, Bamboo Tip & Canvas Case, Leonard & Mills Co., 9 Ft.	600.00
Fly Rod, Bangor Rod, F.E.Thomas, Signed, 9 Ft. 3 In.	250.00
Fly Rod, Berkley Tri–Sport, Leather Case, 5 Piece	50.00
Fly Rod, Chubb, 1895 Model, 9 Ft.	145.00
Fly Rod, Heddon, Bamboo, 9 Ft. 2 In.	75.00
Fly Rod, Phillipson Premium, Split Bamboo, 2 Cases, 9 Ft. 6 In.	250.00
Fly Rod, R.E.Thomas Special, Cane, 9 1/2 Ft.	140.00
Fly Rod, Split Bamboo, Brass Fittings, Concave Case, 9 Ft.	90.00
Fly Rod, Trout, Thomas Dirigo Bangor, German Silver Band, 9 Ft.	200.00
Handlines, Braided Silk, New England, Hooks, 1880–1905, 1 X 20 In.	7.50
Horn, Fog, Lake Superior, Blue Paint Over Brass, 2 Ft.	85.00
Lure, Archer Wakeman, 1886, 4 In.	250.00
Lure, Bates Patent Spinner, Metal, No Hooks, 1865	400.00
Lure, Creek Chub, Bug Wiggler, Bug Finish, 1 1/4 In.	100.00
Lure, Creek Chub, Flip Flap, White & Red, Glass Eyes	65.00

Lure, Creek Chub, Gar Minnow, Green Gar, Scale Finish, Side Weights	145.00
Lure, Creek Chub, Gar Minnow, Natural Gar Finish, Glass Eyes	85.00
Lure, Creek Chub, Husky Plunker, Blue Mullet, Glass Eyes	55.00
Lure, Creek Chub, Jigger, Frog Finish, Glass Eyes	75.00
Lure, Creek Chub, Sarasota, Yellow, Red & Black Spots, Glass Eyes	250.00
Lure, Creek Chub, Sucker, Natural Sucker Scale Finish, Glass Eyes	120.00
Lure, Creek Chub, Surfster, Pikie Humpback, Glass Eyes	40.00
Lure, Creek Chub, Tiny Tim, White Scale Finish, Painted Eyes	25.00
Lure, Creek Chub, Weed Bug, Frog Finish, Glass Eyes	80.00
Lure, Fin–Tail Shiner, Rubberized Cloth Fins & Tail	100.00
Lure, Frog Skin Bait, Shakespeare, 3 3/4 In.	65.00
Lure, Frog, Hastings, Muskelunge Size, Box, C.1900	138.00
Lure, Grass Widow, Yellow, Wilson	68.00
Lure, Keeling Crab, Yellow & Black	100.00
Lure, Little Joe, Shakespeare, Tangerine, Black Back, Yellow Spots	35.00
Lure, Mermaid, W.D.Chapman	45.00
Lure, Minnow, Flexible Copper, 2 1/2 In.	275.00
Lure, Minnow, K & K Animated, 1907	143.00
Lure, Minnow, Kurtz Buckskin	28.00
Lure, Minnow, Peerless, Wooden, Glass Eyes, Brass Front, 3 1/2 In.	70.00
Lure, Minnow, Pflueger, Neverfail, Yellow Perch, Glass Eyes	40.00
Lure, Minnow, Pflueger, Neverfail, Yellow, Brown Crackle Finish	50.00
Lure, Minnow, Pflueger, Neverfail, Green Scale Finish, Glass Eyes	35.00
Lure, Minnow, Pflueger, Neverfail, Rainbow Finish, Glass Eyes, 3 In.	30.00
Lure, Minnow, Pflueger, Red Finish, Glass Eyes, 2 3/4 In.	40.00
Lure, Minnow, Pflueger, Surprise, Luminous, Gold Spots, Glass Eyes	50.00
Lure, Minnow, Pflueger, White Finish, Glass Eyes, Hand Painted Gills	60.00
Lure, Minnow, Shakespeare, Red, Yellow Sides, Glass Eyes	30.00
Lure, Minnow, South Bend Combination, Rainbow Finish, Glass Eyes	40.00
Lure, Minnow, Spinning, John Dineen, Box, 1911, 3 3/8 In.	275.00
Lure, Minnow, Wooden, Bing, 1910	450.00
Lure, Open Mouth Shiner, Painted Eyes	30.00
Lure, Plug, Pflueger, All–In–One, Green Frog Finish, Faceted Eyes	40.00
Lure, Silversides, Torpedo Style Bait, Painted Eyes, C.1960	60.00
Lure, Slim Jim, Shakespeare, Green Back, Black Stripes, Glass Eyes	25.00
Lure, South Bend, Vacuum Bait, Tack Eye, Red Design	40.00
Lure, Whirlwind Spinner, Shakespeare, Notched Props, Red Body	150.00
Net, Trout, Metal Fitting On Wooden Handle, 1924, 12 X 15 In.	35.00
Pail, Minnow, Metal, Falls City, Inner Screen Container, Handle	35.00
Poster, Kingfisher Fishing Tackle, Stand–Up Back, 17 X 25 In.	40.00
Reel, Bait Casting, Julius Vom Hofe, German Silver & Rubber	260.00
Reel, Brass, Mahogany, 1800s, 5 In.	100.00
Reel, Bronson Altoona, Level Winding Casting, No.4200, Box	5.00
Reel, Cased Salt Water, Edward Vom Hofe Co., 12/0 Size	600.00
Reel, Casting, Shakespeare, 1920	9.00
Reel, Conroy & Bisset, S Handle, Brass, 2 3/4 In.	250.00
Reel, Cozzon, C.1920, 60 Yd.	175.00
Reel, Deep Sea, Hardy, Aluminum, German Silver, 12/0 Size	750.00
Reel, Gateway Deluxe, No.1500	25.00
Reel, Haywood, Brass Multiplying, Spool Stop, 1 Piece Foot	60.00
Reel, J.Kopft, 1885 Patent, 40 Yd.	68.00
Reel, Meisselbach No.4, Amateur, 1886 Patent, Front Click	85.00
Reel, Multiplying, Eli Terry, Rim Mounted Stop Latch, 1 3/4 In.	75.00
Reel, Orvis, 1874 Patent	450.00
Reel, Pflueger Medalist No.1492, C.1930	42.00
Reel, Rubber City, 4 Bros.	40.00
Reel, Salmon, Zwarg	300.00
Reel, Shakespeare Marhoff No.1964, Model GE, Nickel Silver	15.00
Reel, Small Bass, German Silver, Hard Rubber, Vom Hofe & Co.	467.50
Reel, Small Surf Casting, Vom Hofe & Co., German Silver, Rubber	44.00
Reel, South Bend, No.400	25.00
Reel, The Kosmic Reel, Nickel Plated, 60 Yard	80.00
Reel, Trout, Edward Vom Hofe Co., German Silver, Rubber, 3 In.	700.00
Reel, Trout, Raised Relief Fishing Scene, Brass, 2 1/2 In.	302.50

Rod Trap, Tool For Making Rods, Brass Inlaid Throat	175.00
Rod, Garrison No.228, Salmon, Cane, 2 Piece, 9 Ft.	2350.00
Rod, Heddon Deluxe No.35, Trout, Cane, 3 Piece, 9 Ft.	255.00
Rod, Jim Payne, Model 102, 2 Piece, 8 Ft.	415.00
Rod, Salmon, Dame, Stoddard & Kendall, Fitted Velvet Case, 9 Ft.	280.00
Rod, South Bend, Lock Joint, Steel, Case, 1900, 4 Piece	75.00
Rod, Split Bamboo, South Bend, No.769–7	27.50
Rod, Trout, Heddon, Deluxe, President No.50, Aluminum Case, 8 Ft.	210.00
Rod, Trout, Payne, Model 96, 6 Ft.	2700.00
Tackle Box, Barton, Cedar, 2 Fitted Trays, 10 X 20 In.	135.00
Trap, Minnow, Bottle Type, Glass, 42 In.	50.00
Trap, Minnow, Shakespeare, Glass	40.00 To 60.00
Weight Mold, Raritan Brand, Bronze, Hinged	95.00

FLAG, see Textile, Flag

Flash Gordon appeared in the Sunday comics in 1934. The daily strip started in 1940. The hero was also in comic books from 1930 to 1970, in books from 1936, in movies from 1938, on the radio in the 1930s and 1940s, and on television from 1953 to 1954. All sorts of memorabilia are collected, but the ray guns and rocket ships are the most popular.

FLASH GORDON, Book, Big Little Book, Forest Kingdom of Mongo	50.00 To 75.00
Book, Big Little Book, On Planet Mongo	45.00
Book, Coloring, Whitman, 1950s	25.00
Figure, Wood Composition, Painted, 5 1/2 In.	250.00
Game, Space Graphics, Target, Tin, Box, 1950s	65.00
Game, Target, Space Graphics, Box, 1950, Tin	65.00
Gun, Space, Battery Powered, Original Package	32.00
Pistol, Arresting Ray, Tin, Litho	150.00
Pistol, Signal, Box	125.00
Ring, Post Toasties	8.50
Space Ship, 1935	85.00
Telephones, 2–Way, On Original Card	150.00
Toy, Flash & Rocket Ship, Mechanical, Tin Litho, Marx, 12 In.	825.00
Toy, Signal Pistol, Marx, Box, 1935	250.00

Flow blue, or flo blue, was made in England about 1830 to 1900. The plates were printed with designs using a cobalt blue coloring. The color flowed from the design to the white plate so that the finished plate has a smeared blue design. The plates were usually made of ironstone china.

FLOW BLUE, Basket, Watteau, Chestnut, 4–Footed, Davenport	275.00
Berry Bowl, Touraine, Stanley	14.00
Bonbon, La Belle, Free–Form, 5 X 5 In.	30.00
Bone Dish, Fleur–De–Lis, Meakin	38.00
Bone Dish, Richmond	27.00
Bowl, Alton, 10 In.	45.00
Bowl, Cambridge, New Wharf Pottery, 9 In.	40.00
Bowl, Cashmere, 10 1/2 In.	138.00
Bowl, Conway, New Wharf Pottery, 7 1/4 In.	48.00 To 55.00
Bowl, Floral, 9 In.	45.00
Bowl, Gladys, New Wharf Pottery, 9 In.	58.00
Bowl, Ivy, 10 In.	45.00
Bowl, La Belle, Assymetrical, 9 1/2 In.	135.00
Bowl, Oregon, 8 In.	50.00
Bowl, Rose, Ridgway, 7 1/4 In.	35.00 To 47.00
Bowl, Vegetable, Burleigh, Burgess & Leigh, Covered, Oval, 9 In.	145.00
Bowl, Vegetable, Clarence, Grindley, Covered, Round, 7 3/4 In.	150.00
Bowl, Vegetable, Mabel, Covered, Oval	75.00
Bowl, Vegetable, Manhattan, Alcock, Covered	115.00 To 125.00
Bowl, Vegetable, Marechal Niel, Covered, Oval	125.00
Bowl, Vegetable, Oriental, Ridgway, Covered, Oval	245.00
Bowl, Vegetable, Rose, Grindley, Covered, 9 1/4 In.	50.00
Bowl, Vegetable, Seville, Wood & Sons, Covered	175.00

Bowl, Vegetable, Touraine, 10 In. 95.00
Bowl, Vegetable, Waldorf, Round, 9 In. 85.00
Bowl, Waste, Temple, Podmore & Walker 165.00
Butter Chip, Blue Danube, Johnson Bros. 22.00
Butter Chip, Clarence, Grindley 30.00
Butter Chip, Dainty, John Maddock & Son 22.00
Butter Chip, Fairy Villas 28.00
Butter Chip, La Belle, Wheeling Pottery 24.00
Butter Chip, Lakewood 25.00
Butter Chip, Marlborough 22.00
Butter Chip, Meissen, Ridgway 20.00
Butter Chip, Melbourne .... 20.00 To 25.00
Butter Chip, Mentone 20.00
Butter Chip, Navarre, Wedgwood 25.00
Butter Chip, Waverly 25.00
Butter, Crumlin, Covered, Liner 125.00
Butter, Oriental, Ridgway, Covered 225.00
Cake Plate, Nonpareil, Burgess, Leigh, 11 In. 65.00
Celery, La Belle, 13 1/2 X 4 1/2 In. 135.00
Chamber Pot, Campion, Grindley, Covered 195.00
Charger, Kyber, Adams, 12 In. 130.00
Charger, Tyrolean, 12 1/4 In. 125.00
Compote, La Belle, Loop Handles 155.00
Compote, Scinde 450.00
Creamer, Bouquet, 5 1/4 X 3 1/2 In. 55.00
Creamer, Geneva, Royal Doulton, 4 3/4 In. 112.50
Creamer, Manilla, Podmore & Walker 275.00
Creamer, Marble, Wedgwood 65.00
Creamer, Rose, Grindley 40.00
Creamer, Scinde, Alcock, 5 1/2 In. 250.00
Creamer, Tonquin, Adams 275.00
Creamer, Touraine .... 100.00 To 165.00
Creamer, Wagon Wheel, 3 1/2 In. 100.00
Cup & Saucer, Arabesque, Mayer 85.00
Cup & Saucer, Cashmere 125.00
Cup & Saucer, Chapoo 95.00
Cup & Saucer, Clifton, Grindley 45.00
Cup & Saucer, Grace, Demitasse 55.00
Cup & Saucer, Monarch 40.00
Cup & Saucer, Normandy 75.00
Cup & Saucer, Persian Moss .... 30.00 To 42.00
Cup & Saucer, Roseville 35.00
Cup & Saucer, Scinde 85.00
Cup & Saucer, Shanghai, Grindley 55.00
Cup & Saucer, Spinach .... 42.00 To 50.00
Cup & Saucer, Temple, Podmore Walker 95.00
Cup & Saucer, Touraine .... 60.00 To 68.00
Cup & Saucer, Tulips & Leaves 50.00
Cup & Saucer, Wagon Wheel 95.00
Cup Plate, Amoy 36.00
Cup, Bouillon, Underplate, Shanghai, Grindley 75.00
Cup, Dahlia, Demitasse 65.00
Cup, Kyber, Adams, 2 Handles 85.00
Eggcup, Madras 50.00
Game Set, La Belle, Platter, 13 X 19 1/2 In., 7 Piece 350.00
Gravy Boat, Argyle, Ford & Sons 55.00
Gravy Boat, Beaufort 65.00
Gravy Boat, Lancaster 65.00
Gravy Boat, Leicester 48.00
Gravy Boat, Lonsdale 75.00
Gravy Boat, Nonpareil 90.00
Gravy Boat, Touraine 145.00
Gravy Boat, Underplate, Rose, Grindley 75.00
Honey Dish, Amoy 55.00

Jardiniere, Briar Rose, Royal Doulton, 8 1/2 X 7 1/8 In. 165.00
Knife Rest, Davenport 135.00
Mug, Dahlia 85.00
Oyster Plate, Spinach 85.00
Pitcher & Bowl, Chapoo, Oval, Pitcher, 12 In. 385.00
Pitcher, Indian Jar, Furnival 175.00
Pitcher, Ivy, 7 1/2 In. 30.00
Pitcher, Madras, Doulton, 2 Qt. 145.00
Pitcher, Milk, Grenada 75.00
Pitcher, Milk, La Belle 150.00
Pitcher, Touraine, 3 Pt. 295.00
Pitcher, Water, Touraine 400.00
Pitcher, Willow, Ashworth, 6 1/2 X 5 1/2 In. 110.00
Plate, Abbey, Geo.Jones & Son, 10 In. 50.00
Plate, Alton, Grindley, 10 In. 40.00
Plate, Alton, Grindley, 7 In. .... 20.00 To 30.00
Plate, Amoy, 8 1/2 In. 40.00
Plate, Ashburton, 10 In. 50.00
Plate, Beatrice, Maddock, 8 In. 25.00
Plate, Blue Danube, 10 In. 45.00
Plate, Candia, 8 In. 35.00
Plate, Canton, Ashworth Bros., 7 1/4 In. 32.50
Plate, Carlton, Alcock, 8 1/4 In. 60.00
Plate, Cashmere, 9 1/2 In. 90.00
Plate, Ceylon, 9 In. 40.00
Plate, Chapoo, Wedgwood, 10 1/2 In. 95.00
Plate, Chusan, 9 1/2 In. 75.00
Plate, Clarence, Grindley, 10 In. 50.00
Plate, Dahlia, 8 1/4 In. 65.00
Plate, Daisy, 10 In. 58.00
Plate, Devon, 9 In. 42.00
Plate, Don, Allerton, 9 In. 45.00
Plate, Fairy Villas, Adams, 10 In. .... 45.00 To 50.00
Plate, Fairy Villas, Adams, 7 3/4 In. .... 27.00 To 35.00
Plate, Gem, Maddock, 10 In., 8 Piece 150.00
Plate, Gironde, Grindley, 9 In. .... 38.00 To 47.00
Plate, Hampton Spray, Grindley, 6 In., 4 Piece 40.00
Plate, Holland, Meakin, 10 In. 42.00
Plate, Indian, Pratt, 7 1/4 In. 35.00
Plate, Indian, Pratt, 9 1/4 In. 65.00
Plate, Iris, Wilkinson, 9 In. 115.00
Plate, Italia, 8 5/8 In. 55.00
Plate, Keele, W.H.Grindley, 9 In. 32.00
Plate, Knox, 9 In. 45.00
Plate, Kyber, Adams, 9 In. 35.00
Plate, Kyber, Adams, 10 In. .... 45.00 To 60.00
Plate, La Belle, 7 1/2 In. 35.00
Plate, La Belle, 9 In. 45.00
Plate, La Belle, Wheeling, 7 1/2 In. 37.00
Plate, Leicester, 9 In. 130.00
Plate, Lorne, Grindley, 9 In. 30.00
Plate, Lorne, Grindley, 10 In. 35.00
Plate, Lucerne, New Wharf, 9 In. 37.00
Plate, Madras, Doulton, 10 1/2 In. 85.00
Plate, Manhattan, Alcock, 7 1/2 In. 32.00
Plate, Manilla, Podmore & Walker, 7 1/2 In. 50.00
Plate, Marechal Niel, 6 3/4 In. 25.00
Plate, Marquis, Grindley, 10 In. 22.00
Plate, Melbourne, 8 In. .... 24.00 To 40.00
Plate, Napier, 9 3/4 In. 32.00
Plate, Nonpareil, 10 In. 50.00
Plate, Normandy, Johnson, 10 In. .... 35.00 To 65.00
Plate, Olympia, Grindley, 9 3/4 In. 38.50
Plate, Oriental, 9 3/4 In. 85.00

Plate, Paris, New Wharf, 9 In. 55.00
Plate, Pelew, Challinor, 9 1/2 In. 70.00
Plate, Pembroke Castle, C.1920, 10 1/2 In. 75.00
Plate, Regent, Meakin, 8 3/4 In. 27.50
Plate, Rose, Grindley, 1893, 10 In. 30.00
Plate, Rose, Grindley, 7 1/2 In. 20.00
Plate, Roseville, 9 In. 25.00
Plate, Scinde, Alcock, 10 1/2 In. 125.00
Plate, Scinde, Alcock, 7 In. 50.00
Plate, Seville, 9 In. 40.00
Plate, Shanghai, Adams, 10 In. 95.00
Plate, Shanghai, Grindley, 10 In. .... 45.00 To 65.00
Plate, Shanghai, W. & E.Corn, 10 In. .... 42.00 To 72.00
Plate, Spinach, 7 1/2 In. 30.00
Plate, St.Louis, Johnson, 9 In. 45.00
Plate, Temple, 9 In. .... 52.00 To 70.00
Plate, Togo, C.1900, 10 In. 35.00
Plate, Touraine, Alcock, 7 3/4 In. 35.00
Plate, Touraine, Alcock, 8 7/8 In. 45.00
Plate, Trent, Ford, 10 1/2 In. 50.00
Plate, Trent, New Wharf, 9 In. 32.00
Plate, Tyrolean, Ridgway, 12 In. 98.00
Plate, Vermont, 10 In. 45.00
Plate, Verona, Ford, 9 In. 35.00
Plate, Verona, Ridgway, 8 In. 28.00
Plate, Versailles, Furnival, 9 In. 70.00
Plate, Waldorf, 10 In. 60.00
Plate, Warwick, Johnson, 8 In. 38.00
Plate, Watteau, Doulton, 7 In. 30.00
Plate, Watteau, Doulton, 10 In. 52.00
Platter, Alaska, Grindley, 14 In. .... 60.00 To 95.00
Platter, Albany, Johnson, 14 1/2 In. 85.00
Platter, Ashburton, Grindley, 16 In. 145.00
Platter, Bacon, Oriental, Ridgway, 11 X 9 In. 90.00
Platter, Belmont, 13 In. 90.00
Platter, Burleigh, Burgess & Leigh, 13 3/4 In. 90.00
Platter, Canton, Maddock, 14 In. 95.00
Platter, Cashmere, 17 1/2 X 14 1/2 In. 495.00
Platter, Catherine, Grindley, 14 X 10 In. 55.00
Platter, Chapoo, Wedgwood, 10 X 14 In. 225.00
Platter, Chen–Si, 14 X 17 1/2 In. 225.00
Platter, Chusan, Clementson, 17 In. 210.00
Platter, Clayton, Johnson Bros., 14 1/4 In. 110.00
Platter, Coburg, 18 In. 395.00
Platter, Cows, Wedgwood, 17 X 13 1/2 In. 175.00
Platter, Gironde, Grindley, 15 In. 80.00
Platter, Grace, 13 In. 75.00
Platter, Hofburg, Grindley, 14 1/2 In. 58.00
Platter, Holland, Johnson Bros., 18 In. 150.00
Platter, Hong Kong, 16 In. 325.00
Platter, Indian Jar, 10 3/4 In. 125.00
Platter, Keele, Grindley, 16 1/2 In. 140.00
Platter, Keswick, Wood & Sons, 12 In. 65.00
Platter, Kyber, Adams, 10 In. 65.00
Platter, Kyber, Adams, 17 In. 225.00
Platter, Landscape, 14 X 10 1/2 In. 125.00
Platter, Leicester, S.Hancock, 15 X 12 In. 115.00
Platter, Linda, Maddock, 17 In. 90.00
Platter, Lorne, Grindley, 16 In. 100.00
Platter, Mandarin, 18 X 13 1/2 In. 215.00
Platter, Manila, 15 In. 195.00
Platter, Meissen, Oval, 16 X 12 In. 95.00
Platter, Melbourne, Grindley, 16 In. 100.00
Platter, Ning PO, 10 X 13 In. 285.00

Platter, Olympia, Grindley, 18 X 21 In. 90.00
Platter, Oriental, Ridgway, 12 1/2 In. 140.00
Platter, Paris, 14 In. 62.00
Platter, Sabraon, 13 1/2 X 10 3/4 In. 160.00
Platter, Scinde, Alcock, 12 1/2 X 16 In. 200.00
Platter, Tonquin, Heath, 15 In. 295.00
Platter, Touraine, 10 In. 75.00
Platter, Touraine, 15 In. 135.00
Platter, Touraine, Alcock, 13 X 9 In. 95.00
Platter, Vincennes, 15 1/2 In. 95.00
Platter, Virginia, 16 5/8 In. 115.00
Relish, La Belle, 13 In. 90.00
Relish, Nelson, New Wharf, 9 In. 68.00
Sauce, Monarch 16.00
Sauce, Osborne, Rathbone, Covered 150.00
Sauceboat, Lonsdale 78.00
Saucer, Ebor, Ridgway 12.50
Saucer, Touraine, Alcock 18.00
Soup, Dish, Alexandria, Hollinshead & Kirkhan .... 20.00 To 35.00
Soup, Dish, Amoy 75.00
Soup, Dish, Astoria, 10 1/2 In. 45.00
Soup, Dish, Athens 36.00
Soup, Dish, Hamilton 20.00
Soup, Dish, Kenworth, Johnson 45.00
Soup, Dish, Marguerite, Grindley 25.00
Soup, Dish, Nonpareil, Burgess & Leigh 55.00
Soup, Dish, Sabraon 75.00
Soup, Dish, Scinde 45.00
Soup, Dish, Shanghai, Grindley, 7 3/4 In. 48.00
Soup, Dish, Waldorf 45.00
Soup, Dish, Watteau, Doulton 495.00
Sugar & Creamer, Amoy 375.00
Sugar & Creamer, Monarch, Covered 75.00
Sugar & Creamer, Mongolia, Johnson 150.00
Sugar & Creamer, Scinde, Walker 165.00
Sugar, Beaufort, Covered 95.00
Sugar, Duchess, Grindley 85.00
Sugar, Georgia, Covered 115.00
Sugar, Melbourne 95.00
Sugar, Touraine 125.00
Sugar, Wagon Wheel, Child's 85.00
Tea Set, Wagon Wheel, Child's, 17 Piece 550.00
Teapot, Amoy 500.00
Teapot, Hindustan 450.00
Teapot, Lobelia, Phillips, C.1845 .... 290.00
Teapot, Monarch 135.00
Teapot, Oregon, Mayer 450.00
Toothbrush Holder, Melba, 6 In. 75.00
Tray, Scinde, Rectangular, 16 In. 280.00
Tureen, Bouquet, Covered 145.00
Tureen, Osborne, Footed, Ford, 12 X 8 1/2 In. 195.00
Tureen, Sauce, Mandarin, Underplate, 9 X 7 In. 240.00
Tureen, Sauce, Oregon 350.00
Tureen, Scinde, Covered, Underplate, Alcock 375.00
Tureen, Soup, Ladle, Roseville 450.00
Tureen, Soup, Mattean, Octagonal 200.00
Tureen, Soup, Paisley, Mercer 295.00
Vase, Babes In Woods, 2 Girls, Purse, Umbrella, Doulton, 6 In. 158.00
Waste Bowl, Keele, W.H.Grindley, C.1891, 5 7/8 X 3 1/4 In. 52.00
    FLYING PHOENIX, see Phoenix Bird

> Folk art is listed in many sections of the book under the actual
> name of the object. See categories such as Box; Cigar Store Figure;
> Weather Vane; Wooden; etc.

FOLK ART, Bank, VFW, Widows & Orphans National Home, Wooden	70.00
Barn, Wooden, Red, Green, Roof Opens, 16 X 10 X 12 In.	69.00
Bird, Carved, Painted, 7 1/2 In.	35.00
Board, Cutting, Pig, Red & Black Trim & Stencil	110.00
Boat & Base, Hand Carved, Wood, Red Paint Traces, 9 In.	87.00
Box, Carved Birds, Deer & Trees, 10 1/2 X 5 3/4 In.	100.00
Box, Splint, Swirl Design, Red, Oval, 8 1/2 In. ....*Illus*	80.00
Box, Wooden, Applied Leather Flowers, Dark Finish, 11 In.	35.00
Buffalo & Calf, Wooly Hide, Wire Moves Head, J.W.Brongart, 9 In.	230.00
Bust, Abraham Lincoln, Hand Carved, 6 In.	65.00
Comb, Whale Shape, Hand Painted, Face, For Combing Wigs, Horsetail	135.00
Figure, 2 Horses, Work Sled, Wooden, Painted, Tailgate, 32 In.	595.00
Figure, Boxer, Carved Wood, Painted, Late 19th Century, 18 In.	2200.00
Figure, Boy, Flowered Robe, Dog, 18th Century, 7 1/2 In.	85.00
Figure, Crow, Wood, Glass Eyes, Black Repaint, 18 In.	105.00
Figure, Eagle Head, Carved, Red & Black Paint, 12 In.	50.00
Figure, Equestrian General, Mounted, Enoch Wood, 9 In.	750.00
Figure, Full–Bodied Indian & Soldier, Wooden, 12 X 18 In.	195.00
Figure, Girl, Standing, Hands On Hips, Bright Paint, 8 In.	45.00
Figure, Gull, Wood, White Paint, 22–In.Wing Span	45.00
Figure, Indian Chief, Squaw, Sandstone, E.Reed, 1974, 48 In., Pair	4400.00
Figure, Man, Dark Finish, 15 1/2 In.	10.00
Figure, Owl, Wood, White Paint, Hoop, Hanger, 20th Century, 27 In.	1870.00
Figure, Rooster, Carved & Polychromed, 20th Century, 12 In.	140.00
Figure, Sperm Whale, Carved Wood, Stamped C.Voorhees, 18 In.	175.00
Mirror, Shaving, Animals At Base, Wooden, Carved, Varnished, 8 In.	500.00
Painting, On Wooden Barrel Head, Barnyard Scene, 18 1/2 In.	150.00
Pipe Rack, Moose Head	125.00
Planter, Wooden Stave, 4 Hanging Buckets, Black Paint, 49 In.	100.00
Silhouette, Man, Polychrome Paint, Wooden, 43 In.	45.00
Stand, Geometric Marquetry, 1 Drawer, 1 Pull–Out Shelf, 28 In.	90.00
Stand, Hardwood, Turned Column, X Shaped Base, Red Paint, 27 In.	90.00
Toilet Paper Holder, Outdoor, Wooden, Man Shape	160.00
Toy, Grasshopper, Wheels, Legs Move, Old Taupe Paint, 6 1/2 In.	60.00
Whirligig, Airplane	175.00
Whirligig, Animated Woodpecker, Painted, 21 1/2 In.	40.00
Whirligig, Carved Man, Cap, Paddle Movable Arms, Block Mount	195.00
Whirligig, Clown, Legs Go Around, Wooden	40.00
Whirligig, Indian, Paddles Canoe, Carved, Painted, 11 1/2 In.	550.00
Whirligig, Indian, Paddles, Wood, Worn Paint, No Headdress, 15 In.	800.00
Whirligig, Kilted Scotsman, Paddle & Knife, C.1900	2300.00
Whirligig, Man Sawing Wood, Painted Red, Blue & Green, 31 In.	375.00
Whirligig, Policeman	1650.00
Whirligig, Standing Figure In Canoe, Wood, 32 In.	350.00
Whirligig, Uncle Sam, C.1900, 34 X 19 In.	350.00
Whirligig, Woman Washing	55.00

Cold feet have been a problem for generations. Our ancestors had many ingenious ways to warm feet with portable foot warmers. Some warmers held charcoal, others held hot water. Pottery, tin, and soapstone were the favored materials to conduct the heat. The warmer was kept under the feet, then the legs and feet were tucked into a blanket, providing welcome warmth in a cold carriage or church.

FOOT WARMER, Advertising, Stoneware	65.00
Brass Cap & Handles, Half Round Shape, Pewter, 10 X 5 In.	95.00
Buggy, Carpet Covered	18.00
Coal, 1880s	195.00
Copper, Brass Cap & Ring Handle, Oval, 11 1/2 X 7 1/2 In.	68.00
Friesian Carved All Sides, Geometric Chip Carving, 8 In.	600.00
Incised Dorchester Pottery Works, Boston, Ma., Dated 1912	125.00
Little Eva, 2 Oven Doors, Ash Pit Door, Cast Iron, C.1860	275.00
Oval, Copper, Initialed E.C.E., Dated 1839	195.00
Pierced, Cherry	260.00

Punched Tin Hearts, Hudson Valley 275.00
Punched Tin, Mortised Wood Frame, Turned Corner Posts, 9 In. 110.00
Punched Tin, Wooden Frame, Charcoal Pan, 1800s 175.00
Rockingham, Cylindrical, 14 In. 60.00
Skater's, Beveled Edges, 5 Rows of Holes, C.1890 .... 90.00
Skater's, Wooden 100.00
Stoneware, Henderson, Blue & White .... 130.00 To 180.00
Tin & Wood 225.00
Tin, New England, 1780–1800 .... 225.00
Turned Wooden Posts & Frame, Square, Pierced Tin 130.00
Victorian Carpeting On Top, Hudson Valley, Heart Design 200.00
Wire Bail, Oblong, Soapstone 23.50

Fostoria glass was made in Fostoria, Ohio, from 1887 to 1891. The factory was moved to Moundsville, West Virginia, and most of the glass seen in shops today is a twentieth–century product. The company was sold in 1983; and new items will be easily identifiable, according to the new owners, Lancaster Colony Corporation.

FOSTORIA, see also Milk Glass

FOSTORIA, Alexis, Salt, Pedestal, Individual, 6 Paneled Bowl, 2 1/8 In. 18.00
American Lady, Cordial, Amethyst 25.00
American Lady, Goblet, Water, Amethyst 22.00
American Lady, Sherbet .... 14.00 To 25.00
American, Ashtray, Square, 2 7/8 In., Set of 4 .... 15.00
American, Bottle, Bitters, Stopper .... 35.00 To 52.00
American, Bottle, Cordial, Label Space, Pinpoint Stopper, Pair 65.00
American, Bowl, 7 1/2 In. 12.00
American, Bowl, 12 In. 35.00
American, Bowl, Centerpiece, 11 1/2 In. 33.00
American, Bowl, Covered, 5 1/2 In. 15.00
American, Bowl, Fruit, 3–Footed, 10 1/2 In. 18.00
American, Bowl, Handle, Footed, 8 In. 35.00
American, Bowl, Shrimp 265.00
American, Bowl, Tricorner 32.00
American, Box, Cigarette, Covered 40.00
American, Butter, Covered, 1/4 Lb. .... 20.00 To 22.00
American, Butter, Covered, Dome 95.00
American, Butter, Round, Covered, Red Flashed 240.00
American, Cake Plate, 12 In. 30.00
American, Cake Plate, Pedestal, Square .... 60.00 To 90.00
American, Candleholder, 2–Light, Pair 35.00
American, Candleholder, Hexagonal Base, 6 In., Pair 45.00
American, Candy Dish, Covered, 6 Sides, 3 Sections 50.00
American, Carafe, Water 275.00
American, Condiment Set, 5 Piece 275.00
American, Condiment Set, 6 Piece 425.00
American, Cookie Jar, Covered .... 245.00 To 350.00
American, Cup & Saucer 6.00
American, Decanter, Cordial, Stopper, 9 Oz. 95.00
American, Decanter, Holder, Lock, Key, 24 Oz. .... 225.00 To 265.00
American, Dish, Lemon, Covered .... 30.00 To 45.00
American, Dish, Olive 22.00
American, Dish, Shrimp 250.00
American, Goblet, Footed, 3 Oz. 8.00
American, Goblet, Iced Tea, Liner 40.00
American, Humidor, Metal Lid, 5 In. 295.00
American, Ice Tub, Underplate 125.00
American, Jug, 42 Oz. 50.00
American, Lamp, Candle 110.00
American, Mayonnaise, Liner & Spoon 45.00
American, Mug, Tom & Jerry .... 25.00 To 30.00
American, Nappy, Square, 4 1/4 In. 20.00
American, Pitcher, 1/2 Gal. 85.00
American, Pitcher, Bulbous, 3 Pt. .... 35.00 To 45.00

American, Pitcher, Footed, 1 Quart 50.00
American, Plate, 18 In. 25.00
American, Platter, Oval, 12 In. 40.00
American, Punch Bowl, High Foot, 14 In. 155.00
American, Punch Cup .... 5.50 To 8.00
American, Punch Set, 13 Piece 250.00
American, Relish, 2 Sections, Handle, 12 In. 20.00
American, Relish, 4 Sections, 9 In. .... 35.00 To 65.00
American, Relish, Oval, 10 In. 20.00
American, Rose Bowl, 5 In. 33.00
American, Salt & Pepper, Tray, Individual, 3 Piece 30.00
American, Sandwich Plate, Handle 35.00
American, Sugar & Creamer .... 10.00 To 25.00
American, Syrup, Metal Handle, Small 40.00
American, Tray, Handles, 9 In. 25.00
American, Tumbler, 2 Oz. 11.50
American, Urn, Square, 6 1/2 In. 42.00
American, Vase, Bud, 8 In. 19.00
American, Vase, Cupped, 10 In. 110.00
American, Vase, Square Base, Flared Top, 10 In. 40.00
American, Vase, Straight Sides, 12 In. .... 65.00 To 80.00
American, Vase, Sweet Pea 85.00
Baroque, Bonbon, Blue 29.50
Baroque, Bowl, 2 Handles, Blue, 9 1/2 In. 47.50
Baroque, Bowl, Handle, Topaz, 10 In. 28.00
Baroque, Candleholder, 2–Light, Pair 45.00
Baroque, Candleholder, 3–Light, Amber, Pair 50.00
Baroque, Cruet, Topaz 250.00
Baroque, Cup & Saucer, Blue 25.00
Baroque, Goblet, Water, Blue, 9 Oz. 35.00
Baroque, Ice Bucket, Chrome Handle, Topaz 53.00
Baroque, Jam Jar, Covered, 7 1/2 In. 35.00
Baroque, Mayonnaise Set, Lido Etch, 3 Piece 35.00
Baroque, Mustard, Covered, Blue 110.00
Baroque, Plate, Blue, 7 1/2 In. 8.50
Baroque, Punch Cup, Blue 38.00
Baroque, Punch Set, 11 Piece 250.00
Baroque, Relish, 2 Sections, Blue, 6 In. 30.00
Baroque, Relish, 3 Sections, Amber 15.00
Baroque, Relish, 3 Sections, Topaz 15.00
Baroque, Salt & Pepper, Topaz 50.00
Baroque, Sherbet, Topaz, 5 Oz. 10.00
Baroque, Torte 10.00
Beverly, Cup & Saucer, Demitasse, Amber 12.00
Beverly, Cup & Saucer, Demitasse, Green 28.00
Beverly, Soup, Cream, Amber 8.00
Beverly, Tumbler, Etched, Amber, 6 In. 115.00
Bookends, Rearing Horse .... 42.00 To 75.00
Brazilian, Tumbler, Gold Rim, Green 20.00
Buttercup, Cup & Saucer 30.00
Buttercup, Goblet, 8 In. 15.00
Buttercup, Sherbet 12.00
Century, Bowl, Oval, 9 1/2 In. 32.00
Century, Candleholder, Trindle, Pair 38.00
Century, Creamer & Tray, Individual 7.50
Century, Cup & Saucer, Footed 32.00
Century, Sugar & Creamer, Footed, 4 In. 25.00
Chintz, Bowl, Handles, Crystal, 10 1/2 In. 30.00
Chintz, Candleholder, 5 1/2 In., Pair 38.00
Chintz, Champagne, Saucer 13.00
Chintz, Creamer 9.00
Chintz, Ice Bucket, Clear 60.00
Chintz, Plate, Torte, 14 In. 42.00
Chintz, Relish, 3 Sections 38.00

Chintz, Sherbet, Low 10.00
Chintz, Sugar & Creamer, 3 1/2 In. 24.00
Chintz, Tumbler, Footed, 12 Oz. 12.00
Cigarette Holder, Green Foot 26.00
Coin, Bowl, Wedding, Covered 40.00
Coin, Cake Plate, Pedestal 55.00
Coin, Candy Dish, Covered, Amber 30.00
Coin, Candy Dish, Covered, Green 30.00
Coin, Cruet, Stopper 38.00
Coin, Lamp, Courting, Amber Handle, Opalescent Chimney, Pair 118.00
Coin, Nappy, Handle, Amber 18.00
Coin, Sugar & Creamer, Covered 30.00
Coin, Sugar & Creamer, Green 45.00
Colony, Ashtray, 3 In. 5.00
Colony, Bowl, 2 Handles, 8 1/2 In. 22.00
Colony, Bowl, 9 In. 22.00
Colony, Bowl, Mayonaisse, Underplate 21.00
Colony, Bowl, Oval, 10 In. 20.00
Colony, Candleholder, Prisms, 9 1/2 In. 32.00
Colony, Compote, Covered, 6 3/8 In. 32.00
Colony, Creamer, 3 1/2 In. 6.00
Colony, Goblet, 9 Oz. 12.50
Colony, Goblet, Water, 9 Oz. 8.00
Colony, Pitcher, 2 Quart 58.00
Colony, Relish, 3 Sections, 13 1/2 X 10 In. 13.00
Colony, Salt 10.00
Colony, Sherbet 10.00
Colony, Sugar & Creamer .... 8.00 To 10.00
Colony, Sugar, Creamer, & Tray 20.00
Colony, Tray, Muffin .... 15.00 To 35.00
Colony, Tumbler, Footed, 5 Oz. 9.00
Colony, Vase, Cupped & Footed, 7 In. 27.50
Colony, Vase, Flared, Footed, 7 1/2 In. 32.00
Cornucopia, Green, 10 In. 8.00
Corsage, Bowl, Flame, Oval 22.00
Corsage, Champagne .... 15.00 To 18.00
Corsage, Cocktail 20.00
Corsage, Relish, 2 Sections, Handle 20.00
Corsage, Tumbler, Iced Tea 18.00
Edgewood, Water Set, Carafe, 7 Piece 120.00
Empire, Cordial, Green, 6 In. 10.00
Engagement, Sherbet 18.50
Fairfax, Cup & Saucer, Blue 15.00
Fairfax, Cup & Saucer, Topaz 5.00
Fairfax, Dish, Mint, Footed, Green 13.00
Fairfax, Goblet, Footed, Blue, 9 Oz. 13.50
Fairfax, Nappy, Green 15.00
Fairfax, Plate, Rose, 7 In. 3.00
Fairfax, Plate, Salad, Green 4.00
Fairfax, Plate, Topaz, 7 1/4 In. 2.00
Fairfax, Platter, Green, 15 In. 45.00
Fairfax, Relish, Divided, 9 In. 8.00
Fairfax, Salt & Pepper, Blue 60.00
Fairfax, Sauceboat, Green 20.00
Fairfax, Soup, Bouillion, Green 7.75
Fairfax, Sugar & Creamer, Blue 20.00
Fairfax, Sugar & Creamer, Ruby 80.00
Figure, Pelican, Frosted 75.00
Figurine, Bear, Frosted 36.00
Figurine, Deer, Blue 35.00
Figurine, Doe, Standing, 4 In. 20.00
Figurine, Pelican, Frosted 75.00
Figurine, Polar Bear, Frosted 55.00
Fleur–De–Lis, Sugar & Creamer 22.00

Fleur–De–Lis, Tray, Luncheon, Handles, 11 In. 28.00
Florentine, Cup & Saucer 7.00
Florentine, Soup, Dish 9.50
Glacier, Candy Dish, Covered 49.00
Heather, Butter, Covered, 1/4 Lb. 45.00
Heather, Plate, 7 In. 8.50
Heather, Relish, 2 Sections, 7 In. 20.00
Heather, Salt & Pepper .... 25.00 To 50.00
Heather, Sugar, Creamer & Tray 40.00
Heirloom, Bowl, Blue, 10 In. 22.00
Heirloom, Plate, Topaz, 9 In. 20.00
Heirloom, Vase, Pink, 12 In. 12.00
Hermitage, Pitcher, Footed, Topaz, 3 Pt. 95.00
Hermitage, Plate, Topaz, 6 In. 2.50
Hermitage, Tumbler, Footed, Topaz, 9 Oz. 7.00
Jamestown, Goblet, 12 Oz. 9.00
Jamestown, Goblet, Amber, 12 Oz. 9.00
Jamestown, Goblet, Wine, 4 Oz. 9.00
Jamestown, Sherbet, Amber 6.50
Jamestown, Sherbet, Ruby 21.00
Jamestown, Tumbler, Footed, Amber, 6 In. 10.00
Jenny Lind, Decanter, Stopper 47.00
Jenny Lind, Dresser Set, Milk Glass, 7 Piece 295.00
June, Bowl, 3–Footed, 10 1/2 In. 52.00
June, Cake Plate, Amber Handle 30.00
June, Cordial, Rose Stem 22.00
June, Cup & Saucer 16.00
June, Cup & Saucer, Demitasse, Topaz 39.50
June, Plate, 9 1/2 In. 5.00
June, Platter, 15 In. 22.00
June, Sandwich Server, Handles, Blue 40.00
June, Sugar & Creamer, Blue, Small 45.00
June, Vase, Flower Frog, Oval, Blue, 13 In. 165.00
Kashmir, Tumbler, Topaz, 10 Oz. 12.00
Lafayette, Bowl, Blue, 7 1/4 In. 15.00
Lafayette, Cocktail 47.50
Lafayette, Plate, 10 1/4 In. 60.00
Legion, Relish, 3 Sections 30.00
Lucerne, Pitcher, 8 In. 40.00
Lyre, Bookends 53.00
Manor, Vase, 6 In. 48.00
Mayfair, Dish, Jelly, Pink 25.00
Mayfair, Relish, Divided, Pink, 10 In. 90.00
Mayflower, Vase, 12 In. 80.00
Meadow Rose, Candleholder, 2–Light, Pair 35.00
Meadow Rose, Cocktail 25.00
Meadow Rose, Cup & Saucer 22.00
Meadow Rose, Goblet, Water 20.00
Meadow Rose, Plate, 9 1/2 In. 27.00
Meadow Rose, Sugar & Creamer 25.00
Meadow Rose, Tumbler, Footed, 12 Oz. 18.00
Midnight Rose, Candleholder, 2–Light 60.00
Midnight Rose, Cup & Saucer 12.00
Midnight Rose, Plate, 7 In. 6.00
Morning Glory, Sugar & Creamer, Green, Etched 30.00
Navarre, Bowl, Oval, 12 In. 31.50
Navarre, Cake Plate, Handles, 10 In. 32.00
Navarre, Candleholder, 4 In., Pair 28.00
Navarre, Champagne, Saucer, 6 Oz. 20.00
Navarre, Cheese & Cracker Set, Etched 20.00
Navarre, Claret, Pink 28.00
Navarre, Cocktail, 3 1/2 Oz. 12.00
Navarre, Compote, 5 1/2 In. 24.00
Navarre, Goblet, Water 18.50

Navarre, Relish, 5 Sections, 13 In. .... 49.50 To 52.50
Navarre, Salt & Pepper 25.00
Navarre, Sugar & Creamer 25.00
Oak Leaf, Biscuit Jar, Copper Lid, Jadite 75.00
Oak Leaf, Bonbon, 2 Handles 14.00
Oak Leaf, Goblet, 6 In. 7.50
Persian, Toothpick 145.00
Pioneer, Cup & Saucer, Blue 5.00
Pioneer, Cup & Saucer, Footed, Green 10.00
Pioneer, Eggcup, Green 6.00
Pioneer, Plate, Blue, 7 1/2 In. 3.00
Priscilla, Pitcher, Green & Gold 110.00
Priscilla, Spooner, Emerald Green 70.00
Priscilla, Syrup, Emerald Green 195.00
Queen Anne, Candleholder, Bobeches, Prisms, 19 1/2 In., Pair 75.00
Raleigh, Sugar & Creamer, Individual 10.00
Richmond, Sherbet 24.50
Rogene, Cocktail 12.00
Rogene, Goblet, 9 Oz. 18.00
Rogene, Plate, 8 In. 10.00
Romance, Champagne, 3 1/2 Oz. 14.00
Romance, Champagne, Saucer 18.00
Romance, Cocktail, 3 1/2 Oz. 22.00
Romance, Cup & Saucer 20.00
Romance, Goblet, 9 Oz. .... 14.00 To 22.00
Romance, Plate, 7 1/2 In. 12.00
Romance, Sherbet, 5 1/2 In. 15.00
Romance, Sugar & Creamer, Covered 30.00
Romance, Tumbler, Footed, 6 1/8 In. 17.00
Royal, Grapefruit, Green 22.00
Royal, Platter, Green, 13 1/2 In. 18.00
Seascape, Sugar & Creamer, Pink 18.00
Seville, Oyster Cocktail, Green 22.00
Seville, Sugar & Creamer, Green 37.00
Seville, Vase, Flared, Green, 8 In. 72.00
Trojan, Bowl, Footed, Topaz, 12 In. 20.00
Trojan, Compote, Topaz, 6 In. 25.00
Trojan, Cup & Saucer, Topaz 20.00
Trojan, Ice Bucket, Topaz 75.00
Trojan, Mayonnaise Set, Topaz, 3 Piece 95.00
Trojan, Oyster Cocktail, Topaz 18.00
Trojan, Sherbet, Low, Topaz 10.00
Trojan, Sugar & Creamer 25.00
Trojan, Sugar & Creamer, Topaz 30.00
Versailles, Bonbon, Pink 14.00
Versailles, Bowl, Blue, 7 1/2 In. 10.00
Versailles, Cocktail, Pink 25.00
Versailles, Ice Bucket, Blue 80.00
Versailles, Ice Bucket, Pink .... 55.00 To 75.00
Versailles, Pitcher, Green 325.00
Versailles, Pitcher, Pink 250.00
Versailles, Plate, Blue, 9 1/2 In. 18.00
Versailles, Plate, Topaz, 10 1/4 In. 32.00
Versailles, Tankard, Topaz 220.00
Versailles, Tumbler, Footed, Blue, 9 Oz. 18.00
Vesper, Berry Bowl, Blue, 5 1/2 In. 18.00
Vesper, Finger Bowl, Amber, 4 1/2 In. 12.00
Vesper, Goblet, Water, Amber 25.00
Vesper, Ice Bucket, Amber 45.00
Vesper, Ice Bucket, Green 55.00
Vesper, Pitcher, Amber .... 188.00 To 275.00
Vesper, Plate, Amber, 8 5/8 In. 9.00
Vesper, Plate, Amber, 9 1/2 In. 7.00
Vintage, Goblet, Wine, Green 7.00

FOVAL, see Fry Foval
FRAME, see Furniture, Frame

Francisware is a named glassware made by Hobbs, Brockunier and Company of Wheeling, West Virginia, in the 1880s. It is a clear or frosted hobnail or swirl pattern glass with amber-stained rim. Some pieces were made by a pressed glass method, others were mold blown.

FRANCISWARE, Chop Plate, Coronado, 12 In.	10.00
Coffeepot, Madeira	45.00
Creamer, Sundance	15.00
Cup & Saucer, Ivy	15.00
Cup & Saucer, Starburst	4.00
Plate, Bread & Butter, Starburst	3.00
Plate, Salad, Cafe Royal	4.00
Sugar Shaker, Swirl, Frosted, Original Lid	145.00
Sugar, Covered, Swirl, Frosted, Amber	85.00
Sugar, Sundance	25.00
Table Set, Hobnail, Frosted, Amber, 4 Piece	325.00
Teapot, Apple	45.00

Frankart, Inc., New York, New York, mass-produced nude "dancing-lady" lamps, ashtrays, and other decorative Art Deco items in the 1920s and 1930s. They were made of white lead composition and spray-painted. "Frankart Inc." and the patent number and year were stamped on the base.

FRANKART, Bookends, 2 Horses' Heads With Flying Manes	75.00
Bookends, Bust, Art Decoy Lady, Pyramid Base, Green Paint	210.00
Bookends, Dog's Head	70.00
Bookends, Dutch Boy & Girl	145.00
Bookends, Gazelle, High Gloss Bronze Finish	75.00
Bookends, Great Dane, Bronze Patina, Signed	145.00
Bookends, Stylized Deer	70.00
Bookends, Woman, Flowers In Hair	125.00
Card Holder, Figural, Nude, Silver Patina, 9 1/2 In. .... 150.00 To	195.00
Lamp, Nude, 9 In.	250.00
Lamp, Silhouette, Original Black Paint	325.00
Lamp, Single Nude, Green Patina, Frosted Glass Insert	290.00

Frankoma Pottery was originally known as The Frank Potteries when John F. Frank opened shop in 1933. The factory is now working in Sapulpa, Oklahoma. Early wares were made from a light cream-colored clay, but in 1956 the company switched to a red burning clay. The firm makes dinnerwares, utilitarian and decorative kitchen wares, figurines, flowerpots, and limited edition and commemorative pieces.

FRANKOMA, Bookends, Charger Horse	65.00
Candleholder, Gracetone	20.00
Character Jug, Uncle Sam, Blue	15.00
Cornucopia, Aqua, 8 In.	6.00
Demitasse Set, Woodland Moss	28.00
Figurine, Bowl Maker, Orange, Paper Label	85.00
Figurine, Coyote	15.00
Figurine, English Setter, Marked	70.00
Figurine, Fan Dancer, Green, Bronze	125.00
Figurine, Fan Dancer, Tan & Rust Glaze	110.00
Figurine, Indian Maiden	20.00
Figurine, Pacing Panther	95.00
Figurine, Prairie Girl, Multicolored	50.00
Figurine, Swan, Green, 3 In.	35.00
Figurine, Weeping Lady, Black, Paper Label	125.00
Flower Frog, Fish, Peacock Blue	85.00
Lazy Susan, Wagon Wheel, Desert Gold	40.00
Mug, Donkey, 1975	12.50

Mug, Elephant, 1968 ....65.00 To 115.00
Mug, Elephant, 1971 .... 30.00
Mug, Elephant, 1972 .... 26.00
Mug, Elephant, 1973 .... 30.00
Mug, Uncle Sam, Red, 1976 .... 12.00
Pitcher, Green, 8 In. 10.00
Pitcher, Green, Art Deco Shape, Circular 19.00
Pitcher, Guernsey, Prairie Green Lid, Large 24.00
Pitcher, Wagon Wheel, Green, 7 1/2 In. 15.00
Planter, Duck 12.50
Plaque, Will Rogers 125.00
Plate, Aztec, Green, 9 In. 4.00
Plate, Buffalo, Box 20.00
Plate, Christmas, 1965 .... 210.00
Plate, Christmas, 1966 .... 145.00
Plate, Christmas, 1967 ....80.00 To 105.00
Plate, Christmas, 1968 .... 43.00
Plate, Christmas, 1969 .... 10.00 To 35.00
Plate, Christmas, 1970 .... 35.00
Plate, Christmas, 1971 .... 12.00
Plate, Christmas, 1974 .... 12.00
Plate, Christmas, 1979 .... 12.00
Plate, Easter, 1972 .... 10.00 To 20.00
Plate, Oklahoma Wildlife, 1973, Bobwhite Quail 27.00
Plate, Oklahoma Wildlife, 1974, Prairie Chicken 27.00
Plate, Oklahoma Wildlife, 1975, Largemouth Bass 27.00
Plate, Oklahoma Wildlife, 1977, Gray Squirrel 27.00
Salt & Pepper, Black Panther 35.00
Sign, Dealer, Desert Gold 25.00
Sugar & Creamer, Leopard Mark 65.00
Sugar & Creamer, Westwind, Flame, Brown Interior 12.50
Sugar, Prairie Green 8.00
Tea Set, Tray, 4 Piece, Blue 25.00
Teapot, Green, 2 Cup 8.00
Trivet, Good Luck, Brown 5.00
Trivet, Orange, Square 8.00
Trivet, Rooster 20.00
Vase, Bottle, Teenagers of The Bible, 1973 .... 10.00
Vase, Bud, Snail 8.00
Vase, Celadon, Signed, 5 In. 60.00
Vase, Spiral Carved, 12 In. 45.00
Vase, Trade Winds, Club, Tulsa, Ok., 8 1/2 In. 22.00
Wall Pocket, Acorn, Blue, Gray, & Jade, Pair 32.00
Wall Pocket, Acorn, Brown 17.50
Wall Pocket, Boot, Green, 7 In. 15.00

> Fry glass was made by the H. C. Fry Glass Company of Rochester,
> Pennsylvania. The company, founded in 1901, first made cut glass
> and other types of fine glasswares. In 1922, they patented a heat–
> resistant glass called "Pearl Oven glass." For two years, 1926–27,
> the company made Fry Foval, an opal ware decorated with colored
> trim. Reproductions of this glass have been made. The company also
> made Depression glass.

FRY FOVAL, Compote, Green Jade Stem, 7 In. 69.50
Creamer, Blue Opalescent Stripe, Cobalt Blue Handle 30.00
Mug, Lemonade, Applied Jade Handle, 5 In. 60.00
Pitcher, Water, Optic, Blue Handle & Finial, Amber, Covered 120.00
Plate, Amber Threading Under Rim, Trapped Bubbles, 1920s, 9 In. 55.00
Tea Set, Opaline, 9 Piece 450.00
Tumbler, Icicle Pattern, Flared Rim, Green Handle, 5 1/4 In. 60.00
    FRY, see also Cut Glass
FRY, Basket, Twisted Handle, Floral & Hobstars, Signed 350.00
Compote, Daisy & Button, Pedestal, 1940, 8 X 12 1/2 In. 180.00
Dish, Refrigerator, 12 1/2 X 4 X 3 1/4 In. 28.00

Grill Plate	25.00
Pan, Bread Loaf, Ovenware	20.00
Platter, Meat, Metal Holder	25.00
Roaster, Lid, 15 X 10 X 6 1/2 In.	65.00
Sugar & Creamer, Signed	40.00

FULPER   Fulper is the mark used by the American Pottery Company of Flemington, New Jersey. The art pottery was made from 1910 to 1929. The firm had been making bottles, jugs, and housewares from 1805. Doll heads were made about 1928. The firm became Stangl Pottery in 1929. Fulper art pottery is admired for its attractive glazes and simple shapes.

FULPER, Bookends, Primitive Man, Blue Matte	150.00
Bookends, Ramses II, Paper Label, Verte Antique Glaze, 8 1/2 In.	650.00
Bowl, Black, Snowflake	80.00
Bowl, Blue Metallic Drip Glaze, Applied Florals, 4 X 7 In.	75.00
Bowl, Crystalline, 16 In.	110.00
Bowl, Effigy, Blue Flambe Over Slate Gray, Stamped, 10 1/2 In.	225.00
Bowl, Handles, Aqua, 15 In.	25.00
Bowl, Lily, Ink Mark, 9 In.	95.00
Bowl, Mushroom Frog, Aqua, 9 In.	65.00
Bowl, Rolled Edge, Green, Gray Drip Glaze	45.00
Bowl, Rolled Rim, Glossy Green Streaks, Marked, 8 1/2 In.	80.00
Candleholder, Blue, 3 1/2 In., Pair	55.00
Candleholder, Custard, Maroon, Rope Stem, 11 1/4 In., Pair	175.00
Candleholder, Flower Shape, 1 Petal Handle, Marked, 5 In., Pair	38.00
Candleholder, Green, Pointed Handle, 2 1/2 X 6 In.	25.00
Candleholder, Hand Thrown, White, 5 1/2 In.	50.00
Candleholder, Ivory, Red, Twisted Rope, 11 1/4 In., Pair	145.00

Fulper, Candleholder, Squat Base, 2 Handles, Blue Glaze, 3 1/2 In.

Fulper, Vase, Bulbous, Short Neck, 3 Handles, Turquoise, 7 1/4 In.

Fulper, Vase, Conical Form, 2 Handles, Green, 11 1/4 In.

Candleholder, Ringed Disc Base, Drip Glaze, 11 In., Pair 225.00
Candleholder, Squat Base, 2 Handles, Blue Glaze, 3 1/2 In. ....*Illus* 40.00
Candleholder, Twist Stem, Pair, 11 In. 98.00
Candleholder, White, Pinched, 5 In. 50.00
Chamberstick, Hooded, Handle 125.00
Creamer, Rose On Green 55.00
Crock, Ice Water, Spigot 100.00
Decanter, Musical, Sterling Silver Overlay, Flat Sides, 10 1/4 In. 75.00
Ewer, Black Over Green, 4 1/2 In. 40.00
Ewer, Green Crystalline, Musical, 12 In. 85.00
Figurine, Frog, Full Figure, Mottled Gray & Brown, Marked, 4 1/4 In. 50.00
Flower Frog, Arrowhead Shape, Purple 11.00
Flower Frog, Lily Pad & Mushroom 35.00
Inkwell, Olive, 2 Piece 135.00
Jardiniere, Black, Gunmetal & Caramel Glaze, 3 Handles, 4 In. 75.00
Jardiniere, Matte Chinese Blue 85.00
Lamp, Bulbous, Double Handle, Blue Crystalline, 21 In. 225.00
Lamp, Mushroom 7700.00
Lamp, Perfume, Art Deco, Ballerina 145.00
Lamp, Perfume, Deco Girl, Curtsying, 5 X 6 1/2 In. 175.00
Pitcher, Gray & Brown, High Glaze, 4 In. 50.00
Pitcher, Mirror Black, Art Deco, 5 In. 45.00
Powder Jar, Art Deco Lady 90.00
Powder Jar, Covered, Girl, Purple Hat, Holding Fan, 6 1/2 In. 155.00
Powder Jar, Oriental Lady, Outstretched Arms Form Cover, Marked 150.00
Tile, Blue & Cream, Round, 6 In. 70.00
Tile, Round, 6 In. 90.00
Urn, 3 Handles, Green To Mauve, Marked, 8 X 6 1/2 In. 95.00
Vase, Ball Shape, Hand Thrown, Blue–Green Drip, Matte White, 7 In. 90.00
Vase, Black Drip Over Green Glaze, Signed, C.1910, 17 1/4 In. 550.00
Vase, Black Glaze, Lamp Hole, 13 In. 200.00
Vase, Blue, Green Crystalline Glaze, Art Nouveau Designs, 8 In. 90.00
Vase, Blue, Green Glaze, 3 Handles, 6 1/4 X 4 1/4 In. 55.00
Vase, Brown & Caramel, 4 In. 30.00
Vase, Brown Crystalline Glaze, Vertical Stamp Mark, 4 In. 50.00
Vase, Bud, 3 Tapered Sides, 8 In. 80.00
Vase, Bud, Blue, 6 3/4 In. 55.00
Vase, Bud, Gun Metal Crystalline, C.1915, 8 1/4 In. 150.00
Vase, Bulbous, Short Neck, 3 Handles, Turquoise, 7 1/4 In. ....*Illus* 20.00
Vase, Buttress, Mottled, 8 1/2 In. 100.00
Vase, Conical Form, 2 Handles, Green, 11 1/4 In. ....*Illus* 90.00
Vase, Crystalline Blue Glazed, Flared Top, 8 In. 65.00
Vase, Crystalline, Art Deco, 4 1/2 In. 45.00
Vase, Fan Shape, 8 In. 70.00
Vase, Gray Flambe, 7 In. 80.00
Vase, Lava Glaze, Rose Over Green, 6 X 7 In. ....60.00 To 125.00
Vase, Leopard Skin, Art Deco, 5 In. 70.00
Vase, Medieval Design, Blue & Green, Square Tapering, 8 1/4 In. 200.00
Vase, Molded Floral, Green, 8 In. 65.00
Vase, Mottled Green, Yellow & Brown, 8 1/2 In. 125.00
Vase, Mushroom Shape, Reticulated Top, 13 Openings, Green, 8 In. 72.00
Vase, Prang, 6 In. 125.00
Vase, Robin, White, 2 1/2 In. 140.00
Vase, Squat, Double Gourd Form, Stamped, C.1915, 6 1/2 In. 850.00

A vase that is drilled for a lamp, even if the hole for the wiring is original, is worth 30 to 50 percent less than the value of the same vase without a hole.

Furniture, Armchair, Belter,
Carved Rosewood, Laminated

Furniture, Armchair, Chinese, Carved,
Marble Leaves & Fruits, Pair

All types of furniture are listed in this section. Examples dating from the seventeenth century to the 1950s are included. Prices for furniture vary in different parts of the country. Oak furniture is most expensive in the West; large pieces over eight feet high are sold for the most money in the South where high ceilings are found in the old homes. Condition is very important when determining prices. These are NOT average prices but rather reports of unique sales. If the description includes the word "style," the piece resembles the old furniture style but was made at a later time. It is not a period piece.

FURNITURE, Armchair, see also Furniture, Chair

FURNITURE, Armchair, 4 Vertical Slats, Cushion Seat, C.1907, 44 In.	500.00
Armchair, Adirondack, On Springs	475.00
Armchair, Adjustable Back, L & JG Stickley, No.471, C.1907, 39 In.	700.00
Armchair, American Chippendale, Ball & Claw Foot, Open, Crest	5800.00
Armchair, Bamboo, Chinese Export, Caned Seat, Cluster Legs	1100.00
Armchair, Bamboo, Windsor, Wide Seat, Green Paint	300.00
Armchair, Banister Back, Black Paint, Pierced Design, Rush Seat	1200.00
Armchair, Banister Back, C.1720, 52 1/2 In.	2750.00
Armchair, Banister Back, New England, Painted, C.1730, 41 In.	300.00
Armchair, Belter, Carved Rosewood, Laminated ....*Illus*	9900.00
Armchair, Biedermeir, Upholstered Backrest, Fruitwood	8250.00
Armchair, Bow Arm, Gustav Stickley, No.336, C.1907, 36 In.	1600.00
Armchair, Charles Baudouine, N.Y., Rosewood, 19th Century, Pair	4400.00
Armchair, Charles II, Oak, Upholstered Seat, C.1700	1800.00
Armchair, Charles X Style, Mahogany Fauteuil, Upholstered Seat	1750.00
Armchair, Child's, Arched Slats, Turned, Blue Paint, New England	175.00
Armchair, Child's, Banister Back, Old Red Paint, 25 In.	625.00
Armchair, Chinese, Carved, Marble Leaves & Fruits, Pair ....*Illus*	550.00
Armchair, Chippendale, Walnut, Pierced Splat, Slip Seat, Pa.	6250.00
Armchair, Chippendale, Walnut, Pierced Splat, Square Legs	2900.00
Armchair, Classical, Upholstered, Boston, Mahogany, C.1830	2200.00
Armchair, Curule–Type, Inlaid Rosewood, Pottier & Stymus, 1870	1100.00
Armchair, Double Tiered Backrest, 18th Century, Elm & Yew, Pair	990.00
Armchair, Empire, Carved Giltwood, Padded Seat, Pair	7250.00
Armchair, Empire, Parcel Gilt, Painted, Napoleon Insignia	850.00
Armchair, Empire, Walnut, Leather Upholstery, English ....*Illus*	900.00
Armchair, Federal, Mahogany, Serpentine Upholstered Back, Seat	1450.00
Armchair, French Provincial, Walnut, Open, Upholstery, Caned Seat	700.00
Armchair, Fruitwood, Art Deco, Paul Frankl, C.1930, Pair	2750.00

Armchair, George III, Mahogany, Waved Cresting Rail, C.1775 .... 13200.00
Armchair, George III, Serpentine Rail, Shaped Arms, C.1775 .... 935.00
Armchair, Gustav Stickley, 4 Horizontal Slats, C.1907 .... 475.00
Armchair, Gustav Stickley, No.1097, Spindle, Upholstered 9500.00
Armchair, Kolomon Moser, Stained Mahogany & Gilt Bronze 2000.00
Armchair, L & JG Stickley, 4 Vertical Slats, C.1907 ....*Illus* 500.00
Armchair, L & JG Stickley, Slat–Sided, No.408, C.1912, 32 In. 1200.00
Armchair, Ladder Back, 4 Slat, Alligatored Black, Rush Seat 2500.00
Armchair, Library Steps, Regency Mahogany, C.1810 ....*Illus* 5500.00
Armchair, Library, Padded Back & Arms, Needlework Upholstery 2975.00
Armchair, Louis XV Style, Giltwood, Carved, C.1870, Pair 6000.00
Armchair, Louis XV Style, Painted & Parcel Giltwood, 4 Piece 2750.00
Armchair, Louis XV, Arched Upholstered, Loose Cushion, Beechwood 2200.00
Armchair, Louis XV, Beechwood, Caned Cartouche Back, Pair 2425.00
Armchair, Louis XV, Central Roseheads, Beechwood, Pair 2850.00
Armchair, Louis XV, CL Burgat, Padded Back & Armrests, Pair 2475.00
Armchair, Louis XV, Padded Backrest, Molded Frame, Beechwood 9350.00
Armchair, Louis XV, Upholstered Backrest, Beechwood, Pair 6325.00
Armchair, Louis XV, Upholstered, Vine & Flower Frame, Beechwood 5775.00
Armchair, Louis XVI, Gray Paint, Upholstered, Padded Arms, Pair 4400.00
Armchair, Man's, Laminated Rosewood, Belter 5000.00
Armchair, Martha Washington, Hepplewhite, Mahogany Frame 7750.00
Armchair, Master's, George III, Pierced Backrest, Mahogany 660.00
Armchair, Neo–Belter Style, Laminated Mahogany, C.1900 .... 550.00
Armchair, Paine Furniture Co., 12–Spindle Back, C.1906, Pair 550.00
Armchair, Reading, George II, Red Walnut, Compartment 4500.00
Armchair, Reading, Pierced Backrest, Bow Front Seat, Mahogany 825.00
Armchair, Regency Style, Black Lacquer & Gilt, Padded Seat, Pair 1900.00
Armchair, Regency Style, Serpentine Rail, Mahogany, 19th Century 990.00
Armchair, Regency, Serpentine Rail, Upholstered Backrest, Beech 3850.00
Armchair, Regency, White Paint, Cushioned Cane Seat, Set of 9 .... 11550.00
Armchair, Slat–Sided, Harden Co., Oak, C.1910, 34 3/4 In., Pair 1000.00
Armchair, Thornden, Stickley, 2 Slat Back, Decal, 1901–02 .... 1100.00
Armchair, Turned Slat Back, Delaware Valley, Shaped Arms, C.1750 .... 800.00
Armchair, Victorian, Carved Walnut, 1870s 395.00
Armchair, Victorian, Rosewood, Padded Arms, Upholstered 5500.00
Armchair, Wallace Nutting, Rush Seat, Maple, No.464 .... 750.00
Armoire, Biedermeier, Birch, Ebonized, Bow Front Top Door, 89 In. 3850.00
Armoire, Biedermeier, Inlaid Cherry 300.00
Armoire, Child's, English, 1920s 175.00
Armoire, Neoclassical, Painted Festoons, 2 Doors, Italy, 86 In. 6975.00

Furniture, Armchair, Empire, Walnut,
Leather Upholstery, English

Furniture, Armchair,
L & JG Stickley,
4 Vertical Slats,
C.1907

Furniture, Stand, Plant,
Limbert, No.251, Box Base,
C.1910, 24 In.

Furniture, Armchair, Library Steps,
Regency Mahogany, C.1810

Furniture, Bed, Dutch Neoclassical,
4 Ft.5 In. X 7 Ft.7 In., Pair

Armoire, Oak, 2 Doors, American 1595.00
Armoire, Oak, Mirror, Drawer On Bottom, 1920s 200.00
Armoire, Oak, Salesman's Sample, Brass Finials, Drawer, 13 In. 295.00
Armoire, Walnut, Burl Inlaid Doors, Mid-1800s 1595.00
Baker's Rack, Brass, Iron, Grille Back, 3 Shelves, France, 96 In. 1200.00
Bed Steps, Leather Inset, Mahogany, C.1870, 27 In. 935.00
Bed, American Renaissance, Carved Walnut, Burled, C.1870 .... 2640.00
Bed, Brass, Full Size 895.00
Bed, Brass, Junior 319.00
Bed, Brass, Ornate, Double Size 1099.00
Bed, Brass, Polished & Lacquered, European, Full Size 1500.00
Bed, Brass, Twin, C.1910 .... 525.00
Bed, Cannonball Rope, Red, Black Grained, Blanket Bar, 49 1/2 In. 175.00
Bed, Cannonball, Rope, Curly Maple Posts, 51 X 68 In. 275.00
Bed, Cannonball, Walnut, Primitive, 1840 .... 595.00
Bed, Canopy, Federal, Mahogany & Maple, C.1800, 58 In. 2100.00
Bed, Canopy, Federal, Maple, 1820, 80 X 50 X 72 In. 1500.00
Bed, Child's, Eastlake, Walnut 265.00
Bed, Child's, Folding, Walnut, 1890s 425.00
Bed, Child's, Iron, Drop Sides, Fancy 275.00
Bed, Child's, Trundle, Rope, High Sides 495.00
Bed, Country Sheraton, Painted, Spool Crest, C.1820, 54 In. 400.00
Bed, Dutch Neoclassical, 4 Ft.5 In. X 7 Ft.7 In., Pair ....*Illus* 8470.00
Bed, Eastlake Style, Walnut, Arched Headboard, 65 3/4 X 57 In. 200.00
Bed, Empire, Birch, Turned Rope Acanthus Posts, Canopy, 67 In. 1300.00
Bed, Empire, Crest Rail, Brass Finials, Painted Metal, 40 In. 750.00
Bed, Federal, Four-Poster, Mahogany, Acanthus, C.1810, 6 Ft.7 In. 2550.00
Bed, Federal, Four-Poster, Turned Maple, C.1810, 4 X 6 Ft. 2650.00
Bed, Federal, Mahogany, Maple, Massachusetts, C.1815, 6 Ft. 8 In. 3520.00
Bed, Federal, Maple, Fluted Faceted Feet, C.1825, 4 Ft.6 In. 3575.00
Bed, Federal, Stained & Turned, C.1810, 6 Ft. 1750.00
Bed, Folding, Child's, Victorian, Bedding 45.00
Bed, Four-Poster, Baltimore Empire, Scrollwork Head & Foot, 1835 .... 1760.00
Bed, Four-Poster, Chippendale, Mahogany, 6 Ft.6 In.X 4 Ft.6 In. 5500.00
Bed, Four-Poster, Federal, Turned Mahogany, C.1800, 4 X 6 Feet 2550.00
Bed, Four-Poster, Sheraton, Birch, Red Finish, Canopy, 65 In. 3700.00
Bed, Four-Poster, Sheraton, New Hampshire 1800.00
Bed, Half-Tester, Carved Walnut, C.1870, Single Size 1550.00
Bed, Half-Tester, Mahogany, Carved Grapes, Net Bars, P.Mallard 7150.00
Bed, Jenny Lind, Walnut, Double 250.00
Bed, Jenny Lind, Walnut, Spindle Head, 3 Ft.11 In. 145.00

Furniture, Bedroom Set, Eastlake Maple,
C.1880, 6 Piece

Furniture, Bureau, 4 Drawers,
Mahogany & Maple, 41 1/2 In.

Bed, Louis XVI, Gray Paint, Rectangular Head & Foot, 81 In. 3300.00
Bed, Low Post, Maple, Blue–Green Paint, New Eng., 1810, 6 Ft. 2850.00
Bed, Majorelle, Fruitwood, Pierced Blossoms Edge, 5 Ft.5 In. 2000.00
Bed, Pencil Post, Maple, New England, 1750–90 .... 4900.00
Bed, Pine, Schulenburg, Dated 1860, Small 895.00
Bed, Post, Rope, Country, Poplar, 54 X 70 X 66 In. 650.00
Bed, Renaissance Revival, Mahogany, Ebonized, Plaques 8800.00
Bed, Renaissance Revival, Oak 4280.00
Bed, Renaissance Revival, Walnut 850.00
Bed, Rope, Blue Painted, Washington Co., Texas, 3/4 Size 895.00
Bed, Rope, Cannon Ball, Curly & Bird's–Eye Maple, 55 X 72 In. 800.00
Bed, Rope, Cannon Ball, Old Yellow Paint Over Red, Single 220.00
Bed, Rope, Cannon Ball, Scrolled Headboard 225.00
Bed, Rope, Goblet Finials, Poplar, Double Size .... 185.00 To 200.00
Bed, Rope, Low Post, Original Red, Ohio, 77 X 52 X 41 In. 745.00
Bed, Rope, Pine & Cherry, C.1820 .... 240.00
Bed, Rope, Turned Posts, Cannon Ball, Poplar, Red Paint, Single 225.00
Bed, Rope, Turned Posts, Original Rails, 53 X 70 X 54 In. 200.00
Bed, Settle, Pine, Scrolled Arms & Crest, Strap Hinges, 68 In. 1000.00
Bed, Sheraton, Inlaid Satinwod, Cherry, American 1600.00
Bed, Sheraton, Post, Rope Rail, Pine Headboard, Birch, 66 1/2 In. 3000.00
Bed, Sleigh, American, Carved, Mahogany 632.00
Bed, Sleigh, Cast Iron, C.1850 .... 4500.00
Bed, Square Head & Footboards, Spindles, Full Size 475.00
Bed, Tall Post, Curly Maple, Canopy Frame, 51 X 71 X 80 In. 4000.00
Bed, Tall Post, Curly Maple, Rope, Canopy Frame, 55 X 72 X 82 In. 1100.00
Bed, Tall Post, Tester, Cherry, Spool, Red, C.1830, 77 X 71 In. 800.00
Bed, Tester, Maple, Sponge, Feathering, Ohio, 1820 .... 4500.00
Bed, Tester, Victorian, Carved Mahogany, Full Size 6050.00
Bed, Victorian, Crest, Paneled Headboard, Rosewood 2530.00
Bed, Walnut, Pierced & Applied Carving, Floral & Leaf, Double 1200.00
Bedroom Set, American Renaissance Revival, Walnut, 1870, 2 Piece 3000.00
Bedroom Set, Art Deco, Light Mahogany, Carved, 6 Piece 675.00
Bedroom Set, Chestnut, Victorian, Carved Fruit Pulls, 3 Piece 1400.00
Bedroom Set, Eastlake, C.1880, 6 Piece ....*Illus* 5775.00
Bedroom Set, Eastlake Style, Walnut & Burl, 1870s, 2 Piece 1700.00
Bedroom Set, Louis XV, Rosewood, With Triple Mirrored Armoire 5800.00
Bedroom Set, Victorian, Cherry, Hand Carved, 1880, 3 Piece 7500.00
Bedroom Set, Victorian, Fruit Pulls, Marble, Walnut, 3 Piece 5000.00
Bedroom Set, Victorian, Oak, 2 Piece 4450.00
Bedroom Set, Walnut, Marble, Dresser, 7 Ft.Bed, Washstand, 3 Pc. 2400.00

Bench, Alligatored Yellow & Green Paint, Pine, 34 X 16 In. 70.00
Bench, Amish, Painted Fruit & Flowers, Pennsylvania 3000.00
Bench, Blue Paint Over Old Red, Cutouts, Long 95.00
Bench, Bootjack Legs, White Paint, 13 X 16 In. 55.00
Bench, Bucket, Pine, Primitive, Top Shelf, Yellow Paint, 43 In. 1000.00
Bench, Chippendale Style, Padded Seat, Rectangular, 34 In. 200.00
Bench, Country, Pine Top, 15 X 65 X 18 In. 100.00
Bench, Cricket, Original Paint, Stenciled 75.00
Bench, Crock, 2 Shelves, Old Red Paint 275.00
Bench, Cutout 1 Side Top, Red, 9 X 51 In. 70.00
Bench, Deacon's, Windsor Style, Pennsylvania, 78 In. 1650.00
Bench, Fireside, Grain Painted, Raised Panels, Shoe Feet, C.1790 .... 4250.00
Bench, Garden, Iron & Wire Mesh, White, 37 In. 95.00
Bench, Garden, Twisted Wire, Vinyl Cushions, Black, 60 In. 125.00
Bench, Garden, Woven Wire, White Paint, 40 In. 225.00
Bench, Green Paint, Cut Out Feet, 13 X 48 X 18 In. 85.00
Bench, Iron, American Rococo, Fern 1550.00
Bench, Iron, Gothic, Arms, Mesh Seat, Medallion Back, C.1830 .... 1050.00
Bench, Kneeling, Primitive, Old Dark Finish, 36 In. 65.00
Bench, Kneeling, Signed J.Revell, Pine, 7 3/4 X 39 1/2 X 8 In. 210.00
Bench, Pine, 3 Sides, Cutout Feet, Front Apron, Brown, 68 In. 245.00
Bench, Pine, Bucket, Green Paint, 33 X 12 X 25 In. 125.00
Bench, Pine, Gray Paint, Cutout Feet, Square Nail, 10 X 112 In. 100.00
Bench, Rocking, Arms, Painted Design 1300.00
Bench, Victorian, Iron, James W.Carr, Richmond Foundry 965.00
Bench, Water, 1 Board Truncated Ends, Poplar, 47 1/4 In. 310.00
Bench, Water, Step Back Shelves, Red Traces, Walnut, 46 1/2 In. 425.00
Bench, Windsor, Bamboo, Dark Green Paint, 77 1/2 In. 625.00
Bench, Windsor, Spindle Back, S Arms, Brown Finish, 96 In. 8500.00
Bench, Windsor, Triple Back, H Stretcher, Arms 6750.00
Bergere, Louis XV, Beechwood, Serpentine, Cushion, Cabriole 3575.00
Bidet, Federal, Mahogany, Canton Blue & White, 1800, 19 In. 2750.00
Billiard Table, Brunswick, Brilliant Novelty, Rosewood, 1885 .... 8500.00
Billiard Table, Brunswick, Slate Top, C.1890, 5 X 9 Ft. 1675.00
Book Shelf, Open, Gustav Stickley, Cutout Handles, 1904, 38 In. 800.00
Bookcase, 2 Doors, Gustav Stickley, Red Decal, C.1903, 56 In. 4500.00
Bookcase, 2 Doors, L & JG Stickley, No.645, 12 Pane Doors, 1912 .... 2500.00
Bookcase, 5 Shelves, Reddish, Roycroft, 65 X 20 X 18 In. 7150.00
Bookcase, 6 Shelves, Red Wash Paint, Pine, 70 3/4 In. 550.00
Bookcase, Biedermeir, Glazed Doors, Fruitwood, 5 Ft. 9 1/4 In. 3575.00
Bookcase, Carved Anthemion Mullions, Feather, Mahogany, 92 In. 3650.00
Bookcase, Cincinnati, Rosewood, 1850s 1650.00
Bookcase, Cylinder Top, Glass Shelves 1400.00
Bookcase, Eastlake, Walnut, Glass Door 575.00
Bookcase, George III, Fan Frieze, Mahogany, C.1830, 8 Ft.8 In. 4400.00
Bookcase, George III, Glazed Doors, C.1780, 2 Parts, 5 Ft.7 In. 1050.00
Bookcase, George III, Glazed Doors, Shelves, Satinwood, 8 Ft. 9075.00
Bookcase, George III, Mahogany, 4 Doors, 8 Ft.8 In. 7150.00
Bookcase, Globe-Wiernicke, Lawyers, 3 Stacks, C.1905 .... 550.00
Bookcase, Globe-Wiernicke, Mahogany, 4 Stacks 425.00
Bookcase, L & J.G.Stickley, Single Glass Door, 1912, 51 In. 1700.00
Bookcase, Leaded Stained Glass Doors, French, Oak, Pair 1450.00
Bookcase, Leaded, 1 Door, G.Stickley, No.700, 1904, 58 In. 7500.00
Bookcase, Leaded, 2 Doors, G.Stickley, No.716, 1904, 55 In. 2200.00
Bookcase, Onondaga, Double Door, Stickley, C.1902, 56 1/2 In. 1900.00
Bookcase, Renaissance, Victorian, Walnut, Glass Door, 7 Ft.10 In. 1500.00
Bookcase, Victorian, 3 Glazed Doors, Mahogany, 1800s, 6 Ft.7 In. 1100.00
Bookcase, Walnut, Crest, Base Drawer, 3 Piece, 9 Ft.6 In. 1700.00
Bookshelf, G.Stickley, Open Slat-Sided, C.1909, 30 In. 800.00
Bookshelf, Standing, 4 Shelves, Mahogany, C.1830, 47 In. 605.00
Bookstand, George III, Revolves, Mahogany, 5 Tiers, 6 Ft.4 In. 13750.00
Breakfront, George III, Mahogany, Satinwood, 6 Ft. 6050.00
Breakfront, Glazed Doors, Shelved, Mahogany, C.1830, 7 Ft.11 In. 6875.00
Buffet, Art Nouveau, Oak, Carved, Refinished, 3 Drawers, 1906 .... 500.00

Buffet, Charles X, 1 Shelf On Supports, Maple, 4 Ft.6 In. 1870.00
Buffet, Empire Style, Glass Pulls, Wine Rack, Mahogany, 6 Ft. 1250.00
Buffet, Louis XV, 3 Frieze Drawers, Carved Oak, 4 Ft.2 1/2 In. 2700.00
Buffet, Mahogany, 6 Drawers, 2 Doors, 1930s, 62 In. 225.00
Buffet, Pine, Grain Painted, Gothic Doors, 19th Century, 21 In. 1100.00
Buffet, Queen Anne Style, 1920s 595.00
Buffet, Victorian, English, Oak, Lions, Columns, Mirror, 6 Ft. 1875.00
Bureau Bookcase, Dutch, Marquetry, Fruitwood, Walnut, 6 Ft. 6 In. 4950.00
Bureau Cabinet, Regency, Mahogany, Glazed Doors, 5 Ft.8 In. 1760.00
Bureau, 4 Drawers, Mahogany & Maple, 41 1/2 In. ....*Illus* 700.00
Bureau, 4 Drawers, Mahogany, Reverse Serpentine, 1780, 37 In. 1800.00
Bureau, 4 Drawers, Walnut, Swell–Front, 39 1/2 In. ....*Illus* 1350.00
Bureau, 4 Graduated Drawers, Curly & Bird's–Eye Maple, C.1800 .... 2600.00
Bureau, Alligatored Grained Paint Over Vinegar Sponge 2700.00
Bureau, Bow Front, Federal, Cherry & Mahogany, C.1800, 36 In. 1900.00
Bureau, Bow Front, Federal, Mahogany, 4 Drawers, 1800, 40 X 21 In. 4750.00
Bureau, Bow Front, Federal, Mahogany, Cockbeaded Drawers, 36 In. 2000.00
Bureau, Bow Front, Hepplewhite, 4 Drawers, Banded Inlay 1875.00
Bureau, Bow Front, New England, Mahogany & Maple Veneer, C.1800 .... 2000.00
Bureau, Chippendale, American, Tiger Maple, C.1780, 38 In. 1600.00
Bureau, Chippendale, Bow Front, Cherry, Beaded Case, 1800, 33 In. 1700.00
Bureau, Chippendale, Cherry, Serpentine, 4 Drawers, C.1780, 32 In. 6000.00
Bureau, Chippendale, Mahogany, Serpentine, 4 Drawers, 1780, 36 In. 5750.00
Bureau, Country Chippendale, Cherry, 4 Drawers, 1780, 35 X 39 In. 4750.00
Bureau, Empire, Mahogany, Serpentine, Cartouche Mirror, 74 In. 450.00
Bureau, Federal, Bow Front, Cherry, 4 Drawers, 1790, 34 X 40 In. 1200.00
Bureau, Federal, Cherry, 4 Tiger Maple Drawers, 1815, 40 In. 900.00
Bureau, Federal, Cherry, Mahogany Inlay, New Eng., 1815, 40 In. 1200.00
Bureau, Federal, Mahogany, Bow Front, 4 Graduated Drawers, 40 In. 950.00
Bureau, Federal, Mahogany, Swell Front, Rope Posts, American, 1815 .... 700.00
Bureau, Federal, Pine, Graduated Drawers, Child's, C.1815, 27 In. 600.00
Bureau, Italian, Fitted Interior, Walnut, C.1740, 39 In. 6500.00
Bureau, Napoleon III, Mahogany, 6 Long Drawers, France, 59 In. 450.00
Bureau, Secretary, Walnut & Burl Veneer, Lock End, 56 X 38 In. 1200.00
Bureau, Swell Front, American, Walnut, C.1805, 39 1/2 In. 1350.00
Bureau, Swell Front, Hepplewhite, Mahogany, 41 In. 1700.00
Butler's Desk & Bookcase, Federal, Mahogany, C.1800, 7 Ft., 2 Pc. 4950.00
Butler's Secretary, Linen Press, Federal, Mahogany, 1790, 92 In. 2300.00
Cabinet, 2 Drawers, Cupboard, Carrying Handles, Mahogany, 29 In. 1450.00
Cabinet, Bedside, Faux Bamboo, Marble Top, Drawer, 34 In., Pair 500.00
Cabinet, Biedermeier, Pedestal, Marble Top, Fruitwood, 29 In. 1100.00

Furniture, Bureau, 4 Drawers, Walnut,
Swell–Front, 39 1/2 In.

Furniture, Chair, Banister Back, Rush Seat,
19th Century

Cabinet, Bombe, Louis XV Style, Gilt Bronze Mounted 6000.00
Cabinet, Bronze, 3 Glass Sides, Paste Jewels, Gold Inside, 8 In. 325.00
Cabinet, Chinoiserie, Black Lacquer, 44 X 74 In. 1500.00
Cabinet, Corner, George III Style, Inlaid Mahogany, 6 Ft.10 In. 1100.00
Cabinet, Corner, Hanging, Pine Bow-Front, 36 X 24 In. 400.00
Cabinet, Corner, Hepplewhite, Mahogany, Mullioned Door, 80 In. 2000.00
Cabinet, Corner, Mahogany, Diamond-Paned Doors, 7 Ft.5 In. 2870.00
Cabinet, Dutch-Indonesian, Amboyna & Ebonized Hardwood, C.1700 .... 8500.00
Cabinet, Filing, Oak, 75 Drawer, Pat.Dated 1875, 1 Piece 1800.00
Cabinet, George III, Inlaid Figured Satinwood Panels, Small 3850.00
Cabinet, George III, Mahogany, Fret Gallery, 7 Ft.2 In. 3575.00
Cabinet, Glazed Door, Curvilinear Bars, Mahogany 1800.00
Cabinet, Gustav Stickley, 4 Shelves 5500.00
Cabinet, Italian, Neoclassical, Satinwood, Bow Top, 2 Doors 7150.00
Cabinet, Library, 3 Fabric Inset Doors, 6 Ft. 6 In. X 42 In. 5775.00
Cabinet, Library, Leather Top, End Bookstands, Maple, 7 Ft. 8800.00
Cabinet, Liquor, Desk Shape, Arts & Crafts, 2 Doors, 1 Drawer 3000.00
Cabinet, Louis XV, Bow Front, 3 Shelves, Marble Top, 55 In. 1400.00
Cabinet, Marquetry, Colored Wood, 20th Century, 53 X 62 In. 625.00
Cabinet, Parcel Gilt, Carved, Painted, Lacquer, China, 59 In. 2100.00
Cabinet, Record, Quarter Oak, C.1915 .... 300.00
Cabinet, Regency, Black, Lacquered Figures, 37 In. 4400.00
Cabinet, Regency, Mahogany, Etagere Top, 2 Part, England, 53 In. 500.00
Cabinet, Renaissance Revival, Inlaid Rosewood, C.1870, 47 In. 1900.00
Cabinet, Sewing, Shaker, Pine, 4 Drawers, 24 X 16 In. 1980.00
Cabinet, Sliding Top, 3 Drawers, Ivory, Enamel & Metal, 16 In. 5500.00
Cabinet, Spice, Hanging, Oak, 8 Drawers 115.00
Cabinet, Spice, Oak, Star Inlaid, Tombstone Door, English 1500.00
Cabinet, Stand, Jacobean Style, Tooled Leather Doors, 66 In. 900.00
Cabinet, Teak, 23 Shelves, Oriental, 18 X 28 In. 420.00
Cabinet, Verni Martin Type, Painted Doors, 4 Ft.7 In. 750.00
Cabinet, William & Mary, Marble Top, C.1870, Oak, 23 In., Pair 775.00
Cabinet, William IV, 1 Door, Adjustable Shelves, Mahogany, 40 In. 1400.00
Canape, Louis XVI, Beechwood, Upholstered, Padded Arms, 60 In. 4400.00
Canape, Louis XVI, Fruitwood, Tapestry, Kidney Seat, 59 In. 225.00
Candlestand, Cherry, Octagon Top, New Eng., 18th Century, 25 In. 1900.00
Candlestand, Cherry, Rose Head Nails, 25 3/4 In. 900.00
Candlestand, Cherry, Tripod, Spider Legs, 26 In. 275.00
Candlestand, Chippendale, Cherry, Octagon, C.1760, 25 X 17 In. 1500.00
Candlestand, Chippendale, Cherry, Square Top, Tripod, 1780, 28 In. 450.00
Candlestand, Chippendale, New England, Painted, C.1780, 29 In. 800.00
Candlestand, Chippendale, Tray Top, Cherry, C.1720, 26 In. 1100.00
Candlestand, Curly Maple, Tripod Base, Snake Feet, 18 X 28 In. 1000.00
Candlestand, Federal, Cherry, Birchwood, Scalloped Top, 27 In. 4675.00
Candlestand, Federal, Mahogany, C.1820, Oblong Top, 29 In. 2420.00
Candlestand, Federal, Mahogany, Reeded Legs, C.1815, 30 In. 2475.00
Candlestand, Federal, Maple, Cherry, 1800, 27 X 20 In. 300.00
Candlestand, Federal, Revolving Tilt Top, Mahogany, 1790, 29 In. 3850.00
Candlestand, Federal, Tiger Maple, Tilt Top, 1800, 28 In. 1700.00
Candlestand, Federal, Tilt Top, Tripod, Country, 1810, 27 5/8 In. 900.00
Candlestand, Hepplewhite, Cherry, Country, 27 In. 250.00
Candlestand, Hepplewhite, Cherry, Spider Legs, Oval, 28 In. 1000.00
Candlestand, Hepplewhite, Maple Base, Cherry Top, 29 In. 800.00
Candlestand, Hepplewhite, Tilt Top, Cherry & Birch, 20 1/8 In. 750.00
Candlestand, Ovolo Corner Top, Cherry, 27 1/2 In. 750.00
Candlestand, Pine & Poplar, Old Red On Underside, 21 X 29 In. 275.00
Candlestand, Queen Anne, Maple, Painted, Country, C.1780, 26 In. 900.00
Candlestand, Rectangular Top, Snake Foot, Cherry, 27 1/2 In. 625.00
Candlestand, Rococo Revival, Giltwood, Dolphins, 39 In., Pair 10450.00
Candlestand, Scalloped, Inlaid Central Medallion, Cherry, 23 In. 400.00
Candlestand, Snake Feet, Cherry, 24 1/2 In. 650.00
Candlestand, Snake Foot, Mahogany & Cherry, C.1780, 25 1/4 In. 725.00
Candlestand, Threaded Post, Adjustable Shelf, Red Paint, 47 In. 1100.00
Candlestand, Threaded Top, Adjustable Arm, Dark Finish, 29 In. 710.00

Candlestand, Tilt Top, 1–Board Top, Curly Maple, 28 In. 300.00
Candlestand, Tilt Top, Birch, Hepplewhite, Inlaid, C.1800, 27 In. 2500.00
Candlestand, Tilt Top, Bulbous Column, Oval Top, 28 1/4 In. 225.00
Candlestand, Tilt Top, Cherry, Spider Legs, Column, 27 1/8 In. 375.00
Candlestand, Tilt Top, Hepplewhite, Mahogany, Spider Legs, 19 In. 325.00
Candlestand, Tilt Top, Mahogany, Column, English, 26 X 18 In. 375.00
Candlestand, Tilt Top, New England, Mahogany, C.1805, 29 In. 1650.00
Candlestand, Tilt Top, Oval Top, Cherry, 28 In. 225.00
Candlestand, Tilt Top, Pennsylvania, Walnut, C.1790, 29 In. 3850.00
Candlestand, Tilt Top, Shod Pad Feet, Mahogany, 1790, 28 In. 1550.00
Candlestand, Tilt Top, Snake Feet, Mahogany, 22 1/2 X 28 In. 250.00
Candlestand, Tilt Top, Snake Feet, Oval Top, Mahogany, 28 1/4 In. 1000.00
Candlestand, Tilt Top, Turned Column, Inlaid Eagle, Walnut 155.00
Candlestand, Tripod, Snake Feet, 8–Sided Top, Cherry, 27 In. 1000.00
Canterbury, 6 Sections, 1 Drawer, Brass Casters, Inlaid Walnut 2000.00
Canterbury, George III, Early 19th Century, Mahogany, 23 In. 1100.00
Canterbury, Pine, Brown Flame Graining, Salmon, Drawer, 17 In. 200.00
Carrier, Book, Satinwood, Handle, 2 Drawers, 44 In. 2860.00
Case, Display, Hanging, Oriental, Teak, 23 Shelves, 20 X 34 In. 250.00
Cellarette, George III, Brass Bound, Mahogany, C.1800, 27 In. 1650.00
Cellarette, George III, Inlaid Mahogany, Frieze Stand, 29 In. 3025.00
Cellarette, George III, Inlaid Mahogany, Hinged Top, 29 In. 1875.00
Cellarette, Inlaid Design On Cover, Mahogany, C.1780, 26 In. 2300.00
Cellarette, Regency, Mahogany, Acanthus Finial, 23 X 34 In. 6600.00
Cellarette, Sloping Sides, Brass Lion's Paw Feet, Mahogany 2000.00
Chair Table, Child's, Salmon Brown Paint, Inscription 425.00
Chair Table, Drawer In Base, Original Paint, 18th Century 550.00
Chair Table, Scrubbed Top, 1 Drawer 995.00
Chair, Acanthus Carved Crest, Gothic Splat, Mahogany, 1770, Pair 5500.00
Chair, Art Nouveau, Mother–of–Pearl Inlay, Velvet Seat 350.00
Chair, Arts & Crafts, Oval Back, Macintosh Design, Oak, C.1910 .... 325.00
Chair, Balloon Back, Walnut, Tufted Back, Man's & Woman's, Pair 700.00
Chair, Banister Back, Maple, Sausage Turnings, Rush Seats, Pair 400.00
Chair, Banister Back, Molded Slats, Yoke Crest, Splint Seat 150.00
Chair, Banister Back, Rush Seat, 19th Century ....*Illus* 200.00
Chair, Banister, Turned Legs, Replaced Splint Seat, Refinished 275.00
Chair, Baroque Style, Carved Crest, Mahogany, 19th Century 160.00
Chair, Batwing, Mahogany, 19th Century 150.00
Chair, Belter, Rosalie Pattern, Arms, Small 7500.00
Chair, Bidet, Regency, Mahogany, Covered Back Box, 32 1/4 In. 250.00
Chair, Bronze, Green Fabric Seat & Back, Giacometti, Pair 825.00
Chair, Captain's, Child's, Pinstripe, Gilt Stencil, Plank Seat 215.00
Chair, Captain's, Child's, Rockers, Painted Design, Arrow Slats 85.00
Chair, Captain's, Turned Spindles 55.00
Chair, Carved Cinnabar, Chinese, Pair 770.00
Chair, Carver, Maple, Hickory, Ladder Back, 1650–1700 .... 700.00
Chair, Child's, Bentwood Arms, Painted Floral On Crest, 21 In. 90.00
Chair, Child's, Bow Back, Saddle Seat, 5 Spindles, Old Red Paint 470.00
Chair, Child's, French Reproduction, Upholstered, 1920s 400.00
Chair, Child's, Gustav Stickley, Leather Seat, C.1907, 23 In. 300.00
Chair, Child's, Hand Carved, Bright Paint, Rust Seat 25.00
Chair, Child's, Old Red Paint, Spindle Back, Wooden, 17 In. 35.00
Chair, Child's, Original Red Paint, Reeded Seat 175.00
Chair, Child's, Queen Anne Style, Wing Back 467.00
Chair, Child's, Shaker, Union Village, Ohio 475.00
Chair, Chippendale, Cedar Wood, Bermuda, Pair 1500.00
Chair, Chippendale, Grain Painted, Country, C.1780, 38 In., Pair 600.00
Chair, Chippendale, Mahogany, Carved Crest, Trapezoidal Seat 650.00
Chair, Chippendale, Mahogany, Crest, Tassle Splat, C.1770 .... 4675.00
Chair, Chippendale, Mahogany, Pierced Splat, Pair 1000.00
Chair, Chippendale, Mahogany, Pierced Splat, Upholstered Seat 550.00
Chair, Chippendale, New York, Beaker Form Splat, Mahogany, C.1770 .... 3400.00
Chair, Chippendale, Pennsylvania, Cherrywood, Tassel Splat, 1780 .... 3300.00
Chair, Chippendale, Ribbon Back, Square Legs, Birch, Slip Seat 600.00

Furniture, Chair, Corner, Child's,
William & Mary, England, C.1750

Furniture, Chair, English Victorian, Walnut,
Set of 6

Chair, Chippendale, Rush Seat, Pierced Vase Splat, Maple, Pair	900.00
Chair, Chippendale, Trefoil Cutout	1650.00
Chair, Corner, 1 Slat Back, Curved Arm Rail, Splint Seat	425.00
Chair, Corner, Child's, William & Mary, England, C.1750 ....*Illus*	2400.00
Chair, Corner, Curved Top Rail, Slip-In Seat, Walnut, C.1870	1775.00
Chair, Corner, George II, Elmwood, Bowed Cresting Rail	2300.00
Chair, Corner, George III, Pierced Splats, Ash, C.1780	1550.00
Chair, Corner, Mahogany, Pierced Splat, Leaf Carved Knees	1900.00
Chair, Corner, New England, Carved Maple, Rush Seat, C.1760	3190.00
Chair, Corner, Queen Anne, Scrolled Hand Holds, Mahogany, C.1765	5175.00
Chair, Corner, Turned Maple, Ash, New England, Refinished, 1730	650.00
Chair, Country Chippendale, Maple, Birch, Arms, New England, 1780	600.00
Chair, Cube, 3 Vertical Slats, Mission Oak, 20th Century	400.00
Chair, Cutout Hearts, Yew Wood, C.1780, 18 X 8 In. ....*Cover*	950.00
Chair, Cypress, Hide Seat, Round Top, Texas, 1917	125.00
Chair, Doll's, Windsor, 4-Spindle Back, Step-Down Crest, 7 In.	185.00
Chair, Duck Feet, Pierced Splat, Yellow Striping, Pair	2300.00
Chair, Empire, Country, Green, Rosette Design, Turned Posts	700.00
Chair, Empire, Parcel Gilt, Painted, Upholstered Back, Seat, Pair	2000.00
Chair, English Victorian, Walnut, Set of 6 ....*Illus*	500.00
Chair, Federal, Inlaid Mahogany, Boston, C.1805, Pair	4950.00
Chair, Federal, Mahogany, X-Form Splat, C.1805, Pair	3300.00
Chair, Federal, N.Y., Plume Carved Splat, Mahogany, C.1800, Pair	7425.00
Chair, Federal, Rush Seat, Baltimore, Painted Red, Gilt, C.1815	1550.00
Chair, Fruitwood, Majorelle, Carved Blossoms, Shaped Seat	1870.00
Chair, Gentleman's, Rococo Revival, Rosewood, Upholstered	400.00
Chair, George I, Pierced Splat, Cypher Inlay, C.1720, Walnut	300.00
Chair, George II, Walnut, Upholstered, Serpentine Back	2200.00
Chair, George III Style, Tall Upholstered Backrest & Seat	300.00
Chair, George III, Ebonized, Parcel Gilt, C.1800, Pair	990.00
Chair, Great, 4 Arched Slats, Sloping Arms, Black Paint, C.1720	450.00
Chair, Green, Gilt, Neo-Gothic Backrest, 19th Century	1550.00
Chair, Gustav Stickley, Spindle, Mahogany, Upholstered Seat	4400.00
Chair, Haggard & Marcuson, F.L.Wright, Chicago Comfort, 1930	650.00
Chair, Hall, Italian Rococo, Painted Flower Urn, Box Base, Pair	3575.00
Chair, Hall, Open Arm, Italian Style, Urn, Putto Crest, Apron	550.00
Chair, Hepplewhite, Martha Washington, C.1780	7800.00
Chair, Hitchcock Type, Gilt Stenciled Design, Rush Seat, Pair	90.00
Chair, Hitchcock, Button Feet, Cutout Splats	150.00
Chair, Hitchcock, Red & Black Graining, Swan On Splat, Rush Seat	175.00
Chair, Ladder Back, 3 Slats, Sausage Turnings, Rush Seat, Brown	275.00

Chair, Ladder Back, 4 Slats, Added Rockers	50.00
Chair, Ladder Back, Child's, Green, Roses, Rush Sheet	195.00
Chair, Ladder Back, Child's, Nipple Finials, Splint Seat	135.00
Chair, Ladder Back, Maple, Rush Seat	190.00
Chair, Ladder Back, Sausage Turnings, New England	1400.00
Chair, Ladder Back, Sausage Turnings, New Rush Seat	525.00
Chair, Ladder Back, Turned Post Finials, 4 Slats, Splint Seat	500.00
Chair, Lavender Paint, Splat & Crest Stenciled	45.00
Chair, Lolling, Mahogany, Upholstered Armrests, England, C.1800	250.00
Chair, Louis XV, Beechwood, Needlepoint Upholstered, Pair	9350.00
Chair, Louis XV, Cartouche Upholstered Back, Loose Cushion, Pair	4950.00
Chair, Louis XV, Corner, Gilt, Square Seat, Cabriole Legs, France	150.00
Chair, Louis XV, Padded Backrest, Armrests, Beechwood, Pair	3850.00
Chair, Lyre Back, Mahogany, Rush Seat, Biedermeier ....*Illus*	575.00
Chair, Lyre Back, Upholstered, 18th Century, Pair	700.00
Chair, Mama & Papa, Rush Seat, Queen Anne, 18th Century, Pair	2600.00
Chair, Morris, Carved Oak	375.00
Chair, Morris, Child's, Oak, Cushions	215.00
Chair, Morris, Turned Feet, Oak	50.00
Chair, Office, Revolving, G.Stickley, C.1904, 36 In.	1300.00
Chair, Papier–Mache, Pearl, Painted, England, 1830, Pair	2400.00
Chair, Parlor, Heywood–Wakefield, White Paint	935.00
Chair, Parlor, Rococo, Walnut, Rose Carved Crest, 45 1/2 In.	550.00
Chair, Philadelphia Chippendale, Needlepoint Seat	7250.00
Chair, Porter's, Gilt, Damask Upholstery, English ....*Illus*	550.00
Chair, Queen Anne Style, Arched Back, Arms, Upholstered Seat, Pr.	3000.00
Chair, Queen Anne, Ball Feet, Carved Crest, Vase Splat, Maple	200.00
Chair, Queen Anne, Mahogany, C.1750, 40 In.	2300.00
Chair, Queen Anne, Maple, C.1730, 40 1/2 In.	800.00
Chair, Queen Anne, Massachusetts, Carved Walnut, C.1760	8800.00
Chair, Queen Anne, New England, Maple, C.1730, 40 1/2 In.	800.00
Chair, Queen Anne, Painted, Rush Seat, Yoke Crest, C.1750	750.00
Chair, Queen Anne, Rush Seat, Cut–Out Heart On Back Splat	300.00
Chair, Queen Anne, Slipper Feet, Upholstered, Rhode Island	1800.00
Chair, Queen Anne, Spanish Feet, Rush Seat, Red Over Black, 1750	1600.00
Chair, Queen Anne, Spanish Feet, Rush Seat, Vase Splat, Maple	275.00
Chair, Queen Anne, Spanish Feet, Vase Splat, Protruding Ears	395.00
Chair, Queen Anne, Traces of Old Red, Vase Splat, Yoke Crest	325.00
Chair, Queen Anne, Vase Splat, Carved Name S.Tyler On Back	300.00
Chair, Queen Anne, Vase Splat, Mahogany, Mass., C.1750	2300.00
Chair, Queen Anne, Vase Splat, Trapezoidal Seat, Walnut, C.1750	1600.00
Chair, Queen Anne, Vase Splat, Yoke Crest, Maple	300.00
Chair, Queen Anne, Walnut, Vase Splat, Slip Seat, Trifid Feet	7425.00
Chair, Queen Anne, Yoked Crestrail, Vase Splat, Slip Seat, Maple	1500.00
Chair, Regency Style, Tub Back, Pair	3600.00
Chair, Regency, Padded Armrest, Loose Cushion, Walnut	6875.00

Furniture, Chair, Lyre Back, Mahogany, Rush Seat, Biedermeier

Furniture, Chair, Porter's, Gilt, Damask Upholstery, English

Furniture, Chair, Shaker, Maple, Tape Seat, Sabbathday, C.1850

Furniture, Chair, Shaker, Maple, Ash, Tape Seat, Harvard, C.1850

Chair, Regency, Serpentine Rail, Padded Armrests, Walnut 3300.00
Chair, Regency, Upholstered Seat, Mahogany, C.1810, Pair 495.00
Chair, Renaissance Revival, Walnut, Cartouche Back, Needlepoint 450.00
    FURNITURE, Chair, Rocker, see Furniture, Rocker
Chair, Rococo Revival, Rosewood, Upholstered, 1855, Pair 1300.00
Chair, Russian, Scrolled Armrest, Upholstered, Birch, 5 Piece 9900.00
Chair, Set, Angelwing, Half Spindle Back, Maple, Poplar, 1830, 4 .... 1599.00
Chair, Set, Arrowback, Country, 4 .... 120.00
Chair, Set, Balloon Back, Old Black Paint, 4 .... 625.00
Chair, Set, Balloon Back, Original Brown Paint, Stencil, 6 .... 1685.00
Chair, Set, Black Paint, Stenciled, By Separatists of Zoar, 4 .... 625.00
Chair, Set, Bow Back, Bamboo Turnings, Saddle Seat, 6 .... 6600.00
Chair, Set, Charles X, Maple & Amaranth Marquetry, French, 6 .... 9350.00
Chair, Set, Chippendale, Brown Finish, Maple, Rush Seat, 4 .... 1100.00
Chair, Set, Curly & Bird's-Eye Maple, Cane Seats, 6 .... 810.00
Chair, Set, Dining, Chippendale, 2 Armchairs, 10 .... 8500.00
Chair, Set, Dining, Classical, Mahogany, Acanthus Backrail, 10 .... 5775.00
Chair, Set, Dining, Federal Style, Mahogany, Shield Back, 12 .... 4500.00
Chair, Set, Dining, Georgian Style, Mahogany, 14 .... 9900.00
Chair, Set, Dining, Hepplewhite, Mahogany, England, C.1780, 10 .... 5000.00
Chair, Set, Dining, Mahogany, Gondola Back, Sabre Legs, 8 .... 1980.00
Chair, Set, Dining, Mahogany, Paneled Crest, Sabre Legs, 12 .... 6875.00
Chair, Set, Dining, V Back, G.Stickley, No.354 1/2, C.1907, 6 .... 2300.00
Chair, Set, Directoire, Blue Paint, Pierced Acanthus Splat, 4 .... 1980.00
Chair, Set, Elmwood, Rush Seat, S.Lancashire, 4 .... 715.00
Chair, Set, Empire, Mahogany Flame Veneer, Cherry, Maple, 6 .... 335.00
Chair, Set, Federal, Mahogany, Serpentine Stiles, 8 .... 4400.00
Chair, Set, Grained Brown, Stencil, Cane Seat, C.1840, 8 .... 6875.00
Chair, Set, Green, Yellow Stripes, Rose On Crest, S.Hartronft, 6 .... 1650.00
Chair, Set, Hepplewhite, Wallace Nutting, Carved, Mahogany, 5 .... 3450.00
Chair, Set, Hitchcock, Black Paint, Gilt Stenciling, 3 .... 450.00
Chair, Set, Ice Cream, Twisted Wire Frame, Wood Seats, 4 .... 275.00
Chair, Set, Ladder Back, 5 Graduated Slats, Split Seats, 6 .... 2100.00
Chair, Set, Louis XVI, Mahogany, Shield Back, Serpentine Seat, 12 .... 5775.00
Chair, Set, Neo-Classical, Iron, Leather Back, Seat, Diederick, 4 .... 3700.00
Chair, Set, Oak, Pressed Back, Medallion Pattern, Caned Seat, 4 .... 675.00
Chair, Set, Plank Seat, Ohio, 6 .... 650.00
Chair, Set, Plank Seat, Painted Pink, Red Flowers, Penn., 6 .... 1495.00
Chair, Set, Plank Seat, Red, Black Graining, Stenciled, 6 .... 750.00
Chair, Set, Queen Anne Style, Balloon-Shaped Back, Walnut, 4 .... 2300.00
Chair, Set, Queen Anne, Birch & Maple, Rush Seats, 7 .... 8500.00
Chair, Set, Regency, Gothic, Carved Mahogany, Set 6 .... 7150.00
Chair, Set, Rush Seat, New England, C.1835, Green, 4 .... 1430.00
Chair, Set, Russian, Scrolled Armrest, Upholstered, Birch, 4 .... 4675.00
Chair, Set, Sheraton, Original Yellow Paint, Striping, 6 .... 5700.00
Chair, Set, Sheraton, Turned & Carved Detail, Curly Maple, 6 .... 3150.00
Chair, Set, Side, Birch, Ebonized, Biedermeier, Sabre Legs, 4 .... 4950.00
Chair, Set, Thumb Back, Mustard Grain Painted, G.P.Folsom, 6 .... 3000.00
Chair, Set, Twisted Spindle Back, Oak, 4 .... 480.00
Chair, Set, Victorian, Walnut, Mid-19th Century, 6 .... 1300.00
Chair, Set, Wallace Nutting, Numbered 326, 5 .... 2500.00
Chair, Set, William & Mary, Banister Back, Rush Seat, 4 .... 950.00
Chair, Set, Windsor, 9 Spindles, Bamboo Turned Legs, Black, 6 .... 2750.00
Chair, Set, Windsor, Bow Back, Bamboo Turnings, Green Paint, 4 .... 5200.00
Chair, Set, Windsor, Bow Back, D.R.Dimes Reproduction, 6 .... 1300.00
Chair, Set, Windsor, H Stretcher, T.Wilson, Halifax, C.1810, 6 .... 4500.00
Chair, Set, Yellow Striping, Polychrome Floral & Seashell, 5 .... 660.00
Chair, Shaker, 3 Legs, Enfield 1800.00
Chair, Shaker, 3 Slats, Cane Seat, Tilters, Enfield, N.H. 1100.00
Chair, Shaker, Ladder Back, 3 Slats, Tape Seat, No.3, N.Y. 375.00
Chair, Shaker, Ladder Back, Enfield, 3 Slats, Cherry, C.1840, Pair 5250.00
Chair, Shaker, Ladder Back, Mt.Lebanon, C.1870, Pair 3450.00
Chair, Shaker, Ladder Back, New York, Maple, C.1840, 41 1/4 In. 475.00
Chair, Shaker, Maple, Ash, Tape Seat, Harvard, C.1850 ....*Illus* 700.00

Furniture, Chair, Teakwood,   Furniture, Chair, Swivel, Oak,   Furniture, Chair–Table, Cherry & Maple,
Vine Design, Elephant Legs, Indian   Coat of Arms, Upholstered Seat   Oval Top, 26 1/2 In.

Chair, Shaker, Maple, Tape Seat, Sabbathday, C.1850 ....*Illus*	500.00
Chair, Shaker, Maple, Turned, Arms, Green, Blue Tape Seat, C.1890	1650.00
Chair, Shaker, No.5, Arms	650.00
Chair, Shaker, Sister's, Rush Seat, Stamped F.W., Watervliet	900.00
Chair, Shaker, Tilter, C.1870	750.00
Chair, Sheraton, Curly Maple Slat & Crest, Country, Maple	45.00
Chair, Sheraton, Gilt Stenciled, Cane Seat, Black Paint	70.00
Chair, Sheraton, Outward Turned Feet, Rush Seat, Maple	85.00
Chair, Sheraton, Red, Black Graining, Yellow Stripes, Cane	135.00
Chair, Spindle Back, Rush Seat, Pair	110.00
Chair, Swivel, Oak, Coat of Arms, Upholstered Seat ....*Illus*	800.00
Chair, Teakwood, Vine Design, Elephant Legs, Indian ....*Illus*	130.00
Chair, Tete–A–Tete, Mahogany	605.00
Chair, Transitional Queen Anne, Green Paint, Rush Seat, Maple	875.00
Chair, Tub, Upholstered, Arched Backrest, Mahogany	1320.00
Chair, Tub, Victorian, 19th Century, Padded Back, Walnut	700.00
Chair, Victorian, Folding, Upholstered, Dated 1865	225.00
Chair, Victorian, Grapes, Meeks, Hartford	2100.00
Chair, Welsh, Dipped Rail, Vertical Splats, Oak, Pair	1540.00
Chair, Wicker, Pillow Seat, Arms, Heywood Brothers Label	1450.00
Chair, William & Mary, Splint Seat, Painted, 17th Century	2000.00
Chair, William IV, Grained & Stenciled, Rosewood	605.00
Chair, Windsor, 7 Spindles, Saddle Seat, 17 1/2 In.	400.00
Chair, Windsor, 8 Spindles, Saddle Seat, Ash, Maple, New England	1300.00
Chair, Windsor, 9 Spindles, Connecticut, Continuous Arm	775.00
Chair, Windsor, Arched Backrest, Yew & Elm, C.1875	1875.00
Chair, Windsor, Ash & Maple, C.1780, 37 1/2 In.	1300.00
Chair, Windsor, Ash & Maple, Fanback, Saddle Seat, C.1780, 37 In.	475.00
Chair, Windsor, Bamboo Turnings, Cage Back, Old Green Paint	600.00
Chair, Windsor, Bamboo, 7 Spindles, Shaped Seat	125.00
Chair, Windsor, Bamboo, Medallion Back, Country, 17 1/4 In., Pair	220.00
Chair, Windsor, Bamboo, Scrolled Arms, 18 In.	135.00
Chair, Windsor, Bamboo, Splayed Base, Shaped Seat	125.00
Chair, Windsor, Birdcage, Old Black Paint	325.00
Chair, Windsor, Birdcage, Painted, Massachusetts, C.1800, Pair	1600.00
Chair, Windsor, Bow Back, 7 Spindles, Ash, Pine, New Eng., C.1780	500.00
Chair, Windsor, Bow Back, 7 Spindles, Bamboo Turnings	270.00
Chair, Windsor, Bow Back, 7 Spindles, Old Red Paint, Tracy School	400.00
Chair, Windsor, Bow Back, 7 Spindles, Saddle Seat, 15 1/4 In.	110.00
Chair, Windsor, Bow Back, 7 Spindles, Saddle Seat, 1780	1000.00
Chair, Windsor, Bow Back, 8 Spindles, American, 19th Century	200.00
Chair, Windsor, Bow Back, 9 Spindles, 17 1/2 In.	900.00
Chair, Windsor, Bow Back, 9 Spindles, Bamboo Turned Legs	145.00
Chair, Windsor, Bow Back, American, Pine Seat, 18th Century	800.00
Chair, Windsor, Bow Back, Bamboo Turnings, Shaped Seat	90.00
Chair, Windsor, Bow Back, Black Paint, Yellow Stripes, Hickory	1000.00

Chair, Windsor, Bow Back, Dark Green Over Red, W.Cox, 1780 .... 39.00
Chair, Windsor, Bow Back, Knuckle Rest, C.1780, 38 In. 1400.00
Chair, Windsor, Bow Back, Maple, Ash & Pine, 7 Spindles, C.1780 .... 800.00
Chair, Windsor, Bow Back, Maple, Ash & Poplar, C.1780, 38 In. 750.00
Chair, Windsor, Bow Back, Painted, Saddle Seat, J.Beal, Jr., 1810 .... 475.00
Chair, Windsor, Bow Back, Saddle Seat, H Stretcher 350.00
Chair, Windsor, Bow Back, Shaped Arms, Paint Remnants 1575.00
Chair, Windsor, Bow Back, Shaped Seat, H Stretcher 775.00
Chair, Windsor, Bow Back, Shaped Seat, Knuckle Arms, Painted 925.00
Chair, Windsor, Bow Back, Shaped Seat, Spindle Back, 18 In. 550.00
Chair, Windsor, Bow Back, Sheet Metal, Black, Ex Hagler 275.00
Chair, Windsor, Bow Back, Splayed Base, H Stretcher 450.00
Chair, Windsor, Bow Back, Splayed Base, Shiny Black Repaint 1200.00
Chair, Windsor, Bow Back, Splayed Base, Worn Brown Paint 975.00
Chair, Windsor, Bow Back, Turned, Painted, C.1800, Pair 3080.00
Chair, Windsor, Bow Back, Turned, Painted, C.1815 .... 550.00
Chair, Windsor, Box Stretcher, Stenciled Back, Country, Pair 265.00
Chair, Windsor, Brace Back, Continuous Arm, H Stretcher 850.00
Chair, Windsor, Brace Back, Potty Seat, Wallace Nutting, R.I. 2100.00
Chair, Windsor, Brace Back, Splayed Base, Dark Varnish, R.I. 2100.00
Chair, Windsor, Cage Back, American, Early 19th Century 175.00
Chair, Windsor, Comb Back, 9 Spindles, Carved, C.1775 .... 4675.00
Chair, Windsor, Comb Back, Lady's, Saddle Seat, Black Paint 900.00
Chair, Windsor, Comb Back, Nutting Paper Label 550.00
Chair, Windsor, Comb Back, Old Black Paint, Yellow Striping 600.00
Chair, Windsor, Comb Back, Splayed Base, H Stretcher .... 14300.00 To 20000.00
Chair, Windsor, Comb Back, Vermont, C.1800, 42 1/2 In. 1500.00
Chair, Windsor, Comb Back, Wallace Nutting, No.415 .... 850.00
Chair, Windsor, Comb Back, Wallace Nutting, Philadelphia 1320.00
Chair, Windsor, Fanback, 6 Spindles, Saddle Seat, Shaped Crest 275.00
Chair, Windsor, Fanback, 7 Spindles, Curved Shaped Crest 200.00
Chair, Windsor, Fanback, 7 Spindles, Saddle Seat, 17 3/4 In. 400.00
Chair, Windsor, Fanback, Connecticut, Green Paint, 1770–90 .... 2850.00
Chair, Windsor, Fanback, New England, Ash & Maple, C.1780, 37 In. 475.00
Chair, Windsor, Fanback, New England, Painted, C.1780, 34 1/2 In. 300.00
Chair, Windsor, Fanback, No.73 Mark, Scrolled Back, Saddle Seat 500.00
Chair, Windsor, Fanback, Painted, New England, C.1780, 36 1/4 In. 600.00
Chair, Windsor, Fanback, Saddle Seat, Shaped Crest, 17 In. 250.00
Chair, Windsor, Fanback, Shaped Crest, Bulbous Legs 200.00
Chair, Windsor, Fanback, Small Saddle Seat, American, 1700s 175.00
Chair, Windsor, Fanback, Splayed Base, H Stretcher 8300.00
Chair, Windsor, Fanback, Splayed Base, Shaped Seat, H Stretcher 450.00
Chair, Windsor, Fanback, Wallace Nutting, Paper Label, C.1920 .... 650.00
Chair, Windsor, Lady's, Gentleman's, Arm Brace Back, Pair 4200.00
Chair, Windsor, Sack Back, 9 Spindles 525.00
Chair, Windsor, Scrolled Seat, Rabbit Ear Back 85.00
Chair, Windsor, Step Down, Bamboo Turnings, Black Paint 420.00
Chair, Windsor, Writing Arm, Late 18th Century 4200.00
Chair, Wing, Chippendale, England, C.1760, 46 In. 4250.00
Chair, Wing, Chippendale, Mahogany, Upholstered, C.1780 .... 7425.00
Chair, Wing, Mahogany Legs, Upholstered, Pa., C.1780 .... 4200.00
Chair, Wing, Queen Anne Style, Pad Feet, Pair 1000.00
Chair, Wing, William & Mary, Walnut, Upholstered, 1700 .... 12100.00
Chair, Wing, William IV, Leather Upholstering, Mahogany, C.1840 .... 3400.00
Chair, Writing, Windsor, Orange, Black Highlights, C.1825 .... 4070.00
Chair–Table, Cherry & Maple, Oval Top, 26 1/2 In. ....*Illus* 5000.00
Chaise, Rocking, Thonet Brothers Label 605.00
Chaise, Wicker 495.00
Chaise, Wire, American, C.1900 .... 975.00
Chest, 2 Drawers, 19th Century, Bombe, Parquetry, 34 In. ....*Illus* 1400.00
Chest, 2 Drawers, Bombe, Marble Top, French, 19th Century, 33 In. 1000.00
Chest, 2 Drawers, Marquetry, Brass Gilt Mounts, Marble, French 2100.00
Chest, 2 Drawers, Mule, 2 Fake Drawers, Pine, 35 X 40 1/4 In. 375.00
Chest, 2 Drawers, Mule, Old Gray Paint, Staple Hinges, Pine 450.00

Chest, 2 Drawers, Mule, Wooden Pulls, Staple Hinges, Pine 575.00
Chest, 2 False & 2 Real Drawers, Grained, Pine & Oak, C.1720 .... 7150.00
Chest, 2 Short & 2 Long Drawers, Roycroft, C.1906, 39 X 44 In. 600.00
Chest, 3 Drawers, Cherry, Splashback, 3 Ft.8 In. 200.00
Chest, 3 Drawers, Graduated, Queen Anne, Walnut, 31 In. 522.00
Chest, 3 Drawers, Linen, Rosewood, Marble, Mitchell & Rammelsberg 600.00
Chest, 3 Short & 5 Long Drawers, Pennsylvania, C.1780, 5 Ft. 4400.00
Chest, 4 Drawers, Applied Beading, Geometric Inlay, 40 In. 1100.00
Chest, 4 Drawers, Beaded, Sheraton, Pineapple Carvings 550.00
Chest, 4 Drawers, Birch, Red Finish, 41 X 37 1/2 In. 2750.00
Chest, 4 Drawers, Cherry, Bonnet Drawer, 4 Ft.X 3 Ft.4 In. 153.00
Chest, 4 Drawers, Child's, New England, C.1820, 13 In. ....*Illus* 950.00
Chest, 4 Drawers, Cockbeaded, Hepplewhite, Inlay, Cherry, 37 In. 900.00
Chest, 4 Drawers, Cockbeaded, Hepplewhite, Maple, 42 X 35 In. 600.00
Chest, 4 Drawers, Cockbeaded, Sheraton, Mahogany, 41 3/4 In. 160.00
Chest, 4 Drawers, Dovetailed, Sheraton, Cherry, Poplar, 41 In. 465.00
Chest, 4 Drawers, Graduated, New England, Cherry, Figured Maple 3500.00
Chest, 4 Drawers, Hepplewhite, Bow Front, Cherry, Inlaid, 1806 .... 1900.00
Chest, 4 Drawers, Hepplewhite, French Feet, Cherry, 37 3/4 In. 900.00
Chest, 4 Drawers, Hepplewhite, Inlay, Cherry, 41 3/8 In. 1500.00
Chest, 4 Drawers, Hepplewhite, Maple, Flame Graining, 37 In. 10750.00
Chest, 4 Drawers, Hepplewhite, Oval Brasses, Cherry, 35 1/4 In. 6000.00
Chest, 4 Drawers, Line Inlay, Cherry, 38 3/4 X 35 3/4 In. 900.00
Chest, 4 Drawers, New Hampshire, Maple, Birch, C.1800, 36 1/4 In. 1400.00
Chest, 4 Drawers, New Hampshire, Tiger Maple & Cherry, C.1830 .... 5000.00
Chest, 4 Drawers, Pine, Wood Pulls, Cutout Feet, Country, 39 In. 275.00
Chest, 4 Drawers, Sheraton, Cherry, Reeded 550.00
Chest, 4 Drawers, Sheraton, New Eng., Red Paint, C.1910 .... 2500.00
Chest, 4 Drawers, Sheraton, Reeded Stiles, Curly Birch, 39 In. 425.00
Chest, 4 Drawers, Sheraton, Walnut, 42 1/2 X 44 3/4 In. 325.00
Chest, 4 Drawers, Tiger Maple & Cherry, 47 X 44 In. 1350.00
Chest, 5 Drawers, Hepplewhite, Eagle Brasses 2850.00
Chest, 5 Drawers, Old Brasses, Curly Maple, 43 X 45 1/2 In. 650.00
Chest, 5 Drawers, Queen Anne, Relief Carvings, Pine, 49 In. 2400.00
Chest, 6 Drawers, Biedermeier, Maple, C.1840, 46 In. 1300.00
Chest, 6 Drawers, Chippendale, Cherry, Batwing Brasses, 55 In. 4000.00
Chest, 6 Drawers, Queen Anne, Walnut, 35 1/2 In. 660.00
Chest, 7 Drawers, Inlaid, Continental, 13 X 44 X 31 In. ....*Illus* 650.00
Chest, 7 Drawers, Maine, Grain Painted, C.1830, 48 X 42 X 19 In. 800.00
Chest, 7 Drawers, Sheraton, Original Brasses 650.00
Chest, 9 Drawers, Dovetailed, Pine, Blue, Labels, 33 X 25 In. 1500.00
Chest, Black Striped Graining, Yellow, Pine 100.00
Chest, Blanket, 1 Bottom Drawer, American, Grained, 18th Century 450.00
Chest, Blanket, 1 Drawer, Cutout Feet, Till, Pine, 35 X 27 In. 525.00
Chest, Blanket, 2 Drawers, Colonial, Maple, Chestnut, Lift Top 8500.00
Chest, Blanket, 2 Drawers, Cutout Legs, Original Paint, C.1830 .... 500.00

Furniture, Chest, 2 Drawers,
19th Century,
Bombe, Parquetry, 34 In.

Furniture, Chest, 4 Drawers,
Child's, New England,
C.1820, 13 In.

Furniture, Chest, 7 Drawers, Inlaid,
Continental, 13 X 44 X 31 In.

Furniture, Chest, Blanket, Lift Top, Till,
Green Paint, 30 In.

Furniture, Chest, Bow Front, Mahogany,
5 Drawers, 38 1/2 In.

Chest, Blanket, 2 Drawers, Original Brasses, 47 3/4 X 30 In.	1300.00
Chest, Blanket, 2 Drawers, Sponge Design, Red & Black Paint	800.00
Chest, Blanket, 3 Drawers, Cherry, Bracket Feet, 49 X 29 In.	900.00
Chest, Blanket, 3 Drawers, Country Empire, Poplar, 49 In.	475.00
Chest, Blanket, 3 Drawers, Pennsylvania, Punchwork Design	2900.00
Chest, Blanket, 4 Drawers, Pine, Oak, Teardrop Pulls, 1720s, 36 In.	6500.00
Chest, Blanket, Applied Herringbone Pattern Over Pine, 22 In.	120.00
Chest, Blanket, Base & Lid Molding, Till, Pine, Miniature	375.00
Chest, Blanket, Blue Paint, Floral, 43 X 18 X 19 3/4 In.	7300.00
Chest, Blanket, Bracket Feet, Poplar, 16 1/2 In.	145.00
Chest, Blanket, Carved & Painted, American, Miniature	350.00
Chest, Blanket, Chippendale, Walnut, Till, Ogee Feet, 24 X 52 In.	1100.00
Chest, Blanket, Connecticut, Scrolled Apron, Till, 46 X 25 In.	300.00
Chest, Blanket, Dovetailed Case, Walnut, 40 X 19 X 24 In.	375.00
Chest, Blanket, Federal, Painted Pine	880.00
Chest, Blanket, Flared Feet, Painted, 1810–20	450.00
Chest, Blanket, Floral Design On Drawer, Cutout Front & Sides	2000.00
Chest, Blanket, Front Bracket Foot, Brown Graining, Canada	200.00
Chest, Blanket, Gray Paint, Brown Graining, Poplar, 43 X 26 In.	190.00
Chest, Blanket, Hepplewhite, False Drawer, Painted, C.1810	1695.00
Chest, Blanket, Hepplewhite, Square Nails, Chamfered Drawer	950.00
Chest, Blanket, Lift Top, Till, Green Paint, 30 In. ....*Illus*	120.00
Chest, Blanket, Mahogany, Bird's–Eye Maple Veneer, Pulls, 12 In.	700.00
Chest, Blanket, Molded Lid, Painted Designs, Pine, 19 X 43 In.	2300.00
Chest, Blanket, New England, Onion Feet, Grain Painted	350.00
Chest, Blanket, New England, Painted & Grained Drawers, 42 In.	3850.00
Chest, Blanket, Oak, 3 Front Panels, 1 Drawer, C.D.B., 49 X 33 In.	900.00
Chest, Blanket, Oak, 4 Front Panels, Maple Top, 58 X 22 In.	900.00
Chest, Blanket, Old Red Paint, Walnut & Poplar, 20 3/4 In.	165.00
Chest, Blanket, Original Sponge Paint, C.1830, 34 In.	750.00
Chest, Blanket, Original Staple Hinges, Curly Maple, Miniature	675.00
Chest, Blanket, Original Yellow Graining, 39 1/2 X 24 In.	225.00
Chest, Blanket, Painted Design & Inscription, 1815, 48 1/2 In.	1150.00
Chest, Blanket, Painted, Massachusetts, Pine & Oak, C.1720, 36 In.	6500.00
Chest, Blanket, Painted, Stenciled L.Quay, Knox, N.Y., 1838	950.00
Chest, Blanket, Pine, 6 Boards, Cutout Feet, 43 X 17 X 23 In.	180.00
Chest, Blanket, Pine, Merrimac Valley, C.1730, 32 X 49 In.	750.00
Chest, Blanket, Pine, Strap Hinges, Refinished, 45 X 19 In.	425.00
Chest, Blanket, Pine, Till, Blue, Bracket Feet, 43 X 18 In.	180.00
Chest, Blanket, Poplar, Walnut, Red Flame Grained, 37 X 18 In.	675.00
Chest, Blanket, Red Flame Graining, Decorated, 37 1/2 X 23 In.	675.00
Chest, Blanket, Removable Baffle, Red–Brown, Poplar, 24 1/2 In.	250.00

Furniture, Chest,
Chippendale, 4 Drawers,
Cherry, 38 X 19 X 40 In.

Furniture, Chest,
Louis XV, 2 Drawers,
Marble Top, 19th Century

Furniture, Chest,
Mahogany, George III,
18th Century

Chest, Blanket, Salmon–Colored Paint, Smoked Graining, Small	235.00
Chest, Blanket, Scalloped Feet, Walnut, 41 2/3 X 20 In.	150.00
Chest, Blanket, Scalloped Rockers & Sides, Poplar, 42 In.	240.00
Chest, Blanket, Scroll Feet, Till, Pine, 39 1/2 X 23 1/2 In.	300.00
Chest, Blanket, Shaker, Molded Drawers, Pine, C.1800, 38 1/2 In.	1800.00
Chest, Blanket, Till, Pine & Poplar, Red Flame Graining, 25 In.	400.00
Chest, Blanket, Till, Walnut, 37 3/4 X 21 1/2 In.	250.00
Chest, Blanket, Tree Design, H Hinges, Feather Design Paint	275.00
Chest, Blanket, Tree Design, Red Paint, 1849, 37 In.	9100.00
Chest, Blanket, Vermont, 6 Boards	1900.00
Chest, Blanket, Victorian, Brass Lifting Handles, Walnut, 21 In.	247.00
Chest, Blanket, William & Mary, Lift Top, New Eng., 1720, 39 In.	1300.00
Chest, Blanket, William & Mary, Pine, Black Paint, 37 In.	6875.00
Chest, Blanket, Yellow Sponged Design, Old Red Paint, Poplar	190.00
Chest, Bow Front, 4 Drawers, Bird's–Eye Maple Drawer Fronts	1700.00
Chest, Bow Front, 4 Drawers, Federal, Mahogany, 1805, 38 In.	3520.00
Chest, Bow Front, 4 Drawers, Flame Veneer, Mahogany, 36 3/4 In.	525.00
Chest, Bow Front, 4 Drawers, Maple & Birch, New Hampshire	2300.00
Chest, Bow Front, Cherry Flame Veneer, Cherry, 40 1/2 X 39 In.	550.00
Chest, Bow Front, Chippendale, Mahogany, Chestnut, C.1780	3400.00
Chest, Bow Front, Hepplewhite, Mahogany, 39 X 20 In.	1600.00
Chest, Bow Front, Mahogany, 5 Drawers, 38 1/2 In. ....*Illus*	2200.00
Chest, Bow Front, Sheraton, Cherry, Curly Maple Veneer	1050.00
Chest, Bow Front, Sheraton, Veneered Facade, Cherry, 44 1/4 In.	850.00
Chest, Campaign, Mahogany, C.1850	1400.00
Chest, Cherry, French Feet, Shaped Apron, 64 X 42 In.	4000.00
Chest, Cherry, Thumb–Molded Drawers, New England, C.1800, 40 In.	550.00
Chest, Child's, Bittersweet & Black Paint, 1887	260.00
Chest, Chinese Export, Painted Pigskin, Camphorwood	3080.00
Chest, Chinese, Black Wood, C.1820	2500.00
Chest, Chinese, Leather Covered & Brass Bound Camphor, 29 In.	275.00
Chest, Chippendale, 2 Drawers Over 4 Drawers, Ogee, 18th Century	1320.00
Chest, Chippendale, 4 Beaded Drawers, Brasses, Cherry, 35 3/4 In.	8500.00
Chest, Chippendale, 4 Drawers, Birch, Red Repaint, 36 X 33 In.	850.00
Chest, Chippendale, 4 Drawers, Cherry, 38 X 19 X 40 In. ....*Illus*	3500.00
Chest, Chippendale, 4 Drawers, Cherry, Bracket Feet, 1790–1820	2000.00
Chest, Chippendale, 4 Drawers, Cherry, C.1780, 36 X 35 In.	2500.00
Chest, Chippendale, 4 Drawers, Connecticut, Cherry, 35 3/4 In.	6300.00
Chest, Chippendale, 4 Drawers, Dovetailed, Walnut, 41 In.	1200.00
Chest, Chippendale, 4 Drawers, Maple, New Hampshire, 1790–1800	4600.00
Chest, Chippendale, 4 Drawers, New England, C.1770, 40 In.	2500.00
Chest, Chippendale, 4 Drawers, Pennsylvania, Mahogany, C.1780	8525.00
Chest, Chippendale, 4 Drawers, Philadelphia, C.1770	1430.00
Chest, Chippendale, 4 Drawers, Walnut, Pennsylvania, 1800–10	1525.00
Chest, Chippendale, 5 Drawers, C.1760, 46 In.	2300.00
Chest, Chippendale, 5 Drawers, Cherry, C.1790, 38 1/4 X 43 In.	1400.00

Chest, Chippendale, 5 Drawers, Country, Poplar, Pennsylvania, Red 2350.00
Chest, Chippendale, 5 Drawers, Maple, Old Red Paint, 39 X 37 In. 1250.00
Chest, Chippendale, 5 Drawers, New England, C.1760, 46 1/2 In. 2300.00
Chest, Chippendale, 6 Drawers, Maple, Brown Finish, 51 In. 3500.00
Chest, Chippendale, 6 Drawers, Walnut, Bracket Feet, Pa., 49 In. 1900.00
Chest, Chippendale, 7 Drawers, Bracket Base, Tiger Maple 2600.00
Chest, Chippendale, 8 Drawers, Dovetailed, Walnut, 38 X 57 In. 575.00
Chest, Chippendale, 8 Drawers, Fluted Frieze, Hardwood, 68 In. 575.00
Chest, Chippendale, 9 Drawers, Walnut, C.1780, 63 1/4 In. 4000.00
Chest, Chippendale, Graduated Drawers, Pine, Chestnut, 59 In. 1700.00
Chest, Chippendale, Grain Painted, Salmon Paint, Drawers, 35 In. 1300.00
Chest, Chippendale, Mahogany, Reverse Serpentine, 31 X 39 In. 11000.00
Chest, Curly Maple Graining, 4 Drawers, Walnut & Cherry, 43 In. 150.00
Chest, Decorated, Grained Pine & Birch, 4 Drawers, C.1835 .... 1700.00
Chest, Dome Top, Strap Hinges, Oak, 46 3/4 In. 270.00
Chest, Dutch Baroque Style, Walnut & Fruitwood, 26 In. 4200.00
Chest, Dutch, Rococo Lacquer, 2 Sets of Short Drawers, 38 In. 3850.00
Chest, Empire, 4 Drawers, Curly Maple Veneer, Country, 47 3/4 In. 625.00
Chest, Empire, 4 Drawers, Flame Grained, Pine, 43 3/4 X 50 In. 3600.00
Chest, Empire, 4 Drawers, Rope Carved Pilasters, Flame Veneer 295.00
Chest, Empire, 5 Drawers, Curly Maple, Tiger Stripe, 48 5/8 In. 700.00
Chest, Empire, 6 Drawers, Black & Red Paint, Turned Legs 4950.00
Chest, Empire, Cherry, Ink Graining, 47 In. 295.00
Chest, Empire, Mahogany, 2 Glove Drawers, Mirror, 1840s 350.00
Chest, Empire, Pine, High Feet, Removable Top, 42 X 51 In. 1900.00
Chest, Empire, Sponged Over Bright Yellow Base 1900.00
Chest, Empire, Tiger Maple Drawer Fronts, Walnut 485.00
Chest, Federal, 4 Drawers, Beaded, Mahogany, 40 X 18 1/4 X 39 In. 375.00
Chest, Federal, 5 Drawers, Mahogany, C.1815, 44 In. 4025.00
Chest, Federal, 6 Drawers, Inlaid Walnut, Mahogany, C.1800, 42 In. 2200.00
Chest, Federal, Bellflower Inlay, Mahogany 3750.00
Chest, Federal, Bow Front, Mahogany Veneer On Pine, 47 In. 400.00
Chest, Gentleman's, Empire, Mahogany, Glass Pulls, 5 Ft. 550.00
Chest, George III, 2 Drawers, Bow Front, Mahogany, C.1790, 47 In. 550.00
Chest, George III, Bow Front, C.1810, Mahogany 1500.00
Chest, German Rococo, Ormolu Mounted Walnut, Parquetry, 38 In. 6050.00
Chest, Hepplewhite, Bow Front, Mahogany, Drop Panel, Inlaid 2500.00
Chest, Hepplewhite, Cherry, Poplar, Maple, Pa., 1800, Miniature 2900.00
Chest, Herb, Shaker, Pine, 9 Drawers 250.00
Chest, Ice, Oak, 24 X 36 In. 450.00
Chest, Ice, Pennsylvania, C.1850 .... 675.00
Chest, Italian Neoclassical, Fruitwood, Walnut, Marquetry, 4 Ft. 5775.00
Chest, Italian Neoclassical, Fruitwood, Walnut, Marquetry, 75 In. 7700.00
Chest, Lift Top, Queen Anne, Tiger Maple 5500.00
Chest, Louis XV, 2 Drawers, Marble Top, 19th Century ....*Illus* 550.00
Chest, Mahogany, George III, 18th Century ....*Illus* 3740.00
Chest, Maple Leaf Door, 4 Drawers, Roycroft, 44 X 25 In. 4950.00
Chest, Maple, Mahogany Banding, Thos.Reed, Mass., C.1800 .... 1750.00
Chest, Mule, Hinged Top, Inlaid Oak, Mahogany, C.1780, 43 In. 770.00
Chest, Mule, Pine, 6 Boards, Worn Gray Paint, Cutout Feet, 41 In. 650.00
Chest, Mule, Pine, Lift Lid, 6 Boards, 37 X 17 X 46 In. 1400.00
Chest, On Stand, Inlaid Oyster, Veneered Laburnum, 5 Ft.3 In. 8250.00
Chest, On Stand, William & Mary, 8 Drawers, Walnut 1200.00
Chest, Oxbow Shape, High Bracket Base, Cherry 5500.00
Chest, Peter Gehron, July 29, 1883, 47 3/4 X 21 In. 200.00
Chest, Pine, Polychrome Flowers, Blue, 39 X 18 In. 250.00
Chest, Pine, Poplar, Tulipwood Top, Beartrap Lock, Green, Pa. 1250.00
Chest, Pine, Stepped Cornice Over Graduated Drawers, 48 In. 800.00
Chest, Reeded Quarter Columns, C.1740, 6 Ft. 2900.00
Chest, Reverse Serpentine, Ball & Claw Feet, Massachusetts 5940.00
Chest, Sea, Walnut, Brass Hardware, Strap Hinges, 40 1/2 In. 145.00
Chest, Sewing, 1–Drawer Top, Thread Holder Bottom 55.00
Chest, Shaker, Pine, 4 Long Drawers, Canted Base, 34 In. 3025.00
Chest, Sheraton, 4 Drawers, Beaded, Cherry, Country, 40 1/4 In. 400.00

Chest, Sheraton, 4 Drawers, Pine, Painted Mahogany Grain, Country 675.00
Chest, Sheraton, Figured Cherry, 2 Over 4 Drawers, Crest 325.00
Chest, Spice, 8 Drawers, Old Blue Paint, Small 245.00
Chest, Spice, Hanging, 4 Dovetailed Drawers, 15 1/2 X 19 In. 380.00
Chest, Spice, Pine, 4 Overlapping Drawers, 19 In. 380.00
Chest, String Inlay, Diagonal Inlay Base, Walnut, C.1800 .... 2420.00
Chest, Swell Front, Cherry, Graduated Drawers, New England, 1780 .... 4200.00
Chest, Tiger Maple Posts, Black Walnut Gallery, Mahogany 595.00
Chest, Tiger Maple, Dovetailed, Original Brass Knobs, Miniature 1700.00
Chest, Till, Pine, Iron Strap Hinges, Worn Old Red Paint, 33 In. 360.00
Chest, Victorian, Mitchell & Ramellsburg, Walnut, 6 Ft.10 In. 725.00
Chest, Victorian, Walnut, 3 Burled Drawer Fronts, Marble Top 250.00
Chest, Walnut, Graduated Drawers, Ogee Feet, Wooden Pins 2500.00
Chest, Wellington, 6 Graduated Drawers, Mahogany, 5 Ft. 3 In. 2750.00
Chest, William & Mary, Grain Painted, 2 Section, 39 X 19 In. 1875.00
Chest, William & Mary, Maple, Pine, Bun Feet, 5 Drawers, 40 In. 6250.00
Chest–On–Chest, 8 Drawers, English, Pine, 74 X 48 X 21 In. 1850.00
Chest-On-Chest, Cherry, 9 Drawers, 36 In.Top 7000.00
Chest–On–Chest, Chippendale, Walnut, 7 Drawers, C.1780, 79 In. 9000.00
Chest-On-Chest, George I, Burl Yew, Walnut, C.1725, 6 Ft. 11000.00
Chest-On-Chest, Hepplewhite, Mahogany, Veneer, 8 Drawers, 78 In. 750.00
Chest–On–Chest, Inlaid Mahogany, Cockbeaded Drawers, C.1780 .... 3850.00
Chest-On-Frame, Queen Anne, Cherry, 5 Drawers, 1770, 54 1/2 In. 7500.00
Chest–On–Frame, Queen Anne, Curly Maple, 4 Graduated Drawers 7700.00
Chest-On-Frame, Queen Anne, Curly Walnut, C.1750, 7 Ft. 3 In. 10450.00
Chest-On-Frame, Queen Anne, New England, Carved Maple, C.1785 .... 1450.00
Chest-On-Frame, Queen Anne, New England, Curly Maple, 1770–90 .... 6600.00
Chest–On–Frame, William & Mary, English Burl Walnut, C.1740 .... 3300.00
Cheval, Federal, Mahogany, Glass, Molded Frame, C.1810, 5 Ft. 3650.00
China Cabinet, Curved Glass, Claw Feet Front & Back, Oak 750.00
China Cabinet, Lion's Head Top, Mirror, Lights, Oak, 48 X 66 In. 800.00
China Cabinet, Oak, Round With Curved Glass, Claw Feet 750.00
China Cabinet, Pressed Carving, Mirror Back, Oak 1600.00
China Cabinet, Victorian, Bowed Sides, Claw Feet, Mahogany 500.00
China Closet & Desk Combination, 3 Drawers, 2 Doors, 1930s 220.00
Clothes Press, Burled Paneled Insets In Doors, Kentucky 3600.00
Commode, Bird's–Eye Maple, Tiger, Gallery, Signed Conroy, 1847 .... 1400.00
Commode, Bombe, Rococo Style, Mahogany, Russell, 1860, 39 X 60 In. 2800.00
Commode, Demilune, Inlaid Fruitwood, Variegated Onyx Top, 48 In. 1200.00
Commode, Demilune, Louis XVI, Mahogany, 3 Center Drawers, 50 In. 9350.00
Commode, Empire, 4 Drawers, Ormolu Keyhole, Fruitwood, 39 In. 4400.00
Commode, Empire, Figured Mahogany, Marble, Frieze Drawer, C.1830 .... 1100.00
Commode, Long Drawer, 2 Half Drawers, Oak, Roycroft, 1906, 38 In. 800.00
Commode, Louis IV, 3 Drawers, Marble, 19th Century, 28 In., Pair 900.00
Commode, Louis Philippe, Flame–Grained Mahogany, Marble, 38 In. 1400.00
Commode, Louis XV, 3 Drawers, French, Walnut, 18th Century, 49 In. 1800.00
Commode, Louis XV, Mahogany, Purplewood Marquetry, Cabriole Legs 5225.00
Commode, Louis XV, Petite, Faux Marble, Cream, France, 32 X 17 In. 425.00
Commode, Louis XV, Signed P.Roussel, Kingwood, Tulipwood, 43 In. 4950.00
Commode, Louis XV, Tulipwood Parquetry, Kingwood, 35 In., Pair 7700.00
Commode, Louis XVI, Brass Mounted, Walnut, Parquetry, Miniature 2530.00
Commode, Louis XVI, Marble Top, Banded Marquetry Panels, 26 In. 525.00
Commode, Mahogany, Marble Top, New Orleans, C.1850 .... 358.00
Commode, Marble Top, 2 Doors, Marquetry Border, 43 3/4 In. 4125.00
Commode, Marble Top, Maple Interior, Rosewood 1320.00
Commode, Ormolu Mounted Walnut, Fruitwood Marquetry, 33 3/4 In. 2475.00
Commode, Regency, Kingwood, D Shape Marble Top, 4 Ft.3 1/2 In. 6875.00
Commode, Victorian, Walnut, Marble Top 800.00
Commode, Walnut, Eastlake Style, Marble Top 150.00
Console, Charles X, Marble Top, Drawer, Maple, Birch, 36 In. 7150.00
Console, Empire, Mahogany, Marble, C.1830, 34 X 35 In. 1300.00
Console, Liver Mottled Marble Top, Center Medallion, Oak, 32 In. 8250.00
Console, Louis XV Style, Marble Top, Gilt Wood, 36 In., Pair 8800.00
Console, Louis XV, Gilt Wood, Marble Top, C Scroll Support, Pair 3850.00

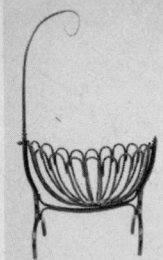

Furniture, Cradle, Ebonized   Furniture, Desk, Chippendale, Maple,   Furniture, Etagere, Belter–Style,
Bentwood, Open Scrolled Sides   Slant Top, American, 36 In.   Rosewood, Marble Base, 57 In.

Console, Louis XVI, Parcel Gilt, Shaped Stretcher, Center Urn 3850.00
Console, Mottled Marble Top, Shell Apron, Gilt Wood, 37 1/4 In. 8525.00
Console, William IV, Porphyry Top, Rosewood, C.1830, 37 In., Pair 6000.00
Couch, Pine Frame, Scrolled Back, Upholstered, Country, 78 In. 775.00
Couch, Rope Frame, Plaid Upholstery, Country, 90 In. 100.00
Couch, Southern, Walnut, Scrolled Arms, Baby Guard, 89 In. 1400.00
Cradle, Amish, Round Sides, Old Red Paint 250.00
Cradle, Arrow Back, H Stretcher, Spindle, C.1820 .... 685.00
Cradle, Ebonized Bentwood, Open Scrolled Sides ....*Illus* 900.00
Cradle, Elongated Finials, Scalloped Headboard, Birch, 37 In. 275.00
Cradle, Hood, New England, Grain Painted, C.1780, 43 X 30 In. 300.00
Cradle, Hood, Stenciled Fruit Baskets, Red, Black, 39 In. 175.00
Cradle, Mahogany, Dovetailed Foot, Refinished, 42 In. 120.00
Cradle, Pine, Primitive, Red Paint, Cutout Foot 225.00
Cradle, Rockers, Heart Cutouts, Red, Black Flame Graining, 38 In. 250.00
Cradle, Scalloped Sides, Cutout Handles, Walnut, 45 1/2 In. 200.00
Cradle, Sheraton, Removable Rockers, Hardwood, 18 3/4 X 42 In. 400.00
Cradle, Spindle, Walnut, Virginia, C.1840 .... 450.00
Cradle, Woven Splint, Blue & Faded Red Design, 19 In. 150.00
Crib, Brass, Canopy 595.00
Cupboard, 2 Raised Panel Doors, Black On Red, 2 Piece 4000.00
Cupboard, 3 Lower Drawers, 3 Upper, Painted Birds, Flowers, Pine 500.00
Cupboard, Amish, Old Blue Paint Over Green, Ohio Valley 5200.00
Cupboard, Apothecary, Pine, 4 Doors, English 700.00
Cupboard, Apothecary, Pine, Overlapping Drawers, 65 1/2 In. 850.00
Cupboard, Arabesque Marquetry, Burr Walnut, German, 6 Ft.11 In. 8800.00
Cupboard, Art Nouveau, Pierced Panels, Liberty, England 1300.00
Cupboard, Baker's Bucket, Original Paint, Pierced Tin, 1840 .... 1400.00
Cupboard, Barrel Back, White Pine Butterfly Shelf, 4 Shelves 3200.00
Cupboard, Biedermeier, Pine, Black Lacquer, Key, C.1800, 5 Ft. 5800.00
Cupboard, Board & Batten Door In Base, Pine, 35 X 73 1/2 In. 300.00
Cupboard, Butternut Panels, Poplar, 1 Piece, 43 X 81 1/4 In. 800.00
Cupboard, Cheese, Shaker, C.1840, Watervliet 2300.00
Cupboard, Cherry, Raised Paneled Doors, 3 Drawers, 86 In. 1550.00

Be sure the big furniture you buy is small enough to go through the door into your room.

Cupboard, Child's, Hand Carved, Beveled Mirror, C.1880, 61 In. 1850.00
Cupboard, Child's, Step Back, Black Hinges, 4 Doors 125.00
Cupboard, Chimney, Light Green Paint, Open, 1 Door, 7 Ft. 1125.00
Cupboard, Chimney, Old Paint, 38 1/2 In. 130.00
Cupboard, Chimney, Shaker, Pine, Red Wash, New Lebanon, 6 Ft. 3500.00
Cupboard, Corner, 4 Doors, Pine, 44 X 75 In. 975.00
Cupboard, Corner, Ball & Claw Feet, Cherry, 101 In. 1400.00
Cupboard, Corner, Blue Paint, C.1840, 6 Ft.6 In. 5400.00
Cupboard, Corner, Carved Fans On Doors, Cherry, 83 In. 1150.00
Cupboard, Corner, Cherry, Bracket Feet, Pegged, Pa., C.1800 .... 4400.00
Cupboard, Corner, Cherry, Top Glass Doors, 1 Piece, 90 In. 1250.00
Cupboard, Corner, Dutch, Mirrored Door, Walnut, 6 Ft. 9 In. 1900.00
Cupboard, Corner, Federal, Glazed Doors, Pine, C.1820, 86 In. 2100.00
Cupboard, Corner, Federal, Grain Painted, 1820, 84 In. 3250.00
Cupboard, Corner, Fluted Pilasters, Pine, C.1790, 6 Ft. 11 In. 1430.00
Cupboard, Corner, Grain Painted, Pennsylvania, C.1850 .... 3850.00
Cupboard, Corner, Hanging, Paneled Door & Base, Pine, 34 In. 325.00
Cupboard, Corner, Hanging, Scalloped Crest, Pine, 30 In. 175.00
Cupboard, Corner, Old Blue Paint, Rosehead Nails, H Hinges 3800.00
Cupboard, Corner, Paneled Doors In Base, Poplar, 81 3/4 In. 510.00
Cupboard, Corner, Pennsylvania, Curly Cherry, 2 Piece, 89 In. 4500.00
Cupboard, Corner, Pennsylvania, Grain Painted, 2 Piece, C.1850 .... 4500.00
Cupboard, Corner, Poplar, Paneled Doors, 83 In., 1 Piece 700.00
Cupboard, Corner, Poplar, Varnish, Orange Inside, 1 Piece, 83 In. 950.00
Cupboard, Corner, Raised Panel Doors, Green, Pine, 95 In. 1300.00
Cupboard, Corner, Reeded Pilasters, 2 Doors, Cherry, 85 In. 1000.00
Cupboard, Corner, Regency, Mahogany, Shelves, Glazed Door, 44 In. 350.00
Cupboard, Corner, Wall, Old Blue Paint, Pine, 39 X 74 In. 900.00
Cupboard, Corner, Walnut, Paneled Beveled Doors, 52 X 86 In. 3000.00
Cupboard, Corner, Walnut, Raised Paneled Doors, 2 Drawers, 85 In. 1300.00
Cupboard, Door, 6 Panels, Side Cutouts, 4 Shelves, Gray Paint 875.00
Cupboard, Foliage Scrolls, Alligatored Red & Green, 76 In. 375.00
Cupboard, Fruit, Peg Construction, Original Red, Cherry, C.1850 .... 600.00
Cupboard, Glazed Doors, Shaped Shelves, Grain Painted 2750.00
Cupboard, Hanging, 2 Doors, Beaded Frames, Grained, 22 X 15 In. 75.00
Cupboard, Hanging, 24 Glass Panes, 3 Shelves, Red, 35 In. 700.00
Cupboard, Hanging, Iron Butterfly Hinges, Pine, 19 1/4 X 30 In. 900.00
Cupboard, Hanging, Pine, 2 Doors, 3 Shelves, Red Paint, 30 In. 475.00
Cupboard, Hanging, Reeded Doors & Stiles, Red Paint, 25 3/8 In. 130.00
Cupboard, Hanging, Scalloped, Paneled Doors, Mahogany, 16 3/4 In. 105.00
Cupboard, Hanging, Single Board Door, Brass Latch, Pine, 35 In. 235.00
Cupboard, Jelly, 2 Dovetailed Drawers, Walnut, 43 X 21 In. 205.00
Cupboard, Jelly, 4 Shelves, Poplar, 20 1/4 X 66 3/4 In. 325.00
Cupboard, Jelly, Batten Doors, Old Green Paint, 35 X 41 1/2 In. 125.00
Cupboard, Jelly, Brown Grained, Batten Doors, Poplar, 49 1/2 In. 350.00
Cupboard, Jelly, Double Doors, Butternut Panels, Cherry, 47 In. 400.00
Cupboard, Jelly, Flame Graining, Pine & Poplar, 52 3/4 In. 1700.00
Cupboard, Jelly, Poplar, Diamond Paneled Door, Blue, 58 In. 2100.00
Cupboard, Jelly, Scalloped Base, Paneled Doors, Poplar, 60 In. 340.00
Cupboard, Kitchen, Step Back, Minnesota, C.1885 .... 695.00
Cupboard, Kitchen, Step Back, Oak, C.1890 .... 585.00
Cupboard, Linen, Mirror, M.Blanchet, France, C.1849, 83 3/4 In. 500.00
Cupboard, Livery, Georgian, Pierced Doors, Oak, 5 Ft.11 In. 1320.00
Cupboard, New England, 3 Open Shelves, Pine, C.1750, 85 1/2 In. 1500.00
Cupboard, Open Pewter, 2 Removable Shelves, Pine, 49 X 75 In. 375.00
Cupboard, Open, 2 Doors, Red & Yellow Flame Graining, 70 1/2 In. 3700.00
Cupboard, Paneled Doors, Drawers, Poplar, 42 1/4 X 42 1/4 In. 350.00
Cupboard, Pennsylvania, Curly Maple, Walnut, Green, 2 Piece 2100.00
Cupboard, Pewter, 3 Open Shelves, Pine, Brown, 46 X 74 3/4 In. 675.00
Cupboard, Pewter, Board & Batten Door, Pine, 45 X 17 X 71 In. 500.00
Cupboard, Pewter, Open, Pine, Batten Door, 55 X 74 In., 1 Piece 2500.00
Cupboard, Pewter, Open, Scalloped Top, Starflowers, Pine, 74 In. 555.00
Cupboard, Pewter, Pine, Open Top, Double Doors, 1 Piece 1800.00
Cupboard, Pewter, Shaker, 3 Open Shelves, Old Red Paint 750.00

Cupboard, Pine, 6 Drawers, 2 Doors, Olive Over Red, 87 In. 550.00
Cupboard, Pine, Poplar, Brown Graining, 2 Paneled Doors, 66 In. 335.00
Cupboard, Pine, Poplar, Yellow Interior, Glass Doors, 89 In. 1300.00
Cupboard, Pine, Primitive, 1 Door, Wavy Glass, 12 1/2 In. 195.00
Cupboard, Pine, Primitive, Batten Doors, Red, 49 X 28 In. 185.00
Cupboard, Poplar, Paneled Door, Molded Cornice, Red Paint, 67 In. 2200.00
Cupboard, Poplar, Paneled Doors, Red Flame Grained, 95 In. 1850.00
Cupboard, Setback, Hardware, Beveled Glass, Pine, 91 In. 1500.00
Cupboard, Shaker, 2 Lower Shelves, Closed Upper Section 5400.00
Cupboard, Shaker, Enfield, Butternut & Pine, 62 X 102 In. 4250.00
Cupboard, Shaker, Step Back, Pine, Red Wash, 1825, 6 Ft. 8800.00
Cupboard, Spice, 3 Step Back Tiers, 14 Drawers, Pine, 25 1/2 In. 810.00
Cupboard, Spice, Drawers, Spoon Slots, Curly Maple, 87 1/2 In. 3000.00
Cupboard, Step Back, American, Pine, C.1860, 76 X 44 In. 1195.00
Cupboard, Step Back, Canadian, Original Paint, C.1870 .... 1450.00
Cupboard, Step Back, Double Drawers, 2 Piece, C.1850 .... 875.00
Cupboard, Step Back, Green & Mustard, Glass Pane Doors, 1830s 3200.00
Cupboard, Step Back, Mustard Over Red Paint, Maryland, C.1835 .... 3500.00
Cupboard, Step Back, New England, Old Green Paint 2950.00
Cupboard, Step Back, New Hampshire, Blue Paint, Early 1800s 3900.00
Cupboard, Step Back, Pine, 4 Doors, 2 Drawers, C.1850 .... 1295.00
Cupboard, Step Back, Pine, Pennsylvania, Red Paint, Pie Shelf 750.00
Cupboard, Step Back, Red & Green Painted, Georgia 495.00
Cupboard, Wall, 2 Door, Brown Paint, Yellow Striping, 1800, 35 In. 700.00
Cupboard, Wall, Beechwood, Walnut, Poplar, 4 Doors, Ohio 995.00
Cupboard, Wall, Cherry, Paneled Doors, 3 Drawers, Shelf, 98 In. 3350.00
Cupboard, Wall, Country, Double Doors Top, Cherry, Walnut, 88 In. 675.00
Cupboard, Wall, Double Doors, 6 Panes, Walnut, 49 3/4 X 86 In. 2100.00
Cupboard, Wall, Paneled Doors, 2 Drawers, Open Top, Brown Paint 625.00
Cupboard, Wall, Scalloped Feet, 2 Drawers, Cherry, 89 3/4 In. 800.00
Cupboard, Walnut, 1 Paneled Door, Blue Repaint, 29 X 11 X 42 In. 345.00
Cupboard, Walnut, Grain Painted, 4 Doors, Ohio, 1830–40 .... 1950.00
Cupboard, Washroom, Hanging, Mirrored Door, 2 Drawers, 38 3/4 In. 115.00
Cupboard, Welsh, Oak, 75 In. 900.00
Cupboard, Welsh, Open Base Shelves, 2 Drawers, Pine, 76 In. 525.00
Cupboard, White & Brown Graining Over Red Stain, Pine, 65 In. 195.00
Cupboard, Yellow Graining, Divided Interior, Poplar, 82 In. 375.00
Curio Cabinet, Marquetry, Tortoiseshell, Scrimshaw, 19th Century 1075.00
Daybed, Biedermeier, Fruitwood 800.00
Daybed, Chinese Export, Caned, 3 Drawers, Mahogany, 7 Ft. 5500.00
Daybed, Sheraton, Mahogany, Reeded Legs, Brown Cushion, 78 In. 450.00
Daybed, Spool, Black Paint, Original Feather Tick, 5 Cushions 390.00
Desk & Bench, Child's, Primitive, Worn Red Paint, C.1800 .... 295.00
Desk & Chair, Art Deco, Madagascar Ebony 4000.00
Desk & Chair, Wicker 250.00
Desk, 2 Large Drawers, 2 Ogee Drawers, Pine, 42 1/2 X 33 In. 300.00
Desk, Architect's, Lift Top, Drawer Each Side, Mahogany, 28 In. 1550.00
Desk, Butler's, Hepplewhite, Curly Cherry, 45 In. 700.00
Desk, Butler's, Hepplewhite, Fitted Interior, Mahogany 1000.00
Desk, Butler's, Mahogany Veneer, Sandwich Knobs, 49 X 45 In. 675.00
Desk, Carlton House, Satinwood, U Form Drawers, 40 In. 7775.00
Desk, Child's, Slant Front, Massachusetts, Maple & Pine, C.1750 .... 3575.00
Desk, Chippendale, 1760, Miniature, 18 X 8 X 14 In. ....*Cover* 6500.00
Desk, Chippendale, Fall Front, Mahogany, Serpentine, 1780, 44 In. 2200.00
Desk, Chippendale, Maple, Slant Top, American, 36 In. ....*Illus* 2750.00
Desk, Chippendale, Oxbow Slant Front, Mahogany, C.1775, 43 In. 7800.00
Desk, Chippendale, Oxbow, English, Late 18th Century, Mahogany 6650.00
Desk, Chippendale, Oxbow, New England, C.1760 .... 5500.00
Desk, Chippendale, Slant Front, 4 Graduated Drawers, American 6000.00
Desk, Chippendale, Slant Front, Curly Birch, 4 Drawers, 42 In. 1000.00
Desk, Country Hepplewhite, Slant Front, Curly Maple, 44 In. 2050.00
Desk, Country, Lift Lid, Bin Interior, Pine, 26 X 30 In. 140.00
Desk, Drop Front, Cabinet Doors, G.Stickley, C.1902, 48 In. 3700.00
Desk, Drop Front, Cabinet Doors, Lifetime Co., C.1910, 44 In. 600.00

Desk, Drop Front, Cherry, 4 Drawers, Federal, C.1800, 43 1/4 In. 1600.00
Desk, Drop Front, Limbert, Curvilinear Cutouts 1980.00
Desk, Empire, Glass, Crotch Mahogany, American, 7 1/2 Ft. 2300.00
Desk, Executive, Walnut, 1930s, 36 X 60 In. 175.00
Desk, Fall Front, Burlwood Interior, Continental 1650.00
Desk, Fall Front, Chippendale, Birch, Serpentine, 4 Drawers, 1780 .... 5000.00
Desk, Fall Front, Eastlake, Appears Like Chest When Closed 1320.00
Desk, Fall Front, Federal, Sliding Lid, Mahogany, C.1820 .... 600.00
Desk, Flat Top, 2 Drawers, Lower Shelf, Limbert, 1912, 30 X 40 In. 350.00
Desk, Flat Top, G.Stickley, Copper Pulls, Red Decal, 29 X 42 In. 450.00
Desk, Fruitwood Marquetry, Leather Top, Galle, 4 Ft.X 40 3/4 In. 3300.00
Desk, Hand Carved, Ivory Eyes, Chair, Teak, Chinese 2500.00
Desk, Hepplewhite, Slant Front, Cherry 4300.00
Desk, Inlaid Ivory & Mother-of-Pearl, Oriental 4500.00
Desk, Kneehole, Chippendale, Block & Shell, Center Door, 36 In. 5775.00
Desk, Lady's, Curly Maple, 1 Drawer, 1855-80 .... 1200.00
Desk, Lady's, Flat Top, Letter Rack, Drawers, Shelf, G.Stickley 450.00
Desk, Lady's, Sheraton, Cylinder Top, Fitted Interior, Mahogany 1200.00
Desk, Lady's, Slant Lid, Fruitwood, Crossbanded, France, 38 In. 950.00
Desk, Lap, Brass Corners, Inside Velvet 65.00
Desk, Lap, Child's, Pirate Scene, Signed Tony Sarg 90.00
Desk, Lap, Interior Writing Surface, Drawers, Mahogany, 19 In. 715.00
Desk, Lap, Pearl Inlay 350.00
Desk, Leather Hinged Top, Mahogany, Federal, C.1790, 34 In. 1210.00
Desk, Louis XVI, H.Dasson, Plum Pudding Mahogany, 5 Ft. X 44 In. 4675.00
Desk, Oxbow, Chippendale, Slant Lid, Mahogany, 37 X 44 5/8 In. 6000.00
Desk, Partners', 3 Frieze Drawers, Cupboard, Mahogany, 44 In. 2200.00
Desk, Partners', Divided Top, Lifts To Both Sides, Mahogany 1450.00
Desk, Partners', George III, 3 Frieze Drawers, Mahogany, 5 Ft. 4750.00
Desk, Partners', George III, Carved Mahogany, 4 Ft.8 In. 3080.00
Desk, Partners', George III, Mahogany, Pedestal, 4 Ft.7 In. 4400.00
Desk, Partners', Jacobean, Oak, Kneehole, Marquetry 600.00
Desk, Partners', Leather Top, 3 Drawers Each, Mahogany, 5 Ft. 880.00
Desk, Partners', Pedestal, Mahogany, 34 X 57 X 40 1/2 In. 7865.00
Desk, Partners', Tyler's Desk Co., St.Louis 1500.00
Desk, Partners', Victorian, 3 Drawers, Cupboard, Mahogany, Small 1450.00
Desk, Pedestal, 3 Drawer, Victorian, Leather, Mahogany, 29 In. 1100.00
Desk, Pedestal, Drawer Above File Drawer Each Side, Mahogany 1000.00
Desk, Pedestal, Tooled Leather Surface, Mahogany, 4 Ft. 7 In. 2200.00
Desk, Pedestal, Victorian, 3 Drawers, Leather, Mahogany, 4 Ft. 1750.00

As a general rule, the drawer bottom of an 18th-century chest was made of two or three pieces of wood, the Victorian drawer bottom was made from a single piece. The Victorian bottom was often screwed in place.

Early (18th-century) glass is thinner than later glass. Early mirrors reflect a darker image than new mirrors.

Gilt frames can be cleaned with beer.

Desk, Plantation, Drop Front, Walnut	550.00
Desk, Queen Anne, Drop Front, Curly Maple	5300.00
Desk, Queen Anne, New England, Maple, 1750–70, 30 1/2 X 36 In.	13750.00
Desk, Regency, Rosewood, Leather Inset, Cabriole Legs, 4 Ft.	7975.00
Desk, Roll Top, Cylinder, Burl	2400.00
Desk, Roll Top, Italian Neoclassical, Russian, Mahogany, 47 In.	3850.00
Desk, Roll Top, Oak, Child's, Swivel Chair	225.00
Desk, Roll Top, Raised Panels	2100.00
Desk, Roll Top, Typewriter Storage Inside, 7 Drawers, Oak, 45 In.	500.00
Desk, S Roll Top, Mahogany, Fitted Interior, Recessed Panels	3000.00
Desk, S Roll Top, Oak, 48 In.	650.00
Desk, S Roll Top, Oak, Double Pedestal, 36 X 60 In.	1300.00
Desk, S Roll Top, Quarter Sawn Oak, 60 In.	2500.00
Desk, S Roll Top, Secret Compartment	1750.00
Desk, School, Shaker, Double Lift Top, Old Gray Paint	125.00
Desk, Schoolmaster's, 3 Drawers, Wooden Drawer Pulls, Yellow	1000.00
Desk, Schoolmaster's, Hepplewhite, Pine, Comb Graining, 44 In.	300.00
Desk, Schoolmaster's, Lift Top, Pine & Poplar, 25 X 35 In.	125.00
Desk, Schoolmaster's, Slant Lid, Pine, 31 X 20 1/2 X 34 In.	295.00
Desk, Shaker, Kneehole, Pine, Red Paint, C.1863, 45 In.	3300.00
Desk, Sheraton, Mahogany, Tambour Doors, 2 Piece, 51 In.	775.00
Desk, Slant Front, Cherry, 10 Interior Drawers, 18th Century	4100.00
Desk, Slant Front, Cherry, 3 Drawers, New York, C.1760	2900.00
Desk, Slant Front, Cherry, 4 Drawers, French Feet	5400.00
Desk, Slant Front, Chippendale, Carved Maple, C.1775, 45 In.	4950.00
Desk, Slant Front, Chippendale, Cherry, 4 Drawers, 40 1/2 In.	2900.00
Desk, Slant Front, Chippendale, Curly Maple, C.1785, 42 In.	7425.00
Desk, Slant Front, Chippendale, Curly Maple, Ogee Feet, 41 In.	6500.00
Desk, Slant Front, Chippendale, Inlaid Birch, C.1770	1320.00
Desk, Slant Front, Chippendale, Maple, C.1780, 41 X 35 In.	4250.00
Desk, Slant Front, Chippendale, New England, Maple, C.1780, 42 In.	2600.00
Desk, Slant Front, Chippendale, Patera Carved Interior, Mass.	3550.00
Desk, Slant Front, Chippendale, Tiger Maple, C.1770, 42 1/2 In.	3700.00
Desk, Slant Front, Country Chippendale, New England, 1790, 42 In.	3000.00
Desk, Slant Front, Country Chippendale, Old Brasses, 48 In.	2700.00
Desk, Slant Front, Curly Maple, Cherry, Inlaid, French Feet	3300.00
Desk, Slant Front, Dovetailed Beaded Drawers, Cherry, 44 In.	1550.00
Desk, Slant Front, Federal, 4 Graduated Drawers, New Eng., 1800	1900.00
Desk, Slant Front, Federal, Walnut, Inlaid, Original Brasses, 1800	4250.00
Desk, Slant Front, Hepplewhite, Inlaid, 4 Drawers	2310.00
Desk, Slant Front, Inlaid Mahogany, 5 Drawers, 39 1/2 X 43 In.	950.00
Desk, Slant Front, Leaded Glass Doors Below, Oak	550.00
Desk, Slant Front, Maple & Birch, New England, C.1800	2500.00
Desk, Slant Front, Overlapping Drawers, Pine, Chestnut, 42 In.	5500.00
Desk, Slant Front, Queen Anne, Curly Maple, 4 Graduated Drawers	4400.00
Desk, Slant Front, Scalloped Apron, Pine, 31 1/2 X 31 1/4 In.	1150.00
Desk, Spinet, Walnut, Turned Spindle Legs, 1 Drawer	225.00
Desk, Table, Victorian, Walnut, Interior Fitted Drawers	250.00
Desk, Tambour, Massachusetts, Inlaid Mahogany & Veneer	2500.00
Desk, Travel, Brass Bound Mahogany, 14 X 19 1/2 In.	400.00
Desk, Venetian Chinoiserie, Pedestal	1875.00
Desk, Victorian, Pedestal, Leather Top, 3 Frieze Drawers, Walnut	3500.00
Desk, Wagon, Shaker, Pine, Bottom Hinged Door, 27 X 26 In.	2310.00
Desk, Wicker, Oak, 1 Drawer, Chair	345.00
Desk, Wooton, Largest Standard Model	6000.00
Desk, Writing, Lady's, Kidney Shape, Kingwood, 5 Ft. 9 In.	8250.00
Desk, Writing, Leather Top, Frieze Drawers, Tulipwood, 30 In.	1430.00
Desk, Writing, Mahogany, Inlaid, Fall Front, 49 X 20 In.	250.00
Desk–Bookcase, Federal, Tiger Maple, 2 Glazed Doors, 1820, 83 In.	4200.00
Dining Set, Art Deco, Walnut & Burl Table, 4 Chairs	270.00
Dining Set, Louis XV, Mahogany, Satinwood, Floral, 10 Piece	1500.00
Dining Set, Mahogany, Paine, 10 Piece	1540.00
Dining Set, Oak, Carved, Refinished, C.1870, 15 Piece	8500.00
Dining Set, Round Table, G.Stickley, Oak, Leaves, 6 Chairs, 9 Pc.	5675.00

Dresser, American Rococo, Marble Top, Rosewood, 19th Century 2310.00
Dresser, Butterfly Mirrors, English, Walnut 1000.00
Dresser, Eastlake–Style, Walnut, Mirror, Brown Marble Top 995.00
Dresser, Mitchell & Rammelsberg, Marble Top, Carved Rosewood 4000.00
Dresser, Oak, Mirror, Carved Drawer Fronts, C.1905 .... 525.00
Dresser, Victorian, 3 Drawer, Oval Mirror, Glove Boxes, Walnut 875.00
Dresser, Victorian, Drop Center, Mirror, 6 Ft.4 In. 475.00
Dresser, Waterfall, Inlaid, Beveled Glass, Mirror, 3 Drawer 375.00
Dresser, Welsh, Oak, Plate Shelves, 3 Drawers, 77 1/2 In. 1500.00
Dresser, Wishbone, Acorn Handles, Walnut 650.00
Dresser, Wooden Knobs, Toe Board, G.Stickley, Decal, C.1907 .... 700.00
Dressing Table, Marble Top, Prudent Mallard Type, Rosewood 4400.00
Dry Sink, Board & Batten Door, Blue Paint, Pine, 30 1/2 In. 275.00
Dry Sink, Country, Pine, 2 Doors, Mid–1800s 595.00
Dry Sink, Drawer, Paneled Doors, Brown, Yellow Graining, Poplar 355.00
Dry Sink, Ohio Dutch, Walnut 715.00
Dry Sink, Pennslyvania, Shelf, Drawers At Top 450.00
Dry Sink, Pine, Country, Diagonal Slat Door, 22 X 24 In. 295.00
Dry Sink, Pine, Primitive, Red Finish, Drawer, 44 X 37 In. 1250.00
Dry Sink, Poplar, Half Open Shelf Top, C.1880, 6 Ft. 1295.00
Dry Sink, Red Paint, Original Zinc Lining 900.00
Dumbwaiter, 2 Tiers, George III, Mahogany, C.1875, 35 In. 2250.00
Dumbwaiter, 3 Tiers, Tripod, George III, Mahogany, C.1820, 45 In. 605.00
Dumbwaiter, 3 Tiers, Tripod, Mahogany, C.1810, 42 In. 550.00
Dumbwaiter, Adjustable, 3 Graduated Shelves, Rosewood, 41 In. 412.00
Etagere, 5 Tiers, Bronze Mounted, Mahogany, C.1825, 5 Ft.4 In. 6600.00
Etagere, Bamboo, 6 Shelves 135.00
Etagere, Belter–Style, Rosewood, Marble Base, 57 In. .... *Illus* 3300.00
Etagere, Charles X, Brass Galleries, 28 In. 4125.00
Etagere, Corner, Dutch, Scrolled Sides, Doors, Red, Gilt Lacquer 3300.00
Etagere, Napoleon III, Hanging, Glass Shelves, Doors, 24 In. 885.00
Etagere, Regency, Shelves, Beading, Rosewood, C.1825, 5 Ft.7 In. 3250.00
Etagere, Renaissance, Marble Shelf, 1 Drawer 1100.00
Etagere, Rosalie, Belter, Rosewood, C.1855 .... 13500.00
Etagere, Rosewood, Mirrored Cabinet Doors, Belter, Small 3250.00
Etagere, Rosewood, Stylized Dolphin Brackets, 6 Shelves, Meeks 880.00
Etagere, Rosewood, Turned Spindle Shelf Support, Roux 10500.00
Fainting Couch & Hide–A–Bed, Red Upholstery, Oak, C.1890 .... 985.00
Fauteuil De Cabinet, Louis XV, Beechwood, Caned, E.Meunier, Pair 4125.00
Footstool, Bootjack Ends, Dark Green Paint, Pine, 15 In. 30.00
Footstool, Bootjack Ends, Scalloped Apron, Walnut, 14 In. 65.00
Footstool, Country Windsor, Old Green Repaint, 12 1/2 X 9 In. 45.00
Footstool, Cow Horn Legs 25.00
Footstool, Cutout Hearts, Red Finish, Black Trim, Pine, 8 In. 400.00
Footstool, Double, Leather Top, Mahogany, Paine, C.1910 .... 225.00
Footstool, George I, Walnut, Slip Seat, Oriental, 1740, 20 In. 4675.00
Footstool, George II Style, Needlepoint Upholstered, Mahogany 1300.00
Footstool, L & JG Stickley, No.391, Leather Top, C.1907, 18 In. 200.00
Footstool, Old Red, Corner Grained Fans Top, 9 3/8 X 13 X 8 In. 65.00
Footstool, Original Red, Black Graining, Stenciled Gold Basket 70.00
Footstool, Oval Seat, Gilt Highlights, Marked A.W.Pratt, Pine 75.00
Footstool, Pine, Bootjack Ends, Brown–Yellow Paint, 10 X 15 In. 35.00
Footstool, Pine, Cutout Legs, Drawer, Black, 10 X 16 In. 175.00
Footstool, Pine, Oval Plank Seat, C.1830, 8 X 13 1/2 In. 75.00
Footstool, Shaker, 2 Steps, Light Gray–Green Paint, 9 1/2 In. 150.00
Footstool, Shaker, Turned Legs, Mt.Lebanon, N.Y. 250.00
Footstool, Slant Top, Bootjack Legs, Pine, 11 3/4 X 6 1/2 In. 38.00
Footstool, Spindle Sides, Gustav Stickley, C.1907, 15 X 16 In. 3000.00
Footstool, Splayed Legs, Beveled Edge Top, 8 X 12 X 6 In. 55.00
Footstool, Upholstered Padded Top, Pine, 15 X 9 X 9 1/4 In. 9.50
Footstool, Victorian, Iron Legs 95.00
Footstool, Wicker, 3 Legs, C.1900 .... 52.50
Footstool, Windsor, Original Green Paint, Striping, Oval, 11 In. 55.00
Footstool, Windsor, Oval Top, Old Blue Paint, 9 1/4 X 16 In. 200.00

Footstool, Woven Cane Top, Black Paint, Yellow Striping, 9 In.	65.00
Frame, Doweled Corners, Stylized Floral Design, 19th Century	125.00
Garden Seat, Baluster Shape, Blue Canton, Pair	5000.00
Garden Seat, Famille Rose, Hexagonal, Greek Key Border, 19 In.	1300.00
Garden Seat, Famille Rose, Oriental Figures, 19 In.	2700.00
Garden Seat, Majolica, Wedgwood	1895.00
Garden Set, 2 Armchairs, Settee, Cast Iron, Old White Paint	150.00
Glider, Victorian, Pressed Back, Oak, Turnings	185.00
Grain Bin, Original Yellow Grained Paint, Miniature	475.00
Gueridon, Louis XVI, Walnut, Marble Top, Diamond Design, 32 In.	8800.00
Gueridon, Mahogany, Painted, Parcel Gilt, Tripod, 27 X 33 In.	7150.00
Gueridon, Neoclassical, Mahogany, 3 Reed Brass Legs, 28 X 20 In.	2850.00
Hall Rack, Walnut, Umbrella Holders, Marble Top, Drawer, Large	875.00
Hall Seat, Oak, Mirror & Hat Hooks	370.00
Hall Seat, Oak, Mirror, Hooks, 1 Drawer, Handles On Sides	195.00
Hall Stand, 6 Branches, Iron, Mirror, Umbrella Tray, 27 In., Pair	700.00
Hall Stand, Animal Horns, Mirror, Wenzel Friederich, 1890s	6500.00
Hall Stand, Bear Holding Tree, Cubs, Austrian, C.1890, 7 Ft.4 In.	4675.00
Hall Stand, Full Mirror, Hooks, Umbrella Holders, Walnut, 100 In.	1700.00
Hall Stand, Iron, Tree Form, Pat.1858, 71 In., Pair	450.00
Hall Stand, Oak, Beveled Mirror, Belgian, 8 Ft.	2295.00
Hall Stand, Quarter Sawn Oak, Beveled Mirror, Hat Hooks, Small	825.00
Hall Stand, Victorian, Marble Top Table, C.1860	2420.00
Hall Stand, Victorian, Pierced Back, Mirror Handles Both Sides	595.00
Hall Stand, Walnut, Twig & Vine, Marble, Iron Basin, 8 1/2 Ft.	5000.00
Hat Rack, Wall, Buffalo Horns	47.50
Highboy, 3 Thumb-Molded Drawers, Maple, C.1760, 36 In.	1400.00
Highboy, Oak, Bonnet Box, Original Brass & Copper Hardware	975.00
Highboy, On Stand, Oak, George I, C.1720	8900.00
Highboy, Queen Anne, Carved Fans, Massachusetts	750.00
Highboy, Queen Anne, Carved, Figured Maple, C.1750, 7 Ft.5 In.	5775.00
Highboy, Queen Anne, Chester County, Figured Maple	7250.00
Highboy, Queen Anne, Maple, Concealed Document Drawer, 5 Ft.	5100.00
Highboy, Queen Anne, Turned Rosettes, Finials, Walnut, 78 1/2 In.	2150.00
Highboy, Queen Anne, Walnut, Cabriole Legs, 40 X 62 In.	11000.00
Highboy, William & Mary, Walnut Veneered, C.1730, 62 1/2 In.	5775.00
Highchair, Ash, Arched Slats, Sloped Arms, Rush Seat, 1800, 32 In.	150.00
Highchair, Regency, Mahogany, Upholstered Seat	495.00
Highchair, Splayed Base, Rush Seat, 19th Century	660.00
Highchair, Spring Mounted, Wooden Base, Yellow Graining, 1857	165.00
Highchair, Windsor Style, Plank Seat, C.1830	125.00
Highchair, Yellow Striping, Spindle Back, Old Red Paint, 34 In.	85.00
Highchair-Stroller, Caned Seat	250.00
Highchair-Stroller, Oak, Pressed Back	495.00
Huntboard, Sheraton, 2 Drawers, Curly Maple, Pine Top, 37 In.	4250.00
Hutch, Child's, Pine, 25 1/2 In.	70.00
Ice Cream Set, Child's, Table, 2 Chairs	150.00
Icebox, Oak, Hinged Top, Original Finish, Small	170.00
Icebox, Oak, Original Brass Hardware, Refinished, 4 Door, Large	300.00
Kas, Butternut, Ohio, 2 Doors, 2 Drawers, 84 In.	3000.00
Kas, Chippendale, Walnut, Pine, 1780–1800, English, 83 In.	6000.00
Kas, Queen Anne, Paneled Doors, Walnut, 1750–80, 7 Ft. 5 In.	11000.00
Kas, Removable Base, Cornice, Pine, Flame Graining, 82 In.	350.00
Ladder, Library, Folding, Brass Mounted, Mahogany, 7 Ft. 8 In.	5775.00
Library Steps, George III Style, Top Shelf, Oak, 5 Ft. 3 In.	4000.00
Library Steps, Regency, Inset Leather Risers, Mahogany	700.00
Library Steps, Victorian, 2 Leather Treads, Mahogany, 53 In.	2000.00
Limbert, Bookcase, Open, 3 Shelves, C.1910, 28 1/2 X 28 In.	300.00
Linen Press, George III, Inlaid Frieze, Inlaid Mahogany, 77 In.	3500.00
Linen Press, George III, Sliding Shelves, Mahogany, 4 Ft. 6 In.	2475.00
Linen Press, Oval Inlaid Paneled Doors, Mahogany, 6 Ft.6 In.	1210.00
Linen Press, Paneled Doors, Mahogany, C.1835, 7 Ft. 3 In.	1980.00
Lounge, Haywood Wakefield, Wicker, Pair	365.00
Lounge, Regency, Cane & Wood, C.1920	875.00

Love Seat, Hand Carved Florals, Green Upholstery, Walnut	600.00
Love Seat, Upholstered, J.& J.Meeks	5000.00
Love Seat, Wicker, 1920s	135.00
Lowboy, Chippendale, American, Mahogany, C.1750, 32 In.	1870.00
Lowboy, English, Oak, 3 Drawers, Spanish Feet	500.00
Lowboy, George I, Inlaid Walnut, 4 Drawers, 29 In.	3850.00
Lowboy, Queen Anne, Mahogany, 5 Drawers, Cutout Scalloped Apron	8800.00
Lowboy, Queen Anne, Walnut, Mahogany, Veneered Drawers, 34 In.	9900.00
Magazine Rack, L & JG Stickley, 3 Open Shelves, C.1910, 42 In.	1100.00
Magazine Rack, Panel Sides, 5 Open Shelves, C.1910, 45 1/2 In.	200.00
Magazine Stand, Victorian, Oak Top, 4 Brass Divisions, 15 In.	425.00
Mirror, Acorns & Flowers, Mid–1870s, 40 X 24 In.	400.00
Mirror, Adams Style, Gilt Gesso, 18th Century, 3 Ft.5 In.	425.00
Mirror, Arched Plate, Pollard Elm & Amaranth, French, 74 In.	2200.00
Mirror, Austrian Rococo, Gilt Wood, Eagles Frame, 57 X 40 In.	5500.00
Mirror, Banister, Gilt, Split, Reverse Painting, 1835, 38 X 18 In.	325.00
Mirror, Baroque, Framed, Acanthus Scrolls, 49 X 35 In.	500.00
Mirror, Baroque, On Marble Top Pedestal, 109 X 31 In.	1800.00
Mirror, Cartouche Shape, Scrolls, Putti, Carved Walnut, 52 In.	4125.00
Mirror, Carved Mahogany, Pierced Scroll Crest, 1840, 45 X 30 In.	350.00
Mirror, Carved Strapwork Cartouche, Gilt, Oval, 75 X 40 In.	650.00
Mirror, Charles X, Amaranth & Maple Marquetry, 24 X 38 In.	770.00
Mirror, Cheval, Charles X, Inlaid Stars Frame, 42 In. X 6 Ft.	2750.00
Mirror, Cheval, George III, Gesso Border, Mahogany, 51 1/2 In.	605.00
Mirror, Cheval, Half Clad Female One Side, On Stand, 9 Ft.4 In.	3850.00
Mirror, Cheval, Tabletop, Domed Top, 4 Drawers, 25 X 23 In.	600.00
Mirror, Chinese Chippendale Style, Gilt Wood, 29 X 61 In.	1000.00
Mirror, Chip Carved Poplar Frame, 5 X 6 1/4 In.	450.00
Mirror, Chippendale, Carved Eagle, Mahogany, 22 X 43 1/2 In.	675.00
Mirror, Chippendale, Carved Gold Eagle, Mahogany, 17 X 34 In.	650.00
Mirror, Chippendale, Gilded Phoenix Top, Mahogany, 1760, 30 In.	200.00
Mirror, Chippendale, Gilded Star Crest, Mahogany, 11 X 20 In.	285.00
Mirror, Chippendale, Gilt Carved Shell, Liner, C.1760, 37 In.	175.00
Mirror, Chippendale, Mahogany Gilt Wood, C.1780, 43 X 27 In.	1300.00
Mirror, Chippendale, Mahogany, 12 1/4 X 20 3/8 In.	375.00
Mirror, Chippendale, Mahogany, Gilt Gesso, 1780, 36 X 19 In.	1000.00
Mirror, Chippendale, Mahogany, Scroll, Molded, 14 X 25 3/4 In.	850.00
Mirror, Chippendale, Mahogany, Shaped Crest, 1760–80, 20 In.	400.00
Mirror, Chippendale, Mahogany, Shaped Crests, 39 X 22 In.	1540.00
Mirror, Chippendale, Molded Frame, Walnut, 11 1/2 X 18 In.	155.00
Mirror, Chippendale, Original Glass, 19th Century, 17 X 36 In.	450.00
Mirror, Chippendale, Original Glass, Mahogany, 15 X 30 In.	575.00
Mirror, Chippendale, Original Glass, Walnut, 12 1/4 X 20 3/4 In.	325.00
Mirror, Chippendale, Scroll, Varnish, Signature, 12 X 18 In.	625.00
Mirror, Chippendale, Scrolled Crest & Base, American, 33 In.	400.00
Mirror, Chippendale, Scrolled Frame, Boston, C.1860, 26 1/2 In.	550.00
Mirror, Chippendale, Walnut, 11 1/2 X 19 1/2 In.	155.00
Mirror, Chippendle, Gilded Liner, Mahogany Veneer, 41 In.	550.00
Mirror, Convex, Gilt Wood, Eagle Top, Round, C.1850, 54 In.	4675.00
Mirror, Courting, Reverse Glass, 1803, 11 1/2 X 16 1/2 In.	825.00
Mirror, Courting, Reverse Painted Inserts, 11 X 20 In.	300.00
Mirror, Crown Etching, Gilded Crest, Ornate	3850.00
Mirror, Dieppe Ivory, Oval Glass, 18th Century, 34 X 22 In.	4750.00
Mirror, Dressing Table, Carved Walnut, 1 Drawer, 41 X 24 In.	4100.00
Mirror, Dressing Table, Regency, 3 Drawers, Mahogany, 19 In.	160.00
Mirror, Dressing, Carved Ivory, Walnut, Europe, Oval, 23 In.	950.00
Mirror, Dressing, Chippendale, Mahogany, 30 X 17 In.	650.00
Mirror, Dressing, Federal, Original Glass, 16 1/2 X 33 In.	750.00
Mirror, Eastlake, Walnut, 25 1/4 X 56 1/2 In.	450.00
Mirror, Eglomise Glass, Molded Frame, 21 X 35 In., 2 Piece	375.00
Mirror, Empire, Acanthus Carved Pilasters, 16 1/2 X 34 In.	85.00
Mirror, Empire, Eglomise Panel, Split Baluster Columns, 35 In.	175.00
Mirror, Empire, Reverse Painting of Sailboat, 14 X 22 In.	60.00
Mirror, Empire, Watercolor of Church, Fisherman, 12 X 24 1/2 In.	75.00

Mirror, Federal, Eglomise, Gilt Wood, Wm.T.Grinnell, R.I. 750.00
Mirror, Federal, Gilt Girandole, New England, C.1795, 31 In. 1100.00
Mirror, Federal, Gilt Wood, Convex Glass, Eagle, 4 Candles, 44 In. 1700.00
Mirror, Federal, Gilt Wood, Girandole, C.1800 .... 6050.00
Mirror, Federal, Gold Leaf Frame, Reverse On Glass Top, 41 In. 235.00
Mirror, Federal, Gold Leaf, Reverse Painting Panel, 25 X 44 In. 2250.00
Mirror, Federal, Inlaid Mahogany, Gilt Wood, Urn Top, 1795, 55 In. 5500.00
Mirror, Federal, Original Glass, Gold Leaf, 30 X 47 In. 850.00
Mirror, French Empire, Crest, 4 Ft.3 In.X 2 Ft.7 In. 175.00
Mirror, George II Style, Parcel Gilt, Walnut, 4 Ft.3 In. 1900.00
Mirror, George II, Parcel Gilt, Walnut, 4 Ft. 6 In. X 27 In. 6600.00
Mirror, George II, Swan Neck Pediment, Walnut, 31 X 56 In. 5250.00
Mirror, George III Style, Gilt Wood, Beveled Glass, 43 In. 1400.00
Mirror, George III, Chippendale, Gold, S Scroll, 44 X 23 In. 1200.00
Mirror, George III, Gesso, Wood, Fluted Columns, Border, 55 In. 550.00
Mirror, George III, Mahogany, Gilt, 19th Century 3520.00
Mirror, Georgian, Partial Gilt Wood, England, C.1760, 27 X 52 In. 4000.00
Mirror, Gilded Acorn & Oakleaf Design, New England, C.1730 .... 1850.00
Mirror, Gilded Eagle, Original Glass, 19th Century, Small 500.00
Mirror, Gilded, London, T.Fentham, Pine, Convex, 1810, 25 X 44 In. 8000.00
Mirror, Gilded, Williams, N.Y., Spiral Cornucopias, C.1840, 50 In. 7800.00
Mirror, Gilt Bronze, Fruits Bottom, Chain Hung, C.1925, 30 In. 2200.00
Mirror, Gilt Carved Frame, Hosea Dugliss, C.1835 .... 2000.00
Mirror, Girandole, Federal, Carved, Gilded, 19th Century, 33 In. 4400.00
Mirror, Gold Leaf, Raised Roses, Oval, 28 X 34 In. 800.00
Mirror, Hall, Beveled Glass, Gold Gilt Frame, 26 X 48 In. 70.00
Mirror, Hall, Oak, Coat Hooks, Hanging 190.00
Mirror, Hall, Queen Anne, Arched Form, Crest, Walnut, 54 In. 950.00
Mirror, Louis XVI, Painted & Parcel Gilt, Trophies, 25 X 46 In. 1430.00
Mirror, Mahogany Scroll, 19th Century, 14 X 26 3/4 In. 230.00
Mirror, Mantel, 3 Beveled Glasses, Walnut 1000.00
Mirror, Mantel, Oval, Rectangular Frame, Parcel Gilt, 4 Ft.4 In. 7150.00
Mirror, Mother-of-Pearl Inlay, Pierced Crest, Hardwood, 61 In. 400.00
Mirror, Napoleon III, Gilt Bronze Mounted, 44 In. 2550.00
Mirror, Neoclassical, Carved Frame, Cornucopia Top, 5 Ft.6 In. 3575.00
Mirror, Neoclassical, Painted & Parcel Gilt, Fruitwood, 4 Ft. 3960.00
Mirror, Neoclassical, Parcel Gilt, Painted Green, 6 Ft.4 In. 1900.00
Mirror, Oval Carved, Bellflower Swags, 19th Century, 64 X 30 In. 750.00
Mirror, Pier, American Rococo Gilt, Matching Console Table 1000.00
Mirror, Pier, Marble Top Base, 9 Ft.6 In. 1275.00
Mirror, Pier, Marble Top, Gilt Highlights, Walnut, 10 Ft. 850.00
Mirror, Pier, Neoclassical, Foliate Scrolls, Vines, 67 In. 2550.00
Mirror, Pier, Neoclassical, Twisted Ribbon Frame, 5 Ft.9 In. 5500.00
Mirror, Pier, Rococo Style, Cartouche, 19th Century, 113 X 32 In. 450.00
Mirror, Pier, Rococo, Carved Mahogany, 9 Ft. 1210.00
Mirror, Pierced Crest, Hoho Bird, Parcel Gilt Mahogany, 37 In. 900.00
Mirror, Pilasters, Reverse Painting, Gold, 10 X 18 In., 2 Piece 200.00
Mirror, Pine, Molded Cornice, Reverse Painted, 11 X 16 In. 125.00
Mirror, Plateau, Beveled, Copper Color Frame, Footed 65.00
Mirror, Plateau, Beveled, Cut Stars, 12 In. 38.00
Mirror, Plateau, Beveled, Leaf & Scroll, Footed, 12 In. 65.00
Mirror, Plateau, Beveled, Pairpoint, Silver Plate 65.00
Mirror, Plateau, Brass Ormolu Base, Footed, 12 In. 125.00
Mirror, Plateau, Fleur-De-Lis & Floral Cut, Rosettes, 15 In. 165.00
Mirror, Plateau, On Stand, Gilt Bronze, C.1860, 5 Ft.8 In. 8250.00
Mirror, Plateau, Ram's Head & Feet, Jutting Handles, 12 In. 205.00
Mirror, Plateau, Recessed Top, Art Deco Engravings, 12 In. 135.00
Mirror, Plateau, Scroll Leaf Forms, Shell Clusters, 12 In. 105.00
Mirror, Plateau, Sheffield, Leaf Rim, Paw Feet, 18 In. 300.00
Mirror, Plateau, Silver Plate, Beveled, Scroll Feet, 14 In. 50.00
Mirror, Plateau, Wreath Figures, Silver Plate, 16 In. 115.00
Mirror, Queen Anne, Carved Walnut & Gilt Wood, C.1740, 19 In. 1045.00
Mirror, Queen Anne, Chinoiserie Design, Pine, 14 X 24 1/2 In. 725.00
Mirror, Queen Anne, Convex Frame, Japanned, English, 34 X 51 In. 3575.00

Mirror, Queen Anne, Country, Walnut Crest & Base, 9 1/2 X 18 In.	500.00
Mirror, Queen Anne, Japanned Bird Forms, English, 3 Ft.3 1/2 In.	850.00
Mirror, Queen Anne, Mahogany, Shaped Crest, C.1750, 18 X 10 In.	550.00
Mirror, Queen Anne, Molded Frame, 18th Century, 15 X 10 In.	250.00
Mirror, Queen Anne, Ogee Molding, Crest, Dark Finish, 8 X 14 In.	800.00
Mirror, Queen Anne, Scroll, Mahogany Veneer, 13 3/4 X 23 3/4 In.	1000.00
Mirror, Queen Anne, Scrolled Whale's Tail, Walnut, 22 X 45 In.	7250.00
Mirror, Queen Anne, Walnut Veneer, Crest, C.1750, 23 X 12 In.	770.00
Mirror, Queen Anne, Walnut, Shaped Crest, 1750, 24 In.	425.00
Mirror, Reflector, Magnifying Lens, Mahogany Stand, 26 In.	175.00
Mirror, Regency, Alternating Cut Glass, Reverse, Irish, 26 In.	3850.00
Mirror, Regency, Indian Bust Top, Branches, 5 Ft. 10 In.	5500.00
Mirror, Rococo, Gilt Italianate, Rectangular, 55 X 30 In.	900.00
Mirror, Scroll, Curly Walnut, 17 3/4 X 30 3/4 In.	175.00
Mirror, Scroll, Walnut, Ogee Frame, Lovebird Crest, 14 X 34 In.	1500.00
Mirror, Shaving, 2 Dovetailed Drawers, Pine, 20 In.	110.00
Mirror, Shaving, Country Empire, Mahogany Veneer, Drawer, 17 In.	35.00
Mirror, Shaving, Federal, Mahogany & Ivory, C.1810, 19 In.	1100.00
Mirror, Shaving, Oval, Beveled Glass, Stand, 8 1/2 In.	20.00
Mirror, Shaving, Quarter Sawn Oak	750.00
Mirror, Shaving, Scrolled Crest, Gilded Liner, 7 5/8 X 4 1/4 In.	115.00
Mirror, Toilet, Queen Anne, 3 Drawers, Walnut	1895.00
Mirror, Toilet, Queen Anne, Japanned, Gilt Design, 35 X 18 In.	770.00
Mirror, Wall, Chippendale, Pendant Below, Mahogany, C.1790, 38 In.	2550.00
Mirror, Wall, Continental, Brass, Beveled Plate, 38 X 23 In.	300.00
Mirror, Wall, Copper & Enamel, England, C.1905, 29 3/4 X 22 In.	500.00
Mirror, William & Mary, Carved Pine, C.1680, 42 X 40 In.	4400.00
Murphy Bed, Oak, Beveled Mirror	450.00
Nightstand, Cherry, Drawer, Splashback, 35 X 24 X 19 In.	150.00
Nightstand, Empire, Mahogany, Marble, Ogee Frieze, Drawer, 1830	275.00
Nightstand, Walnut, Marble, Drawer, Panel Door, France, 32 In.	150.00
Parlor Set, Jelliff, Rosewood, Carved Heads, Arms, Backs, 4 Piece	3950.00
Parlor Set, Louis XVI, Padded Arms & Seat, Gilt Wood, 1900, 5 Pc.	3100.00
Parlor Set, Renaissance Revival, Walnut, 1865, 7 Piece	3400.00
Parlor Set, Rosewood, Sofa, Armchair, 5 Side Chairs, 1850s	8000.00
Parlor Set, Shaped Horn Back & Arms, Upholstered Seat, 3 Piece	6000.00
Parlor Set, Victorian, Walnut, Upholstered, C.1850, 4 Piece	2500.00
Pedestal, Elongated Corbel Sides, Limbert, C.1906, 32 1/2 In.	900.00
Pedestal, George III, Painted, Marble Top, Carved, 43 In., Pair	4950.00
Pedestal, Neoclassical, Fruitwood, Columnar Form, 50 In., Pair	6325.00
Pew, Church, Pine, 9 Ft.	125.00
Pie Safe, 1 Drawer, 12 Punched Star & Circle Panels, Poplar	375.00
Pie Safe, 1 Drawer, 8 Panels, Diamond & Circle Pattern, 54 In.	320.00
Pie Safe, 2 Doors, Punched Tin, Southern	400.00
Pie Safe, Blue & Green Original Paint, Bottom Drawer, C.1860	1150.00
Pie Safe, Blue Over Green Paint, Punched Tin, Ala., 1850s	1450.00
Pie Safe, Glass Sides, 2 Movable Shelves, Columbus, 22 X 17 In.	225.00
Pie Safe, Original Green Paint, Punched Tin, Double Width	2450.00
Pie Safe, Paneled Doors, Screen Panel Ends, Poplar, 50 X 57 In.	285.00
Pie Safe, Punched Tin, Green Paint, 2 Doors, Dated 1820–30	3200.00
Pie Safe, Softwood, 12 Painted Tins	425.00
Plant Stand, Cast Iron, Mid–19th Century, 12 Holders	2100.00
Plant Stand, Louis XV, Brass, Marble	475.00
Plant Stand, Wire	650.00
Potty Chair, Child's, Yellow Paint	70.00
Potty Chair, Gray Graniteware Potty	25.00
Potty Chair, Leatherized Cloth Covered Seat, Pine, 24 1/2 In.	95.00
Potty Chair, Wicker	80.00
Rack, Baker's, Grapevine Sides, Wrought Iron, 1910, 7 X 5 Ft.	325.00
Rack, Drying, 4 Sections, Pine, 33 1/2 X 65 1/2 In.	135.00
Rack, Drying, Center Turned Post, Pine, 4 Sections, 38 X 54 In.	130.00
Rack, Drying, Mortised Pine, 2 Bars, Old Gray Paint, 36 X 40 In.	65.00
Rack, Drying, Shoe Feet, Old Green Paint, 41 1/2 X 40 1/2 In.	175.00
Rack, Magazine, 5 Tiers, 5 Hand Painted Cameo Scenes, 1900s	600.00

Furniture, Recamier, American, Rosewood & Laminated, Pair

Furniture, Rocker, Child's, Shaker, Red & White Seat, Black Paint

Rack, Plate Drying, Dowel Rod Shelves, Castors, 43 1/2 X 54 In.	75.00
Rack, Towel, Turned Posts, Rosewood Graining, 26 X 25 3/4 In.	55.00
Rack, Wall, Telescoping, Oak, 9 Iron Hangers	58.00
Recamier, American Empire, J.& J.Meeks, Mahogany, 86 In.	1400.00
Recamier, American, Rosewood & Laminated, Pair ....*Illus*	9350.00
Recamier, Rosalie With Grapes, Belter, Pair	9900.00
Rocker, Arms, Gustav Stickley, No.323, Vertical Slats, 36 In.	1000.00
Rocker, Arms, Open, 4 Slats, Spring Cushion Seat, C.1907	325.00
Rocker, Arms, Windsor, Comb Back, C.1800	1650.00
Rocker, Arrow Back, Black Paint, Yellow Striping, Scrolled	125.00
Rocker, Arrow Back, Scrolled Arms, Splayed Back, Ink Grained	155.00
Rocker, Black Walnut, Large Lion's Heads, Massive	550.00
Rocker, Boston Style, Solid Curved Pine Seat	145.00
Rocker, Cherry, Carved Dragons Crest, Arms	165.00
Rocker, Child's, Bentwood Arms, Turned Back & Arms, 1 Piece	100.00
Rocker, Child's, Bentwood, Hickory, Pair	375.00
Rocker, Child's, Black Paint, Rush Seat, Arms, 18th Century	125.00
Rocker, Child's, Ladder Back, Sausage Turnings, Rope Seat, Arms	450.00
Rocker, Child's, Pressed Back, Wide Bentwood Arms, Oak	135.00
Rocker, Child's, Rabbit Ear, Spindle Back	95.00
Rocker, Child's, Shaker, Arms, Red & Beige Tape	1100.00
Rocker, Child's, Shaker, Red & White Seat, Black Paint ....*Illus*	350.00
Rocker, Child's, Wicker	175.00
Rocker, Child's, Wicker, Upholstered Seat, 15 X 20 In.	55.00
Rocker, Chippendale, Pierced Splat, Arms, Black, Yellow	250.00
Rocker, Cube, Lifetime Co., Spring Cushion Seat, C.1907	1000.00
Rocker, Glider, Oak, Dated 1888	500.00
Rocker, Heywood Wakefield, Wicker	175.00
Rocker, Hunzinger, Platform, Walnut, 43 In. ....*Illus*	175.00
Rocker, L.& J.G.Stickley, Upholstered Seat & Back, Oak	475.00
Rocker, Ladder Back, 4 Arched Slats, Rush Seat	75.00
Rocker, Ladder Back, 5 Arched Slats, Shaped Arms	1050.00
Rocker, Ladder Back, Scrolled Arms, Woven Cane Seat	150.00
Rocker, Ladder Back, Walnut, Rush Seat, 45 In. ....*Illus*	325.00
Rocker, Oak, Limbert	190.00
Rocker, Oak, Pressed Back, Turned Spindle	235.00
Rocker, Oak, Stick & Ball, Upholstered	595.00
Rocker, Platform, Bird's–Eye Maple	125.00
Rocker, Platform, Wicker, Natural Brown Finish	300.00
Rocker, Red & Black Graining, Yellow Striping, Arrow Spindles	150.00
Rocker, Scrolled Seat & Arms, Gold Foliage & Wheat, Crest	75.00
Rocker, Sewing, 4 Slats, G.Stickley, Red Decal, C.1904, 33 In.	200.00

Rocker, Sewing, Folding, Walnut	200.00
Rocker, Shaker, Armless, Enfield, C.1840, 41 In.	2000.00
Rocker, Shaker, Decal, Arms, Mt.Lebanon, 1930s	675.00
Rocker, Shaker, Maple, Black Over Red Paint, Splint Seat, Arms	1320.00
Rocker, Shaker, Maple, Tape Seat, Lemon Shape Finials, C.1910	715.00
Rocker, Shaker, No.3, Arms, Mt.Lebanon, N.Y.	650.00
Rocker, Shaker, No.3, Interlaken, N.Y.	565.00
Rocker, Shaker, No.4, Arms	446.25
Rocker, Shaker, No.4, Cherry, Splint Seat & Back, Mt.Lebanon	250.00
Rocker, Shaker, No.6, Arms	735.00
Rocker, Shaker, No.6, Bentwood	300.00
Rocker, Shaker, No.6, Interlaken, N.Y.	750.00
Rocker, Shaker, No.7, Arms	472.50
Rocker, Shaker, Shawl Back, Arms, Red & Brown Upholstered	675.00
Rocker, Sheraton, High Back, Old Black Paint, Rush Seat	70.00
Rocker, Signed Stickley, Oak	150.00
Rocker, Spindle Back, Black Paint	75.00
Rocker, Stained Ash, Gustav Stickley, C.1902 ....*Illus*	3300.00
Rocker, Tiger Maple, Arms, Reeded Back & Seat	350.00
Rocker, Windsor, Bamboo, Comb Back, Red Paint Over Black, Arms	170.00
Rocker, Windsor, Bamboo, Step Down Crest, Old Red Paint, Arms	355.00
Rocker, Windsor, Birdcage Maple, Pine, New England, 1810	400.00
Rocker, Windsor, Comb Back, American, C.1815	325.00
Rocker, Windsor, Comb Back, Old Paint, 41 1/2 In.	485.00
Rocker, Windsor, High Back, Bamboo Turnings, Shaped Seat	200.00
Rocker, Windsor, Maple, Ash, Pine, 3 Back, Saddle Seat, Arms, C.1780	1300.00
Salon Suite, Carved Fruitwood, Majorelle, C.1900, 5 Piece	6600.00
Salon Suite, Walnut, Majorelle, Fan Design, C.1900, 5 Piece	6325.00
Screen, 2–Panel, Carving, Ivory & Lacquer, Panel 70 X 32 In.	2700.00
Screen, 2–Panel, Oriental Wormwood, Tiffany Stained Glass	3500.00
Screen, 3–Panel, Louis XVI, Potentate & Europeans, 4 Ft. 9 In.	1100.00
Screen, 3–Panel, Oak, Ball & Stick Design	190.00
Screen, 4–Panel, Wallpaper, Hand Painted, Hunting Party, 86 In.	2500.00
Screen, 5–Panel, Needlepoint, Prunus, Brown, Beige Ground, 6 Ft.	2400.00
Screen, Leaded Glass, Enameled, Rosewood Frame, 1900, 4 Ft.4 In.	3025.00
Screen, Pole, Floral Needlework, England, Mahogany, C.1795, 60 In.	350.00
Screen, Wedding Celebration, Black Lacquer, C.1750, 6 Ft.	3100.00
Secretary Bookcase, Chippendale, Slant Front, Mahogany	8750.00
Secretary Bookcase, Drop Front, Oak	775.00
Secretary Bookcase, Federal, Mahogany, Inlaid Skirt, 7 Ft.4 In.	2300.00
Secretary Bookcase, Federal, Mahogany, Satinwood, C.1810, 80 In.	9075.00
Secretary Bookcase, George II, Inlaid, Mahogany & Satinwood	5500.00
Secretary Bookcase, George III, Mahogany, Glazed Doors, 85 In.	2000.00
Secretary Bookcase, Secret Drawer, Mahogany, Rosewood, C.1835	1325.00
Secretary Bookcase, Victorian, Carved Rosewood	3850.00
Secretary Cabinet, Regency, Mahogany, Satinwood, 7 Ft.	2475.00

Furniture, Rocker,
Hunzinger, Platform,
Walnut, 43 In.

Furniture, Rocker,
Ladder Back, Walnut,
Rush Seat, 45 In.

Furniture, Rocker,
Stained Ash,
Gustav Stickley, C.1902

Furniture, Secretary, Drop Front,
Mahogany, Marble, 6 Ft.10 In.

Furniture, Settee, Triple Chairback,
Black Lacquer, 5 Ft.9 In.

Secretary, Butler's, Carved Grapes, Original Hardware, Rosewood	2250.00
Secretary, Drop Front, Biedermeier, Birch & Ebonized, 6 Ft.	5500.00
Secretary, Drop Front, Mahogany, Marble, 6 Ft.10 In. ....*Illus*	5500.00
Secretary, Empire, Mahogany, Fall Front, Marble, 1800, 4 Ft.9 In.	3575.00
Secretary, Empire, Mahogany, Gothic Revival Panels, 1835, 88 In.	950.00
Secretary, Fall Front, Fitted Interior, Biedermeier, Fruitwood	1200.00
Secretary, Fall Front, Marble Top, Carved Rosewood, C.1850	2420.00
Secretary, Federal, Mahogany, Bird's–Eye Maple, Mass., 1790	6420.00
Secretary, Lady's, Rococo Revival, Rosewood, 77 In.	800.00
Secretary, Mahogany Veneer, D.G.Rollings, 74 X 40 X 19 In.	650.00
Secretary, Mullioned Upper Case, Inlaid Mahogany, Maple, C.1800	1600.00
Secretary, Neoclassical, Various Woods, Alabaster, Sweden, 7 Ft.	8800.00
Secretary, Pine, Double Glass Top Doors, 2 Piece	1500.00
Secretary, Regency, Mahogany, Glazed Doors, 102 X 47 X 21 In.	2700.00
Secretary, Shaker, Butternut & Pine, Fold Down, 2 Doors, 68 In.	2100.00
Secretary, Slant Front, Country, Walnut, 3 Bottom Drawers, Conn.	5500.00
Secretary, Slant Front, English Oak, 18th Century, 3 Piece	2400.00
Secretary, Slant Front, Norwich, Cherry, 1717, 33 In.	4750.00
Server, Chippendale, Rectangular, Mahogany, 35 X 38 X 19 In.	300.00
Server, Country Queen Anne, Cherry, 2 Drawers	2000.00
Server, Empire, Mahogany, Claw Foot, Marble Top, Mirror Back	695.00
Server, Oak, Carved Chalet, Landscape Scene, Winged Column Ends	1000.00
Server, Sheraton, Fluted Legs, Mahogany, American, 33 In.	1600.00
Server, Sheraton, Maple, 2 Drawers, Reeded Legs	4150.00
Settee, 3 Chair Back, Black Lacquer, Shaped Arms, 5 Ft.9 In.	1450.00
Settee, American Rococo, Cast Iron	3300.00
Settee, Arched Padded Back, Cushion Seat, Mahogany, 7 Ft.4 In.	1450.00
Settee, Bentwood, Thonet, Original Gold Leaf, Austria, 1880	1750.00
Settee, Child's, Cane Seat, Bentwood, Thonet Label, 32 In.	850.00
Settee, Classical, Carved Cornucopia, Mahogany, New York	2500.00
Settee, Continental, Leaf Carved Tablet, Mahogany, 7 Ft.	1300.00
Settee, Double Chairback, George III, Mahogany, C.1880, 4 Ft.	3000.00
Settee, Ebonized Birch, Serpentine Upholstered, Biedermeier	4950.00
Settee, Federal, Inlaid, Mahogany, Scrolled Arms, 33 X 75 In.	600.00
Settee, Federal, Scrolled Crest, Upholstered, C.1810, 75 In.	6000.00
Settee, George II, Walnut, Upholstered Scroll Arms, 5 Ft.	6875.00
Settee, Gothic, Oak, American	4000.00
Settee, L.& J.G.Stickley, No.281, Decal, 34 X 76 In.	3000.00
Settee, Louis XVI, Carved Rosewood, A.& H.Lejambre	600.00
Settee, Maple & Pine, Bulbous Turned Legs, C.1920, 51 X 22 In.	600.00
Settee, Medallion Back, Victorian, Walnut Frame, 69 In.	650.00

Settee, Nutting, 3 Block Raised Panels On Arms, Maple, Pine 600.00
Settee, Oak, Saddle Leather Upholstery, Claw Foot 700.00
Settee, Old Hickory Furniture Co. 300.00
Settee, Padded Sides, Loose Cushion, C.1800, 6 Ft. 5 1/2 In. 2090.00
Settee, Regency, Walnut, Serpentine Back, 4 Ft., Pair 400.00
Settee, Rococo Revival, Walnut, Serpentine, Scroll Arms, 66 In. 300.00
Settee, Russian, Scrolled Armrest, Upholstered Seat, Birch 8525.00
Settee, Sheraton, Reeded Legs, Mahogany, Upholstery, 49 In. 250.00
Settee, Triple Chairback, Black Lacquer, 5 Ft.9 In. ....*Illus* 1430.00
Settee, Windsor, Maple, Pine, Rod Back, Plank Seat, C.1810, 71 In. 800.00
Settee, Windsor, New Eng., Painted Black, 18th Century, 78 In. 2000.00
Settee, Windsor, Original Mustard Paint 6000.00
Settee, Winged Griffins, North Wind Faces, Oak, 4 X 4 Ft. 3200.00
Settle, Arms, Brown Graining, Yellow Ground, 72 In., Pair 800.00
Settle, Dark Green, Roses, Pennsylvania 1850.00
Settle, Storage, Chester County, Pa., Original Paint, 1820s 3000.00
Settle, Turned Legs, Arms, Half Arrow Back, Black, 74 In. 225.00
Sewing Desk, Shaker, Enfield, Butternut 22000.00
Shelf, Corner, Shaker, Pine, 3 Graduated Shelves, Red, 37 In. 700.00
Shelf, Folding, Leg Supports, Scrubbed Top, Poplar, 67 X 32 In. 135.00
Shelf, Hanging, Dovetailed, Pine, 24 1/2 In. 125.00
Shelf, Hanging, Jigsaw Back, Cherry Tree, Birds, Dog, Walnut 110.00
Shelf, Hanging, Made March 27, 1873, G.W.Gage, 22 1/2 X 27 In. 425.00
Shelf, Hanging, Mahogany, 2 Drawers, C.1820, 33 X 8 X 26 In. 1100.00
Shelf, Hanging, Mahogany, 3 Shelves, 38 X 35 In. 900.00
Shelf, Hanging, Pine, Scalloped, Drawer, Grained, 23 X 7 In. 250.00
Shelf, Hanging, Poplar, Paneled Doors, Yellow, 20 X 10 In. 55.00
Shelf, Hanging, Poplar, Turned Posts, Red, 26 X 5 X 24 In. 27.50
Shelf, Hanging, Step Back Shelves, Finish Over Red, 24 In. 415.00
Shelf, Pine, Primitive, Cutout Scalloped, 21 X 8 X 23 In., Pr. 1500.00
Shelf, Plate, Hanging, Pine, Scalloped, Brown, 48 X 37 In. 1025.00
Shelf, Regency, Mahogany, 3/4 Upper Gallery, 4 Ft.9 In. 3100.00
Shelf, Whale End, 3 Shelves, Walnut, 24 X 34 1/2 In. 550.00
Sideboard, 8 Legs, No.817, Gustav Stickley, 1904, 50 X 70 In. 7000.00
Sideboard, American, Mahogany, C.1835 .... 880.00
Sideboard, Black Finish, Stickley, 40 X 50 X 23 In. ....*Illus* 5500.00
Sideboard, Carved Game, Fruit, Dog's Head, 2 Mirrors, Walnut 3300.00
Sideboard, Carved, Beveled Mirror, Oak, 6 Ft. 6 In. 975.00
Sideboard, Chippendale, Flat Top, Mahogany, 37 X 68 X 23 In. 550.00
Sideboard, Continental, Carved Oak, Lion Mask Pulls, 29 In. 1700.00
Sideboard, Demilune, Mahogany, Original Brasses, English 4200.00
Sideboard, Empire, Carved, Mahogany, C.1835 .... 1700.00

Furniture, Sideboard, Black Finish, Stickley,
40 X 50 X 23 In.

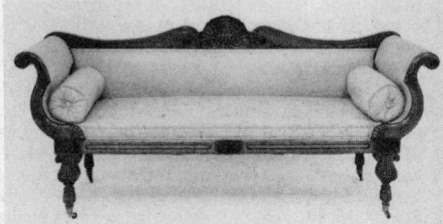

Furniture, Sofa, Classical Revival, Teak, China,
C.1840, 86 In.

Sideboard, Federal, American, Inlaid Mahogany, 1795, 72 X 40 In.	6325.00
Sideboard, Federal, Inlaid Mahogany, Convex Drawer, 1795, 65 In.	4400.00
Sideboard, Federal, Mass., Inlaid Mahogany, C.1815, 42 In.	1550.00
Sideboard, Federal, Massachusetts, C.1819, 69 3/4 X 41 In.	5775.00
Sideboard, George III, Inlaid Mahogany, Cellaret, 4 Ft.6 In.	3960.00
Sideboard, George III–Style, 2 Bottle Drawers, Mahogany, 37 In.	825.00
Sideboard, George III–Style, Heavily Inlaid	4950.00
Sideboard, Hepplewhite, Mahogany, Serpentine, 1800, 69 In.	1750.00
Sideboard, Hepplewhite, Serpentine, Mahogany, English	7150.00
Sideboard, Marble Top, Inlaid Design, Bronze Mounted, C.1850	7700.00
Sideboard, Mission, 6 Drawers, Gustav Stickley, Bottom Shelf	3800.00
Sideboard, New England, Mahogany & Mahogany Veneer, C.1810	3250.00
Sideboard, Plate Rack, 3 Half Drawers, Stickley, 1912, 44 In.	900.00
Sideboard, Rectangular, Stile Feet, Oak, 17th Century, 48 In.	1200.00
Sideboard, Renaissance Revival, Mirror, D Shape	2800.00
Sideboard, Renaissance, Victorian, Walnut, Marble Top	1000.00
Sideboard, Rosewood, Marble Top, Mirror Back, 69 In.	650.00
Sideboard, Serpentine Front, Scotland, C.1790, Mahogany, 7 Ft.	1980.00
Sideboard, Stepped Front, 3 Drawers, Mahogany, 1795, 72 In.	300.00
Sideboard, Victorian, Walnut, Deer's Head	3650.00
Sideboard, William IV, Mahogany, Pedestal, 1830	2200.00
Sofa, American Empire, Gold Stenciling, Mahogany, C.1830, 89 In.	4500.00
Sofa, American Rococo, Belter, Rosalie Pattern, Rosewood	4500.00
Sofa, Carved Mahogany, Curved Arms, New York, C.1825	2300.00
Sofa, Carved, Gold Stenciling On Rail, C.H.& J.F.White, C.1830	5800.00
Sofa, Chippendale, Mahogany, Eggshell Tapestry, 87 In.	1500.00
Sofa, Chippendale, Mahogany, Serpentine, Blue Damask, 1780, 85 In.	5500.00
Sofa, Chippendale, Upholstered, C.1780, 74 3/4 X 37 In.	4000.00
Sofa, Classical Revival, Teak, China, C.1840, 86 In. ....*Illus*	2000.00
Sofa, Empire, Carved Mahogany, Upholstered, C.1830, 87 1/2 In.	450.00
Sofa, Empire, Ormolu Mounts, Upholstered, Fruitwood	3950.00
Sofa, Jeliff, Original Finish & Gilding, Rosewood	2200.00
Sofa, Louis XV, Upholstered, Painted Gray, 18th Century	2300.00
Sofa, Miller, Marguetry	2000.00
Sofa, Rococo Revival, Carved Rosewood, Belter, Upholstered	4950.00
Sofa, Rococo Revival, Rosewood, Serpentine, 66 In.	550.00
Sofa, Rosewood, Laminated, Belter, Rosalie Pattern	5775.00
Sofa, Sheraton, Carved Mahogany, C.1790	3300.00
Sofa, Sheraton, Mahogany, Turned Legs, Open Arms, Satin, 73 In.	1375.00
Sofa, Sheraton–Style, Reeded Legs, Upholstered, Mahogany	850.00
Sofa, Triple Back, Flower, Leaf & Shell Carvings, Rosewood	2750.00
Sofa, Upholstered & Carved, S.Field McIntire, Mahogany, 1825	6600.00
Sofa, Victorian, Medallion Back, Carved	1750.00
Stand, 1 Dovetailed Drawer, Walnut, 28 5/8 In.	90.00
Stand, 2 Dovetailed Drawers, 2 Board Top, Walnut, 28 1/2 In.	325.00
Stand, American, Drawer, Turned Legs, Tiger Maple, 25 X 19 In.	500.00
Stand, Ball & Claw Feet, Chinese, Carved Teak, 14 3/4 In.	150.00
Stand, Basin, Corner, Neoclassical, Mahogany, 18th Cent., 40 In.	275.00
Stand, Basin, Corner, Shelf, Mahogany, C.1810, 38 In.	1760.00
Stand, Bird's–Eye Maple, Turned Legs, 28 In.	275.00
Stand, Black Paint, Pine & Poplar, 30 3/4 In.	65.00
Stand, Bottle, Victorian, Hinged Lid, Mahogany, 18 In.	675.00
Stand, Charles X, Ormolu, Leather Top, Gallery, Paw Feet, 24 In.	1870.00
Stand, Cherry, 1 Drawer, 1 Board Top, Red Glaze Over Yellow	200.00
Stand, Cherry, 1 Drawer, 2 Board Top, 23 X 24 X 29 1/2 In.	125.00
Stand, Cherry, 1 Drawer, Strip Gallery On Edge, 28 5/8 In.	180.00
Stand, Cherry, Sandwich Knobs, 2 Tiger Maple Painted Drawers	795.00
Stand, Chinese, Teak, 2 Shelves, Marble Top, Carving, 32 In.	185.00
Stand, Chinese, Teak, Carved, Octagonal, Marble Insert, 36 In.	475.00
Stand, Curly Maple Top, Cherry, 2 Dovetailed Drawers, 27 3/4 In.	205.00
Stand, Curly Maple, 1 Dovetailed Drawer, Handmade, 29 In.	130.00
Stand, Curly Maple, Cherry Apron, Turned Legs, 25 In.	105.00
Stand, Curly Maple, Drawer, Turned Legs, Refinished, 28 In.	325.00
Stand, Cutout Design On Shoe Feet, Alligatored Finish, 12 In.	25.00

Furniture, Stand, Plant,
2 Tiers, Green Paint,
Circular Top, 32 In.

Furniture, Stand, Sheraton, 2 Drawer,
Blue Paint, 28 1/2 X 18 In.

Furniture, Stand,
Reading, Mahogany,
George III, C.1800, 40 In.

Stand, Dovetailed Drawer, 2 Board Top, Pine, Poplar, 19 X 29 In.	250.00
Stand, Dovetailed Drawer, Curly Maple Front, 20 X 20 X 28 In.	275.00
Stand, Dovetailed Drawer, Dark Finish, Walnut, 28 1/4 In.	135.00
Stand, Dressing, Mustard Paint, Design, Small	2860.00
Stand, Drop Leaf, Red Flame Graining, Drawer, Pine, 29 In.	250.00
Stand, Empire, 1 Drawer, Dark Red Finish, Gallery, 28 X 24 In.	295.00
Stand, Empire, 2 Drawers, 2 Board Top, Cherry, 27 3/4 In.	195.00
Stand, Empire, Curly Maple, Dovetailed Drawer, 21 X 30 In.	350.00
Stand, Empire, Flame Veneer Ogee Apron, Mahogany, 26 X 29 In.	255.00
Stand, Empire, Rope Carved Legs, 2 Drawers, Cherry, 28 1/2 In.	325.00
Stand, Federal, Maple, New Hampshire, 1800, 28 X 18 In.	850.00
Stand, Fern, Eastlake, Walnut	45.00
Stand, Fern, Marble Top, Walnut	70.00
Stand, Folio, Concave Front, 2 Doors, Adjustable, Mahogany	880.00
Stand, Gilt Brass, Onyx, Reeded Handles, Twisted Legs, 33 1/2 In.	250.00
Stand, Hepplewhite Style, Drawer, Cherry, 18 X 28 In., Pair	320.00
Stand, Hepplewhite, Cherry, 1 Drawer, Dovetailed, 28 3/4 In.	250.00
Stand, Hepplewhite, Cherry, Line Inlay, Banding, 15 X 17 In.	200.00
Stand, Hepplewhite, Dovetailed Drawer, Pine Top, 29 In.	170.00
Stand, Hepplewhite, Drawer, Cherry, 26 3/4 In.	150.00
Stand, Hepplewhite, Old Red, 1 Board Top, Hardwood, 28 3/4 In.	450.00
Stand, Hepplewhite, Tapered & Mortised, Poplar, 29 In.	285.00
Stand, Hepplewhite, Worn Red Paint, Black Graining, Pine, Poplar	1100.00
Stand, Lift Top, 2 Drawers, Cherry, New England, C.1820, 31 In.	450.00
Stand, Philadelphia, Empire, Figured Mahogany Tilt Top, 30 In.	320.00
Stand, Pierced Carved Apron, Oriental, Teak, 15 X 15 X 29 In.	75.00
Stand, Pine, Birch, Lower Shelf Added, C.1800, 27 1/2 X 19 In.	450.00
Stand, Pine, Brown Flame Graining, Drawer, Turned Legs, 18 In.	135.00
Stand, Pine, Poplar, Red Paint, Black Graining, 1 Drawer	525.00
Stand, Plant, 2 Tiers, Green Paint, Circular Top, 32 In. ....*Illus*	1900.00
Stand, Plant, 3 Tiers, White Paint, 37 1/2 In.	140.00
Stand, Plant, Hourglass Shape, Wicker	35.00
Stand, Plant, Limbert, No.251, Box Base, C.1910, 24 In. ....*Illus*	1000.00
Stand, Plant, Mission Oak .... 65.00 To	75.00
Stand, Reading, Adjustable, Candle Slide, Mahogany, 1800, 31 In.	2400.00
Stand, Reading, Mahogany, George III, C.1800, 40 In. ....*Illus*	3080.00
Stand, Shaving, Adjustable Mirror, 2 Drawers, 20 X 68 In.	300.00
Stand, Shaving, Carved Walnut, Marble, Mirror, Drawer, 58 In.	1200.00
Stand, Shaving, Empire, Marble Top, Maple Drawer, Rosewood	1155.00
Stand, Sheraton, 2 Drawer, Blue Paint, 28 1/2 X 18 In. ....*Illus*	200.00
Stand, Sheraton, 2 Drawer, Wooden Pulls, Light & Dark Finish	1750.00
Stand, Sheraton, 2 Drawers, Molded Top, Fluted Legs, Mahogany	1100.00
Stand, Sheraton, Cherry, Cookie Corners, Turned Legs	650.00
Stand, Sheraton, Drop Leaf, Flame Veneer Drawer, 27 In.	180.00
Stand, Sheraton, W.Nutting, Label, Drawers, Mahogany, 29 In., Pair	850.00

Stand, Sheraton, Walnut, Maple Bird's–Eye Veneer Drawer, 28 In.	325.00
Stand, Sheraton, Yellow Reeding, Cherry, 28 1/2 In.	325.00
Stand, Smoke, Depression Glass Jar & Ashtray, Cast Iron	22.50
Stand, Smoking, Gustav Stickley, Chamfered	2750.00
Stand, Smoking, Walnut, Copper Lined	59.00
Stand, Snake Feet, 1 Board Top, Cherry, 16 1/2 X 17 In.	950.00
Stand, Teak, 5 Foliage Scroll Legs, Dragons, Chinese, 24 In.	370.00
Stand, Telephone, Gustav Stickley, No.605, C.1907, 30 In.	350.00
Stand, Tiger Maple, Cherry Legs, 1 Drawer	450.00
Stand, Tiger Maple, New England, C.1870	675.00
Stand, Tiger Maple, Striping, 2 Drawer, Midwestern	1400.00
Stand, Tilt Top, Cherry, Candle, Tripod Base, 16 X 16 X 27 In.	1100.00
Stand, Tilt Top, Urn Pedestal, Maple Top, Cherry, C.1790, 23 In.	900.00
Stand, Tripod, William IV, Rosewood & Satinwood, C.1835, 29 In.	1100.00
Stand, Umbrella, Golden Oak, Mission Style, 11 X 11 In.	45.00
Stand, Umbrella, Oak, Wicker Basket	200.00
Stand, Windsor, Birch, 1 Board Poplar Top, 28 X 17 In.	350.00
Stand, Worn Blue Paint, Replaced Drawer, Turned Legs	225.00
Stool, Biedermeier, Mahogany, C.1820, 22 1/2 In., Pair	1700.00
Stool, Cricket Footed, C.1820, 7 X 7 12 In.	130.00
Stool, Empire, Curly Maple, Turned Handles, 7 X 17 In.	375.00
Stool, Folding, Scrolled Arms, Woven Seat, Walnut, 21 1/2 In.	90.00
Stool, Hardwood Legs & Rungs, Round Pine Seat, 27 In.	80.00
Stool, Louis XVI, Mahogany, Needlepoint Covered, Pair	1300.00
Stool, Milking, Walnut	75.00
Stool, Napoleon III, Gilt Wood Rope, Upholstered Seat, C.1860	3300.00
Stool, Organ, Eastlake, Walnut, Needlepoint Top	150.00
Stool, Piano, Glass Claw & Ball Feet	60.00
Stool, Piano, Twist Up Style, Glass Ball & Claw Feet	85.00
Stool, Queen Anne Style, Hinged Top, Mahogany, 20 In.	325.00
Stool, Red & Black Design, Chinese Lacquer, 19 1/4 In.	120.00
Stool, Shoe Fitting, Twisted Wire Legs, Bentwood Seat	24.00
Stool, Windsor, Bamboo Turnings, Upholstered, 15 In., Pair	2800.00
Stool, Work, Charles X, Needlepoint, Maple & Walnut, 17 In.	2000.00
Swing, Porch, Wicker	450.00
Table Set, Cast Iron, Ornate, Blue Paint, 1880s, 2 Chairs	1750.00
Table Set, Ice Cream, Dated 1904, 4 Heart Back Chairs, 5 Piece	235.00
Table Set, Ice Cream, Marble Top, 2 Chairs	215.00
Table Set, Oak, Leaves, Pressback Chairs, 42 X 42 In.Table, 5 Pc.	745.00
Table, 2 Tiers, Piecrust Shelves, Brass Feet, Walnut, 31 In.	85.00
Table, 24 Delft Tiles, Dutch Buttery Scene, 17 X 32 In.	800.00
Table, Altar, Rosewood, Carved Apron, China, 33 X 47 In.	600.00
Table, Architect's, George III, Mahogany, 43 X 25 In.	9900.00
Table, Baker's, 2 Pullout Breadboards, 2 Storage Bins	450.00
Table, Banquet, American Empire, Mahogany, Carved Legs	5000.00
Table, Banquet, Federal, Mahogany, Veneer, D Ends, 1815, 63 In.	500.00
Table, Banquet, Hepplewhite, Drop Leaves, 49 In.	6500.00
Table, Banquet, Hepplewhite, Mahogany, Conn., Extends To 97 In.	3750.00
Table, Banquet, Sheraton, 3 Part, Mahogany, 84 X 30 In.	450.00
Table, Base Shelf, Oak & Poplar, 23 1/2 X 30 1/2 In.	110.00
Table, Bedside, George III, Hinged Top, Mahogany, C.1820, 28 In.	825.00
Table, Bedside, Hinged Top, Mahogany, C.1855, 29 In.	330.00
Table, Biedermeier Style, Walnut Veneer, Ebonized, 29 X 43 In.	200.00
Table, Billiard, Brunswick, Oak, Slate Top, C.1900	1675.00
Table, Billiard, Snooker, Ivory Inlay, Schmidt, C.1904	3500.00
Table, Bird's–Eye & Tiger Maple, Drawer, New Eng., 1825, 18 In.	500.00
Table, Bobbin Turned Legs, Serpentine Stretchers, Oak, C.1690	850.00
Table, Brass, Inlaid Mahogany, Rectangular, 32 X 18 In.	150.00
Table, Breakfast, Crossbanded Mahogany, Tilt, Leaf, 4 Ft.3 In.	2300.00
Table, Breakfast, Federal, Drop Leaf, Mahogany, 1820, 42 In.	475.00
Table, Breakfast, George III, Inlaid Mahogany, 19th Century	2450.00
Table, Breakfast, Plum Pudding Mahogany Top, English	600.00
Table, Breakfast, Queen Anne, Drop Leaf, Maple, 36 X 35 1/2 In.	2200.00
Table, Breakfast, Rectangular, Tilt Top, Faded Mahogany, 4 Ft.	825.00

Table, Breakfast, Sheraton, Mahogany, Drop Leaf, N.Y., 40 In. 900.00
Table, Breakfast, Tilt Top, Lion's Paw Feet, Mahogany, 27 In. 1000.00
Table, Card, Chippendale, Tiger Maple, Marlborough Legs, 1780 .... 1700.00
Table, Card, Classical Revival, Mahogany, Gilt, 1820–30 .... 1300.00
Table, Card, Classical Revival, Mahogany, Veneer, C.1815, 37 In. 450.00
Table, Card, Country Federal, Birch, Mahogany, 1800, 34 X 18 In. 950.00
Table, Card, Empire, Paw Feet, Swing Top, Mahogany, 32 X 30 In. 200.00
Table, Card, Federal, Bird's–Eye Apron, Inlaid Maple, C.1800 .... 1300.00
Table, Card, Federal, Brass Fitted Mahogany, C.1810, 29 In. 9350.00
Table, Card, Federal, Drawer Frieze, Mahogany, C.1825, 29 1/2 In. 1100.00
Table, Card, Federal, Duncan Phyfe, Flame Veneer Top, 29 In. 300.00
Table, Card, Federal, Inlaid Mahogany, C.1810, 29 3/4 In. 5500.00
Table, Card, Federal, Inlaid Mahogany, Maple, 1810, 35 X 17 In. 4950.00
Table, Card, Federal, Mahogany Inlay, New Hamp., 1790, 35 X 17 In. 2000.00
Table, Card, Federal, Mahogany, Brass Mounted, Mass., 1815, 36 In. 3575.00
Table, Card, Federal, Mahogany, Hepplewhite, Banded Rosewood 6000.00
Table, Card, Federal, Mahogany, Ovolo Corners, 1810 .... 2600.00
Table, Card, Federal, Mahogany, Rosewood Cross Banding, Satinwood 2750.00
Table, Card, Federal, Mahogany, Satinwood, Reeded Legs, C.1800 .... 2850.00
Table, Card, Federal, Mahogany, Veneer, C.1795, 30 1/4 In. 1900.00
Table, Card, Federal, Massachusetts, Mahogany, 36 X 29 In. 1700.00
Table, Card, Federal, New England, Inlaid Mahogany, C.1805, 29 In. 3850.00
Table, Card, Federal, New Hampshire 3500.00
Table, Card, Federal, Plume & Acanthus Pedestal, Mahogany, C.1820 .... 1750.00
Table, Card, George III, Satinwood, Painted, D Shape, 36 In. 2750.00
Table, Card, Hepplewhite, Demilune 1700.00
Table, Card, Hepplewhite, Line Inlay, Swing Leg, Walnut, 30 In. 275.00
Table, Card, Inlaid, Fluted Legs, C.1800 .... 5175.00
Table, Card, Louis Philippe, Mahogany, Apron, Drawer, 1840 .... 325.00
Table, Card, Mahogany & Birch, Samuel & William Todd 9000.00
Table, Card, Mahogany, Chippendale, Long Drawer, C.1780, 29 In. 4500.00
Table, Card, New England, Mahogany, Flame Birch, C.1800, 29 In. 4950.00
Table, Card, Regency, Satinwood, Pedestal, D Shape, Pair 8250.00
Table, Card, Sheraton, American, Mahogany, C.1810 .... 1000.00
Table, Card, Sheraton, Mahogany, Flame Veneer Apron, 30 In. 500.00
Table, Card, Sheraton, Mahogany, Serpentine, Cut Corners, C.1800 .... 1900.00
Table, Card, Stringing, Drawer, Inlaid Fans, Walnut, 29 In. 800.00
Table, Card, Tiger Maple Top, Bow Front, Inlaid Mahogany, N.H. 1980.00
Table, Card, Trompe L'Oeil Playing Cards & Fish Tokens 9075.00
Table, Carved Marble, 3 Lion Supports, Paw Feet, 40 In. 9900.00
Table, Carved Oak, Dolphin Feet, Grotesque Face, Drawer, 35 In. 450.00
Table, Center, American Empire, Walnut Veneer, Marble Top, 1820 .... 495.00
Table, Center, American Renaissance, Rosewood, Marble Top, 36 In. 1650.00
Table, Center, Biedermeier, Fruitwood, Lyre Support, 23 1/2 In. 1760.00
Table, Center, Carved Rosewood, Marble Top, X Stretchers, 31 In. 300.00
Table, Center, Charles X, 5 Drawers, Elm & Fruitwood 8250.00
Table, Center, Charles X, Mahogany, Marble, Tripod Base, 34 In. 5225.00
Table, Center, Drop Leaf, 2 Drawers, Mahogany, Opens To 58 In. 935.00
Table, Center, Empire Style, Frieze Drawer, Mahogany, C.1900 .... 4400.00
Table, Center, Fruitwood, Tri–Partite Stretcher, Biedermeier 8525.00
Table, Center, Italian, Mottled Marble, Winged Lion Supports 2650.00
Table, Center, Renaissance Revival, Walnut, 28 X 43 In. ....*Illus* 1800.00
Table, Center, Rosewood, 3 Legs, Marble, Urn, Base Stretcher 775.00
Table, Center, Rosewood, Ebony Specimen Marble, Scroll Feet 7700.00
Table, Center, Tripod, Marquetry, Walnut, 1830–40, 43 In.Diam. 9350.00
Table, Center, Veneered Chevron On Top, Russian, Birch, 31 In. 1650.00
Table, Chair, Pine & Birch, C.1750, 27 X 41 In. 3500.00
Table, Charles X, Faux Marble Top, Cupboard Door, 30 In., Pair 5500.00
Table, Child's ABC, Circus Scene, Nursery Rhymes, Graniteware 90.00
Table, Child's, Oak, Folding, Paris Toy Co. 35.00
Table, Chippendale, Birdcage Carved, Mahogany, C.1750, 30 In. 2000.00
Table, Chippendale, Drop Leaf, Swing Leg, Square Legs, 38 In. 440.00
Table, Chippendale, Maple, Drawer, 1780, 30 X 26 X 17 In. 1900.00
Table, Chippendale, Maple, Marlborough Legs, Pembroke, C.1780 .... 950.00

Furniture, Table, Center,
Renaissance Revival,
Walnut, 28 X 43 In.

Furniture, Table, Dining,
Tiger Maple,
England, C.1820, 49 1/2 In.

Furniture, Table, Drop Leaf,
Queen Anne,
Walnut, 19th Century

Table, Chippendale, Serpentine, Figured Maple, 2 Drawers, C.1770	6500.00
Table, Cinnabar Lacquer, Carved Scene, 12 1/2 X 12 1/2 X 5 In.	490.00
Table, Console, American Gothic, Drawer, Carved Rosewood	600.00
Table, Console, D End, Mahogany, 28 1/4 In.	250.00
Table, Console, Gadrooned Top, 2 Drawers, Mahogany, 4 Ft.	1750.00
Table, Console, George III, Painted Satinwood Verde, 19th Cent.	5720.00
Table, Console, Iron, Marble Top, Cabriole Legs, E.Brandt, 40 In.	6050.00
Table, Console, Italian Neoclassical, Rosette Supports, 31 In.	3025.00
Table, Console, Mahogany, Sheraton, C.1815, 33 In.	2500.00
Table, Console, Marble Top, Gilt Metal Mounted, C.1825, 36 In.	5225.00
Table, Console, Pierced Lift Off Mirror, Serpentine, Drawer	2500.00
Table, Console, Sheraton, Mahogany, C.1800, 56 X 21 In.	650.00
Table, Console, Sheraton, New England, Mahogany, C.1815	2500.00
Table, Continental, Ebonized, Birch & Rosewood Parquetry, 26 In.	2975.00
Table, Country, Scrubbed Top, Ohio, C.1830	1275.00
Table, Cypress, Round Top, Texas, 1917	695.00
Table, Demilune, George III, Inlaid Mahogany, 45 X 22 1/2 In.	1100.00
Table, Demilune, George III, Inlaid Satinwood, 42 In., Pair	9900.00
Table, Dining, 4 Leaves, Red Decal, G.Stickley, C.1907, 54 In.	1200.00
Table, Dining, 9 Leaves, Burl Veneer, Walnut	2000.00
Table, Dining, Carved Walnut, Pedestal, 4 Leaves, 19th Century	1800.00
Table, Dining, Chippendale, 2 Drop Leaves, Mahogany, 36 In.	450.00
Table, Dining, Drop Leaf, Carved Curly Walnut, C.1760, 50 In.	7150.00
Table, Dining, Drop Leaf, Mahogany, Pad Feet, 18th Century, 44 In.	1100.00
Table, Dining, Drop Leaf, Pennsylvania, Walnut, 1780, 5 Ft.3 In.	2975.00
Table, Dining, Drop Leaf, Queen Anne, Maple, Cabriole Legs, 1770	3100.00
Table, Dining, Federal, Cherry, Drop Leaf, New England, 1820	750.00
Table, Dining, Gustav Stickley, No.632, 6 Leaves, C.1907, 54 In.	2600.00
Table, Dining, Mahogany, 3 Leaves, 30 X 45 X 72 In.	625.00
Table, Dining, Mahogany, Center Tripod, 4 Leaves, 6 Ft.4 In.	3300.00
Table, Dining, New England, Mahogany, Mahogany Veneer, C.1835	2400.00
Table, Dining, Pedestal Base, Branded, Limbert, C.1906, 48 In.	550.00
Table, Dining, Quaint Furniture, Oak, Round, C.1908, 54 In.	1400.00
Table, Dining, Queen Anne, Mahogany, Cutout Apron, C.1750, 48 In.	2750.00
Table, Dining, Queen Anne, Maple, Birch, Pad Feet, C.1750, 28 In.	3900.00
Table, Dining, Queen Anne, Maple, New Eng., C.1770, Extends 46 In.	4400.00
Table, Dining, Queen Anne, New England, Maple & Birch, C.1750	3900.00
Table, Dining, Regency, Mahogany, 3 Leaves, 31 X 64 X 32 In.	450.00
Table, Dining, Renaissance Revival, 9 Leaves, Walnut	2200.00
Table, Dining, Sheraton, Mahogany, C.1800, 103 X 51 In.	3500.00
Table, Dining, Swing Leg, Butternut, C.1840	750.00
Table, Dining, Tiger Maple, England, C.1820, 49 1/2 In. ....*Illus*	1900.00
Table, Director's, Mission, Gustav Stickley	6000.00
Table, Dovetailed Drawer, 2 Board Top, Cherry, Poplar, 28 In.	195.00
Table, Drawer, Pullout Leg Support, English, Mahogany, 29 In.	650.00
Table, Dressing, 2 Drawers, Arched Kneehole, Mahogany, 28 In.	885.00

Table, Dressing, 3 Beveled Mirrors, Serpentine Front, Oak	275.00
Table, Dressing, Carved Mahogany, 19th Century	2100.00
Table, Dressing, Cherry, Hinged Mirror, 38 X 20 X 65 In.	650.00
Table, Dressing, Dolphin Carved Mirror Supports, Mahogany	1595.00
Table, Dressing, Duncan Phyfe, Framed Mirror, 56 In.	1975.00
Table, Dressing, Federal, Swivel Mirror, Mahogany, 1800, 54 In.	3850.00
Table, Dressing, Gentleman's, Hinged Lid, Mahogany, 35 In.	385.00
Table, Dressing, Inlaid Faded Mahogany, 18th Century, 30 In.	1200.00
Table, Dressing, Italian Neoclassical, Inlaid Walnut, C.1780	445.00
Table, Dressing, Kneehole, Ogee Feet, Mahogany, 1780, 33 X 32 In.	2300.00
Table, Dressing, Louis XV, Fruitwood Marquetry, Tulipwood, 33 In.	3850.00
Table, Dressing, Louis XV, Kneehole, Brass Gallery, Serpentine	400.00
Table, Dressing, Mirrored, 2 Drawers, Logo, Roycroft, 1906, 56 In.	750.00
Table, Dressing, Scalloped, White Paint, Striping, Stencil, Pine	1600.00
Table, Dressing, Sheraton, Red Flame Graining, Pine, 37 In.	700.00
Table, Drop Leaf, 6 Legs, American, Mahogany, C.1800, 47 1/2 In.	700.00
Table, Drop Leaf, 6 Legs, Leaves, Curly Maple, 48 X 28 In.	2500.00
Table, Drop Leaf, Cherry, 20 1/2 X 41 X 29 In.	150.00
Table, Drop Leaf, Dovetailed Drawer, Cherry, 26 1/2 In.	225.00
Table, Drop Leaf, Drawer, Brass Pull, Curly Maple, 28 3/4 In.	550.00
Table, Drop Leaf, Empire, Mahogany, Drawer, Rope Legs, 20 X 41 In.	250.00
Table, Drop Leaf, France, Walnut, Fluted Legs, 29 X 57 X 41 In.	1200.00
Table, Drop Leaf, George III, Mahogany, C.1820, 27 1/2 In.	1210.00
Table, Drop Leaf, Hepplewhite, Birch, Red Finish, 46 In.	325.00
Table, Drop Leaf, Mahogany, Acanthus Carved Legs	385.00
Table, Drop Leaf, Mahogany, Reeded Legs, 1820, 41 X 21 In.	700.00
Table, Drop Leaf, Mahogany, Turned & Reeded, 6 Legs, C.1810	750.00
Table, Drop Leaf, Old Hickory Furniture Co.	325.00
Table, Drop Leaf, Pembroke, Curly Birch, Drawer, Turned Legs	450.00
Table, Drop Leaf, Pembroke, Mahogany, Drawer, Reeded Legs	1000.00
Table, Drop Leaf, Queen Anne, New England, Tiger Maple, C.1760	1600.00
Table, Drop Leaf, Queen Anne, Oval, Swing Legs, Maple, 28 In.	4200.00
Table, Drop Leaf, Queen Anne, Walnut, 19th Century ....*Illus*	650.00
Table, Drop Leaf, Reeded Legs, C.1820, 41 In.	700.00
Table, Drop Leaf, Sheraton, Swell Turned Legs, Birch, 28 1/2 In.	550.00
Table, Drop Leaf, Swing Leg, Sheraton, Cherry, 29 1/4 In.	200.00
Table, Drop Leaf, Turned Legs, Cherry, 17 1/2 X 36 In.	150.00
Table, Drop Leaf, Walnut, Turned Legs	200.00
Table, Eastlake, Marble Top, Walnut, 19th Century, 29 In.	2640.00
Table, Empire Style, Onyx Top, Gilt Leaf Border, Mahogany, 1890	1875.00
Table, Empire, French Style, Rosewood Veneer, 32 X 32 X 29 In.	275.00
Table, Empire, Marble Top, Bronze Female Figure Supports, 1890	7425.00
Table, Empire, Ormolu, Oval Mirror Top, Gallery, Mahogany, 78 In.	2750.00
Table, English Chippendale, Square Legs, Walnut, 27 In.	275.00
Table, Farm, 2 Drawers, Walnut, C.1820	1290.00
Table, Farm, Cherry, Pullout Breadboard & Drawer, French	2500.00
Table, Farm, Pine, Missouri, 6 Ft.3 In.	650.00
Table, Federal, Cherry, Bird's-Eye Maple, Birch, C.1810	325.00
Table, Federal, Cherry, C.1790, 28 In.	900.00
Table, Federal, Pine, Stencil, Drawer, Tapered Legs, 28 In.	1325.00
Table, French Country, Fruitwood, 1 Drawer, Keyhole, 1740s	1250.00
Table, Fruitwood Marquetry, 2 Tiers, Arctic Shape, Galle, 27 In.	2975.00
Table, Fruitwood Marquetry, Gallery, Galle, C.1900, 28 1/4 In.	4125.00
Table, Fruitwood Marquetry, Majorelle, Tulips, Drawer, 27 In.	2750.00
Table, Fruitwood, 3 Incurved Sabre Legs, Biedermeier, 20 In.	2535.00
Table, Game, American Empire, Mahogany, Winged Carved Feet	445.00
Table, Game, Empire, Lyre Scroll Legs, 3 Ft.X 2 Ft.11 In.	125.00
Table, Game, Empire, Mahogany, R.B.Sykes, New York, C.1840	1540.00
Table, Game, Empire, Mahogany, Shelf, 28 X 38 In.	300.00
Table, Game, George III, Concertina Action, Mahogany, 35 In.	4400.00
Table, Game, Hinged Top, Stringing, Ebony & Mahogany, 29 In.	1430.00
Table, Game, Inlaid Playing Cards, Chips, Cigar, Mahogany	385.00
Table, Game, Italian Neoclassical, Inlay, Walnut, 30 1/2 In	3850.00
Table, Game, Louis XVI, Inlaid, Baize Lined, Mahogany & Brass	1900.00

Table, Game, Lyre Base, Walnut 200.00
Table, Game, Papier–Mache, Mother–of–Pearl Board, 19th Century 125.00
Table, Game, Rosewood, Serpentine 935.00
Table, Game, Tilt Top, Parcheesi Board, 19 X 19 X 26 3/4 In. 1350.00
Table, Game, Triple Top, George II, Walnut, 33 X 30 In. 2000.00
Table, Garden, Victorian, Cast Iron, Circular 385.00
Table, Garden, Victorian, Cast Iron, Marble Top, Rectangular 285.00
Table, Gateleg, Drop Leaf, George II, Mahogany, 1850, 28 In. 1750.00
Table, Gateleg, Georgian, Oval Top, Oak, 18th Century, 4 Ft. 935.00
Table, Gateleg, Mahogany, Spanish Foot, Castor, 47 In. 2800.00
Table, Gateleg, Oak, Turned Legs, Drawer, 29 1/2 In. 350.00
Table, Gateleg, Oak, Turned Legs, Oval Top, 11 X 30 X 14 In. 350.00
Table, Gateleg, Pine Top, Maple & Oak, Iron Butterfly Hinges 700.00
Table, Gateleg, William & Mary, Japanned, Gilt Design, 30 In. 2300.00
Table, George II, Tilt Top, Tripod, Mahogany, C.1740, 29 In. 1200.00
Table, George III, Tilt Top, Dished Top, Mahogany, C.1870, 28 In. 1100.00
Table, Gustav Stickley, No.646, Oak, C.1904, 29 X 40 In. 700.00
Table, Hall, Oak, H Stretcher, 14 X 30 X 30 In. 150.00
Table, Handkerchief, George III, Triangular, Mahogany, 28 In. 1100.00
Table, Handkerchief, Queen Anne, Walnut, C.1730, 27 1/2 In. 2200.00
Table, Harvest, Drop Leaf, Pine, Painted, New England, 1800, 85 In. 2100.00
Table, Harvest, Maple Legs, Ash Apron, Top, 32 1/4 X 30 3/4 In. 200.00
Table, Harvest, Walnut, Turned Legs, 38 X 110 In. 6000.00
Table, Hepplewhite, Brown Graining, Drawer, Pine, 36 X 31 In. 200.00
Table, Hepplewhite, Brown Graining, Wood Inlays, Pine, 31 In. 175.00
Table, Hepplewhite, Mahogany, Apron Drawer, 19 X 28 In. 950.00
Table, Hepplewhite, Pine, Flame Graining, D Shape, 21 X 37 In. 800.00
Table, Hepplewhite, Square Legs, Birch, 27 1/2 X 28 In. 75.00
Table, Hutch, New England, Red Paint, Box Stretcher, C.1820 .... 3650.00
Table, Hutch, Pine, Trestle, Box Stretcher, 1780, 56 In. 1600.00
Table, Ice Cream, Marble Top 175.00
Table, Inlaid Top, Fluted Edge Above Frieze, Mahogany, 31 In. 2000.00
Table, Kitchen, Chrome, Yellow, 1950s 85.00
Table, Kitchen, Drop Leaf, Hardwood 225.00
Table, Lamp, Black Over Red Paint, Scalloped, Nova Scotia 950.00
Table, Lamp, Limbert, Arts & Crafts 850.00
Table, Library, 2 Drawer, Lower Shelf, Logo, Roycroft, 1907, 30 In. 550.00
Table, Library, 2 Drawer, Rohlf 8000.00
Table, Library, Hexagonal Top, Gustav Stickley, No.625, C.1904 .... 900.00
Table, Library, Leather Top, True, False Drawers, Mahogany, Round 1980.00
Table, Library, Oak, Cabriole Legs, Quarter Sawn Top, C.1900 .... 495.00
Table, Louis XV/XVI, Tulipwood, Serpentine, Writing Slide, 30 In. 3300.00
Table, Louis XVI, 1 Drawer, Reeded Legs, Round, 28 X 21 In. 700.00
Table, Marble Top On 3 Winged Herms, Fruitwood, 28 In., Pair 6600.00
Table, Marble Top, Fret Carved Frieze, Mahogany, 29 1/2 In. 1045.00
Table, Marble Top, Ornate Cast Iron Base, Round, 36 In. 375.00
Table, Mosaic Top, Mueller 150.00
Table, Mother–of–Pearl, Bone, Tulipwood Marquetry, 1860 .... 2200.00
Table, Occasional, Empire Style, Marble Top, Mahogany, 25 In., Pr. 1400.00
Table, Occasional, Louis XV Style, Porcelain & Brass, 14 In. 275.00
Table, Occasional, Lyre Form, Inlaid Rosewood, C.1820, 24 In. 665.00

Cigarette burns on wooden furniture are difficult to conceal. Rub the burn with scratch-cover polish. If that does not help, rub the burn with a paste of rottenstone (found in most hardware stores) and linseed oil.

Table, Occasional, Yew, Biedermeier, 31 X 37 In. ....*Illus* 700.00
Table, Parlor, Eastlake, Walnut, Marble, 27 X 19 In. 175.00
Table, Parlor, Iron & Glass Ball Feet, Square, Oak, 24 In. 75.00
Table, Pedestal, Six 9 In.Leaves, Mahogany, Round, 52 In. 800.00
Table, Pembroke, 2 Drawers, Inlaid Mahogany, C.1800, 26 In. 1750.00
Table, Pembroke, 2 Drop Leaves, New York, Mahogany, 1815, 29 In. 1000.00
Table, Pembroke, American, Cherry, C.1790, 37 3/4 In. 650.00
Table, Pembroke, Drop Leaf, Frieze Drawer, Mahogany, C.1780 .... 445.00
Table, Pembroke, Federal, Curly Maple, Shaped Leaves, 37 In. 4400.00
Table, Pembroke, Federal, Mahogany, C.1815, 29 In. 5775.00
Table, Pembroke, Federal, Mahogany, Pedestal, 1815, 24 In. 1000.00
Table, Pembroke, George III, Divided Top, Faded Mahogany, 29 In. 775.00
Table, Pembroke, George III, Mahogany Inlay, Banded, Drawer, 1790 .... 2400.00
Table, Pembroke, Hepplewhite, Drop Leaves, Walnut, 26 3/4 In. 325.00
Table, Pembroke, Mahogany, Drawer, 1810, 26 X 28 In. 700.00
Table, Pembroke, Pierced Brackets, Walnut, C.1780, 28 1/4 In. 9350.00
Table, Pembroke, Regency, Mahogany, Rectangular Top, 29 1/2 In. 350.00
Table, Pembroke, Shaped Drop Leaf, Maple & Birch, 28 1/2 In. 225.00
Table, Pembroke, Square Legs, Original Brasses, Cherry, 27 In. 200.00
Table, Pembroke, W.Nutting, Inlay, Mahogany, 18 X 32 3/4 In. 600.00
Table, Pennsylvania, Cherry, Cabriole Legs, 2 Drawers, 82 In. 925.00
Table, Pier, Art Deco, Iron, Parcel Gilt, Marble, France, 30 In. 950.00
Table, Pier, Classic Revival, Mahogany, Veneer, Marble Top, 1825 .... 1300.00
Table, Pier, Classical, Mahogany, Marble, C.1815, 36 In. 2425.00
Table, Pier, Empire, Mirrored Back, Marble Top, Mahogany, 39 In. 175.00
Table, Pier, Federal, Mahogany, Marble Top, C.1810, 34 In. 9900.00
Table, Pier, Parcel Gilt, Carved, Scroll Ends, China, 32 X 51 In. 1500.00
Table, Pierce Carved, Burmese, Dog On Scrolled Feet, 41 In. 2100.00
Table, Pine, 2 Drawers, Nova Scotia, C.1810 .... 500.00
Table, Pine, Pegged, 3 Board Top, 6 Ft. 650.00
Table, Plant, Cottage Style, 1880s 45.00
Table, Pool, Brunswick, Baby Grand, 1917, 4 X 8 Ft. 1950.00
Table, Pool, Brunswick, Dark Maple, 1880, 4 X 8 Ft. 7500.00
Table, Pool, Brunswick, Oak, 1880, 4 X 8 Ft. 8500.00
Table, Pool, Brunswick, Poplar, 1880, 4 X 8 Ft. 6000.00
Table, Prayer, Carved, Chinese 195.00
Table, Queen Anne, English, Mahogany, 28 X 46 X 40 In. ....*Illus* 500.00
Table, Queen Anne, Philadelphia, Walnut, C.1760, 49 X 28 3/4 In. 3500.00
Table, Queen Anne, Swing Leg, Scalloped Apron 2200.00
Table, Reading, George III, Mahogany 1980.00
Table, Red & Black, Chinese Lacquer, Hexagonal Base, 32 In. 250.00

Furniture , Table, Occasional, Yew,
Biedermeier, 31 X 37 In.

Furniture, Table, Queen Anne, English,
Mahogany, 28 X 46 X 40 In.

Table, Round Apron, 1 Drawer, European, Walnut, 29 X 25 In. 175.00
Table, Sawbuck, Old Red–Brown Paint, Pine, 26 1/2 X 41 1/2 In. 700.00
Table, Sawbuck, Pine, 1 Board Top, Old Color, New England, 59 In. 600.00
Table, Sawbuck, Pine, Cross Brace, Breadboard Top, 25 X 38 In. 850.00
Table, Scagliola Top, Battle Scene, Paw Feet, Mahogany, 32 In. 1430.00
Table, Seat, Telephone, 1940s 145.00
Table, Serving, Federal, Mahogany, C.1815, 37 In. 3350.00
Table, Sewing, Federal, Curly Maple, Mahogany, C.Briggs, 19 In. 6650.00
Table, Sewing, Federal, Original Sewing Bag, Cookie Corners 5775.00
Table, Sewing, Regency, Fitted Drawer, Rosewood, C.1830, 21 In. 800.00
Table, Sewing, Sheraton, Drop Leaves, 2 Drawers, Mahogany 250.00
Table, Sewing, Sheraton, Drop Leaves, Drawers, American, C.1815 .... 400.00
Table, Shaped Top, Graduated Drawers, Tiger & Bird's–Eye Maple 1650.00
Table, Sheraton, 2 Tiers, Red & Black Paint 8250.00
Table, Sheraton, Red Flame Graining, Drawer, 30 In. 550.00
Table, Snooker, Brunswick, Medalist Model, 6 Legs, C.1930 .... 5500.00
Table, Snooker, Brunswick, Royal Model, Rack, Oak, 5 X 10 Ft. 2500.00
Table, Split Pedestal, Quarter Sawn Oak, Claw Feet, 54 In. 2650.00
Table, Square Pedestal, Round, Oak, 48 In. 375.00
Table, Tavern, 1 Board Top, Pegged Ends, 1 Drawer, 42 In. 950.00
Table, Tavern, 3 Board Dish Top, English, Oak, 26 3/8 X 26 In. 350.00
Table, Tavern, American, Cherry, 18th Century, 26 3/4 In. 1000.00
Table, Tavern, Beaded Edge, 1 Drawer, 2 Board Top, Pine, 27 In. 750.00
Table, Tavern, Boxed Stretcher Base, Oval Top, New England 2700.00
Table, Tavern, Button Feet, Round 2 Board Top, Maple, 28 X 25 In. 800.00
Table, Tavern, Cabinetmaker Jim Johnston, Curly Maple, 27 In. 135.00
Table, Tavern, Country Queen Anne, Curly Maple, 22 X 32 In. 9000.00
Table, Tavern, Hepplewhite, Maple, 1 Board Top, 22 X 32 In. 4200.00
Table, Tavern, Hepplewhite, Tiger Maple, C.1790, 44 3/4 X 25 In. 875.00
Table, Tavern, Maple Base, Pine Oval Top, 19 1/2 X 29 X 25 In. 700.00
Table, Tavern, Oval Top, Pine & Birch, 20 3/4 X 31 3/4 In. 1700.00
Table, Tavern, Queen Anne, 1 Drawer, 1 Board Pine Top, 26 In. 1600.00
Table, Tavern, Queen Anne, Maple Base, Pine Top, Drawer, 26 In. 400.00
Table, Tavern, Queen Anne, Maple, Green Repaint, 21 X 28 In. 2695.00
Table, Tavern, Queen Anne, Maple, New England, 1740, 26 In. 6600.00
Table, Tavern, William & Mary, Maple & Pine, C.1730, 26 In. 1600.00
Table, Tavern, William & Mary, Maple, New England, C.1740, 27 In. 750.00
Table, Tavern, William & Mary, New England, C.1700, 41 3/4 In. 5250.00
Table, Tavern, William & Mary, Oval, Painted, C.1740, 25 1/4 In. 6750.00
Table, Tea, Chippendale, Dish Top, Vase Post, Mahogany, 27 In. 1300.00
Table, Tea, Chippendale, Mahogany, Round Tip Top, 30 X 34 In. 175.00
Table, Tea, Chippendale, Tilt Top, Cherry, C.1770, 23 1/2 X 28 In. 800.00
Table, Tea, Chippendale, Tilt Top, Maple, C.1780, 28 1/2 In. 675.00
Table, Tea, George II, Mahogany, Drawer, Carved Apron, 33 In. 2200.00
Table, Tea, Gustav Stickley, No.644, Red Decal, C.1904, 29 In. 700.00
Table, Tea, L & JG Stickley, Round, C.1907, 30 X 29 In. 550.00
Table, Tea, Lower Medial Shelf, G.Stickley, Label, C.1907, 29 In. 600.00
Table, Tea, Mission Oak, C.1910, 19 X 31 3/4 In. 200.00
Table, Tea, Queen Anne, Cabriole Legs, Country, 1770, 30 X 20 In. 1000.00
Table, Tea, Queen Anne, Mahogany, C.1770, 25 1/2 In. 7500.00
Table, Tea, Tilt Top, Cabriole Legs, Mahogany, 31 X 28 1/2 In. 475.00
Table, Tea, Tilt Top, Curly Maple, Maple, 35 X 27 1/2 In. 500.00
Table, Tea, Tilt Top, Tripod, Snake Feet, Birdcage, 28 X 33 In. 550.00
Table, Tilt Top, 1 Board Top, 17 X 23 X 28 In. 225.00
Table, Tilt Top, Chippendale, Ball & Claw Feet, 29 In. 1000.00
Table, Tilt Top, Chippendale, Mahogany, 1780, 26 In. 450.00
Table, Tilt Top, Chippendale, Mahogany, Birdcage, 1880s, 26 In. 375.00
Table, Tilt Top, Chippendale, Mahogany, C.1780, 29 In. ....*Illus* 500.00
Table, Tilt Top, Chippendale, Walnut, Tripod, 27 1/2 In. 350.00
Table, Tilt Top, Game, Mother–of–Pearl, Lacquer 3350.00
Table, Tilt Top, George II, Fluted Standard, Mahogany, C.1760 .... 1045.00
Table, Tilt Top, George III, Mahogany, Birdcage, 30 In. 2475.00
Table, Tilt Top, Mahogany, Turned Post, 20 X 26 In. 1100.00
Table, Tilt Top, Maple, Grained Base, 24 X 27 In. 1250.00

Furniture, Table, Tilt Top, Chippendale,
Mahogany, C.1780, 29 In.

Furniture, Table, Work, Rosewood,
Satinwood Interior, Tray, Mirror

Table, Tilt Top, New England, Mahogany, C.1810, 19 X 29 In.	1300.00
Table, Tilt Top, Queen Anne, Candle Reflector, 19th Century	295.00
Table, Tilt Top, Tripod, George III, Mahogany, 28 /12 In.	440.00
Table, Trestle, L & JG Stickley, No.593, Oak, C.1910, 29 In.	800.00
Table, Trestle, Shoe Foot, 18th Century, 8 Ft.X 3 Ft.4 In.	4500.00
Table, Vanity, Mahogany, Interior Mirror, 26 X 20 X 32 In.	2250.00
Table, Victorian, Carved Walnut, 20 X 32 1/2 In.	385.00
Table, Walnut, C.1880, 22 In.	350.00
Table, Walnut, Round Marble Top, 2 Drawers, 30 X 26 In.	375.00
Table, William & Mary, 1 Drawer, Twisted Legs, Walnut, 28 In.	605.00
Table, William & Mary, Maple, Baluster Legs, 1780, 47 In.	5000.00
Table, William IV, Rosewood, Brass Mounted, 47 In., Pair	9350.00
Table, Work, 1 Drawer, 3 Board Top, Cherry, 29 X 35 X 29 1/2 In.	425.00
Table, Work, 1 Drawer, Removable Top, Traces of Red, 30 In.	190.00
Table, Work, 2 Board Top, Brown Paint Base, Pine, 34 1/2 X 71 In.	350.00
Table, Work, 2 Drawers, Removable Top, Poplar, 33 X 57 1/2 In.	350.00
Table, Work, Birch Base, Breadboard Top, 29 1/2 X 26 1/4 In.	450.00
Table, Work, Birch, Pine Board Top, 8 In.Drop Leaves, 48 In.	500.00
Table, Work, Boston, Inlaid Mahogany, C.1810, 29 1/2 In.	3575.00
Table, Work, Classical Revival, Mahogany, Spooner & Trask, 29 In.	4950.00
Table, Work, Country Heppplewhite, 3 Board Top, 33 1/2 X 50 In.	500.00
Table, Work, Curly Maple Veneer, Shelf, 2 Drawers, 18 X 21 In.	175.00
Table, Work, Curly Maple Veneer, Base Shelf, 18 X 21 In.	175.00
Table, Work, Drop Leaf, 2 Half Drawers, Michigan, C.1910, 29 In.	500.00
Table, Work, Drop Leaf, Rope Legs, 2 Drawers, Mahogany, 30 1/2 In.	525.00
Table, Work, Federal, Mahogany Inlaid, Mass., C.1790, 20 X 16 In.	3740.00
Table, Work, Federal, Mahogany, Bird's–Eye Maple, 1815, 19 In.	4250.00
Table, Work, Federal, Walnut & Tiger Maple, C.1820, 30 3/4 In.	800.00
Table, Work, Hepplewhite, Pine, 2 Board Top, 21 X 29 X 28 In.	325.00
Table, Work, Louis Philippe, Figured Walnut, Leather Top, 25 In.	600.00
Table, Work, Marquetry, Lyre Supports, Elm & Amaranth, 27 In.	2200.00
Table, Work, Mortised & Pinned Apron, Removable Top, 40 In.	350.00
Table, Work, Rosewood, Satinwood Interior, Tray, Mirror ....*Illus*	2200.00
Table, Work, Shaker, 2 Graduated Drawers, Cherry, C.1810, 27 In.	1200.00
Table, Work, Square Legs, 2 Board Top, Pine, 27 X 35 1/2 X 27 In.	175.00
Table, Work, Walnut Base, Pine Breadboard Top, 30 X 48 In.	200.00
Table, Writing, Federal, Lady's, Inlaid Mahogany, C.1810, 52 In.	5225.00
Table, Writing, George III, Mahogany, Kneehole, 36 X 26 In.	2850.00
Table, Writing, George III, Walnut Veneer, 47 X 25 In.	4125.00
Table, Writing, Inlaid Mahogany, C.1790, 4 Ft. 1 In.	2300.00
Table, Writing, Lady's, Federal, Mahogany, C.1805, 31 X 24 In.	5500.00

Table, Writing, Louis XV, Ebonized & Parcel Gilt, 28 1/2 In. 5500.00
Table, Writing, Louis XV, Leather Top, Drawers, Tulipwood, 39 In. 6875.00
Table, Writing, Louis XV, Shaped Top, Kingwood, 4 Ft.10 In. 8850.00
Table, Writing, Louis XVI Style, Mahogany Yew, 44 X 29 In. 1300.00
Table, Writing, Parquetry, Tulipwood, C.1890, 4 Ft. 8 In. 4400.00
Table, Writing, Regency, Rosewood, Ebony, Leather Top, 36 In. 8800.00
Table, Writing, Regency, Rosewood, Leather Top, C.1820 .... 1400.00
Tabouret, Octagonal, L & JG Stickley, Decal, C.1907, 17 In. 275.00
Tea Cart, Drexel, Mahogany, Drop Leaves, 2 Lower Drawers 50.00
Tea Cart, Wicker .... 300.00 To 550.00
Tea Stand, Carved Bats, Fruit, Chinese, Marble Top, 20 In. 200.00
Tea Table, Queen Anne, Scallop Shell Each Knee, Mahogany, 36 In. 900.00
Tray, Butler's, Stand, 19th Century, Mahogany, 27 1/2 In. 100.00
Tray, Butler's, Stand, Victorian, Mahogany, 19th Century 500.00
Tray, Carrying Handle, Inlaid Mahogany, Oval, Satinwood, C.1775 .... 495.00
Tray, On Stand, George III, Inlaid, Scalloped, Satinwood, 23 In. 900.00
Trolley, Meat, Mahogany, Brass Bands, Wheels, Iron Pendant, 1850 .... 4800.00
Umbrella Rack, Art Nouveau Floral, Iron, English, 26 3/4 In. 95.00
Umbrella Stand, Can, Oak, English 48.00
Umbrella Stand, Old Hickory Furniture Co. 150.00
Umbrella Stand, Peasant Girl, Basket of Grapes, Iron, 32 In. 150.00
Umbrella Stand, Wicker 15.00
Urn, Knife, Domed Lid, Inlaid Ebony, Satinwood, C.1800, 26 In. 605.00
Vitrine, Louis XVI, Carved & Painted, 60 X 27 1/2 In. 1400.00
Wardrobe, 2 Doors, 3 Drawers, 37 X 19 1/2 X 63 In. 600.00
Wardrobe, American Classical, Mahogany, Stenciled 6600.00
Wardrobe, Classical, 3 Sections, Mahogany, C.1825, 7 Ft. 2 In. 4450.00
Wardrobe, Mahogany, England, 1890–1900, 86 X 81 X 30 In. 2500.00
Wardrobe, Pine, Poplar, Paneled End Doors, 60 X 86 In. 500.00
Wardrobe, Victorian, Oak, Applied Carvings, 7 Ft. 950.00
Wardrobe, William IV, Inlaid Mahogany, C.1830, 7 Ft. 2 In. 675.00
Washstand, 1 Dovetailed Drawer, Curly Maple, 25 X 29 3/4 In. 325.00
Washstand, 1 Drawer, Dovetailed, Cherry, 19 X 21 X 29 In. 315.00
Washstand, Cherry, Drawer In Shelf, Cutout, Bowl, 28 X 17 In. 140.00
Washstand, Country Federal, 1 Drawer, Red, 1810, 31 X 15 In. 300.00
Washstand, Country Sheraton, Base Shelf, Drawer, Red, 31 In. 310.00
Washstand, Federal, Mahogany, 1 Drawer, New England, 1800, 38 In. 770.00
Washstand, George III, 1 Drawer, Mahogany, C.1830, 38 In. 935.00
Washstand, Red & Black Graining, Striping, Pine, 37 3/4 In. 375.00
Washstand, Scalloped Apron, Accessory Cutouts, Pine, 30 3/4 In. 95.00
Washstand, Yellow Paint, Black Striping, 32 X 17 X 38 In. 175.00
Whatnot, 5 Shelves, Mahogany, C.1860, 4 Ft. 7 In. 1650.00
Whatnot, Classical Style, Mahogany, 19th Century, 45 In. 200.00
Window Seat, Federal, Mahogany, Upholstered, C.1815, 44 In. 14850.00
Wine Cooler, Sarcophagus Form, Mahogany, C.1820 .... 2500.00

G-ARGY-
ROUSSEAU
Gabriel Argy–Rousseau, born in 1885, was a French glass artist who produced a variety of objects in the Art Deco style. His mark, "G. Argy–Rousseau," was usually impressed.

G.ARGY–ROUSSEAU, Bowl, White Rabbits, Pate–De–Verre, C.1925, 3 1/2 In. 8800.00
Box, Covered, Bacchus Mask, Gray, C.1930, 6 1/4 In. 7700.00
Night–Light, Chevrons, Tigers, Pate–De–Verre, 7 3/4 In. 7700.00
Paperweight, Signed, Pate–De–Verre 300.00
Pendant, Art Nouveau, Cord, Pate–De–Verre, 2 X 3 In. 895.00
Vase, Magenta Stars, Gray Ground, C.1925, 3 3/4 In. 3575.00
Vase, Moths, Pate–De–Verre, Bulbous, C.1925, 3 1/8 In. 6600.00

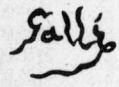 Galle was a designer who made glass, furniture, and other Art Nouveau items, including pottery. Emile Galle founded his factory in France in 1874. After Galle's death in 1904, the firm continued to make glass and furniture until 1931. The name "Galle" was used as a mark, but it was often hidden in the design of the object.

GALLE POTTERY, Dish, Fleur–De–Lis Shape, Victorian Couple, 9 1/2 In. 225.00

Galle Pottery, Figurine,
Pug Dog, Sitting,
Flower Sprigs, 12 In.

Galle, Vase, Cameo, Trees,
3–Color, Signed,
7 3/4 In.

Galle, Vase, Cameo, Floral,
Leaf Design,
3–Color, 16 In.

Duck, Imari Colors, Marked, 15 1/2 X 7 In., Pair	850.00
Figurine, Pug Dog, Sitting, Flower Sprigs, 12 In. ....*Illus*	950.00
Vase, Castle & Field Scene, Flower Shape, Signed, 11 In.	565.00
GALLE, Bottle, Perfume, Cut Orange–Red To Amber–Yellow	330.00
Bottle, Perfume, Enameled, 4 Applied Medallions, Hunter & Dog, Signed	650.00
Decanter Set, Allover Enameled Flowers, Signed, 7 Piece	1550.00
Decanter Set, French Toast On Glass, Enameled, Signed, 7 Piece	1350.00
Ewer, 3 Stages of Poppy Flower, Pinched Sides, Brown, 11 1/2 In.	750.00
Fixture, Hanging, Original Mounts, 3 Chains, 18 In.	2800.00
Lamp, Black Metal Base, Frosted White, Butterflies, Signed, 4 In.	375.00
Lamp, Butterflies On Yellow, Metal Base, Umbrella Shade, 4 1/2 In.	650.00
Lamp, Desk, Amethyst, Brown & Cream Design	715.00
Lamp, Umbrella Shade, Butterflies, Yellow Ground, Signed, 4 1/2 In.	525.00
Tankard, Summer Season, Mill Scene	1000.00
Vase, Aqua, Bullet Form, Enameled Anemone Blossoms, 13 3/4 In.	2750.00
Vase, Brown Water Lily Buds & Pads, Leafy Trees, Signed, 5 3/4 In.	595.00
Vase, Bulbous Bottom, Red Vine On Orange Ground, 5 In.	595.00
Vase, Cameo Brown, Yellow, Frosted Pinecones, Star Marked, 11 3/4 In.	900.00
Vase, Cameo, Floral, Leaf Design, 3–Color, 16 In. ....*Illus*	1500.00
Vase, Cameo, Trees, 3–Color, Signed, 7 3/4 In. ....*Illus*	1550.00
Vase, Carved Wisteria Flowers, Leaves, Signed, 24 In.	1950.00
Vase, Crocus, Teardrop Shape, Yellow, Lavender, 8 1/2 In.	3850.00
Vase, Floating Pond Lilies, Blue To Chartreuse, 11 3/4 In.	1575.00
Vase, Floral On Yellow Ground, Pedestal, Signed, 8 1/4 In.	495.00
Vase, Floral, Orange Frost, Hidden Signature, 7 In.	1175.00
Vase, Floral, Spherical Base, Slender Neck, Flared Lip, 12 In.	1400.00
Vase, Flowers & Vines, Opaque Amber Ground, Signed, 7 In.	875.00
Vase, Grape & Leaf Design, Signed, 13 In.	985.00
Vase, Gray, Mustard Splashes, Foil, Flattened Sides, 6 3/4 In.	1870.00
Vase, Green & Yellow Daffodils, 12 In.	2500.00
Vase, Japanese Irises & Leaves, Water Lilies, Signed, 13 1/8 In.	950.00
Vase, Lake, 2 Boats, Tree At Shore, Cut In Brown, Signed, 4 1/2 In.	695.00
Vase, Landscape, Baluster Form, Amber, Gray, C.1900, 20 1/4 In.	4125.00
Vase, Notre Dame, 1914, Baluster, Marigold, Swirls, 20 In.	4675.00
Vase, Ocher Vegetation On Orange To Lemon, 6 3/4 In.	650.00
Vase, Orange & Chocolate Brown, Signed, 7 1/2 In.	435.00
Vase, Orange Flowers, Aqua Ground, Bulbous, Signed, 7 3/4 In.	700.00
Vase, Orange Poppies, Frosted Ground, Signed, 4 1/2 In.	450.00
Vase, Pinched On 1 Side, Pitcher Shape, Clear, Signed, 4 1/4 In.	2750.00
Vase, Pitcher Shape, Embedded Pieces In Berries, Stand, 4 1/2 In.	1850.00
Vase, Polished Glass, Teardrop, Orange Red, Cameo, 6 In. ....*Illus*	900.00
Vase, Pond Lilies Floating In Water, Scenic, 11 3/4 In.	1350.00
Vase, Purple To Yellow, Signed, 3 In.	400.00
Vase, Raised Floral, Bird, Butterfly, Signed, 9 1/2 In.	385.00
Vase, Raspberry, Ovoid, Yellow, Gray, Mold Blown, 9 1/2 In.	4675.00
Vase, Rust Flowers, Cream Ground, 4 In.	295.00

Vase, Slender Neck, Oval Body, Brown Leaves, Beige, 5 1/2 In. 425.00
Vase, Spherical, Leaves, Vines, Avocado To Yellow, Pink Ground, 12 In. 1200.00
Vase, Starfish & Sea Plants, Burgundy, 12 1/2 In. 1800.00
Vase, Stick, Amber Twist, Footed, Thistle, Cross of Lorraine, 8 In. 595.00
Vase, Stick, Bun Base, Sweet Pea Vine & Flower, Signed, 13 In. 750.00
Vase, Stick, Pansy Type Flowers, 10 In. 500.00
Vase, Stick, Yellow & Green, 17 1/2 In. 1250.00
Vase, Thistle, Frosted, 8 In. 625.00
Vase, Trees, White & Yellow Ground, Cameo, C.1900, Marked, 21 In. 1000.00
Vase, Wisteria, Baluster Form, Green & Blue, Signed, 12 1/4 In. 1000.00
Vase, Wisteria, Frosted Ground, Signed, 12 In. 950.00
Wall Pocket, Butterflies, Sky Blue, Brown, Gold, Fan Shape, 14 In. 450.00
Wall Pocket, Butterflies, Touches of Gold, Fan Shape, 14 In. 395.00
Wine Set, Blue Enamel Cornflowers, Handle, Heart Stopper, 4 Cups 825.00

> Game plates are any make of plate decorated with pictures of birds,
> animals, or fish. The game plates usually came in sets consisting of
> twelve dishes and a serving platter. These sets were most popular
> during the 1880s.

GAME PLATE, Limoges, Coronet, Signed Brussillon, 11 1/2 In. 165.00
GAME SET, Platter, 14 3/4 X 9 3/4 In., 7 Piece 150.00

> Children's games of all sorts are collected. Of special interest are
> any board games or card games. Other games may be found listed
> under Toy, Card, or the name of the character or celebrity featured
> in the game.

GAME, Across The Continent, Train Playing Pieces, Tootsietoy, 1952 .... 95.00
 Admiral Byrd's South Pole, Board, Parker Brothers, C.1934 .... 120.00
 Alfred Hitchcock Presents Why, Milton Bradley, 1958 .... 15.00
 All American Football, Cadaco, 1969, 19 X 12 1/2 In. 10.00
 All In The Family, Milton Bradley, 1972 .... 10.00
 American Ball Game, Marx, Original Box 40.00
 American Flag, 1940 .... 45.00
 Around The World, Tin Board, Flags, Zeppelin, Wolverine, 1930s, 16 In. 30.00
 Assembly Line, Board, Ford, Plymouth, Chevrolet, Studebaker, 1940 .... 47.50
 Atomic Bomb, A.C.Gilbert Co. 50.00
 Attack, C.1900 .... 15.00
 Auto Bridge, Teaches You To Play, Dated 1952, 15 X 10 In. 12.00
 Baseball Pinball, Sheet Metal, Plastic Top, Marbles, Marx, 1950s 15.00
 Baseball, Board, Card, Pastime Games Co., 1930, 4 X 5 3/4 In. 12.00
 Baseball, Roger Maris, Tin, Box, 1962 .... 30.00
 Batman, Ideal, Box, 1966 .... 12.00
 Beany & Cecil, Jumping D J Game, Mattel, 1962 .... 12.00
 Ben Casey ....6.00 To 15.00
 Beverly Hillbillies 20.00
 Bewildered Travelers, Games of John Gilpin, C.1890 .... 30.00
 Billy Whiskers, Board & Box 35.00
 Bingo Cage, Wooden Balls, With Numbers 50.00
 Bingo, Tucker Toy Corp, Wooden & Cardboard Box 12.00
 Black Peter, Pictures Black Man, Pocket 15.00
 Blocks, ABC, Fire Department, Truck, Ladders Pictured, McLoughlin, 1893 .... 350.00
 Blondie Goes To Leisureland, Westinghouse, Box, 1935 .... 25.00
 Board, Canvas, Sailor's, 19th Century, Roll, 8 X 18 In. 2150.00
 Board, Cribbage, Blue Ground, Carved Star & Eye Top, Polychromed 500.00
 Board, Double Game, Football, Baseball, Checkers, 1926 .... 60.00
 Board, Inlaid Backgammon & Chess, Turkish, Inlaid, 1875, 18 In. 150.00
 Board, Parcheesi, Breadboard Ends, C.1900, 18 X 19 In. 1550.00
 Bonanza, 4 Cartwrights, Seated At Ranch, Box, 1964 .... 18.00
 Bowling, 10 Turned Wooden Pins, 2 Balls, Wooden Box, 8 In.Pins 30.00
 Bowling, Sambo, 5 Pins 190.00
 Bowling, Wooden Pins, Tin Man, Baldwin Mfg.Co., 1920s, 6 X 30 In. 55.00
 Boy Scouts, Parker Bros., 1912 .... 45.00
 Break The Bank, Bert Parks, Bettye-B Product, 1955 .... 14.00
 Call Me Lucky, Bing Crosby, Parker Brothers 18.00

Card, Blondie	15.00
Card, Cities	22.00
Card, Elite Conversation, McLaughlin	15.00
Card, Ferdinand The Bull, Whitman, 1938	20.00
Card, Flowers, Cincinnati Game Co., 1899	10.00
Card, Hi–Ho Silver, Parker	22.00
Card, Kennel Club, Dog Pictures, 1939, Box	12.00
Card, Make A Million, 1945	17.50
Card, Man From U.N.C.L.E., 1965 ....6.50 To	12.50
Card, Old Maid, 1924	5.00
Card, Old Maid, Box, C.1920	10.00
Card, Old Maid, Circus Edition	4.00
Card, Pinocchio, Parker, 1932	15.00
Card, Pit, Bull & Bear, Parker Brothers, Dated 1939	5.00
Card, Rook, 1931	19.50
Card, Skippy	15.00
Card, Spoof, Bradley, 1918, Box	20.00
Card, Touring, Auto, Parker	15.00
Cargoes, Board, Ocean Liner Box, Selchow & Righter, 1936	35.00
Casino, James Bond 007, Revolver, Gambling Chips, 1965	18.00
Changeable Charlie, Puzzle Blocks, Nabisco Premium, Box	10.00
Charlie Chan, Box, 1936	150.00
Checkerboard 1 Side, Round Layout Other, Pine, Gallery, 24 In. ..	50.00
Checkerboard, Applied Gallery Edge	175.00
Checkerboard, Black & Natural Pine, 18 1/4 X 26 1/2 In.	100.00
Checkerboard, Black On Unpainted Pine, 19th Century	140.00
Checkerboard, Carved Green & Silver, 20th Century	575.00
Checkerboard, Natural Pine, Black Squares, Tray Edge, 16 X 19 In.	75.00
Checkerboard, Old Black & White Paint, Pine, 12 3/4 X 19 1/4 In.	125.00
Checkerboard, Pocket Size, Leather Case Opens To 8 X 8 In.	20.00
Checkerboard, Red & Black Paint, Beveled Edges, 13 3/4 X 25 In.	145.00
Checkerboard, Red Paint, Natural Pine, Primitive, 17 X 23 1/2 In.	65.00
Checkerboard, Red, Gold Paint 1 Side, Carved Mill Game Other, 13 In.	235.00
Checkerboard, Squares On Back, Wooden, Mustard Paint, 17 X 29 In.	205.00
Checkerboard, Under Drawer To Hold Wooden Checkers, 15 X 13 In.	245.00
Chess Set, Ivory, Silk Lined Teak Case	750.00
Chinese Star Checkers, Board, Milton Bradley, Box	10.00
Chipmunks, Alvin & Friends	10.00
Chopper Strike, Played 2 Levels, Terrain Map, 1976	12.00
Chuck–A–Luck Cage, Nickel Plate, 3 Dice, 11 In.	90.00
Circus Marble, Plastic Case, Tin Litho, Wolverine, Original Box	15.00
Circus Trix, Gotham, Marble, Tin, Glass, 8 X 16 In.	25.00
Colorita, England, C.1890	25.00
Cribbage, Board & Pegs, Says Last Sale Wins Box, Cherries, 1930s	37.50
Cube Anagrams, Parker, Box, 1899	18.00
Dark Shadows ....15.00 To	20.00
Dart, Clowns, Tin Litho, 12 X 15 In.	13.00
Dart, Dragnet, Box	18.00
Dart, Rudolph The Red Nosed Reindeer, Magnetic, 1939	35.00
Dominoes, Advertising, Eagle Oil & Supply, Wooden, Dovetailed Box	48.00
Dominoes, Ivory, Black Base, Brass Pins, Embossing Co., Rules ...	48.00
Dominoes, Set, Red, With Rhinestones	150.00
Dominoes, White, Catalin, Pre–1940	25.00
Double Board Game, Parker Brothers, Baseball, Football, Checkers, 1926	65.00
Dr.Kildare, Richard Chamberlain TV Show Picture, Ideal, 1962	17.00
Dragnet, Board, Transogram, Salesman Sample, 1955	45.00
Easy Money, Milton Bradley, 1936	20.00
Eddie Cantor, Tell It To The Judge, Parker Brothers, Box, 1936 ...	35.00
Elsie The Cow, Where's Elmer?	20.00
Faro Cards	150.00
Fast Mail Train, Milton Bradley, C.1900	150.00
Fess Parker Trail Blazers, Daniel Boone TV, Milton Bradley, Box, 1964	22.00
Fibber McGee, 1930s	20.00
Fibber McGee, Wistful Vista Mystery, 1940	30.00

Fiddlestix, 40 Colored Sticks, Directions, Plaze Mfg. Co.	5.00
Fish Pond, McLoughlin	60.00
Fishing, Magnetic, Celluloid Fish & Swan Pieces, 1900s	40.00
Flintstones, Unused, Box, 1961	38.00
Game of Nations, Milton Bradley, 1908	16.00
Gay Goblins, Paper On Wood, 1800s	125.00
Gee–Wiz Race, Mechanical, Wolverine, 1923	75.00
Get My Goat, Pocket, 1914	17.00
Gilbert Meteor, Clay Marbles, Complete, 1910	50.00
Go–Bang, Signed J.H.	25.00
Golden State Limited, Milton Bradley, 1920s, Box	50.00
Goofy Filipino Twister Yo Yo	6.00
Grandma's Mince Pie, McLoughlin, C.1890	100.00
Great American Baseball, Tin Lithograph, 1925	45.00
Hardy Boys Treasure, Board, Parker Bros.	8.00
Heads & Tails, Parker Bros., Nickel Edition, 4 3/4 X 3 1/2 In.	17.00
Hokum, Parker Bros., 1927	12.00
Horsman Holma, Board, 1885	35.00
In Dixie–Land, 1897	25.00
International Mail, U.S. & Foreign Stamps, 6 Boards, Box	50.00
Jack Daw, Teddy Bear On Cover, Milton Bradley	30.00
James Bond 007 Casino, Milton Bradley, Box, 1965	16.00
John Cameron Swayze, Fold Board, World Map, Milton Bradley, 1954	22.00
Johnny's Historical Game, Geo.S.Parker, C.1890	40.00
Jumeau, Litho of Eiffel Tower Background	400.00
Jump, Peg, Selchow & Righter Co.	15.00
Jungle Target, Marx, Box	25.00
Katch The Kaiser, Pocket, 1917	17.00
Katzenjammer Kids, Punch Out, Original Envelope	15.00
Kentucky Derby, Horseracing, Dice, Metal Box	55.00
Knapp Electric Questioner, H & K	80.00
Krull, Science–Fiction Movie, Parker Bros., 1983	10.00
Kukla, Fran & Ollie	25.00
Ladder, Katzenjammer Kids, Other Comic Figures On Litho	175.00
Laverne & Shirley, 1977	7.00
Li'l Abner, Parker Brothers, Copyright 1969	12.00 To 15.00
Limited Mail & Express, Parker Bros., 1895	150.00
Little Messenger Boy, McLoughlin Bros., C.1890	65.00
Little Word Builder, Samuel Gabriel Sons & Co., C.1910	20.00
Logomachy, McLoughlin, Cards of Children, Victorian Costumes, 1874	75.00
Lotto, Glass Tiles, McLoughlin Bros.	49.00
Mah–Jongg, Bone, Bamboo, Wooden Chest	50.00
Mah–Jongg, Heavy Cardboard, Box, 1923	20.00
Mah–Jongg, Ivory Sticks	65.00
Mah–Jongg, Junior, Instructions, 1923	30.00
Mansion of Happiness, McLoughlin, Dated 1895	250.00
Marble Run, Stencil Design, Victorian	125.00
Mary Poppins	25.00
Merry Goose, McLoughlin Bros., Framed, Wooden Box	65.00
Merry Time Roulette Wheel, Numbered Cloth, Rules, Marx	18.00
Mighty Comics Super Heroes, Transogram, 1966	12.00
Mighty Mouse, Milton Bradley, 1978	7.00
Million Dollar Man	6.00
Monkey Shines, Target, Cardboard, Pistol, American Toy Works	8.00
Monopoly, Complete, 1940s	65.00
Mork & Mindy, Pointing Finger At Ork, 1979, Square, 16 1/2 In.	9.00
Mystery Shooter, Marble	25.00
Name That Tune, Board	11.00
Nancy Drew Mystery, 1957	35.00
National Velvet, Based On TV Show, Transogram, Box, 1961	15.00
Nellie Bly, Board Only	25.00
New Game of Hunting, McLoughlin, 1904	260.00
O'Skeet, Parker Bros., Box, 1935	50.00
Official Radio Baseball, Toy Creations, Box, 1939	35.00

Ole Thousand Face, Schoenhut, 1925	35.00
Options, Colored Cover, 1883	25.00
Ouija Board, Wm.Fuld, Planchette In Own Box	45.00
Our Navy, Dewey, Box	60.00
Over The Rainbow See–Saw, Milton Bradley	25.00
Paddington Lucky Day, 1977	7.00
Parker Wings, Air Mail	25.00
Pegity, Parker	6.50
Peter Coddle Trip To Chicago, Parker	15.00
Peter Rabbit, 1978	10.00
Pick–Up Sticks, Schoenhut .... 13.00 To 15.00
Pin The Tail On The Donkey, C.Zimmerling, 36 X 32 In.	20.00
Pinball, Bat–M–Up	35.50
Pinball, Jet Age	40.00
Pirate & Traveler, Single Fold Board, Milton Bradley, 1910, Box	52.00
Planet of The Apes, Board, Based On Movie, 1974	12.00
Plunder, Milton Bradley, 1939	35.00
Poems, 1898	10.00
Pollyana, Parker Bros., 1940	18.00
Pool Balls, Composition, Box, Dated 1911	55.00
Puss 'N Boots, Litho of Cat Dressed Up, Box, 1920s	72.00
Put Hat On Uncle Wiggily	35.00
Puzzle Maker, Lindstrom Tool & Toy Co., Inc., C.1920	65.00
Puzzle Parties, Gilbert, Box, 1920	22.00
Puzzle, A Spill Out On Snow, Currier & Ives	30.00
Puzzle, Christmas Card, Wooden	12.00
Puzzle, Circus, Framed, Milton Bradley	35.00
Puzzle, Civil War Scene, Original Box	35.00
Puzzle, Flying, Put Plane In Paris, Wooden, 14 Piece	10.00
Puzzle, Grimsel, Wooden	35.00
Puzzle, Happy Family, Kittens, 1902	60.00
Puzzle, Jig Chase, Dog Race, 4 Sets	7.00
Puzzle, Jigsaw, $500 Title Contest, From Famous Painting, 1933	8.00
Puzzle, Jigsaw, Blondie, King Feature, 1933	17.50
Puzzle, Jigsaw, Gasoline Alley, Captain Midnight, 1930s	22.00
Puzzle, Jigsaw, Gone With The Wind, 1972	15.00
Puzzle, Jigsaw, Hood's Sarsaparilla, Double Sided, 15 X 10 In.	45.00
Puzzle, Jigsaw, Munsters, Whitman, 1965, 100 Pieces	12.00
Puzzle, Jigsaw, Norman Rockwell, 1931	15.00
Puzzle, Jigsaw, Winter Moonlight, Original Box, Wooden, 150 Pieces ...	15.00
Puzzle, Jolly Time All Fair, 3 Black Scenes, E.Fairchild, Box	10.00
Puzzle, Katzenjammer Kids, Jaymar, Box	15.00
Puzzle, Little Folks, Parker	75.00
Puzzle, Little Red Riding Hood, Whitman	15.00
Puzzle, Lydia Pinkham	40.00
Puzzle, Map of The Work, Capitol At Washington, McLaughlin	125.00
Puzzle, Map of U.S., McLoughlin Bros., C.1890	85.00
Puzzle, Mooley Cow, Parker Bros., Box	18.00
Puzzle, Our Gang, Saalfield, 1930s, Original Box, Set of 3	35.00
Puzzle, P.T.Barnum Hieroglyphic	50.00
Puzzle, Peter Coddle's Trip To New York, Milton Bradley	13.00
Puzzle, Peter Pan, 1952	8.00
Puzzle, Rainy Day, Hoods Sarsaparilla	25.00
Puzzle, S.W.A.T., Set of 2	6.00
Puzzle, Snow White & 7 Dwarfs, Walt Disney Enterprises, 1938	22.00
Puzzle, Spanish American War, War of 1812, Parker, 4 Piece	55.00
Puzzle, Star Trek, Green Box, Guild, Whitman, 1978	4.00
Puzzle, Steps To Manhood, Boy Scout Saluting Picture of Washington ...	25.00
Puzzle, Three Bears & Three Kittens, Box, Early 1900s	20.00
Puzzle, U.S.Map, Parker Bros.	25.00
Puzzle, Victrola Talking Machine Co., Dated 1908, Nipper	85.00
Puzzle, Young Folks Geographical, McLoughlin	13.00
Radio, Milton Bradley, 1920s	25.00
Raggedy Ann, 1954	5.00

Rin Tin Tin, Single Fold Board, Transogram, Box, 1960s 26.00
Ring–A–Peg, Board, Rings, Square Shooters, E.I.H.Pat.1940s 5.00
Robin Hood, Castle Set, Marx 54.00
Round The World, Joe Parker 24.00
Sanke, McLoughlin, C.1890 .... 85.00
Scapegoat, 1909 .... 11.00
Sea Raider, Single Fold Board, Parker Brothers, Box, 1940 .... 26.00
Secret Agent, Unused 20.00
Seven Keys, Ideal, 1961 .... 6.00
Shoot The Birds Off The Fence, Popgun 40.00
Shoot The Loop, Marble 20.00
Six Million Dollar Man 15.00
Ski Jumper, Schoenhut, Box 295.00
Sliced Birds, Selchow & Righter 30.00
Snake Eyes, Black Subject 35.00
Snap Dragon, Folds Up Into Wooden Box, 1880s 95.00
Snoopy, Fisher Price 20.00
Snow White & Seven Dwarfs, 1937 .... 20.00 To 55.00
Space 1999, Milton Bradley, 1976 .... 16.00
Space Race, Card, Edu–Cards, Unused, 1969, 2 1/2 X 3 1/2 In. 12.00
Spiderweb, Selchow & Righter 35.00
State Capitols 6.00
State Capitols, 1952 .... 7.00
Story of The U.S. Air Force, Transogram 10.00
Strange Game of Forbidden Fruit, Game of Shopping, Parker 25.00
Swayze, Milton Bradley 20.00
Table Croquet, Milton Bradley, C.1920 .... 10.00
Table Tennis Set, Wright–Ditson, Complete 70.00
Table Tennis, McLoughlin 18.00
Target, Little Black Sambo, Gun, Wyandotte, 14 X 23 In. .... 65.00 To 75.00
Target, Planet of The Apes, Darts, 1967 .... 10.00
Target, Untouchables, Arcade, Box 40.00
Target, Untouchables, Marx 85.00
Telegraph Office, 1913 .... 55.00
Ten Pins, Striped, Saginaw Wood Products 42.00
Ten Pins, Wooden Pins, Balls, Box 15.00
They're Off, Horse Race, Parker Bros., 1954 .... 17.00
Tiddlywinks, Peter Pan, Whitman 10.00
Tip The Bellboy, Stand Up Black Bellboy, Balls, All–Fair Toys, 1929 .... 40.00
Tip Top Boxing, Winding Tops, Metal Frame, Original Box 45.00
Tom Hamilton's Football Game, Parker Bros., 1936 .... 30.00
Tom Hamilton's Football, Army–Navy, 1926 .... 35.00
Toonerville Trolley 60.00
Tootsieroll Train, Factory, Candy Shop, Hasbro, 1969 .... 20.00
Uncle Remus, Walt Disney Productions 95.00
Video Village, Milton Bradley 8.00
Wells Fargo, 1959 .... 10.00
What's My Line, TV 35.00
Wild Animals, 1903 .... 8.00
Winnie The Pooh, Parker Bros., 1933 .... 65.00
Wizard of Oz, Cadaco 5.00
Wonderful Joe, McLoughlin 25.00
Young Folks' Geographic, McLoughlin Bros., C.1890 .... 25.00
Zorro, Board, Whitman, Box, 1958 .... 21.00

ГАРДНЕРЪ   The Gardner porcelain works was founded in Verbiki, outside Moscow, by the English–born Francis Gardner in 1766. Gardner made porcelain tablewares, figurines, and faience.

GARDNER, Cup & Saucer, Brown Flowers, Ribbon Handle, Demitasse 125.00
  Group, 2 Merchants Talking, Late 19th Century, Incised Mark, 8 In. 1150.00
  Group, Drunken Man, Helped To Feet By Wife, Incised Mark, 6 1/4 In. 1050.00

Gaudy Dutch pottery was made in England for America from about 1810 to 1820. It is a white earthenware with Imari–style decorations of red, blue, green, yellow, and black. Only sixteen patterns of Gaudy Dutch were made: Butterfly, Carnation, Dahlia, Double Rose, Dove, Grape, Leaf, Oyster, Primrose, Single Rose, Strawflower, Sunflower, Urn, War Bonnet, Zinnia, and No Name. Other similar wares are called "Gaudy Ironstone" and "Gaudy Welsh."

GAUDY DUTCH, Cup & Saucer, Single Rose	75.00
Pitcher & Bowl, Oyster Pattern, C.1840	145.00
Plate, Grape, 8 In.	250.00
Punch Bowl, Floral Design, Blue, Brown, Green, 6 1/4 In.	375.00
Punch Bowl, Stylized Floral Design, Footed, England, 12 In.	375.00

Some collectors have named the ironstone wares with the bright Gaudy Dutchlike patterns "Gaudy Ironstone." There may be other examples found in the listing for Ironstone or under the name of the ceramic factory.

GAUDY IRONSTONE, Bowl, Black Floral Design, J.Heath, 14 X 4 1/2 In.	55.00
Creamer, Allerton	25.00
Cup & Saucer, Seeing Eye	135.00
Jam Jar, Mandarin Pattern	60.00
Pitcher, Embossed Lilies, Purple Luster, 7 1/2 In.	75.00
Pitcher, Polychrome Lilies, Purple Luster, 7 1/2 In.	75.00
Pitcher, Tulips, Blue Underglaze, Luster, 7 3/4 In.	47.50
Plate, 12 Sides, Blue Leaves, Strawberries	65.00
Plate, 9 Flowers, 5 Petals, Copper Outline, 8 1/4 In.	85.00
Plate, Floral, Purple Luster, 9 1/2 In.	25.00 To 40.00
Plate, Toddy, Seeing Eye, 5 In.	225.00

Gaudy Welsh is an Imari–decorated earthenware with red, blue, green, and gold decorations. It was made after 1820.

GAUDY WELSH, Cup & Saucer, Oyster	60.00
Mug, 2 In.	42.50
Plate, Wagon Wheel, 7 1/2 In.	58.00
Potty, Miniature	125.00
Punch Bowl, 1850	325.00
Sugar, Covered	65.00
Tea Set, Flowers, C.1820, Cake Plate, 10 1/2 In., 12 Piece	600.00
Teapot, Sadler	45.00 To 75.00
Tureen, Cornucopia Finial, Ram's Head Handles, 11 1/2 In.	225.00

In the late nineteenth century Geisha Girl porcelain was made in Japan for export. It was an inexpensive porcelain often sold in dime stores or used as free premiums. Pieces are sometimes marked with the name of a store. Japanese ladies in kimonos are pictured on the dishes. Borders of red, blue, green, gold, brown, or several of these colors were used. Modern reproductions are being made.

GEISHA GIRL, Bowl, Red, Scalloped, 7 In.	9.00
Chocolate Pot, 9 1/2 In.	60.00
Chocolate Set, 11 Piece	110.00
Chocolate Set, Rust Trim	85.00
Cookie Jar, Cobalt Blue	65.00
Creamer, Archery, Cobalt Blue Border	24.00
Creamer, Red	7.00
Cup & Saucer, Blue	8.00
Cup & Saucer, Green Trim	8.00
Cup & Saucer, House & Water Scene, Thin	6.50
Cup & Saucer, Red Trim	8.00
Cup & Saucer, Red, Demitasse	6.00
Hatpin Holder, Orange, 4 In.	32.00
Pitcher, Green, 4 In.	6.50

Plate, 3 People In Boat, Mountains, White Ground	25.00
Plate, 6 In.	4.50
Plate, Blue, Scalloped, 7 1/2 In.	6.50
Plate, Green, 7 In.	4.00
Plate, Open Handle, 10 In.	28.00
Plate, Scalloped, 8 1/2 In.	6.00
Powder Jar, Box	78.50 To 89.50
Saki Set, Whistling Bird, 7 Piece	60.00
Salt & Pepper, Red, 2 1/2 In.	8.00 To 10.00
Sugar & Creamer	15.00
Tea Set, Red Trim, 9 Piece	139.00
Teapot, 1–Cup	22.50
Teapot, 4–Cup	35.00
Toothpick, 3 Handles	30.00
Tray, Pin	9.50
Vase, Roses, Brown, 10 In.	60.00

Gene Autry was born in 1907. He began his career as the "Singing Cowboy" in 1928. His first movie appearance was in 1934, his last in 1958.

GENE AUTRY, Book, Coloring, Chuck Wagon Chatter	12.00
Book, Gene Autry Golden Ladder Gang, 1950	35.00
Cap Gun	32.00 To 65.00
Cap Pistol, Gold Finish, Box	95.00
Card, Arcade, Vending Machine Sign, 1 Cent	40.00
Doll, Gene Autry, With Guitar, Marx	60.00
Guitar, Emenee, Case	75.00 To 90.00
Horn, Bicycle, Pistol Shape	35.00
Music Book, 1932	25.00
Phonograph, Columbia, 1950s	55.00
Postcard, Home of Gene Autry, Color, 1940, 3 1/2 X 5 1/2 In.	8.00
Poster, Call of The Canyon, 1942, 14 X 22 In.	15.00
Puzzle, Wooden, Box	42.50
Record, Velvet Tone, 78 RPM	15.00
Sheet Music, Oh Dem Golden Slippers, 1935	10.00
Sheet Music, South of The Border, 1939, 6 Pages	12.00
Song Book, 64 Pages, 1934	10.00
Tablet, Unused, 1940s	5.00
Thermos, Melody Ranch, Litho Metal, Red Plastic, 1950s, 8 In.	15.00
Wallet, Brown Leather, Zippered, ID Card, Badge, Box	50.00
Wristwatch, Animated Pistol, 1940s	225.00

Black and blue decorated Gibson Girl plates were made in the early 1900s. Twenty–four different 10 1/2–inch plates were made by the Royal Doulton Pottery at Lambeth, England. These pictured scenes from the book "A Widow and Her Friends" by Charles Dana Gibson. Another set of twelve 9–inch plates featuring pictures of the heads of Gibson Girls had all–blue decoration. Many other items also pictured the famous Gibson Girl.

GIBSON GIRL, Plate, Fancy Dress Ball, 10 1/2 In.	45.00
Plate, Hostile Criticism, 10 1/2 In.	75.00
Plate, Miss Babbles Brings A Copy, 10 1/2 In.	85.00 To 95.00
Plate, Mr.Waddles Arrives Late, 10 1/2 In.	90.00
Plate, She Contemplates The Cloister, 10 1/2 In.	85.00
Plate, She Goes To Fancy Dress Ball As Juliet, 10 1/2 In.	85.00
Plate, She Is Disturbed By A Vision, 10 1/2 In.	75.00
Plate, They Go Fishing, 10 1/2 In.	90.00
Plate, Winning New Friends	43.00
Plate, Winning New Friends, 10 1/2 In.	95.00

GILLINDER Gillinder pressed glass was first made by William T. Gillinder of Philadelphia in 1863. The company had a working factory on the grounds at the Centennial and made small, marked pieces of glass for sale as souvenirs. They made a variety of decorative glass pieces and tablewares.

GILLINDER, Bust, Lincoln	300.00
Slipper, Glass, Centennial, 1886	29.00

The Girl Scout movement started in 1912, two years after the Boy Scouts. It began under Juliette Gordon Low of Savannah, Georgia. The first Girl Scout cookies were sold in 1928. Collectors search for anything pertaining to the Girl Scouts, including uniforms, publications, and old cookie boxes.

GIRL SCOUT, Cockade, For Beret	4.00
Doll, Georgene, 1930s Uniform, 14 In.	55.00
Doll, Uniform, Yarn Hair, Painted Face, Lenci Type, 12 In.	18.00
Handbook, 1953	5.00
Hatchet, Sheath, Plumb	35.00
Knife, Pocket, Utica, 2 Blades	35.00

GLASS, CONTEMPORARY, see Contemporary Glass

Eyeglasses, or spectacles, were mentioned in a manuscript in 1289 and have been used ever since. The first glasses with rigid side pieces were made in London in 1727. Bifocals were invented by Benjamin Franklin in 1785. Lorgnettes were popular in late Victorian times.

GLASSES, Auto Driving	15.00
Goggles, Willson, Tin Litho Box	8.00
Granny, Sliding Frames, Marked Coin	45.00
Lorgnette, 14K Gold	245.00
Lorgnette, Collapsible, Gold Rimmed	75.00
Lorgnette, Gold Chain, 49 In.	375.00
Lorgnette, Lacy Design Handle, Push Button To Fold, 3 1/2 In.	75.00
Lorgnette, Short Handle, 14K White Gold	65.00
Lorgnette, Silver Sterling, Hanging, Ornate	52.00
Rhinestone, Slight Wing Shape, French, 1940s	20.00
Safety, Wire, Amber Lens, Tin Case	9.00
Spectacles, Church & Rogers, Hartford, Ct., C.1830	95.00
Spectacles, Gold, Octagonal Lenses, Folding, Stamped Richards	335.00
Spectacles, Hyde, Coin Silver, C.1830	125.00
Sterling Silver, Case, Signed J.Peters, 1821	250.00

Goebel W. Goebel Porzellanfabrik of Oeslau, Germany, now Rodental, West Germany, has made many types of figurines and dishes. The firm is still working. The pieces marked "Goebel Hummel" are listed under Hummel in this book.

GOEBEL, Ashtray, Thumper, Disney	125.00
Bottle, Figural, Young Girl Holding Posy Bouquet	45.00
Candy Container, Snowman, With Broom	10.00
Creamer, Elephant, Figural, Orange, Black, White, WG & Crown, 5 In.	85.00
Decanter, Clown Minstrel, Crown Mark	125.00
Dresser Set, Gold Filigree Edge, 17 In.Mirrored Tray, 4 Piece	55.00
Figurine, Blumenkinder, 3 Line Mark	150.00
Figurine, Boy With Fish, Girl Serving Tea, Marked, 7 1/2 In., Pair	30.00
Figurine, Good News & Bag of Sour Balls, 3 Line Mark	45.00
Figurine, Madonna & Child, White Glaze, 13 In.	50.00
Figurine, Nude, Art Deco, Crown Mark, 15 In.	395.00
Figurine, Owl	150.00
Figurine, Pheasant	150.00
Flask, Monk, 3 Line Mark, 5 In.	55.00
Jar, Covered, Monk, No.237	32.00
Mask, Crown, Artist A.Molier, 1935–48, 15 1/4 In.	350.00
Match Holder & Ashtray, With Striker, Scotty Dog, Yellow & Lime	75.00

Napkin Ring, Dutch Boy & Girl, Brown Mark	85.00
Pitcher, Friar Tuck, Stylized Bee, 5 In.	40.00
Pitcher, Monks, Full Bee, 2 1/4 In.	17.00
Salt & Pepper, Friar Tuck, Stylized Bee, 2 1/2 In.	30.00
Sign, Retailer's, Bird On End, 5 In.	70.00
Sugar & Creamer, Friar Tuck	55.00
Sugar, Baby Shape, Pierrette Head, Orange, Handle, Marked, 4 In.	85.00
Table Set, Monk, Full Bee	60.00
Wall Pocket, Cockatoo, Glass Eyes, Crown Mark, Pair	85.00

Goldscheider Wien Porcelain has been made by three branches of the Goldscheider family. The family left Vienna during World War II and started factories in England and in Trenton, New Jersey.

GOLDSCHEIDER, Ashtray, Russian Wolfhound

GOLDSCHEIDER, Ashtray, Russian Wolfhound	38.00
Box, Music, Madonna, 9 In.	55.00
Bust, Female, Art Deco, 12 In.	275.00
Bust, Madonna	90.00 To 150.00
Candlestick, Double, Art Deco Couple Kissing, 11 In.	300.00
Figurine, Art Nouveau Woman, Blue Skirt, 16 In. ....*Illus*	825.00
Figurine, Brown Woman, Turquoise Curls, Signed, 9 In.	350.00
Figurine, Cavalier & Lady, Marked, Pair	150.00
Figurine, Chinese Princess, 9 In.	95.00
Figurine, Colonial Lady, Yellow Hat, 10 1/2 In.	80.00
Figurine, Courting Couple, Signed Motto	175.00
Figurine, Curtsying, Gray, Gold	35.00
Figurine, Dandy & Lady Friend, 9 1/2 In., Pair	65.00
Figurine, Deer, 1940s, 5 1/2 X 7 1/2 In.	42.00
Figurine, Lady Spanish Dancer	200.00 To 225.00
Figurine, Lady, 8 1/2 In.	65.00
Figurine, Lady, With Fan, 10 1/2 In.	75.00
Figurine, Lady, Yellow Hat, 10 1/2 In.	75.00
Figurine, Lorenzi, Girl, In Blue Lace Dress, 8 In.	175.00
Figurine, Madonna In The Clouds, Signed, 15 In.	195.00
Figurine, Merry Christmas	75.00
Figurine, Prince of Wales, 6 1/4 In.	65.00
Figurine, Sing Lo, 7 In.	35.00
Figurine, Southern Lady, 7 1/2 In.	50.00
Figurine, White Christmas	65.00

Galle, Vase, Polished Glass, Teardrop,
Orange Red, Cameo, 6 In.

Goldscheider, Figurine, Art Nouveau Woman,
Blue Skirt, 16 In.

Lawton Gonder opened Gonder Ceramic Arts, Inc. in 1941. He worked in the old Peters and Reed pottery in Zanesville, Ohio. Gonder pieces include lamp bases marked "Eglee" and many wares with Oriental–type glazes.

GONDER, Pitcher, Splotched Yellow & Pink, 7 1/2 In.	12.50
Sugar, Creamer, & Teapot, Mottled Brown	25.00
Vase, Blue & Pink, 7 In.	12.00
Vase, Long Twisted Handles, 9 In.	25.00
Vase, Pansy Shape, Gray & Pink, 7 In.	6.00

Goofus glass was made from about 1900 to 1920 by many American factories. It was originally painted gold, red, green, bronze, pink, purple, or other bright colors. Many pieces are found today with flaking paint and this lowers the value.

GOOFUS GLASS, Basket, 7 1/2 X 5 1/2 In.	38.00
Bowl, Gold Center Design, Fluted & Beaded Rim, 8 3/4 In.	32.00
Bowl, Gold Trim, Flowers, Scalloped, 7 In.	18.00
Bowl, Red & Gold, 9 1/2 In.	35.00
Bowl, Roses In The Snow, 7 In.	10.00
Bowl, Roses, 9 In.	28.00
Bowl, Strawberry, 10 In.	15.00
Cake Plate, Roses In The Snow, 11 In.	20.00
Compote, Strawberries, 10 1/2 X 8 3/4 In.	55.00
Fruit Bowl, Gold, Red Grapes	40.00
Fruit Bowl, Red & Green Roses, Ruffled	28.00
Plate, Flowers, Gold Trim, Scalloped, 10 3/4 In.	16.00
Plate, Grapes, Gold Trim, Scalloped, 10 1/2 In.	16.00
Plate, Red Apple, Gold, 8 In.	15.00
Plate, Roses, 11 In.	30.00
Plate, St.Louis 1904 World's Fair	37.50
Powder Box, Puffy Rose	20.00
Powder Jar, Cabbage Rose	32.00 To 35.00
Powder Jar, Metal Cover, Flowers	80.00
Rose Bowl, Footed, 9 In.	35.00
Vase, Bird & Grapes, Black, Red, Gold, 10 In.	37.50
Vase, Butterfly & Poppy, 3 1/2 In.	14.00
Vase, Cabbage Rose, 7 In.	35.00
Vase, Cabbage Rose, Original Paint, 7 In., Pair	85.00
Vase, Single Rose, 10 In.	15.00

Goss china has been made since 1858. English potter William Henry Goss first made it at the Falcon Pottery in Stoke-on-Trent. The factory name was changed to Goss China Company in 1934 when it was taken over by Cauldon Potteries. Production ceased in 1940. Goss china resembles Irish Belleek in both body and glaze. The company also made popular souvenir china, usually marked with local crests and names.

W.H.COSS

GOSS, Bust, Yorick's Skull	125.00 To 150.00
Ewer, Shrewsbury, 4 In.	30.00
Figurine, Cat, Winking, 4 In.	25.00
Figurine, Manx Cottage	115.00
Plate, Armorial, 10 In.	25.00
Plate, St.Nicholas Chapel	200.00
Vase, Southwold, 6 In.	40.00

PLAZUID
GOUDA
HolLAND
A.M.P.smit.

32V
SCHOONHOVEN
HOLLAND
COREL
E

Pottery has been made in Gouda, Holland, since the seventeenth century. Two firms, the Zenith pottery, established in the eighteenth century, and the Zuid–Hollandsche pottery, made the brightly colored wares marked "Gouda" from 1880 to about 1940. Many pieces featured Art Nouveau or Art Deco designs.

GOUDA, Basket, Regina Rosario, Rope Handle	40.00
Bowl, Black Interior, Rolled-In Rim, Marked, 2 1/2 X 8 In.	55.00
Bowl, Fall Colors, Low, 12 1/2 In.	195.00

Bowl, Rust & Cobalt Blue Scrolls, Green Ground, House Mark, 6 In. 45.00
Candleholder, Shield Back 125.00
Candlestick, Damascus, 11 1/2 In. 185.00
Candlestick, Gaudy, Majestic, 18 1/2 In. 175.00
Candlestick, Swirled Ribbing Center, Flared Foot, 9 1/2 In. 60.00
Jug, Stopper, 11 In. 150.00
Lamp, Ginger Jar Shape, Maasa Mark 125.00
Pitcher, Cylinder, Rooster Bottom, Late 1800s, 10 1/2 In. 175.00
Shoe, Marked Regina, 5 In. 80.00
Smoke Set, Ashtray & Cigarette Box, Covered, Marked, Green 60.00
Smoke Set, Border Pattern, Box, 4 1/2 X 3 3/4 In., 3 Piece 70.00
Tray, Match & Pipe Holder 125.00
Vase, Art Deco Design, 6 In. 95.00
Vase, Art Nouveau, Ocher Dots, Flowers, Green Base, 9 In. 395.00
Vase, Blue, Rust, White, Green Border, 6 1/2 In. 85.00
Vase, Floral, House Mark, 7 1/2 In. 95.00
Vase, Poppies, 4 In. 25.00
Vase, Tekla, House Mark, 12 In. 125.00
Vase, Tulip Design, Handles, Marked, 5 In. 45.00
Wall Pocket, Shoe, Regina 85.00

Graniteware is an enameled tinware that has been used in the kitchen from the late nineteenth century to the present. Earlier graniteware was green or turquoise blue, with white spatters. The later ware was gray with white spatters. Reproductions are being made in all colors.

GRANITEWARE, Basin, Gray Mottled, Salesman Sample 35.00
Berry Bucket, Brown & White Swirl 130.00
Berry Bucket, Covered, Mottled Blue & White, 8 X 5 1/2 In. 70.00
Berry Bucket, Gray, Small 45.00
Berry Bucket, Lid, Turquoise & White Swirl, Tiny 180.00
Boiler, Coffee, Diffused Blues 49.00
Boiler, Double, Lid & Bail, Medium Blue, Oval 45.00
Bowl, Apple Design, Blue, White, 6 1/2 In., Pair 20.00
Bowl, Green & White, Swirl, 8 In. 78.00
Bowl, Swirl, Turquoise, 5 In. 9.00
Box, Salt, Hanging, Blue, Open 42.00
Bread Raiser, Gray 65.00
Camping Set, Green 110.00
Candleholder, Saucer Base, Handle, Pastel Flowers, Leaves 35.00
Chamber Pot, Handle, Gray, 11 In. 25.00
Chocolate Pot, Gray, Tin Lid, 1 Cup 140.00
Churn, Dazey, Original Paper Label, Blue & White, Small 265.00
Coffee Urn, Gray 105.00
Coffeepot, Agateware, Gray, Signed, 3 Gal. 95.00
Coffeepot, Blue Speckled, 3 Gal. 25.00
Coffeepot, Brown & White Swirl, 12 In. 90.00
Coffeepot, Cobalt Blue & White Swirl, Tin Lid 165.00
Coffeepot, Floral Design, Black Handle, Pink 75.00
Coffeepot, Gray, 7 In. 35.00
Coffeepot, Gray, Covered, Top & Bail Handle, 10 In. 30.00
Coffeepot, Gray, Wooden Knob, French Gray Label, 8 In. 40.00
Coffeepot, Green & White Swirl, Large 165.00
Coffeepot, Green & White Swirl, Small 165.00
Coffeepot, Green & White, Crystolite, Small 75.00
Coffeepot, Hinged Tin Lid, Handle, Gray, 9 1/2 In. 32.00
Coffeepot, Metal Lid, Gray & White, Large 38.00
Coffeepot, Pewter Lid, Hinged Spout & Handle, Gray, Large 165.00
Colander, Blue & White 18.00
Colander, Gray, 10 In. 7.00
Colander, Green & Cream, 3–Cornered 15.00
Colander, Mottled Brown 65.00
Cream Can 135.00
Creamer, Pewter Trim 115.00

Cup & Saucer, Green & Ivory 7.50
Cup, Green & White Swirl 35.00
Cup, Handle, Gray & White, Tin, 6 In. 22.00
Cuspidor, Gray 20.00
Double Boiler, Blue & White Swirl 115.00
Double Boiler, Green & White Swirl 135.00
Dustpan, Robin's Egg Blue 50.00
Firkin, Mustard Yellow, Lid, No Handle 50.00
Flask, Cobalt Blue 25.00
Flask, Coffee, Dark Blue 85.00
Flask, Gray 70.00
Frying Pan, Covered, Light Green 20.00
Funnel, Canning, Blue 8.00
Funnel, Canning, Handle, Gray & White 16.00
Funnel, Cobalt Blue & White Swirl 48.00
Funnel, Crimped Edge, Gray, 7 In. 16.00
Funnel, Gray, Handle, Large 12.00
Funnel, Green & White Swirl 65.00
Grater, Blue 75.00
Grater, Gray 130.00
Grater, Sky Blue 55.00
Gravy Boat, Mottled Blue & White 200.00
Jug, Milk, Lid, Chocolate Brown 35.00
Kettle, Canning, Mottled Gray, 4 Gal. 22.00
Ladle, Green & Ivory 8.00
Ladle, Long Handle, Gray 27.00
Ladle, Mottled Gray, Long Handle 12.00
Lunch Pail, 3 Sections, Green & White Swirl 147.00
Lunch Pail, Blue, Covered, Round 40.00
Lunch Pail, Green Swirl, Crystolite, Covered, Oval 65.00
Milk Pan, Gray, 2 1/2 X 11 In. 15.00
Mold, Corn, Gray Mottled, Oval 60.00
Pail, Blue Speckled, 5 In. 20.00
Pail, Gray, 9 In. 10.00
Pail, Gray, Wooden Bail Handle, Savo Sterling Label, 9 1/2 In. 50.00
Pan, Blue & White Swirl, Advertising, Miniature 75.00
Pan, Cake, Gray, 13 X 9 In. 8.00
Pan, Cake, Rectangular, Cobalt & White Swirl 85.00
Pan, Muffin, 8 Cup, Cobalt Blue & White Swirl 128.00
Pan, Muffin, Turquoise & White Swirl 185.00
Pan, Rectangular, Green & Ivory 10.00
Pan, Tube, Dark Blue & White 22.00
Pan, Tube, Gray 30.00
Pie Plate, Cobalt Blue & White Swirl 12.50
Pie Plate, Green, White Spatter, 10 In. 20.00
Pitcher, Gray, Creamer Shape, 4 In. 45.00
Pitcher, Milk, Blue 25.00
Pitcher, Milk, Dark Rose, Black Trim, Germany, 8 3/4 In. 60.00
Pitcher, Molasses, Gray 55.00
Plate, ABC, Green Ombre, Scene 110.00
Plate, Child's, Dutch Boy With Geese, Blue, 7 In. 35.00
Plate, Green & White Swirl, 7 In. 9.00
Platter, Blue, Doll Size 25.00
Roaster, Blue 15.00
Roaster, Blue & White, Large 40.00
Salt Box, Sky Blue, High Back, Lid 55.00
Salt Box, White, Hinged Wooden Lid, Hanging, Early 1900s 75.00
Scoop, Blue, Perforated 28.00
Scoop, Flour, Gray 37.50
Scoop, Strainer, Sky Blue 30.00
Skillet, Cobalt & White Swirl 90.00
Skimmer, Cobalt & White Swirl 55.00
Soap Dish, Hanging, Brown & White Swirl 130.00
Soap Dish, Red 45.00

Spatula, Gray 30.00
Spittoon, Gray, Pewter Trim 350.00
Spoon Rest, Fish, Gray 75.00
Spooner, Turquoise & White Swirl 175.00
Strainer, Round, Gray, 10 1/2 In. 20.00
Sugar Shaker, Blue, White Specks 200.00
Sugar, Open, Gray 180.00
Syrup, Gray, Pewter Trim 175.00
Teakettle, Blue 55.00
Teakettle, Blue & White Swirl 200.00
Teakettle, Gooseneck, Cream & Green 40.00
Teakettle, Wooden Handle, Deep Blue & Light Blue Specks 32.00
Teapot, Bulbous, Pewter Trim 200.00
Teapot, Floral Design, Pewter Handle, Spout, Top, English 225.00
Teapot, Gray, Cast Iron Handle, Tin Lid 45.00
Teapot, Hinged Spout, Silver Plated Handle, Manning–Bowman 85.00
Teapot, Speckled Green, Pewter Lid, Manning–Bowman 95.00
Teapot, White 28.00
Tumbler, Blue & White Swirl 75.00
Washboard 60.00
Washboard, Blue, Advertising 78.00
Washboard, Dark Blue .... 35.00 To 85.00

Greentown glass was made by the Indiana Tumbler and Goblet
Company of Greentown, Indiana, from 1894 to 1903. In 1899, the
factory name was changed to National Glass Company. A variety of
pressed, milk, and chocolate glass was made.

GREENTOWN, see also Chocolate Glass; Custard Glass; Holly Amber; Milk Glass; Pressed Glass

GREENTOWN, Bowl, Rectangular, Clear, Set of 4 .... 45.00
Butter, Covered, Daisy .... 210.00 To 225.00
Butter, Covered, Green, 1/4 Lb. 38.00
Butter, Squirrel, Covered 210.00
Cake Plate, Footed 40.00
Cake Stand, Herringbone Buttress 185.00
Compote, Robin On Nest 195.00
Cordial, Shuttle, Clear 25.00
Creamer, Covered, Daisy, Milk Glass 30.00
Creamer, Dewey, Green, 4 In. 40.00
Creamer, Indian, Nile Green 475.00
Creamer, Teardrop & Tassel, Green 80.00
Cruet, Dewey, Canary, Original Stopper 165.00
Cruet, Leaf Bracket, Stopper 125.00
Dish, Cat On Hamper Cover, Amber 195.00
Dish, Dewey, Round Ribbed Base, Amber 250.00
Dish, Dolphin, Fish Cover, 7 In. 475.00
Dish, Drapery, Blue, 5 In. 40.00
Dish, Hen Cover 30.00
Dish, Honeycomb Pattern, Band of Ovals At Sides, 1 7/8 N. 15.00
Dish, Rabbit Cover, Amber 135.00
Dish, Rabbit Cover, Clear 55.00
Dish, Tall Cat On Hamper Cover, Amber 195.00
Doughnut Stand, Scalloped, 7 1/2 In. 26.00
Dustpan, Blue 80.00
Goblet, Herringbone Buttress 85.00
Goblet, King Vine, Blue 45.00
Match Holder, Indian Head, Milk Glass 125.00
Mug, Chocolate, Herringbone 45.00
Mug, Dewey, Clear 35.00
Mug, Dewey, Nile Green 275.00
Mustard, Fish Finial, 7 In. 475.00
Nappy, Covered, Clear 55.00
Pitcher, Water, Cord Drapery, Amber 168.00
Pitcher, Water, Cord Drapery, Green 225.00

Pitcher, Water, Deer & Oak Tree 150.00
Pitcher, Water, Squirrel With Nut, Scalloped Top 100.00
Relish, Drapery, Clear, 9 1/4 In. 20.00
Salt Dip, Block & Fan 10.00
Salt, Zigzag Band, Starburst Bottom, 1 3/4 In. 10.00
Saltshaker, Shuttle 40.00
Sauce, Daisy & Button Arches, Gold Trim 18.50
Stein, Drinking Scene, Nile Green 275.00
Sugar & Creamer, Shell Pattern, Opalescent Blue 150.00
Syrup, Cord Drapery 165.00
Tumbler, Dewey, Canary 50.00
Tumbler, Dewey, Vaseline .... 39.50 To 70.00
Tumbler, Iced Tea, Cactus 75.00
Tumbler, Teardrop & Tassel, Clear 22.00
Vase, Austrian, 8 In. .... 25.00 To 45.00
Vase, Emerald Green, 6 In. 35.00
Water Set, Brazen Shield, Electric Blue, 7 Piece 450.00
Wine, Austrian, Canary 110.00
Wine, Herringbone Buttress, Green 160.00
Wine, Shuttle 18.00

Grueby Faience Company of Boston, Massachusetts, was incorporated in 1897 by William H. Grueby. Garden statuary, art pottery, and architectural tiles were made until 1920. The company developed a matte green glaze that was so popular it was copied by many other factories making a less expensive type of pottery. This eventually led to the financial problems of the pottery.

GRUEBY, Bowl, Faience, High Glaze Green Swirl, 1 1/2 X 8 In. 250.00
Paperweight, Scarab, Circle & Lotus Mark, C.1908, 4 In. 350.00
Tile, Cherub Playing Tambourine, Blue & Brown, Square, 6 In. 185.00
Tile, Greek Horses Group, White On Blue, Green, 1905, Round, 6 In. 275.00
Tile, Raised Spanish Galleon, Round, C.1905, 8 In. 375.00
Tile, Sailing Ship, Curling Waves, Finished Sides, 4 Colors 385.00
Tile, Stylized Trees, Blue Sky, Label, C.1905, 6 In. 400.00
Tile, Viking Ship, Paper Label, C.1908, 4 In. 200.00
Vase, 2-Color Butterscotch, Leaves, C.1905, 11 In. 2300.00
Vase, Cylindrical Neck, Green, Squat Body, 10 In. 450.00
Vase, Flared Angled Shoulder, Open Flowers, C.1905, 10 In. 450.00
Vase, Light Mustard Yellow Glaze, 4 1/2 In. 95.00
Vase, Molded Leaves & Flowers, Mottled Green, Fluted Top, 7 3/4 In. 200.00
Vase, Yellow Gourd Form, With Leaves, Large 7700.00

Included in this category are shotguns, pistols, and other antique firearms. Rifles are listed in their own section. Be very careful when buying or selling guns because there are special laws governing the sale and ownership. A collector's gun should be displayed in a safe manner, probably with the barrel filled or a part missing to be sure it cannot be accidentally fired.

GUN, 155 mm, Self-Propelled, Tank Chassis, Box 485.00
Air Pistol, Haenel Luger Model 28, 1930s 70.00
Bar Girl's, Holster 350.00
BB, Daisy, Double Barrel, Plastic Stock 200.00
BB, Daisy, Model 118, Blued Finish, 10 In. 25.00
BB, Red Ryder 20.00
Blunderbuss, Elliptical, Muzzle, Dutch, C.1725 .... 860.00
Cane, Percussion, 50 Caliber, 34 In.Barrel 200.00
Carbine, Austrian Werndl Breech Loading, 1870 .... 125.00
Carbine, Evans Lever Action, 44 Caliber, C.1879, 22 In.Barrel 225.00
Carbine, Winchester, .73 Saddle Ring 495.00
Carbine, Winchester, Model 1894, 30–30 .... 660.00
Colt, 36 Caliber, Navy Silver Trigger Guard, Strap, Black Powder 450.00
Colt, Blue Thin Handles, Mold Engraved, Polished 700.00
Flask, Colt Type, Navy, Embossed Spread Eagle & Crossed Pistols 900.00
Flintlock Fowling, C.1830, 16 Gauge 180.00

Flintlock, English Officer's, Brass Barrel, Walnut Stock, C.1790	435.00
Flintlock, Johnson, Model 1836	1400.00
Gambler, Percussion, Belly, Pre–1880	75.00
Luger, American Eagle, DWM Toggle, With Holster	1300.00
Luger, German, Model 493, 1939	500.00
Musket, 1846 Springfield, 69 Caliber, 42 In.Barrel	250.00
Musket, Arabian Miquelet–Flint, 59 Caliber, 44 1/2 In., Barrel	110.00
Musket, Winchester, Low Wall Winder	250.00
Pistol, American Bicentennial, High Standard, 1776–1976, 13 In.	295.00
Pistol, Boot Leg, H.J.Hale, 31 Caliber	290.00
Pistol, Box Lock, Concealed Trigger, Pocket, 50 Caliber, English	132.50
Pistol, Brass Cannon Barrel, 1840s	225.00
Pistol, Derringer, Philadelphia, 44 Caliber, 3 In.Brown Barrel, Pair	1800.00
Pistol, Flintlock, French, Silver Mounted	550.00
Pistol, Iron Barrel, Leaf & Foliage Design, 23 In.	700.00
Pistol, Muff Set, Tools, Powder Flask, Rosewood Veneered Case	1100.00
Pistol, Regimental, Scottish, Metal, 1 Piece Brass Stock, 58 Caliber	850.00
Pistol, Silver Inlaid, Wheel Design Butt, Thomas Caddel, Scott, 11 In.	1425.00
Pistol, Union Firearms Co. Auto., 4 In.Barrel	600.00
Pistol, USA, Liquid, Cast Iron, Nickel Plated, 1896	85.00
Revolver, 1862 Colt, Percussion, 36 Caliber, Walnut Grip	450.00
Revolver, 22 Caliber, Lee Arms, No.2, Blue Jacket, Patent 1897	75.00
Revolver, 32 Caliber, Lee Arms, No.4, Red Jacket, Octagon Barrel	90.00
Revolver, Austrian World War I Military, 32 Caliber, Blue Finish	70.00
Revolver, Belgian Pin Fire, Folding Trigger, Iron, 36 Caliber	30.00
Revolver, Cartridge, Flip Trigger, 32 Caliber, Russian, C.1918	40.00
Revolver, Colt Navy, Allan Jordan, 1851	3000.00
Revolver, Hopkins & Allen, Pearl Handle, 32 Caliber, C.1888	125.00
Revolver, Marlin Spur Trigger	75.00
Revolver, Pin, E.Lefaucheux, Side Ejector, 44 Caliber, Civil War	120.00
Revolver, Savage, 6 Shot, 36 Caliber, C.1860, 7–In.Octagonal Barrel	1400.00
Revolver, Springfield Arms Co., Pocket, Walnut Case, Velvet Lined	700.00
Revolver, Spur Trigger, Hopkins & Allen	105.00
Shotgun, Double Barrel, W.W.Greener, 10 Gauge, 32 In.Barrels	1000.00
Shotgun, Hagadorn–Cole, Detroit, Side–By–Side Percussion, 58 Caliber	750.00
Shotgun, L.C.Smith, Field, 20 Gauge, Pair	1000.00
Shotgun, Purdy, Cased, 10 Gauge Box Lock, 12 Gauge Barrels	4125.00
Shotgun, Washington Arms Pepperbox, 6 Shot, Engraving, 31 Caliber	175.00
Shotgun, Winchester, 12 Gauge, Model 1912	300.00
Winchester, Lee, Straight Pull, Civilian Model, 1897	225.00

Gunderson glass was made at the Gunderson–Pairpoint Glass Works of New Bedford, Massachusetts, from 1952 to 1957. Gunderson Peachblow is especially famous.

GUNDERSON, Basket, Burmese, Rope Handle	925.00
Toothpick, Fluted Top	85.00
Toothpick, Peachblow	135.00

Never put hot glass in cold water or cold glass in hot water. The temperature change can crack the glass.

Gutta–percha was one of the first plastic materials. It was made from a mixture of resins from Malaysian trees. It was molded and used for daguerreotype cases, toilet articles, and picture frames in the nineteenth century.

GUTTA–PERCHA, Case, Child Holding Baby, Tin, 2 1/2 X 3 In.	25.00
Case, Civil War Soldier	45.00
Match Safe, Victoria	95.00

Haeger Potteries, Inc., Dundee, Illinois, started making commercial art wares in 1914. Early pieces were marked with the name "Haeger" written over an "H." About 1938, the mark "Royal Haeger" was used. The firm is still making florist wares and lamp bases.

HAEGER, Ashtray, Century of Progress, Green, 1934	45.00
Compote, Oriental, Royal	24.00
Console Set, Brass Bases, Pebble Texture On Bronze Color, Royal	40.00
Dish, Peacock, No.3008–H, 22 In.	48.00
Figurine, Hen & Rooster, Gold Tweed Glass, Pair	45.00
Head, 6 1/2 In.	45.00
Pitcher & Bowl, 8 X 12 In.	90.00
Pitcher, Rope Handle, Matte Green, Royal	12.00
Planter, Pond Shape, Aqua, 11 1/2 In.	10.00
Vase, Horsehead, Art Deco, 14 In.	45.00
Vase, Horsehead, Art Deco, Gray, 12 In.	25.00

Hall China Company started in East Liverpool, Ohio, in 1903. The firm made all types of wares. Collectors search for the Hall teapots made from the 1920s to the 1950s. The dinnerwares of the same period, especially Autumn Leaf pattern, are also popular. The Hall China Company is still working. Autumn Leaf pattern dishes are listed in their own category in this book.

HALL, Ashtray, Palmer House, Chicago	10.00
Baker, French, Flute	18.00
Baker, French, Richmond, Flute	15.00
Baker, French, Silver	8.00
Bean Pot, Orange Poppy	65.00
Bean Pot, Rose Parade, Tab Handle	40.00
Bowl Set, Sunshine, Autumn Flowers	40.00
Bowl, Banded, Chinese Red, 7 1/2 In.	15.00
Bowl, Cadet Blue, White Daisy, Blue Flowers, No.3	10.00
Bowl, Crocus, 7 1/2 In.	15.00
Bowl, Fruit, Richmond	2.00
Bowl, Morning Glory, Blue, No.3	15.00
Bowl, Nesting, Radiant Ware	50.00
Bowl, Nesting, Star Burst, Blue, Gold Design, 3 Piece	60.00
Bowl, Salad, Orange Poppy	15.00
Bowl, Sunshine, Floral Decal	10.00
Bowl, Vegetable, Oval, Tulip, 10 1/4 In.	12.00
Bowl, Vegetable, Round, Crocus	14.00
Bowl, Wildfire, 9 In.	20.00
Butter, Covered, Aristocrat, Canary	14.00
Cake Plate, Orange Poppy	12.00
Cake Plate, Primrose	10.00
Canister Set, Red Poppy, Round, 3 Piece	18.00
Canister Set, Red Radiance, 4 Piece	250.00
Canister, Sugar, Brown	45.00
Casserole, Basket, Pink	12.00
Casserole, Black Beauty	38.00
Casserole, Blue Willow, Covered, 6 In.	30.00
Casserole, Cactus, Banded	45.00
Casserole, Chinese Red, Covered, 3 Qt.	20.00
Casserole, Crocus	30.00
Casserole, Orange Poppy, Oval, Covered	28.00

Casserole, Pink Morning Glory 30.00
Casserole, Rose Parade 20.00
Casserole, Rose Parade, Covered, 8 1/2 In. 20.00
Casserole, Sundial, Covered, Red, 10 In. 30.00
Coaster, Taverne 6.00
Coffeepot, Autumn Leaf, 8 Cup 30.00
Coffeepot, Covered, Terrace 25.00
Coffeepot, Drip, Sunshine 47.00
Coffeepot, Monarch 35.00
Coffeepot, Red Poppies, Green Leaves 42.00
Coffeepot, Step Down, Ivory, Gold Dot 22.00
Cookie Jar, Chinese Red, Banded 50.00
Cookie Jar, Farmer John, Barn Shape 60.00
Cookie Jar, Gold Dot 20.00
Cookie Jar, Little Red Riding Hood .... 65.00 To 75.00
Cookie Jar, Medallion, Green With Gold 18.00
Creamer, Chinese Red, New York 15.00
Creamer, Floral, Pink, Yellow, Red & Blue 55.00
Creamer, Rose Parade, Red 7.00
Cup & Saucer, Tulip 5.00
Custard, Orange Poppy .... 4.00 To 5.00
Dish, Figural, Lobster, Red, 6 Piece 75.00
Drip-O-Lator, Green & Silver 30.00
Flagon, Monk's Head 28.00
Gravy Boat, Blue Ribbon, Roses 8.00
Jar, Pretzel, Orange Poppy .... 55.00 To 65.00
Jug, Ball, Blossom, Blue, 2 Qt. 50.00
Jug, Ice Lip, Red 25.00
Jug, Rose Parade, 7 1/2 In. .... 25.00 To 30.00
Jug, Sani-Grid, Chinese Red 55.00
Jug, Sunshine, Yellow, Covered 45.00
Jug, Water, Phoenix, Cadet Blue 17.00
Leftover, Sunset, Aristocrat, Oval, Westinghouse 10.00
Marmalade Set, Jewel Tea, 3 Piece 40.00
Matchbox Holder, Taverne, Metal 35.00
Mixing Bowl, Autumn Leaf, 8 1/2 In. 18.00
Mixing Bowl, Orange Poppy, 8 1/4 In. 12.00
Mustard, Open, Underplate, Jewel Tea 45.00
Pie Plate, Mt.Vernon, 8 In. 10.00
Pitcher, Chinese Red, Banded, 5 In. 10.00
Pitcher, Little Red Riding Hood, Side Pour 125.00
Pitcher, Little Red Riding Hood, Top Pour, 8 In. 125.00
Pitcher, Milk, Autumn Leaf, 6 In. 15.00
Pitcher, Primrose 13.00
Pitcher, Water, Garden Emperor 25.00
Pitcher, Whiskey, Ambassador Scotch, Chrome Trim 12.00
Plate, Cameo Rose, 10 In. 7.00
Plate, Cameo Rose, Jewel Tea, 6 In. 3.50
Plate, Cameo Rose, Jewel Tea, 10 In. 6.50
Plate, Orange Poppy, 9 In. 7.00
Plate, Richmond, 9 In. 4.00
Platter, Tulip, 13 In. 14.00
Potato Masher, Taverne, Metal 32.00
Refrigerator Pitcher, Water, Hotpoint, China Tipped Cork 35.00
Refrigerator Pitcher, Water, Phoenix, Westinghouse, Delphinium 22.00
Refrigerator Pitcher, Westinghouse, Blue 100.00
Refrigerator Pitcher, Westinghouse, Blue, Large 25.00
Refrigerator Set, Butter, Water Server, 2 Leftovers, Westinghouse 55.00
Rolling Pin, Autumn Leaf 65.00
Salt & Pepper, Banded, Chinese Red 20.00
Salt & Pepper, Covered, Drip, Flute, Chinese Red 45.00
Salt & Pepper, Little Red Riding Hood .... 15.00 To 25.00
Salt & Pepper, Sani-Grid, White 12.00
Soap Dispenser, Taverne, Metal 35.00

Soup, Dish, Crocus	12.00
Soup, Dish, Taverne	10.00
Spittoon, Green Exterior, White Interior	25.00
Sugar & Creamer, Little Red Riding Hood, Side Pour, 5 1/2 In.	65.00
Sugar & Creamer, Orange Poppy	25.00 To 35.00
Sugar & Creamer, Rose Parade	20.00
Sugar & Creamer, Silhouette	15.00
Sugar, Colonial, Green	16.00
Sugar, Covered, Tulip	12.00
Syrup, Banded, Chinese Red	45.00
Tea Set, Forman Family, Covered, Yellow, 3 Piece	35.00
Tea Tile, Taverne	90.00
Teapot, Airflow, Chinese Red	38.00
Teapot, Airflow, Cobalt With Gold, 6 Cup	40.00
Teapot, Aladdin, Blue Bouquet	45.00
Teapot, Aladdin, Cobalt Blue, Gold Trim	30.00
Teapot, Aladdin, Matte Black, Inverted Spout	30.00
Teapot, Aladdin, Turquoise	32.50
Teapot, Albany, Mahogany With Gold	29.00
Teapot, Autumn Leaf, J–Sunshine	38.00
Teapot, Basketball, Red	400.00
Teapot, Birdcage, Maroon	40.00
Teapot, Boston, Brown & Gold	20.00
Teapot, Boston, Yellow	24.00
Teapot, Classic, Octagonal, Brown, 2 Cup	4.00
Teapot, Cobalt Blue, Gold Roses	28.00
Teapot, Cobalt Blue, Gold Trim	20.00
Teapot, Connie, Celadon	20.00
Teapot, Cube, White	25.00
Teapot, Daffodil, Cozy	30.00
Teapot, Disraeli, Pink	18.00
Teapot, Doughnut, Ivory	40.00
Teapot, Doughnut, Red	110.00
Teapot, French, Cadet Blue & Gold	18.00
Teapot, French, Yellow & Gold, 4 Cup	25.00
Teapot, Globe, Gold Design, Dripless	60.00
Teapot, Hollywood, Maroon	15.00
Teapot, Hook Cover, Oval Opening, Infuser, Cadet Blue, Gold Trim	20.00
Teapot, Leaf & Acorn	24.00
Teapot, Lipton, Wine	12.00
Teapot, Little Red Riding Hood	110.00 To 125.00
Teapot, Los Angeles, Cobalt Blue, Gold Trim	20.00
Teapot, McCormick, Blue Green	12.00
Teapot, Melody, Chinese Red	100.00
Teapot, New York, Maroon, 2 Cup	28.00
Teapot, New York, Red Poppy	45.00
Teapot, Parade, Canary	15.00 To 20.00
Teapot, Philadelphia, Black	24.00
Teapot, Philadelphia, Green & Gold	21.00
Teapot, Philadelphia, Teal & Gold	22.00
Teapot, Plume, Pink	16.00 To 20.00
Teapot, Rhythm, Dusty Dark Blue, Marked	40.00
Teapot, Ronald Reagan	30.00
Teapot, Sani–Grid, Cadet Blue	45.00
Teapot, Sani–Grid, Chinese Red	19.00
Teapot, Star, Teal & Gold	20.00
Teapot, Streamline, Canary	45.00
Teapot, Surfside, Emerald & Gold	60.00
Teapot, Tea–For–Four, White	25.00
Teapot, Windshield, Orange Poppy	95.00
Teapot, Windshield, Turquoise & Gold	45.00
Thermos, Picnic, Autumn Leaf	75.00
Tom & Jerry Set, Covered Bowl, 11 Cups	55.00
Tray, Metal, Oval, Orange Poppy, Large	30.00

Halloween is an ancient holiday that has been changed in the last 200 years. The jack-o'-lantern, witches on broomsticks, and orange decorations seem to be a twentieth-century creation. Collectors started to become serious about collecting Halloween-related items in the late 1970s. The papier-mache decorations, now replaced by plastic, and old costumes are in demand.

HALLOWEEN, Bell, Tin	9.00
Bell, Tin, Painted Cat & Witch Figures	27.00
Book, Songs, Games, 1925	12.00
Booklet, Pranks & Parties, 1927	15.00
Candleholder, Pumpkin, Cardboard, Tissue Face	55.00
Candleholder, Skull, Cardboard, Tissue Face	65.00
Candy Container, Jack-O'-Lantern	88.00
Cat Face, Black, Papier-Mache	8.00
Cat, Black, Playing Banjo, Papier-Mache	20.00
Cat, Pressed Cardboard, Black, 3 1/2 In.	12.00
Centerpiece, Dennison, Box, 1920s	125.00
Clicker, Felix The Cat, Red	55.00
Clicker, Mickey Mouse, Green	50.00
Costume, Archie Bunker	5.00
Costume, Aunt Jemima, Box	30.00
Costume, Batman, Mask & Cape, Box, 1965	18.00
Costume, Chinese Man, Pants, Jacket, Hat & Mask, Yellow, Black, Box	20.00
Costume, Clown, 1930s	45.00
Costume, Flintstones	5.00
Costume, Indian, Pants, Jacket, Feathered Headdress	18.00
Costume, Mickey Mouse, Box, 1934	200.00
Costume, Woody Woodpecker	50.00
Costume, Zorro	15.00
Fan, Orange, Black, German	15.00
Fanny Whacker	40.00
Head, Shrunken, Human Hair, 1/8 In. Scale	15.00
Hood & Cat Mask, Black, Gold, Yellow	20.00
Jack-O'-Lantern, Black Cat Face	55.00
Jack-O'-Lantern, Black, Paper Face, German, 3 In.	35.00
Jack-O'-Lantern, Cardboard Pumpkin Face, 6 X 7 In.	38.00
Jack-O'-Lantern, Cat Face, Green Eyes, Wire Bail, Pressed Paper	30.00
Jack-O'-Lantern, Different Face On Each of 4 Sides	42.00
Jack-O'-Lantern, Double Face, 5 In.	30.00
Jack-O'-Lantern, Papier-Mache, 6 X 7 In.	40.00
Jack-O'-Lantern, Papier-Mache, Tissue Paper, Candle, 3 1/2 In.	75.00
Jack-O'-Lantern, Pouch Shape, German, 5 In.	40.00
Jack-O'-Lantern, Pumpkin Face, Metal, 6 X 5 In.	38.00
Lantern, Black Cat Face, Papier-Mache	35.00
Lantern, Black Cat, Paper	35.00
Lantern, Cat Face, Papier-Mache	15.00
Lantern, Devil, Cardboard Head, Paper Face Forms Lantern	50.00
Lantern, Tissue Face, Black Cat, Cardboard, Pair	65.00
Marionette, Witch	20.00
Mask, Cisco Kid & Pancho, 1953, Pair	30.00
Mask, Joe Palooka, Wheaties	15.00
Mask, Witch, Crepe Paper Black Hat	8.00
Noisemaker, Clown, Tin	5.00
Noisemaker, Devil, Papier-Mache, Wooden	37.00
Noisemaker, Gold, Orange, Black, Czechoslovakia, 6 In.	20.00
Noisemaker, Orange, Black & White, Yellow Clapper	7.00
Noisemaker, Orange, Black, Wooden, 6 In.	16.00
Noisemaker, Pumpkin, Papier-Mache, Wooden	37.00
Noisemaker, Witch, Papier-Mache, Wooden	37.00
Noisemaker, Witch, Pumpkin Face, Metal, T.Cohn Inc., 3 X 5 In.	32.00
Owl, Gray, Pressed Paper, White, Yellow, 13 In.	45.00
Owls, Orange, Paper, 3 In.	15.00
Postcard, 1912, 5 Piece	25.00

Pumpkin, Papier-Mache, Large 25.00
Puppet, Hand, Witch 10.00
Skull, Papier-Mache 15.00
Sparkler, Witch, Tin Litho, Box 65.00
Tambourine, Witch Design, Tin 25.00
Toy, Balancing Witch, Orange, Black, Yellow & Green 25.00
Toy, Black Cat, Movable Eyes, On Stick 25.00
Toy, Cat, Steiff, Large 195.00
Wig, Old Maid, Black Man Picture, Box 15.00
Witch, Figural, Papier-Mache, Germany, 3 In. 15.00
Witch, Flying, Pressed Paper 20.00

 Hampshire pottery was made in Keene, New Hampshire, between 1871 and 1923. Hampshire developed a line of colored glazed wares as early as 1883, including a Royal Worcester-type pink, olive green, blue, and mahogany. Pieces are marked with the printed mark or the impressed name "Hampshire Pottery" or "J.S.T. & Co., Keene, N.H."

HAMPSHIRE, Bonbon, 3 Handles Joined In Center 125.00
Bowl, Cobalt Blue, Glazed, Fan Shell Design 65.00
Chamberstick, Shield Back, Handle, Green 100.00
Chocolate Pot, Worcester Finish 65.00
Ewer, Green, 10 In. .... 60.00 To 65.00
Hair Receiver, Leaf Design, Souvenir, Brown 75.00
Jug, Peanut, Green High Glaze 35.00
Lamp, Green Slag Leaded Shade, Pottery Base, 19 1/2 In. 750.00
Lamp, Leaded Handel Shade, Green Slag Glass, 21 In. ....*Illus* 700.00
Lamp, Matte Green, Embossed Design, Footed, 5 X 8 In. 135.00
Mug, Relief Form Design, Gold, Blue Glaze 75.00
Pitcher, Melon & Vine, Gold & Cream 75.00
Tea Set, Olive High Glaze, Tampa, Fla.In Gold, 3 Piece 68.00
Teapot, Butterfly Finial, Sweeping Handle 55.00
Urn, Blue, Turned Top, 4 1/2 In. 45.00
Vase, Cylindrical, Striated Green, 7 1/2 In. 60.00
Vase, Serpent Handle, 6 In. 150.00
Vase, Signed Cad.Robertson, 10 In. 195.00

Hampshire, Lamp, Leaded Handel Shade, Green Slag Glass, 21 In.

Handel, Lamp, Desk, Pinecone Design Shade, Marked

Philip Handel worked in Meriden, Connecticut, about 1885 and in New York City from about 1900 to the 1930s. His firm made art glass and other types of lamps. Handel shades were made not only of leaded glass in a style reminiscent of Tiffany but also of reverse painted glass.

HANDEL, Humidor, Owl Design, Squat, Silver Plated Lid, Signed, 5 1/2 X 5 In.	395.00
Lamp, Boudoir, Clipper Ship	900.00
Lamp, Bronze Base, Mums, Signed, 16 1/2 In.	2500.00
Lamp, Crackle Ice Shade, Hand Painted Floral Border, 23 In.	975.00
Lamp, Desk, Drab Olive Shade, Signed	340.00
Lamp, Desk, Pinecone Design Shade, Marked ....*Illus*	350.00
Lamp, Desk, Pond Lily	795.00
Lamp, Filigree, Carmel Glass Panels, Signed, 26 X 18 In.	2800.00
Lamp, Hanging, Dome, Marked, 20 In.	3300.00
Lamp, Poppy, Pink Slag Glass, 2 Metal Poppy Buds	850.00
Lamp, Reverse Painted Shade By Palme	2700.00
Lamp, Table, Bronze Base, Green Leaded Shade	3900.00
Lamp, Yellow, Hand Painted Flowers, Signed Base & Shade, 14 In.	425.00
Sugar & Creamer, Green & White, Signed	285.00

HARDWARE, see Architectural

Harker Pottery Company of East Liverpool, Ohio, was founded by Benjamin Harker in 1840. The company made many types of pottery but by the Civil War was making quantities of yellowware from native clays. They also made Rockingham–type brown–glazed pottery and whiteware. The plant was moved to Chester, West Virginia, in 1931. Dinnerwares were made and sold nationally. In 1971 the company was sold to Jeanette Glass Company and all operations ceased in 1972.

HARKER, Bowl, Crazed, 8 In.	8.00
Hot Plate	10.00
Rolling Pin, Amy	50.00
Rolling Pin, Mexican Design	40.00
Teapot, Cameo Ware, Pink & White	20.00

Harlequin dinnerware was produced by the Homer Laughlin Company from 1938 to 1964, and sold without trademark by the F.W. Woolworth Co. It has a concentric ring design like Fiesta, but the rings are separated from the rim by a plain margin. Cup handles are triangular in shape.

HARLEQUIN, Ashtray, Basketweave, Aqua	20.00
Ashtray, Basketweave, Blue	20.00
Ashtray, Maroon	24.00
Ashtray, Red	40.00
Ashtray, Turquoise	35.00
Creamer, High Lip, Yellow	15.00
Creamer, Spruce	17.00
Creamer, Turquoise	7.00
Cup & Saucer, Turquoise	16.00
Duck, Yellow	38.00
Eggcup, Double, Gray	13.00
Eggcup, Double, Turquoise	6.00
Eggcup, Green	4.50
Eggcup, Maroon	20.00
Figurine, Cat, Maverick, Gold	10.00
Figurine, Penguin, Yellow	38.00
Gravy Boat, Turquoise	8.00
Humidor, Clown, Ruffled Collars Are Ashtrays	27.00
Jam Jar, Figural, Orange	60.00
Pitcher, Green, 22 Oz.	20.00
Pitcher, Red	22.50
Pitcher, Water, Light Blue	10.00
Pitcher, Water, Maroon	25.00

Pitcher, Yellow, 22 Oz.	15.00
Plate, Gray, 9 In.	8.00
Plate, Maroon, 9 In.	7.00
Plate, Nautilus, Eggshell, 8 In., Set of 6	14.00
Plate, Red, 10 In.	10.00
Powder Box, Jester, Green	25.00
Rose Bowl, 5 1/2 In.	3.50
Spoon Rest, Double, Yellow	150.00
Spoon Rest, Turquoise	138.00
Spoon Rest, Yellow	138.00
Sugar, Gray, Covered	15.00
Teapot, Red	34.00
Teapot, Spruce	49.50
Tumbler, Spruce	25.00
Tumbler, Yellow	20.00

Hatpins were fashionable from 1860 to 1920 when the large, heavy hat required special long–shanked pins to hold the hat in place. Naturally, hatpin holders were made during the same years. The hatpin holder resembles a large saltshaker, but it often has no opening at the bottom as a shaker does. Hatpin holders were made of all types of ceramics and metal. Look for other prices under the name of specific manufacturers.

HATPIN HOLDER, Art Nouveau, Lavender Bisque, Lady's Face	175.00
Carnival Glass, Grape & Cable Pattern, Purple Base, 7 In.	175.00
Chinese Figures, Gold Beading, Footed, Oriental, C.1900	155.00
Figural, 2 Faces, Man & Lady, Porcelain	265.00
Floral Design, Green Leaves, Germany, 4 7/8 In.	38.00
Hand Painted Roses, Gold Top, Vienna	55.00
Horn, Polished	9.00
Portrait, Hat Lifts Off, Hand Serves As Ring Tree, 6 In.	65.00
Violets, Gold, Nippon, 5 In.	55.00

Hatpins were popular from 1860 to 1920. The long pin, often over four inches, was used to hold the hat in place on the hair. The tops of the pins were made of all materials from solid gold and real gemstones to ceramics and glass. Be careful to buy original hatpins and not recent pieces made by altering old buttons.

HATPIN, Amber Stone, Large	75.00
Banded Hat, Carnival Glass	15.00
Belle, Carnival Glass	35.00
Brass Filigree, Horseshoe & Bit, Rhinestone, 9 In.	20.00
Butterfly, Carnival Glass	10.00
Cattails, Plums & Stems, Carnival Glass	12.00
Coolie Hat, Carnival Glass	10.00
Dogwood Top, Flower, Sterling Silver, 10 In.	45.00
Domed Net, Silver Luster, Carnival Glass	8.00
Flying Bat, Carnival Glass	32.00
Four of Hearts, Carnival Glass	30.00
Golf Club, Sterling Silver, Long Stem	38.00
Heart, Embossed Florals, Brass, 9 In.	30.00
Indian Maiden Bust, 2 Upright Feathers, Braided Hair, Victorian	125.00
Niagara Falls, Enameled, 3 Piece	45.00
Pearl, 11 1/2 In.	15.00
Rhinestone, 9 1/2 In.	20.00
Rooster, Amethyst, Carnival Glass	15.00
Straw Hat, Carnival Glass	15.00
Tufted Throw Pillow, Carnival Glass	25.00
Woman, Egyptian Headdress, Brass, 9 In.	30.00

HAVILAND & CO. Haviland china has been made in Limoges, France, since 1842. The factory was started by the Haviland Brothers of New York City. Other factories worked in the town of Limoges making a similar chinaware. It is possible to match existing sets of dishes through dealers who specialize in Haviland china. Listings of these china matching services can be found in "The Kovels' Collectors' Source Book." Porcelains made by other factories in Limoges, France, are listed in this book under "Limoges."

HAVILAND, Bowl, Vegetable, Princess, Covered	50.00
Butter Chip, Floral, Set of 4	20.00
Butter, Covered, Bretagne	65.00
Chocolate Pot, Apple Blossoms	95.00
Chocolate Pot, Bow Handle, Brushed Gold, Blue Lilacs	140.00
Chocolate Pot, Grapevine Handle, Raised Grapes, Gold, C.1895	175.00
Chocolate Pot, Pink Flowers, 10 In.	135.00
Chop Plate, Pink & Blue Ground, Purple Grapes, Marked, 12 In.	95.00
Coffee Set, Ranson Pattern, Gold Trim, White, 3 Piece	135.00
Compote, Open Basketweave, Violet Design	225.00
Cup & Saucer, Autumn Leaf, No.60	25.00
Cup & Saucer, Princess	25.00
Dinner Set, Cluny Pattern, 85 Piece	400.00
Fish Plate, Signed, 8 1/2 In., Set of 6	270.00
Fish Set, Rectangular Platter, Attached Sauce Dish, 8 Piece	390.00
Ice Cream Set, Leaf Shaped Plates, 1889, 13 Piece	150.00
Oyster Plate, Pink Floral Rim, Set of 12	400.00
Oyster Plate, White, Gold Embossed, 9 1/4 In.	50.00
Plate, Garlands of Flowers, Gold Border, 9 3/4 In.	30.00
Plate, Hand Painted Sparrow, Artist Signed, Dated 1889, 11 In.	65.00
Plate, Napoleon Portrait, Blue, Beehive, 10 In.	125.00
Plate, Rosalinde, 10 In.	8.00
Platter, Child's, 12 X 18 In.	60.00
Platter, Gladiola Pattern, Signed, 16 In.	55.00
Platter, Hand Painted Birds, 13 In.	98.00
Platter, Montgomery, Blue, 14 In.	75.00
Platter, Pink & Lilac Roses, Gold Trim, White, 18 X 24 3/4 In.	90.00
Platter, Tree & Well, Pink Roses, 21 1/2 In.	75.00
Salad Set, Hand Painted Shrimp & Shells, Peach, Artist, 7 Piece	375.00
Sugar & Creamer, Autumn Leaf, No.60	42.00
Sugar, Covered, Blue & Pink Floral, Gold Handles, 4 1/2 In.	18.00
Tobacco Jar, Pink Floral, Gold	110.00
Tray, Dresser, Pink Roses Allover, Gold Trim, 8 1/2 X 10 1/2 In.	38.00
Tureen, Soup, Basketweave Handles, Florals, Signed, 13 1/4 In.	125.00

T. G. Hawkes & Company of Corning, New York, was founded in 1880. The firm cut glass blanks made at other glassworks until 1962. Many pieces are marked with the trademark, a trefoil ring enclosing a fleur-de-lis and two hawks. Cut glass by other manufacturers is listed either under the factory name or the general category "Cut Glass."

HAWKES, Biscuit Jar, Allover Design, Signed, 9 1/2 In.	175.00
Bishop's Hat, Rolled Rim, Signed	1000.00
Bonbon, Scallop & Sawtooth Rim, 7 In.	80.00
Bottle, American Brilliant, Brunswick Pattern, Stopper, 8 In.	165.00
Bottle, Cologne, Allover Intaglio Cut, Sterling Holder, 8 In.	95.00
Bottle, Water, Full Cut, Signed, 7 1/2 In.	125.00
Bottle, Whiskey, 3 Shot Glasses, Signed	675.00
Bowl, Chrysanthemum Pattern, 9 In.	485.00
Bowl, Chrysanthemum Pattern, Square, Signed	595.00
Bowl, Console, Gravic Cut, Floral & Geometrics, 12 In.	185.00
Bowl, Covered, Cut Flowers & Words Chili Sauce	275.00 To 325.00
Bowl, Gravic, Signed, 7 1/2 In.	185.00
Bowl, Hobstar Set Into Scalloped Rim, 24 Point Bottom, 9 In.	395.00

Box, Hinged Top, Oval, Signed 250.00
Bread Tray, Hobstars, Signed, 13 1/2 X 8 1/4 In. 235.00
Candlestick, Engraved Florals, Hollow Stem, Signed, 12 1/4 In., Pair 260.00
Candy, Covered, Rectangular, Signed 135.00
Celery, Allover Cutting, Signed, 10 1/2 In. 140.00
Centerpiece, Sheraton, Signed 750.00
Champagne, Chantilly, Signed, Set of 12 .... 600.00
Cocktail Shaker, Sterling Top & Strainer, Signed 99.00
Compote, Hobstars, Teardrop Stem With Cutting, 9 1/2 In. 195.00
Compote, Petite Cut, Signed, 7 1/2 In. 125.00
Cordial, Adam Pattern, Signed, Set of 6 .... 450.00
Cruet, Engraved, Sterling Silver Stopper 85.00
Cup & Saucer, Signed, Demitasse 300.00
Decanter, Cut Glass, Faceted Stopper, Signed, 8 1/2 In. 235.00
Decanter, Venetian, Cut Glass, 11 1/2 In. 420.00
Decanter, Whiskey, Lines, Sterling Collars, Stopper, Marked, Pair 450.00
Decanter, Whiskey, Owl In Tree, Silver Plated, Trefoil Mark, Pair 600.00
Decanter, Whiskey, Ship's, Sunburst Base, Mushroom Top, Trefoil Mark 400.00
Decanter, Wine, Signed, 10 In. 135.00
Dish, Scalloped Rim, Brilliant Cut, Signed 115.00
Epergne, Lily, 4 .... 350.00
Goblet, Chantilly, Signed, Set of 12 .... 600.00
Goblet, Russian Pattern, Signed, 9 Piece 1170.00
Mayonnaise Jar, Engraved Stopper, Handles, Signed, 4 1/4 In. 110.00
Pitcher, Cider, Signed, 8 In. 165.00
Pitcher, Covered, Flowers, Trefoil Mark, 8 1/2 X 7 1/2 In. 300.00
Pitcher, Milk, Buzz Star, Signed, 6 3/4 In. 175.00
Pitcher, Pinwheel & Star, Signed, 11 1/2 In. 195.00
Pitcher, Queen's Pattern, Signed, 8 1/2 In. 1075.00
Pitcher, Satin Stripes, Sterling Silver Overlay, Signed, 10 In. 325.00
Pitcher, Tankard, Harvard Pattern, Rayed Base, Signed, 11 In. 315.00
Pitcher, Water, Hobstars & Variants, Signed .... 185.00 To 195.00
Punch Bowl, Brazilian, Red, 14 X 12 1/2 In., 2 Piece 1900.00
Punch Bowl, Hobstars Within Vesicas, Strawberry Diamond, Signed 1400.00
Punch Bowl, Hobstars, Vesicas, Signed, 2 Part 750.00
Sherbet, Underplate, Enameled Roses, Forget–Me–Nots, Signed 225.00
Sugar & Creamer, Pedestal Base, Birds, Florals 125.00
Sugar, Allover Cut, Handles, Signed 145.00
Tray, Brunswick, Round, 10 In. 675.00
Vase, Apple Green Iridescent, Cut To Clear, Swags, Signed, 8 In. 175.00
Vase, Blue & White Enameling, Gold Top & Bottom, 10 In. 125.00
Vase, Blue Cut Ribbons & Florals, Sterling Silver Rim, 8 1/2 In. 165.00
Vase, Bud, Engraved Leaves & Flowers, 10 In. 90.00
Vase, Engraved Florals, Signed, 3 1/2 In. 40.00
Vase, Fan, Vintage Pattern, Green To Clear, Signed, 7 1/2 In. 60.00
Vase, Flower Sprays At Shoulder, 88 Bull's–Eyes 150.00
Vase, Intaglio, 9 1/2 In. 95.00
Vase, Inverted Baluster, Geometrics, Sterling Silver Base, 13 In. 150.00
Vase, Trumpet Style, Signed, 13 1/2 In. 175.00
Vase, Trumpet, Queen's 950.00
Water Set, Queen's, 7 Piece 2000.00

 Heintz Art Metal shop made jewelry, copper, silver, and brass in
Buffalo, New York, from 1915 to about 1935. It became Heintz
Brothers Manufacturers about 1935. The most popular items with
collectors today are the copper desk sets and vases made with silver
overlay designs.

HEINTZ ART, Ashtray, Art Deco, Sterling On Bronze 30.00
Candlestick, Metal, 7 1/4 In. 115.00
Lamp, Boudoir, 5 X 11 In. 190.00
Trophy, Golf, Iroquois Brewery, Indian Chief, 1912, 11 In. 450.00
Vase, Grape Leaves, Sterling Silver On Bronze, 10 In. 75.00
Vase, Silver Cattail Design, Green, 8 In. 115.00
Vase, Sterling Silver Overlay, Bronze, Signed, 6 3/4 In. 60.00

Heisey glass was made from 1896 to 1957 in Newark, Ohio, by A. H. Heisey and Co., Inc. The Imperial Glass Company of Bellaire, Ohio, bought some of the molds and the rights to the trademark. Some Heisey patterns have been made by Imperial since 1960. After 1968, they stopped using the "H" trademark. Heisey used romantic names for colors such as "Sahara." Do not confuse color and pattern names.

HEISEY, see also Custard Glass, Ruby Glass

HEISEY, Admiralty, Sherry, Frosted Stem	14.00
Albemarle, Champagne	15.00
Antarctic Etch, Pitcher, Queen Ann, 65 Oz.	80.00
Aristocrat, Candy Jar, Footed, Low, Covered, Cobalt Blue, 1/2 Lb.	375.00
Banded Flute, Chamberstick	45.00
Banded Flute, Champagne, 4 1/2 Oz.	12.00
Banded Flute, Cruet, 4 Oz.	38.00
Banded Flute, Goblet, Marked	137.50
Banded Flute, Tray, 13 In.	68.00
Barcelona Cut, Goblet, Iced Tea, Jamestown, Footed	65.00
Barcelona, Champagne	17.00
Barcelona, Plate, 7 In.	30.00
Beaded Panel & Sunburst, Creamer, Ruby Stained, Individual	65.00
Beaded Panel & Sunburst, Table Set, 4 Piece	130.00
Beaded Swag, Berry Bowl, Milk Glass, 5 In.	22.00
Beaded Swag, Butter, Cornflower Design, Covered, Opalescent	65.00
Beaded Swag, Cruet, Milk Glass	125.00
Beaded Swag, Goblet	75.00
Beaded Swag, Sugar, White, Covered	45.00
Beaded Swag, Syrup, Milk Glass	105.00
Beaded Swag, Tumbler, Opalescent, Pair	55.00
Beaded Swag, Wine, Custard Glass, Marked	58.00
Beehive, Plate, Zircon, 5 In.	75.00
Bookends, Donkey	195.00
Bookends, Fish	90.00 To 195.00
Bookends, Horsehead, Frosted	190.00
Brookville, Sherbet, Handle, Marked, 3 1/2 Oz.	15.00
Buxton Inn, Sherbet, Marked	6.00
Cabochon, Advertising Sign	120.00
Cabochon, Relish, 3 Sections, Dawn, 9 In.	50.00
Cabochon, Tumbler, Iced Tea, Crystal, 12 Oz.	80.00
Carcassone, Cigarette Holder, Footed, Cobalt	75.00
Carcassone, Tankard, Houston Bridge	140.00
Carcassone, Tumbler, Moongleam, Footed	10.00
Carcassonne, Decanter, Flamingo	175.00
Cathedral, Vase, Moongleam, Floral	105.00
Chanticleer, Cocktail, Frosted Stem	85.00
Chateau Cut, Goblet, Albemarle	55.00
Cherub, Candlestick	375.00
Chintz, Dish, Pickle, Chintz Etch, Sahara, 10 In.	32.00
Chintz, Goblet	17.50
Coarse Rib, Celery, Marigold, 9 In.	30.00
Coarse Rib, Nappy, Flamingo, 5 In., Pair	36.00
Coarse Rib, Sherbet, Marked, 6 1/2 Oz.	20.00
Colonial, Berry Bowl, Marked, 7 In.	25.00
Colonial, Bottle, Water, Scalloped Top	30.00
Colonial, Candelabra, 4-Light, No.300	475.00
Colonial, Celery, Etched Flowers & Leaves, Star Cut Base, 12 In.	30.00
Colonial, Compote, Marked, Low, 4 1/2 In.	75.00
Colonial, Compote, Pedestal, 9 1/2 X 7 In., Pair	275.00
Colonial, Cruet, 8 Sides, Marked, Flamingo	590.00
Colonial, Goblet	20.00
Colonial, Punch Cup, 6 Piece	45.00
Colonial, Punch Set, Ladle, 8 1/2 X 11 In., 11 Piece	350.00
Colonial, Sherbet, 6 Piece	75.00

Colonial, Sherbet, Flared, Marked 32.00
Colonial, Sugar & Creamer 25.00
Colonial, Syrup, 8 In. 25.00
Colonial, Tray, Rayed Center, Marked, Round, 10 1/2 In. 15.00
Columbia, Console Set, Crimped Foot Candlesticks, Bowl, 13 In. 85.00
Continental, Bottle, Water, Marked 25.00
Cornucopia, Fruit Bowl, Cobalt Blue, 10 1/2 X 4 1/4 In. 200.00
Courtship, Goblet, Cut 45.00
Coventry, Cocktail, Zircon, 3 Oz. 65.00
Creole, Cocktail, Alexandrite, Crystal Stem 120.00
Creole, Goblet, Soda, Footed, Alexandrite, 12 Oz. 75.00
Cross Lined Flute, Goblet, 7 Oz. 22.50
Crystolite, Bowl, 8 In. 20.00
Crystolite, Bowl, Fruit, 12 In. 25.00
Crystolite, Box, Cigarette, 4 In. 25.00
Crystolite, Cake Plate, Footed 200.00
Crystolite, Candleholder, Ball, Tag 45.00
Crystolite, Candlestick, 3–Light, Pair 35.00
Crystolite, Candlestick, Double, Bobeche & Prisms, Pair 110.00
Crystolite, Cigarette Holder, Oval 9.00
Crystolite, Coaster 4.00
Crystolite, Compote 35.00
Crystolite, Cup & Saucer, Pattern To Rim 22.00
Crystolite, Dish, Covered, Footed, Round, 6 In. 35.00
Crystolite, Dish, Lemon, Flamingo, Marked 35.00
Crystolite, Ice Bucket, Tongs, Chrome Handle 110.00
Crystolite, Lamp, Hurricane 125.00
Crystolite, Mustard 25.00
Crystolite, Plate, 8 In. 10.00
Crystolite, Punch Set, Underplate, Ladle, 13 Piece 315.00
Crystolite, Sugar & Creamer .... 20.00 To 28.00
Decagon, Cup & Saucer, Flamingo 16.00
Decagon, Sugar & Creamer, Flamingo 20.00
Diamond Crystal, Sugar 20.00
Diamond Optic, Cruet 40.00
Diamond Optic, Sugar & Creamer, Flamingo 46.00
Diamond Optic, Sugar & Creamer, Moongleam 48.00
Diamond Optic, Tumbler, Juice, Flamingo, 4 Piece 35.00
Diamond Point & Punty Band, Cruet 70.00
Diamond Swag, Punch Cup 10.00
Dolphin, Bowl, Moongleam, 10 In. 97.50
Dolphin, Candleholder, 5 In. 95.00
Dolphin, Candlestick, Pair 475.00
Double Rib & Panel, Basket, Emerald 65.00
Duck, Ashtray, Flamingo 95.00
Duquesne, Parfait, Tangerine 100.00
Empress, Ashtray, Sahara 85.00
Empress, Berry Set, Flamingo, 7 Piece 120.00
Empress, Bowl, Dolphin Footed, Alexandrite, 11 In. 350.00
Empress, Bowl, Emerald, 2 Handles, 10 In. 30.00
Empress, Bowl, Footed, Flamingo, 11 In. 46.00
Empress, Bowl, Handles, Footed, Sahara, 8 In. 42.50
Empress, Bowl, Moongleam, Oval, 10 In. 40.00
Empress, Celery, Sahara, 13 In. 27.00
Empress, Console, Moongleam 100.00
Empress, Creamer, Sahara 32.00
Empress, Cup & Saucer, Etched, Set of 9 .... 95.00
Empress, Cup & Saucer, Moongleam, Square Saucer, Marked 15.00
Empress, Dish, Covered, Dolphin Handle, Farberware Holder 60.00
Empress, Jam Jar, Covered, 3–Footed, Yellow 100.00
Empress, Jug, Footed, Marked, Sahara, 3 Pt. 150.00
Empress, Nut Cup 13.00
Empress, Pitcher 48.00
Empress, Plate, Sahara, 8 In. 7.50

Empress, Plate, Tangerine, 6 1/2 In.	150.00
Empress, Punch Cup, Yellow	18.00
Empress, Relish, 3 Sections, Sahara	45.00
Empress, Sugar & Creamer, Dolphin Footed, Flamingo	40.00
Empress, Sugar & Creamer, Sahara, 3 Handles, Footed	75.00
Empress, Sugar, Sahara, Individual	28.00
Empress, Tray, Handle, Sahara	20.00
Enchantress Cut, Plate, Waverly, Plate, 14 In.	45.00
Everglade, Tumbler	110.00
Fairacre, Pitcher, Water, Moongleam Base & Handle, Crystal, 54 Oz.	135.00
Fancy Loop, Cruet, Clear	65.00
Fancy Loop, Goblet, Emerald	65.00
Fancy Loop, Punch Bowl, 2 Piece	365.00
Fancy Loop, Punch Cup	15.00
Fancy Loop, Sugar, Open, Individual	40.00
Fancy Loop, Toothpick	40.00 To 65.00
Fancy Loop, Wine, Emerald	75.00
Fandango, Creamer, Individual	25.00
Fandango, Saltshaker, Emerald	65.00
Fandango, Toothpick	65.00
Figurine, Bull, Marked	1100.00 To 1125.00
Figurine, Clydesdale, Imperial, Blue	150.00
Figurine, Colt, Rearing, Cobalt	175.00
Figurine, Colt, Standing, Amber	450.00
Figurine, Donkey, Imperial, Blue	75.00
Figurine, Elephant, Imperial, Blue	75.00
Figurine, Elephant, Marked, Large	295.00
Figurine, Elephant, Marked, Medium	245.00
Figurine, Elephant, Small	145.00 To 165.00
Figurine, Fish, Tropical	1070.00
Figurine, Flying Mare, Amber	500.00
Figurine, Gazelle, Imperial, Blue	150.00
Figurine, Geese, Set of 3	425.00
Figurine, Giraffe, Head Forward	140.00
Figurine, Goose, Halfway Wings	85.00 To 125.00
Figurine, Goose, Wings Down	100.00 To 325.00
Figurine, Goose, Wings Up	60.00 To 100.00
Figurine, Hen	370.00 To 385.00
Figurine, Madonna	99.00
Figurine, Mallard, Halfway Wings	160.00
Figurine, Mallard, Wings Down	105.00
Figurine, Pig & 2 Piglets, Blue, Set	100.00
Figurine, Pig & 2 Piglets, Red	60.00
Figurine, Plug Horse, Amber	550.00
Figurine, Pony, Rearing	120.00 To 150.00
Figurine, Pony, Standing	75.00 To 80.00
Figurine, Pouter Pigeon, Marked	475.00
Figurine, Rooster	450.00
Figurine, Rooster, Fighting	120.00 To 145.00
Figurine, Scotty, Imperial, Blue	60.00
Figurine, Swan & 2 Cygnets	595.00
Figurine, Swan, 7 In.	850.00
Figurine, Wood Duck	475.00 To 480.00
Figurine, Woodchuck, Blue	50.00
Flat Panel, Jar, Cigar, Covered	85.00
Flat Panel, Syrup	32.50
Fox Chase, Cocktail Shaker	145.00
Frontenac Etch, Goblet, Wabash	15.00
Gascony, Candlestick, Yellow, Pair	140.00
Gascony, Sugar & Creamer	52.00
Greek Key, Banana Boat, 4–Footed	27.50
Greek Key, Bottle, Water	86.00
Greek Key, Bowl, 4 1/2 In.	20.00
Greek Key, Celery, 9 In.	25.00 To 27.50

Greek Key, Cocktail, 3 Oz.	30.00 To 45.00
Greek Key, Cordial, 3/4 Oz.	195.00
Greek Key, Cruet, 4 Oz.	60.00
Greek Key, Cruet, 6 Oz.	65.00
Greek Key, Goblet, 7 Oz.	150.00
Greek Key, Ice Bucket, Hotel	95.00 To 265.00
Greek Key, Lamp, Figural, Chanticleer, Silver Plated Base, 8 1/2 In.	350.00
Greek Key, Pitcher, Water	50.00
Greek Key, Punch Bowl, Base, Flamingo	300.00
Greek Key, Punch Cup	10.00
Greek Key, Punch Set, Marked, 16 Piece	450.00
Greek Key, Sherbet, 4 1/2 Oz.	20.00
Greek Key, Sherbet, 6 Oz.	22.50
Greek Key, Tray, French Bread	175.00
Groove & Slash, Cruet	50.00
Horn of Plenty, Vase, Cobalt Blue, 11 In.	350.00
Horsehead, Box, Cigarette	55.00 To 88.00
Horsehead, Cocktail Shaker	135.00
Impromptu, Goblet, 12 Oz.	18.50
Intercepted Flute, Nappy, Flared, Marked, 4 In.	7.00
Ipswich, Bowl, Centerpiece, Footed, Crystal	35.00
Ipswich, Champagne, Sahara	15.00 To 25.00
Ipswich, Cruet	85.00
Ipswich, Goblet, Iced Tea	18.00
Ipswich, Goblet, Water	15.00
Ipswich, Plate, Cocktail, Oyster, Sahara	20.00
Ipswich, Sherbet, 4 Oz.	7.00
Ipswich, Tumbler, Juice	18.00
Jamestown, Cocktail	12.00
Kalonyal, Celery, 11 3/4 In.	68.00
Lariat, Bonbon, Crytal, 7 1/2 In.	15.00
Lariat, Bottle, Perfume, Allover Enameled Flowers, Gold Trim	48.00
Lariat, Bowl, 2 Sections, 7 In.	18.00
Lariat, Bowl, Silver Design, 7 In.	35.00
Lariat, Candleholder, 1 1/2 In., Pair	15.00
Lariat, Candlestick, 3 In.	35.00
Lariat, Candy Dish, Silver Plated Cover, Snail Feet	30.00
Lariat, Coaster	10.00
Lariat, Console Set, Silver Overlay, 2–Light Candleholders	85.00
Lariat, Cruet, Stopper, Handle	45.00
Lariat, Cup	8.00
Lariat, Dish, Turned Edge	24.00
Lariat, Goblet, 10 Oz.	12.50
Lariat, Nappy, 7 In.	17.50
Lariat, Plate, Cuttings, 13 In.	22.00
Lariat, Punch Cup, Marked	60.00
Lariat, Punch Set, Ladle, 15 Piece	235.00
Lariat, Relish, 4 Sections, 9 In.	28.00
Lariat, Sugar & Creamer	10.00 To 25.00
Lariat, Tray, 13 1/2 In.	38.00
Locket On Chain, Cake Plate, Footed	70.00
Locket On Chain, Wine, Ruby Stained	287.00
Lodestar, Pitcher, Dawn	150.00
Maryland, Wine, Cut, 3 Oz.	16.50
Minuet Etch, Candlestick, Trident, Pair	135.00
Minuet Etch, Champagne, Saucer, 6 Oz.	25.00
Minuet Etch, Goblet, Water	26.00
Minuet Etch, Goblet, Water, Label	33.00
Minuet Etch, Sugar & Creamer, Dolphin Footed	90.00
Monte Cristo, Goblet, 9 Oz.	18.00
Moonglo Cut, Candlestick, Lariat, Triple, Pair	95.00
Moonglo, Relish, 3 Sections	40.00
Narcissus, Bell	30.00
Narrow Flute, Butter, Covered, Round	60.00

Narrow Flute, Cocktail, 3 Oz.	10.00
Narrow Flute, Dish, Banana Split	23.00
Narrow Flute, Eggcup, 5 Oz.	15.00
Narrow Flute, Nappy, 4 In.	3.00 To 6.00
Narrow Flute, Nut Cup, Flamingo Rim, Set of 8	100.00
Narrow Flute, Parfait	13.00
Narrow Flute, Punch Bowl, Base	175.00
Narrow Flute, Sugar	55.00
Narrow Flute, Tray, 6 In.	15.00
Navarro, Relish, 3 Sections, 10 In.	37.50
Navarro, Sherbet	16.00
Navarro, Tumbler, Footed	24.00
New Era, Candelabra, Frosted, 2 Branches, Pair	150.00
New Era, Champagne	62.50
Oak Leaf, Coaster	9.00
Oceanic, Relish, Marked, 7 In.	65.00
Octagon, Cheese Dish, Marigold, 6 In.	20.00
Octagon, Ice Bucket, Green	67.50
Octagon, Plate, Flamingo, 6 In.	5.00
Octagon, Sugar & Creamer, Ribbed	20.00
Octagon, Sugar & Creamer, Sahara	25.00
Octagon, Sugar, Flamingo	15.00
Old Colony Etch, Goblet, Carcassone	10.00
Old Colony Etch, Goblet, Duquesne, Tall	10.00
Old Colony, Goblet, Sahara	24.00
Old Colony, Vase, Dolphin Footed, Sahara	95.00
Old Dominion, Goblet, Water	29.00
Old Sandwich, Bottle, Catsup	85.00
Old Sandwich, Candlestick, Emerald, Pair	175.00
Old Sandwich, Cruet	45.00
Old Sandwich, Goblet, Footed, Sahara, 10 Oz.	35.00
Old Sandwich, Mug, Cobalt Blue	250.00
Old Sandwich, Pitcher, Water, Sahara	35.00 To 110.00
Old Sandwich, Plate, Square, 8 In.	9.00
Old Sandwich, Salt & Pepper	30.00
Old Sandwich, Tumbler, Soda, Sahara	23.00
Old Sandwich, Wine, Sahara	25.00
Old Williamsburg, Candelabra, 2–Light, Pair	180.00
Old Williamsburg, Candlestick, Sahara, No.300–3, Pair	595.00
Orchid Etch, Ashtray, Tyrolean, 3 In.	29.50
Orchid Etch, Bowl, 13 In.	39.00 To 40.00
Orchid Etch, Bowl, Crimped, 12 In.	45.00 To 75.00
Orchid Etch, Bowl, Floral, 12 In.	60.00
Orchid Etch, Bowl, Seahorse, 3–Footed, Floral, 10 In.	110.00
Orchid Etch, Butter, Covered, Square, 6 In.	165.00
Orchid Etch, Candleholder, Single	30.00 To 35.00
Orchid Etch, Candlestick, 3–Light, Pair	150.00
Orchid Etch, Candlestick, Waverly, Double, Pair	110.00
Orchid Etch, Compote, Footed, Low, 6 In.	43.00
Orchid Etch, Compote, Jelly, Greek Key, Footed, 6 1/2 In.	55.00
Orchid Etch, Cordial	50.00
Orchid Etch, Cup & Saucer, Queen Ann	48.00
Orchid Etch, Goblet, Marked, 10 Oz.	32.00
Orchid Etch, Goblet, Soda, Footed, 5 1/2 In.	32.00
Orchid Etch, Goblet, Tyrolean, Low, 10 Oz.	29.00
Orchid Etch, Goblet, Tyrolean, Tall, 10 Oz.	33.00
Orchid Etch, Goblet, Water, Seahorse, 10 Oz.	40.00
Orchid Etch, Ice Bucket, Handles	110.00
Orchid Etch, Plate, 8 In.	20.00
Orchid Etch, Plate, Waverly, 8 In.	16.00
Orchid Etch, Sandwich Plate, 14 In.	80.00
Orchid Etch, Sherbet, Seahorse	25.00
Orchid Etch, Sherbet, Tyrolean, 6 Oz.	20.00
Orchid Etch, Sherry	45.00

Orchid Etch, Sugar & Creamer 65.00
Orchid Etch, Sugar & Creamer, Footed 60.00
Orchid Etch, Sugar & Creamer, Individual 50.00
Orchid Etch, Torte Plate, 14 In. 65.00
Orchid Etch, Vase, Footed, 4 In. 67.50
Orchid Etch, Wine, Tyrolean, 3 Oz. .... 45.00 To 95.00
Paneled Cane, Berry Dish 35.00
Park Lane, Goblet, 10 Oz. 21.00
Peerless, Bottle, Bitters, 6 Oz. 15.00
Peerless, Cocktail, 2 Oz. 8.00
Peerless, Eggcup, Marked 18.00
Peerless, Pitcher, 9 1/2 In. 95.00
Peerless, Punch Cup, Set of 6 .... 45.00
Peerless, Sherbet, Marked 30.00
Peerless, Spooner, Printed, 6 In. 40.00
Peerless, Sugar & Creamer, Individual 32.00
Peerless, Syrup 40.00
Peerless, Vase, 12 In. 30.00
Penguin, Decanter 185.00
Pied Piper, Jug, Cut Neck, Squat, 3 Pt. 165.00
Pillows, Bowl, Fruit, Footed, 8 X 8 1/2 In. 100.00
Pillows, Cake Stand .... 95.00 To 110.00
Pillows, Spooner .... 65.00 To 85.00
Pineapple & Fan, Celery, Gold Trim 150.00
Pineapple & Fan, Cruet 75.00
Pineapple & Fan, Mug, Gold Trim, Souvenir 45.00
Pineapple & Fan, Salt & Pepper 45.00
Pineapple & Fan, Table Set, Gold Trim, Emerald, 4 Piece 325.00
Pineapple & Fan, Toothpick, Emerald With Gold 165.00
Pinwheel & Fan, Basket, 11 3/4 In. 325.00
Pinwheel & Fan, Punch Bowl & Base 95.00
Plain Band, Salt, 2 1/4 In. 20.00
Plain Band, Toothpick 65.00
Plain Panel Recessed, Salt, Pedestal, 6 Sides, Scalloped, 1 3/4 In. 15.00
Plantation, Bowl, Low, 10 In. 45.00
Plantation, Butter, Sterling Cover 45.00
Plantation, Candlestick, Blocks, Pair 70.00
Plantation, Compote, Covered, 5 In. 95.00
Plantation, Creamer 15.00
Plantation, Cruet, Full Pineapple Design 100.00
Plantation, Dish, Jelly, Handles, 6 1/2 In. 25.00
Plantation, Epergne Candleholder, Footed, 5 In. 65.00
Plantation, Jam Jar, Covered 68.00
Plantation, Plate, Round, 7 1/2 In. 16.00
Plantation, Punch Bowl, Marked 100.00
Plantation, Relish, 4 Sections, Round, 8 In. 55.00
Plantation, Salt & Pepper .... 35.00 To 45.00
Plantation, Sugar Shaker, Clear 110.00
Plantation, Syrup .... 50.00 To 65.00
Plantation, Tray 35.00
Plantation, Vase, 9 1/4 In. 95.00
Plateau, Rose Bowl, Flamingo, 6 In. 45.00
Pleat & Panel, Compote, Covered, Gold Trim, Flamingo, 7 In. ... 60.00
Pleat & Panel, Cruet, Flamingo 50.00
Pleat & Panel, Cup & Saucer, Flamingo 25.00
Pleat & Panel, Pitcher 60.00
Pleat & Panel, Plate, Flamingo, 7 In. 6.00
Pleat & Panel, Plate, Flamingo, 10 1/2 In. 50.00
Pleat & Panel, Sugar & Creamer, Flamingo 48.00
Pleat & Panel, Vase, Flamingo, 8 In. 37.50
Pointed Oval In Diamond Point, Dish, Glass Balls At Rim, 2 In. ... 11.00
Pointed Oval In Diamond Point, Spooner 15.00
Portsmouth, Goblet, 9 Oz. 30.00
Prince of Wales, Plumes, Punch Cup .... 10.00 To 15.00

Prince of Wales, Plumes, Toothpick, Gold Trim	120.00
Priscilla, Cruet	20.00
Priscilla, Mustard, Covered	25.00
Priscilla, Vase, Basket Shape, 6 In.	25.00
Priscilla, Violet Vase, Flared, Marked, 3 1/2 In.	20.00
Prison Stripe, Nappy, 4 In.	18.00
Prison Stripe, Punch Set, 8 Cups	395.00
Provincial, Candleblock, Pair	37.50
Provincial, Cruet	40.00
Provincial, Goblet, 10 Oz.	15.00
Provincial, Punch Set, Bowl, Platter, Ladle, Marked, 15 Piece	250.00 To 350.00
Provincial, Relish, 4 Sections	35.00
Provincial, Tumbler, Iced Tea, Footed, Zircon, 12 In.	32.00
Provincial, Tumbler, Red, Imperial	12.00
Provincial, Wine, Heather	6.00
Punty & Diamond Point, Nappy, 8 In.	25.00
Punty & Diamond Point, Pitcher, Marked, 1/2 Gal.	125.00
Punty & Diamond Point, Relish, Oblong, 12 In.	40.00
Punty & Diamond Point, Salt & Pepper, Sterling Silver Tops	95.00
Punty & Diamond Point, Sugar Shaker, Silver Top	60.00
Punty & Diamond Point, Tumbler, 8 Oz.	75.00
Punty Band, Mug, Ruby Flash, 1906	35.00
Punty Band, Wine, Red Stain, Coney Island 1908	17.50
Puritan, Ashtray, Horsehead, Square, 4 1/2 In.	55.00
Puritan, Box, Cigarette, Covered, Horsehead, 6 1/4 X 4 In.	55.00
Puritan, Claret, 4 Oz.	11.00
Puritan, Cocktail, 2 Oz.	7.50
Puritan, Dish, Jelly, Footed, 5 In.	32.00
Puritan, Ice Tub, Drainer, Marked	65.00
Puritan, Jug, 3 Qt.	112.50
Puritan, Jug, Squat, Marked, 1/2 Gal.	55.00
Puritan, Punch Cup, Starred Bottom, 4 1/2 Oz.	55.00
Puritan, Salt, 1 3/4 In.	12.00
Puritan, Sherbet, Marked, 4 1/2 Oz.	15.00
Puritan, Sugar & Creamer, Hotel, Oval	35.00
Puritan, Tumbler, 8 Oz.	10.00
Queen Ann, Bowl, 10 In.	35.00
Queen Ann, Bowl, 12 In.	22.00
Queen Ann, Bowl, Dolphin Footed, 11 In.	45.00
Queen Ann, Candleholder, Crystal, Prisms, Pair	110.00
Queen Ann, Candlestick, Pair	28.00
Queen Ann, Ice Bucket, Silver Overlay	75.00
Queen Ann, Plate, Square, Sahara, 6 In.	5.95 To 6.50
Queen Ann, Relish, Divided, 9 In.	35.00
Queen Ann, Soup, Cream, Underplate	27.50
Queen Ann, Sugar & Creamer	135.00
Recessed Panel, Candy Jar, Gold Trim, Ruby Flash	35.00
Regency, Candleblock, Single	40.00
Renaissance Etch, Champagne, Old Glory, 5 Oz.	17.50
Renaissance Etch, Cordial, Old Glory, 1 Oz.	95.00
Revere, Dish, Jelly, 2 Handles, 5 In.	20.00
Revere, Salt, Tab Handles, Flamingo, Marked, 2 In.	15.00
Rib & Panel, Basket, 10 In.	75.00
Rib & Panel, Bowl, Flanged	28.00
Rib & Panel, Cruet, Marked	35.00
Rib & Panel, Pitcher, Glass Lid, 1 Qt.	135.00
Rib & Panel, Relish, 3 Sections, Center Handle	24.00
Rib & Panel, Sugar & Creamer, Hotel	20.00
Rib & Panel, Vase, Etched, 9 1/2 In.	17.50
Ribbed Octagon, Sandwich Plate, Center Handle, Sahara, 10 1/2 In.	45.00
Ridgeleigh, Bonbon, Handles	18.00
Ridgeleigh, Bowl, 12 In.	35.00
Ridgeleigh, Bowl, Oval, 12 In.	30.00
Ridgeleigh, Box, Cigarette, 4 Ashtrays	49.50

Ridgeleigh, Candelabrum, Bobeche, Prisms 60.00
Ridgeleigh, Candlestick, 7 In., Pair 80.00
Ridgeleigh, Cocktail Shaker 90.00
Ridgeleigh, Compote, Jelly, Handle, 6 In. 10.00
Ridgeleigh, Dish, Jelly, 2 Sections, 6 In. 12.00
Ridgeleigh, Ice Tub 42.50
Ridgeleigh, Nappy, 2 Sections, Handle 15.00
Ridgeleigh, Nappy, Flared, 5 1/4 In. 6.50
Ridgeleigh, Plate, 8 1/2 In. 6.00
Ridgeleigh, Plate, Flamingo, 7 1/2 In. 40.00
Ridgeleigh, Punch Cup .... 6.00 To 8.50
Ridgeleigh, Relish, Triangular, Handle, Marked, 6 In. 18.00
Ridgeleigh, Salt & Pepper 45.00
Ridgeleigh, Sherbet, Set of 6 .... 55.00
Ridgeleigh, Sugar & Creamer 30.00
Ridgeleigh, Vase, Zircon, 8 In. .... 140.00 To 185.00
Ring Band, Berry Set, 7 Piece 175.00
Ring Band, Compote, Jelly, Gold Trim .... 115.00 To 125.00
Ring Band, Creamer 65.00
Ring Band, Hat, Custard Glass 295.00
Ring Band, Jar, Horseradish, Gold Trim 28.00
Ring Band, Punch Cup, Souvenir, East Machias, Maine 26.00
Ring Band, Toothpick, Custard Glass, Roses 95.00
Rooster Head, Cocktail Shaker, 2 Qt. 95.00
Rosalie, Bowl, Dolphin Etch, Footed, 10 In. 95.00
Rose Etch, Basket, Lariat, Crystal, 9 In. 175.00
Rose Etch, Bowl, Crimped, Waverly, 10 In. 50.00
Rose Etch, Candleholder, Trident, 2–Light, Crystal, Pair 125.00
Rose Etch, Candlestick, 1–Light, 4 In., Pair 45.00
Rose Etch, Candy Dish, Waverly, Covered, Sea Horse Handle 170.00
Rose Etch, Creamer, Footed 32.00
Rose Etch, Goblet, 7 In. 37.00
Rose Etch, Mayonnaise Set, Waverly, 3 Piece 85.00
Rose Etch, Platter, Waverly, 13 In. 80.00
Rose Etch, Tumbler, Iced Tea, Footed, 12 Oz. 40.00
Rose Etch, Tumbler, Juice, Footed 42.50
Rose Etch, Violet Vase, 4 In. 75.00
Sandwich Star, Plate, 8 In. 135.00
Saturn, Finger Bowl, 4 In., Set of 3 .... 20.00
Sawtooth Band, Table Set, Child's, Ruby Stained, 1903, 4 Piece 550.00
Southwind, Goblet, Cabochon Stem 12.00
Spanish, Champagne, Tangerine Bowl 100.00
Spanish, Goblet, Cobalt Blue Bowl, 10 Oz. 60.00
Sportsman Etch, Plate, Square, 8 In. 42.00
Stanhope, Cup, Black Knob, 1 Handle 15.00
Stanhope, Goblet 23.00
Stanhope, Sugar 15.00
Stanhope, Sugar & Creamer 28.00
Star & Zipper, Bowl, Emerald, 8 In. 175.00
Starflower Cut, Goblet, Omega, Paper Label 68.00
Sunburst, Candy Dish, Footed 23.00
Sunburst, Cruet 30.00
Sunburst, Jug, 3 Qt. 195.00
Sunburst, Nappy, Oval, 7 1/2 In. 20.00
Sunburst, Punch Bowl, Stand 185.00
Sunflower, Butter, Covered 48.00
Swan, Crystolite, Large 28.00
Tally Ho Etch, Goblet, Universal 30.00
Thistle, Wine, Stem, Marked 17.00
Thumbprint & Panel, Candlestick, 2–Light, Flamingo 48.00
Town & Country, Tumbler, Dawn 30.00
Triplex, Candleholder, Flamingo 70.00
Trojan Etch, Tumbler, Iced Tea, 12 Oz. 70.00
Trojan, Candlestick, Pair 100.00

Twist, Bonbon, Rolled–Up Sides, Handle, Flamingo, 6 In.	15.00
Twist, Bowl, Nut, Footed, Marigold	40.00
Twist, Bowl, Rolled Edge, 9 In.	35.00
Twist, Celery, 9 In.	10.00
Twist, Celery, Flamingo, 13 In.	17.50
Twist, Compote, Moongleam, 7 In.	70.00
Twist, Cornucopia, Cobalt Blue, 5 1/2 In.	155.00
Twist, Cruet	40.00
Twist, Goblet, Iced Tea, Footed, Flamingo, Set of 6	125.00
Twist, Ice Bucket, Handle, Crystal	46.50
Twist, Ice Bucket, Handle, Moongleam, Marked	50.00
Twist, Mustard, Covered, Flamingo	67.50
Twist, Nappy, Flamingo, 4 In.	10.00
Twist, Platter, Sahara, 12 In.	50.00
Twist, Relish, 3 Sections, Moongleam, 13 In.	28.00
Twist, Relish, Celery Shape, 3 Sections, Flamingo, 13 In.	23.00
Twist, Tumbler, Marigold, 5 Oz.	33.50
Victorian, Plate, 8 1/4 In.	7.00
Victorian, Shot Glass, 2 Oz.	12.00
Victorian, Sugar & Creamer	50.00
Victorian, Tumbler, Marked	25.00
Victorian, Vase, Flared, 8 1/2 In.	48.00
Victorian, Wine	12.00
Victory, Vase, 4 In.	11.00
Waldorf, Toothpick	44.00 To 60.00
Wampum, Console Set, 12 In.	85.00
Wampum, Plate, 12 In.	35.00
Wampum, Torte Plate, 14 In.	35.00
Warwick, Bowl, Flower, Cobalt	225.00
Warwick, Candlestick, Double, No.1428, Pair	55.00
Warwick, Vase, 5 In., Pair	40.00
Warwick, Vase, Cobalt Blue, 9 In., Pair	425.00
Warwick, Vase, Cornucopia, Cobalt Blue, 9 In.	215.00
Waverly, Compote, Footed, 6 In.	10.00
Waverly, Relish, 2 Sections, Oval	25.00
Waverly, Salt & Pepper, Plastic Tops	39.50
Waverly, Tray, Imperial, 14 In.	30.00
Winged Scroll, Cruet, Gold Trim, Emerald, Original Stopper	265.00 To 350.00
Winged Scroll, Powder Box, Covered, Emerald, Gold Trim	85.00
Winged Scroll, Spooner, Emerald	55.00
Winged Scroll, Sugar & Creamer, Covered, Gold Trim, Emerald	155.00
Winged Scroll, Sugar, Covered, Emerald	65.00
Yeoman, Bowl, 8 In.	35.00
Yeoman, Candelabrum, Sahara, Marked, 20 1/2 In.	395.00
Yeoman, Cruet, Flamingo, 4 Oz.	75.00
Yeoman, Cup & Saucer, Flamingo	12.00 To 17.50
Yeoman, Dish, Banana Split, Footed, Moongleam	35.00
Yeoman, Dish, Cheese, Footed, Flamingo	55.00
Yeoman, Goblet, Sahara	15.00
Yeoman, Sandwich Plate, Gold Overlay, 10 1/2 In.	50.00
Zodiac, Bowl, Imperial, Footed	50.00
Zodiac, Candy Jar, Covered, Marked, Tall	60.00
Zodiac, Nappy	27.50
Zodiac, Plate, 8 In.	23.00

HEREND, see Fischer

Gebruder Heubach, a German firm working from 1820 to 1925, is best known for bisque dolls and doll heads, their principal products. They also manufactured bisque figurines, including piano babies, beginning in the 1880s, and glazed figurines in the 1900s. Dolls are not listed here, but are listed in the doll section.

HEUBACH, Bank, Pig, Drinks From Bottle, Bisque	30.00
Dish, Indian, Dancing, Green Jasperware, Rising Sun Mark, 4 1/4 In.	110.00

HEUBACH, DOLL, see Doll, Gebruder Heubach

Figurine, Baby Lying On Back, 12 In. 375.00
Figurine, Black Baby, Sitting, White Suit, Blue Dots, 4 In. 300.00
Figurine, Black Boy, Polkadot Romper, 5 In. 800.00
Figurine, Boy & Girl, Fishing, 11 1/2 In., Pair 250.00
Figurine, Boy With Cigar, Girl Holding Doll, Marked, 11 In., Pair 350.00
Figurine, Boy, Blue Shift, White Apron, Throwing Ball, 12 In. 500.00
Figurine, Boy, Fez, Glasses & Cigar, Seated, 15 In. 200.00
Figurine, Boy, Holding Chicken, CH Mark, 8 In. 52.00
Figurine, Boy, Sitting On Basket, Playing Drum, Marked, 11 1/2 In. 325.00
Figurine, Boy, Sitting, Wicker Chair, Smoking Cigar, Signed, 14 In. 380.00
Figurine, Boy, Standing, Holding Huge Umbrella, 8 In. 115.00
Figurine, Dog, Beagle, Green Mark, 4 In. 85.00
Figurine, Dog, Puppy With Towel Wrapped Around Head 90.00
Figurine, Dog, Sad-Looking, Lop-Eared, Bisque, Gray & White, 6 In. 235.00
Figurine, Dog, Shaggy, On Hind Legs, Red Collar, Marked, 7 1/4 In. 300.00
Figurine, Dog, Sitting Up, Long Hair, Intaglio Eyes, Marked, 6 In. 75.00
Figurine, Dutch Boy & Girl, 4 3/4 In., Pair 150.00
Figurine, Dutch Couple, Kissing, Marked, 4 1/2 In. 75.00
Figurine, Girl, Dancing, Blond Hair, Pink Dress, 15 In. 725.00
Figurine, Girl, Holding Basket, Marked, 7 In. 85.00
Figurine, Girl, Holding Rabbit, Bisque, 9 1/2 In. 150.00
Figurine, Rabbit Girl, With Egg, Bisque, Signed 145.00
Figurine, Rope Jumpers, Kate Greenaway Children, 9 1/4 In., Pair 600.00
Figurine, Woman, Blue Skirt, Gold Florets, Yellow Gloves, 11 In. 160.00
Plaque, Scalloped, Green & White, 4 3/4 In. 20.00

Higbee glass was made by the J. B. Higbee Company of Bridgeville, Pennsylvania, about 1900. Tablewares were made and it is possible to assemble a full set of dishes and goblets in some Higbee patterns. Most of the glass was clear, not colored.

HIGBEE, see also Pressed Glass
HIGBEE, Berry Set, Child's, Flute, Marked, 5 Piece 45.00
Compote, Open, Yoke & Circle, 8 In. 15.00
Creamer, Paneled Thistle 22.50
Dish, Scalloped Rim, Concave Sides, Marked, 1 3/4 In. 8.00
Salt, Style Pattern, Scalloped, Concave Sides, 1 3/4 In. 8.00
Sugar, Bear, Covered 250.00
Syrup, Tacoma 47.50
Vase, Flared, 5 In. 22.00
Wine, Hawaiian Lei, Marked 10.00
HISTORIC BLUE, see Adams; Clews; Ridgway; Staffordshire

Hobnail glass is a pattern of glass with bumps in an allover pattern. Dozens of hobnail patterns and variants have been made. Clear, colored, and opalescent hobnail have been made and are being reproduced. Other pieces of hobnail are also listed under Carnival Glass, Hobnail.

HOBNAIL, see also Fenton; Francisware
HOBNAIL, Ashtray, Belmont Hills Country Club, 5 In. 35.00
Compote, Flint 45.00
Condiment Set, Child's, English, 4 Piece 42.50
Cordial 20.00
Creamer, Child's 50.00
Cruet, Cranberry Opalescent, Original Stopper, Hobb 275.00
Pitcher, Amber, Cased, Hobbs 150.00
Pitcher, Water, Thumbprint Base 20.00
Punch Cup, Sapphire Blue 5.00
Salt, Closely Spaced Hobbs, Rounded Points, 2 In. 6.00
Spooner, Opalescent, Northwood 20.00

Holly amber, or golden agate, glass was made by the Indiana Tumbler and Goblet Company of Greentown, Indiana from January 1, 1903, to June 13, 1903. It is a pressed glass pattern featuring holly leaves in the amber–shaded glass. The glass was made with shadings that range from creamy opalescent to brown–amber.

HOLLY AMBER, Butter, Covered, 7 In.	1000.00
Cake Plate, Stemmed	1800.00
Cruet	200.00
Sauce, 4 1/4 In.	275.00
Sherbet, 4 3/4 In.	295.00 To 350.00
Tray, Round	595.00
Tumbler, Beaded	425.00
Vase, 6 In.	425.00

Hopalong Cassidy was named William Lawrence Boyd when he was born in Cambridge, Ohio, in 1895. His first movie appearance was in 1919, but the first Hopalong Cassidy film was not until 1934. Sixty–six films were made. In 1948, William Boyd purchased the television rights to the movies, then later made fifty–two new programs. In the 1950s, Hopalong Cassidy was seen in comics, records, toys, and other products. Boyd died in 1972.

HOPALONG CASSIDY, Bank	22.00
Barrette, Girl's, Brass	35.00
Bedspread	145.00
Binoculars, Gray Metal, Hoppy Decals	35.00
Book, Pop–Up, Doubleday, 1950	50.00
Bottle, Hair Trainer, 4 Oz.	5.00
Camera, Box	45.00
Cap Pistol & Holster, Brown Leather, Metal, Nicholas	20.00
Chair, T.V.	65.00
Clock, Alarm, 1950s	120.00
Coffee Cup	12.00
Cookie Jar, Cookie Corral, Hoppy & Horse, Ranch, Ceramic	250.00
Crayon & Stencil Set, Hoppy, Box	65.00
Curtains	30.00
Dart Board, Magnetic, Box	65.00
Dominoes, Unused, Box, 1950	50.00
Film, Border Justice, Castle Films, 16 Mm	40.00
Game, Board, Milton Bradley, 1950	35.00
Glass, Juice	20.00
Gun, Zoomerang	18.00
Handbill, Stick To Your Guns, With Bill Boyd	25.00
Hat, Black Felt, No Chin String	35.00
Horseshoe, Good Luck	15.00
Knife, Pocket	28.00
Lamp, Revolving Action, 1949	125.00
Lunch Box & Thermos	35.00 To 60.00
Member Card, Hoppy Trooper Club, Secret Code	15.00
Mirror, Metal Frame, 4 X 6 In.	18.00
Money Clip, Bar	20.00
Mug	18.00

When the weather is bad, the auction will probably be good. Brave storms and attend the auctions in bad weather when the crowds are small and the prices low.

Mug, Black Design, Milk Glass 10.00
Mug, Red 10.00
Mug, Scene & Logo, Blue Milk Glass 6.00
Neckerchief, Black Satin 20.00
Night–Light, Aladdin, Pistol, Holster, Decal ....95.00 To 125.00
Pen, Fountain 40.00
Pennant, White, Black Felt, 19 1/2 In. 18.00
Pillow Case 20.00
Pin, Daily News, Dated 1950, William Boyd 11.00
Pin, Hawthorne Melody 13.00
Plate, Ceramic 25.00
Pogo Stick 85.00
Poster, Lobby, Strange Gamble, 1947 .... 95.00
Poster, Movie, Doomed Caravan, Color Litho, 1940 .... 175.00
Puzzle, In Envelope 20.00
Puzzle, Original Box, Set of 3 .... 35.00
Radio, Arvin, Red & Silver 125.00
Radio, Black Case 75.00
Ring, Signet, 1940s 20.00
Rug, Bedside, Chenille 65.00
Sheet Music, Knights of The Range, 1939 .... 16.00
Sheet Music, Renegade Trail, 1939 .... 16.00
Sheet Music, Secrets of The Wasteland, 1951 .... 16.00
Slate Board 25.00
Spurs 12.00
Sunglasses 20.00
Target, 2 Sides, Tin, 1950 .... 15.00
Thermos .... 10.00 To 23.00
Thermos, 1950 .... 20.00
Tie, Bolero 8.00
Toy, Rocking Horse, Windup, Tin, Marx 185.00
Tumbler, Milk Glass, Breakfast, Lunch & Dinner, Set of 3 .... 65.00
Tumbler, Welch's, 6 Piece 20.00
Woodburning Set, Hoppy, Box 95.00
Wristwatch, Original Band, Engraved .... 55.00 To 75.00

Howdy Doody and Buffalo Bob were the main characters in a children's series televised from 1947 to 1960. Howdy was a redheaded puppet. The series became popular with college students in the late 1970s when Buffalo Bob began to lecture on the campuses.

HOWDY DOODY, Bank, Bust of Howdy, Ceramic 75.00
Beanie, Cloth 12.00
Book, Little Golden Book 12.00
Clock, Tell Time 45.00
Crayon Set, Milton Bradley 65.00
Dilly Dally, Box, Small 12.00
Doll, Box, 6 1/2 In. 55.00
Doll, Stuffed Body, Composition Head, 20 In. 145.00
Figures, Plastic, Beehlen Art, Box, 5 Piece 55.00
Game, Card, Complete 10.00
Game, T.V., 1949 .... 18.00
Glass, Jelly, Welch's, 1953, Set of 6 .... 30.00
Howdy's Own Game, 1949 .... 40.00
Key Chain, Figural, Plastic 5.00
Lamp 37.00
Lunch Box, Tin 20.00
Marionette, Composition 75.00
Marionette, Composition, 1940s, 17 In. 120.00
Marionette, Princess, From Howdy Doody Show 45.00
Night–Light, Figural .... 45.00 To 58.00
Paint Set, Box, Kagan, Milton Bradley 60.00
Pencil 15.00
Phonograph Doodle, Box 125.00

Puppet, At NBC Microphone, Jointed, Kohner, Box	65.00
Puppet, Clarabelle, String, Red & White Suit, 15 In.	75.00
Puppet, Mr.Bluster	65.00
Puppet, Original Clothes, Mouth Opens, 25 In.	35.00
Puppet, Plastic Head, Hands, Pull String, NBC, 1973, 26 In.	20.00
Puppet, Plastic, Howdy Doody Characters, Display Card	28.00
Record Player	95.00
Ring, Flashlight, Brass, Pink Howdy Head	60.00
Ring, Flub–A–Dub Flip, Original Package	20.00
Ring, Poll Parrot, Raised Head	40.00
Shoe Polish, Bottle, Mid–1950s, 5 In.	25.00
Sign, Ice Cream	12.50
T–Shirt	15.00
Thermos, Red Plastic, 4 Sides, Decal, NBC, No Cap	5.00
Top, Tin	25.00
Toy, Bubble Pipe, Plastic, Yellow	12.00
Toy, Phono–Doodle, Box	125.00
Toy, Pully, Kohner Bros., Box	80.00
Toy, Put–In Head, 3–D Toy, Makes 100 Different Faces	50.00
Toy, Trapeze, Tin Litho, Spring, Arnold West, W.Ger., 12 In.	375.00
Wrapper, Ice Cream	10.00

Hull pottery was made in Crooksville, Ohio, from 1905. Addis E. Hull bought the Acme Pottery Company and started making ceramic wares. In 1917, A. E. Hull Pottery began making art pottery as well as the commercial wares. For a short time, 1921 to 1929, the firm also sold pottery imported from Europe. The dinnerwares of the 1940s, including the Little Red Riding Hood line, the high gloss artwares of the 1950s, and the matte wares of the 1940s, are all popular with collectors. The firm is still in business.

HULL, Ashtray, Deer Center, Brown	10.00
Bank, Little Red Riding Hood	225.00
Bank, Porky Pig, Yellow, Blue, Rose, 5 In.	23.00
Basket, Blossom Flite	13.00
Basket, Bow Knot, 8 1/2 In.	40.00
Basket, Dogwood, 7 1/2 In.	40.00
Basket, Ebb Tide, Green To Pink, 16 1/2 X 11 In.	22.00
Basket, Tulip, 9 In.	50.00
Basket, Woodland, 8 3/4 In.	25.00
Bowl, Pony, Figural	18.00
Butter, Cherry Wreath, Enameled Cherries, Gold Trim, Covered	120.00
Butter, Little Red Riding Hood, Covered	100.00 To 110.00
Candleholder, Serenade, Pink, 6 1/2 In., Pair	32.00
Candy Dish, Serenade, Covered	42.00
Canister Set, Little Red Riding Hood, 5 Piece	700.00
Canister, Coffee, Little Red Riding Hood	200.00 To 235.00
Canister, Flour, Little Red Riding Hood	250.00
Casserole, Sunglow	17.00
Compote, Magnolia, 12 1/2 In.	35.00
Console Set, Butterfly, 3 Piece	38.00
Console Set, Gray & Pink Pattern, 3 Piece	30.00
Console Set, Magnolia, 3 Piece	55.00
Console Set, Open Rose, 3 Piece	150.00
Console Set, Parchment & Pine, 3 Piece	35.00
Cookie Jar, Big Apple	24.00
Cookie Jar, Goldilocks	85.00
Cookie Jar, Little Red Riding Hood, Open Basket	60.00 To 98.00
Cookie Jar, Monk, Thou Shalt Not Steal	15.00
Cornucopia, Athena, Green, 8 1/2 In.	15.00
Cornucopia, Bow Knot, 7 1/2 In.	33.00 To 45.00
Cornucopia, Bow Knot, Double	65.00
Cornucopia, Butterfly, 10 1/2 In.	35.00
Cornucopia, Calla Lily	36.00

Cornucopia, Magnolia, Matte, 8 1/2 In.	15.00
Cornucopia, Open Rose, 8 1/2 In.	25.00
Cornucopia, Parchment & Pine, 22 In.	55.00
Cornucopia, Pink, 11 In.	22.00
Cornucopia, Wild Flower, 8 1/2 In.	32.50
Cornucopia, Woodland, 11 In.	20.00
Creamer, Little Red Riding Hood	35.00 To 65.00
Creamer, Serenade, Pink	5.00
Ewer, Bow Knot, 5 1/2 In.	25.00
Ewer, Butterfly, 13 In.	48.00
Ewer, Calla Lily, 10 In.	75.00
Ewer, Dogwood, 11 1/2 In.	75.00
Ewer, Ebb Tide, Coral & Turquoise, 14 In.	22.00
Ewer, Mardi Gras	26.00
Ewer, Open Rose, 13 In.	175.00
Ewer, Rosella, Pink, 6 1/2 In.	20.00
Ewer, Royal Woodland, 13 1/2 In.	60.00
Ewer, Serenade, Gold Trim	40.00
Ewer, Tulip, 13 In.	65.00
Ewer, Wild Flower, 5 1/2 In.	16.00
Ewer, Woodland, Chartreuse, Marked, 5 1/2 In.	3.00
Jam Jar, Little Red Riding Hood, Wolf Cover	300.00
Jar, Little Red Riding Hood, Covered, 9 1/4 In.	95.00
Jardiniere, Bow Knot, 9 3/8 In.	75.00
Lantern, Parrot	15.00
Match Holder, Little Red Riding Hood	295.00 To 375.00
Mustard, Little Red Riding Hood	75.00
Mustard, Little Red Riding Hood, Spoon	120.00 To 135.00
Pitcher, Little Red Riding Hood, 8 In.	125.00
Pitcher, Little Red Riding Hood, Side Spout, 6 1/2 In.	115.00
Pitcher, Serenade, Blue, 10 1/2 In.	25.00
Pitcher, Water, Serenade	35.00
Planter, Bow Knot, Underplate, Blue, Pink Matte, 6 1/2 In.	30.00
Planter, Butterfly	25.00
Planter, Dachshund, 15 In.	18.00
Planter, Goose, Pink, Gray Green, Polka Dot Kerchief, No.74, Large	30.00
Planter, Kitten, Pink, 7 1/2 In.	15.00
Planter, Parrot Pulling Cart	16.00
Planter, Swan	25.00
Rose Bowl, Iris, 7 In.	36.00
Salt & Pepper, Little Red Riding Hood, Large	22.50 To 27.00
Salt & Pepper, Little Red Riding Hood, Small	15.00 To 25.00
Saltshaker, Little Red Riding Hood, 4 1/2 In.	50.00
Sugar & Creamer, Bow Knot	20.00
Sugar & Creamer, Cherry Wreath, Enameled Cherries, Gold Trim	55.00
Sugar & Creamer, Little Red Riding Hood, Large	65.00
Sugar & Creamer, Little Red Riding Hood, Small	55.00
Teapot, Blossom Flite, With Sugar & Creamer	45.00
Teapot, Little Red Riding Hood	75.00 To 125.00
Teapot, Magnolia	65.00
Teapot, Water Lily	30.00
Vase, Bow Knot, 8 1/2 In.	35.00
Vase, Continental, Persimmon, 14 In.	18.00
Vase, Cornucopia, Magnolia, Matte, 9 In., Pair	55.00
Vase, Ebb Tide, 10 In.	15.00
Vase, Ebb Tide, Angelfish	35.00
Vase, Magnolia, 5 In.	10.00
Vase, Magnolia, 6 1/4 In.	18.00
Vase, Magnolia, 8 1/2 In.	25.00 To 30.00
Vase, Magnolia, Matte, 12 1/2 In.	24.00
Vase, Magnolia, Matte, 15 In.	145.00
Vase, Matte Pastels, 8 1/2 In.	27.50
Vase, Open Rose, 4 In.	12.00
Vase, Orchid, 6 In.	17.00

Vase, Parchment & Pine, 12 In., Pair 35.00
Vase, Ribbed, Tan, 12 In. 14.00
Vase, Rosella, Pink, 8 1/2 In. 15.00
Vase, Royal Ebb Tide, 7 In. 10.00
Vase, Serenade, Yellow 14.00
Vase, Tulip, 16 In. 235.00
Vase, Water Lily, 9 1/2 In. .... 25.00 To 38.50
Vase, Water Lily, Pink Top, Blue Bottom, 5 1/2 In. 20.00
Vase, Wild Flower, 3 Colors, 8 1/2 In. 20.00
Vase, Wild Flower, 9 In. 40.00
Vase, Wild Flower, Matte, 7 1/2 In. 40.00
Vase, Woodland, Blue Shaded To Gray, Handles, 11 In. 25.00
Wall Pocket, Bow Knot .... 20.00 To 25.00
Wall Pocket, Gold Trim 20.00
Wall Pocket, Little Red Riding Hood .... 145.00 To 165.00
Wall Pocket, Open Rose 40.00
Wall Pocket, Sunglow, Pink 15.00
Wall Pocket, Sunglow, Whisk Broom 10.00
Wall Pocket, Woodland, 7 1/2 In. 20.00
Water Set, Cherry Wreath, Enameled Cherries, Gold Trim, 7 Piece 120.00

Hummel figurines, based on the drawings of Berta Hummel, are made by the W. Goebel Porzellanfabrik of Oeslau, Germany, now Rodenthal, West Germany. They were first made in 1934. The mark has changed through the years. The following are the approximate dates for each of the marks: "Crown" mark, 1935 to 1949; "U. S. Zone, Germany," 1946 to 1948; "West Germany," after 1949; "full bee," with variations, 1950 to 1959; "stylized bee," 1960 to 1972; "three line mark," 1968 to 1979; "vee over gee," 1972 to 1979; "new mark," 1979 to present.

HUMMEL, Butter Tub, Covered, Embossed Daisy 85.00
Calendar, 1960 .... 35.00
Calendar, 1965 .... 22.00 To 35.00
Calendar, 1978 .... 8.00
Figurine, No. 1, Puppy Love, Three Line Mark 98.00
Figurine, No. 2/II, Little Fiddler, Stylized Bee 775.00
Figurine, No. 5, Strolling Along, Three Line Mark 92.00
Figurine, No. 6/0, Sensitive Hunter, Crown Mark 375.00
Figurine, No. 6/II, Sensitive Hunter, Stylized Bee 295.00
Figurine, No. 7/II, Merry Wanderer, Full Bee 750.00
Figurine, No. 7/III, Merry Wanderer, Crown Mark 2000.00
Figurine, No. 9, Begging His Share, Without Hole, Full Bee 400.00
Figurine, No. 10/I, Flower Madonna, Stylized Bee 170.00
Figurine, No. 11/0, Merry Wanderer, Full Bee 175.00
Figurine, No. 12/2/0, Chimney Sweep, Three Line Mark 49.00
Figurine, No. 13/0, Meditation, Three Line Mark 98.00
Figurine, No. 18, Christ Child, Stylized Bee 64.00
Figurine, No. 20, Prayer Before Battle, Three Line Mark 92.00
Figurine, No. 21/II, Heavenly Angel, Three Line Mark 230.00
Figurine, No. 28/II, Wayside Devotion, Full Bee 285.00
Figurine, No. 43, March Winds, Full Bee .... 150.00 To 160.00
Figurine, No. 46/0, Madonna, Without Halo, Full Bee, 11 In. 65.00
Figurine, No. 47/0, Goose Girl, Stylized Bee 85.00
Figurine, No. 49/3/0, To Market, Three Line Mark 98.00
Figurine, No. 50/0, Volunteers, Full Bee 280.00
Figurine, No. 50/I, Volunteers, Crown Mark 1330.00
Figurine, No. 51/0, Village Boy, Stylized Bee 115.00
Figurine, No. 51/3/0, Village Boy, Three Line Mark 49.00
Figurine, No. 53, Joyful, Full Bee 100.00
Figurine, No. 53, Joyful, Three Line Mark 55.00
Figurine, No. 56/A, Culprits, Full Bee .... 160.00 To 210.00
Figurine, No. 57/0, Chick Girl, New Mark 41.00
Figurine, No. 57/0, Chick Girl, Three Line Mark 82.00
Figurine, No. 58/0, Playmates, Crown Mark 268.00

Figurine, No. 58/0, Playmates, New Mark	82.00
Figurine, No. 59, Skier, Three Line Mark	110.00
Figurine, No. 66, Farm Boy, Full Bee	220.00
Figurine, No. 66, Farm Boy, Stylized Bee	120.00
Figurine, No. 68/0, Lost Sheep, Stylized Bee	98.00
Figurine, No. 68/2/0, Lost Sheep, New Mark	68.00
Figurine, No. 71, Stormy Weather, Full Bee	310.00 To 325.00
Figurine, No. 73, Little Helper, Full Bee	105.00
Figurine, No. 73, Little Helper, Three Line Mark	68.00
Figurine, No. 74, Little Gardener, Stylized Bee	65.00 To 79.00
Figurine, No. 79, Globe Trotter, Full Bee	110.00
Figurine, No. 80, Little Scholar, Stylized Bee	92.00
Figurine, No. 82/2/0, School Boy, New Mark	68.00
Figurine, No. 84/0, Worship, Full Bee	220.00
Figurine, No. 84/V, Worship, Three Line Mark	775.00
Figurine, No. 87, For Father, Stylized Bee	105.00
Figurine, No. 88/II, Heavenly Protection, Stylized Bee	330.00
Figurine, No. 89/I, Little Cellist, Stylized Bee	150.00
Figurine, No. 94/3/0, Surprise, Three Line Mark	82.00
Figurine, No. 99, Eventide, Three Line Mark	155.00
Figurine, No.110/I, Let's Sing, Three Line Mark	92.00
Figurine, No.111/3/0, Wayside Harmony, Full Bee	155.00
Figurine, No.112/3/0, Just Resting, Stylized Bee	79.00
Figurine, No.112/I, Just Resting, Three Line Mark	89.00
Figurine, No.119, Postman, Stylized Bee	105.00 To 150.00
Figurine, No.123, Max & Moritz, Full Bee	123.00
Figurine, No.124/0, Hello, Stylized Bee	98.00
Figurine, No.124/I, Hello, Full Bee	175.00
Figurine, No.128, Baker, Three Line Mark	92.00
Figurine, No.129, Band Leader, Full Bee	165.00
Figurine, No.129, Band Leader, Three Line Mark	110.00
Figurine, No.132, Star Gazer, Full Bee	200.00
Figurine, No.133, Mother's Helper, Full Bee	200.00
Figurine, No.141/V, Apple Tree Girl, Stylized Bee	660.00
Figurine, No.142/I, Apple Tree Boy, Full Bee	250.00
Figurine, No.143/0, Boots, Stylized Bee	65.00
Figurine, No.150/2/0, Happy Days, Stylized Bee	62.00
Figurine, No.152/A/0, Umbrella Girl, Stylized Bee	330.00
Figurine, No.152/B/0, Umbrella Girl, Three Line Mark	300.00
Figurine, No.170/III, School Boys, Stylized Bee	1000.00
Figurine, No.172, Festival Harmony, Angel, Mandolin, Stylized Bee	900.00
Figurine, No.177/III, School Girls, Stylized Bee	1000.00
Figurine, No.178, Photographer, Three Line Mark	130.00
Figurine, No.179, Coquettes, Stylized Bee	150.00
Figurine, No.182, Good Friends, Stylized Bee	75.00
Figurine, No.183, Forest Shrine, Stylized Bee	340.00
Figurine, No.188, Celestial Musician, Stylized Bee	165.00
Figurine, No.195/2/0, Barnyard Hero, Full Bee	200.00
Figurine, No.195/2/0, Barnyard Hero, Vee Over Gee	85.00
Figurine, No.196/I, Telling Her Secret, Stylized Bee	333.00
Figurine, No.197/II/0, Telling Her Secret, Full Bee	150.00
Figurine, No.198, Home From Market, Full Bee	300.00
Figurine, No.199, Feeding Time, Full Bee	278.00 To 280.00
Figurine, No.200/0, Little Goat Herder, Full Bee	225.00
Figurine, No.203/II, Signs of Spring, Full Bee	225.00
Figurine, No.214, Nativity Set, Plus Stable, 1951, 18 Piece	1500.00
Figurine, No.214/L, Moor King, Stylized Bee	105.00
Figurine, No.217, Boy With Toothache, Three Line Mark	75.00
Figurine, No.218/2/0, Birthday Serenade, Full Bee	325.00
Figurine, No.226, Mail Coach, Stylized Bee	425.00
Figurine, No.226, Mail Coach, Three Line Mark	330.00
Figurine, No.240, Little Drummer, Three Line Mark	60.00
Figurine, No.260, Nativity Set, With Stable	3600.00
Figurine, No.305, The Builder, Three Line Mark	97.00

Figurine, No.307, Good Hunting, Full Bee	1750.00
Figurine, No.321, Wash Day, Three Line Mark	118.00
Figurine, No.322, Little Pharmacist, Three Line Mark	64.00
Figurine, No.333, Blessed Event, Three Line Mark	398.00
Figurine, No.347, Adventure Bound, Three Line Mark	2500.00
Figurine, No.348, Ring Around The Rosie, Three Line Mark	1600.00
Figurine, No.351, The Botanist, New Mark	110.00
Figurine, No.352, Sweet Greetings, New Mark	110.00
Figurine, No.355, Autumn Harvest, New Mark	110.00
Figurine, No.358, Shining Light, New Mark	52.00
Figurine, No.359, Tuneful Angel, Three Line Mark	52.00
Figurine, No.366, Flying Angel, New Mark	68.00
Figurine, No.367, Busy Student, Three Line Mark	90.00
Figurine, No.369, Follow The Leader, Three Line Mark	550.00
Figurine, No.378, Easter Greetings, New Mark	110.00
Figurine, No.383, Going Home, New Mark	155.00
Figurine, No.386, On Secret Path, New Mark	140.00
Figurine, No.389, Girl With Sheet Music, New Mark	38.00
Plaque, No. 30/A & 30/B, Ba–Bee Rings, Crown Mark	494.00
Plaque, No. 30/A, Ba–Bee Rings, Full Bee	68.00
Plaque, No.125, Vacation Time, Stylized Bee	125.00
Plaque, No.690, Smiling Through, Vee Over Gee	80.00
Plate, Anniversary, 1971	140.00
Plate, Anniversary, 1985	150.00
Plate, Annual, 1971	510.00 To 675.00
Plate, Annual, 1972	45.00
Plate, Annual, 1973	100.00
Plate, Annual, 1974	60.00
Plate, Annual, 1982	85.00
Plate, Annual, 1983	99.00

LORENZ
HUTSCHEN REUTER

GERMANY

Hutschenreuther Porcelain Company of Selb, Germany, was established in 1814 and is still working. The company makes fine quality porcelain dinnerwares and figurines. The mark has changed through the years, but the name and the lion insignia appear in most versions.

HUTSCHENREUTHER, Ashtray, Peter Pan, Legs Extended, 5 1/4 In.	145.00
Dinner Set, Maple Leaf, 51 Piece	650.00
Figurine, Bulldog, Sitting, Tan & Brown, 4 X 3 1/2 In.	110.00
Figurine, Elephant, 8 1/2 In.	80.00
Figurine, Elephant, 9 1/2 In.	48.00
Figurine, Fawn, No.2137, 5 X 4 In.	425.00
Figurine, Man Kissing Woman Artist, Artist Mark, 9 In.	195.00
Figurine, Naked Putti With Pipes, 1920, 5 In.	125.00 To 150.00
Figurine, Nude, Dancing, Art Deco, Green Mark	110.00
Figurine, Nude, On Gold Ball, White, 1930	165.00 To 190.00
Figurine, Nude, Playing Flute, Dog, Art Deco, Green Mark	160.00
Figurine, Penguin, 5 In.	45.00
Ginger Jar, Cobalt Blue	95.00
Plate, C.1925, 10 1/2 In., 11 Piece	775.00
Plate, Sparrows, Gunther Granget, 1972	125.00
Salt & Pepper, Figural, Schnauzers, Gray, 6 1/4 X 7 In.	180.00
Tea Set, Child's, 15 Piece	110.00

An icon is a special, revered picture of Jesus, Mary, or a saint. These are usually Russian or Byzantine. The small icons collected today are made of wood and tin or precious metals. Many modern copies have been made in the old style and are being sold to unsuspecting tourists in Russia and Europe.

ICON, Christ Pantocrator, Sides of Saints, Silver Gilt, Enamel, 11 1/2 In.	3350.00
Crucifix Scene, 3–Part Folding, Brass, Russia, 19th Century, 15 In.	450.00
St.Andreas & Nadezhda, Brass, Enameled, Russian Writing, 3 X 2 In.	450.00
St.Nicholas, Miracle Worker, Scenes On Frame, Russian, 21 X 18 In.	2000.00

Imari patterns are named for the Japanese ware decorated with orange and blue stylized flowers. The design on the Japanese ware became so characteristic that the name "Imari" has come to mean any pattern of this type. It was copied by the European factories of the eighteenth and early nineteenth centuries.

IMARI, Bowl, Birds, Floral, Gold, 7 1/2 In.	35.00
Bowl, Deer & Double Gourd, 19th Century, 8 1/2 In.	165.00
Bowl, Fish, Bird & Floral Reserves, Cutout Base, 6 3/4 X 12 In.	350.00
Bowl, Floral Panels, Gold, Scalloped, 6 1/4 In.	60.00
Bowl, Iron Red, Gold Flowers, Trellis Diaper Border, 1725–40, 9 In.	660.00
Chamber Pot, Flowers, Trellis Diaper, Loop Handle, 1725, 9 5/8 In.	1200.00
Charger, Blue, Orange, Gold, Green, 1900s, 10 1/2 In.	69.00
Charger, Blue, Orange, Gold, Scalloped, Ribbed, 1880s, 13 1/2 In., Pair	1500.00
Chop Plate, Blossom Shape, 4 Sections, Floral, Diaper, 12 3/4 In.	150.00
Dish, Scenic Panels, Scalloped, Multicolor, Gold, 5 1/4 In.	40.00
Dish, Shell, Flying Birds, Cherry Blossoms, Red & Blue, C.1800	250.00
Ginger Jar, Animal Cover, Handles, Blue & White	215.00
Jar, Temple, Onion Finial, Domed Cover, Dragon, Japan, 27 In.	400.00
Jardiniere, Floral, Bird Reserves, Chysanthemum Ground, 81 X 21 In.	1700.00
Pitcher, Devil Face, 1820, 5 In.	200.00
Plate, European Figural Design, Diaper Border, C.1720, 9 In., Pair	2975.00
Plate, Polychrome Design, Gilt, 8 1/2 In.	60.00
Platter, Lobster, Floral & Geometric, Blue, White, 14 X 15 3/4 In.	120.00
Tureen, Covered, Sampans, Gilt Shell Handles, C.1740, 10 3/8 In.	1750.00
Vase, Bottle Shape, Early 18th Century, 9 In., Pair	742.50
Vase, C.1840, 12 In.	125.00
Vase, Dragon Handles, Blue & White, Square, 14 In.	185.00
Vase, Signed Zoshuntei, 19th Century, 8 In., Pair	375.00

**IMPE
RIAL**

Imperial Glass Corporation was founded in Bellaire, Ohio, in 1901. It became a division of Lenox, Inc., in 1977 and was sold to Arthur R. Lorch in 1981. It was sold again in 1982. It went bankrupt in 1982 and some of the molds and assets have been offered to other companies. The Imperial glass preferred by the collector is stretch glass, art glass, carnival glass, and the top-quality tablewares.

IMPERIAL, Ashtray & Match Holder, Leaf Shape, Grapes, 2 3/4 In., 2 Piece	15.00
Ashtray, Crystal, Round, 5 In.	8.00
Ashtray, Heart Shape, 4 1/2 In.	10.00
Ashtray, Round, 4 In.	8.00
Beaded Block, Sugar, Open, Pink	12.50
Bowl, Katy, Blue, 6 In.	14.00
Bowl, Katy, Blue, 8 1/2 In.	30.00
Box, Lion, Crystal Satin, Covered	95.00
Candlewick, Ashtray, 3 Piece	15.00
Candlewick, Bowl, 5 1/2 In.	9.00
Candlewick, Bowl, Bell Shape, 10 In.	25.00
Candlewick, Bowl, Float, 10 In.	20.00
Candlewick, Bowl, Heart Shape, 5 In.	10.00
Candlewick, Cake Plate, Birthday Candle	225.00
Candlewick, Cake Stand, Pedestal	60.00
Candlewick, Candleholder, Double, Pair	22.00 To 26.00
Candlewick, Candleholder, Single, Flower & Leaf Etch	10.00
Candlewick, Candlestick, Double, Pair	25.00
Candlewick, Candy Dish, Covered, 3 Sections	50.00
Candlewick, Champagne	17.00
Candlewick, Cigarette Set, 6 Piece	50.00
Candlewick, Coaster, Spoon Rest, 4 1/2 In.	9.00
Candlewick, Cocktail, 4 Oz.	20.00
Candlewick, Compote, 5 1/2 In.	17.50
Candlewick, Compote, Cheese, Low	20.00
Candlewick, Cup & Saucer	5.00
Candlewick, Cup & Saucer, Star Cut	16.00 To 18.00
Candlewick, Decanter, Stopper	180.00

Candlewick, Dish, Lemon 28.00
Candlewick, Figurine, Asiatic Pheasant, Amber 150.00
Candlewick, Goblet, 5 Oz. 16.00
Candlewick, Goblet, Water, 12 Oz., 7 1/2 In. 16.00
Candlewick, Gravy Boat, Underplate 70.00
Candlewick, Jug, 40 Oz. 225.00
Candlewick, Mayonnaise Set, 3 Piece 35.00
Candlewick, Nappy, 5 1/2 In. 13.00
Candlewick, Pitcher, Cocktail, 40 Oz. 145.00
Candlewick, Plate, 2 Handles, 10 In. 20.00
Candlewick, Plate, 7 In. 7.00
Candlewick, Plate, Bread & Butter .... 8.00 To 10.00
Candlewick, Plate, Etched Princess, 12 In. 50.00
Candlewick, Plate, Handles, 9 In. 15.00
Candlewick, Plate, Salad, 8 In. 10.00
Candlewick, Plate, Serving, Open Handle, Round, 11 1/2 In. 35.00
Candlewick, Platter, Oval, 13 In. 60.00
Candlewick, Punch Bowl, 12 Cups, Set 200.00
Candlewick, Punch Cup, Footed 7.50
Candlewick, Relish, 3 Feet 50.00
Candlewick, Relish, 4 Sections .... 10.00 To 28.00
Candlewick, Relish, Footed 50.00
Candlewick, Relish, Leaf Shape 15.00
Candlewick, Rose Bowl, Footed, 7 1/2 In. 140.00
Candlewick, Salt & Pepper 27.00
Candlewick, Salt & Pepper, Sterling Silver Tops 15.00
Candlewick, Salt, 16 Balls Around Rim, 2 1/8 In. 6.00
Candlewick, Sugar & Creamer .... 10.00 To 12.00
Candlewick, Tray, Circle Bottom, 10 In. 50.00
Candlewick, Tray, Handles, Round, 11 1/2 In. 17.00
Candlewick, Tumbler, 10 Oz. 14.00
Candlewick, Tumbler, 12 Oz. 16.00
Candlewick, Tumbler, Whiskey, 2 1/2 Oz. 12.00
Candlewick, Vase, Bud, 6 In. .... 20.00 To 40.00
Candlewick, Vase, Fan, 8 In. 20.00
Cape Cod, Bottle, Hot Saucer, With Tube 48.00
Cape Cod, Bowl, Handles, 9 In. 10.00
Cape Cod, Cake Plate, Birthday, Holes For Candles, 13 In. 155.00
Cape Cod, Candleholder, 2-Light, Pair 50.00
Cape Cod, Cocktail, 3 1/2 Oz. 10.00
Cape Cod, Compote, Footed, 4 1/4 X 6 In. 12.00
Cape Cod, Cruet, Pointed Stopper 50.00
Cape Cod, Figurine, Pig & 2 Piglets, Red 60.00
Cape Cod, Lamp, Hurricane, 9 In., 2 Piece 40.00
Cape Cod, Punch Set, Bowl, Ladle, Underplate, 10 Cups 135.00
Cape Cod, Salt & Pepper 10.00
Cape Cod, Sherbet, Tall, 6 Oz. 10.00
Dish, Duck Cover 8.00
Dubarry, Claret, 5 Oz. 30.00
Figurine, Madonna, Crystal 25.00
Figurine, Owl, Chocolate Slag, Marked, 7 In., 2 Piece 39.00
Figurine, Swan, Chocolate Slag, Open Back, Marked, 9 In. 45.00
Freehand, Vase, Bronze Iridescent, Gray Blue Interior, 11 In. 80.00
Freehand, Vase, Cobalt Blue, Hearts & Vines, Paper Label, 10 In. 250.00
Freehand, Vase, Drag Loop Design, Label, 11 1/2 In. 225.00
Freehand, Vase, Golden Bronze, Blue Interior, 11 1/2 In, ... 95.00
Freehand, Vase, Trailing Vine, Baluster Body, Label, 11 3/4 In. 325.00
Fruit Bowl, Swirl, Pink, Wide Silver Rim 55.00
Gaelic, Water Set, 7 Piece 110.00
Goose & Cat Tails, Console Set 150.00
Goose & Cat Tails, Goblet, Water 34.00
Grape, Pitcher, 6 In. 55.00
Rose of Sharon, Goblet, 12 Oz. 35.00
Rose of Sharon, Wine 32.00

Sugar Cane, Bowl, 6 1/2 In.	9.00
Valley Lily, Champagne, Sherbet, 4 Ball Stems, 6 Oz.	20.00
Valley Lily, Cocktail, 4 Oz.	21.00
Wildflower, Celery, Amber	50.00

> Indian Tree is a china pattern that was popular during the last half of the nineteenth century. It was copied from earlier Indian textile patterns that were very similar. The pattern includes the crooked branch of a tree and a partial landscape with exotic flowers and leaves. Green, blue, pink, and orange were the favored colors used in the design.

INDIAN TREE, Plate, 10 In.	15.00
Platter, Turkey	65.00

> Indian art from North America has attracted the collector for many years. Each tribe has its own distinctive designs and techniques. Baskets, jewelry, pottery, and leatherwork are of greatest collector interest. Eskimo art is listed in another section in this book.

INDIAN, Bag, Pipe, Sioux, Beaded, Fringed, Geometric Designs, C.1860	1100.00
Bag, Plains, Beaded, Turquoise Ground, Floral Design, 1915	350.00
Bag, Sled, Cree, Canadian, Moosehide, Beaded Reindeer Heads, Floral	2860.00
Bag, Yakima, Beaded, Flowers, Turquoise Ground	350.00
Bandolier, Northern Plains, Thunderbirds, Circles, Central Star	2750.00
Basket, Fish, Cherokee, 12 In.	150.00
Basket, Fish, Cherokee, Split Oak	135.00
Basket, Hoopa, Steps To The Mountain, 1910, 5 In.	160.00
Basket, Hopi, Coiled Yucca, C.1950, 8 In.	200.00
Basket, Hopi, Wicker, 3rd Mesa, 1900s, 9 X 9 N.	75.00
Basket, Klamath, 1910, 9 X 5 1/2 In.	125.00
Basket, Klamath, 7 X 4 1/2 In.	120.00
Basket, Koasati, Covered, Pine Needle & Raffia, C.1930, 4 X 2 In.	35.00
Basket, Maine, Sweet Grass, Acorn Shape, Miniature	45.00
Basket, Micmac, Wicker, Wall	45.00
Basket, Navajo, Wedding, Natural Dye Colors, 14 1/2 In.	395.00
Basket, Nootka, Covered, 3 1/2 In.	145.00
Basket, Northeast, Covered, Freehand Design, 14 X 14 X 9 In.	475.00
Basket, Papago, Deep Colors, 9 X 5 In.	95.00
Basket, Papago, Lid, Handle, Allover Brown Bird Design, 12 In.	135.00
Basket, Papago, Yucca & Martynia Geometric Design, 7 X 4 In.	45.00
Basket, Papago, Yucca, Black Martynia Stepped Design, 6 X 4 In.	35.00
Basket, Papaya, C.1900, 10 X 14 1/2 In.	325.00
Basket, Penobscot, Ash Splint & Sweet Grass, 4 X 6 1/2 In.	35.00
Basket, Pima, Willow & Martynia, Geometric Cross, 6 X 2 1/2 In.	45.00
Basket, Pima, Willow & Martynia, Horse Design, 4 X 2 In.	95.00
Basket, Siwash, 9 1/2 X 7 In.	97.50
Basket, Taghanic, 2 Handles, Double Wrapped Rim, Demijohn, 5 1/2 In.	125.00
Basket, Wasco, Hemp, Dyed Grass, Rawhide Rim, 4 1/2 X 5 1/2 In.	100.00
Basket, Washoe, Willow Coil, 8 1/2 X 4 In.	150.00
Basket, Woodland, Woven Splint, 11 1/2 X 4 1/2 In.	25.00
Basket, Woodland, Woven Splint, Domed Lid, Handle, 19 X 14 In.	500.00
Basket, Woodland, Woven Splint, Lid, Potato Print, 12 X 15 In.	75.00
Basket, Woodland, Woven Splint, Orange, Black Design, 12 In.	50.00
Basket, Woodland, Woven Splint, Potato Print, 15 X 22 In.	65.00
Basket, Woodland, Woven Splint, Round, 11 1/2 X 4 1/2 In.	25.00
Basket, Woodland, Woven Splint, Round, 13 1/2 X 8 In.	40.00
Blanket, Chimayo, Multicolored Southwestern Design, 50 X 86 In.	75.00
Blanket, Navajo, Germantown Chief's, Woven, Red, Purple, Black, White	3500.00
Blouse, Navajo, Deerskin, Fringed, Size 5–8	105.00
Bow Case, Cheyenne, Hide, Beaded & Fringed, Quiver	3100.00
Bowl, Catawba, Indian Chief Heads Each End, Sara Ayers, 13 In.	75.00
Bowl, Hopi, Black Polychrome Design, Dark Tan, 2 X 5 1/2 In.	70.00
Bowl, Hopi, Black, Red & Brown Polychrome, 2 3/4 In.	65.00
Bowl, Hopi, Red & Black Polychrome Design, Dated 1934, 3 X 4 In.	95.00
Bowl, San Ildefonso, Feather Design, Buff Ground, 7 1/4 X 4 In.	95.00

Bowl, San Ildefonso, Umber Geometric Design On Red, 8 3/4 In. 185.00
Box, Miwak, Birchbark Covered, Round, 7 /12 In. 90.00
Box, Storage, Northwest Coast, Wooden, Totem Eyes Painted Sides 2750.00
Breastplate, Woman's, Sioux, Dance, Quilled, Bead & Cowrie Strands 5300.00
Canoe, Penobscot, Birch, Quill Florals Design, C.1930, 15 1/2 In. 195.00
Canteen, Water, Hopi, Signed Fannie Nampeyo 90.00
Canteen, Zia, Black & Red, Cream Slip, 19th Century 1325.00
Canteen, Zia, Ceramic, 1910 .... 1250.00
Cradle Board, Apache 45.00
Cradle Board, Nez Perce 650.00
Cradle Board, With Doll, Blackfeet, Cloth, Cover, 22 In. 650.00
Cup, Hopi, Umber Band, Orange Slip, Edith Nash, 3 1/2 X 2 1/4 In. 75.00
Doll, Leather Clothing, Beaded Design, 1930s, 9 In. 40.00
Doll, Navajo, Handmade, Full Skirted, Beaded, 1940s 30.00
Doll, Plains, Cloth, Yarn Hair, Buckskin Clothing, 9 In. 110.00
Doll, Sioux, Rawhide Body & Dress, Beaded Yoke, Moccasins, 21 In. 805.00
Doll, Southern Plains, Beaded, Trade Cloth, Leather Face 550.00
Doll, Wooden Head, Leather Body, In Clay Pot, Miniature 26.00
Dress, Crow, Blue Trade Cloth, False Elk's Teeth Bodice, 1890 .... 2300.00
Dress, Crow, Cowrie Shell Design 200.00
Earrings, Pawn Zuni, Flower Dangle, 17 Turquoise Stones In Each 65.00
Fan, Cherokee, Beaded Handle, 12 In. 45.00
Fetish, Umbilical Cord, Turtle Shape, Stitch Beading, 1910, 5 In. 50.00
Figurine, Hopi, Owl, Carved Wood, 12 In., Pair 40.00
Figurine, Pueblo, Man, Primitive, Unglazed Clay, Mica Flecks, 6 In. 25.00
Gauntlets, Nez Perce, Floral Design On Buckskin, Fringe, 9 In. 75.00
Headband, Penobscot, Red Wool Trade Cloth, Floral, 21 In. 115.00
Headdress, Dyed Feather, 1899 & 1900 Silver Dollars, C.1930 .... 175.00
Headdress, Traditional Style, Loom Beaded Band, Feather, C.1945 .... 50.00
Holster, Ojibwa, Beaded Hide 3525.00
Hymnal, Choctaw, Leather Bound, 1872 .... 275.00
Jar, Acoma, Flaring Rounded Form, Design On White, 13 X 12 In. 2500.00
Jar, Santa Clara, Globular, Geometric, Signed Minnie, 5 X 4 In. 125.00
Jar, Southwest, Pottery, Birds, 11 In. 550.00
Jar, Zia, Geometric Zigzag Design, 36 X 11 In. 975.00
Jug, Water, Hopi, Black & Red Polychrome, Pauline Setalle, 4 In. 90.00
Leggings, Man's, Crow, Stroud Cloth, Beaded Buffalo Hide Strips 4675.00
Leggings, Sioux, Hide, Beaded, Pair 990.00
Maple Sap Catcher, Birchbark, Pegged, C.1800, 5 X 8 X 13 In. 220.00
Mask, Iroquois, Cornhusk 150.00
Mask, Northwest Coast, Braids, 1930s 1400.00
Moccasins, Iroquois, Beading On Vamp & Cuff, 6 1/4 In. 20.00
Moccasins, Sac, Anklets Attached, Beaded, C.1870 .... 75.00
Moccasins, Sioux, Beaded Geometric Cross, Early 1900s 75.00
Moccasins, Sioux, Multicolor Beaded Vamp, 10 1/2 In. 45.00
Moccasins, Sioux, Tab Style, Lazy Stitch, Blue & Red, C.1930 .... 195.00
Moccasins, Southern Cheyenne, Beaded, Fringed 495.00
Moose Calling Horn, Cone Shape, Birchbark, Peg, N.Y., 1800, 22 In. 150.00
Necklace & Earrings, Navajo, Double Squash Blossoms 225.00
Northwest Coast, Bowl, Ceremonial, Carved Elk Handle, 19 X 7 In. 775.00
Pin, Zuni, Silver, 30 Turquoise Stones, Signed On Back 95.00
Pipe, Cherokee, Incised Geometric Design 30.00
Pipe, Crow, Polished Greenstone, Late 1800s 125.00
Pitcher, Mohawk, Red, Design, Small 27.00
Plate, Hopi, Black & Red On Tan Polychrome, 6 1/2 In. 90.00
Pot, Acoma, Black Geometric On White, Birds, Handle, 6 1/2 In. 95.00
Pot, Cooking, Catawba, 3 Legs, Handles, C.1850 .... 225.00
Pot, Zia, Black & Red On Tan, Handles, 3 In. 65.00
Pouch, Northern Plains, Shoulder, Hide & Beaded Martingale Cloth 3850.00
Pouch, Seneca, Velvet, Glass Beadwork, C.1860 .... 75.00
Pouch, Tobacco, Apache, Translucent Beads, Designs, Fringe, 13 In. 275.00
Prayer Stick, Kickapoo, Mnemonic Symbols Both Sides, Maple 3575.00
Rattle, Northwest Coast, Raven 3850.00
Rattle, Peyote, Arapaho, Multicolor Striped, Handle, 15 1/2 In. 100.00

Rattle, Southern Plains, Turtle Shell & Rawhide, 18 In. 35.00
Rug, Navajo, Brown Spider Design, White Triangles, 68 1/2 X 44 In. 225.00
Rug, Navajo, Central Triangles On Red Field, 62 1/2 X 39 1/2 In. 150.00
Rug, Navajo, Ganado Diamond Design, Carded Wool, 41 X 52 In. 125.00
Rug, Navajo, Ganado Terrace Design, C.1930, 48 X 72 In. 225.00
Rug, Navajo, Grays, Ivory & Red, 38 X 66 In. 155.00
Rug, Navajo, Lightning Pattern, Hand Spun, Hand Dyed, 31 X 55 In. 550.00
Rug, Navajo, Orange & Red Dot Medallion, 4 X 4 Ft. 125.00
Rug, Navajo, Red, Brown, & Natural, 82 X 47 In. 255.00
Rug, Navajo, Stepped Design, Terrace Border, 6 X 9 Ft. 750.00
Rug, Navajo, Tan Crosses, Red, Tan Border, 3 Ft.8 In.X 2 Ft.6 In. 145.00
Rug, Navajo, Yeibachi Figures, 66 X 96 In. ....*Illus* 950.00
Rug, Navajo, Zigzag Designs, C.1900, 58 X 29 In. 185.00
Rug, Navajo, Zigzag Pattern, White V Accents, 4 Ft. 9 In. X 10 Ft. 400.00
Rug, Yei, Corn Dancers, 5 X 7 Ft. 200.00
Saddle Pad, Cheyenne, Lazy Stitch Beading, Hide, 28 X 47 In. 425.00
Serape, Mexican, Blue, Black, Red & Natural, Fringed, 56 X 74 In. 55.00
Sheath, Knife, Sioux 4400.00
Sheath, Knife, Sioux, Quilled Buckskin 220.00
Shirt, Plains, Buckskin, Beadwork On Yoke & Lapel 750.00
Snowshoes, Ojibway, Pair 100.00
Sword, Gauntlet, Pata, Scalloped Edge, 18th Century, 36 In.Blade 245.00
Tepèe, Hand Painted, Soft Leather, Large 375.00
Tobacco Bag, Apache, Beaded 125.00
Tobacco Bag, Sioux, Pipe–Keeper's, 1870–80 .... 1850.00
Tomahawk, Pipe, Pierced Steel Head, Wooden Shaft, Beaded Flag 4675.00
Totem Pole, Northwest Coast, Carved Cedar, Natural Finish, 20 Ft. 1550.00
Trade Beads, Clear Red & Blue Glass, Shell Disks, 1921, 29 In. 35.00
Tray, Jicarilla Apache, Winnowing, 1880s, 15 X 17 In. 135.00
Tray, Papago, Whirlwind Design, C.1930, 11 In. 140.00
Tray, Salish, 12 In. 135.00
Trousers, Iroquois, Beaded, Fringed Leather, Matching Belt, C.1880 .... 400.00
Vase, Acoma, Wedding, 2 Spouts, Twisted Handle, Geometrics, 13 In. 150.00
Vest, Child's, Plains, Beaded 225.00
Vest, Sioux, Beaded, Flags & Stars, Double 1350.00
War Club, Iroquois, Tin & Feather Dangle, Wooden, 21 In. 25.00
Watch Fob, Sioux, Beaded Hide, 1910, 6 1/2 In. 35.00

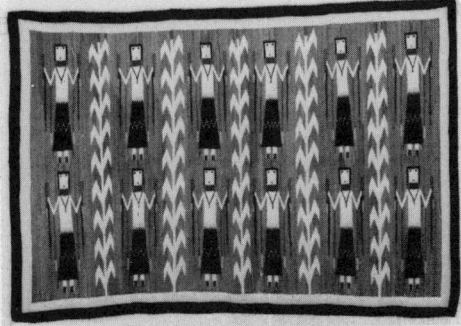

Indian, Rug, Navajo, Yeibachi Figures,
66 X 96 In.

Iron, Stand, Plant,
Battle–Axes, English,
19th Century, 47 In.

An inkstand was made to be placed on a desk. It held some type of container for ink, and possibly a sander, a pen tray, a pen, a holder for pounce, and even a candle to melt the sealing wax. Inkstands date to the eighteenth century and have been made of silver, copper, ceramics, and glass.

INKSTAND, Art Nouveau, Nude Lady, Brass	80.00
Bronze, Running Stag, Cut Glass Bottles, Hinged Top, 9 X 7 In.	160.00
Double, Center Elephant, Raised Trunk, 12 In.	55.00
Figure of Cherub, Paw Feet, Bronze, 19th Century, 8 3/4 In.	250.00
Gondola, 2 Wells, Art Nouveau Lid, Bronzed Metal, Large	80.00
Hinged Cup Inkwell, Papier–Mache, Enameled Design	100.00
Iron, 3 Graduated Pen Holders, 2 Wells, Pat.1879, 8 X 4 In.	115.00
Porcelain, Twin Wells, Bulbous Ribs, Tray, Red Flowers, 6 X 4 In.	85.00
Raised Leaf Bands Around Sides, England, Pewter, 19th Century	60.00
Running Stag, Emerald Eye, Cut Glass Wells, Brass Hinged Tops	220.00
Silver, 2 Cut Glass Bottles, Inscribed, Reily & Storer, 12 In.	1650.00

Inkwells, of course, held ink. Ready–made ink was first made about 1836 and was sold in bottles. The desk inkwell had a narrow hole so the pen would not slip inside. Pottery, glass, pewter, silver, and other materials were used to make inkwells. Look in other sections for more listings of inkwells.

INKWELL, Art Glass, Feather Design, Iridescent Blue & Purple	225.00
Art Nouveau, 2 Figural Birds, French, Brass, 4 X 8 In.	75.00
Art Nouveau, Nude Lady, Brass	60.00
Arts & Crafts, Hammered Copper, Gustave Stickley	350.00
Bakelite, Sengbusch, Maroon, Inverted, Pen	12.00
Beer Bottle Shape, Johann Hoff, Berlin, Crystal Well, Austria	50.00
Black, Gold Trim, Label, Silliman & Co., Wood, 2 1/2 In.	75.00
Blown, Aqua, Applied Foot, New York, 3 1/2 X 2 1/2 In.	200.00
Blue Glass, Square Holder Base	135.00
Cast Iron, Cauldron & Fire, Marble, Lid Hinges, 3 1/4 In.	35.00
Chandelier Pattern	60.00
Clear Dark Green Blown Molded, Bubbles, 1820–35, 2 1/2 In.	950.00
Crab Shape	52.50
Crystal Ball, On 3 Balls, Iridescent, Brass Hinged Lid, Victorian	169.00
Daisy & Button, Amber	145.00
Deer Hoof	25.00
Diamond, Blue	140.00
Dog, Bow At Neck, Hinged At Neck, Crystal	60.00
Dog, With Nursing Bottle, White Metal, Porcelain Insert, 3 In.	95.00
Double Cube, Blue	160.00
Double, Snail, Revolving Frame, Cast Iron	85.00
Glass Dome Top, Pat.1905, Pair	35.00
Glass, Keene, Olive Green	110.00
Greyhound, 1850, Staffordshire	185.00
Marble, 2 Pots, Brass Lids, 6 In.	35.00
Millefiori, Faceted, Letter P, Perthshire, 6 1/2 In.	290.00
Monkey, Ruby Eyed Pirate, Bronze	125.00
Old Lady Head, 1840, Staffordshire, 3 In.	195.00
Olive Amber, New England–Type Pitkin, Ribbed, C.1825, 2 1/2 In.	600.00
Oriental Design, Removable Well & Lid, Porcelain	85.00
Parrot, Hinged At Neck, Pot Metal	35.00
Porcelain, Pink, White, Gold, Attached To Leaf, Hinged Lid, 4 In.	45.00
Pottery, Yellow Glazed, Brown Geometric Design, English, Round	675.00
Pyramid Top, Blue Glass, Hinged Base, White Enamel, 2 X 3 In.	195.00
Reindeer Head, Antlers Hold 5 Pens, Cast Iron, Covered Insert	115.00
Ribbed Clear Glass, Star Band, Sterling Silver Floral Top, 1896	95.00
Single, Snail In Revolving Frame	45.00
Stamp Set, Ink, From Stamp Drawer, 5 Different Scenes, American	16.00
Stoneware, Drum Shape, Impressed C.Boynton, Troy, 1 3/4 X 4 In.	225.00
Teapot Type, Amethyst	260.00
Traveling, Brass, Leather, 1860s, English, 1 3/4 X 1 1/4 In.	195.00

Wooden, 2 Quill Holder, Original Cork Plug, Silliman, Round, 2 In. 40.00
World War I Soldier, Wells Each Side, Front Tray, Teplitz, 10 In. 75.00

Insulators of glass or pottery have been made for use on telegraph or telephone poles since 1844. Thousands of different styles of insulators have been made. Most common are those of clear or aqua glass, most desirable are the threadless types made from 1850 to 1870.

INSULATOR, Alaska Railroad, White Porcelain 13.00
American, No.134, Aqua 9.00
Cable, Hinged Top, Iron & Composition, Patent March '97 .... 14.00
Cable, No.3, Aqua 15.00
California, Yellow Helmet 350.00
Columbia, Aqua 45.00
Diamond, Light Olive 50.00
Double Diamond, Yellow, 2 Piece 10.00
Duquesne Keg, Blue 150.00
ECM, Cobalt Blue 375.00
Gayner, Aqua 6.00
H.G.Co., Sapphire Blue 70.00
Hemingray, Carnival 50.00
Hemingray, Deep Green 30.00
Hemingray, No. 4, Aqua 8.00
Hemingray, No. 9 .... 3.00
Hemingray, No.19, Cobalt Blue 55.00
Hemingray, No.20, Amber 65.00
Klondike Telegraph Line, Canadian Western Union 15.00
Manhattan, Blue 25.00
Marigold 20.00
Ramshorn, Brooks, Aqua Glass Insert 35.00
Threadless Pilgrim's Hat, Transcontinental R.R. 75.00
Whitall Tatum, Purple 9.00
    IRISH BELLEEK, see Belleek

Iron is a metal that has been used by man since prehistoric times. It is a popular metal for tools and decorative items like doorstops that need as much weight as possible. Items are listed here or under other appropriate headings such as Doorstop, Kitchen, or Tool. The tool that is used for ironing clothes, an iron, is listed under Kitchen, Iron; or Kitchen, Sadiron.

IRON, Ashtray, Griswold 20.00
Ashtray, Open Cupped Hands, Grapes, Leaves At Wrist 95.00
Baster, Griswold, Tite Top, Covered, Bail Handle, 1920, 10 X 4 In. 25.00
Bird Feeder, American Gothic Revival 605.00
Birdbath, Fiske 945.00
Boot Scraper, Dachshund 45.00
Boot Scraper, Horse Shape, Iron, Mounted On Board, 11 1/2 In. 195.00
Bootjack, Naughty Nellie 65.00
Bootjack, Naughty Nellie, Red & Gilt Paint 95.00
Box, Lock, Punched, Tooled Brass Face Plate, 6 1/2 In. 16.00
Candle Snuffer, 5 1/2 In. 20.00
Candle Snuffer, Scissors Type, Hand Forged 47.00
Candleholder, Tommy, Sticking, 7 3/4 In. 135.00
Candlestand, Tripod, Penny Feet, Adjustable Arm, 18th Century, 51 In. 4100.00
Candlestick, Dolphin, Old Gold Paint, 9 1/2 In. 60.00
Clipper, Cigar, Eagle's Head, Pocket 45.00
Crusie, Double, Ram's Horn Finial, No Hanger, 6 1/4 In. 65.00
Dog, Lying, Paws Outstretched, White Paint, Life Size, Garden, Pair 5800.00
    IRON, DOORSTOP, see Doorstop
Figurine, Amish Couple, Painted, 5 In., Pair 80.00
Figurine, Dog, Wooden Base, Alligatored Paint, 6 In. 45.00
Figurine, Magellan, White, Old Gilt Finish, 12 1/2 In. 75.00
Footman, Cut Sheet Iron, Queen Anne, Bandy Legs, England, 13 1/4 In. 75.00
Frame, Gilded, Scroll Foot, Ornate, 10 X 7 In. 38.50

Remove the rust by soaking the piece in kerosene for twenty-four hours or use any one of several commercial preparations made for the removal of rust. Wash, dry, and coat the piece with a light oil to protect it.

To test ivory to see if it is real, heat the tip of a needle or pin until it is red hot. Put the point on the ivory in an inconspicuous spot. If it goes in more than a tiny pinprick, it is not ivory.

Frame, Swivel, Old White Repaint, 18 In.	25.00
Grave Marker, Civil War Veteran, G.A.of Republic, Cannon, Large	110.00
Handcuffs, Tower Beans Pattern, No Key	15.00
Hanger, Clothes, Handlebar Mustache Shape Hooks, 12 In., Pair	530.00
Hanger, Trouser, Crow & Son, Hartford, Ct., C.1910	55.00
Hitching Post, Black Boy, No Arms, American, 19th Century	550.00
Hitching Post, Figural, Boy, Standing, Original Paint Traces, C.1860	2200.00
Hitching Post, Horsehead	325.00
Hitching Post, Tree Form, Embossed Bark, Old Black Paint, 65 In.	185.00
Hitching Weight	17.50
Jardiniere, Flat Scalloped Edge, Square Plinth, 44 In., Pair	550.00
Light, Rush, Scrolled Counterbalance, Penny Feet, 8 5/8 In.	250.00
IRON, MATCH HOLDER, see Match Holder	
Meat Hook, Butcher's, 49 In., Pair	35.00
Ornament, Roof, Snow Bird	38.00
Pulley, Well, Iron	12.00
Pump, Salesman's Sample	65.00
Rushlight, Candle Socket Counterbalance, Wooden Base, 11 1/2 In.	135.00
Safe, Balaster Standard, 4 Legs, Hoof Feet, Painted & Gilt, 42 In.	2200.00
Safe, Fred M.Bryant, Floral Design On Door, Small	357.50
Seat, Implement, Eureka	135.00
Shelf, Kettle, Brass Lyre Shaped Shelves, 15 In.	90.00
Shelf, Kettle, Brass Reticulated, 13 1/2 In.	35.00
Soap Saver	8.00
Spittoon, Turtle, Tin Insert, Mechanical, Signed, Dated, 14 In.	165.00
Spurs, Silver Design Inlay, Pair	45.00
Stand, Plant, Battle–Axes, English, 19th Century, 47 In. *Illus*	500.00
Stove Plate, Art Nouveau Scene, Girl In Tree, 20 X 26 3/4 In.	70.00
String Holder, Cone	20.00
Target, Bear, Pitted, 5 1/4 In.	85.00
Target, Double Cat & Dog, Orange, Yellow Repaint, 11 In.	45.00
Target, Running Rabbit, Pitted, 11 3/4 In.	60.00
Tazza, Topless Woman, Riding Panther, Neptune, Man, 8 X 4 In., Pair	145.00
Tool, Lighting, Swivel, Wrought	900.00
Tray, Nail, Cobbler's, Revolving Base, Round	15.00
Tsuba, Chiseled, Gold & Copper Inlay, Samurai, House, 2 3/4 In.	225.00
Tsuba, Warriors Engaged In Battle, Soten School, Japan, 2 15/16 In.	275.00
Urn, Garden, Campana Form, 24 1/2 In., Pair	1700.00
Urn, Garden, Kramer Bros.Fdy., Dayton, O., 2 Sections, 32 1/2 In., Pair	500.00
Urn, Garden, Pedestal, Wallace Lithgow & Co., Louisville, 1852, Pair	3650.00
Urn, Garden, Scrolling Handles, Marked Kramer Bros., Dayton, Ohio, Pair	1375.00
Urn, Garden, Signed M.D.J. & Co., 1879, 16 3/4 X 24 In., Pair	450.00
Urn, Garden, Tulip Shaped Bowl, Square Base, 18 1/4 In.	100.00

Urn, Goblet Shape, Weathered White & Black Paint, 8 1/4 In., Pair	65.00
Windmill Weight, Bobtailed Horse	70.00 To 225.00
Windmill Weight, Bull	325.00
Windmill Weight, Bull, Fairbury, Neb.	525.00
Windmill Weight, Chicken, Hummer, 17 1/2 X 17 In.	450.00
Windmill Weight, Coin Shape, 5 Pointed Star Embossed, 8 In.	295.00
Windmill Weight, Crescent Moon, Embossed Eclipse	195.00
Windmill Weight, Crescent Moon, Fairbanks, Morse	245.00
Windmill Weight, Eclipse of Moon, Signed, 6 1/2 X 10 In.	150.00
Windmill Weight, Half Moon, Eclipse	40.00 To 140.00
Windmill Weight, Horse, 16 1/2 In.	225.00
Windmill Weight, Horse, Dempster, 16 In.	125.00
Windmill Weight, Horse, Short Tail, Marked Dempster	225.00
Windmill Weight, No.2, 10 Ft.	350.00
Windmill Weight, Rooster, Elgin	1200.00
Windmill Weight, Rooster, Hummer	200.00
Windmill Weight, Rooster, Marked Hummer E 184	350.00
Wine Rack, Ornate, Holds 6 Bottles, Pyramid Style, Handle On Top	50.00

Ironstone china was first made in 1813. It gained its greatest popularity during the mid-nineteenth century. The heavy, durable, off-white pottery was made in white or was decorated with any of hundreds of patterns. Much flow blue pottery was made of ironstone. Some of the decorations were raised. Many pieces of ironstone are unmarked but some English and American factories included the word "Ironstone" in their marks.

IRONSTONE, see also Chelsea Grape; Chelsea Sprig; Gaudy Ironstone; Moss Rose; Staffordshire

IRONSTONE, Bowl, Vegetable, Covered, Wheat & Blackberry, Meakin	80.00
Butter Chip, Bramble, Meakin, Set of 6	35.00
Butter, Covered, Hyacinth, Liner	35.00
Cake Stand, Meakin, 14 1/4 X 6 In.	195.00
Chamber Set, Child's, Variant Pattern & Border, C.1840, 4 Piece	595.00
Child's Set, Raised Maple Leaf Design, Coxon & Co., 7 Piece	60.00
Coffeepot, Berlin Swirl	40.00
Coffeepot, Blanke's Coffee Embossed On Side, White, Crazed	60.00
Coffeepot, Ceres Wheat, Luster	275.00
Coffeepot, Domed, J.W.Pankhurst Co.	75.00
Coffeepot, Puritan Prize, T.J.& J.Mayers	85.00
Compote, Fruit, Vista, Red, Mason, 12 In.	85.00
Compote, Oriental Design, Red, Blue, 6 3/4 In. *Illus*	140.00

Ironstone, Compote, Oriental Design, Red, Blue, 6 3/4 In.

Ivory, Figurine, Woman, Holding Barrel, Wooden Base, China, 6 In.; Ivory, Figurine, Old Man, With Monkey, Japan, C.1900, 6 In.

Compote, Pedestal, Pearl Sydenham, Meakin 165.00
Crock, Bail Handle, C.1925 .... 25.00 To 35.00
Cup & Saucer, Oak & Acorn, Pankhurst 25.00
Cuspidor, Lady's, Masked Spout, Side Handles 38.00
Decanter, Embossed Masonic Designs, Gilt Trim, 8 5/8 In. 10.00
Gravy Boat, Blackberry 25.00
Gravy Boat, Vintage 22.00
Gravy Boat, White, Meakin 22.00
Jug, Puzzle, Jester, Cockfight Scene, Thomas Jones, 1860, 8 In. 100.00
Mold, Cauliflower, Alcock 50.00
Mold, Food, Castle, White, 7 7/8 X 5 7/8 In. 32.00
Mold, Lilies Among Leaves, Alcock 75.00
Mold, Rose, Alcock 50.00
Nappy, Prairie Flowers, Livesley Powell 15.00
Pitcher, Castle, Blue, White, Octagonal, Mason, 6 3/4 In. ....*Illus* 35.00
Pitcher, Fat, Brown Transfer, Italy Pattern, England, 10 In. 38.00
Pitcher, Figural, Napoleon, Polychrome Enameling, 10 3/4 In. 95.00
Pitcher, Milk, Paneled Grape, Meigh 75.00
Pitcher, Vista, Pink, Mason's 20.00
Plate, Baker, Tulip, English, 9 In., 4 Piece 200.00
Plate, Birds & Floral Design, 10 1/2 In. 38.00
Plate, Chinese Pavillion, River Scene, Mason's, 1813, 12 Piece 950.00
Platter, Black Stencil Castle & Landscape Scene, 18 In. 60.00
Platter, Blue Feather Edge, 17 3/4 In. 10.00
Platter, Brown Transfer, Meakin 25.00
Platter, Double Landscape, Mason's, C.1883, 13 1/2 X 10 3/4 In. 250.00
Platter, Floral Transfer, Black, Mason's, 19 1/4 In. 200.00
Platter, Hyacinth Border, Baker, Oval, 16 3/4 X 12 1/2 In. 35.00
Platter, J.Edwards–Dale Hall, British Reg., 12 X 15 In. 65.00
Platter, Prairie Shape, White, J.Clementson, 1862, 13 X 10 In. 24.00
Platter, Spring, Grindley, 14 In. 28.00
Platter, Wheat Border, Meakin, 16 1/2 In. 35.00
Punch Bowl, Footed, White, 7 X 12 In. 65.00
Sauce, Ladle & Underplate, Swirl, Covered, Mayer & E.Berlin 125.00
Sauce, Underplate, Covered, Footed, Boote, 5 X 6 1/2 In. 38.00
Sauceboat, Covered, Ladle, Wheat & Blackberry 60.00
Sugar, Corn & Oats 50.00
Sugar, Covered, Budded Vine, Meakin 65.00
Table Set, Child's, Blue Flower, 21 Piece 110.00
    IRONSTONE, TEA LEAF, see Tea Leaf Ironstone
Tea Set, Blue Floral Transfer, Black Striping, 7 Piece 40.00
Tea Set, Brown Transfer, River & Cottages Scene, 15 Piece 55.00
Tea Set, Child's, White, Blue Flowers, 21 Piece 105.00
Tea Set, Polychrome, Service For 6, E.Walley, C.1850, 24 Pc. 995.00
Teapot, Allover Ridges, Cobalt Blue 18.00
Teapot, Berlin Swirl, Mayer 165.00
Teapot, Hyacinth, Wedgwood 85.00
Teapot, Laurel Wreath, Luster 225.00
Tureen, Fruit Finial, Vintage Handles, Red Cliff, 11 1/4 In. 45.00
Tureen, Sauce, Ashworth, Imari, 9 In. 300.00
Tureen, Soup, Covered, Hyacinth, Oval 215.00
Tureen, Soup, Underplate, Vista, Mason's 290.00
Tureen, Tulip, Octagonal, 10 In. 225.00
Vase, Ferrara, Wedgwood, 10 In. 150.00
Vegetable, White, Melon Ribbed, D.P.Co., 1860–1900, 9 X 2 1/2 In. 20.00
Wash Pitcher, Wheat & Blackberry 100.00

Laszlo Ispanky began his American career as a designer for Cybis
Porcelains. In 1966, he established his own studio in Pennington,
New Jersey; and, since 1976, he has worked for Goebel of North
America. He works in stone, wood, or metal, as well as porcelain.
The first limited edition figurines were issued in 1966.

ISPANKY, Figurine, Ballerina, Artist Signed 975.00
    Figurine, Lancelot 375.00

"IVOREX"
OSBORNE-COPYRIGHT.
MADE IN ENGLAND.

Arthur Osborne made Ivorex plaques in England in the beginning of the 1900s. The plaques, made of a material he called "sterine wax," pictured buildings or room interiors modeled in three dimensions. After Osborne's death his daughter Blanche ran the company. It was closed in 1965, then purchased by W.H. Bossons Ltd. in 1971. Production of the plaques started again in 1980.

IVOREX, Plaque, Birthplace of Old Glory, England, 1925	34.00
Plaque, Westminster Abbey	25.00

The tusk of an elephant is ivory; and to many, that is the only true ivory. To most collectors, the term "ivory" also includes such natural materials as walrus, hippopotamus, or whale teeth or tusks, and some of the vegetable materials that are of similar texture and density. Other ivory items are listed under Scrimshaw or Netsuke.

IVORY, Beads, Ojimi, Animals, Household Gods, 19th Century, Japan, 31 Piece	2700.00
Billiard Ball, Oak Case, Set of 3	185.00
Bottle, Snuff, Peaches With Worms, Brocade Box, 20th Century, 3 In.	120.00
Bottle, Snuff, Pearl, Coral, Turquoise Beads, Jade Plaques, 2 3/4 In.	200.00
Box, Work, 2 Hinged Covered Compartments, 4 Claw Feet, 12 In.	200.00
Bust, Happy God, Whale Tooth, Drilled For Pendant, 3 In.	650.00
Case, Needle, Carved, Screw Top Cylinder	95.00
Cigarette Holder, Carved	12.00
Cigarette Holder, Carved Claw	35.00
Cigarette Holder, Cat Chasing Ball	95.00
Doctor's Lady, Lying On Side, Movable Bracelet, 4 In. .... 75.00 To	82.00
Figurine, Basket Seller, Mask, Signed, 5 1/2 In.	175.00
Figurine, Emperor & Empress, 9 In., Pair	3300.00
Figurine, Female Nude, Veil, Late 19th Century, 5 3/4 In.	745.00
Figurine, Hotei & Boy Acrobat, Japan, 5 In.	80.00
Figurine, Japanese Man With Fan, Bird On Stand, 8 In.	185.00
Figurine, Old Man, With Monkey, Japan, C.1900, 6 In. ....*Illus*	180.00
Figurine, Oriental Fisherman, 6 In.	35.00
Figurine, Smiling Man, Chinese, 22 1/2 In.	775.00
Figurine, Sumo Wrestler, Color Applied Hair & Eyes, Japan, 4 In.	90.00
Figurine, Woman, Holding Barrel, Wooden Base, China, 6 In. ....*Illus*	225.00
Memorial Scene, Applied Hair, Tomb, Doves, Framed, 5 1/2 X 5 3/4 In.	50.00
Mirror, Hand, Carved Figure, Young Angel, Beveled, C.1890, 10 3/4 In.	1100.00
Oliphant, Animals, Scrolls, Late 19th Century, French, 41 In.	2475.00
Paper Cutter, Ivory Handle, Marked THS, 6 In.	55.00
Pie Crimper, Female Anatomy Shape Handle, Whalebone, Signed Blanche	2500.00
Poker Chip	10.00
Ruler, Folding, No.90, Brass Hinges	100.00
Screen, Table, Man & Horse, Woods, Scrolled Feet, 17 In.	1100.00
Tankard, Putti, Animals, Scrolled Handle, Continental, 19 1/4 In.	6325.00
Tool, Sector, Stanley of London, C.1860	135.00
Totem Pole, Walrus	175.00
Umbrella Handle, Art Nouveau Woman, Cherub, Sterling Tip, 12 In.	2350.00
Whale Tooth, C.S.Sumter, Confederate Cruiser, June 1, 1861, 5 1/4 In.	1650.00
Writing Set, Child's, Victorian, Velvet Lined, Wooden Egg	85.00

Jack Armstrong, the all–American boy, was the hero of a radio serial from 1933 to 1951. Premiums were offered to the listeners until the mid–1940s. Jack Armstrong's best–known endorsement is for Wheaties.

JACK ARMSTRONG, Flashlight, Blue	30.00
Flashlight, Torpedo	14.00
Hike–O–Meter	18.00
Hike–O–Meter, Original Mailer	28.00
Magic Answer Box, With Box	75.00
Model Airplane Kit, 10 Different Planes, Cut, Mailer, 1944	45.00
Pedometer .... 15.00 To	24.00
Whistle Ring, 1938 .... 42.00 To	45.00

Jack–in–the–pulpit vases were named for their odd trumpetlike shape that resembles the wild plant called jack–in–the–pulpit. The design originated in the late Victorian years. Vases in the jack–in–the–pulpit shape were made of ceramic or glass.

JACK–IN–THE–PULPIT, Vase, Amberina, 6 In.	175.00
Vase, Amethyst To Clear, 17 In.	95.00
Vase, Blue To Vaseline, Ruffled Allover Floral, 7 In.	75.00
Vase, Blue, Applied Crystal Spiral, 16 In.	195.00
Vase, Coil Stem, Petal Feet, Clear To Green, 8 In.	88.00
Vase, Diamond–Quilted, Wishbone Feet, 6 3/8 In.	125.00
Vase, Green, Black Trim, 13 In.	20.00
Vase, Hobnail Ruffle, White Outside, Green, 7 1/2 In.	100.00
Vase, Jade Green Opaque, Ruffled, Gold Trim, 5 In.	70.00
Vase, Opalescent Striped, Petal Top, 5 3/8 In.	85.00
Vase, Petal Top, Blue Opalescent To Vaseline, 9 In.	88.00
Vase, Pink To Vaseline, 5 1/8 In.	95.00
Vase, Ruffled, Chartreuse Green, 7 1/2 In.	70.00
Vase, Ruffled, Green Verre Moire, Loopings, 7 1/2 In.	135.00
Vase, Ruffled, White, Purple Overlay, 7 1/2 In.	100.00
Vase, Transparent Rainbow, 11 In.	325.00
Vase, Vaseline Leaf Foot Base, Coil Stem, 10 In.	88.00
Vase, Vaseline Opalescent, Ruffled, 6 X 3 3/8 In.	58.00
Vase, White Outside, Green Overlay, Clear Feet, 7 In.	88.00
Vase, White, Green Overlay, Hobnail, Ruffled, 7 In.	100.00

Jackfield ware was originally a black glazed pottery made in Jackfield, England, from 1750 to 1775. A yellow glazed ware has also been called Jackfield ware. Most of the pieces referred to as "Jackfield" today are black–glazed, red–clay wares made at the Jackfield Pottery in Shropshire, England, in Victorian times.

JACKFIELD, Creamer, Covered, Cow, 5 X 7 In.	110.00
Pitcher, Enamel & Gilt, 5 3/4, 6 3/4, 7 3/4 In., 3 Piece	45.00
Teapot, Enamel Design	65.00

Two different minerals, nephrite and jadeite, are called jade. Nephrite is the mineral used for most early Oriental carvings. Jade is a very tough stone that is found in many colors from dark green to pale lavender. Jade carvings are still being made in the old styles, so collectors must be careful not to be fooled by recent pieces. Jade jewelry is found in this book under Jewelry.

JADE, Bowl, Fruit, Blown, Blue, Applied Cream Edge, Polished Pontil	145.00
Box, Cigarette, Diamond Set Mounts, Ruby Thumbpiece, C.1910	425.00
Cuspidor, Lady's, Green, 2 1/2 X 5 1/2 In.	195.00
Figurine, Court Lady, Holding Fan, Scarves, Medium Green, 8 1/2 In.	295.00
Figurine, Pheasant, China, 5 In.	75.00
Vase, Trumpet, Green, 10 In.	345.00

Japanese Coralene is a ceramic decorated with small raised beads and dots. It was first made in the nineteenth century. Later wares made to imitate coralene had dots of enamel. There is also another type of coralene that is made with small glass beads on glass containers.

JAPANESE CORALENE, Vase, Water Lily, Leaves On Mottled Blue, Squatty, 4 In.	250.00
Vase, Yellow To Purple, Beading, 2 Handles, 4 1/2 In.	175.00

There are two types of jasperware. Some pieces have raised designs of white or a contrasting color made from colored clay. Other pieces are made by decorating the raised portions with a color.

JASPERWARE, see also various art potteries; Wedgwood

JASPERWARE, Box, Covered, Lady With Cupid, Round	75.00
Humidor, Full Figures In Relief, German, 6 3/4 In.	85.00
Plaque, Boy, 2 Cherubs, White, Green Ground, 8 1/2 X 6 1/2 In.	195.00
Plaque, French Musketeer, White, Green Ground, 9 In.	75.00

Plaque, Lady, Swing, 2 Angels, Blue & White	65.00
Plaque, Milwaukee Library Museum, Green, 5 1/4 In.	25.00
Powder Jar, Blown-Out Woman's Face Each Side, Pink, 3 In.	145.00
Vase, Woman's Face, Lilac, Swans, Topiary Trees Handle, 8 In.	850.00

 Jewelry, if made from gold and precious gems or plastic and colored glass, is still popular with collectors. Values are determined by the intrinsic value of the stones and metal and by the skill of the craftsmen and designers. Victorian and older jewelry has been popular since the 1950s. More recent interests are Art Deco and Edwardian styles, Mexican and Danish silver jewelry, and beads of all kinds. Copies of almost all styles are being made.

JEWELRY, Bar Pin, Garnet, Victorian, 3 In.	42.00
Belt Buckle, Brass, Ceramic, Egyptian Revival, 3 X 2 In.	358.00
Belt Buckle, Empire Revival, Rectangular, 3 X 2 In.	77.00
Belt Buckle, Engraved, 14K Yellow Gold	60.00
Belt Buckle, Ivory, Black Bakelite, Profile, 2 X 3 In.	110.00
Belt, Faux Coral, Lapis & Jade, Gold Mounted, Schreiner, Large	85.00
Belt, Lady's, Allover Rhinestones, Diamond Shaped Buckle, 1920s	75.00
Belt, Rhinestone, 3 Rows, Adjustable	40.00
Box, Cigarette, Abstract Design, Diamond Set Thumbpiece, 14K Gold	800.00
Box, Cigarette, Striped Design, Cabochon Blue Thumbpiece, 14K Gold	900.00
Bracelet & Earring Set, Mexico, Sterling, Opalescent Stones	75.00
Bracelet & Earrings, 18K Gold & Coral, Tiffany & Co.	850.00
Bracelet & Earrings, Large Pink Rhinestone, Schiaparelli	35.00
Bracelet, Bangle, 14K Yellow Gold, Florentine	150.00
Bracelet, Bangle, Bar Claw Set With 3 Red Stones, Gold	175.00
Bracelet, Bangle, Enameled, Rhinestones, Trifari	25.00
Bracelet, Bangle, Engraved, Enamel Leaves, Buckle Design, C.1875	425.00
Bracelet, Bangle, Interlocking Circles, 18K Gold, Cartier	1500.00
Bracelet, Bangle, Rhinestone, Miriam Haskell	55.00
Bracelet, Braided Hair, Ophelia, 14K Gold Fittings, Box	115.00
Bracelet, Charm, Curb Links Chain, Gold Filled Charms	175.00
Bracelet, Chinese Jade, 5 Cabochon Ovals, Silver, Signed	125.00
Bracelet, Coral & Onyx, 18K Gold, Alternately Set Diamonds	1500.00
Bracelet, Earrings, Necklace & Brooch, Sterling, Marcasite, 1920	250.00
Bracelet, Expansion, Rhinestone, 4 Stones Each Bar, Box, 1945	30.00
Bracelet, Fancy Links, Crown Motif, 14K Gold	500.00
Bracelet, Flat Gold Boxes, Side Chain Links, 14K Yellow Gold	95.00
Bracelet, Gold On Platinum, Onyx, Pierced Plaques	175.00
Bracelet, Gold Plated, Buckle Design, Slides Open, 1/2 In.Wide	10.00
Bracelet, Gold Plated, Simmons	95.00
Bracelet, Gold, Ruby, Pearl & Emerald, C.1800	725.00
Bracelet, Identification, Man's, 18K Gold, Heavy, 1920	450.00
Bracelet, Interlocking Links, 9 Diamonds, Tiffany & Co., 18K Gold	2000.00
Bracelet, Man's, Wide, 14K Gold, 1910	575.00
Bracelet, Pear Shape, Crystal Links, 7 In.	35.00
Bracelet, Pearl, Hobe	65.00
Bracelet, Pearls & Rhinestones, Coro	40.00
Bracelet, Plastic Camel, On Plastic Link Chain, Black & Clear	30.00
Bracelet, Rhinestone, Eisenberg	65.00
Bracelet, Rhinestone, Expansion, 4 Rows of Stones	25.00
Bracelet, Rhinestone, Kramer, Huge, Gaudy	40.00
Bracelet, Rose Gold Plated, Engraved, Hinged, C.1916, 5/8 In.Wide	50.00
Bracelet, Sapphire & Diamond, Bezel Set, Platinum Mount	1700.00
Bracelet, Scrolled Links, 18K Gold & Enamel	275.00
Bracelet, Slide, Victorian, Gold & Opal, Mesh Bracelet	225.00
Bracelet, Snake, Antique Gold, Woven Mesh, Coiled Tail	650.00
Bracelet, Snake, Platinum, Whiting & Davis	125.00
Bracelet, Sterling Silver, Georg Jensen, 3/4 In.Wide	195.00
Bracelet, Yellow Link Twist, White Gold Chain, 8 In.	330.00
Brooch & Earrings, Basket, Haskell	60.00
Brooch & Earrings, Satsuma, Metal Mounted	425.00
Brooch, 1 Large & 34 Small Diamonds, Platinum	550.00

You can tell a piece of jade by the feel. It is cold, even in warm weather.

Diamonds clean well in club soda.

Do not clean rhinestones with water. It will tarnish the foil background. Use a Q-Tip or a small, soft brush and glass cleaner. Do not hold the jewelry under running water. Rub dry with a soft cloth.

Perfume and hair spray will damage amber beads and pearls.

If you are having antique jewelry repaired, be sure that the jeweler uses old stones. New ones are cut differently and will seem brighter. Pearls and turquoise change color with age.

Brooch, 3–Dimensional, Resembles Musical Instrument, 15th Century	115.00
Brooch, Bird, Sterling Silver, Danecraft	35.00
Brooch, Bow, 14K Pink Gold, Ruby & Diamond, C.1940, 8 In.	2300.00
Brooch, Chased Gold Spirals, Horses, Seed Pearl Frame, Emeralds	375.00
Brooch, Cluster Paste Stones, Painted Lady, 1850, 3 In.	210.00
Brooch, Colored Rhinestones, Weiss	25.00
Brooch, Copper, Musical, Renoir	12.00
Brooch, Flower Design, 12K Gold Filled, Pearls, Bal Ron, 1 1/4 In.	35.00
Brooch, Flower Design, Sterling Silver, Botticelli, 2 1/2 In.	25.00
Brooch, Flowers, Rhinestone Center, BSK Paper Label, 2 In.	25.00
Brooch, Gold & Garnet, Studded Collet–Set Garnets	400.00
Brooch, Ivory, Cluster of Grapes On Vine	250.00
Brooch, Ivory, Mourning, Woman, At Tomb, Black, Brown, Case, 1 7/8 In.	350.00
Brooch, Jade, Oriental Figure, Pale Green Jade, C.1935	850.00
Brooch, Leaf Shape, 14K Gold, 5 Large Pearls, 1940s	75.00
Brooch, Maltese Cross, Emeralds & Rubies Center, 18K Gold	150.00
Brooch, Marcasite, Art Deco, Rectangular, Inset Flared Initials	48.00
Brooch, Memorial, Pearl, Gold & Enamel Frame, Woman	100.00
Brooch, Mosaic, Flowers, Leaves, 14K Gold Frame, Pietra Dura, 1860	295.00
Brooch, Opalescent White, With Rhinestones, Kramer	12.00
Brooch, Pendant, Cameo, Filigree Frame, C.1890	75.00
Brooch, Pendant, Cameo, Lavender Agate, Woman, 14K Gold Frame	300.00
Brooch, Pendant, Cameo, Marcasite Border, C.1880	175.00
Brooch, Pendant, Shell Cameo, Female Profile, Engraved Frame	125.00
Brooch, Pendant, Silver, Blue Stone, Alpaca, Mexican, 2 1/2 In.	35.00
Brooch, Pink Rhinestones, Sterling Silver	19.00
Brooch, Rhinestone Wings, Eisenberg	200.00
Brooch, Rose–Cut Diamond Petals, Turquoise, Silver & Gold Mount	375.00
Brooch, Shell Cameo, Female Figure, 14K White Gold Frame	100.00
Brooch, Shell Cameo, Female Figure, Gold Frame, My Wife, 1856	300.00
Brooch, Shell Cameo, Horseshoe Shape, Good Luck, Gold Frame	100.00

Brooch, Starburst, Rhinestone, Pink, Gray	8.00
Brooch, Sterling Silver, Eisenberg	35.00
Brooch, Sterling Silver, Nye	15.00
Brooch, Victorian, Filigree, Floral, Gargoyles, Gilt, 3 In.	15.00
Brooch, Winged Horse, Rhinestones, Sterling Silver, Coro, 2 In.	30.00
Brooch, Woven Hair	75.00
Chain, 14K Gold & Turquoise Beads, 1920s, 16 In.	125.00
Chain, 14K Gold, Curb Lengths, 14.5 Grams, 16 1/2 In.	90.00
Chain, Antique Gold & Colored Stone, Carved Plaques	850.00
Chain, Diamond Solitaire, 14K Gold, 15 In.	170.00
Chain, Diamond-Shaped Rubies & Seed Pearl Slide, Gold Filled	45.00
Chain, Fob, Gold & Enamel, Rectangular Links, Blue Flowers	200.00
Chain, Herringbone, 14K Yellow Gold, 17 Gram, 19 In.	200.00
Chain, Penknife, Link Chain, Gold & Diamond Set Knife	125.00
Chain, Rope, 14K Gold, 19 In.	55.00
Chain, Rope, 20 In.	350.00
Chain, Watch, 14K Gold, 19 In.	160.00
Chain, Watch, Braided Hair, Gold Plated Fittings	45.00
Chain, Watch, Enamel, Pearl & Onyx Fobs, Victorian, Gold	850.00
Chain, Watch, Man's, 3 Charms, Gold	45.00
Chain, Watch, Squared Links, Scrolled Slide, 14K Gold	275.00
Chain, Watch, Victorian, Fluted Double Links, Gold Slide, Enameled	950.00
Charm, Cinderella's Pumpkin Coach, 9K Yellow Gold	125.00
Charm, Golf Bag, With Clubs, Silver	25.00
Charm, Horse, Covered Surrey, Silver	25.00
Cigarette Case, 14K Gold & Sterling Silver	55.00
Cigarette Case, 14K Gold, Engine Turned Striped Design	350.00
Clip, Dress, Bakelite, Green Leaf	7.50
Clip, Dress, Rhinestone, Painting, On Porcelain, 1930s, 2 Piece	32.50
Clip, Wirework Brass, Oval Carnelian Center, Czechoslovakia	25.00
Comb, Art Nouveau, Celluloid, Black, Clear, Rhinestones	15.00
Compact, 14K Gold, Engine Turned Striped Pattern, Monogram	150.00
Cross, 10K Gold Filled Chain, C.1901	40.00
Cuff Links, Art Deco, 10K White Gold	28.00
Cuff Links, Black Onyx Center, Threaded Rose Diamonds, Platinum	95.00
Cuff Links, Gold, Monogram B.P., 18th Century, 3/4 In., Pair	713.00
Dickey, Silver, 1940	10.00
Ear Clips, 14K Yellow Gold, Massalone, Starburst Design, C.1940	225.00
Ear Clips, Designed As Fluted Dome, 18K Gold, David Webb	850.00
Earrings, 14K Gold, Onyx, 1920, Large	100.00
Earrings, Crystal Balls, Red Blossom, Cobalt Blue, Kaziun Sterling	450.00
Earrings, Drop, Red & Green Stones, Kenneth Lane	30.00
Earrings, Marcasite Flower, Sterling Silver Bezel, 9/16 In.	35.00
Earrings, Onyx, Dangling, 14K Gold, 1920	100.00
Earrings, Oval Emerald, 14K Gold Mounting	350.00
Earrings, Rhinestone, Clear, Eisenberg, Large	25.00
Earrings, Rhinestone, Dangle, Pink, Green, Weiss, 2 1/2 In.	25.00
Earrings, Rhinestone, Heart Shape, Arlene Francis	18.00
Earrings, Rhinestone, Star Shape	7.00
Earrings, Spinal Hoop, 14K Yellow Gold, Posts	70.00
Earrings, Turquoise, Pearl, Suspended From Curved Bar, Victorian	375.00
Etui, Pendants, Brass, 3 Turquoise Jewels, Chain, 1860, 2 X 1/2 In.	145.00
Etui, Pendants, Brass, 4 Green Stones, 3 Buttons, 2 X 3/4 In.	165.00
Hair Ornament, Gilded Silver, Kingfisher, Pearls, China, 6 In.	175.00
Hair Ornament, Open Heart Shape, Gold Fastener Bar, 18K Gold	575.00
Hat Ornament, Peach Bakelite, Rhinestones, Art Deco	24.00
Holder, Comb, Green Bakelite, Jade Stones, Mirror, Schildkraut	13.00
JEWELRY, INDIAN, see Indian	
Lighter, 14K Gold, Engine Turned Striped Pattern, Monogram	50.00
Locket, 14K Gold, Holds 4 Photos	125.00
Locket, Brass, On Black Silk Cord, C.1880	20.00
Locket, Mourning, Clock Face, Gilt Back, C.1870, Round, 1 1/2 In.	118.00
Locket, Octagonal, Black Incised Designs, 1 3/4 In.	30.00
Locket, Victorian, 4 Mine Cut Diamonds, 18K Gold, C.1870	275.00

Necklace & Bracelet, Brown & Amber Rhinestones, Schiaparelli 60.00
Necklace & Bracelet, Peruzzi, Amethyst Beads, Silver Mounts, Grapes 250.00
Necklace & Bracelet, Rhinestone, Eisenberg 125.00
Necklace & Bracelet, Rhinestone, Green, Box 60.00
Necklace & Drop Earrings, Mesh, Chain, Sarah Coventry 15.00
Necklace & Earrings, Baroque Pearls, Rhinestones, Miriam Haskell 75.00
Necklace & Earrings, Clear, Leaf Design, Gold 15.00
Necklace & Earrings, Fish, Blue Glass Eyes, Los Castillo Taxcos 400.00
Necklace & Earrings, Garnet, Brass Set, With Gold Wash, Bohemian 350.00
Necklace & Earrings, Lapis Beads, Bead Earrings, Screw Back 195.00
Necklace & Earrings, Plique-A-Jour, Pendant, Drop Pearls, French 325.00
Necklace & Earrings, Rhinestone, White Gold, Coro 25.00
Necklace, 14K Gold Rope Chain, Cameo Pendant, Victorian, 19 In. 385.00
Necklace, 15K Gold & Pearl, Braided Chain, Pearl-Set Star 100.00
Necklace, 18K Gold, Coiled Gold Wire 250.00
Necklace, Amber Bead, Stand, Graduated Faceted Beads, 20 In. 75.00
Necklace, Amber, Graduated Faceted Beads, 36 In. 145.00
Necklace, Amethyst, Graduated Faceted Beads, 30 In. 250.00
Necklace, Antique 14K Gold & Sapphire, Pear Shaped Sapphires 1400.00
Necklace, Antique Gold & Amber, Clip Chain, Amber Beads, 18 In. 475.00
Necklace, Antique Gold, Flexible Snake Chain, 15 In. 1600.00
Necklace, Baroque Pearl, Haskell, 29 In. 35.00
Necklace, Bracelet & Earrings, White Stones, Rhinestone, Kramer 40.00
Necklace, Braided Hair, Compass Pendant, Victorian 125.00
Necklace, Carnelian & Gold, 14 1/2mm Beads, 18K Gold Frame 275.00
Necklace, Choker, Rhinestone, Eisenberg 40.00
Necklace, Clear Glass Beads, 1 Strand, 16 In. 5.00
Necklace, Coral, White, Double Strand, 18 In. 125.00
Necklace, Cultured Pearl, 30 In. 700.00
Necklace, Dangle Earrings, 3 Strand Bracelet, Glass Beads, Hobe 120.00
Necklace, Double Snake Chain, Front Slide, Trifari, 12 1/2 In. 45.00
Necklace, Earrings & Bracelet, Leaf, Rhinestone, Yellow, Trifari 40.00
Necklace, Egyptian Revival, 3 Strands Faience Beads, Gold Bail 425.00
Necklace, Flapper, Red Stone, On Brass Filigree Chain 15.00
Necklace, Freshwater Pearl Flowers, Leaves, Gold Plated, 9 In. 35.00
Necklace, Gold Bead, 111 3 1/2mm Beads, 14 1/2 In. 125.00
Necklace, Gold Beads, Graduated, Monet, 10 In. 30.00
Necklace, Heart, 21 Pave Diamonds, 14K White Gold Chain 350.00
Necklace, Jade Beads, 9mm, Jade Pendant Drop, 40 In. 100.00
Necklace, Lapis Lazuli, Beads, Graduated, 32 In. 500.00
Necklace, Marcasite Flower, Sterling Silver, 9 1/2 In. 60.00
Necklace, Opal Beads, 29 Graduated Beads, 8mm To 14mm, 14 In. 1400.00
Necklace, Opal Bead, Graduated Beads, 36 In. 950.00
Necklace, Pearl, 65 Cultured Pearls, 14K Gold Clasp 375.00
Necklace, Pewter, Turquoise, Georg Jensen 28.00
Necklace, Platinum & Diamond, 56 Graduated Diamonds 13000.00
Necklace, Rhinestone, Brown & Amber, Teardrop, Chunky, Large 20.00
Necklace, Rhinestone, Floral, Leaves, Eisenberg, Gray Box 120.00
Necklace, Rhinestone, Large Aquamarine, Crystal Stones 28.00
Necklace, Russian Charms, Moonstone, Diamond Pendant, Cartier 2900.00
Necklace, Satsuma, 30 Medallions, Birds, Flowers, Landscapes, Faces 700.00
Necklace, Silver, 3 Strands, Mother-of-Pearl Birds 45.00
Necklace, Venetian Glass Beads, 52 In. 50.00
Necklace, White Glass, Barrel Shape Beads, Victorian, 38 In. 32.00
Pendant & Earrings, 18K Gold & Wood, Van Cleef & Arpels 950.00
Pendant & Earrings, Shark Tooth, Gold Cap, Gold Bar 100.00
Pendant, 8 Rose Diamonds, Cluster, 14K Gold, White Gold Chain 450.00
Pendant, Art Nouveau, Silver & Enamel, Spaced Enamel Flowers 300.00
Pendant, Cameo, 10K Gold Frame, C.1875 .... 225.00
Pendant, Cameo, 12K Gold Mount, Signed, C.1890 .... 250.00
Pendant, Carved Jade, Apricot, Chain 65.00
Pendant, Coral Cameo, 3 Dimensional, Filigree Frame, 14K Gold 50.00
Pendant, Five Dollar Gold Piece, 10K Gold Bezel, Dated 1887 .... 200.00
Pendant, Gold & Jade, Plaque Chain, Gold Cap, Buddha 175.00

Pendant, Gold, Pearl & Enamel, Madonna, Green, Blue, C.1910 .... 450.00
Pendant, Ivory Heart, Hand Carved, C.1880 .... 38.00
Pendant, Jade, Hand Carved, 14K Gold Loop, 2 X 2 5/8 In. 230.00
Pendant, Pin, Opal & Pearl, Pierced 14K Gold, Opal Rosette 100.00
Pendant, Pink Art Glass, Chain, Whiting Davis 25.00
Pendant, Porcelain Portrait, Fancy Frame, Limoges 22.00
Pin & Earrings, 5 Horse Heads, Sterling Silver, 3 Piece 50.00
Pin & Earrings, Pink Stones, Rhinestones, Eisenberg, Box 80.00
Pin & Earrings, Silver Leaf, Black, Signed Napier 28.00
Pin & Necklace, 14K Gold, Round, Diamond, Sapphire, Pearl, C.1880 .... 325.00
Pin, 14K White Gold, 24 Diamonds 360.00
Pin, 18K Gold, Diamond Buckle, Four Green Stones, Hallmarked 275.00
Pin, Bar, 18K Gold, 3 Diamonds 150.00
Pin, Butterfly, Weiss 35.00
Pin, Cameo, Messenger Mercury, 14K Gold, Seed Pearls, C.1880 .... 275.00
Pin, Cameo, Victorian Lady, 14K Gold, Black & White Onyx, C.1880 .... 275.00
Pin, Cat, Glass Body, Face & Ears, Rhinestone Tail, Whiskers, 2 In. 15.00
Pin, Circle, 14K Yellow Gold, 6 Round Opals 250.00
Pin, Cluster, Victorian, Flowers, Center Pearl, Rubies, Pure Gold 225.00
Pin, Crown, Trifari, Moonstones, Red & Blue, Sterling Silver, 2 In. 35.00
Pin, Dachshund, Sterling Silver 2 1/2 X 1 In. 15.00
Pin, Double Leaf, Jensen, 1 1/8 In. 30.00
Pin, Double Tulip & Berries, Jensen, 1 3/4 X 1 1/4 In. 110.00
Pin, Feather, Blue Rhinestones, 3 In. 15.00
Pin, Flower Spray, Rhinestone, Eisenberg, Gray Hinged Box 85.00
Pin, Gold Sheaths, 2 Amethysts 175.00
Pin, Horse, Bakelite, Inlaid Eyes, Brass Harness 40.00
Pin, Lady's Head, Flowing Hair, Peacock On Top, Unger Bros. 300.00
Pin, Lily-of-The-Valley, Hattie Carnegie 28.00
Pin, Mourning, Willow, Beveled Edge, Urn Center, Enameled & Gilt 200.00
Pin, Multicolored Floral, Sterling, Coro 20.00
Pin, Pinwheel, Rhinestone, Weiss, 2 1/2 In. 17.00
Pin, Puffy Heart Shape, Triple Layered, 60 Garnets, 1 X 1 In. 68.00
Pin, Rhinestone, Black, Hattie Carnegie 35.00
Pin, Rhinestone, Circle, Weiss 22.50
Pin, Rhinestone, Crown Shape, Large 10.00
Pin, Rhinestone, Lacy Bow Shape, Clear, 2 5/8 In. 5.00
Pin, Rhinestone, Wasp, Wings Move, Hattie Carnegie, 2 In., Pair 35.00
Pin, Russian Enamel, Sheathed Sword Silver Gilt, Hallmark 150.00
Pin, Set In Spray of Garnets, Set In 14K Gold 145.00
Pin, Silver, Crystal & Marcasite, Frosted Oval, Silver Frame 350.00
Pin, Sterling Silver, Art Deco, 3 Bells 15.00
Pin, Sterling Silver, Figural, Lady, Siam, 3 X 2 1/2 In. 20.00
Pin, Sunburst, Garnet, C.1890 .... 45.00
Pin, Sweater, Double, Gold On Sterling, Red, White Crowns, Chain 55.00
Pin, Tulip, Coro 30.00
Pin, With Spider, Sterling Silver, Charles Horner 150.00
Ring, 14K White Gold, Agate, 1915 .... 65.00
Ring, 14K Yellow Gold, 6 Round Amethysts 250.00
Ring, 14K Yellow Gold, Art Nouveau, Oval Garnet 75.00
Ring, 18K Gold, Hairwork, Victorian 80.00
Ring, Agate, 14K White Gold, Fancy, 1915 .... 65.00
Ring, Amethyst & Diamond, 10K White Gold Mount 675.00
Ring, Aquamarine, Diamond, 4 Pear Shaped Aquamarines 250.00
Ring, Art Deco, Ruby Flowers, 30 Diamonds, Wide Band, 14K Gold 250.00
Ring, Black Onyx, Diamond In Corner, 14K White Gold 95.00
Ring, Bow Shape, Eisenberg, Signed 65.00
Ring, Cameo, Angel, Harp, Black Ground, Wire Frame 275.00
Ring, Cameo, Gold & Garnet, Ancient Warrior, Snakes 700.00
Ring, Chinese Gold & Jade, Oval Jade Cabochon, Beaded Bezel 275.00
Ring, Citrine, Channel Set Rubies & 2 Diamonds, C.1940 .... 500.00
Ring, Coral, 18K Gold, Oval Pink Coral, Woven Bezel, Italy 75.00
Ring, Diamond, 14K Gold, Wedding Band 250.00
Ring, Diamond, Cushion Cut, .50 Ct., Yellow Gold Setting 275.00

Ring, Diamond, Round, Pierced Yellow Gold Mount, .60 Ct.	425.00
Ring, Diamond, Solitaire, Pear Shape, Platinum Mount	4700.00
Ring, Dinner, Filigree, 20 Diamonds, 14K White Gold	225.00
Ring, Dinner, Lady's, Diamond Center, 14 Small Diamonds On Side	995.00
Ring, Double Qypsy Mount, Pear Shape Synthetic Sapphire	125.00
Ring, Emerald & Diamond Cluster, White Gold	175.00
Ring, Engagement, 3 Large & 4 Small Diamonds, 14K White Gold	425.00
Ring, Engagement, Tiffany Twist Setting, 1 Diamond, Size 7	495.00
Ring, Gold Pearl, Wire Twist, Floral Design, Cultured Pearls	200.00
Ring, Gold, 14K, Opals, Hallmarked, C.1875	145.00
Ring, Gold, Form of Belt Buckle, Diamond & Ruby, Victorian	125.00
Ring, Gold, Mourning, Drawing, Under Glass, Woman, Tomb, Nov.1793	175.00
Ring, Gold, Victorian, Form of Belt, Buckle, Star Diamond & Ruby	125.00
Ring, Gold, Yellow Gold Leaf Design, Blue Stone	225.00
Ring, Half Dome, 21 Square Cut Rubies, Diamonds, C.1940	1900.00
Ring, Lady's Profile, 10K Gold	50.00
Ring, Lady's, Opal & 4 Diamonds, 10K Gold	90.00
Ring, Lady's, Pearl & Emerald Swirl, 14K Gold	130.00
Ring, Man's, Carved Cameo Tiger Eye, 10K Gold, 1930s	45.00
Ring, Man's, Emerald, Cabochon Set, 18K Gold Mount	175.00
Ring, Man's, Intaglio Onyx Warrior, Hand Carved, 10K Gold	125.00
Ring, Mobe Pearl Set, 14K Gold Textured Mount	175.00
Ring, Onyx & Diamond, Fan Shape, Snake Bezel, Diamonds	125.00
Ring, Platinum & Diamond Mount, 4 Prong, 6 Diamonds	175.00
Ring, Platinum & Diamond Mount, 4 Prong, 8 Diamonds	150.00
Ring, Platinum & Diamond, Elongated Pierced Mount	725.00
Ring, Platinum & Emerald, Square Cut, 2 Baguettes	175.00
Ring, Rhinestone, Convertible, 4 Interchangeable Tops	37.50
Ring, Sapphire & Diamond, Ceylon Sapphire, 6 Small Diamonds	1150.00
Ring, Snake, 14K Gold, Cat's Eye Quartz, Coiled Snake Mount	110.00
Ring, Snake, Garnet Eyes, 14K Yellow Gold	70.00
Ring, Sterling Silver Filigree, Central Moonstone, 2 Amethysts	175.00
Ring, Tiger Eye, 10K Gold, 1930s	60.00
Ring, Topaz, Oval Frame, Silver & 18K Gold Mounting, Georgian	300.00
Ring, Turquoise & Diamond, Domed 18K Gold Mount	275.00
Ring, Wedding, 14K White Gold, 3 Diamonds, 1920s	25.00
Scarf Slide, Cupid, Silver	65.00
Stickpin, Amethyst, Greek Key, 14K Gold Filigree	58.00
Stickpin, Sadiron, Figural, Asbestos, Dover Mfg., Canal Dover, Ohio	48.00
Stickpin, Sapphire Surrounded By 6 Diamonds, 14K Gold	225.00
Sweater Clip, Rhinestone, Amethyst	12.00
Sweater Guard, Rhinestone, Blue, 1950	15.00
Thimble Holder, On Chatelaine Chain, Sterling Silver, 2 3/8 In.	55.00
Tiara, Rhinestone	25.00 To 35.00

JEWELRY, WATCH, see Watch

John Rogers statues were made from 1859 to 1892. The originals were bronze, but the thousands of copies made by the Rogers factory were of painted plaster. Eighty different figures were made. Similar painted plaster figures were made by some other factories. Never repaint a Rogers figure because this lowers the value to collectors.

JOHN ROGERS, Group, Checkers At The Farm	475.00
Group, Playing Doctor	700.00
Group, Taking Oath & Drawing Rations, 20 In.	325.00

Any memorabilia that refers to the Jews or the Jewish religion is collected. Interests range from newspaper clippings that mention eighteenth– and nineteenth–century Jewish Americans to religious objects, such as menorahs or spice boxes. Age, condition, and the intrinsic value of the material, as well as the historic and artistic importance, determine the value.

JUDAICA, Container, Esrog, Hinged Lid, Sterling Silver, C.1890, 6 1/2 In.	605.00
Cup, Sterling Silver, Russian	98.00

Kiddush Cup, Embossed Grape Design, Sterling Silver, 6 In.	225.00
Lamp, Hanukkah, Crown At Top, 8 Oil Receptacles, Silver, 10 In.	660.00
Medal, Calendar, 1804, Jewish Year 5565, Silver Edge	300.00
Painting, Rabbinical Ponderings, A.Bender, Framed, 1930s	1400.00

Jugtown Pottery refers to pottery made in North Carolina as far back as the 1750s. In 1915, Juliana and Jacques Busbee set up a training and sales organization for what they named "Jugtown Pottery." In 1921, they built a shop at Jugtown, North Carolina, and hired Ben Owen as a potter in 1923. The Busbees moved the village store where the pottery was sold and promoted to New York City. Juliana Busbee sold the New York store in 1926 and moved into a log cabin near the Jugtown Pottery. The pottery closed in 1958. It reopened and is still working near Seagrove, North Carolina.

JUGTOWN, Bean Pot, Covered, Orange Luster, 5 In.	40.00
Bowl, Chinese Glaze	105.00
Bowl, Gray & Blue, 5 1/4 In.	65.00
Cookie Jar, 10 In.	150.00
Cracker Jar, Covered, Strap Handles, 12 In.	75.00
Cup & Saucer	35.00
Cup & Saucer, 6 Sets	90.00
Inkwell, Art Nouveau, Emerald Green & Black	45.00
Jar, Covered, Orange, Brown, Ear Strap Handles, 11 In.	95.00
Pitcher, Pinched Spout, Bulbous, 8 1/2 In.	60.00
Pitcher, Strap Handle, Salt Glaze, 1 Pint	52.50
Rose Jar, Covered, Olive Drab Glaze, 4 1/2 In.	45.00
Sugar & Creamer, Covered, Mustard Luster	40.00
Tray, Bread, Handles, Large	25.00
Urn, Bonita, Artist Signed, 6 In.	30.00
Vase, Chinese White, Bulbous, Open Handles, 6 1/2 In.	150.00
Vase, Frog Skin Over Redware, 6 In.	90.00

Kate Greenaway, who was a famous illustrator of children's books, drew pictures of children in high-waisted Empire dresses. She lived from 1846 to 1901. Her designs appear on china, glass, and other pieces. Figural napkin rings depicting the Greenaway children are also to be found listed under Napkin Ring, Figural.

KATE GREENAWAY, Book, Pied Piper of Hamlin	56.00
Figurine, Cake Decoration, Bisque, 1 1/4 In.	28.00
Figurine, Girl, Holding Pug Dog, 7 In.	175.00
Match Holder, Girl, Helping Sister Over Log, Striker	85.00
Napkin Ring, Boy, Baseball Bat, Ball, Silver Plate	250.00
Napkin Ring, Drummer Boy, On Bench, Silver Plate	240.00
Napkin Ring, Girl Beside Ring, Silver Plate	100.00
Napkin Ring, Girl, Hands On Ring, Barbour Bros.	175.00
Napkin Ring, Girls Climb Ladders Over Ring, Silver Plate	355.00
Napkin Ring, Infant, Derby Silver Co., 1873	130.00
Picture, Girls Looking Out Window, Framed, 1885, 6 X 5 In.	195.00
Salt & Pepper, Boy & Girl, Silver Plate, 4 1/2 In.	145.00
Salt & Pepper, Girl, Coat, Muff, Silver Plate, 4 1/2 In.	45.00

"Kauffmann" refers to the type of work done by Angelica Kauffmann, a painter and decorative artist for Adam Brothers in England between 1766 and 1781. She designed small-scale pictorial subjects in the neoclassic manner. Most porcelains signed "Kauffmann" were made in the 1800s. She did not do the artwork on all pieces signed with her name.

KAUFFMANN, Bowl, Maidens & Cupid, Gold Rim, Beehive, Square, 10 In.	120.00
Charger, 3 Draped Ladies & Nymph On Portico, Marked, 13 1/4 In.	145.00
Cup & Saucer, Medallion, Classic Ladies, Beehive Mark, Demitasse	55.00
Plate, Lady, Seated, 2 Attendants, Cherub, Beehive	65.00
Plate, Scenic, 22K Gold Border	35.00
KAYSERZINN, see Pewter	

Ironstone, Pitcher, Castle, Blue, White,
Octagonal, Mason, 6 3/4 In.

Kew Blas, Pitcher, Green Feathering,
Silvery Blue Handle, 5 In.

KELVA

Kelva glassware was made by the C. F. Monroe Company of Meriden, Connecticut, about 1904. It is a pale, pastel–painted glass decorated with flowers, designs, or scenes. Kelva resembles Nakara and Wave Crest, two other glasswares made by the same company.

KELVA, Bonbon, Bail Handle, 4 In.	150.00
Bowl, Jewelry, Hand Painted Florals, Brass Ormolu Rim, Marked, 6 In.	495.00
Box, Covered, Blown–Out Rose, Blue	275.00
Box, Green Lining, Ormolu Collar, Mottled Green, 3 X 4 In.	345.00
Box, Hinged Lid, Floral On Gray Mottled Ground	325.00
Box, Hinged Lid, Orange Poppy, Seed Pods, Lined, Signed, 4 1/2 X 3 In.	335.00
Box, Hinged Lid, Raised Design On Collar, Flowers, 4 X 3 In.	345.00
Box, Jewelry, Hinged Lid, Raised Design On Collar, Signed, 8 In.	675.00
Box, Jewelry, Hinged Lid, Raised Flowers, Silk Lining, 8 In.	675.00
Vase, Draping At Side & Bottom, Green Ground, Flowers, 18 In.	1700.00
Vase, Pink Flowers, Green Ground, 13 1/2 In.	600.00
Vase, Pink Flowers, Silver Plated Handles & Feet, 18 In.	1600.00
Vase, Rose Sprays, Mottled Green Ground, Ormolu Brass Feet, 9 In.	450.00
Vase, Single–Petaled Roses, Mottled Green Ground, 9 1/2 In.	385.00

Kemple glass was made by John Kemple of East Palestine, Ohio, and Kenova, West Virginia, from 1945 to 1970. The glass was made from old molds. Many designs and colors were made. Kemple pieces are usually marked with a "K" on the bottom. Many milk glass pieces were made with or without the mark.

KEMPLE, Dish, Cat Cover, Green	55.00
Dish, Hen Cover, Green	22.00

The Kenton Hills Pottery made art wares, including vases and figurines that resembled Rookwood, probably because so many of the original artists and workmen had worked at the Rookwood plant.

KENTON HILLS, Vase, Iridescent Brown, 6 X 7 In.	110.00
Vase, Turquoise	100.00

Kew Blas is the name used by the Union Glass Company of Somerville, Massachusetts. The name refers to an iridescent golden glass made from the 1890s to 1924. The iridescent glass was reminiscent of the Tiffany glass of the period.

KEW BLAS, Compote, Gold, Pink Highlights, Twisted Stem, Ribbed Cup, 7 In.	375.00
Pitcher, Green Feathering, Silvery Blue Handle, 5 In. ....*Illus*	550.00

Plate, Iridescent Gold, Signed, 6 In.	145.00
Vase, Dark Blue, Light Blue Draped Swirls, 6 1/2 In.	775.00
Vase, Gold Feathering, Opal Top, 6 In.	750.00
Vase, Green & Gold Pulled Design, Gold Interior, 5 1/2 In.	750.00

Kewpies, designed by Rose O'Neill, were first pictured in the "Ladies' Home Journal." The pixielike figures were a success, and Kewpie dolls started appearing in 1911. Kewpie pictures and other items soon followed. Collectors search for all items that picture the little winged people.

KEWPIE, Bell, Kewpie On Top, Brass	25.00 To 30.00
Book, Coloring, 1962	20.00
Booklet, Jell-O, 1915	30.00
Card, Doll, Flocked Santa Hat, Cardboard, 1913, 12 In.	26.00
Card, Easter, Rose O'Neill, Gibson	10.00
Card, Merry Christmas, Kewpie In Sock, Rose O'Neill, 1922	15.00
Card, Tying Bow On Box, Rose O'Neill	28.00
Clock, Signed O'Neill, 4 1/2 In.	375.00
Creamer, Signed Rose O'Neill, 3 3/4 In.	85.00
Cup & Saucer, Action Kewpies	85.00
Cup & Saucer, Child's, Rose O'Neill	55.00
Doll, Bisque, Lefton, 1950s, 5 In., Set of 3 Different	14.00
Doll, Bisque, Painted & Molded Tufts of Hair, O'Neill, 6 In.	75.00
Doll, Boy, Bellhop Uniform, Movable Arms, 6 1/4 In.	135.00
Doll, Boy, Box, 26 In.	75.00
Doll, Boy, Celluloid, Rose O'Neill, 6 In.	35.00
Doll, Cameo, Vinyl, Marked, 1966, 28 In.	325.00
Doll, Celluloid, Crepe Paper Outfit, 9 1/2 In.	35.00
Doll, Celluloid, Feather Costume, 15 In.	45.00
Doll, Chalkware, Hands Under Chin, Rose O'Neill, 4 In.	12.00
Doll, Civil War Soldier, Bisque, Action, Signed O'Neill, 4 In.	300.00
Doll, Composition, Heart Sticker, Marked O'Neill, 12 In.	75.00
Doll, Confederate Soldier, Stamp On Foot, 3 1/2 In.	250.00
Doll, Crawling, O'Neill, 2 X 3 3/4 In.	195.00
Doll, Hands On Stomach, O'Neill Label, Pat.1913, 2 1/2 In.	80.00
Doll, Holding Pen, Action, Signed O'Neill	125.00
Doll, Little Confederate Soldier, Signed O'Neill, 4 1/4 In.	345.00
Doll, One Hand Up, One To Side, O'Neill Label, Pat.1913, 2 1/2 In.	80.00
Doll, Rose Red Table, 2 1/2 X 4 In.	45.00
Doll, Seated In Chair, Bisque, C In Circle 43, 4 In.	260.00
Doll, Traveler, Bisque, O'Neill Triple Signed	300.00
Doll, With Book, Bisque, 3 In.	85.00
Doll, With Green Wings, Celluloid, Japan, 3 In.	10.00
Figurine, Bisque, Label On Chest, Signed Foot, 6 In.	125.00
Figurine, Huggers, 3 1/2 In.	80.00
Figurine, Signed, 4 In.	110.00
Letter Opener, Pewter	65.00
Light Bulb, Christmas	45.00
Match Holder, Indian, Amber	18.50
Necklace, Sterling, Ivory Charm, Arms Move	28.00
Paper Doll, Kewpie Kin, Saalfield, Uncut, 2 Sets	20.00
Paper Doll, Kewpies To Color, Saalfield	20.00
Paper Doll, Uncut, 1967	25.00
Perfume Bottle, Little Thinker, Germany, 3 In.	75.00
Planter, Thinker, By Tree Trunk, Blue	35.00
Planter, Winker, 6 In.	20.00
Plaque, Sleeping In Flower, Pink, 5 X 7 In.	45.00
Plate, 7 Figures, O'Neill, Rudolstadt, 6 In.	79.00 To 99.00
Plate, Kewpie Band, 1973, 8 In.	25.00
Plate, Santa Claus, 1973	20.00
Quilt, Appliqued, Crib, 33 X 46 In.	95.00
Tea Set, Pink Luster, Marked, 8 Piece	950.00
Toothpick, Doll, Glass, Original Paint	35.00
Toothpick, Standing, Glass, Marked	60.00

Vase, Kewpie, With Mandolin, Heart Shape, 5 1/2 In. 27.50
KIMBALL, see Cluthra
KING'S ROSE, see Soft Paste

 All types of kitchen utensils, from eggbeaters to bowls, are collected today. Handmade wooden and metal items, like ladles and apple peelers, were made in the early nineteenth century. Mass–produced pieces, like iron apple peelers and graniteware, were made in the nineteenth century. Other kitchen wares are listed under manufacturers' names or under Iron; Advertising; Tool; or Wooden.

KITCHEN, Apple Corer, Tin, T–Shape, 6 X 3 7/8 In. 13.00
Apple Corer, Tin, Wooden Knob, Round 18.50
Bean Pot, Wagner, No.8, Iron 23.00
Beater Jar, Beater, Green, Marked 20.00
Beater Jar, Cast Iron, Glass Bottom, Dated 1885 .... 40.00
Beater Jar, Wesson Oil, Crockery 60.00
Beer Bottle Drainer, Wooden 12.00
Biscuit Pricker, Tin, Round, Dome Top, Iron Teeth, 3 1/4 In. 130.00
Board, Slaw, J.Stamm, Mount Joy, Pa. 39.00
Bottle, Sprinkler, Clothespin, Yellow 30.00
Bowl, Butter, Red Paint, Worn Interior, 11 In. 55.00
Bowl, Butter, Wooden, Blue Paint, 14 3/4 In. 45.00
Bowl, Chopping, Burl, With Spoon 90.00
Bowl, Poplar, Green Over White, 14 1/2 X 4 3/4 In. 40.00
Bowl, Refrigerator, Hazel Atlas, Covered, Round, 5 3/4 In. 6.00
Bowl, Shallow Kettle, Sloping Sides, Bail Handle, Iron, C.1890 .... 36.00
Box, Cutlery, Keen Kutter, Oak, 10 In. 15.00
Box, Pantry, Covered, Bail Handle, Wooden Grip, 10 1/2 X 6 In. 52.00
Box, Recipe, Gold Medal Flour, Oak 12.00
Bread Box, Enamel Ware, Green 55.00
Bread Knife, Rumford, Green Handle 12.50
Bread Knife, Word Bread Carved On Handle 45.00
Bread Maker, Universal No.8, Gray Tin, Lid, Pat.Dec.25, 1906 .... 55.00
Bread Riser, Kneading Handle, No.8 .... 25.00
Broom Holder, Wire, Hangs From Ceiling, 1880s 375.00
Bucket, Blue, 2 Metal Hoops, Wire Handle, 4 3/4 X 7 In. 23.00
Bucket, Grease, Handle & Cover, Mennonite 175.00
Butter Carrier, Covered, Wooden Bail, Natural Finish, 6 X 9 In. 150.00
KITCHEN, BUTTER MOLD, see Kitchen, Mold, Butter
Butter Print, Stylized, Round, 4 3/4 In. 45.00
Butter Stamp, Bird In Flight, Wooden, 4 X 3 1/4 In. 29.00
Butter Stamp, Bird, Small Side Knob Handle 75.00
Butter Stamp, Canada Goose On Water, Wooden, 3 1/2 X 4 1/2 In. 28.50
Butter Stamp, Carved Starflower & Foliage, Wooden, Round, 4 In. 85.00
Butter Stamp, Chicken, Screw–In Handle, Wooden, 4 1/8 In. 155.00
Butter Stamp, Cow, Fence, Grass, Bough 245.00
Butter Stamp, Eagle 175.00
Butter Stamp, Eagle, Turned Handle, 4 3/8 In. 225.00
Butter Stamp, Fern Leaf Pattern, Knob Handle, 19th Century 40.00
Butter Stamp, Fish 375.00
Butter Stamp, Geometric Floral Design, Tin Handle, 4 7/8 In. 100.00
Butter Stamp, Hearts On Starflower, Tulips, Turned Handle, 5 In. 275.00
Butter Stamp, Initials M.S., Nickel Plated Brass Plunger, 5 In. 65.00
Butter Stamp, Lollipop, Double Sides 330.00
Butter Stamp, Lollipop, Star Flower, 12 1/2 In. 400.00
Butter Stamp, Off–Center Pinwheel, Philadelphia, 4 5/8 X 5 In. 180.00
Butter Stamp, Pineapple Design, Turned Handle, 4 In. 135.00
Butter Stamp, Pomegranate, Inserted Handle, 4 1/2 In. 145.00
Butter Stamp, Sheaf of Wheat, Hexagonal, Cherry, C.1850 .... 40.00
Butter Stamp, Sheaf, J.C.& J.P.Sharpless, Turned Handle, 3 3/8 In. 195.00
Butter Stamp, Starflower, Cased, Round, 4 5/8 In. 55.00
Butter Stamp, Strawberry & Leaves, Hand Carved, American, 3 In. 85.00
Butter Stamp, Strawberry, Inserted Handle, 4 In. 155.00
Butter Stamp, Sunflower, Round, Wooden 45.00

Butter Stamp, Wooly Sheep, Germany, Large 80.00
Butter Stamp, Wooly Sheep, Germany, Small 50.00
Butter Worker, Maple, 19th Century, 9 3/4 X 5 In. 26.00
Cabinet, Hoosier, Glass Doors, 21 In. 95.00
Cabinet, Hoosier, Green Slag Glass Door Panels, Oak 485.00
Cabinet, Hoosier, Oak, Pullout Counter, C.1915, 68 X 40 X 24 In. 1100.00
Cabinet, Hoosier, Possum Bellied Bin Lower Section, 2 Part 450.00
Cabinet, Sellers, Painted, Roll Front, Enamel Top 455.00
Can Opener, Bull Head, Figural, Cast Iron, 6 In. 32.00
Can Opener, Bully, Horn, 7 In. 28.00
Can Opener, Pet Milk, Metal, Embossed Cow 15.00
Canister, Blue Agate, White Embossed Coffee 38.00
Canister, Set, Kramer 15.00
Carpet Beater, Braided Wire 17.00
Carpet Beater, Heart Shape, Heavy Wire 16.50
Cart, Shopping, Wicker 85.00
Carving Set, Winchester, Bone Handles, 3 Piece 65.00
Casserole, Pyrex, Metal Frame, Oval 35.00
Cherry Pitter, Enterprise 28.00
Cherry Pitter, Pat.March 31, 1903 .... 18.00
Chimney Cleaner, For Glass Lamp, Wooden, Wire 12.00
Chopper, Double Blade, NRS & Co., Groton, N.Y., May 2, 1899, Iron 12.50
Chopper, Food, Double Wooden Handles, Germany 8.00
Chopper, Food, Horseshoe Shaped Forged Steel Blade, Bar Handle 85.00
Chopper, Food, Iron Blade, Wooden Handle, 6 X 7 In. 36.00
Chopper, Food, Keen Kutter, No.22 .... 25.00
Chopper, Food, Rocker Type, 2 Wooden Handles, 9 In.Curved Blade 27.00
Chopper, Food, Tiller Type, Wooden Handle, 5 In.Blade 10.00
Chopper, Food, Wooden Handles, Marked Wm.Greaves & Sons, 5 3/4 In. .. 30.00
Chopper, Onion, Federal, Label 20.00
Churn, Barrel, Yellow Paint, Side Crank, 16 X 18 X 20 In. 175.00
Churn, Cast Iron Fittings, Stenciled Label, Climas Churn, 34 In. 150.00
Churn, Cherry, Brass Hoops 250.00
Churn, Daisy 55.00
Churn, Danbre, Electric, 3 Gal. 40.00
Churn, Dandy, Glass, 1 Gal. .... 20.00 To 27.00
Churn, Dazey No.40, Decal 75.00
Churn, Dazey No.40, Glass, Embossed 55.00
Churn, Dazey, Glass Bottom, 1 Qt. 200.00
Churn, Dazey, Glass, 1 Gal. .... 15.00 To 42.50
Churn, Gem Dandy, Barrel Shape, Electric 90.00
Churn, Glass, Dazey Type, Wooden Paddles, Crank Handle, 6 Qt. 35.00
Churn, Glass, Standard Churn Co., Paper Sticker, 4 Qt. 35.00
Churn, Glass, Tin Top, Wooden Paddle 35.00
Churn, Illinois Map, 3 Gal. 145.00
Churn, Table, Gray, Wooden, Tin Bottom, Iron Crank, 12 X 10 In. 138.00
Churn, Tin, Handmade, Dasher 80.00
Churn, Tin, Wooden Frame, Hand Or Foot Operated, Kentucky 265.00
Churn, Vermont, Original Red Paint 350.00
Churn, Wagnerware, Glass Bottom, 1/2 Gal. 59.00
Cleaver, Meat, Green River Works, Russel 22.00
Cleaver, Meat, Winchester 55.00
Clothes Bars, Wooden, Favorite Home Dryer 22.00
Clothes Boiler, Enameled 145.00
Clothes Brush, Composition Top, Dog Head, 7 1/2 In. 20.00
Clothes Hanger, Telescopic, Leather Case, 1913 .... 10.00
Clothes Washer, Hand, Tin 40.00
Clothespin, Brass Attachments, Dated 1904 .... 4.50
Clothespin, Set, Klose Klips, Metal Springs, Box, 1940s 15.00
     KITCHEN, COFFEE GRINDER, see Coffee Grinder
Coffee Mill, Arcade, Telephone, Unused, Original Paint 440.00
Coffee Mill, Eagle, Tin, C.1870 .... 35.00
Coffeepot, Brown Enamel 15.00
Coffeepot, Silex, Blue, Large 28.00

Condiment Set, Girl Shape, Tray, Spoon, Germany, 3 In., 3 Piece 50.00
Container, Rice, Blue & White, L & R, Germany 20.00
Cooker, Waterless, Mary Dunbar, With Cookbook, 1936 .... 50.00
Cookie Board, 5 Figures, Each Side, Full Length, 3 X 24 1/2 In. 40.00
Cookie Board, 5 Figures, Pig, Dog, Windmill, Birds, 3 X 26 3/4 In. 35.00
Cookie Board, 6 Figures, Mermaid, Rooster, Ship, 3 1/4 X 26 In. 35.00
Cookie Board, Alpine Figure, Full Length, Both Sides, 6 X 17 In. 100.00
Cookie Board, Cherry, Basket of Flowers, Tulip & Leaves, 6 X 7 In. 495.00
Cookie Board, Couple Arm In Arm, 7 X 12 3/4 In. 105.00
Cookie Board, Double Horse & Cart One Side, Bicycle Other, 14 In. 350.00
Cookie Board, Drummer One Side, Crowned Figure Other, 4 X 9 In. 175.00
Cookie Board, Early Automobile, Driver, 8 3/4 X 14 In. 85.00
Cookie Board, Equestrian Figure One Side, Rooster Other 245.00
Cookie Board, Equestrian Figures Both Sides, 8 1/2 X 12 1/2 In. 195.00
Cookie Board, Full Man One Side, Woman Other, 8 1/4 X 20 3/4 In. 125.00
Cookie Board, Horse & Rider, Dog, 6 5/8 X 16 In. 155.00
Cookie Board, Lion & Tombstone, Koning Van Dieren, 8 3/4 X 14 In. 365.00
Cookie Board, Lion, Horses, & Sleigh, Carved, 4 1/2 X 22 1/2 In. 150.00
Cookie Board, Man On Horseback, Geometric, 11 X 11 5/8 In. 50.00
Cookie Board, Man, Full–Length, Woman Other Side, 6 X 16 1/2 In. 145.00
Cookie Board, Man, Full–Length, Woman Other Side, 6 X 19 In. 45.00
Cookie Board, Pickup Truck, People, Animals, Flowers, 9 X 23 In. 150.00
Cookie Board, Rooster, Carved, 18th Century, Dutch 1495.00
Cookie Board, Rooster, Equestrian Figure One Side, Flowers, Grapes 150.00
Cookie Board, Tombstone, Pine, Old Patina, 12 3/4 X 26 In. 105.00
Cookie Set, Mirro, 9 Tin, 15 Aluminum, With Handles, Unused, Box 32.50
Corer, Apple, A & J Advertising, 6 In. 15.00
Corn Popper, Lightning, Tin, Wooden Handle, Part Label 21.00
Corn Sheller, Fulton 35.00
Cup, Measuring, Kelloggs, Pink Glass 15.00
Cup, Measuring, Metal, Cotolene 8.00
Cup, Measuring, Swansdown Cake Flour, Aluminum .... 6.00 To 8.50
Cutter, Biscuit, Rumford 14.00
Cutter, Cabbage, Cutout Heart, Butternut, 7 1/2 X 20 In. 150.00
Cutter, Cabbage, Fishtail Crest, Arched Base, Butternut, 23 1/4 In. 80.00
Cutter, Cheese, Bow With Wire, Turned Wooden Handle, Iron, 22 In. 125.00
Cutter, Cookie, Camel, Tin 22.00
Cutter, Cookie, Cat, Stylized Features, Crimped Tail, Tin, 6 In. 145.00
Cutter, Cookie, Dog, Standing, Tin, 1920 .... 6.00
Cutter, Cookie, Double End, Scalloped, Gray Tin, 1 3/4 To 3 In. 13.50
Cutter, Cookie, Drum, Tin 2.00
Cutter, Cookie, Eagle, Tin 20.00
Cutter, Cookie, Fish, Back & Strap Handle, Tin 13.50
Cutter, Cookie, Gun, Tin, 3 1/4 In. 65.00
Cutter, Cookie, Halloween, 4 Piece 8.00
Cutter, Cookie, Hatchet, Strap Handle, Open Back, Tin, 5 1/2 In. 11.00
Cutter, Cookie, Hatchet, Tin, Double Arched Handles, Giant 34.00
Cutter, Cookie, Heart, Beaded Strap Handle, Tin, 3 X 3 In. 35.00
Cutter, Cookie, Heart, Tin 12.00
Cutter, Cookie, Hen, Handle, Tin 9.00
Cutter, Cookie, Horse, Back & Strap Handle, Tin 13.50
Cutter, Cookie, Horse, Handle, Tin 9.00
Cutter, Cookie, Horse, Trotting, 6 In. 75.00
Cutter, Cookie, Lion, Flat, Tin 20.00
Cutter, Cookie, Mickey Mouse & Minnie Mouse, Tin 40.00
Cutter, Cookie, Profile Bust, Man Singing, Tin, 3 3/4 In. 100.00
Cutter, Cookie, Rabbit, Upright Position, Tin 11.50
Cutter, Cookie, Scotty, Wooden Handle 7.50
Cutter, Cookie, Star, Tin, Small 5.00
Cutter, Cookie, Woman, Punched Circle Design, Tin, 4 1/2 In. 115.00
Cutter, Cookie, Woman, Tin 9.00
Cutter, Doughnut, Rumford 14.00
Cutter, Kraut, Handmade, 1 Blade, Extra Shredder 40.00
Cutter, Kraut, Whittled Legs, Dovetailed Hopper, Walnut, 37 In. 125.00

Clean the inside of graniteware pots by boiling peeled potatoes in water.

Cookie cutters can be dated by the construction methods. Old ones are soldered in spots, not a long thin solder joint. If the solder joins the cutting-edge piece to the back by a thin, barely visible line, it is less than 50 years old.

Cutter, Pastry, Wooden, Relief Carved Flowers On Handle, 7 In.	175.00
Cutter, Pie Dough, Kreamer, Scalloped Edge, Tin, 10 In.	35.00
Cutter, Sugar, Iron, C.1830	40.00
Cutter, Vegetable, Enterprise Manufacture Co., Cast Iron	100.00
Cutting Board, Fish Shape, 14 In.	15.00
Cutting Board, Pig, Open Curly Tail, Maple, 11 1/2 X 33 In.	140.00
Cutting Board, Rolling Pin, Child's	15.00
Dipper, Iron, Brass, 8 1/4 In.	70.00
Dipper, Iron, Handle Stamped J.Schmidt, 1849. 19 1/2 In.	225.00
Dipper, Iron, Stamped H.W.Weaver, 23 1/2 In.	65.00
Dipper, Pickle, Wooden	48.00
Dipper, Sandwich, Jiffy Ice Cream, Pat.1925	160.00
Dispenser, Iced Tea, Glass Barrel, Metal Spigot, Pottery Base	65.00
Drainer, Green Pottery	145.00
Dryer, Clothes, Perfection, Wall, 8 Arms, 34 In.	25.00
Dryer, Glove, Stretcher, Wooden, American, Pair	50.00
Dryer, Mitten, Wooden, American	12.00
Dryer, Sock, Stretcher, Man's, 5 Holes, American, Pair	62.00
Dryer, Stocking, Wooden, Adult Size 11, Pair	20.00
Duck Press, Aluminum, Stainless Steel, Maryland, Oak Base, 24 In.	475.00
Dutch Oven, Griswold, No.8, Tite Top	38.00
Egg Carrier, Star, Wooden, Lettering, Paper Insert, 1906, 2 Dozen	45.00
Egg Cooker, Electric, Green Porcelain, C.1925	22.50
Egg Cooker, Hankscraft, All Parts, Directions	30.00
Egg Crate, Humpty–Dumpty, Handle, 12 X 12 X 12 In.	28.00
Egg Separator, Rumford	15.00
Egg Slicer, Elephant Hen, With Long Tail, German	45.00
Egg Timer, Iron, Quaker Lady, Sitting On Bench, 4 X 3 In.	10.00
Eggbeater, A & J, Green Handle, Patent 10/9/23	10.00 To 12.00
Eggbeater, Cassidy Fairbanks, Turbine, 1912	18.00
Eggbeater, Dover, 1882	18.00
Eggbeater, Dover, Cast Iron	20.00
Eggbeater, Taplin, Green Handle, 1924	8.00
Flue Cover, Child, Holding Fan, Near Large Vase, Oval	40.00
Flue Cover, Cottage, Flower Garden, Brass, English, 10 In., Pair	25.00
Flue Cover, Courting Couple	28.00
Flue Cover, Farm Scene Center, Stamped Tin	6.00
Flue Cover, Girl, In Rose Garden	3.00
Flue Cover, Horse Picture, Glass	15.00
Flue Cover, Little Girl With Flowers, Glass	28.00
Flue Cover, Maud Humphrey, Signed	47.50
Flue Cover, Seasons, Stamped Tin	13.00
Flue Cover, Swiss Couple, Glass, Chain	15.00
Flue Cover, Victorian Boy & Girl, Holiday Attire, 9 1/2 In.	50.00
Flue Cover, Victorian Children, Dancing, Bug Orchestra, 9 1/2 In.	35.00
Flue Cover, Victorian Courting Couple Picture, Large	28.00

Flue Cover, Woman Holding Flowers, Gold Frame 18.00
Fork, Meat, 3 Tines, Rumford 20.00
Fork, Potato, Winchester 45.00
Fork, Roasting, Iron, Primitive, European, 18 In. 25.00
Freezer, Ice Cream, North Pole 35.00
Freezer, Ice Cream, White Mountain, Wooden, 1/2 Gal. 30.00
Funnel, Marked Pratts Animal Regulator, Tin, 2 1/2 In. 10.00
Funnel, Tin, For Canning Jars, Dated June 19, '97 .... 5.00
Grabber, Long Handle, For Can Or Box 55.00
Grater, Hand Held, Mouli Type 10.00
Grater, Hanging, Tin, 1878 .... 9.00
Grater, Kreamer, Tin, Hinged Lid 15.00
Grater, Nutmeg, Edgar 35.00
Grater, Nutmeg, Mechanical, Boston, Walnut, Brass, 7 1/2 In. 225.00
Grater, Nutmeg, Spring Loaded, Nickeled Steel 50.00
Grater, Nutmeg, Tin & Wood 48.00
Grater, Nutmeg, Tin, 1875 .... 60.00
Grater, Nutmeg, Tin, Turned Wooden Handles, Signed, 5 1/4 In. 55.00
Grater, Nutmeg, Tubular Tin, Knob Handle 125.00
Grater, Spice, Edgar, Dated 1891 .... 45.00
Grater, Tin Handle Over Top, 9 In. 16.00
Grater, Tin, Half Round, Wooden Handle At Top, 11 X 4 X 2 In. 20.00
Grater, Triangular Top, Hole For Hanging, Copper, 3 1/2 22 In. 160.00
Griddle, Griswold, Cast Iron, Round 30.00
Griddle, Hearth, Cast Iron, 3 Footed, 18th Century, 13 X 22 In. 125.00
Griddle, Pancake, Aunt Jemima, Quaker Oats, 25 X 26 In. 400.00
Griddle, Swedish Pancake, Griswold, No.34 .... 35.00
Griddle, Waffle, Stand, Indian Chief, Cast Iron 39.00
Grill, Rotating, Iron, Initials Handle, Curled Feet, 18th Century 385.00
Grinder, Food, Climax, Crank Handle 13.50
Grinder, Food, Griswold, No.4, 1 Round & 2 Cross-Shaped Blades 55.00
Grinder, Food, Hinged, Russian No.2, Folds Down For Cleaning, 1902 .... 32.00
Grinder, Food, Keen Kutter, No.12 .... 15.00
Grinder, Food, Winchester, No.32 .... 57.50
Grinder, Nut, Glass Bottom, Red Tin Top, Flower 15.00
Grinder, Nut, Wooden Top, Germany 13.00
Grinder, Poppyseed, Brass & Iron 35.00
Grinder, Sausage, Clamps On Table 20.00
Grinder, Sausage, Icon, Dated 1899 .... 15.00
Grinder, Sausage, Wooden Case, Wrought Iron, Crank, Red, 20 In. 65.00
Hat Rack, Heart Cutouts, Fancy Footed Base, Nickel Plated 23.00
Holder, Towel, Walnut, Spindle, 4 Porcelain Knobs, 20 In. 50.00
Huller, Strawberry & Pin Feathers, Tin, 1906 .... 4.50
Ice Cube Breaker, Lightning, Cast Iron, Depression Glass Tray 35.00
Ice Pick, Heat With Coal 8.00
Ice Shaver, Griswold 32.50
Ice Tongs, Gifford, 13 In. 12.00
Icebox, 6 Door, Raised Panel, Porcelain Interior, Brass Hinges 500.00
Iron, Brass, Wooden Handle, Original Heating Slug, 4 X 7 In. 98.00
Iron, Charcoal, Cast Iron 40.00
Iron, Charcoal, Chimney, W.B.Cummings, 6 3/4 In. 30.00
Iron, Charcoal, Chinese Bronze, Open Pan Style, 18 Century 138.00
Iron, Charcoal, Flott, German, 8 1/4 In. 65.00
Iron, Charcoal, Marked UG, Raised Tin Panel, Castle 98.00
Iron, Child's, Cast Aluminum 16.00
Iron, Child's, Original Red Paint 26.00
Iron, Colebrookdale, Boyertown, Pa., Detachable Handle, 6 1/4 In. 75.00
Iron, Dover, 2 Piece 32.00
Iron, Electric, International Baby, Small 10.00
Iron, Electric, Wooden Handle, 1930s, Small 20.00
Iron, Flat End Handle, Dover, 4 Piece 40.00
Iron, Fluting, Cast Iron, Aug.2, 1870 .... 69.00
Iron, Fluting, Flat, Hinged At Front, Pair 65.00
Iron, Fluting, Geneva, Top Only 20.00

Iron, Fluting, Hand, Smart & Shephers, Canada, 5 3/4 In.	100.00
Iron, Fluting, Rolling, H.A.Doty, Corrugated Brass Roller, 7 In.	135.00
Iron, Fluting, The Best	65.00
Iron, Gas, Blue Graniteware	30.00
Iron, Gas, Coleman, Blue Graniteware	39.00
Iron, Gas, Coleman, Trivet, Instructions, Fuel Can, Box	65.00
Iron, Gas, Coleman, With Pump, Rest & Fill Can, Original Box	35.00
Iron, Gas, Otto, Bakelite Handle, 6 7/8 In.	85.00
Iron, Heating Slug, Side Knob Rest, 18th Century, 3 1/2 X 8 In.	145.00
Iron, Kerosene, Diamond, Instructions On Tank, 7 1/4 In.	30.00
Iron, Liquid Fuel, Coleman, Model 4–E, 8 In.	60.00
Iron, Sears, 1936	10.00
Iron, Sleeve Presser	40.00
Iron, Sleeve, Dover	28.00
Iron, Sleeve, Sensible, No.1, Detachable, Handle, 7 In.	35.00
Iron, Smoothing, Child's, Detachable Handles, 3 To 5 In., 4 Piece	135.00
Iron, Spirit, French, C.1800	65.00
Iron, Spirit, Nickel Plate, Contrasting Brass Fuel Tank, 5 In.	165.00
Iron, Wire Handle, Embossed O, 1 7/8 In.	30.00
Jar Lifter, Canning, Twisted Wire	9.00
Jar Rack, Canning, Wire, 10 X 19 In.	11.00
Kettle, Child's, Iron, 4 In.	29.50
Kettle, Open, Griswold, No.72, Small	15.00
Ladle, Caribbean, Cobalt Handle	38.00
Ladle, Stamped J.Schmidt, 1857, Iron Handle, 11 1/2 In.	30.00
Lard Press, Wooden, Primitive	50.00
Lemon Reamer, Wooden	35.00
Lemon Squeezer, Beech, Dark, 2 Handles	45.00
Lemon Squeezer, Gilchrist, Iron	5.00
Lemon Squeezer, Hand Held, Hinged Cast Iron, Wooden Insert	19.00
Lemon Squeezer, Wooden	45.00 To 50.00
Lid Lifter, Stove, Cast Iron	14.50
Mangle Board, Beechwood, Cutout Horse Handle, Red, 22 In.	295.00
Masher, Wire, Twisted, Wood Handle	10.00
KITCHEN, MATCH SAFE, see Match Safe	
Measure, Grain, Pennsylvania, 18th Century	850.00
Measure, Ice Cream, Tin, Pt.Cup	40.00
Measure, Kellogg, Pink, 1 Cup	10.00
Measure, Tin Bands, Bentwood, Peck Size	42.00
Measure, Wooden, Red Paint Traces, Daniel Cragin Mfg., 8 7/8 In.	24.00
Meat Cleaver, Steel	28.00
Meat Grinder, Keen Kutter	12.00
Meat Press, Griswold, Pre–1920	70.00
Meat Press, Universal	15.00
Meat Tenderizer, Enameled Flowers, Ironstone, 1890	35.00
Meat Tenderizer, Gray, Blue Trim, Stoneware, 4 3/8 In.	725.00
Meat Tenderizer, Porcelain, Wooden Handle	55.00
Meat Tenderizer, Rocket Type, Pat.1892	22.00
Mixer, Sunbeam, Green Juicer & Bowl, 1930s	40.00
Mixer, Windup Beater, On & Off Lever, Glass Bottom, Metal Top	25.00
KITCHEN, MOLD, see also Pewter, Mold; Tinware, Mold	
Mold, Baking, Cast Iron, Pig, 9 In.	225.00
Mold, Butter, 2 Acorns & Leaves, 1/2 Lb.	75.00
Mold, Butter, 3 Leaves, Miniature	57.00
Mold, Butter, 4 Different Fruits, 1 Lb.	95.00
Mold, Butter, 6–Sided, Sheaf of Wheat, Small	45.00
Mold, Butter, 8–Petal Flower, Hand Carved Wood, 4 In.	45.00
Mold, Butter, Acorn, Varnished, 2 Piece, Penn.Dutch, 1/2 Lb.	99.00
Mold, Butter, Carved Rosette, 2–Sided Lollipop, Short Handle	330.00
Mold, Butter, Cow, Hand Carved Wood, 4 1/4 In.	75.00
Mold, Butter, Cow, Plunger Stick, Round, 3 1/4 In.	24.00
Mold, Butter, Cricket, Flat Back, American	35.00
Mold, Butter, Double Acorn	75.00
Mold, Butter, Fleur–De–Lis, Wooden Handle	45.00

Mold, Butter, Floral Design, Carved By Lewis B.Pert, 1839, 4 In. 150.00
Mold, Butter, Flowers In Bottom, 1 Lb. 65.00
Mold, Butter, Flowers, Square 95.00
Mold, Butter, Folding, 18 Small Houses, 42 In. 305.00
Mold, Butter, Foliage 65.00
Mold, Butter, Glass, Cow Pattern, Wooden Handle, 6 In. 40.00
Mold, Butter, Letters M O, Brass Mechanism 40.00
Mold, Butter, Lollipop With Star Pattern 400.00
Mold, Butter, Peacock, 1/2 Lb. 375.00
Mold, Butter, Peasant Man & Woman, Round 192.00
Mold, Butter, Pinwheel 180.00
Mold, Butter, Rooster, Plunger Stick, 3 1/4 X 3 1/2 In. 24.00
Mold, Butter, Sheaf of Wheat, Pine 45.00
Mold, Butter, Sheep, 1 Piece, Knob, 4 In. 98.00
Mold, Butter, Sheep, Plunger Stick, Round, 3 1/2 In. 27.00
Mold, Butter, Stars, Lines, Removable Bottom, 5 In., 2 Piece 75.00
Mold, Butter, Strawberry & Leaves, Round, C.1850, 1/2 Lb. 95.00
Mold, Butter, Swan ....68.00 To 125.00
Mold, Butter, Thistle On Heart Shape, Wide Flat Back, 3 In. 40.00
Mold, Butter, With Pie Crimper Back 220.00
Mold, Butter, With Ring, Miniature 244.50
Mold, Butter, Word Butter Carved In Wood, Glass Insert 65.00
Mold, Cake, Lamb, Griswold 95.00
Mold, Cake, Lamb, Griswold, No.866, Booklet & Recipes 65.00
Mold, Cake, Rabbit, Sitting, Iron 150.00
Mold, Cake, Santa Claus, Griswold, Cast Iron 235.00
    KITCHEN, MOLD, CANDLE, see Tinware, Mold, Candle
Mold, Candy, 2 Dogs, 3 1/2 X 12 In. 20.00
Mold, Candy, Boy On Pig, Initialed V.E., 4 1/2 X 4 5/8 In. 255.00
Mold, Candy, Flower Design 45.00
Mold, Candy, Indian Chief Bust, Headdress, 2 1/4 In. 15.00
Mold, Cheese, Heart Shape, 3 Footed, Handle, Pa., 4 X 3 In. 165.00
Mold, Cheese, Tin, Heart Shape, Pierced 45.00
Mold, Chocolate Bar, Hershey, 1910 .... 8.50
Mold, Chocolate, 2 Turkeys, 8 In. 30.00
Mold, Chocolate, 4 Rabbits, Tin 55.00
Mold, Chocolate, 6 Lions, In Profile, Copper, Flat 50.00
Mold, Chocolate, Bugs Bunny, Warner Bros. 75.00
Mold, Chocolate, Bunnies, Kissing, 8 In. 30.00
Mold, Chocolate, Bunny With Pack, 11 In. 30.00
Mold, Chocolate, Bunny, Sitting, Turnable Type, 9 In. 30.00
Mold, Chocolate, Camel, 3 1/2 X 5 In. 22.00
Mold, Chocolate, Charlie Chaplin, Flat, 5 Grooves, 4 X 7 In. 135.00
Mold, Chocolate, Harp, Angel, German, Tin 32.00
Mold, Chocolate, Hen, Cooked, Sg.E. & Co., 2 1/2 X 6 1/4 In. 16.00
Mold, Chocolate, Lamb, Wire Clips, Tin, 8 1/2 X 6 In. 70.00
Mold, Chocolate, Mickey Mouse, Tin, 5 1/2 In. 75.00
Mold, Chocolate, Rabbit In Easter Egg 55.00
Mold, Chocolate, Rabbit, Book Style, Hinged, 4 Hole 60.00
Mold, Chocolate, Rabbit, Metal, American, 9 1/2 X 4 1/2 In. 45.00
Mold, Chocolate, Rabbit, Standing, 21 1/2 X 12 In. 325.00
Mold, Chocolate, Rabbits, Sitting, 12 In. 95.00
Mold, Chocolate, Rabbits, Standing, 13 In. 115.00
Mold, Chocolate, Rooster, Tin, 2 1/4 X 1 3/4 In. 6.50
Mold, Chocolate, Rooster, With Top Hat, Tin, 2 Part, 6 3/4 In. 35.00
Mold, Chocolate, Santa Claus, Single, Tin, 3 1/2 X 7 1/2 In. 25.00
Mold, Chocolate, Santa Claus, Warner Bros. 75.00
Mold, Chocolate, Sitting Hen, Tin 45.00
Mold, Chocolate, St.Nicholas, Sg.E.& Co., 8 1/2 X 6 1/4 In. 85.00
Mold, Chocolate, Turkey, 3 Parts, Germany, 7 1/2 In. 60.00
Mold, Chocolate, Turkey, 8 In. 30.00
Mold, Chocolate, Valentine, 9 Victorian Hearts, Flat, 14 X 18 In. 135.00
Mold, Cookie, Horn of Plenty, Iron, Oval, American 78.00
Mold, Cookie, Springerle, Pewter, On Wood, 4 Designs, 3 1/2 X 4 In. 85.00

Mold, Cookie, Springerle, Rabbit, Grapes, House, Hen On Nest 30.00
Mold, Doughnut, Cloverleaf Shape, Hinged, Makes 3, Cast Iron 55.00
Mold, Food, Andy Gump, Nickel Over Copper 90.00
Mold, Food, Apple, With Stem 30.00
Mold, Food, Copper, Round, Embossed Chicken, 8 In. 30.00
Mold, Food, Fleur-De-Lis 25.00
Mold, Food, Odd Fellow Links 30.00
Mold, Food, Oval, Tin, Ear of Corn, Embossed, 4 X 5 In. 50.00
Mold, Food, Rabbit, 5 1/2 X 4 1/2 In. 45.00
Mold, Food, Turk's Head, Copper, Swirled Design, Tin Wash, 10 In. 35.00
Mold, Food, Turk's Head, Swirled Design, Handle, Green, 9 3/4 In. 25.00
Mold, Fruit Jelly, Tin, Oval, C.1880 .... 65.00
Mold, Headcheese 25.00

KITCHEN, MOLD, ICE CREAM, see also Pewter, Mold, Ice Cream

Mold, Ice Cream, Banana, Tin 25.00
Mold, Ice Cream, Bell, Tin 15.00
Mold, Ice Cream, Brick, Tin, 7 1/2 In. 25.00
Mold, Maple Sugar, Duck, 6 1/4 X 5 1/4 In. 8.00
Mold, Maple Sugar, Elephant, Long Trunk, 7 1/2 X 5 1/2 In. 8.00
Mold, Maple Sugar, Heart, Diamond, Spade, C.1850, 4 X 17 X 2 In. 150.00
Mold, Maple Sugar, Horse, 6 1/2 X 5 1/2 In. 8.00
Mold, Maple Sugar, Pine, Strawberry, C.1830, 1 1/2 X 5 X 9 In. 150.00
Mold, Maple Sugar, Rabbit, 6 1/2 X 5 3/4 In. 8.00
Mold, Maple Sugar, Rooster, 6 1/4 X 5 1/2 In. 8.00
Mold, Maple Sugar, Squirrel, 6 1/4 X 6 In. 8.00
Mold, Pudding, Covered, Kreamer, Wire Ring Handle, 9 In. 25.00
Mold, Pudding, Polychrome, English 25.00
Mold, Pudding, Tinned Interior, 3 X 9 In. 130.00
Mold, Sugar, Rabbit, Indiana, 7 1/2 X 6 1/4 In. 34.00
Mortar & Pestle, Curly Maple, 8 1/4 In. 65.00
Mortar & Pestle, Iron, 6 3/4 In. 25.00
Noodle Board, With Backboard, 22 In. 23.00
Opener, Beer, Blaze, Bottle Shape, Wooden 20.00
Opener, Beer, Duquesne, Bottle Shape, Metal 15.00
Opener, Beer, Pabst, Bottle Shape, Metal 15.00
Opener, Beer, Schlitz, Bottle Shape, Metal 15.00
Oven, Reflector, Hearth, Spit, Crank Handle, C.1830, 10 X 12 In. 385.00
Paddle, Applesauce 8.00
Paddle, Butter, Hook End, C.1880 .... 18.00
Pan, Bundt, Cast Iron 40.00
Pan, Cake, Bundt, Fluted, Tin, 9 1/2 In. 10.00
Pan, Corn Muffin, Iron, Crusty Corn Cobs, Pat.1920, 4 X 9 In. 40.00
Pan, Cornstick, Cast Iron, Makes 11, 7 X 14 In. 20.00
Pan, Cornstick, Griswold Crispy Corn, 4 1/4 X 8 1/2 In. 75.00
Pan, Cornstick, Griswold, No.262 .... 65.00
Pan, Cornstick, Griswold, Small, No.252 .... 15.00
Pan, Cornstick, Wagner Ware, Glass, 1920 .... 20.00
Pan, French Roll, Griswold, Cast Iron 20.00
Pan, Frying, Good Health Embossed, Iron, 7 In. 10.00
Pan, Frying, Griswold No. 3 .... 8.00
Pan, Frying, Griswold No. 10 .... 15.00
Pan, Frying, Griswold, No.709, Red Porcelain 28.00
Pan, Heart Shape, Dark Tin, Hand Soldered 47.50
Pan, Jam, Brass, Fixed Handle, Mid-19th Century, 9 In. 40.00
Pan, Muffin, G.F.Filley, No. 5, Cast Iron 75.00
Pan, Muffin, G.F.Filley, No.10, Cast Iron, I Bar Handles 75.00
Pan, Muffin, Griswold, No.10 .... 30.00 To 40.00
Pan, Popover, Griswold, No.10 .... 40.00
Pancake Turner, Rumford 22.00
Pantry Jar, Emerald Glass, Large 20.00
Pasta Maker, Iron, Table Clamp Attachment, 5 Different Rolls 38.00
Pastry Board, Hanging, Tin 190.00
Pastry Roller, Floral Design, Turned Handle, J.Conger, 11 1/2 In. 375.00
Peeler, Apple, Bonanza, Large 125.00

Peeler, Apple, Cast Iron, Pat.1850	45.00
Peeler, Apple, Coons, Holds 3 At Once, Patent 1915, 18 X 36 In.	210.00
Peeler, Apple, Goodell	25.00 To 48.00
Peeler, Apple, Hudson Parer Co., 3 Gears, Dated 1928	48.00
Peeler, Apple, Iron, '72	35.00
Peeler, Apple, Iron, 5 Cogs, Hand Crank, Pat.1865	65.00
Peeler, Apple, Iron, Pat.1868	50.00 To 65.00
Peeler, Apple, Keen Kutter	65.00 To 95.00
Peeler, Apple, Lockey–Howland, Cast Iron, 1856	45.00
Peeler, Apple, Mechanical, 1/2 In.Circle, Cast Iron, 1863	48.00
Peeler, Apple, Mechanical, Iron, 1863	48.00
Peeler, Apple, Reading Hardware Co., Mechanical, Dated 1878	36.00
Peeler, Apple, Rival, No.296, Dated 1889, Hand Crank, 32 X 18 In.	245.00
Peeler, Apple, Sinclair	45.00
Peeler, Apple, Triumph, Geared Motor, Dated 1889	455.00
Peeler, Apple, Triumph, Motor Driven	500.00
Peeler, Apple, White Mountain	23.00 To 32.50
Peeler, Potato, Hamlinite, 1920	30.00
Peeler, Potato, Morton Salt	10.00
Pie Bird, Chef	22.00
Pie Bird, Chick, Pink & Blue, Tall	9.00
Pie Bird, Chick, Yellow	9.00
Pie Bird, Crown, Black Under Glaze	13.00
Pie Bird, Duck, Pink & Gray	9.00
Pie Bird, Duck, Yellow & Brown	9.00
Pie Bird, Peacock, Blue, Green, Rosemead Label, 4 1/2 In.	45.00
Pie Bird, Rooster, Orchid & Green, Blue Tail	10.00
Pie Board, Handle, Pine, 19 3/8 X 3 1/2 In.	85.00
Pie Crimper, Serrated Crimper, Handle, Brass, Patent 1871	45.00
Pie Crimper, Wooden, Wheel, 7 In.	28.00
Pie Pan, Cottolene Shortening, Tin	12.00
Pie Plate, Jane Parker, Tin	5.00
Pitcher, Milk, Lisk Enamelware, Black, White	19.00
Plant Stand, Iron, Graduated Tiers, Scroll Arms, Green, 43 In.	1900.00
Potato Ricer, Cast Iron	18.00
Press, Lard, Primitive, Leather Hinge	14.00
Pump, Water, For Sink, Cast Iron, 18 In.	40.00
Rack, Drying, Country, 2 Bars, Shoe Feet, Gray, 31 X 38 In.	115.00
Rack, Drying, Folding, Beading, Blue Paint, 35 X 44 In.	90.00
Rack, Drying, Pine, Mortised, Primitive, 3 Sections, 48 X 55 In.	85.00
Rack, Egg, Holds 12, Pine	40.00
Rack, Pie, 2 Tier, Tin	27.50
Rack, Pie, 20 1/2 In.	65.00
Rack, Plate Drying, Dowel Rod Shelves, On Wheels, Wooden, 55 1/2 In.	75.00
Rack, Utensil, Pine, Scalloped, 11 Hooks, Stripped Finish, 27 In.	165.00
Rack, Utensil, Scalloped Pine, Old Red Paint, 9 Hooks, 24 In.	235.00
Roller, Cookie, Wooden, Hand Carved, Floral & Leaves, 7 X 2 In.	125.00
Rolling Pin, 6–Sided, Carved Designs	20.00
Rolling Pin, Blown Amber Glass, 15 In.	73.00
Rolling Pin, Blue Striped	68.00 To 185.00
Rolling Pin, Child's, Original Red Painted Handles, C.1910	25.00
Rolling Pin, China, Cork Stopper	45.00
Rolling Pin, Cigar Shape, Button End	25.00
Rolling Pin, Curly Maple	30.00 To 45.00
Rolling Pin, Custard Glass, Sprinkler Closure	125.00
Rolling Pin, Finger Grip, Turned Handle, Maple, 17 1/2 In.	20.00
Rolling Pin, Glass, Amber, 15 In.	85.00
Rolling Pin, Golden Grain Homemade Bread, Pottery, Wooden Handles	35.00
Rolling Pin, Green Handles, Tiger Maple, 15 In.	18.00
Rolling Pin, Harker, Pottery, Flowers	65.00
Rolling Pin, Joseph Reuter, Gilbertville, Iowa, Pottery	190.00
Rolling Pin, Kelvinator, China	50.00
Rolling Pin, Maple, Button Ends, 20th Century, 11 1/2 In.	9.00
Rolling Pin, Maple, Peg Handles	15.00

Rolling Pin, Mule Ear Handles, Maple, 18 1/2 In. 13.00
Rolling Pin, Noodle, Primitive, 1 Piece 45.00
Rolling Pin, Ogilvie's Flour, Nippon, Blue Mark 100.00
Rolling Pin, Pekin Coal, Neb., Milk Glass 135.00
Rolling Pin, Pink, Wooden Handles, 15 1/2 In. 125.00
Rolling Pin, Pottery, Brown, Tan Wooden Handles, 1930s 110.00
Rolling Pin, Pottery, Reuter, Gen.Merchandise, Gilbertsville, Iowa .. 180.00
Rolling Pin, Ravioli 22.00
Rolling Pin, Roll–Rite, Glass 14.00
Rolling Pin, Snow White Grocery, W.Langsdale, Stoneware 175.00
Rolling Pin, Solid Glass, Aqua 110.00
Rolling Pin, Stoneware, Blue Handle 15.00
Rolling Pin, Swirled Enamel Handle 15.00
Rolling Pin, Taverne, China 75.00
Rolling Pin, Tiger Maple, 14 In. 85.00
Rolling Pin, Walnut, Pennsylvania, 13 In. 195.00
Rolling Pin, Wildflower, Blue & White, Pottery, 8 In. 135.00
Sadiron, Child's, C.1920, 3 1/2 X 2 1/2 In. 27.00
Sadiron, Clamp Style, Asbestos, Handle, 3 Piece 30.00
Sadiron, Colbrookdale, Detachable Wooden Handle, Extra Iron 27.00
Sadiron, Dolphin Handle, Heven & Co., 6 1/2 In. 40.00
Sadiron, Enterprise, 2 1/2 In. 30.00
Sadiron, Mrs.Potts, Separate Wooden Handle 16.50
Salt, Hanging, Blue Agate 60.00
Sausage Stuffer, Cast Iron, 1897, 6 Qt. 50.00
Scaler, Fish, Iron, C.1893 .... 8.50
Scoop, Apple Butter, Open D Handle, Wooden 220.00
Scoop, Brass, Wooden Handle, Small 20.00
Scoop, Burl, Blunt End Handle, Checkered Design, 8 1/2 In. 250.00
Scoop, Ice Cream Sandwich, Icy–Pi 110.00
Scoop, Ice Cream Sandwich, Polar–Pak 250.00
Scoop, Ice Cream Sandwich, Reliance 100.00
Scoop, Ice Cream Soda, Gilchrist, Size 12 .... 30.00
Scoop, Ice Cream Soda, Gilchrist, Size 16 .... 50.00
Scoop, Ice Cream Soda, Gilchrist, Size 31 .... 35.00
Scoop, Ice Cream Soda, Gilchrist, Size 40 .... 45.00
Scoop, Ice Cream, Arnold, No.50, Dated 1927 .... 28.00
Scoop, Ice Cream, Banana 475.00
Scoop, Ice Cream, Benedict DeLuxe 17.50
Scoop, Ice Cream, Benedict Indestructo, No.30 .... 22.00
Scoop, Ice Cream, Brass 45.00
Scoop, Ice Cream, Clipper Disher 190.00
Scoop, Ice Cream, Clipper, 1905 .... 125.00
Scoop, Ice Cream, Cone Shape, Gilchrist No.33 .... 85.00
Scoop, Ice Cream, Dairy Fresh 28.00
Scoop, Ice Cream, Dover Mfg.Co., No.20, Nickel Plated Brass 75.00
Scoop, Ice Cream, Dover Mfg.Co., Right & Left Handed, Brass 75.00
Scoop, Ice Cream, Dover, No.10, 2 Way 25.00
Scoop, Ice Cream, Gilchrist No.30, Size 12 .... 48.00
Scoop, Ice Cream, Gilchrist, Brass, Size 20 .... 35.00
Scoop, Ice Cream, Gilchrist, No.30 .... 25.00
Scoop, Ice Cream, Gilchrist, Tin, Smallest Size 32.00
Scoop, Ice Cream, Hamilton Beach, Brass 25.00
Scoop, Ice Cream, Hamilton Beach, Model 60 .... 24.00
Scoop, Ice Cream, Isaly Dairy Skyscraper 45.00
Scoop, Ice Cream, John W.Wallace, Tin 25.00
Scoop, Ice Cream, Wooden Handle 15.00
Scoop, Marrow, Carved Wood, E.I., 1779, 6 1/4 In. 320.00
Scoop, Sugar, Round Oak Stove 40.00
Scraper, Dough, Iron, Initials J.B. On Blade, 4 1/2 In. 145.00
Seeder, Olive 135.00
Seeder, Raisin, Everett 68.00
Seeder, Raisin, Rollman 35.00
Seeder, Raisin, Wooden, Signed & Dated 1860, Small 42.00

Sieve, Horsehair, Woven, Shaker Style, 8 X 4 1/2 In. 49.00
Sieve, Wooden, Tin Hand Punched Bottom, 1800s, 14 X 20 In. 98.00
Sifter, Flour, Blood's Patent, Screen Roller, Crank Handle 130.00
Sifter, Flour, Bromwell's, Wooden Knob, 1930, 1 Cup 10.00
Sifter, Flour, Bromwell's, Wooden Knob, 1930, 3 Cup 7.00
Sifter, Flour, Calumet Baking Powder, Tin, 2 Cup 12.00
Sifter, Flour, Child's, Tin 12.00
Sifter, Flour, Columbia Flour, Landers, Frary, Clard 15.00
Sifter, Flour, Duplex, Gray Tin, Top, Bottom Covers, 5 Cup 25.00
Sifter, Flour, Hoosier Cabinet, Tin 38.00
Sifter, Flour, Horsehair Mesh, Wooden Sides, 11 1/2 In. 67.00
Sifter, Flour, I.G.A. 7.00
Sink Drainer, Corner, Blue, Perforated, Tin, With Hanger 23.00
Sink Drainer, Corner, Lisk Enamelware, Black, White, Labels 21.00
Sink Drainer, Corner, Perforated Tin, Blue, With Hanger 23.00
Skillet, Egg, Griswold, Iron 10.00
Skillet, Griswold, Colonial Breakfast 22.50
Skillet, Griswold, No.768, Square .... 28.00 To 32.00
Skillet, Iron, Double, Griswold, No.80 .... 32.50
Skillet, Iron, Erie, 8 In. 12.00
Skillet, Smoke Ring, Griswold, 13 In. 45.00
Skimmer, Brass & Iron, 18th Century 145.00
Skimmer, Brass, Iron, 19 3/4 In. 70.00
Skimmer, Brass, Iron, Handle, 8 3/4 In. 185.00
Skimmer, Copper, Iron Handles, 17 In. 60.00
Sleeve Board, Pat.1903 .... 10.00
Slicer, Potato, Wooden, Ornate, 15 In. 35.00
Slicer, Vegetable, Feemasters, Box, 1940s 7.00
Slicer, Vegetable, Primitive, Wooden, Long & Narrow, C.1895 .... 55.00
Slicer, Vegetable, Tin, Handmade, Heart Cutout 65.00
Slicer, Vegetable, Wooden, 6 Serrated Blades, Label, 1898, 18 In. 50.00
Slicer, Vegetable, Wooden, Dated 1895 .... 35.00
Soap Dish, Wire, Fits Over Side of Tub 15.00
Soap Shaver, Fels Naphtha, Tin 4.00
Spatula, Marked F.B.S., Canton, Ohio, Iron & Brass, 14 1/4 In. 125.00
Spatula, Rumford .... 6.00 To 15.00
Spatula, Swansdown Flour 14.00
Spice Box, 4 Smaller Containers Inside, Round 65.00
Spice Box, 8 Boxes Inside, Each Marked, Wooden, 3 1/4 X 9 1/2 In. 170.00
Spice Box, 8 Containers, Wooden, Dated 1858 .... 295.00
Spice Box, 8 Drawers, Oak 120.00
Spice Box, Chautauqua Spices, 7 Inside Tins, Round, C.1910 .... 60.00
Spice Box, Hanging, Black Stenciled Labels, 8 Drawer, Chestnut 135.00
Spice Box, Hanging, Tin, 8 Drawers 120.00
Spice Box, Pyramid, 6 Sections, Dark Finish, 12 1/2 In. 175.00
Spice Mill, Enterprise, Wall Mount, Iron 65.00
Spice Set, Barrel, Blue, White, Containing Cans of Spices, Germany 80.00
Spice Set, Green Swirl, 8 Piece 65.00
Spice Set, Wall Hung, Hinged Cover, Black Tole, 6 Cans 37.50
Spoon, Mustard, Wooden, Small 6.00
Spoon, Slotted, Rumford 11.50
Sprinkler, Dutch Boy 15.00
Sprinkler, Siamese Cat, 8 1/2 In. 12.00
Squeezer, Lard, Leather Hinges, Wooden Handle 7.00
Stand, Washtub, Folding 65.00
Stove, Cooking, Combine, Plate Warmers, Cast Iron, 45 X 62 In. 575.00
Strainer Set, Eveready, 1919 .... 22.00
Strainer, Grater & Meat Grinder, Child's, Little Homemaker, 1930s 32.50
Strainer, Maple Syrup, Dustpan Style 17.50
Strainer, Tea, Faultless Starch, Tin 7.00
String Holder, Apple, Chalkware 22.00
String Holder, Beehive, Cast Iron 35.00
String Holder, Bonnet Girl 20.00
String Holder, Boy, Chalkware, Top Hat, Pipe 15.00

String Holder, Chef .... 20.00 To 35.00
String Holder, Chicago String Co., Cast Iron 70.00
String Holder, Dutch Girl, Chalkware 12.00
String Holder, Mermaid, Cast Iron, 12 In. 55.00
String Holder, Postum 145.00
String Holder, Strawberry Face 20.00
Sugar Cutter, Black Iron, 18th Century 795.00
Sugar Cutter, Iron, Spring, Clasp, 9 1/2 In. 85.00
Sugar Nippers, Iron, 8 3/4 In. 85.00
Taster, Brass, Iron Handle, Tooled, Date 1862, 7 3/4 In. 375.00
Taster, Brass, Iron, Tooled Handle, 7 1/2 In. 110.00
Taster, Iron, Brass, Scrolled Hanger, 9 5/8 In. 75.00
Taster, Iron, Brass, Shaped Handle, 10 1/4 In. 165.00
Teakettle, Cast Iron, Label Bottom, 15 In. 75.00
Teakettle, Gooseneck Spout, Iron, 6 X 9 In. 130.00
Teakettle, Tea, Open Hearth, Ball Shape, Gooseneck, Footed 220.00
Teapot, Swing Lid, Porcelain Knob, Griswold, Miniature 95.00
Thermometer, Candy, Green Handle, Taylor, Pat.1931, 1934, 12 In. 10.00
Thermometer, Candy, W.Ragsdale, Candy Specialist, Wooden Box, 12 In. 35.00
Thermometer, Candy, Wexler, Box 10.00
Thermometer, Stove Top, Mercury, Swans Down Cake Flour, Miniature 45.00
Toaster, 4 Slice, Goldberg Type 45.00
Toaster, Cookenette, Electric 17.50
Toaster, Electric, Brass, Fancy Design, 1915 .... 45.00
Toaster, Hotpoint, Art Deco 28.00
Toaster, Knoblock Pyramid, 1909 .... 12.00
Toaster, Pop–Down, Industrial Design, Art Deco 30.00
Toaster, Primitive, Iron, 2 Section Rack, Wooden Handle, 18 In. 65.00
Toaster, Stainless Steel, Art Deco, 1930s 25.00
Toaster, Stainless Steel, Electric, Star, Connecticut .... *Cover* 20.00
Toaster, Toastmaster, 1930 .... 10.00
Toaster, Twisted Wire Handles, Clamps, Homemade, Wire 22.50
Trammel, Sawtooth, Iron, Zigzag Tooling, Adjustable, 1754, 31 In. 350.00
Tub, Dyeing, Staved, Red, Indigo Stain Interior, 3 Hoops, 12 X 13 In. 175.00
Wafer Iron, Cast Iron, Wrought Handles, Diamond Design, 25 In. 90.00
Wafer Iron, Iron, Long Handle, Dated 1706, Paddle, 6 X 35 In. 200.00
Wafer Iron, Lute Pattern 95.00
Wafer Iron, Wrought Handles, Tulip Design, Cast Iron, 30 1/2 In. 115.00
Waffle Iron, Child's, Wagner, 1922 .... 90.00
Waffle Iron, Child's, Wagner, Wooden Handle 55.00
Waffle Iron, Griswold, No. 8, 1908 .... 25.00
Waffle Iron, Griswold, No. 8, Ring Handles 40.00
Waffle Iron, Griswold, No. 8, Stove Poker Type Handle 40.00
Waffle Iron, Griswold, No.11, Square, 1908 .... 60.00
Waffle Iron, Heart 'N Stars, High Base, Griswold 95.00
Waffle Iron, Iron Stand, Nickel Finish, Sidney, Ohio, 4 1/2 In. 100.00
Waffle Iron, Keen Kutter 95.00
Waffle Iron, Stover, Cast Iron, Box, Miniature 150.00
Waffle Iron, Wagner, Cast Iron, 1910 .... 50.00
Waffle Iron, Wagner, Stovetop, Pat.1892 .... 65.00 To 75.00
Washboard, Blue Graniteware 10.00
Washboard, Brass 9.50
Washboard, Circle, For Hand Washables 75.00
Washboard, Graniteware, Blue, Imperial 15.00
Washboard, Hand–E–Washboard, Magic Circles 120.00
Washboard, Mother Hubbard's 70.00
Washboard, National Brass King, Brass, Both Sides 65.00
Washboard, National, No.862, Blue Graniteware 35.00
Washboard, Reversible Spring Protector, Cure For Blue Monday 85.00
Washboard, Rounded Corrugated Scrub Surface, 15 X 27 1/2 In. 175.00
Washboard, Slanted, Arched Footed Ends, C.1800, 20 1/2 X 9 In. 21.50
Washboard, Soap Saver, Glass King, National 26.50
Washboard, Soap Saver, White Hen, National, Pat.1918 .... 39.00
Washboard, Tin, Short Wooden Feet, 12 X 22 In. ....

Washboard, Wooden, Handmade, Soap Tray Top, 24 X 13 1/2 In. 65.00
Washboard, Zinc .... 16.00 To 18.00
Washing Machine, Copper, 1920 .... 250.00
Wax Card, For Sadirons, 1908 .... 9.00
Wedding Cake Figure, Bride & Groom, C.1920 .... 22.50
Whip, Cake Mixer, Rumford, 1908 .... 10.00
Whip, Cream, A.& J.Whippit, Box 10.00
Whip, Cream, Fries, Tin, 4 Legs, Crank, Worn Black Paint, 9 In. 45.00
Whip, Cream, Rumford 12.50
Whip, Cream, Tin, Cone Shape, Pat.Sept.14, 1875, 4 X 14 In. 37.00
Whip, Cream, Tin, Gray, 4 Curved Legs, Center Handle, Lid 60.00
Wringer, Child's, Iron, Wood, Horseshoe Brand 45.00

In the 1960s, the United States government passed a law that required knife manufacturers to mark their knives with the country of origin. This seemed to encourage the collectors, and knife collecting became an interest of a large group of people. All types of knives are collected, from top quality twentieth–century examples to old bone– or pearl–handled knives in excellent condition.

KNIFE, 2 Blades, Marked Western States, Boulder, Colo., 3 In. 18.00
Banana 12.00
Bolo, Folding 150.00
Bowie, Alfred Williams, Sheffield, Bone Grip, 19th Century, 6 In. 57.00
Bowie, Double Scalloped Blade, Brass Guard, Rosewood Grips 80.00
Bowie, Folding, Stag Handle, 12 In. 75.00
Bowie, Spearpoint, Brass & Wood Grip, Inlaid British Lion 145.00
Bread, Christy, Open Handle, Pat.1889–1901 .... 10.00
Butcher's, Shapleigh 15.00
Butcher, Case, XX 10.00
Butcher, German, C.1890, Long Blade 25.00
Camp, Case XX, Red Bone 35.00
Chamfer, Cooper's, 16 In. 28.00
Child's, Primitive, Wooden Handle, Embossed For A Good Girl 8.50
Clip Point, Arnes & Son, Sheffield, Leather & Metal Scabbard, 12 In. 195.00
Draw, Fold Up Handle, Winstead 25.00
Draw, German Pattern 35.00
Draw, Simmons Hardware 15.00
Europa Steamship, Pearlized Handle, Leather Case 75.00
Farrier's, Bone Handle, Sheffield 25.00
First Spice Mixing Co., Pearl Handle, 5 1/2 In. 26.00
Flax, Chestnut, Dark Patina, 23 In. 12.00
Folding, With Spoon, Camillus Cutlery Co., N.Y., Rosewood Handles 40.00
Fruit, Silver Plated Grips, Design, 2 1/2 In.Blade 15.00
Fruit, Silver, Pearl Handle, Ridge In Handle, 9 1/8 In., 8 Piece 125.00
Gentleman's, Silver Plate, Keen Kutter, Single Blade 20.00
Grafting, Henry Sears & Son, 2 Blade, 1865 .... 60.00
Hay, The American, Adjustable Handle, Pat.Sept.5, 1899 .... 22.00
Hunting & Skinning, Cutco, Leather Sheath 20.00
Hunting, Bone Handle, Stag, Germany, Sheath 25.00
Jack, Case, Sodbuster, XX2138 .... 15.00
Jack, Engraved Single Blade, Textured Sides, Coin, 3 1/4 In. 28.00

Clean aluminum with fine steel wool or steel wool soap pads. To remove discoloration, boil two teaspoons of cream of tartar and a quart of water in the utensil. The acid from cooking tomatoes or rhubarb in the pot may also remove the stain.

Jack, Gold Filled, For Watch Chain 18.00
Jack, Sterling Silver 25.00
Jack, Ulster Boy Scout 40.00
Joseph Veiner, Cherokee, Iowa 75.00
King's Holme Cruise, Commemorative, 4 Blade, 3 1/2 In. 38.00
Kris, Carved Ivory Handle, Ornamental Sheath, Japan 550.00
Machete, Legitimus, Collins 30.00
Marilyn Monroe 5.00
Pen, Lawrence Welk 8.00
Pocket, 2 Blades, Nickel Silver Handle, Valley Forge Cutlery, Pair 250.00
Pocket, Boker Tree Brand, Germany, 3 Blades 35.00
Pocket, Buffalo, Case XX, Large 45.00
Pocket, Case, No.2137 .... 20.00
Pocket, Case, No.P172 .... 45.00
Pocket, First National Bank, Webster City, Iowa 12.50
Pocket, High Shoe Shape, Multicolor Handle 22.00
Pocket, Jacoby, Western Germany, Brass Grips, Corkscrew, Can Opener ... 20.00
Pocket, Ka–Bar, Double Blade 22.00
Pocket, Kenney Shoes 10.00
Pocket, Mule Day, No.358, Box, 1983 .... 40.00
Pocket, Remington R4353, Bullet 450.00
Pocket, Remington, Bullet, No.4353 .... 450.00
Pocket, Remington, Purina, 4 Blade 90.00
Pocket, Schlitz Beer, Nickel Silver Finish, Metal Grips 14.00
Pocket, Sod Buster, Case XX 25.00
Pocket, Star Brand Shoes, Shoe Shaped 65.00
Pocket, Travelers Insurance Co. 65.00
Pocket, Winchester, No.2069 .... 85.00
Sacrificial, Bone Scrimshaw Case 160.00
Schrade Cutlery Co., 2 Blade, Celluloid 120.00
Sheath, K–Bar 35.00
Sheath, Remington UMC 50.00
Winchester, 3 Blades 75.00

KNOWLES, TAYLOR & KNOWLES, see KTK; Lotus Ware

The name "Koch" is signed on the front of a series of plates decorated with fruit, vegetables, animals, or birds. The dishes date from the 1910 to 1930 period and were probably decorated in Germany.

KOCH, Bowl, Fruit, Apples, 9 In. 70.00
Bowl, Hand Painted Fruit & Leaves, Signed, 9 In. 30.00
Celery, Scalloped, Enameled Birds, Flowers, Silver Plated Holder 165.00
Cracker Jar, Covered 250.00
Jam Jar 95.00
Pitcher, Lemonade 125.00
Plate, Grapes, 8 1/2 In. .... 25.00 To 35.00
Sugar Shaker 145.00
Tray, Bunches of Grapes, Open Handles, Beaded Rim, 15 In. 85.00

KOREAN WARE, see Sumida

Most dealers and collectors use the term "KPM" to refer to Berlin porcelain, but the same initials were used alone and in combination with other symbols by several German porcelain makers. They include the Konigliche Porzellan Manufaktur of Berlin, initials used in mark 1823–47; Meissen, 1723–24 only; Krister Porzellan Manufaktur in Waldenburg, after 1831; Kranichfelder Porzellan Manufaktur in Kranichfeld, after 1903; and the Kister Porzellan Manufaktur in Scheibe, after 1838.

KPM, Candy Dish, Black Children 125.00

KPM, LITHOPHANE, see Lithophane

Plaque, Boy, White Shirt, Brown Coat, KPM, 1892, 13 In. 550.00
Plaque, Classical Maiden, White Gown, Holding Roses, KPM, 13 In. 1300.00
Plaque, Gitana, After Asti By Wagner, 10 5/8 In. 4400.00
Plaque, Jasperware, Prussian Royal Family Busts, 7 3/4 In. 495.00

A mixture of flour and olive oil can sometimes remove a dull film from a lacquered piece. Rub on the paste, then wipe and polish with a soft cloth.

Chandeliers can be cleaned in place with a new spray cleaner made for that purpose. Cover the floor with paper or cloth to catch the drips. Then spray the chandelier. It will clean and drip dry.

Red powder is an indication of "red rot." It is caused by absorption of sulfur dioxide and cannot be stopped.

Plaque, Man With Guitar, 5 Women, Lithophane, No.332, 7 1/2 X 9 1/2 In. 300.00
Plaque, Penitent Magdalene, 12 1/4 X 16 1/4 In. 3575.00
Plaque, Woodsman, Metal Frame, No.153, Lithophane, 6 X 5 In. 200.00
Punch Bowl, Stand, Ladle, Nymphs, Fruits, Handles, 25 In. 1650.00

K.T.&K. CHINA

KTK are the initials of the Knowles, Taylor and Knowles Company of East Liverpool, Ohio, founded by Isaac W. Knowles in 1853. The company made many types of utilitarian wares, hotel china, and dinnerwares. They made the fine bone china known as Lotus Ware from 1891 to 1896. The company merged with American Ceramic Corporation in 1928. It closed in 1934. Lotus Ware is listed in its own category in this book.

KTK, Chamber Pot, Blue, Gold Trim Molded Leaves, 6 Piece 650.00
Gravy Boat, Tray, Brown Flowers 15.00
Plate, Green, Blue Floral Border, 9 In. 6.00

Any items relating to the Ku Klux Klan are now collected because of their historic importance. Literature, robes, and memorabilia are available. The Klan is still in existence, so new material is found.

KU KLUX KLAN, Banner, Anderson, Ind., Co.1, No.13, Brass Rod, 22 X 28 In. 275.00
Book, A Fool's Errand, By One of The Fools, 1879 .... 22.50
Book, Origin, Meanings & Scope of Operation, 56 Pages, 1922 .... 12.00
Booklet, 1915 .... 25.00
Figurine, Chalkware, KKK Member, In Full Dress, 5 1/2 In. 15.00
Figurine, KKK Figure, Saluting Nazi Style, Chalkware, 1923 .... 89.00
Outfit, Cape, Robe, Hood, Carrying Case, Pamphlet, 1921 .... 300.00
Outfit, Complete 125.00
Pinback, We Belong To KKK, Do You?, Oct.6, 1898, Kansas City 250.00
Sheet Music, Face Behind The Mask 12.00

Kutani ware is a Japanese porcelain made after the mid–seventeenth century. Most of the pieces found today are nineteenth century. Collectors often use the term "kutani" to refer to just the later, colorful pieces decorated with red, gold, and black pictures of warriors, animals, and birds.

KUTANI, Bowl, Orange–Red & Green Glaze, Signed, 7 1/2 In. 75.00
Bowl, Pine Tree, Flared, 7 In. 25.00
Bowl, Polychrome & Gold Flowers, Gold Seal–Form Signature, 4 In. 300.00
Bowl, Rice, Covered, Gold Mushroom Handle, Hand Painted, Box 250.00
Chamberstick, 2 Sockets, Multicolor & Gilt, Fan Shape 38.00
Coffeepot, 1920 .... 25.00 To 35.00

Cup & Saucer, Bird & Flower Design, Hash Mark	20.00
Saucer, Hand Painted, Dragon, Set of 6	13.50
Sugar & Creamer, Footed, Gold Tracery, Bamboo Style Handles	250.00
Tea Set, Child's, Flowers, 15 Piece	55.00
Tea Set, Gold Dragons On White, 13 Piece	85.00
Tea Strainer, Base, Hand Painted, Gold Trim	45.00
Teapot, Blown Out, Floral & Gold, 5 1/2 X 6 In.	65.50
Teapot, Sugar & Creamer, Thousand Flowers, Signed	85.00
Vase, Double Gourd, Diaper, Floral Bands, 19th Century, 14 In.	600.00
Vase, Hanging, Hand Painted Birds, Pre-1900, 8 In.	48.00

> Lacquer is a type of varnish. Collectors are most interested in the Chinese and Japanese lacquer wares made from the Japanese varnish tree. Lacquer wares are made from wood coated with many coats of lacquer. Sometimes the piece is carved or decorated with ivory or metal inlay.

LACQUER, Bowl, Gold Dragons, Chinese, Signed, 5 In.	15.00
Box, Covered, Painted Coastal Scene, Hinged Lid, Gilt, 12 In.	40.00
Box, Sewing, Gold Figures, Black, Domed Cover, China, 5 3/8 In.	450.00
Box, Singing Squirrel, Golden Nut, Foil, Russian, 5 1/2 X 9 In.	725.00
Box, Tavern Scene, Men Drinking, Russian, 3 X 2 1/2 In.	340.00
Box, Troika Design, Russian, 6 X 2 1/2 In.	345.00
Box, Whimsical Scene, 2 Donkeys At Fence, English, 3 X 2 In.	100.00
Box, Writing, Ink Stone, Metal Dropper, Japanese, 9 X 8 1/2 In.	1045.00
Box, Writing, Travel, Stand, Black & Gold, Chinese, 20 X 14 In.	1100.00
Screen, 4-Panel, Painted & Applied Masks, Box, Japan, 7 X 12 In.	125.00
Tray, Black, Gilt & Red Floral Design, Oval, 24 In.	250.00
Tray, Black, Mother-of-Pearl Inlay, Fly Scene, 9 In.	30.00

> Lalique glass was made by Rene Lalique in Paris, France, between the 1890s and his death in 1945. The glass was molded, pressed, and engraved in Art Nouveau and Art Deco styles. Pieces were marked with the signature "R. Lalique." Lalique glass is still being made. Pieces made after 1945 bear the mark "Lalique."

Lalique

LALIQUE, Apple, Pomme, 5 1/8 In.	225.00
Ashtray, 8 Frosted Cherubs, Label	75.00
Ashtray, Bird, 1950	60.00 To 65.00
Ashtray, Cendrier Irene, 3 3/4 In.	60.00
Ashtray, Nudes, Oval, Set of 4	225.00
Ashtray, Scalloped, Partly Clear Base, Marked, 5 1/2 In.	60.00
Ashtray, Sparrow, 3 1/2 In.	135.00
Bell, Clochette Bird, Pinson, 51/2 In.	105.00
Bookends, Swallows, Hirondelles, Pair	325.00
Bottle, Perfume, Birds, Frosted, Atomizer, 4 In.	250.00
Bottle, Perfume, Cobalt Blue, Round, Flat, Signed, 8 Oz.	195.00
Bottle, Perfume, Double Dahlia, Frosted, Dahlia Stopper, Signed	135.00
Bottle, Perfume, Dove, 4 In., Pair	50.00
Bottle, Perfume, Full Figure Female Nudes, Atomizer, Signed	125.00
Bottle, Perfume, L'Air Du Temps, Frosted Bird Stopper, 3 1/2 In.	40.00
Bottle, Perfume, Le Parisian, Dancing Ladies, Box	375.00
Bottle, Perfume, Nina Ricci, Frosted Dove Stopper, Signed, 4 In.	65.00
Bottle, Perfume, Nina Ricci, Heart Shape, Signed	150.00
Bottle, Purse, With 4 Hearts, 3 3/4 In.	145.00
Bowl, Clear, 6 Panels, Frosted Cherry Design, Signed, 4 1/2 In.	200.00
Bowl, Honfleur	185.00
Bowl, Relief Satin Finish, Vintage Design, R.Lalique, 8 In.	100.00
Bowl, Scalloped Swirl Design, 8 In.	155.00
Box, Covered, Flowers, Frosted Ground, Round, 3 1/2 In.	230.00
Carafe, Femmes Antiques	200.00
Carafe, Water Stream Panels, Charcoal Stain, Art Glass, 9 1/2 In.	1650.00
Champagne, 1896 Paris Exposition, Figure Stem	1200.00
Champagne, Golden Thistle, Tulip, Fluted	115.00
Cordial, Golden Thistle	98.00
Cup & Saucer, Cactus	175.00

Lalique, Vase, Serpent, Frosted, Marked,
C.1932, 10 1/4 In.

Lalique, Vase, 6 Figurines Et Masques,
Frosted, C.1932, 9 1/2 In.

Lamp, Electric, Peacock, Beaded Feathers,
Bronze, Marble Base

Figurine, Bird, Underplate, Signed, 3 1/2 X 2 In.	65.00
Figurine, Birds, 6, Base, Signed, 3 1/2 X 11 1/2 In.	2250.00
Figurine, Bison	170.00
Figurine, Boar, Sanglier	75.00
Figurine, Cat, Sitting	400.00
Figurine, Cockatoo, Ara, 11 3/4 In.	950.00
Figurine, Dancing Nudes, Frosted, Textured Clear Base, 10 In.	850.00
Figurine, Deer	85.00
Figurine, Dove, Colombe Charis, 10 1/2 In.	775.00
Figurine, Dove, Double, Ariane, 8 1/2 In.	575.00
Figurine, Duck, Cane, 9 1/2 In.	525.00
Figurine, Fish, Double, Deux Poissons, 11 In.	900.00
Figurine, Kneeling Nude, Flowing Hair, Arm Outstretched, 5 In.	385.00
Figurine, Owl, Baby, Chouette	70.00
Figurine, Owl, Baby, Rapace	65.00
Figurine, Panther	600.00
Figurine, Quail, Perdrix Couchee, 5 1/4 In.	150.00
Figurine, Quail, Perdrix Inquiete3 3/4 In.	150.00
Figurine, Rooster, Paper Label, Script Signature, 5 X 8 In.	90.00
Figurine, Seagull, Mouette Chloe, 8 3/4 In.	295.00
Figurine, Seagull, Mouette Daphnis, 9 1/4 In.	295.00
Figurine, Sparrow, Wings Spread, Head Up, Signed	45.00
Figurine, Stag, Cerf, 10 1/2 In.	675.00
Figurine, Swan, Cygne Tete Baissee, 14 In.	1800.00
Figurine, Virgin & Child, Wooden Base, 20 In.	1250.00
Frame, Lilies of The Valley, Frosted, Clear, Square, 4 In.	455.00
Goblet, Water, Golden Thistle, Set of 6	125.00
Goblet, Wine, Red, Golden Thistle, Set of 6	125.00
Goblet, Wine, White, Golden Thistle, Set of 10	115.00
Holder, Placecard, Floral	95.00
Holder, Placecard, Fruit	95.00
Jar, Fern Pattern, Blue Enameling, Ovoid, Large	1430.00
Jardiniere, Venise, 8 1/4 In.	500.00
Lamp, Bubble Design, Hanging, Adjusting Chain, Signed, 8 X 5 In.	495.00
Lemonade Set, Frosted Band, Crystal, Signed, 9 Piece	250.00
Lighter, Briquet	135.00
Lighter, Cigarette, Lions' Heads	115.00
Liqueur, Nude Stem	35.00
Paperweight, Boulogne	125.00
Paperweight, Vincennes	90.00
Pendant, Nude, Original Cord, Signed	350.00

Plate, Allover Swirled Feather, Blue Opalescent, Signed, 11 In.	153.00
Plate, Annual, 1965	850.00
Plate, Annual, 1968, Gazelle Fantasy .... 60.00 To 95.00	
Plate, Annual, 1970, Peacock	70.00
Plate, Annual, 1976, Eagle	80.00
Plate, Sailing Ship, 8 1/2 In.	90.00
Plate, Tree of Life, Black, 7 In.	150.00
Plate, Tree of Life, Black, 10 1/2 In. .... 100.00 To 175.00	
Powder Box, 3 Dancing Nudes, Frosted, Marked, 1 1/2 X 3 1/2 In.	175.00
Powder Box, 3 Nudes On Cover, Peach, 3 3/4 X 1 1/2 In.	195.00
Powder Box, Agnes, Frosted, Aqua Wash, 3 In.	595.00
Powder Box, Flying Dove Finial On Cover	125.00
Ring Tree, Bird	35.00
Rose Bowl, Aqua–Blue, Grapes, 9 In.	1250.00
Scent Burner, Sirens, Gray, Satin In Recesses	1750.00
Sherbet, Golden Thistle	115.00
Shot Glass, Golden Thistle	98.00
Shot Glass, Overlapping Leaf Pattern, 2 1/4 In.	40.00
Tumbler, Raised Grapes At Base, Vines, Signed, 4 1/2 In., 6 Piece	300.00
Vase, 3 Nude Boys, Clear & Frosted, Signed, 6 In.	525.00
Vase, 6 Figurines Et Masques, Frosted, C.1932, 9 1/2 In. ....*Illus*	2090.00
Vase, 8 Sides At Top & Base, Nude Children, Florals, 3 1/2 In.	165.00
Vase, Amber, Brown, Pierced Bottom For Lamp, 1920s, 9 In.	250.00
Vase, Bacchanal & Revelers, Signed, 8 1/2 In.	3895.00
Vase, Bacchantes, Nude Female Frieze, Amber, Art Glass, 9 1/2 In.	4125.00
Vase, Blown–Out Birds, Frosted, Signed, 6 3/4 In.	260.00
Vase, Blown–Out Petal Design, 1920s	975.00
Vase, Chiraz, 11 1/4 In.	390.00
Vase, Claude, 13 1/2 In.	250.00
Vase, Deux Anemones, 6 1/2 In.	220.00
Vase, Embossed Fan Shaped Wheat Heads, Blue Stained, Marked, 7 In.	495.00
Vase, Embossed Grapes & Vines, Signed, 6 1/4 In.	495.00
Vase, Embossed Protruding Nubs, Marked, 7 1/8 In.	650.00
Vase, Eucalyptus, Molded Leaves & Buds, Signed, C.1920, 6 1/2 In.	615.00
Vase, Eucalyptus, Signed, 7 In. .... 450.00 To 475.00	
Vase, Flower Petal, Stamens Between Petals, Blue, 5 3/4 In.	425.00
Vase, Grasshopper, Green Glass	8000.00
Vase, Rosine, 5 1/8 In.	195.00
Vase, Roxanne, 15 1/2 In.	440.00
Vase, Senlis, 11 1/2 In.	975.00
Vase, Serpent, Frosted, Marked, C.1932, 10 1/4 In. ....*Illus*	5775.00
Vase, Sunflower, Opalescent, Script R.Mark, 4 3/4 In.	375.00
Vase, Sylvie, 8 1/4 In.	300.00
Vase, Thistle, Blue Stain Over Opalescent, Block R Mark, 8 1/2 In.	650.00
Vase, Versailles, 14 1/4 In.	150.00
Vase, Vertical Lines, Frosted Applied Leaves At Top Rim, 1920s	700.00
Vase, White Leaves, With Blue Wash, 5 1/2 In.	675.00
Vase, White Opalescent, Intertwined Rope, Conical, 8 In.	300.00
Vase, Woman Medallion, Cylindrical, Handles, Inscribed, 9 1/4 In. ..../	600.00
Water Set, Grape Design, 5 Tumblers, Tray, Grape Handles, 15 In.	1500.00
Wine Set, Steeple Stopper, 9 Piece	595.00

Interest is strong in lamps of every type, from the early oil–burning Betty and Phoebe lamps to the recent electric lamps with glass or beaded shades. Fuels used in lamps changed through the years; whale oil (1800–40), Argand (1830), lard (1833–63), camphene (1828), turpentine and alcohol (1840s), gas (1850–79), kerosene (1860), and electricity (1879) are the most common. Other lamps are listed by manufacturer or type of material.

LAMP, Airplane, Chrome & Blue Glass	475.00
Alabaster, Birds On Base, Fruit Laced, Beaded Wire Frame, French	650.00
Aladdin, B– 11, Opalescent Shade	215.00
Aladdin, B– 12, Victoria, Model B Nashville Burner	225.00
Aladdin, B– 27, Alacite, Gold Luster	170.00

Aladdin, B– 30, Simplicity, Log Cabin Shade 75.00
Aladdin, B– 39, Washington Drape, Clear 50.00
Aladdin, B– 47, Washington Drape, Clear, Bell Stem, Burner 70.00
Aladdin, B– 50, Washington Drape, Filigree Stem, Clear .... 50.00 To 55.00
Aladdin, B– 53, Washington Drape, Tripod, Clear 40.00
Aladdin, B– 60, Lincoln Drape, Calcite, Short 225.00
Aladdin, B– 61, Lincoln Drape, Short, Amber 1250.00
Aladdin, B– 62, Lincoln Drape, Short, Ruby .... 265.00 To 350.00
Aladdin, B– 75, Lincoln Drape, Ivory Alacite, Scalloped Foot, Tall 70.00
Aladdin, B– 76, Lincoln Drape, Cobalt, Scalloped Foot, Tall 450.00
Aladdin, B– 80, Beehive, Clear 50.00
Aladdin, B– 82, Beehive, Dark Amber, Burner 75.00
Aladdin, B– 83, Beehive, Ruby Beta, Crystal, Burner .... 200.00 To 220.00
Aladdin, B– 86, Diamond Quilt, Green Moonstone 70.00
Aladdin, B– 86, Diamond Quilt, Green Moonstone, Model B Burner 160.00
Aladdin, B– 88, Vertique, Yellow Moonstone 300.00
Aladdin, B– 93, Vertique, White Moonstone, No.11 Burner 75.00
Aladdin, B– 98, Queen, Rose Moonstone 120.00
Aladdin, B–100, Corinthian, Clear 35.00
Aladdin, B–100, Corinthian, Log Cabin Shade 75.00
Aladdin, B–102, Corinthian, Green Beta Crystal 45.00
Aladdin, B–106, Colonial, Amber 225.00
Aladdin, B–107, Cathedral, Clear .... 55.00 To 60.00
Aladdin, B–108, Cathedral, Green 65.00
Aladdin, B–110, Cathedral, White Moonstone, With Burners .... 145.00 To 160.00
Aladdin, B–112, Cathedral, Rose Moonstone, With Burners .... 112.00 To 120.00
Aladdin, B–115, Corinthian, Green Moonstone 70.00
Aladdin, B–122, Majestic, Green Moonstone, With Burners 150.00
Aladdin, B–124, Moonstone, Black & White 80.00
Aladdin, B–132, Orientale, Rose Gold 85.00
Aladdin, B–134, Orientale, Bronze 80.00
Aladdin, B–388, Ducks 75.00
Aladdin, B–501, Shade 60.00
Aladdin, B–750, Student, Papers, Box 250.00
Aladdin, Black Amethyst Glass, Brass Base, Peacock Finial 100.00
Aladdin, Boudoir, Alacite 30.00
Aladdin, Caboose, Shade .... 40.00 To 85.00
Aladdin, Cupid, Alacite .... 75.00 To 95.00
Aladdin, G– 24, Cupid, Alacite, Green Base 90.00
Aladdin, G– 46, Cupid, Blue Base, Original Shade, Pair 125.00
Aladdin, G– 77, Suzie, Figurine, Opalique 375.00
Aladdin, G–376, Urn Lamp, Alacite Sticker, Original Instructions 47.50
Aladdin, Kerosene, Vase, Plum, Iridescent 250.00
Aladdin, Lady With Wolfhound, Alacite 150.00
Aladdin, No. 5, Hanging, High Altitude Chimney 300.00
Aladdin, No. 6, Hanging, With Burners .... 160.00 To 200.00
Aladdin, No. 8, Table, Kerosene, With Burners 175.00
Aladdin, No. 11, Nickel, All Original 120.00
Aladdin, No. 12, Brass Vase 50.00
Aladdin, No.104, Colonial, Clear, Burners 65.00
Aladdin, Phoenix Chimney, Ivory Color 65.00
Amethyst Cut To Clear Font, White Base, Brass Fittings, 11 3/4 In. 550.00
Amethyst Swirled Fonts, Marble Base, Brass Stem, 7 In., Pair 110.00
Argand, Brass Font, 2–Step Marble Base, Electrified, C.1850, 19 In. 325.00
Argand, Cut & Frosted Globes, Bronze, 13 1/2 In., Pair 1100.00
Argand, Cut Shades & Prisms, American, Bronze & Gilt Bronze, C.1840 .... 1450.00
Argand, Gilt Bronze, 1 Arm, Glass Prisms, E.Gardiner & Co., 1840, Pair 3100.00
Argand, Gilt Bronze, Cut Glass, Lewis & Vernon, C.1835, 18 In., Pair 2550.00
Art Deco, Dancing Girls, Globe Between, Green 165.00
Art Deco, Draped Nude, Frosted Glass, Black Metal Base, 10 In., Pair 175.00
Art Deco, Girl Seated, Knee Raised, Globe Other End, Green 100.00
Art Deco, Harlequin, Bronze, Ivory Face, Ball Shade, 9 In. 375.00
Art Deco, Lady, On Chair, Kicking Legs, Skirt Raised, Ball Shade Side 195.00
Art Deco, Minstrels, Lamppost, Plaster, Hobnail Glass Shade, 1936 .... 70.00

Art Deco, Nude, Chrome 45.00
Art Deco, Opaline, 6 Sided Vase Shape, Nude On 3 Panels 65.00
Art Deco, Sea Gulls, Aluminum Paint Finish, 8 X 10 1/2 In. 100.00
Art Deco, Woman, Sitting In Large Circle, Iron, Black, Flame Bulb 35.00
Art Deco, Women Holding Fruit Basket, Pot Metal, 10 X 13 In.Shade 75.00
Art Nouveau, Bronze, Leo Laporte Blairsy 2500.00
Art Nouveau, Cherubs On Base, 2 White Opaque Etched Shades, Pair 200.00
Art Nouveau, Table, Pairpoint Taffy Slag Shade, Cone Shape 295.00
Art Nouveau, Woman, Kneeling 65.00
Artichoke, Burner, Miniature 45.00
Astral, American Gothic, Gilt Bronze, Cut Glass Shade 2420.00
Astral, Gilt Bronze, Lyre Cut Shade, C.1820 .... 2310.00
Banquet, Enameled Outdoor Scene, Milk Glass, 36 In. 200.00
Banquet, Girl Holding Rabbit Font, Pewter & Brass, 18 In. 140.00
Banquet, Peach Font, Brass Stem, Pottery Base, 23 In. 695.00
Bed, Fashion Doll, Chiffon Dress Shade, Hooks On Bed, Munzerla, 1920s 95.00
Betty, Brass & Iron, Hanger, Pick, 1847, 4 1/2 In. 1550.00
Betty, Brass, Iron Hanger, Jack & Chain, D.P.1845, 6 In. 1800.00
Betty, Copper & Iron, Hanger, Pick, 1839, 5 In. 1800.00
Betty, Crimped Top Plate, Tin 68.00
Betty, Iron, Hanger, Pick, 4 1/2 In. 170.00
Betty, Miner's, Brass Shield With Crossed Picks, Initials IS, Iron 150.00
Betty, Stand, Tin, 8 In. 150.00
Betty, Standing, 2 Iron Arms, Wooden, H.& R.Boker, 53 In. 250.00
Betty, Wire Hanger, Tin, 19th Century 55.00
Boudoir, Cambridge, Ebony, Gold Trim, No Shade 155.00
Boudoir, Moe Bridges, Reverse Painted Shade, Landscape 110.00
Boudoir, Reverse Painted Glass Shade, Lake Scene 275.00
Bouillotte, Brass, Toleware, Baker, Arnold & Co., C.1810, 26 In. 3300.00
Bouillotte, Louis XVI, 3 Scrolled Branches, Green Tole Shade, 25 In. 1320.00
Bouillotte, Louis XVI, Silvered Metal, 3 Arms, Tole Shade, 24 In. 950.00
LAMP, BRADLEY & HUBBARD, see Bradley & Hubbard, Lamp
Brass, Double Chmimney, Green & Blue Shapes 125.00
Bronze, Table, Bas Relief School of Fish, 22 3/8 In. 475.00
Camphene, Hand, Brass, Pat.1856 D.Symonds 110.00
Camphene, Pear Shaped Font, Etched Grape Design, C.1845, 12 In., Pair 150.00
Camphene, Peg, C.1815 .... 150.00
Candle, Hanging, Enameled Flowers, Height Adjustment, 11 In. 700.00
Candle, Hanging, Red Satin Glass 175.00
Candle, Hurricane, Wire Frame, Bail, Tin Base, R.Givens, Texas, 16 In. 85.00
Candle, Louis XVI, Phoenix Supporting Drip Pan & Nozzle, Pair 935.00
Carbide, Autolite, 4 In. 30.00
Ceiling, Slag, 6 Quezal Shades 1100.00
Chandelier, 2–Light, Quezal Diamond–Quilted Gold Shades 375.00
Chandelier, 3–Light, Charles X, Swan Form Candle Branch, 10 In., Pair 1760.00
Chandelier, 4–Light, Brass 75.00
Chandelier, 4–Light, Signed Shades, C.1912 .... 750.00
Chandelier, 5–Light, Brass, 14 X 20 In., 12 In.Drop 150.00
Chandelier, 6–Light, Beads & Prisms, Glass, 5 Ft. 3 In. 3025.00
Chandelier, 6–Light, Charles X, Bronze, Swan, Horn Branches, 13 In. 1540.00
Chandelier, 6–Light, Cornelius, Original Shades, C.1857 .... 6500.00
Chandelier, 6–Light, Cut Glass, Neoclassical, Ormolu, 39 X 29 In. 3575.00
Chandelier, 6–Light, Empire, Silver Metal, Electrified, 34 In. 1430.00
Chandelier, 6–Light, Queen Anne, Scrolling Arms, 21 In. 1100.00
Chandelier, 8–Light, Empire Style, Gilt Bronze & Cut Glass, 45 In. 2750.00
Chandelier, 8–Light, Louis XV, Rock Crystal, Drip Pans, 28 In. 7750.00
Chandelier, 8–Light, Regency, First Quarter 19th Century, 38 In. 4500.00
Chandelier, 12–Light, Cut Glass & Bronze, Spires, Teardrop Pendants 4400.00
Chandelier, 12–Light, Louis XV, Brass, Iron & Cut Glass, 4 Ft. 3500.00
Chandelier, 12–Light, Louis XVI, Prisms, Gilt Brass, 42 In. 2250.00
Chandelier, 12–Light, Ormolu & Cut Glass, 2 Tiers, 38 In. ....*Illus* 3960.00
Chandelier, 14–Light, Cut Glass & Gilt Bronze, C.1870, 49 In. 8250.00
Chandelier, 15–Light, Bronze & Glass, Amethyst Glass Drops, 5 Ft. 2200.00
Chandelier, 15–Light, Iron & Cut Glass, Italian Rococo, 4 Ft. 4950.00

Lamp, Chandelier, 12–Light,
Ormolu & Cut Glass,
2 Tiers, 38 In.

Lamp, Copper & Slag Shade,
Gun Metal Over Green,
C.1905, 14 In.

Lamp, Dirk Van Erp, Table,
4 Sockets, Hammered Copper,
18 In.

Chandelier, 16–Light, George II, Urn Form, Silvered Bronze, 32 In.	2750.00
Chandelier, 20–Light, William & Mary, Sphere Form Body, 43 In.	1045.00
Chandelier, 24–Light, 3 Tiers, Central Glass Balusters, 4 Ft.3 In.	3850.00
Chandelier, Bronze Turtle Back, Glass, Chains, Tiffany, 4 Ft.5 In.	6325.00
Chandelier, Louis XVI Style, Beads & Prisms, Cut Glass Swags, 41 In.	5500.00
Copper & Slag Shade, Gun Metal Over Green, C.1905, 14 In. ....*Illus*	600.00
Crusie, Double, Iron, 19th Century	35.00
Desk, Cast Iron, Amber Glass, Pair	75.00
Desk, Emeralite, No.873K	400.00
Desk, Gooseneck, Gold Aurene Melon Ribbed Steuben Shade, Inkwell	185.00
Desk, Gooseneck, Paper Label On Shade, French	85.00
Desk, Verdelite, Double	275.00
Dirk Van Erp, Copper, Mica	7700.00
Dirk Van Erp, Table, 4 Sockets, Hammered Copper, 18 In. ....*Illus*	14300.00
Electric, Amber, Reverse Painted Shade, Autumn Leaves, Pittsburgh	775.00
Electric, Art Glass, Floral Shade, Spelter Urn Shaped Base, 23 In.	400.00
Electric, Bent Panel, 3 Colors of Glass, 1910 ....*Illus*	1000.00
Electric, Buhl Conquest, Blue Globe	175.00
Electric, Cameo Glass, Gilt Bronze Shade, 3 Putti, C.1900, 37 In.	1760.00
Electric, Charlie Tuna, Sunkist	10.00
Electric, Cloisonne, Blue & Green Dragons, Geometric, No Shade, 15 In.	575.00
Electric, Cut Glass, Mushroom, 6 In.Prisms, 12 In.	150.00
Electric, Degue, Table, Signed Shade	375.00
Electric, E.Miller, Nickel Over Brass, White Opalescent Shade	75.00
Electric, Emeralite No.8734TW, Double Knuckle, Extension Arm, Clamp	345.00
Electric, Emeralite, No.8734, Type L, Rolltop, Clamp On	225.00
Electric, Empire, Maiden Support, Black Basalt & Gilt Metal, 34 In.	300.00
Electric, Flintstone, With Shade	45.00
Electric, Fruit, Bronzed Rococo Plateau Mirror Base, Figural Fruits	330.00

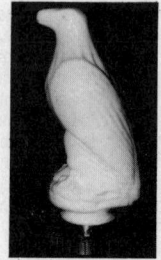

Lamp, Electric, Bent Panel,
3 Colors of Glass,
1910

Lamp, Electric, Maiden,
Marble Base, French,
24 In.

Lamp, Electric,
White Eagle

Electric, Goosegirl, Chalkware, Original Shade 20.00
Electric, H & B, No.193 .... 750.00
Electric, Half Doll, Hands Away, Plumed Hat, Victorian Dress 100.00
Electric, Jefferson, Bronze Base, Doone Landscape Shade, 10 In. 495.00
Electric, Jefferson, Reverse Painted Scene, Bell Shaped Base, Signed 1050.00
Electric, Jefferson, Reverse Painted Shade, Landscape Scene, 18 In. 880.00
Electric, Lady, Kneeling, Holding Gold Glass Shade Over Head, Spelter 75.00
Electric, Lady, Standing, Arms Over Head, Marble Base, Spelter 95.00
Electric, Maiden, Marble Base, French, 24 In. ....*Illus*   850.00
Electric, Millefiori, Bronze, La Jongleuse 650.00
Electric, Millefiori, Dome Top, 18 In. 435.00
Electric, Millefiori, Iron Hanger, Melon Shaped Shade, 1915, 24 In. 325.00
Electric, Moe Bridges, Autumn Sunset, 18 In. 1550.00
Electric, Moe Bridges, Brass Base, Blue Frosted Floral Shade, 13 In. 325.00
Electric, Moving, Action, Little Boy Relieving Himself, 1950s 20.00
Electric, Olympic Games, St.Louis, Woman Holding Torch, Wreath, 1904 .... 275.00
Electric, Owl, Brown Enamel Over Ivory, Cambridge 600.00
Electric, Papier-Mache, Advertising, Liberty Bodice, Children & Owl 400.00
Electric, Parrot, Green, Red Comb, U.S.Glass Co. 250.00
Electric, Peacock, Beaded Feathers, Bronze, Marble Base ....*Illus*   700.00
Electric, Reverse Painted, Winter Scene, Orange Shade, 24 X 16 In. 425.00
Electric, Rock Crystal, Hexagonal Baluster, Ormolu Base, 16 In., Pair 2475.00
Electric, Snoopy, Glass Globe, United Features Syndicate, Inc., 15 In. 35.00
Electric, Statue of Liberty, Rotating, Dated 1957 .... 45.00
Electric, Tiffany Type, Grapes & Leaves, Leaded Dome Shade 700.00
Electric, Tiffin, Boudoir, Orange Parrot, U.S.Glass 295.00
Electric, TV, Black Panther, Ceramic, 1950s, 21 In. 20.00
Electric, TV, Green Panther 10.00
Electric, TV, Siamese Cat, 1950s 28.50
Electric, White Eagle ....*Illus*   350.00
Electric, White Overlay Cut To Clear, Marble Base, 1840, 10 1/2 In. 225.00
Electric, Wicker Shade, Gustav Stickley, Oak, C.1910, 22 In. 1100.00
Fairy, 3 Faces, Owl, Cat, Dog, Porcelain 150.00
Fairy, Art Deco Pottery, Cottage On Saucer Base, English, 3 X 5 In. 110.00
Fairy, Blue Glass Shade, Enameled Blue Metal Pedestal Base, 6 In. 110.00
Fairy, Blue Opalescent, Pyramid, Clear Marked Clarke Base, 3 3/4 In. 85.00
Fairy, Burmese, Clarke, Clear Base, 4 In. 90.00
Fairy, Clarke Clear Base, Green Satin Top, 3 X 4 In. 30.00
Fairy, Cobweb, Jeweled, Brass 165.00
Fairy, Lithophane Shade, Forest Scene, C.1840 .... 300.00
Fairy, Marked Clarke Base, Pale Pink, Pyramid, 4 In. 110.00
Fairy, Owl, Frosted, Painted Eyes, Clarke Base, 5 In. 225.00
Fairy, Pyramid, Cranberry, Clear Glass Applied Petals 160.00
Fairy, Sheffield Silver Plate, Clarke 4-Lamp Holder, Signed 685.00
Fairy, Silver Plated Holder, Clarke Cup, Cricklite Shade, 24 In., Pair 450.00
Fairy, Verre Moire, Blue, White Loopings, Ruffled Base, Pyramid, 5 In. 375.00
Fairy, Verre Moire, Cranberry, White Loopings, Dome Shade, 5 1/2 In. 450.00
Fairy, Verre Moire & Red Crystal, Sawtoothed Inner Rim, 6 In. 265.00
Fairy, Verre Moire, White Loopings, Fluted Base, 5 1/4 X 6 1/4 In. 395.00
Finger, Coin Dot, Flat, Blue Opalescent 375.00
Finger, Coolidge Drape, Footed, Cobalt Blue 225.00
Finger, Emerald Green Glass, English, C.1870 .... 68.00
Finger, Fishscale, Reflectory & Chimney, Purple 175.00
Finger, Heart & Thumbprint, Pedestal 88.00
Finger, Heart, Green Custard Glass 355.00
Finger, Hobbs-Bruckinier, Cobalt Blue, Princess Feather Design 175.00
Finger, Peach & White Spatter Glass, Clear Applied Handle, 6 1/4 In. 100.00
Finger, Peanut Pattern 45.00
Finger, Ribbed, Crystal Handle, Cranberry, 9 1/2 In. 165.00
Fluid, Cut Glass, Pale Green, Brass Stem Font, Marble Base, 8 1/4 In. 220.00
Fluid, Forest Green, Small, Pair 1760.00
Fluid, Glass Font, White Opaque, Cobalt Blue Windows, Marble, 7 In. 450.00
Fluid, Papier-Mache, Fibre Ware Co., C.1875, 10 In. 125.00
Fluid, Reed & Barton, Double Camphene Burner, Pewter, 10 In. 200.00

Fluid, Wheel Engraved Fonts, Frosted, Ball Shades, 19 In., Pair 825.00
Gas, Converted, Victorian, Cupid Base, Double Pink Satin Glass Shades 125.00
Gasolier, 4–Light, 5 Tiers of Prisms, American, Crystal, 58 In. 2860.00
Gasolier, 6–Light, Rococo, Gilt Bronze, Foliage, Birds, Cherubs, 6 Ft. 8250.00
Gone With The Wind, Beaded Drape, Red Satin ....*Illus* 500.00
Gone With The Wind, Blown Out Regal Iris, Ruffled Shade, 27 In. 750.00
Gone With The Wind, Face of Arab On Base & Shade 850.00
Gone With The Wind, Floral Ball Shade, 12 In. 300.00
Gone With The Wind, Grape & Leaf, All Original, 25 In. 700.00
Gone With The Wind, Grape Pattern 350.00
Gone With The Wind, Green, Gold Dragons On Globe & Base 1000.00
Gone With The Wind, Hanging, Green Satin Glass Ball Shade 495.00
Gone With The Wind, Pink Lilies, Orange To Mahogany Ground, 19 In. 240.00
Gone With The Wind, Pink To Burgundy Ground, Large Owls, Large 895.00
Gone With The Wind, Pink, Flowers, Mottled Pink & White Ground 350.00
Gone With The Wind, Red Satin Glass, B & H., 1890s 700.00
Gone With The Wind, Red Satin Glass, Beaded Drape, Shade, Miniature 295.00
Gone With The Wind, Roses, 23 In. 215.00
Gone With The Wind, Satin Finish Crystal, Roses, Electrified, 24 In. 640.00
Gone With The Wind, Water Lilies, Tan 300.00
Gone With The Wind, White Puffy, Hand Painted Pink Floral 100.00
Grease, Bronze, Primitive, Chinese, 15th Century, 16 In. 1250.00
Grease, Hanging, Sawtooth Trammel, 3–Part Pan, Iron, 35 In. 600.00
Grease, Pottery, Primitive, Green Glaze, 6 In.Saucer, 8 In. 300.00
Grease, Saucer Base, Dark Brown Glaze, Zanesville, Ohio, 4 1/4 In. 450.00
Hall, Diamond–Quilted, Pear Shape, Amberina 495.00
Hand, Brass, Tin Bottom, E.F.Rogers, Pat.Jan.30, 1866, 4 In. 175.00
Hand, Currier & Ives Pattern, Original Burner & Blown Chimney 100.00
Hand, Eyewinker 75.00
Hand, Morey & Smith, Bell Shape, Pewter, 3 1/2 In. 125.00
Hand, Smith & Co., Boston, Brass Single Drop Burner, C.1852, 3 3/8 In. 300.00
Hand, Sun With Face Pattern, Applied Handle, Dated 1860, 2 1/2 In. 130.00
LAMP, HANDEL, see Handel, Lamp
Hanging, Double Greek Key Shade, White Opalescent, Electrifed, 8 In. 395.00
Hanging, Frosted, Cranberry Glass, Allover Oval Eyes, Chain, 5 In. 378.00
Hanging, Hobnail, Ruby, Fluted, 8 In.Base 295.00
Hanging, Leaded, Lily Pad 1250.00
Hanging, Rochester, Jeweled, Original Shade & Prisms 750.00
Hanging, Slag Glass, Light Caramel, 6 Panels, Tulip Type, 11 In. 45.00
Hurricane, Blown Amethyst Glass, Cast Metal, Bowl Shape Bottom 3575.00
Hurricane, Sterling Base, Etched Chimney, 15 In. 35.00
Kerosene, Angle, Hanging, 4 Arms, Brass & Copper Finish 725.00
Kerosene, Astral, Marble Base 285.00
Kerosene, Bristol, Gold Over White, Pair 200.00
Kerosene, Climax, Brass, 1906 .... 45.00
Kerosene, Coolidge Drape, Burner 75.00
Kerosene, Coolidge Drape, Tall Stem 60.00
Kerosene, Cosmos, Gone With The Wind Ball Shade 120.00
Kerosene, Cosmos, Miniature 125.00
Kerosene, Cranberry, Spanish Lace, Pair 600.00
Kerosene, Dewey, Artillery Shell Shape, Copper, Brass, Iron, 13 In. 325.00
Kerosene, Dietz Royal 28.00
Kerosene, Dragon Handle, White Metal, Brass, Oriental Style, 15 In. 105.00
Kerosene, Embossed Roses & Scalloped Design, Metal Base, Milk Glass 125.00
Kerosene, Figural, Girl With Puppies On Lap, Stone Base, 9 1/2 In. 100.00
Kerosene, Florals, Brass Well & Base, 31 In. 425.00
Kerosene, Green Opalescent Font, Art Nouveau, Cosmos Burner, 20 In. 295.00
Kerosene, Gustav Stickley, Copper, Wicker Shade 3500.00
Kerosene, Miller ....200.00 To 275.00
Kerosene, Moon & Stars, Blue & Amber 275.00
Kerosene, Pickwick On Saucer Base, Ring Handle, Tin, 9 1/4 In. 110.00
Kerosene, Rayo, Nickel Plated Brass, Green Ribbed Shade, Chimney 175.00
Kerosene, Ruffled Bull's–Eye, 9 In. 40.00
Kerosene, Sapphire Blue, Full Figure Stem, Girl In Party Dress 70.00

Kerosene, Saucer Base, Ring Handle, Tin, 7 1/8 In. 75.00
Kerosene, Serrated Loop, Clear 45.00
Kerosene, Student, Manhattan, Brass, Original Shade, Pat.1876–79 .... 425.00
Kerosene, Thuro Burner & Chimney, Diamond Band & Shield 64.00
Kerosene, Tin & Brass, Red Stenciled Swans, French, 22 In. 2530.00
Kerosene, Tiny Juno, Original Opaque Shade & Chimney, 12 In. 125.00
Lace Maker's, Blown Glass 275.00
Lard, Cast Iron Foot, Brass Font Label, S.N.& H.C.Ufford, 8 In. 45.00
Lard, Painted Tin, Gilt Borders, American, 9 In. 100.00
Lard, Tin, Finger Handle 100.00
Loom, Hanging, Trammel Adjustment, Brass Candle Socket, 42 1/2 In. 300.00
Marriage, Double Opaque Fonts, Joined Clambroth Match Holder 975.00
Marriage, Opaque Blue Fonts, Opaque White Base, Ripley, 1870 .... 760.00
Miner's, Brass Plate For Pole, Wire Loop Handles, Ferguson, N.Y., 1878 .... 150.00
Miner's, Carbide, Autolite, 4 In.Reflector 11.00
Miner's, Carbide, Brass, Justrite Reflector, 7 1/2 In. .... 27.00 To 35.00
Miner's, Carbide, Complete 15.00
Miner's, Iron, Brass Heart Shaped Finial, 3 3/4 In. 180.00
Miner's, Porcelain, Woman's Hands Holding Lamp, Flowers, 10 In. 22.50
Oil, 2–Light, Empire, Urn Form, Suspending Foliate, 8 3/4 In., Pair 1045.00
Oil, Aladdin Shape, Bird's Head Handle, Sterling Silver, 3 X 5 In. 150.00
Oil, Baccarat, Pewter, Silver Plate, Swirl Font, Presentation 1898 .... 550.00
Oil, Blue Swirl Font, Fluted Brass Shaft, Marble Base, C.1850, 9 In. 195.00
Oil, Boudoir, Ruffled Top, Hand Painted Flowers, Robins, 21 In. 250.00
Oil, Canadian Heart 175.00
Oil, Cast Iron, Green Slag Glass, C.1900 .... 295.00
Oil, Central Glass Co., 1880–90 .... 75.00
Oil, Ceramic, Crown Point, Volkmar 125.00
Oil, Circles, Copper Wheel Engraved Foliage, Brass, Marble, 11 In. 400.00
Oil, Clarissa, Matching Shade, 22 In. 595.00
Oil, Clear Font, Flattened Chimney, Ripley & Co., Pat.1877 .... 125.00
Oil, Continental, Pedestal Base, Hinged Lid, Hanger, Pewter, 6 In. 360.00
Oil, Cosmos Variant, Green Band, Matching Shade, Milk Glass 325.00
Oil, Cosmos, Miniature 145.00
Oil, Cut, Cranberry Font, Opaque White Base, Brass Collar, 12 In. 325.00
Oil, Double Marriage, Blue Fonts, White Milk Glass Base 775.00
Oil, Enameled On Green Glass, Iron Base, Stourbridge 175.00
Oil, Figural, Girl In Bloomers, Blue Shade, White Metal, 23 1/2 In. 90.00
Oil, Giant Sawtooth Pattern, 10 In., Pair 350.00
Oil, Gold, Cranberry Ball Shade, Pink, White, Gold Porcelain Base 295.00
Oil, Greek Key, 9 In. 65.00
Oil, Hanging, Country Store, Pat.1895 .... 180.00
Oil, Hanging, French, Chanticleer Finial, 19th Century, 29 In. 250.00
Oil, Heart Pattern, Custard Glass Font, Frosted Stem & Base 250.00
Oil, Heart Top Panel Font, Marble Stepped Base 135.00
Oil, Kadota Pattern, Original Burner, 8 In. 135.00
Oil, Leaf Mold, Pink & Green, Miniature 125.00
Oil, Little Duchess, Miniature 155.00
Oil, Logan Pattern, Vaseline, 10 In. 155.00
Oil, Milk Glass, Allover Protruding Pink Rosebuds, 8 In., Pair 20.00
Oil, Milk Glass, Netted Ground, Fired Pink & Blue Flowers, Miniature 275.00
Oil, Milk Glass, Nutmeg, Burner, Brass Band Forms Handle, Miniature 35.00
Oil, Milk Glass, Orange Fired On Flowers, Miniature 195.00
Oil, Nutmeg, Blue, 6 In. 75.00
Oil, Peg, Cranberry, Carnival Glass, Brass Holder 300.00
Oil, Pineapple & Basket, Flashed Gold, Emerald Green 275.00
Oil, Pink Overlay Satin, Yellow Mother–of–Pearl Base, Miniature 65.00
Oil, Pressed Glass, Giant Sawtooth, Flint, 9 1/2 In. 145.00
Oil, Princess Feather, Opaque Blue, Burner Dated 1879 .... 425.00
Oil, Rosa, Emerald Green, Satin Bowl 95.00
Oil, Sandwich, Engraved, Ball Shade, 19th Century, 16 1/2 In. .... *Illus* 150.00
Oil, Sandwich, Milk Glass Cut To Cranberry, 16 In. .... *Illus* 425.00
Oil, Thousand Eye With Diamond & Dot Green Font, Clear Base, 14 In. 395.00
Oil, World's Fair, Woman's & Government Building Scenes, Shade 85.00

LAMP, PAIRPOINT, see Pairpoint, Lamp

Pan, Hanging, Adjustable, Iron, Original Hook, 13 In.	165.00
Pan, Hanging, Spout Holder, Brass Hanger	100.00
Peg, Amethystine, Paneled, Brass Collar, Snuffer Cap, 4 In.	85.00
Peg, Brass Base, Embossed Design, 15 In., Pair	1475.00
Peg, Brass Candlestick, Satin Glass, Flowers On Font, Etched Shade	250.00
Peg, Etched Design On Shade, Silver Plated Holder, 12 1/2 In.	615.00
Peg, Mother–of–Pearl, Brass Holder, 13 In.	525.00
Peg, Satin Glass, Yellow Overlay, Original Candlestick	485.00
Perfume, Art Deco, Brass Dome Top, Jewels, Sphinx Holder	165.00
Perfume, Art Deco, Porcelain, Japan, 6 In.	85.00
Perfume, Ballerina	125.00
Piano, Rococo Revival	522.50
Rushlight Holder, Candle Socket Counterbalance, Iron, 18 In.	25.00
Rushlight Holder, Iron, Pine Trammel Base, Adjustable To 40 1/2 In.	550.00
Rushlight Holder, Iron, Twisted Stem, 11 1/2 In.	400.00
Rushlight Holder, Scrolled Arm, Curled Up Toes, Iron, 10 1/2 In.	32.00
Rushlight Holder, Splint Lighting, Spring Loaded, Iron, 12 In.	125.00
Rushlight Holder, Turned Base, 18th Century	180.00
Rushlight Holder, Wooden Standard, Iron Top, Push Up, 37 In.	525.00
Safety, Perkins & House, Brass, Iron Stand, Patent 1857	65.00
Sconce, 2–Light, Empire, Gilt Bronze, Winged Female, 23 In., Pair	715.00
Sconce, 2–Light, George III, Gilt Wood & Gesso, C.1870, 43 In., Pair	5280.00
Sconce, 2–Light, George III, Gilt Wood, 2 Bowed Shelves, 46 X 22 In.	1045.00
Sconce, 2–Light, George III, Mirrored Backplate, Brass, 18 In., Pair	2200.00
Sconce, 3–Light, Louis XV, Gilt Bronze, Leaf Drip Pans, 22 In., Pair	1100.00
Sconce, 4–Light, Louis XVI, Marble & Rock Crystal, 26 In., Pair	3575.00
Sconce, 5–Light, Ribbon of Snake Wrap, C.1900, 24 In., Pair	1760.00
Sconce, 5–Light, William & Mary, Scrolling Arms, Brass, 22 In., Pair	2100.00
Sconce, Candle, Oval Reflector Back, Crimped Pan, Tin, 12 In., Pair	1050.00
Sconce, Reflectors, Tin, American, 18th Century, 8 1/2 In., Pair	895.00
Sconce, Triple, Attached Drawer With Punchwork, Brass, 18th Century	275.00
Skater's, Bail Handle, Glass Globe, 7 In.	15.00
Skater's, Bulbous Globe, Kerosene Burner, 11 In.	120.00
Skater's, Lacy Cast Iron, Clear Globe, Coal Oil Burner, Wire Bail	220.00
Skater's, Perko Wonder Jr.	35.00
Skater's, Red Paint, Tin	12.00
Solar, Labeled Philadelphia, Etched Shade	605.00
Solar, Leaf Support, Gothic Base, Cut Shade, Gilt Bronze, C.1850	935.00
Solar, Rococo Gilt Bronze, Prisms, Cut Shade	1045.00
Sparking, Globular Font, Miniature Cup Plate Base, Handle, 4 In.	400.00
Sparking, Tube Burner, Flint, 3 3/4 In.	35.00
Student, ACB Ivrene Shade, Single	590.00
Student, Brass, All Original, Manhattan, 1876–79	345.00
Student, Brass, Green Shade, Manhattan Brass Co., Pat.'76, 20 In.	245.00
Student, Brass, Single, Adjustable, Shade, Pat.Sept.23, 1890	155.00

Lamp, Gone With The Wind,   Lamp, Oil, Sandwich,   Lamp, Oil, Sandwich,
Beaded Drape, Red Satin   Engraved, Ball Shade,   Milk Glass Cut
        19th Century, 16 1/2 In.   To Cranberry, 16 In.

Student, Brass, White Milk Glass Shade, Electrified, 19 In. 280.00
Student, Dosmos Brenner, Kerosene Burner, Milk Glass Shade, 18 In. 250.00
Student, Double, Lithophane, Various Scenes, Germany, 23 In. 2850.00
Student, Lincoln, C.1879 .... 595.00
Student, Manhattan, Burnished, Rewired, Pat.Date 1887 .... 350.00
Student, Miller No. 2, Cased Green 10 In.Shade, All Original 545.00
Student, Original Red Roses On Pink Shade, Not Wired 425.00
    LAMP, TIFFANY, see Tiffany, Lamp
Torchere, Blackamoor, Gilt Branch, Pillowed Base, 6 Ft. 5 In., Pair 7425.00
Vapo–Cresolene, Dated 1879, Box 85.00
Vapo–Cresolene, Pink Shade, 10 In. 15.00
Wall, 3–Light, Neoclassical, Cobalt Blue, Bobeche, Russia, 27 In., Pair 8850.00
Wall, Hammered Copper, Gustav Stickley, C.1905, 17 In. 800.00
Whale Oil, Aqua Glass, Embossed London Lamp, Tin Shield, 6 In. 75.00
Whale Oil, Bakewell Pattern, Pressed Glass Base 1155.00
Whale Oil, Banded Apple Font, Maine, 19th Century, 7 In. 100.00
Whale Oil, Blown Font, Pressed Lemon Squeeze Base, 1835–45, 9 In. 50.00
Whale Oil, Blown Glass, Square Base, Pewter Burner, 1830–45, 8 In. 150.00
Whale Oil, Brass, Acorn Shaped Fonts, Pair 725.00
Whale Oil, Bull's–Eye & Star, Flint 90.00
Whale Oil, Double Burner, Pewter 160.00
Whale Oil, Double Magnifying Lens, Pewter Collar, Striping, 9 In. 260.00
Whale Oil, Free Blown, Spherical Font, Claw Feet, 9 In., Pair 150.00
Whale Oil, French, Brass, 10 In., Pair 300.00
Whale Oil, Loop & Bull's–Eye Pattern, Canary Yellow, Pewter, 11 In. 500.00
Whale Oil, Sandwich Glass, Paneled Waffle, 1840, 11 1/2 In., Pair 250.00
Whale Oil, Saucer Base, Dolphin Form Handle, Double Burners, Brass 250.00
Whale Oil, Saucer Base, Removable Shade, Dark Green Tole, 12 In. 250.00
Whale Oil, Silver Plate, Brass Snuffer Cap & Ring Handle, Small 45.00
Whale Oil, Standing, Saucer Base, Double Burner, 6 1/2 In. 220.00
Whale Oil, Tin, Shelf, Black Repaint, Box Shape, 10 X 12 1/2 In. 400.00

A lantern is a special type of lighting device. It has a light source, usually a candle, totally hidden inside the walls of the lantern. Light is seen through holes or glass sections.

LANTERN, Barn, Dietz, Red Globe 18.00
  Blown Glass, Tin Leaf Design, 19th Century, Pair 950.00
  Buggy, Rayo, Pony No.2, Bull's–Eye, 1911 .... 55.00
  Candle, 4 Glass Sides, Curved Wire Braces, Flat Bail, Tin 150.00
  Candle, Handmade, Scalloped Finial Vent, Wooden Handle, 9 In. 120.00
  Candle, Jack–O'–Lantern Shape, Tin, Original Orange Paint, 6 In. 525.00
  Candle, McKinley Campaign, Signed R.Givens, Corpus Christi, 1894 .... 95.00
  Candle, Paul Revere Type, 1822 Punched In Door, Tin, 14 In. 150.00
  Candle, Pierced Brass, Cut Foliate Design, 12 1/2 In. 90.00
  Carriage, Dietz 65.00
  Carriage, Victorian, Silver & Black, Glass Panels, 28 In., Pair 605.00
  Child's, Feverhand, West Germany, Tin, 8 In. 30.00
  Dietz, Fire King F.D., Brass 160.00
  Dietz, No. 2, Farm, D–Lite 45.00
  Dietz, No.100, Red Globe 20.00
  Dietz, Red Globe, Glass Font, Tin, 6 1/2 In. 95.00
  Embry, No.40, Red Globe 22.50
  Empire Style, Ormolu, Hexagonal, Acanthus Surrounds Candle, 24 In. 495.00
  Hall, George III, 6 Candles, Gilt Bronze & Glass, 28 In. 900.00
  Hall, Louis XV, Cage Form, 5 Glazed Sides, Mid–18th Century, 32 In. 5225.00
  Hall, Pressed Tin, Hexagonal, 1 Candle, Etched Glass Panels, 12 In. 200.00
  Hall, Regency Style, 6 Arms, Gilt Metal & Glass, 29 1/4 In. 750.00
  Hanging, Hexagonal, Black, Tin, 20 In. 35.00
  Kerosene, Metal, Red, Globe, Bail Handle, Winged Wheel, 7 1/2 In. 5.00
  Onion, Burner, Hand Punched Tin, C.1800 .... 325.00
  Paul Revere, Punched Tin, Candle Socket, Ring Handle, 11 In. 125.00
  Policeman's, Crimped Cone Top, Bull'–Eye Lens, Revolving Lights 45.00
  Skater's, Justrite, Carbide, 9 In. 95.00
  Switch, Bull's–Eye 100.00

Vintage Pattern, Leaded Cased Glass, Oak Arm, Standard, 13 1/4 In. 450.00
Walnut, Punched Tin Top, Ring Handle, Crimped Tin Pan, 16 In. 525.00
Whale Oil, Perforated Tin Base & Top, 13 1/2 In. 185.00

> Le Verre Francais is one of the many types of cameo glass made in France. The glass was made by the C. Schneider factory in Epinay–sur–Seine from 1920 to 1933. It is a mottled glass, usually decorated with floral designs, and bears the incised signature "Le Verre Francais."

LE VERRE FRANCAIS, Night–Light, 3 1/2 In. 300.00
Vase, Blue & Orange Stylized Flowers, Signed, 6 1/2 In. 375.00
Vase, Etched Morning Glory Design, 8 1/2 In. 325.00
Vase, Flying Geese, Cameo, 3 Colors, Pedestal, 12 In. 585.00
Vase, Red, Orange & Yellow, Amethyst Base, 21 In. 1750.00

> Leather is tanned animal hide and it has been used to make decorative and useful objects for centuries. Leather objects must be carefully preserved with proper humidity and oiling or the leather will deteriorate and crack. This damage cannot be repaired.

LEATHER, Blackjack, Leather Strap, 1900 .... 48.00
Cowboy Cuff, Gopher Brand, Pair 16.00
Desk Set, Scissors & Letter Opener 20.00
Hat Box, C.1860 .... 175.00
Holster Rig, Cowboy, Hand Tooled, Double, Fits Colt, 4440 Loops 350.00
Holster, Shoulder, Harness, Black, 45 Caliber, U.S.Bucheimer 26.00
Horse Collar, With Mirror 28.00
Lederhosen, Lady's, Austrian, Size 12 .... 50.00
Lederhosen, Man's, Austrian, Size 40 .... 58.00
Magazine Rack, Tooled, Wall 65.00
Pouch, Smoker's, Snakeskin, 4 Folding Tools, 2 1/2 X 3 1/2 In. 250.00
Razor Strop, Marked U.S.Cavalry 28.00
Shaving Kit, Brush, Comb, Mug, Art Nouveau Design 40.00
Shucking Peg, Large 27.00
Sidesaddle, Embossed, Carpet, Multicolored 75.00
Strop, Horse, 4 Brass Insignia, 16 In. 25.00
Toilet Case, Man's, Fitted, 1940s 28.00
Travel Case, Pigskin, Art Deco 25.00

> Leeds pottery was made at Leeds, Yorkshire, England, from 1774 to 1878. Most Leeds ware was not marked. Early Leeds pieces had
LEEDS POTTERY. distinctive twisted handles with a greenish glaze on part of the creamy ware. Later ware often had blue borders on the creamy pottery.

LEEDS, Bowl, Oriental Design, 8 3/4 X 3 5/8 In. 175.00
Bowl, Peafowl, 6 In. 95.00
Charger, Urn of Flowers, Scalloped Edge, 14 In. 880.00
Charger, Water Scene, 13 In. 577.50
Mug, Pearlware, Cross–Hatched Diamond Border, Pagoda Scene, 6 In 300.00
Pitcher, Peafowl, Sponged Foliage, Soft Paste, 2 1/16 In. 225.00
Platter, Blue Willow, Reticulated Border, Oval, 10 1/2 In. 265.00
Saucer, Peafowl, Green Spatter Tree, 6 In. 75.00
Sugar, Blue & White Floral, Pearlware, Bulbous, Shell Handles, 5 In. 130.00

> The Geo. Zoltan Lefton Company has imported porcelains to be sold in America since 1940. The pieces are often marked with the Lefton name. The firm is still in business. The company mark has changed through the years and objects can be dated accurately by the shape of the mark.

LEFTON, Cigarette Set, 3 Piece 15.00
Cookie Jar, Santa Claus 85.00
Cookie Jar, Vista Train 45.00
Figurine, Ayrshire Cow 18.00
Pitcher & Bowl, Roses On Green Ground, Gold Trim, Small 15.00
Plate, Goldfinch, Cardinals, Chickadees, Set of 3 .... 45.00

A Special Survey: 20 years of Antiques Prices

Tiffany lamp, table, crocus, yellow & green shade...........$750
RS Prussia, plate, cake, dice throwers, 10 in., red mark....$180
Majolica, Etruscan, 9 in. leaf dish, pink, green & yellow....$10

Would you like to buy at these prices? It's hard to believe it was ever possible, but these were the prices 20 years ago when our first price book was published. In that price book there was no Royal Doulton, only two makers of art pottery, no Depression glass, and no folk art. A careful reader might have noticed hints of things to come in the collecting world. There were 4 quilts, 2 tin advertising signs, 39 tin toys, 16 iron doorstops, a decoy worth $45, and a Larkin oak fall-front desk for $25.

Most collectors in 1950 wanted only items that were made before 1850; antiques that were at least 100 years old. "Collectibles," as such, didn't exist at the antiques shows. Now collectors want items made before 1960. Twenty years ago who would have considered buying old clothes? Used kitchenware or tools were junk to most, and few people used the terms "folk art," "Fiestaware," "Art Nouveau," or "Art Deco." Some Mission furniture was used for kindling wood. Collectibles such as radio premiums or Mickey Mouse watches were purchased as novelties and not considered part of a serious collection.

What are the reasons for the changing market? There are more people collecting today than in 1968. There are fewer available 100-year-old items, and they have become so expensive that new collectors usually start with more recent objects. Fifties items are popular with the under-40-year-olds. Housing styles have changed. Now everything from rehabbed lofts and restored Victorian houses to modern high-ceiling, multi-window houses and condos are furnished with antiques and collectibles. The physical dimensions of a home partially determine the furnishings, just as the number of windows and light intensity make some colors more suitable.

There have been more than 10,000 books on collecting written since 1969. One can now feel comfortable buying Shaker furniture or American art pottery because there are books that explain the marks, design, and the quality. Museums have had exhibits displaying and explaining everything from Eva Zeisel dishes to dummy boards. New technology makes it easier to spot fakes or repairs. Leisure

Solid-colored dinnerwares from the 1930s regained favor in the 1970s. In 1941 this blue Hall pitcher was included with the refrigerator. Today it sells for $20, more expensive than the red Hall or yellow Alamo pitchers.

Decoy prices have taken off. They range from $10 for this papier-mâché example to $319,000 for a rare, carved wooden model.

Toys delight collectors of all ages. This 1950s tin guitar-playing monkey sells for $85.

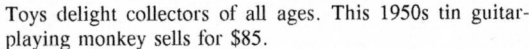

time and extra money make collecting possible at all levels. Today the $2 milk bottle, as well as the $319,000 duck decoy, is in demand. There are more shows, more publications, and more lectures. Collecting has status and is a recognized sign of good taste and intelligence.

We love antiques and have collected since our college days. A combination of factors made it possible for us to report on the changing world of collecting through this series of price books. In 1968 we were writing a national newspaper column and reading hundreds of letters a week written by perplexed collectors. The computer was a reality. We decided to do an up-to-date price book about antiques using modern methods. The result was a hardcover book printed in computer type. There were no pictures, just 30,000 prices of items offered for sale that year. We decided *not* to include any items priced over $9,999 because the book was for the average collector. Now *Kovels' Antiques & Collectibles Price List* has over 50,000 prices, hundreds of pictures, company histories, trademarks, the advantage of computer technology, new type styles, and a complete index. We also include a report of prices that have set records each year because these prices influence the less expensive items.

We have never been dealers, but we have always been buyers. We have followed the changes in prices and objects sold in antiques shops and shows during the past 20 years. Our prices are reported from actual sales, so we quickly learn which items are gaining or losing in popularity. Depression glass was not given a name and a section in our book until 1971. The smaller American art potteries started to be listed in their own sections by 1974. Tin toys have gone from inexpensive (many under $10) to expensive (many over $500) in just a few years. Plastic costume jewelry of the 1950s has gone from throw-it-away to $150 for a choice piece. Somewhere hidden in this 20th edition of *Kovels'* must be clues as to what will be the next "hot" collectibles. Will '50s furniture and glass continue to go up or is the interest just a brief fad?

We are often asked whether a special antique will be a "good investment." We can't predict the future any better than a stockbroker who gives an educated guess as to the future value of a stock. What we did here is analyze the past 20 years of prices, including the factor for inflation. Which antiques have done better than dollars in an average bank savings account? Which have outperformed the Dow Jones averages for the stock market?

It is true that some antiques have been excellent investments over the past 20 years. Top price for a piece of American furniture has gone from $25,000 to $2,275,000, a remarkable jump. During the same time period, English 18th-century porcelain prices have not even kept pace with inflation. Comic art, advertising art, and iron doorstops have skyrocketed, while collector plates have gone up and then down. Like any investment, antiques are subject to cyclical influences, inflation rates, interest rates, new decorating trends, and even color preferences. A rhinestone pin has gone up in price from $5 to $100 in three years. However, it may go down again if designers decree that pearls are more fashionable. It may stay in style because new pieces are expensive and real jewelry has too much mugger appeal. Who could have predicted that rubies and emeralds would go up in price while diamonds would go down?

Antiques are *always* a good investment if you use them. The chair for the dining room, the picture on the wall, the jewelry or clothes you wear, have, for the past 20 years, always been priced lower than comparable modern examples. Quality of workmanship of older pieces is frequently better. But best of all, a collector feels special pride in selection and connoisseurship that no non-collector could ever understand. There is a joy of ownership that gives a value well beyond the price tag. Collectors should buy because they like the item, not because it may be worth more money some day.

This 20-year analysis of the market gave us several surprises. Although prices continue to rise, the realities of interest rates, comparative purchasing power of the dollar, and changing tastes have resulted in both good and bad "dollar investments." Through it all, more people have joined us and the groups of collectors who buy for enjoyment and consider the eventual high resale price a bonus. It is pleasant to verify that wise choices have been made.

INFLATION VALUE CHART

Antiques prices and profits or losses are not always what they seem. You may buy a dish for $10 and ten years later sell it for $20. Was that a profit or did inflation make it look like a profit? You must consider the actual buying power a dollar represents. To simplify this concept, we are ignoring all the other factors that make an investment good or bad: interest you could have gotten from a bank, expenses of

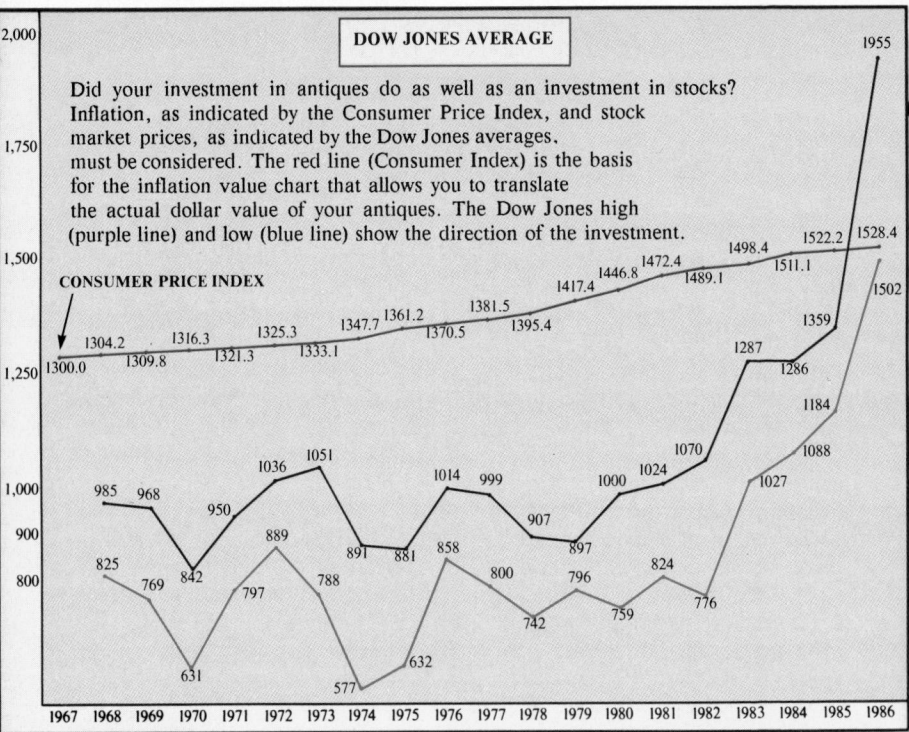

DOW JONES AVERAGE

Did your investment in antiques do as well as an investment in stocks?
Inflation, as indicated by the Consumer Price Index, and stock
market prices, as indicated by the Dow Jones averages,
must be considered. The red line (Consumer Index) is the basis
for the inflation value chart that allows you to translate
the actual dollar value of your antiques. The Dow Jones high
(purple line) and low (blue line) show the direction of the investment.

CONSUMER PRICE INDEX

maintaining a collection, and the enjoyment and recreational advantages.

By using our inflation value chart based on the Consumer Price Index, you can determine what a 1967 price (as reported in a *1968* price book) really means today. Because of inflation, each $1 in 1967 has the equivalent buying power of $3.284 in 1986. To determine the actual current value of your antique, find the year of purchase and multiply the corresponding inflation value by the original purchase price. This is today's price adjusted for inflation.

If you purchased a Bing and Grondahl 1915 Christmas plate as a collectible in 1968, you would have paid $54.75. In the 1986 price book, almost 20 years later, the listed price is $120. However, inflation made your original $54.75 worth $172.51 (the 1968 inflation value of 3.151 times $54.75), so you actually lost money. If you had sold the plate in 1972, the plate would have brought $84 (listed price book dollar value in 1972 dollars). To compare these two numbers, translate both to 1986 buying power numbers. The results indicate that you paid $172.51 (3.284 times $54.75) and sold for $220.08 (2.620 times $84) and you made money. In 1986 the price you would have gotten for your Bing and Grondahl plate was $120 (listed price book dollar value in 1986). Your purchase 20 years ago translated to 1986 dollars was $172.51, so the plate was not a profitable investment. You lost money.

Antiques, like stocks, have highs and lows and go through cycles.

There is a best time to buy, a best time to sell. But you must also consider that you had the pleasure of owning the item. What is that worth to you?

To determine the actual purchase power value of your antique, find the year of purchase and multiply it by the inflation value. That is today's price adjusted for inflation.

━━━ INFLATION VALUE CHART ━━━

These numbers are based on the Consumer Price Index. To find the actual current value of your antique, find the year of purchase and multiply the corresponding inflation value by the original purchase price.

Take this chart into consideration when looking at the prices in the tables below, where we have followed items from the 1st through the 20th price books.

1967	3.284	1974	2.223	1981	1.205
1968	3.151	1975	2.037	1982	1.135
1969	2.990	1976	1.926	1983	1.100
1970	2.823	1977	1.809	1984	1.055
1971	2.707	1978	1.680	1985	1.019
1972	2.620	1979	1.510	1986	1.000
1973	2.467	1980	1.330		

 # ADVERTISING (STORE)

I n 1968 items listed under "store" were primarily fixtures, counters, whip holders, and bins. Expensive signs listed were early, one-of-a-kind, wooden and metal, three-dimensional shop signs that pictured objects such as eyeglasses or clockfaces. These are now listed and sold as folk art. The first major advertising collectible show was held in 1973, the year of *Kovels'* fifth price guide. Many prices listed in the book came from that show. The major dealers and collectors interested in advertising were there. Prices were at the top of the market. At the same time the theme restaurants began to feature old ads and the decorating magazines recognized the possibilities of an old sign. American advertising items, especially if they feature name brands such as Coca-Cola and Planters Peanuts, have been one of the best invest-

Advertising collectibles, ignored by collectors in the 1950s, now bring high prices, especially large signs and lithographed tins.

ments of the past 20 years. We bought the famous tin Grapenuts sign picturing a girl and a St. Bernard in 1956 for $18. Today it sells for $1,400.

Collector interest has dictated that cash registers (first listed in 1979), lunch boxes (1984), and some other advertising items be listed in their own sections. We now list many signs selling for over $2,000.

TINS

	1ST ED.	5TH ED.	10TH ED.	15TH ED.	20TH ED.
Chesterfield flat fifty	$1	$4	$4.50	—	$8.50
Nigger Hair tobacco pail	—	$65–$85	$75	$105	$145
Sweet Cuba bin	$22.50	$38	$150	$135	$80–$145
Dan Patch can	—	$12	$15	$22.50–$28	$30

ASSORTED ADVERTISING ITEMS

	1ST ED.	5TH ED.	10TH ED.	15TH ED.	20TH ED.
Diamond Dye cabinet with tin front	$55	$50	$135–$425	$425–$650	$550–$750
Putnam Dye cabinet with horseback rider on tin	$18	$32	$38.50	$135	$125
Boye Needle case	$5	$48	$60	$85	$85
Hires Mettlach mug	$5	$14–$20	$95–$135	—	$65
Ward's Lemon dispenser	$30	—	$165	$345	$275

 ART POTTERY

Art pottery was first made in America in the 1870s. The works of some factories, such as Rookwood, were immediately accepted by the art-trained world and examples of the pottery were purchased by many museums. Other factories were popular in limited areas for limited years, and were out of favor when our first price book appeared in 1968. The most popular collected art potteries then were Rookwood, Weller, Roseville; these companies are still in demand.

In 1974 *The Kovels' Collector's Guide to American Art Pottery* and Paul Evans's *Art Pottery of the United States* were published. Informed collectors became interested in smaller factories. Potteries were in their own categories in the years when prices became available. The first year for Fulper was 1968; Newcomb, 1970; Grueby, 1971; Teco, 1973; Ohr, 1973; Paul Revere, 1974; Pewabic, 1975;

and Overbeck, 1980. Sometimes the interest was created by a museum exhibit and catalog (Newcomb), sometimes by a new book (Overbeck), and sometimes it was because of a special display by a dealer (Ohr). All art pottery purchased before 1968 has been an excellent investment. Many types purchased since then have been good investments.

The tables below show the relative prices for Rookwood, Weller, and Roseville. Roseville pieces were selling for over $600. Because of the random selection system used for the book, none of these top quality examples happened to be listed in the price book. Other potteries have had dramatic rises in price, especially Ohr and Newcomb. Only

George Ohr pottery prices are rising quickly. This puzzle jug sold for $15 in 1974. Today it is worth over $3,000.

one pottery was erratic. Fulper went up until 1980, then down, then up a little. Pottery that is silver-mounted or otherwise embellished has been excluded. Prices are rounded to the nearest dollar. Because the market is very high for choice pieces, low for the ordinary, the range may seem strange.

——— ART POTTERY ———

	1ST ED.	5TH ED.	10TH ED.	15TH ED.	20TH ED.
Rookwood	$5–$85	$8–$325	$13–$550	$20–$3850	$6–$5720
Weller	$4–$100	$7–$275	$7–$695	$16–$1500	$5–$2200
Roseville	$5–$13	$4–$98	$7–$145	$14–$225	$8–$2200

—— RECENT RECORD PRICES FOR ART POTTERIES ——

Anna Pottery	jug, applied snakes	$11,660
Grueby	vase, green with three yellow narcissus, rolled lip, 1902, 12 x 8 in.	$14,300
Grueby	tiles, pinetree landscape frieze, 8 tiles, 48 x 6 in.	$13,200
Newcomb	vase, high glaze, blossoms, 10½ x 6 in.	$ 4,700
Overbeck	vase, carved men, landscape, 7½ x 3 in.	$ 4,675
Pewabic	vase, matte green, carved leaves, 12½ x 8½ in.	$ 4,950
Rookwood*	vase, iris glaze, Shirayamadani, storks in flight	$15,400
Rookwood	plaque, windmill and canal scene	$ 5,720
Teco	jar, octagonal, green to black, shield embossed	$ 4,675

*In 1980 an 1899 vase decorated with a Sioux warrior, painted by Matthew Daly, sold for $32,000. Rookwood "Indians" have always been very high priced.

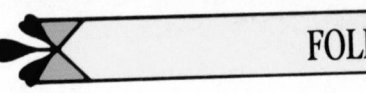 

The folk art market has changed from the 1960s to the 1980s, not only in price but also in definition. Early collectors of folk art searched for stiff, formal American portraits done by itinerant painters of the 17th and 18th centuries. Ships' carved mastheads, cigar store figures (preferably Indians), weather vanes, and Schimmel eagles were bought for high prices. The Abby Aldrich Rockefeller collection now at Williamsburg, the Electra Webb collection at the Shelburne Museum, and the Garbisch collection at the National Gallery of Art in Washington, D.C., are typical of folk art collectors' choices before the 1960s. In 1974 important books on folk sculpture and paintings were published. The major collections had become public in the 1950s and had been seen by thousands, museums began to publicize folk art, and tastes gradually changed.

One collector, Herbert W. Hemphill, Jr., began buying large, very decorative pieces for his collection. Age did not matter, just appearance and style. Soon dealers were featuring pieces with the "Hemphill" look. That collection was obtained by the Smithsonian this year. Three-dimensional objects became more popular. The definition of folk art included decoys, boxes, painted furniture, tramp art, certain toys, quilts, and even wooden gates.

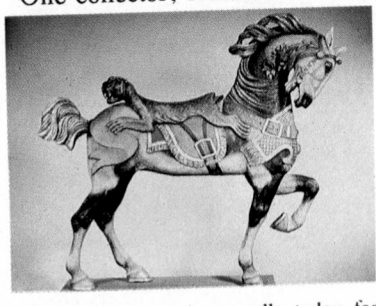

The best carousel horse sells today for over $20,000; an average example is worth more than $5,000. This fine horse was made by Stein and Goldstein of New York about 1915.

By the 1980s the favored pieces had a sculptured, almost modern, look. Dapper Dan, a slick cigar store dandy, sold in 1980 for $55,000, then again for a record $258,500 in 1986. The most expensive cigar store figure we could find in 1968 was an 1880, five-foot-high, Baltimore figure that sold for $4,100. An expensive decoy in 1968 brought $250 at auction. The record in 1986 was $319,000 for a preening pintail drake carved by A.E. Crowell in 1915. Certainly the best investment in folk art in the past 20 years has been top quality decoys. Another good investment has been quilts, selling for $100 or less in 1968, up to $176,000 for the record-setting Baltimore Album quilt sold in 1987.

Today folk art is a term that can mean many things. It is still stiff portraits and cigar store figures. It is also such handcrafts as pop bottle cap baskets, carved whales' teeth, enormous sculptures assembled from old light bulbs and foil, and primitive Grandma Moses-type landscape paintings. Some even include decorated stoneware containers, plaster figures called "chalkware," wooden horses made commercially for merry-go-rounds, or very special advertising signs. They have all been rising in price for at least ten years. Decorators, museums, and magazine articles feature the large, colorful, imaginative folk art and these are the pieces that have been the best recent investment.

FURNITURE

E xperts say that American furniture has been one of the best investments of the past 20 years. In 1967 Federal period and earlier furniture were the choices of collectors. *Kovels'* listed a good Hepplewhite mahogany serpentine front sideboard for $4,500; a Boston rocker for $30; a one drawer cherry stand, c.1810, for $45; a fall-front Larkin oak desk for $25. Today the sideboard would sell for $10,000, the Boston rocker for $400, the cherry stand for $200, and a Larkin desk for $350. The expensive Hepplewhite sideboard did not keep up with inflation, but the others have been good investments. If the sideboard had been of museum quality, it too would have done better than inflation.

The very expensive and rare pieces and the then-out-of-favor furniture have gained the most in value. We did not even list rolltop desks, Shaker chairs, '50s furniture, or even much Victorian furniture. There was little buyer interest.

Shaker furniture began to excite collectors in 1967 when the World's Fair featured pieces in an exhibit. A Shaker chair that sold for $125 in 1972 was worth $500 in 1982 and is worth $1,650 today. In the last

Victorian rococo revival furniture like this Potier and Stymus chair rose in price when collectors could identify the makers.

The "country look" became a rage in 1980 and chairs like this rush-back rocker tripled in price in less than seven years.

two years the prices for painted Shaker furniture have been rising even faster than for natural wood pieces.

A Belter-style armchair sold in 1972 for $650. Today the Belter pieces can be identified with more authority, and an armchair is worth $10,000. Other Victorian pieces that have more than tripled in value in the past ten years (inflation would account for prices doubling, any amount over that is ''profit'') are Renaissance revival bedroom sets, Herter, Roux, and Potier and Stymus furniture, Wooton desks, and, recently, ebonized pieces. The rolltop oak desk of 1900 has gone from a few hundred dollars to over $2,000.

''Country'' came into fashion in 1980. There had been collectors before that, but suddenly ''American country'' became a style. Blue-painted furniture, wicker, tavern tables, plank chairs, and other primitive pieces quickly went up in price to about four times their 1980 value. Pieces bought before 1980 have been a good to great investment.

Art Nouveau pieces by makers like Gallé, Art Deco furniture of extreme design, and name designer pieces of the 20th century by Marcel Breuer, Charles Eames, Le Corbusier, Thonet, and Mies van der Rohe, top quality Mission furniture by makers like Gustav Stickley, or Rohlfs, have increased in value by four to ten times since 1980.

In 1985 the auctions began getting higher prices for fine 18th- and 19th-century English furniture and today records are being set. From 1967 to the 1980s, English pieces rose about 400 percent, about three times the rate of inflation.

AMERICAN FURNITURE

Almost every piece of furniture is unique, so comparisons are difficult. To analyze the American furniture market, it is necessary to look at the highs and lows. The most expensive piece of American furniture sold in 1967 was a Philadelphia Federal inlaid mahogany breakfront secretary bookcase, c.1790. It sold for $25,000. In 1987 an upholstered carved mahogany Philadelphia Chippendale chair, c.1770, sold for $2,750,000. That is an astounding gain of over 10,000 percent. The following chart shows other record prices.

——— **AMERICAN FURNITURE** ———	
Inlaid Honduras mahogany desk, designed by Greene and Greene for Charles M. Pratt, a record for a piece of 20th-century furniture.	$220,000
Chippendale chest-on-chest, carved mahogany, scroll-top, attributed to Thomas Affleck.	$308,000
Pair of drop-leaf Philadelphia Chippendale carved mahogany tables	$583,000
Pair of upholstered, mahogany, barrel-back Federal armchairs, attributed to Duncan Phyfe, New York, c. 1830.	$104,500
De Witt Clinton carved mahogany Federal sofa, attributed to Duncan Phyfe, New York, c. 1810, 78 in.	$82,500
Pie safe decorated with urn and grape tin panels, Wayne County, Virginia, c. 1840.	$4,200

cont.

Cadwalader Chippendale carved mahogany, hairy paw, winged armchair, 1770, by Thomas Affleck, record for any piece of furniture.	$2,750,000
Frank Lloyd Wright chair, from Willits house, Highland Park, Illinois, 1901.	$198,000
Aesthetic movement Herter table, inlaid rectangular top, stylized flowers, vases, carved paw feet, stretcher base	$40,700
Chippendale carved mahogany bonnet-top highboy, Philadelphia, William Savery, c. 1765, 94 by 45 by 24 in.	$418,000
Chippendale carved mahogany marble-top table, Philadelphia, John Penn, 1765–1775, 31 by 44 by 21 in.	$605,000
Unupholstered armchair, wainscot, carved oak, Essex County, Massachusetts, c. 1675.	$528,000

 PRESSED GLASS

From the 1920s to the 1950s pressed glass was a popular collectible. Collections were assembled for use or display. We often saw shelves filled with Sandwich glass or enjoyed luncheon for 12 served on vaseline pressed glass dishes. The major books about pressed glass by Ruth Webb Lee, Minnie Watson Kamm, and Alice Hulett Metz were written before 1958. As prices rose, the interest dwindled, and by the 1970s pressed glass was no longer a major part of many antiques dealers' stock. Patriotic glass such as U.S. Coin and Liberty Bell have kept their value, probably because the coin and political collectors buy these. Actress pattern became a favorite of show business personalities. Prices on pieces with frosted figural knobs and stems have remained high. A few standard patterns remain popular, particularly Bellflower and the banded patterns. Other, less distinctive, patterns have not gained in monetary value. They compete with Depression glass, which has been very inexpensive. In 1985 we noticed that pressed glass prices were again starting to rise, probably because Depression glass, Heisey, and other glasswares were becoming expensive

Pressed glass like this cornucopia pitcher has not been an investment that kept up with inflation.

and it once again made good, economic sense to assemble a set of pressed glass dishes.

Prices for a selected list of goblets that were listed in each of these editions.

PATTERN	1ST ED.	5TH ED.	10TH ED.	15TH ED.	20TH ED.
Buckle	$7.50–$11.50	$15	$14.50–$22	$15–$28.50	$22.50
Diamond Point	$16	$9–$20	$47.50	$45–$65	$48–$52
Frosted Lion	$21.50	$37.50	$45–$55	$48	$55–$65
Honeycomb	$2.50–$6.50	$4–$6	$20	$12–$15	$22.50
Horn of Plenty	$20–$25	$15–$39.50	$57.50	$65	$50–$75
New England Pineapple	$17	$20–$25	$45–$52.50	$35–$65	$30

 DEPRESSION GLASS

Prices for Depression glass have gone from so unimportant they were not even mentioned in the first book to a range that goes up to thousands of dollars for a few great rarities. It has been a good investment.

———— **DEPRESSION GLASS** ————

Prices for the Miss America pink grill plate from each of these editions.

EDITION	1ST ED.	5TH ED.	10TH ED.	15TH ED.	20TH ED.
—		$3.75	$5–$7.25	$10	$12

 ROYAL DOULTON FIGURINES AND JUGS

In the first *Kovels'* in 1968, Royal Doulton was of so little interest to the antiques collector, it was almost ignored. We listed Doulton stoneware and pieces made before 1900. Less than 100 items were included, most priced under $50, and only two over $100. The figurines were not items described by name and HN number. By the 7th edition the HN numbers that identify the figurines were included. Prices were beginning to rise. It was not until the 9th edition that character jugs and toby mugs were carefully described. The first major books about figurines and character jugs had been published by the Royal Doulton factory and information about rarity, variations, and quantities was available for collectors. *The Kovels' Illustrated Price Guide to Royal Doulton* (1980) listed all known figurines and jugs, plus animals, flambé, and other pieces. Prices continued to rise until the 17th edition and now, with the exception of rare, limited edition figurines, the prices seem to be steady. Some pieces were a good investment; some are worth less in actual dollars. Royal Doulton has gone up in value but it seems to have passed its peak, at least for the present.

ROYAL DOULTON

Every piece was not listed in every edition. This is a list of prices for pieces that appeared in several editions.

FIGURINE — EDITIONS

Hostess from Williamsburg	2nd, $35		19th, $125	20th, $125
Balloon man	2nd, $30		18th, $125	
Wigmaker of Williamsburg	3rd, $25		18th, $120	
Silks and Ribbons	3rd, $25		17th, $ 80	

CHARACTER JUG

Granny, small	3rd, $18.50	9th, $23.50	17th, $80	20th, $30
John Peel, small	3rd, $18.50	10th, $62	17th, $80	20th, $65
'Arriet, mini	3rd, $15.50	10th, $90	19th, $60	

TOBY

Fat Boy	2nd, $19.50	7th, $45	12th, $185	
Sir Winston Churchill	5th, $55		15th, $100	
Happy John	5th, $22	11th, $29	19th, $ 98	

SERIES WARE

Bowman, plate	1st, $12.50	18th, $30	
Dickens teapot, Bill Sykes	1st, $15	18th, $225	20th, $225

 **SILVER**

The price of silverware is influenced by many things. Raw silver has a value on the international market. In 1967 silver was $1.55 an ounce, in 1972 it was $1.69, in 1974 up to $4.39. By September 1979 the price was $16 an ounce. The Hunt brothers started to buy silver futures and forced the price of raw silver to over $44 an ounce. They tried and failed to corner the market, and by June 1980, silver was back to the $16 range. At the end of 1986 it was $5.30 per

AMERICAN COIN SILVER

Price ranges for selected items

	1ST ED.	5TH ED.	10TH ED.	15TH ED.	20TH ED.
teaspoon	$1–$6	$5–$17	$8–$60*	$16.50–$60	$16–$80
coffeepot	$500–$1120	$500	—	$1400	$450–$8800

*Basket of Flowers pattern, now one of the most expensive patterns.

ounce. Appraisers for many years estimated the value of good, but not exceptional, quality silver at roughly 2½ times the meltdown or raw silver value of the piece. When the price rose in 1979, it became more profitable to melt ordinary silver than to sell it for the antique value.

Another factor influenced the silver market. Prices for antique silver were pushed up quickly in England in the early 1970s. Then the craze cooled and in 1972 there was a sudden drop in prices in the London market. This lowered prices for antique silver in other parts of the world.

American silver has not all been a good investment. This nineteenth century coffeepot by John Adams of Virginia is the type of quality silver that is now gaining in value.

Design and makers' names also have affected prices. Silver pieces by famous makers, like Paul Storr or Paul Revere, have risen in value faster than similar pieces by lesser well-known makers. Art Deco, Art Nouveau, Arts and Crafts, and other schools of design have gained in interest and price in recent years. There were no Art Nouveau items listed until 1973; Arts and Crafts appeared in 1979. Today the fastest rising prices are for Chinese Export silver, pieces in the japonisme tradition, and early examples of wares by Georg Jensen.

Silver flatware has become a special type of collecting in recent years. Because of the high cost of silver sets, there are now matching services that sell used spoons or forks in your pattern at a price lower than that charged for new pieces at a retail store. They can also find pieces that are no longer made. The antiques store price of flatware has been higher than meltdown, lower than new retail, and has followed the lead of these two prices.

——— ENGLISH SILVER ———

Prices listed here are for
the *most* expensive piece of silver listed for each year.

	1ST ED.	5TH ED.	10TH ED.	15TH ED.	20TH ED.
game dish	$1386				
tea urn	$1850				
candlesticks		$4500			$7700
tureen		$4000	$5500	$5000	
epergne				$6000	
urn				$5600	
platter					$9350

In 1968 silver-plated Britannia ware was considered inexpensive, not very desirable Victoriana. The elaborate tea sets, card holders, serving pieces, tilting water pitchers, napkin rings, and vases were abhorred by the expensive antiques shops, neglected by the others. The best place to buy these pieces was from a scrap metal dealer. The one exception was the figural spoon. Although most collectors preferred sterling silver spoons, many collected plated examples.

The 1st edition of *Kovels'* listed 123 spoons, about 1/3 silver plate. Rainwater's *Encyclopedia of American Silver Manufacturers* had been published in 1966, so pieces could be identified, and then *American Silverplate* appeared in 1969. *American Victorian Figural Napkin Rings* by Victor Schnadig, picturing hundreds of examples, was published in 1971. Prices began to rise. Today a good plated napkin ring is worth five to ten times as much as it was in 1968.

Tastes changed in the past ten years and elaborate Victorian furniture and silver are back in style. The rococo silver tea set and elaborate fanciful épergne are selling for high prices. If purchased before 1977, they have been a very good investment.

——— AMERICAN SILVER PLATE ———

	1ST ED.	5TH ED.	10TH ED.	15TH ED.	20TH ED.
napkin ring	$6–$35	$15–$80	$32–$225	$36–$275	$9–$245
tilting water pitcher*	$85	$65	$275	$475	$325

*The highest priced piece of silver plate in the 1st, 5th, 10th, and 15th editions was a tilting water pitcher.

 # TIFFANY

One of the most volatile collecting areas of the past 20 years has been the work of Louis Comfort Tiffany. In the 1950s when we first began to collect, the leaded glass Tiffany lampshade could be found in a Salvation Army store for a few dollars. The first serious collectors of Tiffany became evident in the early 1960s. A lamp, even in New York City, sold for under $100. In 1969 we listed 30 lamps, from $75 to $1,900. Just five years later there were 47 lamps, from $375 to $7,000. A daffodil lamp went from $900 in the first book to $4,800 in the fifth. Lamps listed in later editions included only the lower end of the market because *Kovels'* didn't include any antiques

The Tiffany lamp peaked in price in 1980. It is still a high priced antique, but has not shown recent gains in price.

selling for over $9,999. But the Tiffany lamp continued to rise in price until, in 1980, the record of $360,000 was set for a spider web table lamp. Nine other Tiffany lamps set records that year, selling from $26,000 to $240,000. Then in 1981 the price for Tiffany lamps dropped, and it has gone up only a little since that time. The year to sell a Tiffany lamp was 1980. The time to buy was before 1964, when *Louis C. Tiffany, Rebel in Glass* by Koch was published. Prices took another leap after the Metropolitan Museum of Art show of 1970.

The rest of the Tiffany market has responded in very different ways. Gold-colored Tiffany glass vases were the first type to sell, and in the 1960s small pieces of Tiffany could be found in house sales for under $10. Rare forms of Tiffany art glass began to sell well during the art glass craze years of the late 1960s. Tiffany pottery was almost unknown until the late 1970s. It was not mentioned in *Kovels'* until the 7th edition. A fine vase sold for about $200 to $500. Tiffany silverware did not have a listing until the 8th edition. For the past three years the japonisme designs have become extremely popular and are rapidly rising in price.

Glass and bronze desk sets made by Tiffany have always been useful and in demand with sophisticated collectors. Prices took a big jump about 1975, probably because of the rising interest in the lamps. Prices have been going up steadily each year, and analysis of the charted prices shows the best time to have bought was before 1970, the best time to have sold was between 1978 and 1983. If the pattern continues, Tiffany will qualify as an investment that kept pace with inflation.

——— TIFFANY INKWELLS ———

High and low prices for any Tiffany inkwells listed in these editions.

1ST ED.	5TH ED.	10TH ED.	15TH ED.	19TH ED.	20TH ED.
$27–$40	$85–$110	$110–$250	$190–$1000	$395–$550	$130–$1500

——— ZODIAC DESIGN INKWELL ———

Prices for the Tiffany Zodiac design inkwell in these editions.

1ST ED.	5TH ED.	10TH ED.	15TH ED.	19TH ED.	20TH ED.
$40	$41–$65	$110	$295	$550	$350

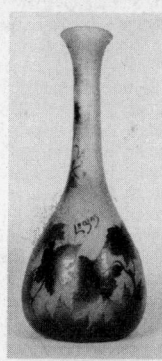

Legras, Vase, Amber, Art Deco, Etched, Bulbous, Signed, 9 In.

Legras, Vase, Vine Design, Cameo, Signed, 15 In.

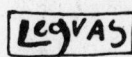

Legras was founded in 1864 by Auguste Legras at St. Denis, France. It is best known for cameo glass and enamel–decorated glass with Art Nouveau designs. Legras merged with Pantin in 1920 and became the Verreries et Cristalleries de St. Denis et de Pantin Reunies.

LEGRAS, Vase, Amber, Art Deco, Etched, Bulbous, Signed, 9 In. ....*Illus*   450.00
Vase, Cameo, Forest Scene, Enameled, 10 1/2 In., Pair 1200.00
Vase, Cameo, Lavender & Brown Flowers, Blue, Signed, 20 1/2 In. 950.00
Vase, Chipped Ice, Cascading Leaves, Dogs, Signed, 9 1/2 In. 1250.00
Vase, Chipped Ice, Orange Trees, Grass, Dogs, Signed, 9 In. 850.00
Vase, Cockleshells, Carved Murex, Cream Ground, Signed, 23 In. 1550.00
Vase, Design Blown Into Glass, Painted Swans, Signed, 14 In. 475.00
Vase, Enameled Scene, Trees, Lake, Boats, Boat Shape, 6 1/4 In. 600.00
Vase, Forest Scene, 6 In. 495.00
Vase, Girl & Sheep Scene, Signed, 7 3/4 In. 349.00
Vase, Green Owl, In Tree, Frosted Green & Red Ground, Signed, 9 In. 550.00
Vase, House & Trees, Red, Green, & Blue Overlay, Signed, 6 In. 550.00
Vase, Intaglio Cut Art Nouveau Design, Floral, 15 1/2 In., Pair 950.00
Vase, Lake Scene, Forest, Orange, Green, Brown, Signed, 14 In., Pair 950.00
Vase, Leaves & Berries, Yellow Ground, Signed, 5 X 4 3/4 In. 350.00
Vase, Quatrefoil, Leaves & Fruit, Signed, 5 In. 200.00
Vase, Shepherdess Scene, Cameo, Carved, Enameled, Signed, 7 3/4 In. 385.00
Vase, Vine Design, Cameo, Signed, 15 In. ....*Illus*   525.00

Walter Scott Lenox and Jonathan Cox founded the Ceramic Art Company in Trenton, New Jersey, in 1889. In 1906, Lenox left and started his own company. The company makes a porcelain that is similar to Irish Belleek. The marks used by the firm have changed through the years and collectors prefer the earlier examples.

LENOX, see also Ceramic Art Co.

LENOX, Ashtray, Brown Hunting Scene, 8 In. 35.00
Ashtray, Schooner, Columbia, 8 In. 30.00
Bouillon, Pewter Holder, Set of 11 .... 250.00
Bowl, Art Nouveau, Sterling Overlay, Footed, Blue 145.00
Bowl, Lemon Yellow, Marked, 16 In. 100.00
Box, Covered, White Finial, Green, Gold Trim, 7 In. 100.00
Bust, Woman's Profile, 4 In. 125.00
Butter Chip, Oriental Style Floral, Cream Ground, 3 1/2 In., 8 Piece 45.00
Butter, Covered, Rose 50.00
Coaster, Art Nouveau Silver Gilt Overlay, 3 In. 55.00

Cocoa Set, Raised Flowers, 24K Gold Trim, Green Mark, 25 Piece 1200.00
Coffee Pot, Sterling Overlay, Gooseneck Spout, Palette, 7 In. 195.00
Coffee Set, Pink Roses, Foliage, Square Based, Gold Spout, 3 Piece 225.00
Coffeepot, Ming, Gold Mark, Individual 65.00
Creamer, Noblesse 40.00
Creamer, Reverse C Handle, Pink, 5 In. 30.00
Cup & Saucer, Antoinette, Gold Mark 25.00
Cup & Saucer, Art Nouveau Sterling Overlay, Cobalt Blue, Demitasse 125.00
Cup & Saucer, Engagement Pattern, Foot Rim, Coral, Demitasse 60.00
Cup & Saucer, Fluted & Flared, Coral & White Handle, Demitasse 60.00
Cup & Saucer, Harvest 20.00
Cup & Saucer, Weatherly 35.00
Dish, Pin, World's Fair Logo, Coral & White, 1939 .... 45.00
Figurine, Ballerina, White Dress, Green Mark, 6 In. 450.00
Figurine, Bird, Pedestal, Open Back, Pink, 7 In. 95.00
Figurine, Floradora 225.00
Figurine, Madonna, Green Mark, 11 In. 500.00
Figurine, Natchez Belle 225.00
Figurine, Prima Donna 225.00
Figurine, Swan, Pink 43.00
Gravy, Attached Tray, Weatherly 710.00
Ice Bucket, Green Stamp 55.00
Jam Jar, Laurel Wreath, Sterling Silver Overlay, Square 65.00
Jam Jar, Underplate, Covered, Fairmount 60.00
Lamp, Boudoir, Urn Shape, Handle, Pair 150.00
Lamp, Figural, Lady, Full Skirt, Holding Silk Shade, Dated 1929 .... 325.00
Mug, Friendship, 3 Handles, Sterling Collar, Roses, Signed 220.00
Mug, Friendship, Sterling Silver Collar, Repousse Roses, 3 Handles 145.00
Mug, Friendship, Sterling Silver Collar, Wine Cellar Scene 220.00
Mug, Grapevines & Grapes, Sterling Silver Overlay, 7 1/2 In. 225.00
Night-Light, Angel Head, Metal Base, Green Mark, 5 In. 185.00
Oyster Plate, Hand Painted Nautical Scene, 8 1/2 In. 80.00
Pitcher, Dimpled, Mask Spout, Pink 115.00
Pitcher, Lemonade, Clusters of Lemons, Leaves, Marked, 10 3/4 In. 235.00
Pitcher, Lemonade, Leaves, Blossoms, Lemons, Palette Mark, 11 In. 275.00
Pitcher, Lemonade, Lemons, Leaves, Blossoms, Palette Mark, 10 3/4 In. 50.00
Pitcher, Lemons, Blossoms & Leaves, Artist Signed, 10 3/4 In. 250.00
Pitcher, Pink, Mask Spout, White Handle, Green Mark, 7 1/4 In. 130.00
Pitcher, Water, Windmills, Pink 45.00
Planter, Bird, Tail Up, Green Wreath, 5 1/4 In. 38.00
Plate, Alaris, 10 1/2 In. 20.00
Plate, Ballad, Wide Sterling Band, Gold Mark, 11 3/4 In. 55.00
Plate, Dinner, Cretan 20.00
Plate, Dinner, Harvest 12.00
Plate, Hunt Scene, Artist Signed, 8 In. 69.00
Plate, Oyster Shell, Nautical Scene, Hand Painted, Belleek, 8 1/2 In. 75.00
Plate, Thoroughbred Horse, Gold Rim, Green Mark 35.00
Plate, Weatherly, 10 1/2 In. 25.00
Platter, Cretan, Oval, Large 80.00
Platter, Rose, 13 1/2 In. 60.00
Platter, Scalloped, Gold Effect, Draped Handles, 16 1/2 X 12 In. 60.00
Salt & Pepper, Nipper 32.50
Salt, Hand Painted Roses, Green Leaves, Forget-Me-Nots, Wreath Mark 10.00
Salt, Oyster Shell Shape, Painted Flowers, Gold Rim, Green Mark 13.50
Salt, Swan, Pink 30.00
Salt, Wreath & Lyre, Forget-Me-Nots, Gold Trim, Set of 6 .... 48.00
Sugar & Creamer, Covered, Rose 60.00
Sugar & Creamer, Open, Bowl of Flowers, Top Blue Band, Gold Handle 30.00
Sugar, Covered, Noblesse 45.00
Sugar, Weatherly 38.50
Tankard, Grapes, Belleek 325.00
Tankard, Silver Overlay, Brown & Green Ground, Grape & Vine, 7 In. 225.00
Tea Set, Artist Signed, C.1917, 4 Piece 180.00
Teapot, Mansfield 65.00

Teapot, Ming, Gold Mark, Individual	65.00
Teapot, White, Silver Overlay, Reticulated Insert	130.00
Toby Jug, William Penn, Green Mark	135.00
Vase, Embossed Design, Red Glaze, 10 In.	125.00
Vase, Embossed Morning Glories, Gold Tim, Gold Wreath Mark, 7 In.	45.00
Vase, Empire, Swan Handles, Green Mark, 11 In.	135.00
Vase, Ivory Fluted Top & Handles, Dusty Rose, 8 In.	35.00
Vase, Pink Rose, White, Signed, 8 1/2 In.	22.00
Vase, Rose Design, Green Wreath Mark, 7 1/4 In.	85.00
Vase, White Sprigs, Green, 7 1/2 In.	85.00

Letter openers have been used since the eighteenth century. Ivory and silver were favored by the well–to–do. In the late nineteenth century, the letter opener was popular as an advertising giveaway and many were made of metal or celluloid. Brass openers with figural handles were also popular.

LETTER OPENER, Advertising, Cheney Silk Yarns	7.00
Advertising, John Deere, Hanging Type	40.00
Barnsdall Distributor, Etched Eagle, Brass	6.00
Bone, Scrimshaw Design, Elk On Blade, 20th Century, 10 In.	50.00
Bronze, Benjamin Franklin At Top, Monroe F.Dreher, Inc.	50.00
Buffalo, Brass, Pan American, 1901	32.00
Carved Bear's Head, Glass Eyes, Wooden, 14 3/4 In.	45.00
Cathedral	10.00
Clown Face In Relief, Brass	18.00
Dog Handle, Sterling Silver, Celluloid	47.50
Duo Escohol Injection Fluid, Embalmer's Supply Co., Bronze	35.00
E.R.Squibb & Sons, Silver Plate	15.00
Fish, Silver Plate	18.00
Fort Smith & Western Railway Co., Brass	35.00
Golfer, Silver Plate	8.00
Pole Shape, Brass, National Pole Co., Escanaba, Mi.	15.00
RCA, Metal, Plastic, Floating Radio Tube In Handle	30.00
Roland Electric Co., 1930s Train On Celluloid Handle	15.00
Ruler, Sterling, 4 In.	40.00
Smiling Black Boy In Tattered Hat, Brass, 13 In.	100.00
Standard Paint Co., Celluloid, 7 In.	10.00
Sunbonnet, Cast Iron, Original Colors	45.00
Sword, Siam Dancer, Sterling Silver	16.00
Tiger Maple Inlaid Handle, Curved Blade, C.1870, 8 1/4 In.	19.00
Union Station, Kansas City, Sterling Silver	9.00
Wells Stamp Co., Philadelphia, Brass Handle, 8 3/4 In.	15.00
Woman, Art Nouveau, Pewter	25.00
Yale Lock, Figural	30.00

The Libbey Glass Company has made glass of many types since 1892. Libbey made cut glass and tablewares that are collected today. The stemwares of the 1930s and 1940s are once again in style. The Toledo, Ohio, firm was purchased by Owens–Illinois in 1935 and is still working under the name "Libbey" as a division of that company.

LIBBEY, see also Amberina; Cut Glass; Maize

LIBBEY, Basket, Amberina, Signed, 7 In.	1200.00
Bowl, Aztec Pattern, Flared, Signed, 3 X 9 3/4 In.	2095.00
Bowl, Crosscut Diamonds, Fans, Hobstar, 8 In.	90.00
Bowl, Intaglio Grapes, Branches, Leaves, Signed, 9 X 2 In.	150.00
Bowl, Kimberly, 3 Corners, Turned–In Sides, 10 In.	350.00
Bowl, Pinwheel, Footed, Oval, Signed, 11 X 6 In.	125.00
Butter, Domed Cover, Signed, 8 In.	350.00
Candleholder, Camel Opalescent, Signed, 5 1/2 In., Pair	495.00
Candlestick, Figural, Camel, Opalescent, Pair	380.00
Celery, Green To Clear, Teardrop Stem, Signed	150.00
Champagne, Green Concentric Circles At Top, Twisted Stem	125.00
Champagne, Squirrel	135.00

Cocktail, Giraffe Stem, Opalescent, Signed, C.1930	145.00
Cocktail, Kangaroo Stem, Black, Signed	135.00
Cocktail, Kangaroo Stem, Opalescent, Signed	125.00
Compote, Amberina, Signed, 5 X 5 In.	250.00
Compote, Cut Daisies & Foliage, 8 In.	85.00
Compote, Expanded Zipper Pattern, Twisted Stem, Turquoise	275.00
Compote, Feathered Star, Teardrop Stem, 9 In.	125.00
Compote, Jelly, No.408, Signed, 8 In.	185.00
Compote, Sword Mark, 8 1/2 In.	165.00
Cruet, Hobstar Chain, Signed	60.00
Cup, Overlapping Petals, Embossed Company Name	85.00
Dish, Cheese, Harvard Pattern, 9 X 8 In.	785.00
Dish, Holly Engraving, Ruffled, Signed, 7 In.	65.00
Dish, Ice Cream, Signed, 14 In.	195.00
Figurine, Menagerie Animal Series, 8 Piece	700.00
Fruit Bowl, Oblong, Marked, 7 1/2 In.	170.00
Goblet, Cat, Opalescent	100.00 To 135.00
Humidor, Middlesex Pattern, Hobstar & Vesicas	400.00
Ice Cream Set, Cut Glass, Marked, 11 Piece	500.00
Jug, Spirit, Harvard Pattern, Handle, 13 1/2 In.	425.00
Nappy, 2 Handles, Signed, 11 In.	165.00
Paperweight, Woman, Flowing Hair, Columbian Exposition, 1893	225.00
Paperweight, World's Columbian Exposition, Building, Dated 1893	45.00
Pin Dish, World's Fair 1893, Leaf Shape, Frosted Glass, Signed	22.00
Pitcher, Blue Nailsea Type Design, Strap Handle, C.1930, Signed	155.00
Pitcher, Notched Rim, Sunburst Each Side, Hobstars, Signed, 8 In.	275.00
Pitcher, Tankard, Hobstars, Fans, Diamond Point, Signed, 7 1/2 In.	260.00
Plate, Cut Glass, Aztec Pattern, Marked, 7 In.	360.00
Punch Bowl, Harvard Pattern, 12 1/4 X 6 In.	475.00
Punch Bowl, Hobstars & Strawberry, 24 Point Hobstar Base	1200.00
Punch Set, Low Pedestal Base, Signed, 9 Piece	3750.00
Relish, Round, Signed, 6 X 2 1/2 In.	150.00
Salad Set, Spillane Pattern, Bowl & Underplate, Signed, 11 1/2 In.	1950.00
Salt, Satin Design	98.00
Saltshaker, Columbian Exhibition, Signed, 1893	85.00
Smoke Set, Floor Ashtray, Aluminum Stem, 2 Coasters, 28 In.	225.00
Sugar & Creamer, Ellsmere Pattern	1100.00
Toothpick, Fluted, Prisms	42.00
Tray, Ice Cream, Ellsmere Pattern, 12 In.	850.00
Vase, Amberina, 11 1/2 In.	395.00
Vase, Amberina, Ruffled Lip, Ribbed Swirl, Bulbous, 10 In.	200.00
Vase, Cut Glass, Daisy & Button, Stepped Square Base, 16 1/2 In.	250.00
Vase, Ripple Top, Cut Floral Design, Signed, 8 In.	225.00
Vase, Trumpet Shape, Mignon Pattern, Scalloped, Signed, 9 1/2 In.	155.00
Vase, Twisted Stem, Engraved, Signed, 7 1/4 In.	75.00

Cigarettes became popular in the late nineteenth century and with the cigarette came matches and cigarette lighters. All types of lighters are collected, from solid gold to the first of the recent disposable lighters. Most examples found were made after 1940.

LIGHTER, Chesterfield Cigarette	9.50
Cigar, Counter, Electric, Needs Coil	25.00
Cigar, Donkey, Sitting, Cast Iron	35.00
Cigar, Electric, Cobalt Blue, Porcelain, Needs Cord	35.00
Cigar, Hawkeye, 1910	225.00
Cigar, Midland Spark Jump	165.00
Cigar, Snuffer On Chain, Footed, Sterling Silver, 4 1/2 X 3 In.	125.00
Cigar, Sterling Silver Font, Wooden Handle	115.00
Cigar, Tinder, Pistol Grip, Wooden Grip Replaced, 6 7/8 In.	70.00
Cigarette, Advertising, Camel, World's Fair, 1933	75.00
Cigarette, Akro Agate, Dome Shape, Silk Electric Cord	22.50
Cigarette, Aladdin's Magic Lamp, Occupied Japan	18.00
Cigarette, Armored Man, Music Box	28.00
Cigarette, Art Deco Nude, Dunhill	25.00

Cigarette, Ashtray, Akro Agate, Green 10.00
Cigarette, Brass, Round, German 100.00
Cigarette, Canadian National Railways, Logo Both Sides, Box 10.00
Cigarette, Chase Brass Co., Brass, Table 18.50
Cigarette, Chesterfield 10.00
Cigarette, Chrome Airplane, Art Deco .... 27.00 To 45.00
Cigarette, Chrome, Schlitz, Table, 1961 .... 20.00
Cigarette, Colt, Marked 12.50
Cigarette, Demley Surelite, Austria, Brass 35.00
Cigarette, Dr Pepper 20.00
Cigarette, Dunhill 10.00
Cigarette, Golf Ball Between 2 Crossed Clubs 10.00
Cigarette, Grapette, Miniature, 1940s 15.00
Cigarette, Gun Shape, Mother-of-Pearl Inserts, Occupied Japan 18.00
Cigarette, Hobnail, Dark Amber, Table, Square, 2 1/4 X 3 In. 15.00
Cigarette, Imari 55.00
Cigarette, L & M 9.50
Cigarette, Lalique, Lions' Heads 115.00
Cigarette, Manning Bowman, 115 Volt, Electric, Patent 1911 .... 45.00
Cigarette, Newport 5.00
Cigarette, Pack of Cigarettes, Box 18.00
Cigarette, Pistol, Occupied Japan 10.00
Cigarette, Planters Peanuts 75.00
Cigarette, Pre-Civil War Derringer, Wooden Stand, 6 In. 27.00
Cigarette, Ronson & Evans, Combination Case & Lighter 20.00
Cigarette, Ronson, Sterling Silver, Case, Pocket 23.00
Cigarette, Rooster & Eagle, World War I 45.00
Cigarette, Rosecut Diamonds & Rubies, 14K Gold, 1920s, 4 3/8 In. 495.00
Cigarette, Roulette Wheel 50.00
Cigarette, Savings Bank, Slot Machine Shape, 2 1/4 X 4 1/4 In. 125.00
Cigarette, Ship's Wheel .... 20.00 To 30.00
Cigarette, Silver Crown, Wm.Rogers 20.00
Cigarette, Swiss, Disk 75.00
Cigarette, Tareyton 5.00
Cigarette, Valve Stem 10.00
Cigarette, Wind King, Absolutely Can't Be Blown Out, Wick, 7 In. 10.00
Cigarette, World War I, Gott Mit Uns 15.00
Cigarette, Zippo, Display, Action Light, Advertising 160.00
Cigarette, Zippo, Etched 10.00
Cigarette, Zippo, Winchester Commemorative Logo, 1866-1966 .... 20.00
Compact, Schildkraut, Foil Cloisonne, Enameled Violets 42.00

Lightning rods were placed on barns and wooden houses to protect
the building from fire. Lightning rods are now favored by the folk
art collectors, although most were commercially made. The glass
balls added to the rods were for decorative purposes only. The
earliest glass balls for lightning rods date from the 1840s. Today
most lightning rods have plastic instead of glass balls.

LIGHTNING ROD, Ball, Milk Glass, Stars, Amber 20.00
Ball, White 12.50
With Vane, Ruby Ball, Electra Arrow 120.00

Limoges porcelain has been made in Limoges, France, since the
mid-nineteenth century. Fine porcelains were made by many
factories including Haviland, Ahrenfeldt, Guerin, Pouyat, Elite, and
others. Modern porcelains are being made at Limoges and the word
"Limoges" as part of the mark is not an indication of age. Haviland
is listed as a separate category in this book.

LIMOGES, Biscuit Jar, Orange & Violet Poppies, Gold Trim 150.00
Bowl, Fish Finial Cover, Chrysanthemums, Foliage, Handles, 5 3/4 In. 485.00
Bowl, Hand Painted Roses, Green Ground, Green Mark, 9 1/4 In. 85.00
Box, Cupids On Cover, Cobalt Blue & White, Square, 4 1/4 In. 180.00
Box, Gilt Metal Collar, Cherub Scene On Lid 30.00
Box, Pate-Sur-Pate Design Lid, Wedgwood Blue, Square, 4 1/4 In. 185.00

Box, Portrait On Cover, Signed, 8 1/2 In.	325.00
Celery, Leaf Design, Gold Trim, 12 X 5 3/4 In.	40.00
Charger, Allover Yellow Roses, Gold & Black Rim, Signed, 12 In.	85.00
Charger, Peasant Couple, Field, D & C Mark, 14 1/2 In.	160.00
Charger, Portrait, Madame Pompadour, Garlands, Roses, 12 1/2 In.	70.00
Chocolate Pot, Hand Painted, Artist Signed, 9 In.	125.00
Chocolate Pot, Pale Green, Pink Flowers, 11 In.	95.00
Chocolate Set, Cascading Lilacs, Green Ground, Gold Trim, 7 Piece	275.00
Chocolate Set, Scattered Pink Roses, 14 In.Tray, 15 Piece	595.00
Coffee Set, Armorial, Hand Painted, Paris, Dated 1870, 7 Piece	250.00
Cookie Jar, Sprays of Flowers, Gold Trim, Blue Ground, 7 1/2 In.	125.00
Creamer, Roses, Crimped, Elite, 5 1/2 In.	30.00
Cup & Saucer, Roses Inside & Out, 2 Handles	18.00
Cuspidor, Lady's, Flowered Rim, Gold Trim, Handle, 3 X 2 In.	45.00
Custard Cup, Liners, Pastel Rose Design, Jean Pouyat	65.00
Dinner Service, Guerin & Co., 75 Piece	800.00
Dish, 3 Sections, Gold Trim, Peach To White Roses, Marked, 12 In.	135.00
Dish, Art Nouveau, Gold Tracery, White, Gold Handle, 7 X 10 In.	160.00
Dish, Cavalier & Lady Scene, 2 Sections, 14 1/4 X 4 In.	165.00
Dish, Cheese, Dome Cover, Gold Tracery Border, Leaves, Marked, 6 In.	325.00
Dish, Pancake, Covered	315.00
Dish, Sardine, Shell Shape	155.00
Dresser Set, Violets, 6 Piece	285.00
Fish Set, Beaded Scalloped Borders, Hand Painted, 24 Piece	1700.00
Fish Set, Rectangular Platter, 9 X 24 In., 13 Piece	550.00
Fish Set, Sauceboat, Platter, Hand Painted, Imperial, 14 Piece	1300.00
Fish Set, Scalloped Borders, Artist Baumy, 9 In.Plate, 13 Piece	700.00
Fish Set, Water Lilies, Gold Trim, Signed, C.1870, 12 Piece	2500.00
Game Set, Stylized Birds, Hand Painted, Artist Signed, 13 Piece	495.00
Hatpin Holder, Cream, Gold Embossed Border	28.50
Humidor, Indians Smoking Peace Pipe	275.00
Inkwell, Double, Pen Tray	38.00
Jam Jar, Underplate, Celadon Green, Florals & Gilding, C.1850	125.00
Match Holder, Attached Underplate, All White, T & V	15.00
Nappy, Serving, Maple Leaf Shape, Handle, Roses, 10 In.	55.00
Oyster Plate, 5 Sections, Salmon Pink, Gold Trim, 8 5/8 In.	55.00
Oyster Plate, Molded Shell, Brown Shaded, For Pres.Hayes, Set of 6	1430.00
Pitcher, Dancing Couples, 2 Sides, Painted, Gold Trim, 1890, 5 In.	190.00
Pitcher, Hanging Grapes, Brown, Yellow, Rust, Marked, 12 In.	185.00
Pitcher, Lemonade, Grape Design, Dated 1905	125.00
Pitcher, Melon Shape, Allover Pink Floral, Scalloped Base, 9 In.	70.00
Pitcher, Tankard, Hanging Grapes, Marked, 6 1/2 In.	185.00
Plaque, Allover Yellow Roses, Gold & Black Rim, Signed, 12 In.	85.00
Plaque, Carp, Morning Glories, Rococo Gold Border, Artist, 14 In.	265.00
Plaque, Deer, Artist Tuville	275.00
Plaque, Game, Gold Rococo Border, Marked, 13 1/2 In.	225.00
Plaque, Hunting Dog Scene, Oval, Artist Signed, 10 X 14 1/2 In.	275.00
Plaque, Scenes of French Countryside, 5 1/2 X 7 1/2 In., Pair	120.00
Plaque, Woman Bust, On Green, Rococo Gold Border, LePic, 10 In.	175.00
Plate, 2 Fighting Boars, Signed Pradet, 10 In.	85.00
Plate, 3 Ducks, Pierced, Signed Bald	100.00

Modern bleach can damage 18th-century and some 19th-century dishes. To clean old dishes, try hydrogen peroxide or bicarbonate of soda. Each removes a different type of stain.

Plate, Bust of Lady, Green Ground, Signed LePic, 10 In. 175.00
Plate, Cavalier Portrait, Coronet 65.00
Plate, Deer In Forest Scene, Artist Signed, 9 In. .... 165.00 To 175.00
Plate, Dutch Harbor Scene, Rococo & Gold Rim, Hanging, 10 In. 115.00
Plate, Game, Scalloped Gold Rim, Pierced, Artist Signed, 10 In. 48.00
Plate, Hand Painted, Chrysanthemums, Scalloped Gold Rim, 7 In. 85.00
Plate, Iris, Lake Scene Ground, Rococo Gold, Pierced, Marked, 11 In. 175.00
Plate, Lady, Scalloped Border, Marked, 13 1/8 In. 275.00
Plate, Lighthouse, Ships, Fisherman, Signed, Gold Rim, 10 In. 85.00
Plate, Peasant Girl, Standing, Hand Painted, Coronet, 10 In. 65.00
Plate, Pheasant & Quail, Hand Painted, 10 1/2 In., Pair 350.00
Plate, Pheasants, 10 In., Pair 60.00
Plate, Pheasants, Green Ground, Scalloped, Marked 75.00
Plate, Pheasants, Green Ground, Scalloped, Signed, Pair 75.00
Plate, Pheasants, Quail, Rococo Gold Rim, 13 In., Pair 495.00
Plate, Pink, Scalloped, Floral Design, 8 In. 12.00
Plate, Quail, Gold Border, Marked, 8 1/2 In. 75.00
Plate, Quail, Pheasants, Marked, 12 1/2 In., Pair 495.00
Plate, Quail, Rococo Gold, L.Coudert, 10 1/8 In., Pair 275.00
Plate, Raspberries, Gold Scalloped Rim, Artist Signed, 8 1/2 In. 45.00
Plate, Scene, Gold Scalloped Border, 13 In., Pair 425.00
Plate, Violets, Ahrenfeldt, 9 1/2 In. 90.00
Platter, Dog & 4 Puppies, Grassy Knoll, Sky & Clouds, 17 1/2 In. 605.00
Platter, Game Birds, Gold Edging, Landscape, Marked, 14 X 20 In. 375.00
Platter, Pheasant In Flight, Cornet Mark, Signed 225.00
Salad Set, Shells, Seaweed, Gold Tracery, C.1897, 7 Piece 295.00
Salt, Iridescent White Interior, Beige, Hexagonal, Marked, 2 In. 8.00
Sugar & Creamer, Coronet, Floral 30.00
Tankard, Fruit, 11 In. 135.00
Tankard, Raised Gold, Green, Pink, Gold Handle, Signed, 14 1/2 In. 225.00
Tankard, Roses, 14 In. 150.00
Tea Set, Blue Forget–Me–Nots, F.C.Richards Artist, 15 Piece 200.00
Tea Set, Child's, Portrait, 14 Piece 75.00
Tray, Comb, Hand Painted 22.00
Tray, Heart Shape, Roses, Scalloped Edge, 6 X 6 3/4 In. 65.00
Tray, Musical Instruments, Flowers, Gold Rim, 9 X 16 1/2 In. 265.00
Tray, Pink Flowers, Gold Trim, 8 X 6 In. 125.00
Vase, 3 Rococo Shaped Handles, Corset Shape 95.00
Vase, Bulbous On Top, Roses & Bud On Shaded Ground, Marked, 12 In. 145.00
Vase, Floral, Greeen & Gold Trim, Entwined Handles, 12 1/2 In. 325.00
Vase, Gold Iris Pattern, 3 Ovals, Scenes, 34 In. 1200.00

In 1927, Charles Lindbergh, the aviator, became the first man to fly across the Atlantic Ocean. He was a national hero. In 1932, his son was kidnapped and murdered, and Lindbergh was again the center of public interest. He died in 1974. All types of Lindbergh memorabilia are collected.

LINDBERGH, Ashtray, Our National Hero, Portrait, Furniture Store, 5 In. 20.00
Book, Lone Eagle, 21 Pages, 1929, 8 X 9 In. 18.00
Bookends, Bronze Wash .... 30.00 To 50.00
Bookends, Bust, Verona, Cast Iron 25.00
Bookends, Figural, Flight Jacket, Helmet, Copper Over Metal 49.00
Bookends, The Aviator, Bronze, Dated 1928 .... 85.00
Button, Bond Bread 22.00
Button, Welcome Lindy 18.00
Case, Pencil, Portrait, Tin 45.00
Game, Lindy Flying Game 26.00
Game, New Lindy Flying 26.00
Label, Cigar Box, World's Greatest Flyer 14.00
Look Magazine, Cover & Story, April 11, 1939 .... 12.50
Pencil Box, Metal 37.50
Pin, Spirit of St. Louis, Figural, Brass 20.00
Pinback, Plucky Lindy, Gold Horseshoe 35.00
Plate, Commemorative, Limoges, 1927 .... 28.00 To 45.00

Postcard, Lindbergh & Mother, Timetable Back, C.1927 .... 12.00
Program, Fargo, Dated 35.00
Quilt, Commemorative, 36 Planes, Geometrics, Handmade, C.1930 .... 450.00
Ribbon, Woven, 7 In. 100.00
Sheet Music, Lone Eagle March, Photo of Lindy 10.00
Sheet Music, Lucky Lindy, With Airplane 8.50
Soap, Hand, Lindy, Paper Label, Unopened 45.00
Toy, Paint Box 45.00
Toy, Plane, Spirit of St.Louis, Tin 490.00
Watch, With Fob 150.00

> Lithophanes are porcelain pictures made by casting clay in layers of various thicknesses. When a piece is held to the light, a picture of light and shadow is seen through it. Most lithophanes date from the 1825–75 period. A few are still being made. Many lithophanes sold today were originally panels for lampshades.

LITHOPHANE, Cup & Saucer, Geisha, Demitasse 25.00
Cup & Saucer, Nude, Moriage Dragon Design 45.00
Cup, Souvenir, Mannequin In Bottom, 1 7/8 X 1 1/2 In. 45.00
Cup, With Lid, Russian Scene, Russian Wording, C.1860 .... 275.00
Lamp, 4 Panels, Brass Pedestal, 13 1/4 X 5 In. 595.00
Lamp, Candle, 4 Scenes, White Porcelain, Gold Legs, 7 X 5 In. 500.00
Lamp, Kerosene, 4 Scenes, Electrified, 3 Piece 850.00
Panel, Boy In Disgrace, Mother Repairing Pants, Trapezoid 135.00
Panel, Girl & Dog, Stained Glass Frame, 7 X 8 1/8 In. 275.00
Panel, Girl, Under Tree, Approaching Girl & Boy, 7 5/8 X 6 In. 310.00
Panel, Lady On Prayer Stool, Red Case Glass, 6 3/8 X 5 1/2 In. 275.00
Panel, Mill With Trees, Glaze, 7 X 5 1/8 In. 250.00
Panel, Mother Teaching Girl To Knit, Framed, 5 1/2 X 4 3/8 In. 295.00
Panel, Napoleon, 7 5/8 X 8 3/8 In. 295.00
Panel, Paterson Falls, Trapezoid, 5 1/2 In.At Bottom, 5 1/4 In. 135.00
Panel, Regimental, 10 In. 110.00
Panel, Schoolmaster With Mother & Boy, 6 3/8 X 5 3/8 In. 285.00
Panel, Seated Mother, Boy At Side, Kitchen, 7 1/4 X 5 3/4 In. 325.00
Panel, Soldiers & Fire, Marked, 5 7/8 X 7 1/2 In. 285.00
Panel, Springtime, Couple On Swing, Metal Frame, 5 1/2 X 5 In. 225.00
Panel, St.Sextus, Madonna, Iron Frame, White, 7 1/2 X 19 1/2 In. 425.00
Panel, Tell's Chapel, Stained Glass Sides, 8 3/4 X 10 1/2 In. 375.00
Panel, Victorian Lady, Kneeler, Red Panes, Holder, 6 3/4 In. 150.00
Panel, Waves Against Craggy Shore, Moon, 4 1/4 X 5 1/8 In. 125.00
Panel, Woman In Front of Mirror, 11 7/8 X 9 1/2 In. 375.00
Plaque, Lady With Baby, White Frame, Marked PPM, 8 1/2 X 9 In. 150.00
Plaque, The Storm, Black Ebony Frame, 9 1/8 X 12 In. 325.00
Plaque, Two Young Ladies With Fan, 5 1/8 X 6 1/4 In. 240.00
Stein, Man, Game Scene, Pewter Lid, Dove Finial 155.00
Stein, Regimental, Pair 660.00
Stein, Tavern Scene 80.00
Tea Set, Dragon Moriage, 9 Piece 145.00
Vase, Grandmother Teaching Child To Knit, Marked PPM, 8 In. 150.00

> Liverpool, England, was the site of several pottery and porcelain factories from 1716 to 1785. Some earthenware was made with transfer decorations. Sadler and Green made print–decorated wares from 1756. Many of the pieces were made for the American market and feature patriotic emblems, such as eagles, flags, and other special–interest motifs.

LIVERPOOL, Bowl, Black Masonic Transfer, 4 1/2 X 9 7/8 In. 165.00
Jug, Farmer's Arms, Black & White Transfer, 11 1/2 In. 700.00
Mug, American Eagle, James Leech, Black Transfer, 4 7/8 In. 105.00
Mug, Farmer's Arms, God Speed The Plow, Black Transfer, 5 In. 175.00
Plaque, George Washington, Black Transfer, Gilt Frame, 8 X 9 In. 650.00
Plate, Feather Pattern, Black, American Ship, 10 In., 4 Piece 550.00

Juan, Jose, and Vicente Lladro opened a ceramics workshop in Almacera, Spain, in 1951. They soon began making figurines in a distinctive, elongated style. In 1958 the factory moved to Tabernes Blanques, Spain. The company makes stoneware and porcelain vases and figurines in limited and nonlimited editions.

LLADRO, Figurine, Girl With Lamb	100.00
Figurine, Japanese Girl With Purse, 11 In.	150.00
Figurine, Mother & Child	110.00
Figurine, Oriental Girl	185.00
Figurine, Poodle, Nursing 5 Puppies, 6 1/2 X 6 In.	125.00
Figurine, Umbrella Girl & Boy	265.00
Plate, Mother's Day, 1971	30.00

Locke Art is a trademark found on glass of the early twentieth century. Joseph Locke worked at many English and American firms. He designed and etched his own glass in Pittsburgh, Pennsylvania, starting in the 1880s. Some pieces were marked "Joe Locke," but most were marked with the words "Locke Art." The mark is hidden in the pattern on the glass.

LOCKE ART, Goblet, Brandy, Engraved Florals	95.00
Pitcher, Leaf & Berry Design, Clear, 8 In.	375.00
Tumbler, Ribbed, Cherry Design, Signed, 5 1/4 In.	140.00
Tumbler, Vintage Pattern, Signed, 3 5/8 In.	80.00

Johann Loetz bought a glassworks in Austria in 1840. He died in 1848 and his widow ran the company; then in 1879, his grandson took over. Loetz glass was varied. Most collectors recognize the iridescent gold glass similar to Tiffany, but many other types were made. The firm closed during World War II.

LOETZ, Biscuit Barrel, Vertical Ribs, Intertwined Crisscross Threads	175.00
Bowl, Cup Form, Iridescent Gold, Bronze Holder, 4 1/2 In. ....*Illus*	800.00
Bowl, Green Iridescent, Signed, 4 1/4 In.	275.00
Bowl, Pleated, Wavy Rim, Purple Branches On Amber, 8 In.	200.00
Bowl, Scalloped, Crinkle Finish, Signed, Green, 9 1/4 In.	175.00
Box, Enamel Thistles On Hinged Cover, Round, Oil Stained, 5 1/2 In.	350.00
Bride's Bowl, Red To Green, Ruffled, Iridescent	185.00
Bride's Bowl, Sterling Silver Cherub Stand	800.00
Candleholder, Gold Iridescent, Signed, 17 1/2 In.	235.00
Compote, Iridescent Green, Scalloped, Metal Base, Signed, 9 In.Diam.	210.00
Cuspidor, Melon Ribbed, Green Iridescent	90.00
Dish, Sweetmeat, Random Threads, Swirled Ribs, Silver Plated Rim	195.00
Epergne, Figural Cupid Holder	185.00
Inkwell, Brass Cover, Iridescent, 2 X 5 1/4 In.	325.00
Inkwell, Threaded Glass, Brass Hinged Lid, Iridescent	195.00
Lamp, Art Glass, Upright, Brass Base, 9 1/4 In.	110.00
Rose Bowl, Iridescent Green, Scalloped, Signed, 6 In.	175.00
Urn, Green & Amethyst, Overall Threading, Fluted Neck, 11 In.	140.00
Vase, Amber, Iridescent, Dimpled Sides, Blue Feathering, 4 1/2 In.	550.00
Vase, Blown Out, Silver–Green Outside, Brown Inside, Signed, 10 In.	215.00
Vase, Blue Oil Spot On Green, 18 1/2 In.	750.00
Vase, Cameo, Flowers & Leaves, Green, Lavender, Pink, Signed, 11 In.	675.00
Vase, Cobalt Blue, Purple & Green Iridescent, 4 Ribbed, 11 X 6 In.	210.00
Vase, Dimpled Surface, Blue–Green & Silver On Green, 5 X 5 In.	610.00
Vase, Flared Rim, Light Gold & Blue, Signed, 5 1/2 X 3 In.	115.00
Vase, Fluted, Green, Signed, 5 1/2 In.	55.00
Vase, Free–Form, Squat, Pinched Sides, 4 X 2 1/4 In.	110.00
Vase, Gold, Red Iridescent, Signed, 8 1/4 In.	195.00
Vase, Gooseneck, Pinched Bottom, Green, 9 In.	450.00
Vase, Gooseneck, Pinched Bulbous Bottom, Blue Iridescent, 9 In.	450.00
Vase, Green Crinkle, Triangle Indents, Signed, 9 1/2 In.	175.00
Vase, Green Iridescent, Signed, 12 1/2 In.	150.00
Vase, Green Lava Exterior, Purple Interior, Signed, 6 In.	125.00
Vase, Green, Allover Satin Ribbon Design, 12 In.	650.00

Loetz, Bowl, Cup Form,
   Iridescent Gold,
Bronze Holder, 4 1/2 In.

Loetz, Vase, Purple, Blue, Pewter Holder,
5 1/2 In.

Vase, Green, Bulbous, Gold Blown–Out Leaves, Berries, Signed, 7 In. 185.00
Vase, Green, Indented, Square, Signed, 11 In. 185.00
Vase, Indented On 4 Sides, Gold, 9 In. .... 295.00 To 450.00
Vase, Indented, Triangular, Iridescent, Signed, 8 In. 165.00
Vase, Iridescent Blues, Silver Overlay Floral Spray Center, 5 In. 350.00
Vase, Lime Yellow To Blue, Iridescent, Signed, 8 1/4 In. 240.00
Vase, Maroon, Ribbed, Flared 5 In.Base, Signed, 13 In. 165.00
Vase, Peacock Blue, Gold Iridescent, Signed, 4 In. 250.00
Vase, Peacock, Gold Dimples, 4 In. 165.00
Vase, Peacock, Scaled Green, Dimples, Quatrefoil Rim, 7 X 6 In. 400.00
Vase, Pinched, Silver Dragonflies At Rim, Signed, 5 X 4 In. 295.00
Vase, Pulled Feathering, Ruffled Top, Polished Pontil, 9 1/2 In. 285.00
Vase, Purple Shaded To Green, Handle, Tall 990.00
Vase, Purple, Blue, Pewter Holder, 5 1/2 In. ....*Illus* 275.00
Vase, Purple, Iridescent, Squat, 15 In. 550.00
Vase, Purple, Red, Blue, Threaded Trailings, Handles, 7 In. 295.00
Vase, Purple, Shaded To Green, Handle, Tall 1090.00
Vase, Red & Blue, Iridescent, Flower Opening, Pedestal, 8 In. 200.00
Vase, Red, Cobalt Blue Loopings & Trailings, 11 1/4 In. 1210.00
Vase, Ribbed, Scalloped, Dark Green, Signed, 6 1/2 In. 110.00
Vase, Ribbed, Triangle Indented Design, Green, Signed, 9 1/2 In. 185.00
Vase, Ruby Top, Blue Iridescent To Yellow, Thumbprint, 12 1/2 In. 295.00
Vase, Ruffled Lip, Green Over Cranberry, Irregular Stripes, 11 In. 385.00
Vase, Ruffled Top, Pulled Feathering, 9 1/2 In. 185.00
Vase, Scaled Green Peacock, Dimples, Quatrefoil Rim, 7 X 6 In. 350.00
Vase, Scalloped, Gold Iridescent, Signed, 7 1/2 In. 135.00
Vase, Silver–Blue Bands, Amber & Peach Ground, 5 In. 935.00
Vase, Snakeskin Pattern, Pinched On 4 Sides, Purple & Green, 9 In. 450.00
Vase, Striated Blue & Burgundy, Blue Ground, 8 3/4 In. 1210.00
Vase, Triangle Top, Indented, Green, Signed 325.00
Vase, Twist Shape, Encased In Metal, Pulled Thread Design 195.00

The Lone Ranger is a fictional character introduced on the radio in 1932. Over three thousand shows were produced before the series ended in 1954. In 1938, the first Lone Ranger movie was made. Television shows were started in 1949 and are still seen on some stations. The Lone Ranger appears on many products and was even the name of a restaurant chain for several years.

LONE RANGER, Badge, Bond Bread 36.00
  Badge, Shield 46.00
  Binoculars 35.00
  Blanket, Red, Brown, Beige, Cotton 65.00
  Blotter, Bond Bread 15.00
  Book Bag 25.00
  Book, Bond Bread 14.00
  Book, By Fran Striker, C.1940 .... 10.00

Book, Lone Ranger Desert Storm, Whitman	7.00
Brush, Boy's, 1939	12.00
Cap Pistol & Holster Set, Leather, Metal, Nichols Stallion	35.00
Clock, Alarm, Double Bell, Bradley, Box	30.00
Coloring Book, Tonto, Unused	9.00
Doll, Composition, 1938	250.00
Figurine, Horse, Saddle, Hat & Guns, Hartland, 1950s	90.00
Figurine, Lone Ranger, Standing, Carnival	35.00
Figurine, Tonto, Hartland, 1950s	80.00
Flashlight, Signal Siren, Usalite, Box	38.00
Game, Lone Ranger, Hi-Ho Silver, Board, Parker Brothers, 1938	52.00
Game, Round-Up, Lone Ranger Trying To Rope Calf	55.00
Game, Target Board, Tin, 28 In.	75.00
Holster Set, Box, 1980, 6 Piece	25.00
Key Chain, Silver Bullet	15.00
Knife, Bullet On Handle	75.00
Lamp, Gun In Holster, Ceramic, Aladdin, Pair	15.00
Mask, Cheerios Premium, Cardboard, Late 1940s, 8 1/2 In.	20.00
Paperweight, Glass, With Snow, Roping Steer	65.00
Pedometer, Wheaties Official, Silvered Metal, 1948, Box, 3 In.	35.00
Pen Set, Silver Bullet, Ranger, Silver, & Tonto, Bullet Shape	35.00
Pin, Safety Scout	6.00
Pistol, Tin, 1938	18.00
Ring, Atom Bomb	32.00
Ring, Colt 45	65.00
Ring, Flashlight, Bulb & Battery	30.00
Sign, Merita Bread, Embossed, Tin, 24 X 36 In.	475.00
Soap Dish, Silver, Lid, Engraved	10.00
Toy, Hi-Ho Silver, Windup, Tin, Marx	160.00 To 250.00
Vest & Chaps	125.00
Viewer, Movie, 3 Films, Box	85.00
Watch, Pocket, New Haven, Portrait, Silver Rearing	110.00
Wristwatch, Leather Strap, Ranger Saying Hi-Ho Silver	30.00

The Longwy Workshop of Longwy, France, first made ceramic wares in 1798. The workshop is still in business. Most of the ceramic pieces found today are glazed with many colors to resemble cloisonne or other enameled metal. The factory used a variety of marks.

LONGWY, Charger, 12 In.	325.00
Charger, Coat of Arms	250.00
Pitcher, Bird Design, 10 In.	150.00
Saltshaker, Pewter Top	35.00
Tray, Yellow & Black, 11 In.	200.00

The Lonhuda Pottery Company of Steubenville, Ohio, was organized in 1892 by William Long, W. H. Hunter, and Alfred Day. Brown underglaze slip-decorated pottery was made. The firm closed in 1896. The company used many marks; the earliest included the letters "LPCO."

LONHUDA, Vase, Portrait, 3 Trout In Water, Signed, 8 X 8 In.	1100.00
Vase, Spider Mum Design, Long Neck, Artist Signed, 10 3/4 In.	395.00

Lotus Ware was made by the Knowles, Taylor & Knowles Company of East Liverpool, Ohio, from 1890 to 1900. Lotus Ware is a thin, Belleek-like porcelain. It was sometimes decorated outside the factory. Other types of ceramics that were made by Knowles, Taylor & Knowles Company are listed under "KTK."

LOTUS WARE, Bowl, Pink, Green, & Gold, Signed, 5 X 4 In.	525.00
Bowl, Reticulated Ends, Beaded Rim, White, Signed, 4 1/4 In.	525.00
Dish, Shell, 3 Coral Feet, 2 1/2 X 8 In.	65.00
Rose Bowl, Ruffled, Hand Painted Roses, Gold Design, 4 1/4 In.	225.00
Vase, Pastel Floral Sprays, Bulbous, Narrow Neck, Handles, 9 In.	550.00

J.&J.G.LOW

Low art tiles were made by the J. and J. G. Low Art Tile Works of Chelsea, Massachusetts, from 1877 to 1902. A variety of art and other tiles were made. Some of the tiles were made by a process called "natural," some were hand-modeled, and some made mechanically.

LOW, Tile, Birds, Brown, 7 1/2 In.	250.00
Tile, Man's Hand, Green, 7 1/2 In.	550.00
Tile, Relief Bearded Man, Green Glaze	150.00

The Lowestoft factory in Suffolk, England, worked from 1757 to 1802. They made many commemorative gift pieces and small, dated, inscribed pieces of soft paste porcelain.

LOWESTOFT, see also Chinese Export

LOWESTOFT, Cup & Saucer, Raised Leaf & Enameled Fruit Design, C.1770	55.00
Plate, Woman With Wreath Center, Swag Border, C.1780, 9 In.	250.00

LOY-NEL-ART, see McCoy

Lunch pails and lunch boxes have been used to carry lunches to school or work since the nineteenth century. Today, most collectors want either early advertising boxes or children's lunch boxes made since the 1930s. The original Thermos bottle must be inside the box for the collector to consider it complete.

LUNCH BOX, Beatles, Yellow Submarine	45.00
Blue Tin, Art Deco, Handles, Contains 18 ABC Blocks	25.00
Brotherhood Tobacco, Tin	95.00
Burley Boy Tobacco	200.00
Campus Queen, With Thermos, 1967	8.00
Child's, Spaceship 1999	100.00
Cracker Jack	12.00
Crow-Mo-Smokers	105.00
Daniel Boone, Thermos, 1955	30.00
Dixie Kid, Black	450.00
Dixie Queen, Portrait	110.00
Dr.Seuss	10.00
Friends Tobacco, Dogs	250.00
George Washington Tobacco, Dark Blue	45.00
Graniteware, Cobalt Blue	40.00
Green Hornet	20.00
Green Turtle Cigars	135.00
Gunsmoke, 1972	13.00
Hand Bag Tobacco	195.00
Joe Palooka .... 45.00 To	50.00
Just Suits Tobacco, 8 X 5 X 4 In. .... 30.00 To	55.00
Laredo Cut Plug	70.00
Little House On The Prairie	12.00
Mayo's Cut Plug	25.00
Mickey Mouse, Land of Giants	25.00
Mickey Mouse, School Bus	10.00
Old Glory Cigars, Eagle	60.00
Patterson Tobacco, Cane Litho, Handle	19.00
Patterson's Seal, Basketweave, Tobacco	25.00
Pedro Tobacco	55.00
Penny Post	10.00
Penny Post, Dark Red	95.00
Peter Rabbit Candy	55.00
Pinocchio, Early 1940s	135.00
Rat Patrol, Thermos	15.00
Red Crest Tobacco, Leather, Rooster, 1890s	100.00
Robin Hood, Thermos, 1956	35.00
Runkels Cocoa	75.00
Salerno Cookie, Tin, 12 X 7 X 5 3/4 In.	24.00
Sensation Tobacco, Yellow Basket .... 45.00 To	65.00
Snow White, Aladdin	12.00

Sunset Trail Tobacco, Blue	125.00
Tom Corbett, Space Cadet, C.1952	19.50
U.S.Marine, Basket Weave	165.00
Walt Disney, School Bus	32.50
White Hen Cigar	175.00
Winner, Silver With Red Letters	100.00
LUNCH PAIL, Kandies For Kiddies	85.00
Mickey Mouse Club, With Annette, Bobby	15.00

Luneville, a French faience factory, was established in 1731 by Jacques Chambrette. It is best known for its fine biscuit figures and groups and for large faience dogs and lions. The early pieces were unmarked. The firm was acquired by Keller and Guerin and is still working.

LUNEVILLE, Jardiniere, Cranes In Wooded Landscape, 14 1/2 In.	525.00
Vase, Mottled Orange Ground, Berries, Leaves, Enameled, 7 3/4 In.	750.00
Vase, Scenic, Yellow Ground, Outer Blue Layer, Signed, 11 3/4 In.	575.00

Lusterware was meant to resemble copper, silver, or gold. It has been used since the sixteenth century. Most of the luster found today was made during the nineteenth century. The metallic glazes are applied on pottery. The finished color depends on the combination of the clay color and the glaze.

LUSTER, Canary, Pitcher, House, 4 1/2 In.	48.00
Copper & Pink, Mustard, Sand Bands	95.00
Copper, Creamer, Dark Blue, Gold Band	15.00
Copper, Goblet, Band of Flowers In Pink, Green & Yellow, 4 1/2 In.	75.00
Copper, Mug, Blue Band, Orange Stripe, 4 In.	25.00
Copper, Pitcher, Blue Band, Figures, Allerton & Longton, 3 5/8 In.	45.00
Copper, Pitcher, Boy & Girl In Forest, Red Transfer, 4 1/2 In.	47.50
Copper, Pitcher, Pink Flowers, Lancaster, England, 3 In.	38.00
Copper, Pitcher, Raised English Hunt Scene	50.00
Copper, Salt, Sanded Band, Pedestal Base, 1850s	45.00
Copper, Sugar & Creamer, England	25.00
LUSTER, COPPER, TEA LEAF, see Tea Leaf Ironstone	
Copper, Teapot	90.00
Copper, Tumbler, Blue Band & Floral Enameled Band, 3 3/8 In.	20.00
Copper, Vase, Dutch Children In Relief, Hand Painted	20.00
LUSTER, FAIRYLAND, see Wedgwood	
Mustard, Tea Set, Child's, Roses, Dauphine, Wedding Ring, 21 Piece	250.00
Orange, Vase, Metallic Looping, 7 7/8 In.	150.00
Pink, Mug & Saucer, Child's, Copper Luster Bands, Pink Mottling	125.00
Pink, Mug, House Pattern, 2 In.	95.00
Pink, Mug, House Pattern, Soft Paste, C.1820, 3 In.	75.00
Pink, Pitcher, Nautical Transfer Front & Back	50.00
Pink, Plate, AYP, 4 Buildings, 1909, 8 In.	42.00
Pink, Plate, Shepherd Boy, Transfer of Boy Center, C.1825, 7 In.	45.00
Pink, Punch Bowl, Scenic Design Inside, Floral Exterior, 11 In.	425.00
Pink, Tea Set, Child's, 3 Pigs, Japan, 18 Piece	225.00
Pink, Tea Set, Child's, Noah's Ark, Czechoslovakia, 11 Piece	150.00
Purple, Figurine, Frog, 5 In.	200.00
Rose, Cup, Souvenir, Salisbury, Mass.	18.00
Silver, Pitcher, Mulberry Transfer	95.00
LUSTER, SUNDERLAND, see Sunderland	

Lustre Art Glass Company was founded in Long Island, New York, in 1920 by Conrad Vahlsing and Paul Frank. The company made lampshades and globes that are almost indistinguishable from those made by Quezal. Most of the shades made by the company were unmarked.

LUSTRE ART, Shade, Gold Threading, On Pulled Feathers, Signed	110.00
Shade, Top White, Gold Swirls, Bottom Green & Gold, Set of 5	675.00

Lustres are mantel decorations, or pedestal vases, with many hanging glass prisms. The name really refers to the prisms, and it is proper to refer to a single glass prism as a lustre. Either spelling, luster or lustre, is correct.

LUSTRES, Cut Prisms, Polychrome Floral, Pink, 14 3/4 In., Pair	330.00
Hanging Prisms, Crystal, 12 In., Pair	175.00
Milk Glass, Enameled, Spear Point Prisms, Pair	450.00
Satin Glass, Green, Floral & Ribbon Swags, 12 In., Pair	200.00
Scalloped, Pink Overlay, Bristol, Gold Design, 15 5/8 In., Pair	850.00
White Cut To Clear, Floral Clusters, Bohemian, 10 1/2 In., Pair	850.00

Nicolas Lutz worked at the Boston and Sandwich Glass Company from 1869 to 1888. He made delicate and intricate threaded glass of several colors. Other similar wares made by other makers are now known by the generic name "Lutz."

LUTZ, Finger Bowl, 7 In. Underplate, 4 1/4 In.	115.00
Whiskey Tumbler, White Latticino, Pink & Gold Stripes	58.00

Petrus Regout established the De Sphinx pottery in Maastricht, Holland, in 1836. The firm was noted for its transfer-printed earthenware. Many factories in Maastricht are still making ceramics.

MAASTRICHT, Bowl, Oriental Scene, 8 In.	40.00
Bowl, Sphinx, Leaf Design	32.00
Charger, Stick Spatter	60.00
Pitcher, Milk, Polychrome Design	40.00
Plate, Abbey, 8 In.	20.00
Soup, Dish, Oriental Pattern	12.00
Waste Bowl, Polychrome Marbelized Design, Ironstone, 5 In.	20.00

Maize glass was made by W. L. Libbey & Son Company of Toledo, Ohio, after 1889. The glass resembled an ear of corn. The leaves were usually green, but some pieces were made with blue or red leaves. The kernels of "corn" were light yellow, white, or light green.

MAIZE, Butter, Ear of Corn Finial, Gold Outlined, Covered, 7 1/2 X 6 In.	485.00
Carafe, Pale Gold Leaves, Gold Highlights, Bulbous Base, 8 In.	300.00
Celery, Clear Blue Leaves	115.00
Cruet, Molded-In Leaves, Turned-Up Handle, 7 In.	945.00
Pitcher, Water, Barrel Shape, Strap Handle, 8 3/4 In.	335.00
Sugar Shaker, Blue-Gray, Gold-Edged Yellow Leaves, Liberty 1889	195.00
Water Set, 7 Piece	200.00

Majolica is a general term for any pottery glazed with an opaque tin enamel that conceals the color of the clay body. It has been made since the fourteenth century. Today's collector is most likely to find Victorian majolica. The heavy, colorful ware is rarely marked. Some famous makers include Wedgwood; Minton; Griffen, Smith and Hill (marked "Etruscan"); and Chesapeake Pottery (marked "Avalon" or "Clifton").

MAJOLICA, Bank, Dog Standing On Hind Legs, Blue Hat & Bow	75.00
Bottle, Water, Wedgwood, Dated 1879, 10 In.	300.00
Bowl, Etruscan, Marked, 9 3/4 In.	125.00
Bowl, Figural, Classical Bust & Garlands, Cobalt Blue ....*Illus*	400.00
Bowl, Green, Cream, Leaf Border & Center, 9 1/2 In.	65.00
Bowl, Men & Women Picking Grapes, Handles, Marked, 7 1/2 In.	120.00
Box, Sardine, Pink Flower, Brown Twig Handles, 1876 Eng. Reg. Mark	225.00
Box, Sardine, Swan Finial	375.00
Bread Tray, Basket Weave, 14 X 10 1/2 In.	190.00
Bread Tray, Etruscan Leaf, 11 In.	20.00
Bread Tray, Etruscan, Oak Leaf	90.00
Bread Tray, Pond Lily	75.00
Butter Chip, Begonia	20.00
Butter Chip, Etruscan, Pansy, Marked	35.00

Majolica, Bowl, Figural,
Classical Bust & Garlands, Cobalt Blue

Majolica, Jardiniere,
Pedestal, Royal Blue,
Floral Design, 40 In.

Majolica, Figurine,
Shakespeare, 16 In.

Butter Chip, Geranium, Set of 6	165.00
Butter Chip, Smilax, Etruscan	25.00
Butter Chip, Strawberry, Gray, Green, 3 1/2 In.	12.00
Butter, Flower & Wheat Pattern, Twig Handle, Covered, Ice Liner	98.00
Butter, Strawberry, Covered	185.00
Cake Stand, Begonia Leaves, Green, Brown & Yellow	90.00
Cake Stand, Etruscan Classical Series, Rose	65.00
Cake Stand, Maple Leaf, Etruscan	135.00
Candlestick, Brownie, Palmer Cox	285.00
Candy Dish, Green Leaf, 7 In.	20.00
Cracker Jar, Roses, Brown & White Leaves & Flowers	160.00
Creamer, Blackberry, 4 In.	55.00
Creamer, Brown Bird, Green Ground, 5 In.	28.00
Creamer, Cauliflower	95.00
Creamer, Cow, Brown Sponged, 1850	150.00
Creamer, Pineapple, Bulbous, Brown Handle	90.00
Cup & Saucer, Bird & Fan, Wardle, English Registry Mark	55.00
Cup & Saucer, Etruscan, Bamboo	75.00
Cup & Saucer, Leaf & Basket Weave	39.00
Cuspidor, Lady's, Flowers, Leaves, Pink Interior, Marked, 7 1/2 In.	225.00
Dish, Pickle, Begonia Leaf	35.00
Figurine, 2 Cats, Seated, Blue Sofa, 1 3/4 In.	125.00
Figurine, Black Girl, Reclining, Aqua Hat, Pink Skirt, 5 1/2 In.	85.00
Figurine, Dog & Frog, 5 In.	60.00
Figurine, Quail, Italian, 5 1/2 In.	48.00
Figurine, Shakespeare, 16 In. ....*Illus*	250.00
Humidor, Art Nouveau Flowers, Inscribed Lid, Take A Pipe	110.00
Humidor, Bison Head, Brown	145.00
Humidor, Brownie, Palmer Cox	285.00
Humidor, Figural Pipe On Lid, Portrait of Dutch Children, 4 In.	48.00
Humidor, Indian, 7 In.	80.00
Humidor, Pipe On Cover, Man Smoking, Horse On Side	245.00
Inkwell, 2 Stacked Books, Lady's Hand On Top, With Sander	95.00
Jardiniere, Blackberries, Pink Flowers On White, 5 1/2 X 6 In.	175.00
Jardiniere, Deer & Fawn, Mottled Ground, Pink Interior, 9 3/4 In.	140.00
Jardiniere, Pedestal, Art Nouveau Style, 43 In.	350.00
Jardiniere, Pedestal, Royal Blue, Floral Design, 40 In. ....*Illus*	400.00
Jardiniere, Pedestal, Serpent, 29 In.	350.00
Jardiniere, Pedestal, Serpent, 34 In.	350.00
Lamp, Oil, Mottled Ground, Applied Leaves, Cast Metal Base, 12 In.	230.00
Lampshade, Lamp, Bird & Fan, Lavender Interior, 9 In.	34.50
Match Holder, Figural, Comic Character & Dog	95.00
Match Holder, Hanging, Woven Basket, Acorns, Leaves, 4 X 3 In.	195.00
Match Holder, Palmer Cox Brownie On Striker Dish	130.00
Match Holder, Sailboat, With Sailor Boy, Turquoise Interior	60.00
Match Striker, Comical Singer, Standing, Open Book, Numbers	85.00

Map, Globe, Library,
Newton's, C.1830,
36 In., Pair

Majolica, Vase,
Musician In Relief, English,
31 In.

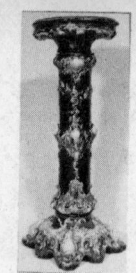

Majolica, Pedestal,
Royal Blue, 33 In.

Match Striker, Handsome Man, Mustache, Brimmed Hat	75.00
Match Striker, Mottled Green & Brown, Wedgwood, 3 1/4 In.	55.00
Match Striker, Wedgwood	220.00
Mug, Bamboo, Floral, Handle, English Reg.Mark	95.00
Mug, Etruscan, Acorn	160.00
Mug, Hunt Scene, 6 1/2 X 4 In.	65.00 To 85.00
Mug, Tan Treebark, Brown Handle, Green Leaves	45.00
Oyster Plate, 7 Wells, Seaweed Separations, Marked	100.00
Oyster Plate, Minton	125.00
Oyster Plate, Multicolor Shell Pattern, Marked, 9 1/2 In.	95.00
Pedestal, Royal Blue, 33 In. ....*Illus*	300.00
Pitcher, Begonia Leaf, 7 1/4 In.	75.00
Pitcher, Bird & Floral, 5 1/2 In.	48.00
Pitcher, Bird On Branch, 8 In.	135.00
Pitcher, Birds & Fan, Wedgwood, 4 In.	85.00
Pitcher, Blackberry, Yellow, Marked, 5 1/2 In.	110.00
Pitcher, Brown & Aqua Floral, 6 In.	85.00
Pitcher, Brown, Green & Pink Flowers, 5 In.	25.00
Pitcher, Cider, Shell & Seaweed	375.00
Pitcher, Conch Shell, Wedgwood, Dated 1878, 9 3/4 In.	550.00
Pitcher, Corn, 4 1/2 In.	65.00
Pitcher, Corn, Pewter Top, 6 In.	150.00
Pitcher, Dark Brown Bark Pattern, Pouring Slot, 9 In.	145.00
Pitcher, Dogwood, Tree Branch Handle, Yellow, 8 In.	100.00
Pitcher, Elephant	190.00
Pitcher, Etruscan, Brown Ground, Green, Lavender, Bulbous, 8 In.	190.00
Pitcher, Fish, 10 In.	75.00
Pitcher, Floral, Butterfly Lip, Wedgwood	125.00
Pitcher, Floral, Yellow, Brown, C Mark, 7 3/4 In.	90.00
Pitcher, Frog On Cantaloupe, Mouth Pouring	225.00
Pitcher, Ivory Basket Weave, Grapes, Gold Trim, Chesapeake, 11 In.	70.00
Pitcher, Milk, Florals, Pink Interior, Beige	75.00
Pitcher, New England Astor, 8 In.	150.00
Pitcher, Owl, Morley, Unsigned, 10 In.	165.00
Pitcher, Parrot, Beak Pouring, Marked, 11 In.	90.00
Pitcher, Pineapple, 1850, 5 1/2 In.	125.00
Pitcher, Pineapple, 7 In.	150.00
Pitcher, Printed Legend, Turquoise Jeweling, 8 1/2 In.	350.00
Pitcher, Pug, Mouth Pouring, Teeth Showing, 10 1/2 In.	250.00
Pitcher, Rooster & Hens	65.00
Pitcher, Shell & Seaweed, 5 3/4 In.	195.00
Pitcher, Songbird, Brown, Pink & Green	85.00
Pitcher, Wild Rose, Butterfly Spout, Etruscan, 7 In.	85.00
Pitcher, Wine, Star of David	65.00
Pitcher, Yellow, Twisted Rope Floral In Middle, 5 1/2 In.	55.00
Planter, Turquoise Lining, Embossed Fence Design, Minton	125.00

Plate, Apple Blossoms, Bee, Butterfly, Wedgwood, 9 In.	35.00
Plate, Aster, New England, 8 1/2 In.	35.00
Plate, Basket Weave Border, Asparagus Spears Center, 9 1/2 In.	45.00
Plate, Basket Weave, Blue, Green, Raised Cherries, Plums, 9 In.	55.00
Plate, Bird & Grapes, 6 1/2 In.	24.00
Plate, Bird In Flight, Turquoise, Monogram, Jos.Holdcroft, 8 In.	65.00
Plate, Brown & Yellow Leaves, Turquoise Ground, 7 3/4 In.	24.00
Plate, Cauliflower, Etruscan, 9 In.	165.00
Plate, Cherries & Tulips, 6 In.	20.00
Plate, Dog & Doghouse, Scalloped Edge, 10 In.	110.00
Plate, Etruscan Rose, Mottled Center, 7 In.	55.00
Plate, Fern & Bow, 10 1/2 In.	30.00
Plate, Grapes, 6 1/2 In.	20.00
Plate, Grapes, Leaves, 7 3/4 In.	35.00
Plate, Large Leaf, Brown & Cream, Wedgwood, 7 3/4 In.	50.00
Plate, Leaf & Basket Weave, 9 In.	75.00
Plate, Lettuce Leaf, 8 1/2 In.	65.00
Plate, Napkin, George Jones, 8 In.	150.00
Plate, Overlapping Begonia Leaves, Greens, Marked, 8 In.	35.00
Plate, Pink Flowers, Green Leaves, Handles, Etruscan, 12 In.	90.00
Plate, Rabbit, 9 In.	45.00
Plate, Shell & Milkweed, Etruscan, 9 In.	150.00
Plate, White Basket Weave, Pale Green Leaves, Etruscan	100.00
Plate, Yellow Sunflower, Green, 7 In.	25.00
Platter, Asparagus & Artichoke, Marked, 17 X 10 In.	185.00
Platter, Basket Weave Center, Bamboo Edge, Wedgwood, 12 1/2 In.	100.00
Platter, Flying Crane & Water Lily, 10 1/2 In.	110.00
Platter, Grapes, Multicolored Leaves, Wedgwood, 10 X 12 In.	250.00
Platter, Tulip, Handles, 15 In.	48.00
Smoke Set, Brownie Policeman, Candle In Hat, 3 Jars	245.00
Spooner, Bamboo, Etruscan, Marked	100.00
Stein, Art Nouveau, Molded Woman's Face, Floral Design, 1/2 Liter	340.00
Stein, Black Man, Smoking Pipe, Hoop Earrings, 7 1/2 In.	325.00
Sugar, Bamboo, Etruscan, 6 In.	95.00
Sugar, Cauliflower, Etruscan	20.00
Sugar, Covered, Shell & Seaweed, Albino, Etruscan	125.00
Syrup, Daisies, Brown Twigs, Brown Handle, Pewter Top, 6 In.	125.00
Syrup, Hinged Tin Cover, Designs, Lattice Bands, 4 1/8 In.	55.00
Syrup, Pewter Lid, Green Leaf, Tan Bark, Basket Weave Base	140.00
Syrup, Pewter Lid, Sunflower Design, Signed Bennetts	125.00
Syrup, Sunflower, Etruscan, Marked GSH, No Lid	150.00
Tea Set, Cobalt Blue Ground, 11 Piece	300.00
Teapot & Sugar, Bird & Iris, Blue Ground, Etruscan	300.00
Teapot Stand, Pink & White, Etruscan, Marked	175.00
Teapot, Bamboo Handle, Leaves	130.00
Teapot, Bird & Fan	175.00
Teapot, Pineapple	150.00
Teapot, Rose & Rope, Aqua	150.00
Tile, Center Medallion, Woman Gathering In Apron, Leaf & Branch	65.00
Tobacco Jar, Elephant	375.00
Tobacco Jar, Hunter, Fox, Marked BM, 7 3/4 In.	130.00
Tobacco Jar, Little Blue Fox	50.00
Tobacco Set, Dog, Boxer, By Gate, Stump Match Holder, 8 In.	95.00
Toby Jug, Monk, 1860, 10 In.	150.00
Toothpick, Sunflower Pattern	95.00
Tray, Basket Weave, Handles, Wheat Stalks, Butterfly, 13 X 10 In.	300.00
Tray, Begonia Leaf Shape, 7 3/4 In.	17.00
Tray, Fan Shape, Bird In Flight, Flowers, Wardle & Co.	185.00
Tray, Leaf & Acorn, 12 In.	95.00
Tray, Leaf, Etruscan, 12 In.	115.00
Umbrella Stand, Embossed Pattern, Brown, Greens & Pinks	200.00
Urn, George Jones, Rams' Heads, C.1870, 22 1/2 In., Pair ....*Illus*	2750.00
Vase, Daisies, Leaves, Strawberry Color Inside, 8 1/2 X 6 1/2 In.	95.00
Vase, Fish, 8 1/2 In.	95.00

Marble Carving, Bust,
Young Augustus, White,
Roman, 16 In.

Meissen, Figurine, Pug,
Seated, Blue Collar,
Signed, 6 1/2 In.

Majolica, Urn, George Jones,
Rams' Heads,
C.1870, 22 1/2 In., Pair

Vase, Musician In Relief, English, 31 In. ....*Illus* 300.00
Vase, Peacock Nested On Monument, W.S.& S., 13 3/4 In., Pair 675.00
Vase, Pink Flowers, 6 In. 25.00

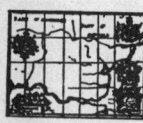

Maps of all types have been collected for centuries. The earliest
known printed maps were made in 1478. The first printed street
map showed London in 1559. The first road maps for use by drivers
of automobiles were made in 1901. Collectors buy maps that were
pages of old books, as well as the multifolded road maps popular in
this century.

MAP, Atlas, British Empire, French & Spanish Settlements, London 1733 .... 7000.00
Atlas, Philadelphia, 22nd Ward, Published By F.M.Hopkins, 1876 .... 150.00
Beloit College Campus, Wisc., Pictorial, Framed, 1930s, 14 X 15 In. 15.00
Boston, Print, July 4, 1870, F.Fuchs, Walnut Frame, 25 X 35 In. 3500.00
British & French Dominions In North America, 1775, 27 X 38 In. 10.00
British Possessions In North America, Dated 1809, 10 X 16 In. 25.00
Cambridgeshire, England, Speed, Engraved, 1612–16, 16 5/8 X 21 1/4 In. 1500.00
Carte De La Nouvelle, France, N.A., Chatelain, Engraved, 20 X 24 In. 1800.00
Chicago's Gangland, 1930s 200.00
Colorado, Township Subdivisions, Forts, Trail Routes, 1862 .... 30.00
Eastern Hemisphere, From Mitchell's Geography, 1880s, 8 X 11 In. 10.00
England, Drawn & Engraved, Thomson's New Gen.Atlas, 27 X 32 In. 35.00
Georgia & Alabama, Hand Colored, 1865, 18 X 20 In. 18.00
Globe, Celestial, C.Smith & Co., C.1830 .... 4500.00
Globe, Library, Newton's, C.1830, 36 In., Pair ....*Illus* 15950.00
Hartfordshire & Devonshire, Hand Colored, Engraved, Frame, 10 X 11 In. 70.00
Illinois Central Railroad, Wall, 48 X 60 In. 5.00
Iowa, Auto, Huebinger, 1917 .... 12.50
Michigan, Hand Colored By Silas Farmer, 1869, 21 X 33 In. 35.00
Mining, Tonopah County, Nevada, Linen, 1912 .... 35.00
Newark, N.J., Charles Magnus, Color, 1853 .... 20.00
Nova Virginiae Tabula, Virginia, Blaeu, Engraved, 1630, 14 3/4 X 19 In. 2400.00
Pacific Theater, Esso 15.00
Pennsylvania, Nash Premium, Foldout, 1920s, 3 X 4 1/2 In. 10.00
Peoria, Ill., Color, 1873, 18 X 30 In. 35.00
Road, Mexico, Conoco, 1930s 4.00
Road, Sinclair, 2 Old Cars & Pump With Globe On Top 11.00
Salt Lake, Mormon, Pamphlet, Colored, 1899 .... 15.00
Street, Haverhill, Mass., Groveland & Merrimac, 1933 .... 2.00
Texas, Oregon & California, Foldout, Mitchell, 1846, 22 5/8 X 21 In. 4500.00
United States & Possessions, Roll–Up, 1936, 4 Ft. 55.00
Virginia & West Virginia, Hand Colored, Engraved, Framed, 1867 .... 65.00
War, With Booklet, 1862, 25 1/2 X 25 1/2 In. 35.00
Yellowstone & Missouri Rivers, War Department, 1876, 30 X 40 In. 10.00

Marble Carving, Venus, Italian, 40 In.

Marble Carving, 2 Classical Maidens,
Nicolas Coustou, 29 In.

Marble is used in many ways on antiques. Marble tops are popular for tables because they resist stains and damage. Listed here are marble carvings, large or small figurines, and groups of people or animals that have been a special art form since the time of the ancient Greeks. Reproductions, especially of large Victorian groups, are being made of a mixture using marble dust. These are very difficult to detect and collectors should be careful. Other carvings are listed under Alabaster.

MARBLE CARVING, 2 Classical Maidens, Nicolas Coustou, 29 In. ....*Illus*	1800.00
Allegorical Woman, Clutching Drapery, 48 3/4 In.	2475.00
Apollo & Daphne, Black Marble Pedestal, 7 Ft.8 In.	6000.00
Bather, Ready To Dive, 4 Ft. 9 In.	3300.00
Bust, Apollo, S.Amore, Italian, 19th Century, 15 In.	275.00
Bust, Charles X, Queen Josephine, W.Theed, 1834, 44 In., Pair	2530.00
Bust, Woman, Gilt Bronze Drapery, A.Gory, 28 3/4 In.	3850.00
Bust, Woman, Long Wavy Hair, G.Besli, 15 In.	880.00
Bust, Woman, Turned Left, E.H.Baily, C.1840, 14 3/4 In.	1100.00
Bust, Young Augustus, White, Roman, 16 In. ....*Illus*	850.00
Bust, Young Lady, Smiling, Straw Hat, C.1890, 25 In.	2860.00
Bust, Young Woman, Rose In Hair, John Gibson, C.1855, 27 In.	7500.00
Child With Puppy, C.1855, 4 Ft.1 In.	8360.00
Cleopatra, Reclining, Dagger At Side, 31 In.	5225.00
Marie Antoinette, Hinged Skirt, Scene, 9 In.	880.00
Mary Magdalene, Caroline Wilson, C.1860, 36 1/4 In.	6500.00
Napoleon, Overcoat, Prof.A.Petrilli, 44 In.	7155.00
Nude, Allegorical, Draped With Lion Pelt, 28 In.	7700.00
Nymph, Nude, Foliate Headband, C.1900, 4 Ft. 3 In.	5775.00
Nymph, On Sphere, Flanked By Flowers, C.1900, 4 Ft. 2 In.	6600.00
Paperweight, Porcelain Knob, Initials L.E., 4 3/4 In.	17.50
Pedestal, Corinthian Column, Pierced Bronze Base, 30 In.	625.00
Plaque, Voices of The Dead, M.K.Potter, C.1902, 6 Ft. 3 In.	9900.00
Putti Playing Musical Instruments, 38 In.	3575.00
Reclining Cupid, Nude, Quiver & Bow, 22 In.	1100.00
Reclining Hermaphrodite, 19th Century, 35 In.	3300.00
Salt & Pepper, White, Spool of Thread Shape, 1 7/8 In.	10.00
Seated Greyhound, Late 19th Century, 14 1/2 X 24 In.	1600.00
Three Graces, Antonio Canova, Glass Dome, 9 In.	2200.00
Venus De Milo, F.Romanelli, Italian, 19th Century, 47 In.	1700.00
Venus, Italian, 40 In. ....*Illus*	1600.00
Woman, Sunamitis, Braided Hair, Half Clad, 35 In.	3575.00

The game of marbles has been popular since the days of the ancient Romans. American children were able to buy marbles by the mid–eighteenth century. Dutch glazed clay marbles were least expensive. Glazed pottery marbles, attributed to the Bennington potteries in Vermont, were of a better quality. Marbles made of pink marble were also available by the 1830s. Glass marbles seem to have been made later. By 1880, Samuel C. Dyke of South Akron, Ohio, was making clay marbles and The National Onyx Marble Company was making marbles of onyx. The Navarre Glass Marble Company of Navarre, Ohio, and M. B. Mishler of Ravenna, Ohio, made the glass marbles. Ohio remained the center of the marble industry and the Akron–made Akro Agate brand became nationally known. The most expensive marbles collected today are the sulfides. These are glass marbles with frosted white figures in the center.

MARBLE, Blue & White Swirl Stripes, White Latticinio Swirl Core, 7 In.	85.00
Candy Stripe, 2 In.	50.00
Candy Swirl, Wide Twist Core, 1 1/16 In.	16.00
Comic, Emma	35.00
Comic, Koko	35.00
Latticinio Core Swirl, 2 1/4 In.	95.00
Marblestone, 1 7/8 In.	15.00
Onionskin, Red & White, Found At Sandwich Glass Co., 1930s	15.00
Pontil Swirl	13.00
Stoneware, Blue & White, 1 7/8 In.	65.00
Sulfide, Baby In Cradle	225.00
Sulfide, Clown, Standing, Hands In Pockets, 2 1/4 In.	525.00
Sulfide, Dog, 1 3/4 In.	85.00
Sulfide, Eagle, 1 5/8 In.	110.00
Sulfide, Flying Goose, 1 3/4 In.	325.00
Sulfide, Goldfish, Gold & Silver, Large	95.00
Sulfide, Lamb, 1 3/4 In.	65.00
Sulfide, Lion, 2 In.	210.00
Sulfide, Mica Flakes, End–of–Day, 1 3/4 In.	425.00
Sulfide, Mule, 1 3/4 In.	135.00
Sulfide, Onionskin, 2 1/2 In.	700.00
Sulfide, Poodle, 1 3/4 In.	95.00 To 125.00
Sulfide, Poodle, 1 7/8 In.	85.00
Sulfide, Ram, 2 1/4 In.	35.00
Sulfide, Rearing Horse, 2 1/8 In.	85.00
Sulfide, White Tiger, 2 3/16 In.	125.00
Swirl, Split Ribbon Core, 1 9/16 In.	48.00
Swirling Bands, Wide Latticinio Center, 1 In.	20.00
White Latticinio Swirl Core, Blue & White Stripes, 7 In.	85.00

The Marblehead Pottery was founded in 1905 by Dr. J. Hall as a rehabilitative program for the patients of a Marblehead, Massachusetts, sanitarium. Two years later it was separated from the sanitarium and it continued operations until 1936. Many of the pieces were decorated with marine motifs.

MARBLEHEAD, Bowl, Blue, 4 In.	25.00
Bowl, Green, 4 X 5 In.	45.00
Flower Frog, Green, 2 1/4 In.	15.00
Tile, Blue & White Sailing Ship, 4 3/4 In.	140.00
Tile, Ship, Waves, Multicolored, 4 In.	400.00
Vase, 4–Color Geometric Design, Corset Shape, AEB, 8 1/2 In.	3575.00
Vase, Blue Matte, 7 In.	150.00
Vase, Blue, 7 In., Pair	190.00
Vase, Brown & Green Ground, Ebony Panthers, H.Tutt, 7 In.	3850.00
Vase, Bulbous, Blue, 6 1/4 In.	85.00
Vase, Bulbous, Gray, 7 In.	60.00
Vase, Bulbous, Lavender, 4 In.	125.00
Vase, Carved Design of Branch, Trees, Signed, C.1905, 4 1/2 In.	600.00
Vase, Funnel Shape, Blue, 6 In.	100.00

Vase, Gray, Speckled, 5 In.Opening, 4 In.	85.00
Vase, Gray, Swollen, 7 In.	38.00
Vase, Green, 3 1/2 In.	70.00
Vase, Squatty, Blue, Marked, Sticker, 3 X 6 In.	175.00
Vase, Wisteria To Powder Blue, 3 1/2 In.	115.00
Wall Pocket, Cobalt Blue, Signed	100.00

R W Marten
London
Martinware is a salt–glazed stoneware made by the Martin Brothers of Middlesex, England, between 1873 and 1915. Many figural jugs and vases were made by the three brothers. Of special interest are the fanciful birds, usually made with removable heads.

MARTIN BROTHERS, Inkwell, Birds	125.00
Match Holder, 2 In.	100.00
Pitcher, Blue Foliage, Monogram, 5 In.	50.00
Pitcher, Peacock, 11 In.	300.00 To 350.00
Pitcher, Snake Handle, 5 In.	75.00 To 85.00
Tile, Fish, 3 In.	125.00
Tobacco Jar, Incised Birds, 1880	175.00 To 215.00
Vase, Cranes, 11 In.	200.00
Vase, Grotesque Fish, 5 In.	200.00
Vase, Grotesque, 4 Necks, Claw Feet, 13 In.	550.00
Vase, Palmettes, 10 In.	135.00 To 175.00
Vase, Smiling Crow, Miniature	135.00
Vase, Squash, Red Luster, 7 In.	155.00 To 200.00

Mary Gregory glass is identified by a characteristic white figure painted on dark glass. It was made from 1870 to 1910. The name refers to any glass decorated with a white silhouette figure and not just to the Sandwich glass originally painted by Miss Mary Gregory. Many reproductions have been made and there are new pieces being sold in gift shops today.

MARY GREGORY, Biscuit Barrel, Diamond–Quilted, Green, Silver Plated Lid	350.00
Bottle, Barber, Cobalt Blue	180.00
Bottle, Barber, Green, Pair	410.00
Bottle, Boy & Flowers, Green, Inside Ribbing, 7 1/4 In.	135.00
Bottle, Girl Playing	120.00
Bottle, Girl, Bubble Stopper, Sapphire Blue, 9 In.	165.00
Bottle, Perfume, Sapphire, White Girl, No Atomizer, 6 1/2 In.	135.00
Box, Girl Feeding Bird, Sapphire Blue, Covered, 6 X 5 5/8 In.	475.00
Box, Hinged Lid, Girl Blowing Bubbles, Amethyst, 3 3/4 X 3 In.	245.00
Box, Hinged Lid, Girl By Fence, Cobalt Blue, 3 3/4 In.	235.00
Box, Hinged Lid, Girl Running, Cranberry, 3 In.	160.00
Box, Hinged Lid, Oriental Boy, Blowing Bubbles, 5 X 5 1/2 In.	395.00
Box, Lift–Off Lid, Boy By Fence, Sprays, Cranberry, 2 In.	145.00
Cookie Jar, Young Girl, Seated On Fence, Cranberry 7 1/2 In.	425.00
Creamer, All White Girl, Blue Ground, Clear Handle	120.00
Cruet, Boy Holding Flower, Clear, 8 In.	60.00
Cruet, Little Boy, Clear Handle & Stopper, Cranberry	77.50
Cruet, Young Boy Sitting On Fence, Birds, Amethyst, 8 1/2 In.	375.00
Cup, Young Girl In White Enamel, Glass Handle, Amber, 4 In.	75.00
Decanter, Girl Playing, Emerald, Clear Handle	140.00
Decanter, Wine, Boy, Pink Suit, Emerald Green, Bubble Stopper	165.00
Liqueur Set, Girl, Hat, Holding Flower, Sapphire Blue, 9 Piece	495.00
Mug, Boy, Applied Handle, Sapphire Blue, 3 3/8 In.	88.00
Mug, Liqueur, Young Boy, Amethyst, 1 3/4 In.	50.00
Mug, Marked From Georgie 1890, Clear	95.00
Mug, White Enameled Boy, Amethyst, 1 1/2 In.	78.00
Mug, Young Boy, Clear Handle, Cranberry, 3 In.	75.00
Mug, Young Boy, Ribbed, Clear Handle, Cranberry, 3 5/8 In.	75.00
Patch Box, Enameled Dots, Leaves, Sapphire Blue, 2 In.	95.00
Patch Box, Hinged Lid, Boy & Foliage, 1 3/4 X 1 1/8 In.	135.00
Patch Box, Young Boy On Lid, Cobalt Blue, 2 1/8 In.	155.00
Perfume Bottle, Flowers, Bird, Butterfly, Blue, 3 In.	235.00
Pitcher, Blue, Clear Handle, 12 In.	260.00

Pitcher, Boy In Garden, Signed L.Nappen, Cranberry, 4 In.	135.00
Pitcher, Boy With Sailboat, Sapphire Blue, 6 In.	210.00
Pitcher, Clear Paneled, Scalloped Spout, Garden Scene, 12 In.	100.00
Pitcher, Clear, Ribbed, Girl Holding Bird, 1870, 10 1/2 In.	155.00
Pitcher, Girl Catching Butterfly, Gold Trim, 12 1/2 In.	410.00
Pitcher, Milk, Clear, 6 In.	60.00
Pitcher, Water, Girl, Fancy Dress, Olive Amber, 11 1/8 In.	235.00
Pitcher, Water, Green, 14 In.	85.00
Powder Jar, Cranberry	250.00
Punch Cup, Blue, Gold Rim, Thumbprints, Reeded Handle	70.00
Rose Bowl, All White Girl, Gold Trim, Cranberry, Miniature	135.00
Rose Bowl, Young Boy, White, Gold Trim, Amethyst, 4 3/8 X 4 In.	265.00
Stein, Inverted Thumbprint, White Boy, Green, 5 5/8 X 3 In.	135.00
Sugar & Creamer, Boy On Creamer, Girl On Sugar, Cranberry	198.00
Toothpick, Young Boy, Clear, 2 1/2 In.	65.00
Tray, Dresser, 2 Boys, Riding, Pulling Branch, Blue, 7 In.	265.00
Tray, Dresser, Double Figure, Cobalt Blue, 6 3/4 X 9 3/4 In.	225.00
Tumble–Up, Boy & Girl, Green, 5 In.	235.00
Tumble–Up, Underplate, Cranberry, Lady, Victorian	195.00
Tumbler, Cranberry Crackle, Girl, With Flowers, 3 3/8 In.	30.00
Tumbler, Girl Feeding Birds, Amber, 7 In.	75.00
Tumbler, Juice, Boy In White, Tinted Features, Cranberry	48.00
Tumbler, White Enameled Girl, Cranberry, 4 X 2 1/2 In.	65.00
Vase, Ball Shape, Lime Green, Young Girl, 2 1/2 X 2 5/8 In.	78.00
Vase, Black Amethyst, White Enameled Boy, 9 3/4 In.	188.00
Vase, Boy & Girl, Scalloped Top, Honey Amber, 10 In., Pair	495.00
Vase, Boy & Horse, Under Tree, Emerald Green, 9 3/4 In.	125.00
Vase, Boy Flying Kite, Girl Holding Flowers, 13 In., Pair	475.00
Vase, Boy With Hat, Clear Handle, Lime Green, 6 3/4 In.	100.00
Vase, Boy, Cobalt Blue, 7 1/4 In.	110.00
Vase, Bud, Young Boy, Pedestal Foot, Cranberry, 8 1/2 In.	118.00
Vase, Child, Holding Bird, Cranberry, Ruffled, 10 In.	175.00
Vase, Enameled Boy Piper, Green, 8 In.	130.00
Vase, Enameled Boy, Amber, Snail Handles, 7 3/8 In.	145.00
Vase, Enameled Boy, Ruffled, Sapphire Blue, 8 3/4 In.	195.00
Vase, Facing Girls, With Hats, Electric Blue, 12 2/8 In., Pair	575.00
Vase, Facing Pair, Young Ladies, All White, 9 1/2 In., Pair	300.00
Vase, Girl In Garden, Cranberry, 3 In.	230.00
Vase, Girl In White, Cranberry, 6 1/2 In.	95.00
Vase, Girl Sitting On Ground, Cranberry, 3 7/8 In.	100.00
Vase, Girl With Hat, Feeding Bird, Green, 6 1/4 In.	125.00
Vase, Girl, Bird Nest In Tree, Metal Rim, Handles, 16 3/4 In.	1010.00
Vase, Girl, Flowers In Hand & On Apron, Emerald Green, 9 In.	145.00
Vase, Girl, Ruby, 3 X 2 In.	58.00
Vase, Inverted Thumbprint, Ruffled, 4 1/4 In.	110.00
Vase, Running Boy, Hat, Girl, Cranberry, 8 3/4 In., Pair	365.00
Vase, Scenes of House, Fluted, Amethyst, 14 1/4 In., Pair	315.00
Vase, White Enameling, Cranberry, 10 1/2 In.	195.00
Vase, Young Boy, Holding Bird, Shaded Green, 5 7/8 In.	118.00
Vase, Young Girl, Cranberry, 8 3/4 In.	175.00
Vase, Young Girl, Holding Plate, Orange Swirl, 6 3/4 In.	110.00
Vase, Young Girl, Shell Trim, Cranberry, 7 1/2 In.	168.00

Modern Freemasonry started in seventeenth–century England. The fraternal order was introduced in the American colonies in the 1730s. Symbols, including the trowel, square, level, plumb rule, pillars, columns, arches, the letter "G," beehive, five–pointed star, compass, and eye, have special meaning and are often pictured on Masonic material. Masonic Shrine glassware was made from 1893 to 1917.

MASONIC, Apron, Gold & Silver Braid, 1926	45.00
Armchair, Masonic Crest, Eastlake	110.00
Ashtray, Shriners, Gold, Lenox, 1959	18.00
Belt, Ceremonial, AOKMC, Leather, With Brass Figures	55.00

Bill Case, Sterling Silver	20.00
Bookends, Shriner, Head With Scimitar, Ed Star, 1922	45.00
Bowl, Pillars of Hercules Interior, Chinese, 1795, 11 In.	550.00
Carte De Visite, Mason, In Sash, Apron & Pins	12.50
Champagne, Louisville, Tobacco Leaf, 1909	45.00
Champagne, Paper Label, 1911	70.00
Champagne, San Francisco, 1902	65.00
Champagne, Swords & Tobacco Leaf Base, 1909	75.00
Charm, Compass Emblem, FLT Enameled At Bottom, Gold, 1 1/4 In.	20.00
Cup, Fraternal Shriner, Pittsburgh, 3 Handles, 1905	65.00
Goblet, Gilt Sabers, St.Paul, Minn., 1908	60.00
Goblet, Man On Camel, Pittsburgh, Pa.& Rochester, N.Y., 1911	67.50
Humidor, Yaarab Temple, Atlanta, Insignia Finial	75.00
Lamp, Wooden	32.00
Letter Opener, Metal	12.00
Loving Cup, Knights Templar, Philadelphia, 1898, Toronto, Ohio	75.00
Match Safe, Sterling Silver, 1904	85.00
Matchbox, Wall, Old Paint	30.00
Mug, Saratoga, 1903	75.00
Napkin Ring, Veiled Prophet, St.Louis, 1901	45.00
Nodder, Figural	30.00
Paperweight, Symbol, Brass	35.00
Plate, Caliper, Eye, Square Edge, 8 1/2 In.	40.00
Plate, Portrait, Dated 1906, 8 1/4 In.	30.00
Print, Odd Fellowship Illustrated, Pictures, 1894, 22 X 28 In.	10.00
Ring, Black Stone, 10K Gold	50.00
Ring, Lady's, White Cross Through Star, 14K Gold	135.00
Shaving Mug, Gold Emblem, Blue Ground, Iridescent Luster	65.00
Shot Glass, K.C.C.H., Cranberry	35.00
Tray, Lu Lu Patrol of Philadelphia, Bronze, 1911, 6 X 7 In.	59.00
Trivet, Cast Brass, 8 3/8 In.	42.50
Trunk, Costume	50.00
Tumbler, Victorian Woman, I Want To Be A Shriner, Dated 1897	110.00
Watch Fob, Dated 1906	20.00
Wine, Syria Temple Pittsburgh, 1893	95.00

Massier pottery is iridescent French art pottery made by Clement Massier in Golfe–Juan, France, in the late nineteenth and early twentieth centuries. It has an iridescent metallic luster glaze that resembles the Weller Sicard pottery glaze. Most pieces are marked "J. Massier."

MASSIER, Vase, Handles, Plum, Gray & Iridescent, Marked, 6 1/2 In.	325.00
Vase, Swirl Design, Signed, 4 1/4 In.	200.00

Large wooden matches were used in the nineteenth and twentieth centuries for a variety of purposes. The kitchen stove and the fireplace or furnace had to be lit regularly. One type of match holder was made to hang on the wall, another was designed to be kept on a tabletop. Of special interest today are match holders that have advertisements as part of the design.

MATCH HOLDER, Acorn & Leaf, Hanging, Self–Closing Hinged Top, Iron, C.1865	85.00
Alligator Skin Pattern, Valise Shape	65.00
Bay State Rangers, Hanging, Wooden	40.00
Black Boys, Pumpkin & Cotton Bale, Metal, Painted, 2 1/2 In.	25.00
Black Glass Pipe, Figural, Norwich, Conn.	23.00
Black Man, Fishing On Rock, Man With Pipe, China, Pair	95.00
Bulldog, Cut Plug	700.00
Buster Brown Bread	220.00
Ceresota Flour, Rectangular Box	200.00
Clover Brand Shoes, Tin	30.00
DeLaval Separator, Tin	80.00
Devil's Face	50.00
Dog On Base, Brass, 3 3/4 X 4 In.	29.50
Double, 2 Mules, When Shall We Three Meet Again, Iron, 10 In.	25.00

Double, Open Scrollwork, Cast Iron, Dated 1867	55.00
Double, Wall, Art Nouveau Woman, Brass, 4 X 6 In.	85.00
Dr.Shoop's Health Coffee, Wall, Pictures Box, Tin	80.00
Dutch Boy, Figural, Wall	225.00
Easel Type, Striker, Brass	55.00
Eclipse Stoves, Cast Iron, Wall, Large	175.00
Elwood Steel Fences	70.00
Game, Double Pouch, Cast Iron, Old Paint, 4 1/2 X 8 In.	85.00
Hotel Statler	10.00
Hunting Dog, Rushes On Hinged Cover, Wall, Cast Iron	85.00
Hunting Scene, Cast Iron, Germany	60.00
Indian Basketry, Wall	45.00
Indians, Dragon & Flowers, Wall, Covered, Tin	48.00
Jasperware, Art Nouveau Lady, Blue & White, 3 Chains	95.00
Kelly's Famous Flour, Tin	35.00
Ken–L–Ration, Plastic	6.00
Lighthouse, Painted Tin, Open Pocket, 3 1/2 X 8 In.	65.00
Man Riding Horse, Silver Plate, Pocket	85.00
Michigan Stove Co., Wall	65.00
Milwaukee Harvesting Machines, Tin	25.00
New Process Range	30.00
Old Judson Whiskey	85.00
Pig, Figural, Brass, Pocket	110.00
Pig, Gray, Blue, Stoneware	58.00
Seminude Woman Running, Silver Plate, Pocket	85.00
Sharples Cream	60.00
Shoebrush, Figural	55.00
Smith Wallace Shoe Co., Tin	35.00
Stamped Tin, Red, Green	23.00
Stick, Advertising Grocery Store, Liberty, N.Y., Hanging	7.00
Summit Pike's Peak, Metal	12.00
Universal Stove, Wall, Tin	65.00
Venus & Cupid Kissing, Wall, Hanging, Cast Iron, 1915	95.00
Vulcan Machinery	425.00
Wagon, With 2 Horses, Porcelain	20.00
Wall, Tin, Crimped Shell Top, Natural Surface, 4 1/2 X 7 In.	15.00
Workman's Pants, Pocket, Figural	98.00

Early matches were made with phosphorus and could ignite unexpectedly. Match safes were designed to be carried in the pocket. The matches were safely stored in the tightly closed container. Examples were made in sterling silver, plated silver, or other metals. The English call these "vesta boxes."

MATCH SAFE, Anheuser–Busch, Brass, Logo, Dated 1899, St.Louis, Mo.	40.00
Arm & Hammer Soda	75.00
Atlantic City, Bright Cut, Aluminum, 1907	8.00
Berlin Iron Bridge Co., Celluloid	75.00
Blatz Beer, Chrome	45.00
Bridge, Hampton Beach, N.H.	24.00
Bright Cut Butterfly, Sterling Silver	68.00
C.Parker, Cast Iron, C.1870	60.00
Christopher Columbus	145.00
Coin Silver, Ornately Engraved, 4 X 3 In.	57.50
Cotton States Exposition, 1895	55.00
Creel & Rod Incised	20.00
Dancing Nude, Flowers & Scrolls, Art Nouveau, Sterling Silver	75.00
Domo Separator, Celluloid	20.00
Economy Clothing	45.00
Embossed Men, Canoe, Fishing, Brass, Silver Finish, Advertising	40.00
Engraved Harry From Lady Mullen, Sterling Silver	60.00
Flower Design, Embossed, Sterling Silver, Chain	110.00
Gillette Razors	10.00
Glasgow Intern.Exhib., Horseshoe Shape, Gutta Percha, 1901	42.00
Gold Dust Twins, Gold Metal, Engraved, 2 3/4 X 1 1/2 In.	275.00

Horse Design, Aluminum, Pocket, 1904	12.00
Hunter & Dog, Moose On Reverse, Brass	45.00
Juicy Fruit, Tin	65.00
Knights of Columbus, 1919	95.00
Little Red Riding Hood	365.00
Log Cabin Pattern, Tecumseh Embossed, Frosted Glass, 2 In.	95.00
Majestic Alleys & Billiard Parlors, Silver Finish, 2 X 5 In.	6.50
Mt. Vernon Pure Rye Whiskey	45.00
Nation Lead Co., St.Louis, Enameled Wrap–Around, Striker End	38.00
Old Hickory, Tin	140.00
Pepsin Bitters, Celluloid Picture of General	40.00
Pig, Figural, Brown Glaze, Pottery, C.1900, 7 3/4 In.	250.00
Queen Victoria, Brass Medallion, Metal, 1880s, 2 X 1 3/8 In.	85.00
Red Top Rye	65.00
Rochester	55.00
Rosana Vokes Cigars, Cincinnati	65.00
Schlitz Beer, Leather & Chrome	65.00
Scroll Repousse, Sterling Silver, Gorham, 4 3/8 In.	48.00
Silver, Monogram, Gathered Bottom, Gorham	50.00
Spaniel Center, Celluloid Trim, Chrome	40.00
St. Louis Fair, 1904	65.00
Sterling Silver, Dated 1898	60.00
Sterling Silver, Design, Initials, Striker Bottom, 2 1/4 In.	25.00
World's Fair, St.Louis, Advertising, 1904	65.00

Matsu–no–ke was a type of applied decoration for glass patented by Frederick Carder in 1922. There is clear evidence that pieces were made before that date at the Steuben glassworks. Stevens & Williams of England also made an applied decoration by the same name.

MATSU–NO–KE, Rose Bowl, Brown To Cream Outside, Crystal Trim, 4 3/4 In.	885.00
Vase, Applied Flowers, Handles, Stevens & Williams, 8 In.	275.00
Vase, Blush Pink, Floral, Handles, Stevens & Williams, 8 In.	285.00

MATT MORGAN
–CIN. O–
ART POTTERY Cᵒ

Matt Morgan, an English artist, was making pottery in Cincinnati, Ohio, by 1883. His pieces were decorated to resemble Moorish wares. Incised designs and colors were applied to raised panels on the pottery. Shiny or matt glazes were used. The company lasted only a few years.

MATT MORGAN, Vase, Blue, Incised Design, 4 In.	200.00
Vase, Flowers, Blue, White, 6 In.	250.00

McCoy pottery is made in Roseville, Ohio. The J. W. McCoy Pottery was founded in 1899. It became the Brush McCoy Pottery Company in 1911. The name changed to the Brush Pottery in 1925. The word "Brush" was usually included in the mark on their pieces. The Nelson McCoy Sanitary and Stoneware Company, a different firm, was founded in Roseville, Ohio, in 1910. The firm made art pottery after 1926. In 1933 it became the Nelson McCoy Pottery. Pieces marked "McCoy" were made by the Nelson McCoy Company.

MCCOY, Ashtray, Between 2 Frogs	12.00
Bookends, Dog	20.00
Bookends, Lily	18.00
Clothes Sprinkler, Chinaman	20.00
Coffeepot, El Rancho	30.00
Cookie Jar, Aunt Jemima	40.00 To 95.00
Cookie Jar, Basket of Fruit	35.00
Cookie Jar, Bobby Baker	18.00 To 30.00
Cookie Jar, Brown Owl	17.00
Cookie Jar, Bunch of Bananas, Marked	27.00
Cookie Jar, Cat On Basket	29.50
Cookie Jar, Christmas Tree	235.00 To 300.00
Cookie Jar, Circus Horse	40.00 To 65.00

Cookie Jar, Clown, In Green Barrel 34.50
Cookie Jar, Colby Cat 57.00
Cookie Jar, Cookie Boy, Yellow 75.00
Cookie Jar, Cookstove 15.00
Cookie Jar, Dalmatians ....75.00 To 135.00
Cookie Jar, Davy Crockett, Bust 145.00
Cookie Jar, Doughboy, White 45.00
Cookie Jar, Duck On Basket 15.00
Cookie Jar, Dutch Treat Barn 30.00
Cookie Jar, Farmer Pig, Green Clover Leaves, Marked 75.00
Cookie Jar, Fireplace 45.00
Cookie Jar, Fortune Cookies, Marked 39.00
Cookie Jar, Frontier Family 25.00
Cookie Jar, Globe ....85.00 To 125.00
Cookie Jar, Grandfather Clock ....40.00 To 45.00
Cookie Jar, Green Pepper ....11.00 To 15.00
Cookie Jar, Hamm's Bear 60.00
Cookie Jar, Happy Face ....10.00 To 22.00
Cookie Jar, Have Happy Day 10.00
Cookie Jar, Hippo With Monkey On Back 95.00
Cookie Jar, Honey Bear 30.00
Cookie Jar, Indian ....52.00 To 135.00
Cookie Jar, Kangaroo, Blue 95.00
Cookie Jar, Keebler Tree House, Elf In Tree, Green 62.00
Cookie Jar, Kettle 12.00
Cookie Jar, Lamb In Basket 25.00
Cookie Jar, Log Cabin 25.00
Cookie Jar, Mammy 90.00
Cookie Jar, Mammy, With Cauliflower 395.00
Cookie Jar, Mouse On Clock 24.00
Cookie Jar, Old King Cole 35.00
Cookie Jar, Orange Shape, Yellow 12.00
Cookie Jar, Pears, On Basket Weave 25.00
Cookie Jar, Picnic Basket 35.00
Cookie Jar, Pineapple ....28.00 To 35.00
Cookie Jar, Popeye 65.00
Cookie Jar, Pot–Bellied Stove, Black, Marked 33.00
Cookie Jar, Raggedy Ann ....25.00 To 32.00
Cookie Jar, Red Barn 115.00
Cookie Jar, Rooster 55.00
Cookie Jar, Snoopy ....40.00 To 60.00
Cookie Jar, Squirrel On Log, Marked 24.00
Cookie Jar, Teapot Shape, 9 1/2 In. 30.00
Cookie Jar, Tepee ....60.00 To 155.00
Cookie Jar, Thinking Puppy 15.00
Cookie Jar, Timmy Tortoise ....15.00 To 30.00
Cookie Jar, Touring Car 35.00
Cookie Jar, Train ....45.00 To 50.00
Cookie Jar, Turkey ....45.00 To 80.00
Cookie Jar, W.C.Fields ....52.00 To 95.00
Cookie Jar, Wishing Well 20.00

For emergency repairs to chipped pottery, try coloring the spot with a wax crayon or oil or paint. It will look a little better.

Cookie Jar, Woodsy Owl	95.00
Cookie Jar, Wren House, Brown Bird	50.00
Crock, Butter	45.00
Decanter, Apollo	25.00
Flower Frog, Duck, Green	35.00
Jar, Grease, Head of Lettuce	30.00
Jardiniere, Chrysanthemums, Brown Light Glaze, Loy–Nel–Art, 13 In.	90.00
Jardiniere, Tulip Design, 4 Feet, Marked Loy–Nel–Art, 11 3/4 In.	160.00
Jug, Gray & Dark Green	14.00
Lamp, Boot Shape	25.00
Mixing Bowl, Green, 8 1/2 In.	18.00
Mug, Buccaneer, Shield Mark	25.00
Mug, Little Red Riding Hood	22.50
Pitcher, Brush	240.00
Pitcher, Grapes & Leaves, Green & Brown, 9 1/2 In.	30.00
Pitcher, No.4, Brown Glaze, Shield Mark, 1926	20.00
Planter, Cowboy Boots	7.00
Planter, Down By The Old Mill Stream, Green & Tan	13.00
Planter, Dutch Shoe	4.00
Planter, Fawns, Forest, 11 1/2 X 8 In.	25.00
Planter, Hunting Bird Dog	65.00
Planter, Log, Dark Brown, 7 In.	5.00
Planter, Shell, Pair	20.00
Planter, Turtle, Green	10.00
Planter, Wishing Well	5.00 To 7.00
Planter, Yellow Birds On Nest	20.00
Tea Set, Ivy Pattern, 3 Piece	30.00
Tea Set, Pinecone	34.00
Teapot, Pinecone	12.00
Teapot, White	10.00
Vase, 10 Sides, Italian Green, 7 1/4 In.	7.00
Vase, Berries, Leaves, 2 Handles, Loy–Nel–Art, 10 1/2 In.	185.00
Vase, Calla Lilies, Handles, Olympia, 1905, 11 3/4 In.	150.00
Vase, Hyacinth, Purple Flowers	20.00
Vase, Red Poppies, Green Stems, Loy–Nel–Art, 8 1/2 In.	68.00
Vase, Rosewood, 9 In.	35.00
Vase, Tulips, Handle, Loy–Nel–Art, 11 1/2 In.	95.00
Vase, Wishing Well	6.50
Wall Pocket, Sunburst Gold, Fan Shape	15.00
Wall Pocket, Umbrella	14.00

PRESCUT   The McKee name has been associated with various glass enterprises in the United States since 1836, including J. & F. McKee (1850), Bryce, McKee & Co. (1850 to 1854), McKee and Brothers (1865), and National Glass Co. (1899). In 1903, the McKee Glass Company was formed in Jeanette, Pennsylvania. It became McKee Division of the Thatcher Glass Co. in 1951 and was bought out by the Jeanette Corporation in 1961. Pressed glass, kitchenwares, and tablewares were produced.

MCKEE, see also Custard Glass

MCKEE, Autumn, Banana Bowl, Green	20.00
Bowl, Lattice, 8 X 5 1/2 In.	14.00
Bowl, Rock Crystal, Footed, Pink, 12 In.	35.00
Butter, Quintec, Covered	23.00
Butter, Red Ships	15.00
Cake Stand, Chain With Star, 10 3/4 In.	42.50
Cake Stand, Plume, 9 In.	25.00
Candlestick, Custard, Laurel	25.00
Canister, Coffee, Jadite	28.00
Champagne, Ruby	25.00
Clock, Green	200.00
Cocktail, Rock Crystal, Footed, 3 1/2 Oz.	12.00
Compote, Crystal, 8 In.	40.00
Compote, Jelly, Spearpoint Band, Open, Scalloped, 4 3/4 In.	15.00

Creamer, Comet	40.00
Cruet, Rock Crystal	45.00
Cup & Saucer, Laurel, Blue	9.00
Cup, Lorain, Amber	10.00
Dish, Rainbow Pattern, Panels of Cane, Separated By Flutes, 2 In.	10.00
Goblet, Rock Crystal, 9 Oz.	12.00
Jar, Straw, Best Design	60.00
Plate, Rock Crystal, 7 1/2 In.	6.00
Punch Set, Tom & Jerry	34.00
Relish, 5 Sections, Rock Crystal	6.00
Salt & Pepper, Roman Arches, Black	25.00
Sherbet, Sylvan, Amber	12.00
Sugar & Creamer, Rock Crystal, Ruby, Covered	180.00
Sugar, Covered, Comet	50.00
Toothpick, Diamond Crystal	20.00
Tray, Footed, Rock Crystal, Round	40.00
Tumble–Up, Custard	55.00
Tumble–Up, Nude	20.00
Tumbler, Bottoms–Up	55.00
Tumbler, Flower Band, Green, 3 1/2 In.	6.00
Tumbler, Rock Crystal, 5 Oz.	10.00
Tumbler, With Coaster, Jadite	100.00
Vase, Flapper, Art Deco, Green, 8 1/2 In.	65.00
Vase, Footed, Rock Crystal, 8 1/2 In.	12.50
Water Set, Jug Has Star Cutting, 6 Piece	75.00

MECHANICAL BANK, see Bank, Mechanical

 All types of equipment used by doctors or hospitals are included in this section. Medical office furniture, operating tools, microscopes, thermometers, and other paraphernalia used by doctors are included. Medicine bottles are listed under Bottle. There are related collectibles listed under Dental.

MEDICAL, Apothecary Jar, Lid, U.S.Army, White, Red Emblem, Carr China	15.00
Aspirating Set, Potain's, Metal Case, Marked Wocher, C.1890	125.00
Atomizer, Mercury Glass, Bulb	30.00
Audiometer, Otarion Pure Tone, Complete, Case, C.1930, 13 X 10 In.	30.00
Bag, Doctor's, Leather, Lilly	32.50
Bag, Doctor's, Leather, Mulford Co., C.1897	60.00
Bag, Saddle, Doctor's, Folding, With Locks, Dated 1870	145.50
Bedpan, Gooseneck Spout, Ironstone, White	20.00
Birth Control Wheel, Prof.H.Marston, Natural Birth Control, 1948	10.00
Bleeder, 2 Blades, Brass	45.00
Bleeder, 3 Blades, Brass, All Different Sized, 3 1/2 In.	75.00

Be very careful when handling old bottles or medical equipment. The remains of old drugs, even toxic materials, may still cling to the surface. A broken bit of glass or a sliver could let these toxic materials reach your bloodstream.

Metal saltshaker tops can be kept from rusting or oxidizing if they are cleaned or sprayed with a silicone product. Wax will also help.

Old milk glass is slightly opalescent at the edge if held up to a strong light; new glass is not.

Bleeder, 3 Blades, Shark's Teeth Shaped, Cast Steel, Horn Grips 55.00
Bleeder, 12 Blades, Spring Loaded, Brass, Case 150.00
Bleeder, 13 Blades 325.00
Bleeder, Brass, Spring Loaded, Carved Wooden Box, Marked Pol, 1842 .... 70.00
Bleeder, Full Figural Handle, Hunter, Pheasant, Sterling Silver 135.00
Book, Journal of Chemotherapy, Jan.1929 .... 7.00
Breast Pump, Bestmaid, Box 15.00
Breast Pump, Glass Trumpet Shape, Rubber Bulb 15.00
Breast Pump, Tyler Rubber Co., Rubber Bulb, English, 1920s, Box 35.00
Cabinet, 50 Original Blood Samples On Glass Slides, Small, 1912 .... 40.00
Cabinet, File, Pharmacy, Oak, 5 Drawers, Original Files, Small 150.00
Cabinet, Optician's, Lens, Oak, 2 Drawers 75.00
Case, Pharmacist, 11 McKesson & Robbins Drug Bottles, 10 X 6 In. 65.00
Casting Device, Brass Ring With Chain Inlay, C.1930 .... 20.00
Chest, Apothecary, 45 Vials, Patent 1890 .... 55.00
Coffin, With Skeleton 275.00
Cork Press, Apothecary, Cast Iron, Leaf Design, 9 In. 55.00
Electro–Magnetic Machine, Dr.Jerome Kidder, Pat.Aug.10, 1869 .... 150.00
Embalming Kit, Complete 100.00
Enema Syringe, Pewter, Ivory, Fitted Mahogany Case, 1800s, 9 In. 125.00
Enema, Cased Pewter, 1800s 285.00
Eyecup, Cobalt Blue, 8 Panels 14.00
Eyecup, John Bull, Green .... 50.00 To 85.00
Eyecup, Milk Glass 20.00
Eyecup, Pairpoint, Red, Pedestal 50.00
Eyecup, Wyeth 12.00
Feeder, Invalid, Graniteware 20.00
Fleam, Spring Driven, 11 Piece 900.00
Fumigator, Formaldehyde, Johnson & Johnson, Metal, Box, 1930s 20.00
Glass, Dose, Druggist, Butler & Evans, Yate's Center, Kansas 25.00
Glass, Medicine, World's Dispensary Medical Association, 1 Oz. 12.00
Head, Says Phrenology On Base, English 1850.00
Herb Cutter, Druggist 185.00
Hot Water Bottle, Child's, Blue, Figural, Dog, Bowtie, England 20.00
Hot Water Bottle, Metal, Pat. 1912 .... 18.00
Inhaler, Tin, Round, Removable Spout, Benzoinol Mfg.Co., N.Y. 18.00
Instrument, Opthalmo & Otoscope, 1918, Set 40.00
Ledger, Prescription, Long Island, N.Y.Drug Store, 1921 .... 85.00
Machine, Pill Making, Druggist 275.00
Mannikin, Male Body, Philip's Anatomy, Color, 104 Folding Parts 75.00
Medicine Glass, Normal Temp 98, Adult Pulse 72 .... 7.00
Microscope, 2 Objectives, Carl Zeiss Jena, Wooden Case 155.00
Microscope, 3 Lens Turret, Brass, Mahogany Case, 1920s 195.00
Microscope, American Professions Supply Co., Chicago, Brass 115.00
Microscope, McAllister, Brass & Iron 55.00
Microscope, R.J.Beck, Brass, London, Triangular Base, 4 X 6 In. 450.00
Microscope, Spencer, Buffalo, N.Y., Iron & Brass, 12 In. 120.00
Mortar & Pestle, Goldfield, Nev., Cast Iron 49.50
Mortar & Pestle, Incised Lines, Maple, C.1850 .... 55.00
Mortar & Pestle, No.1, Wedgwood 25.00
Mortar & Pestle, No.8, Schering Commemorative, 1970 .... 25.00
Nasal Douche, Glass, Birmington Type, C.1900, Box, 4 In. 15.00
Nipple Shield, Ivory, 1800s 175.00
OB Perforator, 1800s 175.00
Optical Kit, C.1910 .... 88.00
Optician's Set, Half Case, With Frames & 200 Lenses, Pat.1895 .... 115.00
Pill Case, Doctor's, 6 Bottles, 5 In. 15.00
Pill Roller, Walnut & Brass, American, 1880, 13 X 5 In. 195.00
Pill Tile, Glass, 0–24 Cutting Scale, 20th Century, 10 X 8 In. 35.00
Prescription, For Whiskey, Richmond Doctor, Prohibition, 1934 .... 18.50
Probe, Down Bros., Fitted Case, 1900, 12 Piece, 15 In. 90.00
Quack, Renu Life Ultra–Violet Rays, Beasley–Eastman, 1919 .... 40.00
Saw, Surgeon's, 1800s 275.00
Sharpener, Hypodermic Needle 45.00

Sphygmomanometer, C.1917	40.00
Spray Tube, Ethyl Chloride, Glass, Metal Squeeze Device, 7 In.	20.00
Sterilizer, Hypodermic Needle, Nickel Plated Brass, Folding, 1918	35.00
Stethoscope, Monaural, 1800s	275.00
Surgical Kit, Travel, Leather, Tools, Blanc Firm, 18th Century	950.00
Tester, Blood Pressure, Accoson Dominion, Case	50.00
Thermometer, Rectal, Nickel Plated Brass Case	6.95
Tin, Botanic Herb, Parke Davis, Hinged Lid, Green, 5 X 5 X 9 In.	35.00
Tin, Drefs' Gout & Rheumatism Cure, Buffalo, N.Y., Round, 2 In.	7.00
Tin, Phoenix Herb, Whitall Tatum Co., Green, Brass Holder, 4 In.	32.00
Vaporizer, Tin, Box	40.00
Vial Case, Homeopathic, F.C.Stiefel Druggist, 3 X 4 In.	35.00
Vial Case, J.A.Meller Drug Co., Boscobel, Wis., 6 Glass Vials	20.00

Meerschaum pipes and other pieces of carved meerschaum, a soft mineral, date from the nineteenth century to the present.

MEERSCHAUM, Cigarette Holder, Hand Carved Dragon	55.00
Holder, Cheroot, Black Man's Head, Amber Stem, 3 In.	300.00
Holder, Cheroot, Carved Ivory, Dog, Case	55.00
Holder, Cigar, Amber Stem, Gold Shield	45.00
Holder, Cigar, Bull, Matador, Leather Case, 4 13/16 In.	200.00
Holder, Cigar, Carved Horse, Amber Stem, Case	85.00
Pipe, Bearded Civil War Figure, 4 1/2 In.	90.00
Pipe, Black Boy, Full Head, Silver Band, Amber Stem, 6 In.	300.00
Pipe, Bulldog Head, Smoke Comes Out of Ears, Mouth, 6 1/2 In.	575.00
Pipe, Dog & House Bowl, 3 Footed, Cherrywood Stem, 1820	175.00
Pipe, Dog Walking Along Stem, Amber Top, 5 In.	70.00
Pipe, Dogs, Walking Around Tree Stump, Amber Stem, 7 In.	175.00
Pipe, Elf On Bowl, Amber Stem, Case	95.00
Pipe, Farmer Harnessing Horse, Tree Stump Bowl, 6 In.	225.00
Pipe, Female Nude Holding Bowl, Amber Top, 6 In.	145.00
Pipe, Female Nude, Flowing Drapery, Amber Stem, 9 In.	500.00
Pipe, Four Racing Horses, Amber Stem, 8 1/2 In.	250.00
Pipe, Gibson Girl's Head, Flowing Hair, Case, 5 X 2 1/2 In.	170.00
Pipe, Gypsy Boy, Curly Hair & Hat, Amber Stem, 7 In.	95.00
Pipe, Horse With Lioness On Back, Amber Stem, 8 In.	175.00
Pipe, Horses Anchored To Urn, Amber Stem, 5 In.	200.00
Pipe, Hunter Seated, Rifle, 2 Hunting Dogs, Amber Stem, 7 In.	250.00
Pipe, Hunter, With Dog On Hind Legs, Case, 2 1/4 X 6 In.	200.00
Pipe, Jockey Cap, Racing Horse, Amber Stem, Case, 4 1/4 In.	75.00
Pipe, Jockey Holding Whip, Amber Stem, Case, 5 X 2 In.	85.00
Pipe, Lady Bareback Rider, Amber Stem, Case, 4 3/8 In.	375.00
Pipe, Lady's Hand Holding Stein, Elf, Silver Cap, 8 In.	175.00
Pipe, Lady's Hand, Bowl Draped With Leaves, Nude Cherub, 5 In.	130.00
Pipe, Lady's Hand, Bowl Draped With Vines, Case, 7 X 3 In.	250.00
Pipe, Lady's Hand, Vines, Amber Bowl, Case, 4 X 3 In.	100.00
Pipe, Nude Woman, Arabian Headdress, Half Portrait, 6 In.	300.00
Pipe, Old Salt Fisherman, Rain Hat, Case, 4 X 6 In.	375.00
Pipe, Pineapples, Stag Hunt Scene, 39 In.	500.00
Pipe, Prancing Horse, Amber Tip, 4 1/2 In.	55.00
Pipe, Reindeer, Yellow Amber Stem, Case, 19 In.	350.00
Pipe, Running Deer & Cottage	60.00
Pipe, Tree Trunk, Rearing Horse, Snake, Case, 4 3/4 In.	750.00
Pipe, Victorian Fallen Female Next To Flower Bowl, 10 In.	800.00
Pipe, Victorian Lady's Head, Hat, Case, 3 1/4 In.	400.00

Meissen is a town in Germany where porcelain has been made since 1710. Any china made in the town can be called Meissen, although the famous Meissen factory made the finest porcelains of the area. The crossed swords mark of the great Meissen factory has been copied by many other firms in Germany and other parts of the world.

Meissen, Figurine, Classical Woman, Cupid,
Arrows, Marked, 8 In.

Meissen, Figurine, Man, Standing, Wine Keg,
Lavender Pants, 7 In.

Meissen, Figurine, Putti, Birds In Cage,
5 1/4 In.

MEISSEN, Bowl, Center, Pierced, Maiden & Man Playing Hide & Seek, 20 In. 1875.00
Bowl, Covered, Basket Weave Mold, Floral, Crossed Swords, 8 In. 250.00
Bowl, Covered, Landscape Scene, Floral Design, C.1760, 4 1/2 In. 225.00
Bowl, Reticulated, Children Dancing, Crossed Swords, 13 In. 825.00
Box, Covered, Mythological Scenes, Bronze Hinges, 11 X 7 X 6 In. 1100.00
Candelabra, Lady, Child, 3 Arms, Center Holder, Roses, 20 In. 450.00
Centerpiece, Basket Weave, Flowers, Crossed Swords, 12 X 8 In. 395.00
Charger, Roses & Leaves Center, Crossed Swords, 10 1/2 In. 300.00
Chocolate Pot, Floral Bouquets Each Side, Marked, C.1923, 12 In. 215.00
Chocolate Set, Hand Painted Roses, Marked, 13 Piece 695.00
Clock, Figures of Father Time & Jupiter, 2 Putti, Gilt, 25 3/8 In. 2530.00
Clock, Mantel, Armorial, Maiden, Stand, Crossed Swords, 28 In. 1650.00
Coffee Can & Saucer, Tulip, White Ground, Marcolini, C.1800 .... 275.00
Cup & Saucer, Cobalt Blue & White Panels, Flowers, Gold Trim 95.00
Cup & Saucer, Floral, Leaf Form Handles, Demitasse, 11 Piece 110.00
Cup & Saucer, Floral, Swan Handle, Crossed Swords, Demitasse, 1760 .... 50.00
Cup, Covered, Hand Painted Insects, Flowers, Pastoral Scene 75.00
Dish, Poultry, Molded Flora & Leaf, C.1770, 4 3/4 In. 110.00
Dish, Sweetmeat, Maiden Or Man Reclining At Side, 20 In., Pair 1430.00
Ewer, Allover White Florets, Oriole On Branches, Marked, 23 In. 2750.00
Figurine, Boy, Holding Flower Wreath, Marked, 4 3/4 In. 225.00
Figurine, Boy, Seated, Holding Pot of Roses, One Rose In Hand 275.00
Figurine, Boy, With Hoe On Shoulder, Carrying Basket, 5 1/2 In. 160.00
Figurine, Carriage, Forget-Me-Nots, 19th Century, 10 In. 495.00
Figurine, Cherub, 1840-60, 7 In. 375.00
Figurine, Classical Woman, Cupid, Arrows, Marked, 8 In. ....*Illus*   275.00
Figurine, Count Bruhl's Tailor, Tools of Trade, 17 1/4 In. 2975.00
Figurine, Dove, 19th Century, Miniature 85.00
Figurine, Flower Girl, Barefoot, Carrying Basket, 5 In. 175.00
Figurine, Girl, Flowers In Apron, Marked, 5 In. 225.00
Figurine, Girl, Yellow Skirt, Floral Apron, Marked, 5 In. 200.00
Figurine, Lady, By Tall Pedestal, Flowers In Urn, 7 1/2 In. 250.00
Figurine, Lady, Singer, C.1924 .... 450.00
Figurine, Malabar Musicians, Fur-Lined Kimonas, 12 1/4 In., Pair 1200.00
Figurine, Man, Flute Player, C.1814 .... 450.00
Figurine, Man, Standing, Wine Keg, Lavender Pants, 7 In. ....*Illus*   375.00
Figurine, Monkey Band, Marked, C.1860, 10 Piece 675.00
Figurine, Polar Bear, 4 X 9 In. 245.00
Figurine, Pug, Seated, Blue Collar, Signed, 6 1/2 In. ....*Illus*   1870.00
Figurine, Putti, Birds In Cage, 5 1/4 In. ....*Illus*   300.00
Figurine, Triangle Player, C.1814 .... 450.00

Figurine, Turbaned Rider & Rearing White Stallion, 11 In.	700.00
Figurine, Wagtail, Sweeping Tail, Marked, 8 3/4 In., Pair	825.00
Girandole, Mirror Backplate, Branch Arm, Floral, 19 In., Pair	1100.00
Group, Dancing Couple, Crossed Swords, 7 In.	250.00
Group, Juno, 3 Cupids, Crossed Swords, 8 3/4 In.	935.00
Group, Jupiter, Eagle Drawn Chariot, Crossed Swords, 19 In.	770.00
Group, Lovers On Settee, Musical Instruments, Marked, 5 7/8 In.	1425.00
Group, Maidens Casting For Baby, Crossed Swords, 11 3/4 In.	770.00
Group, Mercury, Cupid & Venus, Crossed Swords, 8 1/4 In.	330.00
Group, Summer, 4 Putti, Crossed Swords, No.2490, 6 In.	770.00
Inkwell, Square, 4 In.	35.00
Match Holder, Striker Bottom	30.00
Plate, Blue & White Inserts, Flower Center, Late 19th Century	85.00
Plate, Christmas, Blue, White, House & Trees, 20th Century, 10 In.	155.00
Plate, Courting Figures, Applied Blue & White Flowers, 10 In.	450.00
Plate, Courting Scene Center, Reticulated Edge, 7 In., Set of 8	345.00
Plate, Floral Center, Embossed Swirled Border, Marked, 11 In.	125.00
Plate, Floral Center, Embossed, Scalloped, 11 1/4 In.	78.00
Plate, Hand Painted Courting Scene, Reticulated Border, 7 In.	48.00
Plate, Oriental Design, Crossed Swords Mark, 10 In.	40.00
Plate, White, Gold, Leaf Shape, C.1860, 10 In.	110.00
Salt, Open, Floral, Fluted, Divided, Center Ring Handle	45.00
Sprinkler, Rosewater, Flower Clusters, Gilding, Marked, 6 In.	125.00
Tea Caddy, Grapevines, Clusters of Fruit, C.1745, 4 1/8 In.	165.00
Tureen, Covered, Swan Shape, Crossed Swords, 14 1/2 In.	1760.00
Urn, Twin Coiled Snake Handles, Gold, White, 19 In. ....Illus	650.00
Vase, 3 Birds, Schneeballen, Crossed Swords, 19 In.	2530.00
Vase, Putti, Covered, 8 In.	250.00

Mercury, or silvered, glass was first made in the 1850s. It lost favor for a while but became popular again about 1910. It looks like a piece of silver.

MERCURY GLASS, Candelabra, 2-Branch, Pair	150.00
Candlestick, Floral Enameling, 7 In.	40.00
Console Set, Aqua, Bowl, 9 1/2 In.	110.00
Creamer, Clear Applied Handle, 6 3/8 In.	65.00
Figurine, Rooster, Paper Label, Germany, 5 1/2 In.	25.00
Jug, Brown Top, Stenciled Blue Center, 5 In.	35.00
Salt, Pedestal, Silver Coated Interior, 1 3/4 In.	15.00
Sugar, Open, 5 1/4 In.	65.00
Tieback, Vintage Engraved, 4 1/2 & 4 In., 7 Piece	65.00
Vase, Floral Design, 6 1/2 In., Pair	25.00
Vase, Spherical, Silver, 7 3/4 In.	50.00

Mettlach, Germany, is a city where the Villeroy and Boch factories worked. Steins from the firm are known as Mettlach steins. They date from about 1842. PUG means "painted under glaze." The steins can be dated from the marks on the bottom which include a date-number code. Other pieces may be listed in the Villeroy & Boch category.

METTLACH, Beaker, No.2327/1025, Barmaid, PUG	125.00
Beaker, No.2327/1192, Fisherman With Net	38.00
Beaker, No.2327/1214, 1/4 Liter, Woman Smoking Handle, PUG	71.00
Beaker, No.2327/1215, 1/4 Liter, Woman Holding Fruit Basket, PUG	72.00
Butter, Shamrock & Rectangular Pattern, Marked, Covered, 18 In.	125.00
Cup & Saucer, No.153, Floral Pattern, Silver Inlay	95.00
Dish, No.377, Leaf	45.00
Mug, No.2001, Rows of Books, 4 1/2 In.	125.00
Mug, No.2333, 3/10 Liter, Elves, PUG	55.00
Pitcher, Green Leaves, Gray, Birch Handle, Seal Mark, 1890, 9 In.	210.00
Pitcher, Wind, Flowers, Birds, Band of Dancing People, 13 In.	450.00
Planter, Art Nouveau, Iris Design, 5 1/2 X 12 X 7 In. ....Illus	300.00
Plaque, Classical Maidens, Kneeling Man, Gear Wheel, 18 In.	650.00
Plaque, No. 307, Dutch Girl, Scenic, 12 In.	100.00

Plaque, No.1044/1206, Drinking Scene, PUG, 17 1/2 In.	335.00
Plaque, No.1106, 3 Men With Staffs, Jewels, Gold Trim, 16 1/2 In.	850.00
Plaque, No.2148, Snow White	1400.00
Plaque, No.2350, 2351, Facing Pair, Dated 1897, 17 1/2 In., Pair	1450.00
Plaque, No.2375, Classical Women & Man, Green, 17 1/2 In.	695.00
Plaque, No.2621, Cavalier, Pouring Wine	175.00
Plate, Boat Scene, Matte Finish, Drilled For Hanging, 10 1/4 In.	95.00
Plate, No.3096, Art Deco Design In Burnt Gold	65.00
Pokal, No.2058, 3 Liter, Monkeys At Play, Etched & Relief	2915.00
Punch Set, Grape & Leaf Incised Design, Geometric, 13 Piece	990.00
Stein, No. 368, 1/2 Liter, Tree Trunk, Leaf & Branch Design	180.00
Stein, No.1001C, 1/2 Liter, Owl Perched On Books, Marked, 6 In.	550.00
Stein, No.1005, 1/2 Liter, 3 Cavalier Scenes	88.00
Stein, No.1028, 1/2 Liter, Man & Woman Harvesters, Marked, 7 In.	225.00
Stein, No.1146, 1/2 Liter, Students In Tavern	500.00
Stein, No.1266, 1/2 Liter, 3 Panels, Drinking Scene, 5 1/2 In.	185.00
Stein, No.1403, 1/2 Liter, Bowling Scene, Inlaid Lid, 7 1/8 In.	525.00
Stein, No.1467, 1/2 Liter, Tavern Scene	102.00
Stein, No.1471, 1/2 Liter, Musicians, Etched, Signed Warth	342.00
Stein, No.1526, 1/2 Liter, Dueling Student Crest	184.00
Stein, No.1526, 1/2 Liter, Fraternal Emblem	140.00
Stein, No.1526, 1/2 Liter, Yale University, PUG	170.00
Stein, No.1526/600, 1 Liter, Cavalier & Verse, Gray Ground, PUG	264.00
Stein, No.1526/604, 1/2 Liter, Fireman Implements In Shield, PUG	245.00
Stein, No.1530, 1 Liter, Robed Man, Smoking Pipe, Signed, 8 3/4 In.	375.00
Stein, No.1642, 1/2 Liter, Man Drinking	275.00 To 450.00
Stein, No.1675, 1/2 Liter, Heidelberg Scene, Pewter Lid	450.00
Stein, No.1725, 1/2 Liter, Young Couple, Signed WARTH	222.00
Stein, No.1740, 1/4 Liter, Floral Design	225.00 To 325.00
Stein, No.1786, 1/2 Liter, St.Florian, Dragon Handle	467.00
Stein, No.1794, 1/2 Liter, Bismarck In Uniform, Etched	450.00
Stein, No.1801, 1/4 Liter, Geometric Design, Mosaic	110.00
Stein, No.1863, 1/2 Liter, Stuttgart Scene, Pewter Lid, 10 In.	550.00
Stein, No.1892, 1 Liter, Floral Design, Pewter Lid, 9 In.	120.00
Stein, No.1909/ 727, 1/2 Liter, Dwarfs Bowling, PUG	286.00
Stein, No.1909/ 979, 1/2 Liter, Dwarfs	165.00
Stein, No.1909/1058, 1/2 Liter, Frogs Drinking At Dock, PUG	374.00
Stein, No.1909/1176, 1/2 Liter, Dice Players, PUG	218.00
Stein, No.1997, 1/2 Liter, George Ehret Brewer	225.00
Stein, No.2002, 1/2 Liter, Munich Scene	325.00 To 390.00
Stein, No.2007, 1/2 Liter, Black Cat, Etched	399.00
Stein, No.2008, 1/2 Liter, Trumpeter On Black Horse	291.00
Stein, No.2009, 1/2 Liter, Lovers, Etched	485.00
Stein, No.2024, 1/2 Liter, Shield of Berlin	495.00
Stein, No.2025, 1/2 Liter, Cherubs	396.00
Stein, No.2028, 1/2 Liter, Outdoor Drinking Scene	414.00
Stein, No.2036, 1/2 Liter, Owl	895.00
Stein, No.2051, 1/2 Liter, Students Drinking	495.00
Stein, No.2077, 3/10 Liter, Scene of 3 Different Shields	126.00
Stein, No.2082, 1/2 Liter, William Tell, Pewter Lid	756.00
Stein, No.2086, 1/2 Liter, People Dancing, Pewter Lid	126.00
Stein, No.2106, 2/5 Liter, Monkeys In Cage	2860.00
Stein, No.2134, 1/2 Liter, Gnome In Nest, Holding 2 Steins	1600.00
Stein, No.2140/942, 1/2 Liter, Night Watchman & Rooster, PUG	341.00
Stein, No.2184/967, 3/10 Liter, Dwarfs Drinking, PUG	247.00
Stein, No.2204, 1 Liter, Black German Eagle	695.00
Stein, No.2271/1020, 1/2 Liter, Tavern People & Verse, PUG	341.00
Stein, No.2271/1055, 1/2 Liter, Drunk Cavaliers, Wine Cellar, PUG	269.00
Stein, No.2327/1050, 1/4 Liter, Woman With Jug, PUG	83.00
Stein, No.2327/1189, 1/4 Liter, Woman At Seashore.PUG	44.00
Stein, No.2327/1288, 1/4 Liter, Fox With Stein, PUG	121.00
Stein, No.2382, 1/2 Liter, Thirsty Knight	610.00
Stein, No.2441, 1/2 Liter, 2 Dice Players, Music Box In Base	595.00
Stein, No.2556, 1/2 Liter, Drinking & Card Playing Scene	220.00

Stein, No.2582, 1/2 Liter, Jester, Performing On Table, Etched 373.00
Stein, No.2608, 3/10 Liter, Cavaliers, Cameo 345.00
Stein, No.2631, 2.5 Liter, Boar Hunt Scene, Cameo, Stahl 1400.00
Stein, No.2691, 2.75 Liter, Inlaid Man, With Guitar, In Cellar 1100.00
Stein, No.2725, 1/2 Liter, Artist 3740.00
Stein, No.2729, 1/2 Liter, Blacksmith 2640.00
Stein, No.2753, 1/2 Liter, Man, Woman & Musicians, 3 Panels 595.00
Stein, No.2776, 1/2 Liter, Keeper of Wine Cellar 875.00
Stein, No.2778, 1 Liter, Carnival Player & Drinkers, Schlitt 1350.00
Stein, No.2785/6130, Man Playing Bagpipes, PUG, 14 In. 625.00
Stein, No.2829, .5 Liter, PUG 1800.00
Stein, No.2900, 1/2 Liter, Argentina Quilmas, 1904 .... 375.00
Stein, No.2959, 1/2 Liter, Boy Bowling .... 295.00 To 435.00
Stein, No.5394, 1 Liter, Mercury & Pegasus 1980.00
Sugar, No.2948, Covered, Stylized Trees, Ivory Ground, Marked 95.00
Vase, No.1591, Boys Playing Instruments, Florals, 12 3/4 In. 695.00
Vase, No.1808, 10 In. 100.00
Vase, No.1870, Elephant Handles, 14 In. 275.00

> Milk glass was named for its milky–white color. It was first made in
> England during the 1700s. The height of its popularity in the United
> States was from 1870 to 1880. It is now correct to refer to some
> colored glass as blue milk glass, black milk glass, etc. Reproductions
> of milk glass are being made and sold in many stores.

MILK GLASS, Ashtray, Beaded Grape, 6 1/2 In. 20.00
Basket, Chick Emerging From Egg, Handle, 3 1/2 In. 40.00
Basket, English Hobnail, Handle, 9 1/2 In. 30.00
Bonbon, English Hobnail, Covered, Footed, 4 1/2 In. 20.00
Bone Dish, Crescent Shape, Openwork Border 20.00
Bottle, Figural, Statue of Liberty 175.00
Bottle, Joan of Arc, Figural Head Stopper, 16 1/2 In. 285.00
Bottle, Perfume, Block, Miniature 110.00
Bowl, Bulb, Phoenix Bird Feet 15.00
Bowl, Ivy, Paneled Grape, Footed, Westmoreland, 6 1/2 In. 35.00
Bowl, Maple Leaf, Fluted, Westmoreland, 5 1/2 X 9 1/2 In. 25.00
Box, Duck Cover, Amethyst Head, Atterbury, C.1887, 10 3/4 In. 215.00
Box, Jewel, Heart, 8 1/2 In. .... 20.00 To 25.00
Bread Plate, Wheat, Give Us This Day, Beaded Edge 36.00
Butter, Cosmos, Covered, Pink Band .... 125.00 To 250.00
Butter, Covered, Guttate, White, Gold Trim 65.00
Butter, Tree of Life, Covered .... 70.00 To 125.00
Butter, Wild Rose, Covered, Child's 65.00
Butter, Wild Rose, Covered, Silver Trim 30.00
Cake Plate, Grape, 13 X 4 1/2 In. 40.00
Candlestick, Crucifix, L.E.Smith, 9 In., Pair 25.00
Candlestick, Dutch, Child's, Boudoir, Blue 145.00
Candy Dish, Dolphin, Antique Blue, Shell Finial 38.00
Celery Vase, Jewel, 9 In. 110.00
Celery Vase, Old Quilt Roses & Bows 35.00
Compote, Atlas, Scalloped .... 110.00 To 125.00
Compote, Paneled Grape, Westmoreland .... 38.00 To 49.00
Compote, Shell, Dolphin Base 25.00
Condiment Set, Cosmos, Original Holder 475.00
Condiment Set, Forget–Me–Not, PeeWee 50.00
Creamer, Paneled Flower 35.00
Creamer, Wild Rose, Silver Trim, Child's 35.00
Cruet, Paneled Grape, Westmoreland 20.00
Cruet, Tree of Life, Original Stopper 75.00
Cup & Saucer, Banded Raindrop 12.50
Custard, Corn 90.00
Dish, American Hen Cover .... 55.00 To 60.00
Dish, Battleship Maine Cover 40.00
Dish, Bird On Nest Cover, Tripod Footed Base 195.00

Dish, Cat Cover, Glass Eyes, Westmoreland, 8 X 5 In. 75.00
Dish, Cat Cover, White Head, Blue, Ribbed Base, 5 1/4 In. 50.00
Dish, Chick On Sleigh Cover 45.00
Dish, Chicks In Square Basket Cover 90.00
Dish, Deer On Fallen Tree Cover, White, Marked 95.00
Dish, Dewey, Tile Base 35.00
Dish, Dolphin Cover 47.00
Dish, Easter Egg, 6 In. 22.00
Dish, Easter Egg, Embossed Greetings, 4 1/2 In. 18.00
Dish, Entwined Fish Cover, 1889 .... 115.00
Dish, Fish Cover, Boat Shape, 7 1/2 In. 20.00
Dish, Fish Cover, Challinor Taylor 200.00
Dish, Fox Cover, Atterbury, Dated August 6, '89 .... 155.00
Dish, Hand–In–Dove Cover, White, Ring & Bird's–Eye Stones 125.00
Dish, Hen Cover, Basket Weave Base, Blue 40.00
Dish, Hen Cover, Blue Head, Lacy Edge, Atterbury, 7 1/2 In. 127.00
Dish, Hen Cover, Lacy Base, White 95.00
Dish, Hen On Nest Cover, Dark Amber 135.00
Dish, Hen On Nest Cover, Red Comb, Westmoreland, 5 1/2 In. 35.00
Dish, Honey, Beaded Grape, Gold Relief, Covered, Footed, Square 25.00
Dish, Lamb On Picket Base Cover, Blue 40.00
Dish, Leaf, Westmoreland 7.50
Dish, Lion Cover, Basketweave Base 50.00
Dish, Oregon Cruiser Cover 45.00
Dish, Rabbit Cover, Lacy Rim, Colored Eggs, Westmoreland, Large 65.00
Dish, Ribbed Lion Cover, Lacy, Dated 8/6/89 .... 135.00
Dish, Robin On Pedestal Cover 40.00
Dish, Santa Claus In Sleigh Cover ....60.00 To 110.00
Dish, Sitting Frog Cover 125.00
Dish, Squirrel On Acorn Cover 65.00
Dish, Stag On Fallen Tree Cover 65.00
Dish, Turtle Cover 57.00
Dish, Uncle Sam On Battleship Cover 60.00
Eggcup, Basket Weave 30.00
Eggcup, Leaf Garland, Double 12.50
Epergne, Hobnail 32.00
Figurine, Cat, Lacy Base, Atterbury, Date On Lid, 8 X 5 X 6 In. 145.00
Figurine, Victorian Girl, 4 3/4 In. 38.00
Goblet, Princess Feather 40.00
Gravy Boat, Dolphin Finial, Beading, Covered 45.00
Humidor, Screw Top, Figural Pouch, Tied With Bow, Dated 1886 .... 65.00
Jar, Remember The Maine, Scene, Bulbous, Covered, 5 1/2 X 4 In. 195.00
Jar, Rib & Scallop, Red, Original Metal Top 85.00
Jardiniere, Paneled Grape, Westmoreland, 6 X 6 1/2 In. 30.00
Lamp, Block & Dot ....55.00 To 100.00
Lamp, Dresser, Cranberry Glass Shade, Hanging Bobbles, Pair 135.00
Lamp, Kerosene, Blackberry 155.00
Lamp, Nutmeg, Cobalt Blue Shade, Miniature 75.00
Lamp, Oil, Versailles 145.00
Lamp, Pedestal, Banner Stars Improved, 2 1/2 In. 95.00
Match Holder, Kettle, Hanging 18.00
Mug, Washington, Lafayette, 3 1/4 In. 25.00
Mustard, Bull's Head Cover, Spoon For Tongue ....130.00 To 150.00
Mustard, English Hobnail, Spoon, Footed 20.00
Paperweight, Washington Monument 75.00
Pepper Pot, Blue, Tin Top, 6 In. 6.00
Pitcher, Milk, Block & Daisy, 7 In. 35.00
Pitcher, Milk, Windmill, Imperial 26.50
Pitcher, Water, Guttate, Pink Cased 350.00
Pitcher, Water, Paneled Grape, Westmoreland, 1 Qt. 35.00
Plaque, Gen.U.S.Grant Profile, 10 1/4 In. 260.00
Plaque, Lincoln, Original Brown Stain 200.00
Plate, Admiral Dewey, Club, Loop, Shell 28.00
Plate, Battleship Maine, Gothic Border 28.00

Plate, Bryan Campaign 55.00
Plate, Chick & Eggs 25.00
Plate, Eagles Rim, Blue, Dated 1903 .... 25.00
Plate, Easter Greetings, 7 In. 35.00
Plate, Owl Lovers, 7 1/2 In. 45.00
Plate, Rabbit & Horseshoe, Original Paint 32.00
Plate, Robin On Nest 40.00
Plate, Serenade, 6 In. 12.00
Plate, Spring Meets Winter 55.00
Plate, Taft Campaign 55.00
Plate, Three Kittens, Openwork, Blue, 7 In. 35.00
Plate, Trumpet Vine Lattice, Flower Design, 10 1/2 In. 30.00
Plate, Winged Cherub, Blue 75.00
Platter, Retriever 70.00
Punch Bowl, English Hobnail, Painted, 6 Piece 30.00
Punch Cup, Nursery Rhyme, Child's 8.00
Punch Cup, Wild Rose, Child's 15.00
Punch Set, Little Red Riding Hood, Child's, 5 Piece 240.00
Punch Set, Nursery Rhymes, Blue, 7 Piece 595.00
Range Set, General Electric Refrigerator, 3 Piece 69.00
Range Set, Hotpoint, Set of 4 .... 40.00
Relish, Blackberry, Egg Shape 35.00
Relish, Fish, Divided, White 27.50
Salt & Pepper, Challinor 55.00
Salt & Pepper, Cosmos, Pink Band 120.00
Salt & Pepper, Diamond Point & Leaf 100.00
Salt & Pepper, Heart, Pink 90.00
Salt & Pepper, Leaf & Flower 60.00
Salt & Pepper, Swag With Brackets, Amethyst, Gold 80.00
Salt, Birch Leaf, Footed, Flint, Master 18.00
Salt, Diamond Faceted, Star Bottom, 1 7/8 In. 12.00
Salt, Double Basket, Loop Handle, Rope Rim, Dated 1874, 4 In. ... 50.00
Salt, Double Cord & Tassel 13.50
Salt, Lacy Daisy, Westmoreland, 2 1/4 In. 12.00
Saltshaker, Cactus, Blue 40.00
Saltshaker, Cotton Bale, Blue 30.00
Saltshaker, Hen & Rabbit 30.00
Saltshaker, Thrush Wing 70.00
Sauce, Blackberry 5.00
Sauce, Paneled Grape, Footed, Westmoreland 11.50
Sauce, Wheat 5.00
Shoe, Baby Bootie 45.00
Shoe, Lady's, White, Iridescent Lion Head On Top, 9 In. 45.00
Spooner, Apple Blossom 18.00
Spooner, Blackberry .... 25.00 To 45.00
Spooner, Cosmos 85.00
Spooner, Sawtooth 25.00
Spooner, Waffle, Green 60.00
Sugar & Creamer, Baltimore Pear, Shell Pink 48.00
Sugar & Creamer, English Hobnail, Footed 25.00
Sugar & Creamer, Fan & File, Westmoreland, Child's 16.00
Sugar & Creamer, Feather, Gold Trim 50.00
Sugar & Creamer, Paneled Grape, Westmoreland 20.00
Sugar Shaker, Beaded Twist 22.00
Sugar Shaker, Blown-Out Tulip 30.00
Sugar Shaker, Blue, 4 Sides, Aluminum Top, Word Sugar, 5 In. ... 15.00
Sugar Shaker, Guttate, Cranberry 125.00
Sugar Shaker, Ice Blue 75.00
Sugar, Strawberry, Salamander Finial, Covered, Gold Trim, 5 In. ... 70.00
Syrup, Clamp-On Lid, Paneled Lower Half, Hobnail Above 55.00
Syrup, Daisy & Fern, Blue 95.00
Syrup, Fishnet & Poppies, Colored Flowers 52.00
Syrup, Floral Design, Original Metal Top 39.00
Syrup, Hand Painted Florals, Metal Dome Shape Lid 125.00

Syrup, Tree of Life 75.00
Syrup, Wild Rose, Hinged Cover 110.00
Table Set, Child's, Wild Rose, 4 Piece 250.00
Toothpick, 3 Swan's Heads Around Body 45.00
Toothpick, Chick In Egg 85.00
Toothpick, Horseshoe & Clover 25.00
Toothpick, Owl, Westmoreland 18.00
Toothpick, Pansy, 3 Handles 18.00
Toothpick, Snake Around Barrel 40.00
Toothpick, Tramp Shoe 45.00
Tray, Calling Card, Welcome Hand, Victorian 45.00
Tray, Dresser, Monkey's Head 43.00
Tray, Lady & Fan 95.00
Tray, Shell, Child's 90.00
Tumbler, Buttermilk, Paneled Grape, Westmoreland 15.00
Tumbler, Guttate, Glossy White 27.00
Tumbler, Iced Tea, Old Quilt, Westmoreland 17.00
Tumbler, Scroll 25.00
Tumbler, Single Rose 23.50
Vase, Fan, English Hobnail, Footed, 5 1/2 X 6 In. 18.00
Vase, Fan, Old Quilt Roses & Bows, Gold Trim, 6 1/2 X 8 1/2 In. 30.00
Vase, Grape, Footed, Westmoreland, 6 In. 19.00
Vase, Grape, Westmoreland, 5 3/4 In. 15.00
Vase, Hobnail, 12 X 12 In. 18.00
Vase, Poppy, 5 In. 20.00

> Millefiori means, literally, a thousand flowers. It is a type of
> glasswork popular in paperweights. Many small flowerlike pieces of
> glass are grouped together to form a design.

MILLEFIORI, Coffeepot, Cobalt Blue, White Flowers, Applied Handle, 6 In. 225.00
Creamer, Cobalt Blue, White Flowers, 4 1/4 X 3 In. 100.00
Cruet, Ribbed Camphor Handle, Stopper 89.50
Cup & Saucer, Cobalt Blue, White Flowers, 4 1/8 In.Saucer 85.00
Lamp, Boudoir, 19th Century, 14 In., Pair ....*Illus* 200.00
Sugar, Covered, Cobalt Blue, White Flowers, 3 1/2 X 4 In. 110.00
Tumbler, 3 1/2 In. 85.00

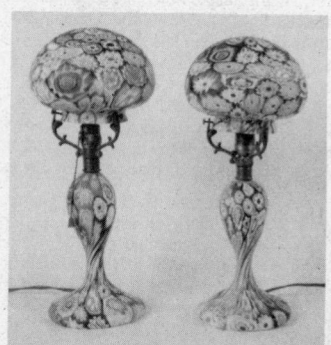

Meissen, Urn, Twin Coiled Snake Handles,   Millefiori, Lamp, Boudoir, 19th Century,
Gold, White, 19 In.   14 In., Pair

Minton china has been made in the Staffordshire region of England from 1793 to the present. The firm became part of the Royal Doulton Tableware Group in 1968, but the wares continued to be marked "Minton." Many marks have been used. The one shown dates from about 1873 to 1891, when the word "England" was added.

MINTON, Box, Nun Pigeon Cover, Black & White, Marked, C.1820, 7 3/4 In., Pair	600.00
Cup & Saucer, Birds & Insects, Pate-Sur-Pate, Signed D.Leroy	200.00
Eggcup, Roses, Blue Jeweled Design	25.00
Figurine, Ariadne On Panther, Parian, 1864, 16 In.	300.00
Garden Seat, Barrel Shape, Yellow, Chrysanthemum, Rings, 18 In.	325.00
Jam Jar, Butterfly, Blue, 1920 .... 35.00 To 45.00	
Jardiniere, Cherub Handles, 1880s, 10 1/2 In.	375.00
Pitcher, Salt Glaze	170.00
Plate, Clam, Fish Design, White, Staffordshire Salt Glaze, 11 In.	69.00
Plate, Garden Pinks, 10 1/2 In.	20.00
Plate, Warwick Castle, 9 1/2 In.	24.00
Salt, Figural, Boy In Green Costume Holding Dish	425.00
Sugar & Creamer, Audley	40.00
Teapot, Chinaman, Majolica	995.00
Tile, Cream & Brown Floral, 6 X 6 In.	25.00
Tile, Fish, C.1880, 6 X 6 In.	35.00
Tile, Scenic, Flow Blue, Square, 5 In.	25.00
Tile, Seahorse, C.1880, 6 X 6 In.	35.00
Trivet, Twisted Iron Frame, Footed, 1842 Mark	70.00
Vase, Secessionist, Flambe, Green, 10 In. .... 125.00 To 150.00	

MIRROR, see Furniture, Mirror

Mochaware is an English-made product that was sold in America during the early 1800s. It is a heavy pottery with pale coffee-and-cream coloring. Designs of blue, brown, green, orange, black, or white were added to the pottery.

MOCHA, Bowl, Blue Band, 2 Black Lines Either Side, 4 3/4 X 2 3/4 In.	45.00
Bowl, Rust With Brown, Blue & White Earthworms, 5 X 3 In.	300.00
Butter, Green Seaweed On Cream Band, Yellowware Cover, 6 1/2 In.	160.00
Compote, Marbelized Design, Blue, Black, White, Brown, Footed, 4 In.	100.00
Cup Plate, Yellow, Black Seaweed Design, 3 1/2 In.	375.00
Measure, Seaweed Design, Blue & Brown Bands, 1 Qt.	200.00
Mug, Porringer, Balloon Design, Tan, Brown Stripes, 4 1/4 X 3 In.	600.00
Pitcher, Cider, Covered, Blue Bands, Earthworm Design, 6 In.	425.00
Salt, Master, Blue Band, Stripes, Earthworm Design, 3 X 2 1/4 In.	200.00
Shaker, Acorn Shape, Marked Pepper, English Registry Mark, 2 In.	77.50
Shaker, Earthworm & Cat's Eye Design, Blue Bands, 4 5/8 In.	450.00
Sugar Shaker, White Dots, Dark Blue Top, White, Blue & Black, 5 In.	140.00
Sugar, Bands of Sand Texture, Blue Bands, Cream Ground, Covered	80.00
Sugar, Creamware, Beige Band, Brown Striping, Seaweed, 6 1/2 In.	450.00
Syrup, Blue, Brown, Metal Top	75.00
Teapot, Blue & White, Brown & White Checkered Border, Child's	175.00
Tumbler, Marbelized, Brown, White, Black & Yellow, 3 3/4 In.	350.00
Waste Bowl, Blue Band, Black Stripes, Green Rim, 4 5/8 X 3 In.	120.00

Monmouth Pottery Company started working in Monmouth, Illinois, in 1892. The pottery made a variety of utilitarian wares. They became part of Western Stoneware Company in 1906. The maple leaf mark was used until 1930. If the word "Co." appears as part of the mark, the piece was made before 1906.

MONMOUTH, Cookie Jar, Yellow & Brown	15.00
Jardiniere, Egyptian, 8 3/4 In.	50.00
Jug, Brown Glaze, 6 In.	15.00
Mug, Hound Handle	60.00
Pitcher, Brown, 6 1/4 In.	8.00
Salt, Hanging, Lid, Colonial Design	300.00
Vase, Leaf Shape, Sticker, 6 1/2 In., Pair	35.00

Vase, Pink, Small Ear Handles, Sticker, 6 In. 15.00
MONT JOYE, see Mt. Joye

William Moorcroft managed the art pottery department for James
MacIntyre & Company of England from 1898 to 1913. In 1913, he
started his own company, Moorcroft Pottery, in Burslem, England.
He died in 1945, but the company continues. The earlier wares are
similar to those made today, but color and marking will help
indicate the age.

MOORCROFT, Ashtray, Leaf & Berry, 6 In. .... 110.00 To 120.00
Biscuit Jar, Crocus, Sterling Silver Mounts 350.00
Bowl, Leaf & Berries, 10 In. .... 190.00 To 225.00
Box, Rose & Pansies, Cobalt Blue Ground, Round, Covered 250.00
Candlestick, Dark Blue & Yellow, Fruits, 4 3/4 In., Pair 110.00
Candlestick, Pomegranate, Cobalt Blue, 7 In. 85.00
Compote, Burslem, Handles, Footed, 5 1/4 X 5 1/2 In. 295.00
Cup & Saucer, Florian, Blue 255.00
Dish, Fruit On Blue Ground, Marked, 7 1/4 In. 55.00
Dish, Pomegranate, 8 1/2 In. .... 90.00 To 100.00
Dish, Poppies, Green Ground, 11 X 2 In. 205.00
Goblet, Painted Panels, Gilding, Signed, 5 3/4 In. 525.00
Jardiniere, MacIntyre, Aurelian, 7 X 8 In. 275.00
Mug, 1911 Coronation 195.00
Mug, 1937 Coronation 165.00
Pitcher, Berries, Leaves, 7 In. 200.00
Pitcher, Florian, Silver Rim, 8 In. 500.00
Pitcher, Gesso Faience, MacIntyre, 6 In. 200.00
Plate, Aurelian Ware, Poppies, Blue & Gold Panels, 6 1/2 In. 75.00
Plate, Moonlight Blue, Brass Handle, 9 In. 355.00
Plate, Waving Corn, 8 In. .... 90.00 To 135.00
Tazza, Pomegranate, Plated Stem .... 190.00 To 200.00
Tazza, Wisteria, Stand 190.00
Tray, Store Display, Green Letters On White, 8 1/4 X 3 5/8 In. 75.00
Vase, Allover Peach Poppies, Green, 7 1/2 In. 195.00
Vase, Bara Ware, 4 In. 100.00
Vase, Blue Fruit Design, 12 1/2 In. 265.00
Vase, Blue To Green, Berries & Leaves, Signed, 5 1/4 In. 45.00
Vase, Blue, Natural Ware, 1930, 7 In. 70.00
Vase, Chrysanthemum, Painted, 6 In. 75.00
Vase, Cornflower, 8 In. 350.00
Vase, Cornflower, Mottled Green Ground, Signed, 5 1/2 In. 495.00
Vase, Flambe, 12 In. 150.00
Vase, Floral, Cobalt Blue Ground, Marked, 5 In. 35.00
Vase, Florian, Art Nouveau, Poppies, Tulips, 12 In. 500.00
Vase, Florian, Blue Poppies, 13 In. 650.00
Vase, Florian, Blue, 9 1/2 In. .... 315.00 To 325.00
Vase, Florian, Cornflowers, 11 In. 500.00
Vase, Florian, Globular, Chevrons, Flowers, 8 In. 285.00
Vase, Florian, Lilies, Blue, 12 In. .... 325.00 To 400.00
Vase, Florian, Poppies, 10 In. .... 350.00 To 450.00
Vase, Florian, Poppies, Blue & Green, 12 In. .... 600.00 To 700.00
Vase, Hazeldene, Squat, Olive Green, 4 In. 450.00
Vase, Hibiscus, Cobalt Ground, Corset Shape, Paper Label, 7 In. 45.00
Vase, Hibiscus, Dark Luster, 3 3/4 In. 75.00
Vase, Moonlight Blue, 11 In. 600.00
Vase, Mottled Yellow Trees, Blue Hills, Signed, 10 In. 1050.00
Vase, Narrow Base, Wide Middle, Narrow Neck, Orange, 14 In. 195.00
Vase, Natural Ware, Blue, 1930, 7 In. 75.00
Vase, Orange Luster, 8 In. 50.00
Vase, Orchid Flower, Cobalt Blue, Blue Print Mark, 2 In. 38.00
Vase, Pansy, 8 In. 200.00
Vase, Pink Hibiscus, Dark Blue Ground, Green Wreath, 10 In. 425.00
Vase, Poppy, Blue Background, Marked, 7 In. 360.00
Vase, White Flower Panels, Speckled Blue, 8 In. 165.00

Vase, Wisteria, Mottled Green Top, Blue Base, Signed, 14 1/2 In. 2200.00

> Some types of Japanese pottery and porcelain are decorated with a special type of raised decoration known as moriage. Sometimes pieces of clay were shaped by hand and applied to the item; sometimes the clay was squeezed from a tube in the way we apply cake frosting. One type of moriage is called dragonware and is listed under that name.

MORIAGE, Biscuit Jar, Lacy Slip Work, 7 1/4 In. 290.00
Candlestick, Red Flowers, Pastel Green 85.00
Decanter, Wine, Wheat Design, 7 3/4 In. 275.00
Ewer, Floral Medallion, Green, Allover Turquoise Beading, 9 In. 179.00
Humidor, House & Trees 75.00
Incense Burner, Dragon, Gold Finial, Handles, 3 X 4 In. 120.00
Jug, Wine, Monk Drinking From Jug, Stopper 525.00
Mug, Dragon, Green Wreath Mark 90.00
Mug, Lacy Slip Over Pink Roses, 5 1/2 In. 85.00
Pitcher, Turquoise Beading, Raised Enamel Design, 6 In. 250.00
Sugar & Creamer, Allover Roses, Applied Flowers 225.00
Sugar & Creamer, Rose Cover 200.00
Sugar Shaker, Pastel Flowers .... 85.00 To 95.00
Sugar, Beading 40.00
Sugar, Covered, Scalloped, Paste Design 45.00
Tankard, Floral Panels, Cobalt, Yellow & Green, 10 In. 290.00
Tea Set, Fuchsia Flowers, Green Trim, Mauve Ground, 13 Piece 675.00
Tea Set, White Cottages & Trees, Gray Matte, 3 Piece 165.00
Urn, Floral, Greens & Browns, Scalloped, 2 Handles 275.00
Vase, Allover Lacy Design, Handles, 7 1/4 In. 185.00
Vase, Corset Shape, Handles, Allover Slip Work, 11 1/2 In. 150.00
Vase, Deep Maroon, Floral, Applied Rigaree, Signed, 10 In. 135.00
Vase, Flowers, Grapes, Swallow, Double Handled, 12 In. 295.00
Vase, Green, Blue & Pink Trim, Floral Sprays, 2 3/4 In. 35.00
Vase, Hummingbird & Flowers, 16 In. 285.00
Vase, Medallion & Scene, Beaded, 2 1/2 In. 38.00
Vase, Peony, Turquoise Ground, Pink Jeweling 195.00
Vase, Pink & Blue Raised Work, Florals, Handle, Miniature 40.00
Vase, Swan Scene, 4 Sides, Grapes, 9 1/2 In. 225.00

> The Mosaic Tile Company of Zanesville, Ohio, was started by Karl Langerbeck and Herman Mueller in 1894. Many types of plain and ornamental tiles were made until 1959. The company closed in 1967. The company also made some ashtrays, bookends, and related gift wares. Most pieces are marked with the entwined MTC monogram.

MOSAIC TILE CO., Box, Cigarette, Dog On Cover, Shades of Green 200.00
Cookie Jar, Mammy .... 200.00 To 250.00
Tile, Bear, Black Glaze, 10 X 6 In. 68.00
Tile, General Pershing, Blue Jasperware, Oval 40.00

> Moser glass is made by Ludwig Moser und Sohne, a Bohemian glasshouse founded in 1857. Art Nouveau–type glassware and iridescent glassware were made. The most famous Moser glass is decorated with heavy enameling in gold and bright colors. The firm is still working in Czechoslovakia. Few pieces of Moser glass are marked.

MOSER, Bishop's Hat, Amber Gold Leaf, Green Design, Signed, 11 In. 110.00
Bowl, Blue Floral, Crystal, Triangular, 9 In. 175.00
Bowl, Pink Opalescent, Jewels Around Band, Signed, 7 1/4 X 9 In. 950.00
Bowl, Ribbed Base, Gold Greek Design, Signed, Pale Green, 10 In. 575.00
Box, Boy Feeding Ducks In Pond, Royal Blue, 5 1/2 In. 630.00
Box, Pink Berries, Gold Leaves, Green Glass, Covered, 2 X 3 3/8 In. 245.00
Box, Salamander On Hinged Lid & Forming Feet, Gold Trim, 4 1/2 In. 605.00
Celery Vase, Cranberry, Raised Florals, Square Top, Signed, 8 In. 175.00
Celery Vase, Gold Enameling, Cranberry, Signed, 6 In. 135.00
Celery Vase, Raised Enameled Daisies, Amberina, Signed, 6 1/2 In. 195.00

Chalice, Gold Design, Cranberry, Signed, 6 1/2 In.	145.00
Champagne, Gold Figural Design, Cupids At Play, Jewels, 6 In.	145.00
Compote, Cranberry Floral Etching, Signed, 7 1/2 In.	185.00
Compote, Floral Panels, Scalloped, Green, 7 In.	180.00
Compote, White Overlay Cut To Cranberry, Metal Base, Signed, 10 In.	395.00
Cordial, Green Cut To Clear	45.00
Creamer, Opalescent Blue, Allover Multicolored Leaves, Handle, 3 In.	450.00
Cruet, Amber & White Enameling, Applied Handles, 8 In., Pair	140.00
Cruet, Amber, Raised Florals, Square, Signed, 8 In.	125.00
Cruet, Gold Overlay, Faceted Stopper, Signed	125.00
Cruet, Portraits All Around, Clear Stopper & Base, Signed, 9 In.	165.00
Cup & Saucer, Dolphin Handle, Gold Trim, Cobalt Blue	140.00
Cup & Saucer, Enamel Filigree Flowers & Curliques, Blue	165.00
Cup & Saucer, Gold Cameo Etching, Extruded Ruby Panels, Signed	375.00
Decanter, Brandy, Gold Medallions, Ornate Stopper, Signed, 11 1/2 In.	210.00
Decanter, Wine, Raised Floral Enamel, Faceted Stopper, Signed	185.00
Ewer, Yellow Spatter, Appplied Gold Acorns, 9 In.	375.00
Finger Bowl, Underplate, Amberina, Enamel Design On Border	485.00
Finger Bowl, Underplate, Purple To Clear, Set of 12	400.00
Goblet, Water, Flower Form, Purple To Clear, 12 Piece	480.00
Goblet, Wine, Allover Gold, Prunts, Turquoise To Clear	369.00
Lamp, Crystal Prisms, Brass Base, Floral, Cranberry, 13 1/2 In., Pair	325.00
Lamp, Portrait, Brass Base, Cranberry, Electrified, Signed	275.00
Lamp, Portrait, Cranberry, Applied Porcelain Medallion, 15 1/2 In.	275.00
Mug, Amberina, Corset Shape, Enameled Flowers & Butterflies	125.00
Mug, Measuring, Rubina, Enameled Bird, Flowers, Millimeter Marks	175.00
Mug, Olive Amber, Gold Flowers & Leaves, Amber Handle, 1 In.	35.00
Nut Set, Leaf Shaped Bowls, 24K Gold Design, 7 Piece	750.00
Perfume Bottle, Cranberry, Portrait Medallion, Stopper, Pair	375.00
Perfume Bottle, Floral, Porcelain Medallions, Paneled Stem, 9 In.	235.00
Pitcher, Clear Handle, Floral Enameling, Handle, Signed, 4 1/2 In.	175.00
Pitcher, Cranberry Crackle, Clear Handle, Floral, Signed, 4 1/2 In.	175.00
Pitcher, Intaglio, Clear To Pale Peach, Metal Handle & Top, Marked	325.00
Pitcher, Lily of The Valley, Gold Trim, 12 In.	600.00
Pitcher, Raised Floral Enamel, Gold Trim, Signed, 8 1/2 In.	135.00
Pitcher, Raised Floral, Applied Handle, 10 In.	210.00
Pitcher, Tyrolian Youths, Beer Scene, Gold Tracery, 10 3/4 In.	445.00
Pitcher, Water, Grid Pattern, Gold Band, Amber, 1920s	300.00
Pitcher, Wine, Applied Amber Handle, Floral, Signed, 11 In.	245.00
Plate, Amberina, Gold Enamel Design, 7 3/8 In.	125.00
Plate, Scalloped, Deep Green, Signed, 12 In.	165.00
Powder Box, Gold & Enamel Design, Green	210.00
Rose Bowl, Enameled Flowers & Scrolls, Gold Design, Flared, Ruffled	165.00
Rose Bowl, Purple, Gilt Garden Scene, Ribbed, Crimped Top, 5 In.	105.00
Rose Bowl, Raised Enamel, Signed, Amber, 8 X 7 In.	285.00
Tea Caddy, Cranberry, Enameled Flowers, 4 Paw Feet, 4 X 6 X 7 In.	450.00
Urn, Intaglio Band of Scholars, Amethyst	250.00
Vase, 3 Colored Flowers, Applied Intaglio Cut Buds, Karlsbad, 7 In.	1250.00
Vase, 33 Jewels, Gold, Small Jewels Encircling Neck, Signed, 16 In.	265.00
Vase, Acorn & Acorn Leaf, Covered, Gold Berry Prunts, 26 1/2 In.	6000.00
Vase, Allover Gold Enameling, Cranberry, Signed, 11 1/4 In.	295.00
Vase, Amberina, Scalloped Top, Gold Design, Signed, 11 In.	260.00
Vase, Amethyst, Intaglio, Signed, 12 In.	225.00
Vase, Amethyst, Square Top, Floral Enameling, Signed, 11 In.	185.00
Vase, Amethyst, White Floral Overlay, Enameling, Pedestal, 10 In.	195.00
Vase, Applied Fish, Enameled Flowers, 5 In.	175.00
Vase, Birds In Flight, Cranberry, Crimped, Signed, 14 In.	315.00
Vase, Bud, Green Cut To Clear, 3 3/4 In.	145.00
Vase, Bulbous, Cranberry, Raised Gold, Signed, 16 In.	210.00
Vase, Clear To Deep Amethyst, Ruffled, Enameled Flowers, 7 In.	320.00
Vase, Cranberry To Clear Swirl, Floral Enameling, Signed, 13 1/2 In.	325.00
Vase, Cranberry, Gold Encrusted, Signed, 8 In.	175.00
Vase, Cranberry, Gold Overlay, Pedestal, Fluted, Signed, 16 1/2 In.	285.00
Vase, Cranberry, Scalloped, Signed, 14 In.	235.00

Vase, Cut Flower Panels, Presentation Piece, Moser–Karlsbad, 10 In.	175.00
Vase, Deep Amber, Gold Grecian Overlay, Signed, 8 3/4 In.	250.00
Vase, Enameled Flowers, Double Handles, Green, 10 In.	150.00
Vase, Frosted Pink With Gold, White, Signed, 11 In.	160.00
Vase, Gold Bird, Scalloped, Enameling, Cranberry, Signed, 14 In.	235.00
Vase, Gold Cut Back To Frosted White, Green, Metal Stand, 10 In.	365.00
Vase, Gold Design, Green, Signed, 15 1/2 In.	175.00
Vase, Gold Leaf Elephants, Signed, 8 In.	1250.00
Vase, Gold Lions & Palm Trees, Amber, Signed, 5 1/2 X 5 In.	210.00
Vase, Gold Tracery, Emerald Green, 13 In.	400.00
Vase, Green Cut, Heavy Gold, Signed, 9 In.	135.00
Vase, Green Reeds At Base, Fish Each Side, Crackle Glass, 5 1/4 In.	138.00
Vase, Green, White Enameling, Gold, Marked, 10 In.	135.00
Vase, Multicolored Animals, Pedestal, Artist Signed, 9 In.	235.00
Vase, Multicolored Enamel & Gilt, Triangular Pedestal, 8 1/4 In.	165.00
Vase, Pedestal, Cranberry, Gold, Signed, 15 In.	325.00
Vase, Pedestal, Scalloped, Cranberry, Signed, 9 In.	145.00
Vase, Portrait In Gold Scrolls, Allover Florals, Blue, 21 In., Pair	400.00
Vase, Portrait, Child, Gold, Signed, 8 1/2 In.	325.00
Vase, Portrait, Cranberry, Porcelain Medallion, Pedestal, 10 In., Pr.	825.00
Vase, Portrait, Gold Enameling, Pedestal, Porcelain Medallion, 14 In.	375.00
Vase, Portrait, Porcelain Medallion, Signed, 10 In.	235.00
Vase, Portrait, Woman On Oval, Gold Design On Green, Signed, 12 In.	395.00
Vase, Portrait, Woman On Oval, Overall Gold Design, Signed, 14 In.	525.00
Vase, Portrait, Young Woman, Applied Oval, Green, Signed, 10 3/4 In.	285.00
Vase, Raised Enamel Floral & Butterfly, Signed, 14 In.	145.00
Vase, Raised Floral & Gold, Signed, 9 In.	125.00
Vase, Raised Floral, Twist Shape, Signed, 13 1/2 In.	310.00
Vase, Raised Gold Enamel, Amethyst, Signed, 9 In.	130.00
Vase, Raised Gold, Clear To Cranberry, Pedestal, 13 1/2 In.	215.00
Vase, Salamander, 3 Salamander Feet, Enameled Bird, Signed, 9 1/2 In.	625.00
Vase, Scenic, Gold Leaf, Enameled, Amber, 11 In.	750.00
Vase, Swirl Design, 2 Fish Swimming, Topaz, 9 In. ....*Illus*	250.00
Vase, Trophy, Acorns, 3 Handles, Frosted To Crystal, 7 In.	325.00
Vase, Trumpet, Gold Enamel, Cranberry To Clear, 8 3/4 In.	195.00
Vase, Warrior, Amber, 12 Panel, 14 1/2 In.	195.00
Vase, White Ornaments, Opaque Green, Lavender, Beige, Signed, 11 In.	125.00
Vase, White Overlay, Cut To Cranberry, Gold, Signed, 13 1/2 In.	265.00
Water Set, Floral, Clear Applied Handle, Signed, 7 1/2 In., 3 Piece	200.00
Wine, Allover Gold Leaf, Designed Prunts, Turquoise To Clear	369.00
Wine, Flower Form, Purple To Clear, 12 Piece	450.00
Wine, Pale Green Etched Top, Clear Pedestal Base, Signed, 4 Piece	185.00

> Moss rose china was made by many firms from 1808 to 1900. It has
> a typical moss rose pictured as the design. The plant is not as
> popular now as it was in Victorian gardens, so the fuzz–covered bud
> is unfamiliar to most collectors. The dishes were usually decorated
> with pink and green flowers.

MOSS ROSE, Cup & Saucer, Demitasse, Japan	4.00
Plate & Platter Set, Child's, Japan	7.00
Plate, Ironstone, Meakin, 7 In.	12.50
Syrup, Stone China, Dated Pewter Lid, Marked	85.00
Tea Set, Demitasse, Japan, 11 Piece	22.00
Tray, Tiered	15.00

> Mother–of–pearl glass, or pearl satin glass, was first made in the
> 1850s in England and in Massachusetts. It was a special type of
> mold–blown satin glass with air bubbles in the glass, giving it a
> pearlized color. It has been reproduced. Mother–of–pearl shell
> objects are listed under Pearl.

MOTHER–OF–PEARL, Basket, Raindrop, White, Rose, 7 In.	295.00
Biscuit Jar, Herringbone, Gold Ferns, Flowers, 9 1/2 In.	600.00
Bottle, Perfume, Diamond–Quilted, Knobby Stopper, 4 In.	385.00
Bowl, 3 Frosted Feet & Neck, White Lining, Ruffled, 6 In.	245.00

Creamer, Frosted Handle, Wafer Foot, Blue, 2 3/4 In. 675.00
Cruet, Air Trap Swirl, Pinks, Original Stopper, 5 1/2 In. 435.00
Finger Bowl, Diamond-Quilted, Blue, Ground Pontil 85.00
Finger Bowl, Underplate, Diamond-Quilted, Striped, 6 In. 950.00
Mug, Diamond-Quilted, Flowers, Reeded Handle 375.00
Pitcher, Blue, Satin, Frosted Wafer Foot, Handle, 3 1/2 In. 245.00
Rose Bowl, Diamond-Quilted, Rose, Pink, 5 In. 295.00
Rose Bowl, Flower & Acorn, White Lining, 10 Crimp, 3 In. 265.00
Rose Bowl, Pink, Herringbone, White Lining, 3 1/4 In. 165.00
Rose Bowl, Satin Glass, 3 Crimp Top, White Lining, 3 In. 118.00
Saltshaker, Diamond-Quilted, Enamel Floral Branches 215.00
Saltshaker, Diamond-Quilted, Flower Branch, Blue 215.00
      MOTHER-OF-PEARL, SATIN GLASS, see Satin Glass; Smith Brothers; etc.
Tumbler, Diamond-Quilted, Pink To White ....92.00 To 127.00
Tumbler, Diamond-Quilted, Pink, 4 In. 75.00
Tumbler, Herringbone, Blue To White, 3 3/4 In. 85.00
Vase, Bulbous, Flared & Fluted Top, Satin Glass, 4 1/4 In. 225.00
Vase, Chartreuse, Ribbon, Frosted Wafer Foot, 2 1/2 In. 195.00
Vase, Diamond-Quilted, Gold To White, Egg Shape, 6 1/2 In. 245.00
Vase, Diamond-Quilted, Pink, Handle, 13 In. 365.00
Vase, Diamond-Quited, Pink Lining, 10 In. 495.00
Vase, Dimpled, American Beauty Rose, 4 5/8 In. 525.00
Vase, Gold Prunus, Blossoms, Branches, 4 1/8 In. 325.00
Vase, Gold Prunus, Frosted Foot, White Lining, 3 In. 350.00
Vase, Herringbone, Blue, 7 In. 110.00
Vase, Herringbone, Coralene Design, Butterflies, 10 In. 535.00
Vase, Herringbone, Ruffled, Florals, Butterfly, 6 1/4 In. 245.00
Vase, Medium Blue To Light Blue, Pedestal, 7 1/2 In. 195.00
Vase, Rivulet Pattern, White Lining, Petal Top, 5 3/8 In. 210.00
Vase, Satin, Star Coralene Pattern, White Lining, 4 In. 450.00
Vase, White Lining, Diamond-Quilted, Melon Ribbed, 9 In. 165.00
Vase, White Ribbon Pattern, Gilded, Medallions, 6 1/2 In. 1100.00
Water Set, Diamond-Quilted, Apricot To White, 7 Piece 1275.00
MOUSTACHE CUP, see Mustache Cup

Mt. Joye is an enameled cameo glass made in the late nineteenth and the twentieth centuries by Saint-Hilaire Touvoir de Varraux and Co. of Pantin, France. This same company made De Vez glass. Pieces were usually decorated with enameling. Most pieces are not marked.

MT.JOYE, Bottle, Perfume, Eggshell, Silver Plated Hinged Top, 5 1/2 In. 160.00
Pitcher, Brass Spout & Handle, Crystal, Green, Gold, Signed 485.00
Vase, Enameled Leaves, Poppies On Chipped Ice Ground, 8 1/2 In. 385.00
Vase, Open Flower On Stem, Leaves, Gold Outline, Amber, 12 In. 375.00

The Mt. Washington Glass Works started in 1837 in South Boston, Massachusetts. In 1869 the company moved to New Bedford, Massachusetts. Many types of art glass were made there to the 1890s. These included Burmese, Crown Milano, Royal Flemish, and others.

MT.WASHINGTON, Berry Set, Inverted Thumbprint, Amberina, 5 Piece 225.00
Biscuit Jar, Floral Enameling, Silver Plated Top, 7 In. 195.00
Biscuit Jar, Flowers, Silver Plated Bail, Cover, Pairpoint 350.00
Biscuit Jar, Gold Flowers, Stems, Silver Plated Lid, Handle 400.00
Bowl, Burmese, Yellow Rim, 3 3/4 X 2 1/2 In. 225.00
Bowl, Cream Lining, Footed, 5 In. 130.00
Bowl, Peppermint, 8 3/4 X 2 5/8 In. 125.00
Bowl, Winged Animals, Pink To Red Cased On White, 8 1/2 In. 225.00
Box, Covered, Metal, Christmas Holly, Berries, Signed, 5 In. 325.00
Box, Enameled Floral, Word Handkerchief, White, 5 X 6 In. 95.00
Box, Jewelry, Hinged Lid, Raised Floral, Signed, 5 1/2 In. 210.00
Box, Raised Enameling, Metal Trim, Footed, Signed, 4 In. 295.00
Box, Shell Design On Hinged Cover, Lined, 3 1/2 In. 125.00

Compote, Enameling, Silver Plated Base, Signed, 9 1/4 In. 275.00
Compote, Ribbed Top, Metal Stand, Beige, Signed, 8 1/2 In. 285.00
Cracker Jar, Burmese, Oak Leaves & Acorns 595.00
Creamer, Burmese, Wishbone Feet, Water Scene 975.00
Cruet, Ribbed, Yellow Handle, Ribbed Stopper, 7 In. 795.00
Cuspidor, Amberina, Optic Ribbing, 2 1/2 In. 250.00
Dish, Sweetmeat, Cornflowers, Gold Design, 4 1/2 In. 275.00
Ewer, Burmese, Rigaree Handle, 6 1/4 In. 225.00
Ewer, Egyptian Style Duckbill 2500.00
Finger Bowl, 9 Crimp Top, Salmon Pink To Yellow, 5 In. 195.00
Flower Frog, Mushroom, Roses, White Satin 135.00
Lamp, Kerosene, Lava Glass 1500.00
Mustard, Bristol Ring Neck, Pansy Design 75.00
Mustard, Fig Mold, Pagoda Lid .... 165.00 To 235.00
Pitcher, Amberina, Reed Handle 300.00
Pitcher, Burmese Duckbill, 12 In. 985.00
Pitcher, Burmese, Squatty, 2 Qt. 585.00
Pitcher, Mother-of-Pearl, Blue, 7 1/2 In. 735.00
Powder Box, Brass Rim, Raised Flower On Hinged Lid, 5 In. 325.00
Powder Box, Frosted Pink, Elephant Finial, Round, 6 1/2 In. 45.00
Rose Bowl, Applied Burmese Icing 925.00
Rose Jar, Covered, White, Ovoid, Berry Pontil, 5 In. 185.00
Salt & Pepper, 6 Lobes, Floral Design, Pair 185.00
Salt & Pepper, Amberina, Fuchsia, C.1880, Pair 275.00
Salt & Pepper, Burmese, Pansies 470.00
Salt & Pepper, Egg Shape, Flat Side, 1893 Centennial 100.00
Saltshaker, Burmese, Pink Roses 235.00
Saltshaker, Fig Shape, Cobalt Blue & Lavender Florals 135.00
Saltshaker, Figural, Hand Painted Flowers, White Satin 70.00
Saltshaker, Flat Sided Egg, 1893 Expo., White .... 85.00 To 115.00
Saltshaker, Tomato, Red Holly Berries, Leaves, Original Top 58.00
Sugar & Creamer, Burmese, Rigaree Handles 425.00
Sugar & Creamer, Burmese, Squat, Yellow Rim 575.00
Sugar Shaker, Egg Shape, Pink, Enameled Flowers 185.00
Sugar Shaker, Egg Shape, White, Blue Flower Design 185.00
Sugar Shaker, Pansies & Leaves, Egg Shape .... 145.00 To 185.00
Sugar Shaker, Salt & Pepper, Enameled Asters, Leaves, Vines 325.00
Toothpick, Burmese, Enameled Flowers, 2 In. 465.00
Toothpick, Fig Mold, Pink To White Ground 245.00
Tumbler, Diamond-Quilted, Fuchsia Amberina 175.00
Tumbler, Expanded Diamond, Fuchsia Amberina 275.00
Tumbler, Peachblow, Pink Upper Area, Blue Band At Base 1150.00
Tumbler, Whiskey, Diamond-Quilted, 2 5/8 In. 325.00
Vase, Burmese, Elongated Egg Shape, Daisy Blossoms, 9 In. 785.00
Vase, Burmese, Queen's Design, 8 In. 1085.00
Vase, Gourd Shape, Foliage, Buds, Traceries, 12 In. 1475.00
Vase, Mother-of-Pearl, Blue Diamond Pattern, 11 1/2 In. 825.00
Vase, Pelicans, Marsh, Square, Blue, Frame, 10 In., Pair 475.00
Vase, Queen's Design, Gourd Shape, 7 In. 1850.00
Vase, Ribbed Lily, Fuchsia Amberina, 7 In. 350.00
Vase, Tea Roses Both Sides, Shell Handles, Square Top 1050.00

Mud figures are small Chinese pottery figures made in the twentieth
century. The figures usually represent workers, scholars, farmers, or
merchants. Other pieces are trees, houses, and similar parts of the
landscape. The figures have unglazed faces and hands but glazed
clothing. They were originally made for fish tanks or planters. Mud
figures were of little interest and brought low prices until the 1980s.
When the prices rose, reproductions appeared.

MUD FIGURE, 2 Elders, 1 Holding Quiver & 1 Holding Plate, 5 In. 42.00
Chinese Elder, Coin Carrier, 10 In. 87.50
Chinese Elder, Holding Quiver On Shoulders 38.00
Chinese Elder, Plate In Hand 38.00
Chinese Elder, Yoke Across Shoulders, Green Robe, 3 In. 32.00

Chinese Man With Book, 3 In. 24.00
Chinese Man, Sitting, Robed, 5 1/2 In. 45.00
Man, Robed, Bearded, Standing, Impressed China, 9 In. 70.00
Man, Sitting, Holding Basket of Flowers, 6 1/2 In. 50.00
Man, Standing, Robed, Bearded, Marked China, 9 In. 70.00
Men, Various Positions, Brown Enamel, 1 To 1/4 In., Set of 7 .... 85.00

> Mulberry ware was made in the Staffordshire district of England from about 1850 to 1860. The dishes were decorated with a transfer design of a reddish brown, now called "mulberry." Many of the patterns are similar to those used for flow blue and other Staffordshire transfer wares.

MULBERRY, Bowl, Vegetable, Covered, Jeddo 250.00
Creamer, Brush Stroke 85.00
Creamer, Jeddo, Adams 110.00
Creamer, Vincennes, Alcock 80.00
Cup & Saucer, Castle Scenery, Handleless 50.00
Cup & Saucer, Hyson, Handleless 55.00
Cup & Saucer, Jeddo, Handleless 60.00
Cup & Saucer, Royal Rose 45.00
Cup & Saucer, Temple, Podmore Walker 40.00
Cup & Saucer, Vincennes, Alcock, Handleless 55.00
Gravy Boat, Peru, Holcroft 65.00
Nappy, Tivili, Meigh 18.00
Nappy, Washington, Podmore Walker 25.00
Pitcher, Cyprus, Davenport, 12 In. 125.00
Pitcher, Jeddo, 1 Qt. 165.00
Pitcher, Milk, Washington, Podmore Walker 250.00
Plate, Allegheny, 9 In. 40.00
Plate, Calcutta, 10 In. 50.00
Plate, Corean, 9 In. 40.00
Plate, Corean, Clementson, 12 Sides, Set of 10 .... 250.00
Plate, Jeddo, 9 1/2 In. 50.00
Plate, Medina, 8 In. 35.00
Plate, Napoleon Portrait, 8 1/2 In. 25.00
Plate, New York University, Wedgwood, 1932, Set of 10 .... 90.00
Plate, Ning PO, 9 1/2 In. 70.00
Plate, Percy, 9 1/2 In. 45.00
Plate, Rhone Scenery, 9 1/2 In. 45.00
Plate, Venus, Podmore Walker, 9 1/2 In. 38.00
Plate, Vincennes, Alcock, 10 In. 50.00
Plate, Washington Vase, 9 In. 40.00
Platter, Bochara, 14 In. 95.00
Platter, Corean, Davenport, 8 Sides, 13 3/4 X 10 3/8 In. 95.00
Platter, Heath's Flower, 13 1/2 In. 95.00
Platter, Marble, 15 1/2 X 12 In. 85.00
Platter, Vincennes, Alcock, 15 1/2 X 11 1/2 In. 125.00
Platter, Washington Vase, 16 X 12 1/2 In. 100.00
Relish, Corean 65.00
Saucer, Washington Vase 25.00
Soup, Dish, Cypress, 9 1/4 In. 42.00
Soup, Dish, Pelew, 9 7/8 In. 65.00
Sugar, Corean, Lion Head Handles 125.00
Sugar, Covered, Vincennes, Alcock 135.00
Teapot, Corean 225.00
Teapot, Jeddo 250.00
Wash Bowl, Bochara 95.00

> Muller Freres, French for Muller Brothers, made cameo and other glass from the early 1900s to the late 1930s. Their factory was first located in Luneville, then in nearby Croismaire, France. Pieces were usually marked with the company name.

MULLER FRERES, Lamp, Glass and Iron, Dome Shade, C.1920, 13 3/4 In. 7700.00
Lamp, Glass and Iron, Helmet Form, C.1920, 10 1/4 In. 6325.00

Moser, Vase, Swirl Design,
2 Fish Swimming,
Topaz, 9 In.

Muller Freres, Vase, Landscape, Signed,
C.1910, 10 1/2 In.

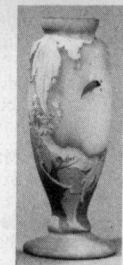

Muller Freres, Vase,
Berry Laden Branches,
C.1920, 11 3/4 In.

Lamp, Iron Stem, Signed, Dome Shade, 16 In.	625.00
Lamp, Metal Openwork Base, Dome Glass Shade, Mauve	450.00
Vase, Berry Laden Branches, C.1920, 11 3/4 In. ....*Illus*	2970.00
Vase, Boats, Mountains, Peach Ground, Signed, 10 In.	650.00
Vase, Cameo, Branches, Moth, C.1920, 11 3/4in.	2970.00
Vase, Cameo, Landscape, C.1920, 15 1/2 In	5775.00
Vase, Fisherman In Boat Scene, 4 Layers, Squat, 3 In.	550.00
Vase, Landscape, Signed, C.1910, 10 1/2 In. ....*Illus*	4675.00
Vase, Mottled Orange To Brown At Base, Signed, 6 In.	150.00
Vase, Mountain & Waterfall Scene, Signed, 9 1/2 In.	2650.00
Vase, Purple Crocuses Over White Milk Glass, Signed, 8 In.	450.00
Vase, Shepherd & Flock of Sheep, Signed, 6 1/2 In.	1175.00
Vase, Windmill & Cottages By Shore, Signed, 13 1/4 In.	1195.00

MUNCIE   The Muncie Clay Products Company was established by Charles Benham in Muncie, Indiana, in 1922. The company made pottery for the florist and gift shop trade. The company closed by 1939. Pieces are marked with the name "Muncie" or just with a system of numbers and letters like "1A."

MUNCIE, Vase, Charcoal, Rust Flambe, 4 In.	25.00
Vase, Mottled Orange Glaze, 3 1/4 In.	25.00
Vase, Red Orange, Signed, 4 In.	30.00

Music boxes, musical instruments, and sheet music are listed in this section. Phonograph records, jukeboxes, and phonographs are listed in other sections in this book.

MUSIC, Accordion, Brass Keys, German	60.00
Accordion, Dallape Special, 1932	1000.00
Accordion, Hohner, 1900s, Marked	250.00
Accordion, Kahn & Uhlmann	65.00
Aeolian Orchestrelle, Style A	2900.00
Automaton, 2 Singing Birds In Cage, French, 1900, 21 X 11 In.	1000.00
Automaton, Bicyclist, Decamps, Bisque Head, C.1880, 13 1/2 In.	4675.00
Automaton, Bird In Cage, Windup, Flaps Wings, Tin, 7 X 9 1/2 In.	395.00

If you have an old piano, beware of moths. They sometimes infest the interior fabrics.

Automaton, Birds In Shadow Box, Gilded Gesso, Swiss, 16 X 20 In. 1600.00
Automaton, Black Lute Player, Decamps, Papier–Mache Head, 26 In. 5500.00
Automaton, Carousel, Mirrored Standard, 3 Figures, C.1890, 20 In. 3025.00
Automaton, Dancing Monkey, Kicking Leg, Swinging Arms, French, 32 In. 2750.00
Automaton, Doll, Bisque Face, Playing Harp, C.1850, 8 X 18 In. 1000.00
Automaton, Girl With Bird In Basket, Jumeau Head, Lambert, 21 In. 3300.00
Automaton, Gymnast, Bisque Head, All Original, Working, 27 In. 1150.00
Automaton, Lady Playing Guitar, Theroude, Silk Dress, C.1870, 15 In. 6050.00
Automaton, Lady Playing Tambourine, Head Turns, Hand Shakes, 17 In. 3575.00
Automaton, Lady, Basket & Dog, Bisque Head, Nods, Dog Peers Twice 3575.00
Automaton, Magician, Renou, Bisque Head, 19th Century, 24 In. 7425.00
Automaton, Monkey Harpist, Silk Waistcoat, Blinking Eyes, 20 In. 3300.00
Automaton, Pierrot Playing Violin, Nodding Head, 25 In. 3575.00
Automaton, Pierrot Serenading Moon, French 5500.00
Automaton, Polar Bear, French, Early 1900s 1600.00
Automaton, Tree, Birds Hop Branch To Branch, Ship, Clock Base, French 5775.00
Banjo, 1910 .... 125.00
Box, 3 Monkeys, Playing Instruments, Mahogany, Phalibois, C.1880 .... 3500.00
Box, Ariston Organette, 23 Discs 650.00
Box, Autograph Album, After The Ball & Oh Promise Me, Celluloid 200.00
Box, Bird, Blue & White Enameled, Brass, Lapis Corners, German, 1930 .... 995.00
Box, Cartel, Green Tole, 14 Piece Comb, 5 Tooth Sections 500.00
Box, Christmas Carousel, Wooden, German 20.00
Box, Console Disc, Rookwood Case, Paintings, 20 3/4 In. 9500.00
Box, Criterion, 76 Note, Carved Mahogany Case 2350.00
Box, Criterion, Gold Anodized Design, Adeste Fideles, 11 1/2 In. 20.00
Box, Fortuna, Upright, 6 Discs, 21 1/4 In. 3250.00
Box, Lecoultre, Key Wind, 8 Tune, Maple Case, 19th Century, 20 In. 885.00
Box, M.Bolivillier, 6 Tunes On Original Card, 18 In. 885.00
Box, Mermod Bros., Cylinder, 12 Tunes, Original Program Card, 1895 .... 2200.00
Box, Mermod Freres, 3 Interchangeable Cylinders, 11 In. 2800.00
Box, Mermod Freres, Interchangeable Cylinder, Carved Oak 1800.00
Box, Mermod Ideal Guitare, 8 Cylinders, Drawer, Base 4800.00
Box, Mira, Disc, 15 1/2 In. 3300.00
Box, Monopol, Coin–Operated, Double Comb, Oak Case, Discs, 42 In. 1750.00
Box, Monopol, Double Comb, Walnut Case 2400.00
Box, New Century, 2 Tunes Each Disc 6500.00
Box, New Haven Lohengrin, Mantel, C.1890 .... 275.00
Box, Nicole Freres, Model P41 .... 2900.00
Box, Ohio Art, Children & Animals, Litho, 9 In. 12.00
Box, Orchestral, 6 Cylinders, Matching Table, Large 7000.00
Box, Paillard, Cylinder, Organ Section, Coin–Operated, Walnut Case 6500.00
Box, Perfection, Oak Case 2200.00
Box, Perfection, Oak Case, 2 Discs, 14 In. 1250.00
Box, Pirouette, Cigarette In Mouth, Mandolin, Valencia, German, 24 In. 255.00
Box, Polyphon, Coin–Operated, Crank, Glazed Mahogany Case, 38 In. 1750.00
Box, Polyphon, Upright, Base, 8 Ft. 8500.00
Box, Regina, 28 Discs, 20 In. 3900.00
Box, Regina, Crank, 15 1/2 In. 45.00
Box, Regina, Disc, 15 In. 1250.00
Box, Regina, Double Comb, Oak Case 3200.00
Box, Regina, Mahogany, Serpentine, 23 Discs, 20 3/4 In. 3400.00
Box, Regina, No.20, Rookwood Case, With Paintings 9500.00
Box, Regina, No.50, Double Comb, Table Model, Oak 3500.00
Box, Regina, Orchestral, Upright, 20 Discs 5495.00
Box, Regina, Stop–Start Switch, Oak Box, 13 Discs, 13 In. 880.00
Box, Regina, Sublima, Coin–Operated, C.1900, 70 In. 6600.00
Box, Regina, Table Model, 35 Discs, 22 1/2 X 20 In. 4000.00
Box, Reginaphone, No.246 .... 3500.00
Box, Reuge, Sublime Harmonie, Hymn Box 1250.00
Box, Stellia–Thornwall, Disc 2000.00
Box, Swiss, 3 Interchangeable Cylinders, Rosewood Case, 34 In. 3520.00
Box, Swiss, 8 Tunes, Inlaid, R.Giler Mechanism, C.1880, 28 X 11 In. 2195.00
Box, Swiss, Brass Cylinder Roll, 11 In. 500.00

Box, Swiss, Brass Cylinder Roll, 20 In.	1000.00
Box, Swiss, Cylinder, 6 Tunes, Late 19th Century, 18 1/4 In.	275.00
Box, Swiss, Key Wind, 8 Tunes, C.1840, 19 In.	550.00
Box, Swiss, Piccolo Zither	550.00
Box, Symphonion, Center Crank, Ebonized Box, 13 Discs, 12 1/2 In.	550.00
Box, Symphonion, Eroica, Triple Disc	8000.00
Box, Symphonion, No.345361, Oak & Walnut Case, 10 Discs, 19 In.	1210.00
Box, Wooden, Amber Bakelite Feet, Mirror Lid, Plays Anchors Aweigh	35.00
Bugle, Army, U.S.Regulator	25.00
Calliaphone, Tangley CA–43, Rootes Blower, Roll Or Keyboard	9000.00
Calliope Pipes, Eastlake, Blue, Yellow, Brown & Gold Paint, 1860s	895.00
Calliope, Kozak Player Piano Co., Vacuum Motor, Control Stack	495.00
Cigar Box Instrument, Maybell, Folk Art, No Strings	25.00
Clarinet, Boxwood & Ivory, C.1830	275.00
Clarinet, Cavalier, Silver	25.00
Concertina, Abalone Ornate Work	90.00
Doll, Clown, Musical, Dressed In Red, White & Blue, Holding U.S.Flag	14.95
Drum, American Eagle, Shields, Flags, Original Paint, 23 X 25 In.	500.00
Duster, Record, Columbia, Round, Embossed In Wood	15.00
Flute, Haynes, Sterling Silver, Case, 1909	2200.00
Guitar, Alvarez, Case, 1950s	80.00
Guitar, Buck Jones	55.00
Guitar, C.F.Martin, Abalone Trim, C.1920	1500.00
Guitar, Gibson, Flat Top, Mahogany, Tortoiseshell Binding, Pick Guard	265.00
Guitar, Gibson, Les Paul Custom, 1960	2500.00
Guitar, Martin, D–35	750.00
Guitar, Martin, No.00021, 6 String	1250.00
Harmonica, Butterfly, Occupied Japan	18.00
Harmonica, Hohner's Best, Case	65.00
Harmonica, Hohner, Little Lady, Box	18.00
Harmonica, Hohner, Marine Band, No.1896, Box	27.00
Harmonica, Kromer, Case, 8 In.	30.00
Harmonica, Tuckaway, Late 1920s, Box	15.00
Harmonium, Wooden Case, English	85.00
Harp, Deacon, Bells, 37 Note	1200.00
Harp, Fluted Post, Tin Resonator, Blue & Gold Paint, Pat.1874, 31 In.	750.00
Harpsichord, Zuckerman	500.00
Hexaphone, Regina, Oak	4500.00
Horn, Fox Hunter, Brass, Leather Case, English, 3 1/2 Ft.	150.00
Hurdy–Gurdy, Piano Shape, 6 Tunes, Late 1800s, Barcelona, 23 In.	1800.00
Jew's Harp, Iron, Brass Skimmer, 18th Century	135.00
Kit, Piano Tuner's, 1902	195.00
Losche Orchestrion, 15 Mirrors, 4 Lamps	5000.00
Mandolin Harp, Music & Tuning Key, Original Box	1200.00
Mandolin, Gibson, Style A, Blond Face, Mahogany Back, 1910	400.00
Mandolin, Label, M.E.Schoening	75.00
Mandolin, Lyon & Healy, Style A	570.00
Mandolin, Martha, Model 0–28, 1929	750.00
Melodeon, Geo.A.Price Co., Rosewood, Books, 1848	1250.00
Melodeon, Rosewood, Tapered Octagon Legs, Stool	950.00
Metronome, DeMaelzel, Seth Thomas, Windup, Wooden Case	35.00
Metronome, Mahogany, 1800s	80.00
Metronome, Seth Thomas, Walnut, Key	38.00
Nickelodeon, Fox Pianotainer, 30 Rolls	1250.00
Nickelodeon, Link, Model 2E	8900.00
Nickelodeon, National	3000.00
Nickelodeon, Seeburg, Cabinet Style, Stained Glass, Oak	7500.00
Nickelodeon, Seeburg, Leaded Glass Panels, 2 Instruments, 7 Rolls	6655.00
Nickelodeon, Seeburg, Model A, Oak, Restored	2950.00
Nickelodeon, Seeburg, Model L, Stained Glass, Mahogany Case	5750.00
Nickelodeon, Standard, Upright, Oak, Art Glass, Restored, 25 Cents	6500.00
Nickelodeon, Weiser & Sons, Art Glass, 1917	5000.00
Nickelodeon, Western Electric, Mascot, Oak	6800.00
Organ, Aeolian, Style 17, Player, Stool, 44 Rolls, Walnut Case	2500.00

Piano keys can be cleaned with yogurt.

The label of Antonius Stradivarius has been forged and appears in many 19th- and 20th-century violins of low value. One type of labeled violin was offered in the Sears catalog for $7.

Organ, Bandola, Band, 125 Rolls	8500.00
Organ, Barrel, On Pushcart	3960.00
Organ, Clarion, Paper Roll	295.00
Organ, Clough & Warren, Pump, Burl Trim, Patent 1884	1600.00
Organ, Cornish, Parlor, Walnut, Hutch Top, Scalloped Mirror	450.00
Organ, Crown, Mirror, 1900	2250.00
Organ, Estey, Church, 2 Keyboards, Floor Pedals, Oak, Electrified	3000.00
Organ, Estey, Pump, Candlestand, 13 Stops, Walnut	1200.00
Organ, Gem, Roller, 10 Cobs	400.00
Organ, Gulbransen, Preacher's, 4 Octave Keyboard, Case	165.00
Organ, Hammond, B–3, Leslie Speaker	3500.00
Organ, Kilgan, Theater, 88 Note, Roll Player, 3 Ranks	2000.00
Organ, Kimball, Pump, Oak, 1890s	1100.00
Organ, Mandolina, Roll	500.00
Organ, Mason Hamlin, Pump, 2 Keyboards, External Air Connection, 1896	1500.00
Organ, National, Parlor, Oak	300.00
Organ, Perlee of Amsterdam, Front Panels, 25 Notes, Books	6500.00
Organ, Pipe, Hook & Hastings, 1914	500.00
Organ, Playrola, With Music	250.00
Organ, Prinsen, Table Top, 32 Key, Book–Operated, Dutch, 6 Books	5950.00
Organ, Story & Clark, Walnut, 7 Ft.	1750.00
Organ, Trumpet Hurdy–Gurdy, Barrel Pipe	6000.00
Organ, Wurlitzer, No.103, Band, Restored	9500.00
Organ, Wurlitzer, No.146, Band	6500.00
Organ, Wurlitzer, No.4430, Reed Electronic, French Provincial	650.00
Organette, C.Ariona, 5 Rolls	350.00
Piano Roll, Old Black Joe, Original Box	22.00
Piano, Bloomfield & Otis, Grand, Square, Rosewood	500.00
Piano, Boardman & Gray, Grand, Square, Rosewood, Early 1800s	600.00
Piano, Charles Steiff, Grand, Square, Rosewood, C.1870, 82 X 39 In.	3200.00
Piano, Chickering & Mackay, Grand, Square, No.3988	2500.00
Piano, Chickering, Grand, Square, Rosewood	500.00
Piano, English Cottage, 6 1/2 Octave, Carved Rosewood, 1860	1500.00
Piano, Haines, Ampico, Reproducing, Upright	900.00
Piano, Hallet & Davis, Grand, Square, Rosewood, C.1850	1000.00
Piano, Hallet, Davis & Co., Grand, Carved Rosewood Case, Chair, 1898	5000.00
Piano, Henry F.Miller, Grand, Rosewood Legs, Late 1800s	5000.00
Piano, J.& C.Fischer Ampico, Reproducing, Rebuilt	2000.00
Piano, J.& C.Fischer, Grand, Square, Rosewood	500.00
Piano, Kimball, Baby Grand	800.00
Piano, Kimball, Grand, Square, Stool, Walnut	2500.00
Piano, Knabe Ampico, Reproducing Grand, William & Mary Walnut Case	9500.00
Piano, Lauberger & Gloss, Baby Grand, Beech Parquetry, 5 Ft.7 In.	5500.00

Piano, Marshall & Wendell Ampico, Reproducing, Walnut, 5 Ft.8 In.	7900.00
Piano, Niendorf, Baby Grand, Louis XVI Style, Painted, Stool, C.1915	7700.00
Piano, Player, Adam Schaff, 88 Note, 40 Rolls	3000.00
Piano, Player, Baldwin Manualo	2000.00
Piano, Player, Cecilian Farrand	650.00
Piano, Player, Chickering, Baby Grand, 1912	5000.00
Piano, Player, Chickering, Baby Grand, Stoddard Ampico, Mahogany	6900.00
Piano, Player, Cremona, Coin–Operated, 1905	3500.00
Piano, Player, Everette Orchestrion, Upright, 1905	5000.00
Piano, Player, Howard, Baldwin, Motorized, Burled Walnut	3000.00
Piano, Player, Jesse French, Simplex Action, Electric, Restored	2300.00
Piano, Player, Kimball, Grand, 25 Rolls	3500.00
Piano, Player, Knabe, Grand, Ampico, 1923, 5 Ft.3 In.	3500.00
Piano, Player, Steck, Duo–Art, Queen Anne, Walnut	6200.00
Piano, Player, Story & Clark, Coin–Operated, Oak, Electrified	1050.00
Piano, Player, Stroud Duo–Art, Upright, Electric, 25 Rolls	4500.00
Piano, Player, Studio Figure, Fancy Legs, Walnut, 1926, 45 In.	1750.00
Piano, Player, Sublima, Regina, Oval Window, Coin–Operated, Oak	5500.00
Piano, Player, Weber Duo–Art, Figured Mahogany, 6 Ft.	4800.00
Piano, Steinway & Sons, Carved Rosewood, C.1850	1045.00
Piano, Steinway, Grand, Square, Rosewood, C.1875	5900.00
Piano, Welte, Ellington, Upright	3200.00
Piano, Welte, Vorsetzer, Polished Ebony, 1926	4500.00
Piano, Wing & Son, Grand, Concert, 5 Pedal	600.00
Piano, Wurlitzer, Baby Grand, Celluloid Keys, Bench, C.1932	925.00
Stafford Orchestrion, Leaded Glass, Lamps	8000.00
Tambourine, Painted Black Face, Li'1 Savannah Minstrel Co., 11 In.	350.00
Violin, Flame Maple Back, Original Varnish, Jais, Germany, C.1848	3250.00
Violin, Klingenthal, Restored, Germany, C.1860	5000.00
Violin, Stradivarius, Anton Winter Copy, Bow, Case, 1917	3000.00

The mustache cup was popular from 1850 to 1900 when the large, flowing mustache was in style. A ledge of china or silver held the hair out of the liquid in the cup. This kept the mustache tidy and also kept the mustache wax from melting. Left–handed mustache cups are rare but are being reproduced.

MUSTACHE CUP, Blue Onion, Brandenburg	35.00
Comic Actor, Holding Banner, Barber Supply Co.	325.00
Floral Engraving, Tufts, Inscribed, 1869–87	85.00
Saucer, Blue Flowers, Pink Scroll, Gold Handle, Haviland	125.00
Saucer, Leaf & Bow Design, Figural Handle, Gold Rim, 1902	95.00
Saucer, Left–Handed, Pink & White Roses	48.00
Saucer, Red Roses On Green, Germany	55.00
Silver Plate, Saucer, Tufts, Engraved Floral	75.00

"MZ Austria" is the wording on a mark used by Moritz Zdekauer on porcelains made at his works from about 1900. The firm worked in the town of Alt–Rohlau, Austria. The pieces were decorated with lavish floral patterns and overglaze gold decoration. Full sets of dishes were made as well as vases, toilet sets, and other wares.

Mz Austria

MZ AUSTRIA, Bowl, Oriental Bird, On Branch, Square, 7 3/4 In.	30.00
Chocolate Set, Floral, 6 Sides, Signed, 13 Piece	175.00
Dish, Child's, Dog, Cat, Chicken, Ducks, Rim, 7 In.	165.00
Fish Set, Scalloped Plate, Gravy Boat, Underplate, 10 Piece	115.00
Sugar Shaker, Blue Border of Roses, Double Eagle Mark	55.00
Teapot, Rose Design, Flower Finial, Marked, 6 1/2 In.	120.00

Nailsea glass was made in the Bristol district in England from 1788 to 1873. It was made by many different factories, not just the Nailsea Glass House. Many pieces were made with loopings of either white or colored glass as decoration.

NAILSEA, Bottle, Perfume, Glass Stopper, 3 In.	45.00
Cup, Cordial, Pair	75.00
Flask, Blue, White Looping, 9 In.	125.00
Flask, Chestnut, Deep Red, White Looping, 4 5/8 In.	160.00
Flask, Opalescent Looping, 7 5/8 In.	50.00
Flask, Pink & White, 1800, 8 In.	115.00
Flask, Red & White, Blue Looping, 6 1/4 In.	110.00
Lamp, Crystal, White Looping, Cranberry Threading Top, 13 In.	995.00
Pipe, Cranberry Swirl Glass, Hand Blown, 19 In.	150.00
Rolling Pin, Clear, Red Looping, 12 In.	110.00
Rolling Pin, Red & White, 17 In.	135.00
Rolling Pin, White, Red Looping, 14 1/2 In.	118.00
Rolling Pin, White, Red Looping, 17 In.	125.00
Vase, Red, White Looping, Black Glass Foot, Handles, 9 1/2 In.	275.00
Vase, Trumpet Form, Blue & White, Double Ring, 14 In., Pair	660.00

NAKARA

Nakara is a trade name for a white glassware made about 1900 by the C. F. Monroe Company of Meriden, Connecticut. It was decorated in pastel colors. The glass was very similar to another glass made by the company called "Wave Crest." The company closed in 1916. Boxes for use on a dressing table are the most commonly found Nakara pieces. The mark is not found on every piece.

NAKARA, Basket, Blue, 3 1/2 In.	250.00
Bowl, Radish, Underplate, 5 In.	100.00
Box, Collar & Cuff, Pale Blue Flowers, Leaves, Beading, 8 1/2 In.	675.00
Box, Cupids On Lid, Holding Harp & Music, Red, 3 3/4 In.	350.00
Box, Hinged Lid, Octagonal, Hand Painted Iris, Signed, 6 In.	625.00
Box, Hinged Lid, Pink, Blue, & White Floral, 8 X 5 In.	1295.00
Box, Jewelry, Glass, Floral Design, Hinged, Lined, Round, 2 3/4 In.	245.00
Box, Pink Satin, Cupids On Lid, 3 1/2 In.	375.00
Box, Ring, Portrait	495.00
Creamer, Old Man In The Mountain	70.00
Humidor, Indian Chief, Dark Green, Brass Rim & Cover	495.00
Letter Holder, Indian Portrait, Footed, 5 X 4 1/2 In.	465.00
Vase, Enameled Floral, Metal Handles, Green, Dolphin Feet, 12 In.	725.00
Vase, Hexagonal Base, Hand Painted Florals, Beading, Signed, 13 In.	865.00
Vase, Ormolu Foot, Green Center, Applied Pink Flowers, 13 7/8 In.	350.00
Vase, Pink To Gray, Beading, Roses, Footed, 14 In.	525.00
Vase, Rose Sprays, Ormolu Collar, Green Ground, Footed, 9 1/2 In.	485.00

Nanking is a type of blue–and–white porcelain made in Canton, China, since the late eighteenth century. It is very similar to Canton, which is listed under its own name in this book. Both Nanking and Canton are part of a larger group now called "Chinese Export" porcelain. Nanking has a spear–and–post border and may have gold decoration.

NANKING, Bowl, Mountain Scene, Blue, White, C.1850, 6 X 14 1/2 In. ....*Illus*	1300.00
Dish, Covered, Bud Finial, Draped Shield, Monogram, 12 1/2 In.	325.00
Platter, Dart Border, 17 In.	500.00

Napkin rings were in fashion from 1869 to about 1900. They were made of silver, porcelain, wood, and other materials. They are still being made today. The most popular rings with collectors are the figural napkin rings of silver plate. Small, realistic figures were made to hold the ring. Good and poor reproductions of the more expensive rings are now being made and collectors must be very careful, especially when buying any of the Kate Greenaway rings.

NAPKIN RING, Bakelite, Ribbed, 3 Yellow, 2 Green, 1 Red, Set	25.00
Coin Silver, Engraved Eliza	19.50
Dutch Boy & Girl, Ceramic, Goebel, Crown Mark	125.00
Engraved Mother, Sterling Silver, 1 3/8 In.	35.00
Figural, 2 Birds, Tulips, Beaded Base, Silver Plate	80.00
Figural, Acorn Form, Squirrels On Branch Handle, 10 In.	67.00

Figural, Baby In Cradle, James Tufts 295.00
Figural, Baby, Ring On Back, Silver Plate 100.00
Figural, Barrel With Cherubs 40.00
Figural, Baying Wolf, Ring Base, Signed 220.00
Figural, Bird On Branch, Meriden .... 45.00 To 75.00
Figural, Boy On Knees, Bird Protecting Nest, Meriden 175.00
Figural, Boy, Holding Foot, Triple Plate 65.00
Figural, Boy, Kicking Ball, Silver Plate 49.00
Figural, Boy, Large Hat, Silver Plate, 3 In. 125.00
Figural, Cherub, Holding Vase, Rockford, Silver Plate 150.00
Figural, Chick On Wishbone, Derby 42.00
Figural, Child Erecting Pole, Ring On Top, Silver Plate, 5 In. 225.00
Figural, Child Riding Fish, Silver Plate 155.00
Figural, Children In Pixie Hats, Reed & Barton, Sterling 200.00
Figural, Cockatoo, Meriden 155.00
Figural, Cow, Standing, Bird Design On Ring, Silver Plate 70.00
Figural, Crossed Fans, Open Salts On Ring, Derby 155.00
Figural, Dog Pulling Sled, Silver Plate, Ring On Top, Meriden 235.00
Figural, Dogs Barking At Bird, Tree Trunk Base, Silver Plate 155.00
Figural, Double Eagle, Meriden 25.00
Figural, Drummer Boy, On Bench, Ring Is Drum, Silver Plate 240.00
Figural, Emu & Kangaroo, Australian Map, Silver Plate 65.00
Figural, Engraved Floral, Embossed Horseshoe, Silver Plate 70.00
Figural, Flower Form, On Top Of Pyramid, Silver Plate 30.00
Figural, Girl, Pushing Ring, Silver Plate, Middletown 75.00
Figural, Girl, Sitting Beside Toothpick Holder, Silver Plate 100.00
Figural, Horseshoe, Engraved Bonheur, Tufts 58.00
Figural, Insects, Flowers, Birds 9.00
Figural, Lily Pad & Bud, Silver Plate, Rogers 65.00
Figural, Lion, Prone, Ring On Back, Silver Plate 60.00
Figural, Little Miss Muffet 95.00
Figural, Peacock Perched On Top 50.00
Figural, Ring Sits On Victorian Chair, Silver Plate 90.00
Figural, Sitting Squirrel Next To Fluted Ring, Silver Plate 70.00
Figural, Sleeping Boy, Seated, Pairpoint 165.00
Figural, Stag, Ring On Back, Rogers Bros. 200.00
Figural, Tennis Player, Knickers, Engraved, Silver Plate 255.00
Figural, Water Lily 30.00
Figural, Wolf, Embossed Rococo Base 245.00
Man Holding Barrel, Bisque, Germany 15.00
Top Hatted Dandy, Art Deco, Noritake 25.00

Nash glass was made in Corona, New York, after 1919 by Arthur
Nash and his sons. He worked at the Webb factory in England and
for the Tiffany Glassworks in the United States.

NASH, Bowl, Centerpiece, Silver Chintz, Red, Signed 425.00
Bowl, Jewel, Gold Phantom Luster, 2 1/4 X 7 3/4 In. 275.00
Candlestick, Chintz, Ball Stem, Red, Signed, 4 In., Pair .... 435.00 To 450.00
Goblet, Chintz, Ball Stem, Green & Blue, 6 1/4 In. 110.00
Vase, Irregular Ribbed, Ground Pontil, Signed, Blue, 6 3/4 In. 525.00

Nautical antiques are listed in this section. Any of the many objects
that were made or used by the seafaring trade, including ship parts,
models, and tools, are included. Other pieces may be found listed
under Scrimshaw.

NAUTICAL, Ashtray, Queen Mary, Brass, Enameled Flags & Insignia 25.00
Ashtray, Sabina, Black Pregnant Woman, Humorous Saying, 6 In. 42.00
Bell, Chelsea, Brass, 6 In. 425.00
Bell, Ship's, With Mount, 8 In. 65.00
Booklet, Steamboat Excursion, St.Louis, Tenn.River Packet, 1900 .... 22.50
Box, Candy, Normandie 350.00
Card, Playing, Eastern Steamship Lines, House Flag & Logo, Deck 7.00
Card, Playing, Olympia, Portrait, Box, Double 15.00
Card, Playing, Orient Line, Gilt Edge, Box, Double, Miniature 10.00

Card, Playing, Queen Mary, Portrait At Sea, Single	15.00
Chart, Marquesas Islands, 4th Edition, 1917, 30 X 41 In.	3.00
Chart, Marshall Islands, Colored, 1944, Revised 1974, 36 X 54 In.	2.00
Chest, Blanket, Seaman's, Canted, C.1800	325.00
Chest, Grommet Handles, Original Green Paint, 23 3/4 In.	325.00
Chest, Rope Handles, New England, Blue	365.00
Chronometer, 2–Day, 2–Tier Mahogany, Mid–19th Century, 6 1/2 In.	1450.00
Chronometer, 2–Day, 2–Tier, Mahogany, C.1860, German, 6 In.	2750.00
Chronometer, 2–Day, 2–Tier, Mahogany, J.J.Sewill, 7 3/8 & 7 In.	2300.00
Chronometer, 8–Day, Brass, Drum Shape, Arnold, London, 1800, 4 In.	3525.00
Clock, Bell, Brass, 6 In.	245.00
Clock, Chelsea, Mahogany	265.00
Clock, Chelsea, Sweep Second Hand, 24–Hour Dial, 5–In.Dial	140.00
Clock, Chelsea, U.S.Maritime Commission, Second Hand, W.W. II	225.00
Clock, Chelsea, U.S.Maritime, Sweep Hand, 1930s, 5–In.Dial	140.00
Clock, Schaffer & Budenberg, Porcelain Dial, Brass, 1890	250.00
Clock, Seth Thomas, Brass Case	300.00
Clock, Seth Thomas, Inside Bell	265.00
Clock, Seth Thomas, Navy, 24–Hr., Sweep Second, 7 1/2–In.Dial	150.00
Clock, Seth Thomas, U.S.Maritime, 3 Hands, Sweep Hand, 5–In.Dial	140.00
Compass, Attached Lamp, Brass, 6 X 8 X 10 In.	250.00
Compass, Brass Rim, T & G Wooden Carrying Case	130.00
Compass, Brass, Gimbaled, Mahogany Box	75.00
Compass, Brass, U.S.Navy, Dated 1941	225.00
Compass, Gruchon & Emmons, Berne, U.S.Engineer Corps	100.00
Compass, Hinged Sun Dial, Brass	395.00
Compass, Mariner's, Pink, Green, C.1900	375.00
Creamer, Great Northern Steamship Co.	55.00
Decanter, Ship's, Pressed Glass, Jigger Top, 8 In.	20.00
Document, American Line, For Ship Saluda, Dated 1919, 10 X 14 In.	6.00
Hat, Sailor's, R.M.S.Queen Mary	22.00
Helmet, Deep Sea Diving, Brass & Copper, Early 1900s, 16 In.	395.00
Helmet, Diving, A.J.Morse, Boston, Mass., Copper & Brass	1500.00
Label, Baggage, New Zealand Line, Leaf Shape, 1930s, 6 1/2 In.	3.00
Lamp, Anchor, Schooner, 1880s, 24 In.	80.00
Lamp, Ship's Pulley, Wood, Iron, No Shade, 14 1/2 In.	27.50
Lantern, Night Watch, Red, Dietz, 8 In.	75.00
Light, Running, Red Lens	15.00
Light, Stern, Purple Glass	20.00
List, Passenger, Saloon, Inman Line, City of Berlin, 1889	20.00
Log, Ship's, Whaling Stamps, New Bedford To Pacific, 1851, 7 Pages	1300.00
Manual, Caille Portable Boat Motor, 1900	10.00
Match Safe, Aquitania Steamship	85.00
Menu, S.S.Europa, German Lloyd, 1937	15.00
Menu, U.S.S.President Wilson, 1923	8.00
Model, 3–Masted Schooner, American Flag, Blown Glass, 13 1/2 In.	325.00
Model, Battleship Utah, Signed David A.Strausser, 1904, 4 Ft.	2600.00
Model, Felicity, Frazer & Sons, Half Model, 44 1/4 X 9 In.	450.00
Model, Gun Ship, Prisoner of War, Bone	2000.00
Model, McKay Clipper Ship, Sovereign of Seas, Mahogany, 49 In.	2850.00
Model, Plank Construction, Female Figurehead, Case, 43 In.	1870.00
Model, Santa Maria, Early 20th Century, 3 Ft.	1500.00
Model, Steam Engine, Paddle, 19th Century	2035.00
Musket Balls, From Atocha Shipwreck, 1622, 2 Piece	25.00
Porthole, 8 Sides, Brass	50.00
Porthole, Ship's, Glass, 1920s, Round, 15 In.	85.00
Postcard, Cunard, Color Print, Port Side, 1925	2.00
Postcard, Quebec Steamship, Color Print, Hamilton, Bermuda, 1904	2.50
Poster, Antilles, Color Cutaway, M.Lezla, 19 X 47 In.	15.00
Poster, Bergensfjord I, Ship At North Cape, 17 1/2 X 23 In.	15.00
Poster, France III, At Sea, Laminated On Masonite, 21 1/2 X 30 In.	40.00
Poster, Grace Line, 2 Pirates At Ping-Pong Table, 28 X 40 In.	40.00
Poster, Norway, Map of Caribbean	7.00
Ruler, Marine, C.1880	115.00

Schedule, Mallory Steamship Line, New York To Key West, 1888	10.00
Sign, Ship Chandler's, Carved Pine, Telescope Shape, 34 In.	550.00
Stove, Whaling Ship's, Soapstone Griddle, Cast Iron	175.00
Sugar, Transylvania Steamship, Silver Plate	18.00
Telescope, 3 Brass Sections, Pigskin Case, Extends To 22 1/2 In.	115.00
Telescope, 3 Draw Pocket, Leather, 1800s, 17 In.	110.00
Telescope, 360 Degree, Andrew Yeates, London, Brass, 22 1/2 In.	110.00
Telescope, 4 Brass Sections, Mahogany & Brass, Extends To 36 In.	235.00
Telescope, Extra Lens, Dated 1917	95.00
Telescope, Green Vellum, Brass Rings, England, C.1730	1150.00
Telescope, J.Atwood & Co., London, Day Or Night, 1 Drawer, 20 In.	300.00
Tip Tray, American Line, Ship Picture	65.00
Toothpick, Cedric Steamship	15.00
Trunk, Ship's, Tools, C.1790	1300.00
Wheel, Steering, Riverboat, 1890s, 5 Ft.	1350.00
Whistle, Bosuns', Pewter, Sign of Office	175.00
Whistle, Steamboat, Brass, Wooden Handle, Great Lakes Region	225.00

Small ivory, wood, metal, or porcelain pieces were used as buttons on the end of the cord that held a Japanese money pouch. These were called "Netsuke." The earliest date from the sixteenth century. Many are miniature, carved works of art.

NETSUKE, Ebony, South Sea Islander, Ryomin, 1 3/4 In.	1500.00
Ivory, 2 Men, Wrestling, Kazumasa, 1 1/8 In.	130.00
Ivory, Ball of Animals of Zodiac, Signed, 20th Century, 1 7/16 In.	130.00
Ivory, Bearded Man, Crouching On Turtle Boy	85.00
Ivory, Bird, Late 19th Century	360.00
Ivory, Boy, Crouched Atop Plump Pony, Signed Tomotada	440.00
Ivory, Cockerel, Seated, Head Turned Right	1650.00
Ivory, Dragon, Coiled Tail, Signed, 2 In.	50.00
Ivory, Duck, Sitting, Hakusen, 2 1/16 In.	50.00
Ivory, Elephant, 1 In.	700.00
Ivory, God of Luck, Mitsuhiro	650.00
Ivory, Group of Shishi, 1 3/4 In.	3000.00
Ivory, Guardian, Shunkoku, Dressed In Dhoti, Shoulder Bar	220.00
Ivory, Man With Fish On Shoulder, 20th Century, 1 1/4 In.	40.00
Ivory, Man, Baskets On Shoulder Bar, Children, Signed, 1 15/16 In.	150.00
Ivory, Man, Puppet & Boy, Hidemasa, 1 3/4 In.	3300.00
Ivory, Man, Seated, Spoon & Bowl In Hands	80.00
Ivory, Mare & Foal, Inset Jet Eyes, Signed, 1 3/8 In.	90.00
Ivory, Mask, Yushida	231.00
Ivory, Men, Standing, Lighting Pipes	85.00
Ivory, Monkey, Kaigyokusai Masatsugu	1210.00
Ivory, Perforated With Tree & Rock Landscapes	425.00
Ivory, Puppy, Inro Cord Fasteners	220.00
Ivory, Quail, In Millet, Tadamitsu, 15/16 In.	200.00
Ivory, Quail, Millet, Leaves	249.00
Ivory, Saddled Horse, Yoshiyuki, Late 19th Century	358.00
Ivory, Scholar, Reclining, With Book	90.00
Ivory, Shishi Playing With Brocade Ball, Ball Inside, 1 1/2 In.	75.00
Ivory, Snake Coiled On Back of Turtle, Signed	50.00
Ivory, Stag, 19th Century, Oval Plinth	165.00
Ivory, Tiger, 19th Century, Inlaid Eyes	990.00
Ivory, Tiger, Sitting, Cub	425.00
Ivory, Turtle, Pouring Water, Gourd Held By Man, Mitsu, 1 3/16 In.	275.00
Ivory, Woman Bathing, Signed Ryushi	825.00
Ivory, Zodiac Animals Group, Toshitsugu, 20th Century	715.00
Sterling Silver, Monkey	990.00
Sterling Silver, Sparrow	210.00
Wood, Fisherwoman, Searching For Shells, Seiyodo	220.00
Wood, Fukurokuju, God of Longevity	450.00
Wood, Group of Toads, Masanao, 1 3/4 In.	1500.00
Wood, House At Lake, Brass & Silver Trim, 5 Piece	450.00
Wood, Mask of A Demon	100.00

Wood, Men Playing Go, 1 3/4 In. 450.00
Wood, Monkey Mask, Tomochika, Inlaid Eyes 325.00
Wood, Rat Catcher, 19th Century 550.00
Wood, Rat, On Bamboo Shoot, Sensui, 2 3/16 In. 40.00
Wood, Rats, Climbing A Treasure Sack, Masakiyo 660.00
Wood, Rope Maker, Stretching Rope With His Foot, Cherry 425.00
Wood, Seal Form, Horse Finial, 19th Century, 1 5/8 In. 50.00
Wood, Tiger, Masanobu, 19th Century 357.50
Wood, Wasp, On Decaying Pear, Yosue 522.00
Wood, Wise Man, Riding On Carp, Lacquered 75.00
Wood, Witch Hannya, Wrapped Around A Temple Bell, Masanao 660.00
Wood, Women, With Ivory Head & Hands 990.00
Wood, Wrestling Match 4290.00

New Hall Porcelain Manufactory was started at Newhall, Shelton, Staffordshire, England, in 1782. Simple decorated wares were made. Between 1810 and 1825, the factory made a glassy bone porcelain sometimes marked with the factory name. Do not confuse New Hall porcelain with the pieces made by the New Hall Pottery Company, Ltd., a twentieth-century firm.

NEW HALL, Bowl, Elongated Chinese Figures, Orange, Blue, Green, 8 In. 125.00
    Cup & Saucer, Orange, Blue Flowers 75.00

The New Martinsville Glass Manufacturing Company was established in 1901 in New Martinsville, West Virginia. It was bought and renamed the Viking Glass Company in 1944 and is still producing fine glasswares.

NEW MARTINSVILLE, Ashtray, Moondrops, Red 20.00
Basket, Footed, Crystal, 5 X 8 3/4 In. 24.00
Bookends, Nautilus .... 30.00 To 46.00
Bookends, Rearing Horse 30.00
Bookends, Squirrel, 5 1/2 In. 29.00
Bookends, Starfish 55.00
Bowl, Sun Glow, Ruffled, Melon Ribbed, 4 In. 65.00
Bowl, Sunburst, Peachblow, Ruffled, 10 3/4 In. 110.00
Bowl, Sunburst, Ribbed, Flared & Ruffled, 1901, 7 1/2 In. 345.00
Bride's Bowl, Burmese, Pairpoint Frame 200.00
Candleholder, Moondrops, Red, 3–Light, Pair 75.00
Candlestick, Etched, Wing, Amber, 5 In., Pair 30.00
Cigarette Holder, Judy, Green 24.00
Console Set, Radiance 40.00
Console Set, Swan, Amber, Crystal Necks, 3 Piece 55.00
Cordial, Prelude 11.00
Cordial, Radiance, Amber 3.50
Creamer, Swan Handle, Sterling Base 22.00
Cruet, Janice, Blue 40.00
Cruet, Radiance, Red .... 60.00 To 65.00
Cup, Janice, Red 8.00
Decanter, Stopper, Amber, 7 3/4 In. 23.00
Decanter, Stopper, Cobalt Blue, 11 1/4 In. 88.00
Figurine, Baby Bear .... 30.00 To 50.00
Figurine, Elephant, Pair 95.00
Figurine, German Shepherd 40.00
Figurine, Papa Bear .... 95.00 To 175.00
Figurine, Rooster 45.00
Figurine, Squirrel .... 28.00 To 40.00
Figurine, Wolfhound, 7 In. 75.00
Mustard, Covered, Janice, Blue 28.00
Powder Jar, Black Glass Cover 18.00
Punch Set, Cobalt Blue Cups, Chrome Holder, 16 Piece 65.00
Relish, Prelude, 5 Sections, 13 1/4 In. 12.00
Salt, Master, Florene 45.00
Sugar & Creamer, Eagle, Green 22.00
Sugar, Moondrops, Hand Painted Flowers 22.50

Vase, Radiance, Crimped, Red, 12 In.	40.00
Wine, Moondrops, Red, 4 In.	12.00

Newcomb Pottery was founded by Ellsworth and William Woodward at Sophie Newcomb College, New Orleans, Louisiana, in 1896. The work continued through the 1940s. Pieces of this art pottery are marked with the printed letters "NC" and often have the incised initials of the artist as well. Most pieces have a matte glaze and incised decoration.

NEWCOMB, Bowl, Blue, Incised Floral Design, 2 1/2 X 5 3/4 In.	300.00
Coaster, Floral, Paper Label, A.F.Simpson, 4 In.	325.00
Plaque, Southern Pines, Full Moon, Blue, Green, 10 X 6 In.	2750.00
Tile, Spanish Moss On Tree, A.F.Simpson, Framed, 1917, 3 1/2 In.	800.00
Vase, 2 Handles, College Scene	2000.00
Vase, Blue Hanging Moss Scene, Sadie Irvine, 5 1/2 In.	650.00
Vase, Dark Green, A.F.S., 9 In.	700.00
Vase, Floral Border, 3 X 5 1/2 In.	550.00
Vase, Floral Design, Leaves, Flowers, Matte Glaze, Bailey, 5 1/2 In.	350.00
Vase, Hi–Glaze Floral, 5 In.	2800.00
Vase, Landscape, Blue Trees, Green Moss, 10 X 7 In.	1980.00
Vase, Louisiana Iris, Blue & Green Matte, Sadie Irvine, 13 1/2 In.	2975.00
Vase, Matte Blue & Green, Glazed, J.Myers, 3 3/4 In.	90.00
Vase, Moss Scene, Greenish Blue, Yellow Ground, Simpson, 3 1/4 In.	400.00
Vase, Pink On White Flowers Around Top, Signed, 6 1/4 In.	450.00
Vase, White, Yellow Iris Blossom, Leaves, 11 X 6 In.	4675.00

𝒩𝐼𝐿𝒪𝒜𝒦

Niloak Pottery (Kaolin spelled backward) was made at the Hyten Brothers Pottery in Benton, Arkansas, between 1909 and 1946. Although the factory did make cast and molded wares, collectors are most interested in the marbelized art pottery line made of colored swirls of clay. It was called "Mission Ware."

NILOAK, Candlestick, Mission, 8 In.	110.00
Ewer, Blue & Terra–Cotta Swirls, Flared, Ruffled, Handle, 11 In.	125.00
Figurine, Elephant, On Circus Tub, Citron, 5 1/2 In.	20.00
Pitcher, Batter, Geometric Design, Open Handle, 6 In.	32.00
Planter & Flower Frog, Blue	37.00
Planter, Brown Bear	15.00
Planter, Deer, Fawn, Glossy Maroon	12.00
Planter, Elephant, Blue	16.00
Planter, Fawn	8.00
Planter, Squirrel, Blue .... 10.00 To 27.50
Sugar & Creamer, Marbelized	25.00
Vase, Aqua, Paper Label, 8 In.	21.00
Vase, Gourd, 10 In.	105.00
Vase, Marbelized, 3 In.	35.00
Vase, Marbelized, 4 1/2 In. .... 28.00 To 37.50
Vase, Marbelized, 6 1/2 In.	40.00
Vase, Marbelized, 6 In. .... 45.00 To 50.00
Vase, Marbelized, 8 In. .... 40.00 To 70.00
Vase, Marbelized, 10 1/4 In.	200.00
Vase, Marbelized, 16 1/2 In.	400.00
Vase, Marbelized, Cylindrical, Thrown Form, 9 In.	155.00
Vase, Marbelized, Multicolor, Bulbous, 8 1/2 X 8 1/2 In.	60.00
Vase, Marbelized, Red & Brown, 4 1/2 In.	55.00
Vase, Maroon, 2 Handles, 7 In.	16.00

Nippon–marked porcelain was made in Japan from 1891 to 1921. "Nippon" is the Japanese word for "Japan." A few firms continued to use the word "Nippon" on ceramics after 1921 as a part of the company name more than as an identification of the country of origin. More pieces marked Nippon will be found in the Dragonware, Moriage, and Noritake sections.

NIPPON, Ashtray, Blown Out, Cigar & Box of Matches, Green Mark	200.00
Ashtray, Blown–Out Hunting Dog	295.00

Ashtray, Grape Leaves, Enameled Bunches of Grapes 250.00
Ashtray, Kingfisher 600.00
Ashtray, Lake & House, Gold Outlining, 5 1/4 In. 72.50
Ashtray, Owl In Flight, Blue Ground, Beaded Brown Rim 75.00
Ashtray, Sailboat Scene, Marked 35.00
Basket, Hand Painted, Dogwood, Gold Trim, 5 X 9 In. 65.00
Berry Bowl, Underplate, Leaf Shape, Blue Trim, Pink Roses, Gold 65.00
Berry Set, Cobalt Blue On Gold Design, Gold Trim, 7 Piece 135.00
Berry Set, Flowers & Leaves, Green Mark, 7 Piece 45.00
Berry Set, Swans On Pond, Bowl, 10 1/2 In., 6 Piece 125.00
Biscuit Jar, Blown–Out Portrait Old Man, Metal Cover, Signed, 8 In. 210.00
Bottle, Perfume, Jeweled, Stopper, Gold, Green, Pink 75.00
Bottle, Perfume, Pink & Red Roses, Cobalt Trim, Gold, 5 In. 75.00
Bowl, Acorn Scene, Allover Bisque, 6 In. 35.00
Bowl, Blown–Out Squirrel, Footed, Green Mark, 9 In. 525.00
Bowl, Child, Googly Eyes, 6 In. 35.00
Bowl, Hand Painted, Purple Flowers, Yellow Inside, Handles, 9 In. 65.00
Bowl, Pink Roses, Gold Trim, Blue Border, 10 1/2 X 2 3/4 In. 200.00
Bowl, Red Poppies, Gold Trim, Crown Mark, 10 1/2 In. 50.00
Bowl, River Scene, Man On Sailboat, Open Handles, Peach, 9 In. 115.00
Bowl, Strawberries, Wide Gold Rim, 9 In. 95.00
Bowl, Tomatoes & Leaves Allover Design, Pierced Handles, 9 In. 45.00
Bowl, Water Scene, Square, 7 1/2 In. 35.00
Bowl, Woodlands Scene, Footed, Maple Leaf, 7 3/4 In. 169.00
Butter, Covered, Pink & Green Flowers, Raised Gold, Green Mark 55.00
Butter, Covered, Sampan, 2 People, Mountain 120.00
Cake Set, Floral, Gold, Blue Trim, Rising Sun, 7 Piece .... 65.00 To 80.00
Cake Set, Flying Geese, Jewels, Gold Trim, Aqua, 7 Piece 175.00
Candlestick, Purple, Black, Gold Tracing, Medallions, Beading, 8 In. 115.00
Candy Dish, Hunt Scene, Open Pierced Handle, Large 185.00
Cheese Dish, Roses Around Top, Gold Band, Marked 50.00
Chocolate Pot, Floral Over Deep Green, Signed, 9 In. 125.00
Chocolate Pot, White, Gold Trim 68.00
Chocolate Set, Boating Scene, White Ground, 7 Piece 100.00
Chocolate Set, Cobalt Blue, Gold, Large Flowers, 11 Piece 135.00
Chocolate Set, Gold Floral Band, White, Marked, 9 Piece 160.00
Chocolate Set, Gold Trim, Hand Painted Pink Roses, Marked, 5 Piece 265.00
Chocolate Set, Purple Flowers, Gold Stippling, 11 Piece 175.00
Cider Set, Camel & Desert Scene, 7 Piece 230.00
Cookie Jar, 4 Gold Feet, 3 Handles 195.00
Creamer, Blown–Out Child's Face 40.00
Creamer, Floral On Lavender, Gray Ground 14.00
Cup & Plate, Fat Boy, 6 In.Plate 100.00
Cup & Saucer, Wedgwood Style 110.00
Dinner Set, Blue Crane, 30 Piece 350.00
Dish, Cucumber, Underplate, Roses, Marked 65.00
Dish, Dessert, Village Scenes, Gold Rim, Maple Leaf Mark, Set of 6 .... 55.00
Doll, Boy, Black Pants & Jacket 115.00
Dresser Set, Cobalt Banding, Looped Beading, Marked, 8 Piece 160.00
Ewer, Red, Yellow Roses, Blue, Squatty, Marked, 5 1/2 In. 65.00
Fernery, Flowers, Gold Beading, Ivory Feet, Maple Leaf, 7 1/2 In. 195.00
Fernery, Lion & Palm Tree Scenic, Green Wreath Mark 95.00
Fernery, Pink & Red Flowers, Gold Beading, Blue Ivory Feet 185.00
Fernery, Scenic, Enameled, Jeweled Feet, Green Mark, 5 1/2 In. 47.00
Fernery, Windmill Scene, Cobalt Blue Border, 10 In. 195.00
Figurine, Clog Shoe, Signed 89.00
Figurine, Colonial Couple, Dancing, Dresden Type Lace On Both 145.00
Goblet, Loganberry & Grape 25.00
Hair Receiver, Green & Gold, Marked, 4 1/2 In. 27.00
Hair Receiver, Hand Painted Florals, 3 Footed 30.00
Hatpin Holder, Beaded, Green & White, Maple Leaf Mark, 4 3/4 In. 48.00
Hatpin Holder, Hanging, Cornucopia Shape, Floral, Leaf Mark, 7 In. 75.00
Hatpin Holder, Pink Roses, Gold Trim, 4 In. 45.00
Hatpin Holder, Violets, Green & Gold Attached Saucer, 4 1/4 In. 50.00

Humidor, Blown Out, Indian Chief On Horse, Tortoiseshell Ground	850.00
Humidor, Blown–Out Dog	800.00
Humidor, Brown, Tan Classic Roman Figures	150.00
Humidor, Dark Green Trees, Yellow	225.00
Humidor, Deer Picture, Green	275.00
Humidor, Indian, Canoe, Flying Geese On Lid, 6 Sides, Marked, 6 In.	215.00
Humidor, Jeweled, Scenic Panel ....*Illus*	110.00
Humidor, Lakeside Scene, 4 Sides, 4 3/4 In.	225.00
Humidor, Leaping Stag, Enameled Knob Design, 3 Feet, Wreath Mark	395.00
Humidor, Lion & Lioness	850.00
Humidor, Man On Camel, 4 In.	175.00
Humidor, Windmill Scene, 6 Sides, 5 1/2 In.	225.00
Jug, Whiskey, Windmill & House Scene, Enameled Flowers, 7 1/2 In.	350.00
Juicer, White, Gold Trim, 2 Sections	45.00
Lemonade Set, Covered Pitcher, Geese In Flight, Aqua Ground, 7 Pc.	600.00
Lemonade Set, Hand Painted Raspberries, TE–OH Mark, 7 Piece	95.00
Loving Cup, Turquoise Beading, Roses, Gold Ground, 3 Handles	95.00
Match Holder, On Ashtray, Lavender & Gray	85.00
Mug & Plate, Child's, Fat Boy Picture, 6 In.Plate	120.00
Mug, Baby's, Clowns & Rabbits, 2 1/4 In.	28.00
Mug, Gold Beading, Lake Scene, 4 1/2 In.	60.00
Mustard, Attached Underplate, Pink Roses, Gold	30.00
Mustard, Covered, Attached Underplate, Spoon, Roses, Gold Trim	35.00
Mustard, Salt & Pepper, Blue, Beaded Trim, 3 Piece	18.50
Mustard, Spoon, Floral, Gold Trim	16.00
Nut Set, Scenic, Blue Leaf Mark, 7 Piece	90.00
Nut Set, Tree In Meadow, 6 Piece	45.00
Pancake Server, Floral, Gold Trim, Maple Leaf Mark	150.00
Pitcher, Lemonade, Royal Nishiki Mark	195.00
Pitcher, Milk, Gold Handle, Orange Poppies, 7 1/2 In.	85.00
Pitcher, Underplate, Covered, Floral, Gold, Signed, 7 In.	130.00
Pitcher, Water, Roses On Green, Gold Overlay, Marked	145.00
Plaque, Blown–Out Dogs, Green Mark, 10 5/8 In.	500.00
Plaque, Blown–Out Indian On Horseback	575.00
Plaque, Bulldog, Hanging, 10 In.	375.00
Plaque, Fruit In Compote, Pierced, 11 In.	75.00
Plaque, Gray & Pink Moriage Bird On Cherry Blossoms, 10 1/2 In.	65.00
Plaque, Lion & Lioness, Molded In Relief, 10 1/2 In.	650.00
Plaque, Lions, Blown Out, Pair ....*Illus*	1200.00
Plaque, Oriental Junk, Continental Scene, Marked, 10 1/2 In.	185.00
Plaque, Sailboat Scene, Applied Moriage, 2 Fishermen, 11 In.	275.00
Plaque, Sailing Ship, Enameled, 10 In.	175.00
Plate, Blown–Out Lions, 10 3/4 In.	625.00
Plate, Floral Border, Gold Handles, Octagonal, 10 In.	32.00
Plate, Hand Painted, Plums, Pomegranate, Green Wreath, 10 In.	40.00
Plate, Lake Scene, Beaded Border, Green Leaf Mark, 8 1/2 In.	45.00

Nanking, Bowl, Mountain Scene,
Blue, White,
C.1850, 6 X 14 1/2 In.

Nippon, Humidor,
Jeweled, Scenic Panel

Nippon, Plaque, Lions,
Blown Out, Pair

Plate, Multicolored Poppies, Green M, 10 In.	65.00
Plate, Tapestry, Castle, Footed, Square Handles, Green Mark, 8 In.	525.00
Pot, Hanging, Gold Figural, Ram's Head	345.00
Punch Bowl, Stand, Geese In Water, Gold Outlining, Marked	375.00
Relish, 2 Sections, Center Handle, Blue, Maple Leaf Mark	95.00
Relish, 3 Sections, Yellow Roses, 9 1/2 In.	85.00
Salt & Pepper, Butterflies, Green, Gold Trim	25.00
Salt, Celery, Hand Painted Flower & Leaves, Marked, 2 3/4 In.	5.00
Salt, Sunset Scene, Gold Trim, Marked, 2 In.	12.00
Server, Pancake, Floral, Hand Painted	110.00
Sugar & Creamer, Cobalt Blue, Gold Dragons, Marked	185.00
Sugar & Creamer, Floral Enameling, Signed	70.00
Sugar & Creamer, Hand Painted Gold Dogwood, Green Wreath Mark	24.00
Sugar & Creamer, Violets, Gold Trim, Green M	25.00
Sugar Shaker, Gold Flowers, Bows, Bells, Swags, Marked	75.00
Sugar Shaker, Roses With Thorns, RC Mark	45.00
Syrup, Covered, Underplate, Pastoral Scene, Marked	70.00
Syrup, Octagonal Underplate, Gold Grapes & Trim, Marked, 4 1/4 In.	70.00
Syrup, Underplate, Palm Trees, Gold Outlining	75.00
Tankard & 2 Mugs, Elk ....Illus	850.00
Tankard Set, Moriage Dragon, Marked, 5 Piece	485.00
Tankard, Cobalt Blue, Gaudy, 16 In.	450.00
Tankard, Feathered Handle, Grapes, Autumnal Scene, 11 In.	180.00
Tea Caddy, Indian Signs, Triangular, Footed, Green Wreath, 6 In.	175.00
Tea Set, Earth Tones, Signed, 10 Piece	225.00
Tea Strainer, Flowers, Green Ground	40.00
Teapot, Aladdin's Lamp, Gold Design	40.00
Teapot, Flying Geese, Jewels, Gold Trim, Aqua	125.00
Toothpick, Hexagon Shape, VP Mark	50.00
Toothpick, Pyramids & Palm Trees	45.00
Toothpick, Truncated Cube	45.00
Tray, Basket of Flowers, Hand Painted, 5 1/2 In.	15.00
Tray, R.C.A.Victor Dog	185.00
Tray, Woodland Scene, 8 Sides, 9 X 13 In.	95.00
Trivet, Oranges With Trees	55.00
Vase, Allover Florals, Butterflies, Label, C.1905, 16 In.	625.00
Vase, Beaded Panels, Blue Ground, Gold Trim, 9 In.	175.00
Vase, Bird & Flower, Coppertone, 4 In.	25.00
Vase, Cowboy On Horse, Handles, 8 In.	195.00
Vase, Cowboy, Blue Mark, 12 In.	550.00
Vase, Cylindrical, Impressionistic Boat Scene, 3 Handles, 12 In.	175.00
Vase, Encrusted Gold Dots, 12 In.	265.00
Vase, Floral Panels, Gold, Bulbous, 6 In.	60.00
Vase, Floral Pattern, Gold Leaves & Beading, C.1891, 13 1/2 In.	245.00
Vase, Forest Scene With Deer, Handles, 12 In.	175.00
Vase, Gold Beading, Roses, Handles, Maple Leaf, 4 1/2 X 10 In.	60.00

Mettlach, Planter, Art Nouveau, Iris Design,
5 1/2 X 12 X 7 In.

Nippon, Tankard & 2 Mugs, Elk

Vase, Gold Moriage Flowers, Vines, Green Mark, 12 In. 225.00
Vase, Gold Phoenix Bird, Black Border, Double Handles, 13 In. 235.00
Vase, Hand Painted Scene, Pink Roses, Raised Gold, Marked, 7 1/2 In. 80.00
Vase, Hand Painted White Blooming Roses, 12 In. 85.00
Vase, Hand Painted, M In Wreath Mark, 13 3/4 In. 330.00
Vase, Large Sailing Ship, 10 In. 165.00
Vase, Lavender, Gold & Orange Irises, Green Tapestry, 12 In. 250.00
Vase, Man Poling Boat, River Scene, Beaded Gold Trim, 6 3/4 In. 75.00
Vase, Peacock & Geometrics Allover, Green Wreath, 7 1/2 In. 95.00
Vase, Raised Floral At Top, Floral Band Bottom, Green Mark, 11 In. 200.00
Vase, Red, Yellow Roses, Flaring Gold Handles, Marked, 7 In. 125.00
Vase, Sailing Boat Scene, Jewels, Gold, Beading, Marked, 12 In. 295.00
Vase, Sailing Ship Center Medallion, 10 In. 275.00
Vase, Scene, Melon Shape, Gold, Handle, 8 1/2 In. 95.00
Vase, Scenic Panels Front & Back, Green Mark, 7 1/2 In. 200.00
Vase, Stippling, Beading, Dahlias, Handle, 12 In. 200.00
Vase, Tapestry, Roses, Maple Leaf Mark, 9 1/4 In. 325.00
Vase, White Clematis, Violets Down Front, Green Ground, 9 In. 115.00
Vase, Woman Walking, Forest House, Twin Beaded Handles, 8 1/2 In. 195.00
Vase, Woman, Holding Baby, Child, By River, 5 1/2 In. 215.00
Vase, Woodland & Water Scene, Gold Handles, Green Mark, 9 1/4 In. 145.00
Vase, Woodland Scene, Ram's Head Handles, 11 1/2 In. 325.00

> Nodders, or nodding figures, or pagods, are porcelain figures with heads and hands that are attached to wires. Any slight movement causes the parts to move up and down. They were made in many countries during the eighteenth and nineteenth centuries. A few Art Deco designs are also known. Copies are being made.

NODDER, 2 Ladies On Divan, Knitting, Bisque, 4 X 2 1/2 In. 175.00
2–Faced Boy, Reversible Head, 1 Black, 1 White 125.00
Advertising Display, Clockwork, Glass Eyes, C.1890, 27 In. 2200.00
Andy Gump, Porcelain, 4 In. 125.00
Birds, German, Pair, 7 In. 150.00
Black Baby, Bank, Porcelain 35.00
Black Boy, Sitting, Bisque, Gold Cane, Red Turban, Germany 50.00
Black Boy, Smoking Cigar, Hat & Overalls, Metal, 4 1/2 In. 125.00
Black Oriental, Seated, 4 1/2 In. 125.00
Blackamoors, Male & Female, Bisque, 1880, 4 1/2 In. 150.00
Bobie–Mae Swing & Sway, Composition 70.00
Boy & Girl Pigs, Dressed 22.50
Buttercup, Bisque, Germany 175.00
Cat, Papier–Mache 85.00
Ching Chow, German, 3 1/2 In. 65.00
Daddy Warbucks, Bisque, Germany 150.00
Detroit Tigers, Baseball, Composition, Sports Specialties, 7 In. 10.00
Dog, Glass Eyes, Brass Collar, Papier–Mache 20.00
Donkey, Celluloid, Bobblehead, 3 In. 28.00
Duck, Plastic, Germany 15.00
Elephant, Composition, 6 1/2 In. 33.00
Football Player, Plastic 2.50
Foxy Grandpa, Hand Painted 89.00
Goose, Celluloid, Bobblehead, 3 In. 35.00
Group, Colonial Ladies & Men, Nodding Heads, 10 In. 175.00
Gump Family, Germany 125.00
Kaiser Wilhelm, Clockwork 1275.00
Kitten, Celluloid, Bobblehead, Wide–Eyed, 3 1/2 In. 58.00
Little Orphan Annie, Bisque, Germany 135.00
Lord Plushbottom, Bisque, Germany 125.00
Los Angeles Dodgers 15.00
Mickey McGuire, German, 2 In. 50.00
Monkey, Celluloid, Bobblehead, Jointed Arms & Legs, 6 1/2 In. 65.00
Moon Mullins, German 45.00
Moose, Bobblehead, Celluoid, 8 In. 55.00
Mushmouth, German, 3 1/2 In. 60.00

Oriental, Man Juggles, Lady Plays Drums, Pair 450.00
Pheasant, Salt & Pepper 14.00
Philadelphia Phillies, Baseball, 1962 .... 20.00
Pittsburgh Pirates, Baseball, Composition, 7 In. 10.00
Puppy, Fake Fur On Papier–Mache Composition, Moving Eyes, 6 In. 30.00
Rabbit, Ears, Head, Mouth Move, Top Hat, Monocle, Boutonniere, 18 In. 1750.00
Rachel, German, 3 1/2 In. 60.00
Reindeer, Windup, 14 1/4 X 16 In. 450.00
Salt & Pepper, Fish, Green 12.00
Santa Claus, Celluloid, Tin, Windup, Japan, 1930s, 7 In. 275.00
Snoopy, Papier–Mache 7.50
Sultan & Sultaness, Black, Moving Tongues, 2 1/2 X 4 1/2 In., Pair 245.00
Uncle Bim, Germany 125.00
Uncle Walt, Bisque, 3 1/2 In. 45.00
Winking Figure, Glass Eye, Papier–Mache, Germany, 5 3/4 In. 65.00
Woman, Plucking Goose, Porcelain, German, 6 1/2 In. 125.00

Noritake–marked porcelain was made in Japan after 1904 by Nippon Toki Kaisha. The best–known Noritake pieces are marked with the M in a wreath for the Morimura Brothers, a New York City distributing company. This mark was used until 1941. Another famous Noritake china was made for the Larkin Soap Company from 1916 through the 1930s. This dinnerware, decorated with azaleas, was sold or given away as a premium. There may be some helpful price information in the Nippon category since prices are comparable.

NORITAKE, Ashtray, Black Spade In Center 25.00
Ashtray, Figural, Bird On Clover 75.00
Ashtray, Figural, Cat, Luster, 3 X 4 In. 110.00
Ashtray, Figural, Clown, Art Deco 150.00
Ashtray, Figural, Polar Bear, Blue Luster, 4 1/2 In. 98.00
Ashtray, Hand Painted Tree By Stream, Marked, Nested Pair 45.00
Ashtray, Spade Shape, Figural Pipe 75.00
Asparagus Set, Pearlized Colors, 7 Piece 175.00
Bottle, Perfume, Gold Design, Hexagonal Gold Stopper, Pair 95.00
Bowl, Art Deco, Butterfly & Wild Rainbow, 7 In. 24.00
Bowl, Azalea, 10 In. 30.00
Bowl, Butterfly, Blue, Orange & Yellow Flowers, Marked, 8 In. 35.00
Bowl, Molded Ram's Head Handle, Blue & Gold Luster, 11 In. 125.00
Bowl, Orange Butterfly, Orange & Yellow Flowers, 8 In. 30.00
Bowl, Pearl Luster, Pink, Blue Flowers, Black Flowers Rim, 7 In. 30.00
Bowl, Salad, Underplate, Flower Shape, Orange, Blue–Green Luster 70.00
Bowl, Stylized Scene, Square, 6 1/2 In. 35.00
Bowl, Vegetable, Covered, Floral 40.00
Box, Powder, Floral, Blue Luster Cover, Black Accents, Marked 75.00
Box, Powder, Spanish Lady, 3 3/4 In. 110.00
Cake Plate, Autumnal Scene, Gold Handles & Rim, 10 In. 75.00
Cake Plate, Azalea, Handles, 9 1/2 In. 20.00
Cake Plate, Tree In Meadow, Pierced Handles .... 18.00 To 28.00
Cake Set, Tree In Meadow, 7 Piece 40.00
Cake Set, White Prunus Blossoms, Black Ground, 7 Piece 65.00
Candlestick, Green & White Striped Border, Black & Orange 35.00
Candlestick, Tan Luster, Art Deco, 5 In., Pair 75.00
Candy Dish, Covered, Red Roses, Blue Ground, Gold Knob, Marked 75.00
Card Holder, Figural, Swan, Orange Head, Tail, & Wings, Green Stand 135.00
Chamberstick, Underplate, Black, Green, White Cup, Marked 35.00
Chocolate Set, Multicolored Flowers In Panels, Marked, 6 Piece 275.00
Coffeepot, Tree In Meadow 160.00
Compote, Cobalt & Gold Grapes, Marked, 3 1/2 X 9 In. 75.00
Cup & Saucer, Azalea 15.00
Cup, Tree In Meadow 12.00
Demitasse Set, Multicolored Flowers, Center Band, 12 Piece 395.00
Dinner Set, Warrington Pattern, Service For 8 .... 450.00
Dish, Cheese, Slanted, Figural Parrot Handle, Blue Luster 85.00

Dish, Lemon, Azalea 16.50
Dish, Trinket, Orange Luster, Blue–Green Interior & Handle 25.00
Dresser Set, Egyptian Figures & Symbols, Hand Painted, 7 Piece 325.00
Figurine, Tohi Kaiska Lady, Holding Fan, Blond, Marked, 7 In. 250.00
Flower Frog, Blue Luster 15.00
Hatpin Holder, Azalea 50.00
Humidor, Blown–Out Camel & Rider, Signed, 7 1/2 In. 595.00
Humidor, Figural, Owl, Signed 375.00
Humidor, Golfer 188.00
Ice Cream Set, Art Deco Parrot Design, Red Mark, 7 Piece 125.00
Incense Burner, Figural, Foo Dog, Orange Luster, Marked 35.00
Jam Jar, Azalea, Covered, Ladle 110.00
Jam Jar, Tree In Meadow, Cherry Finial, Covered, Plate & Ladle 65.00
Jam Jar, Underplate, Figural Rose Finial, Green Mark 42.50
Lamp, Candle, Floral Design, Black, 6 1/4 In. 45.00
Luncheon Set, Gaudy, 20 Piece 175.00
Match Holder, Striker On Both Sides, Floral Bouquet 55.00
Mayonnaise Set, Art Deco, Wild Flowers, Ladle, 2 Piece 23.00
Mayonnaise Set, Azalea, 3 Piece 30.00
Mayonnaise Set, Orange, Yellow, White, Man In Gondola, Venice 85.00
Mustard, Swan In Lake Scene, Covered, Spoon 38.00
Napkin Ring, Art Deco Lady, Muff, Signed 35.00
Napkin Ring, Tree In Meadow 35.00
Plate & Mug, Child's, Boy & Girl, Sitting At Table 50.00
Plate, Art Deco, Butterfly Center, 8 In. 27.00
Plate, Azalea, 7 1/2 In. 6.00
Plate, Azalea, 10 In. 15.00
Plate, House & Pond, Geese, Hand Painted, Hanging Hole, 9 In. 15.00
Platter, Figural, Cat, Marked 85.00
Platter, Floral, 11 1/2 In. 28.00
Powder Jar, Art Deco, White Center, Daisies, Blue Border 70.00
Punch Bowl, Stand, Flying Geese, Water Scenes, 12 In. 175.00
Relish, Azalea, Oval 16.50
Relish, Tree In Meadow, Divided 20.00
Salt & Papper, Azalea 20.00
Salt & Pepper, Tree In Meadow 14.00
Salt, Blue–Green Exterior, Orange Luster Interior, Individual 30.00
Saucer, Azalea 4.00
Soup, Dish, Azalea 13.00
Spooner, Art Deco Palm Tree, Coconut Handles 48.00
Spooner, Figural, Birds On Top of Handle 72.00
Sugar & Creamer, Butterfly, Blue, Orange Flowers 20.00
Sugar & Creamer, Covered, Azalea .... 22.00 To 25.00
Sugar & Creamer, Faye 9.00
Sugar & Creamer, Tree In Meadow .... 18.00 To 35.00
Sugar Shaker, Orange Top, Blue Bottom, Orange Flowers, Butterfly 20.00
Sugar Shaker, Tree In Meadow 35.00
Tea Set, Child's, Silhouette of Girl, Doll, Tea Party, 21 Piece 275.00
Tea Set, Otter, 21 Piece 500.00
Tea Set, Tree In Meadow, 15 Piece 125.00
Teapot, Tree In Meadow 75.00
Toothpick, Azalea 75.00
Toothpick, Tree In Meadow 35.00
Tray, Sandwich, Bird Finial, Fruit Design, 8 In. 155.00
Vase, Art Nouveau, Hand Painted Landscape, Handles, 10 In. 185.00
Vase, Bird, Florals, Signed, 13 1/2 In. 110.00
Vase, Black & Gold Flowers, Gold Trim, Marked, 8 1/2 In. 55.00
Vase, Country Scene, Autumn Colors, Handle, 10 X 5 1/2 In. 65.00
Vase, Flapper, Footed, 7 1/2 In. 95.00
Vase, Gray Dragon On Dark Green, Handles, Green M, 5 In. 75.00
Vase, Scenic Top, Blue Luster, 10 In. 75.00
Vase, Tree In Meadow, 8 1/2 In. 55.00
Wall Pocket, Birds, Cream With Gold Trim, 8 In. 45.00
Wall Pocket, Butterfly Design, Flared, 9 In. 110.00

Wall Pocket, Japanese Lanterns, Blue Luster, Marked, 8 In. 65.00

The Norse Pottery Company started in Edgerton, Wisconsin, in 1903. In 1904 the company moved to Rockford, Illinois. The company made a black pottery which resembled early bronze relics of the Scandinavian countries. The firm went out of business in 1913.

NORSE, Bowl, Footed, No.101, 2 3/4 X 8 In. 130.00
Bowl, Otter's Head Handles, 3 In. 85.00
Bowl, Owls, 4 In. 165.00
Vase, Gunmetal Black, Gold Geometric Design, 9 In. 140.00
Vase, Incised Line, Snake Design, 3–Footed, Marked, 3 3/4 In. 140.00

The North Dakota School of Mines was established in 1892 at the University of North Dakota. A ceramic course was included and pieces were made from the clays found in the region. Students at the university made pieces from 1909 to 1949. Although very early pieces were marked "U.N.D.," most pieces were stamped with the university seal.

NORTH DAKOTA SCHOOL OF MINES, Bookends, Planters 150.00
Figurine, Cowboy, No.13, Gun Toting 230.00
Paperweight, Rebecca, Turquoise .... 55.00 To 65.00
Pitcher, Incised Flower, Maroon, 9 In. 130.00
Pitcher, Maroon, 8 1/2 In. 120.00
Planter, Flat Side, Grape Leaf, 3 3/4 In. 100.00
Tile, 6 Colors, Scene, Mattson, 1928 .... 350.00
Vase, Green To Purple, Cable, 3 1/4 In. 50.00
Vase, Green, Cable, 6 1/2 In. 95.00
Vase, Huck & Mattson, 3 1/2 In. 95.00
Vase, Incised Wheat, Glossy Blue, 4 In. 165.00
Vase, Navy Blue, 3 In. 70.00
Vase, Raised Viking Ship, Stamped, 3 In. 150.00
Vase, Turquoise, 7 1/2 In. 90.00

The Harry Northwood Glass Company was founded by Harry Northwood, a glassmaker who worked for Hobbs, Brockunier and Company, La Belle Glass Company, and Buckeye Glass Company before founding his own firm. He opened one factory in Sinclaire, Pennsylvania, in 1896, and another in Wheeling, West Virginia, in 1902. Northwood closed when Mr. Northwood died in 1923. Many types of glass were made, including carnival, custard, goofus, and pressed. The underlined N mark was used on some pieces.

NORTHWOOD, Basket, Basketweave, Blue Opalescent 95.00
Berry Set, Cable & Cherries, Gold Design, Colored Fruit, 7 Piece 100.00
Berry Set, Jeweled Heart, Aqua, 10 Piece 225.00
Berry Set, Leaf Medallion, Gold Trim, Amethyst, 6 Piece 195.00
Berry Set, Memphis, Gold Design, 7 Piece 95.00
Berry Set, Peach Pattern, 5 Piece 160.00
Berry Set, Shell Pattern, Blue, 7 Piece 395.00
Bowl, Beaded Cable & Rays, Blue & Marigold, 7 In. 90.00
Bowl, Fruit, Memphis, Furniture Store Advertising, 2 Piece 390.00
Bowl, Grape & Cable, 7 1/2 In. .... 52.50 To 67.50
Bowl, Strawberry Pattern, Amethyst 115.00
Butter, Cherry Thumbprint, Covered 125.00
Butter, Peach Pattern, Green, Gold Trim, Covered 115.00
Candlestick, Grape & Cable, Sea Green, Marked, 5 5/8 In., Pair 85.00
Compote, Jelly, Shell Pattern, Gold Trim, Green 190.00
Creamer, Regal, Blue 95.00
Cruet, Buzz Saw, Green 525.00
Cruet, Leaf Mold, Cased Mica Flakes, Pink & White 225.00
Epergne, Single, Metal Stand, Rose, 13 In. 110.00
Lampshade, Cased, Dark Pink, Miniature 195.00
Pitcher, Water, Regent, Aquamarine 155.00
Pitcher, Water, Royal Oak, Square Top, Applied Handle 200.00

Plate, Amethyst, Davidson Chocolates, 2 Sides Turned Up, 6 In.	295.00
Powder Jar, Grape & Cable, Purple	100.00
Rose Bowl, Feather, Blue Inside, Tan Outside, Crimped, 3 1/8 In.	950.00
Rose Bowl, Pull–Up Feathers, Blue Inside, Marked, 3 In.	1100.00
Salt & Pepper, Leaf Umbrella, Mauve	90.00
Spooner, Peach Pattern, Green	75.00
Spooner, Regal, Blue	65.00
Sugar Shaker, Daisy & Fern, Cranberry Opalescent	125.00
Sugar Shaker, Netted Oak	80.00
Sugar Shaker, Parian Swirl, White Opaque	75.00
Sugar Shaker, Spatter Leaf Mold, Vaseline	160.00
Sugar, Covered, Peach Pattern, Green	110.00
Syrup, Apple Blossom	175.00
Syrup, Netted Oak	195.00
Table Set, Paneled Holly, 4 Piece	345.00
Table Set, Regal, Opalescent Green, Gold Trim, 4 Piece	450.00
Tumbler, Blue Opalescent, Drapery	45.00
Tumbler, Grape & Cable, Marigold, Set of 6	190.00
Vase, 6 Crimp Top, Cream Lining, 8 1/8 In.	595.00
Vase, Brown Pull–Up Feather, Blue Lining, 3 X 5 1/2 In.	750.00
Water Set, Cherry Lattice, Embossed Cherries, Leaves, 3 Piece	70.00
Water Set, Concave Diamond, Celeste Blue, 7 Piece	395.00
Water Set, Drape, Blue, 5 Piece	235.00
Water Set, Inverted Fan & Feather, Gold Trim, Green, 7 Piece	495.00
Water Set, Leaf Mold, Vaseline, Spatter Glass, 7 Piece	395.00
Water Set, Oriental Poppy, Green, Gold Trim, 7 Piece	395.00
Water Set, Peach Pattern, Gold Trim, Green, 7 Piece	325.00

NU–ART   Nu–Art was a trademark registered by the Imperial Glass Company of Bellaire, Ohio, about 1920.

NU–ART, Ashtray, Black Amethyst Insert, Art Deco Nude, Gun Metal	165.00
Ashtray, Sitting Nude, 8 In.	85.00
Bookends, Gold Dancing Ladies	65.00
Bookends, Sailing Ship, Pearlized Finish	55.00

Nutcrackers of many types have been used through the centuries. At first the nutcracker was a fancy hammer; but by the nineteenth century, many elaborate and ingenious types were made. Levers, screws, and hammer adaptations were the most popular. Because nutcrackers are still useful, they are still being made, some in the old styles.

NUTCRACKER, Alligator, Brass	135.00
Alligator, Cast Iron	125.00
Counter, Sargeant's, Iron & Wood	28.00
Crocodile, Brass	15.00
Dog, Brass	110.00
Dog, Cast Iron	49.00 To 78.00
Dog, Pull–Down Tail, Nut In Mouth, Aluminum	25.00
Elephant, Brass	95.00
Elephant, Cast Iron	60.00
Jester Head, Brass	75.00
Lady's Legs, Brass, 4 In.	35.00
Mr.Pickwick, Gilded Iron	39.00
Parrot, Brass, 5 1/2 In.	12.50
Parrot, Green, Cast Iron	75.00
Perfection, Cast Iron, 1914	18.00
Pheasant, Bronze, France	100.00
Rooster Head, Brass	20.00
Screw Type, Mounted In Center of Butternut Bowl, C.1920	35.00
Squirrel, Cast Iron, Black	28.00 To 35.00

The Nymphenburg porcelain factory was established at Neudeck-ob–der–Au, Germany, in 1753 and moved to Nymphenburg in 1761. The company is still in existence. Modern marks include a checkered shield topped by a crown, and a crowned "CT" with the year and a contemporary shield mark on reproductions of eighteenth–century porcelain.

NYMPHENBURG, Figurine, Donkey, Cutout Eyes, Signed, 5 X 5 In.	95.00
Figurine, German Shepherd, Stamped, No.398, 9 X 5 In.	195.00
Figurine, Lady, Regional Costume, C.1946, 8 In.	100.00
Urn, White, Devil Figural Side Handles, 6 In.	25.00

The words "Occupied Japan" were used on pottery, porcelain, toys, and other goods made during the American occupation of Japan after World War II, from 1945 to 1952. Collectors now search for these pieces. The items were made for export.

OCCUPIED JAPAN, Candy Dish, Metal Frame & Lid, Cobalt Blue Glass, 6 In.	40.00
Dish Set, Child's, Blue, White, Floral, 15 Piece	95.00
Figurine, 4 Bears, Base, Porcelain, 7 In.	27.50
Figurine, Colonial Man & Woman, Bisque, 5 1/2 In., Pair	45.00
Figurine, Girl, Blue Delft, 5 1/4 In.	30.00
Figurine, Little Boy, Scotty Dog Pulling On Shirt, 8 In.	25.00
Figurine, Young Man & Woman, Fence, Bisque, 11 In., Pair	145.00
Lamp, Double Colonial Couple, 8 In.	45.00
Nut Set, Swans Floating, Pond Near Cottage, Box, 7 Piece	75.00
Planter, Bisque, Colonial Couple, Rabbits, 9 X 5 In.	75.00
Plate, Floral, Lattice Border, 8 1/4 In.	25.00
Salt & Pepper, Drunks On Stand	30.00
Salt & Pepper, Mermaid	22.00
Shelf Sitter, Musical Instrument, 6 In.	20.00
Tea Set, Child's, Floral, Cream Ground, Service For 6	90.00
Teapot, Tomato, Red Cover	35.00
Toby Jug, Full Figure Man, 5 In.	40.00

George E. Ohr, a true eccentric, made pottery in Biloxi, Mississippi, between 1883 and 1918. The pottery was made of very thin clay that was twisted, folded, and dented into odd, graceful shapes. Some pieces were lifelike models of hats, animal heads, or even a potato. Some pieces were decorated with folded clay "snakes." Although reproductions would be almost impossible to make, there have been some reworked pieces appearing on the market. These have been reglazed, or snakes and other embellishments have been added.

OHR, Bowl, Bulbous, 2 Colors, Stamped, 4 In.	250.00
Bowl, Ruffled, Crumpled White Clay Body, 3 X 5 In. ....*Illus*	2475.00
Candlestick, Ring Handle, Stamped	150.00
Jug, Tree of Life, Family History On Each of Many Handles	950.00
Pitcher, Strap Handle, Stamped, 6 1/2 In.	325.00
Teapot, S–Shaped Spout, Chrome To Black Glaze, 7 X 8 In. ....*Illus*	2640.00
Vase, 2 Side Handles, Stamped, 4 In.	200.00
Vase, Applied Coiled Snake, Gunmetal Glaze, 2 Handles, 8 In.	2800.00
Vase, Bulbous, Metallic Black To Brown, 2 1/2 X 3 In. ....*Illus*	715.00
Vase, Dark Green Matte Glaze, Stamped, 5 1/2 In.	480.00
Vase, Pushed & Ruffled Form, Marble Glaze, 8 In.	2600.00
Vase, Twisted Cylindrical Body, Mottled Brown & Green Glaze, 4 3/4 In.	500.00
Vase, Unglazed, Bulbous, 1 Large, 2 Small Handles, Expo Clay 1904, 4 In.	295.00
Vase, Urn Shape, Green, Red Spots, 4 1/2 In.	150.00
Vase, Yellow Gloss, Kelly Green Speckles, Folded Rim, 4 X 3 1/2 In.	880.00

OLD IVORY
84

Old Ivory china was made in Silesia, Germany, at the end of the nineteenth century. It is often marked with a crown and the word "Silesia." Some pieces are also marked with the words "Old Ivory." The pattern numbers appear on the base of each piece.

OLD IVORY, Berry Bowl, No.11, 9 1/2 In.	25.00
Berry Set, No.16, 7 Piece	195.00

Ohr, Vase, Bulbous,
Metallic Black To Brown,
2 1/2 X 3 In.

Ohr, Teapot, S–Shaped Spout,
Chrome To Black Glaze,
7 X 8 In.

Ohr, Bowl, Ruffled,
Crumpled White Clay
Body, 3 X 5 In.

Orrefors, Vase, Bulbous,
Vertical Purple Lines,
8 1/2 In.

Berry Set, No.69, 5 Piece	150.00
Berry Set, No.75, 7 Piece	175.00 To 195.00
Berry Set, No.84, 7 Piece	225.00
Bowl, No.10, Open Handle, 10 In.	65.00
Bowl, No.16, 10 In.	85.00
Bowl, No.28, Silesia, 9 1/2 In.	85.00
Bowl, No.84, 8 1/2 In.	35.00
Bowl, No.84, 10 In.	85.00
Bowl, Vegetable, No.11, 10 1/2 In.	35.00
Cake Plate, No. 16, Pierced Handles, 10 In.	85.00
Cake Plate, No. 63, Pierced Handles	65.00
Cake Plate, No. 73, Pierced Handles, Ruffled Poppies, 10 In.	85.00
Cake Plate, No. 75, 11 1/2 In.	95.00
Cake Plate, No. 84, 11 In.	95.00
Cake Plate, No. 84, Pierced Handle, 6 1/4 In., Set of 6	225.00
Cake Plate, No.122, Silesia, 10 In.	90.00
Cake Set, No.16, 7 Piece	75.00
Cake Set, No.75, Open Handles, 5 Piece	175.00
Cake Set, No.84, 7 Piece	225.00
Cake Set, No.84, Pierced Handles, 10 1/4 In., 7 Piece	225.00
Celery, No. 11, 11 3/4 X 6 In.	35.00
Celery, No. 16, 11 X 5 3/4 In.	75.00 To 115.00
Celery, No. 84, 11 X 5 1/2 In.	85.00
Celery, No.200, 11 3/4 X 5 1/2 In.	65.00
Charger, No.11, 12 3/4 In.	55.00
Chocolate Pot, No.11, Clarion, Scalloped Foot	195.00
Chocolate Pot, No.16	295.00
Chocolate Set, No.16, 7 Piece	650.00
Chocolate Set, No.84, 11 Piece	535.00 To 550.00

Don't store dishes for long periods of time in old newspaper wrappings. The ink can make indelible stains on the china.

Cracker Jar, No.16 .... 350.00
Creamer, No.11, Silesia 60.00
Creamer, No.16 .... 62.50
Creamer, No.33, Covered 35.00
Creamer, No.75 .... 35.00
Creamer, No.84 .... 35.00
Cup & Saucer, No. 16 .... 45.00
Cup & Saucer, No. 33 .... 30.00
Cup & Saucer, No. 84 .... 48.00
Cup & Saucer, No.122 .... 25.00
Dish, Pickle, No.11, Oval, 8 1/2 In. 25.00
Dish, Soup, No.16, 9 1/2 In., Set of 6 .... 625.00
Muffineer, No.84 .... 195.00
Nappy, No.84, Self–Handle 110.00
Pepper Shaker, No.16 .... 45.00
Plate, Chantilly, Silesia, 6 In. 25.00
Plate, No. 7, 7 1/2 In. 42.50
Plate, No. 10, 8 In. 35.00
Plate, No. 11, Clarion, 7 1/2 In. .... 24.00 To 25.00
Plate, No. 11, Open Handles, 10 3/4 In. 40.00
Plate, No. 15, Silesia, 8 In. 20.00
Plate, No. 16, 6 3/4 In. 24.00
Plate, No. 16, 8 1/4 In. 40.00
Plate, No. 78, Scalloped, Roses, Raised Gold Scrolls, 13 In. 80.00
Plate, No. 82, 6 In. 24.00
Plate, No. 84, 8 1/2 In. .... 35.00 To 40.00
Plate, No.200, 6 In. .... 10.00 To 20.00
Plate, Shalimar Pattern, Syracuse, 8 In. 10.00
Plate, Thistle Pattern, Corn Mark, 6 1/4 In. 14.00
Platter, No.16, 8 X 11 In. 40.00
Platter, No.84, Oval 110.00
Relish, No. 11, Oval, 6 1/4 In. 15.00
Relish, No. 84, 5 X 8 1/2 In. 85.00
Relish, No.200 .... 50.00 To 55.00
Salt & Pepper, No.15 .... 110.00
Salt & Pepper, Yellow Rose 75.00
Soup, Dish, No.84, 9 1/2 In., 6 Piece 625.00
Sugar & Creamer, No. 11, Silesia 75.00
Sugar & Creamer, No.200 .... 120.00
Sugar, No.11, Silesia, Covered 65.00
Sugar, No.16 .... 62.50
Tea Set, No.84, Silesia, 11 Piece .... 550.00 To 650.00
Toothpick, No.75 .... 40.00 To 65.00
Tray, Dresser, 9 X 7 In. 75.00
Tray, No.11, Oval, 11 1/2 In. 50.00

OLD SLEEPY EYE, see Sleepy Eye

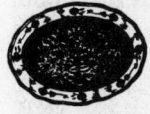

Onion pattern, originally named "bulb pattern," is a white ware decorated with cobalt blue or pink. Although it is commonly associated with Meissen, other companies made the pattern in the late nineteenth and the twentieth centuries. A rare type is called "red bud" because there are added red accents on the blue and white dishes.

ONION, Bowl, Corners Scalloped & Crimped, Meissen, 9 In. 165.00
Bowl, Crossed Swords, 11 X 2 1/2 In. 165.00
Bowl, Oval With Star, Meissen, Square, 10 In. 90.00
Butter Chip, Leaf Shape 25.00
Candlestick, Variation, 7 In., Pair 75.00
Canister, Barrel Shape, Pepper, 3 1/2 In. 35.00
Centerpiece, Stand, Man, Woman, 22 In. 935.00
Cup & Saucer, Crossed Swords, Demitasse, 1900 .... 55.00
Cup & Saucer, Twig Handle, Deep Saucer, Demitasse, Crossed Swords 45.00
Dish, 2 Sections, Handle, Marked, Meissen, 11 In. 225.00
Dish, Tricornered, Meissen, 9 In. 75.00

Eggcup, Saucer, Meissen	35.00
Funnel	45.00
Invalid Feeder	25.00 To 30.00
Knife, Fruit, Porcelain Handle, Meissen	25.00
Match Holder	45.00
Mustard	35.00 To 45.00
Pestle, Wooden Handle, 19th Century	145.00
Pitcher, Crossed Swords Mark, C.1860, 7 In.	125.00
Plate, Crossed Swords, 9 1/4 In.	50.00
Plate, Oval With Star, Meissen, 10 In.	42.00
Plate, Scalloped Rim, Pierced Work, Marked, Meissen, 8 In.	110.00
Plate, Villeroy & Boch, 8 In.	25.00
Platter, Scalloped, Well & Tree Center, Crossed Swords, 21 In.	300.00
Rolling Pin	165.00
Salt Box	95.00
Salt, Crossed Swords, 1 3/4 In.	45.00
Salt, Double, Crossed Swords, Meissen	85.00
Saltshaker, Blue, C.1900	35.00
Soup, Dish, Oval With Star, Meissen, 9 In.	38.00
Sugar & Creamer, Crossed Swords, C.1900	175.00
Tray, Flat, Crossed Swords, 15 X 9 In.	165.00
Trivet, Meissen, Round, 6 In.	75.00

Opalescent glass is translucent glass that has the bluish–white tones of the opal gemstone. It is often found in pressed glassware made in Victorian times. Some dealers use the terms "opaline" and "opalescent" for any of the bluish–white translucent wares.

OPALESCENT, see also Northwood, Pressed Glass, Spanish Lace

OPALESCENT, Basket, Diamond–Quilted, Vaseline To Pink, Pink Handle, 7 In.	145.00
Basket, Floral, Blue Edge, Vaseline Thorn Handle, 8 1/2 In.	195.00
Basket, Green Edging, Clear Handle, Vaseline, 8 3/4 In.	175.00
Basket, Richelieu, English, Blue, 6 1/2 X 4 1/4 In.	70.00
Basket, Ruffled, Amber Handle, Applied Flowers, Vaseline, 8 In.	195.00
Berry Bowl, Circle Scroll, Blue, Large	75.00
Berry Bowl, Everglades, White, 5 In.	15.00
Berry Bowl, Fan & Feather, 6 1/2 In.	35.00
Berry Bowl, Honeycomb & Clover, Blue	20.00
Berry Bowl, Inverted Fan & Feather, White, 6 1/2 In.	35.00
Berry Bowl, Jewel & Fan, Oval, 8 1/2 In.	25.00
Berry Bowl, Master, Dolly Madison, Green	48.00
Berry Bowl, Master, Iris With Meander, Green	25.00
Berry Bowl, Master, Winged Scroll, Green	125.00
Berry Bowl, Tokyo, Green, 6 1/2 In.	18.50
Berry Set, Argonaut Shell, Blue, 7 Piece	395.00
Berry Set, Everglades, Vaseline, 7 Piece	375.00
Berry Set, Fluted Scrolls, Vaseline, 6 Piece	300.00
Berry Set, Hobnail With Thumbprint, Vaseline, 7 Piece	140.00
Berry Set, Iris With Meander, Vaseline, 6 Piece	220.00
Berry Set, Jewel & Flower, Gold, Cranberry Flashed, 7 Piece	235.00
Berry Set, Jeweled Heart, Blue, 5 Piece	125.00
Berry Set, Palm Beach, Vaseline, 7 Piece	295.00
Berry Set, Regal, Green, 5 Piece	165.00
Berry Set, Wreath & Shell, Vaseline, 5 Piece	150.00
Bonbon, Jackson, Blue, 8 In.	20.00
Bottle, Daisy & Fern, Cranberry	100.00
Bowl, Child's, Beaded Key, Blue, 9 In.	49.50
Bowl, Daisy & Button, 8 X 5 In.	45.00
Bowl, Dragon & Lotus, Collar Base, Green, 9 In.	485.00
Bowl, Honeycomb & Clover, 8 3/16 In.	25.00
Bowl, Jeweled Heart, Ruffled, Blue, 9 1/2 In.	35.00
Bowl, Lily & Cattails, Crimped, Amethyst, 9 In.	35.00
Bowl, Loop, Blue, Pittsburgh, 9 1/4 X 2 7/8 In.	425.00
Bowl, Meander, Spatula Feet, Blue, 9 In.	30.00
Bowl, Reverse Drapes, Green, 8 In.	30.00

Bowl, Ribbed Spiral, Ruffled, Yellow, 8 In. .... 35.00 To 45.00
Bowl, Ruffles & Rings, White, 8 In. .... 15.00 To 20.00
Bowl, Seaweed, Ruffled, Footed, Green, 12 In. 35.00
Bowl, Water Lily & Cattail, Amethyst, 11 In. 52.00
Butter, Covered, Circle Scroll, Green 135.00
Butter, Covered, Floral, Vaseline 225.00
Butter, Covered, Fluted Scrolls, Blue .... 150.00 To 175.00
Butter, Covered, Holly With Cord & Tassel, Twig Finial, 1845 .... 147.50
Butter, Covered, Intaglio, Gold Trim, Green 85.00
Butter, Covered, Iris With Meander, Blue 300.00
Butter, Covered, Iris With Meander, Vaseline 190.00
Butter, Covered, Jewel & Flower, Vaseline 180.00
Butter, Covered, Scroll With Acanthus, Blue Design 95.00
Butter, Covered, Swag & Bracket, Green 145.00
Butter, Holly With Cord & Tassel, Covered, 1845 .... 147.50
Cake Plate, Berry Patch, White 65.00
Cake Stand, Embossed Rib, Low Foot, Blue, 3 1/8 X 8 1/2 In. 85.00
Candy Dish, Barbells, White 15.00
Candy Dish, Many Loops, Green 25.00
Celery, Beatty Swirl, Blue .... 45.00 To 75.00
Celery, Block, Vaseline, 7 In. 40.00
Celery, Hobnail, Vaseline, 3–Footed 95.00
Celery, Red Block 58.00
Celery, Regal, Northwood, Blue 125.00
Celery, Sunburst & Shield, Blue, 10 In. 65.00
Compote, Beaded Panel, Openwork Base, 7 In. .... 40.00 To 45.00
Compote, Colonial, Footed, 5 3/4 In. 550.00
Compote, Covered, Diamond Spearhead, Vaseline 60.00
Compote, Diamond Pressed, Scalloped, Blue, 4 1/4 X 5 1/8 In. 58.00
Compote, Fine Cut & Panel, Blue, 10 X 6 1/2 In. 65.00
Compote, Jelly, Cottage, Green 33.00
Compote, Jelly, Everglades 28.00
Compote, Jelly, Everglades, Vaseline .... 65.00 To 115.00
Compote, Jelly, Intaglio .... 28.00 To 40.00
Compote, Jelly, Iris With Meander, Vaseline .... 65.00 To 75.00
Compote, Jelly, Scroll With Acanthus 28.00
Compote, Jelly, Swag With Bracket, Blue 38.00
Compote, Jelly, Swag With Bracket, Green 30.00
Compote, Jelly, Tokyo, Green 25.00
Cracker Jar, Wreath & Shell, Blue 325.00
Creamer, Alaska, Vaseline 70.00
Creamer, Argonaut Shell, Blue .... 95.00 To 140.00
Creamer, Cactus, Vaseline 35.00
Creamer, Circled Scroll, Green .... 48.00 To 60.00
Creamer, Diamond Spearhead, Vaseline 45.00
Creamer, Dot Optic, Cranberry, Fenton 25.00
Creamer, Everglades, Gold Trim, Vaseline 60.00
Creamer, Everglades, White 40.00
Creamer, Flower & Jewel, Vaseline 75.00
Creamer, Fluted Scrolls, Vaseline .... 38.00 To 55.00
Creamer, Intaglio, Blue 24.00
Creamer, Inverted Fan & Feather, Blue, Gold Trim 95.00
Creamer, Jackson, Blue 55.00
Creamer, Jewel & Flower, Clear 35.00
Creamer, Water Lily & Cattails, Blue 52.00
Creamer, Wild Flower, Blue 32.00
Cruet, Block & Lattice 45.00
Cruet, Coin Dot, Cranberry, Smooth Handle 55.00
Cruet, Daisy & Fern, Blue 70.00
Cruet, Daisy & Fern, Blue, Nettled Blossom Mold 110.00
Cruet, Daisy & Fern, White 55.00
Cruet, Everglades, Vaseline .... 325.00 To 500.00
Cruet, Herringbone, Clear Ball Stopper, Blue, 7 5/8 In. 110.00
Cruet, Intaglio 95.00

Cruet, Intaglio, Blue ......65.00 To 155.00
Cruet, Intaglio, White 75.00
Cruet, Paneled Sprig & Lattice 65.00
Cruet, Regal, Green 395.00
Cruet, Ribbed Lattice, Blue 175.00
Cruet, Scroll & Acanthus, Clear Stopper, Blue 195.00
Cruet, Seaweed, Blue ...... 125.00 To 140.00
Cruet, Swag With Bracket, Original Stopper, Vaseline 245.00
Cruet, Waffle, Peach, Original Stopper 90.00
Cruet, Wild Bouquet, Original Stopper 125.00
Dish, Sweetmeat, Vaseline, Scalloped, Silver Plate Holder, 6 In. 95.00
Epergne, Single Lily, Fluted Pedestal, Fluted Bowl, Blue 75.00
Finger Bowl, Seaweed, Blue 45.00
Goblet, Honeycomb, 6 Piece 100.00
Goblet, Scalloped Fan & Daisy, Green 35.00
Gravy Boat, Fan, Green 45.00
Jam Jar, Iris & Meander, Vaseline 40.00
Lamp Shade, Gas, White, Swirl, 8 In. 60.00
Lamp, Finger, Snowflake, Cranberry 365.00
Muffineer, Chrysanthemum, Cranberry 125.00
Mug, Peacock & Crane, Pink, 2 5/8 In. 15.00
Mug, Rose In Snow, In Fond Remembrance 25.00
Pitcher, Buttons & Braids, Pale Blue, C.1910 ...... 140.00
Pitcher, Fern, Square Mouth, Blue 160.00
Pitcher, Intaglio, Blue 125.00
Pitcher, Iris With Meander, Vaseline 250.00
Pitcher, Water, Alaska, Blue 295.00
Pitcher, Water, Beatty Swirl, Blue 175.00
Pitcher, Water, Circle Scroll, Green 195.00
Pitcher, Water, Daisy & Fern, White 85.00
Pitcher, Water, Drape, Blue 195.00
Pitcher, Water, Everglades, Vaseline 375.00
Pitcher, Water, Jeweled Heart, White 1265.00
Pitcher, Water, Klondike, Round 900.00
Pitcher, Water, Raindrop 125.00
Pitcher, Water, Reverse Swirl, Bulbous, Blue 145.00
Pitcher, Water, Seaweed 165.00
Pitcher, Water, Swag With Bracket, Blue 250.00
Pitcher, Water, Swirl, Crimped, White, 9 In. 75.00
Pitcher, Water, Tokyo, Green 125.00
Pitcher, Water, Water Lily & Cattails, Amethyst ...... 195.00 To 250.00
Pitcher, Water, Wavering Quill, Green 65.00
Pitcher, Water, White Swirl, Bulbous, Crimped Top, Clear Handle 85.00
Pitcher, Water, Wild Bouquet, Blue ...... 235.00 To 250.00
Plate, Raindrop, Blue, 11 In. 25.00
Plate, Tokyo, Rimmed, Footed, Green, 8 1/2 In. 35.00
Powder Box, Fluted Scrolls, Vaseline 45.00
Powder Jar, Fluted Scrolls, Blue 55.00
Powder Jar, Fluted Scrolls, Vaseline ...... 30.00 To 45.00
Relish, Mitered Diamond, Blue 22.00
Rose Bowl, Beaded Cable, Aqua 275.00
Rose Bowl, Daisy & Fern, Blue 100.00
Rose Bowl, Dotted Loops, Blue, Footed 45.00
Rose Bowl, Drapery, Pastel 345.00
Rose Bowl, Jewel & Fan, Blue 60.00
Rose Bowl, Pearls & Scales, Green 45.00
Salt & Pepper, Daisy & Fern, Swirl Ribbed Mold, Cranberry 125.00
Salt & Pepper, Windows 125.00
Saltshaker, Alaska, Blue 42.00
Saltshaker, Paneled Forget–Me–Not, Pewter Lid, White 65.00
Saltshaker, Swag With Bracket, Blue 75.00
Sauce, Daisy & Greek Key, Blue 35.00
Sauce, Dugan Fan, Footed, Green 30.00
Sauce, Inverted Fan & Feather, Blue 30.00

Sauce, Palm Beach, Vaseline	18.00
Shot Glass, Reverse Swirl, White	45.00
Spittoon, Wreath Shell, Vaseline	78.00
Spooner, Alaska, Blue	95.00
Spooner, Alaska, Vaseline .... 35.00 To 50.00
Spooner, Beaded Oval Holly, Blue	110.00
Spooner, Circled Scroll, Green	45.00
Spooner, Diamond Spearhead, Cobalt Blue	100.00
Spooner, Everglades, Vaseline .... 60.00 To 115.00
Spooner, Grape & Gothic Arches, Gold Trim, Green	35.00
Spooner, Intaglio, Blue	48.00
Spooner, Inverted Fan & Feather	40.00
Spooner, Iris With Meander, Vaseline	46.00
Spooner, Scroll & Acanthus, Vaseline	95.00
Spooner, Wreath & Shell, Blue	75.00
Sugar & Creamer, Covered, Bead Swag, Cornflower Design	165.00
Sugar & Creamer, Covered, Palm Beach, Blue	105.00
Sugar & Creamer, Intaglio, Blue	75.00
Sugar Shaker, Daisy & Fern, Original Top, Vaseline	85.00
Sugar Shaker, Ribbed Lattice	60.00
Sugar Shaker, Ribbed Lattice, Original Lid, Cranberry	135.00
Sugar, Covered, Alaska, Vaseline	125.00
Sugar, Covered, Circled Scroll, Green	80.00
Sugar, Covered, Diamond With Spearhead, Vaseline	115.00
Sugar, Covered, Regal, Northwood, Green	65.00
Sugar, Everglades, Gold Trim, Vaseline	95.00
Sugar, Fluted Scrolls, Covered, Blue	100.00
Sugar, Fluted Scrolls, Vaseline	35.00
Sugar, Wild Bouquet, Vaseline	35.00
Syrup, Coin Dot	110.00
Syrup, Klondike	850.00
Syrup, Plain Windows, Cranberry, 7 In.	195.00
Syrup, Poinsettia, Blue	450.00
Syrup, Seaweed, Square Base, Cranberry	165.00
Table Set, Fluted Scrolls, Northwood, Vaseline, 4 Piece	350.00
Table Set, Grape & Gothic Arches, Gold Trim, Green, 4 Piece	195.00
Table Set, Intaglio, 4 Piece	195.00
Table Set, Leaf Medallion, Gold Trim, Purple, 4 Piece	500.00
Table Set, Swag With Bracket, Vaseline, 4 Piece	355.00
Tankard, Poinsettia, Blue	180.00
Toothpick, Beatty Honeycomb	24.00
Toothpick, Beatty Honeycomb, Blue .... 38.00 To 45.00
Toothpick, Beatty Rib	20.00
Toothpick, Beatty Rib, Cobalt Blue	35.00
Toothpick, Diamond Spearhead, Vaseline	65.00
Toothpick, Diamond, Peach	110.00
Toothpick, Iris With Meander, Green .... 38.00 To 65.00
Toothpick, Iris With Meander, Vaseline .... 75.00 To 100.00
Toothpick, Iris With Meander, White	35.00
Toothpick, Ribbed Lattice, Cranberry	125.00
Toothpick, Ribbed Spiral, Vaseline .... 55.00 To 65.00
Toothpick, Swirl, Amber Rim	135.00
Toothpick, Windows, Blue .... 75.00 To 125.00
Tray, Card, Fluted Scrolls, 3–Footed	35.00
Tray, Water, Beatty Swirl, Vaseline	55.00
Tray, Water, Swirled, Blue, 10 1/2 In.	55.00
Tumbler, Beatty Swirl, White To Blue	55.00
Tumbler, Colonial, Footed	50.00
Tumbler, Daisy & Fern, Blue	35.00
Tumbler, Daisy & Fern, Cranberry	40.00
Tumbler, Tokyo	22.00
Tumbler, Wreath & Shell, Blue	50.00
Vase, Block, Cranberry Edge, 7 In.	35.00
Vase, Diamond Point, Green, 10 3/4 In.	30.00

Vase, Double Greek Key Design, Blue, 6 In.	130.00
Vase, Jack–In–The–Pulpit, Rainbow Stripe, Pedestal, 8 1/4 In.	100.00
Vase, Leaf & Scroll, Vaseline, 4 5/8 In.	90.00
Vase, Lined Heart, Aqua, 12 In.	32.00
Vase, Swirl, Cranberry, 5 1/2 In.	45.00
Vase, Vaseline, Thorny Tree Trunk, Applied Feet, 5 5/8 In.	50.00
Water Set, Blue Swirl, Ruffled, Applied Clear Handle, 5 Piece	90.00
Water Set, Buttons & Braids, Blue, 6 Piece	250.00
Water Set, Coin Dot, Blue, 7 Piece	185.00
Water Set, Fluted Scrolls, 7 Piece	375.00
Water Set, Jeweled Heart, Blue, 7 Piece	850.00
Water Set, Panel & Holly, Blue, Gold Trim, Northwood, 7 Piece	375.00
Water Set, Polka Dot, Fenton, Cranberry, 10 Piece	375.00
Water Set, Swag With Bracket, Vaseline, 7 Piece	389.00
Wine, Thousand Eye, Amber	25.00

Opaline, or opal glass, was made in white, green, and other colors. The glass had a matte surface and a lack of transparency. It was often gilded or painted. It was a popular mid–nineteenth–century European glassware.

OPALINE, Biscuit Jar, Dore Handle & Finial, Hand Painted Flower	125.00
Bottle, Perfume, Cut Panels, Lavender Stopper, 5 3/4 In.	75.00
Bottle, Perfume, Gold & Cream Leaves, White Stopper, 6 1/4 In.	110.00
Chandelier, 6–Light, Charles X, Stylized Feather Design, 28 In.	2525.00
Cruet, Clear Hollow Stopper, Clear Leaves, Pink	97.50
Finger Bowl, Blue Floral Border, Gilt Bands, 4 5/8 In., 6 Piece	485.00
Lamp, Fairy, 4 Faceted Jewels, Filigree Brass, Blue, 17 In.	275.00
Lamp, Oil, Charles X, Turquoise, Bronze Mounted, 16 In., Pair	1980.00
Sugar, Covered, Gold Enameled Trim, Wafered Stem, 1815–30, 7 In.	1025.00
Vase, Flattened Oval Shape, Floral Enameling, French, 8 In., Pair	135.00
Vase, Napoleon III, Gilt Bronze Mount, Baluster Shape, 46 In.	1875.00

The stage is a long way from some of the seats at a play or an opera, so the patrons sometimes carried special opera glasses in the nineteenth and early twentieth centuries. Mother–of–pearl was a popular decoration.

OPERA GLASSES, Almer Coe & Co., Opticians, Chicago, Leather Case	35.00
Bird & Berries Design, French Label	24.00
Gold, Pearl, Velvet Case	125.00
Ivory, French, Leather Case	110.00
Mother–of–Pearl, Case, 1894	35.00
Pearl, Handle, France	42.50
Rose Enameled, Floral & Foliage Design, Carrying Case	75.00

Little Orphan Annie first appeared in the comics in 1924. The redheaded girl and her friends have been on the radio and are still on the comic pages. A Broadway musical show and a movie in the 1980s made Annie popular again and many toys, dishes, and other memorabilia are being made.

ORPHAN ANNIE, Bank, Dime	50.00
Belt, Decoder	90.00
Book, Big Little Book, 1935	25.00
Book, Haunted House, 1928	10.00
Book, Never Say Die, 1930	20.00
Book, Pop–Up, Orphan Annie & Jumbo, 1935	45.00
Book, Shipwrecked, 1931	30.00
Bracelet, Enameled	30.00
Bracelet, ID	30.00 To 35.00
Compass & Sun Watch, Ovaltine Premium, Symbols, 1938	30.00
Cup, Ovaltine, Beetleware, Decal, 1930s, 3 In.	25.00
Decoder, 1937	20.00
Decoder, Radio, 1936	11.00 To 18.00
Doll, Movie Star, Locket, Extra Dress, Knickerbocker, 11 In.	12.00
Doll, Oilcloth	46.00

Doll, Porcelain, Box, 10 In.	50.00
Doll, With Dog Sandy In Pocket, Knickerbocker, Box, 16 In.	65.00
Doll, With Dog Sandy, Cloth, 17 In.	45.00
Doll, Wood Jointed, Elastic Cord, Dressed, 1930s, 5 In.	45.00
Figurine, Sandy, Bisque	9.00
Figurine, With Sandy & Daddy Warbucks, Metal	15.00
Game, Pursuit, S.& R.Games, 1978	8.00
Game, To The Rescue, Bradley	65.00
Knitting Machine, Wooden	25.00
Map, Simmons Corners, Paper, Radio Premium, 1936, 19 X 24 In.	85.00
Mug, Ovaltine, 1937 Radio Premium	20.00
Mug, Shake-Up, Dome Lid	45.00
Nodder, Annie & Sandy, Bisque, German, 3 In., Pair	175.00
Paint Box, Crayons, Sheets of Pictures, 16 X 10 In.Box	65.00
Pin, Decoder, Round, 1935	22.00
Pin, Decoder, Secret Compartment, 1936	22.00
Puzzle, No.1, Box	22.00
Ring, Face	10.00
Salt & Pepper, Annie & Sandy, Chalkware	28.00
Sheet Music, Ovaltine Orphan Annie Song, 1931	25.00
Stove, 2 Oven Doors Open, Annie, Sandy Lithos, 9 1/2 X 8 In.	65.00
Stove, Tin, Blue, 4 1/2 X 4 3/4 In.	20.00
Telephone, Hard Plastic	40.00
Toothbrush Holder, Annie & Sandy, Bisque, 1930s	90.00
Toothbrush Holder, Porcelain	135.00
Toy, Sandy Dog, Mechanical, Tin, Marx, Box, 1930s	75.00
Watch, 1940s, Box	165.00
Watch, Aztec Sun	25.00
Wristwatch, 1934 .... 55.00 To 60.00	

The Orrefors Glassworks, located in the Swedish province of Smaaland, was established in 1916. The company is still making glass for use on the table or as decorations. There is renewed interest in the glass made in the modern styles of the 1940s and 1950s. Most vases and decorative pieces are signed with the etched name.

ORREFORS, Ashtray, Clear, Signed, 8 In.	45.00
Ashtray, Red, 1950s, Signed, 3 X 6 In.	75.00
Bottle, Perfume, Flat Front & Back, Engraved Swan, Stopper, 2 In.	85.00
Bottle, Perfume, Flat Front & Back, Inside Teardrop, 4 In.	70.00
Bowl, Canoe Shape, Inner Speckled Blue Spheres, Signed, 5 1/4 In.	220.00
Candleholder, Ball Shape, Pair	75.00
Decanter, Signed, 9 In.	85.00
Salt, Blue	10.00
Vase, Blue Air Trap Design, Female Profile, Ohrstrom, 7 In.	2200.00
Vase, Bud, Smoke Case, Clear, 8 In.	95.00
Vase, Bulbous, Vertical Purple Lines, 8 1/2 In. ....*Illus*	150.00
Vase, Butterflies, Flowers, Signed, 6 1/4 In.	68.50
Vase, Child With Bird & Goose, Signed, Paper Label, 8 In.	150.00
Vase, Deep Ruby & Clear, Teardrop, Paperweight, 4 In.	85.00
Vase, Engraved Children, Basket of Flowers, Oblong, 6 X 4 3/4 In.	375.00
Vase, Paperweight, Bullet Shape, Interior Design of Fish, 5 In.	325.00
Vase, Squatty, Light Blue Cast, 3 In.	38.00
Vase, Swirl, 8 In.	175.00

Ott & Brewer Company operated the Etruria Pottery at Trenton, New Jersey, from 1863 to 1893. It was under the direction of William Bromley, Sr., who had worked at the Belleek factory at Belleek, Ireland, from 1883. The firm used a variety of marks that incorporated the initials O & B.

OTT & BREWER, Cake Plate, Tridacna, Brushed Gold Design, 9 1/2 In.	225.00
Creamer, Allover Pansies, Gold Handle, Wide Lip, 3 In.	172.00
Cup & Saucer, Cactus Pattern, Gold Paste Thistle & Leaves	150.00
Cup & Saucer, Floral Sprays, Blue & Pink Flowers	125.00

Dish, Sweetmeat, Fluted Gold Design, 5 In.	175.00
Plate, Tulip, Gold Sponged Design, Blue & White, 8 In.	25.00
Tray, Pin, Ruffled Rim, Leaves, Enameled Flowers, 4 1/4 In.	145.00
Vase, Yellow Pansies, 10 In.	695.00

The four Overbeck sisters started a pottery in Cambridge City, Indiana, in 1911. They made all types of vases, each one-of-a-kind. Small, hand–modeled figurines are the most popular pieces with today's collectors. The factory continued until 1955 when the last of the four sisters died.

OVERBECK, Figurine, Charles Dickens Man, Blues, Yellow, Brown, 4 1/2 In.	125.00
Figurine, Indian With Club, Green, Turquoise, Brown, Pink, 5 In.	110.00
Figurine, Lady, Long Pink Dress, Hat, 4 In.	375.00
Vase, Oriental Design, Yellow Glaze, Green Design, 4 In.	375.00
Vase, Seahorses, Green, Yellow, 7 In.	1000.00

OWENS UTOPIAN

Owens Pottery was made in Zanesville, Ohio, from 1891 to 1928. The first art pottery was made after 1896. Utopian Ware, Cyrano, Navarre, Feroza, and Henri Deux were made. Pieces were usually marked with a form of the name "Owens." About 1907, the firm began to make tile and discontinued the art pottery wares.

OWENS, Chamber Pot, Art Nouveau	165.00
Creamer, Utopian, Footed, Metal Rim & Handle, Artist Signed	100.00
Jug, Coralene On Gold, Hand Painted Pansies, 5 X 6 In.	350.00
Lamp, Sudanese	195.00
Lamp, Utopian	125.00
Mug, Utopian, Artist Signed	130.00
Pitcher, Cider, Embossed Lady, Flowing Hair	85.00
Plate, Bluebird	15.00
Tankard, Portrait, Gold Medal, St.Louis, Minerva	250.00
Vase, Brown Cherries, Matte Finish, 10 In.	195.00
Vase, Henri Deux Mold, Matte Green, 8 1/2 In.	68.00
Vase, Indian Gourd, Signed, 5 1/2 In.	135.00
Vase, Opalesque, Oval, 12 In.	325.00
Vase, Stylized Florals & Leaves, Inlaid Opalescent, 12 In.	295.00
Vase, Utopian, Harvey, 3 3/4 X 5 3/4 In.	95.00
Vase, Utopian, High Glaze Floral, 4 In.	110.00
Vase, Utopian, Roses, Flat Spheroid Shape, Signed, 9 1/2 In.	275.00
Vase, Utopian, Twisted Shape, 5 In.	140.00
Vase, Utopian, Wild Rose, Matte, 9 In.	195.00
Vase, Yellow Magnolia, Brown Glaze, Artist Signed, 13 In.	110.00

Oyster plates were popular from the 1880s. Each course at dinner was served in a special dish. The oyster plate had indentations shaped like oysters. Usually six oysters were held on a plate. There is no greater value to a plate with more oysters although that myth continues to haunt antiques dealers. There are other plates for shellfish including cockle plates and whelk plates. The appropriately shaped indentations are part of the design of these dishes.

OYSTER PLATE, 5 Indentations, Blue, Green, CFH	60.00
6 Indentations, Green Seaweed	75.00

Paden City Glass Manufacturing Company was established in 1916 at Paden City, West Virginia. It is best known for glasswares but also produced a pottery line. The firm closed in 1951.

PADEN CITY, Bowl, Irwin Pattern, Ruby, 12 In.	85.00
Cake Plate, Peacock Reverse, Ruby	52.00
Cake Plate, Yorktown, Pedestal, 12 In.	130.00
Candy Dish, Covered, Crow's Foot, Red	45.00
Candy Jar, Covered, Red, 10 In.	125.00
Compote, Footed, Amber, 8 In.	15.00
Compote, Gothic Garden, Pink	35.00
Console Set, Triumph Green, 12 In.Bowl, 3 In.Candlestick, 3 Pc.	35.00
Cookie Jar, Patrician, Crystal	90.00

Painting, On Glass, Chinese Export, Maidens,
28 X 20 In., Pair

Painting, Reverse On Glass,
Chinese Lady Musicians, 20 X 29 In.

Creamer, Crow's Foot, Amber	6.00
Creamer, Hummingbird, Blue	52.00
Figurine, Chanticleer, Crystal	65.00
Figurine, Chinese Pheasants, Clear, 13 3/4 In.	55.00
Figurine, Cottontail Bunny, Blue	50.00
Figurine, Fighting Cock, Clear, 9 In.	150.00 To 160.00
Figurine, Pony, Standing, Crystal	45.00
Figurine, Pouter Pigeon, 7 In., Pair	100.00
Figurine, Squirrel On Log, Crystal	40.00
Goblet, Water, Gothic Garden, 8 In.	25.00
Mixing Bowl, Yellow, Caliente Pottery, 8 In.	8.00
Pitcher, Covered, Party Line, Green	60.00
Platter, Morning Glory	9.00
Platter, Spring Blossom, 12 1/2 In.	6.00
Server, Peacock Reverse, Center Handle, Amber	65.00
Server, Sandwich, Peacock & Wild Rose, Center Handle, Green	35.00
Server, Swan Handle, Silver Overlay, Cupped	30.00
Sherbet, Patrician, Amber	8.50
Soup, Cream, Patrician, Amber	9.00
Sugar & Creamer, Flying Peacock, Pink	50.00
Sugar & Creamer, Patrician, Amber	12.50
Tray, Crow's Foot, Center Handle, Amber	18.00
Tumble–Up, Tray, Pnk	75.00
Tumbler, Iced Tea, Patrician, Crystal	25.00
Vase, Cupid, Pink, 10 In.	135.00
Vase, Orchid Pattern, Black, 10 In.	85.00
Vase, Peacock & Roses, Apple Green, 10 In.	40.00

The paintings listed in this book are not works by major artists but rather decorative paintings on ivory, board, or glass that would be of interest to the average collector. To learn the value of an oil painting by a listed artist you must contact an expert in that area.

PAINTING, On Board, Gentleman, Gray Coat, Henry Smith, 20 5/8 X 24 5/8 In.	950.00
On Board, Melville Smith, Greeting The Indians, 22 1/2 X 36 In.	1100.00
On Board, Snow Covered Mountains, J.A.Brown, 11 X 10 In.	750.00
On Canvas, 2 Children, Flowers, Primitive, Oil, 27 X 35 1/2 In.	4850.00
On Canvas, Lake, Mountains, Shadowbox Frame, Oil, 25 X 31 In.	145.00
On Canvas, Young Gentleman, On Masonite, Oil, Frame, 23 X 30 In.	140.00
On Enamel, Jenny Lind, Signed Carmona, Limoges, 4 X 5 1/2 In.	350.00
On Glass, Chinese Export, Maidens, 28 X 20 In., Pair *Illus*	3850.00
On Glass, Madame Labrun & Daughter, Gold Dust Frame, Miniature	65.00

A miniature painting should not be washed. Most miniatures are painted on ivory and the paint will wash off.

Don't hang an oil painting above a fireplace that is used frequently.

Store paintings under the bed. It's dark, has good air circulation, and the paintings can be kept horizontal.

On Glass, Reverse, George Washington, Oval Frame, 5 X 6 In.	205.00
On Ivory, Child, Auburn Curly Hair, Esther Shelton, 3 X 4 In.	148.00
On Ivory, Court Lady, Tiara, Signed, Miniature	125.00
On Ivory, Duchess De Bourbon, Signed Fazi, C.1830, 1 3/4 In.	90.00
On Ivory, Elizabethan Man, Miniature	145.00
On Ivory, Front View, Young Girl, Moses B.Russell, 1840, 2 1/4 In.	1200.00
On Ivory, Gentleman In High Stock Collar, 3/4 View, 2 X 2 In.	150.00
On Ivory, Girl, Off–Shoulder Dress, American, C.1820, 2 1/2 In.	750.00
On Ivory, Lady, Blue Gown, 8 X 7 In. ....*Illus*	200.00
On Ivory, Lady, Seated, Lace Cap, Paisley Shawl, Signed Fette	250.00
On Ivory, Man, Black Coat, Ebony Frame, C.1800, 2 1/2 X 2 In.	85.00
On Ivory, Man, Whiskers, Gold Frame, Braided Hair Back, 2 In.	325.00
On Ivory, Mother & 2 Children, Red Ground, Gilt Frame, 8 X 9 In.	200.00
On Ivory, Mother With Young Daughter, Holding Flowers, Framed	350.00
On Ivory, Napoleon, Family Scene	375.00
On Ivory, Othello Defending Himself Before Ongen, 7 1/2 In.	1980.00
On Ivory, Plump Young Man, Gold Wash Frame, 1820s, 3 X 2 1/2 In.	325.00
On Ivory, Princess Sophie, Signed Faci, C.1830, 1 3/4 In.	90.00
On Ivory, Victorian Lady, Plumes On Hat, 5 X 4 1/4 In.	89.00
On Ivory, Wife of Charles II, Spain, Collar, Pendant, 1 3/4 In.	195.00
On Ivory, Woman's Bust, Drop Earrings, Sept.15, 1835, 2 X 2 In.	500.00
On Ivory, Woman, Blue, Hair Flowers, Square Ebony Frame, 3 In.	80.00
On Ivory, Woman, Braided Hair, 5 3/4 X 4 3/4 In.	160.00
On Ivory, Woman, Mother–of–Pearl Matte, Pierre A.Hall, 3 In.	150.00
On Panel, Young Man With Spyglass, Framed, 1830s, 11 X 9 1/2 In.	800.00
On Paper, Indian, Waterfall, Black Alligatored Paint, 13 X 17 In.	265.00
On Paper, Theorem, Watercolor, Harrison Family, C.1830, 9 X 12 In.	950.00
On Paper, Watercolor, Young Girl, Scenery, Frame, 19 3/4 X 22 In.	875.00
On Porcelain, Artists Painting Boy, Brass Frame, C.1875, 4 In.	250.00
On Porcelain, Colonial Lady, Gentleman, Unframed, 4 X 5 In., Pair	95.00
On Porcelain, Madonna, Flowing Hair, C.1780, Oval, 3 3/8 In.	486.00
On Porcelain, Woman & Man, Bust, Crown & Hat, Easel, 3 In., Pair	300.00
On Porcelain, Woman In Ball Gown, Jewels, Signed, 5 X 6 In.	200.00
On Silk, 2 Cranes, Meiji Period, Faux Bamboo Frame, 44 X 21 In.	150.00
On Silk, Oriental Lady, 10 X 18 In.	25.00
On Silk, U.S.S.Chattanooga, C.1890	455.00
On Tin, Landscape, 5 3/4 X 7 In., Pair	500.00
On Velvet, Blue Compote, C.1840, 19 X 21 In.	1300.00
On Velvet, Fruit, Painted Ground, Gold Frame, C.1835, 24 X 31 In.	1800.00
On Velvet, Fruits, Basket, D.Ellinger, Framed, 17 X 22 In., Pair	395.00
On Velvet, Theorem, Peaches, Strawberries, C.1840, 5 X 7 In.	100.00
On Wood, Gentleman, Ogee Bird's–Eye Frame, Oil, 28 X 33 In.	275.00
On Wood, Keg Lid, Mountain Landscape, Cabin, 12 3/4 In.	45.00

On Wood, Portrait, Young Woman, English, 25 X 19 In.	4200.00
Reverse On Glass, Castle In Belgium, Curved, Frame, 1817	25.00
Reverse On Glass, Chinese Lady Musicians, 20 X 29 In. *Illus*	500.00
Reverse On Glass, Chinese Mandarin, Attendants, 18 X 24 3/4 In.	1300.00
Reverse On Glass, Hummingbird & Rose, Walnut Frame, 10 X 11 In.	55.00
Reverse On Glass, Lady Musicians, Men, Bridge, China, 10 X 29 In.	500.00
Reverse On Glass, Majestic Radios, Family, C.1920, 15 X 18 In.	725.00
Reverse On Glass, Ship Tennessee of Portland, 21 X 27 3/4 In.	5400.00
Reverse On Glass, Statue of Liberty, 19 X 13 In.	88.00
Reverse On Glass, Statue of Liberty, Folk Art, Bubble Frame	85.00
Reverse On Glass, Washington, Writing Table, 10 3/8 X 12 3/8 In.	925.00

The Pairpoint Manufacturing Company started in 1880 in New Bedford, Massachusetts. It soon joined with the glassworks nearby and made glass, silver plated pieces, and lamps. Reverse–painted glass shades and molded shades known as "puffies" were part of the production until the 1930s. The company reorganized and changed its name several times but is still working today.

PAIRPOINT, Basket, Silver Plated Handle, Cutout Pattern, Ruby Glass	85.00
Biscuit Jar, Burnt Orange Ground, Floral Design, Signed, 9 In.	325.00
Biscuit Jar, Floral Enameling, Burnt Orange, Bail, 9 1/2 In.	285.00
Bowl, Blown–Out Roses, Tennis Racquet Base, Nouveau, 3 1/2 In.	45.00
Bowl, Egyptian Silhouette, Double Handle, Shallow, 10 In.	95.00
Bowl, Fish Finial Cover, Chrysanthemums, 5 3/4 X 6 1/2 In.	485.00
Bowl, Peppermint Stick, Cutting, 8 1/2 In.	125.00
Box, Collar & Cuff, Flowers, Gold Trim, Hinged Lid, Round	235.00
Box, Covered, Hand Painted, Oval, Brass & China, Signed	225.00
Box, Hairpin, Woman's Friend, Silver Plate, Hinged Cover	35.00
Box, Hinged Lid, Gold Flowers & Leaves, Cream, Signed, 6 In.	425.00
Box, Hinged, Gold Flowers & Leaves, Signed, 6 X 7 1/2 In.	425.00
Box, Hinged, Opalescent, Biscuit, Gold & Silver Iris, Signed	455.00
Candelabrum, 5–Light, Victorian, Silver Plate, 15 X 15 In.	195.00
Candleholder, Controlled Bubble Base, Light Green, 11 In., Pair	185.00
Candleholder, Paperweight, Clear Bubble Ball, 4 1/2 In.	45.00
Candlestick, 4 Spindles On Flaring Base, C.1920, 11 1/4 In.	100.00
Candlestick, Bull's–Eye & Miter, Hollow Stem, 12 In., Pair	215.00
Candlestick, Floral & Whiplash Design, Marked, 11 In., Pair	155.00
Candlestick, Mushroom Top, Clear Bubbles, Green, 4 1/2 X 5 In.	95.00
Candlestick, Sterling Overlay, Bubble Base, Black, 12 In., Pair	225.00
Castor, Pickle, Enameled Flowers, Raised Design, Fluted	135.00
Center Set, Crystal, Diamond Ruby Cut Rim, 12 In.Vase, 3 Piece	500.00
Coffeepot, Silver, Serpent Spout, No.300	275.00
Compote, Amber, Vintage, 6 In.	42.00
Compote, Bubble Stem, Italian Green, 6 X 6 1/2 In.	75.00
Compote, Controlled Bubble Base, Ruby, Low, 5 In.	125.00
Compote, Dolphin Metal Base, Marked, 6 In.	185.00
Compote, Nottingham Pattern, 6 1/2 X 6 1/4 In.	125.00
Console Set, Controlled Bubble, Aurora, 3 Piece	275.00
Console, Controlled Bubble Base, Light Green, 12 In.	145.00
Cracker Jar, Daisy Design, Apricot Bulbous Base, 7 X 6 In.	295.00
Cup, Folding, Quadruple Plate	17.50
Dish, Covered, Raised Enameling, Metal Holder, Signed, 10 In.	365.00
Lamp, Floral Shade, Urn, Raised Human Figures, White, 23 In.	380.00
Lamp, Poppies, Roses, Black Ground, 8 In.Berkeley Shade, Boudoir	1095.00
Lamp, Poppy Shade, Rose Base, Brass, Marked, 21 In.	3500.00
Lamp, Puffy, Butterflies, Yellow Roses, 14 In. *Illus*	2750.00
Lamp, Puffy, Butterfly, Flowers, Boudoir *Illus*	900.00
Lamp, Puffy, Flowers, Red, Purple, Tree Form Base, 18 In. *Illus*	5500.00
Lamp, Puffy, Roses, Magenta, Green, Brown, 21 In. *Illus*	4950.00
Lamp, Reverse Painted Exeter Shade, Farmer On Horse, 23 1/2 In.	1650.00
Lamp, Reverse Painted Exeter Shade, Urn Shape, W.Macey, 3 In.	1650.00
Lamp, Reverse Painted Jungle Birds, 4 Parrots, Marked	2600.00
Lamp, Reverse Painted Winter Scene Shade, Brass, 22 3/4 In.	1500.00
Lamp, Swan, Marked Base	1000.00

Pairpoint, Lamp, Puffy,
Butterfly, Flowers,
Boudoir

Pairpoint, Lamp, Puffy, Butterflies,
Yellow Roses, 14 In.

Pairpoint, Lamp,
Puffy, Roses, Magenta,
Green, Brown, 21 In.

Lamp, Tropical Trees, Parrots, Orange, Blue, 21 In. ....*Illus* 1760.00
Match Safe, Exposition, 1893 .... 95.00
Mirror, Plateau, Beveled & Cut, Claw Feet, 12 In. 65.00
Paperweight, Multifaceted Yellow Rose, J.Irving, 3 1/8 In. 250.00
Perfume Bottle, Controlled Bubble Base & Stopper, 5 1/2 In. 110.00
Platter, 2 Mallard Ducks, Blazing Gold Sun, 12 X 8 1/2 In. 485.00
Shade, Scenic, Artist Fisher, 20 In. 1500.00
Shaving Mug, Roses, Quadruple Plate 35.00
Swan, Ruby, Gunderson, 8 In. 185.00
Swan, Ruby, Gunderson, 14 In. 325.00
Toothpick, Figural, Rat That Ate The Malt 45.00
Tray, Sandwich, Hook Handle, Handcut 60.00
Urn, Swirl Connector, Covered, 18 In., Pair 295.00
Vase, Clear, Bubble Ball Connector, Handles, Blue, 8 In. 85.00
Vase, Cobalt Blue, Light Swirls, Bubble Connector, 13 In., Pair 25.00
Vase, Colias Pattern, Green Base, 12 In. 95.00
Vase, Controlled Bubble Base, Ruby, Flared, 13 In. 225.00
Vase, Controlled Bubble Base, Ruby, Rolled Rim, 8 In. 110.00
Vase, Cornucopia, Controlled Bubble Base, Ruby, 9 In. 125.00
Vase, Cranberry, Flared, Bubble Ball Connector, 12 In. 135.00
Vase, Engraved Vintage Pattern, Amethyst, 12 In. 150.00
Vase, Jack-In-The-Pulpit, Ruby Enameled Bird, 7 3/4 In. 155.00
Vase, Swirl Ball, Marine Blue, Flared, 13 In. 150.00

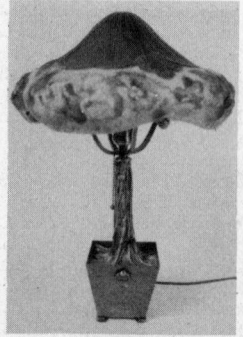

Pairpoint, Lamp, Puffy, Flowers, Red, Purple,
Tree Form Base, 18 In.

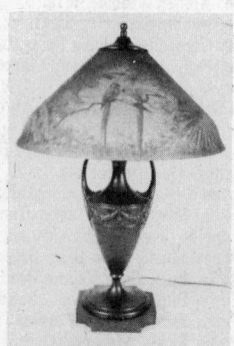

Pairpoint, Lamp,
Tropical Trees, Parrots,
Orange, Blue, 21 In.

Vase, Trumpet Shape, Colias, Intaglio Flower Bottom, 8 In. 80.00
Vase, Trumpet Shape, Crystal Bubble Ball Connector, 8 In. 65.00
Vase, Urn Shape, Green Grapes, 2 Handles, 11 In., Pair 500.00
Wine Coaster, Pierced Silver Plate, Sheffield 20.00
       PALMER COX, BROWNIES, see Brownies

 The first paper dolls were probably the pantins, or jumping jacks, made in eighteenth–century Europe. By the 1880s, sheets of printed paper dolls and clothes were being made. The first paper doll books were made in the 1920s. Collectors prefer uncut sheets or books or boxed sets of paper dolls. Prices are about half as much if the pages have been cut.

PAPER DOLL, American Lady & Her Children, Kimmel & Foster 425.00
  Amy Carter, Uncut, Box 9.00
  Amy Jo, Doll & Her Baby, Rand McNally, 1972 .... 5.00
  Ann Blyth 10.00
  Ann Sothern, 1943, Uncut 40.00
  Annette Funicello, Uncut 20.00
  Arlene Dahl, Book, 1953, Uncut 25.00
  Ava Gardner, Cut 25.00
  Baby, McLoughlin Bros., Cut, Envelope 125.00
  Barbara Britton, 1954, Uncut, Box 20.00
  Barbie & Ken, Whitman, 1970, Uncut 12.00
  Barbie's Boutique, Whitman, 1973 .... 20.00
  Barbie, Western, 1982, Uncut 4.00
  Betty Bonnet's College Sister, 1915, Uncut 15.00
  Betty Bonnet's Rainy Day Party, 1918 .... 15.00
  Betty Bonnet, Next Door Neighbor, Patriotic Party, 1917 .... 16.00
  Betty Campbell, Round About Dolls, 3 Folders, McLoughlin, 1936 .... 38.00
  Betty Fields, Uncut 35.00
  Betty Grable, 8 Pages, Whitman, 1946, Uncut 140.00
  Betty Grable, Merrill, Uncut .... 110.00 To 140.00
  Blue Feather Indian, 1944, Uncut 22.00
  Bonnie Bill, Tuck's 100.00
  Boston Sunday Globe, Cutouts, Aug.2, 1896 .... 30.00
  Brady Bunch, Whitman, 1973 .... 20.00
  Bridal Party, Whitman, 1950 .... 30.00
  Brunette Girl, In Figural Tree & St.Nicholas Folder, S & C 450.00
  Buffy, 1969, Uncut 10.00
  Campbell's Wedding Party, Uncut 8.00
  Carmen Miranda, 1940s 55.00
  Cher, Back & Front, Vinyl Doll 6.00
  Clark's Spool Cotton, 9 Different 80.00
  Claudette Colbert Celebrity Book, 1943, Uncut 110.00
  Connie Francis, Uncut 25.00
  Coronation, Coloring Book, Uncut 30.00
  Cousin Anne, May I Be Your Valentine, Good Housekeeping, 1924 .... 9.00
  Deanna Durbin, Merrill, 1940, Uncut 150.00
  Debbie Reynolds, Clothes In Folder 15.00
  Delie, C.1896 .... 65.00
  Dennis The Menace, 1960s, Uncut 10.00
  Diahann Carrol, Uncut 12.00
  Diane The Bride, McLoughlin, Original Folder 225.00
  Die Kaiserliche Familie, German Royal Family, Portfolio, W & S 1300.00
  Dinah Shore & George Montgomery, Uncut 35.00
  Dolly Dingle Celebrates Halloween, Pictorial Review, 1918 .... 25.00
  Dolly Dingle Joins Red Cross, Pictorial Review, 1918, Uncut 25.00
  Dolly Dingle's Birthday Cards For All The Family, 1919, Uncut 14.00
  Dolly Dingle's Christmas Party, Pictorial Review, 1916, Uncut 35.00
  Dolly Dingle's Trip Around World, Spanish Dons, 1917, Uncut 25.00
  Dolly Dingle, 1920s, Cut 5.00
  Dolly Dingle, 4 Dolls, Clothes, 1920 .... 18.00
  Dolly Dingle, As Bridesmaid, Pictorial Review, 1929 .... 20.00
  Dolly Dingle, Sheet, 1917 .... 17.50

Doris Day, Original Folder, Whitman	40.00
Dotty Dimples, Dimple Triplets, 2 Packages, Uncut, McLoughlin	30.00
Double Wedding, 1939	55.00
Dr.Miles Heart Cure, With 3 Hats & Dresses	125.00
Dresses Worn By 1st Ladies, Maybelle Mercer, Saalfield, 1937	20.00
Ed Byrnes, Uncut	25.00
Elizabeth Taylor, Whitman	45.00
Elsie, Box, 1969	7.00
Esther Williams, Merrill, Uncut	140.00
Eugenia, McLoughlin, Original Booklet	125.00
Eve Arden, Uncut	25.00
Fairy Tales Series, Raphael Tuck Series VIII, 1894	65.00
Family Affair, Box, Uncut	6.00
Fanny Brice, Baby Snooks, Queen Holden, Whitman, Uncut	275.00
Fanny Gray, History of Her Life, Crosby, Nichols & Co.	475.00
Faye Emerson, Uncut	25.00
Flying Kewpies, Woman's Home Companion, May 1913, Uncut	28.00
Gale Storm, Dell, 1957, Uncut	65.00
Ginny, Box	20.00
Girl Scout, Uncut, Cellophane Bag	25.00
Goldilocks & The Three Bears, Punch Out, 1953	27.00
Gone With The Wind, 18 Figures, Merrill, Uncut	375.00 To 550.00
Gone With The Wind, Main Characters	65.00
Grace Kelly, 6 Pages, Whitman, 1956, Uncut	80.00
Green Acres, Eddie Albert, Eva Gabor, Box	22.00
Greer Garson, Cut	50.00
Hayley Mills, 1965, Cut	10.00
Hedy Lamarr, Saalfield, Uncut	70.00
Here's The Bride, 1950s, Uncut	10.00
Holden Hair–Do Dolls	50.00
Honeymooners, Ralph, Alice, Ed & Trixie, VIP Corp., 1956	70.00
Hood's Sarsaparilla, 1903	25.00
Jane Powell, Uncut	12.00 To 17.50
Jane Russell, Cut	10.00
Jane Visits France, Dean & Sons, London	5.00
Janet Leigh, 1958, Uncut	25.00
Jeannette MacDonald, Clothes Uncut, Cover Picture, Cut	85.00
Judy Garland, Queen Holden No.996, Uncut	225.00
Judy Garland, Queen Holden No.999, Cut	185.00
June Allyson, Whitman, 1957	20.00
Kachina, Blue & White, Ejkabi, 1952	8.00
Katie, Selchow & Richter, 9 In.Doll	80.00
Kelly Sisters, 1944, Saalfield, Uncut	20.00
Kewpie Nurse & Better Baby, Woman's Home Companion, 1913	28.00
Lettie Lane's Around The World Party, Japanese, 1910, Uncut	15.00
Li'l Abner, Uncut	25.00
Lilly Beers, McLoughlin, Original Booklet	175.00
Linda Darnell	25.00
Little Jack Horner, Lion Coffee, 3 Piece	4.00
Little Laddie, Selchow & Richter, 8 In.Doll	80.00
Little Sunbeam, Cut–Craft, Envelope	170.00
Little Women, Rachel Ward Taft, C.1934	60.00
Lucille Ball, Cut	20.00
Lucinda Lee, Margaret Evans Price, Envelope, Copyright 1920	250.00
Marcie, 1950s, Box	25.00
Margaret O'Brien, Whitman Pub., 1946, Uncut	190.00
Marilyn Monroe, Saalfield, 1953, Uncut	100.00
Mary & Her Little Lamb, Ottman Lithography, N.Y.	375.00
Mary Hartline, Uncut	12.50
Mary Martin, Saalfield, 1942	16.00
Mary Poppins, Box, Cut	12.50
Mickey Rooney, Stand Ups, Merrill, 1941	55.00
Mini Mods, Box, 1968	7.50
Miriam Has A Happy Easter	20.00

Miss America, Lilja, Florence Salter, 1941, Uncut	45.00
Miss American, Whitman, 1973	20.00
Miss Hollywood	15.00
Mother Goose's New Broomstick, McCalls, Jan.1923, Uncut	7.00
My Book of Paper Dolls, Frances Brundage, Saalfield	45.00
My Favorite Dressing Dolls, Richard, American Colortype, Box	100.00
Nancy, Dennison, Crepe Paper Clothes, Package, 6 Sets, 1931	30.00
Nipper In Italy, McCall's, Apr.1925, Uncut	7.00
Nonesuch Mince Meat, Russian & Spanish Dresses, 1895, 7 In.	18.00
Nursery Favorite, Hays, 1913	20.00
Overall Boys, 1915	45.00
Pajama Party, No.2229, Stephens	6.00
Paper Soldiers, Tents & Stands, McLoughlin, Box, 1891	180.00
Pat & Tricia Nixon, White House, Artcraft	18.00
Pat Boone, Uncut	25.00
Patti Page, 1958, Uncut	25.00
Patty Duke, 1965, Uncut	25.00
Peggy Perkins' Friend, Margie Martin, Black & White, 1918	8.00
Pinocchio, Clothes, Attachable Nose, Walt Disney	18.00
Polly's Paper Playmates, Folk Dances, C.1911, Uncut	40.00
Princess Elizabeth, Margaret Rose, Saalfield, 1939, Uncut	275.00
Princess Leia, Star Wars, Box, 12 In.	65.00
Queen Elizabeth, Coronation, Coloring Section, 1952, Uncut	25.00
Rag–Bag Dolls, John Wanamaker, Philadelpha, C.1900, 5 Dolls	250.00
Raggedy Andy, Lacing Doll, 3 Outfits, 1 For Ann	3.00
Raggy–Doodle, Parachute, Box	65.00
Raphael Tuck, No.653, Articulated	30.00
Rhonda Fleming, Magic Stay Costume, Saalfield, Uncut, Box	30.00
Rita Hayworth, Cut	50.00
Robin Hood, Uncut	8.00
Rock Hudson, Uncut	40.00
Roly Poly, On Ice Skates, From N.Y.World Newspaper, 1906	25.00
Rosemary Clooney, Uncut	85.00
Rosey Ruth, Tuck, Dolls For All Seasons, Box	90.00
Roy Rogers, Cut	20.00
Ruth, Peter Thomas, 4 In.Doll, Uncut	200.00
Sally Field, Flying Nun, 1968, Uncut	22.00
Sandra Dee, Uncut	20.00
Sherree North, Uncut	25.00
Shirley Temple, Cut, 36 In.	70.00
Snow White, Whitman, 1972	20.00
Sonja Henie, Merrill, 1939, Uncut	170.00
Sonja, Little Gypsy, Good Housekeeping, Feb.1925, Uncut	9.00
Sparkle Plenty, Blue Cover, 1948, Uncut	50.00
Spear's, 6 Interchangeable Heads, 9 In.Doll, C.1900	250.00
Spear's, Dorothy & Her Dresses, 10 In.Doll	130.00
Stage Door Canteen, Army, Navy, Partially Cut	25.00
Sunbonnet Babies Primer, 1902	50.00
Sweet Alice, Tuck Artistic Series No.503	100.00
Teddy Bear, Selchow & Richter, 10 1/2 In.	80.00
Texas Tom, Woman's Home Companion, Nov.1926, Uncut	12.00
Tricia Nixon, Saalfield	18.00
Tyrone Power, Cut	35.00
Unsere Kaiserin & Prinzesschen, Gesetslich, Geschutzt, Box	800.00
Victorian Baby, Layette	550.00
Waltons, Whitman, 1975	10.00
Welcome Back Kotter, Box	4.00
Ziegfeld Follies Celebrity Dolls, 11 Dolls, 1940	90.00
Ziegfeld Girl, Queen Holden, No.3466, Uncut	410.00

 Paper collectibles, including almanacs, catalogs, children's books, stock certificates, and other paper ephemera, are listed here. Paper calendars are listed separately under Calendar Paper.

PAPER, Album, Captain Tim's Ivory Stamp Club, Radio Program, 1936	12.50

Almanac, 1956 Pocket Baseball 1.50
Almanac, Barker's, Illustrated, 1918 .... 11.00
Almanac, Christian Family, 1862 .... 7.00
Almanac, Civil War 1863, Boston, Lists Members of Mass.Regiments 12.00
Almanac, Diamond Dye, Household Guide, 1887 .... 4.00
Almanac, Dr.Ayer, 1879, 34 Pages 12.00
Almanac, Dr.D.Jayne, 1904 .... 7.00
Almanac, Dr.J.H.McLean, 1894 .... 7.00
Almanac, Dr.Jayne, 1912 .... 4.00
Almanac, Herricks Almanac, 1863 .... 8.00
Almanac, Hostetter's, Information About Illnesses, 1888, 36 Pages 9.00
Almanac, Hostetter, 1904 .... 5.00
Almanac, Housewife's, Kellogg's All–Bran 10.00
Almanac, Lincoln Farm Almanac, 1909 .... 5.50
Almanac, Warner's Safe Cure, 1809 .... 10.00
Atlas, Iowa & The World, Fayette Co., 1927 .... 22.50
Ballot, Election, Cavendish, Vt., McKinley & Roosevelt, Nov.6, 1900 .... 15.00
Bond, Louisiana, State, 1890s Building, Cherubs, Sword & Scales 22.95
Bond, Mohawk Gold Mining Co., Watertown, N.Y., 1906 .... 16.95
Book, Adventures of Mutt & Jeff, Copyright 1920 .... 50.00
Book, Alice In Philcoland, Hard Cover, 50 Pages, 12 1/2 X 15 In. 35.00
Book, American Soldier & Sailor At War, Stanley, 1889 .... 150.00
Book, Arthur Rackham Fairy Book, J.B.Lippincott Co. 35.00
Book, Audubon's Western Journal, 1849–50, 1852 Edition 135.00
Book, Big Little Book, Bonanza 8.00
Book, Big Little Book, Jack The Giantkiller, Pop–Up 22.00
Book, Big Little Book, Red Ryder 8.00
Book, Big Little Book, Shooting Sheriffs of The Wild West 5.00
Book, Big Little Book, Tarzan 40.00
Book, Borden's, With Elsie, Cartoon 13.00
Book, Brave Men, Ernie Pyle, 1944 .... 3.00
Book, Charlie Chan Carries On, Pocket 14.00
Book, Cinderella, Holiday House 6.00
Book, Coloring, Charlie Chaplin, 1917 .... 10.00
Book, Coloring, Chiquita Banana 8.00
Book, Coloring, Rin Tin Tin, 1957, 6 X 7 In. 15.00
Book, Coloring, Watergate, Political, 1973 .... 5.00
Book, Evening Street, Harlequin 5.00
Book, Gingerbread Man, Whitman Pub.Co., 1930 .... 20.00
Book, Gone With The Wind, 2nd Printing, June 1936 .... 250.00
Book, Gone With The Wind, Motion Picture Edition, Dated 1939 .... 35.00
Book, Jack In The Beanstalk, Holiday House, 1935 .... 6.00
Book, Jolly Animal ABC, McLoughlin, 1890 .... 12.00
Book, Jolly Box of Animal Stories, Platt & Munk Co., 1920s 40.00
Book, Kinky Kids, Color Illustrations, Artist Signed, 1908, 6 Pages 30.00
Book, Knave of Hearts, Parrish Cover & Illustrations 325.00

Although paper is acid, ink fades, and insects and light cause damage, it is still possible to preserve paper antiques. Keep paper dry, cool, and sealed away from oxygen and ultraviolet light. Mylar plastic bags are the best. Important papers should be deacidified by an expert. Dirt and other damage can be repaired.

Book, Knickerbocker's History of New York, Parrish Illustrations 350.00
Book, Laughs With Little Lulu, 60 Pages, David McKay Co., 7 X 6 In. 18.00
Book, Life of P.T.Barnum, 1889 .... 13.00
Book, Light of Western Stars, Zane Grey, C.1914 .... 4.00
Book, Little Black Sambo, 1932 .... 23.00
Book, Little Black Sambo, 1950s 18.00
Book, Little Black Sambo, Pop–Up 22.00
Book, Little Red Riding Hood, 1920, George Sully & Co. 45.00
Book, Maelstrom, Harlequin 35.00
Book, Martian Chronicles, Bantam 25.00
Book, Mary Ware Doll Book, Little Colonel Series, 48 Pages 425.00
Book, McGuffey's 1st German Reader, 1853 .... 30.00
Book, McGuffey's 4th Reader 14.00
Book, Merry Rhymes For Happy Times, Parker Bros, 1901, 14 Pages 19.00
Book, Mother Goose Rhymes, Holiday House, 1939 .... 6.00
Book, Moving Picture Teddies, 1907 .... 75.00
Book, Poll Parrot Shoes, Comic, 1950s 10.00
Book, Puss In Boots, Henry Altenus Co., 1922 .... 45.00
Book, Raggedy Ann, In The Magic Book, Johnny Gruelle Co. 30.00
Book, Red Riding Hood, McLoughlin, 1891 .... 28.00
Book, Return of Tarzan, Burroughs, 1915 .... 15.00
Book, Roosevelt Bears, 15 Color Plates, 1907 .... 75.00
Book, Schoenhut Doll Hospital, 1912 .... 60.00
Book, Sex Education, Chas.Atlas, 1928, 10 Volumes 18.00
Book, Story of Lucky Strike, 1939 .... 15.00
Book, Susie Sunbonnet, Ullman, 1907 .... 35.00
Book, Tarzan & The Silver Globe, Goldstar 15.00
Book, Tarzan, Pop–Up, 1935 .... 80.00
Book, Terry & The Pirates, Pop–Up 60.00
Book, Three Bears, M.A.Donohue & Co. 25.00
Book, Tin Woodman of Oz, 1918 .... 250.00
Book, Tiny Teddies, Story Four Teddy Bears, Linette, 1928 .... 25.00
Book, Tom Thumb, Rand McNally & Co., 1931 .... 8.00
Book, Uncle Remus, Ethnic Language, 1905 .... 30.00
Book, Uncle Tom's Cabin, Harriet Beecher Stowe, Copyright 1882 .... 80.00
Book, Weather Bird Shoes, Bag of Tricks 6.00
Book, White House Cookbook, 1911 .... 45.00
Book, Wizard of Oz, Denslow Illustrations, 1915 .... 110.00
Booklet, Boston Automobile Show, 64 Pages, 1910 .... 60.00
Booklet, Buffalo Bill's Museum, Colorado 10.00
Booklet, Magic, Dated 1921 .... 3.00
Booklet, Niloak, 1916 .... 60.00
Booklet, Postal Telegraph Service Bureau, 1930s 8.00
Booklet, Ventriloquism, 1920 .... 5.00
Catalog, Agricultural Implements & Machinery, 1893, 175 Pages 75.00
Catalog, Bicycles, Mead & Prentiss, Lady, Riding Skirt, 1899, 20 Pages 40.00
Catalog, Brown & Sharpe, Small Tools, 448 Pages, 1926 .... 20.00
Catalog, Brown Shoe Co., Fall–Winter, 1932–33, 128 Pages 25.00
Catalog, Cissna Toys, Illustrations, 1890s 50.00
Catalog, Coffin, Coffin Pictures, Salesman, 100 Pages 95.00
Catalog, Dental, John Hood Co., 775 Illustrations, 1911 .... 200.00
Catalog, Diamond Tool, 1942 Price List, Pictures of Tools, 1940 .... 30.00
Catalog, Excelsior Furniture Co., C.1900, 40 Pages 100.00
Catalog, Favorite Stoves & Ranges, Hardcover, 1914, 320 Pages 75.00
Catalog, Guns, Colt Pistol, 28 Pages, 1960 .... 15.00
Catalog, Kodak, 1917 .... 12.00
Catalog, L.L.Bean, Inc., Sportsmen's, Fall, 1947, 80 Pages 7.00
Catalog, Lexington Horse Auction, 1936 .... 20.50
Catalog, Macy's, Foldout Photos, 1906 .... 48.00
Catalog, Marietta Chair Co., Eastlake Style, 1889 .... 95.00
Catalog, Minnesota Knoll Casket Co., Engravings, 1890, 136 Pages 100.00
Catalog, Montgomery Ward, 1949 .... 2.75
Catalog, Montgomery Ward, Christmas, 1934 .... 45.00
Catalog, Montgomery Ward, Fall–Winter, 1923–24 .... 30.00

Catalog, Morley Saddlery, Sleigh Bells, 1899–1900, 16 Pages 22.00
Catalog, O.T.Moses & Co., Fall–Winter, 1903–4, 31 Pages 25.00
Catalog, Piedmont Wagon Co., 48 Pages, Fully Illustrated 30.00
Catalog, Plumbing & Heating Supplies, Hardin–Lavin, 224 Pages, 1918 .... 45.00
Catalog, Sears, Christmas, 1945 .... 40.00
Catalog, Sears, Philadelphia, Golden Jubilee, 1936 .... 25.00 To 30.00
Catalog, Sears, Roebuck, Fall–Winter, 1942–1943 .... 20.00
Catalog, Sears, Roebuck, Spring–Summer, 1954 .... 12.00
Catalog, Sperry Gyro Compass & Pilot, C.1930 .... 40.00
Catalog, Spiegel, 324 Pages, 1936 .... 18.00
Catalog, Steam Engines & Boilers, Ilustrated, 1894 .... 15.00
Catalog, Trade, Garland Ranges, 168 Pages, 1892 .... 120.00
Catalog, Western Electric Telephone Apparatus & Supplies, 1917 .... 100.00
Catalog, Winchester, Tools, Guns & Knives, 1911 .... 75.00
Catalog, Winchester, Tools, Guns & Knives, 1931 .... 95.00
Catalog, Wireless & Electrical, C.1918 .... 20.00
Cutout, Basket of Flowers, Foliage, Oddfellows Symbol, 9 X 11 In. 125.00
Cutout, Watercolor Design, Black Ground, 9 5/8 X 11 5/8 In. 695.00
Deed, Handwritten, On Laid Paper, Cranston, R.I., 1756, 12 X 15 In. 45.00
Deed, Handwritten, Parchment, Millersburg, Pa., 1765, 16 X 19 In. 45.00
Deed, Land, Texas, 1904 .... 8.00
Deed, Parchment, Commonwealth of Penna., Dated 1801, 14 3/4 X 22 In. 95.00
Fraktur, Baptismal Certificate, Pa.Dutch, 1820, 12 X 15 In. 315.00
Fraktur, Birth Certificate, Northampton County, 1801, 18 X 20 In. 3450.00
Fraktur, Birth Certificate, Susana Herrin, 1814, 11 X 13 In. 925.00
Fraktur, Bookplate, Esther Weber, Pa.German, 1815, 7 X 10 In. 1850.00
Fraktur, Born In 1861, John Tout, Pa., Framed, 10 X 12 In. 275.00
Fraktur, Geburts & Taufschein, 1809 Birth, Pa., Framed, 12 X 15 In. 120.00
Fraktur, Georg Miller, Watercolor, German, Dated 1786, 12 X 14 In. 1925.00
Magazine, Playboy, May 1954 .... 150.00
Magazine, Ring, Joe Louis, 1938 .... 10.00
Magazine, Youth Temperance Advocate, April 1, 1849 .... 18.00
Menu, Izaak Walton Hotel, Essex, Mt., Today's Specials, July 3, 1946 .... 20.00
Menu, S.S.Columbus, 1938 .... 2.75
Menu, Stork Club, 1943 .... 18.00
Pamphlet, Agricultural Implements, Osborne Co., Machinery, 1881 .... 30.00
Program, Football, Penn State Vs.Pitt., 1927 .... 15.00
Program, Madison Square Garden, 6 Day Bike Race, 1926 .... 10.00
Program, Martin Bros.Circus, 1936 .... 5.00
Program, Metropolitan Opera House, April 22, 1893 .... 6.00
Program, Movie, D.W.Griffith's Way Down East, 1920, 8 Pages 15.00
Program, Movie, Gone With The Wind, Illustrated, 1939 .... 35.00
Program, Movie, Walt Disney, Fantasia, 1940 .... 15.00
Program, Olympics, 1936 .... 35.00
Program, Tournament of Roses, 1938 .... 12.50
Stock Certificate, Anaconda Mining Co., Cripple Creek, 1902 .... 13.00
Stock Certificate, Baltimore & Ohio R.R., Liberty Allegory, 1900 .... 18.95
Stock Certificate, Colorado Yule Marble Co., 1910 .... 12.00
Stock Certificate, Marconi Wireless Telegraph Co., 1913 .... 16.00
Stock Certificate, North American Gold Dredging Co., 1899 .... 10.00
Stock Certificate, Northwestern Oils, Nev., Oilfield Vignette, 1951 .... 8.95
Stock Certificate, Ruby Hill Tunnel & Mining Co., 1886 .... 27.00
Stock Certificate, Straus Brothers Co., Allegorical Figure, 1929 .... 9.95
Stock Certificate, United Petroleum Co., Texas, Eagle On Globe, 1920 .... 10.95
Stock, Northern Liberties Gas Co., Philadelphia, 1856 .... 10.00
Ticket, Trolley Car, San Francisco, Kentucky Street, 1900s 3.00

Paperweights must have first appeared along with paper in ancient Egypt. Today's collectors search for every type from the very expensive French weights of the nineteenth century to the modern artist weights or advertising pieces. The glass tops of the paperweights sometimes have been nicked or scratched and this type of damage can be removed by polishing. Some serious collectors think this type of repair is an alteration and will not buy a repolished weight; others think it is an acceptable technique of restoration that does not change the value. Baccarat paperweights are listed separately under Baccarat.

PAPERWEIGHT, Advertising, Alligator, Independent Stove Co., Enamelware	40.00
Advertising, Baby In Womb, Parke–Davis, Lead	45.00
Advertising, Badger Insurance, Cast Iron	20.00
Advertising, Barrel On Base, St.Louis Cooperage, Copper	15.00
Advertising, Bear, Wallis, Cast Iron	125.00
Advertising, Boyt Harness Co., Des Moines, Glass, Leather	37.50
Advertising, Brown & Williamson Tobacco, Glass	12.00
Advertising, Dutch Boy Paints, Phoenix Metal	22.00
Advertising, Elephant, Independent Stove Co., Cast Iron	62.50
Advertising, Glass, Sweet Gum & Mullein, Victorian Girl, Dog	15.00
Advertising, International Harvester, Canton Plow, 1975	28.00
Advertising, Lehigh Foundries, Iron, Round, 1947	10.00
Advertising, Logan–Kanawha Coal, Mirror, 3 1/2 In.	24.00
Advertising, Merchants Motor Freight, Brass, 3 1/2 In.	48.00
Advertising, Missouri–Kansas Telephone, Cobalt Blue	50.00
Advertising, National Cash Register, Cast Iron, Miniature	40.00
Advertising, Nationwide Insurance Co., Glass	20.00
Advertising, Ohio Knife Co., Mirror Picture Stork, Grindstone	48.50
Advertising, Orange Crush, Figural, Bottle	20.00
Advertising, Reeves Stoves	35.00
Advertising, Schaffer Electric Co., Motor Shape	35.00
Advertising, Scottish Union Insurance Co., Brass, Rectangular	75.00
Advertising, Smith Brothers, Cast Iron, 2 1/4 In.	35.00
Advertising, Social Tea Biscuit, Japanese Girl, Glass	15.00
Advertising, Swigart Insurance Assoc., Fireman's Helmet, Iron	35.00
Ayotte, Butterfly With Daffodils, Buds, 3 3/8 In.	450.00
Ayotte, Magpie Jay, Wild Rhododendron, 3 3/4 In.	550.00
Ayotte, Yellow Jacket Nest, Wasps, Apple Blossoms, 3 In.	475.00
Banford, Cardinal, On Limb, With Eggs, White Ground	300.00
Bohemian, 4 Flowers, Central Swirl, White Ground, 3 In.	45.00
Bohemian, Millefiori, Outer Ring Canes, 5 Center Roses, 3 In.	500.00
Bohemian, Outer Ring of Canes, 2 With Silhouettes, 2 3/4 In.	575.00
Book Shape, Cut Glass, Russian Pattern, 3 7/8 X 2 X 1 5/8 In.	195.00
Clichy, Canes In Millefiori Design, Rose Center	950.00
Clichy, Concentric Millefiori, 6 Outer Pastry Rings, 3 In.	1100.00
Clichy, Flat Bouquet, 3 Different Flowers Tied With Ribbon	3200.00
Clichy, Floral Canes, Emerald Green & White Ground, 2 3/4 In.	7250.00
Clichy, Patterned Millefiori, Canes Around Pastry Mold, 3 In.	1000.00
Clichy, Quatrefoil Set On Muslin & Latticinio Tubes, 3 In.	850.00
Cloisonne, Floral, Butterfly, Brass, Rep.China, 3 3/8 In.	100.00
Czechoslovakia, 3 Pink Flowers, Controlled Bubbles, 3 In.	48.00
Eagle, Red, Glass, 1776–1976	12.00
Ernest Borell Watch, On Golf Tee	50.00
General Pershing, Cast Iron, 3 3/4 In.	65.00
Gentile, Spirit of '76	75.00
Gillinder, Abe Lincoln	400.00
Golf Ball, Frosted, 2 1/2 In.	50.00
Hanson, Peach, Red Ground, White Underlay, Marked, 1 3/4 In.	75.00
James A.Garfield, Inauguration 1881, Bronze Medallion, 3 In.	95.00
Kaziun, Cameo Silhouette, Hunter & Dogs, Canes, Signed, 2 In.	1000.00
Kaziun, Millefiore, Light Blue Ground, Miniature	750.00
Kaziun, Poinsettia, Red & Rose Petals, White, Gold K, 2 In.	1600.00

If using a glass shelf to display a paperweight collection, be sure it is strong enough. Ideal size is 18 inches long, 4 inches deep, ¼ inch thick. Paperweights are very heavy and collectors tend to add "just one more" and overload a shelf. Glass will become more fragile with age.

If your papier-mache doll heads or furniture are cracking, you might try arresting the cracks with a thin coat of white household glue.

Pen collectors look for quality workmanship. A gold pen nib is good. The iridium ball fused to some nibs should be intact. The filling system should work or have only a minor problem like a bad ink sac. Large pens usually bring higher prices than small pens.

Kaziun, Purple & White Pansy, Shaded Yellow, Gold K, 2 In.	750.00
Kaziun, Red, Red Rose	1700.00
Kaziun, Sapphire Morning Glory, Yellow, Gold K, 2 In.	1000.00
Kaziun, Snake, Red & White Stripe, Black Head, 1940s, 2 In.	1200.00
Kaziun, Upright Rose	700.00
Kontes, Fruit, White Latticinio, Blue Ground, Signed, 2 3/4 In.	600.00
Kosta, Blue Flower, Clear Ground, Signed	80.00
Lundberg, Daffodil, Green Stems, Dark Blue, 3 1/8 In.	225.00
Lundberg, Fish In Reeds, 3 Flowers, Translucent Water Ground	225.00
Lundberg, Peace Rose, Signed & Dated, 3 In.	300.00
Lundberg, Upright Tiger Lily, Leaves, Footed, 3 1/2 In.	250.00
Lutz, Deep Red Rose, 2 1/8 In.	140.00
Manson, Harry Truman, Blue & White, Sulfide Overlay	200.00
Millefiori, Teapot Shape	125.00
New England Glass Co., Apple	1400.00
New England, Pear, Lying On Side, Clear Wafer Base, 2 1/2 In.	800.00
New England, Pears & Cherries, Latticework Ground	440.00
Pegasus, Bronze	165.00
Perthshire, Bluebell, 1978	155.00
Perthshire, Christmas Flower, 1975	175.00
Perthshire, Christmas Holly Overlay, 1978	195.00
Perthshire, Christmas Poinsettia, 1976	200.00
Perthshire, Ducks In Pond, Apple Green Cased, Faceted, 1983	295.00
Perthshire, Florets, Silhouette Canes, White Muslin, 2 3/4 In.	100.00
Perthshire, Flower & Buds On Lilac, 1974	165.00
Perthshire, Golfer, Latticinio, Millefiore Canes, 3 In.	160.00
Perthshire, Millefiori, Italian Garden, Dated 1978	52.00
Perthshire, Millefiori, Signed, 3 In.	38.00
Perthshire, Millefiori, Signed, Dated 1978	52.00
Perthshire, Miniature Faceted Flowers, 1976	160.00
Perthshire, Moss Ground, 1976	185.00
Perthshire, Scattered Millefiori, 1974	155.00

Don't clean badly tarnished pewter with lye unless you are aware of the physical dangers involved. The pewter won't be hurt but you might be.

Perthshire, Spaced Millefiori, 9 Canes, 4 Silhouettes	155.00
Perthshire, Triple Overlay, 1977	250.00
Perthshire, Tudor Rose, 1975	225.00
Perthshire, Upright Dragonfly, Leaves, Faceted, 2 5/8 In.	400.00
Plymouth Rock, Glass, 3 3/4 In.	80.00
President McKinley, Brass	35.00
Rookwood, Potter At Wheel, Green Matte, Art Pottery, 1935	65.00
Rosenfield, Strawberry	145.00
Shell, Souvenir of Portland, Oregon	8.50
St.Louis, 2 Radishes, 1 Has Bite Out Of It	1350.00
St.Louis, Looped Garlands, Aqua Ground, 28 Point Center, 3 In.	1500.00
St.Louis, Mushroom	2200.00
St.Louis, Pompom Latticinio	2750.00
St.Louis, President Jimmy Carter, Red & White, 2 7/8 In.	120.00
St.Louis, Queen Elizabeth 1950 Coronation, Canes, 2 3/4 In.	350.00
St.Louis, White Spikes, Jasper Ground, Complex Cane, 3 In.	1200.00
Stankard, Berries & Blossoms, Flower Spray, 3 1/4 In.	1000.00
Stankard, Cattleya Epiphytic Orchid, 2 Buds, 3 1/4 In.	800.00
Stankard, Forget-Me-Not, Flowers & Bud On Vine, 3 In.	750.00
Stankard, Herbal Bouquet, Blue Flash Ground, 1979, 2 In.	750.00
Stoneware, McKinley, Dated 1901	48.00
Whitefriars, 5 Faceted Windows, Mushroom Shape, Cane, 1972	200.00
Whitefriars, American Flag, Blue Ring, Dated 1776-1976, 3 In.	450.00
Whitefriars, Concentric Millefiori, Grapes & Leaves, 3 In.	450.00
Whitefriars, Faceted Concentric, Dated 1970, 3 In.	175.00
Whitefriars, Silver Jubilee, Signed, White, 1952-77, 3 In.	350.00
Yellow Lily, Amethyst Ground, Miniature	225.00
Yellowstone Park Sepia Picture, Dome Type, 4 In.	15.00
Ysart, Brown Fish, Multicolored Ground	385.00

Papier-mache is made from paper mixed with glue, chalk, and other ingredients, then molded and baked. It becomes very hard and can be painted. Boxes, trays, and furniture were made of papier-mache. Some of the nineteenth-century pieces were decorated with mother-of-pearl.

PAPIER-MACHE, see also Furniture

PAPIER-MACHE, Box, Koran, Domed Top, Court & Hunting Scenes, Persian, 17 In.	175.00
Caddy, Russian, Kremlin On Cover, Lacquered, C.1860, 4 7/8 In.	1320.00
Desk, Lap, Mother-of-Pearl	165.00
Dish, Original Black Lacquer & Gilt Design, 7 1/4 In.	30.00
Easter Egg, Opens, 5 In.	15.00
Figurine, Bulldog, 14 In.	35.00
Figurine, Duck, Original Polychrome Paint On White, 4 In.	35.00
Figurine, Easter Bunny, In Egg, Carrot In Mouth, 9 In.	28.00
Figurine, Elephant, 32 In.	375.00
Garden Guard, Blackbird, Glass Eyes, 15 In.	12.00
Head, Milliner's, Blue Paint, Leather Head, French, 15 1/4 In.	300.00
Powder Box, Art Deco Flapper, Over Bearskin Rug, French	129.00
Powder Box, Oriental, Black Figures On Lid, Sides, Gold, Pink	30.00
Puppet, New York State Political Figure, Late 19th Century	150.00
Scoop, Duck Shape, Gold & Black Design, Marked Russia, 8 In.	35.00
Table, Tilt Top, Mother-of-Pearl Inlay	250.00
Table, Work, Mother-of-Pearl Inlay	690.00
Tray, Black Lacquer Design, 19th Century, 23 X 18 1/2 In.	1000.00
Tray, Black Lacquer, Bamboo Stand, 1850, 31 X 24 X 19 In.	750.00
Tray, Black Lacquer, Oriental Battle Scene, 15 1/2 X 20 In.	55.00
Tray, Black, Gilt Flower & Butterflies Design, 9 X 14 In.	20.00
Tray, Gilt Design, Butterflies, Insects, On Stand, 30 In.	1400.00

PARASOL, see Umbrella

Parian is a fine-grained, hard-paste porcelain named for the marble it resembles. It was first made in England in 1846 and gained in favor in the United States about 1860. Figures, tea sets, vases, and other items were made of Parian at many English and American factories.

PARIAN, Bust, Apollo, Germany, 7 In. 75.00
Bust, Charles Dickens, Impressed Dickens, 13 In. 150.00
Bust, Charles Sumner, 13 1/2 In. 605.00
Bust, General Grant, 15 1/2 In. 1100.00
Bust, Longfellow, Robinson & Ledbetter, 8 In. 60.00
Bust, Lord Derby, Beard, Suit, E.W.Wyon, 1867, 13 1/2 In. 185.00
Bust, Lord George Bentinck, Count D'Orsay, 1848, 9 3/4 In. 155.00
Bust, Pope Leo XIII, Robinson & Ledbetter, 8 In. 90.00
Bust, Princess Alexandra, When Married, Feb., 1863, Copeland, 12 In. 180.00
Bust, Reverend C.H.Spurgeon, Robinson & Ledbetter, 1878, 13 In. 140.00
Bust, Schiller, German Poet, Impressed J & TB, 7 In. 45.00
Bust, Shakespeare, Impressed J & TB, 7 1/2 In. 55.00
Bust, Shakespeare, Pedestal, 5 X 7 1/2 In. 65.00
Bust, Sir Walter Scott, Copeland, 16 1/2 In. 200.00
Bust, William Thackeray, Wearing Glasses, No Plinth, 10 In. 165.00
Cup & Saucer, Pond Lily, Marked, Cup 3 1/2 In. 85.00
Dish, Scalloped, Vintage Design, Stippled Ground, 8 1/2 In. 90.00
Figurine, 3 Maidens, 5 In. 15.00
Figurine, Boy, Colonial Dress, On Rock, Holding Bird, 9 1/2 In. 95.00
Figurine, Fisherman, Leaning Against Rockwork, Minton, 12 In. 225.00
Figurine, Grape Harvester, Man, 9 In. 90.00
Figurine, Greek Slave, Nude Woman, Chain, Wrists, 21 In. 185.00
Figurine, John Wilson, Standing, Holding Papers, Copeland, 18 In. 250.00
Figurine, Little Red Riding Hood, Copeland, C.1848, 11 1/2 In. 175.00
Figurine, Maidenhood, Inspired By Longfellow's Poem, 22 In. 325.00
Figurine, Man With Cello, Pastel, Capo-Di-Monte, 8 1/2 In. 35.00
Figurine, Nude Boy, With Shell, 12 In. 65.00
Figurine, Nude, Standing, Hand On Pillar, Chignon Hairdo, 12 In. 115.00
Figurine, Paul, Birds In Hat, With Axe, Copeland, 1849, 14 1/4 In. 350.00
Figurine, Ruth, Deep Ivory, 13 3/4 In. 175.00
Figurine, Woman In Classical Robes, Crown, 13 1/2 In. 150.00
Figurine, Young Immigrant, Boy, Knapsack, Copeland, 1863, 20 1/4 In. 375.00
Group, 3 Dancing Girls, 10 In. 75.00
Group, Hagar & Ishmael, C.1860, 15 1/2 In. 285.00
Group, Leda, Companion & Swan, White, 12 In. 150.00
Group, Richard The Lionhearted, Queen, Farewell, 17 3/4 In. 375.00
Jug, Lavender, Bark In Relief, White Inside, C.1847, 7 5/8 In. 145.00
Jug, Sam Alcock, Brown Ground, Raised White Leaf, Man 175.00
Pitcher, Boys Fighting Eagles, Rocky Cliff, 7 X 13 In. 250.00
Pitcher, Cupid & Psyche, 4 In. 45.00
Pitcher, Lily Pad, English Registry April 1857, 11 In. 200.00
Vase, 3 Small Birds, Open Beaks, English, 5 In. 40.00
Vase, Spill, Sage Green, Babes In Woods, T.J.& J.Mayer, C.1850 .... 85.00

Vieux Paris, or Old Paris, is porcelain ware that is known to have been made in Paris in the eighteenth or early nineteenth century. These porcelains have no identifying mark but can be identified by the whiteness of the porcelain and the lines and decorations.

PARIS, Candleholder, Woman, Holding Flower, Ornate, 21 3/4 In., Pair 5500.00
Coffee Can, Golden Maidens, Deep Blue Ground 150.00
Coffeepot, Pink 65.00
Dinner Set, Floral, Blue Border, Old English Initial, 90 Piece 1000.00
Tea Set, Child's, Colored Butterflies, 6 Piece 175.00
Tea Set, Gold & Cobalt Blue Trim, 33 Piece 1000.00
Tray, Battle Scene, Attaque De L'Hotel De Ville, C.1830, 10 1/2 In. 1300.00
Tureen, Gold Design, Beaded Panels, Handles, 1800s, 13 X 15 In. 300.00
Tureen, Sauce, Twig Handles, Domed Cover, Floral Sprays, 8 3/4 In. 275.00
Tureen, Soup, Floral Cartouches, Green Bands, Handles 160.00

Urn, Countryside Scene, Mythical Head Handles, Cobalt Blue, 9 In.	350.00
Vase, Children, Turquoise Landscape, 7 1/2 X 14 1/2 In., Pair	450.00
Vase, Figural Reserve, Teal Ground, Gilt Handles, 16 3/4 In.	200.00
Vase, Frieze, Couple Strolling, Boy Fishing, Mask Handles, 12 3/4 In.	990.00
Vase, Gilt Neck Handles, Urn Shape, C.1820, 28 3/8 In., Pair	2200.00
Vase, Peasants, Flying Kite, Reverse, Girl, Tambourine, 9 1/4 In., Pair	935.00
Vase, Poppies, Surrounded By Open Frontwork, Floral, 10 In.	100.00
Vase, Rustic Cottage, Mountainous Landscape, C.1830, 14 3/4 In., Pair	1210.00

Pate-sur-pate means paste on paste. The design was made by painting layers of slip on the ceramic piece until a relief decoration was formed. The method was developed at the Sevres factory in France about 1850. It became even more famous at the English Minton factory about 1870. It has since been used by many potters to make both pottery and porcelain wares.

PATE-SUR-PATE, Box, Blue & White Ground, Cupids, Signed, 4 X 4 In.	190.00
Box, Cobalt & White, Square, 4 1/4 In.	169.00
Plaque, Girl, Holds Basket, Picks Flowers, Marked, 10 1/4 In.	225.00
Plate, Blue, White Roses, Gold Gilt Edge, 9 In.	40.00
Vase, Classical Figures, Ring Handle, Artist Signed, 6 In.	650.00

Paul Revere pottery was made at several locations in and around Boston, Massachusetts, between 1906 and 1942. The pottery was operated as a settlement house program for teen-aged girls. Many pieces were signed "S.E.G." for Saturday Evening Girls. The artists concentrated on children's dishes and tiles. Decorations were outlined in black and filled with color.

PAUL REVERE POTTERY, Bowl, Blue, Floral Between Bands, 1 1/2 X 6 In.	125.00 To 140.00
Bowl, Footed, Glossy Black, 7 1/2 X 3 In.	96.00
Creamer, Covered, Hen & Chick Medallion, SEG, 1919, 4 3/4 In.	175.00
Creamer, Rabbits Facing Each Other, C.1910, SEG, 3 In.	850.00
Cup, 3 Color Floral Design, Dated 1912	66.00
Cup, 3 Color Iris, Edith Querrier, 1912	60.00
Cup, Floral, 3 Colors, 1912	55.00
Inkwell, Square Cover, Rectangular Form, Signed SEG, 4 In.	275.00
Jug, Blue & White	495.00
Lamp Base, Paper Label	70.00
Mug, Motto, Young Rabbit With Basket, 1917, 3 1/2 In.	325.00
Pitcher, Ovoid, Viking Ships, Bands, Signed SEG, 9 1/2 In.	4900.00
Plate, Center Bunny Medallion, Fanny Levine, 1924, 7 1/2 In.	325.00
Tile, Green Landscape	200.00
Vase, Checkered Band, Wide Mouth, SEG, 1922, 5 1/2 In.	100.00
Vase, Signed E.G.T., 11 In.	220.00

Peachblow glass originated about 1883 at Hobbs, Brockunier and Company of Wheeling, West Virginia. It is a glass that shades from yellow to peach. It was lined with white glass. New England peachblow is a one-layer glass shading from red to white. Mt. Washington peachblow shades from pink to blue. Reproductions of all types of peachblow have been made. Some are poor and easy to identify as copies, others are very accurate reproductions and could fool the unwary.

PEACHBLOW, Bowl, Prunus Leaves, Pie Crust Edge, Webb, 9 1/2 In.	300.00
Bowl, Raindrop Air Traps, Ruffled, Sandwich, Small	235.00
Bowl, Ruffled, New Martinsville, 9 In.	110.00
Butter, Victorian, Silver Plate Bottom, New England	195.00
Creamer, Wheeling, 3 1/4 In.	385.00
Cruet, Teardrop, Mahogany To Pink Base, Amber Handle, Wheeling	1185.00
Cruet, Wheeling	1285.00
Cruet, Wheeling, Teardop	1185.00
Decanter, Wine, Ball Stopper, Leaves, Blue Flowers, 11 In.	495.00
PEACHBLOW, GUNDERSON, see Gunderson	
Lamp, Kerosene, Brass Base, Raised Florals, 24 In.	225.00
Pear, New England	115.00

Pear, New England, Crooked Neck	300.00
Pitcher, Claret, Mahogany To Fuchsia, Wheeling, 10 In.	1735.00
Pitcher, Lemonade, Slightly Tapered, Wheeling, 10 3/4 In.	1950.00
Pitcher, Milk, Art Glass, Wheeling, Large	550.00
Pitcher, Milk, Blue To White, Crimped, New England, 6 1/8 In.	1285.00
Pitcher, Milk, Crimped Top, New England, 6 1/4 In.	1285.00
Pitcher, Triangular, Glossy Finish, 8 In.	1695.00
Pitcher, Water, Mustard Yellow To Mahogany, Wheeling	1250.00
Pitcher, Wheeling, 7 In.	850.00
Punch Cup, New England, Reeded Handle, 2 3/4 In.	385.00
Rose Bowl, New England, 7 Crimps, 3 X 2 1/2 In.	295.00
Salt & Pepper, Original Lids, Wheeling	650.00
Sugar & Creamer, White Handles, New England	865.00
Syrup, Pewter Cover, Wheeling	1450.00
Toothpick, Wheeling, Ball Shape, 2 3/8 In.	280.00
Toothpick, Wheeling, Oxheart Cherry .... 385.00 To	485.00
Tumbler, New England, Wild Rose Pattern, 3 3/4 In.	450.00
Tumbler, Wheeling, Cream Lining, Rose Red To Yellow, 3 7/8 In.	350.00
Tumbler, Wild Rose, Raspberry To Pink, New England, 3 3/4 In.	450.00
Vase, Acorn & Leaves, Yellow To Pink, 4 1/2 In.	375.00
Vase, Bud, Wheeling, 8 3/4 In. .... 525.00 To	577.00
Vase, Bulbous, Mt.Washington, 8 In.	1250.00
Vase, Bulbous, Wheeling, 3 1/2 X 2 3/8 In.	230.00
Vase, Flower Petal Top, Shaded To Blue, Mt.Washington, 3 In.	895.00
Vase, Lily, New England, Paper Label, 7 In.	785.00
Vase, New England, 9 Crimped Rim, 4 1/2 In.	485.00
Vase, Stick, Wheeling, Acid Finish, 8 1/4 In.	950.00
Vase, Swirl Stick Neck, Cream Bulbous Base, 11 1/2 In.	40.00
Vase, Wheeling, Bud, 9 In.	395.00
Vase, Wheeling, Morgan, 8 In.	950.00
Vase, Wheeling, Opaque White Interior, Bottle Shape, 15 1/2 In.	2000.00

PEACHBLOW, WEBB, see Webb Peachblow

Listed under Pearl are items made of the natural mother-of-pearl from shells. The glassware known as mother-of-pearl is listed by that name. Opera glasses made with natural pearl shell are listed under Opera Glasses. Natural pearl has been used to decorate furniture and small utilitarian objects for centuries.

PEARL, Cake Lifter, Sugar Shell, Slotted Server, Sterling Silver, 3 Piece	24.00
Case, Calling Card, Victorian	85.00
Fish Set, 8 Knives, 8 Forks, Silver Trim	85.00
Knife Set, Sterling Silver Trim, Box, 12	30.00
Pen, Gold Tip	25.00

Peking glass is a Chinese cameo glass first made popular in the eighteenth century. The Chinese have continued to make this layered glass in the old manner, and many new pieces are now available that could confuse the average buyer.

PEKING GLASS, Beads, Green, 18 In.Strand	35.00
Bottle, Perfume, Green, White, Cameo, Leaves, No Stopper, 3 In.	50.00
Bottle, Snuff, Flowers, Vines On Milk Glass, 5 Color, 4 In.	800.00
Bottle, Snuff, Green Horses, Clear Ground, Agate Top, 3 In.	350.00
Bottle, Snuff, Objects On Snowflake Ground, 5 Color, 3 In.	1350.00
Bottle, Snuff, Yellow Basket Weave, Amethyst Top, 2 7/8 In.	700.00
Bottle, Snuff, Yellow Birds, Trees, On Clear, Coral Top, 3 In.	500.00
Bowl, Tree, Peonies & Butterfly, Green To White, 6 1/4 In.	145.00
Bowl, White, Butterfly, Flowers, Leaves, Stand, 7 X 3 In.	285.00
Vase, Blue Flowers, White Ground, 6 1/4 In.	185.00
Vase, Green, White, Dogwood Tree, With Birds, Cameo, 8 In.	140.00
Vase, Honeycomb, Green Over White, 8 In.	165.00
Vase, Magenta Flowers, Birds, White Ground, 6 In., Pair	1400.00
Vase, Turquoise Over White, 9 In., Pair	500.00

Peloton glass is a European glass with small threads of colored glass rolled onto the surface of clear or colored glass. It is sometimes called spaghetti, or shredded coconut, glass. Most pieces found today were made in the nineteenth century.

PELOTON, Biscuit Jar, Allover Coconut Strings, White Cased, 5 1/2 In.	595.00
Biscuit Jar, Multicolored Strands, Ribbed, 6 3/4 In.	600.00
Biscuit Jar, Ribbed & Satin Exterior, White Interior, 6 3/4 In.	600.00
Dish, Dessert, Threaded	75.00
Rose Bowl, Coconut Strings, Crimped, White Cased, 2 1/4 In.	245.00
Rose Bowl, Colored Coconut Strings On Body, 6 Crimp Top, 2 In.	245.00
Vase, Orchid Pink Cased, Ruffled, Ball Shape, Strings, 3 1/4 In.	175.00
Vase, Orchid Pink Cased, Ruffled, Coconut Strings, 5 In.	295.00
Vase, Orchid Pink, Coconut Strings, Clear Wafer Foot, 6 1/4 In.	275.00
Vase, Stick, White Lining, Yellow Coconut Strings, 6 3/4 In.	225.00
Vase, White Threading, Clear Rigaree, 4–Pointed Rim, 3 3/4 In.	265.00
Vase, White Threading, Clear, 3 In.	125.00

The first steel pen point was made in England in 1780 to replace the hand–cut quill as a writing instrument. It was 100 years before the commercial pen was a common item. The fountain pen was invented in the 1830s but was not made in quantity until the 1880s. All types of old pens are collected.

PEN, Aurora, Thesi Ballpen, Escosteel, Design, Box, 1983	16.00
Blown Glass, Fairlaigh Shoe Co., Use This Pen When Ordering, Case	75.00
Conklin, Man's, Crescent Gothic Design, Gold Filled	175.00
Conklin, No.30, Crescent Filler, Chased Hard Rubber, 1918	27.00
Dip Style, Scrimshaw	12.00
Drexel, With Pencil, 14K Gold, No.4, Box	35.00
Drexel, With Pencil, Mottled Light Green & Brown, Box	30.00
Esterbrook, Ball Shape, Desk, Bakelite	29.00
Eversharp, Fountain, Desk Set, 14K Gold Nib, Onyx Base, Paper Label	32.00
Eversharp, Gold Filled Cap	12.50
Fairchild, No.5, Black, Brass	10.00
Gold, Relief Rose Design, 5 In.	75.00
John Holland, Hatchet Filler, Gold Filled, Engraved Design, 1915	165.00
Mickey Mouse, Fountain, 1930s	125.00
Mont Blanc, Masterpiece, 14K Gold	130.00
Mont Blanc, No.146, Glossy Black Finish, 14K Gold Nib, 1983	105.00
Mont Blanc, Red Ripple, No.12 Safety Nib	3500.00
Parker, Arrow, Brushed Stainless Steel, Box, 1981	10.00
Parker, Blue Diamond, Unused	40.00
Parker, Challenger, Desk	15.00
Parker, Disappearing Clip, Black, Fountain, 18 1/2 In.	180.00
Parker, Duofold, Green	40.00
Parker, Duofold, Yellow, Fountain	65.00
Parker, Lucky Curve Jr., Green	40.00
Parker, No.45, Black, Gold End Tip, Gold Plated, 1962	30.00
Parker, No.50B, Matte Black, Unitary Steel Nib, Box, 1979	13.00
Parker, No.75, Geometric Design, 14K Gold Filled, Box, 1964	125.00
Parker, Parkette Deluxe, Black Marbled, Box	15.00
Parker, Vacuumatic, Pencil, 1947, 2 Piece	35.00
Pearl Handle, With Carved Fish, Metal Nib	10.00
Sheaffer, Desk, White Dot, 1969	7.50
Sheaffer, Double, Set In Marble Vase, Desk, 1930	50.00
Sheaffer, Feather Touch, Label	8.50
Sheaffer, Green, Gold, Black Striped, Fountain, No.3	16.00
Sheaffer, Lifetime, 1914	35.00
Sheaffer, Lifetime, Military Clip, Brown, 14K Gold	25.00
Sheaffer, No.642, Gold Webbing, Stainless Steel, Box, 1979	13.00
Sheaffer, No.875, Admiral, Green, Price Stickers, 1954	9.00
Stanhope, Full Figural Carved Ivory, Flowers, Deer, 3 Parts, 8 In.	55.00
Surety, Oversized, Orange Celluloid	20.00
Wahl, 14K Gold Nib & Trim, Brown	35.00

Wahl, Gold Filled, 3 1/2 In.	20.00
Wahl, Lady's, Ribbon Ring, Gold Filled, Midget, 1920	23.00
Wahl, Sterling Silver	95.00
Waterman, Fountain, 14K Gold Tip, Black, Silver Cap	9.00
Waterman, Fountain, No.18	50.00
Waterman, Ideal, Black, 1909	85.00
Waterman, No.15, Black Chrome, Eyedropper Filler, 1913	30.00
Waterman, No.55, Orange	150.00
Waterman, Patrician, Lady's, Sterling Silver	200.00
Zorro, Fountain	12.50

The pencil was invented, so it is said, in 1565. The eraser was not added to the pencil until 1858. The automatic pencil was invented in 1863. Collectors today want advertising pencils or automatic pencils of unusual design. Boxes and sharpeners for pencils are also collectible.

PENCIL, Box, Felix The Cat, Graphics, 1931	30.00
Bullet, Chicago Stockyards	2.25
Bullet, Oxydol, Orange	12.00
Buy Pillsbury's Best Flour	5.00
Eversharp, Art Deco, Gold Filled	20.00
Ingersoll, Redipoint, Lady's	12.50
Mechanical, Chevrolet, You're Up, Bat Shape	25.00
Mechanical, Falls City, Floating Bottle	15.00
Mechanical, Oldsmobile Car Floating In Top	15.00
Mechanical, Wooden, Popeye Picture, Large	10.00
Moxie, Red & White	3.50
Rifle, Marked Germany	14.00
Sharpener, Climax No.3, 1921	30.00
Sharpener, Figural, National Cash Register	25.00
Sharpener, Signed Boston, Cast Iron	25.00
Sharpener, U.S.Automatic, Pat.1907	25.00
Sheaffer, Lifetime	15.00
Sheaffer, Marble	70.00
Telescoping, Quincy Stove Mfg.Co., Metal	18.00
Wahl, Eversharp, Gold Filled, Mechanical	15.00

Pennsbury Pottery The Pennsbury Pottery worked in Morrisville, Pennsylvania, from 1950 to 1971. Full sets of dinnerware were made as well as many decorative items. Pieces are marked with the name of the factory.

PENNSBURY, Ashtray, 7 3/4 In.	14.00
Ashtray, Advertising, Fairless Works	15.00
Ashtray, Dog Head Center, Gray, 7 1/2 In.	20.00
Ashtray, Outen The Light, 5 In.	10.00
Bread Plate, Give Us This Day Our Daily Bread, Wheathead	28.00
Cake Plate, Footed, Rooster	20.00
Creamer, Pink Spongeware On White, 4 In.	35.00
Cruet, Amish Man Stopper	25.00
Cup & Saucer, Rooster	15.00
Dish, Washington Crossing Inn	25.00
Figurine, Ducks, 1 Seated, 1 Standing, Yellow, 6 1/2 In., Pair	175.00
Figurine, Nuthatch, No.110	48.00
Mug, Amish Couple, 4 1/2 In.	19.50
Mug, Rooster	15.00
Mug, Sweet Adeline	15.00 To 17.00
Pie Plate, Wire Rack	35.00
Pitcher, Eagle	15.00
Pitcher, Milk, Eagle, With Banner	28.00
Pitcher, Milk, Rooster, Red & Green, 6 In.	35.00
Pitcher, Rooster, 4 In.	9.00
Pitcher, Sweet Adeline, 2 Mugs	50.00
Plaque, Baltimore & Ohio R.R., 6 X 8 In.	45.00
Plate, Christmas, 1970	25.00 To 35.00
Plate, Rooster, Black, 10 In.	18.00

Saucer, Rooster, Red & Green, 6 In.	22.00
Snack Set, Rooster, 9 Piece	85.00
Sugar, Covered, Hex Design, 2 1/2 In.	15.00
Trivet, Amish Lady & Girl, Sunflowers, 6 In.	30.00
Trivet, Amish Scene, 6 In.	20.00
Wall Pocket, Sailboat Design, Artist Signed, 6 1/2 X 6 1/2 In.	65.00

PEPSI-COLA

Pepsi-Cola, the drink and the name, was invented in 1898 but was not trademarked until 1903. The logo was changed from an elaborate script to the modern block letters in the 1970 Pepsi label. All types of advertising memorabilia are collected and reproductions are being made.

PEPSI-COLA, Apron, Carpenter's	5.00
Bank, Vending Machine, 6 Bottle, Cardboard Carrier, Box	25.00
Belt Buckle	25.00
Billboard, Cereal Premium, Miniature	20.00
Bottle Carrier, Tin	14.00
Bottle Opener, Bottle Shape, 1940	15.00
Bottle, 6 1/2 Oz.	5.00
Bottle, Contents, Capped In Space 3, Early 1930s	29.50
Button, Red, White & Blue, 1930s, 2 1/8 In.	10.00
Cake Holder, Tin	30.00
Can, Flat Top, Big Cap Picture	30.00
Clock, Electric	30.00
Display, Figural, Santa Claus, Holding Bottle, Rockwell, 20 In.	35.00
Display, Mickey Mouse As Santa Claus, 36 In.	245.00
Figure, Santa Claus, Pepsi In Hand, Cardboard, 20 In.	30.00
Hat, Say Pepsi Please	12.00
Hat, Take The Pepsi Challenge, Autograph of Don The Snake	20.00
Radio, Bottle Shape, 23 In.	300.00
Sign, Bottle Cap Shape, Drink Pepsi-Cola, Cardboard, 9 In.Diam.	20.00
Thermometer, 1940s	35.00
Thermometer, Bigger-Better, Bottle Picture	55.00
Thermometer, Girl Sipping, With Straw	165.00
Tray, 1909, Girl At Soda Fountain	850.00
Tray, 1940s, Hits The Spot	15.00
Tray, Victorian Lady At Soda Fountain, 13 In.	340.00
Tumbler, Wonder Woman, Super Hero	4.00

PERFUME BOTTLE

Cut glass, pressed glass, art glass, silver, metal, enamel, and even plastic or porcelain perfume bottles have been made. Although the small bottle to hold perfume was first made before the time of ancient Egypt, it is the nineteenth- and twentieth-century examples that interest today's collector. Examples with the atomizer top marked "DeVilbiss" are listed under that name. Glass or porcelain examples will be found under the appropriate name such as Lalique, Czechoslovakia, etc.

PERFUME BOTTLE, Amber Beveled Glass, Brass, With Glass Applicator, 4 In.	95.00
Amber Inverted Thumbprint, Blue Stopper, Leaves, 8 In.	98.00
Amethyst, Applied Rings, Paneled Stopper, European, 8 In.	115.00
An Trice Product, 3 1/2 In.	17.50
Art Deco, Carved Tiger Eye, Leaves Design	185.00
Art Deco, Cut Glass, Geometric Rays, Fan Stopper, 3 1/4 In.	30.00
Art Deco, Head of Egyptian Pharaoh, Marked Napier	30.00
Art Glass, Ground Glass Stopper, Artist Signed, Large	65.00
Art Nouveau Lady, Silver Plated Mount, Chain, 2 1/8 In.	85.00
Art Nouveau, Nymph Amid Morning Glories, Ruby, 6 5/8 In.	265.00
Atomizer, Cut Glass, Travel, 4 1/2 In.	115.00
Atomizer, Pinecones & Scene, Daum Nancy, Cameo, 8 1/4 In.	250.00
Baccarat, Amberina Shell, Original Stopper, 5 1/2 In.	65.00
Black Glass, Atomizer, Gold Top, 5 In.	25.00 To 35.00
Blown Mold, Aqua, Embossed Flowers, Blank Panel, 4 3/8 In.	65.00
Blown Mold, Clear, Rectangular, Fern, Paper Label, 6 In.	50.00
Blown Mold, Pale Aqua, Hourglass Shape, Blank Panels, 4 In.	60.00

Blue To Clear, Mistletoe Pattern, Daum Nancy, 5 In.	550.00
Bohemian Glass, Frosted Floral, Stopper, 5 1/2 In., Pair	10.00
California Perfume Co., American Ideal Sachet, 1915	85.00
California Perfume Co., Lily of The Valley, 1914	125.00
California Perfume, Violet Sachet, Clear, 1912, 3 1/4 In.	125.00
Cambridge, Bird Figural Stopper, Pair	55.00
Chatelaine, Soldier, Womans's Head Reverse, Coin Silver	175.00
Cobalt Blue, 8 Sides, Collared Lip, 6 In.	400.00
Cobalt Blue, Pagoda Shape, Acorn Stopper, 6 5/8 In.	70.00
Crown Shape, Gold, Prince Matchabelli Stradivari, 2 In.	8.00
Cut Glass, Gold Top, Enameled Girl Portrait, 4 In.	350.00
Czechoslovakia, Art Deco Shape, Blue, Stopper, 6 In.	55.00
Czechoslovakia, Art Deco, Purple Cut Glass, 6 Sides, 4 In.	65.00
Czechoslovakia, Blue, Cylinder Shape, Enameled Roses, 6 In.	36.00
Czechoslovakia, Cobalt Blue, Atomizer, Enameled, 8 In.	85.00
Czechoslovakia, Gold Design, Cobalt Blue	38.00
Dabrooks, Embossed Colorful Label	15.00
Deep Amethyst, 12 Panel, Flanged Lip, 7 1/2 In.	180.00
Deep Amethyst, 12 Panel, Rolled Rim, 5 In.	60.00
Diamond Point Trim, Ground Stopper, Clear, 4 1/2 In.	22.00
Enameled On Copper, France, C.1860	75.00
Evening In Paris, 3 3/4 In.	4.50
Evening In Paris, Cobalt Blue, Tapered, Black Cap, Purse	15.00
Evening In Paris, Gift Set, Silver Art Deco Lid, 5 Piece	20.00
Faberge, Music Cologne, Stopper Is Whistle, 3 In.	30.00
Figural, Dog	25.00
Figural, Doll, Holding Mirror, Blue, Germany, 6 3/4 In.	75.00
Figural, Doll, Pink Dress, Holding Envelope, Germany, 3 1/2 In.	35.00
Figural, Doll, Yellow Dress, Pin, White Fan, Germany, 3 In.	35.00
Figural, Eiffel Tower	9.50
Figural, Girl, Umbrella, Clear, Babs Creations, 4 1/4 In.	18.00
Figural, Lady, Cork Blond Hair, Envelope, Germany, 3 1/2 In.	22.00
Figural, Lady, Gold Wash, Glass Skirt, Paris, 7 1/2 In.	40.00
Figural, Rose, Frosted, Butterfly Stopper, 3 1/2 In., Pair	25.00
Figural, Sailor, Frosted, Hat Closure, Rumania, 2 3/4 In.	95.00
Flask, Monkey, Chein Children, Drum, Teddy Bears, Glass Eyes	70.00
Flat, Pink & Light Blue, Matching Stopper, 4 X 4 1/2 In.	27.00
Gold Overlay, Amber Rhinestones, Crystal Stopper, 5 In.	50.00
Green Cased Glass, Atomizer, Floral, West Germany, 8 In.	39.00
Hochst, Woman, Gown, Stopper, Porcelain, 3 In.	100.00
Loop Pattern, Sandwich, Emerald Green, C.1840, 4 3/4 In.	325.00
Lucien Lelong, Brass, With 6 Bells	35.00
Mary Chess, 3 Piece	12.00
Mary Dunhill, Art Deco, Purse, Gold Plated Case, 2 1/2 In.	28.00
Mason, Yellow Stripes On Clear, Dabber Stopper, 3 3/4 In.	30.00
Max Factor, Sophisti–Cat, Blue Velour Cat, In Dome, 4 In.	3.00
Millefiori, Canes In Center & Stopper, 5 1/2 In.	175.00
Moonstone, Paper Label	20.00
Opalescent, Large Front & Back Panels, 8 Sides, 4 1/4 In.	150.00
Opaque White, Bead Design Panel Sides, Flared Lip, 6 In.	25.00
Peacock, Crown Top, Red Mark, Germany	50.00
Pearl, Tube, Lipstick Compartment, 3 3/8 In.	35.00
Pink Opaline Glass, Fleur–De–Lis, Pink Stopper, 8 1/2 In.	150.00
Pressed Glass, Canary, 6 Panel Stopper, C.1850, 5 3/8 In.	160.00
Pressed Glass, Cane Pattern, Original Stopper, 5 In.	32.00
Purse, Silver Plate, Heart Shape, Screw Cap, Dabber, 3 In.	22.00
Rexall Drugs, Glass Atomizer, Knight On Horseback, Box	10.00
Ruby Flashed, Blown, Acorn Stopper, 19th Century, 8 3/8 In.	55.00
Ruby, Victorian, Original Stopper, Bohemian, 9 In.	65.00
Russian Cut, Lay Down, Sterling Silver Top, 10 In.	165.00
Satin Glass, Shaded Deep Teal, Floral, Silver Top, 6 In.	325.00
Satin Glass, Tomato Shape, Shaded Butterscotch, Brass Cap	75.00
Schiaparelli, Brass Design, Red Stones, Tagged Silk Bag	45.00
Venetian Stripe, Blue, Green, Goldstone	48.00

Peters & Reed Pottery Company of Zanesville, Ohio, was founded by John D. Peters and Adam Reed in 1897. Chromal, Landsun, Montene, Pereco, and Persian are some of the art lines that were made. The company became Zane Pottery in 1920, Gonder Pottery in 1941, and closed in 1957. Peters & Reed was unmarked.

PETERS & REED, Jug, Ball Shape, Brown Glaze, Grapes & Leaves	50.00
Jug, Cavalier, High Glaze	35.00
Jug, Garland Design, Squatty, Dark Brown Glaze, 4 1/2 In.	48.00
Jug, Grapes & Leaves In Relief, Brown Glaze	55.00
Loving Cup, Lion's Head, Sprigged Florals	165.00
Pitcher, Sprigged, Man With Banjo, 4 In.	35.00
Pitcher, Wreath Design, 4 1/2 In.	40.00
Rose Bowl, Sprig Pattern, 3 Feet	40.00
Tankard, Portraits of Lincoln & Washington, 12 1/2 In.	185.00
Vase, Chromal, Scenic, 10 In.	95.00
Vase, Floral Medallions, Pinched, 6 Sides, 4 X 6 In.	60.00
Vase, Landsun, 5 1/2 In.	55.00
Vase, Pinched, 6 Sides, Flower Medallions, 4 X 6 In.	60.00
Vase, Wreath With Cherubs, Standard Glaze, 12 1/2 In.	45.00
Vase, Zigzag Lines, Greens, Browns, Blue, Yellows, 3 In.	45.00
Wall Pocket, Moss Aztec, 9 In.	45.00
Wall Pocket, Moss Aztec, Ferrell, 7 1/2 In.	38.00
Wall Pocket, Moss Aztec, Grapes	50.00

PETRUS REGOUT, see Maastricht

The Pewabic Pottery was founded by Mary Chase Perry Stratton in 1903 in Detroit, Michigan. The company made many types of art pottery including pieces with matte green glaze and an iridescent crystalline glaze. The company continued working until the death of Mary Stratton in 1961. It was reactivated by Michigan State University in 1968.

PEWABIC, Ashtray	75.00 To 110.00
Bowl, Console Style, Blue Matte, Green Glaze Interior, Flat	145.00
Bowl, Pink Iridescent, 4 X 2 In.	150.00
Pitcher, Green	250.00
Tile, Embossed Fish, Square, 3 In.	100.00
Vase, Green Leaves, Maple Leaf Mark, 12 In.	2500.00
Vase, Iridescent Blue, Tapering Form, C.1905, 10 In.	700.00
Vase, Veined Leaves, Green Matte, Leaf Mark, 13 X 8 In. ......*Illus*	4950.00

Pewter is a metal alloy of tin and lead. Some of the pewter made after 1840 has a slightly different composition and is called "Britannia metal." This later type of pewter was worked by machine; the earlier pieces were made by hand.

PEWTER, Ashtray, Art Nouveau, Raised Vines, Liberty & Co., 6 1/2 In.	55.00
Baluster, Hammerhead Thumbpiece, Initials R.R., C.1670, 1 Pt.	1500.00
Baptismal Bowl & Communion Plate, Leonard, Reed & Barton, 1835–40	200.00
Basin, Gershom Jones, C.1780, 7 3/4 In.	355.00
Basin, Molded Rim, Deep Rounded Sides, Thomas Badger, C.1800, 8 In.	425.00
Basin, Nathaniel Austin, 1763–1800, 9 1/8 In.	550.00
Basin, Richard Lee, C.1800, 7 3/4 In.	1400.00
Basin, Townsend & Compton, London, 3 1/2 X 13 1/4 In.	425.00
Basket, Art Nouveau, Liberty & Co., 9 In.	60.00
Basket, Floral & Leaf Design Inside, Kayserzinn, 10 In.	215.00
Beaker, Flared Body, Dark, W.I.& 2 Daggers Mark, C.1650, 6 1/2 In.	740.00
Beaker, James Weekes, Footed, 1820–35, 3 3/4 In.	600.00
Beaker, Portrait, King William III, Queen Mary, C.1695, 6 3/4 In.	2450.00
Bedpan, Thomas Danforth Boardman, 1805–50	400.00
Bonbon, Shell Shape, Art Nouveau Nude Woman, Kayserzinn, 8 In.	175.00
Bowl, Art Nouveau, Paneled, Beaded Handles, Nekrasoff, 14 1/2 In.	75.00
Bowl, Footed, Leonard, Reed & Barton, 6 1/4 In.	175.00
Bowl, Hammered, Ring Handles, Marked Trol-Zinn, 9 X 3 1/2 In.	30.00
Bowl, Thomas Danforth III, Footed, 5 In.	40.00

Box, Shoe Form, Hinged Lid, Chased Design	50.00
Buckle, Butterfly Shape, Art Nouveau, C.1890	20.00
Candleholder, Kayserzinn	75.00
Candlestick, Henry Hopper, 10 In.	275.00
Candlestick, Ostrander & Norris, Saucer Base, 4 In.	150.00
Candlestick, Pricket, Germany, 17th Century, 16 1/2 In.	1650.00
Candlestick, Removable Bobeche, Worn Silvering, 10 5/8 In., Pair	100.00
Candlestick, Romanesque, Dark, 13th Century, English, 4 1/2 In.	4500.00
Candlestick, Roswell Gleason, 6 1/2 In.	250.00
Candlestick, Smith & Co., Curved Line Touch, 6 1/8 In.	150.00
Candlestick, Thomas Wildes, Bobeche, 10 In.	200.00
Castor Set, 4–Bottle, Eben Smith, Beverly, Mass., 1813–56	250.00
Castor Set, 4–Bottle, Quilted, Child's	110.00
Chalice, Communion, Leonard, Reed & Barton, Britannia, 7 1/8 In.	140.00
Chalice, Knopped Stem, English, C.1750, 8 In.	255.00
Charger, Continental, Crowned Rose Touch, 13 1/4 In.	130.00
Charger, English, 16 1/2 In.	175.00
Charger, Incised Line On Rim & Base, Henry Will, N, Y., 1765, 15 In. ..	1000.00
Charger, Samuel Hamlin, 18th Century, 13 1/2 In.	750.00
Charger, Signed Flagg & Homan, Pre–1854, 14 In.	75.00
Charger, Triple Reeded, William Wetter, 1670–80, 23 In.	2025.00
Coffee Urn, Cast Brass Spout, Ivory Handle, 19th Century, Large	675.00
Coffeepot, Copper Bottom, Dated 1864, 10 1/2 In.	85.00
Coffeepot, Domed Lid, Straight Tapered, Roswell Gleason, 11 In.	225.00
Coffeepot, Lighthouse Shape, Hiram Yale & Co., C.1828, 9 3/4 In.	425.00
Coffeepot, Signed W.B.Ward	189.00
Creamer, Cast Fruit Finial, Hinged Lid, Homan & Co., Cinci., 6 In.	65.00
Dish, Elizabethan, Crowned Rose Mark, Bird On Reverse, 12 3/4 In.	3265.00
Dish, Medallion, Punch Gadrooned Border, 16th Cent., German, 16 In. ..	4875.00
Dish, Samuel Danforth, Conn., 1795–1816, Marked, 13 1/4 In.	425.00
Flagon, Beefeater, Cromwellian, Twin Cusp Thumbpiece, 12 1/2 In.	4200.00
Flagon, Communion, Lighthouse Shape, Eben Smith, C.1830.10 1/2 In. ..	425.00
Flagon, James I, Knopped Lid, Light, C.1620, English, 10 1/2 In.	2250.00
Flagon, Thomas Boardman, C.1825	1450.00
Flask, James Dixon & Sons	75.00
Flask, Lady's, Cane Covered, 1890	30.00
Funnel, Wine, C.1840	195.00
Goblet, 4 1/2 In., Set of 6	75.00
Inkstand, Georgian, 2 Drawers, Sanding Tray In Lower, C.1770, 3 In. ..	265.00
Inkwell, Embossed Florals & Leaves, Kayserzinn, 8 X 5 In.	115.00
Inkwell, Figural Frog, Kayserzinn	475.00
Jug, Handle, Pointed Spout, Llewllyn, Bristol, C.1835, 5 In.	210.00
Lamp, Acorn Font, Marked R.Gleason, 8 In.	250.00
Lamp, Camphene, 2 Spouts, Brass Burner, C Scroll Handle, 10 In.	225.00
Lamp, Spout, Flat Saucer Base, Strap Handle, English, 10 3/4 In.	250.00
Lamp, Spout, Glass Font, Saucer Base, English, 19th Century, 14 In. ...	325.00
Lamp, Whale Oil, Saucer Base, 6 1/4 In.	135.00
Measure Set, Haystack, Graduated, Irish, 4 Piece	350.00
Measure, Ale, English	36.00
Measure, Bellied, James Yates, 1/2 Pint, 3 3/4 In.	45.00
Measure, Covered, Scotland, 1 Gill	225.00
Measure, Double Volute, 18th Century, 1/2 Gill	300.00
Measure, England, Signed, C.1840, 1/2 Pint	38.00
Measure, Irish Haystack, Austin & Sons, 1850–75, 1/2 Noggin–1 Gal. ..	2600.00
Measure, Tankard, Marked Quart, English, 6 1/2 In.	15.00
Measure, Tappit Hen, Scottish, Crested Chopin, 9 1/2 In.	1200.00
Mold, Candle, 24 Tube, Pine Frame, 19 1/4 In.	400.00
Mold, Cupid, On Wedding Bell, Eppelsheimer	32.00
Mold, Ice Cream, Airplane	45.00
Mold, Ice Cream, American Beauty Rose	40.00
Mold, Ice Cream, Baby Shoe	26.00
Mold, Ice Cream, Banana	40.00
Mold, Ice Cream, Banquet, Champagne Bottle	110.00
Mold, Ice Cream, Basket, Wicker, 3 Sections, K.& Co.	29.00

Mold, Ice Cream, Bell, K.& Co. 22.00
Mold, Ice Cream, Billiken, God of Good Fortune, Dated 1908, K.& Co. 65.00
Mold, Ice Cream, Bride, With Long Flowing Veil, Eppelsheimer 56.00
Mold, Ice Cream, Brownie, Dude In Tuxedo, Palmer Cox, Anton Reiche 65.00
Mold, Ice Cream, Brownie, Palmer Cox, Eppelsheimer 75.00
Mold, Ice Cream, Calla Lily, 3 Sections, E & Co. 35.00
Mold, Ice Cream, Clover On Heart 22.00
Mold, Ice Cream, Cupid, On Rose 35.00
Mold, Ice Cream, Donkey Head, 3 Piece 35.00
Mold, Ice Cream, Eagle, With Shield & Swords 50.00
Mold, Ice Cream, Easter Lily 45.00
Mold, Ice Cream, Elephant, E & Co., N Y. 40.00
Mold, Ice Cream, Flag 65.00
Mold, Ice Cream, Fleur–De–Lis 35.00
Mold, Ice Cream, Football, 3 Parts 25.00
Mold, Ice Cream, George Washington 65.00
Mold, Ice Cream, Horseless Carriage 45.00
Mold, Ice Cream, Kewpie, 3 In. 16.00
Mold, Ice Cream, Leaf & Clover 22.00
Mold, Ice Cream, Liberty Bell, E & Co., No.605 .... 37.50
Mold, Ice Cream, Lily 50.00
Mold, Ice Cream, Locomotive 65.00
Mold, Ice Cream, Man, With Cross & Sword 45.00
Mold, Ice Cream, Mandolin, Pat.1888 .... 45.00
Mold, Ice Cream, Masonic Emblem, E & Co. 35.00
Mold, Ice Cream, Mother Hubbard, Copyright 1890 .... 65.00
Mold, Ice Cream, Potato .... 45.00 To 50.00
Mold, Ice Cream, Pretzel 30.00
Mold, Ice Cream, Rose 25.00
Mold, Ice Cream, Santa Claus, Standing 65.00
Mold, Ice Cream, Turkey 35.00
Mold, Ice Cream, Twin Eagles 50.00
Mold, Ice Cream, Wedding Bell 30.00
Mug, Barrel Shape, Samuel Turner, 1810–20, 4 3/4 In. 300.00
Mug, C Handle, Double Band, Rufus Dunham, 1 Pint, 3 1/2 In. 350.00
Mug, Child's, Handle, 3 In. 65.00
Mug, Edward Danforth, 1788–90, 1 Qt. 2750.00
Mug, Side Spout, James Yates, England, 1 Qt. 175.00
Mug, Tooled Strap Handle, Parkin, 2 3/8 In. 175.00
Mug, Waukesha Old Ale 125.00
Pepper Castor, Banded Body, C.1720, 4 1/2 In. 130.00
Pitcher, Fish, Cattails, Water Lilies, Kayserzinn, C.1900, 8 In. 150.00
Pitcher, Mephistopheles, Kayserzinn, 12 In. 250.00
Pitcher, Tavern, Victorian, Side Spout, English 75.00
Plate, Amos Treadway, Smooth Rim, 18th Century, 7 7/8 In. 550.00
Plate, Angel Touchmarks, F.Rhodius, Engl Zinn, 9 In., Pair 170.00
Plate, Bear Baiting Scene In Center, English, C.1740, 9 3/4 In. 270.00
Plate, Broad Rim, Dark, Nicolas Kelk, London, C.1670, 10 In. 2035.00
Plate, Charles II, Triple Reeded, Robert Marsh, C.1670, 8 3/4 In. 435.00
Plate, Cleeve, London, 1700s, 9 1/4 In. 85.00
Plate, Compton, London, 8 In., Pair 100.00
Plate, Continental, 9 3/8 In. 55.00
Plate, D.Melville, American, 8 1/4 In. 375.00
Plate, Deep Center, Thomas Danforth Boardman, 9 1/4 In. 225.00
Plate, Francis Piggott, English, 9 3/8 In. 65.00
Plate, Frederick Bassett, C.1790, 8 7/16 In. 850.00
Plate, Gatesby, London, 8 1/2 In. 75.00
Plate, George Frenfell, London, 9 3/8 In. 60.00
Plate, Incised Rim Line, Nathaniel Austin, 1763–1800, 8 In. 300.00
Plate, Narrow Single Line Rim, 1763–1800, 8 In. 300.00
Plate, Richard Austin, C.1810, 8 3/4 In. 350.00
Plate, Roses, Floral Border, 1/2-In.Flange, Kayserzinn, 10 1/2 In. 65.00
Plate, Samuel Kilbourn, 1814–39, 7 3/4 In. .... 340.00 To 600.00
Plate, Thomas Badger, 8 7/16 In. 350.00

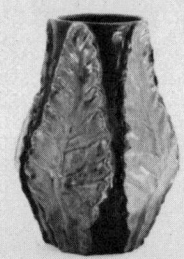

Pewabic, Vase, Veined
Leaves, Green Matte,
Leaf Mark, 13 X 8 In.

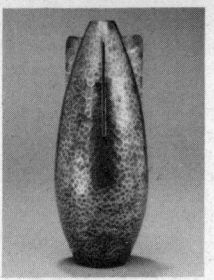

Pewter, Vase, Hammered,
3 Fin–Form Handles,
Signed, C.1930, 9 In.

Purse, Mesh,
Orange, Red, Purple, Fringe,
Chain Handles

Plate, Thomas Danforth II, Hammered, 7 15/16 In.	250.00
Plate, Townsend, English, 8 3/8 In.	65.00
Plate, Triple Reeded, Charles II, C.1680, English, 8 3/4 In.	440.00
Plate, Tudor, Sloping Sides, Fleur–De–Lis, 16th Century, 10 In.	1500.00
Plate, Wriggle Work, Goat, Francis Kingston, C.1730, 8 1/2 In.	1275.00
Plate, Wriggle Work, Peacock Design, J.Hitchman, C.1720, 8 1/3 In.	2025.00
Platter, Scalloped Rim, Oval, Continental, 18 X 11 1/4 In.	35.00
Platter, Turkey, Kayserzinn, 16 In.	150.00
Porringer, Cast Handle, 3 3/8 In.	45.00
Porringer, Crown Handle, Danforth & Boardman, 1820, 5 In.	450.00
Porringer, Crown Handle, Reversed GS Signature, 5 1/2 In.	425.00
Porringer, Elisha Kirk, York, Pa., 5 1/4 In.	660.00
Porringer, Samuel Danforth, Hartford, Conn.	800.00
Salt Box, Hanging, Floral Design, M.A.H., 1645, Continental, 9 In.	500.00
Salt, 6 Petals Folded Up, Make Flower Shape, Chanal	16.00
Salt, Footed, C.1780, 1 3/4 In.	90.00
Salt, Rounded Trencher, C.1680, Round, 2 1/3 In.	300.00
Salt, Trencher, Late 17th Century	800.00
Salt, William & Mary Capstan, Light, English, 3 In.	1350.00
Salver, George III, Henry Cowper, 1789	1900.00
Saucer, Broad Rim, Shallow Central Boss, English, C.1630, 5 3/4 In.	1650.00
Smoking Set, Commemorative, Dated 1869, Burma, 1 Piece	100.00
Snuff Mull, Deer's Foot, Pewter Mounts, Scotland, C.1820, 3 In.	85.00
Spoon, Acorn Knop, Initialed R N, 16th Century, 5 1/2 In.	725.00
Spoon, Chocolate, Marked, Late 17th Century, 4 In., Pair	485.00
Spoon, Corinthian Stem, Brass, C.1500, 4 3/4 In.	240.00
Spoon, Diamond Point, England, 15th Century, 5 1/2 In.	400.00
Spoon, File Knop, Mandolin Shaped Bowl, C.1400, 5 3/4 In.	325.00
Spoon, Hammered Flat Stem, 14th Century, 7 In.	280.00
Spoon, William Bradford, 1719–85, Round Bowl, 6 5/8 In.	1600.00
Sugar & Creamer, Thomas Danforth Boardman, X Mark On Sugar	650.00
Sugar Castor, Shaped Pouring Holes, Late 18th Century, 5 1/4 In.	125.00
Sugar, Open, Dragon Ship Shape, Kayserzinn, 8 In.	150.00
Sundial, Windowsill, New England, C.1790, Small	240.00
Tankard, Domed Lid, George I, John Spicer, C.1720, 7 In.	3000.00
Tankard, Swiss Eagle, Neuchatel, Beaked Spout, Relief Design, 14 In.	325.00
Tankard, Tulip Style, Domed Cover, 8 In.	150.00
Tankard, Wriggle Work, Ball On Thumbpiece, Hallmarked, German, 1808	295.00
Tappit Hen, Scotland, C.1820, 11 1/4 In.	300.00
Tea Set, Child's, Ornate, 10 Piece	120.00
Teapot, Allen Porter, 7 In.	150.00
Teapot, Dixon & Smith, Dated Dec.30, 1841	180.00
Teapot, Eben Smith, Engraved	125.00
Teapot, Globular, Luther Boardman	325.00
Teapot, James H.Putnam, 1830–55	250.00
Teapot, Josiah Danforth, Globular, Ivory Ring On Finial, 7 3/4 In.	250.00

Teapot, Lighthouse Shape, Freeman Porter, C.1840, 6 1/4 In. 300.00
Teapot, Onion Shape, Thomas Danforth Boardman, C.1830 .... 325.00
Teapot, P.Porter, Westbrook, 8 3/4 In. 250.00
Teapot, Roswell Gleason, Globe Shape, C.1840, 7 1/4 In. 400.00
Teapot, Samuel Simpson, No., 6 In. 350.00
Teapot, Swan Neck Spout, Wooden Handle, Finial, English, 7 In. 2400.00
Teapot, Wooden Handle & Finial, Roswell Gleason, 10 In. 125.00
Teaspoon, T.R.Holt, 1845–49, 5 1/2 In., Pair 60.00
Tray, 3 Children In Relief, Moreau, Tudric, 12 In. 130.00
Tray, Leaf, Cricket On Handle, Kayserzinn 45.00
Tumbler, Lizard & Shamrock Design, Engraved Lill, Kayserzinn 40.00
Urn, Lion & Ring Handle, Spigot, Cover, Red, Gold Leaves, 15 In. 935.00
Vase, Hammered, 3 Fin–Form Handles, Signed, C.1930, 9 In. ....*Illus* 770.00
Wine Taster, Shaker Forms Handle, 2 Winged Griffins Interior 95.00

Phoenix Bird, or Flying Phoenix, is the name given to a blue–and–white kitchenware popular between 1900 and World War II. A variant is known as Flying Turkey. Most of this dinnerware was made in Japan for sale in the dime stores in America. It is still being made.

PHOENIX BIRD, Bowl, 5 3/8 In. 10.00
Butter Chip 12.00
Casserole, Covered, Oval, 2 1/2 X 4 1/2 X 6 1/4 In. 47.50
Chocolate Pot, Oriental Mark 85.00
Cup & Saucer .... 11.00 To 18.00
Cup, Bouillon 20.00
Cup, Child's, Green 12.00
Eggcup, Double .... 8.95 To 15.00
Ginger Jar, 4 1/2 In. 8.50
Hot Plate, Blue 55.00
Match Safe, Table 55.00
Pitcher 17.50
Plate, 6 In. 4.50
Platter, Blue, 12 In. 15.00
Relish, 3 Birds, 4 1/2 X 8 1/4 In. 25.00
Salt & Pepper, Flying Turkey 20.00
Salt & Pepper, Japan 15.00
Salt & Pepper, Lighthouse 20.00
Sugar, Covered 17.00
Tea Set, 3 Piece 75.00
Tea Strainer, Base 65.00
Teapot .... 25.00 To 30.00
Tumbler, 2 1/2 In. 15.00

Phoenix Glass Company was founded in 1880 in Pennsylvania. The firm made commercial products such as lampshades, bottles, and glassware. Collectors today are interested in the sculptured glassware made by the company from the 1930s until the mid–1950s. The company is still working.

PHOENIX, Bowl, Blue, Cherries, On Branches, 8 In. 65.00
Bowl, Overall Orchids, Pedestal, Green, 10 1/2 In. 68.00
Box, Covered, Multifloral, Bird of Paradise, Oval, 10 1/2 In. 95.00
Box, Scalloped Oval, White Opalescent, Fruits, 7 1/4 In. 75.00
Dish, Covered, Hummingbird, Blue 85.00
Fruit Boat, Lovebirds All Around, Vines, Green Birds, 15 In. 295.00
Lamp, Amber Grasshoppers 1388.00
Plate, Bird & Flower Pattern, Orchid, 8 1/4 In. 85.00
Plate, Dancing Nudes, Pink 95.00
Powder Box, Blue Hummingbird .... 75.00 To 90.00
Rose Bowl, Sculptured White Star, Flowers, Green Ground, 7 X 7 In. 85.00
Vase, Bird On Branch, Blue, 7 In. 75.00
Vase, Bittersweet, Cream & Melon, 9 1/2 In. 200.00
Vase, Ferns, Blue, White, 7 In. 85.00

Vase, Ferns, White, Blue Ground, Signed, 7 In.	75.00
Vase, Floral, White Satin, Tan, Turquoise, Lamp Hole, 7 X 11 In.	100.00
Vase, Flying Geese, White Satin Ground, 9 1/2 X 12 In.	210.00
Vase, Peonies & Buds, Brown Stems, Aqua Leaves, White, 12 1/4 In.	135.00
Vase, Philodendron Leaves, Blue Ground, 11 1/2 In.	89.00
Vase, Pillow Shape, White Flying Geese, Label, Large	150.00
Vase, Praying Mantis, Pink, 8 In.	80.00
Vase, Praying Mantis, White & Blue, 7 1/2 In.	105.00
Vase, Red Berries, White Ground, 9 1/4 In.	125.00
Vase, Turquoise Leaves, Red Berries, White Ground, 9 1/4 In.	125.00
Vase, White Geese, Brown Ground, Pillow, 8 In.	175.00

The tin cases that held phonograph needles are collected today by music and phonograph enthusiasts and advertising addicts. The tins are very small, about 2 inches across, and often have attractive graphic designs lithographed on the tin.

PHONOGRAPH NEEDLE, Best Talking Machines, Morning Glory Horn, 1920s	10.00
Parrot, 78 RPM	8.00
RCA Victor, Cardboard, Silver Overlay Nipper, Black	15.00
Songster Phonograph Needles, Bird Picture	25.00
Victor, Full Tone, Nipper, Phonograph, 3 X 1/2 In.	30.00

The phonograph, invented by Thomas Edison in the 1880s, has been made by many firms. This section also includes other items associated with the phonograph. Records are listed in their own section.

PHONOGRAPH, Album, Victorian, Plays 2 Tunes	88.00
Aretino, Disc, Outside Horn	350.00
Bendix, Radio Combination, 1940s	250.00
Brunswick, 1920s	195.00
Busy Bee, Cylinder	275.00
Columbia AD Graphophone, Aluminum Horn, 2 In.Cylinders	3100.00
Columbia AH, Large Brass Horn	600.00
Columbia, Model Q, C.1898	400.00
Columbia, Regent, Desk	450.00
Dancer, Siam Soo, 1909 Label	595.00
Eagle Lock Co., Portable, Hand Crank	65.00
Edison, Amberola, Model 50, C.1910	340.00
Edison, Amberola, Model A, Floor Model, Drawers With Cylinders	995.00
Edison, Concert, Standard X, Front Drawer	1400.00
Edison, Eclipse, Penny Operated, Floor Model, Battery	3800.00
Edison, Fireside A, With No.10 Cygnet Horn, 1909	468.00
Edison, Hand Painted Garland of Roses, 30 Cylinders	575.00
Edison, Home, With Diamond B & Wood Grained Cygnet	500.00
Edison, Little Gem, Cylinder, Outside Horn, Records	275.00
Edison, Model 50, Lift Top, Oak	200.00
Edison, Standard, 2 To 4 Minute, Cygnet Horn	650.00
Edison, Standard, Cylinder	350.00
Edison, Standard, With 2 Reproducers	300.00
Edison, Triumph, Blue Morning Glory Horn, Oak	700.00
Federal, Radio Combination	85.00
Garrand, Hand Crafted Snakeskin Horn, 1920	1250.00
Grafonola–Columbia, Oak	465.00
Graphaphone, Model B Base & Lid, Model Q Player	185.00
Jukebox, AMI A, Plastic, 1946	1850.00
Jukebox, Capehart, Orchestrope, 1929	1500.00
Jukebox, Holcomb & Hoke, Electromuse, 1928	1200.00
Jukebox, Mills, Ferris Wheel	450.00
Jukebox, Mills, Panoram Video, 1940	2500.00
Jukebox, Mills, Throne	850.00
Jukebox, Packard, Manhattan, Pla–Mor Wall Speaker	1950.00
Jukebox, Ristacrat, Table Model	500.00
Jukebox, Rockola Model 1426	2000.00
Jukebox, Rockola Model 1428	650.00

Jukebox, Rockola, Model 1448, 1954 .... 1400.00
Jukebox, Rockola, Monarch, 1938 .... 850.00
Jukebox, Seeburg, C–Art 4850.00
Jukebox, Seeburg, Model 146 .... 2000.00
Jukebox, Seeburg, Plaza 750.00
Jukebox, Wurlitzer, Model 750 .... 4900.00 To 5000.00
Jukebox, Wurlitzer, Model 850 .... 9500.00 To 9800.00
Jukebox, Wurlitzer, Model 1015 .... 4500.00 To 7500.00
Jukebox, Wurlitzer, Model 1050 .... 4800.00 To 5000.00
Jukebox, Wurlitzer, Model 1059 .... 4800.00
Jukebox, Wurlitzer, Model 1100, 24 Selections, 57 In. 4400.00
Jukebox, Wurlitzer, Model 1400 .... 750.00
Jukebox, Wurlitzer, Model 1650A, 1954 .... 1400.00
Jukebox, Wurlitzer, Model P–12, 1934 .... 2800.00
Jukebox, Wurlitzer, Model P–500, Rotating Color Cylinders 3000.00
Kinetoscope, Edison 600.00
M.S.Victor, Wooden Horn 1150.00
Mills, Automatic ....750.00 To 1000.00
Pathe, Leather Horn 550.00
Regina, Tabletop, Mahogany, Single Comb, 5 Cent, 26 Discs 3500.00
Rishell Victrola, Upright 450.00
Rishell, Floor Model 375.00
Sousa Talkaphone 1200.00
Stella, Console, 40 Records, Oak 3600.00
Tinfoil, Brass Works, Walnut Handle & Base, 18 In. 7500.00
Victor, Model I, Morning Glory Horn 600.00
Victor, Model III, Morning Glory Horn, Original Paint 700.00
Victor, Model III, Original Petalled Horn 650.00
Victor, Model IV, Mahogany Horn 1200.00
Victor, Model IV, Matching Mahogany Record Cabinet Base 900.00
Victor, Model P 500.00
Victrola, General Phonograph Mfg.Co., Baby Cabinet, 17 X 9 In. 120.00
Victrola, Model XVIII 900.00
Victrola, Victor Mechanism, Hand Carved 950.00
Victrola, VTLA, Flat Top Model 790.00
Wicker, Floor Model, 1920 .... 350.00

The first photograph was a view from a window in France taken in 1826. The commercially successful photograph started with the daguerreotype introduced in 1839. Today all sorts of photographs and photographic equipment are collected. Albums were popular in Victorian times. Cartes de visite were cardboard–mounted photographs popular in the years after the Civil War. Stereo views are listed under Stereo Card.

PHOTOGRAPHY, Ambrotype, Civil War Soldier, Hand Colored, Oval Frame 45.00
Ambrotype, Civil War Soldier, Not In Uniform, Burial Record 50.00
Ambrotype, Man Playing Violin, Framed, 1/2 Plate 35.00
Ambrotype, Man With Dog, Hand Colored, Framed, 1/4 Plate 20.00
Ambrotype, Niagara, Full Plate 345.00
Cabinet Card, Annie Oakley 350.00
Cabinet Card, Buffalo Bill 45.00
Cabinet Card, C.C.Farren, Child, Seated On Horse, Dayton, Pa. 15.00
Cabinet Card, George Turner, Chief Justice of Nevada, 1860–64 .... 10.00
Cabinet Card, Interior Lady's Hat Shop, Hats of 1800s 9.00
Cabinet Card, John Wilkes Booth, 1865 .... 30.00
Cabinet Card, Miner, Whittemore, S.D. 35.00
Cabinet Card, Mrs.Grover Cleveland, Photographer J.E.Hale 10.00
Cabinet Card, Scarface Charlie, Geological Survey 115.00
Camera, Ansco Flash Clipper, Pullout Front, Marked 7.00
Camera, Argus C–3, Matchmatic, 2 Tone, With Meter 19.50
Camera, Box, Brownie Jr. 6.00
Camera, Brownie Bullet 3.00
Camera, Brownie, 2A, Instructions, Box 12.00
Camera, Century, No.8, 1912, 11 X 14 To 45 In. 3500.00

Camera, Conley, No.2, Box, Kewpie	8.00
Camera, Eastman, Model 1898, Wooden Box, Small	110.00
Camera, Graflex, Series II, Case	90.00
Camera, Kodak, Brownie, Flash 620	6.00 To 20.00
Camera, Kodak, Diomatic, No.0	45.00
Camera, Kodak, Duaflex 2	15.00
Camera, Kodak, Folding, Pigskin Case, 1924	25.00
Camera, Kodak, Jr., Autographic	75.00
Camera, Kodak, No.1, Diodak, Folding, Case	50.00
Camera, Kodak, No.1, Pocket	20.00
Camera, Kodak, No.2, Brownie, Box	25.00
Camera, Kodak, No.2, Hawkeye, Folding, Box	12.00
Camera, Kodak, No.3A, Autographic	32.00 To 50.00
Camera, Kodak, No.4, Pocket, Folding, Bellows, Mahogany On Red	75.00
Camera, Kodak, Petite, Green, 1930	75.00
Camera, Kodak, Pocket, Boy Scout, With Case	100.00
Camera, Kodak, Rainbow Hawkeye, Pocket, Blue & White Bellows	55.00
Camera, Kodak, Retina III, 35 Mm	60.00
Camera, Linhof, Film Sheath, Range Finder, Xenar, 10 X 15 In.	165.00
Camera, Mickey Mouse, Mick–A–Matic, Ear Actuated, Box	70.00
Camera, Petite, Blue, Box, Instructions, 1929	80.00
Camera, Petri, 35 Mm	45.00
Camera, Premo Reflex, Hooded Box	95.00
Camera, Seroco Camera Studio	350.00
Camera, Spy, Expo Watch, View Finder, Instructions, Box	125.00
Camera, Stereoscopic, Powell, Collapsible Body	750.00
Camera, Thornton Pickard Special Ruby Reflex, 1/4 Plate	125.00
Camera, Universal Minute 16	55.00
Camera, Wardflex II, Biokor F3	47.50
Camera, Wardflex II, Synchro MX	60.00
Camera, Yashica, Model A, 120	90.00
Camera, Zeiss Ikon, Bellows, Black Leatherette, Carrying Case	20.00
Camera, Zeiss Ikon, Super Ikonta 532/16	80.00
Camera, Ziess Ikon–Icarette, Pompar Lenses, Leather Box	45.00
Carte De Visite, Abraham Lincoln & Son Tad	55.00
Carte De Visite, Butcher	15.00
Carte De Visite, Chinese Man, Edouart & Cobb, San Francisco	25.00
Carte De Visite, Grant & Colfax, Presidential Campaign, 1868	15.00
Carte De Visite, High Falls, N.Y., Moore	14.00
Carte De Visite, Lincoln, By Warren, 1865	125.00
Carte De Visite, Mrs.Lincoln, Mumler	8.00
Carte De Visite, R.C.Wyllie, In Uniform	40.00
Carte De Visite, Sailboat In White Bear Lake, Minn.	20.00
Carte De Visite, Union Officer	18.00
Daguerreotype Case, Civil War, Cannon Balls, Flag, 3 1/2 In.	45.00
Daguerreotype Case, Fortune Teller Scene, 4 X 5 In.	125.00
Daguerreotype Case, Meditating Monk	65.00
Daguerreotype, Daniel Webster's Nephew	35.00
Daguerreotype, Indian, Eastern Dress, 1/6 Plate	150.00
Daguerreotype, Lady Holding Open Book, Backdrop	25.00
Daguerreotype, M.P.Simons, Photographer, Framed	4400.00
Daguerreotype, Man On Sulky	250.00
Daguerreotype, Man Playing Accordion, Oval Mount, 2 X 3 In.	75.00
Daguerreotype, Mexican War Soldier, 1/9 Plate	27.50
Daguerreotype, P.T.Barnum's Museum, Hand Colored, 1857	440.00
Daguerreotype, Woman, With Wooden Arms, 1/6 Plate	65.00
Enlarger, Elwood, Early 1900s	145.00
Film Processing Kit, Black Bakelite, Burgundy Knobs, Box	50.00
Lantern, Darkroom, Kerosene, Ideal	28.00
Lens, Camera, For Box, Brass, Pat.1867, English	92.50
Magic Lantern, Wooden Carrying Case, Germany, C.1890	275.00
Mirroscope, Magnifies On Wall Screen, Electric, Tin	36.00
Photograph, 3 Chiefs, Edward S.Curtis	500.00
Photograph, Abraham Lincoln, Beardless, Springfield, Ill.	175.00

Photograph, Abraham Lincoln, C.S.German, Oval Frame 1750.00
Photograph, Aerial View, Dayton, O., Fire, 1909, 7 X 9 In. 40.00
Photograph, Amelia Earhart, Aviation Uniform, Print Signed 19.00
Photograph, Bride's Portrait, Full, Sepia, 6 1/2 X 8 1/2 In. 14.00
Photograph, Cabinet Card, James Garfield & Family 12.00
Photograph, Cabinet Card, President & Mrs.McKinley 12.00
Photograph, Cabinet Card, Wm.J.Bryan 12.00
Photograph, Chinese Actor, Oriental Backdrop, 5 X 7 In. 15.00
Photograph, Christmas Tree, Fence, Santa Beneath, 20th Century 60.00
Photograph, Electrical Experiment, Inventor Nikola Telsa 220.00
Photograph, Hawaiian, 7 Different Scenes, 1900, 8 X 10 In. 175.00
Photograph, Indian Portrait, F.A.Rhinehart, 5 Piece 660.00
Photograph, Lincoln At Antietam, Alexander Gardener, 1862 .... 3960.00
Photograph, Mission Inn, With Photo Stamp 50.00
Photograph, Panorama of W.Va., U.S.50, 1920s, 8 X 44 In. 65.00
Photograph, Parade, Chinatown, San Francisco, 1920s, 5 X 7 In. 18.00
Photograph, San Francisco Cable Car, By Watkins, 1870s 65.00
Photograph, School Football Team, Junior Champs, 1913 .... 15.00
Photograph, Steam Yacht Satanella, Stebbins, With Story 15.00
Photogravure, Old Man of Cheyenne Tribe, Edward Curtis 99.00
Projector, Keystone, Model 535, Catalog, Film & Tickets, 1923 .... 75.00
Projector, Mirroscope, Postcard 40.00
Scale, Eastman Studio, Box 75.00
Tank, Film, Kodak, Model B2, Box 40.00
Thermometer, Darkroom, Case, Kodak 20.00
Tintype, 1907 Reunion BPOE 60.00
Tintype, 2 Ballplayers, Studio 110.00
Tintype, Black Man, In Civil War Uniform, Hull 250.00
Tintype, Civil War Soldiers, 13 Piece 100.00
Tintype, Horse Drawn Buggy, Black Driver, 5 X 7 In. 50.00
Tintype, Mother & Daughter 18.00
Tintype, Train Engine Seymour, Danforth, Cooke & Co., 1875 .... 605.00
Tintype, Union Soldier, With Musket 85.00
Tintype, Young Girl Holding China Doll, 3 X 4 In. 50.00

> About 1880, the well-decorated home had a shawl on the piano.
> Bisque piano babies were designed to help hold the shawl in place.
> They range in size from 6 to 18 inches. Most of the figures were
> made in Germany. Reproductions are being made. Other piano
> babies are listed under manufacturers' names.

PIANO BABY, Boy, Nude, Holding Sponge, In Porcelain Tub, 5 X 4 1/4 In. 200.00
Child, Putting Thumb In Mouth, 10 X 6 In. 225.00
Crawling, Sunburst, Heubach, 11 1/2 In. 375.00
Holdng Toy Bear, Green Cap & Dress, Kneeling, 8 1/2 X 5 In. 295.00
Intaglio Blue Eyes, Molded Blond Hair, Starburst, 4 1/2 In. 195.00
Lying On Back, Sunburst Mark, 8 1/2 In. 300.00
Lying On Stomach, Holds Pillow, Pacifier In Mouth, 6 3/4 In. 155.00
On Tummy, Flowing Nighty, 17 In. 525.00
On Tummy, Holding Lamb, 6 1/2 In. 128.00
Papa's Darling 50.00
Smiling, Ready To Put Finger In Mouth, One Foot Up, 13 1/2 In. 395.00
With Cat, 10 In. 100.00

> Pickard China Company was started in 1898 by Wilder Pickard.
> Hand-painted designs were used on china purchased from other
> sources. In the 1930s, the company began to make its own china
> wares. The company now makes many types of porcelains including
> a successful line of limited edition collector plates.

PICKARD, Bonbon, Ring Handles, Gold Etched, 6 1/2 In. 18.00
Bowl, Acorns, Gold Trim, Artist Signed, 9 In. 120.00
Bowl, Berries, Gold Leaves, Interior Band, Leroy, 3 X 9 3/4 In. 175.00
Bowl, Covered, Garden Fruit, Gold Trim, Signed, 9 In. 350.00
Bowl, Currant Design, Rust, Yellow Ground, Gold Rim, 10 3/4 In. 150.00
Bowl, Fruit, Poppies & Leaves, Artist Signed, 1898, 10 In. 135.00

Bowl, Gold Finish, Footed, Marked, 7 1/4 X 3 In.	30.00
Bowl, Hazelnut Design, Footed, C.1898, 8 1/4 In.	175.00
Bowl, Pink Flowers Above Apples, Yellow Ground, Gold Rim, 7 In.	80.00
Bowl, Scalloped, Bulging Sides, Gooseberries, Signed, 8 1/2 In.	145.00
Bowl, Strawberries, Tinted Ground, Gold Trim, 1898 Mark, 9 In.	225.00
Candlestick, Etched Gold, 4 1/2 X 3 In., Pair	40.00
Chocolate Pot, Hand Painted, Artist Signed, 12 In.	175.00
Cup & Saucer, Bouillon, Cornflower Pattern, 4 Sets	80.00
Cup & Saucer, Demitasse, Etched Gold Florals	45.00
Cup & Tray, Gold Gilded & Etched, Signed, 9 1/4 In.	45.00
Demitasse Pot, Christmas Poinsettia, Artist Signed, 1910 Mark	195.00
Dish, Condiment, Artist Signed, 6 In.	49.00
Dish, Leaf, Foliage, Pink & Green, Gold Trim, 1912, 5 3/4 In.	35.00
Dish, Mayonnaise, Violets, Gold, Wagner, 2 Piece	75.00
Ewer, Gold Spout, Handle, Blueberries, Marked, 6 1/2 In.	325.00
Hatpin Holder, Violets	60.00
Jam Jar, Blackberries, Signed, 7 In.	78.00
Jug, Indian Corn Design, Stopper, Circle Mark, 7 1/2 In.	265.00
Jug, Rum, Stopper, Stylized Pattern, Gold, 1905 Mark, 6 X 5 In.	265.00
Nappy, Lemons, Cherries, Gold Center & Handle, 3 3/4 In.	90.00
Pitcher, Hand Painted, Orange, Gold Grapes, Marked, 1905, 7 1/4 In.	188.00
Pitcher, Lemonade, Cherry Design, Gold Trim, Artist Signed, 7 In.	195.00
Pitcher, Milk, Pansy Design, Gold Handle, Signed, 4 1/2 In.	195.00
Pitcher, Yellow Tulip Design, Artist Signed, 8 1/2 In.	340.00
Plate, American Bald Eagle, James Lockhart, 1974	750.00
Plate, Annual, 1970, Ruffled Grouse	195.00
Plate, Apple Green, On Ivory, Gold, 1930–38, 10 7/8 In., 12 Piece	550.00
Plate, Currants, Otto Goess, 1898, 7 1/2 In.	75.00
Plate, Gooseberries, Tinted Ground, Scalloped, 1895 Mark, 9 In.	140.00
Plate, Hand Painted, Leaf Mark, 1912, 8 1/2 In.	35.00
Plate, Nut, Signed Wight, 7 In.	30.00
Plate, Roses, Signed, 1898, 8 1/2 In.	85.00
Plate, Scenic, Signed, 8 3/4 In.	175.00
Rose Bowl, Peaches, Gold, Handles, 1905 Mark, 6 3/4 X 8 1/4 In.	190.00
Salt & Pepper, Mother–of–Pearl Ground, Florals, 1905 Mark	110.00
Saltshaker, Poppy Design, Gold Trim, Signed Fox	65.00
Sugar & Creamer, All Gold, No.598	60.00
Sugar & Creamer, Birds, Flowers, Gold Trim, Signed	70.00
Sugar & Creamer, Covered, Autumn, Gooseberries, Gold Trim	60.00
Sugar & Creamer, Dutch Girl, Bisque, F.James, 3 3/4 X 4 3/4 In.	110.00
Sugar & Creamer, Fruit Design, Gold Bands, Marked	250.00
Sugar, Etched Gold, Marked	32.00
Tea Set, Dolphin Head Spout, Gold Rims, Handles, Feet, 3 Piece	650.00
Teapot, Gold Etched, Tapered Body, 9 In.	135.00
Tray, Boat Shape, Bunches of Grapes & Leaves, Signed, 13 1/2 In.	135.00
Vase, Birch Tree & Lake Scene, Pastel, E.Challinor, 11 1/2 In.	400.00
Vase, Gold & Yellow Flowers, Signed, 5 In.	65.00
Vase, Gold Handles & Trim, Red Tracery, Marked, 9 3/4 In.	130.00
Vase, Golden Mums, Green Leaves, Signed, 9 In.	295.00
Vase, Lake Scene, Matte Finish, Handles, Leaf Mark, Challinor, 6 In.	265.00
Vase, Moonlit Scene, 2 Handles, Challinor, 8 In.	150.00
Vase, Scenic, Floral, Scalloped Base & Top, Gold Trim, 8 1/4 In.	275.00
Vase, Scenic, Garden, Bridge, Gold Handles, 7 In.	250.00
Vase, Scenic, Moonlit Lake, Pine Trees, Leaf Mark, 7 3/4 In.	245.00

PICTURE FRAME, see Furniture, Frame

Pictures like silhouettes and small decorative pictures are listed here.
Some other types of pictures are listed under Print or Painting.

PICTURE, Cutwork, J.J.Metzger Family Record, Pa., 1894, Framed, 22 X 27 In.	3960.00
Foil, Floral & Leaf Spray, Black Ground, Victorian, 7 X 10 In.	15.00
Hair Wreath, Flowers, With Beads, Shadowbox Frame, 19 X 21 In.	35.00
Hair Wreath, Shadowbox Frame, 1850s	66.00
Needlework, Silk, Woman At Tomb, Larkin Family, 1801, 14 X 15 In.	375.00
Needlework, Steamship & Sailing Vessels, Wool, Framed, 22 X 29 In.	2310.00

Reverse Painting, Glass, Girl, Flowers, Metallic Paper, 11 In.	45.00
Silhouette, Andrew Jackson, Gilt Highlights, Framed, 9 X 10 In.	350.00
Silhouette, Chauncey B.Culor, Primitive, 1889, 2 3/4 X 3 1/2 In.	37.50
Silhouette, Child, Hollow Cut, Eulogizing Letter Back, 8 X 10 In.	37.50
Silhouette, Couple & 3 Children, Full Length, 11 1/4 X 15 In.	130.00
Silhouette, Full Figure, Gentleman, Frock Coat, Top Hat, 11 In.	85.00
Silhouette, Gentleman, Black Lacquer Frame, Brass, 4 X 5 In.	85.00
Silhouette, Hollow Cut, Gentleman, Gilt Frame, 4 5/8 X 6 In.	45.00
Silhouette, Hollow Cut, Woman, Black Frame, 5 1/2 X 6 In.	75.00
Silhouette, Mary Rice, Born 1782, Frame, 4 1/2 X 6 1/2 In.	175.00
Silhouette, Parson, Painted, Beveled Frame, 7 X 8 1/4 In.	70.00
Silhouette, Reverend Joseph Willard, President Harvard	185.00
Silhouette, Ruth & Anjanette Johnson, Pewter Frame, 3 In., Pair	475.00
Silhouette, Woman, Gilded Highlights, Framed, 8 1/4 X 9 1/4 In.	75.00
Silhouette, Woman, Hollow Cut, Eglomise Matte, Framed, 6 X 7 In.	155.00
Silhouette, Woman, J.Turner, June 3, 1853, Framed, 8 X 8 In.	25.00
Silhouette, Woman, White, On Black Ground, Framed, 4 3/8 X 5 In.	25.00
Silhouette, Young Boy, Oilcloth Frame, Brass Liner, 3 X 5 In.	50.00
Silhouette, Young Woman, Black Reeded Frame, 4 X 5 In.	60.00
Silhouette, Young Woman, Hollow Cut, Framed, 3 1/2 X 4 1/2 In.	150.00
Silhouette, Young Woman, Hollow Cut, Initialed, 4 1/4 X 6 In.	25.00
Theorem, On Velvet, Fruit, F.Grinnel & Sons, C.1840, 15 X 13 In.	200.00
Tinsel, Stylized Urn of Flowers, S.J.Gilkey, Framed, 21 X 17 In.	345.00

The Pigeon Forge Pottery was started in Pigeon Forge, Tennessee, in 1946. Red clay found near the pottery was used to make the pieces. Molded or thrown pottery with matte glaze and slip decoration was made. The pottery is still working.

PIGEON FORGE, Bowl, 3 3/4 In.	10.00
Bowl, Rim Flowers, Gray, Low	14.00
Bowl, Wooden Lid, Green, 1940s	35.00
Candle Bowl, Mottled Brown Glaze	12.00
Figurine, Owl, Artist Signed, 4 1/2 In.	10.00
Sugar & Creamer, Aqua, Small	13.00
Vase, Dogwood, 3 1/2 In.	12.00
Vase, Matte Green, Marked, 5 In.	20.00

The Pilkington Tile and Pottery Company was established in 1892 in England. The company made small pottery wares like buttons and hatpin heads but soon started decorating vases purchased from other potteries. By 1903, the company had discovered an opalescent glaze that became popular on the Lancastrian pottery line. The manufacture of pottery ended in 1937 but decorating continued until 1948.

PILKINGTON, Lamp Base, Royal Lancastrian, Drilled, 9 In.	300.00
Vase, C.Cundall, 1910, 7 1/2 In.	300.00

The pincushion doll is not really a doll and often was not even a pincushion. The top half of a doll was made of porcelain. The edge of the half-doll was made with several small holes for thread, and the doll was stitched to a fabric body with a voluminous skirt. The finished figure was used to cover a hot pot of tea, a powder box, a pincushion, a whiskbroom, or a lamp. They were made in sizes from less than an inch to over 9 inches high. Most date from the early 1900s to the 1950s.

PINCUSHION DOLL, Antoinette Hairdo, Arms Away, Hands To Nude Bust, 4 In.	50.00
Antoinette Hairdo, Green Hat, Hands To Bust, 1 5/8 In.	15.00
Applied Roses In Hair, Arms Away, Gray Hair, 4 7/8 In.	145.00
Arms Akimbo, Sandy Hair, Yellow, Germany, 2 3/4 In.	55.00
Arms Akimbo, Yellow Basket, Black Dress, Blond, 3 1/2 In.	55.00
Arms Away, Fancy Hairdo, Eyeliner, 5 1/4 In.	148.00
Arms Away, Pink Floral Wreath In Hair, Germany, 3 In.	110.00
Arms Extended, Fancy Hairdo, Goebel, 4 In.	150.00
Arms On Chest, Blue Hair Ribbon, Signed, 4 In.	50.00

Art Deco, Black Hair, Turned Head, Arms Away, 2 7/8 In. 25.00
Beige Skirt Cushion, Gold Slippered Feet, Hat, 2 In. 25.00
Bisque, Jointed Arms, Blond Mohair, 2 In. 125.00
Blond, Kate Greenaway Type, Germany, 2 1/2 In. 48.00
Blue Bodice, White Ruffles, Floral Wreath In Hair, 2 In. 30.00
Blue Shawl, Holds Cup To Breast, 2 In. 21.00
Bobbed Hair, Holding Hands Below Bosom, Germany, 3 In. 40.00
Boy, Full Figure, Top Hat, Carrying Bouquet, 3 In. 35.00
Child, Pink Derby Hat, Holding Bouquet, Germany, 2 In. 35.00
Child, Side Curls, Magenta Party Dress, Germany, 3 In. 75.00
Child, White, Pink Bouquet, Kate Greenaway, 2 1/8 In. 65.00
Colonial Lady, Arms Away, Feathers In Hair, 4 3/4 In. 90.00
Cropped Black Hair, Red Dangle Earrings, Germany, 2 In. 35.00
Dog, Schnauzer, Red Bow, 3/4 X 1 1/4 In. 40.00
Dutch Child, Pink Hat, Bouquet, Nippon, 3 1/2 In. 85.00
Flapper, Bald, Green Dress, Gold Bangles, Germany, 4 In. 110.00
Flapper, Black Hair, White Bodice, Germany, 2 In. 30.00
Flapper, Maroon Coat, Fur Collar, Germany, 4 In. 98.00
Flapper, Pleated Skirt, Stamped Germany, 1 1/2 In. 48.00
Flapper, Rust Coat, Ermine Collar, Hat, Germany, 4 In. 125.00
Flapper, Tulip Hat, Ostrich Fan, Germany, 4 In. 85.00
Flapper, White Dress, With Gray & Green, 2 1/2 In. 10.00
Flower Petal Hat, Germany, 2 3/8 In. 10.00
Girl, Clown Outfit, Germany, 1 3/4 In. 25.00
Girl, Holding Mirror, Orange Cushion, Japan, 2 In. 30.00
Gray Hair, Aqua Gown, Hands Clasped At Neck, 2 3/4 In. 25.00
Gray Hair, Blue Feathers, Nude, 5 In. 125.00
Hand At Forehead, Other Over Breast, Germany, 4 In. 185.00
Holding Fan & Pink Rose, Germany, 2 In. 30.00
Holding Fan, Russet Hat, Yellow Blouse, 2 3/4 In. 55.00
Lady, Gaucho Dress, Germany, 4 In. 50.00
Lady, Holding Mirror, Court Hairdo, Germany, 2 In. 35.00
Mardi Gras, Green Dress, Hat, Orange Brush, 4 In. 40.00
Mardi Gras, Pink Bodice, Pink Tulip Hat, Japan, 3 In. 35.00
Mermaid, Bathing, Occupied Japan, 3 1/2 In. 20.00
Molded Hair, Braids, Pink Porcelain, Germany, 4 1/2 In. 58.00
Molded White Camisole, Golden–Brown Hair, 2 5/8 In. 42.00
Nude, Arms Away, Maroon Beads In Hair, Germany, 2 1/2 In. 55.00
Nude, Gray Hair & Eyebrows, 4 1/4 In. 75.00
Nude, Gray Hair, Blue Feathers, 5 In. 125.00
Opaque China, Poke Bonnet, Ruffled Dress, Germany, 3 3/4 In 62.00
Pierrette, Nude Flapper, V Waistline, Germany, 2 In. 65.00
Quaker Girl, Hands Crossed, Dome Base, All White, 2 In. 35.00
Ruffled Cushion, Hands Clasped Under Chin, 2 3/4 In. 32.00
Salome, Arms Away, 4 In. 125.00
Spanish Dancer, Opaque China, Germany, 3 1/2 In. 15.00
Spanish Lady, Black Hair, Comb, Arms Away, Germany, 3 In. 24.00
Spanish, Legs, Yellow Dress, Gold Slippers, Germany 60.00
    PINK SLAG, see Slag, Pink

Put up glass shelves and fill them with inexpensive colorful bottles. A burglar would have to break all the bottles, with accompanying noise, to get in.

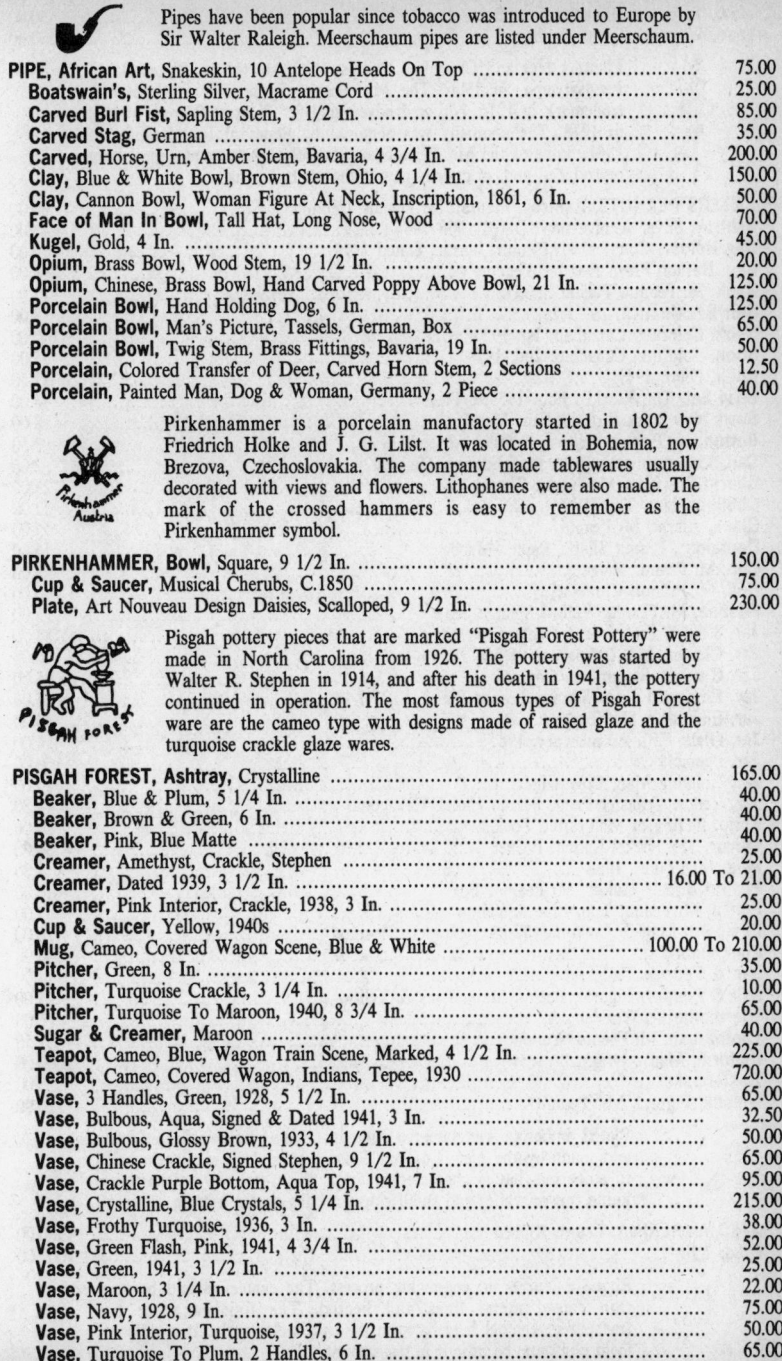

Pipes have been popular since tobacco was introduced to Europe by Sir Walter Raleigh. Meerschaum pipes are listed under Meerschaum.

PIPE, African Art, Snakeskin, 10 Antelope Heads On Top	75.00
Boatswain's, Sterling Silver, Macrame Cord	25.00
Carved Burl Fist, Sapling Stem, 3 1/2 In.	85.00
Carved Stag, German	35.00
Carved, Horse, Urn, Amber Stem, Bavaria, 4 3/4 In.	200.00
Clay, Blue & White Bowl, Brown Stem, Ohio, 4 1/4 In.	150.00
Clay, Cannon Bowl, Woman Figure At Neck, Inscription, 1861, 6 In.	50.00
Face of Man In Bowl, Tall Hat, Long Nose, Wood	70.00
Kugel, Gold, 4 In.	45.00
Opium, Brass Bowl, Wood Stem, 19 1/2 In.	20.00
Opium, Chinese, Brass Bowl, Hand Carved Poppy Above Bowl, 21 In.	125.00
Porcelain Bowl, Hand Holding Dog, 6 In.	125.00
Porcelain Bowl, Man's Picture, Tassels, German, Box	65.00
Porcelain Bowl, Twig Stem, Brass Fittings, Bavaria, 19 In.	50.00
Porcelain, Colored Transfer of Deer, Carved Horn Stem, 2 Sections	12.50
Porcelain, Painted Man, Dog & Woman, Germany, 2 Piece	40.00

Pirkenhammer is a porcelain manufactory started in 1802 by Friedrich Holke and J. G. Lilst. It was located in Bohemia, now Brezova, Czechoslovakia. The company made tablewares usually decorated with views and flowers. Lithophanes were also made. The mark of the crossed hammers is easy to remember as the Pirkenhammer symbol.

PIRKENHAMMER, Bowl, Square, 9 1/2 In.	150.00
Cup & Saucer, Musical Cherubs, C.1850	75.00
Plate, Art Nouveau Design Daisies, Scalloped, 9 1/2 In.	230.00

Pisgah pottery pieces that are marked "Pisgah Forest Pottery" were made in North Carolina from 1926. The pottery was started by Walter R. Stephen in 1914, and after his death in 1941, the pottery continued in operation. The most famous types of Pisgah Forest ware are the cameo type with designs made of raised glaze and the turquoise crackle glaze wares.

PISGAH FOREST, Ashtray, Crystalline	165.00
Beaker, Blue & Plum, 5 1/4 In.	40.00
Beaker, Brown & Green, 6 In.	40.00
Beaker, Pink, Blue Matte	40.00
Creamer, Amethyst, Crackle, Stephen	25.00
Creamer, Dated 1939, 3 1/2 In.	16.00 To 21.00
Creamer, Pink Interior, Crackle, 1938, 3 In.	25.00
Cup & Saucer, Yellow, 1940s	20.00
Mug, Cameo, Covered Wagon Scene, Blue & White	100.00 To 210.00
Pitcher, Green, 8 In.	35.00
Pitcher, Turquoise Crackle, 3 1/4 In.	10.00
Pitcher, Turquoise To Maroon, 1940, 8 3/4 In.	65.00
Sugar & Creamer, Maroon	40.00
Teapot, Cameo, Blue, Wagon Train Scene, Marked, 4 1/2 In.	225.00
Teapot, Cameo, Covered Wagon, Indians, Tepee, 1930	720.00
Vase, 3 Handles, Green, 1928, 5 1/2 In.	65.00
Vase, Bulbous, Aqua, Signed & Dated 1941, 3 In.	32.50
Vase, Bulbous, Glossy Brown, 1933, 4 1/2 In.	50.00
Vase, Chinese Crackle, Signed Stephen, 9 1/2 In.	65.00
Vase, Crackle Purple Bottom, Aqua Top, 1941, 7 In.	95.00
Vase, Crystalline, Blue Crystals, 5 1/4 In.	215.00
Vase, Frothy Turquoise, 1936, 3 In.	38.00
Vase, Green Flash, Pink, 1941, 4 3/4 In.	52.00
Vase, Green, 1941, 3 1/2 In.	25.00
Vase, Maroon, 3 1/4 In.	22.00
Vase, Navy, 1928, 9 In.	75.00
Vase, Pink Interior, Turquoise, 1937, 3 1/2 In.	50.00
Vase, Turquoise To Plum, 2 Handles, 6 In.	65.00

Vase, Turquoise, Pink Interior, 5 1/2 In.	30.00
Vase, Wagons, Signed Stephen, 8 In.	500.00

Planters Nut and Chocolate Company was started in Wilkes–Barre, Pennsylvania, in 1906. The Mr. Peanut figure was adopted as a trademark in 1916. National advertising for Planters Peanuts started in 1918. The company was acquired by Standard Brands, Inc., in 1961. Some of the Mr. Peanut jars and other memorabilia have been reproduced and, of course, new items are being made.

PLANTERS PEANUTS, Ashtray, Figural, Mr.Peanut, Ceramic	60.00
Ashtray, Silver Anniversary, Dated 1906–1956	45.00
Bag Holder, Counter, Mr.Peanut, Plastic, Dated 1979	12.00
Bag, Burlap, Fresh Roasted Peanuts	6.00
Bank, Mr.Peanut, Plastic	7.50
Belt Buckle	8.00
Book, Coloring, Canadian, 1st, 1920s	100.00
Book, Coloring, Canadian, 2nd, 1929	75.00
Book, Paint, 1949	12.50
Bowl Set, Tin, World's Fair, 1939, 5 Piece	45.00
Bowl, New York World's Fair, Metal	8.00
Button, Mr.Peanut, Yellow, Celluloid, Metal, 1930s, 1 In.	3.50
Can, 75th Anniversary, Limited Edition, Tin, 1982	2.00
Charm Bracelet, Mr.Peanut Charm	25.00
Chopper, Nut, Tin, 1938	22.00
Clock, Alarm, Mr.Peanut	55.00
Container, Peanut Shape, Papier–Mache	15.00
Cup, Mr.Peanut, Beige	3.00
Doll, Mr.Peanut, Cloth	10.00
Frisbee, Mr.Peanut, Yellow Sponge	2.00
Jar, 8 Sides, Embossed 5 Cents, Covered	85.00
Jar, Clipper, Lid, Lithograph of Mr. Peanut	70.00
Jar, Counter, Streamline, Covered	50.00 To 65.00
Jar, Embossed Sides, Square, Peanut Finial, 10 X 7 In.	65.00
Jar, Embossed, Slat Top	45.00
Jar, Glass, 75th Anniversary, 1981	4.00
Jar, Pennant	150.00
Jar, Running Man, Covered	120.00
Jar, Yellow Transfer Print, Peanut Finial, Hexagonal	49.50
Knife, Picture of Mr.Peanut, Pocket	20.00
Mirror, The Nickel Lunch, Pocket	30.00
Mug, Mr.Peanut, Blue	4.00
Peanut Butter Maker, Mr.Peanut, Box	10.00
Pencil, Mr.Peanut Top, Blue & Yellow	3.00
Postcard, Man In Costume, Visiting Child In Hospital	20.00
Punchboard	200.00
Salt & Pepper, Celluloid	13.00
Salt & Pepper, Figural, Peanut Man, Black & Yellow	25.00
Thermometer, Wooden	15.00
Toothbrush, Mr.Peanut, Yellow	1.50
Uniform, Man's, Original	1000.00
Wastebasket	5.00
Whistle, Figural, Mr. Peanut	15.00

Plated amberina was patented June 15, 1886, by Edward D. Libbey and made by the New England Glass Works. It is similar in color to amberina, but is characterized by a cream–colored or chartreuse lining (never white) and small ridges or ribs on the outside.

PLATED AMBERINA, Cruet, Ribbed	4000.00
Vase, 7 In.	2000.00

Plique–a–jour is an enameling process. The enamel is laid between thin raised metal lines and heated. The finished piece has transparent enamel held between the thin metal wires. It is different from cloisonne because it is transparent.

PLIQUE–A–JOUR, Salt, Multicolored Band, 3 Twisted Wire Feet, 2 1/8 In. 510.00
Spoon, Wire Twist Handle, Enameled Bowl & Handle 75.00
Tray, Snuff, Blue Flowers, Pink Snowflake Ground, 1 7/8 In. 150.00
Tray, Snuff, Multicolored Flowers, Brocade Box, Stand, 4 In. 300.00
Vase, Various Flowers, Green Ground, C.1930, 4 In. 550.00

All types of political memorabilia are collected, from buttons to banners. Items related to presidential candidates are the most popular, but collectors also search for material related to state and local offices. Many reproductions have been made.

POLITICAL, Badge, LBJ, USA, Lyndon Baines Johnson 9.00
Badge, Souvenir, McKinley Memorial, 1907 .... 15.00
Badge, Wheelman's Club, McKinley 30.00
Ballot, Sample, President, W.Scott & W.English, 1880, 3 X 12 In. 25.00
Bandana, Hoover, Center Picture, 14 X 19 In. 20.00
Bandana, Our Candidates, Grover Cleveland & Allen G.Thurman 195.00
Bank, F.D.Roosevelt, New Deal, Cast Iron 210.00
Banner, George Washington Figure Print, Linen, C.1876, Framed 200.00
Book, Coloring, John F.Kennedy & Friends, Funny Verses, 1962 .... 25.00
Book, Dwight D.Eisenhower, Relman Morin, 256 Pages, C.1967 .... 3.00
Book, Richard Nixon, Monarch 600.00
Bottle, Tippecanoe Extract, Harrison Pres.Campaign, 2 In. 300.00
Box, Cigar, Our President Franklin Roosevelt, New Deal Cigar 25.00
Bracelet, Inaugural Ball, Pres.Richard Nixon 45.00
Bracelet, Johnson, Humphrey, Inaugural Ball, Portraits, 1965 .... 30.00
Bracelet, Memorial, John F.Kennedy, Original Card 10.00
Button, Alfred E.Smith 22.00
Button, Bryan & Stevenson, Jugate, 1900 .... 34.00
Button, Bryan, Silver & Black, Celluloid 16.50
Button, Campaign, Harding, Picture, Red, 1920 .... 15.00
Button, Carry On With Roosevelt, 1 In. 3.00
Button, Carter & Mondale, Flasher, 2 In. 12.00
Button, Cox, Ohio, Celluloid, Small 80.00
Button, Cox, Pictured, Black & White, Celluloid 200.00
Button, Cox, Rooster, Pewter 15.00
Button, Eisenhower, Brown & White, 1 3/4 In. 4.00
Button, Eisenhower, More Than Ever I Like Ike, Flasher 12.00
Button, F.D.Roosevelt, 1 1/4 In. 6.00
Button, Geraldine Ferraro, America's 1st Woman VP, 3 1/2 In. 1.50
Button, Goldwater, Our Nation Needs Goldwater, Litho 2.00
Button, Hanet & Landwirth, Prohibition, Jugate, 1916 .... 64.00
Button, Hoover, For Lapel 25.00
Button, Hughes, Pennsylvania, Celluloid 10.00
Button, Jackson For President, Follow The Rainbow, 1984, 3 In. 1.25
Button, Jimmy Carter For President, 1976, 3 1/2 In. 3.00
Button, John Glenn For President, 1984, 2 1/4 In. 1.00
Button, Johnson & Humphrey, Jugate, 3 1/2 In. 4.00
Button, Johnson For President, Picture, Red, White & Blue, 6 In. 9.00
Button, Kennedy & Johnson, Jugate, 2 1/2 In. 3.50
Button, Louis Abolafia For President, 1968, 2 1/2 In. 35.00
Button, Lyndon Johnson, President, 1964 .... 2.50
Button, McKinley & Hobart, Jugate, 3/4 In. 25.00
Button, Mondale & Ferraro, Oval, 2 3/4 In. 1.25
Button, Naughty Nixon, Celluloid, 3 1/2 In. 40.00
Button, Nixon & Agnew, 1968 .... 1.00
Button, Nixon, Dump Humph, Celluloid, 1 1/4 In. 8.00
Button, Pat For 1st Lady, Pat Nixon Picture 6.50
Button, Re-Elect Hoover, Speed Up Recovery, Keep Him On The Job 4.00
Button, Reagan & Bush, Bringing America Back, 1984, 6 In. 5.00
Button, Reagan, America Needs Reagan, Color, 1984, 3 1/2 In. 1.50
Button, Richard M. Nixon For President, 1 3/4 In. 1.00
Button, Roosevelt & Fairbanks, Jugate, 1904, 7/8 In. 10.00
Button, Roosevelt & Wallace, Jugate 20.00
Button, Taft, Bloomington, Illinois, Club No.1 .... 1000.00

Button, Taft, Multicolor, Oval	50.00
Button, Taft, Multicolor, U–N–I–T–E–D	300.00
Button, Teddy Roosevelt, Campaign	15.00
Button, Teddy Roosevelt, State Delegate, Ribbon, 1902	22.50
Button, Viva Eisenhower–Me Gusta Ike, 1956, 3 1/2 In.	4.00
Button, Wilson & Marshall, Portrait	12.00
Button, Wilson, Celluloid, 1916	12.50
Button, Wilson, Pictured, Black & White, Celluloid	14.00
Car, Pro–Hoover, An Elephant's Job, Nov.8, 1932, 2 X 4 In.	2.00
Cards, Playing, Kennedy Presidental Years, Entire Family	22.00
Clock, Captain At Helm, Roosevelt, United Electric Clock Co.	175.00
Figurine, Elephant, Stratton For Governor, Morton Pottery	35.00
Handkerchief, Teddy Roosevelt, Silk, 1904 Expo	22.50
Handle, Walking Stick, James G.Blaine, Post No.3, GAR, 1884	150.00
Hat, I Like Ike	12.00
Jackknife, Reagan & Bush, 1980	5.00
Jewelry, Lyndon Baines Johnson, 5 Piece	20.00
License Plate, Hoover	15.00
Lighter, Cigarette, Airplane Trip, Harold Stassen, 1948	20.00
Mirror, New Deal, FDR, Pocket	20.00
Mirror, Woodrow Wilson, Green & Sepia, Pocket	125.00
Money Clip, Lyndon Baines Johnson	5.00
Mug, Roosevelt, The New Deal, Profile, Barrel Shape, 4 1/4 In.	18.00
Paddle, Ping–Pong, Nixon, Chairman Mao, Wooden	12.00
Paperweight, John W.Davis For President, Gold Paint	130.00
Paperweight, McKinley & Roosevelt, Eagle, Scalloped, Glass	30.00
Paperweight, President McKinley, Brass	35.00
Pencil Box, Herbert Hoover, Large	35.00
Pencil, Hoover For President, Head of Hoover, 1928	30.00
Pennant, Kennedy & Johnson, 30 In.	20.00
Pennant, Lyndon B.Johnson, Our 36th President, Felt, 18 In.	1.50
Pennant, Republican 1956 Convention, Eisenhower	5.00
Pin, Flag, Franklin Delano Roosevelt	15.00
Pin, Flag, Teddy Roosevelt	15.00
Plate, Bryan Campaign, Milk Glass	70.00
Plate, Dewey, New York State Fair, 1949, White, 6 1/2 In.	10.00
Plate, Eisenhower's 1st Birthday, White House, 13 Piece	95.00
Plate, President Franklin Roosevelt, Somo Pottery, 9 In.	20.00
Plate, President Harrison, Vice President Morton, 8 In., Pair	110.00
Plate, Republican National Convention, Miami Beach, Fla., 1968	15.00
Plate, Taft Campaign, Flags, Stars, Milk Glass	85.00
Plate, Teddy Roosevelt, Birth & Death Date In Black, 10 In.	42.00
Postcard, Dwight Eisenhower, Presidential, Dated 1953	1.00
Postcard, John F.Kennedy, Portrait, Plain Back	.75
Postcard, Mechanical, McKinley, Taft, Bryan, Pull Jackass Tail	50.00
Postcard, Nixon, At Piano, Back Has FRC Signature, 5 X 7 In.	1.50
Postcard, Roosevelt Bears	15.00
Postcard, Teddy Roosevelt & U.S.Capitol	5.00
Postcard, We Miss Ike, We Even Miss Harry, Donkey & Elephant	.75
Postcard, Wm.Jennings Bryan, Star of The West, Round, Red Star	10.00
Poster, Humphrey Initials & Muskie, 1968, 14 X 22 In.	6.00
Poster, Humphrey, Year of The People, '72, 10 X 15 In.	5.00
Poster, Ike & Nixon, Black & White Print, 1952, 11 X 17 In.	7.00
Poster, Landon & Knox, Red, White & Blue, Photos, 15 X 22 In.	36.00
Poster, Nixon, Re–Election, 34 X 22 In.	3.00
Poster, Roosevelt & Truman, 15 X 11 In.	17.50
Purse, Change, President Harding	45.00
Razor, Straight, Teddy Roosevelt	45.00
Ribbon, Harrison Photograph, Frame, Dated 1888	75.00
Ribbon, Lincoln's Picture, Johnson, Textile, 1864	264.00
Ribbon, Reagan & Bush, White Plastic Elephant, 1984, 2 In.	2.00
Ribbon, Reagan Inaugural, White Plastic Elephant, 1981, 2 In.	1.50
Ribbon, Vote Reagan For President, 1980, 2 1/4 In.	1.50
Ribbon, Wallace, Silk–Like Silver, Picture, 1968, 3 X 7 In.	8.00

Ring, Inaugural Ball, Pres.Richard Nixon, Triangle Inscription 45.00
Sheet Music, Man of The Hour, William Howard Taft 25.00
Sheet Music, March On With Roosevelt, 1936 .... 28.00
Spoon, Teddy Roosevelt, On Hose Handle, Sterling Silver 125.00
Stanhope Viewer, Cleveland's Campaign 150.00
Sticker, Window, Truman, Black & White, Photo, 1948, 4 X 5 1/2 In. 5.00
Stickpin, William McKinley, Black & White Photo, Brass, 3/4 In. 12.00
Teddy Bear, Lyndon B.Johnson, Political Pin, Remco, 1964, 6 In. 20.00
Ticket, Inauguration Ball, Grover Cleveland, Pension Bldg. 12.00
Ticket, Lincoln & Johnson, Union Republican, 1864 .... 75.00
Tie Bar, Spiro Agnew 25.00
Toy, Pres.Grant, Smoking, Windup, Bellows Action, Ives, C.1890 .... 4500.00
Tumbler, Busts of McKinley & Hobart, Integrity, Industry 65.00
Tumbler, Busts of McKinley & Teddy Roosevelt, Prosperity 65.00
Watch Fob, Bryan, Kern On Reverse, Celluloid 75.00
Watch Fob, G.O.P., Elephant 15.00
Watch Fob, McKinley 20.00
Watch Fob, Teddy Roosevelt, 4 Scenic Panels & Portrait 50.00
Watch Fob, William Jennings Bryan, Celluloid & Leather 225.00
Watch, Nixon, I'm Not A Crook 225.00

Pomona glass is a clear glass with a soft amber border decorated with pale blue or rose–colored flowers and leaves. The colors are very, very pale. The background of the glass is covered with a network of fine lines. It was made from 1885 to 1888 by the New England Glass Company. First grind was made from April 1885 to June 1886. It was made by cutting a wax surface on the glass, then dipping it in acid. Second grind was a less expensive method of acid etching that was then developed.

POMONA, Bowl, Cornflower Blue, 2nd Grind, 5 In. 125.00
Bowl, Ruffled Amber Rim, 2nd Grind, Large 145.00
Castor, Pickle, Cornflower Insert, 1st Grind, 11 3/4 In. 4800.00
Creamer, Inverted Thumbprint, Ruffled Top, Amber Handle, 1st Grind 115.00
Creamer, Square Top, 1st Grind, 4 1/2 In. 125.00
Cruet, Blown Glass, Globular Stopper, 19th Century, 6 In. 110.00
Finger Bowl, Blueberries, 2nd Grind 125.00
Finger Bowl, Cornflower, 2nd Grind, 5 1/2 X 2 1/2 In. 95.00
Finger Bowl, Inverted Thumbprint, 2nd Grind, 5 1/8 X 2 1/4 In. 75.00
Pitcher, Blue Cornflower Stain, 1st Grind, 7 In. 250.00
Pitcher, Diamond Quilted, Tapered, 2nd Grind, 12 In. 325.00
Pitcher, Ferns & Flowers, Squatty 135.00
Pitcher, Inverted Thumbprint, Square Top, 1st Grind, 6 1/4 In. 300.00
Pitcher, Pansy & Butterfly, Amber Handle, Border, 2nd Grind 365.00
Punch Cup, Art Glass, Hand Drawn Curlicues, 1st Grind 35.00
Punch Cup, Cornflower, 1st Grind 65.00
Punch Cup, Diamond Quilted, 1st Grind 90.00
Sugar, Inverted Thumbprint, Square Top, 2nd Grind, 4 1/2 In. 100.00
Syrup, Fish & Seaweed 275.00
Toothpick, Enameled Daisies & Ferns, Square Mouth 150.00
Toothpick, Frosted Yellow Tricornered Top 175.00
Toothpick, Rigaree Collar, Maude Feld Label, 1st Grind 265.00
Tumbler, Acorn 135.00
Tumbler, Inverted Thumbprint, 1st Grind, 3 5/8 In. 90.00
Tumbler, Water, Cornflower, 2nd Grind, 3 5/8 In. 145.00
Vase, Cornflower Blue, Scalloped, Amber Top, 2nd Grind, 6 In. 469.00
Water Set, 2 Rows of Cornflowers, 2nd Grind, Amber & Blue, 7 Piece 1500.00
PONTYPOOL, see Tole

Popeye was introduced to the Thimble Theater comic strip in 1929. The character became a favorite of readers. In 1932, an animated cartoon featuring Popeye was made by Paramount Studios. The cartoon series continued and became even more popular when the old movies were used on television starting in the 1950s. The full–length movie with Robin Williams as Popeye was made in 1980.

POPEYE, Bank, Dime Register, Tin Litho, 1929 .... 35.00 To 50.00
Bank, Dime, Tin, King Features 52.00
Bank, Quarter, 1950s 100.00
Bank, Tin, Square 60.00
Belt, Boy's, Embossed Leather, Metal Hardware, King Features, 1929 .... 20.00
Belt, Boy's, Full Color, Characters, Brass Buckle, Card, 12 X 6 In. 50.00
Bike Bobber, Popeye & Olive Oyl, Pair 10.00
Book, Adventures of Popeye, Saalfield, 1934 .... 35.00
Book, Big Little Book, Popeye & The Spinach Eater 17.50
Book, Coloring, 1930s, Large 25.00
Book, King Features, Color, 1937, 9 X 13 In. 30.00
Book, Linen, 1936, Large 38.00
Bubble Set, 2 Wooden Pipes, Metal Soap Tray 25.00
Bubble Set, On Card, 1936 .... 25.00
Christmas Light Set, 1930s 75.00
Cookie Jar, King Features Syndicate 65.00
Dish, Soap, Tin 15.00
Doll, Olive Oyl & Popeye, Rubber, Squeeze, 8 In., Pair 30.00
Doll, Pop–Up, Tin Can of Spinach, Mattel, 1957 .... 30.00
Figurine, Wimpy, Wooden, Scirocco 35.00
Game, Bingo, 1929 .... 40.00
Game, Juggler 40.00
Game, Pin The Pipe On Popeye, Whitman, 1937 .... 25.00
Game, Pipe Toss, King Features Syndicate, Box, 1935 .... 20.00
Game, Skeet Shoot, Box 125.00
Game, Wher's Me Pipy, Uncut In Box, 1930s 50.00
Kazoo, 1930s 20.00
Lamp 180.00
Lantern, 1950s, Linemar 125.00
Lunch Box, Thermos, 1964 .... 11.00
Paint Set, American Crayon Co., Unused, 1949 .... 19.00
Pencil Box, Contents, Ruler 20.00
Pencil Box, Eagle, Large 45.00
Pencil Sharpener, Desk, 1929 .... 100.00
Pencil, Mechanical, 1930s 50.00
Pin, Brass 16.00
Pin, Enamel, 1930s 30.00
Ponytail Holder, Olive Oyl's, On Card, 1958 .... 10.00
Punching Bag 375.00
Puppet, Hand, Olive Oyl 25.00
Roller Skates, Linemar 295.00
Salt & Pepper, Popeye & Olive, Tall 25.00
Soap, Figural, 4 In. 10.00
Soap, Figural, Box 45.00
Soap, Popeye's Head Shape 7.00
Thermos, Litho Metal, Red Plastic Cap, 1964, 7 In. 12.00
Toothbrush Holder, 1920s 175.00
Toy, Boatmobile, Olive, Sweetpea, Mechanical, Plastic, Japan, 8 1/2 In. 135.00
Toy, Dippy Dumper, Mechanical, Tin, Celluloid Popeye, Marx, 9 In. 475.00
Toy, Honeymoon Express, Mechanical, Tin Litho, Marx, Box, 9 1/2 In. 650.00
Toy, Mechanical, Vibrates, Arms Jiggle, Japan, Box, 1930s, 8 1/2 In. 750.00
Toy, Moving Van, Mechanical, Tin Litho, Linemar, 12 1/2 In. 325.00
Toy, Overhead Puncher, Arms Move To Hit Cell, Tin, Chein, 9 In. 2250.00
Toy, Paint–O–Graph, Box, Unused 45.00
Toy, Parrot In Carrying Cage, Windup, Tin, Marx 170.00
Toy, Popeye Express, Parrot & Wheelbarrow 300.00
Toy, Popeye Hitting A Punching Bag, J.Chein & Co. 850.00
Toy, Popeye In Barrel, Chein 275.00
Toy, Popeye In Barrel, Mechanical, Celluloid, Tin, Japan, 5 In. 450.00
Toy, Popeye In Roadster, Friction, Linemar 650.00
Toy, Popeye Shooting Basketball 950.00
Toy, Popeye, Carrying 2 Birdcages, Windup, Marx, 1938 .... 250.00
Toy, Walking Wimpy, Papier–Mache 69.00
Toy, Xylophone Player, Pull Toy, Noma 60.00

Tray, Black On White, 9 X 12 In. 25.00

Major porcelain factories are listed in this book under the factory name. This section lists pieces that are by the less well-known factories.

PORCELAIN, Ashtray, Figural, Dog, Calif. 250.00
Basin, Wreath Center, 18th Century, Niderviller, 16 3/4 In. 1045.00
Basket, Floral, Spiderweb, Frog, Blue Star & Moon Mark, 3 1/2 In. 49.00
Bell, Woman Shape, Art Deco, Japan 75.00
Biscuit Barrel, Stabler & Adams, England, 1930s 155.00
Bowl, Domed Cover, Butterfly Borders, Mandarin, C.1800, 5 1/4 In. 250.00
Bowl, Girl, Burgundy, Green Clover, Crown Royal Saxe, 11 In. 85.00
Bowl, Nut, Double Shell, Mother-of-Pearl, French 45.00
Bowl, Salad, Thousand Butterfly, Bands Inside & Out, 10 1/4 In. 750.00
Box, Bird Shape, Polychrome Enameling, 7 3/4 In. 145.00
Box, Cranes, Plants Painted Top, Brass Trim, Chantilly, 3 X 5 In. 55.00
Box, Dresser, Figural, Girl, Holding Umbrella, Erphila, No.6 .... 58.00
Box, Dresser, Figural, Lady, At Dressing Table, Japan, 8 In. 95.00
Box, Trinket, Child Astride Top, German 95.00
Bust, Shakespeare, Nescht, 18th Century, 6 1/4 In. 325.00
Cabaret Set, Floral, Hand Painted, Gold, Paris Type, 8 Piece 150.00
Candleholder, Applied Roses & Leaves, Sitzendorf, Pair 285.00
Candlesnuffer, Lavender Pink, Medallions, Gold Handle & Knob 38.00
Chair, Enameled, Paintings, Metal Frame, Viennese, 3 In., Pair 350.00
Chamber Pot, Domed Cover, Blue Chrysanthemum, China, 6 1/2 In. 300.00
Console Set, Flowers, Crown Over D, Germany, 3 Piece 120.00
Creamer, Cow, Hoan, France 149.00
Cup & Saucer, Raised Polychrome Insects, Gilt Ferns, Turquoise 50.00
Dish, Leaf, Double Twisted Handle, Longton Hall, C.1755, 5 In. 1900.00
Dish, Scene Medallions Around Edge, Edme Samson & Cie, C.1870 .... 475.00
Ewer, Floral, Opaque White, Brown, 17 In., Pair 135.00
Figurine, Boy, Berries, Jacket, Knickers, Sitzendorf, 4 1/4 In. 80.00
Figurine, Boy, Coat, Holding Flower Garland, Sitzendorf, 6 In. 100.00
Figurine, Clown, Pucci, 12 In., Pair 135.00
Figurine, Flower Girl, Magenta Top, Apron, Sitzendorf, 4 In. 70.00
Figurine, Girl Curtsying, Orange Dress, Sitzendorf, 4 1/4 In. 70.00
Figurine, Girl, Rocking Chair, Applied Flowers, Cats, 7 3/4 In. 210.00
Figurine, Grandmama, Paisley Shawl, Paragon, 8 In. 165.00
Figurine, Lady Sybil, Blue Dress, Paragon, 7 5/8 In. 175.00
Figurine, Maiden, Basket of Fruit, 8 1/2 In. .... *Illus* 250.00
Figurine, Maiden, Man, With Dog, 12 In., Pair .... *Illus* 450.00
Figurine, Man & Woman, Seated, French Style, Sitzendorf, Pair 38.00

Porcelain, Figurine, Maiden, Man, With Dog,
12 In., Pair

Porcelain, Figurine, Maiden,
Basket of Fruit,
8 1/2 In.

Figurine, Man & Woman, Seated, U.S.Zone, Germany, 6 X 6 1/2 In. 23.00
Figurine, Man, Smiling, Holding Vase, Polychrome Enamel, 18 In. 105.00
Figurine, Quail, On Flowered Hill, Dynasty Mark, 12 1/2 In., Pair 250.00
Figurine, Rat Catcher, Man, Holding Pole, Box of Poison, 8 In. 125.00
Figurine, Stag, Head Twisted To Left, Wood, C.1770, 6 3/4 In. 4200.00
Figurine, Street Vendor, Man, Holding Bellows, Umbrella, 7 In. 50.00
Figurine, Street Vendor, Woman, Rustic Dress, Basket, 7 In. 75.00
Font, Holy Water, Cross & 2 Disciples, Germany 10.00
Garden Seat, Blue, White, Hexagonal, Pierced, China, 15 X 9 In. 650.00
Garden Seat, Elephant, China, 21 X 22 X 9 In. 175.00
Hat Stand, Black & White Foo Dog Design, C.1870, 11 1/4 In. 195.00
Jam Jar, Covered, Carter, Stabler & Adams, England, 1930s 90.00
Jar, Covered, Stag Amid Flowers, 19th Century, 13 In. 350.00
Jar, Polychrome Enameled Birds On Flowers, Oriental, 12 In. 65.00
Jar, Soccer Ball Shape, Player's Cap Lid, England 135.00
Jardiniere, Blue & White Floral, Oriental, 15 1/2 X 12 In. 325.00
Jug, Corn, England, Miniature, C.1870 .... 140.00
Jug, Milk, Hunting, Figural Dog Handle, English, 7 In. 60.00
Lamp, Table, Exotic Fowl, Tree, Teak Stand, Chinese, 19 In., Pair 300.00
Lemon Set, Reamer & Grater, Blue Forget–Me–Nots, Artist Signed 110.00
Mug, Blown–Out Stag, Autumn Colors 35.00
Mug, Clown & Circus Elephant Transfer, 3 1/8 In. 22.60
Opium Pillow, Blue & White Foo Dog Design, C.1870, 5 1/4 In. 245.00
Penholder, Oriental Women In Garden, Trees, 5 X 11 In. 125.00
Pillow, Polychrome Garden Figures, Chinese, 4 3/4 In. 50.00
Pipe, Monkey, Tricorn, Seated, Tail Forms Stem, C.1800, 5 1/8 In. 1975.00
Planter, Girl's Head, Hand Painted, Dated 1959, 6 X 6 In. 12.00
Plaque, Ladies In Courtyard, Wooden Frame, 7 X 10 In., Pair 200.00
Plaque, Victorian Figures, Metal Filigree Frame, 5 X 7 In. 38.00
Plate, 4 Floral Panels, Diapered Ground, Incised N, 9 In. 70.00
Plate, Battle Scene, Polychrome Enamel, Montereau, 7 Piece 935.00
Plate, Kremlin Service, Russian, 1825–55, 8 3/4 In., Pair 1870.00
Plate, Lake of Killarney & Wilderme, R.Abbott, 9 In., Pair 210.00
Plate, Peacock & Peonies, C.1900, Japan, 10 In. 20.00
Platter, White, Turquoise Trim, Art Nouveau, Round, 15 In. 80.00
Pot, Pink & Purple Luster Design, English, 11 3/4 In. 35.00
Pot–De–Creme, Memory, Bird & Leaf Design, 1735–79, Set of 4 .... 100.00
Powder Box, Figural, Court Lady, On Bench, Fan, Germany, 5 X 4 In. 55.00
Powder Box, Figural, Madame Pompadour, Fan, U.S.Zone, Germany 55.00
Powder Box, Figural, Pierrette, Costume, Goldcastle, 6 In. 52.00
Salt, 3 Buttress Legs, Impressed Shamrocks, Ireland, 2 3/4 In. 4.00

Porcelain, Vase, Floral, Figures, Covered,
Wurttemberg, 24 1/2 In.

Royal Doulton, Figurine, Cobbler, HN 1706

Sconce, 2–Light, Maidens Playing Backgammon, German, 15 1/4 In.	495.00
Stein, Pewter Lid, Saint George Slaying Dragon, 6 In.	65.00
Sweetmeat, Flowers & Leaves, Silver Plated Handle & Lid, 4 In.	118.00
Teapot, Farmer & Oxen Scenes, Gray & Brown, Oriental, 5 In.	125.00
Teapot, Side Handle, Multicolored Flower Design, 1774, 4 X 9 In.	175.00
Urn, Cobalt Blue, Gold Trim, Pastoral Scene	125.00
Urn, Two Human Masks, Ormolu Mounted, C.1841, 18 1/4 In.	300.00
Vase, Blue & White, Carved Wooden Stand, Chinese, 13 3/4 In.	365.00
Vase, Bud, Boxer Dogs, Next To Tree Trunk, 5 1/2 In., Pair	60.00
Vase, Chinese Figures, Mask Handles, C.1880, 22 In., Pair	9900.00
Vase, Floral, Figures, Covered, Wurttemberg, 24 1/2 In. ....*Illus*	1300.00
Vase, Pale Celadon, Blue Floral, Oriental, 23 1/4 In.	65.00
Vase, Panels of Birds & Flowers, Japanese, 17 In., Pair	450.00
Vase, Rozenburg Haag, 6 In.	325.00
Wig Stand, Orange Peel Glaze, Blue & White, 11 In., Pair	550.00

Postcards were first legally permitted in Austria on October 1, 1869. The United States passed postal regulations allowing the card in 1872. Most of the picture postcards collected today date after 1910. The amount of postage can help to date a card. The years the rates changed and the rates are: 1872 (1 cent), 1917 (2 cents), 1919 (1 cent), 1925 (2 cents), 1928 (1 cent), 1952 (2 cents), 1959 (3 cents), 1963 (4 cents), 1968 (5 cents), 1973 (8 cents), 1975 (7 cents), 1976 (9 cents), 1978 (10 cents), 1981 (12 cents), 1981 (13 cents), 1985 (14 cents).

POSTCARD, Alaska–Yukon–Pacific Exposition, Seattle, Wash., 1909	5.00
American Boat Express, Tuck	5.00
American Flag, Clapsaddle	4.00
Apollo 8, Earth, Moon Surface Photo, Unused, 5 1/2 X 7 In.	5.00
Atlantic City, Easter Parade	4.00
Atlantic City, Views, 1909	5.00
Auto, Cobb–Shinn Ford, Set of 6	27.00
Auto, Driven By Cupid, Lovers In Back Seat, Sepia	2.00
Auto, Nash Ambassador, 1941, Set of 3	15.00
Auto, Touring Car, Man & Woman In Back Seat, Black & White	5.00
Bakery Shop Photo, 1912	6.00
Berlin, 10 Card View Folder, Unused, 1936	12.00
Best Wishes, Printed In Color	3.00
Birthday Wishes, 2 Girls, Basket, Flowers Between, 1900 Clothes	3.00
Birthday, Boy Playing Violin, Girl Popping Out, Pumpkin	2.00
Birthday, Children In Hot Air Balloon, Amid Flowers	3.00
Birthday, Floral Stalk, Child's Head At Top, Embossed	5.00
Birthday, Girl In Pinafore, Sailor Hat, Boy In Knickers	3.00
Birthday, Lily of The Valley, Embossed	4.00
Black Child In Tub of Water, Grinning, Color	3.00
Brooklyn Bridge, Hold To Light	25.00
C.D.Durkee & Co., Marine Goods, Couple In Boat	3.00
California Desert Scene, 2 Cent Stamp, 1917	3.00
Centennial Exposition Ground, Texas, 1836	3.00
Century of Progress, Chicago, Museum of Natural History, 1933	3.25
Child Standing On Wicker Settee, Long Curls, Black & White	3.00
Christmas Wishes, Child Toting Tree, Embossed	3.00
Christmas, 2 Kewpies Next To Tree, Signed R.O'Neill, 1918	20.00
Christmas, 3 Young Children Delivering Presents, Color	3.00
Christmas, Boy, With Presents, Brundage	2.00
Christmas, John Rapp, San Francisco Rainier, Agent, 1913	20.00
Christmas, Santa Claus Smoking Pipe, Smoke Forms Greetings	6.00
Christmas, Santa, C.1910	5.00
Christmas, Santa, In Car, With Angel, German	10.00
Columbian Exposition, Agricultural Building, 1893, Set of 4	12.00
Comic, Dentist Pulling Teeth, C.1907	5.00
Comic, Flowers, Views, Leather, 25 Piece	50.00
Coney Island, 1920, Set of 13	32.00
Devil Theme, From One To Another, Shows Red Devil, C.1908	7.50

Easter Greetings, Black Chick In Straw Hat, Next To Pumpkin	5.00
Easter Greetings, Boy & Girl Carrying Flowers, Embossed	3.00
Easter Greetings, Woman In 1890s Long Dress, Plumed Hat	5.00
Easter, Chick Coming Out of Shell, 4 Chicks Around	4.00
Easter, Chicks & Flowers Emerging From Egg	2.00
Easter, Girl With Dog On Leash, Drayton	20.00
Easter, Hold To Light, Girl, Scolding Rabbit, With Chicks	35.00
Expo Universelle, Paris, Pioneer	15.00
Gen.Jas.F.Rusling, Trenton, N.J., 1892, 1 Cent, Allentown	2.00
Gift of Love, Blue Boy Type Outfit, Girl, Long Frock, Embossed	2.00
Girl, Yellow Bird, Purple Flowers, Maud Humphrey, 1909	25.00
Golliwog, Tuck	15.00
Halloween, Jack-O'-Lantern, Woods	15.00
Halloween, Listen Little One, Man Blowing Out Candle	6.00
Halloween, Scarecrow At Door	6.00
Hands Across The Sea, Silk	25.00
Happy New Year, 3 Children Leaning Over Fence, Calendar Date	5.00
Happy New Year, Kewpie Ringing Bell, Rose O'Neill	20.00
Happy New Year, Year 1909 Filled In With Flowers, Embossed	2.00
Hitler Shaking Hands With Nazi Youth Group, World War II	25.00
Hummel, Framed, 1950s	20.00
I Can't Understand Why He Buys From Me, Scantily Dressed Girl	2.00
In God We Trust To Save America, 1941	3.50
Katzenjammer Kids, Uncut	80.00
Lipton Tea, Various Flowers	8.00
Little Red Riding Hood, Ullman, 6 Piece	35.00
Man In Sleigh, Pulled By 2 Horses, Black & White	4.00
Mechanical, French, Pull Tab & Faces Change	35.00
Memorial, Enrico Caruso	10.00
Merry Christmas & Happy New Year, Santa Claus & Mistletoe	2.00
Mexican Border War, Black & White, Woods	25.00
Mining Scene, Copperhill, Lamar Dodd, Georgia, 1939	12.50
Moxie, Man, Weather Prophet Strip, Predicts The Weather	15.00
New York Skyscraper, Original Wrapper, Set of 4	15.00
New York World's Fair, 1939, Set of 10	15.00
North Pole, Cook & Perry	10.00
Nude, Young Girls Show All, 8 Piece	50.00
Official Souvenir Mailing Card, Graphic Arts Building, 1901	10.00
Ottmar Zieher, Embossed, Unused, 9 Piece	60.00
Our Old Nursery Rhymes, Oranges & Lemons, LeMar	12.00
Photograph, Beachey Airship, Contest Winner, St.Louis, 1907	15.00
President, Rutherford B.Hayes, Tuck	10.00
Prospect Park Entrance, Brooklyn, N.Y., Hold To Light, 1907	10.00
Purchase Monument, St.Louis World's Fair, Woven Silk, 1904	150.00
Puzzle, Race Car, 1908	15.00
Railroad, Handcar & Workers, Photograph	7.00
Rock Island Railroad, Advertising, Signed O'Neill	75.00
Roosevelt Bears At Country School, Brown Bear, C.1905	10.00
Russo-Japanese War, 1905	20.00
Sergeant Clapsaddle, Mechanical	50.00
Smith Bros.Cough Drops, Shows Both Brothers, 1910	8.00
Snuffy Smith, World War II, King Features, Unused, Set of 3	14.00
Speculatro Mine, Butte, Mont., Published In Detroit	4.50
St.Louis World's Fair, Cascade Gardens, Woven Silk, 1904	150.00
St.Louis World's Fair, Government Building, See-Through, 1904	20.00
St.Louis World's Fair, Palace of Transportation, 1904	10.00
St.Patrick's Day, People, Scenery	16.00
Teddy Bear, Twelvetrees, Large	15.00
Teddy Roosevelt, Jamestown Exposition, 1907	15.00
Thanksgiving, 4 Young Children, Strutting Turkeys	2.00
Thanksgiving, Boy & Girl Carrying Pumpkin	2.00
Thanksgiving, Child In Headdress Chasing Turkey	3.00
Thanksgiving, Couple Seated At Spinning Wheel, Embossed	3.00
Thanksgiving, Turkey Talking To Pumpkin, Once More	4.00

Valentine, Arrows Through Heart, Cupid Nearby 3.00
Valentine, Boy Teasing Crying Girl, Printed In Color 4.00
Valentine, Children Dressed As Clowns, Hearts Allover 4.00
Valentine, Dutch Children Kissing, Brundage 8.00
Valentine, Love's Fine Message, Heart With Girl In Bonnet 4.00
Valentine, My Heart's Message, Girl's Head Out of Envelope 5.00
Valentine, Pretty Woman Amid Flowers, Embossed 2.00
Valentine, Western Union, Embossed 20.00
Valentine, With Fond Love, Winged Children, Ribbon 3.00
Woman, In Carriage Pulled By Horse, Black & White 3.00
Woman, White Hair & Flowers, Varga 16.00
Yale, 2 College Girls, Signed Earl Christie 12.00
Your Fortune Teller, 4 Circles, Instructions For Assembly, 1910 .... 8.00

> Posters have informed the public about news and entertainment
> events since ancient times. Nineteenth–century advertising or
> theatrical posters and twentieth–century movie and war posters are
> of special interest today. The price is determined by the artist, the
> condition, and the rarity. Other posters are listed under Advertising,
> World War I, and World War II.

POSTER, All Fuel Is Scarce, Plan For Winter Now, 1954, 20 X 28 In. 40.00
American Legion Poppy Days Sale, Red, White, Blue, 1942, 11 X 21 In. 11.00
Arm & Hammer, Birds, Insects, Migration Routes, 1938, 20 X 42 In. 35.00
Arm & Hammer, Colored Birds, 17 X 25 In. 25.00
Babbits Soap, Little Lord Fauntleroy, 1890s, 14 X 30 In. 120.00
Baseball, Major League Centennial, 1969, 15 X 40 In. 25.00
Buchner & Co., One of The Finest Smoking & Chewing Tobaccos 2200.00
Careless Words May Cause Disaster, 1944, 17 X 24 In. 40.00
Champion Harvesting Machines, Framed, 16 X 19 In. 65.00
Chief Horace Rose, Cardboard, 22 X 14 In. 22.00
Circus, Barnum & Bailey, Clown, Black Horse, 1900, 28 X 40 In. 600.00
Circus, Clyde Beatty, Cole Bros., Artist Signed, 28 X 21 In. 95.00
Circus, Inman Bros.Flying Circus, Inman Autograph, 25 X 39 In. 425.00
Circus, Parker Amusement Co., World's Fair On Wheels, 1900 .... 75.00
Circus, Ringling Ros., Barnum & Bailey, Lion & Tiger, 28 X 46 In. 20.00
Ferry's Seeds, Girl Vegetable Vender, 1922, 21 X 28 In. 25.00
Girl, Reading St.Nicholas Magazine, Borders, C.1896 .... 65.00
God's Angels Are Everywhere, Black Angel, 2 Black Kids, 20 X 27 In. 125.00
Good Natured Map of Alaska, 30 X 22 In. 30.00
Harper's Magazine, Framed, Christmas, 1898, 11 1/2 X 16 1/2 In. 350.00
I Want You, 1917, Blond In Sailor Suit, Join Navy, 27 X 41 In. 500.00
Jr.Red Cross, Boy Holding Flags, 1949 .... 10.00
Kraft Products, Gorilla, 19 X 24 In. 25.00
Longchamps Race Track, French, Signed MB, 19 1/4 X 41 1/4 In. 150.00
Movie, Big Town Girl, Claire Trevor, In Mask, 1937, 27 X 40 In. 100.00
Movie, East Side of Heaven, Crosby, Blondell, 1939, 27 X 41 In. 100.00
Movie, Yank At Eton, Mickey Rooney, 27 X 41 In. 100.00
Nouveau Theater Scaramouche, Litho, Linen Backed, 48 X 34 In. 100.00
Osborne Harvester, Auburn 410.00
Problem Cigarettes, Litho, Hans Rudi Erdt, 1912, 27 1/2 X 38 In. 660.00
Schlitz Beer, Horse Festival Parade, 40 Horses, 49 X 22 In. 20.00
Sego Milk, 1930s, 14 X 21 In. 17.50
Sheffield Farms Dairy, Pure Milk, Healthy Cows, 24 X 18 In. 15.00
Sky King, TV Show, Kirby Grant Picture 35.00
Smokey The Bear, 1947, 18 X 26 In. 20.00
The Winner, Billy Sullivan, 1920, 27 X 40 In. 175.00
Third Army Carnival, Coblenz, Germany, 1919 .... 95.00
U.S.Cadet Nurse Corps, 1943, 20 X 28 In. 35.00
United Nations Fight For Freedom, 1942, 28 X 40 In. 25.00
Woodstock Rock Concert 252.00

A potlid is just that, a lid for a pot. Transfer–printed potlids had their heyday from the 1840s to the early 1900s. The English Staffordshire potteries made ceramic containers with decorative lids for bear's grease, shrimp or meat paste, cold cream, and toothpaste. Printed advertising and pictures of historical events, portraits of famous people, or scenic views were designed in black and white or color. Reproductions have been made. The most famous potlids were made by Pratt and are listed in that section.

POTLID, American Dentifrice, Manchester, Dr.Coffin, 3 1/2 In.	75.00
Boot's Toothpaste, Nottingham Chemists, 2 3/4 In.	60.00
Cherry Toothpaste, 2 1/2 In.	50.00
Cracroft's Areca Nut, By John Pepper, 2 3/4 In.	60.00
Sponaceous Tooth Powder, 3 1/2 In.	60.00
Wood's Areca Nut Toothpaste, Plymouth, 3 1/4 In.	60.00

Pottery and porcelain are different. Pottery is opaque; you can't see through it. Porcelain is translucent. If you hold a porcelain dish in front of a strong light you will see the light through the dish. Porcelain is colder to the touch. Pottery is softer and easier to break and will stain more easily because it is porous. Porcelain is thinner, lighter, and more durable. Majolica, faience, and stoneware are all pottery. Many types of pottery are listed in this book under the factory name.

POTTERY, Ashtray, Cowboy Hat, Blue, Catalina	15.00
Ashtray, Hydrant, Gray & Green, Kuekel China Co., 5 X 9 In.	15.00
Ashtray, Rolled Designed Lip, Wood Tone, Heidi Schoop	32.00
Ashtray, With Igloo, Sascha Brastoff	15.00
Bank, Panda, Kay Finch	35.00
Basket, Green, Caliente	18.50
Bean Pot, Apple Pattern, Cover, Watt	59.00
Bean Pot, Bleeding Heart Pattern, Cover, Watt	43.00
Biscuit Jar, Floral, Deep Pink, Silver Plated Lid, English, 8 In.	118.00
Biscuit Jar, Floral, Green Glazed Ground, Imperial Bonn, 6 1/2 In.	88.00
Bookends, Rearing Horse, Pyburn	25.00
Bowl, Blue & Purple Band, Compliments of Farmers' Co–Op, 7 In.	19.00
Bowl, Closed Form, Red Warty Finish, Van Erp	880.00
Bowl, Raggedy Ann & Raggedy Andy, Crooksville, 8 7/8 In.	10.00
Bowl, Turquoise Inside, Ivory, Catalina, 15 In.	35.00
Bowl, Underplate, Kansas State College, Artist Signed, 4 1/4 In.	34.00
Bowl, Wedding Ring, Blue & White, 10 In.	110.00
Box, Salt, Blue & White, Wooden Lid, Floral & Leaf Design	95.00
Candleholder, Jug Shape, Blue, North State, 9 In.	38.00
Candleholder, Matte Pink & Blue, Winfield–Pasadena, Square, 5 In.	8.00
Candlestick, Glossy Orange, Catalina Island, 5 In.	44.00
Candlestick, Handle, Matte Blue, Prang, 3 1/2 In.	65.00
Carafe, Rancho, Yellow, Catalina	35.00
Casserole, Apple Pattern, Cover, Watt	45.00
Charger, Brown Glaze, Yellow Design, White Coggled Edge, 14 In.	1400.00
Coffee Set, Poppy Trail, Metlox, 7 Piece	35.00
Crock, Brown Brothers, Huntington, Double Tulip, 2 Gal.	412.50
Cup & Saucer, Shearwater	19.00
Decanter, Figural, Chimpanzee In Suit, Hat Stopper, Germany	100.00
Dish, Tidbit, 2–Tier, Bamboo Pattern, Weil Ware	12.00
Figurine, Bear, Sitting, Green Glaze, Louis Abel, 7 1/2 In.	195.00
Figurine, Bear, Tan Glaze, 1 3/4 In.	40.00
Figurine, Dove, Worn White Paint, Yellow & Black Detail, 8 1/2 In.	65.00
Figurine, Duck, Green Glaze, Incised Kellogg, 3 1/4 In.	100.00
Figurine, Flamingo, Pink, 2 1/2 & 1 3/4 In., 3 Piece	25.00
Figurine, Foo Dog, Stand, Seated, Movable Eyes, China, 29 In.	1600.00
Figurine, German Shepherd, Reclining, Oval Rug, 6 X 10 1/2 In.	27.50
Figurine, Lion, Magodore Ohio Pottery, 15 In.	750.00
Figurine, Oriental Children, Florence Ceramics, Sticker, 7 In., Pr.	65.00
Figurine, Rooster, Edwin Meaders, Mossy Creek, Ga.	85.00

Figurine, Singing Frog, 6 In.	50.00
Figurine, Southern Belle, Florence Ceramics, 7 In.	40.00
Flowerpot, Attached Saucer, Buff, Green Glaze, John Bell, 5 In.	775.00
Flowerpot, Brown Glaze, Name Nannie Carry, New Geneva, 8 In.	500.00
Flowerpot, Gray Glaze, Flared, Vertical Stripes, Shenandoah, 5 In.	75.00
Flowerpot, Saucer, Buff Clay, Dark Brown–Green Glaze, 9 In.	155.00
Humidor, Figural, Burlap Money Bag, $100, 000 Front	78.00
Jar, Brown Glazed Flowers, Red Clay, New Geneva, 10 1/8 In.	775.00
Jar, Green Ash Glaze, Applied Vintage, Lanier Meaders, 11 1/4 In.	160.00
Jardiniere, Flowers, Gilt Bronze Mount, Handles, 20 In.	990.00
Jardiniere, Iridescent Blue, Hexagonal, Squatty, Putti, 12 1/2 In.	600.00
Jug, Bloomfield Art Pottery, 4 In.	70.00
Jug, Embossed Seaweed, Deep Rose Ground, Beech & Hancock, 9 In.	95.00
Jug, Grotesque, Contempory Southern, Green Ash Glaze, 6 1/2 In.	35.00
Jug, Grotesque, Lanier Meaders, Green Ash Glaze, 9 In.	170.00
Mixing Bowl, Apple Pattern, Farmers Co–Op, Iowa, Watt, 7 In.	19.00
Mixing Bowl, Apple Pattern, Watt, 5 In.	14.00
Mixing Bowl, Apple, Miller's Food Market, Hebr., Watt, 6 In.	25.00
Mixing Bowl, Blue & Purple Band, Watt, No.6, 6 In.	14.00
Mug, Barrel Shape, Green Drip, Dryden	6.00
Mug, Underglaze Indian Design, Rick Wisecarver	45.00
Mug, With Frog, White Clay, Dark Green–Brown Glaze, Ohio, 2 5/8 In.	100.00
Pie Plate, Apple Pattern, Wilkin's Hardware, Watt, 9 1/2 In.	42.00
Pitcher & Bowl Set, Blue Flowers, Wheeling Pottery, 5 Piece	145.00
Pitcher, Apple Pattern, Pay's Produce & Feed, Watt, 5 1/2 In.	28.00
Pitcher, Apple Pattern, Thank You From Singular's, Watt, 5 1/2 In.	36.00
Pitcher, Bleeding Heart Pattern, Watt, 5 1/2 In.	23.00
Pitcher, Brown Foliage Design, Red Clay, Handle, 8 5/8 In.	550.00
Pitcher, Brown Foliage, Red Clay, Handle, New Geneva, 4 3/4 In.	650.00
Pitcher, Churchill, Medalta, 1940	78.00
Pitcher, Cobalt Blue Foliage, Scrolled Design, Somerset, 2 Gal.	12.00
Pitcher, Cylinder, Pink Drip On White Ground, A.R.Cole, 7 In.	25.00
Pitcher, Embossed Art Nouveau Floral, Teal Blue, German, 9 1/2 In.	55.00
Pitcher, Embossed Flying Birds, Blue & White	185.00
Pitcher, Gray & Green, Rushmore Pottery, 4 3/4 In.	30.00
Pitcher, Hunting Scene, Hound Handles, Cobalt Blue, 12 In.	75.00
Pitcher, Pinched Spout, Green Glaze, T.J.Henry, 6 3/8 In.	150.00
Pitcher, Poinsettia Pattern, Watt, No.15, 5 1/2 In.	24.00
Pitcher, Serpent Handle, Pauline	450.00
Pitcher, Sgraffito Type Design, Arabs On Horses, Haynesware	190.00
Pitcher, Starflower Pattern, Watt, 5 1/2 In.	23.00
Pitcher, Vintage & Stags, Brown Glaze, Geo.W.Doane, 7 7/8 In.	200.00
Pitcher, White, Albany Slip Glaze, Inscription, 1895, 9 In.	575.00
Planter, Black Panther, 1950s, 15 3/4 In.	20.00
Planter, Woman's Head, Florence Ceramics, 7 In.	52.00
Pot, Covered, Lobster Finial, Black, Kenwood	12.00
Salt & Pepper, Acorn	4.50
Salt & Pepper, Apple, Farmers Lumber, Hourglass Shape, 5 In.	75.00
Salt & Pepper, Bears, Huggies, Van Tellingen	10.00
Salt & Pepper, Boy & Dog, Van Tellingen	38.00
Salt & Pepper, Bunnies, Huggies, White, Van Tellingen	10.00
Salt & Pepper, Bunnies, Yellow & Pink, Van Tellingen, 3 In.	9.00
Salt & Pepper, Corn With Husk, White	30.00
Salt & Pepper, Duck, Van Tellingen	14.00
Salt & Pepper, Ducks, Huggies, Van Tellingen, Yellow & Black	22.00
Salt & Pepper, Dutch Boy & Girl, Ceramic Arts, 3 In.	10.00
Salt & Pepper, Dutch Couple, Huggies, Van Tellingen	22.00
Salt & Pepper, Jug Shape, Inscribed Black Hills, S.D., Dryden	18.00
Salt & Pepper, Kangaroo, Mom & Baby	15.00
Salt & Pepper, Knickerbocker, Box	10.00
Salt & Pepper, Love Bugs, Van Tellingen	45.00
Salt & Pepper, Maggie & Jiggs	15.00
Salt & Pepper, Mary & Lamb, Van Tellingen	10.00
Salt & Pepper, Millie & Willie Penguin, Plastic, F & F Works	5.00

Salt & Pepper, Pheasants, Rosemead Paper Label	12.00
Salt & Pepper, Rabbit, Van Tellingen	14.00
Salt & Pepper, Snuggle Bunnies, Van Tellingen	8.00
Shaker, Love Bug, Maroon, Van Tellingen, Large	35.00
Shaker, Pig, Van Tellingen, 7 In.	45.00
Shoe, Daisy & Button Design, Brown Glaze, 5 1/2 In.	55.00
Sugar Bowl, Apple Pattern, Farmers Lumber Co., Iowa, Watt, 4 In.	52.00
Tape Dispenser, Clown, On Hands & Knees	37.50
Vase, Ball, Yellow Speckled, Glidden, 5 In.	18.00
Vase, Black, Gold Streaks, Dryden Ozark Pottery, 8 1/2 In.	22.50
Vase, Blue, York, 5 3/4 In.	15.00
Vase, Bud, Figural, Frances, Brayton, 8 1/4 In.	24.00
Vase, Gold & Cream, Hand Thrown, Rushmore Pottery, 4 1/4 In.	40.00
Vase, Gracetone, Cinnamon, 10 In.	20.00
Vase, Grape Design, Marked W.G., 12 In.	85.00
Vase, Gray Specks, Wheel Thrown, Moutainside Pottery, 1920s, 7 In.	37.00
Vase, Hand Thrown, Gray & Blue, Shearwater, 4 In.	30.00
Vase, Round, Handle, Sunset Mountain, 6 1/2 In.	38.00
Vase, Rushmore Pottery, Black Hills, S.D., 1930s, 5 In.	18.00
Vase, Turquoise Ringed, Rushmore Pottery, 3 1/2 In.	60.00
Vase, Twisted Handle, Dark Green Matte, Hywood, 6 In.	10.00
Vase, What Cheer, Indian Head, Iowa	47.50
Wall Pocket, Oriental Girl, Weil	10.00
Wall Pocket, Pink & Blue, West Coast Pottery	11.00
Whistle, Figural, Bird	55.00

Powder flasks and powder horns were made to hold the gunpowder used in antique firearms. The early examples were made of horn or wood, later ones were of copper or brass.

POWDER HORN, Curly Maple Top, Brass Tong Fitting, Brass Fanned At Center	55.00
Eagle & Banner, Tim Tensel, E.Pluribus Unum, 8 1/2 In.	300.00
Engraved, James, Feb 1774, Amasa Newton, Geometrics, 9 1/4 In.	170.00
Engraved, Tree, Animal, Indian, A.Nutt, Oct.22, 1806, 10 In.	1300.00
Hunter, Dog, Deer, J.Emmons, Born 1804, Scrimshaw, 16 1/2 In.	450.00
Leather & Hemp Carrier, From Masterton's Home, 19th Century	175.00
Original Hewn Plugs, 10 In.	45.00
Ships, Flowers, Building, Barnabas Webb, April 1776, 13 In.	950.00
Soldier With Rifle, Dog, S.H.Ginkinger 1865, Scrimshaw, 13 In.	550.00

PRATT
FENTON

Pratt ware means two different things. It was an early Staffordshire pottery, cream-colored with colored decorations, made by Felix Pratt during the late eighteenth century. There was also Pratt ware made with transfer designs during the mid-nineteenth century in Fenton, England. Reproductions of the transfer-printed Pratt are being made.

PRATT, Compote, Highland Music, Acorn Border, Handles, Oval	275.00
Inkwell, Greyhound, 1850	155.00
Jar, Boar Hunt, Blue Ground, 4 1/4 In.	30.00 To 38.00
Jug, Angry Pinocchio Face, 1830, 4 In.	130.00
Mug, 2 Scenes, Aqua Ground, 3 1/4 In.	98.00
Mug, 2 Scenes, Maroon Ground, 4 1/4 In.	135.00
Pipe, Monkey In Top Hat, Smoking Church Warden's Pipe, C.1800, 5 In.	1950.00
Pitcher, Boys Playing Cards, 1820, 8 In.	105.00
Pitcher, Embossed Polychrome Drinking Scenes, 9 1/8 In.	120.00
Plate, Old State House, 1876 Centennial, Signed	65.00
Plate, Rural Scene Center, Plum Border, Gold Stencil, Handle, 9 In.	70.00
Potlid, Outdoor Scene, Wolves, Dated 1860	55.00
Potlid, Shakespeare's House, Dr.Johnson, 3 1/4 In.	75.00
Potlid, Wimbleton Scene, Dated 1860	70.00
Potlid, Yellow Primroses	45.00
Tazza, Spanish Dancers, Scrolled Gold Border, 1850, 11 In.	165.00

Pressed glass was first made in the United States in the 1820s after the invention of glass pressing machines. Hundreds of patterns of pressed glass were made in complete table settings. Although the Boston and Sandwich Works was the most famous of the pressed glass factories, there were about sixteen other factories making pressed glass from 1830 to 1850, and still more from 1850 to 1900, when pressed glass reached its greatest popularity. It is now being widely reproduced.

100–EYE, see Hundred Eye
1000–EYE, see Thousand Eye
101, see One–O–One
ACANTHUS, see Ribbed Palm
PRESSED GLASS, Acorn Band, Goblet 35.00
    ACORN MEDALLION, BEADED, see Beaded Acorn Medallion
Acorn, Creamer 45.00
Acorn, Creamer, Child's 110.00
Acorn, Spooner 22.00
Actress, Bread Plate, Miss Neilson 60.00
Actress, Butter, Covered 80.00
Actress, Cake Stand .... 125.00 To 130.00
Actress, Compote, 11 In. 130.00
Actress, Compote, Covered, 7 In. 85.00
Actress, Compote, Covered, Frosted Dome, 9 1/2 X 6 1/4 In. 125.00
Actress, Compote, Covered, Frosted, 11 In. 120.00
Actress, Compote, Open, 6 X 3 1/2 In. 30.00
Actress, Creamer 95.00
Actress, Cruet 52.50
Actress, Dish, Cheese, Frosted .... 195.00 To 245.00
Actress, Goblet .... 40.00 To 85.00
Actress, Relish 32.50
Actress, Saltshaker 55.00
Actress, Sauce, Footed, 5 In. 95.00
Actress, Sherbet 29.50
Actress, Spooner 70.00
Actress, Sugar, Covered 135.00
Admiral Dewey, Pitcher, Water 65.00
Admiral Dewey, Tumbler 35.00
Aida, Pitcher, Water, Etched 95.00
Alabama, Creamer 36.00
Alabama, Syrup .... 80.00 To 110.00
Alaska, Berry Bowl, Green Design, Ruffled Edge 68.00
Alaska, Berry Set, Vaseline 350.00
Alaska, Bowl, Blue, Square 95.00
Alaska, Creamer, Clear To Opalescent 45.00
Alaska, Pitcher, Water, Green 125.00
Alaska, Pitcher, Water, Vaseline .... 295.00 To 325.00
Alaska, Sauce, White Opalescent 25.00
Alaska, Sugar, Covered, Vaseline Opalescent 120.00
Alaska, Table Set, Vaseline, Enameled 500.00
Alligator Scales With Spearpoint, Sugar, Covered 35.00
Alligator, Toothpick 95.00
Almond Thumbprint, Sugar, Open, Flint 15.00
Amazon, Bowl, 7 In. 12.00
Amazon, Butter, Covered, Child's 65.00
Amazon, Compote, Scalloped, Footed, 6 3/4 In. 18.00
Amazon, Creamer, Child's 20.00
Amazon, Salt, Master, 3 1/4 In. 16.00
Amazon, Spooner, Child's .... 22.00 To 35.00
    AMBERETTE, see Klondike
American Flag, Bread Plate, 38 Stars, 11 X 8 In. 50.00
Anthemion, Pitcher, Water 48.00
Anthemion, Plate, Ruffled, 10 In. 14.00
Apollo, Cake Stand, 9 In. 45.00

Actress   Arched Fleur–de–Lis   Artichoke, Frosted

Apollo, Compote, 5 In.	32.50
Apollo, Compote, Covered, 6 In.	55.00
Apple Blossom, Sugar Shaker	85.00
Aquarium, Pitcher, Water	145.00 To 195.00
Arched Leaf, Bread Plate	20.00
Arched Leaf, Plate, 10 In.	28.50
Arched Ovals, Butter, Covered, Gold Trim	35.00
Argus, Creamer, Flint	70.00
Argus, Goblet	48.00
Art, Banana Stand	95.00
Art, Berry Bowl, Set of 8	50.00
Art, Bowl, Rectangular	20.00
Art, Cake Stand, 9 In.	50.00
Art, Celery	28.00
Art, Cruet	110.00
Art, Goblet, Footed	20.00
Art, Sugar, Covered	45.00
Artichoke, Butter, Covered, Frosted	38.00
Artichoke, Celery, Frosted	55.00
Artichoke, Vase, Cylinder, Frosted, 12 In.	125.00
Artichoke, Water Set, Bulbous Pitcher, Clear, Frosted, 7 Pc.	265.00
Ashburton, Decanter, Yellow, Silver Plated Stopper, 1850s	325.00
Ashburton, Eggcup, Flint	18.00

Atlas   Austrian   Barberry

Ashburton, Goblet, Flint, 6 In. .... 15.00 To 25.00
Ashburton, Wine, Barrel Shape, Flint 41.50
Atlanta, Bowl, 7 In. 35.00
Atlanta, Cake Stand 72.50
Atlanta, Toothpick 42.50
Atlas, Goblet, Etched 35.00
Atlas, Salt, 10 Balls Form Feet, 2 1/2 In. 8.00
Aurora, Tray, 11 In. 24.00
Aurora, Wine Set, Ruby Stained, 6 Piece 375.00
Austrian, Cordial 55.00
Austrian, Sugar, Covered 30.00
Austrian, Wine 35.00
Aztec, Sugar, Open 25.00
Aztec, Wine 14.00
Baby Face, Celery 75.00
Baby Face, Spooner, Frosted 160.00
      BABY THUMBPRINT, see Dakota
Bag Ware, Table Set, Amber, 4 Piece 185.00
      BALDER, see also Pennsylvania
Balder, Bowl, Gold Trim, 9 In. 20.00
Balder, Butter, Covered, Large 55.00
Balder, Punch Cup 18.50
Balder, Salt & Pepper, Metal Frame 36.00
Balder, Sugar & Creamer, Open 35.00
Balder, Table Set, 4 Piece 125.00
Balder, Toothpick, Gold Trim 25.00
      BALKY MULE, see Currier & Ives
Ball & Swirl, Tankard, Milk, Applied Handle, 10 1/2 In. 30.00
Balloon, Sugar, Covered, Flint 100.00
Baltimore Pear, Butter, Covered 75.00
      BAMBOO, see Broken Column
Banded Buckle, Spooner 16.00
      BANDED FINE CUT, see Fine Cut Band
      BANDED PORTLAND, when flashed with pink, is sometimes called
      "Maiden Blush."
Banded Portland, Goblet, Hexagonal Base 30.00
Banded Portland, Powder Jar 35.00
Banded Portland, Sugar Shaker 38.00
Banded Portland, Toothpick, Gold Trim 18.00
Banded Star, Celery, Footed 25.00
Banded Star, Creamer 45.00
      BAR & DIAMOND, see Kokomo
Barberry, Celery, Oval 35.50
Barberry, Compote, Covered 45.00
Barberry, Goblet .... 23.00 To 25.00
      BARLEY & OATS, see Wheat & Barley
      BARLEY & WHEAT, see Wheat & Barley
Barley, Bread Plate 21.00
Barley, Pitcher, Water .... 40.00 To 45.00
Barley, Plate, 6 In. 17.50
Barley, Salt, Wheelbarrow, Metal Wheel, 4 In. 50.00
Barred Forget-Me-Not, Cake Stand 41.50
Barred Oval, Celery, Flat, Ruby Stained 42.50
      BARRED OVALS, see Banded Portland
      BARRELED BLOCK, see Red Block
Basket Weave, Cup, Amber 5.00
Basket Weave, Pitcher, Water, Vaseline 55.00
Basket Weave, Tray, Water, Scenic Center, Vaseline 50.00
Bead & Scroll, Butter, Covered, Gold Trim, Green 110.00
Bead & Scroll, Spooner, Gold Trim, Green .... 55.00 To 60.00
Bead & Scroll, Table Set, Child's, 4 Piece .... 325.00 To 345.00
Beaded Acorn Medallion, Goblet .... 28.00 To 34.00
Beaded Acorn, Goblet 15.00
      BEADED BULL'S-EYE & DRAPE, see Alabama

Block & Fan

Buckle

Beaded Grape

Beaded Dewdrop, Bowl, 7 In.	37.00
Beaded Dewdrop, Cake Stand, 8 1/2 In.	42.00
Beaded Dewdrop, Compote, Jelly	32.00
Beaded Dewdrop, Mug, 3 7/8 In.	38.00
Beaded Dewdrop, Sugar Shaker	65.00
Beaded Dewdrop, Toothpick	50.00 To 55.00
Beaded Dewdrop, Wine	48.00
Beaded Grape Medallion, Eggcup	29.00
Beaded Grape Medallion, Goblet	30.00
Beaded Grape Medallion, Sauce	9.00
Beaded Grape Medallion, Spooner	28.00
Beaded Grape, Bowl, Green, 5 1/2 In.	15.00
Beaded Grape, Bowl, Square, 8 In.	25.00
Beaded Grape, Butter, Green	95.00
Beaded Grape, Celery	38.00
Beaded Grape, Cruet, Original Stopper, Green	125.00
Beaded Grape, Pitcher, Water	85.00
Beaded Grape, Water Set, Green, 7 Piece	255.00
Beaded Loop, Mug, Flashed	25.00
Beaded Oval & Scroll, Creamer	10.00
Beaded Swirl & Disc, Salt & Pepper	18.00
Beaded Swirl, Spooner, Green, Gold Trim	38.00
Beaded Swirl, Table Set, Child's, 4 Piece	95.00
BEARDED MAN, see Viking	
Beatty Rib, Pitcher, Water, Blue	195.00
Bellflower Double Vine & Fine Rib, Creamer, Flint	190.00
Bellflower, Compote, Open, Scalloped, Flint, 8 1/2 In.	95.00
Bellflower, Goblet, Flint	45.00 To 50.00
Bellflower, Sugar, Open, Flint, 5 1/2 In.	35.00
Ben Franklin, Saltshaker, Figural	125.00
BENT BUCKLE, see New Hampshire	
Bethlehem Star, Compote, Covered, 6 In.	55.00
Bethlehem Star, Pitcher, Water	52.00
Beveled Diamond & Star, Butter, Covered	36.00
Beveled Diamond & Star, Celery	28.50
Beveled Star, Compote, Jelly	30.00
Beveled Star, Spooner, Green	40.00
Big Block, Tumbler	19.00
Bigler, Goblet	42.50
Bird & Strawberry, Butter, Covered	100.00
Bird & Strawberry, Cake Plate	65.00
Bird & Strawberry, Cake Stand, 9 In.	45.00
Bird & Strawberry, Creamer, Gold Trim	100.00
Bird & Strawberry, Pitcher, Water	155.00
Bird & Strawberry, Pitcher, Water, Gilt	255.00
Bird & Strawberry, Wine	35.00

Birds At Fountain, Goblet	50.00
Blackberry, Goblet	25.00
Blackberry, Salt, Master	22.00
Blackberry, Spooner	10.00
Bleeding Heart, Goblet	20.00 To 30.00
Bleeding Heart, Spooner	25.00 To 32.00
Bleeding Heart, Sugar, Open	25.00
Bleeding Heart, Table Set, 4 Piece	325.00
Bleeding Heart, Wine	175.00
Block & Fan, Celery	20.00
Block & Fan, Sauce	9.75
BLOCK & FINE CUT, see Fine Cut & Block	
Block & Honeycomb, Celery, Footed	18.00
Block & Lattice, Cruet	45.00
Block & Lattice, Cruet, Ruby Stained	75.00
BLOCK & STAR, see Valencia Waffle	
BLOCK WITH STARS, see Hanover	
Block, Punch Cup	20.00
BLOCKHOUSE, see Hanover	
BLUEBIRD, see Bird & Strawberry	
Bohemian, Sugar & Creamer, Cranberry, Gold Trim	165.00
Bow Tie, Butter, Covered	80.00
Bow Tie, Cup, Rose Decal	85.00
Box–In–Box, Tumbler, Ruby Flashed	28.50
Brickwork, Creamer	27.00
Britannic, Pitcher, Water, Amber Stained	95.00
Britannic, Sherbet, 6 Piece	50.00
Broken Column, Berry Bowl, 4 1/4 In.	12.00
Broken Column, Bowl, Flat, 7 In.	35.00
Broken Column, Cake Stand, 9 In.	47.50
Broken Column, Cake Stand, Footed	70.00
Broken Column, Celery	42.50
Broken Column, Compote, Covered, Square	80.00
Broken Column, Compote, Jelly, Red Flashed	195.00
Broken Column, Compote, Open, Small	45.00
Broken Column, Cruet, Original Stopper	52.00 To 65.00
Broken Column, Goblet	67.50
Broken Column, Pitcher, Water	75.00 To 85.00
Broken Column, Punch Cup, Cobalt Blue	32.00
Broken Column, Spooner	45.00 To 65.00
Broken Column, Tumbler, Ruby Stained	55.00
Broughton, Berry Bowl, Child's	10.00
Broughton, Creamer, Ruby	50.00
Broughton, Tumbler, Child's	8.00 To 9.00
Broughton, Water Set, Child's, 7 Piece	100.00
BRYCE, see Ribbon Candy	
BUCKET, see Wooden Pail	
Buckingham, Fruit Bowl, Pedestal	65.00
Buckle & Star, Wine	21.00
Buckle, Spooner, Flint	35.00
Buckle, Sugar, Covered, 8 In.	20.00
Budded Ivy, Spooner	28.50
Bull's–Eye & Daisy, Butter, Gold	50.00
Bull's–Eye & Daisy, Decanter, Wine, Gold Eyes	55.00
Bull's–Eye & Daisy, Pitcher, Water, Green Spots	94.00
BULL'S–EYE & FAN, see Daisies In Oval Panels	
Bull's–Eye & Rosette, Spill Holder	68.00
Bull's–Eye & Spearhead, Pitcher, Water	35.00
BULL'S–EYE BAND, see Reverse Torpedo	
BULL'S–EYE VARIANT, see Texas Bull's–Eye	
Bull's–Eye, Carafe, Water, Cranberry Opalescent	150.00
Bull's–Eye, Celery, Flint	85.00
Bull's–Eye, Cruet, Pair	75.00
Bull's–Eye, Goblet	17.00

Cable Rose

Bull's–Eye & Daisy

Bullet Emblem, Butter, Covered	250.00
Bullet Emblem, Sugar, Covered	160.00
Bullet Emblem, Sugar, Open	100.00
Butterfly Handles, Sugar, Covered	55.00
Butterfly, Sugar, Covered, 2 Handles	25.00
Button & Star, Cruet	225.00
Button Arches, Creamer, Child's, Ruby	24.00
Button Arches, Spooner	10.00 To 30.00
Button Arches, Table Set, 4 Piece	135.00
Button Arches, Tumbler, Ruby Stained	42.50
Button Arches, Tumbler, Ruby Trim, Frosted Band, Souvenir	60.00
Button Panel, Table Set, Child's	195.00
Buzz Saw, Butter, Child's, Covered	25.00
Buzz Saw, Table Set, Child's, 4 Piece	85.00
By Jingo, Mug, Child's	40.00
Cabbage Leaf, Creamer, Frosted	85.00
Cabbage Rose, Cake Stand, 11 In.	55.00
Cabbage Rose, Goblet	45.00
Cable, Celery, Flint	60.00
Cable, Goblet, Flint	45.00 To 65.00
Cable, Spooner, Flint	35.00
CALIFORNIA, see Beaded Grape	
Camel Caravan, Goblet	75.00
Camel Caravan, Goblet, 6 Piece	250.00
CAMEO, see Ceres	
CANADIAN DRAPE, see Garfield Drape	
Canadian, Butter, Covered	85.00
Canadian, Compote, Covered, 8 In.	150.00
Canadian, Creamer	55.00
Canadian, Goblet, Set of 4	185.00
Canadian, Pitcher, Water	85.00 To 90.00
Canadian, Spooner	45.00
Canadian, Wine, Set of 4	160.00

The early 1840s were the time of the pressed-glass table settings. The early patterns were simple, with heavy loops or ribbed effects. The 1870s meant more elaborate naturalistic patterns. Clear and frosted patterns with figures were in style during the 1870s. Overall patterns that were slightly geometric in feeling were in style by 1880, and patterns such as Daisy and Button and Hobnail came into vogue. Colored pressed-glass patterns became popular after the Civil War.

Ceres   Columbian Coin   Cathedral

There is also a pattern called "Candlewick" which has been made by Imperial Glass Corporation since 1936. It is listed in this book under Imperial, Candlewick.

CANDY RIBBON, see Ribbon Candy

Cane, Creamer	25.00
Cane, Goblet, Amber	32.00
Cane, Pitcher, Water, Blue	60.00
Cane, Plate, Toddy, Amber	14.00
Cape Cod, Compote, Open, Low Stand, 7 In.	30.00
Cape Cod, Pitcher, Water	45.00
Cardinal Bird, Creamer	35.00
Carnation, Pitcher, Water, 1895	35.00
Carolina, Relish	12.00
Cat & Dog, Cup & Saucer, Child's	45.00
Cat's Eye & Fan, Spooner	24.00
Cathedral, Compote, Covered, 7 1/4 In.	75.00
Cathedral, Compote, Scalloped Top, Blue, 9 1/2 In.	65.00
Cathedral, Wine, Amber	40.00

CENTENNIAL, see also Liberty Bell; Washington Centennial

Centennial, Goblet	20.00
Centennial, Pitcher, Applied Handle, 1776–1876	50.00
Centennial, Platter, George Washington, Bear Paw Handles	75.00
Ceres, Creamer	26.50

CHAIN WITH DIAMONDS, see Washington Centennial

Chain With Star, Cake Stand, Pedestal, 10 3/4 In.	42.50
Chain With Star, Goblet	25.00
Chain, Goblet	15.00
Chain, Sugar, Covered	40.00
Champion, Cake Stand, 8 1/2 In.	20.00
Champion, Toothpick	28.00
Chandelier, Cake Stand, Large	65.00
Chandelier, Sugar Shaker	60.00
Chandelier, Sugar, Covered, Etched	35.00
Checkerboard, Honey, Covered, Footed, Square, 5 In.	20.00
Cherry, Goblet	30.00
Chrysanthemum Leaf, Toothpick	20.00
Chrysanthemum Sprig, Wine	35.00
Chrysanthemum, Berry Bowl, Opalescent, Master	60.00
Chrysanthemum, Celery, Opalescent Satin	29.50
Circle, Cake Stand, Frosted	40.00
Circle, Compote, Frosted, 10 In.	44.00
Circle, Syrup, Frosted, Original Lid	110.00
Circle, Table Set, Frosted, 4 Piece	145.00
Circled Scroll, Cruet, Green	245.00
Classic Medallion, Creamer, Footed	20.00
Classic Medallion, Spooner	30.00

Classic, Bowl, 8 In. 145.00
Classic, Bowl, Hexagonal, 7 In. 110.00
Classic, Bowl, Log Feet, 8 In. 100.00
Classic, Butter, Covered 245.00
Classic, Celery, Log Feet 165.00
Classic, Compote, Hexagonal, Footed, Covered, 7 In. 185.00
Classic, Creamer 125.00
Classic, Goblet .... 195.00 To 235.00
Classic, Jam Jar 350.00
Classic, Pitcher, Water 350.00
Classic, Sauce, Log Feet 35.00
Classic, Spooner, Log Feet 85.00
Clematis, Spooner 25.00
Coarse Rib, Eggcup, Double, Flint 32.00
    COIN SPOT, see Coin Spot Category
Colorado, Butter, Covered, Footed, Green 77.00
Colorado, Butter, Covered, Gold 95.00
Colorado, Butter, Covered, Green, Gold Trim .... 85.00 To 125.00
Colorado, Compote, Open, Fluted Rim, 6 1/2 In. 16.50
Colorado, Compote, Ruffled Top, Cobalt Blue, Gold Trim 215.00
Colorado, Custard, Green, Gold Trim 30.00
Colorado, Pitcher, Water, Green, Gold Trim 180.00
Colorado, Punch Cup 30.00
Colorado, Sugar, Emerald Green, Covered, 7 1/2 In. 65.00
Colorado, Table Set, Green, Gold Trim, 4 Piece 350.00
Colorado, Toothpick, Green, Gold Trim 28.00
Colorado, Vase, Blue, 10 1/2 In. 80.00
Colorado, Vase, Cobalt Blue, 12 1/2 In. 80.00
Columbian Coin, Butter, Covered, Frosted 125.00
Columbian Coin, Spooner 45.00
    COMPACT, see Snail
Continental Hall, Bread Plate 42.00
Cord Drapery, Butter, Covered 60.00
Cordova, Toothpick 17.00
Cornucopia, Pitcher, Various High Relief Fruits 35.00
Corona, Decanter, Original Stopper, Ruby Stained 60.00
    COSMOS, see Cosmos Category
Cottage, Butter, Covered, Green 78.00
Cottage, Cake Stand, 9 In. 25.00
Cottage, Creamer 20.00
Cottage, Tray, Water 10.00
    CRANE, see Stork
Crescent & Fan, Rose Bowl 21.00
    CRISSCROSS, see Rexford
Croesus, Berry Set, Purple, 7 Piece 420.00
Croesus, Butter, Covered, Green, Gold Trim 175.00

Deer & Dog

Dahlia

Classic

Croesus, Condiment Set, Green, Gold Trim, 4 Piece 365.00
Croesus, Creamer, Amethyst 125.00
Croesus, Creamer, Purple, Gold Trim, Small 75.00
Croesus, Cruet, Gold Trim 210.00
Croesus, Cruet, Green, Gold Trim 255.00
Croesus, Cruet, Green, Small 85.00
Croesus, Pitcher, Purple, Gold 200.00
Croesus, Spooner, Green 40.00
Croesus, Spooner, Green, Gold Trim 55.00
Croesus, Sugar, Covered, Green, Gold Trim 110.00
Croesus, Sugar, Open 10.00
Croesus, Table Set, Green, Gold, 4 Piece 385.00
Croesus, Tumbler, Purple, Gold Trim 40.00
Crossed Pressed Leaf, Spooner 22.00
Crowfoot, Cake Stand, 9 In. 48.00
Crowfoot, Creamer 20.00
Crowfoot, Spooner 35.00
Crowfoot, Tumbler 20.00
   CROWN JEWELS, see Chandelier; Queen's Necklace
Crusader Cross, Goblet 15.00
Crystal Rock, Pitcher, Water, Pink & Blue Trim 45.00
Crystal Wedding, Cake Stand 55.00
Crystal Wedding, Compote, Covered, Frosted, 5 In. 52.50
Crystal Wedding, Saltshaker, Original Cover 65.00
   CUBE WITH FAN, see Pineapple & Fan
   CUPID & PSYCHE, see Psyche & Cupid
Cupid & Venus, Bread Plate, Amber 30.00
Cupid & Venus, Butter, Covered 55.00
Cupid & Venus, Celery, Ruffled, 8 1/2 In. 48.00
Cupid & Venus, Cordial 85.00
Cupid & Venus, Creamer 36.50
Cupid & Venus, Jam Jar 85.00
Cupid & Venus, Mug, 3 1/2 In. 15.00
Cupid & Venus, Pitcher, Milk 65.00
Cupid & Venus, Pitcher, Water, 9 1/4 In. 50.00
Cupid & Venus, Plate, Handles, 11 1/4 In. 40.00
Cupid & Venus, Spooner .... 35.00 To 45.00
Cupid & Venus, Wine 85.00
Currant, Cake Stand, 11 In. 58.00
Currant, Creamer 35.00
Currant, Spooner 26.00
Currier & Ives, Bread Plate, Balky Mule .... 45.00 To 55.00
Currier & Ives, Goblet 22.00
Currier & Ives, Pitcher, Water .... 30.00 To 65.00
Currier & Ives, Pitcher, Water, Amber 125.00
Currier & Ives, Plate, 9 1/2 In. 50.00
Currier & Ives, Salt & Pepper 58.00
Currier & Ives, Syrup 110.00
Currier & Ives, Waste Bowl, Footed 45.00
Curtain Tieback, Goblet .... 25.00 To 35.00
Curtain, Bowl, Footed, 8 In. 25.00
Curtain, Celery 28.50
Cut Log, Cake Stand, 10 In. .... 45.00 To 95.00
Cut Log, Creamer 38.50
Cut Log, Cruet 40.00
Cut Log, Pitcher, Water, Tankard 75.00
Cut Log, Sugar, Covered 47.50
Cut Log, Wine 24.00
Dahlia, Goblet 25.00
Dahlia, Pitcher, Water, Blue 95.00
Dahlia, Plate, 12 In. 25.00
Dahlia, Sauce, Blue .... 11.00 To 27.00
Dahlia, Sugar, Covered, Green 28.00
Daisies In Oval Panels, Relish, Oval 7.00

Daisy & Bluebell, Creamer	32.50
Daisy & Button With Crossbar, Celery, Pedestal Base, 7 In.	65.00
Daisy & Button With Crossbar, Cruet, Amber	115.00
Daisy & Button With Crossbar, Goblet, Amber	35.00
Daisy & Button With Crossbar, Pitcher, Water, Amber	90.00
Daisy & Button With Crossbar, Tray, Vaseline Handles	50.00
Daisy & Button With Crossbar, Tumbler, Blue	30.00
Daisy & Button With Thin Bars, Salt, Apple Green, 2 1/4 In.	5.00
Daisy & Button, Boot, Lady's, 4 X 4 In.	30.00
Daisy & Button, Bottle, Vinegar, Vaseline	36.50
Daisy & Button, Butter, Square	45.00
Daisy & Button, Candy Dish, Domed Cover, Footed, Blue, 7 In.	65.00
Daisy & Button, Celery, Flared, Tulip Lip, Green, 9 In.	35.00
Daisy & Button, Creamer, Applied Handle, 5 In.	37.50
Daisy & Button, Match Holder, 2 Sections, Cobalt Blue	75.00
Daisy & Button, Pitcher, 8 In.	68.00
Daisy & Button, Pitcher, Water, Blue	90.00
Daisy & Button, Pitcher, Water, Spiral Handle	35.00
Daisy & Button, Powder Jar, Flat Lid, Amber, 3 3/4 In.	30.00
Daisy & Button, Rose Bowl, Vaseline, 4 In.	15.00
Daisy & Button, Salt, Boat Shape, 4 1/2 In.	15.00
Daisy & Button, Slipper, Blue, Dated 1888, 7 1/4 In.	28.00
Daisy & Button, Smoke Bell, Amber	55.00
Daisy & Button, Spooner, Hat, Amber	32.00
Daisy & Button, Spooner, Squared, Footed, Cut Corners, Amber	35.00
Dakota, Butter, Covered	45.00
Dakota, Butter, Covered, Etched	65.00
Dakota, Butter, Covered, Fern & Berry Etched	60.00
Dakota, Cake Stand, Child's, 3 In. .... 100.00 To 125.00	
Dakota, Celery, Flat	35.00
Dakota, Compote, Open, 6 In.	18.00
Dakota, Goblet, Donovan Etched, Ruby Flashed	30.00
Dakota, Pitcher, Water, Etched	65.00
Dakota, Salt & Pepper	35.00
Dakota, Sherbet, Stemmed, Etched	14.00
Dakota, Sugar, Covered, Etched .... 45.00 To 52.00	
Dakota, Tray, Water, Etched	45.00
Dakota, Tumbler, Etched, Ruby Flashed, 3 In.	28.50
Dakota, Wine, Etched	25.00
Dart, Creamer, Footed	35.00
Deep Stars & Octagons, Water Set, Child's, 7 Piece	80.00
Deer & Dog, Compote, Covered	200.00
Deer & Dog, Goblet, Etched, Oval Bowl	65.00
Deer & Dog, Jam Jar, Covered, Etched	90.00
Deer & Dog, Pitcher, Etched	150.00
Deer & Dog, Sauce, Footed	12.00
Deer & Oak Tree, Pitcher	125.00
Deer & Pine Tree, Bread Plate .... 35.00 To 65.00	
Deer & Pine Tree, Celery	95.00
Deer & Pine Tree, Compote, Covered .... 85.00 To 175.00	
Deer & Pine Tree, Mug, Blue	43.00
Deer & Pine Tree, Sauce, Footed	25.00
Deer & Pine Tree, Tray, Amber, 13 X 7 3/4 In.	45.00
Deer Alert, Pitcher	127.50
Deflating Balloon, Goblet	13.00
Delaware, Banana Boat, Green, Gold Trim, 7 1/2 X 11 In.	50.00
Delaware, Banana Boat, Rose, Gold Trim, Flint	60.00
Delaware, Banana Bowl, Green, Gold Trim	40.00
Delaware, Berry Bowl, Green, 8 In.	65.00
Delaware, Berry Bowl, Green, Gold Trim, 8 In.	65.00
Delaware, Bowl, Cranberry, Gold Trim, 8 In.	68.00
Delaware, Bowl, Green, Gold Trim, Oval, 12 In.	65.00
Delaware, Butter, Covered	90.00
Delaware, Butter, Covered, Green	75.00

Delaware, Butter, Covered, Rose 145.00
Delaware, Creamer 68.00
Delaware, Cruet, Green, Gold Trim 85.00
Delaware, Pitcher, Green, Gold Trim 80.00
Delaware, Pitcher, Water, Cranberry, Gold Trim 85.00
Delaware, Powder Box, Jeweled Cover, Rose, Gold Trim 145.00
Delaware, Salt & Pepper, Gold Trim 65.00
Delaware, Spooner, Green, Gold Trim 50.00
Delaware, Spooner, Rose, Gold Trim 55.00
Delaware, Sugar, Covered 100.00
Delaware, Sugar, Covered, Green, Gold Trim 110.00
Delaware, Table Set, Green, 4 Piece 130.00
Delaware, Table Set, Green, Gold Trim, 4 Piece 365.00
Delaware, Tankard 165.00
Delaware, Toothpick, Green, Gold Trim .... 45.00 To 95.00
Delaware, Toothpick, Rose, Gold Trim ....85.00 To 110.00
Delaware, Tray, Dresser, Serpentine, Rose 60.00
Delaware, Tray, Green, Gold Trim, 8 7/8 In. 35.00
Delaware, Tumbler, 4 Piece 160.00
Delaware, Tumbler, Cranberry, Gold Trim 28.00
Delaware, Tumbler, Green, Gold Trim 52.50
Delaware, Tumbler, Rose, Gold Trim 45.00
Delaware, Vase, Rose Flash On Flowers 150.00
Delaware, Water Set, Gold Trim, 6 Piece 245.00
Delaware, Water Set, Green, 7 Piece 675.00
Delaware, Water Set, Rose, 7 Piece 295.00
Delaware, Water Set, Tankard & 6 Tumblers, Ruby 315.00
Dew & Raindrop, Goblet 30.00
Dew & Raindrop, Pitcher, Water .... 29.50 To 50.00
Dewberry, Goblet, Gold 12.50
Dewdrop Drapery, Goblet 21.00
Dewdrop With Sheaf of Wheat, Bread Plate 22.00
Dewdrop With Star, Pitcher, Water 32.00
Dewdrop With Star, Plate, 5 1/4 In. 18.50
Dewdrop, Goblet, Amber 25.00
    DEWEY, see also Admiral Dewey
Dewey, Butter, Covered, Green .... 35.00 To 85.00
Dewey, Creamer, Yellow 35.00
Dewey, Cruet, Amber, Original Stopper 135.00
Dewey, Pitcher, Water .... 55.00 To 65.00
Dewey, Pitcher, Water, Cannonballs 55.00
Dewey, Sauce, Amber 20.00
Dewey, Sugar, Nile Green 85.00
Dewey, Tray, Amber, Serpentine, Large 65.00
Dewey, Tumbler, Green 47.50
Diagonal Band & Fan, Celery 20.00
Diagonal Band & Fan, Compote, 7 In. 28.00
Diagonal Band & Fan, Goblet 18.00
Diagonal Band & Fan, Pitcher, Water 60.00
Diagonal Band & Fan, Plate, 7 In. 12.00
Diagonal Band & Fan, Spooner 19.00
Diamond & Button, Salt, Apple Green, Square, 1 5/8 In. 15.00
Diamond & Button, Saltshaker, Blue 25.00
    DIAMOND & SUNBURST, see Flattened Diamond & Sunburst
Diamond Block With V, Spooner, Amber 25.00
Diamond Cut With Leaf, Sugar, Covered, Amber 65.00
    DIAMOND HORSESHOE, see Aurora
Diamond Medallion, Bread Plate 21.50
Diamond Medallion, Cake Stand, 9 1/2 In. 35.00
Diamond Medallion, Cake Stand, Green 34.00
    DIAMOND POINT DISCS, see Eyewinker
Diamond Point With Flutes, Compote, Covered, 11 1/2 In. 95.00
Diamond Point, Butter, Covered, Flint 75.00
Diamond Point, Champagne 67.50

Excelsior with Maltese Cross   Diamond Thumbprint   Diamond Point

Diamond Point, Champagne, Flint 67.50
Diamond Point, Compote, Flint 65.00
Diamond Point, Eggcup .... 35.00 To 37.50
Diamond Point, Goblet .... 50.00 To 52.00
Diamond Point, Goblet, Flint .... 48.00 To 50.00
Diamond Point, Spooner 30.00
Diamond Prisms, Sugar, Covered 15.00
Diamond Quilted, Bowl, Amber, 8 In. 27.50
Diamond Quilted, Butter, Covered, Vaseline 75.00
Diamond Quilted, Creamer, Amber 38.00
Diamond Quilted, Goblet, Amber 40.00
Diamond Quilted, Goblet, Amethyst 34.50
Diamond Quilted, Goblet, Blue 30.00
Diamond Quilted, Sugar, Covered, Vaseline 60.00
Diamond Ridge, Water Set, 7 Piece 175.00
Diamond Thumbprint, Compote, Scalloped, Low Standard, 8 In. 45.00
Diamond Thumbprint, Creamer, Scalloped Foot, Flint, 6 In. 165.00
Diamond Thumbprint, Spooner 85.00
Diamond Whirl, Bowl, 9 In. 12.00
Diamond, Vase 55.00
Diamonds & Clubs, Tumbler, Emerald Green, Gold Trim 42.50
Dice & Block, Cruet, Original Stopper, Amber 65.00
Dickinson, Compote, Flint, 7 3/8 X 4 7/8 In. 22.50
Divided Hearts, Celery, Pedestal 65.00
Dogwood, Banana Boat, Green, Gold Trim 35.00
Dolphin, Compote, 5 1/2 In. 65.00
    DORIC, see Feather
Dotted Loop, Wine 15.00
Double Beetle Band, Creamer, Blue 35.00
Double Dahlia & Lens, Berry Set, Cranberry, 6 Piece 150.00
Double Dahlia & Lens, Creamer, Gold Trim 45.00
    DOUBLE DAISY, See Rosette Band
Doyle's 500, Creamer, Amber 62.00
Doyle's 500, Table Set, Child's, Amber, Tray, 5 Piece 325.00
Drum, Butter, Child's, Covered 125.00
Drum, Sugar & Creamer, Child's 60.00
Drum, Table Set, Child's 300.00
Duke, Ball & Swirl, Pitcher, Water 45.00
Eagle, Humidor, Cigar 35.00
    EARL, see Spirea Band
Egg In Sand, Tray, Water 35.00
Egyptian, Bread Plate, Cleopatra Center 35.00
Egyptian, Celery .... 70.00 To 85.00
Egyptian, Compote, Covered, Sphinx, 8 In. 225.00
Egyptian, Compote, Open, 8 In. 65.00
Egyptian, Creamer .... 28.00 To 35.00

Frosted Eagle   Fine Cut & Block   Fan with Diamond

Egyptian, Goblet	32.00 To 48.50
Egyptian, Pitcher, Water	95.00 To 225.00
Egyptian, Sauce, Footed	17.50
Electric, Compote, Jelly, Green	25.00
Elk Medallion, Castor, Pickle	65.00
Elson's Block, Celery	21.00
Elson's Block, Sugar, Covered	35.00
Empress, Butter, Covered, Green, Gold Trim	95.00
Empress, Cruet, Green, Etched, Original Stopper	295.00
Empress, Cruet, Green, Original Stopper	78.50
Empress, Salt & Pepper, Green	160.00
Empress, Sugar, Covered, Green	95.00
Empress, Syrup, Emerald Green	225.00
Empress, Table Set, Gold Trim, 4 Piece	595.00
Empress, Table Set, Green, Gold Trim, 4 Piece	625.00
Empress, Toothpick, Gold Trim	55.00 To 68.00
ENGLISH HOBNAIL CROSS, see Klondike	
Esther, Berry Set, Green, Gold Trim, 7 Piece	285.00
Esther, Compote, Jelly, Green	40.00
Esther, Spooner, Emerald Green	75.00
Esther, Tumbler, Green, Gold Trim	40.00
Esther, Water Set, Green, Gold Trim, 6 Piece	295.00
ETCHED BAND, see Dakota	
ETCHED DAKOTA, see Dakota	
Eureka, Bread Plate, 11 1/4 In.	32.00
Eureka, Goblet	28.00
Eureka, Sugar, Open, Flint	15.00
Eureka, Toothpick, Red Flashed	85.00
Excelsior, Cake Stand, Maltese Cross, Flint	175.00
Eyewinker, Butter, Covered	60.00
Eyewinker, Cake Stand	28.00
Eyewinker, Cracker Jar, Covered	125.00
Eyewinker, Creamer	95.00
Eyewinker, Jam Jar	110.00
Eyewinker, Plate, Turned Up, 9 In.	28.00
Eyewinker, Saltshaker, Original Pewter Lid	45.00
Eyewinker, Spooner	34.00 To 45.00
Eyewinker, Syrup	125.00
Faceted Flower, Pitcher, Water	38.00
Falling Leaves, Sugar, Covered, 6 In.	23.00
Fan With Diamond, Butter, Covered	38.00
Fan With Diamond, Creamer	20.00
Fan With Diamond, Goblet	20.00
Fancy Loop, Toothpick, Gold Trim	65.00
Feather Duster, Celery	15.00

Feather Duster, Tumbler, Round Tray, Green, 3 1/2 In., 3 Pc. 30.00
Feather, Butter, Covered .... 35.00 To 45.00
Feather, Cake Stand, 8 1/2 In. 36.50
Feather, Cake Stand, Green 175.00
Feather, Compote, Covered, 8 1/2 In. 90.00
Feather, Creamer 36.00
Feather, Cruet 45.00
Feather, Pitcher, Milk 40.00
Feather, Pitcher, Water .... 48.00 To 55.00
Feather, Sugar, Covered 37.00
Feather, Wine .... 24.00 To 45.00
Fern Garland, Wine 22.00
    FESTOON & GRAPE, see Grape & Festoon
Festoon, Berry Bowl, Master 30.00
Festoon, Compote, Open 58.00
Festoon, Pitcher, Water .... 58.00 To 68.00
Festoon, Relish, 8 1/4 X 5 In. 18.00
Festoon, Sugar, Covered 58.00
Festoon, Water Set, Tray, 7 Piece 250.00
Fickle Block, Cordial 12.00
Fickle Block, Wine 12.00
Fine Cut & Block, Celery, Fancy Rim 65.00
Fine Cut & Block, Goblet, Amber Blocks 75.00
Fine Cut & Block, Relish, Canary Blocks 140.00
Fine Cut Band, Spooner 18.00
    FINE CUT MEDALLION, see Austrian
Fine Rib, Wine, Flint 43.50
Fishscale, Butter, Covered 45.00
Fishscale, Cake Stand, 10 In. 35.00
Flamingo Habitat, Celery, Etched 70.00
Flamingo Habitat, Compote, 8 X 7 In. 45.00
Flamingo Habitat, Sugar, Covered 40.00
Flat Diamond, Creamer, Blue 34.00
Flat Diamond, Goblet, 8 In. 10.00
Flatiron, Butter, Covered, Amber 75.00
Flattened Diamond & Sunburst, Punch Set, Child's, 7 Piece 60.00
Fleur–De–Lis & Drape, Pitcher, Green 40.00
Fleur–De–Lis & Drape, Sugar, Green 44.00
Floradora, Butter, Covered, Green, Gold Trim 165.00
Floradora, Spooner, Cranberry, Gold Trim 65.00
Florette, Butter, Covered, Pink 125.00
Florida Palm, Wine 16.00
    FLORIDA, see also Herringbone
Florida, Nappy, Handle 14.50
Florida, Pitcher, Water, Green 60.00
Flower & Pleat, Pitcher, Water, Ruby Stained 95.00

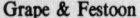

Grape & Festoon

Flattened Diamond & Sunburst

Frosted Circle

FLOWER FLANGE, see Dewey
Flower Medallion, Butter, Covered 35.00
Flower Medallion, Tumbler 10.00
Flower Pot, Sugar, Covered, Vaseline 85.00
Flower With Cane, Toothpick, 3 Handles, Footed 25.00
Flowered Scroll, Butter, Covered, Green, Gold Trim 115.00
Flute & Cane, Pitcher, Tankard 30.00
Flute, Celery, Flint 20.00
FLYING ROBIN, see Hummingbird
Flying Stork, Compote, Covered 85.00
FORGET–ME–NOT IN SNOW, see Stippled Forget–Me–Not
Forget–Me–Not, Table Set, 6 Piece 150.00
Four Petal, Sugar, Covered, Flint 75.00
Fringed Drape, Spooner, Green 25.00
Frost Crystal, Pitcher, Water, Ruby Stained 145.00
FROSTED PATTERNS, see also under name of main pattern
Frosted Circle, Compote, Open, 8 In. 25.00
Frosted Circle, Pitcher, Water 75.00
Frosted Circle, Sugar, Covered 47.50
FROSTED CRANE, see Frosted Stork
Frosted Eagle, Butter, Covered 195.00
Frosted Eagle, Creamer, Etched 48.00
Frosted Eagle, Sugar, Covered 145.00
Frosted Eagle, Sugar, Covered, Etched 145.00
Frosted Fruits, Pitcher, Water, Squirrel In Branches 135.00
Frosted Fruits, Tumbler, Water 65.00
Frosted Leaf, Sugar, Open, Flint 35.00
Frosted Leaf, Tumbler, Footed, Flint 95.00
Frosted Lion, Bread Plate ....32.00 To 110.00
Frosted Lion, Bread Plate, Cable Border, Rampant Lion 95.00
Frosted Lion, Butter, Covered, Child's 125.00
Frosted Lion, Butter, Covered, Rampant Lion 65.00
Frosted Lion, Celery ....65.00 To 72.00
Frosted Lion, Compote, Covered, 5 X 8 In. 150.00
Frosted Lion, Compote, Covered, 8 3/4 X 5 1/2 In. 185.00
Frosted Lion, Compote, Covered, Head Finial, 11 3/4 In. 145.00
Frosted Lion, Compote, Covered, Rampant Lion, 8 In. 145.00
Frosted Lion, Compote, Rampant Lion Finial, 13 In. 150.00
Frosted Lion, Creamer, Child's 75.00
Frosted Lion, Eggcup 65.00
Frosted Lion, Goblet ....55.00 To 65.00
Frosted Lion, Pitcher, 6 1/2 In. 92.50
Frosted Lion, Pitcher, Water 285.00
Frosted Lion, Sauce 10.00
Frosted Lion, Spooner 65.00
Frosted Lion, Sugar, Creamer, Spooner 225.00
Frosted Medallion, Relish 11.00
Frosted Ribbon, Spooner 28.00
Frosted Ribbon, Sugar, Covered 40.00
Frosted St.Bernard, Butter, Pedestal 100.00
Frosted Stork, Bowl, 4 1/2 In. 32.00
Frosted Stork, Castor, Pickle, Double 195.00
Frosted Stork, Spooner, Egg & Dart Border 55.00
Frosted Stork, Sugar, Open 85.00
Frosted Stork, Tray, Water ....105.00 To 125.00
Fruit Panels, Toothpick 30.00
G.A.R., Bread Plate 110.00
Gaelic, Goblet 25.00
Gaelic, Toothpick ....22.00 To 26.50
Galaxy, Goblet 24.00
Galloway, Pitcher, Child's, Gold Trim 24.00
Galloway, Vase, 12 In., Pair 35.00
Galloway, Wine, 6 Piece 250.00

Horn of Plenty   Hamilton   Garfield Drape

GARDEN OF EDEN, see also Lotus & Serpent

Garden of Eden, Compote, 7 1/2 In.	58.00
Garden of Eden, Creamer, Serpent	35.00
Garfield Drape, Bread Plate	45.00
Garfield Drape, Creamer	29.00
Garfield Drape, Pitcher, Water	65.00 To 75.00
Garfield Memorial, Bread Plate	26.00 To 65.00
Gathered Knot, Wine	18.00
Geneva, Bowl, Footed, Green, Gold Trim, 11 In.	65.00
Georgia Belle, Card Tray, 5 3/4 In.	8.00
Gibson Girl, Spooner	50.00
Girl With Goose, Cake Stand	125.00
Gloria, Pitcher, Water, Ruby Stained, Gold Trim	185.00
Gloria, Tumbler, Ruby Stained, Gold Trim	45.00
Gonterman Swirl, Toothpick	150.00

GOOD LUCK, see Horseshoe

Gooseberry, Goblet	25.00
Gothic, Compote, Open, Flint, 8 In.	65.00
Gothic, Creamer, Round Base, Flint, 5 3/4 In.	90.00

GRAND, see Diamond Medallion
GRAND ARMY OF THE REPUBLIC, see G.A.R.
GRAPE, see also Beaded Grape; Beaded Grape Medallion; Magnet & Grape; Paneled Grape; Paneled Grape Band

Grape & Festoon With Small American Shield, Goblet	38.00
Grape & Festoon, Goblet	22.00
Grape & Gothic Arches, Tumbler, Green	12.00
Grape & Magnet, Compote, Frosted, 9 X 8 In.	95.00
Grasshopper With Insect, Spooner, Insects & Fern Etch	38.00
Gridley, Pitcher, You May Fire When Ready	125.00
Hairpin, Goblet	27.50
Halley's Comet, Pitcher, Water, Etched	98.00

HAMILTON WITH CLEAR LEAF, see Hamilton with Leaf

Hamilton With Frosted Leaf, Tumbler, Bar	125.00
Hamilton With Leaf, Compote, Covered, Flint	250.00
Hamilton, Bottle, Bar, Qt.	135.00
Hamilton, Compote, Open, Flint	46.00
Hamilton, Pitcher, Water	205.00

HAND, see Pennsylvania Hand

Hanover, Cake Stand	40.00
Harp, Salt, Footed, Round, Flint	65.00
Hawaiian Lei With Bee, Cake Stand, Child's	35.00
Hawaiian Lei, Cake Stand	25.00
Heart Band, Mug	12.00
Heart Stem, Creamer	32.00
Heart With Thumbprint, Berry Set, Gold Trim, 7 Piece	85.00
Heart With Thumbprint, Bowl, Barrel Shape, 8 3/4 In.	30.00

Heart With Thumbprint, Cruet, Original Stopper 65.00
Heart With Thumbprint, Plate, Scalloped, 10 In. 24.00
Heart With Thumbprint, Sugar, Open, Handles, Green 24.00
Heart With Thumbprint, Syrup, Original Pewter Lid 125.00
Heart, Creamer 45.00
     HEARTS OF LOCH LAVEN, see Shuttle
Henrietta, Berry Set, 5 Piece 100.00
Hercules Pillar, Syrup, Original Lid, Amber 130.00
Heron, Pitcher, Water 125.00
Herringbone Buttress, Wine, Deep Green 160.00
Herringbone, Butter, Covered, Green 35.00
Herringbone, Cruet, Original Stopper, Emerald Green 90.00
Herringbone, Rose Bowl, Purple To Lavender 350.00
Herringbone, Syrup, Emerald Green 175.00
Herringbone, Table Set, Emerald Green, 4 Piece .... 150.00 To 175.00
Herringbone, Tumbler, Green 27.00
Hexagon Block, Pitcher, Water, Ruby Stained 135.00
Hexagon Block, Sauce, Ruby Stained 12.00
Hickman, Bowl, 8 In. 20.00
Hickman, Celery Tray 18.00
Hickman, Compote, 9 In. 45.00
Hickman, Condiment Set, Child's, Green, 3 Piece 75.00
Hobb's Block, Butter, Covered, Amber 95.00
Hobb's Block, Creamer, Frosted, Amber 75.00
Hobble Skirt, Pitcher, Water 50.00
Hobnail With Ornamental Band, Creamer 18.00
Hobnail With Thumbprint Base, Table Set, Child's, 4 Piece 150.00
     HOLBROOK, see Pineapple & Fan
Holly, Butter, Covered, Green, Gold Trim 195.00
Holly, Sugar, Covered, Red Berry, Gold Trim 40.00
Honeycomb Band, Spooner 15.00
Honeycomb With Star, Pitcher, Large 25.00
Honeycomb, Celery, Flint 36.00
Honeycomb, Decanter, 10 In. 75.00
Honeycomb, Goblet, 6 Piece 100.00
Honeycomb, Goblet, Flint 22.50
Hops Band, Sugar, Covered 38.50
Horn of Plenty, Bottle, Sauce, Embossed H.E.Swan, 11 In. 235.00
Horn of Plenty, Butter, Washington Head 750.00
Horn of Plenty, Compote, Flint, 7 1/4 In. 55.00
Horn of Plenty, Compote, Open, 8 X 7 In. 110.00
Horn of Plenty, Creamer, Flint 120.00
Horn of Plenty, Eggcup, 6 Piece 240.00
Horn of Plenty, Eggcup, Flint 40.00
Horn of Plenty, Sugar, Covered, Flint 195.00
Horse & Cart, Toothpick, Amber 75.00
Horsemint, Nappy, Ring Handle 10.00
Horsemint, Sugar, Covered 22.00
Horseshoe, Bowl, 9 In. 45.00
Horseshoe, Bread Plate, Double Horseshoe Handles, 14 In. 35.00
Horseshoe, Butter, Covered 42.00
Horseshoe, Cake Stand, 10 In. 90.00
Horseshoe, Celery 38.00
Horseshoe, Creamer 40.00
Horseshoe, Dish, Cheese 225.00
Horseshoe, Goblet, Knob Stem 25.00
Horseshoe, Pitcher, Water 68.00
Horseshoe, Plate, 10 In. 42.00
Horseshoe, Relish 28.00
Horseshoe, Salt, Shoe Is Rim, Word Luck At End, 2 3/4 In. 20.00
Horseshoe, Wine .... 110.00 To 150.00
Huber, Cordial, Flint 75.00
Huber, Eggcup, Flint 14.00
     HUCKLE, see Feather Duster

Hummingbird, Butter, Covered 48.00
Hummingbird, Celery, Amber .... 65.00 To 78.00
Hummingbird, Goblet, Blue 65.00
Hummingbird, Pitcher, Water, Blue .... 100.00 To 110.00
Hummingbird, Spooner 50.00
Hummingbird, Tumbler, Amber .... 48.00 To 55.00
Humpty–Dumpty, Mug 28.00
Hundred Eye, Goblet 10.00
Ibex, Goblet 50.00
Icicle With Loops, Goblet, Flint 25.00
    IDA, see Sheraton
    IDAHO, see Snail
Idyll, Butter, Covered, Apple Green, Gold Trim 100.00
Idyll, Spooner, Apple Green, Gold Trim 50.00
Idyll, Table Set, Apple Green, Gold, Covered Sugar, 3 Piece 95.00
Illinois, Basket 135.00
Illinois, Toothpick 29.50
    INDIAN TREE, see Sprig
    INDIANA SWIRL, see Feather
Intaglio Sunflower, Pitcher, Water, Large 45.00
Intaglio, Compote, Open, Green 22.00
Interlocked Hearts, Butter, Covered .... 30.00 To 37.00
Interlocked Hearts, Creamer 15.00
Inverted Fern, Goblet, Flint 40.00
Inverted Fern, Sugar, Covered, Flint .... 40.00 To 65.00
Inverted Prism, Creamer 25.00
Inverted Prism, Goblet, Etched .... 15.00 To 20.00
Inverted Strawberry, Punch Set, Child's, 7 Piece 150.00
    INVERTED THISTLE, see Late Thistle
Inverted Thumbprint, Pitcher, Water, Blue Handle, Amber 145.00
Inverted Thumbprint, Syrup, Blue, Pewter, Pat.Jan.29, '84 .... 85.00
Inverted Thumbprint, Tumbler, Amberina 50.00
Inverted Thumbprint, Vase, Medium Blue, 8 1/8 In., Pair 90.00
Iowa, Cruet, Original Stopper 55.00
Iowa, Toothpick 20.00
Iowa, Wine 35.00
Iris With Meander, Compote, Jelly, Gold Trim 35.00
Iris With Meander, Creamer, Gold Trim 45.00
Iris With Meander, Pitcher, Vaseline 300.00
Iris With Meander, Salt & Pepper, Opalescent Canary 45.00
Iris With Meander, Saltshaker, Gold Trim 30.00
Iris With Meander, Spooner, Vaseline 65.00
Iris With Meander, Toothpick, Amethyst .... 38.00 To 45.00
Iris With Meander, Tumbler, Vaseline 45.00
Isis, Cake Stand, 9 In. 17.00
Ivanhoe, Compote, Footed, 8 In. 35.00

Jumbo   Jeweled Heart   Inverted Fern

Jacob's Coat, Creamer, Green 35.00
Jacob's Ladder, Castor, Pickle, Original Frame 110.00
Jacob's Ladder, Celery, Footed, 9 In. 22.50
Jacob's Ladder, Compote, Open, Scalloped, 8 1/2 In. 27.50
Jacob's Ladder, Pitcher, Water 65.00
Jacob's Ladder, Plate, 6 1/2 In. 19.00
Jacob's Ladder, Spooner 30.00
Jacob's Ladder, Syrup .... 75.00 To 85.00
Jacob's Ladder, Wine, Set of 8 .... 195.00
Jefferson Optic, Creamer, Green, Gold, Enameled 32.00
Jenny Lind, Compote, Amber 175.00
Jersey Swirl, Goblet 16.00
Jersey Swirl, Salt, Swirled Prisms On Side, Amber, 1 7/8 In. 15.00
Jewel & Dewdrop, Bread Plate .... 38.00 To 65.00
Jewel & Dewdrop, Cake Stand, 8 In. 60.00
Jewel & Dewdrop, Mug, Vaseline 22.50
Jewel & Dewdrop, Pitcher, 8 In. 47.50
Jewel & Dewdrop, Pitcher, Water 44.50
Jewel & Dewdrop, Toothpick 55.00
Jewel & Dewdrop, Tumbler, Juice, Handle 20.00
Jewel & Flower, Berry Set, Vaseline 325.00
Jewel & Flower, Table Set, Blue 500.00
    JEWEL BAND, see Scalloped Tape
Jeweled Heart, Pitcher, Water, Blue 245.00
Jeweled Moon & Star, Carafe 41.50
Jeweled Moon & Star, Celery 18.50
Jeweled Moon & Star, Compote, Covered, 12 1/2 In. 60.00
Jeweled Moon & Star, Saltshaker, Amber 20.00
    JOB'S TEARS, see Art
Josephine's Fan, Toothpick 35.00
    JUBILEE, see Hickman
Jumbo & Barnum, Sugar, Covered 145.00
Jumbo, Spooner, Dated 650.00
Jumbo, Spooner, Frosted, Dated Sept.23, 1884 .... 275.00
Jumbo, Sugar, Covered, Etched 375.00
Kaleidoscope, Celery 20.00
    KAMONI, see Pennsylvania
    KANSAS, see Jewel & Dewdrop
King's 500, Cruet, Stopper, Blue 200.00
King's 500, Spooner 70.00
King's Crown, Butter, Covered 95.00
King's Crown, Castor Set, 4–Bottle, Stoppers, Glass Holder 100.00
King's Crown, Creamer .... 40.00 To 65.00
King's Crown, Cup & Saucer 55.00
King's Crown, Goblet, Green Eyes, Gold Trim 25.00
King's Crown, Mustard, Covered 58.00
King's Crown, Spooner 55.00
King's Crown, Sugar & Creamer, Amber 15.00
King's Crown, Toothpick, Ruby Flashed, Leaf Pattern 25.00
King's Crown, Tumbler, Footed, Amber 38.00
King's Crown, Water Set, Bulbous, 7 Piece 225.00
King's Crown, Wine, Yellow Stain 25.00
Klondike, Bowl, 8 In. 37.00
Klondike, Butter, Covered, Frosted, Amber Stained .... 300.00 To 365.00
Klondike, Relish, Scalloped Rim, Boat Shape, 4 X 9 In. 110.00
Klondike, Sauce, Scalloped Rim, 1 3/4 X 4 In. 58.00
Klondike, Sugar Shaker, Frosted 65.00
Klondike, Toothpick, Frosted, Amber 85.00
Knights of Labor, Mug 35.00
Kokomo, Decanter 18.00
Kokomo, Tankard 35.00
Kokomo, Wine .... 13.50 To 25.00
Lacy Daisy, Bowl, 9 In. 45.00
Lacy Daisy, Fruit Set, Child's, U.S.Glass, 5 Piece .... 50.00 To 60.00

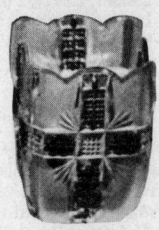

Liberty Bell   Leaf & Dart   Klondike

Lacy Medallion, Salt & Pepper, Green	25.00
Lacy Medallion, Tumbler, Green	27.00
Ladder With Diamonds, Cruet	30.00
Lamb, Butter, Child's, Covered	75.00 To 150.00
Lamb, Creamer, Child's	62.50 To 65.00
Lamb, Table Set, Child's, 4 Piece	275.00
Late Thistle, Salt, 1 3/4 In.	20.00
Lattice Leaf, Creamer	15.00
Leaf & Dart, Goblet	18.00 To 27.50
Leaf & Dart, Pitcher, Water	95.00 To 125.00
Leaf & Flower, Pitcher, Water, Amber	85.00
Leaf & Flower, Tankard, Amber, 14 In.	75.00
Leaf & Rib, Creamer, Amber	35.00
Leaf & Star, Compote, Jelly	22.00
Leaf Bracket, Berry Bowl	32.50
Leaf Medallion, Berry Bowl, Master, Green, Gold Trim	65.00
Leaf Medallion, Creamer, Green, Gold Trim	60.00
Leaf Medallion, Spooner, Green, Gold Trim	60.00
Leaf Medallion, Sugar Shaker, Cranberry, Vaseline Spatter	115.00
Leaf Medallion, Sugar, Covered, Green, Gold Trim	175.00
Leaf Mold, Syrup, Vaseline	245.00
Leaf Umbrella, Toothpick, Cranberry	110.00
Leaf, Goblet	25.00
Lens & Block, Sugar, Flint	18.00
LENS & STAR, see Star & Oval	
Liberty Bell, Bread Plate, Signers, 1776–1876	50.00 To 145.00
Liberty Bell, Butter, Child's, Covered	150.00
Liberty Bell, Butter, Covered	110.00
Liberty Bell, Creamer, Child's	80.00
Liberty Bell, Creamer, Reeded Handle	75.00
Liberty Bell, Goblet	40.00 To 45.00
Liberty Bell, Plate, 8 In.	40.00
Liberty Bell, Plate, Child's	60.00
Liberty Bell, Sauce, Footed	22.00
Liberty Bell, Spooner	70.00 To 92.50
Liberty Bell, Sugar, Covered	95.00 To 135.00
Lily–of–The–Valley, Creamer, Tripod	60.00
Lincoln Drape, Compote, Open, Scalloped, 8 In.	75.00
Lincoln Drape, Eggcup	40.00
Lincoln Drape, Syrup	95.00
Lincoln Drape, Syrup, Flint	120.00
Lion's Head, Butter, Covered	100.00
Lion's Head, Creamer	48.00
LION'S LEG, see Alaska	
LION, see also Frosted Lion	
Lion, Bowl, Gold Outlined Pansies, 8 In.	175.00

Lion, Bread Plate	46.00
Lion, Butter, Child's, Covered	110.00
Lion, Cake Stand, Square	82.50
Lion, Compote, Covered, Rampant Lion Finial, 8 1/4 In.	110.00
Lion, Creamer	55.00
Lion, Creamer, Child's, Commemorative, Pedestal	95.00
Lion, Cup, Child's	30.00
Lion, Goblet	40.00
Lion, Saucer, Child's	38.00
Lion, Spooner, Child's	75.00
Lion, Sugar, Covered, Child's	95.00
Lion, Table Set, 5 Piece	295.00
Lion, Table Set, Child's, 4 Piece	300.00 To 385.00
LIPPMAN, see Flat Diamond	
Log & Star, Cruet Set, Amber, Pedestal Tray, Salt & Pepper	155.00
Log Cabin, Butter, Covered	250.00
Log Cabin, Compote, Covered, High Standard	295.00
Log Cabin, Creamer	125.00
Log Cabin, Mustard, Covered	85.00
Log Cabin, Pitcher, Water	335.00
Log Cabin, Salt, Master	110.00
Loop & Block, Wine, Ruby Stained	25.00
Loop & Dart With Diamond Ornament, Spooner	14.00
Loop & Dart, Eggcup, Pedestal, Flint	25.00
Loop With Dewdrop, Goblet	20.00
LOOP WITH STIPPLED PANELS, see Texas	
LOOP, see also Seneca Loop; Yuma Loop	
Loop, Compote, Flint, 8 X 5 In.	27.50
Loop, Cordial	20.00
LOOPS & DROPS, see New Jersey	
Lotus & Serpent, Bread Plate, Our Daily Bread, 12 3/4 In.	38.00
Lotus & Serpent, Butter, Covered, Snake Head Stem, Finial	125.00
Lotus & Serpent, Mug	48.00
Lotus & Serpent, Plate, 6 1/2 In.	7.00
Lotus, Salt, Apple Green, Flower Shape, Westmoreland, 2 In.	11.00
Lotus, Tray, Ice Cream, Oval, Large	40.00
Louisiana, Cake Stand	45.00
Louisiana, Relish	58.00
Lucere, Toothpick	18.00
Madison, Sugar, Covered, Flint	125.00
Magnet & Grape With Stippled Leaf, Goblet	13.00
Magnet & Grape With Stippled Leaf, Spooner	24.00
Magnet & Grape, Goblet, 6 1/4 In.	7.50
Magnet & Grape, Spooner	22.00
MAIDEN BLUSH, see Banded Portland	
Maine, Bowl, 6 In.	32.00
Maine, Bread Plate, Oval	38.00
Maine, Cake Stand, Green, 8 In.	58.00
Maine, Pitcher, 8 1/2 In.	85.00
Maine, Syrup	125.00
Maltese Cross In Circles, Bread Plate	15.00
Manhattan, Bowl, 9 In.	10.00
Manhattan, Bread Plate, Gold Trim	25.00
Manhattan, Cake Stand, 10 In.	47.50
Manhattan, Plate, Green, 6 In.	22.50
Manhattan, Toothpick, Blue Dots	55.00
Manhattan, Toothpick, Green Eyes	22.00
Maple Leaf, Goblet, Amber	85.00
Mardi Gras, Butter Chip, 6 Piece	50.00
Martha's Tears, Goblet, Amber	15.00
Martyrs, Mug, Lincoln & Garfield, Green	55.00
Maryland, Celery, 11 In.	13.50
Maryland, Toothpick	25.00
Mascotte, Butter	40.00 To 45.00

Mascotte, Celery, Etched 32.00
Mascotte, Creamer 32.00
Mascotte, Sugar, Covered 42.00
Mascotte, Wine 35.00
Masonic, Pitcher, Water, Silver Plated Pouring Lip 75.00
Massachusetts, Creamer, Individual, Gold Trim 15.00
Massachusetts, Mug, Handle, Advertising 30.00
Massachusetts, Punch Cup 12.00
Massachusetts, Sugar, Open, Individual, Gold Trim 15.00
Massachusetts, Toothpick, Metal Filigree Top & Bottom Rims 55.00
Massachusetts, Tumbler, Gold Trim, Flared, 3 1/2 In. 20.00
Massachusetts, Wine 35.00
McKinley Memorial, Bread Plate 23.00
McKinley, Plate 28.00
Medallion Sunburst, Banana Stand 40.00
Medallion, Goblet, Amber 35.00
Medallion, Goblet, Vaseline 40.00
Medallion, Spooner, Apple Green 45.00
Melon & Leaf, Creamer, Electric Blue 55.00
Melrose, Goblet 12.00
Melrose, Salt, 1 3/4 In. 6.00
Melton, Celery, 9 1/8 In. 24.00
Memphis, Spooner, Green, Gold Trim 55.00
Memphis, Table Set, Green, 4 Piece 360.00
Memphis, Water Set, Green, Gold Trim, 5 Piece 225.00
Menagerie, Butter, Covered, Bear, Child's 125.00
Menagerie, Spooner, Fish, Amber, Child's .... 55.00 To 60.00
Michigan, Compote, Open, 9 1/4 In. 62.50
Michigan, Creamer, Pink Blush 85.00
Michigan, Pitcher, Water 55.00
Michigan, Syrup 60.00
Michigan, Table Set, Gold Trim, 4 Piece 225.00
Michigan, Toothpick, Painted Flower, Yellow Stain 50.00
Michigan, Tumbler 25.00
Michigan, Water Set, Pink Blush, Gold Trim, 5 Piece 235.00
Michigan, Water Set, Pink Blush, Gold Trim, 7 Piece 325.00
Minerva, Bread Plate 45.00
Minerva, Bread Plate, Motto, Portrait Center 70.00
Minerva, Cake Stand, 11 In. 90.00
Minerva, Creamer 55.00
Minerva, Goblet 85.00
Minerva, Pitcher 150.00
Minerva, Relish, Motto, Love's Request 30.00
Minerva, Sauce, Footed 14.00
Minerva, Sauce, Portrait In Circles, Footed, 4 In. 15.00
Minnesota, Toothpick, 3 Handles 35.00

Magnet & Grape
with Stippled Leaf

Moon & Star

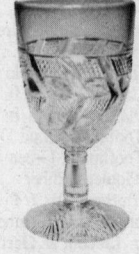

Mitered Diamond

Minnesota, Wine .... 16.50 To 25.00
Mirror, Compote, Standard, Hexagon Paneled Base, 6 1/2 In. 25.00
Missouri, Compote, Jelly 24.50
Missouri, Cruet, Stopper 25.00
Mitered Bars, Celery 25.00
    MITERED DIAMOND POINT, see Mitered Bars
Mitered Diamond, Wine, 4 Piece 100.00
Mitered Frieze, Celery, C.1880 .... 30.00
Mitered Prisms, Wine 16.00
Monkey, Bowl, Open, 8 X 4 1/2 In. 400.00
Monkey, Spooner 95.00
Monkey, Sugar, Flint, Clear, 7 1/8 In. 50.00
Moon & Star, Berry Bowl, 8 In. 25.00
Moon & Star, Bowl, Footed, 6 1/2 In. 25.00
Moon & Star, Compote, 8 In., Pair 50.00
Moon & Star, Cruet, Twisted Applied Handle, Stopper 48.00
Moon & Star, Lamp, Whale Oil, Flint 200.00
Moon & Star, Sauce, Footed 6.00
Moon & Star, Syrup 85.00
Moon & Star, Toothpick 15.00
    MOON & STORK, see Ostrich Looking At Moon
Morning Glory, Eggcup, Flint 65.00
Nail, Butter, Covered, Etched 72.50
Nail, Goblet, Ruby Stained, Set of 4 .... 160.00
Nail, Pitcher, Water 65.00
Nailhead, Butter, Covered 46.50
Nailhead, Cake Stand 22.00
Nailhead, Pitcher, Water 32.50
Nailhead, Plate, 10 In. 10.00
Nailhead, Sugar, Covered .... 20.00 To 24.00
Narrow Swirl, Creamer, 6 In. 16.00
Nellie Bly, Bread Plate, Dated 110.00
Nestor, Creamer, Gold Trim, Enameled 38.00
Nestor, Table Set, Amethyst, 4 Piece 385.00
Nestor, Table Set, Green, 4 Piece 295.00
Nevada, Sugar & Spooner, Covered 35.00
New England Pineapple, Creamer, Footed, Flint, 6 1/2 In. 165.00
New England Pineapple, Eggcup, Flint 30.00
New England Pineapple, Goblet, Flint 30.00
New England Pineapple, Honey, Flint 17.00
New England Pineapple, Spooner, Flint 30.00
New Hampshire, Bowl, 5 3/4 In. 7.00
New Hampshire, Butter, Pink Stained, Gold Trim 125.00
New Hampshire, Saltshaker, Pink Stained, Original Top 18.00
New Hampshire, Spooner 40.00
New Hampshire, Spooner, Ruby Stained 45.00

Maine

Lincoln Drape

New England Pineapple

Pleat & Panel

Open Rose

Paneled Forget–Me–Not

New Hampshire, Sugar, Covered	48.00
New Hampshire, Syrup	48.00
New Hampshire, Water Set, Pink Stained, Gold Trim, 7 Piece	75.00
New Jersey, Berry Set, Gold Trim, Scalloped Saucer, 7 Piece	125.00
New Jersey, Butter, Covered, Gold Trim	68.00
New Jersey, Goblet, Gold Trim	36.50
New Jersey, Pitcher, Water, Gold	45.00
New Jersey, Plate, 10 1/2 In.	16.00
New Jersey, Plate, 11 In.	22.50
Newport, Berry Bowl, Amethyst, Large	23.00
Niagara Falls, Tray, Water, Frosted Scene	125.00
Niagara, Goblet, Gold Trim	16.00
Nursery Rhymes, Berry Set, Child's, 7 Piece	145.00
Nursery Rhymes, Butter, Child's, Covered	55.00
Nursery Rhymes, Mug, Child's, Little Miss Muffet	18.00
Nursery Rhymes, Punch Bowl, Blue	225.00
Nursery Rhymes, Punch Cup, Child's	16.00
Nursery Rhymes, Punch Set, 6 Piece	190.00
Nursery Rhymes, Punch Set, Child's, 7 Piece	225.00
Nursery Rhymes, Sugar, Covered, Child's	50.00
Nursery Rhymes, Table Set, Child's, 4 Piece	225.00 To 300.00
Nursery Rhymes, Tumbler	18.00
Nursery Rhymes, Water Set, Child's, 7 Piece	250.00 To 260.00
O'Hara Diamond, Cruet, Matching Stopper, Ruby Stained	175.00
OAKEN BUCKET, see Wooden Pail	
Odd Fellows, Goblet	28.00
Ohio, Goblet	55.00
ONE HUNDRED ONE, see One–O–One	
One–O–One, Butter, Covered, C.1870	65.00
One–O–One, Creamer, C.1870	45.00
One–O–One, Goblet, C.1870	40.00
One–O–One, Lamp, Oil	85.00
One–O–One, Pitcher, Water	115.00 To 145.00
One–O–One, Plate, C.1870, 7 In.	25.00
One–O–One, Plate, C.1870, 8 In.	30.00
One–O–One, Relish, Oval, C.1870	15.00
One–O–One, Spooner, C.1870	45.00
One–O–One, Sugar, Covered, C.1870	55.00
ONE–THOUSAND EYE, see Thousand Eye	
Open Rose, Eggcup	20.00
Open Rose, Goblet	18.00
Opposing Pyramids, Pitcher, Water	48.00
OREGON, see also Beaded Loop; Skilton	
Oregon, Bread Plate	25.00
Oregon, Pitcher, Water	35.00 To 40.00
Oregon, Saltshaker	15.00

Oregon, Sugar, Open 18.00
    ORION, see Cathedral
Ostrich Looking At Moon, Goblet 50.00
Oval Miter, Goblet 25.00
Oval Star, Spooner, Child's 17.00
Oval Star, Table Set, Child's, 4 Piece .... 67.50 To 85.00
Oval Star, Tankard, Child's 65.00
Oval Star, Water Set, Child's, 7 Piece 95.00
Owl & Possum, Goblet ....80.00 To 125.00
Owl & Pussy Cat, Dish, Cheese ....290.00 To 300.00
Paddlewheel, Sugar, Open 20.00
Paisley, Creamer, Green Eyes, Gold Traces 21.00
Paling, Creamer 18.00
Palm Beach, Tumbler, Vaseline 85.00
Palm Leaf Fan, Bowl, 7 In. 8.00
Palmette, Compote, 7 3/4 X 8 In. 30.00
Palmette, Sauce, 3 3/8 In. 5.00
Palmette, Sugar, Open 20.00
Paneled Daisy, Bowl, Serving, Nested, Set of 3 .... 49.00
Paneled Daisy, Plate, Flint, Square, 9 In. 20.00
Paneled Daisy, Relish 15.00
Paneled Daisy, Tray, Water, 11 In. 20.00
Paneled Diamond Point, Compote, Open, 9 1/2 In. 35.00
Paneled Diamond–Cut & Fan, Creamer 17.00
Paneled Diamonds, Goblet 22.50
    PANELED DOGWOOD, see Dogwood
Paneled Fern, Spooner 20.00
Paneled Forget–Me–Not, Cake Stand, Blue 50.00
Paneled Forget–Me–Not, Compote, Covered, Pedestal 48.00
Paneled Forget–Me–Not, Pitcher, Milk 60.00
Paneled Forget–Me–Not, Pitcher, Water 48.00
Paneled Forget–Me–Not, Spooner 25.00
Paneled Forty–Four, Pitcher, Rose & Gold Flashed, 12 In. 75.00
Paneled Grape Band, Compote, Frosted, Open, 9 In. 45.00
Paneled Grape Band, Eggcup 18.50
Paneled Grape, Cake Stand, Skirted 45.00
Paneled Grape, Pitcher, Vine Handle, 8 3/4 In. 65.00
Paneled Heather, Bowl, 9 X 3 In. 28.50
Paneled Heather, Compote, Covered, Jelly 30.00
Paneled Iris, Wine 12.00
Paneled Jewel, Wine, Vaseline 25.00
Paneled Nightshade, Goblet, Amber 35.00
Paneled Nightshade, Wine 20.00
Paneled Star & Square, Wine 10.00
Paneled Stippled Scroll, Celery 28.50
Paneled Thistle, Bowl, 6 In. 7.50
Paneled Thistle, Bowl, 9 In. 16.00
Paneled Thistle, Cake Stand 18.00
Paneled Thistle, Rose Bowl 16.00
Paneled Thistle, Tumbler, Ruby & Gold Trim On Panels 45.00
Paneled Wheat, Spooner, Scalloped Rim 45.00
Parrot, Goblet 35.00
Parrot, Hearts & Berries, Tankard, Wheel Engraved 75.00
    PATTEE CROSS, see Broughton
Pavonia, Cake Stand, 9 In. 35.00
Pavonia, Celery 25.00
Pavonia, Creamer, Etched 42.50
Pavonia, Goblet 30.00
Pavonia, Pitcher, Water, Ruby Stained 95.00
Pavonia, Table Set, Ruby Stained, 4 Piece 265.00
Pavonia, Tumbler, Etched 24.00
Pavonia, Tumbler, Ruby Stained 47.50
Pavonia, Water Set, Flashed, 7 Piece 350.00
Peace & Plenty, Relish, Deep Blue, Grape Handles 55.00

Peacock Feather, Butter, Covered 60.00
Peacock Feather, Cruet, Decanter, 10 1/2 In. 50.00
    PEACOCK'S EYE, see Peacock Feather
Peek–A–Boo, Toothpick, Amber 30.00
    PENNSYLVANIA HAND, see also Pennsylvania
Pennsylvania Hand, Compote, Covered, 8 In. 92.50
Pennsylvania Hand, Goblet 25.00
    PENNSYLVANIA, see also Balder; Pennsylvania Hand
Pennsylvania, Butter, Child's 65.00
Pennsylvania, Butter, Covered, Child's 60.00
Pennsylvania, Creamer, Green 40.00
Pennsylvania, Goblet 19.00
Pennsylvania, Shot Glass, Gold Trim 18.00
Pennsylvania, Table Set, Child's, 4 Piece .... 175.00 To 210.00
Pennsylvania, Tumbler 15.00
Pennsylvania, Tumbler, Red Flashed 48.00
Pennsylvania, Wine, Green .... 30.00 To 35.00
Pequot, Saucer, Footed, Amber 14.00
Periwinkle, Cruet, Pink 110.00
Perkins, Compote, 5 1/4 In. 12.00
Persian Spear, Goblet, Flint 85.00
Pert, Butter, Child's, Covered 65.00
Petticoat, Cruet, Vaseline, Gold Trim, Original Stopper 275.00
Petticoat, Sugar, Covered, Vaseline, Gold Trim 65.00
Petticoat, Toothpick, Vaseline 65.00
Pigs In Corn, Goblet 350.00
    PILLAR & BULL'S–EYE, see Thistle
Pillow Encircled, Bowl, Ruby Flashed, 3 X 7 In. 27.00
Pillow Encircled, Butter, Ruby Flashed 95.00
    PINAFORE, see Actress
Pineapple & Fan, Syrup, Emerald Green 475.00
    PITT HONEYCOMB, see Honeycomb
    PLAIN SMOCKING, see Smocking
Pleat & Panel, Cake Stand, 11 In. 45.00
Pleat & Panel, Plate, 7 In. 22.00
Plume, Bowl, 6 In. 25.00
Plume, Cake Stand 45.00
Plume, Compote, Crimped, 7 In. 25.00
Plume, Compote, Open, Crimped Edge, 8 In. 32.00
Plume, Tumbler, Ruby Flashed, Word Papa & Date 1898 .... 25.00
Plume, Water Set, Vertical Plumes, 5 Piece 125.00
    POINTED PANELED DAISY & BUTTON, see Queen
    POINTED THUMBPRINT, see Almond Thumbprint
Polar Bear, Bowl, Waste 85.00
Polar Bear, Goblet .... 100.00 To 110.00
Polar Bear, Pitcher, Water 250.00
Polar Bear, Tray, Water, Frosted, Marked 185.00
Polar Bear, Tray, Water, Frosted, Oval 125.00
Popcorn, Cake Stand, 11 In. 78.00
Popcorn, Creamer, With Ears 47.50
Pope Leo XIII, Bread Plate 30.00

If you move glass in cold weather be sure to let it sit at room temperature for several hours before you try unpacking it. The glass will break more easily if there is an abrupt temperature change.

Rose in Snow   Ribbon Candy   Princess Feather

PORTLAND WITH DIAMOND POINT BAND, see Galloway; Virginia

Portland, Butter, Covered	30.00
Portland, Cruet, Original Stopper	17.50
Portland, Tumbler	12.00

POTTED PLANT, see Flower Pot

Powder & Shot, Eggcup, Flint	45.00
Powder & Shot, Goblet	58.00
Powder & Shot, Spooner, Flint	48.00
Powder & Shot, Sugar, Covered, Flint	80.00

PRAYER RUG, see Horseshoe

Pressed Diamond, Bowl, Blue, 7 1/2 In.	20.00
Pressed Leaf, Eggcup, Flint	21.50
Primrose, Wine	22.00

PRINCESS FEATHER, see also Lacy Medallion

Princess Feather, Butter, Covered	50.00
Princess Feather, Celery	28.00 To 38.00
Princess Feather, Creamer	45.00
Princess Feather, Sugar, Covered	45.00 To 65.00
Princess Feather, Sugar, Open	14.00
Priscilla, Tumbler	32.00
Prism & Flute, Goblet, Flint	32.00
Prism & Sawtooth, Compote, Low, Flint	80.00
Prism & Sawtooth, Goblet	22.50
Prism With Diamond Points, Goblet, Flint	25.00
Prize, Spooner, Ruby Stained	65.00
Prize, Table Set, Ruby Stained, 4 Piece	278.00
Psyche & Cupid, Celery	35.00
Psyche & Cupid, Goblet	47.50
Quaker Lady, Cake Stand, 10 1/4 In.	50.00

Roman Rosette   Rexford   Primrose

Quartered Block, Toothpick 24.50
    QUEEN ANNE, see Viking
Queen's Necklace, Vase, 8 3/4 In. 40.00
Queen, Goblet, Amber 24.00
Quintec, Cake Stand 20.00
Quixote, Wine 14.50
Racing Deer, Pitcher, Water 110.00
Railroad Train, Bread Plate, Clear, 12 In. 205.00
Raindrop, Tumbler 6.00
Rebecca At The Well, Teapot 85.00
Red Block, Butter, Covered, Ruby Stained 70.00
Red Block, Creamer 60.00
Red Block, Goblet, Ruby Stained 30.00
Red Block, Pitcher, Water, Ruby Stained .... 115.00 To 125.00
Red Block, Spooner, Ruby Stained 28.00
Red Block, Sugar, Covered 75.00
Red Block, Tumbler, Ruby Stained 22.00
Red Block, Wine, Ruby Stained 37.50
Regal Block, Wine, Gold 12.00
    REGENT, see Leaf Medallion
Reticulated Cord, Compote, Covered, Amber, Pedestal 58.00
Reticulated Cord, Pitcher, Amber, 9 In. 95.00
Reverse 44, Berry Set, Platinum Trim, 5 Piece 125.00
Reverse 44, Tumbler, Pink & Gold Design 18.00
Reverse Torpedo, Berry Bowl, Crimped Edge, 10 3/4 In. 65.00
Reverse Torpedo, Bowl, Ruby Stained, 7 In. 22.50
Reverse Torpedo, Bowl, Shallow, 12 In. 75.00
Reverse Torpedo, Cake Stand 85.00
Reverse Torpedo, Compote, Jelly 40.00
Reverse Torpedo, Dish, Ruffled, 11 3/4 X 2 3/4 In. 85.00
Reverse Torpedo, Salt & Pepper 55.00
Rex, Spooner 30.00
Rex, Water Set, Child's, 7 Piece 85.00
Rexford, Bowl, 8 3/4 In. 12.00
Ribbed Ellipse, Rose Bowl, Large 20.00
Ribbed Grape, Goblet, Buttermilk, Flint, 5 1/4 In. 15.00
    RIBBED OPAL, see Beatty Rib
Ribbed Palm, Goblet, Flint, 6 1/4 In. 12.50
Ribbed Palm, Spooner 45.00
Ribbed Palm, Sugar, Open, Flint 15.00
Ribbed Sawtooth, Table Set, 4 Piece 175.00
Ribbon Candy, Cake Stand .... 20.00 To 25.00
Ribbon Candy, Cake Stand, Child's, Green 55.00
Ribbon Candy, Sugar, Footed 12.00
Ribbon Candy, Syrup, Original Lid 75.00
Ribbon, Cake Stand, Green 45.00
Ribbon, Compote, Open, Dolphin Pedestal 95.00
Ribbon, Sugar, Covered 58.00
Rising Sun, Water Set, Gold Trim, 7 Piece .... 85.00 To 95.00
Rising Sun, Water Set, Green, Gold, 5 Piece 195.00
Roanoke Star, Relish 18.00
Robin Hood, Tumbler 20.00
    ROCHELLE, see Princess Feather
Rock of Ages, Bread Plate 60.00
Roman Rosette, Bread Plate, Oval 35.00
Roman Rosette, Compote, Jelly, Covered 68.00
Roman Rosette, Pitcher, Water, Miniature 65.00
Roman Rosette, Wine .... 24.00 To 30.00
Rooster, Butter, Covered, Child's .... 160.00 To 170.00
Rooster, Creamer, Child's .... 100.00 To 120.00
Rope & Thumbprint, Compote, Open, Amber 30.00
Rope & Thumbprint, Creamer, Vaseline 35.00
Rope Bands, Wine 18.50
Rose In Snow, Bread Plate 35.00

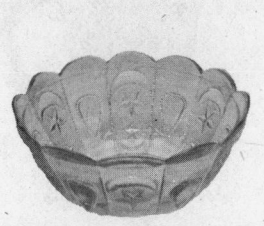  

Shrine   Shell & Tassel   Sawtooth

Rose In Snow, Cake Stand	85.00
Rose In Snow, Compote, Open, Low Standard, 7 In.	40.00
Rose In Snow, Goblet, Amber	40.00
Rose In Snow, Pickle, Handles	19.50
Rose In Snow, Pitcher, Water, Amber	115.00
Rose In Snow, Plate, Handles, 10 In.	33.00
Rose In Snow, Spooner	28.50
Rose Leaves, Goblet	20.00
Rose Sprig, Tumbler, Blue	30.00
Rosette & Palms, Banana Stand	35.00
Rosette Band, Compote, 6 1/4 In.	16.00
Rosette Band, Creamer, Ruby Stained	60.00
ROSETTE MEDALLION, see Feather Duster	
Rosette With Palms, Celery, Flat	10.00
Rosette, Compote, 4 1/2 In.	8.00
Rosette, Compote, Jelly	10.00 To 22.00
Rosette, Pitcher, Milk	40.00
Rosette, Relish	12.00
Rosette, Saltshaker	23.00
Royal Crystal, Syrup	48.00
Royal Ivy, Butter, Clear To Cranberry, Covered	150.00
Royal Ivy, Pitcher, Water, Clear To Cranberry	175.00 To 265.00
Royal Ivy, Salt & Pepper	125.00
Royal Ivy, Saltshaker	55.00
Royal Ivy, Sugar Shaker, Cased Rainbow	175.00
Royal Ivy, Sugar Shaker, Frosted, Clear To Cranberry	135.00
Royal Ivy, Syrup, Cased Rainbow	395.00
Royal Lady, Pitcher, Water	45.00
Royal Oak, Pitcher, Water, Clear To Cranberry	275.00
Royal Oak, Saltshaker	55.00
Royal Oak, Sauce, Clear To Cranberry	45.00
Royal Oak, Sugar Shaker, Frosted, Clear To Cranberry	165.00
Royal Oak, Toothpick, Frosted, Clear To Cranberry	105.00
Royal Oak, Tumbler, Clear To Cranberry	80.00
Royal, Spooner, Ruby Stained	32.00
RUBY ROSETTE, see Pillow Encircled	
RUBY THUMBPRINT, see King's Crown	
S–Repeat, Cruet, Original Top, Green	75.00
S–Repeat, Salt & Pepper, Green, Gold Trim	45.00
S–Repeat, Tray, Condiment, Green	25.00
S–Repeat, Wine, Blue, Gold Trim	30.00
Sandwich Ivy, Creamer, Large	180.00
SANDWICH LOOP, see Hairpin	
SAWTOOTH BAND, see Amazon	
Sawtooth Circle, Salt	27.50
Sawtooth, Compote, Covered, Flint	125.00

Three Face   Star Medallion   Squirrel

Sawtooth, Spooner, Cobalt Blue	65.00
Sawtoothed Honeycomb, Celery	21.00
Scalloped Diamond Point, Berry Bowl, 5 Piece	28.00
Scalloped Tape, Bread Plate, Bread Is Staff of Life	45.00
Scarab, Goblet, Flint	110.00
Scroll With Acanthus, Berry Bowl, Master, Blue Opal	58.00
Scroll With Flowers, Eggcup, Handle	22.50
Scroll With Flowers, Pitcher, Milk	42.00
Scroll, Sugar, Covered	25.00
Seed Pod, Creamer, Blue, Gold Trim	70.00
Seed Pod, Salt & Pepper, Blue	47.50
Seneca Loop, Celery, Flint, 10 In.	45.00
Seneca Loop, Goblet	16.00
Sequoia, Goblet	20.00
Serrated Teardrop, Cracker Jar, Covered	75.00
SHEAF & DIAMOND, see Fickle Block	
Shell & Jewel, Bowl, 7 3/4 In.	20.00
Shell & Jewel, Pitcher, Water	25.00 To 45.00
Shell & Jewel, Tumbler, Blue	35.00
Shell & Jewel, Water Set, 7 Piece	135.00
Shell & Tassel, Bowl, Oval, 10 In.	16.00
Shell & Tassel, Cake Stand, Square, 8 In.	48.00
Shell & Tassel, Compote, Jelly	18.50
Shell & Tassel, Compote, Square, Large	40.00
Shell & Tassel, Oyster Plate	195.00
Shell & Tassel, Spooner	38.00
Shell & Tassel, Sugar, Covered, Dog Finial	95.00
Sheraton, Compote, Open, 7 In.	28.00
Sheraton, Creamer	20.00
Sheraton, Sugar, Covered	28.00
Shield, Celery, Frosted	28.50
Shield, Cruet, Original Stopper	65.00
Shoshone, Cake Stand, Green	38.00
Shoshone, Compote, Jelly, Green	27.00
Shoshone, Cruet, Original Stopper, Green	95.00
Shoshone, Salt, Double Scalloped, 1 3/4 In.	6.00
Shoshone, Syrup, Gold Trim	110.00
Shoshone, Toothpick, Gold Trim	20.00 To 25.00
Shovel, Goblet	15.00
Shrine, Pitcher, Water	45.00
Shrine, Relish	14.50 To 27.00
Shuttle, Mug, Handle, 3 1/4 In.	35.00
Shuttle, Punch Cup	8.50
Skilton, Tumbler, Ruby Flashed	35.00
Slewed Horseshoe, Punch Set, 1909, 13 Piece	75.00
Smocking, Butter, Covered, Design	55.00

Smocking, Spooner 25.00
Smooth Diamond, Creamer 26.00
Smooth Diamond, Pitcher, Water 50.00
Snail, Celery .... 45.00 To 50.00
Snail, Pitcher, Water 88.00
    SPANISH AMERICAN, see Admiral Dewey
    SPANISH COIN, see Columbian Coin
Spearhead, Goblet 16.00
Spearpoint Band, Toothpick, Ruby Stained 125.00
Spearpoint, Creamer, Frosted Band, Ruby Stained 42.00
Spinning Star, Tumbler 19.00
Spirea Band, Goblet, Amber .... 18.00 To 25.00
Split Log, Compote, Covered, 7 1/2 In. 58.00
Sprig, Celery 36.50
Squared Ashburton, Wine, Flint 32.00
Squat Pineapple, Sugar, Open, Flint 35.00
Squirrel In Bower, Pitcher, Water 165.00
Squirrel, Celery 175.00
Squirrel, Teapot 39.50
Star & Crescent, Table Set, 4 Piece 150.00
Star & Oval, Tumbler 9.00
    STAR & PUNTY, see Moon & Star
Star Band, Butter, Covered 22.00
Star In Bull's-Eye, Toothpick 24.50
Star Medallion, Compote, Jelly 10.00
Star of Bethlehem, Relish, 8 1/2 In. 18.50
Star of David, Spooner, Footed, Child's 32.00
Star Rosette, Creamer 22.00
Star Rosetted, Bread Plate 25.00
Star Rosetted, Relish 12.00
Starred Cosmos, Water Set, 6 Piece 115.00
Stars & Bars, Table Set, Amber, 4 Piece 195.00
    STATES, see The States
Stippled Arrow, Mug, Child's 12.00
Stippled Cherry, Plate, 9 1/4 In. 18.00
    STIPPLED DAHLIA, see Dahlia
Stippled Daisy, Tray, Water, 10 In. 17.00
Stippled Fans, Bread Plate 25.00
Stippled Forget-Me-Not, Plate, Baby, Ball Center, 7 In. 60.00
Stippled Grape & Festoon, Spooner .... 24.00 To 30.00
Stippled Grape & Festoon, Sugar, Open 14.00
    STIPPLED PANELED FLOWER, see Maine
Stippled Peppers, Creamer 28.00
    STIPPLED SCROLL, see Scroll
Stippled Star, Spooner 24.00
    STORK LOOKING AT THE MOON, see Ostrich Looking At Moon
Stork, Spooner, Iowa City 50.00
Strawberry & Fan Variant, Compote, Open, 8 X 9 In. 95.00
Strawberry, Spooner 15.00
Strigil, Table Set, 4 Piece 85.00
Sunbeam, Toothpick, Green 25.00
Sunflower, Creamer 25.00
Sunk Honeycomb, Goblet, Etched 38.00
Sunk Honeycomb, Wine, Ruby Flashed 35.00
    SUNKEN BUTTONS, see Mitered Diamond
    SUNRISE, see Rising Sun
Swag Block, Goblet 35.00
Swag With Brackets, Compote, Jelly, Green 40.00
Swag With Brackets, Table Set, Vaseline 460.00
Swan, Butter, Covered 150.00
Swan, Creamer 35.00
Sweetheart, Table Set, 4 Piece, Child's 110.00
Swirl & Panel, Toothpick 22.00
Tacoma, Butter, Covered, Ruby Stained 90.00

Tacoma, Spooner, Amber Stained	60.00
Tandem Bicycle, Goblet	35.00
Tappan, Butter, Child's, Covered, Amber	35.00
Tappan, Creamer, Child's, Amber	15.00
Tappan, Spooner, Child's	12.00
Tarentum's Victoria, Bottle, Water	35.00
Tarentum's Victoria, Jug, Stopper	55.00
Teardrop & Tassel, Butter	50.00
Teardrop & Tassel, Compote, Open	45.00
Teardrop & Tassel, Tumbler, Cobalt Blue	50.00
TEARDROP & THUMBPRINT, see Teardrop	
Teardrop, Butter, Covered, Blue	85.00
Teardrop, Plate, 8 1/2 In.	6.00
Teardrop, Sherbet	6.00
Teardrop, Tumbler, Water, Footed	7.00
Tennessee, Bowl, Flat, 6 1/2 In.	30.00
Tennessee, Pitcher, Milk, 7 In.	68.00
Tennessee, Relish	27.50
Tepee, Dish, Design On Sides, Flat Rim, 1 3/4 In.	10.00
Texas Bull's–Eye, Goblet	22.00
Texas Bull's–Eye, Wine	15.00
Texas, Creamer, Individual	10.00
Texas, Cruet, Original Stopper	65.00
Texas, Toothpick, Gold Trim	25.00 To 38.00
The States, Compote, 9 1/2 In.	80.00
The States, Toothpick, Gold Trim, Rectangular	30.00
The States, Tumbler, Gold Trim	18.50
Theodore Roosevelt, Bread Plate, Frosted Center	120.00
Theodore Roosevelt, Bread Plate, Square Deal	85.00
Thistle, Bowl, 8 In.	10.00
Thistle, Candlestick, Pewter Insert, 9 1/2 In., Pair	125.00
Thistle, Pitcher, Water	75.00
Thousand Eye, Butter, Covered, Knob Finial, Green	75.00 To 85.00
Thousand Eye, Celery, Knob Stem, Green	55.00 To 65.00
Thousand Eye, Honey, Covered, Green	125.00
Thousand Eye, Mug, Amber	18.00
Thousand Eye, Mug, Vaseline	25.00
Thousand Eye, Pitcher, Milk, 7 1/4 In.	20.00
Thousand Eye, Plate, Folded Corners, 10 In.	30.00
Thousand Eye, Plate, Vaseline, 8 In.	26.00
Thousand Eye, Saltshaker, Amber	20.00
Thousand Eye, Spooner, Blue	35.00
Thousand Eye, String Holder	35.00
Thousand Eye, Syrup	140.00
Thousand Eye, Toothpick, Vaseline	42.50
Thousand Eye, Tumbler, Cranberry	37.00
Thousand Eye, Wine, Blue	40.00
Three Birds, Mug	60.00
Three Face, Butter, Pedestal, Satin Stem, Finial, Covered	160.00
Three Face, Cake Stand, 9 In.	125.00
Three Face, Celery, Etched	110.00
Three Face, Compote, Covered, Low Standard, Frosted	75.00
Three Face, Compote, Pedestal	110.00
Three Face, Creamer, Frosted Stem	115.00 To 135.00
Three Face, Goblet	65.00
Three Face, Sugar, Open	75.00
THREE GRACES, see also Three Face	
Three Graces, Bread Plate	52.50 To 78.00
Three Panel, Butter, Covered, Amber	45.00
Three Panel, Compote, Amber, 7 3/4 X 4 In.	38.00
Three Panel, Compote, Open, Footed, Blue, 9 In.	48.50
Three Panel, Compote, Open, Low Foot	12.50
Three Panel, Creamer, Canary	28.00
Three Panel, Pitcher, Water, Amber	85.00

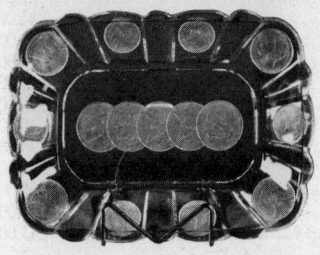

U.S. Coin   Tree of Life   Thumbprint

Three Panel, Spooner, Vaseline	26.00
Three Presidents, Bread Plate, Frosted	55.00
THREE SISTERS, see Three Face	
Thumbprint & Twirl Stem, Wine	14.00
Thumbprint, Bowl, Footed, Flint, 5 1/4 In.	15.00
Thumbprint, Goblet, Flint	55.00
Thumbprint, Goblet, Ruby Stained	25.00
Thumbprint, Pitcher, Water, Ruby Stained	125.00
Thumbprint, Toothpick, Ruby Stained	22.00
Thumbprint, Tumbler, Footed, Flint	39.50
Thumbprint, Water Set, Ruby Stained, 6 Piece	285.00
Thumbprint, Wine	23.00
Tiny Finecut, Decanter Set, Ruby Stained, Gold Trim, 7 Piece	200.00
TOBIN, see Leaf & Star	
Tokyo, Spooner, Green	35.00
TOM THUMB, see Humpty–Dumpty	
Torpedo, Banana Stand	55.00
Torpedo, Bowl, 9 In.	30.00
Torpedo, Celery, 6 1/2 In.	45.00
Torpedo, Compote, Jelly	43.00
Torpedo, Creamer	25.00
Torpedo, Decanter, 1 Qt.	135.00
Torpedo, Pitcher, Milk	50.00
Torpedo, Pitcher, Tankard, Ruby Stained	65.00
Torpedo, Salt, 8 Notched Teardrops, 1 1/2 In.	20.00
Tree of Life With Hand, Compote, Open, Frosted, 5 1/4 In.	50.00
Tree of Life, Butter, Covered	125.00
Tree of Life, Cake Stand, Frosted, 10 In.	95.00
Tree of Life, Compote, Open, 10 In.	95.00
Tree of Life, Creamer, Frosted Base & Stem	55.00
Tree of Life, Dish, 4–Leaf Clover Shape, Blue	10.00
Tree of Life, Pitcher, Water	72.50
Tree of Life, Pittsburgh, Sauce, Star Shape, 8 In.	30.00
Tree of Life, Portland, Cake Stand	45.00
Tree of Life, Portland, Compote, Open, Child's, 8 In.	200.00
Tree of Life, Portland, Compote, Signed Davis, 11 In.	135.00
Tree of Life, Portland, Sauce, 4 In.	22.00
Triple Thumbprint, Sugar, Covered, Gilded	38.00
Triple Triangle, Goblet, Ruby Stained	42.50
Triple Triangle, Pitcher, Water, Ruby Stained	85.00
Triple Triangle, Sugar, Ruby Stained	45.00
Truncated Cube, Decanter Set, Tray, 4 Wines, Ruby Stained	260.00
Truncated Cube, Saltshaker	25.00
Truncated Cube, Toothpick	23.00
Truncated Cube, Wine, Ruby Stained	25.00
Tulip & Honeycomb, Butter, Covered, Oval, Child's	35.00

Tulip & Honeycomb, Creamer, Child's 18.00
Tulip & Honeycomb, Punch Bowl, Child's 32.00
Tulip & Honeycomb, Punch Set, Child's, 7 Piece 85.00
Tulip & Honeycomb, Spooner, Child's 18.00
Tulip & Honeycomb, Table Set, Child's, 4 Piece .... 85.00 To 95.00
Tulip & Honeycomb, Vegetable, Oval, Child's 75.00
Tulip With Sawtooth, Butter, Covered 75.00
Tulip With Sawtooth, Salt, Tulip Shape On Pedestal, 3 In. 20.00
Tulip With Sawtooth, Wine 20.00
Tulip, Compote, Covered, Flint, 7 1/4 X 12 1/2 In. 45.00
Tulip, Toothpick 65.00
Twin Snowshoes, Creamer, Child's 20.00
Twin Snowshoes, Table Set, Child's, 4 Piece 245.00
      TWINKLE STAR, see Utah
Twist, Table Set, Child's, 4 Piece 75.00
Two Panel, Goblet, Apple Green 38.00
Two Panel, Pitcher, Water, Amber 50.00
U.S.Coin, Bread Plate 345.00
U.S.Coin, Butter, Covered 525.00
U.S.Coin, Cake Plate, Frosted Coins, 7 In. 485.00
U.S.Coin, Compote, High Standard, Covered, 8 In. 535.00
U.S.Coin, Lamp, Dollar Stem, Clear Font 850.00
U.S.Coin, Mug, Handle, Dollar Medallions 345.00
U.S.Coin, Pitcher, Water 500.00
U.S.Coin, Sauce, Flat 90.00
U.S.Coin, Sauce, Footed 120.00
U.S.Coin, Spooner, Quarter Dollar Medallions 225.00
U.S.Coin, Tray, Water, Dollars 425.00
U.S.Grant, Bread Plate, Frosted Bust 65.00
U.S.Grant, Peace, Plate, Green 40.00
U.S.Rib, Butter, Covered, Square, Green 66.00
U.S.Rib, Table Set, Gold Trim, 4 Piece 150.00
U.S.Rib, Toothpick, Green, Gold Trim 50.00
Utah, Pitcher, Water .... 28.00 To 45.00
Valencia Waffle, Cake Stand, Amber 65.00
Valencia Waffle, Compote, Covered, 8 In. 45.00
Valencia Waffle, Goblet 24.00
Vermont, Toothpick, Green 35.00
Vermont, Toothpick, Green, Gold Trim 38.00
Vermont, Tumbler, Green, Gold Trim 47.00
Victoria, Compote, Flint, 10 1/4 X 15 1/4 In. 215.00
Viking, Butter, Covered 25.00
Viking, Compote, Covered, Low, 7 1/2 In. 95.00
Viking, Creamer .... 29.00 To 35.00
Viking, Goblet, Amber 24.00
Viking, Pitcher 80.00

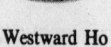

Westward Ho

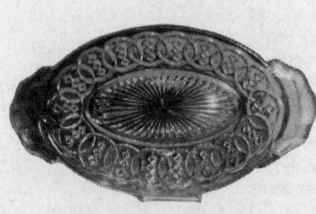

Washington Centennial

Waffle & Thumbprint

Viking, Spooner	40.00
Viking, Sugar, Covered	28.00 To 70.00
Viking, Syrup, Pewter Top, Dated 1871	65.00
Vine & Beads, Creamer, Child's, Teal Green	85.00
Vine & Beads, Spooner, Stippled, Child's	60.00
Vine & Beads, Sugar, Child's, Covered, Teal Green	105.00
VIRGINIA, see also Galloway	
Virginia, Pitcher, Water, Child's	25.00
Virginia, Spooner, Yellow Flashed	35.00
Waffle & Thumbprint, Bottle, Bar, Flint	30.00
Waffle & Thumbprint, Sugar, Covered, Flint	50.00
Waffle & Thumbprint, Tumbler, Whiskey	75.00
Waffle, Cruet	35.00
Washington Centennial, Cake Stand	35.00 To 60.00
Washington Centennial, Relish, Bearclaw Handles, 9 5/8 In.	22.00
Washington, Salt, New England Glass, 2 In.	15.00
Washington, Sugar, Covered, Frosted, 7 3/4 In.	65.00
Waterford, Goblet, 8 1/2 In.	46.00
Way's Currant, Goblet	16.00
Wedding Bells, Spooner, Gold Trim	40.00
Wedding Ring, Goblet	40.00 To 55.00
Wee Branches, Cup & Saucer	65.00
Wee Branches, Cup, Child's	15.00
Wee Branches, Plate, Child's, 3 1/2 In.	55.00 To 60.00
Wee Branches, Plate, Child's, Set of 6	150.00
Wee Branches, Table Set, Child's, 4 Piece	250.00 To 385.00
Westward Ho, Bread Plate, Frosted Deer Handles	90.00
Westward Ho, Compote, 6 In.	90.00
Westward Ho, Compote, 8 In.	70.00
Westward Ho, Compote, Covered, 6 In.	90.00 To 165.00
Westward Ho, Compote, Covered, 7 X 10 1/2 In.	130.00
Westward Ho, Compote, Covered, 8 In.	250.00
Westward Ho, Compote, Open, Low, 8 In.	75.00
Westward Ho, Compote, Oval, 8 3/4 X 6 1/4 In.	125.00
Westward Ho, Creamer, Dog Handle	70.00
Westward Ho, Goblet	48.00 To 95.00
Westward Ho, Jar, Covered, 7 In.	95.00
Westward Ho, Pitcher, Water, Dog's Head Handle	185.00
Westward Ho, Relish	65.00 To 75.00
Westward Ho, Sauce, Footed, 4 In.	23.00
Westward Ho, Saucer	30.00
Westward Ho, Spooner	30.00
Westward Ho, Sugar, Covered	85.00
Westward Ho, Sugar, Open	35.00
Wheat & Barley, Creamer	20.00 To 22.00
Wheat & Barley, Pitcher, Amber	65.00
Wheat & Barley, Saltshaker, Blue	45.00
Wheat & Barley, Sugar, Covered	28.00 To 32.00
Wheat & Barley, Tumbler, Footed, Blue	28.00
Wheat Sheaf, Dish, Beaded Rim, Prisms & Stars Sides, 2 In.	8.00
Wheat Sheaf, Punch Cup, Doll's	23.00
Wheel & Comma, Compote, Covered	75.00
Wheel & Comma, Pitcher, Water	30.00
Wheeling, Plate, 3 Lacy Hearts, 5 3/4 In.	35.00
Whirligig, Butter	20.00
Whirligig, Butter, Child's, Covered	22.00
Whirligig, Creamer, Child's	18.00
Whirligig, Punch Bowl, Child's	20.00
Whirligig, Punch Cup, Child's	8.00
Whirligig, Table Set, Gold Trim, 4 Piece	160.00
Wild Bouquet, Cruet, Blue	285.00
Wild Bouquet, Spooner, Green	65.00
Wild Rose With Scrolling, Creamer, Child's, Emerald Green	125.00
Wildflower, Bread Plate, Square	28.00

Wedding Ring   Wildflower   Westward Ho

Wildflower, Celery 28.00
Wildflower, Compote, Jelly, Green 65.00
Wildflower, Creamer, Amber ....22.50 To 45.00
Wildflower, Goblet, Amber 37.00
Wildflower, Goblet, Vaseline ....40.00 To 45.00
Wildflower, Pitcher, Water ....40.00 To 47.50
Wildflower, Spooner, Amber 35.00
Wildflower, Sugar, Covered 32.50
Wildflower, Syrup, Amber ....155.00 To 200.00
Wildflower, Syrup, Blue 165.00
Wildflower, Tray, Water 42.50
Wildflower, Tumbler 22.00
Wildflower, Water Set, Green, 7 Piece 325.00
Willow Oak, Cake Stand, Amber, 10 In. 60.00
Willow Oak, Compote, Open, Pedestal, Amber 45.00
Willow Oak, Creamer 21.00
Willow Oak, Goblet 33.50
Willow Oak, Pitcher, Milk 40.00
Willow Oak, Pitcher, Water 45.00
Willow Oak, Table Set, 4 Piece 175.00
Willow Oak, Tray, Water 28.00
Willow Oak, Tumbler 45.00
Windflower, Bowl, Oval, 5 X 7 In. 27.50
Windflower, Compote, Open 25.00
Windflower, Creamer ....22.50 To 27.50
WISCONSIN, see Beaded Dewdrop
Wooden Pail, Butter, Covered, Blue 90.00
Wooden Pail, Creamer, Child's 24.00
Wooden Pail, Pitcher 45.00
Wooden Pail, Pitcher, Water, 8 1/2 In. 45.00
Wooden Pail, Pitcher, Water, Amethyst 120.00
Wooden Pail, Pitcher, Water, Blue 48.00
Wooden Pail, Spooner, Blue ....40.00 To 55.00
Wreath & Shell, Berry Set, Blue 300.00
Wreath & Shell, Cracker Jar, Covered, Large 125.00
Wreath & Shell, Pitcher, Vaseline 500.00
Wreath & Shell, Table Set, Blue 500.00
Wreath & Shell, Tumbler, Blue 60.00
Wreathed Cherry, Toothpick, Clear With Red & Gold 120.00
Wyoming, Cake Stand, 9 In. 32.00
X–Ray, Berry Set, Green, Gold Trim, 7 Piece 125.00
X–Ray, Butter, Covered, Green ....50.00 To 110.00
X–Ray, Compote, Jelly, Green 25.00
X–Ray, Creamer ....45.00 To 75.00
X–Ray, Salt & Pepper, Green 25.00
X–Ray, Spooner, Green 17.50

X–Ray, Sugar, Covered, Green 40.00
X–Ray, Sugar, Covered, Green, Gold Trim 55.00
X–Ray, Toothpick, Green 50.00
X–Ray, Tray, Condiment, Green, For Salt & Pepper 48.00
X–Ray, Tumbler, Green, Gold Trim 45.00
X–Ray, Water Set, Green, 7 Piece .... 185.00 To 235.00
    YALE, see Crowfoot
Yuma Loop, Goblet 25.00
Yuma Loop, Spooner 20.00
Zipper, Bottle, Oil, Stopper, Bulbous, 6 In. 37.50
Zippered Swirl & Diamond, Water Set, Ruby Stained, 7 Piece 395.00

 Print, in this listing, means any of many printed images produced on paper by one of the more common methods, such as lithography. The prints listed here are those of interest to the average collector, not the art collector. Many of these prints were originally part of books. Other prints will be found in the sections headed Currier & Ives, Advertising, and Poster.

PRINT, A.Calbet, Reclining Nudes, Pencil Signed 135.00
  Armstrong, Ruby Lips, 1929, 9 X 12 In. 13.00
  Art Deco, Young Woman Portrait, Hat, 11 1/2 X 11 1/4 In. 29.00
  Audubon, American Crossbill, Hand Colored, 29 1/2 X 39 1/2 In. 2500.00
  Audubon, Common Or Virginian Deer, Hand Colored, 21 1/2 X 27 In. 7500.00
  Audubon, Florida Cormorant, C.1835 ....*Illus* 2600.00
  Audubon, Northern Hare, Hand Colored, 21 1/2 X 27 In. 1500.00
  Audubon, Richardson's Columbian Squirrel, Colored, 21 1/2 X 27 In. 600.00
  Aylward, New York, Colored, Framed, 17 X 26 In. 50.00
  Barefoot Indian Maiden, On Rock, Framed, 13 1/2 X 16 1/2 In. 27.00
  Benecke, Sleighing In New York, Lithograph, 1855, 24 1/2 X 34 In. 3500.00
  Bodmer, Mandeh Pachu, Young Mandan Indian, Hand Colored, 17 X 23 In. 1200.00
  Boydell, View of Greenwich, Hand Colored, 12 1/2 X 16 In. 450.00
  Brookshaw, Melon, Hand Colored, 1812, 22 1/2 X 18 In. 3850.00
  Brundage, Returning From Market 40.00
  C.E.Monroe, Fishing, Signed, 27 X 23 In. 25.00
  Catlin, Catching The Wild Horse, Hand Colored, 1844, 12 X 18 In. 2500.00
  Chandler, Skating, Moonlight, Framed, Copyright 1895, 8 X 20 In. 90.00
  Cheret, Musician, Dancer, Paper, Linen Back, 48 3/8 X 34 1/2 In. 825.00
  Christy, Man & Girl In Boat, Framed, 24 X 20 In. 55.00
  Courtship To First Baby, Framed, 9 X 28 In. 55.00
  Curtis, Pinks, Beauty of Flora, Hand Colored, Engraving, 28 X 23 In. 7500.00
  DeLongpre, Lily of The Valley & Carnations 40.00

Painting, On Ivory, Lady, Blue Gown, 8 X 7 In.

Print, Audubon, Florida Cormorant, C.1835

Divine Comedy, Wood Engraving, Signed, Framed	500.00
Edwin Megaree, English Hunting Dog, 10 X 12 In.	35.00
Elliott, Red Grouse, Framed	850.00
Falls By Moonlight, Framed	85.00
Fisher, A Study, Lady's Face, Matted	20.00
Fisher, American Beauties	175.00
Fisher, Song of Hiawatha	150.00
Fox, Good Morning, Horses, Fence	30.00
Fox, In Meditation Fancy Free, Framed	300.00
Fox, Moonlight & Roses, Framed, 14 X 18 In.	35.00
Fox, Perfect Day, Framed, Signed, 19 1/2 X 15 1/2 In.	60.00
Fox, Sunny South, 14 X 10 In.	10.00
Fox, Sunset Dreams, Framed, Medium	42.50
Fox, Twilight Dreams	45.00
Fox, Victorian Girls, Original Frames, 1907, Pair	125.00
Fox, Where Nature Beats In Perfect Time, 16 X 20 In.	75.00
Frost, English Snipe, N.Y., Chromolithograph, 1888, 13 X 20 In.	1200.00
George Rees, St.Blaise, Modern Bird's-Eye Frame, 29 X 39 1/2 In.	130.00
Gould, Little Egret, Hand Colored, 14 1/2 X 21 In.	1500.00
Gunn, Cupid, Framed, 1911	85.00
Gutmann, A Little Bit of Heaven, Original Frame, 14 X 18 In.	90.00
Gutmann, Awakening, Original Frame, 14 X 18 In.	90.00
Gutmann, Babies, 1932	47.50
Gutmann, Bobby, Asleep, Oval, C.1930	52.00
Gutmann, Fairest of The Flowers	135.00
Gutmann, Happy Dreams	20.00
Gutmann, His Majesty, Framed, 15 X 19 1/2 In.	40.00
Gutmann, Message of The Roses, Framed	70.00
Gutmann, Mighty Like A Rose	20.00
Gutmann, My Darling, 1910	200.00
Gutmann, Our Alarm Clock	125.00
Gutmann, Sun Kissed	20.00
Gutmann, The Reward, Framed, 15 X 19 1/2 In.	40.00
Gutmann, The Sampler	55.00
Gutmann, Wedding March, Original Frame, 16 X 21 In.	85.00
Gutmann, Winged Aureole	70.00
Harper's Weekly, Searching Chinese Immigrants, Woodcut, 1882, 9 In.	75.00
Harper's Weekly, Whaling Station, Calif., Woodcut, 1877, 11 X 17 In.	80.00
Haskell & Allen, Summer In The Country	60.00
Henry McDaniel, Anticipation, Signed, 28 X 21 In.	70.00
Henry McDaniel, Best Time of Day, Signed, 28 X 22 In.	80.00
Humphrey, Baby's First Birthday, 1898	85.00
Humphrey, Little Red Riding Hood	135.00
Icart, Apple Girl, Framed, C.1928, 18 X 24 In.	250.00 To 400.00
Icart, Bird Seller, Original Etching, Framed	1850.00
Icart, Bubbles, Framed, C.1928	125.00
Icart, Coursing, Matted & Framed	125.00
Icart, Four Seasons, Framed, Set of 4	245.00
Icart, Illusions, Framed, C.1960	45.00 To 55.00
Icart, Joy of Life, Lady, 20 X 28 In.	10.00
Icart, La Lettre, Original Print, Matted, Framed, C.1928, 18 X 24 In.	285.00
Icart, Lady of The Camellias, Oval, Signed, Frame, 1927	900.00
Icart, Letter, 14 Colors, Matted & Framed, C.1928	285.00
Icart, Sleeping Beauty	500.00
Icart, Speed, Matted & Framed	125.00
Icart, Summer, Triple Matted, Gold Frame	600.00
Indian Chief, In Canoe, Wooden Frame, Signed	20.00
J.Baillie, General Washington, Beveled Frame, 12 1/2 X 16 1/2 In.	55.00
J.Baillie, Rival Favorites, Framed, 13 X 17 1/4 In.	45.00
J.Gemmell, Summer Morning, Grained Frame, 12 3/8 X 16 In.	20.00

Japanese prints are listed as follows: Print, Japanese, name of artist, title or description, type, and size. Dealers use the following terms: Tate–e is a vertical composition. Yoko–e is a horizontal composition. The words Aiban (13 by 9 inches), Chuban (10 by 7 1/2 inches), Hosoban (12 by 6 inches), Oban (15 by 10 inches), and Koban (7 by 4 inches) denote size.

Japanese, 4 Birds On Bough, Framed, 4 1/2 X 6 1/2 In.	40.00
Japanese, Chikanobu, Kunichika, C.1865	400.00
Japanese, Chikanobu, Toyokuni III, 1864	500.00
Japanese, Hasui, Chuzenji Lake At Nikko, 1930, 16 1/4 X 11 1/8 In.	250.00
Japanese, Hasui, Ueno, Toshogu In Snow, 1929, 15 3/4 X 11 In.	250.00
Japanese, Hiroshige, Cherry Blossoms, 1856	4000.00
Japanese, Hiroshige, Fujikawa, 1834	3600.00
Japanese, Hiroshige, Futagawa, 1834	2000.00
Japanese, Hiroshige, Goyu, 1834	4500.00
Japanese, Hiroshige, Hachiman Shrine, 1857	2000.00
Japanese, Hiroshige, Hamamatsu, 1834	4000.00
Japanese, Hiroshige, Kanbara, 1834	4500.00
Japanese, Hiroshige, Kuniyoshi, C.1840	1500.00
Japanese, Hiroshige, Numazu, 1834	4000.00
Japanese, Hiroshige, Sakai Ferry, 1857	2200.00
Japanese, Hiroshige, Shono, 1834	6000.00
Japanese, Hiroshige, Toyokuni III, C.1850	1700.00
Japanese, Hiroshige, Waterfall At Oji, 1856	2500.00
Japanese, Hokusai, Jit Tenno, 1839	3000.00
Japanese, Hokusai, Michizane, 1839	5500.00
Japanese, Hokusai, Mii Temple, C.1800	2100.00
Japanese, Hokusai, Mt.Hira, C.1800	2100.00
Japanese, Hokusai, Seta, C.1800	2100.00
Japanese, Hokusai, Snow At Koishikawa, C.1830	7000.00
Japanese, Izuno, Sacred Mountain, 15 3/4 X 10 1/2 In.	90.00
Japanese, Kuniyoshi, Heroes of Suikoden, C.1830	1200.00
Japanese, Kuniyoshi, Mountain & Oceans, 1852	1200.00
Japanese, Kuniyoshi, The 47 Ronin, C.1847	700.00
Japanese, Kuniyoshi, Two Warriors, C.1850	1200.00
Japanese, Kuniyoshi, Yoshitsune & Benkel Before Battle, Triptych	2100.00
Japanese, Sadanobu III, Dancer At Mt.Arashi, 15 3/8 X 10 1/4 In.	125.00
Japanese, Sadanobu III, Musashi–Bo Benkei, 17 X 12 In.	125.00
Japanese, Shinsui, Snow, 1926, 15 1/4 X 10 1/4 In.	300.00
Japanese, Shoson, Owl, 1926, 15 3/4 X 10 1/4 In.	225.00
Japanese, Yoshida, Bridge At Kameido, 1927, 15 3/4 X 10 3/4 In.	250.00
Japanese, Yoshida, Hirosaki Castle, 1935, 15 3/4 X 10 3/4 In.	250.00
Japanese, Yoshida, Pagoda In Kyoto, 1942, 10 1/2 X 8 In.	95.00
Japanese, Yoshida, Umbrella, 1940, 10 1/2 X 8 In.	95.00
Japanese, Yoshitoshi, Enjoyable Type, 1888	1500.00
Japanese, Yoshitoshi, Flute Players, 1886	1500.00
Japanese, Yoshitoshi, Gentoku Visiting Komei In Snowstorm, Triptych	3000.00
Johnson, Same Old Game, Cupid & Cards, Bathing Beauty, 13 X 20 In.	80.00
Judge, Mulligan's Masquerade Party, Caricature, 1895, 9 X 12 In.	22.50
Judge, Zim Meets Old Friends, St.Patrick's Day, 1903, 9 X 12 In.	22.50
Kellogg & Comstock, Washington, Frame, 12 X 16 In.	45.00
Kellogg, Evening Prayer, Beveled Frame, 10 X 15 In.	35.00
Kellogg, Gardener's Pet, Framed, 11 5/8 X 15 5/8 In.	22.50
Kellogg, He Who Marries Does Well, Framed, 14 3/4 X 19 In.	45.00
Kellogg, Little Drummer, Blue, Red, 12 X 16 In.	130.00
Kip, Chatsworth House, London, 1707–12, Engraving, 16 X 21 In.	275.00
Kurtz & Allison, Perry's Victory On Lake Erie, Framed	165.00
Lyman Powell, Man Holding Woman, Oval of Roses, Framed, 18 X 12 In.	55.00
McKenney & Hall, Peskelchaco, Indian, Hand Colored, 1844, 20 X 14 In.	575.00
McQueen, International Sculling Match, Uncolored, 27 1/2 X 40 In.	850.00
Moore, Girlie, Blond, On Blue Ground, 1950s, 8 1/2 X 11 1/2 In.	6.00
Moran, Grand Canyon, Chromolithograph, 1912, 25 1/2 X 34 1/2 In.	5500.00
Morgan, Children, C.1900, 34 X 24 In.	55.00

Print, Parrish, Three Ladies, With Mandolins,
15 X 11 1/2 In.

Print, Parrish, Woman, Seated, Bubbles,
Framed, 14 1/2 X 11 1/2 In.

Mucha, Sarah Bernhardt, Olive Green, Gold, 1896, 24 1/2 X 16 In.	660.00
Mugaini, The Tower, Matted & Framed, 18 1/4 X 24 1/4 In.	45.00
Muller Luchsinger & Co., After Marriage, Copyright 1895, Framed	90.00
Munson, Girlie, Nude, Lovely To Look At, 1930s, 7 X 9 1/2 In.	8.50
Nutting, A New Hampshire Road	48.00
Nutting, At The Fender, Original Gold Frame, 15 X 17 1/2 In.	125.00
Nutting, Lambs At Rest, Frame, 10 1/2 X 12 1/2 In.	90.00
Nutting, Maple Sugar Cupboard, Framed, 6 X 9 1/2 In.	75.00
Nutting, Swirling Seas, Signed, Framed, 12 X 15 In.	75.00
Nutting, The Burre Brook, Matted, Framed, Signed	35.00
Our Martyrs, Lincoln, Garfield, McKinley, Framed, 1901, 20 X 16 In.	180.00
Parkinson, Cupid Awake & Cupid Asleep, Oval Frames, 1897, Pair	50.00
Parrish, 3 Italian Villas	75.00
Parrish, 6 Little Ingredients	85.00
Parrish, Air Castles	110.00 To 185.00
Parrish, Brazen Boatman, Framed	95.00
Parrish, Broadmoor Hotel, Framed	750.00
Parrish, Cassim In The Cave of 40 Thieves, 1905	45.00
Parrish, Chancellor & The King	95.00
Parrish, Cleopatra	35.00
Parrish, Contentment, Framed, Small	65.00
Parrish, Daybreak, Art Deco Frame, 19 1/2 X 12 1/2 In.	135.00
Parrish, Daybreak, Framed, 10 1/2 X 18 In.	80.00
Parrish, Dinkey Bird, 12 X 16 In.	195.00
Parrish, Dinkey Bird, 5 X 7 In.	20.00
Parrish, Dreaming, C.1960, 10 X 18 In.	55.00
Parrish, Eve Eating The Apple, Framed	18.00
Parrish, Evening, Framed, 11 X 15 In.	155.00
Parrish, Garden of Allah, 9 X 18 In.	80.00
Parrish, Garden of Allah, Framed, 4 1/2 X 8 1/2 In.	35.00
Parrish, Garden of Allah, Framed, 5 3/4 X 9 3/4 In.	50.00
Parrish, Garden of Allah, Framed, 11 1/2 X 20 1/2 In.	75.00
Parrish, Golden Hours, Edison Mazda Calendar Top	65.00
Parrish, Golden Hours, Small	145.00
Parrish, Hilltop, Framed, 12 X 20 In.	475.00
Parrish, King Tastes The Tarts, 3 Figures, 11 X 12 In.	95.00
Parrish, Knave of Hearts, Lady Violetta Making Tarts, 11 X 12 In.	85.00
Parrish, Lady Violetta	85.00
Parrish, Little Princess, Matted	35.00
Parrish, Lute Players, 18 X 30 In.	450.00
Parrish, Morning, Framed, 13 X 16 In.	45.00

Parrish, Old Glen Mill, 13 1/4 X 16 3/4 In.	150.00
Parrish, Old King Cole Tobacco Co., 1st Commission	30.00
Parrish, Peaceful Valley, 13 1/2 X 17 In.	90.00 To 125.00
Parrish, Quiet Solitude, 16 X 19 In.	45.00
Parrish, Reveries, Small	65.00 To 95.00
Parrish, Romance, Framed, 14 X 23 1/2 In.	475.00
Parrish, Rubaiyat, C.1917, 30 1/2 X 8 1/2 In.	295.00
Parrish, Sheltering Oaks, 16 X 19 In.	45.00
Parrish, Stars, Frame, 12 X 20 In.	450.00
Parrish, Sunup, Matted, Framed, 10 3/4 X 14 3/4 In.	75.00
Parrish, The City of Brass	15.00
Parrish, Three Ladies, With Mandolins, 15 X 11 1/2 In. ....*Illus*	120.00
Parrish, Thy Templed Hills	120.00
Parrish, Twilight, 1935, 18 X 24 In.	95.00
Parrish, Under Summer Skies, 16 X 19 In.	45.00
Parrish, Violetta & Knave Examining Tarts, 11 X 12 In.	85.00
Parrish, Waterfall, Framed, 7 X 10 In.	75.00
Parrish, Where The Dinkey Bird Is Singing, Signed, Sticker	100.00
Parrish, Wild Geese, Framed, 10 X 18 In.	125.00
Parrish, Woman, Seated, Bubbles, Framed, 14 1/2 X 11 1/2 In. ....*Illus*	90.00
Parrish, Yellow Hose, Blue Hose	60.00
Pope, Bluebill Duck, Dated 1879, 14 X 20 In.	250.00
Pope, Valley Quail, Dated 1879, 14 X 20 In.	250.00
Prang, Battle of Kenesaw Mountain, Ga., 1887, Civil War, Large	35.00
Prang, George Washington, Bust, Metal Frame, 2 3/4 X 4 1/2 In.	75.00
Prang, Woman, With Holly Border, 5 1/2 X 7 In.	11.00
Pyne, Rose Satin Drawing Room, Colored Engraving, 1819, 11 X 13 In.	125.00
Remington, His First Lesson, 1908	87.50
Rockwell, Christmas, 1931	10.00
Rockwell, Grace, Mahogany Frame	75.00
Rockwell, Song of Bernadette, Movie, 1943, 10 X 14 In.	17.50
Roseland, The Old Mammy, Oak Frame, 11 X 15 In.	165.00
Sebron, Winter Scene In Broadway, N.Y., Aquatint, 1857, 30 X 38 In.	4500.00
Selby, Common Wild Goose, Colored Engraving, 25 1/2 X 20 1/2 In.	900.00
Seligmann, Nightingale, Hand Colored Engraving, 11 1/4 X 9 In.	300.00
Shreyer, A Kabyle, Arabian Horse, 14 X 17 In.	45.00
Shreyer, Imperial Courier, Arabian Horse, 10 X 18 In.	45.00
Silhouette, Ink, Woman, In Chair, Gilt Frame, 5 1/4 X 7 1/2 In.	65.00
Smith, and A Little Child Shall Lead Them, 1919, 11 X 14 In.	20.00
Smith, Last Drake, Signed & Numbered, 27 X 23 In.	150.00
Smith, Mother & Child, 1917, 11 X 14 In.	20.00
Smith, Pease Porridge Hot, Framed	35.00
Smith, Peter, Peter, Pumpkin Eater, Framed	35.00
Smith, The Last Drake, Signed, 19 X 23 In.	110.00
Thomas Kelly, A Home In The Country, 25 X 32 In.	135.00
Thornton, Night–Blowing Cereus, Engraving, 23 X 18 1/2 In.	8500.00
Tuck, A Day With The Harriers, 1882	325.00
Turner, Royal Cockatoos, Framed, 24 X 30 In.	65.00
W.M.Murrell, Map On Temperance, 1846, 23 1/2 X 28 In.	55.00
Whitefield, Tulip, Lily, Fuchsia, For T.Whitman, 1850, 5 X 8 In.	25.00
Williamson, Tiger Springing From An Elephant, 1818, 17 1/2 X 22 In.	1275.00

How to carry a handkerchief and lipstick is a problem today for every woman, including the Queen of England. The purse has been recognizable since the eighteenth century. Leather and needlework purses were preferred. Beaded purses became popular in the nineteenth century, went out of style, but are again in use. Mesh purses date from the 1880s and are still being made.

PURSE, Alligator, Brown, 1940s, Large	40.00
Art Deco, Yellow Celluloid, Geometric, Amber Rhinestones, 3 X 5 In.	65.00
Beaded, Beadwork Roses, C.1890, 7 X 12 In.	85.00
Beaded, Looped Panels, Midnight Blue, Silver Filigree Frame, 6 In.	30.00
Beaded, Peacock On Tree Branch, Ornate Closure, Chain, 7 X 10 In.	75.00
Beaded, Red, White & Blue, Floral, Chain, 1920s, Germany, 8 X 7 In.	40.00

Beaded, Violet, Crystal Loops, Metal Chain, Frame, 1920–30, 5 X 6 In. 60.00
Clutch, Black & Gray Glass Bead Design, Czechoslovakia, 1930s 45.00
Clutch, Lucite, With Rhinestones 35.00
Clutch, Petit Point Roses 15.00
Coin, Maroon Suede, Accordian Closure, 3 1/2 In. 15.00
Coin, On Chain, Sterling Silver, 1920s, 2 In. 49.00
Drawstring, Black Beaded, Blue & Green, Gold Flowers, 6 1/2 X 5 In. 55.00
Evening, Art Deco, Muskrat, Celluloid Top 25.00
Evening, Black Beaded, Fringed, Pouch Type 35.00
Evening, Brown Antelope, Marcasites Around Frame 12.00
Evening, Gold Plated, Rope Design On Front, Rhinestones, Evans 45.00
Evening, Multicolored Beads, Chain 25.00
Evening, Tapestry, Rhinestone Clasp, Volupte 30.00
Evening, Victorian, Beaded, France 125.00
Leather, Alligator Head & Feet 18.00
Looped Beading, Blue, Metal Frame & Chain, 1920–30, 4 1/2 X 6 In. 65.00
Makeup, Art Deco, Evans, Metal, Gold & Copper Chain 30.00
Mesh, Art Deco, Pink, Yellow & Blue, Whiting & Davis 120.00
Mesh, Clark Gable, Whiting & Davis 275.00
Mesh, Enameled, Beige & Brown, Whiting & Davis, 1920s 38.00
Mesh, Enameled, Silver Plated Frame, Fringed, Chain, C.1920, 6 X 4 In. 50.00
Mesh, German Silver, Chain Handle, Ball Trim, 5 1/2 X 7 In. 65.00
Mesh, German Silver, White Leather Lining, Chain, 6 X 6 In. 20.00
Mesh, Gold, Rhinestone Clasp, Whiting & Davis 60.00
Mesh, Orange, Lime, Aqua, Whiting & Davis 20.00
Mesh, Orange, Red, Purple, Fringe, Chain Handles ....*Illus* 80.00
Mesh, Silver Mesh, Floral 1 Side, Chain, 1920s, Germany, 5 X 7 In. 65.00
Mesh, Sterling Silver, Chain Handle, 4 X 4 In. 48.00
Mesh, Sterling Silver, English, Dated 1919 .... 125.00
Mesh, Sterling Silver, Signed Tiffany, C.1900 .... 850.00
Needlepoint, Flame Stitch, Silver Clasp, Sarah E.Pope, 5 In. 325.00
Pouch, Miser's, Blue Bugle Beads, Drawstring 20.00
Sterling Silver, Floral Design, Blue Leather, Russia, C.1880 .... 250.00
Straw, Art Deco, Flowers, C.1937, Large 18.00
Straw, Doll Shape, With Mask Face, Child's, 1940s 15.00
White Metallic, Bakelite Handles, Whiting & Davis 15.00
Wrist, Art Deco, Celluloid 35.00

Quezal   Quezal glass was made from 1901 to 1920 by Martin Bach, Sr., in Brooklyn, New York. Other glassware by other firms, such as Loetz, Steuben, and Tiffany, resembles this gold–colored iridescent glass. After Martin Bach's death in 1920, his son continued the manufacture of a similar glass under the name "Lustre Art Glass."

QUEZAL, Bowl, Iridescent Rose, Gold & Green, Signed, 2 1/2 In. 235.00
Candlestick, Blue Aurene, Footed, Stem, Marked, 7 3/4 In. 150.00
Candy Dish, Thin Stem, Gold Iridescent, Signed, 5 In. 250.00
Compote, Green Swirls, Gold Stem, Foot & Ground, Signed, 6 3/4 In. 725.00
Cup, Curved Body, Scroll Handle, Signed 195.00
Finger Bowl, Gold Iridescent, 2 1/2 X 4 In. 225.00
Lamp, Desk, 2–Light 450.00
Lamp, Desk, Hooked Feather & Heart & Chain, 7 In.Shade 1400.00
Lamp, Gold Paneled Shade, Marked The Twilight, Signed, Miniature 1200.00
Lamp, Pulled Feather, 15 In. 1500.00
Salt, Gold Outside, Bluish Inside, Signed, 2 1/2 X 1 In. 150.00
Salt, Raised Ribbed Body, Gold Iridescent 110.00
Shade, 10 Ribs, Gold Inside & Out, Signed 80.00
Shade, 5 Feathers, Gold Borders, Signed, 5 In. 285.00
Shade, Baluster Shape, Flared, Ribbed, Golden Yellow, Signed, 7 In. 185.00
Shade, Gold Outlining, Gold Interior, Pearly Calcite, 6 1/2 In. 195.00
Shade, Gold Pulled Feathers, Iridescent Gold Interior, 5 In. 165.00
Shade, Gold Trellis, Gold Interior, Ruffled, 6 7/8 In. 765.00
Shade, Iridescent, Gold, Green, Snakeskin, Signed 100.00
Shade, King Tut 160.00

Shade, Paperweight, Yellow & White	500.00
Shade, Platinum Feather, Gold Lined, Green Ground, Signed	475.00
Shade, Snakeskin, Green Top, Butterscotch	155.00
Shade, Zipper Pattern, Allover Gold, Signed, 6 Piece	900.00
Toothpick, Petal Top, Marked	385.00
Vase, Allover Lattice, Gold Pulls At Base, Tricornered, 6 In.	675.00
Vase, Aurene Type, Baluster Form, Dimples, Signed, 4 1/2 In.	265.00
Vase, Bud, Gold, Marked, 11 1/2 In., Pair	825.00 To 850.00
Vase, Gold Inside, Yellow & Green Outside, Signed, 7 1/2 In.	1575.00
Vase, Green & Gold Pulled Feather, Gold Interior, Signed, 5 In.	850.00
Vase, Heart & Trailing Vine, Silver & Purple, Signed, 12 1/4 In.	2100.00
Vase, Pinched, 10 In.	450.00

Quilts have been made since the seventeenth century. Early textiles were very precious and every scrap was saved to be reused. A quilt is a combination of fabrics joined to a filler and a backing by small stitched designs known as quilting. An appliqued quilt has pieces stitched to the top of a large piece of background fabric. A patchwork, or pieced, quilt is made of many small pieces stitched together. Embroidery can be added to either type.

QUILT, Appliqued, 4 Oak Leaf Medallions, Calico On White, 92 X 94 In.	495.00
Appliqued, Allover Floral, Scalloped, Pink, Green, 82 X 100 In.	300.00
Appliqued, Barn Raising, Red, White & Yellow Calico, C.1860, 84 In.	370.00
Appliqued, Basket of Flowers, Vine Border, 70 X 83 In.	195.00
Appliqued, Basket, Red & Blue Triangles, White, 5 1/2 X 6 1/2 Ft.	125.00
Appliqued, Blue Baskets, Vining Border, White Homespun, 75 X 75 In.	1100.00
Appliqued, Brown & White Calico, 9-Patch, 19th Century, 18 X 18 In.	165.00
Appliqued, Central Pinwheel, Smaller Each Corner, Crib Size	375.00
Appliqued, Columbia Star, Blue & White, 1920s, 82 X 69 In.	225.00
Appliqued, Crazy, Dated 1893, Wyoming Documented, 67 X 51 In.	200.00
Appliqued, Dutch Boy Britches, 56 X 71 In.	175.00
Appliqued, Floral Design In Red & Green, 70 X 89 In.	500.00
Appliqued, Floral Medallions, Lavender, White, 68 X 84 In.	270.00
Appliqued, Flower Garden, Diamond, Peach, Blue, 75 X 84 In.	165.00
Appliqued, Flower Garden, Multicolored, Scalloped, 41 X 29 In.	125.00
Appliqued, Garden Wreath, Martha H.Sanborn, C.1850, 84 X 102 In.	275.00
Appliqued, Geometric, Red & White, Sawtooth Border, 64 X 74 In.	250.00
Appliqued, Green Leaves, 2 Shades of Pink, C.1915, Square, 92 In.	660.00
Appliqued, Hearts, Flowers, Foliage, Unused, 83 X 84 In.	500.00
Appliqued, Irish Chain, Blue & White, 74 X 88 In.	250.00
Appliqued, Jacob's Ladder, Hand Sewn, Doll's	45.00
Appliqued, Log Cabin, Hand Sewn, Doll's	45.00
Appliqued, Lone Star, Brown, Blue Calico, 19th Century, 65 X 70 In.	795.00
Appliqued, Medallions In Greens, Green Backing, 92 X 107 In.	150.00
Appliqued, Mennonite Log Cabin Variation, 19th Century, 79 X 79 In.	850.00
Appliqued, Oak Leaf Variant, Calico On White, 81 X 83 In.	260.00
Appliqued, Patch, Red & White, Goldenrod Ground, 1935, 68 X 68 In.	425.00
Appliqued, Pieced, Reversible, Floral Checkerboard, 74 X 78 In.	105.00
Appliqued, Pine Tree, 2 Calico & Olive Green Borders, 77 X 92 In.	1600.00
Appliqued, Pinwheels, Alphabet, Chain Border, 1860, 86 X 89 In.	625.00
Appliqued, Poinsettias, White Ground, 20th Century, 80 X 92 In.	295.00
Appliqued, Red & Green Calico, White Ground, C.1845, 80 X 108 In.	550.00
Appliqued, Red Flower, On White, Tulip & Swag Border, 86 X 88 In.	500.00
Appliqued, Rose of Sharon, Green, Red, 1870s, 72 X 100 In.	525.00
Appliqued, Sawtooth Diamond, Mennonite, Dated 1860, Square, 7 Ft.	1000.00
Appliqued, Snowball Pattern, 69 X 72 In.	145.00
Appliqued, Snowflakes, Stars, Calico, J.M.Merritt, 1860, 30 X 35 In.	1430.00
Appliqued, Steeplechase, Blue Calico, White, C.1910, 29 X 32 In.	450.00
Appliqued, Stylized Floral Medallions, Zigzag Border, 71 X 85 In.	100.00
Appliqued, Stylized Floral Pinwheels, Red, Fabric Faded, 70 X 82 In.	175.00
Appliqued, Stylized Pine Trees, Flowers, Floral Wreaths, 78 X 90 In.	175.00
Appliqued, Stylized Rosebud Medallion, 78 X 78 In.	200.00
Appliqued, The Disk, Green Ground, 1920s, 87 X 74 In.	175.00

Appliqued, White On White, Star Medallion, 76 X 78 In. 185.00
Appliqued, White Stars, Blue Calico, Late 19th Century, 77 In. 895.00
Appliqued, Yellow, White, 75 X 94 In. 245.00
Cross–Stitch, American Sample, Embroidered, 81 X 97 In. 235.00
Cross–Stitch, Apricot, Ivory Cotton Sateen, 80 X 95 In. 135.00
Embroidered Babies & Teddy Bears, 20 Squares, Crib, 1920s 95.00
Patchwork, 4 Red Squares, Multicolored Stars, Calico, 76 X 76 In. 135.00
Patchwork, 4–Point Star, Prints On Green Calico, 70 X 82 In. 50.00
Patchwork, 4–Point Stars, Sawtooth Edge, White Ground, 70 X 84 In. 175.00
Patchwork, 9 Stars On White Calico Ground, 70 X 76 In. 225.00
Patchwork, 9–Patch Pattern, Calico Sawtooth Border, 56 X 56 In. 95.00
Patchwork, 9–Patch Pattern, Chintz, 114 X 118 In. 350.00
Patchwork, 9–Patch, Prints, 66 X 78 In. 120.00
Patchwork, 16 Stars, Red & Green Calico, White, 80 X 94 In. 155.00
Patchwork, 25–Patch Pattern, Crib 25.00
Patchwork, 30 Stars On Squares, Lycoming Co., Pa., 72 X 80 In. 300.00
Patchwork, 36 Multicolored Stars, Calico, 1840s, 96 X 96 In. 300.00
Patchwork, 99 Stars, Checkerboard Placement, N.Y.State, 68 X 78 In. 125.00
Patchwork, Album Pattern, Red & White, Vining Foliage, 88 X 90 In. 95.00
Patchwork, Amish, 3 Shades of Blue Satin, Pink Binding, 72 X 87 In. 550.00
Patchwork, Amish, Blue–Slate, Rose, Lavender & Pink, Square, 72 In. 4200.00
Patchwork, Amish, Log Cabin, 69 X 74 In. 185.00
Patchwork, Amish, Lone Star, Clarion Co., Pa., 68 X 86 In. 150.00
Patchwork, Amish, Ocean Wave Pattern, Indiana, 66 X 72 In. 325.00
Patchwork, Amish, Sunshine & Shadow, 80 X 81 In. 1150.00
Patchwork, Bar Pattern, Prints On Red Calico, C.1890, 80 X 90 In. 160.00
Patchwork, Barn Raising Pattern, Calico, Pink Border, 80 X 81 In. 250.00
Patchwork, Basket Pattern, Calico, 78 X 92 In. 225.00
Patchwork, Basket Pattern, Red Calico On White, 84 X 88 In. 200.00
Patchwork, Bear's Paw, 79 X 71 In. 195.00
Patchwork, Block Pattern, 4–Patch, Greek Key Border, 76 X86 In. 150.00
Patchwork, Block Pattern, Floral Chintz Border, Back, C.1856, 40 In. 700.00
Patchwork, Block Pattern, Union County, Pa., C.1940, 72 X 78 In. 25.00
Patchwork, Bowtie Pattern, Green Border, 40 X 41 In. 125.00
Patchwork, Bowtie, Blue & White, 69 X 80 In. 275.00
Patchwork, Brown, White, Red, Pink Calico, 86 X 92 In. 300.00
Patchwork, Butterfly, Handmade, 70 X72 In. 135.00
Patchwork, Calico, 8–Pointed Stars, Floral, 118–In.Square 3200.00
Patchwork, Checkerboard, Print Border, Lehigh Co., Pa., 68 X 78 In. 150.00
Patchwork, Crazy Quilt, Velvet, C.1910, 72 X 80 In. 275.00
Patchwork, Crazy, Silks, Satins & Velvet, Painted Design, 72 X 72 In. 65.00
Patchwork, Double Irish Chain, Cotton, Hand Quilted, 80 X 71 In. 225.00
Patchwork, Double X Pattern, Yates County, New York, 74 X 88 In. 355.00
Patchwork, Dresden Plate, Handmade, Red Field, 63 X 74 In. 375.00
Patchwork, Dresden Plate, Pastels, 72 X 87 In. 95.00
Patchwork, Drunkard's Path, 63 X 82 In. 150.00
Patchwork, Drunkard's Path, Crib 135.00
Patchwork, Drunkard's Path, Light Green, Pink, 70 X 82 In. 210.00
Patchwork, Embroidered Floral Squares, 93 X 94 In. 125.00
Patchwork, Floral Medallions, Swag Border, Fringe, 91 X 103 In. 1200.00
Patchwork, Flower Garden, 72 X 92 In. 225.00
Patchwork, Flower Garden, Blue, 75 X 84 In. 165.00
Patchwork, Flower Garden, Multicolored Prints, 84 X 86 In. 150.00
Patchwork, Flower Garden, Yellow Edging, 102 X 832 In. 195.00
Patchwork, Flying Geese, Homespun, Blue, 19th Century, 52 X 61 In. 395.00
Patchwork, Four–In–Four Patch, Maroon Border, 76 X 76 In. 375.00
Patchwork, Four–In–Four Pattern, Pennsylvania, C.1935, 68 X 68 In. 425.00
Patchwork, Four–In–Four, Sawtooth Border, C.1935, 68 X 68 In. 425.00
Patchwork, Goose In Pond, Darks On White, 80 X 72 In. 190.00
Patchwork, Grandmother's Flower Garden, C.1930, 82 X 86 In. 90.00
Patchwork, Irish Chain, 86 X 72 In. 300.00
Patchwork, Irish Chain, Calico, Lebanon Co., Pa., 74 X 74 In. 150.00
Patchwork, Irish Chain, Calico, White Ground, 74 X 84 In. 250.00
Patchwork, Irish Chain, Solid Red, Golden Rod, White, 86 X 86 In. 250.00

Patchwork, Irish Chain, Yellow & White, Quilted Flowers, 78 X 88 In. 200.00
Patchwork, Leaf Designs, Blue & White Checkerboard, 84 X 84 In. 275.00
Patchwork, Log Cabin, Paisley Back, 19th Century, 77 X 77 In. 400.00
Patchwork, Log Cabin, Prints & Solids, C.1935, 72 X 74 In. 135.00
Patchwork, Log Cabin, Red, Green, Brown, Gray, & White, 68 X 78 In. 155.00
Patchwork, Log Cabin, Straight Furrows, Wools, 86 X 71 In. 185.00
Patchwork, Lone Star, Beige Ground, 82 X 84 In. 250.00
Patchwork, Lone Star, Red Center, C.1900, 72 X75 In. 265.00
Patchwork, Meandering Feather Pattern, Ecru, Stripes, 98 X 96 In. 75.00
Patchwork, Medallion, Border of Narrow Strips, 79 X 96 In. 295.00
Patchwork, Mennonite, 4–Patch Chain, 79 X 91 In. 300.00
Patchwork, Mennonite, Beige Bars, Green Ground, Unused, 74 X 78 In. 1525.00
Patchwork, Monkey Wrench Pattern, Calico, Berks Co., Pa., 82 X 90 In. 250.00
Patchwork, Multicolored Print Stars On White Squares, 74 X 82 In. 275.00
Patchwork, Pigs In A Blanket, 9–Patch Configuration, 80 X 80 In. 345.00
Patchwork, Pinwheel, Calico, Lebanon Co., Pa., 77 X 77 In. 350.00
Patchwork, Pinwheel, Multicolored, Reversible, C.1890, Crib 250.00
Patchwork, Pinwheel, Pink Calico Ground, 80 X 82 In. 175.00
Patchwork, Princess Feather, Red & Green, C.1850, 77 X 90 In. 850.00
Patchwork, Puss In The Corner, Calico, Lehigh County, 66 X 84 In. 80.00
Patchwork, Rainbow Star, Flannel Back, 1880, 65 X 80 In. 275.00
Patchwork, Red & Green Calico, Signed Susana A.Baughman 1854, Crib 650.00
Patchwork, Red & White Optical Pattern, 74 X 90 In. 350.00
Patchwork, Red Squares, Leaves In Corners, 84 X 100 In. 450.00
Patchwork, Red, White Flowers, 20 Large Squares, C.1910, 80 X 64 In. 185.00
Patchwork, Rocky Road To Kansas, Kentucky, 66 X 82 In. 90.00
Patchwork, Rolling Stone, Calico, Berks Co., Pa., 86 In. Sq. 175.00
Patchwork, Rolling Stone, Lebanon, Pa., 72 X 80 In. 250.00
Patchwork, Sawtooth Edge Triangles, Homespun Back, 80 X 82 In. 35.00
Patchwork, Sawtooth Medallion, White Ground, 102 X 104 In. 925.00
Patchwork, Shaded Roses, Buds, Scalloped, 82 X 72 In. 395.00
Patchwork, Snowball, Calicos On White, 76 X 82 In. 125.00
Patchwork, Star, Calico, 76 X 76 In. 140.00
Patchwork, Star, Calico, Berks County, Pa., 72 X 84 In. 300.00
Patchwork, Star, Feather Quilting, 83 X 85 In. 250.00
Patchwork, Star, Machine Sewn Binding, 68 X 92 In. 325.00
Patchwork, Star, Pink Calico, White Ground, 72 X 80 In. 225.00
Patchwork, Star, Red & Black, 76 X 88 In. 75.00
Patchwork, Star, Stenciled L.A.L. On Corner, 64 X 71 In. 250.00
Patchwork, Starflowers, Stylized, Star Corners, 86 X 94 In. 350.00
Patchwork, Steeplechase, Blue Calico, White, 1900, 68 X 84 In. 525.00
Patchwork, T Square, Yellow & White, 72 X 96 In. 160.00
Patchwork, Triangle, Multicolored Prints, 82 X 84 In. 95.00
Patchwork, Trip Around The World, Prints & Solids, 72 X 88 In. 210.00
Patchwork, Tulips In A Pot, Lavender Ground, C.1920, 78 X 67 In. 185.00
Patchwork, Turkey Track, Berks County, Pa., 68 X 90 In. 350.00
Patchwork, Wedding Ring, Sunflower Pattern, Ring, 64 X 78 In. 195.00
Patchwork, Wedding Ring, Yellow, Green & Pink, C.1930, 77 X 77 In. 350.00
Patchwork, Windmill, Multicolored Prints, 76 X 76 In. 300.00
Patchwork, Windmill, Prints & Solids, 72 X 72 In. 255.00
Patchwork, Windmill, Yellow Calico Ground, 72 X 72 In. 255.00
Patchwork, X Pattern, Red & 2 Shades of Green, 72 X 82 In. 205.00
Patchwork, Yo–Yo, Pink Diamond Design, 51 X 103 In. 220.00
Patchwork, Young Man's Fancy, Red, White & Blue Calico, 67 X 72 In. 325.00

A quilt that is not in use should be aired each year. Open up the quilt and place it flat on the floor for a few days. A quilt that is used on a bed or hung should be taken down and rested every six months.

Tin–glazed, hand–painted pottery has been made in Quimper, France, since the late seventeenth century. The earliest firm, founded in 1685 by Jean Baptiste Bousquet, was known as HB Quimper. Another firm, founded in 1772 by Francois Eloury, was known as Porquier. The third firm, founded by Guillaume Dumaine in 1778, was known as HR or Henriot Quimper. All three firms made similar pottery decorated with designs of Breton peasants and sea and flower motifs. The Eloury (Porquier) and Dumaine (Henriot) firms merged in 1913. Bousquet (HB) merged with the others in 1968. The group was sold to a United States family in 1984. The American holding company is Quimper Faience Inc., located in Stonington, Connecticut. The French firm has been called Societe Nouvelle des Faienceries de Quimper HB Henriot since March 1984.

HR
Quimper

QUIMPER, Bowl, Breton Woman & Man, Dolphin Handles, 17 In.	750.00
Bowl, Portrait, Handles, Henriot, Oval, 11 X 7 1/2 In.	225.00
Cake Stand, Man With Flute, 9 1/2 X 4 1/2 In.	185.00
Charger, Signed, 12 1/2 In.	90.00
Cup & Saucer, Man With Flute, 6 Sides	55.00
Cup & Saucer, Yellow, HB Mark	32.00
Dish, Dolphins Handle, Blue Art Deco Border, Divided, 12 In.	275.00
Figurine, Breton Girl, With Umbrella, 10 In.	275.00
Figurine, Seaman, Net On Shoulder, Artist Fanch, 4 1/2 In.	155.00
Inkwell, Rolled Side of Rim, Acorn Finial, Signed	95.00
Inkwell, Yellow Ground, Signed, 3 Piece	120.00
Jug, Breton Lady, Handle, 6 In.	220.00
Knife Rest, Breton Man & Flowers, 3 1/2 In.	50.00
Knife Rest, Peasant Girl	35.00
Match Holder, Wall, HB, 2 X 3 3/4 In.	85.00
Mug, Peasant Girl, Marked	35.00
Pitcher, Peasant, 6 In.	25.00
Plate, Peasant Man & Woman, Henriot Quimper 99, 10 1/4 In., Pair	95.00
Plate, Yellow, HB Mark, 9 In.	30.00
Relish, Tray, 3 Piece	245.00
Salt, Master, Man Playing Bagpipes	200.00
Salt, Swan	30.00
Saltshaker, Shoe Shape, Flowers, 3 1/4 X 1 5/8 In.	28.00
Snuff Bottle, HR	325.00
Tray, Pastel Flowers, Bird, Insects, 12 In.	650.00
Trivet, Square, 6 In.	72.00
Vase, Hanging, Wall, Bellows Shape, Peasant Woman, Miniature	65.00
Vase, Portrait, Odetta Design, Long Handles, 15 1/4 In., Pair	165.00
Wine Casket, Henriot, 5 In.	125.00

RADFORD
JASPER

Radford pottery was made by Alfred Radford in Broadway, Virginia, Tiffin and Zanesville, Ohio, and Clarksburg, West Virginia, from 1891 until 1912. Jasperware, Ruko, Thera, Radera, and Velvety Art Ware were made. The jasperware resembles the famous Wedgwood ware of the same name.

RADFORD, Jardiniere, Wild Rose, Ruffled, 8 X 10 1/2 In.	175.00
Jardiniere, Winged Figures, Green, 33 1/2 In.	500.00

Figurines are often damaged. Examine the fingers, toes, and other protruding parts for damages or repairs.

Vase, Lincoln, Jasperware, Marked 175.00

> The first radio broadcast receiving sets were sold in New York City in 1910. They were used to pick up the experimental broadcasts of the day. The first commercial radios were made by Westinghouse Company for listeners of the experimental shows on KDKA Pittsburgh in 1920. Collectors today are interested in all early radios, especially those made of Bakelite plastic or decorated with blue mirrors.

RADIO, Admiral, Bakelite, White 20.00
  Air King Products, Table Model, Curved Wooden Cabinet, Model 824 .... 150.00
  American Bosch 219.00
  Arbor Phone, Model 29, 5 Tube 80.00
  Atwater Kent, Cathedral, Model 217 .... 65.00
  Atwater Kent, Model 10, Breadboard, Power Cord Battery, 1922 .... 365.00
  Atwater Kent, Model 20, Big Box, 1924 .... 78.00
  Atwater Kent, Model 30 .... 60.00
  Atwater Kent, Model 90, Cathedral, 1901 .... 225.00
  Auto, Ford Thunderbird, Figural 60.00
  Bendix, Table Model, 0526E, Wooden, 1946 .... 25.00
  Bozo The Clown, Box 25.00
  Buckingham, Table, Battery, Walnut, 3 Dials, Inside Speaker 115.00
  Cascade, Round Top, 13 In. 125.00
  Champion Spark Plug, Spark Plug Shape 95.00
  Columbia, 1928 .... 300.00
  Columbia, Battery 135.00
  Console, Airline, 1930s 295.00
  Crosley, Cathedral 100.00
  Crosley, Clock, White Plastic, 1940s 45.00
  Crosley, Console, T.V., Radio & Record Player, Model 348CP 500.00
  Crosley, Model 11–123U, Maroon, Plastic 46.00
  Crosley, Model 52 SD, 3 Tube, 1923 .... 65.00
  Crosley, Model YJ, 1922 .... 150.00
  Crosley, Show Box, 8 Tube, Speaker 80.00
  Crystal Set, Federal 250.00
  Crystal Set, Flower, 4 X 5 1/2 In. 65.00
  Crystal Set, Howe 200.00
  Crystal Set, Philmore, Glass Dome, Green, Box, 4 X 5 1/2 In. 150.00
  Delco, Magnascope, Wood Cabinet 35.00
  Detrola, Tube, Light Wood, 1943 .... 30.00
  Emerson, 2 Tone, Miracle Wand 65.00
  Emerson, Blue–Green Bakelite 125.00
  Emerson, Maroon, Table 45.00
  Emerson, Mickey Mouse Playing Instruments On Sides, 1934 .... 900.00
  Emerson, Molded Wood, Table Model 65.00
  Emerson, Pocket, Explorer 888, Red 22.00
  Emerson, Violin Shaped Case, Burl Walnut, C.1940 .... 135.00
  Fada, Art Deco Design, Shelf, Mustard Yellow, C.1935, 10 In. 225.00
  Fada, Bakelite, Model 652, Yellow, Red Trim 450.00
  Fada, Neutrodyne, Model 175A, 5 Tube 100.00
  Federal AD 150.00
  Federal, Model A–10, 5 Tube 125.00
  Firestone, Bakelite, White 45.00
  Franklin, Plastic, Baby Grand Piano Shape 40.00
  Freshman Masterpiece 155.00
  General Electric, Cathedral 165.00
  General Electric, Floor Model H–77, Wooden, Push Button Tuning 350.00
  General Electric, Model 408, Bakelite 35.00
  General Electric, Model K63 .... 180.00
  Globe, RCA Globe Trotter, Metal 40.00
  Grebe Syncrophase 155.00
  Grundig Majestic, Plastic, Table Model, Late 1940s 75.00
  Hallicrafter, Model S–41G, Skyrider, Jr. 55.00
  Hallicrafter, Sky Champion Overseas Bands, 1960s 95.00

Jukebox Shape, With Bank, Mirrored Top, 64 Songs, 16 Buttons, 5 In.	100.00
L.O.A.Sunwatch, Original Packing	75.00
Magnavox, Horn	45.00
Majestic, Walnut, 1936	195.00
Metrodyne, Super 7	250.00
Microphone, Fixed To 1340KC, Local Station	230.00
Midwest Consolette	175.00
Montgomery Ward, Single Tube, Copper Coil, 1914	100.00
Motorola, Chevrolet, Manual Control, 1951	18.00
Motorola, Model 52R	25.00
Motorola, Model 65L12, Portable	55.00
Motorola, Red Bakelite	25.00
Musaphonic, Brown Plastic	17.00
Music Master, Horn Speaker, Mahogany Bell	85.00
Neutrowood, 6 Tube, Black Metal	125.00
Northome, Model VI, Speaker, 1925–28	75.00
Old Crow, Crow Shape, Transister, Box	75.00
Packard Bell, Console, 1939	200.00
Peerless Reproducer, Cathedral Cabinet, Fabric Both Sides	65.00
Philco, Model 70, Super Heterodyne 7	150.00
Philco, Model 84, Cathedral	130.00
Philco, Model 510	390.00
Philco, Model B570, Red	50.00
Philco, Transitone, 1950s	65.00
Poodle, Stuffed, 1950s	30.00
Radiola, 3A	125.00
RCA Victor, Model 1089	50.00
RCA, Model AR 927, Battery Operated, Receiver	95.00
RCA, Model CGR 30, 6 Tubes, High Frequency, 1930	100.00
RCA, Portable, Satchel–Like, 1947	30.00
Sentinel, White Plastic, 1930s	75.00
Silver Marshall, Cathedral	280.00
Silvertone Neutrodyne, 5 Tube, 1924	85.00
Silvertone, Cathedral, Battery Operated, Model 1291	110.00
Spartan, Blue Mirror	800.00
Stewart Warner, Model 325, 5 Tubes, 1925	85.00
Stewart Warner, Model 51T136	40.00
Stewart Warner, White Plastic	45.00
Stromberg–Carlson, Bakelite	25.00
Stromberg–Carlson, Corner, Cabinet	165.00
Supreme Radio Analyzer, Model 333, Oak	40.00
Sylvania, Pink	25.00
Trutone, Bakelite, 1930s	35.00
Trutone, Red Bakelite	40.00
Westinghouse, Grandfather Clock	325.00
Westinghouse, Turquoise, 1950s	35.00
Wood Coronado	25.00
Zenith, 1940s	25.00
Zenith, Am/Fm, Table Model	65.00
Zenith, Bakelite, Brown, Handle	25.00
Zenith, Model 5S338, Table	135.00
Zenith, Transoceanic, Model 3000–1, Royal Works	120.00

Railroad enthusiasts collect any train memorabilia. Everything is wanted, from oilcans to whole train cars. The Chessie system has a store that sells many reproductions of their old dinnerware and uniforms.

RAILROAD, Almanac, Santa Fe R.R., 1948	3.00
Ashtray, Chessie, Glass	25.00
Ashtray, Cotton Belt R.R., Metal	10.00
Badge, Brakeman's Cap, New York City	15.00
Badge, Conductor's Cap	5.00
Bell, Bronze, 12 In.	125.00
Bell, Dinner, With Mallet	110.00

Bell, Locomotive, Brass, With Yoke, 300 Lb. 1050.00
Bell, Steam Engine, Bronze, Marked Santa Fe 300.00
Bell, Steam Locomotive, Bronze, Yoke & Cradle, 17 In. 875.00
Bench, Dining Car, Cherry, High Back, Coat Rack On Side 500.00
Blanket, Great Northern, Salmon, Goat Logo, 64 X 84 In. 100.00
Blanket, Lap, Northwest Orient 15.00
Blanket, Pullman Logo, Wool 45.00
Bobber, Caboose, D & R.G. 1900.00
Bottle, Water, S.S.Pullman 35.00
Bowl, Cereal, Pennsylvania R.R., Purple Laurel Design 27.00
Brochure, Illinois Central Green Diamond, 1936 .... 9.50
Butter Chip, N.Y.& N.H., Blue 14.00
Butter Chip, Union Pacific Streamliner .... 20.00 To 30.00
Butter, Union Pacific R.R., White, Trenton China, 3 1/2 In. 10.00
Button, New Haven R.R., Yellow, 7/8 In. 45.00
Button, Rock Island R.R. 12.00
Caboose Marker, Kerosene, S.P.R.R. 175.00
Caboose Marker, S.P.R.R., Kerosene, Adlake Nonsweating, 14 In. 200.00
Caboose Marker, Wabash R.R. 175.00
Calendar, C.& N.W. R.R., 1937, 12 X 24 In. 18.00
Can, Kerosene, N.& W.R.R. 22.00
Castor Set, 3–Bottle, California Zephyr, Silver Plate 150.00
Chamber Pot, Central Pacific, Brass 100.00
Coal Scuttle, Santa Fe R.R., Embossed 20.00
Coffeepot, Great Northern R.R., Silver Plate, C.1910 .... 75.00
Coffeepot, Marked The Challenger, Sterling Silver, 32 Oz. 250.00
Cold Chisel, Atchison, Topeka & Santa Fe R.R. 10.00
Compote, Baltimore & Ohio R.R., Shenango Pattern 50.00
Compote, Union Pacific 17.50
Cordial, Engraved Santa Fe, 3 1/4 In., Set of 4 .... 50.00
Creamer, Covered, Great Northern R.R., Silver Plate, 4 Oz. 55.00
Creamer, Grand Central Depot, Cincinnati, Ohio, Souvenir 18.00
Crock, Rock Island R.R., 1 Gal. 100.00
Cup & Saucer, Southern Pacific, Prairie Mountain Wild Flowers 90.00
Cup & Saucer, Wabash R.R. 250.00
Cup, Santa Fe, California Poppy 35.00
Cuspidor, C.R.I. & P., Brass 225.00
Cuspidor, Pullman Co., Nickel Plated Brass 65.00
Desk, Pay, Mahogany, 5 Ft. 395.00
Dinner, Santa Fe, California Poppy, 10 In. 50.00
Dish, Soup, U.P.R.R., Flying Streamliner 12.00
Door Lock, Caboose. Brass, 2 Knobs, Plate, Skeleton Key, 6 X 4 In. ... 12.00
Door Plate, C & O R.R., Tin, Chessie The Cat 10.00
Eggcup, C.& N. 12.00
Eggcup, Union Pacific Streamliner 60.00
Fan, Burlington Route, Baseball Game, Map, 1888, 10 X 16 In. 15.00
Finger Bowl, Golden Rocket, Silver, Rock Island 85.00
Fire Extinguisher, C.M.St.P & P, Brass 47.50
First Aid Kit, NYC R.R., Complete 25.00
Globe, N.Y.C.S., Red Marked Globe 30.00
Globe, Union Pacific, Tall 85.00
Hammer, Ball Pean, Erie R.R. 15.00
Headlight, Great Northern Steam Engine 950.00
Headlight, Reading Locomotive No.2115 .... 400.00
Holder, Bottle, Ginger Ale, New York Central 42.00
Jug, Baltimore & Ohio, Dated 1927, 14 Oz. 48.00
Jug, Deodorizer, Pullman Co. 50.00
Jug, Water, Pottery, Baltimore & Ohio R.R. 85.00
Knife, Missouri Pacific, Souvenir 30.00
Ladle, Gravy, Fred Harvey, Silver Plate 40.00
Lamp Filler, Kerosene, Pennsylvania R.R., Tin 40.00
Lamp, Caboose Marker, N.Y.C.S., Bull's Eye & Ribbed Lens, Pair 260.00
Lamp, Caboose, Adams & Westlake, Kerosene 55.00
Lamp, Coach, Brass, Midi R.R., Butin Paris, Pair 1200.00

Lamp, Oxweld, Model 2, Carbide 45.00
Lamp, Wall, Student, Boston, Mass., 1871 .... 1400.00
Lantern, A.B.& O.Logo Globe 85.00
Lantern, Boston & Albany, Clear Marked Globe, 4 1/2 In. 45.00
Lantern, Boston–Maine, Red 90.00
Lantern, C.& N.W., Tall Globe 65.00
Lantern, Caboose, Handlan, St.Louis 45.00
Lantern, Cincinnati Union Terminal R.R., Adlake, Green Globe 37.50
Lantern, Clear Globe, Brass Bell Bottom, Meyrose 285.00
Lantern, Delaware & Hudson R.R., Embossed Globe 17.50
Lantern, Depot, Dietz, Beason 75.00
Lantern, Dietz–Monarch 55.00
Lantern, Erie R.R., Reliable, Clear Embossed Globe 35.00
Lantern, Federal Signal Co., Electric, 1913 .... 35.00
Lantern, Green Over Clear Globe, C.T.Ham, Brass, 3 1/2 In. 600.00
Lantern, Hand, High Globe, Chicago & Northwestern R.R. 65.00
Lantern, Hand, High Globe, Double Markings, N.Y.C. R.R. 65.00
Lantern, Hand, Railway Motors, Reflector, Battery Operated, 10 In. 45.00
Lantern, Inspector's, Pennsylvania Railroad, Black Paint 60.00
Lantern, Long Island Railroad, Armspear Type, Ruby Globe 19.00
Lantern, New Haven R.R., Adlake Reliable, Clear Globe, 1908–13 .... 45.00
Lantern, New Haven R.R., Red Globe, 4 1/4 In. 30.00
Lantern, New York Central, Red, Embossed, 6 In. 58.00
Lantern, Northwestern Line, Cast Globe 225.00
Lantern, Northwestern, Logo Globe 225.00
Lantern, Orange Globe, N.Y.C. R.R. 45.00
Lantern, P.R.R., Dressel, Red Globe 65.00
Lantern, Penn Central, Kero 20.00
Lantern, Reading Co. Transportation Dept., Ruby Globe, 1928 .... 35.00
Lantern, Red Dietz Glass Globe, Eclipse 30.00
Lantern, Rock Island, Red Globe 57.00
Lantern, Soo Line, Clear 55.00
Lantern, Switchman's, Wabash R.R., Short Globe 85.00
Lantern, Union Pacific, Cast Globe 225.00
Lantern, Union Pacific, Etched Shield 150.00
Lantern, Union Pacific, Tall Globe 85.00
Lock, Chain, CBQ R.R., 1920 .... 20.00
Matchbook Cover, Union Pacific R.R., 1940s 2.00
Menu, AMTRAK, Breakfast, Empire Builder, Scenes On Cover 8.00
Menu, Cook's Streamliner, Figural, 1940s 10.00
Menu, S.T.S.& F., Dinner, Super Chief, Arrow Maker Cover, 1968 .... 10.00
Menu, San Francisco Overland Limited, Folded, Writing, Dated 1944 ..... 5.00
Menu, Union Pacific, Breakfast, Trains, Postcard Tear–Off Top 12.00
Menu, Union Pacific, Colored Western View, C.1928 .... 12.00
Mug, Rock Island Line, Green & White Swirl, Graniteware, Marked 135.00
Mustard, New York Central 19.00
Oil Can, Great Northern Railway, Long Spout 35.00
Oil Can, N.K.P. R.R., Nickel Plate 42.00
Oil Can, N.Y.Central System 35.00
Oyster Plate, Union Pacific 65.00
Pail, Coal, Great Northern Railway 10.00
Paperweight, Illinois Central R.R., Bronze, 1951 .... 15.00
Paperweight, Milwaukee R.R., Grizzly Bear 55.00
Paperweight, N.P.R.R., Figural, Bronze 80.00
Paperweight, Pennsylvania Keystone Logo, Square, 3 In. 48.00
Paperweight, S.M.& St.P.R.R.Electric Locomotive 50.00
Plate, B. & O.R.R.Diesel Electric 65.00
Plate, B. & O., Thomas Viaduct, 7 In. 55.00
Plate, Bread, Wabash R.R., Banner China 47.50
Plate, Dinner, Santa Fe, California Poppy, 10 In. 50.00
Plate, Florida East Coast, Mystick, 6 In. 15.00
Plate, Missouri & Pacific Diesel, Syracuse China, 10 1/2 In. 195.00
Plate, Missouri Pacific, State Capitols, Diesel Service 275.00
Plate, Missouri Pacific, State Flower 190.00

Plate, Mountain Laurel, P.R.R., 9 1/2 In.	30.00
Plate, New York, New Haven & Hartford R.R., Indian Tree Pattern	32.50
Plate, New York, New Haven & Hartford R.R., Platinum Blue	32.50
Plate, P.R.R., Mt.Laurel, 7 In.	18.00
Plate, Salad, Santa Fe, California Poppy, 7 In.	30.00
Plate, Santa Fe, California Poppy, 10 In.	50.00
Plate, Santa Fe, Membrenos Design, Syracuse China, 10 In.	90.00
Plate, Southern Pacific, Sunset Logo, 7 1/4 In.	37.50
Plate, Union Pacific R.R., 7 In.	28.50
Plate, Western Pacific, 5 1/2 In.	32.00
Plate, Western Pacific, 7 1/4 In.	48.00
Plate, Western Pacific, 9 1/2 In.	215.00
Platter, Union Pacific, Harriman Blue, Oval, Logo, 11 In.	50.00
Platter, Union Pacific, Oval, 6 X 8 In.	20.00
Postcard, Railroad Scene, 1910	5.00
Postcard, Union Pacific Overland, Unused, Set of 12	32.00
Poster, Boston & Albany R.R., Promoting Autumn Excursion	6.00
Poster, Northern Pacific, Mt.St.Helens, 40 X 30 In.	35.00
Print, B & O, Chessie Cat, Framed	35.00
Print, Hinkley Locomotive, C.H.Crosby & Co., 1870, 19 X 28 In.	750.00
Rack, Timetable, Fonda, Johnstown & Gloversville Line, Wooden	160.00
Relish, Square, Union Pacific Streamliner	80.00
Sauceboat, Santa Fe Mimbreno	125.00
Schedule, National Railways Mexico Centenary, 1910	17.50
Sheet Music, In A Little Cottage By The Railroad Track	8.00
Sheet Music, Make That Engine Stop At Louisville, 1913	10.00
Sheet Music, Palm Limited March Two Step	8.00
Sheet Music, San Francisco Bound	8.00
Sherbet, Footed, Great Northern R.R., Silver Plate	45.00
Shovel, Coal, St.L.& Santa Fe	38.00
Sign, Crossing, Cast Iron, Original Paint	160.00
Sign, Do Not Open Door, Train Stops, German, Porcelain, 3 X 18 In.	45.00
Sign, Invalid Car, Hand Painted, With Red Cross, World War I	132.50
Sign, Lake Shore & Michigan Southern R.R., 8 X 9 1/2 In.	8.00
Sign, Warning, Stop, Look & Listen, Cast Iron, White Lettering	285.00
Sign, Wyndmoor, Reading Co., Porcelain Enameled, On Wood, 52 In.	70.00
Silent Butler, Chessie, Wooden Inlay	45.00
Soup, Dish, Union Pacific, 9 In.	28.00
Spittoon, Canadian Pacific R.R., Cast Iron	85.00
Spittoon, Property of Pullman Silver Palace Car Co., 11 In.	125.00
Spittoon, Union Pacific, Brass	100.00
Spoon, Northern Pacific	12.00
Spoon, Soup, Norfolk & Western R.R., Silver	20.00
Step Stool, A.T.S.F., 13 X 18 In.	175.00
Step Stool, Morton, A.T.S.F., 13 X 18 In.	175.00
Step Stool, N.Y.C., Gray & Green, 18 X 20 In.	150.00
Step, Steel, Northern Pacific	85.00
Stock Certificate, Chicago, Burlington & Quincy, 1884	15.00
Stock Certificate, Denver & Santa Fe, Colorado	20.00
Sugar & Creamer, Canadian Pacific R.R., Silver Plate	60.00
Sugar, Northern Pacific, Sterling Silver	75.00
Switchstand, Harp Type, Narrow Gauge East Broad Top R.R., 7 Ft.	725.00
Teapot, Centennial Pattern, Shenango, B.& O., 1927	118.00
Teapot, Union Pacific Streamliner	95.00 To 120.00
Thermos, Pullman, Chrome, 1930s, 1 Qt.	40.00
Timetable, Burlington, 1905	35.00
Timetable, Missouri Pacific Lines, Eagles, 1958	5.00
Timetable, San Francisco, 1911	35.00
Timetable, Seaboard, World War II, Dec.6, 1942	3.50
Tool, Lineman's, Western Union, Marked W.U.T.Co.	15.00
Torch, D & H, Iron	17.50
Traffic Light, Dietz, Syracuse, N.Y.	40.00
Tumbler, Highball, Southern Railroad, Train Picture	10.00
Tumbler, Santa Fe, Etched, 4 In.	12.00

Tumbler, Union Pacific, Footed, 11 Oz. 10.00
Uniform, Conductor's Jacket & Vest, Union Pacific 45.00
Uniform, Conductor's, C.M.St.P & P. 140.00
Whistle, B & O, Brass 16.50
Whistle, Chime, Brass, Fulton Co. 65.00
Wrench, Stillson, New Haven, 18 In. 30.00

The razor was used in ancient Egypt and subsequently wherever shaving was in fashion. The metal razor used in America until about 1870 was made in Sheffield, England. After 1870, machine–made hollow–ground razors were made in Germany or America. Plastic or bone handles were popular. The razor was often sold in a set of seven, one for each day of the week. The set was often kept by the barber who shaved the well–to–do man each day in the shop.

RAZOR, Blue, Box, 1940s, Tiny 10.00
Curvfit Woman's, Case 15.00
Evans, Velvet Lined Flat Tin, Miniature 12.00
Eversharp Schick Injector, 1937 .... 7.50
Gem, Celluloid Box 26.00
Gem, Set, Box 5.00
Geo.Wolstenholm & Sons, Ebony Handle, Incised W–American, Civil War 55.00
Gillette, Safety, Milady, Original Display Box 45.00
Imperial Rolls, English Demonstration Model, Box 17.50
Lafayette Cutlery, White Handle Has Full Peacock, Germany 30.00
Royal, Keen Kutter 35.00
Safety, Nickel Plated Brass, Days of Week Case 37.50
Safety, Winchester, Box 35.00
Schick Injector, Yellow Bakelite 12.00
Schick, Crown Jewel, Electric, Leather Box 40.00
Sharpener, Blade, Automatic Kriss Kross 12.50
Sharpener, Glass, Pink, Advertising 12.50
Shears Type Card Shaver 750.00
Straight, Bone Handle, Sheffield, Original Papier–Mache Case, C.1860 .... 19.50
Straight, Celluloid Handle, Jockey On Horseback, Jumping Fence 75.00
Straight, Crosson, Saginaw, Pictorials 30.00
Straight, Ear of Corn, Ivory 65.00
Straight, Figural, Bamboo Stalk 15.00
Straight, Horse With Rider, Germany 22.00
Straight, Imperial, Eagle With Spread Wings On Blade, Germany 17.00
Straight, Ivory Handle, Germany, Box 20.00
Straight, Keen Kutter, Directions 25.00
Straight, Mother–of–Pearl Handle, Case .... 15.00 To 75.00
Straight, Old Car Etched On Blade 36.00
Straight, Original Pipe Razor, Celluloid Holder 28.00
Straight, Plymouth Rock Etched On Blade 30.00
Straight, Sheffield, 7 Days of The Week 225.00
Straight, Teddy Roosevelt 85.00
Straight, Union Stockyards, Chicago 23.00
Straight, Wade & Butcher, Black Handle 13.00
Straight, Winchester 50.00
The Real, Box, Dated Feb.10, 1903 .... 22.00
Wade & Butcher, Black Horn Handle, Bright Blade, Box 5.00

Reamers, or juice squeezers, have been known since 1767, although most of those collected today date from the twentieth century. Figural reamers are among the most prized.

REAMER, Boss, Lemon, Cast Iron 24.00
Cast Iron, Lemon 60.00
Child's Face Pouring Spout, Handled Base, China 55.00
Clown .... 25.00 To 35.00
Crisscross, Green 12.00
Easley, Glass, 1900 .... 12.00
Fleur–De–Lis, Orange Slag 300.00
Fluted Bowl, Lemon, Cast Iron, 8 In. 22.50

Hazel Atlas	8.00
Iron & Stoneware, Lemon	68.00
Ironstone Insert, 1868	30.00
Ironstone Insert, Iron, 1868	25.00
Jade Clambroth	75.00
McKee, Green Opaque	27.00
Oak Base, Brass & Silver Plate, 12 In.	75.00
Pear, Luster, 3 Piece	45.00
Silver Plate, Meriden	65.00
Sunkist, Chatelaine	185.00
Sunkist, Green Opalescent	35.00
Sunkist, Milk Glass	15.00 To 40.00
Sunkist, Opalescent	18.50
Sunkist, Seville Yellow	50.00
Sunkist, Transparent Green	28.00
Sunkist, Yellow	55.00
Will & Finck, Lime	150.00

The cylinder–shaped phonograph record for use with the early Edison phonograph was made about 1889. Disc records were first made by 1894; the double–sided disc by 1904. The high–fidelity records were first issued in 1944, the first vinyl disc in 1946, the first stereo record in 1958. The 78 RPM became the standard in 1926 but was discontinued in 1957. In 1932, the first 33 1/3 RPM was made but was not sold commercially until 1948. In 1949, the 45 RPM was introduced.

RECORD, Al Jolson, Columbia, 78 RPM	26.50
Album, Country Music Connie Style, Connie Francis, MGM	8.00
Alex Jackson & His Plantation Serenaders, Gennett, 78 RPM	67.00
Beale Street Washboard Band, Vocalion	66.00
Billy The Kid Emerson, Sun 195, 45 RPM	147.00
Bing Crosby, Bells of St. Mary's	15.00
Bing Crosby, Brunswick, 78 RPM	11.00
Buddy Holly, Decca, Promotional Copy, 45 RPM	104.00
Carmen Miranda, 78 RPM	10.00
Casper, Golden Record, 1962	5.00
Charley Skeete & His Orchestra, Edison, 78 RPM	87.50
Chubby Checker, Slow Twist, La Paloma Twist, 45 RPM	5.00
Cinderella, Let's Pretend, Columbia, 3 Piece	12.00
Clarence Williams' Stompers, Okeh	11.00
Cylinder, Edison, 4 Minute	3.50
Dick Tracy & Sparkle Plenty, 78 RPM, 1947	75.00
Duke Ellington & His Orchestra, Brunswick, 78 RPM	25.00
Eddie Cochran, Liberty, 45 RPM	14.00
Edison, Diamond Disc, 1/4 In. Thick	2.50
Fabulous Fabian, LP, Chancellor, Foldout	25.00
Fats Domino, Imperial, 45 RPM	50.00
Ferdinand The Bull, 1950s, 6 In.	12.00
Fritz Kreisler, Violin, With Orchestra	5.00
Goofus Five, Okeh, 78 RPM	11.00
Hotsy Totsy Gang, Brunswick, 78 RPM	16.00
If I Didn't Believe In You, Frankie Laine, ABC	2.00
Island In The Sky, John Wayne, 78 Rpm, 1953	35.00
Jimmie Davis, Bluebird, 78 RPM	7.25
Jimmie Rodgers, Victor, 78 RPM	70.00
John Phillip Sousa, Hands Across The Sea, Decca	5.00
Kate Smith, Diva, 78 RPM	8.25
Kiddy Carnival Review, Narrated By Keener Haynes, 3 Piece	15.00
Kissin' Time, Bobby Rydell, Cameo	2.00
Lena Wilson, Brunswick	15.00
Little Black Sambo, RCA Victor, 45 RPM, Set of 2, Book	35.00
Little Eddie Boyd, RCA Victor, 45 RPM	32.00
Louella, Pat Boone, Dot	2.00
Mae West, Brunswick, 78 RPM	15.00

Martha Drinking Song, Columbia, Henri Scott, 1915 .... 20.00
Mickey Gilley, Lynn 503, 45 RPM 15.00
Paul Whiteman & His Orchestra, Columbia, 78 RPM 12.00
Peggy Sue, Buddy Holly, 45 RPM, 1950s 10.00
Red Lewis & His Band, Columbia, 78 RPM 10.50
Red Nichols & 5 Pennies, Brunswick, 78 RPM 8.50
Red Onion Jazz Babies, Gennett, 78 RPM 90.00
Ripley's Believe It Or Not, Interview, Set of 2, 1939 .... 100.00
Rudy Vallee, Diva, 78 RPM 8.50
Stormy Weather, Four Freshmen, Capitol 2.00
The First Family, Vaughn Meader, Spoof of J.F.Kennedy 25.00
Three For The Show, Soundtrack, 45 RPM, 1955 .... 10.00
Uncle Dave Macon, Bluebird, 78 RPM 23.00
Uncle Don's Playland, Album, 78 RPM, 1927, Set of 3 .... 10.00
Whiteman's Rhythm Boys, Columbia, 78 RPM 7.00
Young World, Rick Nelson, Imperial 2.00

The Red Wing Pottery of Red Wing, Minnesota, was a firm started in 1878. It was not until the 1920s that art pottery was made. It closed in 1967. Rumrill pottery was made for George Rumrill by the Red Wing Pottery and other firms. It was sold in the 1930s.

RED WING, Ashtray, 1965 World Series 55.00
Ashtray, Maroon, 75th Anniversary, 1953 .... 35.00
Ashtray, Twins, 1965 .... 37.00
Bean Pot, Advertising Blue Letters 85.00
Bean Pot, Saffron, Sponged 90.00
Beater Jar, Cheese, Blue Band, Heinrich & Koehler 175.00
Beater Jar, Clearfield, Iowa 66.00
Beater Jar, Cream, Salad Dressing Logo 120.00
Beater Jar, Harley, Iowa 70.00
Beater Jar, Muller & Lohr, Rudd, Iowa, Marked 67.50
Beater Jar, Ribbed Sides, 2 Blue Bands 55.00
Beater Jar, Solid Blue 40.00
Beverage Server, Futura, Organ Grinder 28.00
Bill, Envelope, 1919 .... 10.00
Bird, Hors D'Oeuvres, Bobwhite 32.50
Bowl, Blue & Rust Spongeware, Signed, 7 In. 65.00
Bowl, Blue Bands, Red Sponge, 5 In. 100.00
Bowl, Magnolia, 8 1/2 In. 8.00
Bowl, Mixing, Wide Shoulder, White, 11 In. 35.00
Bowl, Paneled, Spongeware, 4 1/4 X 9 In. 55.00
Bowl, Sponge Band, No.4 .... 175.00
Bowl, Sponge Band, No.6 .... 175.00
Bowl, Spongeware, 7 In. .... 67.50 To 88.00
Bowl, Spongeware, Blue, Rust, Cream, 6 In. 50.00
Bowl, Spongeware, Paneled, Blue, Rust, Cream, 6 In. 75.00
Bowl, Stick Handle, Covered, 8 1/2 In. 12.50
Bowl, Tampico, 9 In. 8.00
Bowl, Vegetable, Magnolia, Divided, 11 1/4 In. 8.00
Bowl, Yellow Geometric Moths, 8 In. 20.00
Butter Churn, Bails On Side, Lid, Patent 1913, 6 Gal. 165.00
Butter, Advertising, 10 Lb. 40.00
Cake Plate, Random Harvest 20.00
Casserole, Covered, Orleans 20.00
Casserole, Provincial, Glazed Interior & Lid, 4 1/2 In. 25.00
Chamber Pot, Blue Stripe 137.50
Chamber Pot, Lily 115.00
Churn, Birch Leaf, 4 Gal. 190.00
Churn, Commemorative, 1979 .... 170.00
Churn, Dated, Small Wing, 3 Gal. 70.00
Churn, Large Wing, 3 Gal. 110.00
Churn, Large Wing, Lid, Dasher, 5 Gal. 135.00
Churn, Leaf, Salt Glaze, Signed, 6 Gal. 850.00
Clock, Black Mammy, Electric, Murcen 60.00

Cookie Jar, Baker, Blue .... 20.00 To 30.00
Cookie Jar, Chef, Blue 25.00
Cookie Jar, Cookies On Front, Floral Design, 8 1/2 In. 75.00
Cookie Jar, Dutch Girl, Blue 45.00
Cookie Jar, French Chef, Yellow 30.00
Cookie Jar, Katrina 42.00
Cookie Jar, King of Tarts .... 52.50 To 135.00
Cookie Jar, Monk .... 15.00 To 45.00
Cookie Jar, Moondrops, Thou Shalt Not Steal 15.00
Cookie Jar, Pear, Turquoise 25.00
Cookie Jar, Sponge Band 125.00
Cookie Jar, Umbrella Kids 26.00
Crock, 3 Gal. 30.00
Crock, 6 Gal. 40.00
Crock, Big Wing, 1 Gal. 45.00
Crock, Butter, 10 Lb. 265.00
Crock, C.Daffenbach & Gisseke, New Ulm, Brown, 2 Gal. 60.00
Crock, Drink 3 Star Coffee, Sioux City, Iowa, 1/2 Gal. 150.00
Crock, Salt Glaze, Cyclone, 3 In.Blue Band, 5 Gal. 75.00
Crock, Salt, Lid, White, Carnation Front 45.00
Crock, Wooden Handle, Large Wing, Dated 1915, 15 Gal. 145.00
Cup & Saucer, Bobwhite 200.00
Cup & Saucer, Village, Green 7.00
Dinner Set, Pepe, 8 Place Settings, Serving Pieces 6.50
Figurine, Accordion Player, 10 In. 998.00
Figurine, Boy, 7 In. 55.00
Figurine, Cowgirl, Reddish Brown Monochrome, 10 1/2 In. 135.00
Figurine, Lady, With Tambourine, 8 In. 45.00
Figurine, Man, With Accordion, 10 In. 65.00
Football, Wisc.Badger, Signed 35.00
Gravy Boat, Covered, Bobwhite 85.00
Jar, Applesauce, 3 Gal. 26.00
Jar, Fruit, Mason, 1 Gal. 70.00
Jar, Fruit, Stone Mason, 1 Qt. .... 260.00 To 295.00
Jar, Pantry, 1 Lb. 110.00
Jar, Pantry, 3 Lb. 125.00
Jar, Perfection Sanitary Self Draining, Stand, 25 Gal. 550.00
Jar, Refrigerator, 5 1/2 In. 195.00
Jar, Snuff, Signed, 2 Pt. 85.00
Jug, Albany Slip Bird Molded, 1/2 Gal. 80.00
Jug, Beehive, Brown, 1/2 Gal. 125.00
Jug, Beehive, Fairfield, Iowa, 5 Gal. 50.00
Jug, Beehive, Mason House, Colfax, Iowa, 5 Gal. 450.00
Jug, Beehive, Salt Glaze, Lazy 8, 5 Gal. 400.00
Jug, Commemorative, 1981 .... 300.00
Jug, Commemorative, 1984 .... 140.00
Jug, Eleda Vinegar, Milwaukee 80.00
Jug, Henry Bosquet, 1/8 Pt. 125.00
Jug, Mason House, Iowa, 5 Gal. 100.00
Jug, R.W.S.W.Co., 1/2 Pt. 350.00
Jug, Salt Glaze, Double P Ribcage, 3 Gal. 300.00
Jug, Salt Glaze, Lazy 8 Beehive, 5 Gal. 275.00
Jug, Sterling Wine House, 1 Gal. 300.00
Jug, Wide Mouth, 1 Gal. 90.00
Jug, Wing In Center, Brown Top, 1/2 Gal. 150.00
Mug, Bobwhite 110.00
Nappy, Random Harvest 50.00
Pitcher & Bowl, Lily 6.00
Pitcher, Bobwhite, 7 In. 275.00
Pitcher, Bobwhite, 12 In. .... 12.50 To 20.00
Pitcher, Bobwhite, 14 In. 20.00
Pitcher, Cherry Band 60.00
Pitcher, Grape & Trellis, Brown, North Star On Base, Blue & White .... 95.00 To 120.00
Pitcher, Grayline, Horstman's Cash Store, Bigelow, Minn. 75.00
      160.00

Pitcher, Saffron .... 68.00 To 80.00
Pitcher, Sponge Band, Compliments Marek's Grocery, Wis., 2 Qt. 160.00
Pitcher, Spongeware, Peterson Co. 575.00
Plate, Bobwhite, 6 1/2 In. 3.00
Plate, Bobwhite, 11 In. 8.00
Plate, Capistrano, 10 In. 7.50
Plate, Driftwood, 6 1/2 In. 2.50
Plate, Driftwood, 10 3/4 In. 7.50
Plate, Lexington, 10 1/2 In. 5.00
Plate, Lotus, 10 1/2 In. 5.00
Plate, Town & Country, 8 In. 4.00
Plate, Town & Country, 10 1/2 In. 6.00
Platter, Bobwhite, 13 In. 17.50
Platter, Magnolia, Green, 13 In. 8.00
Poultry Drinking Fount & Buttermilk Feeder 40.00
Relish, Bobwhite, 3 Sections 18.50
Salt & Pepper, Bird .... 12.00 To 16.00
Salt Crock, Lid, White, Carnation Front 145.00
Saltshaker, Grayline 185.00
Soap Dish, Carnation, Blue & White 140.00
Soup, Cream, Moondrops, Red 20.00
Spittoon, Salt Glaze .... 250.00 To 270.00
Sugar & Creamer, Moondrops, Red, Individual 20.00
Sugar, Driftwood, Covered 12.00
Toothpick, Gopher On Log, Dated 1939 .... 100.00
Trivet, Minnesota Centennial, Green, 1858–1958 .... 25.00
Vase, Brushware, Flowers, 8 1/2 In. 45.00
Vase, Bud, Triple, Green, 7 3/4 In. 13.00
Vase, Green, 12 In. .... 20.00 To 32.50
Vase, Maroon, Handles, 8 1/4 In. 18.00
Vase, Roman Design, No.159, 9 In. 90.00
Vase, Star, Pink, 11 1/2 In. 15.00
Water Cooler, 3 Gal. 190.00
Water Cooler, 4 Gal., Covered 385.00
Water Cooler, 5 Gal. .... 195.00 To 250.00
Water Cooler, 15 Gal. 250.00
Water Cooler, Glass Ball Filter Bulb, 15 Gal. 350.00
Water Cooler, Small Wing, 3 Gal. 300.00
Water Cooler, Spigot 95.00

Redware is a hard, red stoneware that originated in the late 1600s
and continues to be made. The term is also used to describe any
common clay pottery that is reddish in color.

REDWARE, Bank, Light Rust Glaze, Flat Round Finial Top, 3 1/2 X 4 In. 75.00
Bank, Scroddleware, Empire Bureau Shape, 19th Century, 5 3/8 In. 200.00
Basket, 4 1/2 X 3 1/2 In. 28.00
Bean Pot, Rust Glazed Interior Handle, Unglazed Exterior, C.1830 .... 45.00
Bottle, Red Glaze, Dark Splotches, 7 In. 130.00
Bowl, Glaze, Brown Sponging, 3 1/4 In. 165.00
Bowl, Orange Interior, Brown Streaks, Pinched Edge, 13 X 4 In. 180.00
Bowl, Pennsylvania, Yellow Slip Design, Serrated Rim, 13 In. 375.00
Bowl, Rolled Rim, Pennsylvania, Mid–19th Century, 8 1/4 X 3 In. 155.00
Bowl, Tooled Lines, Brown Spots, 7 3/4 In. 110.00
Bowl, White Slip In Lines & Squiggles, Brown Wavy Line, 11 In. 145.00
Bowl, Wooden Tub Shape, Flared, Embossed, Bell Pottery, 10 In. 475.00
Bowl, Yellow Slip Combware, Green Stripes, 10 1/8 X 3 1/4 In. 850.00
Bowl, Yellow Slip Design, 7 In. 35.00
Bowl, Yellow Slip Design, European, 5 X 2 In. 45.00
Cooler, Punch, Figural, Civil War Soldier, C.1860, 25 In. 7000.00
Creamer, Arc & Leaf, Paneled 60.00
Crock, Slip, Dated 1830, 2 Gal. 225.00
Crock, Tooled Bands, Brown Running Splotches, New England, 6 In. 265.00
Cup Plate, Coggled Edge, Yellow Combware Design, 3 7/8 In. 375.00

Cuspidor, Running Brown Flecks, Orange, 9 In. 22.50
Dish, Brown Spotted Glaze, Oval, 8 1/4 X 10 3/4 In. 125.00
Dish, Covered, Handles, Green Glaze, Orange, Brown Splotches, 9 In. 165.00
Dish, Script Inscription In Yellow Slip, Greenish Glaze, 9 In. 300.00
Dish, Stylized Brown Slip Flower, 5 3/4 X 8 In. 875.00
Figurine, Rooster, Orange Brown Glaze, 19th Century, 14 1/2 In. 1760.00
Figurine, Shore Bird, Primitive, Incised Hazel, 10 3/4 In. 215.00
Flowerpot, Attached Saucer, Black Glaze, 4 3/8 In. 25.00
Flowerpot, Attached Saucer, Brown Glaze, Egg Shape, 6 1/2 In. 25.00
Flowerpot, Attached Saucer, Dots of Yellow Slip, 4 1/2 In. 90.00
Flowerpot, Attached Saucer, Tooled Rim, Orange & Brown Spots 275.00
Flowerpot, Attached Saucer, White Slip, Brown Sponging, 4 In. 80.00
Flowerpot, Running Brown Glaze 105.00
Flowerpot, Tooled Bands & Stripes of Yellow Slip, 6 In. 160.00
Jar, Amber Dots, Green, Egg Shape, 8 1/2 In. 250.00
Jar, Cream Colored Glaze, Running Brownish Amber, Egg Shape, 9 In. 500.00
Jar, Green Glaze, V.Rudolph, Egg Shape, 4 3/4 In. 45.00
Jar, Green–Brown Glaze, Yellow Slip Compass Star, 7 1/2 In. 300.00
Jar, Greenish Glaze, Brown Splotches, Egg Shape, 9 In. 55.00
Jar, Incised Wavy Lines, Brown Splotches, Egg Shape, 8 3/4 In. 525.00
Jar, Orange Spots, Brown Splotches, Egg Shape, 7 3/8 In. 575.00
Jar, Preserving, Clear Glaze, Brown Splotches, 12 1/2 In. 290.00
Jar, Preserving, Green Glaze, Amber Spots, Galena, 9 In. 100.00
Jug, Dark Glaze, Ribbed Strap Handle, Drilled For Lamp, 10 In. 55.00
Jug, Green & Orange Spotted Glaze, New Hampshire, Egg Shape, 9 In. 500.00
Jug, Green Glaze, Running Brown, Handle, 9 1/4 In. 275.00
Jug, Lid, Strap Handle, Dripping Yellow Slip, Egg Shape, 9 1/2 In. 1875.00
Jug, Puzzle, Yellow Slip Design, 4 1/2 In. 200.00
Jug, Ribbed Handle, Tooled Shoulder Line, Orange Spots, 7 1/4 In. 100.00
Jug, Ribbed Strap Handle, Tooled Lines, No.18, 8 1/4 X 9 In. 165.00
Jug, Rolled Rim, Ribbed Handle, Egg Shape, 19th Century, 1 Gal. 1400.00
Jug, Strap Handle, Egg Shape, 15 1/2 In. 65.00
Jug, Strap Handle, Flared Lip, Mottled Glaze, Sponging, 8 1/2 In. 350.00
Jug, Strap Handle, Incised At Shoulder, Tan Glaze, Egg Shape, 7 In. 95.00
Jug, Strap Handle, Tooled Line At Midpoint, Egg Shape, 5 1/2 In. 275.00
Jug, Tooled Shoulder Line, Dark Green Glaze, Tan Spots, 6 1/2 In. 225.00
Jug, Tooled Shoulder Lines, Ribbed Strap Handle, Egg Shape, 6 In. 65.00
Lamp, Grease, Brown Glaze, Saucer Base, Strap Handle, Ohio, 4 In. 375.00
Loaf Pan, Coggled Edge, Line Yellow Slip Design, 16 1/4 In. 1250.00
Loaf Pan, White Slip Combware Design, Coggled Edge, 15 1/2 In. 550.00
Mold, Bundt, Light Rust & Green Glaze, 7 In. 130.00
Mold, Cake, Swirl, Black Glaze 65.00
Mold, Turk's Head, Brown Sponging, Clear Glaze, 7 1/2 In. 55.00
Mold, Turk's Head, Scalloped, Dark Glaze, 10 3/4 In. 60.00
Mug, 3 Brown Daubs, Clear Glaze, 5 In. 65.00
Mug, Child's, Brown Glaze, Rust Accents, Handle, 2 1/2 X 3 1/4 In. 75.00
Mug, Strap Handle, Brown, Green & Orange Splotches, 5 1/4 In. 150.00
Pie Plate, 3 Line Yellow Slip Design, Coggled Edge, 11 1/2 In. 425.00
Pie Plate, Coggled Edge, 3 Line Slip Design, Green Glaze, 11 In. 275.00
Pie Plate, Coggled Edge, 3 Line Yellow Slip Design, 8 1/2 In. 250.00
Pie Plate, Coggled Edge, 3 Line Yellow Slip Design, 9 1/4 In. 400.00
Pie Plate, Coggled Edge, Yellow Design, 11 3/4 In. 1450.00
Pie Plate, Coggled Edge, Yellow Line Slip Design, 8 In. 475.00
Pie Plate, Coggled Edge, Yellow Slip Crow's Foot, 7 3/4 In. 65.00
Pie Plate, Coggled Edge, Yellow Slip Design, Reliance, 12 1/4 In. 475.00
Pie Plate, Coggled Edge, Zigzag Design, 10 1/2 In. 400.00
Pie Plate, Coggled, Yellow Slip Dots & Line Design, 11 1/4 In. 90.00
Pie Plate, Crisscross Yellow & Brown Slip, Clear Glaze, 7 In. 400.00
Pie Plate, Green, Yellow Slip S Curves, W.Smith Womelsdorf, 8 In. 400.00
Pie Plate, Outer Black Patina, 9 In. 135.00
Pie Plate, Yellow Slip Commas, Brown Glaze, 7 7/8 In. 125.00
Pitcher, Amber Glaze, Brown Brush Marks, Lines At Lip, 8 In. 675.00
Pitcher, Brown Flecks, Clear Glaze, 5 In. 85.00
Pitcher, Brown Spots, Tan Glaze, Mary Allis, 7 In. 90.00

Pitcher, Butterfly, Blue & White 180.00
Pitcher, Dark Brown Glaze, Egg Shape, 4 1/2 In. 85.00
Pitcher, Embossed Collar, Strap Handle, Green Spots, Flecks, 7 In. 300.00
Pitcher, Greenish Orange Glaze, Circular Mark, J.Owen, 5 3/4 In. 35.00
Pitcher, Strap Handle, 3 Tooled Bands, Pennsylvania, 6 1/2 In. 395.00
Pitcher, Strap Handle, Pinched Spout, 3 Rows of Stripes, 10 In. 700.00
Pitcher, Water, White Slip, Running Brown, Green, Shenandoah, 10 In. 700.00
Pitcher, White Slip, Running Brown, Green, Handle, Shenandoah, 6 In. 550.00
Plaque, Comic Couple Fishing, Embossed Leaf Border, 11 In. 100.00
Plaque, Comic Scene, Man & Woman Fighting, English, 8 X 11 In. 15.00
Plate, Yellow Slip Design of Script Letters NE, 9 1/4 In. 225.00
Plate, Yellow Slip Design of Zigzag & Parallel Lines, 8 1/2 In. 225.00
Salt, White Slip, Mottled Green & Brown Glaze, Shenandoah, 3 In. 325.00
Soap Dish, Lion Head 75.00
Teapot, Green Glaze Design, Twigs, Flowers, Marked, Squat 27.50
Top Hat, Scroddleware, W.Dawson, Preston 1889, 4 1/8 In. 100.00
Vase, 5-Arm, Brown Sponging On Clear, Zigzag Lip Each Arm, 7 In. 850.00
REGOUT, see Maastricht

Richard "Richard" was the mark used on acid-etched cameo glass vases, bowls, night-lights, and lamps made in Lorraine, France, during the 1920s. The pieces were very similar to the other French cameo glasswares made by Daum, Galle, and others.

RICHARD, Jar, Castle, 2 Lakes, Mountains, Reflected In Lake, Signed, 6 In. 455.00
Vase, Black & Orange, Pedestal, Signed, 6 In. 145.00
Vase, Castle, Bridge, Mountains, Blue To Yellow, 8 In. 400.00
Vase, House On River, Bride, Navy Blue, Signed, 8 In. 550.00

Ridgway pottery has been made in the Staffordshire district in England since 1808 by a series of companies with the name Ridgway. The transfer-design dinner sets are the most widely known product. They are still being made. Other pieces of Ridgway are listed under Flow Blue.

RIDGWAY, Chop Plate, Anglesey Pattern, 11 1/2 In. 65.00
Chop Plate, Coaching Days, Christmas Visitor, June, 1907, 12 In. 118.00
Chop Plate, Coaching Days, In A Snow Drift, 1905, 13 1/2 In. 125.00
Coffeepot, Coaching Days, 7 1/2 In. 85.00
Dinner Set, Child's, White, Red, Green Stripes, C.1850, 38 Piece 285.00
Dish, Vegetable, Bow & Quiver, Pattern On Inside, Covered, 9 In. 75.00
Jug, Bamboo Cane Form, Rope Bandings, Rope Handle, 1835, 9 In. 150.00
Jug, Pickwick, Scene In Black, Silver Luster Trim, 7 5/8 In. 70.00
Mug, Coaching Days, Silver Luster Band & Handle, 4 3/4 In. 40.00
Pitcher, Coaching Days, 9 1/2 In. 98.00
Pitcher, Pickwick, Black Scenes, Silver Luster Trim, 9 1/2 In. 100.00
Pitcher, Pickwick, Silver Luster Trim, 12 5/8 In. 125.00
Pitcher, Tavern Scene, Handles, Dated 1835, 9 In. 115.00
Plate, Anglesey Pattern, 10 In. 45.00
Plate, Coaching Days, Capitol, Washington, D.C., 9 In. 42.00
Plate, Coaching Days, Charles Recognized, 7 3/4 In. 45.00
Plate, Coaching Days, Eloped, 9 In. 45.00
Platter, Palestine, Medium Blue, 10 X 12 In. 110.00
Platter, Tyrolian, Green, 14 3/4 In. 95.00
Sugar, Oriental Pattern, Covered, Handles, 5 1/2 X 7 In. 30.00
Syrup, Pewter Top, Yellowware 145.00
Tankard, Coaching Days, Brown, Silver Trim, 6 Oz. 175.00
Tumbler, Coaching Days, Black Scenes, Silver Luster Band 30.00

A rifle is a firearm that has a rifled bore and that is intended to be fired from the shoulder. Other firearms are listed under Gun.

RIFLE, 1864 Springfield 300.00
A.M.Hagadorn, Double Barrel, Percussion, 58 Cal., 32 In.Barrel 1100.00
Bell-Wingert Hawkin Style, 45 Cal., Silver Tip & Stock 550.00
Billinghurst, Buggy, Skeleton Stock, Accessories 2200.00
Chief Crazy Horse Commemorative, Box, Papers 550.00

Eli Whitney, U.S.Percussion, 1841	650.00
Ethan Allen, Drop Breech	400.00
Golcher Hawkin, Percussion, 50 Cal, 29 In.Barrel	175.00
James Golcher, Percussion, Curly Maple, Octagonal Barrel, 56 In.	750.00
Kentucky, Cherrywood, Full Stock, Brass, Patch Box, Handmade, 1835	395.00
Kentucky, Flintlock, Jacob Bloom, Octagonal Barrel, 44 Caliber	1000.00
Kentucky, Flintlock, Richards & Co., German Silver Trim, 54 1/2 In.	775.00
Kentucky, Full Stock, Burned On Curl, Marked R.Ashmore, 59 In.	400.00
Kentucky, Lock Signed T.Neave & Sons, Cincinnati, J.Zink On Barrel	375.00
Kentucky, Maple Half Stock, Percussion, Brass Trigger, 47 In.	250.00
Kentucky, Percussion Lock, M.Sheets, Curly Maple Stock, 58 1/2 In.	450.00
Kentucky, Striped Maple, Half Stock, Jos.Golcher, C.1835	595.00
Mosberg, 22 Bolt Action, 1932	87.00
Peabody Martini, Mid-Range Creedmore	1800.00
Pennsylvania, 36 Caliber, 1840	210.00
Pope, Etched Floral & Deer Pattern Each Side	9000.00
Remington Hepburn No.3	425.00
Sharps Borchardt	850.00
Sharps, Model 1878, Long Range 45 Cal., Engraved	7500.00
Shotgun, Browning Remington, Dual Barrel, With Case, 1903	275.00
Sliding Breech Action, 50 Caliber, Rimfire, Double Set Trigger	225.00
Smith & Wesson, Model 44, Triple Lock	650.00
Springfield, 59 Caliber, 1870	250.00
Springfield, Allin, 1866	400.00
Springfield, Trap Door, 45–70 Caliber, 1873	300.00
Swedish Army, Bolt Action, 1880s	160.00
Westley Richards, Accessories, Dated 1883	6000.00
Winchester, 45/70, 1886	850.00
Winchester–Lee Straight Pull, U.S. Navy Issue	300.00
Wingert Side–By–Side, Percussion, Detroit, 45 Cal., 30 In.Barrel	1100.00

Riviera dinnerware was made by the Homer Laughlin Co. of Newell, West Virginia, from 1938 to 1950. The pattern was similar in coloring and in mood to Fiesta and Harlequin. The Riviera plates and cup handles were square.

RIVIERA, Butter Top, Yellow	30.00
Jug, Green, Covered	40.00
Mug, Green	40.00
Pitcher, Juice, Yellow	36.00
Plate, Ivory, 9 In.	2.50
Platter, Red, 11 1/4 In.	12.00
Sauce Boat, Light Blue	4.00
Syrup, Red	20.00
Tumbler, Blue, Handle	35.00

Roblin Art Pottery was founded in 1898 by Alexander W. Robertson and Linna Irelan in San Francisco, California. The pottery closed in 1906. The firm made faience with green, tan, dull blue, or gray glazes. Decorations were usually animal shapes. Some red clay pieces were made.

ROBLIN, Vase, Allover Blue Glaze, 8 In.	250.00
Vase, Beige Mushrooms, 5 In.	300.00

Rockingham, in the United States, is a brown glazed pottery with a tortoiseshell–like glaze. It was made from 1840 to 1900 by many American potteries. Mottled brown Rockingham wares were first made in England at the Rockingham factory. Other types of ceramics were also made by the English firm.

ROCKINGHAM, Bottle, Shoe, Embossed Laces, 6 1/4 In.	65.00
Bowl, 9 1/2 X 4 1/4 In.	65.00
Bowl, Mixing, Brown & Yellow, 10 In.	110.00
Bowl, Mixing, Embossed Arched Panels, 14 3/4 X 7 1/4 In.	125.00
Bowl, Yellowware, 8 In.	135.00
Candlestick, Baluster Shaft, Domed Base, 8 3/4 In., Pair	200.00

Coffeepot, Rebecca At The Well, 1 Gal. 145.00
Compote, Floral, Hand Painted, Pierced Border, C.1840 .... 350.00
Cuspidor, Classical Bust, 12 1/2 In. 20.00
Cuspidor, Shell Pattern 75.00
Flask, Hanging Game, Gun, Dogs, Buckeye Fiske Co., New York 355.00
Flask, Morning Glory & Eagle, 7 1/4 In. 255.00
Inkwell, Smiling Face, 3 3/8 In. 60.00
Mold, Food, Turk's–Head, 8 1/4 In. 65.00
Pitcher, Anchor, 8 1/2 In. 115.00
Pitcher, Anchor, 19 7/8 In. 55.00
Pitcher, Covered, Embossed Animals, Hound Handle, 10 3/4 In. 140.00
Pitcher, Covered, Old Woman Taking Snuff, Man With Pipe, 9 In. 35.00
Pitcher, Embossed American Eagle, 8 3/8 In. 55.00
Pitcher, Embossed Peacock Design, 8 In. 65.00
Pitcher, Embossed Scene of Cherubs & Vintage, 7 In. 55.00
Pitcher, George Washington, 8 5/8 In. 155.00
Pitcher, George Washington, Dark Brown, 8 In. 110.00
Pitcher, Hound Handle, Embossed Eagle, Boar & Stag, 10 In. 55.00
Pitcher, Hound Handle, Embossed Hunt Scenes, 6 3/4 In. 45.00
Pitcher, Toby, 8 5/8 In. 50.00
Pitcher, Toby, Vintage Handle, 6 1/4 In. 30.00
Pitcher, Vintage & Hunt Scenes, 9 In. 65.00
Pitcher, Vintage, Cherubs, Brown, 7 1/2 In. 85.00
Soap Dish, Acanthus Leaf Design, 6 In. 65.00
Spittoon, 4 1/2 In. 150.00
Teapot, Individual, 5 1/2 In. 10.00
Teapot, Rebekah At The Well, 10 In. 88.00
Window Stop, Lion Head, 5 In. 175.00
ROGERS, see John Rogers

 Rookwood pottery was made in Cincinnati, Ohio, from 1880 to 1960. All of this art pottery is marked, most with the famous flame mark. The R is reversed and placed back to back with the letter P. Flames surround the letters. After 1900, a Roman numeral was added to the mark to indicate the year. The name and some of the molds were purchased in 1984; new items will be clearly marked.

ROOKWOOD, Ashtray, Fish Shape, Aqua 47.00
Ashtray, Frog, Blue Matte Glaze, 1934, 3 X 7 In. 125.00
Ashtray, Heart Shape, Red 26.00
Ashtray, Lyre & Panpipes, Black, 1927 .... 45.00
Ashtray, Owl, Green Matte, 1943 .... 75.00
Ashtray, Reclining Nude, Matte Yellow, 1946 .... 65.00
Ashtray, Rook, Blue Wax Matte 225.00
Ashtray, Rook, Green 85.00
Basket, Footed, 2 Handles, Floral Glaze, 1897, 6 3/4 In. 350.00
Bookends, Elephant, Dark Blue, 1929 .... 90.00
Bookends, Elephant, White Matte Glaze, 1921, 7 1/2 In. 155.00
Bookends, Florals, High Glaze 185.00
Bookends, Pond Lily, Blue 98.00
Bookends, Rook, Chocolate Brown, W.McDonald 165.00
Bookends, Rook, White 110.00
Bookends, Sphinx, Blue, 1920 .... 135.00
Bookends, Tree, Multicolored, McDonald 250.00
Bowl, 3 Handles, Dated 1918, 9 1/4 In. 90.00
Bowl, C.S.Todd, 1920, 8 In. 200.00
Bowl, Cerise Poppies, Green Leaves, Brown, 1905, 7 In. 180.00
Bowl, Cut Corners, Pink Blossoms, 1882, 3 1/2 X 8 In. 450.00
Bowl, Purple Blue, Deep Rose Interior, C.1919, 5 X 9 1/2 In. 100.00
Bowl, Raised Bird–Dog Design, Pedestal, 13 In. 37.50
Bowl, Yellow Matte, Molded Arts & Crafts Design, 1940, 2 1/2 In. 50.00
Candleholder, Curved Handle, Floral Design, Signed, 1892 .... 250.00
Candleholder, Egyptian Ladies, Turquoise, 10 In., Pair 150.00
Candleholder, Lily, Ivory, 1927 .... 25.00
Candlestick, Vellum, White Dogwood, Leaves, 8 In. 210.00

Chamberstick, Hooded, Pink To Olive, Matte, 1915, 7 3/4 In. 65.00
Chocolate Pot, Standard Glaze, Slip Painted, Enameled, AMV 1890 .... 750.00
Compote, 3 Elephant Supports, Green Glaze, C.1929, 11 In. 175.00
Creamer, Footed, Yellow Matte, 1918 .... 55.00
Creamer, Holly Berries, Leaves, Pinched Neck, Fechheimer, 1898 .... 355.00
Creamer, Leaf & Berry Design, Sallie E.Coyne, 1903, 3 In. 245.00
Ewer, Black & Yellow Flowers, 1902, 7 In. 500.00
Ewer, Brownish Green Matte, 6 In. 475.00
Ewer, Clustered Leaves, Berries, 1900, 9 1/4 In. 495.00
Ewer, Floral Brown Glaze, Handles, 1902, 8 In. 350.00
Ewer, Glazed, Gorham Silver Overlay, 5 In. 3575.00
Ewer, Leaves & Berries, Brown To Orange, 1900, 9 1/4 In. 455.00
Ewer, Red Clay Body, Incised Leaves, Gold Around Top, 1882, 11 In. 350.00
Ewer, Rozane, 8 In. 200.00
Ewer, Ruffled Spout, Rust To Brown, Handle, 1900, 8 In. 250.00
Ewer, Sterling Silver Overlay, Trefoil Shape, 1892, 10 1/4 In. 2800.00
Figurine, Cat, Green High Glaze, L.Abel, 1946 .... 195.00
Figurine, Pheasant, Lime Green 195.00
Flower Frog, Blue Matte, 1921 .... 6.00
Flower Frog, Figural, Raven, Black, 1923, 6 In. 200.00
Humidor, Butterfly Finial, Floral Design, Gilt, 1887, 6 In. 425.00
Humidor, Yellow Matte, Molded Design On Lid & Neck, 1921, 8 In. 90.00
Jug, Flattened, Loop Handle, Dragonfly & Wheat, 1882, 6 3/4 In. 150.00
Jug, Palmer Cox Figure, Loop Handle, 1891, 6 In. 955.00
Lamp, Base, White Tulips, Curving Stems, Iris Glaze, 1903, 14 In. 650.00
Mug, Dated 1914, 4 1/4 In. 100.00
Mug, Ear of Corn, Deep Blue To Green, 5 1/4 In. 155.00
Paperweight, Doll, White, 1946, 3 1/2 X 5 In. 100.00
Paperweight, Duck, White, Paper Label, 1965 .... 65.00
Paperweight, Fruit Basket 75.00
Paperweight, Nude, Creamy White, Louise Abel 325.00
Paperweight, Open Book, Harvard University, 1905 .... 60.00
Pitcher, Berries, Van Horne, 1908, 4 In. 375.00
Pitcher, Parade of 8 Frogs, A.Valentien, 1898 .... 3400.00
Planter, Green Matte Glaze, Fern Frond Design, 1905, 9 In. 150.00
Plaque, Boats, C.Schmidt 5720.00
Plaque, Mountain Lake, Rothenbusch, 1912, 8 X 10 In. 1500.00
Plaque, Scene, McDonald, 9 X 5 In. 875.00
Plaque, Vellum, Lake & Mountain Scene, 1847 .... 2000.00
Plaque, Vellum, Vertical Tree Scene, 12 1/2 X 8 1/2 In. 800.00
Plate, Hand Painted Center Grapes, Foliage, 1885, 10 In. 375.00
Plate, Sailing Ships, 10 In. 45.00
Ramekin, Birds Flying Through Clouds, Rettig, 1883 .... 285.00
Sugar & Creamer, Blue Ships 85.00
Sugar & Creamer, Light Caramel, 1945 .... 55.00
Sugar, Rust Leaves, Brown & Rust, Sallie Coyne, 1900 .... 175.00
Tea Set, Bright Yellow, Ship Design 135.00
Tea Tile, Dutch Seaside Scene 125.00
Teapot, Iris Glaze, Butterfly Handle Lid, Fruit Blossoms, 1904 .... 225.00
Tile, 5 Yellow Flying Rooks, 1953, 6 In. 55.00
Tile, Crow On Branch, 9 X 4 1/2 In. 650.00
Tile, Geometric Design, Pastels 75.00
Tile, Grape Design, 1950 .... 95.00
Tile, Parrot Design, 1921, 5 1/2 In. 65.00
Tile, Stylized Bellflower, White Bubbly Glaze, Square, 5 In. 150.00
Tile, Tea, Duck Pattern, 1925 .... 60.00
Tray, Peacock Feather 45.00
Trivet, Floral Basket, Butterflies, Paper Label 110.00
Trivet, Lady With Umbrella, Multicolored, 1922 .... 150.00
Trivet, Red Tulips, 1922 .... 70.00
Vase, 8 Color, Margaret McDonald, Vellum, 1920, 11 In. 360.00
Vase, Apple Bough & Blossoms, Hurley, Vellum, 1910, 11 In. 700.00
Vase, Aqua Unevenly Brushed Over Yellow & Tan, 1930, 3 In. 150.00
Vase, Art Deco Shape, C.1900, 8 In. 75.00

Rookwood, Vase, Chrysanthemum Blossoms,
Green, 9 X 6 In.; Yellow Tulips, Green Leaves, 14 X 5 In.;
Marine Scene, Corset Shape, Boats, 11 X 6 In.

Rookwood, Vase, Deep Umber To Sienna,
Spiral Mold, 5 1/2 In.

Vase, Aventurine, Gold Dust, C.1932, 6 1/4 In.	350.00
Vase, Blue & Green Matte Glaze, Sadie Irvine, 1914, 13 In.	2700.00
Vase, Blue Matte, 1921, 9 In.	65.00
Vase, Blue Matte, Molded Flowers, 1925, 4 1/4 In.	44.00
Vase, Blue, 1930, 5 1/2 In.	45.00
Vase, Braided Handles, Ribbed, Roses Top Third, 1893, 8 In.	450.00
Vase, Brown Glaze, Brown To Orange, Leaves, 1904, 7 In.	195.00
Vase, Brown Glaze, Dark Green, Brown To Orange, 1895, 8 In.	425.00
Vase, Brown Glaze, Yellow, Green To Brown, 1902, 7 1/2 In.	200.00
Vase, Brown Gloss Butterfly, 1950, 4 1/2 In.	58.00
Vase, Brown Water Lilies, Green Mica Drip, Barrett, 1934, 5 In.	295.00
Vase, Bud, Pink, 1921, 7 1/2 In.	55.00
Vase, Bud, Speckled Gray, 1952	40.00
Vase, Burgundy High Glaze, Black Interior, 1928, 7 1/8 In.	80.00
Vase, Chrysanthemum Blossoms, Green, 9 X 6 In. ....*Illus*	5500.00
Vase, Circling Fish, 3 Handles, 1905, 7 In.	160.00
Vase, Daffodil, Matte, D.W., 1927, 9 In.	290.00
Vase, Deep Umber To Sienna, Spiral Mold, 5 1/2 In. ....*Illus*	550.00
Vase, Dragonfly, 9 In.	60.00
Vase, Ducks & Stars In Relief, Blue, 5 3/4 In.	55.00
Vase, Etched, Seahorses In Relief, In Water, 6 1/2 In.	295.00
Vase, Floral Design, Wax Matte, Margaret H.McDonald, 7 1/2 In.	295.00
Vase, Floral, Aqua, 1963, 6 3/4 In.	47.50
Vase, Floral, Dibrowski, 1893, 5 X 7 In.	525.00
Vase, Floral, Vellum, 1905, 7 In.	170.00
Vase, Flowering Almond, Pink, Ivory, Gray Ground, 1905, 8 1/2 In.	325.00
Vase, Fluted Top, Mary Mourse, 1892, 8 1/2 In.	1200.00
Vase, Goldstone, 1939, 4 1/2 In.	200.00
Vase, Green Glaze, Molded Flower & Leaf Design, 1945, 12 In.	100.00
Vase, Green Glaze, Molded Geometric Line Design, 1956, 7 1/4 In.	45.00
Vase, Green Matte, 1929, 6 1/2 In.	45.00
Vase, Holly Berries & Leaves, 9 1/2 In.	200.00
Vase, Holly, Brown Glaze, Bulbous, L.E.H., 3 In.	150.00
Vase, Impressed Stylized Florals, Pink, 1927, 7 In.	45.00
Vase, Incised Wax Matte, Yellow, Red, Feather Design, 1917, 3 In.	180.00
Vase, Iris Glaze, Shirayamadani, 6 1/2 X 9 1/2 In.	950.00
Vase, Iris, Pastel Florals, Beige Ground, 4 In.	550.00
Vase, Large Pelicans, Deep Aqua, 6 X 4 In.	250.00
Vase, Lavender Iris, White, Purple Pansies, Sarah Sax, 1904, 6 In.	325.00
Vase, Lavender, 3 Panels Stylized Leaves & Berries, 1925, 7 In.	130.00
Vase, Lime Green Glazed, Embossed Tiger Lilies, 1946, 7 In.	59.00
Vase, Marine Scene, Corset Shape, Boats, 11 X 6 In. ....*Illus*	3300.00

Vase, Matte Blue, Molded Fruit, Leaves, 1928, 4 1/2 In. 42.00
Vase, Matte Green, L.M.C., 10-1-02, 7 In. 1050.00
Vase, Matte Turquoise Glaze, 1934, 5 1/2 In. 185.00
Vase, Mexican Figures, Turquoise, 1943, 6 In. 75.00
Vase, Molded Flower & Line Design, Green Matte Glaze, 12 In. 215.00
Vase, O.G.Reed, 10 In. 1670.00
Vase, Open Flowers At Top, 1917, 6 1/2 In. 47.50
Vase, Oriental Type Blossoms, Navy, White, Gold, 1918, 7 In. 210.00
Vase, Peacock Feather, Medium Rose, 1919, 9 In. 60.00
Vase, Pink Matte, Green Molded Leaf, 1934, 5 1/2 In. 40.00
Vase, Pink To Gray, 1922, 7 In. 45.00
Vase, Plum Design, 1924, 5 1/2 In. 45.00
Vase, Purple, Embossed Rooks, 1925, 4 1/2 X 4 In. 70.00
Vase, Raised Fruit, Matte, Hentschell, 1911, 10 In. 260.00
Vase, Red Matte, Molded Geometric Design Around Neck, 1916, 9 In. 70.00
Vase, Roman Key, Turquoise, 1927, 6 In. 52.50
Vase, Rose Bud Shape, Pink To Green, 6 In. 65.00
Vase, Roses, J.Swing, 1903, 8 In. 400.00
Vase, Rubens Portrait, Artus Van Briggle, 1893, 14 1/2 In. 2420.00
Vase, Sailing Ships, Tan, 4 1/2 In. 50.00
Vase, Scenic Vellum, E.T.Hurley, 1913, 9 1/2 In. 950.00
Vase, Scenic, Landscape Band, Initialed, Vellum, 1921, 7 1/4 In. 400.00
Vase, Scroll, Medium Blue, 1925, 6 1/2 In. 55.00
Vase, Silver Overlay, Silver Handles, Gold Ferns, 1894, 5 5/8 In. 1300.00
Vase, Spirit of The Summit, Incised Title, 1894, 14 1/2 In. 400.00
Vase, Standard Glaze, Handles, Ovoid Body, 1892, 8 In. 700.00
Vase, Standard Glaze, Steinle, 5 1/2 In. 250.00
Vase, Sterling Silver Overlay, Fluted & Crimped, 1892, 6 1/2 In. 2300.00
Vase, Stylized Floral, Vellum, 1915, 9 In. 325.00
Vase, Stylized Flowers, Blue Matte, 6 In. 50.00
Vase, Stylized Flowers, Blue-Green, 8 1/2 In. 85.00
Vase, Stylized Flowers, Leaves, Hentschell, 1924, 10 In. 525.00
Vase, Thistle, Standard Glaze, Swing, 1904, 5 1/2 In. 295.00
Vase, Thorny Branches, Blossoms, Leaves, Bottle Neck, 6 In. 400.00
Vase, Tiger Eye, M.A.Daly, 6 In. 4125.00
Vase, Tree Scene, Vellum, Blue, Green, Brown, 1930, 8 1/4 In. 1000.00
Vase, Turquoise, Blue Molded Bleeding Hearts, Glazed, 11 In. 110.00
Vase, White Glaze, Red Cherry Design, 5 1/2 In. 80.00
Vase, Yellow Tulips, Green Leaves, 14 X 5 In. ....*Illus* 3850.00
Wall Pocket, Iris Flowers, Green Matte Glaze, 1924, 13 In. 135.00
ROSALINE, see Steuben

Rose bowls were popular during the 1880s. Rose petals were kept in the open bowl to add fragrance to a room, a popular idea in a time of limited personal hygiene. The glass bowls were made with crimped tops, which kept the petals inside. Many types of Victorian art glass were made into rose bowls.

ROSE BOWL, Hobnail, Vaseline Glass, 4 1/2 In. 10.00
  Satin Swirled, Amethyst, 3 3/4 In. 195.00

Rose Canton china is similar to Rose Medallion, except no people are pictured in the decoration. It was made during the nineteenth and twentieth centuries in greens, pinks, and other colors.

ROSE CANTON, Charger, Birds, Bats, Bugs, Butterflies, 16 In. 675.00
  Spittoon 250.00
  Tazza, 1830, 9 In. 100.00
  Teapot, Cylinder Shape, Reed Handle 100.00
  Vase, 12 In., Pair 450.00

Rose Medallion china was made in China during the nineteenth and twentieth centuries. It is a distinctive design picturing people, flowers, birds, and butterflies. Pieces are colored in greens, pinks, and other colors.

ROSE MEDALLION, Bottle, Water, Spherical Body, Genre Panels, 13 In. 500.00

Bowl, Birds, Gilt, 19th Century, C.1900, 12 In.	65.00
Bowl, Covered, Wafer Finial, Genre Scenes, Florals, 10 In.	500.00
Bowl, Geisha Girls, Phoenix Birds, Floral, 13 In.	500.00
Bowl, Lotus, Scalloped, 6 1/2 X 2 1/4 In.	50.00
Bowl, Panels, People, Birds, Flowers, C.1850, 7 In.	90.00
Bowl, Rice, Trivet Base, 4 1/2 X 2 1/2 In.	30.00
Butter Chip	28.00
Charger, 13 1/2 In.	150.00
Creamer, Helmet	120.00
Creamer, Marked, C.1920, 4 In.	42.00
Cup & Saucer, Alternating Panels, Demitasse, C.1850	60.00
Cup & Saucer, Bouillon	38.00
Cup & Saucer, Handleless, Covered	70.00
Cup & Saucer, Octagonal Shape, Eggshell Porcelain	50.00
Cup & Saucer, Scalloped Rim	45.00
Cup & Underplate, Bouillon, Covered, 4 Sets	300.00
Dish, Lemon Peel Glaze, 10 1/2 In.	180.00
Inkwell, Double	125.00
Lamp, Urn Shape, Foo Dog Handles, Genre Scenes, 14 In., Pair	1000.00
Pitcher, Chinese Men, Geisha Girls, 1800s, Large	250.00
Plate, 10 In.	55.00
Plate, 4 Panels, Birds, People, Flowers, 19th Century	125.00
Plate, Alternating Panels, Concave, C.1850, 8 In.	95.00
Platter, Center Rondel, Bird & Tree Peony, Oval, 20 In.	525.00
Platter, Genre Scenes, Floral Panels, 9 1/2 X 13 1/2 In.	250.00
Platter, Mountain Scenes, Famille Rose, 18 X 15 In.	300.00
Platter, Orange Peel Glaze, Genre Scenes, Oval, 13 X 18 In.	250.00
Punch Bowl, Floral & Bird Panels, Genre Scenes, 14 In.	975.00
Punch Bowl, Floral Border, Genre Scene Inside Rim, 16 In.	1400.00
Punch Bowl, Sand, Rose Border, Butterflies, 6 In.	500.00
Punch Bowl, Stand, Rose Border Inside & Out, 19th Century	500.00
Soup Tureen, Stand, 19th Century	275.00
Sugar & Creamer, Domed Cover, Genre Scenes, 5 3/4 In.	125.00
Tea Set, Red Chop Mark, Tray 10 In., 6 Piece	285.00
Teapot, Bulbous, 4 1/2 In.	95.00
Teapot, Cups, Basket, 19th Century, 3 Piece	150.00
Teapot, Cups, Wicker Basket, Brass Hardware, C.1895, 3 Pc.	310.00
Teapot, Early 19th Century, Miniature	80.00
Teapot, People, Birds, Butterflies Panels, C.1830, 5 1/2 In.	150.00
Tray, Hexagonal, Marked, 11 1/4 In.	55.00
Umbrella Stand, 3 Bands Genre Scenes, Floral, 23 3/4 In.	1100.00
Umbrella Stand, 3 Rows of Scenes, In Blocks, 24 In.	800.00
Vase, 16 In., Pair	850.00
Vase, 18 In., Pair	295.00
Vase, Raised Gilt Dragon, Stand, 8 In.	145.00

ROSE O'NEILL, see Kewpie

Rose Tapestry porcelain was made by the Royal Bayreuth factory of Tettau, Germany, during the late nineteenth century. The surface of the porcelain was pressed against a coarse fabric while it was still damp, and the impressions remained on the finished porcelain. It looks and feels like a textured cloth. Very skillful reproductions are being made that even include a variation of the Royal Bayreuth mark, so be careful when buying.

ROSE TAPESTRY, Basket, Orange, Gold Handle, 5 1/2 In.	375.00
Basket, Purple & White Chrysanthemums, 6 In.	310.00
Berry Bowl, Royal Bayreuth, 6 In.	135.00
Box, Portrait On Cover, Royal Bayreuth, Square, 4 1/2 In.	245.00
Box, Trinket, Covered, Free Form, 3 1/2 X 2 1/2 In.	175.00
Creamer, Corset Shape, Blue Mark, 3 3/4 In.	180.00
Creamer, Pinched Spout, Royal Bayreuth, 4 In.	145.00
Creamer, Pinched Spout, 4 Color Roses, 3 1/2 In.	165.00
Creamer, Roses, Pinched Spout, 4 1/2 In.	195.00
Dish, Leaf, Pink Roses, Blue Mark	180.00

Dresser Set, Tray, Hair Receiver & Powder Box 600.00
Hatpin Holder, Pink Roses, Royal Bayreuth 300.00
Jar, Sweetmeat, Scenic 225.00
Match Holder, Hanging, Roses, Leaves, Gold Trim, 4 1/2 In. 195.00
Mug, Blue Mark, 3 3/8 In. 110.00
Nappy, For Lemon Wedges, Arab, Horse, Gold Handle, Marked 150.00
Pitcher, Corset Shape, Royal Bayreuth, 5 In. 135.00
Pitcher, Maiden With Dark Hair, Pinched Spout, 3 1/2 In. 195.00
Pitcher, Tapestry, Pinched Spout, Royal Bayreuth, 3 1/4 In. 170.00
Powder Box, Footed, Royal Bayreuth, 4 1/2 In. 155.00
Ring Tree, Saucer Base, Signed, Royal Bayreuth 495.00
Sugar & Creamer, Royal Bayreuth 350.00
Teapot, Pink Roses, Blue Mark, 6 3/4 X 3 1/2 In. 350.00
Toothpick, Woman With Horse, Royal Bayreuth, Blue Mark 165.00
Tray, 3 Roses, Blue Mark 125.00
Tray, Dresser, House, Castle, Train On Bridge, Blue Mark 185.00
Tray, Scenic, Royal Bayreuth, 11 X 8 In. 280.00
Vase, 2 Handles, Royal Bayreuth, 9 1/2 In. 325.00
Vase, Castle Scene, 4 In. 195.00
Vase, Lady With Bonnet, Blue Mark, 6 1/4 In. 275.00
Vase, Tavern Scene, 2 Handles, Royal Bayreuth, 8 In. 235.00
Vase, Urn Shape, Marked, 4 1/4 In. 225.00

MARKE
Rosenthal

Rosenthal porcelain was made at the factory established in Selb, Bavaria, in 1880. The factory is still making fine–quality tablewares and figurines. A series of Christmas plates was made from 1910. Other limited edition plates have been made since 1971.

ROSENTHAL, Bowl, Vegetable, Covered, Moss Rose, Footed 75.00
Chocolate Set, Isolde, 9 Piece 75.00
Figurine, Bear & Cub, Walking, 4 1/2 X 7 1/4 In. 160.00
Figurine, Bird, Outstretched Wings, Waves, Signed, 7 X 9 In. 95.00
Figurine, Bulldog, Standing, Black & White 195.00
Figurine, Dachshund, Sitting, 6 In. 150.00
Figurine, Deer, Reclining, Marked, 10 X 6 X 5 In. 350.00
Figurine, Doe & Fawn 195.00
Figurine, Finch, Yellow & Gray, Branch With Pods, 5 1/2 In. 115.00
Figurine, Frog, Marked, 3 X 2 In. 65.00
Figurine, Girl, Braids, Holding Bouquet & Hat, Signed, 7 3/4 In. 160.00
Figurine, Nude Boy & English Wolfhound, Green Mark 300.00
Figurine, Poodle, Standing, Gray, 6 In. 110.00
Figurine, Poodle, Standing, White, Green Collar, Marked, 8 X 8 In. 230.00
Figurine, Princess & Frog, 10 In. 295.00
Figurine, Seminude, 9 In. 225.00
Figurine, Squirrel 35.00
Figurine, Turtle, Marked, 2 X 3 In. 55.00
Figurine, Two Satyrs, On Pedestal, 1930, 10 In. 250.00
Figurine, White Rabbit 70.00
Gravy Boat, Attached Underplate, Moss Rose .... 35.00 To 40.00
Plaque, Christmas, Polychrome, 1970 .... 75.00
Plate, Christmas, 1922, Pierced For Hanging 120.00
Plate, Rose Design, Cobalt Blue Border, 8 In. 42.00
Platter, Nazi Logo, Dated 1940 .... 50.00
Syrup, Design, Covered 65.00
Vase, 90's Lady, Parasol, Pillow Shape, Artist Signed, 10 In. 85.00
Vase, Crackle, Rust Foliage, Stockmayer, 1946, 7 In. ....80.00 To 100.00
Vase, Moss Rose, 7 In. 30.00
Vase, Portrait, Crimson, Green, & Gold, 8 In. 145.00

Roseville
U.S.A.

The Roseville Pottery Company was organized in Roseville, Ohio, in 1890. Another plant was opened in Zanesville, Ohio, in 1898. Many types of pottery were made. Early wares include sgraffito, Olympic, and Rozane. Later lines were often made with molded decorations, especially flowers and fruit. Pieces are marked "Roseville."

ROSEVILLE, Ashtray, Donatello .... 60.00 To 80.00

Ashtray, Fatima, Turkish	125.00
Ashtray, Pine Cone	45.00
Ashtray, Snowberry	30.00
Ashtray, Zephyr Lily, Green	35.00
Basket, Apple Blossom, Green, 8 In.	45.00
Basket, Bittersweet, Gray, 6 In.	31.50
Basket, Bittersweet, Yellow, Tan, 6 In.	35.00
Basket, Blackberry, 7 1/2 In.	325.00
Basket, Bleeding Heart, Blue, 10 In.	85.00
Basket, Bleeding Heart, Frog, Green, 12 In.	90.00
Basket, Bleeding Heart, Green, 8 In.	80.00
Basket, Bushberry, Blue, 8 In.	80.00
Basket, Bushberry, Green, 12 X 12 In.	80.00
Basket, Clematis, Brown, 7 In.	32.50
Basket, Foxglove, Blue	95.00
Basket, Freesia, 8 In.	55.00
Basket, Hanging, Apple Blossom, Green	75.00
Basket, Hanging, Blackberry, 7 In.	250.00
Basket, Hanging, Clematis, 6 In.	85.00
Basket, Hanging, Corinthian, 9 In.	100.00
Basket, Hanging, Cosmos, Blue, 5 In.	135.00
Basket, Hanging, Dahlrose, 8 In.	98.00
Basket, Hanging, Freesia, Green	50.00 To 58.00
Basket, Hanging, Futura	125.00 To 150.00
Basket, Hanging, Ming Tree, Green	72.00
Basket, Hanging, Peony, Yellow	95.00
Basket, Hanging, Pine Cone, Brown	165.00
Basket, Hanging, Rozane, 1917, 6 X 9 In.	110.00
Basket, Hanging, Silhouette	35.00
Basket, Imperial I, 6 In.	50.00
Basket, Imperial I, 10 In.	75.00
Basket, Imperial I, 13 In.	65.00
Basket, Imperial II, 7 X 6 In.	55.00
Basket, Jonquil, 8 In.	150.00
Basket, Ming Tree, White	125.00
Basket, Mock Orange, 8 In.	55.00
Basket, Monticello, Brown, 6 In.	185.00
Basket, Monticello, Orange	140.00
Basket, Pine Cone, Brown, 6 In.	195.00
Basket, Rosecraft, Shades of Mauve & Ivory, 10 In.	95.00
Basket, Silhouette, White, Turquoise, 6 In.	23.00
Basket, Snowberry, 8 In.	35.00 To 45.00
Basket, Snowberry, Brown, 7 In.	40.00
Basket, Vista, 6 In.	55.00
Basket, White Rose, 8 In.	65.00
Basket, White Rose, 10 In.	65.00
Basket, Zephyr Lily, 8 In.	50.00
Bookends, Apple Blossom	50.00
Bookends, Burmese, Green	32.00
Bookends, Clematis	60.00
Bookends, Clematis, Blue	12.00

It is easy to glue pieces of broken china. Use a new fast setting but not instant glue. Position the pieces correctly, then use tape to hold the parts together. If the piece needs special support, lean it in a suitable position in a box filled with sand.

Bookends, Magnolia, 13 In. 43.00
Bookends, Magnolia, Green .... 55.00 To 85.00
Bookends, Pine Cone, Brown .... 105.00 To 165.00
Bookends, Snowberry, Blue .... 55.00 To 65.00
Bookends, Wincraft, Apricot 44.00
Bookends, Zephyr Lily, Rust 70.00
Bowl, Baneda, Handle, 8 1/2 In. 35.00
Bowl, Carnelian, Blue & Gray, 8 X 2 3/4 In. 22.00
Bowl, Centerpiece, Thornapple, Pink 98.00
Bowl, Console, Bushberry, Green, 14 In. 95.00
Bowl, Console, Freesia, Brown, Handles, 11 In. 40.00
Bowl, Console, Fuchsia, 8 In. 50.00
Bowl, Console, Pine Cone, Blue, 12 1/2 In. 75.00
Bowl, Console, Topeo, Blue Green Glaze, 13 X 9 In. 58.00
Bowl, Console, Water Lily, Brown, 14 In. 40.00
Bowl, Console, Wisteria, 12 In. 85.00
Bowl, Console, Wisteria, 13 In. 85.00
Bowl, Corinthian, 6 3/4 X 3 1/2 In. 35.00
Bowl, Cremona, Pink, 9 In. 32.00
Bowl, Donatello, Original Stoneware Liner, 8 1/2 X 3 1/4 In. 70.00
Bowl, Dutch, C.1900, 10 1/2 In. 100.00
Bowl, Falline, Terra–Cotta, 10 In. 250.00
Bowl, Ferrella, 10 In. 135.00
Bowl, Ferrella, Raspberry, 12 In. 205.00
Bowl, Florentine, Brown, 8 In. 45.00
Bowl, Foxglove, 10 In. 35.00
Bowl, Freesia, Tangerine, Brown, Handles, 8 In. 40.00
Bowl, Fuchsia, Bulbous, 5 X 3 5/8 In. 22.00
Bowl, Gardenia, 10 In. 60.00
Bowl, Imperial I, Handles, 6 3/4 In. 32.00
Bowl, Imperial II, 10 In. 135.00
Bowl, Laurel, 13 In. 80.00
Bowl, Mock Orange, Pink, 6 In. 25.00
Bowl, Monticello, Turquoise, Tan, 3 X 7 1/2 X 13 In. 55.00
Bowl, Morning Glory, White, 5 X 10 In. 90.00
Bowl, Mostique, Glossy Pattern, Matte Gray, 8 1/2 X 3 1/2 In. 30.00
Bowl, Peony, Green, Handles, 4 In. 30.00
Bowl, Pine Cone, 16 In. 125.00
Bowl, Pine Cone, Blue, 6 In. 58.00
Bowl, Poppy, 4 In. 33.00
Bowl, Silhouette, Blue, Leaf Design, 2 Ear Handles, 4 1/2 In. 12.50
Bowl, Snowberry, Handles, Rose, 10 In. 40.00
Bowl, Topeo, Red, 3 X 11 1/2 In. 85.00
Bowl, Velmoss Scroll, 8 In. .... 35.00 To 40.00
Bowl, Water Lily, Blue, 12 In. 30.00
Bowl, Water Lily, Blue, 18 In. 30.00
Bowl, Wincraft, 10 In. 30.00
Bowl, Wincraft, Yellow Matte, 6 X 4 In. 30.00
Bowl, Windsor, Green Leaves, Yellow Flowers, Blue, 10 In. 125.00
Candleholder, Fuchsia, 5 In. 125.00
Candleholder, Ixia, Green, 7 In., Pair 45.00
Candleholder, La Rose, 4 In. 35.00
Candleholder, Wisteria, 10 In., Pair 125.00
Candlestick, Donatello, 6 1/4 In. 65.00
Candlestick, Florentine 35.00
Candlestick, Freesia, Rust 38.00
Candlestick, Ixia, Double, Yellow 25.00
Candlestick, Magnolia, 2 1/2 In. 20.00
Candlestick, Ming Tree, White, Pair 25.00
Candlestick, Moderne, Pair 75.00
Candlestick, Moderne, Triple, Aqua 75.00
Candlestick, Peony, Double, Yellow, Pair 60.00
Candlestick, Rosecraft, Blue, 10 In., Pair 85.00
Casserole, Venetian, Covered, Large 40.00

Chamberstick, Donatello .... 40.00 To 65.00
Cider Set, Bushberry, Blue, 7 Piece 325.00
Cider Set, Magnolia, Blue, 7 Piece 285.00
Coffeepot, Landscape 85.00
Compote, Donatello, 3 In. 45.00
Compote, Donatello, Chalice Shape, 9 In. 145.00
Conch Shell, Water Lily, Pink, Green, 9 In. 60.00
Console Set, Clematis, 3 Piece 60.00
Console Set, Ixia, 3 Piece 40.00
Console Set, Lotus, Blue, 3 Piece 65.00
Console Set, Magnolia, Blue, 3 Piece 32.00
Console Set, Tuscany, Pink, 3 Piece 70.00
Console Set, Water Lily, 14 In.Bowl, Low Candles, 3 Piece 52.00
Console, Wisteria, Blue, 5 X 9 In. 80.00
Console, Zephyr Lily, Green 24.00
Cookie Jar, Clematis, Blue, 8 In. 115.00
Cookie Jar, Freesia, Green 95.00
Cookie Jar, Magnolia ....85.00 To 115.00
Cookie Jar, Water Lily 175.00
Cookie Jar, Zephyr Lily, Green 65.00
Cornucopia, Bittersweet, Green .... 56.00 To 58.00
Cornucopia, Bleeding Heart, 6 In. 55.00
Cornucopia, Bleeding Heart, 8 In. 75.00
Cornucopia, Bushberry, Blue, 6 In. 20.00
Cornucopia, Bushberry, Brown, 8 In. 55.00
Cornucopia, Magnolia, 6 In. 30.00
Cornucopia, Pine Cone, Blue, 8 In., Pair 125.00
Cornucopia, Russco, Blue, 8 In. 30.00
Creamer, Landscape, Blue Ship 52.00
Creamer, Landscape, Brown 35.00
Creamer, Medallion 40.00
Creamer, Zephyr Lily, Green, 3 In. 27.00
Cuspidor, Donatello ....150.00 To 225.00
Dinner Set, Raymor, Dark Avocado Green, Autumn Brown, 28 Piece 300.00
Ewer, Apple Blossom, 15 In. 135.00
Ewer, Bleeding Heart, Blue, 10 In. 45.00
Ewer, Clematis, Blue, 15 In. 125.00
Ewer, Columbine, 7 In. 50.00
Ewer, Foxglove, 6 1/2 In. 60.00
Ewer, Foxglove, Pink, 15 In. 150.00
Ewer, Freesia, 6 In. 45.00
Ewer, Freesia, Brown, 16 In. 42.00
Ewer, Peony, Green, 6 In. 35.00
Ewer, Peony, Yellow, 10 In. 55.00
Ewer, Pine Cone, Blue, 10 In. 250.00
Ewer, Silhouette, 10 In. ....45.00 To 50.00
Ewer, Snowberry, Blue, 6 In. 25.00
Ewer, Snowberry, Blue, 10 In. ....70.00 To 75.00
Ewer, Tokay, Pink, Green, 6 In. 15.00
Ewer, Wincraft, 8 In. 25.00
Ewer, Zephyr Lily, Green, 10 In. 40.00
Flower Frog, Bushberry, Brown 35.00
Flower Frog, Columbine, Pink 25.00
Flower Frog, Magnolia, Tan 22.00
Flower Frog, Peony 45.00
Flower Frog, Teasel 25.00
Flowerpot, Florane, Blue, 4 In. 20.00
Jardiniere, Apple Blossom, Blue, 6 In. 75.00
Jardiniere, Blackberry, 4 In. 100.00
Jardiniere, Blackberry, 6 In. 95.00
Jardiniere, Blackberry, 9 In. 250.00
Jardiniere, Cherry Blossom, 8 X 6 In. 135.00
Jardiniere, Cherry Blossom, Blue, 4 In. 100.00
Jardiniere, Columbine, Pink, 5 In. 65.00

Jardiniere, Dahlrose, Neck Handles, 6 In. 50.00
Jardiniere, Donatello, 11 X 9 In. 90.00
Jardiniere, Earlam, Art Deco 85.00
Jardiniere, Florentine, 5 In. 28.00
Jardiniere, Futura, 7 1/2 In. 175.00
Jardiniere, Futura, Brown, Pedestal, 28 In. 650.00
Jardiniere, Gardenia, 4 1/2 In. 26.00
Jardiniere, Landscape, Pedestal, 44 In. 2200.00
Jardiniere, Mostique, Pedestal, Mottled Green 265.00
Jardiniere, Persian, 6 In. 150.00
Jardiniere, Pine Cone, Green, 4 In. 30.00
Jardiniere, Pine Cone, Twig Handle, Green, 6 In. 40.00
Jardiniere, Rozane, 1917, 8 In. 65.00
Jardiniere, Rozane, Pedestal, 1917 .... 350.00 To 375.00
Jardiniere, Snowberry, Green, 6 In. 65.00
Jardiniere, Wisteria, Blue, 6 In. 110.00
Jardiniere, Zephyr Lily, Green, 6 In. 65.00
Lamp, Florane, 3 Socket, Paper Label, 11 X 15 In. 145.00
Lamp, Sunflower, 2 Socket, 20 In. 125.00
Match Holder, Pine Cone, Blue 125.00
Mug, Holland 75.00
Mug, Quaker 140.00
Mug, Rozane, Standard Glaze, 4 1/2 In. 125.00
Pitcher, Aztec 48.00
Pitcher, Freesia, Blue, 10 In. 60.00
Pitcher, Holly, Creamware, 3 1/2 In. 125.00
Pitcher, Juvenile, Chick, 3 1/2 In. 48.00
Pitcher, Landscape .... 45.00 To 55.00
Pitcher, Lily, Cobalt Blue, Cream Ground, Pre–1916, 9 In. 60.00
Pitcher, Pine Cone, Green, Ice Lip 150.00
Pitcher, Tulip, 7 1/2 In. 100.00
Planter, Apple Blossom, 8 In. 18.00
Planter, Apple Blossom, Blue, 12 In. 40.00
Planter, Apple Blossom, Pink, 15 In. 45.00
Planter, Donatello, 1915, 8 In. 80.00
Planter, Gardenia, Brown, 8 In. 25.00
Planter, Gardenia, Tan 20.00
Planter, Lotus, 12 In. 75.00
Planter, Lotus, Blue & Tan, 4 In. 65.00
Planter, Ming Tree, 8 In. 23.00
Planter, Snowberry, Green To Brown, Hanging Chain 57.50
Planter, Zephyr Lily, Green, 8 In. 40.00
Plate, Juvenile, 4 Rabbits, Rolled Edge 32.00
Plate, Juvenile, A Piper's Son 35.00
Plate, Juvenile, Chicks 45.00
Plate, Juvenile, Nursery Rhyme 25.00
Plate, Juvenile, Rabbit & Baby 40.00
Platter, Carnelian I, Gold On Green, 12 1/2 In. 90.00
Smoke Set, Creamware, Indian Chief, Label, C.1915, 3 Piece 175.00
Smoke Set, Dutch 200.00
Soap Dish, Holland, Insert 65.00
Spittoon, Rozane, Ivory, 1917 .... 90.00
Sugar & Creamer, White Rose 25.00
Sugar & Creamer, Wincraft, Green 23.00
Sugar & Creamer, Zephyr Lily 25.00
Sugar, Wincraft, Blue 22.00
Tankard Set, Holland, 7 Piece 350.00
Tankard Set, Knights of Pithias, 12 In. 425.00
Tea Set, Blossom Flight 55.00
Tea Set, Clematis, Green ....85.00 To 110.00
Tea Set, Freesia, Green, 4 Piece 90.00
Tea Set, Landscape, Brown, 3 Piece 225.00
Tea Set, Magnolia, Blue 110.00
Teapot, Apple Blossom, Blue 105.00

Teapot, Peony 65.00
Teapot, Wincraft 43.00
Tray, Creamware, 2 Dutchmen, 11 In. 100.00
Tray, Foxglove, 8 1/2 In. 45.00
Tray, Pine Cone, 12 In. 110.00
Tray, Pine Cone, Brown, 12 In. 175.00
Tray, Zephyr Lily, Blue, 14 1/2 In. 32.00
Urn, Baneda, Volcano Shape, Pink, 5 1/2 X 4 1/2 In. 62.00
Urn, Blackberry, 12 1/2 In. 335.00
Urn, Carnelian, Green, Ink Stamped 45.00
Urn, Moss, 6 In. 60.00
Urn, Silhouette, Nude, 8 In. 95.00
Urn, Sunflower, Handles, 5 3/4 In. 35.00
Urn, Thornapple, 6 In. 30.00
Urn, Tourmaline, 2 Handles, Label, 6 In. 60.00
Urn, Volpato, 12 In. 60.00
Urn, Wisteria, Blue, 7 1/2 In. 165.00
Vase, Apple Blossom, Bark Handles, Green, 7 In. 37.50
Vase, Apple Blossom, Blue, 6 In. 35.00
Vase, Apple Blossom, Green, 10 In. 45.00
Vase, Aztec, 10 In. 250.00
Vase, Baneda, Handles At Base, Green, 8 1/4 In. 50.00
Vase, Baneda, Red, 7 1/2 X 6 1/4 In. 70.00
Vase, Bittersweet, Gray, 8 In. 37.50
Vase, Blackberry, 2 Handles, 8 1/2 X 12 1/4 In. 225.00
Vase, Blackberry, 4 In. 75.00
Vase, Blackberry, 6 In. 145.00
Vase, Blackberry, 8 In. 265.00
Vase, Bleeding Heart, Blue, 4 In. 39.00
Vase, Bleeding Heart, Green, 6 In. 42.00
Vase, Bleeding Heart, Rose, 9 In. 45.00
Vase, Bushberry, 12 In. 100.00
Vase, Bushberry, Blue, 6 In. 84.00
Vase, Bushberry, Bud, Brown Berries, Green, 7 In. 22.50
Vase, Bushberry, Green, 4 In. 30.00
Vase, Carnelian II, Fan, Rose, 8 In. 37.00
Vase, Carnelian, 7 In. 25.00
Vase, Carnelian, Handles, 10 In. 58.00
Vase, Cherry Blossom, 4 In. 85.00
Vase, Cherry Blossom, Brown, 5 In. 75.00
Vase, Cherry Blossom, Ear Handles, Brown, 7 1/4 In. 85.00
Vase, Clemana, Green, 6 1/4 In. 75.00
Vase, Clematis, Handles, Green, 7 1/2 In. 42.00
Vase, Columbine, Blue, 3 In. 18.00
Vase, Columbine, Blue, 6 In. 37.50
Vase, Corinthian, Green & White, 8 1/2 In. 60.00
Vase, Cosmos, Green, 8 In. 35.00
Vase, Dahlrose, 6 In. .... 22.50 To 40.00
Vase, Dahlrose, 10 In. 45.00
Vase, Dahlrose, Bud, Double Connected, 7 3/4 X 6 1/4 In. 28.00
Vase, Dahlrose, Handles, 12 In. 75.00
Vase, Dawn, 8 In. .... 30.00 To 45.00
Vase, Della Robbia, Incised & Carved Roman Chariot, 12 In. 1900.00
Vase, Della Robbia, Obelisk Shape, Tree On Each Side, 9 In. 800.00
Vase, Dogwood I, 7 In. 85.00
Vase, Donatello, 10 In. 100.00
Vase, Donatello, 12 In. 100.00
Vase, Earlam, 2 Handles, 7 In. 60.00
Vase, Ebb Tide, Apricot, 10 In. 18.00
Vase, Falline, 6 In. 125.00
Vase, Falline, Brown, 7 In. 120.00
Vase, Falline, Handles, Paper Label, 6 X 7 In. 200.00
Vase, Ferrella, Brown, 10 In. 300.00
Vase, Ferrella, Brown, Handles, 5 1/4 In. 125.00

Vase, Ferrella, Handle, 4 In.	115.00
Vase, Ferrella, Raspberry, 8 In.	188.00
Vase, Ferrella, Red, 6 In.	195.00
Vase, Florentine, 6 In.	25.00
Vase, Florentine, Handles, Ivory, 8 1/2 In.	40.00
Vase, Foxglove, 3 In.	18.00
Vase, Foxglove, Blue, 4 1/4 In.	25.00
Vase, Freesia, 8 In., Pair	75.00
Vase, Freesia, Fan, Brown, 6 In.	25.00
Vase, Freesia, Green, 9 In.	35.00 To 45.00
Vase, Fuchsia, 8 In.	55.00
Vase, Fuchsia, Ball Shape, 5 X 4 In.	24.00
Vase, Fuchsia, Brown, 8 In.	62.00
Vase, Futura, 9 In.	350.00
Vase, Futura, 10 In.	375.00
Vase, Futura, Double Handles, 7 1/2 In.	110.00
Vase, Futura, Pillow, 4 In.	95.00
Vase, Futura, Tiered Neck, Green Glaze, 12 1/2 In.	200.00
Vase, Imperial I, 10 In.	40.00
Vase, Imperial II, Red Flambe, Green Band At Top, 7 In.	160.00
Vase, Iris, 7 In.	30.00
Vase, Iris, Pink, 6 In.	30.00
Vase, Ixia, 7 In.	30.00
Vase, Ixia, Green, 8 In.	35.00
Vase, Ixia, Yellow, 6 In.	25.00
Vase, Ixia, Yellow, 9 1/2 In.	50.00
Vase, Jonquil, 4 1/4 In.	32.00
Vase, Jonquil, 7 In.	45.00
Vase, Jonquil, 8 In.	55.00
Vase, La Rose, 9 1/2 In.	45.00
Vase, Laurel, Handles, Rust Color, 7 1/4 In.	85.00
Vase, Laurel, Orange, 6 In.	30.00
Vase, Lotus, Light Blue, 10 In.	135.00
Vase, Lotus, Turquoise & Beige, 10 In.	100.00
Vase, Luffa, Fluorescent Green, 7 1/2 X 10 1/2 In.	95.00
Vase, Magnolia, 6 In.	37.00
Vase, Magnolia, 7 1/4 In.	28.00
Vase, Magnolia, 14 In.	95.00
Vase, Magnolia, Medium Blue, Marked, 14 In.	100.00
Vase, Ming Tree, White, 6 In.	40.00
Vase, Mock Orange, 7 In.	35.00
Vase, Monticello, 5 In.	38.00
Vase, Monticello, 9 In.	90.00
Vase, Monticello, Bulbous, 5 In.	48.00
Vase, Monticello, Green, 6 In.	38.00
Vase, Morning Glory, Green, Ear Handle, 6 1/2 In.	135.00
Vase, Morning Glory, Low Handles, 7 1/4 In.	120.00
Vase, Morning Glory, White Relief, Handles, 10 In.	350.00
Vase, Mostique, 8 In.	65.00
Vase, Orian Tan, Blue Drip, Gold Label, 8 In.	45.00
Vase, Orian, Gray Blue, Handles, Sticker, 7 In.	45.00
Vase, Orian, Red, 10 1/4 In.	75.00
Vase, Panel, Bud, 8 In.	130.00
Vase, Pauleo, Splotchy Matte Greens Over Rust, 18 1/2 In.	695.00
Vase, Peony, 18 In.	175.00
Vase, Pine Cone, 6 1/2 In.	45.00
Vase, Pine Cone, Brown, 10 In.	95.00
Vase, Pine Cone, Pillow, Brown, 8 In.	85.00
Vase, Poppy, 3 In.	22.00
Vase, Poppy, Handles, Blue, 10 1/2 In.	60.00
Vase, Poppy, Pink, 8 In.	35.00 To 40.00
Vase, Primrose, Brown, 7 In.	25.00
Vase, Primrose, Sticker, Blue, 6 In.	40.00
Vase, Rosecraft, Black, 9 In.	48.00

Vase, Rozane, 10 In.	26.00
Vase, Rozane, Leaves, Bulbous, 8 In.	125.00
Vase, Rozane, Nasturtiums, Artist Signed, 18 1/2 In.	275.00
Vase, Rozane, Twisted Body, Flowers, 5 In.	90.00
Vase, Russco, Crystalline, 8 1/2 In.	68.00
Vase, Savona, Outstretched Handles, Pink, 11 1/2 In.	225.00
Vase, Silhouette, Fan, Green Panel of Reclining Nude, 7 In.	95.00
Vase, Snowberry, Bulbous, 5 In.	27.50
Vase, Sunflower, 5 1/2 In.	55.00
Vase, Sunflower, 7 In.	50.00
Vase, Teasel, Blue Crystalline On Green Glaze, 12 In.	140.00
Vase, Teasel, Bulbous, Cream, 8 In.	45.00
Vase, Thornapple, 15 In.	200.00
Vase, Thornapple, Blue, 15 In.	220.00
Vase, Thornapple, Pink, Green, 8 1/2 In.	85.00
Vase, Topeo, 9 In.	80.00
Vase, Topeo, Red, 11 In.	150.00
Vase, Tourist, Touring Car & Bucking Horse Scene, 9 In.	1100.00
Vase, Tourmaline, Blue, 5 In.	30.00 To 60.00
Vase, Tourmaline, Pink & Blue, 8 1/4 In.	47.50
Vase, Tuscany, 4 X 6 In.	30.00
Vase, Tuscany, Bulbous, Handles, Gray, 8 In.	40.00
Vase, Tuscany, Pink, Handles, 6 In.	22.00
Vase, Velmoss, 2 Handles, 6 1/2 In.	38.00
Vase, Velmoss, 2 Handles, Raspberry Red, 14 1/2 In.	105.00
Vase, Velmoss, 5 In.	35.00
Vase, Velmoss, Aqua, 14 1/2 In.	175.00
Vase, Volpato, 6 1/2 In.	55.00
Vase, Water Lily, Blue, 9 In.	35.00
Vase, Water Lily, Blue, 15 In.	145.00
Vase, Water Lily, Blue, 18 In.	300.00
Vase, Water Lily, Brown, Pitcher Shape, 6 1/4 In.	38.00
Vase, Water Lily, Pink & Green, 14 In.	175.00
Vase, White Rose, 7 In.	34.00 To 40.00
Vase, White Rose, Brown, 9 In.	45.00
Vase, Wincraft, 10 In.	35.00 To 75.00
Vase, Wincraft, Green, 12 In.	50.00
Vase, Wincraft, Yellow, 8 In.	32.00
Vase, Wisteria, 6 In.	75.00
Vase, Wisteria, Blue, 5 In.	90.00
Vase, Wisteria, Shades Brown To Green, 10 1/2 In.	195.00
Vase, Zephyr Lily, 7 In.	25.00
Vase, Zephyr Lily, Green, Brown, 6 In.	45.00
Wall Pocket, Blackberry, Sticker, 8 1/2 X 6 3/4 In.	310.00 To 325.00
Wall Pocket, Carnelian I	45.00
Wall Pocket, Corinthian, 8 In.	50.00 To 65.00
Wall Pocket, Dahlrose, 8 1/2 In.	60.00 To 65.00
Wall Pocket, Donatello, 10 In.	65.00 To 95.00
Wall Pocket, Ferrella, 12 1/2 In.	80.00
Wall Pocket, Florane	85.00
Wall Pocket, Florentine, 7 In.	35.00
Wall Pocket, Freesia, Green & Purple	75.00
Wall Pocket, Futura	145.00 To 225.00
Wall Pocket, Imperial II, Orange & Green, Art Pottery	90.00
Wall Pocket, Jonquil	195.00
Wall Pocket, La Rose, 9 In.	50.00
Wall Pocket, Lily, 8 In., Pair	30.00
Wall Pocket, Lombardy	200.00
Wall Pocket, Luffa	115.00 To 225.00
Wall Pocket, Magnolia, Brown	60.00
Wall Pocket, Ming Tree	110.00
Wall Pocket, Mostique, 10 1/2 In.	45.00 To 55.00
Wall Pocket, Panel, Green, Daisies, 9 In.	85.00
Wall Pocket, Rosecraft, Daisies, Green, 9 In.	95.00

Wall Pocket, Silhouette, Rose 60.00
Wall Pocket, Snowberry, Green 58.00
Wall Pocket, Sunflower .... 165.00 To 200.00
Wall Pocket, Tuscany, Gray, 8 1/2 In. 60.00
Wall Pocket, Velmoss Scroll, 11 In. .... 130.00 To 150.00
Wall Pocket, Wincraft, Caramel 65.00
Wall Pocket, Wisteria 175.00
Wall Pocket, Zephyr Lily, Brown & Green 45.00
Window Box, Apple Blossom, Blue 27.00
Window Box, Gardenia, Gray, 8 X 3 1/2 In. 20.00
Window Box, Pine Cone, Blue, 8 In. 42.00

Rowland & Marsellus Company is a mark which appears on historical Staffordshire dating from the late nineteenth and early twentieth centuries. Rowland & Marsellus is believed to be the mark used by the British Anchor Pottery Co. of Longton, England, for some pieces made for export to a New York firm. Many American views were made. Of special interest to collectors are the rolled edge, blue and white plates.

ROWLAND & MARSELLUS, Cup & Saucer, Seaweed, Handleless 40.00
Plate, British At Concord 40.00
Plate, Indianapolis, Souvenir, 10 In. 38.00
Plate, Plymouth Rock, Deep Blue, Rolled Edge 39.00
Plate, Ride of Paul Revere 40.00
Plate, San Francisco, Cobalt Blue, 10 In. 45.00
Plate, World's Fair, Jefferson Center, 1904, 10 In. 50.00

Roy Rogers was born in 1911 in Cincinnati, Ohio. In the 1930s, he made a living as a singer; and in 1935, his group started work at a Los Angeles radio station. He appeared in his first movie in 1937. From 1952 to 1957, he made 101 television shows. Roy Rogers memorabilia is collected, including items from the Roy Rogers restaurants.

ROY ROGERS, Archery Set, Box 45.00
Badge, Deputy, Secret Compartment 35.00
Bandana, Silk 13.00
Bank, Horseshoe, Picture, Tin, 6 X 8 X 1 In. 32.00
Bank, Trigger, Ceramic 65.00
Billfold, Fur Chaps 20.00
Binoculars .... 15.00 To 40.00
Bolero, Tie, On Card 25.00
Bolo Slide 12.00
Buckle, Belt, With Trigger 65.00
Buckle, Child's 22.00
Camera .... 15.00 To 27.00
Camera, Flash, Box 45.00
Cap Pistol, Cast Metal 20.00
Chaps, Adult Size 40.00
Chaps, Child's 25.00
Cup, Figural 15.00
Figurine, Brave Eagle 125.00
Figurine, Dale Evans, Hartland, 1950s 75.00
Figurine, Roy & Dale Evans, Bisque, Occupied Japan, 6 In., Pair 32.50
Flashlight, Roy Rogers & Trigger, With Secret Code, Box 65.00
Game, Puzzle, 1950 .... 15.00
Guitar .... 45.00 To 55.00
Gun & Holster .... 50.00 To 100.00
Handkerchief 18.00
Harmonica 16.00
Hat, Quick Shooter 60.00
Jewelry Set, Dale Evans, Mother-of-Pearl 10.00
Jigsaw Puzzle, 3–D Viewer 12.00
Key Chain, Good Luck, Brass 7.00
Lantern, Ohio Art, Metal 30.00

Lucky Horseshoe, Black Rubber, Trigger, 5 In.	8.00
Lunch Box, Thermos, Double R Ranch, C.1960	32.00
Lunch Box, Trigger	12.00
Mug, FF Dieworks, 1950s	15.00
Pencil Box	15.00
Play Set, Rodeo Ranch, Complete, 1950s	45.00
Puzzle, Original Package, 1950, Round, 12 X 15 In.	25.00
Raincoat, Child's, Yellow & Black Rubber, Original Tag Inside	95.00
Record, 45 RPM	4.00
Ring, Microscope	30.00
Rodeo Ranch Play Set, Box	95.00
Songbook, 1952	12.00
Star, Deputy, Secret Compartment For Whistle	10.00
Sundial, Original Card	30.00
Tablet, Roy Rogers, With Trigger, Autographed, 10 Cent, 1940s	6.00
Tent, Tepee, Yellow, Red Lettering, 4 X 6 X 4 Ft.	125.00
Toy, Pull, With Trigger, Wooden, Original Tag, Box	225.00
Toy, Stagecoach Train, Marx, Windup	50.00
Toy, Stagecoach, Fix–It, Ideal	50.00 To 75.00
Watch, Pocket	120.00
Wristwatch	22.00
Yo–Yo, Box	45.00

 The Royal Bayreuth factory was founded in Tettau, Bavaria, in 1794. It has continued to modern times. The marks have changed through the years. A stylized crest, the name "Royal Bayreuth," and the word "Bavaria" appear in slightly different forms from 1870 to about 1919. Later dishes may include the words "U.S. Zone," the year of the issue, or the word "Germany" instead of "Bavaria."

ROYAL BAYREUTH, see also Rose Tapestry; Sand Babies; Snow Babies; Sunbonnet Babies

ROYAL BAYREUTH, Ashtray, 2 Men In Tyrolean Costume, Blue Mark	35.00 To 65.00
Ashtray, Devil & Cards, Green Mark	125.00
Ashtray, Elk	60.00
Basket, Gold Handle, 5 1/2 In.	375.00
Bowl, Cattle In Pasture Scene, Blue Mark, 10 In.	85.00
Bowl, Dutch Children, Windmill, Sailboats, Blue Mark, 3 In.	45.00
Bowl, Lobster, Blue Mark, 7 3/4 X 6 In.	150.00
Bowl, Molded Leaf & Grape Border, Inside Vines, 10 1/2 In.	250.00
Candleholder, Hunt Scene, Blue Mark, 4 1/2 In., Pair	260.00
Candleholder, Shield Back, Hunt Scene, Blue Mark	245.00
Candleholder, Shield, Little Boy Blue, Ginger, Blue Mark	150.00
Candy Dish, Figural, Red Clown, Blue Mark	260.00
Candy Dish, Scalloped, Grape Design, Blue Mark, 7 1/2 In.	70.00
Celery, Carnation, Pink, Lavender, Satin	185.00
Celery, Oak Leaf, White, Blue Mark, 5 1/2 X 13 In.	125.00
Chop Plate, Pink Roses, Cream, 13 In.	125.00
Cracker Jar, Shell, Blue Mark	295.00 To 365.00
Cracker Jar, White Mother–of–Pearl	150.00
Creamer, 2 Cavaliers, 3 3/4 In.	35.00
Creamer, Alligator	138.00 To 185.00
Creamer, Apple	65.00 To 80.00
Creamer, Art Nouveau, Satinized, Blue Mark	325.00
Creamer, Bear, Blue Mark	295.00
Creamer, Bird	50.00
Creamer, Black Cat	60.00 To 125.00
Creamer, Boat Head, Signed	90.00
Creamer, Brittany Girl, Sailboat In Background, Blue Mark	55.00
Creamer, Buffalo	90.00
Creamer, Bull's Head, Black	85.00
Creamer, Cat, Blue Mark	125.00
Creamer, Cavaliers, Blue Mark, 3 1/2 In.	45.00
Creamer, Child's, Nursery Rhymes	45.00
Creamer, Coachman	150.00 To 175.00

Creamer, Crow ....75.00 To 110.00
Creamer, Dachshund, Blue Mark .... 125.00 To 135.00
Creamer, Devil & Cards .... 115.00 To 130.00
Creamer, Duck, Blue Mark 105.00
Creamer, Dutch Children, Blue Mark, 4 In. 40.00
Creamer, Eagle .... 125.00 To 135.00
Creamer, Elk, Blue Mark .... 50.00 To 55.00
Creamer, Fish Head, Blue Mark 93.00
Creamer, Fox Hunt 50.00
Creamer, French Poodle, Marked 170.00
Creamer, Frog, Green & Orange 75.00
Creamer, Kangaroo, Blue Mark 650.00
Creamer, Little Jack Horner, Marked 53.00
Creamer, Lobster .... 35.00 To 60.00
Creamer, Melon, Black Mark 85.00
Creamer, Melon, Blue Mark 115.00
Creamer, Monkey, Green .... 185.00 To 195.00
Creamer, Moose Head .... 165.00 To 200.00
Creamer, Mother-of-Pearl Oak Leaf, Blue Mark 135.00
Creamer, Mountain Goat, Marked .... 145.00 To 225.00
Creamer, Oak Leaf, Marked 125.00
Creamer, Old Man of The Mountain, Marked 100.00
Creamer, Owl .... 125.00 To 195.00
Creamer, Pansy, Marked 140.00
Creamer, Parakeet 160.00
Creamer, Pastoral Scene 35.00
Creamer, Pelican 95.00
Creamer, Perch, Blue Mark 135.00
Creamer, Pig 155.00
Creamer, Pig, Blue Mark 350.00
Creamer, Platypus 325.00
Creamer, Poodle 100.00
Creamer, Poodle, Blue Mark .... 135.00 To 165.00
Creamer, Poppy, Lavender, Green, Blue Mark 110.00
Creamer, Poppy, Pink, Blue Mark 125.00
Creamer, Poppy, Red .... 60.00 To 75.00
Creamer, Rooster, Blue Mark .... 160.00 To 165.00
Creamer, Rose, Blue Mark 185.00
Creamer, Santa Claus 500.00
Creamer, Seal, Blue Mark 135.00
Creamer, Sheep, Scenic, 5 In. 110.00
Creamer, Spiky Shell, Coral Handle 65.00
Creamer, St.Bernard, Blue Mark 165.00
Creamer, Strawberry, Signed 125.00
Creamer, Swans On Lake, Pinched Spout, Blue Mark 45.00
Creamer, Trees, Cows Grazing, Gold Rim, Blue Mark 70.00
Creamer, Water Buffalo, Portsmouth, N.H., Blue Mark 95.00
Cup & Saucer, Grape Pattern, Grape Leaf Saucer, Pale Blue 55.00
Cup & Saucer, Jack Horner 150.00
Cup & Saucer, Pansy, Blue Mark, Demitasse 135.00
Cup & Saucer, Pastoral Scene, Footed 65.00
Cup & Saucer, Poppy, Apricot Matte Finish 135.00
Dessert Set, Strawberry Design 500.00
Dish, Mayonnaise, Red Lobster, Underplate, Blue Mark 80.00
Ewer, Swan Scene, Blue Mark, 3 1/2 X 5 1/4 In. 65.00
Figurine, Bavarian Musicians 48.00
Gravy Boat, Tomato, Covered 40.00
Hatpin Holder, Cattle, Attached Tray 185.00
Hatpin Holder, Poppy, Marked 275.00
Humidor, Devil & Card, Winged Devil Finial, Marked, 8 In. 675.00
Humidor, Tobacco, Large 175.00
Inkwell, Elk, Large 245.00
Jar, Frog Cover, Hunt Scene, Blue Mark, 4 X 4 1/4 In. 88.00
Jar, Lobster, Cover, 4 In. 50.00

Jug, Babes In Woods, Handle, Girls Taking Stroll, 6 1/2 In.	295.00
Ladle, Shell	60.00
Loving Cup, Corinthian	45.00
Match Holder, Girl, Dog	200.00
Match Holder, Mountain Goat, Blue Mark	275.00
Match Holder, Poppy, Red, Hanging .... 110.00 To	210.00
Matchbox, Musicians	60.00
Mug, Beer, Elk, Blue Mark	225.00
Mug, Devil & Cards, Large	150.00
Mustard, Pink Poppy, Blue Mark	110.00
Mustard, Rose	195.00
Mustard, Yellow Grape, Blue Mark	85.00
Nappy, Elk, Scenic, Marked	140.00
Nappy, Pansy, Purple, Handle	40.00
Pipe Rest, Basset Hound, Blue Mark	295.00
Pitcher, Arab & Horses, Blue Mark, 5 1/2 In.	50.00
Pitcher, Cavalier, Blue Mark, 3 1/2 In.	80.00
Pitcher, Clown, Red, 5 In.	155.00
Pitcher, Cows Scene, Blue Mark, 6 In.	145.00
Pitcher, Devil & Cards, Blue Mark, 5 1/4 In.	140.00
Pitcher, Devil & Cards, Devil Handle, Green Mark, 7 In.	595.00
Pitcher, Elk, 5 In. ....95.00 To	125.00
Pitcher, Elk, 7 In.	295.00
Pitcher, Figural, Black Water Buffalo, Blue Mark, 6 X 4 In.	135.00
Pitcher, Frog, Red, Blue Mark, 7 In.	525.00
Pitcher, Grape, Green, Blue Mark, 7 In.	325.00
Pitcher, Grape, Yellow, Blue Mark, 7 In.	395.00
Pitcher, Jester, Inscription, Artist Signed, 7 In.	250.00
Pitcher, Lamplighter, 8 In.	185.00
Pitcher, Lemon, 7 In.	175.00
Pitcher, Lobster, Red, 7 In.	250.00
Pitcher, Monkey, Green, 5 In.	295.00
Pitcher, Musician Figures, Hand Painted, 6 In.	220.00
Pitcher, Orange, Signed, 5 In.	125.00
Pitcher, Pansy, Purple, Blue Mark, 5 In.	235.00
Pitcher, Pearl Grape, Blue Mark, 7 In.	375.00
Pitcher, Pearl, Blue Mark, 5 In.	195.00
Pitcher, Robin, 5 In.	75.00
Pitcher, Shell, Blue Mark, 7 In.	295.00
Pitcher, St.Bernard, 7 In. ....300.00 To	395.00
Pitcher, Tomato, Marked, 5 In.	85.00
Pitcher, White Grape, Blue Mark, 5 In.	155.00
Pitcher, White Poppy, Blue Mark, 7 In.	375.00
Plaque, Peacock, 11 In.	165.00
Plate, Arab On Horseback, Blue Mark, 6 In.	24.00
Plate, Center Gold Medallion, Lady & Horse, Gold, 10 In.	75.00
Plate, Jack & The Beanstalk, 7 In.	135.00
Plate, Lady & Horse, Center Medallion, Roses, 9 3/4 In.	75.00
Plate, Leaf, With Handle, Blue Mark, 5 1/2 In.	18.00
Plate, Little Miss Muffet, 6 In.	55.00
Plate, Musicians, 9 In.	125.00
Plate, Pink Roses, Gold, 8 In.	75.00
Plate, Poppy, 7 1/2 In. ....30.00 To	35.00
Plate, Portrait, Gold Border, 10 In.	175.00
Plate, Snow Girls, Signed, 6 In.	55.00
Powder Box, Oyster & Pearl Cover, Blue Mark	125.00
Salt & Pepper, Devil & Cards	350.00
Salt & Pepper, Grape, Green, Tettau Mark	65.00
Salt & Pepper, Lettuce Head, With Lobster, Blue Mark	40.00
Stand, Pipe, Goose Girl, 2 3/4 In.	95.00
String Holder, Rooster, Blue Mark	125.00
Sugar & Creamer, Covered, Lobster, Blue Mark	125.00
Sugar & Creamer, Dogwood Pattern, Gold Handles, Blue Mark	98.00
Sugar & Creamer, Grape	225.00

Sugar & Creamer, Rose Florals 375.00
Sugar & Creamer, Tomato 135.00
Sugar & Creamer, White Floral, Gold Handles, Blue Mark 80.00
Sugar, Cattle In Field, Tab Handles, Oval, 5 1/2 In. 55.00
Sugar, Devil & Cards, Covered 150.00
Sugar, Pansy, Green Mark 145.00
Sugar, Rooster, Blue Mark 165.00
Sugar, Tomato, Blue Mark .... 20.00 To 28.00
Syrup, Carnation, Pink, Yellow, Red Mark, Satin 125.00
Teapot, Old Man of The Mountain 80.00
Teapot, Poppy, Marked 475.00
Teapot, Sunset Scene, Sailboat, Trees, Marked, 3 7/8 In. 95.00
Toothpick, Cavaliers 55.00
Toothpick, Elk ....80.00 To 125.00
Tray, Hunter & Dog 90.00
Tray, Pin, Floral 30.00
Vase, Arab & Horse Scene, Silver Top Band, Blue Mark, 3 In. 40.00
Vase, Boy With Donkeys, Blue Mark, 4 In. 85.00
Vase, Colonial Couple Dancing, 5 1/2 In. 60.00
Vase, Cows In Pasture, 11 In. 85.00
Vase, Dutch Boy & Girl Scene, 3 Handles, Blue Mark, 3 In. 40.00
Vase, Lady & Candle Portrait, Blue Mark, 3 1/2 In. 80.00
Vase, Mountain Castle Scene, Handles, Blue Mark, 8 1/2 In. 145.00
Vase, Pink Roses, Gold Design, 10 In., Pair 85.00
Wall Pocket, Strawberry, Blue Mark 225.00

Royal Bonn is the nineteenth– and twentieth–century trade name for the Bonn China Manufactory. It was established in 1755 in Bonn, Germany. A general line of porcelain was made. Many marks were used, most including the name "Bonn," the initials "FM," and a crown.

ROYAL BONN, Biscuit Jar, Pink, Blue Flowers, Green Leaves, Brass Rim, 7 In. 100.00
Bowl, Hand Painted Floral, Silver Plated Trim, Signed, 8 In. 145.00
Chop Plate, Sheep Scene, Blue & White, Delft, 14 In. 25.00
Ewer, Florals, Turquoise & Ivory, 13 In. 110.00
Ewer, Hand Painted Scene, Signed, 15 In. 120.00
Jardiniere, Multicolor, Castle Mark, 16 In. 375.00
Urn, Covered, Floral, Green, Yellow, Handles, Artist, 13 In. 85.00
Urn, Tapestry, Bulbous, Brass Base & Top, 9 1/2 In. 245.00
Vase, Autumnal Colors, Gold & Orange Flowers, Marked, 8 In. 95.00
Vase, Boy & Girl Sledding, Fuchsia Ground, 5 1/2 In. 65.00
Vase, Bulbous, Flowers, Handles, 15 1/4 In. 195.00
Vase, Flowers, Gold Tracery, Cream Ground, 15 In. 145.00
Vase, Gilt Collar, Shoulder Handles, Pastel Florals, 7 1/2 In. 225.00
Vase, Hand Painted Orchids, Onion Shape, 5 1/2 In. 75.00
Vase, Handles, Purple & Yellow Flowers, Cream Ground, 14 In. 118.00
Vase, Herons, 8 In. 38.00
Vase, Large Florals, Deep Green, Brown, Signed, 11 In. 115.00
Vase, Multifloral Color, Signed, 11 In. 115.00
Vase, Pink, Yellow, & White Roses, Yellow Ground, 8 In. 88.00
Vase, Portrait, Artist Signed, 13 1/2 In. 550.00
Vase, Portrait, Maiden, Long Brown Hair, Artist, 13 1/2 In. 595.00
Vase, Portrait, Signed & Numbered, 12 In. 250.00
Vase, Purple Iris, 12 1/2 In., Pair 195.00
Vase, Raised Gold, Green Ground, 13 1/2 In. 345.00
Vase, Rose Design, White, Scalloped, Cobalt Trim, Marked, 23 In. 120.00
Vase, Roses, Gold Design, 6 In. 95.00
Vase, Squatty, Pink & White Floral, 8 In. 75.00
Vase, Tapestry, Signed, 11 In. 195.00
Vase, Tulips, 8 In. 65.00
Vase, Wheat Fields, Poppies, Daisies, Footed, Wagner, 14 In. 165.00

Royal Copenhagen porcelain and pottery have been made in Denmark since 1772. The Christmas plate series started in 1908. The figurines with pale blue and gray glazes have remained popular in this century and are still being made. Many other old and new style porcelains are made today.

ROYAL COPENHAGEN, Butter Chip, Flowered	18.00
Butter Chip, Girls In Hats, Multicolors, 2 1/2 In., Pair	40.00
Butter Chip, Symphony, Floral, Set of 6	18.00
Carving Set, Flora, Fitted Presentation Case	1100.00
Compote, Crackleware, Gray, Gold Trim, Peaches, 10 X 6 In.	45.00
Cup & Saucer, Flora Danica, Demitasse, Marked, Set of 12	4950.00
Cup & Saucer, Fluted, Blue, Half Lace	25.00
Cup & Saucer, Frijsenborg	26.00
Dinner Service, Blue Fluted Open Lace Pattern, 100 Pc.	3600.00
Dish, Floral Design, 3 In.	15.00
Dish, Ice Cream, Reticulated Cover, Stand, 10 1/4 In.	3025.00
Figurine, Boy Holding Puppy, No.1747	85.00
Figurine, Boy Kissing Girl, No.2162	115.00
Figurine, Boy With Calf, No. 772	195.00
Figurine, Boy, With Teddy Bear, No.3468	185.00
Figurine, Cat, On Back, Tail, Gray, No.1025	95.00
Figurine, Dachshund, Sleeping, No.1234/781, 7 3/4 In.	250.00
Figurine, Duck, No.1933, Brown & Blue, 6 1/2 In.	110.00
Figurine, Elephant, No.599, 4 X 6 In.	130.00
Figurine, European Pheasant, 7 1/2 X 13 1/2 In.	150.00
Figurine, Fawn, Seated, 1930s, 6 In.	145.00
Figurine, French Poodle, No.4757, Gray	75.00
Figurine, German Shepherd Dog, Sitting, 8 In.	225.00
Figurine, Girls With Doll, Dr.Thomsen, 6 In., Pair	185.00
Figurine, Great Horned Owl, 14 In.	775.00
Figurine, Greenland Eskimo, No.2414	75.00
Figurine, Monkeys Huddled Together, No.1581	90.00
Figurine, Nude Infant With Sock, No.1739	90.00
Figurine, Pan With Rabbit, No. 439	200.00
Figurine, Pan, Playing Pipes, No.1736	185.00
Figurine, Pan, Seated, Snake Held In Hand, 4 1/4 In.	315.00
Figurine, Pekingese, White & Tan, No.1772, 5 In.	145.00
Figurine, Penguin, No.417, 9 In.	200.00
Figurine, Penguin, Standing, No.1283, 3 3/4 In.	45.00
Figurine, Pintail Duck, No.1939	125.00
Fish Set, Each With Different Center Fish, 13 Piece	2750.00
Group, Couple Caressing, Nude Woman, Fan, 7 In.	850.00
Group, Couple Caressing, Turkish Clothes, 7 In.	800.00
Group, St.Matthew, With Angel, 1857, Parian, 12 3/4 In.	250.00
Plate, Bicentennial, 1775–1975	25.00
Plate, Christmas, 1951	290.00
Plate, Napoleon & Josephine, Gold Edge, 10 In., Pair	250.00
Plate, Stag, Christmas, 1960	65.00
Platter, Botanical Specimens, 17 1/4 In., Pair	1450.00
Platter, Botanical Specimens, Marked, 14 1/4 In., Pair	885.00
Tureen, Soup, Stand, Botanical Specimen, Round, 11 3/8 In.	3550.00
Vase, White Rose, 1900, 9 In.	130.00
Vegetable, Covered, Flora Danica, Marked, 9 3/8 In.	2750.00

Royal Copley china was made by the Spaulding China Company of Sebring, Ohio, from 1939 to 1960. The figural planters and the small figurines, especially those with Art Deco designs, are of great collector interest.

ROYAL COPLEY, Ashtray, Bluebird & Flower	12.00
Bank, Cadillac, 7 1/2 In.	19.00
Bank, Rooster, 7 1/2 In.	26.00
Bookends, Hen & Rooster	9.00
Bookends, Wolf	9.00

Figurine, Barefoot Boy, 6 In.	9.00
Figurine, Hen & Rooster, 8 In.	45.00
Figurine, Mallard Duck, 6 In., Pair	22.00
Figurine, Sparrow, 5 In.	7.00
Figurine, Vireos, 4 1/2 In.	7.00
Figurine, Wrens, 6 1/4 In.	8.00
Planter, Chinese Boy & Girl, Hat Shape, 7 1/2 In., Pair	24.00
Planter, Deer & Fawn	15.00
Planter, Dog Pulling Wagon	10.00
Planter, Girl In Pigtails, Pink Hat, 7 In.	14.00
Planter, Peter Rabbit	12.00
Planter, Rooster, 8 In.	12.00
Vase, Deer, 7 1/2 In.	14.00
Wall Pocket, Oriental Girl, With Big Hat	18.50
Wall Pocket, Pirate	18.00
Wall Pocket, Rooster	12.00

Royal Crown Derby Company, Ltd., was established in England in 1876. There is a complex family tree that includes the Derby, Crown Derby, Worcester, and Royal Crown Derby porcelains. The Royal Crown Derby mark includes the name and a crown. The words "Made in England" were used after 1921.

ROYAL CROWN DERBY, Bone Dish, Allover Flowers, Gold, 9 X 5 In., Set of 8	75.00
Box, Pheasant, 11 In.	200.00 To 225.00
Cup & Saucer, Cobalt & Red, Gold Trim, Demitasse, 1929	25.00
Figurine, Lady With Bird, Signed	165.00
Ginger Jar, Overall Gold & Enameled Flowers, 9 In.	395.00
Knife & Fork Set, Porcelain Handle, Sheffield, 9 Piece	60.00
Paperweight, Figural, Pig, Marked	58.00
Plate, Dinner, Olde Avesbury	55.00
Plate, Flowers, Scalloped, Green Mark, 8 1/2 In., 8 Piece	95.00
Vase, Hand Painted Scene, Bird, Signed, 5 1/2 In.	325.00

"Royal Doulton" is the name used on Doulton and Company pottery made from 1902 to the present. Doulton and Company of England was founded in 1853. Pieces made before 1902 are listed under Doulton. Royal Doulton collectors search for the out-of-production figurines, character jugs, and series wares. For a complete listing, see "Kovels' Illustrated Price Guide to Royal Doulton."

ROYAL DOULTON, Ashtray, Flambe	25.00
Biscuit Box, Nursery Rhyme, Hey Diddle, Cat & Fiddle On Lid	400.00
Biscuit Jar, Dickens Ware, Tony Weller, 7 In.	300.00
Biscuit Jar, Gaffers Series, Man In Smock, Basket, 7 In.	245.00
Biscuit Jar, Shakespeare Series, Ophelia, Marked, 7 1/4 In.	245.00
Bowl, Blue Swag & Fuchsia Flowers, Glazed Interior, 9 In.	490.00
Bowl, Cereal, Old Woman Who Lived In Shoe, 5 1/4 In.	40.00
Bowl, Coaching Days, 5 In.	30.00
Bowl, Cotswold Shepherd, Man, Dog, Sheep, Square	125.00
Bowl, Lambeth, Blue & Green Stripes, Marked, 9 1/2 X 4 In.	55.00
Bowl, Old Moreton, Oval, 11 In.	45.00 To 60.00
Bowl, Rustic England, Pedestal, 7 1/2 In.	75.00
Box, Smiling Jester Lid, Welcome Is Best Cheer, 4 X 3 In.	100.00
Butter Chip, Elaine, Square	15.00
Cake Set, Strawberry Cream, 21 Piece	140.00
Candlestick, Bill Sykes	255.00
Candlestick, Bodiam Castle, 1925, 6 1/4 In., Pair	95.00
Candlestick, Dickens Ware, Artful Dodger, 7 In.	100.00
Candlestick, Old Moreton, 6 1/2 In.	70.00 To 85.00
Chamberstick, Farm & Woodland Scenes	85.00

Character jugs are the modeled head and shoulders of the subject. They are made in four sizes: large, 5 1/4 to 7 inches; small, 3 1/4 to 4 inches; miniature, 2 1/4 to 2 1/2 inches; and tiny, 1 1/4 inches. Toby jugs depict a seated, full figure.

Character Jug, 'Ard of 'Earing, Large	995.00
Character Jug, 'Ard of 'Earing, Miniature	1150.00
Character Jug, 'Arriet, A Mark, Small	75.00
Character Jug, 'Arry, Large	165.00
Character Jug, 'Arry, Small	165.00
Character Jug, Auld Mac, A Mark, Large	95.00
Character Jug, Auld Mac, Tiny	200.00 To 210.00
Character Jug, Beefeater, Large	75.00 To 110.00
Character Jug, Beefeater, Miniature	45.00
Character Jug, Buz Fuz, A Mark, Small	65.00
Character Jug, Captain Ahab, Large	45.00 To 55.00
Character Jug, Captain Ahab, Miniature	20.00
Character Jug, Captain Hook, Large	395.00
Character Jug, Captain Hook, Miniature	320.00 To 350.00
Character Jug, Cardinal, A Mark, Large	120.00
Character Jug, Cardinal, A Mark, Miniature	40.00 To 55.00
Character Jug, Cardinal, Large	130.00
Character Jug, Cardinal, Tiny	205.00
Character Jug, Cavalier, A Mark, Small	60.00
Character Jug, Cavalier, Large	130.00
Character Jug, Clown, White Hair, Large	1050.00
Character Jug, Dick Turpin, A Mark, Large	125.00
Character Jug, Dick Whittington, Large	375.00 To 395.00
Character Jug, Drake, A Mark, Large	130.00
Character Jug, Farmer John, A Mark, Small	75.00
Character Jug, Fat Boy, A Mark, Miniature	45.00
Character Jug, Fat Boy, Tiny	75.00 To 95.00
Character Jug, Fortune Teller, Large	395.00 To 495.00
Character Jug, Fortune Teller, Miniature	325.00 To 390.00
Character Jug, Fortune Teller, Small	295.00 To 310.00
Character Jug, Friar Tuck, Large	365.00
Character Jug, Gladiator, Large	595.00
Character Jug, Gondolier, Large	550.00
Character Jug, Gone Away, Miniature	25.00
Character Jug, Granny, A Mark, Small	30.00
Character Jug, Granny, Miniature	25.00
Character Jug, Guardsman, Large	50.00
Character Jug, Gulliver, Miniature	325.00
Character Jug, Gulliver, Small	375.00
Character Jug, Henry Morgan, Miniature	20.00 To 40.00
Character Jug, Henry Morgan, Small	35.00
Character Jug, Izaak Walton, Large	55.00
Character Jug, Jarge, Large	260.00
Character Jug, Jester, A Mark, Small	80.00
Character Jug, Jockey, Large	110.00
Character Jug, John Barleycorn, A Mark, Large	120.00
Character Jug, John Barleycorn, A Mark, Miniature	42.00
Character Jug, John Peel, A Mark, Large	120.00
Character Jug, John Peel, A Mark, Miniature	42.00
Character Jug, Lord Nelson, Large	275.00 To 350.00
Character Jug, Lumberjack, Large	55.00
Character Jug, Mephistopheles, Large	2200.00
Character Jug, Mephistopheles, Small	875.00 To 975.00
Character Jug, Mikado, Large	475.00
Character Jug, Mikado, Miniature	295.00
Character Jug, Mine Host, Miniature	25.00
Character Jug, Mr.Micawber, A Mark, Miniature	45.00 To 50.00
Character Jug, Mr.Micawber, Tiny	85.00
Character Jug, Mr.Pickwick, Tiny	195.00 To 210.00

Character Jug, Old Charley, Miniature 20.00
Character Jug, Old Charley, Small 35.00
Character Jug, Old Charley, Tiny .... 60.00 To 95.00
Character Jug, Old King Cole, Large 240.00
Character Jug, Paddy, A Mark, Miniature 45.00
Character Jug, Paddy, Large 120.00
Character Jug, Paddy, Tiny .... 75.00 To 85.00
Character Jug, Parson Brown, Large 120.00
Character Jug, President Reagan, Large .... 335.00 To 395.00
Character Jug, Punch & Judy Man, Large 565.00
Character Jug, Punch & Judy Man, Miniature 325.00
Character Jug, Regency Beau, Large .... 895.00 To 975.00
Character Jug, Regency Beau, Small .... 550.00 To 575.00
Character Jug, Sairey Gamp, A Mark, Large 75.00
Character Jug, Sairey Gamp, A Mark, Miniature 20.00
Character Jug, Sam Johnson, Large 235.00
Character Jug, Sam Johnson, Small .... 165.00 To 175.00
Character Jug, Sam Weller, A Mark, Miniature .... 40.00 To 45.00
Character Jug, Sam Weller, Tiny .... 75.00 To 95.00
Character Jug, Scaramouche, Miniature .... 395.00 To 400.00
Character Jug, Scaramouche, Small 475.00
Character Jug, Simon The Cellarer, Large 110.00
Character Jug, Simple Simon, Large 490.00
Character Jug, Tam O'Shanter, Small 30.00
Character Jug, Toby Philpots, A Mark, Large 115.00
Character Jug, Tony Weller, Miniature 50.00
Character Jug, Touchstone, Large 210.00
Character Jug, Town Crier, A Mark, Small 75.00
Character Jug, Ugly Duchess, Small 275.00
Character Jug, Viking, Miniature .... 95.00 To 125.00
Charger, Jackdaw of Rheims, Dated 1943, 15 In. 225.00
Charger, Pembroke Castle, Blue & White, 13 1/4 In. 95.00
Chop Plate, Jackdaw of Rheims, 13 In. 80.00
Coffeepot, Reynard The Fox 80.00
Compote, Under The Greenwood Tree, Footed, 1903, 8 X 4 In. .. 100.00
Creamer, Bayeux Tapestry, C.1915, 5 In. 90.00
Creamer, Coaching Days, 3 1/4 In. 45.00
Cup & Saucer, Clarendon, Demitasse, Set of 8 .... 150.00
Cup & Saucer, Dickens Ware, Tony Weller, Marked 65.00
Cup & Saucer, Landscape, Flambe, Demitasse 70.00
Decanter, Black Crow In Tuxedo 165.00
Decanter, Rip Van Winkle 95.00
Dish, Child's, Feeding, Little Miss Muffet .... 45.00 To 60.00
Dresser Set, Dickens Ware, Bill Sykes, 4 Piece 295.00
Figurine, A'Courting, HN 2004 .... 435.00 To 450.00
Figurine, Abdullah, HN 2104 .... 375.00 To 550.00
Figurine, Afternoon Tea, HN 1747 .... 215.00 To 255.00
Figurine, Aileen, HN 1645 .... 1500.00
Figurine, Alchemist, HN 1282 .... 1150.00
Figurine, Alice, HN 2158 .... 88.00 To 155.00
Figurine, All–A–Blooming, HN 1466 .... 1400.00
Figurine, Alsatian, Benign of Picardy, Medium, HN 1116 .... 125.00
Figurine, Angela, HN 1204 .... 1075.00
Figurine, Angelina, HN 2013 .... 600.00
Figurine, Annabella, HN 1871 .... 300.00 To 375.00
Figurine, Annette, HN 1471 .... 375.00
Figurine, Anthea, HN 1527 .... 695.00
Figurine, Apple Maid, HN 2160 .... 275.00
Figurine, Ascot, HN 2356 .... 125.00
Figurine, Autumn Breezes, HN 2147 .... 90.00
Figurine, Babette, HN 1423 .... 675.00
Figurine, Baby Bunting, HN 2180 .... 200.00
Figurine, Bachelor, HN 2319 .... 395.00
Figurine, Balinese Dancer, HN 2808 .... 300.00 To 750.00

Figurine, Ballerina, HN 2116 .... 175.00
Figurine, Baltimore Oriole, HN 2612 .... 10.00
Figurine, Barbara, HN 1432 .... 595.00
Figurine, Basket Weaver, HN 2245 .... 350.00
Figurine, Beachcomber, HN 2487 .... 125.00 To 175.00
Figurine, Beggar, HN 2175 .... 375.00 To 400.00
Figurine, Bernice, HN 2071 .... 750.00
Figurine, Biddy, HN 1513 .... 140.00
Figurine, Blithe Morning, HN 2021 .... 150.00
Figurine, Bluebeard, HN 2105 .... 200.00 To 270.00
Figurine, Bon Jour, HN 1888 .... 695.00
Figurine, Boxer Warlord of Mazelaine, HN 2643 .... 52.00 To 65.00
Figurine, Bridget, HN 2070 .... 250.00
Figurine, Broken Lance, HN 2041 .... 395.00 To 430.00
Figurine, Calumet, HN 1689 .... 575.00 To 695.00
Figurine, Camellia, HN 2222 .... 305.00
Figurine, Camille, HN 1586 .... 600.00
Figurine, Captain, 2nd New York Regiment, 1775, HN 2755 .... 850.00
Figurine, Captain, HN 2260 .... 160.00
Figurine, Carmen, HN 1267 .... 800.00
Figurine, Carolyn, HN 2112 .... 185.00
Figurine, Carpet Seller, HN 1464 .... 200.00 To 275.00
Figurine, Cat, Persian, HN 999 .... 60.00
Figurine, Cellist, HN 2226 .... 380.00
Figurine, Child Study, HN 603A 200.00
Figurine, Chinese Dancer, HN 2840 .... 750.00
Figurine, Christine, HN 1839 .... 725.00
Figurine, Christmas Parcels, HN 2851 .... 110.00
Figurine, Cicely, HN 1516 .... 1100.00
Figurine, Clarinda, HN 2724 .... 175.00
Figurine, Clemency, HN 1643 .... 650.00
Figurine, Cobbler, HN 1706 ....*Illus* 120.00
Figurine, Cocker Spaniel & Pheasant, 5 1/4 In., HN 1028 .... 67.00
Figurine, Cocker Spaniel, 6 1/2 In., HN 1002 .... 210.00
Figurine, Collinette, HN 1999 .... 375.00
Figurine, Coppelia, HN 2115 .... 555.00 To 590.00
Figurine, Cup of Tea, HN 2322 .... 95.00
Figurine, Cymbals, HN 2699 .... 475.00 To 500.00
Figurine, Daffy Down Dilly, HN 1712 .... 200.00 To 275.00
Figurine, Dainty May, HN 1639 .... 280.00 To 305.00
Figurine, Dalmatian, Goworth Victor, HN 1113 .... 59.00
Figurine, Dancing Years, HN 2235 .... 250.00 To 325.00
Figurine, Darling, HN 1319 .... 90.00 To 130.00
Figurine, Dawn, HN 1858 .... 875.00 To 1200.00
Figurine, Daydreams, HN 1944 .... 375.00
Figurine, Debutante, HN 2210 .... 300.00
Figurine, Delicia, HN 1681 .... 500.00
Figurine, Delphine, HN 2136 .... 170.00 To 275.00
Figurine, Dog of Foo, Black & White, Basalt 135.00
Figurine, Dog, Lying Down, HN 1101 .... 65.00
Figurine, Dorcas, HN 1558 .... 250.00
Figurine, Doreen, HN 1389 .... 675.00 To 695.00
Figurine, Dragoons, Virginia, 1779, HN 2844 .... 2700.00
Figurine, Drake, HN 806 .... 50.00 To 65.00
Figurine, Dulcinea, HN 1343 .... 1195.00 To 1650.00
Figurine, Dulcinea, HN 1419 .... 1295.00 To 1850.00
Figurine, Easter Day, HN 1976 .... 325.00
Figurine, Easter Day, HN 2039 .... 235.00 To 240.00
Figurine, Eugene, HN 1520 .... 975.00
Figurine, Fair Lady, HN 2835 .... 75.00
Figurine, Family Album, HN 2321 .... 350.00
Figurine, Farmer's Boy, HN 2520 .... 850.00
Figurine, Favourite, HN 2249 .... 150.00
Figurine, First Steps, HN 2242 .... 420.00

Figurine, Fleurette, HN 1587 .... 445.00 To 500.00
Figurine, Flora, HN 2349 .... 225.00
Figurine, Foaming Quart, HN 2162 .... 90.00
Figurine, Folly, HN 1750 .... 1400.00
Figurine, Forget–Me–Not, HN 1813 .... 525.00
Figurine, Fortune Teller, HN 2159 .... 375.00
Figurine, French Peasant, HN 2075 .... 435.00 To 535.00
Figurine, Friar Tuck, HN 2143 .... 360.00 To 450.00
Figurine, Geisha, HN 1234 .... 950.00
Figurine, Genevieve, HN 1962 .... 195.00
Figurine, Giselle, Forest Glade, HN 2140 .... 295.00
Figurine, Gordon Setter, Small, HN 1081 .... 100.00
Figurine, Granny's Shawl, HN 1647 .... 340.00
Figurine, Greta, HN 1485 .... 225.00
Figurine, Griselda, HN 1993 .... 525.00 To 750.00
Figurine, Gude Grey Mare, Medium, HN 2569 .... 285.00
Figurine, Gwynneth, HN 1980 .... 205.00
Figurine, Harlequinade, HN 585 .... 650.00
Figurine, Heart To Heart, HN 2276 .... 325.00
Figurine, Helen of Troy, HN 2387 .... 615.00 To 900.00
Figurine, Henrietta Maria, HN 2005 .... 575.00
Figurine, Her Ladyship, HN 1977 .... 285.00
Figurine, Honey, HN 1909 .... 350.00
Figurine, Hornpipe, HN 2161 .... 650.00
Figurine, Hostess From Williamsburg, HN 2209 .... 125.00
Figurine, Huntsman, HN 2492 .... 155.00
Figurine, In The Stocks, HN 2163 .... 650.00
Figurine, Indian Temple Dancer, HN 2830 .... 750.00
Figurine, Irish Setter, 3 3/4 In., HN 1056 .... 60.00
Figurine, Ivy, HN 1768 .... 58.00 To 70.00
Figurine, Jack Point, HN 2080 .... 660.00
Figurine, Janice, HN 2165 .... 450.00
Figurine, Jennifer, HN 1484 .... 450.00
Figurine, Jersey Milkmaid, HN 2057 .... 210.00
Figurine, Joan, HN 1422 .... 225.00
Figurine, Jolly Sailor, HN 2172 .... 470.00 To 495.00
Figurine, Jovial Monk, HN 2144 .... 150.00
Figurine, Judith, HN 2089 .... 195.00 To 275.00
Figurine, Julia, HN 2705 .... 75.00
Figurine, Kate Hardcastle, HN 2028 .... 500.00
Figurine, Katrina, HN 2327 .... 250.00
Figurine, Kitten, Licking Hind Paw, HN 2580 .... 45.00
Figurine, Lady April, HN 1958 .... 215.00
Figurine, Lady Betty, HN 1967 .... 335.00
Figurine, Lady Charmian, HN 1948 .... 195.00 To 250.00
Figurine, Lady Clare, HN 1465 .... 595.00 To 725.00
Figurine, Lady Jester, HN 1221 .... 1750.00
Figurine, Leopard On Rock, HN 2638 .... 740.00
Figurine, Lido Lady, HN 1220 .... 950.00
Figurine, Lilac Time, HN 2137 .... 215.00 To 265.00
Figurine, Lion On Rock, HN 2641 .... 740.00
Figurine, Little Bridesmaid, HN 1433 .... 120.00
Figurine, Little Miss Muffet, HN 2727 .... 125.00
Figurine, Lobster Man, HN 2317 .... 225.00
Figurine, Long John Silver, HN 2204 .... 375.00 To 425.00
Figurine, Lorna, HN 2311 .... 95.00
Figurine, Lucy Lockett, HN 524 .... 375.00
Figurine, Maisie, HN 1619 .... 350.00
Figurine, Major, 3rd New Jersey Regiment, 1776, HN 2752 .... 1500.00
Figurine, Marietta, HN 1341 .... 550.00
Figurine, Marjorie, HN 2788 .... 85.00
Figurine, Masquerade, HN 2251 .... 250.00
Figurine, Master Sweep, HN 2205 .... 495.00 To 500.00
Figurine, Master, HN 2325 .... 150.00

Figurine, Memories, HN 2030 .... 265.00
Figurine, Mendicant, HN 1365 .... 200.00
Figurine, Merely A Minor, Brown, Medium, HN 2537 .... 225.00 To 325.00
Figurine, Merely A Minor, Brown, Small, HN 2571 .... 275.00
Figurine, Midinette, HN 2090 .... 205.00 To 295.00
Figurine, Midsummer Noon, HN 2033 .... 500.00
Figurine, Milkmaid, HN 2057A 85.00
Figurine, Minuet, HN 2019 .... 260.00
Figurine, Mother's Help, HN 2151 .... 180.00
Figurine, Mr.Micawber, HN 1895 .... 300.00
Figurine, Nadine, HN 1886 .... 650.00
Figurine, Negligee, HN 1454 .... 1450.00
Figurine, New Bonnet, HN 1728 .... 650.00
Figurine, Old King Cole, HN 2217 .... 500.00 To 650.00
Figurine, Old Mother Hubbard, HN 2314 .... 275.00
Figurine, Olivia, HN 1995 .... 450.00 To 525.00
Figurine, Once Upon A Time, HN 2047 .... 235.00
Figurine, One That Got Away, HN 2153 .... 275.00
Figurine, Orange Lady, HN 1953 .... 250.00
Figurine, Orange Vendor, HN 72 .... 950.00
Figurine, Organ Grinder, HN 2173 .... 525.00
Figurine, Paisley Shawl, HN 1391 .... 365.00
Figurine, Paisley Shawl, HN 1987 .... 225.00
Figurine, Paisley Shawl, HN 1988 .... 140.00 To 175.00
Figurine, Pantalettes, HN 1362 .... 300.00 To 347.00
Figurine, Parisian, HN 2445 .... 95.00
Figurine, Past Glory, HN 2484 .... 165.00
Figurine, Patricia, HN 1414 .... 550.00
Figurine, Pied Piper, HN 2102 .... 225.00
Figurine, Pointer, HN 2624 .... 156.00
Figurine, Polka, HN 2156 .... 300.00
Figurine, Polly Peachum, HN 489 .... 366.00
Figurine, Polly Peachum, HN 549 .... 300.00
Figurine, Potter, HN 1493 .... 275.00
Figurine, Pride of The Shires, HN 2564 .... 300.00
Figurine, Private, 2nd Carolina Regiment, HN 2717 .... 1050.00
Figurine, Private, Connecticut Regiment, 1776, HN 2845 .... 750.00
Figurine, Private, Georgia 1st Regiment, 1777, HN 2779 .... 850.00
Figurine, Private, Massachusetts Regiment, 1778, HN 2760 .... 750.00
Figurine, Private, Penn.Rifle Battalion, 1776, HN 2846 .... 750.00
Figurine, Professor, HN 2281 .... 140.00
Figurine, Prue, HN 1996 .... 295.00
Figurine, Puppetmaker, HN 2253 .... 380.00
Figurine, Queen Elizabeth II, HN 2878 .... 380.00 To 395.00
Figurine, Queen of Sheba, HN 2328 .... 600.00
Figurine, Rita, HN 1450 .... 995.00
Figurine, Romany Sue, HN 1757 .... 500.00
Figurine, Rosamund, HN 1320 .... 1350.00
Figurine, Rowena, HN 2077 .... 625.00
Figurine, Royal Governor's Cook, HN 2233 .... 160.00
Figurine, Sabbath Morn, HN 1982 .... 195.00
Figurine, Scottish Terrier, Albourne Arthur, HN 1014 .... 33.00
Figurine, Scottish Terrier, Albourne Arthur, HN 1016 .... 33.00
Figurine, Sealyham, Scotia Stylist, HN 1032 .... 95.00
Figurine, Siesta, HN 1305 .... 1750.00
Figurine, Soiree, HN 2312 .... 125.00
Figurine, Spring Flowers, HN 1807 .... 195.00
Figurine, Springer Spaniel, Dry Toast, HN 2517 .... 48.00
Figurine, Springtime, HN 3033 .... 250.00
Figurine, Summer's Day, HN 2181 .... 375.00
Figurine, Susanna, HN 1233 .... 750.00
Figurine, Sweet Anne, HN 1318 .... 225.00
Figurine, Sweet Anne, HN 1496 .... 200.00 To 275.00
Figurine, Sweet April, HN 2215 .... 310.00

Figurine, Sweet Lavender, HN 1373	550.00
Figurine, Tall Story, HN 2248	210.00
Figurine, Teenager, HN 2203	200.00
Figurine, Terrier, Head Turned, HN 2508	90.00
Figurine, Tiger On Rock, HN 2639	740.00
Figurine, Tootles, HN 1680	90.00
Figurine, Town Crier, HN 2119	180.00 To 235.00
Figurine, Toymaker, HN 2250	300.00
Figurine, Tz'u–Hsi Empress Dowager, HN 2391	490.00 To 640.00
Figurine, Uriah Heep, HN 2101	275.00
Figurine, Vanessa, HN 1836	950.00
Figurine, Vera, HN 1730	795.00
Figurine, Veronica, HN 1943	536.00
Figurine, Viking, HN 2375	150.00
Figurine, Votes For Women, HN 2816	145.00 To 170.00
Figurine, Wandering Minstrel, HN 1224	2950.00
Figurine, Wardrobe Mistress, HN 2145	340.00 To 395.00
Figurine, Welsh Corgi, Spring Robin, HN 2559	33.00
Figurine, Winter, HN 2088	300.00 To 350.00
Figurine, Young Widow, HN 1399	2500.00
Flask, Mr.Micawber, Kingsware, Stopper	195.00 To 225.00
Flask, Oyez, Kingsware	225.00
Jardiniere, 2 Little Girls Under Tree, 8 In.	650.00
Jug, Children's Scenes, Westcott Shape, 5 In.	95.00
Jug, Eglington Tournament, Castle Shape, 5 In.	90.00
Jug, Gleaners, Corinth Shape, 5 1/2 In.	90.00
Jug, Gleaners, Marked, 4 X 5 1/2 In.	80.00
Jug, Jester, Noke, 6 In.	185.00
Jug, Milk, Dickens Ware, Captain Cuttle, 6 1/2 In.	90.00
Jug, Monks In The Cellar, Friar Shape, 7 In.	110.00
Jug, Robin Hood	50.00
Jug, Welsh Ladies, Simon Shape, 6 1/2 In.	100.00
Jug, William Ye Driver Series, Coachman, Whip, 8 3/4 In.	145.00
Loving Cup, Huntsman In Red, Dogs, Kingsware, 6 1/4 In.	110.00
Match Holder, Santa Claus	85.00
Pitcher, Brown Hunting Scene, Beige Relief, 7 In.	125.00
Pitcher, Coaching Days, Man Walking By Coach, 6 3/4 In.	145.00
Pitcher, Dickens Ware, Alfred Jingle, Marked, 9 In.	175.00
Pitcher, Dickens Ware, Arabian Nights, 6 In.	225.00
Pitcher, Dickens Ware, Fagin, Square Shape, Marked, 6 3/4 In.	135.00
Pitcher, Dickens Ware, Old London, Square	195.00
Pitcher, Dickens Ware, Sidney Carton, Marked, 8 7/8 In.	150.00
Pitcher, Falstaff, Sword, Ornate Top, C.1920, 6 3/4 In.	125.00
Pitcher, Hot Water, Covered, Zunday Zmocks, 7 In.	155.00
Pitcher, Jack's The Lad For Work, Old Sea Dogs	130.00
Pitcher, Man On White Horse, Black Mark, 4 1/2 In.	85.00
Pitcher, Milk, Coaching Days	65.00
Pitcher, Milk, Dickens Ware, Cap'N Cuttle, 7 In.	75.00
Pitcher, Mother Goose, 3 In.	39.00
Pitcher, Old Bob Ye Guard, Pinched In, 8 In.	125.00
Pitcher, Rosalind, Dated 1930, 5 In.	85.00
Pitcher, Roses, Green To Pink, Marked, 13 1/2 In.	100.00
Pitcher, Series Ware, Izaak Walton, Saying, Marked, 6 1/2 In.	225.00
Pitcher, Water, Green Glaze, Blue Leaves, Initials, 3 In.	65.00
Plaque, Babes In The Woods, Gold Leaf Frame, 19 X 16 In.	1075.00
Plaque, Dr.Johnson At The Cheshire Cheese, Signed, 13 In.	135.00
Plate, Babes In The Woods, Mother & Child, 9 In.	350.00
Plate, Bayeux Tapestry, 10 In.	65.00
Plate, Bunnykins, Teacher & Class, 1954, 8 1/2 In.	25.00
Plate, Cavalier, Signed Noke, 8 In.	65.00
Plate, Christmas In Mexico, 1973	28.00
Plate, Dickens Portrait, 10 In.	75.00
Plate, Diversions of Uncle Toby As A Toxophilite, 10 In.	65.00
Plate, Every Dog Has His Day, Golf Scene, Marked, 10 1/2 In.	175.00

Plate, Gallant Fishers, Izaak Walton, 10 In.	70.00
Plate, Jester, 10 In.	70.00
Plate, Maritime Provinces, 10 In.	24.00
Plate, Mayor, 10 In.	55.00
Plate, Mother & Child Playing In Yard, 9 In.	350.00
Plate, Nursery Rhymes, Father William, 6 In.	45.00
Plate, Parson, 10 In.	55.00
Plate, Poughkeepsie College, 1917	40.00
Plate, Rip Van Winkle, 10 1/2 In.	75.00
Plate, Shakespeare Ware, Anne Page, Red Dress, 9 In.	60.00
Plate, Sir Francis Drake, Historic England	50.00
Plate, Squire, 10 1/2 In.	58.00
Plate, Town Officials, Night Watchman, Lantern, 10 In.	65.00
Platter, Pomeroy, Blue & White, 13 In.	78.00
Soap Dish, Shakespeare Series, Shylock, Marked, 4 X 5 In.	105.00
Soap Tray, Butterfly Shape, Wright's Coal–Tar Soap, 6 In.	80.00
Tankard, Fisherfolk, 5 1/2 In.	75.00
Tankard, Oliver Twist	195.00
Teapot, Dickens Ware, Bill Sykes, Marked, 4 1/4 X 6 In.	195.00
Teapot, Dickens Ware, Fat Boy	225.00
Teapot, Moorish Gate, Marked, 5 3/4 In.	88.00
Tile, Tea, Mr.Micawber, Marked, Round, 6 In.	60.00
Toby Jug, Cliff Cornell, Blue, 9 In.	350.00
Tray, Dickens Ware, Bill Sykes, Signed, 8 1/2 X 8 1/4 In.	200.00
Tray, Egyptian, 7 1/2 X 12 In.	95.00
Tray, Minstrels, 7 1/2 X 8 1/2 In.	40.00
Tray, Rustic England, 5 X 10 1/2 In.	50.00
Tumbler, Coaching Scene, 1890–1900	30.00
Tumbler, Dickens Ware, Alfred Jingle, Marked, 3 3/4 In.	88.00
Vase, Alfred Jingle, Handles, 5 3/8 X 7 3/4 In.	148.00
Vase, Artful Dodger, 3 1/4 In.	60.00
Vase, Babes In Woods, Girl Holding Doll, 5 1/4 In.	250.00
Vase, Babes In Woods, Lady, Basket, Young Girl, 6 X 7 In.	175.00
Vase, Babes In Woods, Lady, Children & Dog, 10 7/8 In.	295.00
Vase, Bill Sykes, Square, Marked, 2 X 3 7/8 In.	65.00
Vase, Blue & White Flowers, Silicon Coffee Color, 3 In.	65.00
Vase, Bluebell Gatherers, Tapered, Handles, 1920, 7 In.	95.00
Vase, Bud, Coaching Days, 1922, 5 1/2 In.	90.00
Vase, Coaching Days, Man Standing By Fence, 5 1/4 In.	75.00
Vase, Dickens Ware, Alfred Jingle, Square, Handles, 7 5/8 In.	145.00
Vase, Dickens Ware, Barnaby Rudge, Square, Marked, 4 3/4 In.	70.00
Vase, Dickens Ware, Cap'N Cuttle, Flared, Marked, 9 1/2 In.	175.00
Vase, Dickens Ware, Mr.Squeers, Marked, 7 3/4 In.	155.00
Vase, Dickens Ware, Sam Weller, Handles, Marked, 7 1/2 In.	148.00
Vase, Donkeys, Hannah Barlow, 12 In.	400.00
Vase, Flambe, Cottage Scene, 4 1/2 In.	75.00
Vase, Flambe, Country Scene, Artist Signed, 7 In.	300.00
Vase, Flambe, Gnomes & Toadstools, 6 3/4 In.	565.00
Vase, Flambe, Seascape With Ships, C.1901, 6 1/2 In.	155.00
Vase, Flambe, Woodcut Landscape, No.8362, C.1930, Pair	595.00
Vase, Fuchsia Design, Green Glazed Interior, Marked, 6 In.	450.00

Future Royal Doulton collectors will be able to easily identify character jugs and figurines made before 1984. As of this year, the words "hand made" and "hand decorated" are added above the lion and crown mark in the shape of an arch.

Vase, Geneva, Hexagonal, 11 In. 200.00
Vase, Horse, Sheep, Hannah Barlow, 12 In. 385.00
Vase, Moon Shining On Hare, 3 1/2 In. 275.00
Vase, Peacock In Thrush, Signed, 8 1/2 In. 850.00
Vase, Portrait, Flow Blue, 6 Sides, 8 In. 95.00
Vase, Tony Weller, 2 Handles, 5 1/2 In. 150.00
Vase, Urn Shape, Blue Interior, Maple Leaves, 12 In. 450.00
Vase, Venetian Scene, Flambe, 1922–27, 6 1/2 In. 150.00
Vase, Welsh Ladies Series, Walking On Path To House, 7 In. 165.00

The Duxer Porzellanmanufaktur was founded in Dux, Bohemia, in 1860 by E. Eichler. By the turn of the century, the firm specialized in porcelain statuary and busts of Art Nouveau–style maidens, large porcelain figures, and ornate vases with three–dimensional figures climbing on the sides. After 1918, the word "Bohemia" was taken out of the mark because the city had become Duchcov, Czechoslovakia. The firm is still in business.

ROYAL DUX, Basket, Girl On Each Side, Marked, Large 350.00
Bowl, Centerpiece, Lily Pond, Green, 16 In. 550.00
Bowl, Shell, Swelling Waves, Maiden, Burnished Gold, 14 3/4 In. 575.00
Bust, Young Roman, Laurel Wreath Crown, Toga, Marked, 8 1/2 In. 275.00
Centerpiece, Figural, Maiden On Shell Bowl, C.1900, 15 In. 575.00
Centerpiece, Shell, Maiden and Two Cherubs, 12 X 15 X 20 In. 875.00
Figurine, 2 Women On Shell, Triangle Mark, 12 X 14 In. 475.00
Figurine, Bohemian Peasant Boy, Carrying Game, Pre–1918, 21 In. 425.00
Figurine, Boy On Donkey, 12 In. 395.00
Figurine, Classical Lady, Cupid On Shoulder, 1900, 14 In. 275.00
Figurine, Cockatiel, 15 7/8 In. 495.00
Figurine, Cockatoo, 7 In. 65.00
Figurine, Dancing Couple, Blue, White, Gold, Pink Triangle, 8 In. 150.00
Figurine, Dancing Lady, Man Playing Violin, Marked, 16 In. 575.00
Figurine, Deer, 2 3/4 In. 40.00
Figurine, Fish, No.604, Triangle Mark, 7 1/2 X 11 In. 65.00
Figurine, Fruit Gatherers, Man & Woman, 10 In., Pair 990.00
Figurine, Greek Youth, On 2 Horses, 14 In. .... 450.00 To 550.00
Figurine, Hindu Water Carriers, Pink Mark, 27 3/4 In., Pair 950.00
Figurine, Lady With Basket, Acorn Mark, 11 In. 350.00
Figurine, Lady, Sitting, Reading Book, 10 In. 225.00
Figurine, Maiden, Filling Lamp, Man Holding Hourglass, 15 In. 575.00
Figurine, Maiden, Water Carrier, 8 In. 90.00
Figurine, Maiden, With Bird, 9 In. 75.00
Figurine, Maiden, With Robe, 9 In. 80.00
Figurine, Maiden, With Tambourine, 14 In. .... 160.00 To 180.00
Figurine, Man, Mandolin, Girl, Fan, Earth Tones, Triangle Mark, Pr. 550.00
Figurine, Man, With Guitar, Marked, 12 1/2 In. 230.00
Figurine, Nude, Art Nouveau, Wave Base, 9 X 7 In. 300.00
Figurine, Nude, Butterfly On Knee, 9 In. 150.00
Figurine, Peasant Boy, Basket On Shoulder, Marked, 16 In. 450.00
Figurine, Peasant Couple, Binding Sheaves, Pink Triangle, 19 In. 825.00
Figurine, Peasant, Satin Finish, Triangle Mark, 11 1/2 In., Pair 550.00
Figurine, Potter, Seated, At Work, 7 1/2 In. 415.00
Figurine, Siren, Centerpiece, Art Nouveau, Green, 16 In. 650.00
Figurine, Three Maidens, Standing, Centerpiece, 1900, 12 In. 500.00
Figurine, Tiger, Stalking, 15 In. 150.00
Figurine, Woman With Basket of Fish, Triangle Mark, 16 In. 345.00
Figurine, Woman, At Potter's Task, Green, Pink, Triangle, 8 In. 450.00
Figurine, Woman, Watching Potter At Work, 15 1/2 In. 880.00
Tray, Pin, Art Nouveau Girl 300.00
Vase, Applied Full Figured Woman, Pastels, Marked, 18 In. 400.00
Vase, Art Nouveau, Stylized Flowers, Gold Tracery, 14 In. 240.00
Vase, Blown–Out Figurines & Flowers, Marked, 12 In., Pair 525.00
Vase, Female Head Handles, 14 In. .... 135.00 To 150.00
Vase, Woman, Art Nouveau, Blue–Green, Triangle Mark, 14 In. 350.00

Royal Flemish glass was made during the late 1880s in New Bedford, Massachusetts, by the Mt. Washington Glass Works. It is a colored satin glass decorated with dark colors and raised gold designs. The glass was patented in 1894. It was supposed to resemble stained glass windows.

ROYAL FLEMISH, Biscuit Jar, Scrolls In Circles, Silver Plated Fittings 1750.00
  Bottle, Cologne, Blue Daisies, Mt.Washington, 5 3/4 In. 2750.00
  Cracker Jar, Roses 750.00
  Lamp, Banquet, Shields, Gold Lions, 42 In. .... 1950.00 To 2250.00
  Vase, Gold Bordered Pansies, 7 1/4 X 5 3/4 In. 1250.00
  Vase, Mythical Winged Gargoyle, Gold Panel Dividers, 8 In. 2450.00
  Vase, Panels Divided By Raised Gold, Medallions, 1890, 8 In. 1985.00
    ROYAL HAEGER, see Haeger
    ROYAL IVY, see Pressed Glass, Royal Ivy
    ROYAL OAK, see Pressed Glass, Royal Oak
    ROYAL RUDOLSTADT, see Rudolstadt

Royal Vienna was established in Vienna, Austria, by Claude Innocentius du Paquier in 1719. In 1744, the firm began using a shield mark taken from the coat of arms of the Hapsburg royal family. Viewed upside down, the shield looks like a beehive; it became known as the "beehive mark." The factory closed in 1864. Since then, many German, Austrian, and Japanese factories have reproduced Royal Vienna wares, complete with the original shield or "beehive" mark.

ROYAL VIENNA, Charger, Return of Columbus, 1494, Shield Mark, 20 1/8 In. 1100.00
  Coffee Set, Transfer, Cobalt Blue, Shield Mark, 16 Piece 1760.00
  Cup & Saucer, Angelica Kauffmann–Like Scenes, Beehive Mark 85.00
  Plaque, Mignon & Der Harfner, Signed R.Dettrich 2300.00
  Plate, 2 Young Ladies, Feeding Birds, Raised Gold, 9 1/2 In. 650.00
  Plate, Cabinet, Maidens, C.1900, Shield Mark, 10 In., 4 Piece 1980.00
  Plate, Dutch Children, Border, Gold Tracery, Beehive Mark 85.00
  Plate, Girls Feeding Birds In Garden, Beehive Mark, 9 In. 650.00
  Plate, People, Gold Ground, Cobalt Blue Rim, Beehive, 8 In. 250.00
  Plate, Portrait, Musik, Blue Beehive Mark, 13 In. 350.00
  Teapot, Design On Front & Back, A.Kauffmann 65.00
  Tray, Reticulated, Rape of Europa, C.1806, 15 In. 605.00
  Urn, Figures Both Sections, Square Base, Beehive Mark, 16 In. 425.00
  Urn, Peasant Scene, Beehive Mark, 12 In. 130.00
  Vase, Covered, Maiden & Mandolin Panel, C.1900, 6 5/8 In. 275.00
  Vase, Floral, Green To Peach, Hand Painted, 15 In. 195.00
  Vase, Lid, Gold Handles, Scenic Classical Portrait, 14 In. 285.00
  Vase, Madame Lebrun, Signed Wagner, 6 1/2 In. 550.00
  Vase, Portrait, Maroon Ground, Beehive, 5 In. 450.00
  Vase, Purple Irises, Purple Ground, Hand Painted, 15 In. 295.00
  Vase, Stand, Classical Scholars, Cobalt Blue, Covered, 21 In. 1210.00
  Vase, Young Maiden Panels, Donath, C.1890, 17 In., Pair 3000.00

Worcester porcelains were made in Worcester, England, from about 1751. The firm went through many different periods and name changes. It became the Worcester Royal Porcelain Company, Ltd., in 1862. Today collectors call the porcelains made after 1862 "Royal Worcester." In 1976, the firm merged with W. T. Copeland to become Royal Worcester Spode. Some early products of the factory are listed under Worcester.

ROYAL WORCESTER, Ashtray & Cigarette Holder, Bird, Crossed Swords 45.00
  Biscuit Box, Silver Cover & Handle, Signed, 5 1/2 In. 275.00
  Bowl, Florals, Gold Trim, Earthenware, C.1878, 13 1/2 In. 145.00
  Bowl, Fluted, Scalloped, Gold Trim, 9 1/2 X 9 1/2 In. 125.00
  Box, Covered, Floral Design, 1903 Mark, 2 1/2 In. 70.00
  Box, Pin, Bluebird On Cover, Marked 55.00
  Candleholder, Gold Mouse, Marked, 1892, 5 3/4 X 2 1/2 In. 395.00

Royal Worcester, Ewer, Floral, Ivory,
Branch Handle, Marked, 6 In.

Royal Worcester, Figurine,
Girl & Boy Carrying Bucket, 9 In., Pr.

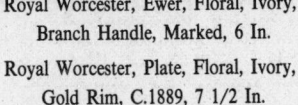

Royal Worcester, Plate, Floral, Ivory,
Gold Rim, C.1889, 7 1/2 In.

Candlesnuffer, Jenny Lind, C.1888	160.00
Candlesnuffer, Plumed Hat, Marked, C.1901	110.00
Candlesnuffer, Woman Warming Hands	60.00
Candlestick, Classical Design, Ram's Head, 10 In., Pair	195.00
Coffee Set, Geometric Band, Blue Mottled, Handles, 11 Pc.	275.00
Coffeepot, Gold Chantilly	125.00
Cracker Jar & Plate, Satin Finish, Dated 1902	595.00
Creamer, Leaf Body & Handle, Ivory	75.00
Creamer, Twig Handle, Gold Leaf Spout, Purple Mark	80.00
Cup & Saucer, Castle Scenes, Yellow Ground, Rushton	250.00
Cup & Saucer, Gnomes, C.1904, 2 1/4 In.	150.00
Dish, Leaf Shape, Beige, Gold Scalloped, 1908, 3 X 4 In.	50.00
Eggcup, Plum Design	9.00
Ewer, Barn Owl Design, Stag Handle, Dated 1887, 7 1/2 In.	420.00
Ewer, Floral, Gold Leaf On Neck, Bulbous, C.1903, 6 In.	175.00
Ewer, Floral, Ivory, Branch Handle, Marked, 6 In. ....*Illus*	80.00
Ewer, Gold On Yellow Ground, Dragon Handle, Signed, 7 In.	225.00
Ewer, Gold, Cream Ground, Horn Handle, Purple Mark, 8 In.	150.00
Figurine, Appaloosa, Doris Lindner	775.00
Figurine, Babes In Woods, No.3302, 1940	295.00
Figurine, Boy With Basket, Marked, 1893, 8 1/2 In.	525.00
Figurine, Boy With Dog, No.3456, Doughty	105.00
Figurine, Boy With Parakeet	75.00
Figurine, Bullfinch, No.1940, 3 1/2 In.	45.00
Figurine, Bullfinch, No.3238	45.00
Figurine, Butterfly, No.3157	395.00
Figurine, Columbine, No.2999, Doris Lindner	325.00
Figurine, December	85.00
Figurine, Dreaming, No.2875, Phoebe Stabler, 1931	450.00
Figurine, England, No.3075, 1934	225.00
Figurine, First Dance	150.00
Figurine, Fortune Teller, No.2924, Doughty	495.00
Figurine, Friday	85.00
Figurine, Girl & Boy Carrying Bucket, 9 In., Pr. ....*Illus*	500.00
Figurine, Goldfinch, No.3239	50.00
Figurine, Goosie Goosie Gander, No.3304	150.00
Figurine, Grandmother's Dress, Yellow, No.3081	75.00
Figurine, Hackney Stallion, Doris Lindner	1575.00
Figurine, Hedge Sparrow, No.3333	50.00
Figurine, Hindu, No.838	400.00
Figurine, Holland, No.3074, 1934	225.00

Figurine, In The Ring, Rider On 3 Circus Horses 1850.00
Figurine, Joy & Sorrow, Allover Florals, 9 7/8 In., Pair 850.00
Figurine, June, No.2908, Sybil Williams & Jess Bray 295.00
Figurine, Kate Greenaway Girl, Basket, 1882, 6 3/4 In. 375.00
Figurine, Madeleine 550.00
Figurine, Man & Woman Holding Jar On Shoulders, 10 In. 700.00
Figurine, Mermaid, Small 55.00
Figurine, Michael, No.2912, Doughty 65.00
Figurine, Mischief, No.2914, 1931 .... 225.00
Figurine, My Favorite, No.3014, Girl With Rabbit 295.00
Figurine, Only Me, No.3226, White Dress, Pink Bows 195.00
Figurine, Palomino, Doris Lindner 1155.00
Figurine, Pansy, No.2930, Anne Acheson 295.00
Figurine, Parakeet, 1930, 7 In. 80.00
Figurine, Parula Warblers, 1957, Pair 1700.00
Figurine, Peter Pan, No.3011, F.Gertner, 8 In. .... 225.00 To 300.00
Figurine, Poor Teddy, Small 55.00
Figurine, Quarter Horse, Doris Lindner 875.00
Figurine, Saturday's Child, Sand, Bucket, Shovel, 5 In. 115.00
Figurine, Scotland, No.3104, 1935 .... 225.00
Figurine, Seaside, Small 55.00
Figurine, Spade Fish, No.3579, Artist Signed 200.00
Figurine, Spanish Lady, No.2936, Anne Acheson 495.00
Figurine, Sparrow, No.3236 .... 50.00
Figurine, Spring, No.3012, Doughty 350.00
Figurine, Sweet Anne 100.00
Figurine, Thrush, No.3234, C.1938, E.Soper, 4 1/2 In. 95.00
Figurine, Thursday's Child, No.3260 .... 115.00
Figurine, Water Baby, No.3151 .... 175.00 To 350.00
Figurine, Wednesday's Child 100.00
Figurine, Wood Warbler, No.3200 .... 50.00
Figurine, Woodland Dance, Doughty 175.00
Figurine, Yankee, No. 836 .... 450.00
Figurine, Young Farmer, No.3433 .... 155.00
Ginger Jar, Blue & Mottled Gold, Dated 1903 .... 225.00
Gravy Boat, Liner, Elephant Head Handle 145.00
Jardiniere, Parian Ware, Cranes & Foliage, C.1873, 13 In. 1750.00
Jug, Chrysanthemums, Artist Signed, Dated 1889, 7 1/2 In. 145.00
Jug, Claret, Allover Floral, Cream Ground, C.1887, 8 In. 175.00
Jug, Double Opening, Floral Sprays, Gold, 1884, 8 In. 295.00
Jug, Owl On Branch, Sky, Serpent Handle, 1885, 8 In. 925.00
Jug, Vines, Berries, Cream Ground, Horn Handle, 1885, 6 In. 160.00
Mustache Cup & Saucer, Band of Violets, Impressed Mark 55.00
Pitcher, Colored Floral, Gold Leaves, Rim, Marked, 8 In. 240.00
Pitcher, Flat Back, 5 Floral Arrangements, Marked, 9 In. 245.00
Pitcher, Flowers, 2 Butterflies, Gilding, C.1884, 8 3/4 In. 175.00
Pitcher, Flowers, Blue & Gold Handle, 1899, 4 1/4 In. 175.00
Pitcher, Gold Overlay, Beaded Flowers, Bulbous, 15 1/4 In. 295.00
Pitcher, Roses, Flared Top & Bottom, 1926, 7 3/4 In. 90.00
Planter, Lizard Around Side, Round, 1852 Mark .... 195.00 To 225.00
Plate, Floral, Ivory, Gold Rim, C.1889, 7 1/2 In. ....*Illus* 60.00
Plate, Geometric, Gold Circles, Apple Blossoms, 1876, 8 In. 70.00
Potpourri Jar, Inner & Outer Lid, C.1917, 13 In. 1275.00
Powder Box, Little Girl Finial, Mischief 125.00
Tea Caddy, Gold Trim, Peach To Cream, 4 1/2 In. 85.00
Teapot, Brown Pattern, White Ground, Stand, C.1887 .... 75.00
Toby Jug, Toby Philpot, 1929 Mark, 1 3/4 In. 95.00
Tureen, Underplate, Elephant Handles, 1886, 9 1/2 X 6 In. 98.00
Vase, 3 Floral Panels, Torch Design, C.1894, 5 3/4 In. 295.00
Vase, 3 Turtles In Relief, Crawling Around Vase, 3 In. 130.00
Vase, Covered, Egg Shape, 3 Hoofed Feet, C.1908, 6 In. 560.00
Vase, Nautilus Shell, Supported By Coral Branches, 9 In. 450.00
Vase, Pink & Yellow Roses, Artist Signed, 3 1/2 In. 125.00
Wall Pocket, Cherubs, Grapevine, Signed, C.1870, Pair 550.00

Wall Pocket, Large Bow With Streamers, Green Mark, 9 In. 150.00

Roycroft products were made by the Roycrofter community of East Aurora, New York, in the late nineteenth and early twentieth centuries. The community was founded by Elbert Hubbard, famous philosopher, writer, and artist. The workshops owned by the community made furniture, metalware, leatherwork, embroidery, and jewelry. A printshop produced many signs, books, and the magazines that promoted the sayings of Elbert Hubbard. Furniture by the Roycroft community is listed in the furniture section.

ROYCROFT, Ashtray, Octagonal, Marked, 4 In. 32.00
Base, Lamp, Patinated, 12 In. 235.00
Bean Pot, Signed, Covered, 4 1/2 In. 20.00
Bookends, Open Square 45.00
Bookends, Star Design, 3 In. 30.00
Bookends, Strap Design & Loop Handle, 4 X 5 In. 80.00
Box, Storage, Marked Hardware, 23 X 12 X 10 In. 460.00
Broadside, Motto, An American Religion, 15 1/2 X 11 1/2 In. 200.00
Calendar, Perpetual 70.00
Chafing Dish, Hammered Copper 1000.00
Crumb Set 60.00
Desk Set, Shop's, Crystal Inkwell, Marked 800.00
Holder, Calendar, Half–Moon Shape, Stylized Floral Design 35.00
Humidor, Enamel Abstract Geometric & Rope Design, Logo, 6 In. 175.00
Jar, Apothecary, Covered 20.00
Jug, Brown Glaze, Handles, 5 In. 15.00
Lamp, Electric, Copper & Mica, C.1910, 14 3/4 In. 1300.00
Matchbox Holder, Copper, Marked 18.00
Mug, Kicking Bird, Twin, 1974, 7 In. 60.00
Nut Set, Hammered Copper, No.809, C.1910, Bowl & 6 Picks 325.00
Tray, Brass Washed, Oval, Stylized Fleur–De–Lis, 22 In. 100.00
Tray, Hammered Copper, Loop Handles, Logo, 15 3/4 In. 150.00
Tray, Silver Plate, Round, 3 1/2 In. 45.00
Vase, Bud, Old Glass Insert, Marked, 9 In. 45.00
Vase, Scalloped Rim, Vertical Lines of Bellflowers, Marked, 9 In. 200.00
   ROZANE, see Roseville

RRP is the mark used by the firm of Robinson–Ransbottom. It is not a mark of the more famous Roseville Pottery. The Ransbottom brothers started a pottery in 1900 in Ironspot, Ohio. In 1920, they merged with the Robinson Clay Product Company of Akron, Ohio, to become Robinson–Ransbottom. The factory is still working.

RRP, Bowl, Embossed Brown Stripes, Yellowware, 10 In. 35.00
Cookie Jar, Peter Pumpkin Eater 45.00
Vase, Blue, 6 In. 20.00

The RS Germany mark was used on porcelain made at the factory of Reinhold Schlegelmilch from about 1910 to 1956 in Tillowitz, Germany. It was sold decorated and undecorated. The Schlegelmilch family made porcelains marked in many ways. Each type is listed separately. See also ES Germany, RS Poland, RS Prussia, RS Silesia, RS Suhl, and RS Tillowitz.

RS GERMANY, Berry Bowl, Calla Lilies, 5 In., Set of 6 .... 55.00
Berry Set, Variegated Roses, Brown To Green, Blue Mark, 5 Piece 95.00
Bonbon, Pointed End, Looped Handle, Peonies, Blue Mark, 8 In. 48.00
Bowl, 4 Seasons Summer, Blown–Out Iris, Handles, 13 X 8 In. 495.00
Bowl, Cotton Plant Design, Gold Trim, Blue Mark, 9 1/2 In. 150.00
Bowl, Fuchsia, 10 In. .... 115.00 To 125.00
Bowl, Lettuce Mold, Red Roses, Marked 145.00
Bowl, Sailing Boats, Mountains, Trees, Green Mark, 10 In. 185.00
Bowl, Swan Scene, Foliage, 10 3/4 In. 95.00
Cake Plate, Dogwood, Shaded Green To Brown, Gold Trim, 10 In. 38.00
Cake Plate, Handles, White Flowers, Gold & Green 55.00
Cake Plate, Poppies, 10 In. 45.00

Cake Plate, Tulips, Green Ground, 10 In.	45.00
Cake Set, Orange & Yellow Roses, Lacy Gold Design, 6 Piece	110.00
Candy Dish, Cloverleaf, Floral, 3 Handles	42.00
Celery, Lily Design, Open Handles, Blue Label, 11 X 5 3/4 In.	95.00
Celery, Maple Leaves, White–Yellow Ground, Open Handle	28.00
Celery, Mill Scene, Luster Finish	88.00
Celery, Poppy Design, Gold Rim, Open Handles, 9 X 4 In.	65.00
Chocolate Set, Lilies, Lacy Gold Borders, Blue Mark, 11 Piece	325.00
Chocolate Set, Portrait, Allover Gold Leaves, 5 Piece	250.00
Chocolate Set, Ruffled Lilies, Green Leaves, 7 Piece	285.00
Chocolate Set, Snowbird Pattern, 19 Piece	1250.00
Chocolate Set, Yellow Daffodils, 9 Piece	185.00
Cookie Jar, Floral, Cream, Covered, Handles, Marked, 6 1/2 In.	118.00
Cracker Jar, Peach, Yellow Roses, Lavender Trim, Marked	275.00
Cup & Saucer, Chocolate, Hand Painted Daisy, Fluted, 1914	30.00
Fernery, Design Gold Outlined, Scalloped, Marked	165.00
Fernery, Floral, Yellows, Green, Lavender	75.00
Gravy Boat, Underplate, Red Flowers, Gold Trim	20.00
Hair Receiver, Pink Flowers	30.00
Hatpin Holder, Gold Top, Floral	52.00
Hatpin Holder, Large Lily Design	75.00
Hatpin Holder, Pink, Green Floral On White, Hexagonal, 5 In.	60.00
Inkwell, Lily–of–The–Valley, Covered	65.00
Jam Jar, Covered, Double Handled, Poppies & Foliage, 4 In.	55.00
Lamp, Fairy, Owl, Pair	525.00
Mustard Pot, Matte Glaze, Rose Design	30.00
Nappy, Violets, 6 In.	38.00
Pitcher, Lemonade, Lily, Gold Trim	98.00
Plaque, Portrait, Steeple Mark, 9 1/2 X 12 1/2 In.	1000.00
Plate, Cheese & Cracker, Roses	50.00
Plate, Man With Horses, 10 In.	95.00
Plate, Petunias, Hand Painted, C.Pate, 10 In.	40.00
Plate, Sweet Pea Design, 6 In.	7.00
Ramekin, Pink Roses	30.00
Relish, Bird of Paradise, 8 In.	75.00
Relish, Floral, 8 1/2 In.	22.00
Relish, White Roses, 11 In.	34.00
Relish, Wild Rose Pattern, Hand Painted, 7 In.	25.00
Sugar & Creamer, Cottage & Mill Scene, Brown Tones, Red Mark	350.00
Sugar & Creamer, Covered, Lavender, Yellow Roses, Blue Mark	125.00
Toothpick, Azaleas, 3 Gold Handles	55.00
Toothpick, Red Cross & American Flags, 3 Handles	45.00
Vase, Acorns, Tan, Bulbous, 3 In.	50.00
Vase, Cottage Scene, 4 In.	40.00
Vase, Roses, 6 In.	35.00

 The RS Poland (German) mark was used by the Reinhold Schlegelmilch factory at Tillowitz from about 1945 to 1956. This is one of many of the RS marks used. See also ES Germany, RS Germany, RS Prussia, RS Silesia, RS Suhl, and RS Tillowitz.

RS POLAND, Bowl, Heart Mold, Poppies, 10 1/2 In.	230.00
Sugar, Roses, Teal Blue Pedestal, Scalloped Rim	95.00
Teapot, Roses, Pedestal	95.00
Tray, Leaf Shape, 10 In.	125.00
Vase, Pink & White Roses, Cream, Gold Top Band, Marked, 8 3/4 In.	165.00

"RS Prussia" is a mark that appears on porcelain made at the factory of Reinhold Schlegelmilch from the late 1870s to 1914 in Tillowitz, Germany, or on items made at the Erdmann Schlegelmilch factory in Suhl, Germany, from about 1910 to 1956. It was sold decorated or undecorated. The factories were owned by brothers. See also ES Germany, RS Germany, RS Poland, RS Silesia, RS Suhl, and RS Tillowitz.

RS PRUSSIA, Barrel, Cookie, Brownstone Cottage Scene	850.00

Berry Bowl, Crimped Floral Edge, Rose Center, Marked, 10 In. 250.00
Berry Bowl, Peacock & Bluebirds, Red Mark, 5 1/2 In. 70.00
Berry Bowl, Stag In Center, 5 In. 285.00
Berry Set, Blue Medallion, Florals, Red Mark, 5 Piece 295.00
Berry Set, Dark Pink Roses, Red Mark, Bowl, 10 3/4 In., 7 Piece 250.00
Berry Set, Roses & Snowballs, Red Mark, 5 Piece 395.00
Berry Set, Snowball, Luster, 7 Piece 285.00
Biscuit Jar, Dogwood Pattern, Red Mark 275.00
Biscuit Jar, Point & Clover, Pink, Flower Finial, Red Mark 275.00
Biscuit Jar, Swallows & Water Lilies, Red Mark 500.00
Bowl, 6 Blown–Out Panels, Roses, Ribbons, Red Mark, 10 1/2 In. 175.00
Bowl, 8 Scrolls, Flowers, Leaves, Berry Bunches, Red Mark, 11 In. 235.00
Bowl, Bluebird, Floral Center, Pink Tones, Marked, 10 In. 420.00
Bowl, Brown, Gold Trim, Pink, Apricot, Yellow, Marked, 6 In. 65.00
Bowl, Clover Mold, Roses, Gold, Sapphire Jewels, Mark, 10 In. 150.00
Bowl, Cottage Scene, Red Mark, 12 In. 900.00
Bowl, Dogwood, Green Tints, Red Mark, 10 X 3 In. 179.00
Bowl, Double Season, Winter & Summer, Floral, 10 1/2 In. 1050.00
Bowl, Ducks, Turkeys & Swallows, 11 In. 600.00
Bowl, Embossed Feathers, 9 1/2 In. 95.00
Bowl, Embossed Rococo, Floral Inside, Gold, Red Mark, 11 In. 165.00
Bowl, Floral Center, Black, Gold Trim, Steeple Mark, 10 X 3 In. 239.00
Bowl, Flowers Around, Scalloped, Pearlized, Red Mark, 8 1/2 In. 125.00
Bowl, Fruit Design, 10 Panels, Raised Rim Design, 7 5/8 In. 175.00
Bowl, Fruit, Floral Border, Green Ground, Red Mark, 3 1/4 In. 195.00
Bowl, Gold Trim, Roses, Red Mark, 11 1/2 In. 250.00
Bowl, Hidden Image, Blown–Out Head of Woman, 9 1/2 In. 225.00
Bowl, Icicle Mold, Lilies, Reflected In Pond, Red Mark, 9 In. 180.00
Bowl, Lady With Fan, Shaded Peach, Blue Iris, 10 In. 850.00
Bowl, Lily & Maidenhair Fern, Red Mark, 11 In. 200.00
Bowl, Multicolored Florals, Pink Ground, 10 1/2 In. 65.00
Bowl, Oak Leaves & Acorn Design, Red Mark, 9 1/4 In. 135.00
Bowl, Pierced Handles, Crimped & Scalloped, Red Mark, 11 In. 195.00
Bowl, Pink Poppies, Floral Mold, Red Mark, 10 In. 180.00
Bowl, Pink Rose Cluster, Deep Pleat, Red Mark, 10 3/4 In. 250.00
Bowl, Pink Roses, Pearlized, Shell Mold, Red Mark, 10 1/2 In. 150.00
Bowl, Pink Roses, Snowballs, Black Edge, Red Mark, 10 1/2 In. 450.00
Bowl, Poppies & Leaves, Beaded Rim, Red Mark, 9 1/4 In. 175.00
Bowl, Poppies, Daisies Reflecting On Water, Red Mark, 11 In. 375.00
Bowl, Poppy Mold, Yellow, Rose, Turquoise, Red Mark, 9 3/4 In. 135.00
Bowl, Portrait, Madame Recamier, Ripple Mold, 10 1/2 In. 595.00
Bowl, Quiet Cove Scene, Marked, 10 In. 395.00
Bowl, Roses, Carnations, Blown–Out Panels, Red Mark, 10 In. 195.00
Bowl, Schooner, Orange, Yellow, Brown & Gold, Red Mark, 9 1/8 In. 495.00
Bowl, Scroll & Floral, Molded Flowers, Floral Center, 10 In. 120.00
Bowl, Shaded Lavender, Pink Roses, Jeweled, Red Mark, 10 In. 160.00
Bowl, Spring Season, Iris Mold, Red Mark, 10 1/2 In. 1200.00
Bowl, Stippled Floral, Poppies, Green Ground, Leaves, 10 In. 120.00
Bowl, Strawberry Blossom Pattern, Gold Trim, Red Mark, 10 In. 125.00
Bowl, Summer Season, 10 1/2 In. 550.00
Bowl, Swallows & Swans, Turkeys & Pheasant Scenes, 11 In. 900.00
Bowl, Swan & Gazebo, Red Mark, 10 1/2 In. 395.00
Bowl, Swan, Satin, Marked, 10 In. 225.00
Bowl, Turkey, Swan & Bluebird Scenes, 11 In. 300.00
Bowl, Winter Scene, Flower Border, Mother–of–Pearl, 10 1/2 In. 850.00
Bowl, Winter, Woman, Red Mark, 9 1/2 In. 695.00
Bowl–In–Bowl, Flower Center, Gold Tracery, Jewels, 10 1/2 In. 275.00
Box, Pin, Pink Floral, Red Mark 60.00
Bread Plate, 6 Green Sections, Roses In Center, 13 1/2 In. 165.00
Butter Chip, Floral, Red Mark 35.00
Butter, Covered, Melon Ribbed, Pink Flowers, Petal Base Rim 185.00
Cake Plate, Barnyard Animals, Pheasant, Icicle Mold, 10 In. 795.00
Cake Plate, Blown–Out Sunflower, Floral, Red Mark, 11 In. 180.00
Cake Plate, Center Roses, Satin, Marked, 11 In. 225.00

RS Prussia, Chocolate Set, Lebrun Portrait

RS Prussia, Chocolate Set,
Jeweled Melon Eaters

Cake Plate, Dice Throwers, Open Handles, Red Mark, 11 In. 1050.00
Cake Plate, Dogwood Blossoms, Gold Enameling, 11 In. 175.00
Cake Plate, Icicle & Poppies, 10 In., Marked 175.00
Cake Plate, Melon Boy, Red Mark, 10 In. 645.00
Cake Plate, Open Handle, Mill, Gold Design On Brown, Red Mark 275.00
Cake Plate, Oriental Poppies, Open Handles, Marked 230.00
Cake Plate, Pheasant In Wood, Open Handles 375.00
Cake Plate, Pink Tulips, Red Mark, 11 In. 200.00
Cake Plate, Scalloped Rim, Poppies, Shaded Leaves, 11 1/4 In. 155.00
Candy Dish, Covered, Heart Shape, Red Mark 75.00
Celery, Basket of Roses In Bottom, Pearlized Ground 165.00
Celery, Green Shadows, Pink & Yellow Roses, Red Mark, 12 In. 125.00
Celery, Lavender & Pink Floral, Red Mark, 12 In. 175.00
Celery, Old Man of The Mountain, Red Mark, 12 X 6 In. 350.00
Celery, White Lilies, Beaded, Satin, Scalloped, 12 1/4 In. 88.00
Cheese Dish, Covered, Red Mark 195.00
Chocolate Pot, Cottage Scene, Ball Feet 550.00
Chocolate Pot, Dogwood, Red Mark 240.00
Chocolate Pot, Green Garland, Red Mark, 9 1/2 In. 125.00
Chocolate Pot, Hand Painted Floral, Red Mark, 11 In. 225.00
Chocolate Pot, Pierced Handle, Variegated Roses, Gold Trim 235.00
Chocolate Pot, Pin & Red Floral, Red Mark 185.00
Chocolate Pot, Pink & Yellow Roses, Gold 195.00
Chocolate Pot, Scallop & Fan Mold, Colored Roses 125.00
Chocolate Pot, Swans & Pine Trees, Red Mark 395.00
Chocolate Set, Carnation Mold, 12 In.Pot, Red Mark, 5 Piece 600.00
Chocolate Set, Five Flower Design, 7 Cups & Saucers, Red Mark 1200.00
Chocolate Set, Jeweled Melon Eaters ....*Illus* 3100.00
Chocolate Set, Lebrun Portrait ....*Illus* 2800.00
Chocolate Set, Lily of The Valley, Red Mark, 5 Piece 250.00
Chocolate Set, Melon Eaters, 6 Cups & Saucers 3000.00
Chocolate Set, Snowball & Roses, Pink, Red Mark, 7 Piece 1200.00
Coffee Set, Swans, Demitasse, 9 Piece 1295.00
Coffeepot, Footed, White & Pink Florals, Green Ground, Red Mark 150.00
Cookie Jar, Cobalt Blue Paint, Red Mark 650.00
Cookie Jar, Covered, Rose Floral, Ball Feet, 2 Handles 300.00
Cracker Jar, Gold Trim, Pink Roses, Red Mark, 9 1/2 In. 275.00
Cracker Jar, Loop Handles, Green Ground, Roses, Red Mark 275.00
Cracker Jar, Roses, Gold Trim, Side Handles, Red Mark, 7 X 8 In. 225.00
Creamer, Swans & Evergreens, Pearl Luster, Hexagonal, 3 3/4 In. 70.00
Cup & Saucer, California Poppy, Marked 75.00

Cup & Saucer, Pink Swan, Red Mark, Demitasse 75.00
Cup, Tulips, Footed 65.00
Dish, Pickle, Scroll & Bead, Mauve Poppies, Red Mark, 9 1/2 In. 60.00
Ferner, Castle Scene 350.00
Hair Receiver, Snowbird, Small 175.00
Hair Receiver, White Roses, Green Ground, Red Mark 140.00
Hatpin Holder, Attached Tray, Pink Roses, Red Mark 95.00
Hatpin Holder, Castle Scene 600.00
Mustard, Drape Mold, Roses Finial, White Satin, Red Mark 135.00
Mustard, Flower Finial, Pink Floral, Red Mark 125.00
Mustard, Ladle, White Flowers, Pink Roses, Green, Red Mark 85.00
Mustard, Molded Blown-Out Rim, Flower Finial 45.00
Pin Jar, Pink Floral, Covered, Red Mark 75.00
Pitcher, Cider, Peeled Orange & Fruit Design, 6 1/2 In. 875.00
Pitcher, Lemonade, Floral, Red Mark 475.00
Pitcher, Milk, Hidden Images, Icicles, Floral, 4 5/8 In. 175.00
Plaque, Portrait, Steeple Mark ....*Illus* 1000.00
Plate, 2 Ravens, Snow Scene, 8 3/4 In. 650.00
Plate, Castle Scene, Iris Mold, 9 1/2 In. 600.00
Plate, Fall Season, Blown-Out Flowers, Gold, Red Mark, 12 In. 2800.00
Plate, Fleur-De-Lis, Poppy, Marked, 11 In. 160.00
Plate, Floral, Maroon Edge, Cream Ground, Red Mark, 8 1/2 In. 125.00
Plate, Floral, Satin Finish, Red Mark, 8 In. 150.00
Plate, Floral, Swallows & Swan Medallions, Gold Border, 8 In. 325.00
Plate, Hidden Images, Floral Form, Icicle Mold, 9 3/4 In. 245.00
Plate, Iris Mold, Summer Season, Open Handle, 11 In. 450.00
Plate, Melon Eaters & Dice Players, 10 In. 575.00
Plate, Mill Scene, Handles, Fleur-De-Lis Mold, 10 1/4 In. 525.00
Plate, Narcissus Trimmed In Gold, Scalloped, Red Mark, 6 In. 60.00
Plate, Old Man of Mountain, Sailboat, Cove, Embossed, 10 In. 335.00
Plate, Pink Roses, Snowballs, Pierced Handles, Red Mark, 10 In. 450.00
Plate, Plumes, Molded Poppies, Gold Outlining, 9 In. 80.00
Plate, Pond Lilies, Red Mark, 8 1/2 In. 125.00
Plate, Poppies Reflected, Pond, Feather Mold, Marked, 9 In. 130.00
Plate, Quiet Cove, Red Mark, 10 1/2 In. 295.00
Plate, Raised Clover, Iris Mold, Red Mark, 10 1/2 In. 235.00
Plate, Snow Scene, 2 Birds ....*Illus* 650.00
Plate, Spring Season Keyhole, 9 In. 700.00
Plate, Swans, Reflecting Flowers, 8 1/2 In. 260.00
Plate, Winter Portrait Lady, Iris Mold, Iris Border, 8 3/4 In. 375.00
Powder Box, Floral, 2 Shades of Green, Gold Trim, Red Mark 190.00

RS Prussia, Plaque, Portrait, Steeple Mark   RS Prussia, Plate, Snow Scene, 2 Birds

Powder Box, Tiger Design, Covered, Square, 4 1/2 In. 1850.00
Relish, Acorn & Oak Leaves, Luster Finish, 4 X 9 1/2 In. 95.00
Relish, Cobalt Blue, Poppies, Open Handle, 3 X 6 1/2 In. 1000.00
Relish, Lilies, Open Handles, 11 In. 75.00
Relish, Opalescent Jewels, Pink Roses, 9 1/2 In. 220.00
Relish, Quiet Cove Scene, Marked, 12 In. 325.00
Relish, Shadow Flowers, Roses, Yellow, Green, 4 1/2 X 9 1/2 In. 85.00
Shaving Mug, Blue Carnation, Red Mark 165.00
Shaving Mug, Melon Eaters, Footed 525.00
Sugar & Creamer, Bellflower 190.00
Sugar & Creamer, Castle Scene, Red Mark 395.00
Sugar & Creamer, Daisies & Poppies, Red Mark 195.00
Sugar & Creamer, Floral, Gold, Pedestal, Marked 200.00
Sugar & Creamer, Flower Spout, Roses On Blue, Gold Trim 210.00
Sugar & Creamer, Fuchsia Flowers, Green 295.00
Sugar & Creamer, Lebrun Portrait, Handles, Red Star Mark 375.00
Sugar & Creamer, Luster Carnations, Handles, Covered, Red Mark 100.00
Sugar & Creamer, Mill Scene 280.00
Sugar & Creamer, Pink Poppies, Pedestal, Footed 150.00
Sugar & Creamer, Pink Roses, Shadow Leaf, Red Mark 250.00
Sugar & Creamer, Swan, Pedestal, Satin, Red Mark 295.00
Sugar & Creamer, White Flowers, Luster Green, Covered, Red Mark 165.00
Sugar Shaker, Colonial Figures, Red Mark .... 225.00 To 275.00
Sugar Shaker, Roses, Red Mark 165.00
Sugar, Pedestal, Floral, Open, Red Mark 45.00
Syrup, Underplate, Blue To Lavender, Gold 165.00
Syrup, Underplate, Floral, Satin Finish 275.00
Tankard, Blown–Out Leaf & Gold Cherries At Base, Red Mark 675.00
Tankard, Carnation Mold, 11 1/2 In. 475.00
Tankard, Icicle Mold, Barnyard, 14 In. 2050.00
Tankard, Icicle Mold, Red Mark, 14 In. 625.00
Tankard, Roses, 13 In. 900.00
Tea Set, Mill Scene, Browns, 3 Piece 700.00
Tea Set, Pink Roses, Gold Trim, Red Mark, 3 Piece 375.00
Toothpick, Pearlized, Pink & Red Roses, Footed, Red Mark 95.00
Toothpick, Reflecting Water Lilies, Double Handles, 3 In. 85.00
Toothpick, Scalloped, Flowers, Gold Tracery, Red Mark, 2 1/2 In. 350.00
Toothpick, Swallows, 2 Handles 325.00
Tray, Animal Portrait, Open Handles, Red Mark, 13 3/4 X 7 In. 400.00
Tray, Bread, Dice Players, Open Handle, Red Border, 7 X 13 In. 725.00
Tray, Bun, Open Handles, 12 In. 135.00
Tray, Florals, Pierced Handles, Red Mark, 11 1/2 X 7 1/4 In. 115.00
Tray, Iris Mold, Roses, Handles, 9 1/2 In. 79.00
Tray, Pheasant, Medallions, Handles, Red Mark, 14 X 7 In. 475.00
Tray, Pickle, Beige Rim, White Center, Roses, Blue Mark, 8 In. 45.00
Tray, Point & Clover Mold, Roses, Hydrangeas, 12 X 8 In. 140.00
Tray, Portrait, Blown–Out Iris, Lavender, Yellow, 12 X 6 In. 850.00
Vase, 4 Medallions At Bottom, Gold Footed, Roses, 9 In. 450.00
Vase, Bird of Paradise Design, Bulbous, 3 In. 250.00
Vase, Castle Scene, Red Mark, 10 In. 800.00
Vase, Cobalt Blue Scene, Lady With Fan, Vienna Mark, 8 1/4 In. 650.00
Vase, Courting Couple, At Well, Red Mark, 8 In. 795.00
Vase, Flowers, Cream, Green, Gold Trim, Jewels, Handles, 8 In. 325.00
Vase, Melon Eaters, Jeweled, Handles, 10 1/2 In. 995.00
Vase, Old Mill, Red Mark, 6 1/2 In. 335.00
Vase, Ostrich, 7 1/2 In. 800.00
Vase, Sheepherder, 2 Handles, Red Mark, 10 In. 575.00
Vase, Spring Portrait, Pearlized, Tracery, Red Mark, 5 1/4 In. 355.00
Vase, Summer Season, Red Mark, 11 1/2 In. 850.00

The RS Silesia mark appears on porcelain made at the Reinhold Schlegelmilch factory in Tillowitz, Germany, from about 1920 to the mid–1930s. The Schlegelmilch family made porcelains marked in many ways. Each type is listed separately. See also ES Germany, RS Germany, RS Poland, RS Prussia, RS Suhl, and RS Tillowitz.

RS SILESIA, Bowl, Lily, Gold Trim, 11 In.	400.00
Vase, Roses, Green, Blue, 10 In.	350.00

RS Suhl was a mark used by the Erdmann Schlegelmilch factory in Suhl, Germany, from c. 1900 to the mid–1920s. The factory worked from 1861 to 1925. The Schlegelmilch family made porcelains in many places. See also ES Germany, RS Germany, RS Poland, RS Prussia, RS Silesia, and RS Tillowitz.

RS SUHL, Cake Plate, Floral Design, Handles, Floral Border, 10 In.	115.00
Ewer, Flowers, Gold Handle, Green, 13 1/4 In.	295.00
Plaque, Wall, Daisies, 10 1/2 In.	60.00

The RS Tillowitz mark was used by the Reinhold Schlegelmilch factory at Tillowitz, near Silesia, from about 1920 to the mid–1930s. Table services and ornamental pieces were made. See also ES Germany, RS Germany, RS Poland, RS Prussia, RS Silesia, and RS Suhl.

RS TILLOWITZ, Berry Set, Poinsettia, Marked, 7 Piece	95.00
Bowl, Lilacs, Blue & Gold Border, 7 1/2 X 7 In.	35.00
Bowl, White Poppies, Cutout Handles, Footed, 6 X 5 1/2 In.	28.00
Relish, Gold Rim, Pierced Corners Form Handles, Green, 8 In.	23.00

Rubena Verde is a Victorian glassware that was shaded from red to green. It was first made by Hobbs, Brockunier and Company of Wheeling, West Virginia, about 1890.

RUBENA VERDE, Basket, Diamond–Quilted, White Scalloped, Thorn Handle, 9 In.	265.00
Bowl, Ruffled, Footed, 9 X 3 1/2 In.	135.00
Pickle Castor, Inverted Thumbprint, Bowed	150.00
Pitcher, Inverted Thumbprint, Bulbous	300.00
Pitcher, Triangular, 8 In.	295.00
Shade, Shell Pattern, Large	275.00
Syrup, Cranberry, Vaseline Hobnails, Clear Handle	685.00
Tumbler, 10–Row Hobnail	185.00 To 225.00

Rubena is a glassware that shades from red to clear. It was first made by George Duncan and Sons of Pittsburgh, Pennsylvania, about 1885. This coloring was used on many types of glassware. The pressed glass patterns of Royal Ivy and Royal Oak are listed under Pressed Glass.

RUBENA, Basket, Honeycomb, Clear Thorn Handle	225.00
Berry Dish, Hobnail, Frosted, Square	25.00
Bride's Bowl, Fluted, Silver Plated Stand, Flowers, 11 1/8 In.	295.00
Jam Jar, Silver Plated, Cover, Holder	150.00
Lamp, Peg, Flower & Leaves, Cranberry To Clear, 5 5/8 3 3/8 In.	70.00
Lemonade Set, Mother–of–Pearl, Diamond–Quilted, Tankard, 5 Mugs	695.00
Pitcher, Diamond–Quilted, Clear Handle, 6 In.	75.00
Pitcher, Water, 8 Panels, Clear Handle, 9 In.	95.00 To 115.00
Salt, Crystal Applique, Silver Plated Holder, Shell Trim, 3 In.	95.00
Sugar Shaker, Coin Spot	110.00
Syrup, Hobnail, Opalescent	220.00
Vase, Melon Sections, Threaded, Gold Trim, 10 1/2 In., Pair	295.00

Ruby glass is the dark red color of the precious gemstone known as a ruby. It was a popular Victorian color that never went completely out of style. The glass was shaped by many different processes to make many different types of ruby glass. There was a revival of interest in the 1940s when modern shaped ruby table glassware became fashionable. Sometimes the red color is added to clear glass by a process called flashing or staining. Pieces of glass colored this way are indicated by the word "stained" in the description.

RUBY GLASS, see also Cranberry Glass; Pressed Glass; Souvenir

RUBY GLASS, Berry Set, Carnation, New Martinsville, Gold Trim, 7 Piece	175.00
Bottle, Cologne, Jeweled, Gold Design, Enameled Foliage, 7 In.	125.00
Bottle, Wine, Loop & Block, Original Stopper, Stained	75.00
Bowl, Block Design, 4 Flashed Panels, Square, 9 X 3 1/2 In.	20.00
Bowl, English Hobnail, Oval, Crimped, 12 In.	24.50
Bowl, Ruffled Pleated, Polished Pontil, 10 In.	95.00
Butter, Covered, Button Arches, Souvenir, Atlantic City, 1919	65.00
Butter, Covered, Dutchess Loop, Gold Trim	75.00
Carafe, Block	35.00
Compote, Jelly, Roman Rosette, Stained	38.00
Condiment Set, Pillow Encircled, Original Tray, 4 Piece	210.00
Creamer, Coney Island, Enameled Flowers, 5 In.	45.00
Creamer, Thumbprint	25.00
Cruet, Beaded Swirl & Lens, Original Stopper	95.00
Cruet, Block & Lattice, Stained	75.00
Decanter, Clear Stopper, 10 1/2 In.	110.00
Decanter, Tiny Finecut, Gold Trim, Stained	75.00
Dish, Soup, Seattle Expo, 1909, Stained	20.00
Goblet, Loop & Block	40.00
Goblet, Thumbprint, Stained	35.00
Jug, Heart Band, Scranton, Pa., 3 In.	13.00
Mug, Seattle Expo, Stained, 1909	15.00
Pitcher, Aventurine, Pulled Feather, Clear Handle	200.00
Pitcher, Milk, King's Crown, Stained	75.00
Pitcher, Milk, Zipper Slash	45.00
Pitcher, Omaha Exposition, 1898, 2 3/4 In.	20.00
Pitcher, Souvenir, Boone, Iowa	32.00
Pitcher, Water, Corona, Gold, Enameled, Stained	110.00
Pitcher, Water, Minnesota State Fair, 1917	100.00
Pitcher, Water, Thumbprint, Stained	145.00
Salt & Pepper, Block & Scroll	115.00
Salt & Pepper, O'Hara Star, Stained	45.00
Spooner, Gothic Style, Footed, Stained, 4 1/2 In.	37.00
Spooner, Triple Triangle	30.00
Sugar, Open, Thumbprint	25.00
Syrup, Majestic	145.00
Syrup, Sunk Honeycomb, Stained	65.00 To 98.00
Table Set, Broken Column, Stained, 4 Piece	365.00
Table Set, Red Block, Stained, 4 Piece	235.00
Tankard, Button Arches, Stained	125.00
Toothpick, Beaded Swag, Heisey, Flashed	40.00
Toothpick, Beaded Swag, Revere Beach, Flashed, 1903	45.00
Toothpick, Bulging Loop	125.00
Toothpick, Serrated Ribs & Panels	45.00
Tray, Water, Beveled Star, Stained	65.00
Tumbler, Beaded Swirl, Stained	30.00
Tumbler, Block & Lattice	42.50
Tumbler, Cathedral	42.50
Tumbler, Diamond Band With Panels	47.50
Tumbler, Enameled	125.00
Tumbler, English Hobnail, Westmoreland, 8 Oz.	9.00
Tumbler, Gloria	47.50
Tumbler, King's Crown, Etched	37.50
Urn, Parcel Gilt Floral, Lamp Mounted, Bohemian, 29 In., Pr.	1100.00

Vase, Bud, Christmas Greetings, Stained, 1901	35.00
Vase, Enameled Birds, 1850, 14 In.	80.00
Water Set, Bar & Diamond, 6 Piece, Stained	265.00
Water Set, Button Arches, Frosted Band, Gold Trim, 7 Piece	275.00
Water Set, Checkerboard, Traces of Gold, 5 Piece	175.00
Water Set, Red Block, Stained, 7 Piece	225.00
Water Set, Thumbprint, 6 Piece	315.00
Water Set, Triple Triangle, 6 Piece	285.00
Wine, Red Block, Stained	25.00
Wine, Sunk Honeycomb, Stained	30.00
Wine, Truncated Cube, Stained	35.00

Rudolstadt was a faience factory in the Thuringia region of Germany from 1720 to about 1791. In 1854, Ernst Bohne began working in the area. From about 1887 to 1918, the New York and Rudolstadt Pottery made decorated porcelain marked with the RW and crown familiar to collectors. This porcelain was imported by Lewis Straus and Sons of New York, which later became Nathan Straus and Sons. The word "Royal" was included in their import mark. Collectors often call it "Royal Rudolstadt." Late nineteenth– and early twentieth–century pieces are most commonly found today.

RUDOLSTADT, see also Kewpie

RUDOLSTADT, Bowl, Floral, Royal, 9 1/2 In.	45.00
Bowl, Polychrome Floral, Silver Rim, R.W.With Crown, 9 3/4 In.	60.00
Bust, Queen Louise, 8 1/2 In.	195.00
Chocolate Pot, Pink Roses, White Flowers, Gold Trim, 10 In.	150.00
Chop Plate, Floral, Royal, 13 In.	120.00
Creamer, Roses	15.00
Cup & Saucer, Pedestal, Hand Painted Roses, Set of 8	150.00
Dish, Feeding, Kewpie Design, O'Neill, Wilson Co., 8 In.	235.00
Dresser Set, Pastel Florals, Blue, Royal, 3 Piece	225.00
Jar, Porcelain, Silver Plated Lid	60.00
Nappy, Flower Spray, Tan Ground, 8 Petals, Handle, Royal, 6 In.	35.00
Pitcher, Raised Gold Leaf Over White, Signed, 15 1/2 In.	275.00
Plate, Iris, Royal, 8 1/2 In.	40.00
Plate, White, Lavender Pansies, Green To White, Royal, 8 1/4 In.	75.00
Platter, Pastels, Signed, 13 In.	125.00
Sugar, Covered, Florals, Gold Handles, 6 1/4 In.	25.00
Tea Set, Royal, Golliwogs	225.00
Tray, Dresser, Violets, Royal, 7 1/2 X 10 In.	62.00
Urn, Covered, Hector & Andro Mache, Gold Trim, Signed, 10 In.	250.00
Vase, Bird, Dragon Feet & Handle, Marked, 16 In.	550.00
Vase, Dragon Heads, Footed, Bird, Earth Tones, Royal, 16 1/2 In.	525.00
Vase, Fern & Flower Sprays, Folded Over Ruffle Rim, 13 1/2 In.	150.00
Vase, Flowers, Blown–Out Leaves, Yellow & Beige Ground, 12 In.	90.00
Vase, Flowers, Cream, Art Nouveau, Blown–Out Leaves, 12 In.	75.00
Vase, Lavender & Coral Flowers, Gold Trim, Marked, 11 5/8 In.	145.00
Vase, Orange Flowers, Cream Ground, Red Mark, 16 In.	150.00

Rugs have been used in the American home since the seventeenth century. The Oriental rug of that time was often used on a table, not on the floor. Rag rugs, hooked rugs, and braided rugs were made by housewives from scraps of material.

RUG, Anatolian, Medallions, Ivory, Blue, Red Field, 3 Ft.11 In.X 9 Ft.8 In.	850.00
Aubusson, Scattered Flowers, Circular Medallions, 13 Ft.9 In.X 8 Ft.	1200.00
Aushak, 17 Ft. 4 In. X 14 Ft. 4 In.	4100.00
Bahktiari, 3 Center Medallions, Dated 1323, 14 Ft. 4 In. X 12 Ft.	5250.00
Bahktiari, Abstract Floral, Vine Border, 5 Ft.2 In.X 10 Ft.2 In.	1500.00
Bahktiari, Black Field, Allover Floral, 8 Ft.2 In.X 11 Ft.6 In.	1400.00
Bahktiari, Center Medallion, Pendants, 1980s, 4 Ft. 10 In. X 6 Ft.	2300.00
Bahktiari, Ivory Field, Allover Design, C.1900, 16 Ft.9 In. X 12 Ft.	6600.00
Bakshaish, Geometric, Stylized Floral, 1920s, 8 Ft. 8 In. X 12 Ft.	1800.00
Baluch, Allover Stepped Medallions, Leaf Border, 3 Ft.7 In.X 7 Ft.	500.00
Baluch, Pattern of Medallions, Allover Boteh, 3 Ft. 10 In. X 7 Ft.	625.00

Baluch, Sawtoothed Medallions On Poles, 2 Ft.9 In.X 4 Ft.9 In.	300.00
Belgium, Multicolor Floral, Machine Made, 9 X 12 Ft.	425.00
Bergamo, 5 Ft. 1 In. X 4 Ft.	600.00
Bidjar, Allover Stylized Tree Pattern, Blue, 7 Ft.6 In.X 11 Ft.	3800.00
Bidjar, Central Directional Medallion, C.1900, 20 Ft.X 12 Ft.2 In.	6600.00
Bidjar-Kurd, Sarouk Style Floral, Blue Ground, 2 Ft.9 In.X 7 Ft.	550.00
Bordjalou Kazak, Red Field, Medallion Shield, 5 Ft.10 In.X 8 Ft.6 In.	800.00
Caucasian, Black Field, Colored Boteh, 3 Ft.11 In. X 11 Ft.6 In.	700.00
Caucasian, Blue-Green Ground, Red Hook Medallions, 3 X 5 Ft.	500.00
Caucasian, Rust Field, Geometrical Palmettes, Red, Aqua, Blue, 6 X 7 Ft.	550.00
Caucasian, Rust, Repeating Geometrical Design, 5 Ft.X 6 Ft. 11 In.	550.00
Chi-Chi, Horizontal Rows of Memling Guls, 4 Ft. X 6 Ft. 4 In.	4400.00
Chinese, Allover Fret Design, Dark Blue, 9 Ft.8 In.X 11 Ft.8 In.	400.00
Chinese, Art Deco Swirls, Florals, C.1925, 8 Ft. 10 In. X 11 Ft. 9 In.	3500.00
Chinese, Art Deco, Mauve, Cranberry, 8 Ft.10 In.X 11 Ft.9 In. ....*Illus*	3500.00
Chinese, Blue & Ivory, Butterflies In Border, 4 Ft.2 In.X 8 Ft.	425.00
Chinese, Gold Field, Birds, Green Border, 8 Ft.10 In. X 11 Ft.5 In.	700.00
Chopor, Trellis Or Ertmen Guls, C.1880, 7 Ft. 11 In. X 11 Ft. 6 In.	2200.00
Drugget, Central Diamond, Neutral Ground, C.1910, 58 1/2 X 32 In.	75.00
Drugget, Latticework, Neutral Ground, 14 Ft.7 In.X 9 Ft.2 1/2 In.	600.00
Drugget, Nile Pattern, C.1910, 9 Ft. 10 In. X 7 Ft. 8 1/2 In.	475.00
Drugget, Overall Zigzag Pattern, Triangles, 9 Ft.2 In.X 11 Ft.8 In.	900.00
Ersari, 3 Rows of Blue Octagonal Guls, Early 20th Century, 8 X 12 Ft.	1200.00
Ersari, Afghanistan, Guls, Dark Red Ground, 8 X 12 Ft.	1200.00
Ersari, Guls, Stepped Medallion Border, C.1875, 7 Ft. 3 In. X 9 Ft.	2100.00
Feraghan, Allover Stylized Floral, C.1915, 4 Ft. 2 In. X 6 Ft. 6 In.	2750.00
Feraghan, Stepped Diamond Field, 1890s, 4 Ft. 4 In. X 6 Ft. 6 In.	4800.00
Floorcloth, Canvas, American Flag, Sailor Made	1750.00
Hamadan, Blue Allover Trellis, Camel, Border, 3 Ft.2 In.X 9 Ft.5 In.	500.00
Hamadan, Classical Design, 20th Century, 4 Ft.1 In.X 6 Ft.8 In.	550.00
Herati, Deep Blue, Stylized Flowers, 3 Stripe Border, 55 X 77 In.	1200.00
Herati, Deep Blue, Stylized Flowers, 7 Stripe Border, 77 X 44 In.	1400.00
Heriz, 8 Point Medallion, Rust Red Field, 8 Ft.11 In.X 11 Ft.2 In.	1800.00
Heriz, Area, Red Field, 8 Point Blue & Ivory Medallion, 9 X 11 Ft.	4000.00
Heriz, Center Medallion, Allover Floral, 8 Ft.9 In. X 11 Ft.8 In.	1300.00
Heriz, Center Medallion, Pendants On Red Field, 7 Ft.X 10 Ft.2 In.	1900.00
Heriz, Central Directional Medallion, C.1900, 12 Ft. 9 In. X 10 Ft.	6325.00
Heriz, Dark Blue Medallion, Rust Field, 6 Ft.9 In.X 9 Ft.3 In.	2000.00
Heriz, Geometric Floral Design, 5 X 7 Ft.	3500.00
Heriz, Geometric Pattern, Red, Ivory, Blue, 8 Ft.7 In.X 6 Ft.4 In.	1150.00
Heriz, Geometric, 10 Ft.7 In.X 18 Ft.8 In.	9250.00
Heriz, Midnight Blue Medallion, Brown Red Field, 9 Ft.2 In.X 12 Ft.	4200.00
Heriz, Midnight Blue Medallion, Red Field, 9 Ft.2 In.X 12 Ft.6 In.	2500.00
Heriz, Pendant Medallion, Turtle Border, 9 Ft.11 In.X 19 Ft.	5000.00
Heriz, Red Field, Lobed Medallion, Spandrels, 9 Ft.9 In.X 11 Ft.	4750.00
Heriz, Wine Field, Flowering Vines, C.1900, 11 Ft. X 9 Ft. 9 In.	9350.00
Hooked, 3 Kittens In Basket, 25 X 40 In.	350.00
Hooked, Acorn Design, Browns, Greens, Amish, Signed, 1935, 25 X 41 In.	125.00
Hooked, Bear & Rabbit, Brown, Gray, & Black, 25 X 32 In.	185.00
Hooked, Bird Scene, Gold, Red & Blue, 69 In.	1150.00
Hooked, Blue, Brown, Yellow & White, 9 X 12 Ft.	225.00
Hooked, Concentric Oval Design, Maroon Corners, 33 X 54 In.	35.00
Hooked, Concentric Stripes, 36 X 60 In.	10.00
Hooked, Cottage, Fence, Trees, 15 X 24 In.	235.00
Hooked, Country Scene, Figures, Cart, Horse, House, 34 In. Square	175.00
Hooked, Deer, Beige Ground, Framed, 27 X 53 In.	45.00
Hooked, Dennis The Menace, 1950s, 3 X 5 Ft.	65.00
Hooked, Dog, 18 X 31 In.	275.00
Hooked, Facing Rabbits, Feather Border, 19th Century, 23 X 43 In.	595.00
Hooked, Farm Scene, 18 1/2 X 38 In.	145.00
Hooked, Farm Scene, Forest Green Border, Signed Quebec, 18 X 35 In.	450.00
Hooked, Figural, Squirrels In Tree & Barn, 18 X 36 In.	65.00
Hooked, Floral & Leaf Border, Center Medallion, Hearth, 35 X 50 In.	650.00
Hooked, Floral Design, Brown & Pastels, Green Ground, 47 X 69 In.	25.00

Hooked,	Floral Design, Pink & Green Center, 33 X 20 In.	65.00
Hooked,	Floral, Geometric, Bright Colors, 38 X 54 In.	30.00
Hooked,	Flower Basket, 33 X 44 In.	700.00
Hooked,	Flowerpots, Zigzag Border, Stylized Design, 23 1/2 X 40 In.	65.00
Hooked,	Fox & Crow, Aesop's Fable, 19th Century, 48 X 26 In.	1250.00
Hooked,	Fruits, Flowers Center, Oval, Wool, 9 Ft. 10 In. X 7 Ft. 11 In.	1540.00
Hooked,	Geometric Checkerboard, Roses, 29 X 40 In.	45.00
Hooked,	Geometric Floral Design, Gray Ground, 26 X 69 In.	35.00
Hooked,	Geometric Leaf Design, 24 X 47 In.	30.00
Hooked,	Golden Brown Scotty, Red Ribbon, Ivy Border, 27 X 40 In.	185.00
Hooked,	Heart Center, Gray Ground, Stylized Design, 31 X 49 In.	95.00
Hooked,	Horse & Colt, C.1890, 34 X 42 In.	595.00
Hooked,	Horse Head, Geometric Foliage Border, 31 1/2 X 49 In.	325.00
Hooked,	House, Garden, Trees, 36 X 19 In.	90.00
Hooked,	Houses, Birds, Flowers, C.1920, 9 X 16 In.	40.00
Hooked,	Hunting Dogs, Roses In Corners, 33 X 22 In.	300.00
Hooked,	Large Dog Center, 25 X 38 In.	1250.00
Hooked,	Leaping Deer, Black Ground, 22 X 35 In.	125.00
Hooked,	Leaping Deer, Solid Colors, Yarn Binding, 24 X 38 In.	85.00
Hooked,	Lines Forming Rectangles Inside Rectangles, 61 X 36 In.	75.00
Hooked,	Little Bopeep, Pink, White, Black Outlined, 19 X 38 In.	105.00
Hooked,	Little Bopeep, Sheep, Morning Glories, 25 X 38 In.	75.00
Hooked,	Multicolored Center, Floral Border, 5 Ft.10 In.X 8 Ft.10 In.	650.00
Hooked,	Multicolored Stripes, Wooden Stretcher, 24 X 38 In.	55.00
Hooked,	Oriental Geometric Pattern, Amber, Blue, Gray, Reds, 3 X 6 Ft.	400.00
Hooked,	Oval Wreath Florals, Multicolor, Beige Ground, 1885, 8 Ft.3 In.	2200.00
Hooked,	Peacock, 8 Colors, 30 X 20 In.	95.00
Hooked,	Rectangles of Stripes & Squares, 26 X 38 In.	45.00
Hooked,	Red Flowers, Green & Brown Ground, 37 X 24 In.	85.00
Hooked,	Runner, Acorn & Oak Leaf Border, Gray Field, 28 X 90 In.	85.00
Hooked,	Running Horses, Amish, Sadie Fisher, 1925, 25 X 44 In.	200.00
Hooked,	Thanksgiving Scene, Woman, Fireplace, Man Eating, 29 X 37 In.	395.00
Hooked,	Varicolored Stripes, 22 X 42 In.	45.00
Hooked,	Variegated Band of Fruit & Florals, Oval, 9 Ft.10 In.X 8 Ft.	1400.00
Hooked,	Winter Scene, 4 Dogs, House, Smoking Chimney, 41 X 26 In.	275.00
Hooked,	Winter Scene, Houses, Barn, Sleigh, C.1910, 15 X 20 In.	110.00
Joshagan,	Blue Center Diamond, Rust Field, 7 Ft.2 In.X 10 Ft.2 In.	1400.00
Karabagh,	Repeat Sawtoothed Medallions, Animal Figures	550.00
Karadje,	Rows of Red & Blue Medallions, 2 Ft. 4 In. X 8 Ft. 6 In.	90.00
Karistan,	Kirman Pattern, Dark Colors, 6 Ft.3 In.X 9 Ft.	350.00
Kashan,	Lobed Center Medallion, C.1920, 4 Ft. 6 In. X 6 Ft. 8 In.	1700.00
Kashan,	Red Field, Blue & Ivory Medallion, 7 X 9 Ft.	3600.00
Kashgar,	Moss Green, Allover Flowers, 15 Ft.5 In.X 11 In.	8800.00
Kasvin,	Allover Floral Sprays, Tomato Red Field, 12 Ft.2 In.X 14 Ft.	2400.00
Kasvin,	Lobed Center Medallion, Floral, Red, 9 Ft.X 8 Ft.10 In.	2000.00
Kazak,	Caucasian, Lasghi–Star Field, Border, 3 X 4 Ft.10 In. ....*Illus*	1300.00
Kazak,	Medallions, Corner Animal Figures, 4 Ft. 7 In. X 7 Ft.	2700.00
Kazak,	Shield Medallions, Ram–Horn Hooks, 4 Ft. 11 In. X 7 Ft. 2 In.	2200.00
Kelim,	Center & Corner Swans, Fretwork Corners, 5 Ft. 1 In. X 7 Ft.	1000.00
Keshan,	Floral, Medallion Pattern, Brick Red, 11 Ft.6 In X 8 Ft.9 In.	4250.00
Keshan,	Silk, Red Urn, Ivory Field, Floral, 4 Ft.X 7 Ft.6 In., Pair	4500.00
Kirman,	Allover Palmette Arabesque, Cream, 9 Ft.2 In.X 11 Ft.7 In.	1600.00
Kirman,	Ivory Field, Magenta, Blue, Lobed Medallion, 4 Ft.X 6 Ft.9 In.	300.00
Kirman,	Midnight Blue Medallion, 14 Ft.4 In.X 10 Ft.11 In.	8800.00
Knotted Wool,	Art Nouveau Border, Rust, Continental, 16 Ft.X 11 Ft.	6325.00
Kuba,	Black Field, Trellis of Plants, 3 Ft. 3 In. X 4 Ft. 10 In.	1400.00
Kuba,	Center Rust Medallion, Dark Blue Field, 4 Ft.X 5 Ft.9 In.	1100.00
Kuba,	Colored Medallions, Chalice, Leaf Edge, 41 In. X 69 In.	1600.00
Kuba,	Crab Medallions, Pale To Medium Blue, 4 Ft.7 In.X 3 Ft.3 In.	2400.00
Kuba,	Medallions, Midnight Blue Field, 1900, 4 Ft.X 5 Ft.4 In.	1000.00
Kurdish,	Bands of Stylized Blossoms, 3 Ft. 6 In. X 8 Ft. 11 In.	750.00
Kurdish,	Elliptical Medallions, 3 Ft. 9 In. X 8 Ft. 11 In.	900.00
Kurdish,	Herati Pattern, Red Borders, 5 Ft. 10 In. X 11 Ft. 9 In.	475.00
Lillihan,	Floral Spray, Rose Red Field, 5 Ft.X 3 Ft.9 In.	425.00

Rug, Chinese, Art Deco, Mauve, Cranberry, 8 Ft.10 In.X 11 Ft.9 In.

Rug, Kazak, Caucasian, Lasghi–Star Field, Border, 3 X 4 Ft.10 In.

Lillihan, Floral, Wine Ground, 8 Ft.11 In.X 11 Ft.5 In.	1800.00
Mahal, Allover Palmette & Arabesque, Rust Red, 10 Ft.X 17 Ft.7 In.	2900.00
Mahal, Blue Field, Herati Filled Medallion, 11 Ft.8 In.X 17 Ft.	5000.00
Mahal, Floral On Wine Red Ground, 4 Ft. 4 In. X 6 Ft. 6 In.	500.00
Mahal, Floral, Animals, Maroon Ground, 9 Ft.X 14 Ft.4 In.	1850.00
Malayer Sarouk, Herati, Dark Blue Field, 4 Ft.2 In.X 6 Ft.3 In.	450.00
Mashad, 19 Point Center Medallion, 1925, 8 Ft. 11 In. X 11 Ft. 8 In.	2700.00
Mashad, Center Medallion, Magenta, 1930, 11 Ft.5 In.X 15 Ft.7 In.	1500.00
Melas, Wing–Like Leaves On Pole, C.1880, 3 Ft. 3 In. X 4 Ft. 6 In.	3750.00
Needlepoint, Ivory, Diamond Reserves, 17 Ft.6 In.X 9 Ft.7 In.	3300.00
Needlepoint, Rows of Flowers, Border, English, 13 Ft.4 X 6 Ft.6 In.	1100.00
Oushak Kilim, Dusty Rose Trellis, 12 Ft.X9 Ft.5 In.	880.00
Sarouk, Center Diamond, Allover Floral, Border, 4 Ft.1 In.X 6 Ft.5 In.	950.00
Sarouk, Center Medallion, Corner Spandrels, 4 Ft.4 In. X 6 Ft.6 In.	900.00
Sarouk, Center Medallion, Red Field, Cluster Border, 40 In.X 60 In.	600.00
Sarouk, Floral Sprays, Blue, Gold, Yellow, 6 Ft.6 In. X 4 Ft.2 In.	300.00
Sarouk, Ivory Diamond Center, Blue Boteh, 2 Ft.2 In.X 2 Ft.6 In.	300.00
Sarouk, Red Field, Blue Medallion, Green, Blue, Cream, 3 X 4 Ft.	600.00
Sarouk, Symmetrical Floral, Mulberry, C.1925, 2 Ft.7 In.X 5 Ft.2 In.	460.00
Senna, Rows of Boteh, Ivory Field, 4 Ft. 5 In. X 6 Ft. 6 In.	1900.00
Shiraz, Central Medallions, C.1900, 8 Ft.8 In. X 4 Ft.10 In.	1320.00
Shirvan Kelim, Bands, Stepped Medallions, 4 Ft. 9 In. X 9 Ft. 4 In.	1700.00
Shirvan, Abstract Plants, 19th Century, 3 Ft. 6 In. X 9 Ft. 1 In.	650.00
Shirvan, Boteh In Black Trellis, Beige Field, 4 Ft.4 In.X 7 Ft. 5 In.	1100.00
Shirvan, Contiguous Medallions, C.1875, 4 Ft. 6 In. X 9 Ft. 1 In.	2100.00
Shirvan, Dark Blue Field, 3 Sawtoothed Medallions, 3 Ft.9 In. X 5 Ft.	650.00
Shirvan, Prayer, Abstract Floral Trellis, C.1900, 10 Ft. X 4 Ft. 5 In.	3400.00
Shirvan, Prayer, Ivory Field, Dated 1314, 3 Ft.8 In.X 4 Ft.3 In.	1700.00
Soumak, 4 Starburst Medallions, 1880s, 4 Ft. 2 In. X 8 Ft. 8 In.	5500.00
Soumak, Medallion, Animal Figures, Bag Face, 19th Century, 1 Ft.7 In.	650.00
Sultanabad, Blue Center Medallion, Red Field, 14 Ft.8 In.X 16 Ft.	3750.00
Tabriz, Allover Herati Design, C.1920, 3 Ft. 10 In. X 5 Ft. 9 In.	1800.00
Tabriz, Medallion Design Allover, 4 Ft. 2 In. X 5 Ft. 6 In.	1300.00
Tabriz, Repeating Rows of Palmettes, 8 Ft.6 In.X 11 Ft.3 In.	1900.00
Tabriz, Rose, Center Gold Medallion, 12 Ft.2 In.X 8 Ft.8 In.	9900.00
Tabriz, Rust Red, Open Field, Green, Pale Blue, 4 Ft.1 In.X 5 Ft.8 In.	475.00
Tekke Chuval, 9 Rust Salor Guls, Magenta, 4 Ft.8 In.X 2 Ft.9 In.	250.00
Tekke Torba, 4 Rows of Chuval Guls, C.1880, 2 Ft. 5 In. X 1 Ft. 1 In.	500.00
Tekke, 3 Rows Guls, Ivory, Blue, Earth Red Field, 45 In. X 54 In.	500.00
Tekke, Brick Red Field, Tekke Guls, C.1900, 9 Ft.11 In. X 6 Ft.9 In.	2750.00
Turkoman Ensi, Candelabra Rows, 19th Century, 4 Ft.4 In.X 5 Ft.4 In.	825.00

Ushak, Arabesque Design, C.1920, 8 Ft. 11 In. X 11 Ft. 9 In.	2900.00
Yomud, 3 Rows of Nauska Guls, C.1860, 4 Ft. 8 In. X 7 Ft. 1 In.	600.00
Yomud, Rows of Chuval Guls, 4 Ft. 10 In. X 8 Ft. 11 In.	3750.00
Yoruk, Directional Panel, Medallion Border, 3 Ft. 1 In. X 4 Ft. 8 In.	325.00
Zili, Lobed Medallion, Peacock Ends, 1890, 3 Ft. 11 In. X 6 Ft. 10 In.	7250.00

RumRill Rumrill Pottery was designed by George Rumrill of Little Rock, Arkansas. From 1930 to 1933, it was produced by the Red Wing Pottery of Red Wing, Minnesota. In 1938, production was transferred to the Shawnee Pottery in Zanesville, Ohio. Production ceased in the 1940s.

RUMRILL, Bookends, Polar Bear, Matte Black	65.00
Candlestick, Cream, 3 In., Pair	10.00
Fruit Boat, White Outside, Blue Interior	25.00
Jug, Water, Covered, Blue To Violet	20.00
Pitcher, Ball, Burnt Orange, 5 1/2 In.	18.00
Pitcher, Tilt, Green	15.00
Vase, Cherry & Leaf Design In Relief, White Matte, 8 1/2 In.	25.00
Vase, Double Nude Pedestal, 8 In.	95.00
Vase, Matte Green & Cream, 6 1/2 In.	14.00
Vase, Orange & Brown Outside, Yellow Inside, 2 Handles, 13 In. ...	7.00
Vase, Side Handles, Green, 9 In.	25.00

RUSKIN POTTERY WEST SMETHWICK Ruskin is a British art pottery of the twentieth century. The Ruskin Pottery was started by William Howson Taylor; his name was used as the mark until about 1899. The factory, at West Smethwick, Birmingham, England, stopped making new pieces in 1933 but continued to glaze and sell the remaining wares until 1935. The art pottery is noted for the exceptional glazes.

RUSKIN, Vase, Blue Crystalline, Tan, Gourd Shape, 6 In.	90.00
Vase, Blue, Red Striated Glaze, Cylinder, 10 In.	250.00

Russel Wright MFG. BY STEUBENVILLE Russel Wright designed dinnerwares in modern shapes for four companies. Iroquois China Company, Harker China Company, Steubenville Pottery, and Justin Therod and Sons made dishes marked "Russel Wright." The Steubenville wares, first made in 1938, are the most common today. This section lists the dinnerwares by Wright. He was a designer of domestic and industrial wares, including furniture, aluminum, radios, interiors, and glassware.

RUSSEL WRIGHT, Ashtray, Bauer .... 185.00 To 195.00	
Beanpot, American Modern, Brown	45.00
Bowl, Iroquois, Ice Blue, 5 1/4 In.	15.00
Bowl, Vegetable, Open, American Modern, Coral	15.00
Butter, Covered, American Modern, Coral	125.00
Butter, Iroquois, Covered	52.00
Carafe, Iroquois, White, 10 1/4 In.	40.00
Carafe, Wine, Charcoal	45.00
Carafe, Wine, Chartreuse	45.00
Casserole, American Modern, Coral, Covered	35.00
Casserole, Covered, Glacier	45.00
Celery, American Modern, Coral	22.00
Celery, Cantaloupe	22.00
Celery, Chartreuse	10.50
Chop Plate, American Modern, Coral	20.00
Chop Plate, Chartreuse, 13 In.	18.00
Chop Plate, Coral	15.00
Chop Plate, Green	20.00
Clock, G.E., Charcoal	50.00
Coffeepot, American Modern, Coral	35.00
Coffeepot, Chartreuse	40.00
Creamer, American Modern, Coral	15.00
Creamer, Coral	12.00
Creamer, Stack, Ice Blue	9.00
Cup & Saucer, After Dinner, Green	14.00

Cup & Saucer, American Modern, Seafoam	6.50
Cup & Saucer, Chartreuse	7.00
Cup & Saucer, Gray	9.00
Cup & Saucer, Iroquois, Ice Blue	9.50
Cup & Saucer, Rose	13.00
Cup, American Modern, White	6.50
Cup, Chartreuse	5.00 To 7.00
Gravy Boat, Chartreuse	15.00
Gravy Boat, Gray	15.00
Pitcher, American Modern, Chartreuse	40.00
Pitcher, Cantaloupe	47.00
Pitcher, Water, American Modern, Chartreuse	28.00 To 40.00
Plate, American Modern, Seafoam Green, 8 In.	4.00
Plate, American Modern, White, 10 1/2 In.	5.00
Plate, Bread & Butter, Gray, 6 In.	2.50
Plate, Brown, 6 In.	3.00
Plate, Chartreuse, 7 In.	4.00
Plate, Dinner, Black, 9 1/2 In.	34.00
Plate, Dinner, Gray, 10 In.	6.00
Plate, Gray, 8 In.	4.00
Plate, Salad, Chartreuse, 8 In.	4.50
Platter, Chartreuse, 13 3/4 In.	15.00
Platter, Divided, Steubenville, Pink, 13 1/2 In.	24.00
Platter, Seafoam, 13 1/2 In.	12.00
Stack Set, Charcoal	10.00
Sugar & Creamer, Cantaloupe	17.00
Sugar & Creamer, Stacked, Chartreuse	15.00
Teapot, American Modern, Coral	45.00

SABINO FRANCE

Sabino
France

Sabino glass was made in the 1920s and 1930s in Paris, France. Founded by Marius–Ernest Sabino, the firm was noted for Art Deco lamps, vases, figurines, and animals in clear, colored, and opalescent glass. Production stopped during World War II but resumed in the 1960s with the manufacture of nude figurines and small opalescent glass animals. The new pieces are a slightly different color and can be recognized.

SABINO, Figurine, Nude, Flowing Hair, Signed, 6 1/2 In.	175.00
Lamp, Opal Draped Nude, 1930s, 8 In.	275.00
Perfume Bottle, Nude, 6 In.	130.00
Vase, Allover Floral Design, Opalescent, 1920s, 6 In.	60.00
Vase, Allover Leaves, Small Berries, Frosted, 1920s, 4 1/2 In.	75.00
Vase, Amethyst Wisteria, White Ground, Serrated Leaf Rim, 8 In.	250.00
Vase, Beehive, Bulbous, Signed, 8 In.	450.00
Vase, Bulbous, Wild Turkeys Dancing, Allover Design, Signed, 9 In.	650.00

Salopian ware was made by the Caughley factory of England during the eighteenth century. The early pieces were blue and white with some colored decorations. Another ware called "Salopian" today is a tableware elaborately decorated with color transfers. This ware was made during the late nineteenth century.

SALOPIAN, Cup & Saucer, Handleless, Cow Pattern	77.50
Vase, Gold Floral Design, Green	80.00

SALT & PEPPER, see Porcelain; Pressed Glass; etc.

Salt glaze has a grayish–white, pitted, orange–peel–textured surface. It is a method of decoration that has been used since the eighteenth century. Salt–glazed pieces are still being made.

SALT GLAZE, Butter Churn, Complete, C.1875	47.50
Crock, Blue Flower, No.3, Handles, 3 Gal.	65.00
Crock, Greensboro, Pa., Light Brown, Signed, 1 Gal.	90.00
Crock, Stamped With 3, 3 Gal.	40.00
Dish, Baking, Bail Handle	25.00
Figurine, Shepherdess With Lamb, Tight Bodice, C.1750, 4 In.	4200.00
Jug, Argyle, Gray Ground, Blue Trim, 1865, 7 7/8 In.	85.00

Jug, E.E.Hynes, Merrimack St., Haverhill, Blue Incised, 1 Gal.	150.00
Jug, Foliate Design, Cobalt Blue, Bulbous, Dutch, 7 In.	412.00
Jug, Goodale, Stedman, Hartford, Pear Shape	140.00
Jug, Leaves Near Base, Wm.Brownfield, White, 1864, 8 In.	100.00
Jug, Milk, Pear Shape, Grooved Strap Handle, C.1760, 5 1/4 In.	1500.00
Jug, Tam O'Shanter & Souter Johnnie, Grape Vines, 7 3/8 In.	125.00
Mug, Barrel Shape, Blue & White	65.00
Mug, Pink & Rose	58.00
Pitcher, Bluebird, Large	195.00
Pitcher, Peacocks, Large	225.00
Pitcher, Pewter Lid, Dated 1844, Meigh	125.00
Pitcher, Pewter Lid, Oak Leaf, Acorn & Fern Pattern, Marked	140.00
Pitcher, White, Pewter Lid, Embossed Sheaf, Lilies, 10 1/2 In.	95.00
Platter, Basketweave Panels, England, 18th Century, 12 X 15 In.	125.00
Salt, Hanging, Lid, Rose & Daisy	185.00
Soap Dish, Cat Face, Blue	90.00
Syrup, Apostle Paul	225.00
Tankard, Bell Shape, Oriental Landscapes, C.1760, 2 3/4 In.	2500.00
Tankard, Peasant Lass, Pink Scalloped, Handle, C.1760, 5 1/4 In.	2000.00
Tea Set, Spherical, Allover Punched Design, England, 1850, 3 Pc.	100.00
Teapot, Bell Shape, Serpent Spout & Handle, C.1750	3000.00
Teapot, Blue Enamel Ground, Foliage & Buds, C.1760, 4 3/4 In.	3500.00
Teapot, Compressed Globular Form, Inset Cover, C.1760, 3 In.	1650.00
Teapot, Inverted Ovoid Form, Colored Enamels, C.1760, 5 3/4 In.	1900.00
Teapot, Leaf & Vine Design, Rosette Band, 1800, 6 X 10 In.	100.00

ABCDE Samplers were made in America from the early 1700s. The best examples were made from 1790 to 1840. Long, narrow samplers are usually older than square ones. Early samplers just had stitching or alphabets. The later examples had numerals, borders, and pictorial decorations. Those with mottoes are mid–Victorian.

SAMPLER, 3 Pots of Flowers, E.Updegraff, A.D.1838, 20 1/4 X 20 1/2 In.	425.00
Almena Lester, Age 14, Wine Is A Mocker, 20 5/8 X 21 3/8 In.	270.00
Alphabet, 12 Pictures, Punch Paper, Signed, 1854, 7 1/4 X 10 In.	125.00
Alphabet, Abigail H.Cook, Age 11, Nov.1827, Framed, 17 X 16 In.	4180.00
Alphabet, Birds, 1796, 11 1/2 X 14 In.	275.00
Alphabet, Capitals, Gothic, Jane Westwood, 1880, 11 X 14 In.	250.00
Alphabet, Deborah Weeks, Age 9, 1785, Framed, 7 X 10 1/2 In.	550.00
Alphabet, Floral Crest, Names, Linen, Europe, 1810, 11 X 20 In.	250.00
Alphabet, Homespun, Mary Bowmar Wragby, 1809, 8 X 10 3/4 In.	325.00
Alphabet, House, Elizabeth, Born July 20, 1804, Linen, 16 X 16 In.	800.00
Alphabet, Melissa Barker Stone, 8 Years, 1830, 13 1/2 X 21 In.	1500.00
Alphabet, Numbers, Rebekah Halder, 1759, 15 X 9 X 7 In.	325.00
Alphabet, Pictorial, Sara A.Crumes, Born 1827, 23 X 15 1/2 In.	850.00
Alphabet, Stylized Flowers, Homespun, C.E.U.F., 1831, 18 X 23 In.	175.00
Alphabet, Verse, Eliza Ann Bacon, Age 9, 1831, 17 X 17 In.	1800.00
Alphabet, Verse, Landscape, 18th Century, 17 X 17 In.	7400.00
Alphabet, Verse, Mary Ann Brown, AD 1823, Framed, 21 X 17 In.	400.00
Alphabet, Verse, Mason Family, 1846, Framed, 21 1/2 X 21 1/2 In.	400.00
Alphabet, Verses, Framed, Dated 1869, 12 X 16 In.	145.00
Alphabets, Nancy Jane Whitten, July 12, 1810, Framed, 12 X 16 In.	850.00
American Beauty, Roses & 48–Star Flag, 22 X 20 In.	37.50
Ann Morris, Bands of Floral Vines, 1790, 13 X 10 In.	350.00
Anna Atwater, 1773, Age 9, 10 1/4 X 16 In.	5500.00
Buildings, American Flag, Embroidered Wool, Red, 14 X 12 In.	670.00
Caroline Woodbury, Born 1807, Cape Elizabeth, Me., 10 X 16 1/2 In.	1200.00
Cross–Stitch, Mary Barker, Age 11, 1820, 13 X 21 In.	400.00
Elizabeth Heberton, Misspelling, Trees, Urns, 11 1/4 X 16 1/4 In.	1800.00
Elizabeth Lamb, Framed, C.1825, 14 3/4 X 16 3/4 In.	150.00
Frances Amelia Parcelle, Age 13, 1851, 10 1/4 X 10 1/4 In.	235.00
George E.Mayton, Age 7, Died Sept.1, 1867, 9 X 15 1/2 In.	200.00
Harriet A.Brady, Finished July 23, 1836, 11 X 8 3/4 In.	600.00
Harriet A.Silberts, Age 10, April 1840, 14 X 20 1/2 In.	250.00
Home Sweet Home, Crewel, Cottage, Flowers, Framed, Square, 20 In.	45.00

Satsuma, Jar, Carved
Teak Cover, Dragon,
19th Century, 13 In.

Sampler, Susanah Cadmore,
Silk Yarn Landscape, 1805, 12 X 13 In.

Johanna Weisingh, Seated Stag, Rampant Lions, 1702, 15 X 12 In. 500.00
Liquid Embroidery, Words, Children, Tree, Strawberry Border, 1920 .... 34.00
Lovebirds, Flowers, Amy Wilds, July 31, 1758, 14 X 8 3/4 In. 225.00
Map, England & Wales, Maria, Bobby, 1838, Framed, 18 X 20 In. 225.00
Mary Law Work, House, Animals, 19th Century, Framed, 16 X 18 In. 1000.00
Narcessa M.Peirce, 14 Years, A.D.1826, Garden Walk, 16 X 21 In. 400.00
Polly Symond, Age 12, Year 1792, Sawtooth Border, 11 1/2 X 13 In. 850.00
Rebecca Miers, Verses, Strawberry Border, C.1830, 22 X 21 In. 700.00
Sara Jubb, Age 9, 1809, England, Solomon's Temple, 17 1/2 X 19 In. 475.00
Susanah Cadmore, Silk Yarn Landscape, 1805, 12 X 13 In. ....*Illus* 500.00
Tug of War, Victorian, Walnut Frame, C.1900, 2 X 4 Ft. 125.00

Samson and Company, a French firm specializing in the
reproduction of collectible wares of many countries and periods, was
founded in Paris in the early nineteenth century. Chelsea, Meissen,
Famille Verte, and Chinese Export porcelain are some of the wares
that have been reproduced by the company. The firm uses a variety
of marks on the reproductions. It is still in operation.

SAMSON, Figurine, Dwarf, Mansion House, 5 In. 120.00
Jar, Oriental Export Style Design, Ovoid, 19th Century, 10 In., Pair 425.00
Saltshaker, Figural, Hand Painted, 7 In., Pair 320.00
Tea Caddy, Porcelain, C.1870 .... 150.00

Sand Babies were used as decorations on a line of children's dishes
made by the Royal Bayreuth China Company. The children are
playing at the seaside. Collectors use the names "Sand Babies" and
"Beach Babies" interchangeably.

SAND BABIES, Plate, Royal Bayreuth, 6 1/4 In. 85.00

To test the age of engraving on glass, place a white handkerchief on
the inside. If the engraving is old, the lines will usually show up darker
than the rest of the glass. New engraving has a bright powderlike
surface.

Sandwich glass is any one of the myriad types of glass made by the Boston and Sandwich Glass Works in Sandwich, Massachusetts, between 1825 and 1888. It is often very difficult to be sure whether a piece was really made at the Sandwich factory because so many types were made there and similar pieces were made at other glass factories.

SANDWICH GLASS, see also Pressed Glass, etc.

SANDWICH GLASS, Bell, Stork Standing, Cattails, Original Clapper, 5 1/2 In.	195.00
Bottle, Perfume, Sapphire Blue, Ground Mouth, 5 1/2 In.	125.00
Bowl, Fleur–De–Lis & Thistle, 9 In.	500.00
Bowl, Floral, Moongleam, Footed, Oval, 11 In.	120.00
Bowl, Hairpin, 6 1/4 In.	100.00
Bowl, Hairpin, Hexagonal, 5 1/2 In.	100.00
Bowl, Heart With Leaf, 10 1/2 X 2 1/2 In.	700.00
Bowl, Industry, Serrated Border, 6 1/4 In.	350.00
Bowl, Leaf & Gothic Arch, Rectangular, 8 3/8 X 6 3/8 In.	135.00
Bowl, Peacock Eye, 9 In.	275.00
Bowl, Tulip & Acanthus Leaf, 8 1/2 In.	50.00
Candlestick, Amber, 9 In., Pair	75.00
Candlestick, Clambroth Loop Base, Sapphire Blue Top, Pair	570.00
Candlestick, Dolphin, Pair	450.00
Candlestick, Loop Pattern, Bobeche, Blue, C.1835, 7 In., Pair	225.00
Candlestick, Petal & Loop, Canary, Pair	250.00
Candlestick, Sapphire, Hexagonal, Pair	475.00
Candlestick, Single Step, Canary, Pair	850.00
Candlestick, Square Base, Fluted Stem, 10 In., Pair	90.00
Celery, Waffle, Scalloped, Knob Stem, 9 1/4 In.	45.00
Compote, Pineapple, New England, Covered, 9 In.	75.00
Compote, Princess Feather, 4 X 6 1/2 In.	360.00
Compote, Rose In Snow, Blue, Open Low Stand, 4 1/2 In.	95.00
Creamer, Dolphin	135.00
Creamer, Gothic With Chain, 4 1/2 In.	525.00
Creamer, Heart	90.00
Cruet, 3–Mold, Swirled Cobalt, C.1850, 7 In.	325.00
Cruet, Amber, Blown, Applied Handle, Hollow Stopper, 6 In.	66.00
Cruet, Chrysanthemum Leaf, Original Stopper	65.00
Decanter, 3–Mold Geometric, C.1840, 1 Qt.	140.00
Decanter, Clear, 12 In., Pair	225.00
Dish, Beehive Pattern, 9 1/8 In.	95.00
Dish, Feather, Quatrefoil Center, Serrated, 9 1/2 In.	275.00
Iron, Clear, 1 1/4 In.	175.00
Lamp, Amber, Opalescent White	195.00
Lamp, Brass Column, Marble Base, Ruby To Clear, 25 1/2 In.	395.00
Lamp, Fluid, Inverted Font, Brass Stem, Marble Base, 1860s	375.00
Lamp, Hurricane, Vintage Globe, Prisms & Drops, 22 In.	475.00
Lamp, Oil, Deep Blue Acanthus Font, Brass Connector, 13 In.	395.00
Lamp, Pear–Shaped Font, White To Ruby, Black Base, 14 In.	1300.00
Lamp, Whale Oil, Acanthus Leaf Font, Brass, 13 1/2 In.	175.00
Lamp, White To Clear, Traces Of Slag, Overlay, 19 3/4 In.	1000.00
Pitcher, Inverted Thumbprint, Enameled Flowers, 9 In.	295.00
Pitcher, Tankard, Sahara	140.00
Pitcher, Water, Beaded Ovals, Green, Gold Trim	75.00
Plate, Eagle & 13 Stars, Octagon, Deep, 7 In.	275.00
Plate, Grapevine & Harp, Medium Blue, 4 1/4 In.	235.00
Plate, Peacock Feather & Thistle, 8 In.	85.00
Plate, Plume & Diamond, Emerald Green, 4 5/8 In.	295.00
Plate, Toddy, Lacy, Medium Blue, 4 3/8 In.	70.00
Platter, Commemorative, Embossed Train, 1880s	85.00
Salt, Boat Shape, Opaque Blue	500.00
Salt, Cable Rim & Bottom, Flint, 2 In.	9.00
Salt, Chariot, Silvery Opaque Blue	600.00
Salt, Christmas, Amber, Pewter Top, Agitator, Dated 1877	95.00
Salt, Eagle, Opalescent	425.00

Salt, H.Clay, Railroad, Footed 1100.00
Salt, Lafayette, Boat Shape, Sapphire, Opaque 800.00
Salt, Thistle Base, Lacy, Clear 195.00
Sauce, Winged Scroll, Custard, Gold, 4 3/4 In. 30.00
Spillholder, Star 425.00
Sugar & Creamer, Ivy, Black Amethyst 200.00
Tieback, Amberina, Ruby Center, Pewter Shank, 3 In., Pair 75.00
Tieback, Opaque White, Pewter Shank, Small, Pair 35.00
Tray, Butterfly, Lacy, 8 In. 225.00
Tray, Card, Scrolled Leaf & Fleur–De–Lis, 7 In. 85.00
Vase, Block & Punty, Goffered Top, Amethyst, 9 1/4 In., Pr. 1200.00
Water Set, Amber Reed Handle, World's Fair, 1893, 6 Pc. 400.00
Whiskey Taster, Vaseline, Loop With Variant 85.00

Utzschneider and Company, a porcelain factory, made ceramics in
Sarreguemines, Lorraine, France, from 1770. Transfer–printed wares
and majolica were made in the nineteenth century. The nineteenth–
century pieces, most often found today, usually had colorful
transfer–printed decorations showing peasants in local costumes.

SARREGUEMINES, Dish, Covered, Underplate, Marked, Gaudy, 10 In. 95.00
Jug, Jolly Man's Face, Turquoise Inside, 6 3/4 In. 60.00
Pitcher, Pink Blossoms & Leaves, 12 In. 45.00
Pitcher, Water, Random Underglaze, Silver Circles, Marked 65.00
Pitcher, Water, Xenia 70.00
Plaque, Hanging, Floral, Majolica 24.00
Plate, Boy & Girl Scene, 8 In. 25.00
Plate, Cherries & Strawberres, Gold Ground, 9 In., 6 Piece 145.00
Plate, Floral, Majolica, Purple, Green, White, 8 In. 17.00
Wall Pocket, Beetle, Iridescent, 9 1/2 In. 95.00

Satin glass is a late nineteenth–century art glass. It has a dull finish
that is caused by a hydrofluoric acid vapor treatment. Satin glass
was made in many colors and sometimes had applied decorations.
Satin glass is also listed by factory name or in the mother–of–pearl
category in this book.

SATIN GLASS, Basket, Green, Gold Ruffled Edge, Reeded Handle, 6 3/4 In. 165.00
Basket, Ruffled, Twisted Rope Handle, Yellow, 6 X 5 In. 145.00
Basket, Water Lily, Blue, 7 In. 30.00
Biscuit Jar, Flowers, Silver Plate Cover, James Tufts Co. 125.00
Biscuit Jar, Gold Bamboo Design, Green To Yellow, 9 In. 900.00
Biscuit, Florette, Puffy, Quilt, Pink To Dark Pink 100.00
Bottle, Perfume, Gold Prunus, Green To Yellow, Webb, 3 1/2 In. 325.00
Bowl, Rose To White To Salmon, Air Traps, Mt.Washington 210.00
Butter, Bead & Drape Pattern, Covered, Red 610.00
Candlestick, Water Lily, White, Pair 30.00
Cracker Jar, Florette, Puffy Pink, Silver Plated Collar, Bail 215.00
Cruet, Blue, Design, 9 In., Pair 265.00
Decanter, Flat Stopper, Engraved Grasses, Leaves, 10 1/2 In. 135.00
Ewer, Enameled Flowers, Frosted Handle, 3 Petal Top, 9 1/4 In. 98.00
Ewer, Melon Sections, Frosted Handle, Jewels, Blue, 10 3/4 In. 135.00
Ewer, Quilted, Yellow, Green Vine & Leaves, Handle, 6 In. 295.00
Finger Bowl, Pink Lining, Moss Roses, White 42.50
Lamp, Drape Pattern, 28 In. 900.00
Pitcher, Enameled Flowers, Foliage, Frosted Handle, Blue, 6 In. 210.00
Rose Bowl, 4 Crimp Top, Flowers, Butterfly, Blue, 5 1/2 In. 135.00
Rose Bowl, 8 Crimp Top, Shaded Blues, Enameled Flowers, Leaves ... 75.00
Rose Bowl, Blue Overlay, Diamond–Quilted, White, 3 1/8 In. 145.00
Rose Bowl, Petit Point Enamel, Dots, Rose Color, 4 In. 325.00
Rose Bowl, Pink, White Enameled Flowers, Maroon Leaves, 5 In. 145.00
Rose Bowl, White Lining, 8 Crimp Top, Leaf Feet, 4 3/4 In. 135.00
Shade, Beaded Drape, Red, 10 In. 200.00
Spooner, Bee & Florals, Enameled 125.00
Syrup, Green Frosted Handle, Enameled Flowers, Red 495.00
Tumbler, Diamond–Quilted, Blue, 4 Oz. 65.00

Tumbler, Diamond–Quilted, Cranberry Shaded To White	80.00
Vase, Art Nouveau Girl, Green, Silver Overlay Is Hair, 4 In.	375.00
Vase, Black, Silver Overlay, 6 3/4 In., Pair	150.00
Vase, Branches, Cherries, Leaves, Outlined In Gold, 8 3/8 In.	150.00
Vase, Crimped, Cranberry With White Loops, Bulbous, 7 In.	175.00
Vase, Crimped, Frosted Handle, Gold Trim, Flowers, Blue, 9 In.	95.00
Vase, Diamond–Quilted, Pink, 5 1/2 In.	98.00
Vase, Frosted Rim Ruffle, Enameled Flowers, 9 1/4 In.	95.00
Vase, Jack–In–The–Pulpit, Pink, White, 6 In.	68.00
Vase, Pink & White, Cornflower Blue Zigzag, C.1890, 8 In.	247.00
Vase, Quatrefoil Mouth, Vine Feet, Enameled Ivy, 3 3/4 In.	65.00
Vase, Rose Overlay, Ribbed, White Lining, Square, 7 3/4 In.	145.00
Vase, Ruffled, Lavender & Gold Foliage, 10 5/8 In.	225.00
Vase, Shaded Peach Overlay, Melon Ribbed, Handle, 12 3/4 In.	210.00
Vase, Wavy Gold Branch Base, Enameled Gold, Foliage, 4 In.	125.00
Water Set, Cane, Yellow, 7 Piece	265.00

SATIN GLASS, WEBB, see Webb

> Satsuma is a Japanese pottery with a distinctive creamy beige
> crackled glaze. Most of the pieces were decorated with blue, red,
> green, orange, or gold. Almost all the Satsuma found today was
> made after 1860. During World War I, Americans could not buy
> undecorated European porcelains. Women who liked to make hand–
> painted porcelains at home began to decorate plain Satsuma. These
> pieces are known today as "American Satsuma."

SATSUMA, Bowl, Design Inside & Out, 10 Lobes Each Quarter, 5 7/16 In.	300.00
Bowl, Ladies of Court In & Out, Gold, Fitted Stand, 1/4 X 1/2 In.	75.00
Bowl, Thousand Faces, Fluted, Scalloped, Gold, Signed, 9 In.	175.00
Buckle, Butterflies, Silver Back	50.00
Creamer, Child's, Child Playing Shuttlecock Scene	25.00
Cricket Cage, Seven Gods of Good Fortune, C.1830, 8 In.	350.00
Dish, Geometric & Flower Design, Oval, 7 7/8 In.	75.00
Dish, Polychrome Fruits & Flowers, Square, 8 1/4 In.	175.00
Eggcup, Florals & Gold, Kinkozan	45.00
Hatpin, Reticulated, Round	135.00
Incense Burner, Thousand Faces, Foo Dog, Elephant Handles, C.1880	350.00
Jar, Carved Teak Cover, Dragon, 19th Century, 13 In. ....*Illus*	950.00
Jar, Warriors, Covered, 18 In.	300.00
Match Holder, Ashtray, Elephant, Brown, Orange, Gold	35.00
Mug, Gold Pagoda, Scenery, Black Matte Finish, 4 5/8 In.	48.00
Plaque, Florals, Hanging Wisteria, Waterbird, C.1900, 9 3/4 In.	190.00
Plate, Bird of Paradise, Flower Design, Underglaze Seal, 7 1/8 In.	75.00
Plate, Gold Florals, Greek Key Border, C.1860, 10 In.	775.00
Plate, Mother & Children In Garden, Floral Border, Signed, 9 In.	290.00
Platter, Floral Design, Gold Trim, Marked, 16 1/4 In.	20.00
Powder Jar, Covered	225.00
Saki Pot, Bamboo Design, Woven Reed Handle, Signed, Miniature	80.00
Salt, Different Flower Center, Set of 4	75.00
Salt, Thousand Faces, 1925	59.00
Teabowl, Thinly Potted, Family Crest, 18th Century, 3 3/4 In.	302.50
Teapot, Brown Speckle, Miniature	15.00
Teapot, Children Playing In Garden, Signed, 4 1/4 X 3 In.	585.00
Teapot, Dragon Shape, C.1880, 8 In.	275.00
Teapot, Enameled Flowers, Meiji Period, C.1900, 3 1/2 In.	275.00
Toothpick, Gold Scrolling, Nishiki Border, C.1868	250.00
Vase, 1000 Butterflies, 6 In.	345.00
Vase, Baluster Shape, Rolled Rim, Enamels, C.1915, 7 X 13 In.	480.00
Vase, Blown–Out Geese, Blue Beading, 12 In.	295.00
Vase, Cobalt, Gold Floral Panel Scene, Bulbous, 2 3/4 In.	42.00
Vase, Disciples, Dragon, Cobalt Blue Ground, 9 1/2 In.	85.00
Vase, Dragon Handles, Meiji Period, 3 5/8 In., Pair	400.00
Vase, Figure Panels, Blue, 5 In.	80.00
Vase, Flared, Handles, Raised Enameling, 12 In.	155.00
Vase, Floral Enameling, Flared, 2 Handles, 20 In.	175.00

Vase, Flowers, Butterflies, Meiji Period, 8 In.	75.00
Vase, Orange To Red, Diaper Design, Bulbous, C.1885, 7 In.	75.00
Vase, Panel of Women In Group, Playing Children, Signed, 5 In.	675.00
Vase, Samurai, 9 1/2 In.	85.00
Vase, Scenic Panels, Ladies, Children, Gilt On Cobalt, 3 1/2 In.	90.00
Vase, Thousand Butterflies, 6 In.	375.00
Vase, Tiger, 3 Molded Figures, With Halos, 9 1/2 In.	190.00
Vase, Warrior, Pottery, 1900, 14 In.	145.00
Vase, Warriors, Green, Gold Trim, Taisho Period, 12 In.	250.00
Vase, Women, C.1900, 8 In.	80.00

Special scales have been made to weigh everything from babies to gold. Collectors search for all types. Most popular are small gold-dust scales and special grocery scales.

SCALE, Alsace–Lorraine, Set Into Wooden Box, 5 X 2 1/2 In.	115.00
American Family, 1902	25.00
Apothecary, Beveled Glass, Brass Pans, Weights, Oak Frame, 1891	335.00
Apothecary, Brass Pans, Marble Top, 19 X 6 X 5 3/8 In.	110.00
Apothecary, Free Standing, Brass, Germany	35.00
Apothecary, Marble & Brass, Patent 1866, 5 Weights	250.00
Apothecary, Marble, Oak Base, 2 Pans, 4 Weights, 18 1/2 X 7 1/4 In.	175.00
Baby, Victorian, Wicker	18.00
Balance, Brass, Mahogany Base, H.P.Crofts & Co., 1 Weight, 24 In.	125.00
Balance, Turned Shaft, Acorn Top, Original Paint, Heart Indicator	390.00
Brass & Iron, Spring, 8 In.	35.00
Chainomatic, Christian Becker, Marble Base, Glass Case, Gold	165.00
Chainomatic, Marble Base, Glass Case, Cherry Trim, Gold	275.00
Chatillon, Milk Scale, Brass Face, Spring, Iron Hooks, 12 In.	40.00
Child's, Iron, Scoop, 3 Weights	35.00
Cotton, Beam, Iron	25.00
Dayton, Model 166, Candy, 1 Lb.	185.00
Egg, Jiffy Way, Red	12.50
Egg, Reliable	18.00
Egg, Zenith, Cast Iron	24.00
Fairbanks, Brass, Postal	65.00
Fairbanks, Upright	100.00
Fribo, Marca Reg., Graduated, Hide, Set	45.00
Gem Postal, Wooden	18.00
Gifford Wood Co., Up To 200 Lbs., Ice	30.00
Grapette Soda, 1 Cent	2200.00
H.Poole & Son Ltd., Birmingham, Stand, Brass, 44 1/2 In.	225.00
Hanson No.1509, Postal, Stainless Steel, 1963	12.00
Henry Troemer, Brass, Patent 1877, Kitchen, 3 Ft.	2500.00
Lollipop, Cast Iron	450.00
Majestic, Counter, Black Paint, Patent 1912	13.00
Miner's, Gold, Improved, Case	195.00
National Specialty No.4, Ornate, Candy	160.00
No.20T, Salter's Spring Balance, British Made, Iron, 23 In.	85.00
Peddler's, Brass Scoop, 3 Iron Weights, 1920s	40.00
Purina, Brass–Faced	85.00
R.C.Cola, Coin–Operated, 1 Cent, Floor Model	850.00
Red Buffalo, Brass Pan, Candy	40.00
Steelyard, 16 In.Arm	25.00
Steelyard, Iron, 3 Hooks, Weight, 22 In.	23.00
Stempson, Grocery	600.00
Store, Hangs From 3 Chains, Round Dial, Tin Scoop	98.00
Tester, Diamond	175.00
Tin Hopper, 8 Brass Weights In Case, Cast Iron, 14 In.	55.00
Toledo, Style 345, Store, Patented 12/25/06	250.00
Winchester Howe, No.47, Brass, Grain	250.00
Wrigley's Gum, Brass Pan & Face, Decals	185.00
Wrigley's Spearmint Pepsin Gum, Brass Scoop, 4 Lb.	225.00

Schafer & Vater, makers of small ceramic items, are best known for their amusing figurals. The factory was located in Volkstedt–Rudolstadt, Germany, from 1890 to 1962. Some pieces are marked with the crown and R mark, but many are unmarked.

SCHAFER & VATER, Ashtray, Figural, Pierced Bald Head	55.00
Bell, Jewels, Crystalline Glaze	100.00
Bottle, Twig Handle, Cherries	30.00
Cigarette Holder, Elephant, Howdah, White	40.00
Creamer, Child With Scarf & Hat, Blue & White	65.00
Creamer, Comical Black Man	95.00
Creamer, Dutch Girl, Basket On Back, Marked	48.00
Creamer, Mother Goose, Bisque, Small	85.00
Dresser Set, Jeweled, Green Trim, 3 Piece	67.50
Figurine, Blue Dog, Says I Am A Gay Dog, 5 1/4 In.	100.00
Flask, A Wee Scotch	55.00
Hair Receiver, Triangular	50.00
Hatpin Holder, Art Nouveau, Lady's Face, Lavender & Green	175.00
Hatpin Holder, Egyptian Series, Pink	95.00 To 125.00
Match Holder, Striker, Green Elephant, Marked, 3 1/4 In.	75.00
Nodder, Bug–Eyed Boy, Fat Cheeks, China, Marked, 4 1/2 In.	110.00
Nodder, Girl With Cat, 4 1/4 In.	195.00
Perfume Bottle, Roses On Green, Figural Stopper, 7 In.	70.00
Pitcher, Bear Holding Muff, 5 In.	95.00
Pitcher, Chinaman Holding Screaming Child, 6 In.	150.00
Pitcher, Comic Black Man	98.00
Pitcher, Jester, Blue & White, Glazed, 5 In.	130.00
Pitcher, Kneeling Witch, Cape & Fan	70.00
Pitcher, Lady, Kerchief, Holding Pitcher, All Blue	70.00
Pitcher, Milk, Chinaman Holding Large Bird, 6 1/4 In.	145.00
Vase, Adam & Eve, Marked, 5 1/4 In.	40.00
Vase, Art Nouveau, Cupid Musicians, Birds, Marked, 5 In.	175.00
Vase, Googly–Eyed Girl Shape, With Teddy Bear, 3 1/2 In.	75.00
Vase, Pink Jasper Upper, Cupid Musicians, Birds, 5 3/8 In.	90.00

Schneider

Schneider Glassworks was founded in 1903 at Epinay–sur–Seine, France, by Charles and Ernest Schneider. Art glass was made between 1903 and 1930. The company still produces clear crystal glass.

SCHNEIDER, Candleholder, Double, Paperweight Base, Clematis, Signed	145.00
Compote, Orange To Yellow Top, Purple Stripe, Signed, 13 In.	350.00
Compote, Orange, Black Base, Signed, Covered, 9 In.	195.00
Compote, Red Stem, Amethyst Bowl, Signed, 10 X 12 In.	650.00
Compote, Tortoise, Burnt Orange, 8 In.	350.00
Inkwell, Yellow & Blue	135.00
Vase, Internal Design, Pedestal Foot, Spatter, 15 3/4 In.	1200.00
Vase, Mottled Rose & Yellow Body, Amethyst Base, Signed, 7 In.	375.00
Vase, Pedestal Base, Orange, Signed, 9 In.	115.00

Scrimshaw is bone or ivory or whale's teeth carved by sailors and others for entertainment during the sailing–ship days. Some scrimshaw was carved as early as 1800. There are modern scrimshanders making pieces today on bone, ivory, or plastic.

SCRIMSHAW, Cribbage Board, Engraved On Tusk, Walrus & Fish, 11 In.	135.00
Ship, Model, Prisoner of War, Case, 14 1/2 In.	3600.00
Swift, 21 In.	700.00
Tooth, Paddlewheeler & Vicksburg, Eagle, Guns, Flag	200.00
Tooth, Peacock, On Stand, Boy & Girl Marching Other Side	1095.00
Tooth, Ship Scene, 9 In.	600.00
Tooth, Ship, Clouds, Gulls, Walnut Base, 2 1/4 In.	50.00
Tooth, Wall Basket, Flowers, Tree, Leaning Ladder Other Side	795.00
Tusk, Ivory, Whaling Scene, Dated 1841	1250.00
Walrus Tusk, John Paul Jones, Battle Scene, War of 1779	500.00

Walrus Tusk, Whaling Ship, Birds, American Flags, 1842, 24 In. 2000.00

Prescott W. Baston made the first Sebastian miniatures in 1938 in Marblehead, Massachusetts. More than 400 different designs have been made and the collectors search for the out–of–production models. The mark may say "Copr. P. W. Baston U.S.A.," or "P. W. Baston, U.S.A.," or "Prescott W. Baston." Sometimes a paper label was used.

SEBASTIAN MINIATURES, Amish Folk, Green Label 20.00
  Annie Oakley & Buffalo Bill, Pair 85.00
  Betsy Ross 48.00
  Bob Cratchit & Tiny Tim 55.00
  Clown, No.30B 70.00
  Cranberry Picker 10.00
  Drummer Boy, Green Label 20.00
  Family Picnic, Yellow Label 40.00
  George Washington, Yellow Label 28.00
  James Monroe & Elizabeth Monroe, Pair 195.00
  John Smith & Pocahontas 195.00
  Lion, 1947 .... 25.00
  Lobsterman, 1947 .... 45.00
  Madonna of The Chair 48.00
  Martha Washington 45.00
  Mayflower 75.00
  Mrs.Cratchit & The Pudding, Green 75.00
  Old Salt, 1950 .... 100.00
  Paul Bunyan, Green Label 100.00
  Paul Revere, Marblehead Label 95.00
  Penny Shop, 1951 .... 100.00
  Peter Stuyvesant, Orange Label, Signed R.Burrows 20.00
  Piano Player, Blue Label 20.00
  Pilgrims 60.00
  Rip Van Winkle, Box 25.00
  Sailing Days, Orange Label, Pair 35.00
  Sam Houston & Margaret Houston, Pair 110.00
  Santa Claus, Green Label .... 17.00 To 35.00
  School Days 25.00
  Scrooge, Blue Label 17.00
  Shaker Man & Woman, Pair 125.00
  Sidewalk Days, Green Label, Pair 60.00
  Snow Days 25.00
  Speak For It, 7 X 3 1/2 In. 35.00
  Spirit of '76, Marblehead Label 100.00
  Uncle Sam, Blue Label 20.00
  SEG, see Paul Revere Pottery

Sevres porcelain has been made in Sevres, France, since 1769. Many copies of the famous ware have been made. The name originally referred to the works of the Royal Porcelain factory. The name now includes any of the wares made in the town of Sevres, France. The entwined lines with a center letter used as the mark is one of the most forged marks in antiques. Be very careful to identify Sevres by quality, not just by mark.

SEVRES, Bowl, Blue, Fluted, Silver Pedestal, 8 In. 150.00
  Bowl, Flowers, Gilt Border, Bronze Handles & Feet, Marked, 17 In. 715.00
  Bowl, Start of The Hunt Scene, Holly Leaves, 7 In. 30.00
  Box, Roses On Cover, Brass Hinges & Mounts, Round, 2 3/4 In. 150.00
  Candelabra, 4–Light, Putti, Jeweled, Bronze Handles, 26 In., Pair 3300.00
  Candelabra, Bronze Mounted, Louis XVI Style, 4–Candle, 35 In., Pair 3850.00
  Candelabra, Jewel Mounted, Gilt Bronze Fittings, 25 In., Pair 2750.00
  Cup & Saucer, Cupids, 1800s .... 70.00 To 75.00
  Garniture, Clock, Candelabra, Courting Couples, 19th Century, 3 Pc. 1540.00
  Jar, Trinket, Floral Inside & Out, Lady Portrait, Signed, 4 In. 450.00
  Lamp, Crystal Spiral, Pale Green, C.1920 .... 120.00

Sevres, Vase, Couples Sitting On Ground,
Marked, 31 1/8 In.

Silver–Danish, Compote, Vine Stem,
Georg Jensen, C.1949, 12 In.

Sevres, Vase, Classical Figures, 36 In.

Mug, Champion Dog On Side, Brown Tones, 5 In.		45.00
Plate, Center Court Picture, Signed Delacroix, 10 In., Set of 12		2300.00
Plate, Doves, Flowers, Ribbons, Scalloped, Signed, 1846		200.00
Plate, Hunting Scenes, Sprays of Holly Leaves, 6 In., Set of 6		95.00
Plate, Napoleon, Putti, Monogram, C.1859, 9 1/2 In.		90.00
Plate, Napoleon, Various Scenes, C.1900, Guillou, 9 3/8 In., Set of 6		1750.00
Plate, Portrait, Duchess De Bourgogne, Gold Trim, Blue, 9 1/2 In.		135.00
Plate, Portrait, Madame DuBarry		125.00
Plate, Rai De Rome, Gold Trim, Signed		175.00
Platter, 2 Maidens, Monument, Gilt Metal, Froger, Oval, 21 1/2 In.		995.00
Potpourri, Louis XVI, Covered, Snake Handles, Socle, 12 In., Pair		3575.00
Tabletop, Louis XVI Center, Marie Antoinette Top, C.1880, 19 In.		1025.00
Tray, Maidens Strolling, River, Gilt Metal, Poitevin, 23 1/2 In.		2090.00
Urn, Colonial Maiden Scene, Ormolu Handles, Brass Footed, 9 1/4 In.		185.00
Urn, Covered, Raised Gold Lily Pads Over Body, Signed, 10 In.		425.00
Urn, Napoleon Battlefield Scene, Ormolu, Desprez, 38 In.		1000.00
Urn, Portrait & Scene, Pastels, Gold Ornaments, Brass Base, 28 In.		775.00
Urn, Portrait Front, 2 Handles, Marked, 8 1/2 In.		135.00
Urn, Portrait, Marked, 7 1/2 In.		225.00
Urn, Portrait, Scene, Gold Ornaments, Brass Base & Top, 28 In.		775.00
Vase, Butterflies, Mauve Ground, Ribbon At Neck, 8 In.		690.00
Vase, Classical Figures, 36 In.	*Illus*	1650.00
Vase, Couple, Country Scene, Bronze Handles, Marked, 25 In., Pr.		2860.00
Vase, Couples Sitting On Ground, Marked, 31 1/8 In.	*Illus*	1760.00
Vase, Covered, Courting Couple, Bronze Mount, 1900, Marked, 40 In.		2310.00
Vase, Covered, Gilt Bronze, Coy Maiden Panels, 31 3/4 In., Pair		5775.00
Vase, Covered, Maiden & Putto, Gilt Bronze, Lamp Mounted, 36 In.		880.00
Vase, Covered, Shepherd Lovers, Gilt Borders, 28 3/8 In., Pair		5775.00
Vase, Frieze, Maiden On Staircase, Joins Lover In Gondola, 33 In.		1870.00
Vase, Gilt Bronze Mounted, Flared Rim, Metal Figure Putto, 21 In.		1210.00
Vase, Gilt Bronze Mounted, Ladies & Gentlemen, Strolling, 36 In.		1320.00
Vase, Hand Painted Scenes, 1800s, 12 In.		150.00
Vase, Napoleon Scene, Swan's Neck Handles, Gilt Bronze, 23 In.		1320.00
Vase, Napoleon, Covered, Gilt Bronze Handles, Vigion, 23 In., Pair		1540.00
Vase, Pinched Sides, Hexagon Shape, Paper & Label, 5 X 10 1/2 In.		350.00
Vase, Stand, Frieze, Coy Maiden, Landscape, Marked, C.1900, 27 3/4 In.		2420.00
Vase, Woodland Scene, Reverse Painted, Mounted As Lamp, 22 1/2 In.		1540.00

Sewer tile figures were made by workers at the sewer tile and pipe factories in the Ohio area during the late nineteenth and early twentieth centuries. Figurines, small vases, and cemetery vases were favored. Often the finished vase was a piece of the original pipe with added decorations and markings. All types of sewer tile work are now considered folk art by collectors.

SEWER TILE, Bank, Frog, Ohio Sewer Tile, 6 X 9 In. 65.00
  Collander, Curved Handle, 7 3/4 X 13 In. 55.00
  Collie, Standing, Square Base, Incised Kyte, 11 1/4 In. 220.00
  Dog, Seated, Dark Brown Glaze, 7 3/4 In. 100.00
  Dog, Seated, Incised Head, Collar, Feet, Brown Glaze, 10 In. 85.00
  Figurine, Dog, Seated, Tooled Coat, 3 In. 195.00
  Figurine, Naughty Frog, What Cheer, Iowa 90.00
  Lamp Base, Nude, Lying, Lion, Square Base 850.00
  Lion, Brown Glaze, Rectangular Base, 8 In. 125.00
  Match Holder, Squat Bell Tile Shape, Impressed Label, 2 In. 10.00
  Peasant Girl, With Water Jug, Gray Salt Glaze, 17 3/4 In. 850.00
  Squirrel, With Nut, 7 1/2 In. 15.00
  Trunk, Lion & Nude Lady, J.W.Moore, 1928, 25 X 14 In. 850.00
  Whimsey, Fly Swatter Shape, Bust of Man At Base, 5 3/4 In. 55.00

All types of sewing equipment are collected, from sewing birds that held the cloth to old wooden spools.

SEWING, Basket, Fitted, Thimble, Woven Needle & Scissors Case, Scissors 85.00
  Basket, Reed, Splint, Basketweave Design Interior & Cover, 9 In. 22.00
  Basket, Wicker, Heywood–Wakefield Tag 225.00
  Bird Clamp, Brass, Dated 1853 .... 175.00
  Bird, Brass, Pincushion, Dated Feb.15, 1853 .... 150.00
  Bird, Double Cushions, Twist Knob, Patent 1854 .... 85.00
  Bird, Double Pincushion, Brass, Dated 1853, 5 1/2 In. 165.00
  Bird, Original Cushion, Brass, 1853 .... 175.00
  Bird, Table Clamp, Silver Gilt, Red Plush Pincushion, 5 In. 190.00
  Bird, Wooden, Ivory 35.00
  Bodkin, Folding Scrimshaw, Triple 52.00
  Box, Bird's–Eye Maple, Hinged Cover, Ring Handles, 4 X 9 X 12 In. 200.00
  Box, Figural, Perambulator, American, C.1890 .... 400.00
  Box, Lacquer, Claw Feet, Allover Oriental Screws, Ivory Fittings 425.00
  Box, Lacquer, Fitted Interior, China, Mid–19th Century, 22 X 8 In. 150.00
  Box, Scrimshaw, Inlaid, Dovetailed, Wooden, 1850 .... 70.00
  Box, Velvet Covered Lid, Heart Shape, 5 In. 125.00
  Cabinet, Spool, Clark's, 6 Drawers, Ruby Glass, Walnut 795.00
  Cabinet, Spool, Slant Front, Shelf, 1 Drawer, 1830, 6 X 9 X 10 In. 175.00
  Caddy, 4 Drawers, Pedestal Base, Turned Wood, 9 X 11 In. 55.00
  Caddy, Thread, Drawer, Pincushion, Dark Finish, 7 5/8 In. 25.00
  Case, Needle & Shuttle, Boye 100.00
  Case, Needle, Glass & Wooden Case 55.00
  Case, Needle, New Simplicity, Tin 28.00
  Casket, Pin, Footed, Figural Leaf Slide Lid, English, Brass, C.1882 .... 135.00
  Darner, Foot Form, Amethyst Glass 25.00
  Darner, Glove, 4 Rows of Beading, Applied Ring, Sterling Silver 45.00
  Darner, Glove, Attached Top, 4 Rows of Beading, Sterling Silver 48.00
  Darner, Glove, Embossed Mums, Sterling Silver, Marked, 4 In. 40.00
  Darner, Glove, Repousse Nouveau Design, Sterling Silver, 4 1/2 In. 42.00
  Dress Form, Child's, Rear, Iron Stand, Size 4 .... 195.00
  Gauge, Dressmaker's, Picken, Metal, Dated 1915, 6 In. 8.00
  Gauge, Skirt, Simplicity, Box, 1929 .... 7.00
  Machine, Jones & Co., With Cover 85.00
  Machine, Kayanee, Metal, 8 In. 45.00
  Machine, Kenmore, Treadle, Oak 175.00
  Machine, Little Comfort Improved, 1896, Cast Iron, Chrome, Miniature 125.00
  Machine, National, Cast Iron, Small 275.00
  Machine, Naumann, England 298.00
  Machine, Western Electric, Gooseneck 40.00

Machine, Wilcox & Gibbs, Instruction Booklet, Papers 65.00
Machine, Wilcox Gibbs, Mounted On Wood 95.00
Needle Case, Carved Vegetable Ivory, Acorn Shape Each End, 3 In. 95.00
Needle Case, Figural, Umbrella, Ivory 115.00
Needle Case, Quadruple Golden Casket, Hinged Top, C.1880 .... 125.00
Needle Case, R.J.Roberts, Cardboard, Brass Binding, Sliding Board 5.00
Needle Case, Wooden, Carved Boxwood, 1820–40 .... 85.00
Needle Roll, Drawstring Pouch & Tape Ties, C.1800, 14 3/4 In. 195.00
Needle, Shuttle, Bobbin Tin, With Contents, Boye 45.00
Needlepoint Frame, Walnut, Handmade Attached Note Pad, 1877 .... 77.50
Pincushion & Pin Box, Collingbourne's Pure Silk, Tin 14.00
Pincushion & Tape Measure, Pot–Bellied Stove, Porcelain 9.00
SEWING, PINCUSHION DOLL, see Pincushion Doll
Pincushion, Bisque Boy, Holding Dog, Sits On Cushion 18.00
Pincushion, Butterfly, Brass, Worn Silver Finish, Pat.1852, 5 In. 485.00
Pincushion, Coolie, Occupied Japan 20.00
Pincushion, Cowrie Shell, Steel, 6 1/2 In. 155.00
Pincushion, Indian's Head, Metal, Occupied Japan 10.00
Pincushion, Jockey Cap 30.00
Pincushion, Pig, Brass 85.00
Pincushion, Pillsbury 12.00
Pincushion, Seated Black Woman, Watermelon In Lap, 5 In. 30.00
Pincushion, Victorian, Heart Shape, Beading 65.00
Punch, Eyelet, With Gauge, Sterling Silver, Engraved Handle 30.00
Punch, Floral Handle, Silver 35.00
Scissors, Buttonhole 20.00
Scissors, Embroidery, Repousse & Beading, Marked, Sterling Silver 32.00
Scissors, Embroidery, Stork Figure, Germany 20.00
Shuttle, Engraved Floral, Sterling Silver 85.00
Shuttle, Engraved, Sterling, Marked 80.00
Shuttle, Tatting, Ivory, 19th Century 34.00
Spool Holder, 2–Tier, Drawer Pull Finial, Wire Support, Black Paint 200.00
Spool Holder, Ivory Butter Churn, 1890s, 1 3/4 X 1 In. 84.00
Tape Measure, Airlington Skirt, Colored Petticoats, N.Y.C. 45.00
Tape Measure, Alligator, Pink, Green & Black, 7 1/2 In. 18.00
Tape Measure, Baseball Player, Celluloid 24.00
Tape Measure, Bear, Plush, 1930s 22.00
Tape Measure, Black Mammy, Ladybug Pull, Celluloid 48.00
Tape Measure, Carter's Paper, Boston, Celluloid 20.00
Tape Measure, Cat, Playing With Brass Ball, Wind Tail, Metal 75.00
Tape Measure, DeLaval 40.00
Tape Measure, Donald Duck, Celluloid 100.00
Tape Measure, Dutch Girl, Pottery, German 22.00
Tape Measure, Dutch Lady, Celluloid 35.00
Tape Measure, Egg, Fly Pull, Tin 30.00
Tape Measure, Fab, Celluloid 23.00
Tape Measure, Flamingo 40.00
Tape Measure, Frigidaire, Iceman 32.50
Tape Measure, Fruit Basket, Celluloid 15.00
Tape Measure, I Made Kentucky Famous In A Measure, Cap Pulls Out 65.00
Tape Measure, Kangaroo, Celluloid 15.00
Tape Measure, Lewis Lye .... 25.00 To 35.00
Tape Measure, Lydia Pinkham, Celluloid 35.00
Tape Measure, Madame Pompadour Style Lady On Top, Celluloid 17.50
Tape Measure, Model of Ship In Full Sail, Celluloid, Japan 50.00
Tape Measure, Pig, Brass, With Coin In Mouth 89.00
Tape Measure, Pig, Celluloid .... 22.00 To 35.00
Tape Measure, Reclining Bathing Beauty, Green Shoes, Germany 35.00
Tape Measure, Sailing Ship 40.00
Tape Measure, Ship, Celluloid 25.00
Tape Measure, Straw Hat Shape, Says Hats Cover Head, Covers Feet 55.00
Tape Measure, Swift & Co. 28.00
Tape Measure, Swiss Cleansing Co., Celluloid, Swiss Maid 28.00
Tape Measure, Turtle, Pull My Head, Not My Leg, Metal, 1 1/2 In. 85.00

Tape Measure, Vacha FDA Florist 15.00
Tatting Shuttle, Ivory 32.00
Tatting Shuttle, Sterling Silver 25.00
Thimble Case & Thimble, Carvings, Acorn Design, Vegetable Ivory 95.00
Thimble Holder, Crocheted Basket, Applied Flowers 5.00
Thimble Holder, Festival Hall Shape, Brass, St.Louis, 1904 .... 120.00
Thimble, 12–Sided, Engraved, 14K Gold, Size 7 .... 90.00
Thimble, 14k Gold, Panels, Engraved Initials, Wicker Holder, Size 7 .... 75.00
Thimble, 14K Gold, Simon Bros., Philadelphia 98.00
Thimble, Allover Daisy Pattern, Royal Spa, Sterling, Horner, 1938 .... 69.00
Thimble, Blue Willow, Bone China, Staffordshire 8.00
Thimble, Child's, For A Good Girl 4.00
Thimble, Circles With Star Centers, Shield With S Mark, Size 11 .... 30.00
Thimble, House Scene, Marked, Sterling Silver 40.00
Thimble, Ivory, Scrimshaw, Ship, Flowers 15.00
Thimble, Scene of House, Mountains, Sterling Silver, Size 7 .... 40.00
Thimble, Scissors & Pincushion, Sterling, C.1870, Miniature, 3 Piece 184.00
Thimble, Silver Sterling, Floral Border, No.8, Box 30.00
Thimble, Simon Bros., 14K Gold 100.00

Shaker–produced items are characterized by simplicity, functionalism, and orderliness. There were many Shaker communities in America from the eighteenth century to the present day. The religious order made furniture, small wooden pieces, and packaged medicines, herbs, and jellies to sell to "outsiders." Other useful objects were made for use by members of the community.

SHAKER, Baker's Box, Pine, Turned Maple Rolling Pin, 2 Piece 500.00
Basket, Berry, Metal Rims Top & Bottom, Dated 1859, 3 1/4 X 3 In. 150.00
Basket, Cheese, Support Rails, Hexagonal Weave, Round, 9 In. 185.00
Basket, Handle, Covered, 10 X 9 In. 65.00
Basket, Maple Splint, Side Handles, Large 400.00
Basket, Picnic, Enfield, Oval, 12 In. 165.00
Basket, Sewing, Fully Fitted, Sabbathday Lake, Maine 150.00
Basket, Sewing, Round Top, Octagon Base, Brown Patterns, 10 In. 150.00
Beater, Carpet, Bentwood 65.00
Bonnet, Black, Machine Sewn, 12 1/2 In. 17.50
Bonnet, Folding, Cotton, With Polar Stays 65.00
Bonnet, Palm & Straw, Black Ribbons, Silk Flounce, S.Union, Ky. 385.00
Box, 1–Finger, Copper Tacks, Oval, 6 1/2 In. 55.00
Box, 4–Finger, Oval, 10 In. 235.00
Box, Copper Fasteners, Oval, Fingered, Small 120.00
Box, Covered, Labeled Thread, Chalk Measures For Quilt, Cherry, Pine 500.00
Box, Knife, Gray Paint 50.00
Box, Pantry, 5 1/4 In. 85.00
Box, Red, Oval, 8 In. 65.00
Box, Sewing, 2 Drawers, Fitted, Butternut, C.1820, 7 1/2 X 8 In. 7750.00
Box, Sewing, Various Hardwoods, Natural, 1 Drawer, 7 In. 45.00
Box, Shaker Vegetable Seed Co., Wooden 750.00
Box, Storage, 1–Finger Fitted Cover, Cherry, 5 1/2 X 9 1/2 X 13 In. 450.00
Box, Utility, Poplar, Breadboard Ends, Well, 5 X 14 In. 330.00
Box, Wooden, Oval, 5 In. 20.00
Bucket, Berry, Bail Handle, Design 225.00
Bucket, Fixed Bail Handle, Oak, Pine, Stained Red, Signed, C.1850 .... 350.00
Bucket, Sap, Stave, Iron Bands & Hanger, Impressed Mark, 11 In. 145.00
Bucket, Stave, Wooden Handle, Wire Bale, Yellow, No.21, 9 1/4 In. 350.00
Carrier, Maple, Pine, Oval, 2 Tapered Fingers, Handle, 8 X 15 In. 330.00
Clothespin 10.00
Coffeepot, Sabbathday Lake, Maine, Tin, 5 3/4 In. 125.00
Creel, Sabbathday Lake, Maine, Late 19th Century 310.00
Darner, 5 In. 75.00
Doll, Pen Wiper 75.00
Drainer, Cheese, Tin, 1 In.Holes, Handles, 6 X 18 In.Diam. 125.00
Firkin, Pine, Maple, 1–Finger Over Lid, Gray Paint, C.1860, 22 In. 440.00

Funnel, Great Barn, Large 125.00
SHAKER, FURNITURE, see Furniture
Grater, Corn 325.00
Hanger, Marked, Set of 4 .... 350.00
Herb Ladder, Cabinet Finish, 7 1/2 X 18 1/4 In. 260.00
Kettle, Apple Butter, Iron Handle, Copper, Large 285.00
Masher, Herb, Mushroom Shape, Wooden, Round, 5 In. 37.50
Pail, Covered, Mt.Lebanon, Original Old Green Paint 85.00
Pie Lifter 32.50
Pincushion, Alfred, Me. 75.00
Print, Shakers Near Lebanon, Hand Colored, Framed, 13 X 16 In. 635.00
Rack, Drying, Gray Paint, Shoe Feet, C.1830, 26 X 42 In. 192.00
Rake, Hay, Mt.Lebanon, Detachable Handle 275.00
Shelf, Wall, Birch, New Hampshire, 6 Shelves, C.1840, 48 X 34 In. 825.00
Sieve, Horsehair, 6 X 13 In. 150.00
Tape, New Lebanon, New York, Blue & White, 1874–1900, 13 Yards 40.00
Tool, Corn Sheller, Red Finish, Fastens On Bench, 8 X 21 In. 145.00
Tool, Straight Edge, Elliptical Cutouts, Double Beveled Edge 225.00
Trivet, Cast Iron, Geometric, 3 1/2 X 4 5/8 In. 25.00
Whip, Ivory Handle 40.00

Shaving mugs were popular from 1860 to 1900. Many types were made, including occupational mugs featuring pictures of men's jobs. There were scuttle mugs, silver plated mugs, glass-lined mugs, and others.

SHAVING MUG, A.O.U.W., Fraternal 225.00
American Legion 200.00
Ancient Order of United Workmen, Name In Gold 95.00
Avon, Train, Full Color Iron Horse 25.00
BPOE, Elk's Head, Owner's Name, Limoges 60.00
Brushed Blue Floral Design, Stoneware 2400.00
Bulldog Head, Cream & Gray, Black Trim, S.J.Johore Mark, 4 In. 118.00
Bust of President Garfield & Wife, 2 Cups 185.00
English Hunt Scene, Blue & White, Early 19th Century 95.00
F.O.E., Fraternal .... 200.00 To 225.00
Foley Scuttle 35.00
Horsedrawn Fire Wagon, Germany .... 195.00 To 295.00
Horsehead Transfer, Aqua Rim 19.50
Jasperware, 3 Grooming Scenes 145.00
Knights of Columbus, Name In Gold 110.00
M.W.A., Fraternal 130.00
Masonic, 32nd Degree 275.00
Occupational, 2 Horses, Lightning, Name 100.00
Occupational, Bartender .... 250.00 To 350.00
Occupational, Batter & Catcher 200.00
Occupational, Boiler Maker, Man With Sledge 375.00
Occupational, Bootmaker 350.00
Occupational, Brewmaster, Wooden Vat, Tools, Barley, Hops 500.00
Occupational, Brotherhood of Railroad Trainmen, Flags 75.00
Occupational, Bull's Head & Tools, C.A.Cole 125.00
Occupational, Butcher 275.00
Occupational, Caboose 350.00
Occupational, Carpenter 275.00
Occupational, Comic Actor, Holding Banner, His Name On It 325.00
Occupational, Doctor 100.00
Occupational, Draper, Barrett & Harley, N.Y., Gold Rod, Tassel 178.00
Occupational, Druggist 200.00
Occupational, Farrier 475.00
Occupational, Fruit & Vegetable Wagon 375.00
Occupational, Fruit Wagon 375.00
Occupational, Grocery Store 375.00
Occupational, House Mover 250.00
Occupational, Hunter With Bird Dog, Shooting Bird 275.00
Occupational, L.& N. R.R., Steam Locomotive 400.00

Occupational, Oilman 300.00
Occupational, Pool Player 75.00
Occupational, Printer .... 275.00 To 400.00
Occupational, Sewing Machine Salesman 275.00
Occupational, Square, Saw, Plane, Chisel 150.00
Occupational, Steam Engine & Ender, B.of L.F. & E. 400.00
Occupational, Telegrapher .... 325.00 To 350.00
Occupational, Tinsmith, Stove & Tools, Name In Gold 225.00
Occupational, Train Picture 100.00
Occupational, Trumpet 250.00
Occupational, Union Official, UMW 325.00
Oddfellow, Fraternal 175.00
Pearlized Floral, Germany 45.00
Redware, Strap Handle, Holder For Soap & Brush, 4 3/8 In. 200.00
Remember Me, Gilt Trim, Germany 23.00
Royal Arcanum 250.00
Scuttle, Elephant 65.00
Scuttle, Hand Painted Florals, Marked Union Shaving Mug, 1870 .... 45.00
Skull 50.00
Snow Flower, Pine Ground, With Gold Overlay, R.S.Prussia 98.00
St.Bernard Dog, German· 27.50
Think of Me, Gilt Trim, Germany 23.00
Tin, Civil War Handles, Open Side Pocket 57.00
Vicks Vaporub 70.00

Shawnee USA The Shawnee Pottery was started in Zanesville, Ohio, in 1935. The company made vases, novelty ware, flowerpots, figurines, dinnerwares, and cookie jars. Shawnee produced pottery for George Rumrill during the late 1930s. The company stopped working in 1961.

SHAWNEE, Ashtray, Squirrel 12.00
Bank, Owl 50.00
Bank, Smiley Pig, Gold 155.00
Bank, Winnie Pig 85.00
Bowl, Corn King, 6 1/2 In. .... 17.00 To 20.00
Bowl, Corn King, Round, 8 In. 22.00
Bowl, King Corn, No.5 .... 9.00
Candleholder, Green 8.00
Casserole, Corn King, Individual 22.50
Casserole, Corn King, No.74 .... 35.00
Casserole, Covered, Corn King, Large 18.00
Casserole, Individual, Corn King 30.00
Cookie Jar, Clown 75.00
Cookie Jar, Cookie House .... 200.00 To 250.00
Cookie Jar, Cookie Monster 20.00
Cookie Jar, Corn King .... 55.00 To 75.00
Cookie Jar, Drummer Boy 85.00
Cookie Jar, Dutch Boy .... 32.00 To 55.00
Cookie Jar, Dutch Boy, Patches & Gold Trim .... 95.00 To 125.00
Cookie Jar, Dutch Boy, Striped Pants 55.00
Cookie Jar, Dutch Girl .... 35.00 To 55.00
Cookie Jar, Dutch Girl, Tulip, Gold Trim, Decals 115.00
Cookie Jar, Elephant, Pink .... 38.00 To 50.00
Cookie Jar, Farmer Pig .... 35.00 To 65.00
Cookie Jar, Fruit Basket 38.00
Cookie Jar, Ma & Pa Pig, Pair 85.00
Cookie Jar, Mugsey .... 50.00 To 100.00
Cookie Jar, Owl 75.00
Cookie Jar, Pig 20.00
Cookie Jar, Puss 'N Boots .... 35.00 To 45.00
Cookie Jar, Puss 'N Boots, White Bow, Gold Trim, Decals 110.00
Cookie Jar, Sailor Boy .... 25.00 To 30.00
Cookie Jar, Smiley Pig, Blue Bandana 60.00
Cookie Jar, Smiley Pig, Blue Bandana, Gold Trim, Decals 100.00

Cookie Jar, Smiley Pig, Red Bandana, Gold Trim, Decals 115.00
Cookie Jar, Smiley Pig, Shamrocks 60.00
Cookie Jar, Winking Owl 55.00
Cookie Jar, Winnie Pig, Gold, Red & Gold Trim 225.00
Cookie Jar, Winnie Pig, Green Collar .... 50.00 To 69.00
Creamer, Corn King .... 6.00 To 10.00
Creamer, Elephant .... 10.00 To 18.00
Creamer, Pig, Yellow 22.00
Creamer, Puss 'N Boots .... 8.00 To 20.00
Creamer, Puss 'N Boots, Green & Yellow, Gold Trim 49.00
Creamer, Smiley Pig, Yellow & Blue 12.00
Dish, Corn King, Set of 6 .... 25.00
Figurine, Rabbit 22.00
Mug, Corn King 15.00
Pitcher, Bopeep, Gold Trim 75.00
Pitcher, Bopeep, Gold, Hand Painted, Decals 90.00
Pitcher, Bopeep, Peach Trim 44.00
Pitcher, Cat .... 10.00 To 15.00
Pitcher, Chanticleer 27.00
Pitcher, Chanticleer, Gold Decals .... 75.00 To 100.00
Pitcher, Chicken, Large 19.00
Pitcher, Corn King, 5 In. 17.00
Pitcher, Fruit Design, Tilted 19.00
Pitcher, Granny 35.00
Pitcher, Little Boy Blue, Gold Trim 75.00
Pitcher, Smiley Pig 55.00
Planter, Baby Buggy 7.50
Planter, Baby Shoe 3.00
Planter, Bird .... 11.00 To 35.00
Planter, Boy, With Wheelbarrow 14.00
Planter, Bull 35.00
Planter, Burro, No.722 .... 15.00
Planter, Caboose 8.00
Planter, Duck, Gold Trim 10.00
Planter, Elephant, Black, Pink Base 20.00
Planter, Fawn & Doe, No.669 .... 12.00
Planter, Giraffe 9.00
Planter, Man, With Pushcart, No.621 .... 12.00
Planter, Pump 9.00
Planter, Skunk 9.00
Planter, Watering Can, Pink 8.00
Planter, Wishing Well, Dutch Boy & Girl .... 12.00 To 15.00
Plate, Corn King, 6 In. 20.00
Relish, Corn Queen 10.00
Salt & Pepper, Bopeep, Gold Trim 18.00
Salt & Pepper, Cat 15.00
Salt & Pepper, Corn King, 6 In. 22.00
Salt & Pepper, Cowboy 14.00
Salt & Pepper, Duck 18.00
Salt & Pepper, Dutch Boy & Girl 12.00
Salt & Pepper, Milk Pail 7.50
Salt & Pepper, Mugsey 12.00
Salt & Pepper, Owl .... 5.00 To 12.50
Salt & Pepper, Puss 'N Boots, Gold 85.00
Salt & Pepper, Rooster, Large 18.00
Salt & Pepper, Sailor, Gold Trim 18.00
Salt & Pepper, Swiss Children 20.00
Saucer, Corn King, 8 1/2 In. 20.00
Teapot, Blue Floral 18.00
Teapot, Cookie House 200.00
Teapot, Corn King 28.00
Teapot, Corn Queen 58.00
Teapot, Elephant, Yellow 50.00
Teapot, Granny Ann, Lavender Apron 44.00

Teapot, Rose & Green Floral	18.00
Teapot, Tom Tom The Piper's Son, White & Brown Base	40.00
Toothbrush Holder, Dutch Boy	35.00
Toothbrush Holder, Elephant, Pink	65.00
Vase, Cameo, Green & White, 9 In.	15.00
Wall Pocket, Bird House	10.00
Wall Pocket, Girl & Rag Doll, No.810	15.00
Wall Pocket, Grandfather Clock, Gold Trim	20.00

The Shearwater pottery is a family business started by Mr. and Mrs. G. W. Anderson, Sr., and their three sons. The local Ocean Springs, Mississippi, clays were used to make the wares in the 1930s.

SHEARWATER, Candlestick, 5 1/2 In.	55.00
Cup & Saucer, Oriental, Mint Green, Marked	36.00
Figurine, Pirate, Standing, Hands Crossed, 5 In.	23.00
Teapot, Blue	125.00
Tumbler, 4 1/4 In.	35.00
Vase, Blue & Gray Gloss, 4 In.	18.00
Vase, Blue Flambe, 5 1/2 In.	150.00
Vase, Bulbous, Handles, Green, 5 1/4 In.	135.00
Vase, Funnel, Blue Flambe Glaze, Olive Green, 5 In.	45.00
Vase, Gunmetal Green, Circle Mark, 6 X 8 1/2 In.	70.00
Vase, Olive Green, Beige & Blue Drip, Circular Mark, 5 In.	85.00

Sheet music from the past centuries is now collected. The favorites are examples with covers with artistic or historic pictures. Early sheet music covers were lithographed but by the 1900s photographic reproductions were used. The early music was larger than more recent sheets and you must watch out for examples that were trimmed to fit in a twentieth–century piano bench.

SHEET MUSIC, Abide Wih Me, Nick Manoloff, 1935	1.00
Allegheny Moon, Patti Page, 1956	5.00
Alone, A Night At The Opera, Marx Brothers, 1935	10.00
Amos & Andy	12.00
As Time Goes By, Bogart & Bergman, Casablanca	30.00
Autumn of My Life, Bobby Goldsboro, 1968	1.25
Barney Google, Spark Plug On Cover, 1923	8.00 To 15.00
Beautiful Blue Danube, J.Strauss, 1926	1.00
Beautiful Star of Heaven, Louis A.Drumheller, 1906	1.50
Begin The Beguine, Cole Porter, 1935	1.00
Black Hawk Waltz, Picture of Indian, 1908	5.00
Black Smoke, 1903	12.50
Blue Hawaii, 1929	.50
Blue Hawaii, Leo Robin, Ralph Rainger, 1937	1.00
Break The News To Mother, Battle Scene Drawings, 1898	10.00
By Radio Phone, Girl Operator On Cover, 1922	15.00
By The Sad Potomac Shore Or Death of Col.Baker, Civil War	9.00
By The Saskatchewan, C.M.S.McLellan, Ivan Caryll, 1910	1.00
By The Watermelon Vine Lindy Lou, 1904, Large	4.50
Call Me Irresponsible, Jackie Gleason Picture Cover, 1962	6.00
Canadian Sunset, Gimbel & Heywood, 1956	1.75
Cascades, View of St.Louis Expo On Cover, Scott Joplin	27.50
Charley My Boy, Boy In Collegiate Clothes, 1924	.75
Chicago Day Waltz, Columbian Exposition, 10–9–1893	35.00
Chicken Reel, Black Dancers On Cover	15.00
Come Kiss Yo Charcoal Baby, Framed, Horton, 15 X 16 In.	25.00
Come On You Athletics, Philadelphia A's Baseball Team, 1928	2.00
Cool Places, Ron Mael, Russell Mael, 1983	1.50
Cubs On Parade, Frank Chance, Picture, Framed, 1907	85.00
Dancing With Tears In My Eyes, Rudy Vallee, 1929	7.50
Daybreak, Ferde Grofe, Harold Adamson, 1942	1.25
Dearie, B.Hilliard, D.Mann, 1950	1.25

Deep Purple, Peter DeRose, Piano Solo, 1934	1.00
Down By The Old Mill Stream, Will Oakland Photo, 1905	1.25
Father of The Land We Love, George M.Cohan, Washington, 1932	4.00
First Performance By Kate Smith, Armistice Day, 1938	5.00
Follow The Fleet, Fred Astaire, Ginger Rogers, 1936	8.00
Friendly Enemies, Gutmann Print, 11 X 14 In.	35.00
Go To Sleep My Little Pickaninny, Black Baby	5.50
Gold Mine In The Sky, Kate Smith, 1937	6.00
Good Night Sweetheart, Rudy Vallee, 1931	7.50
Grand Triumphal March, Admiral Dewey, 1898	8.00
Grizzly Bear, Irving Berlin, 1910	20.00
Hand Me Down My Walkin' Cane, Joe Davis Production, 1928	1.50
He's A Rag Picker, Irving Berlin, 1914	5.00
Heartaches, Jimmy Lucas, Albert Gumble, 1919	1.00
Hello Lindy, 1927	20.00
Hello My Dearie, Ziegfeld Follies, 1917	25.00
I Didn't Raise My Boy To Be A Soldier, Ed Morton Photo, 1915	5.00
I Never Had But One Love, John J.Niles, 1955	1.00
I Still Love To Kiss You Goodnight, ZaSu Pitts	3.75
I'd Give A Million Tomorrows, Arthur Godfrey, 1948	10.00
I'd Love To Call You My Sweetheart, Eddie Cantor, 1924	6.00
I'll Have You All Over Again, T.Earl Christy, 1920	15.00
I'll Tell The World, Harold B.Freeman, 1919	1.50
I'm Forever Blowing Bubbles, 1919	1.75
I'm In Love With A Mystic Shriner, H.Murtagh, W.Davis, 1920	1.00
I'm Nooby's Baby, Andy Hardy, Rooney & Garland	10.00
If You Can't Afford A Ford, 1915	8.00
In The Shadows, Herman Finck, 1911	1.50
It Looks Like Rain, Cherry Blossom Lane, 1937	1.25
It's A Long Way To Belring, Show of 1917	6.00
Japanese Sandman, Raymond B.Egan, Richard A.Whiting, 1920	1.00
Jeepers Creepers, Going Places, Ronald Reagan's Name, 1938	50.00
Joyville Jingles, John A.Allen, 1915	1.50
Laugh Clown Laugh, Lon Chaney	10.00
Let Me Call You Sweetheart, Beth Whitson, Leo Friedman, 1910	1.00
Let Us Waltz As We Say Goodbye, Art L.Beiner, 1925	.50
Lilac, Gustave Kline, 1888	6.00
Little French Mother, N.Rockwell Cover, 1919	5.00
Lonesome At Twilight, Milton Charles, 1923	1.75
Lost, P.Ohman, J.Mercer, M.Teetor, 1936	1.00
Louise, Maurice Chevalier, 1929	12.00
Love In Bloom, From She Loves Me Not, Bing Crosby, 1933	1.75
Mammy Jinny's Jubilee, Black, 1913	20.00
Maple Leaf Rag, Scott Joplin, 1902	25.00
March To Eisenhower, 1953, Inauguration Souvenir, Ike, Flag	1.50
Memories of The South, Black Man, Chair Picture, 1908	2.50
Mother Wore Tights, Betty Grable & Dan Dailey, 1947	2.00
Moxie Fox Trot, 1930	22.00
Mutt & Jeff Musical Comedy Song Book, 1916, Large	8.50
My Doughnut Girl, Salvation Army, 1919	10.00
My Old Kentucky Home, Black Woman At Window of House, 1902	1.75
Nigger War Bride Blues	22.00
Orphan Annie, Framed	45.00
Over There, Rockwell Cover, 1918	17.00
Pagan Love Song, Arthur Freed, Nacio H.Brown, 1920	1.00
Paper Doll, Johnny Black, 1942	1.00
Paper Doll, Mills Brothers, 1933	10.00
Parrish Reveries, 1926, 15 X 23 In.	350.00
Perfect Day, Carrie Jacobs-Bone, 1910	1.00
Play A Simple Melody, Irving Berlin, 1942	1.00
Rag Baby Rag, Picture of Black Rag Doll Cover, 1909	25.00
Ragging The Scale, Ed.B.Claypoole, 1915	5.00

Ragtime Violin, Irving Berlin, 1911 .... 5.00
Red River Valley, Gene Autry, 1935 .... 10.00
Red Wing, Indian Maiden, Headdress Picture, 1907 .... 3.00
Roll Along Cowboy, Smith Ballew, 1947 .... 4.00
Rooster Dance, Pictures Rooster, 1903 .... 15.00
Rose of No Man's Land, 1918 .... 1.00
Serenade of The Violet, Benjamin Richmond, 1911 .... 1.50
Short'nin Bread, Mammy Figure, 1928 .... 12.50
Smile Through Your Tears, Bernard Hamblen, 1919 .... 1.00
Smilin' Through, 1919 .... 2.00
Somebody Stole My Gal, 1922 .... 1.75
Someone To Watch Over Me, Ira & George Gershwin, 1926 .... 1.00
Sonny Boy, From Singing Fool, Al Jolson, 1936 .... 2.00
South of The Border, Gene Autry, Autry On Cover, 1939 .... 5.00
Sparkling Jewels, Sydney P.Harris, 1905 .... 1.50
Steal Away, Black Spiritual, H.Burleigh, 1921 .... 10.00
Stein Song, Rudy Vallee, 1930 .... 10.00
Stray Sunbeam, Roy Hatfield, 1906 .... 1.50
Sweet Dreams Sweetheart, From Movie Hollywood Canteen, 1945 .... 1.75
Teddy Bear Blues, 1922 .... 10.00
That Ragtime Symphony, E.G.James, Blacks On Cover, 1914 .... 7.50
That's An Irish Lullaby, J.R.Shannon, 1944 .... 2.00
The Army's Full of Irish, Doughboy Bust Center, 1917, Large 1.75
The Invincible Eagle March, Sousa Picture, 1901 .... 1.75
The Sheik of Araby, Color, 1921 .... 1.00
Theme Song, Amos 'N Andy, Pepsodent Hour, 1924 .... 10.00
There Is A Tavern In The Town, Wm.H.Hills, 1911 .... 1.00
There's A Cabin In The Pines, 1933 .... 1.00
Third Man Theme, Anton Karas, 1949 .... 2.00
Through The Courtesy of Love, Jack Scholl, 1936 .... 2.00
Too Young, 1951 .... 1.00
Tripoli, On The Shores of Tripoli, 1920 .... 1.00
Tulip Time, Ziegfeld Follies, 1919 .... 1.75
Two Sleepy People, Bob Hope, 1938 .... 10.00
Veteran's Dream, Civil War, McClellan's 1864 Candidacy 8.00
Victory Polka, 1943 .... 1.00
We Just Couldn't Say Goodbye, 1932 .... 1.00
Wedding Bells Are Breaking Up That Old Gang of Mine 1.00
What Are You Going To Do To Help The Boys, 1918 .... 2.25
What's The Matter With Father, Harry Bulger Photo, 1910 .... 1.75
When That Midnight Choo Choo Leaves For Alabam, Berlin, 1912 .... 13.50
When You Wish Upon A Star, Pinocchio, 1939, Walt Disney Prod. 15.00
Where Do We Go From Here, W.J.Reilly Photo, 1917 .... 2.50
Yankee Doodle Dandy, James Cagney, 1931 .... 10.00
Yes We Have No Bananas, 1923 .... 2.50
SHEFFIELD, see Silver–English; Silver Plate

Shirley Temple, the famous movie star, was born in 1928. She made her first movie in 1932. Thousands of items picturing Shirley have been and still are being made. Shirley Temple dolls were first made in 1934 by Ideal Toy Company. Millions of Shirley Temple cobalt blue glass dishes were made by Hazel Atlas Glass Company and U.S. Glass Company from 1934 to 1942. They were given away as premiums for Wheaties and Bisquick. A bowl, mug, and pitcher were made as a breakfast set. Some pieces were decorated with the picture of a very young Shirley, others used a picture of Shirley in her 1936 "Captain January" costume. Although collectors refer to a cobalt creamer it is actually the 4 1/2 inch high milk pitcher from the breakfast set. Many of these items are being reproduced today.

SHIRLEY TEMPLE, Book, Captain January & Little Colonel, Random House 10.00
Book, Coloring & Drawing, No.1724 .... 18.00
Book, Heidi, Saalfield, 1937 .... 15.00

Book, How I Raised Shirley Temple, 1935 .... 30.00
Book, Little Princess 20.00
Book, Now I Am Eight 25.00
Book, On The Movie Lot 20.00
Book, Real Little Girl, 1938 .... 22.50
Book, Shirley Temple Through The Day, 1936 .... 40.00
Book, Sunnybrook Farm, Movie 7.00
Book, Through The Day, Saalfield, 1936 .... 35.00
Bowl, Cereal, 6 1/2 In. .... 10.00 To 32.50
Buggy, Wooden, Hubcaps, Canvas Hood, Sides Marked 400.00
Button, My Friend Shirley Temple, Pink, 1930s, 1 1/4 In. 25.00
Calendar, 1936 .... 60.00
Card, Lobby, Kiss & Tell, 1950s Reissue, 22 X 28 In. 6.00
Cover, San Francisco Examiner, May 29, 1946, Colored 9.00
Doll, Brown, Hawaiian Skirt, Lei, Marked, 18 In. 285.00
Doll, Composition, Red & White Dress, Crazed, 22 In. 365.00
Doll, Composition, Sleep Eyes, Clothes, Ideal Button, 17 In. 330.00
Doll, Flirty Eyes, 1957, 19 In. 195.00
Doll, Heidi, Plastic, 14 In. 95.00
Doll, Heidi, Wooden Shoes, Ideal, 8 In. 25.00
Doll, Ideal No.585, 16 In. 295.00
Doll, Sleep Eyes, Open Mouth, Composition, Ideal, 14 1/2 In. 70.00
Doll, Snow White, Cape, Dress, Walt Disney, 1939, 13 In. 225.00
Embroidery Kit, 4 Potholders 20.00
Film Picture, Wheaties, Colored, Set of 12 .... 150.00
Mirror, 3 X 2 In. 15.00
Mirror, Quaker Puffed Wheat 15.00
Mug, Picture 20.00
Paper Doll, Masquerade Costumes, Saalfield 200.00
Paper Doll, No.1761, 2 Large Dolls, 1937 .... 45.00
Paper Doll, Saalfield, 1936, 34 In. 165.00
Pitcher, Cobalt Blue, 4 1/2 In. 50.00
Plate, Photograph Center, Cobalt Blue 275.00
Playing Cards, Drummer 40.00
Saltshaker, Figural 45.00
Sheet Music, Good Ship Lollipop 16.00
Sheet Music, Goodnight My Love, Shirley On Cover 8.00
Soap, Box 45.00
String Holder, Plaster 35.00
Trunk, Doll's 52.50
SHRINER, see Masonic

Silver deposit glass was made during the late nineteenth and early twentieth centuries. Solid sterling silver was applied to the glass by a chemical method so that a cutout design of silver metal appeared against a clear or colored glass. It is sometimes called silver overlay.

SILVER DEPOSIT, Bowl, Black Amethyst, Floral, Handles, 4 X 8 In. 35.00
Coffeepot Set, Silver Birds, Bavarian, 18 Piece 145.00
Decanter, Rooster 1 Side, Cherries Other, 12 In. 150.00

Listed in this section are many of the current and out-of-production silver and silver plated flatware patterns made in the past eighty years. Other silver is listed under Silver-American, Silver-English, etc. Most silver flatware sets that are missing a few pieces can be completed through the help of one of the many silver matching services listed in "The Kovels' Collectors' Source Book."

SILVER FLATWARE SILVER PLATE, Arundell, Cheese Scoop, Rogers 25.00
Berkshire, Butter Server, Twist, 1847 Rogers 10.00
Berkshire, Lettuce Fork, Rogers 25.00
Berkshire, Meat Fork, Rogers 25.00
Berkshire, Pastry Server, Rogers 25.00
Berkshire, Spreader, 1847 Rogers, 6 Piece 48.00
Carnation, Soup Spoon, Rogers 10.00
Carolina, Teaspoon, Holmes & Edwards 8.50

Colony, Tablespoon, Rogers 15.00
Devonshire, 54 Piece 250.00
Fantasy, Service For 8, Oneida, Case, 64 Pc. 96.00
Gardenia, Service For 8, Rogers, 1941, 50 Pc. 125.00
Grape, Demitasse Spoon, Wallace, 8 Piece 35.00
Grenoble, Butter Server, Twist, 1847 Rogers 10.00
Lilyta, Teaspoon, Stratford 7.50
Mayflower, Fruit Spoon, Rogers 12.00
Muscatel, Teaspoon 5.00
Mystic, Dinner Fork, Rogers, Set of 6 .... 24.00
New Century, Teaspoon 7.00
Newport, Mustard Spoon, Rogers 5.00
Old Colony, Service For 12, 65 Piece 250.00
Orange Blossom, Butter Spreader, Rogers, 4 .... 14.00
Priscilla, Knife, Hollow Handle, Wm.Rogers 12.50
Vesta, Butter Knife, Roger Bros., Individual 16.00
Vesta, Spoon, Rogers 8.00
Warwick, Butter Pick, Rogers 22.00
Wild Rose, Teaspoon, Niagara Falls 7.50
Yale, Butter Pick, Rogers 12.00
SILVER FLATWARE STERLING, Adam, Berry Spoon, Whiting 90.00
Adolphus, Sugar Shell, Mt.Vernon 20.00
Alexandra, Bouillon Spoon, Dominick & Haff, 6 .... 90.00
American Beauty, Tomato Server, Shiebler 90.00
Andante, Fork, Gorham, 7 1/8 In. 22.00
Andante, Knife, Gorham 15.00
Asparagus Fork, Marie Antoinette 285.00
Asparagus Tongs, Monogram, Canfield Bros., 1850 .... 450.00
Baronial, Demitasse Spoon, Gorham, Set of 6 .... 60.00
Baronial, Soup Ladle, Gorham 250.00
Bridal Rose, Fork, Alvin 24.00
Bridal Rose, Tea Infuser, Alvin 225.00
Buttercup, Tablespoon, 8 3/8 In. 45.00
Buttercup, Youth Set, Gorham, 3 Piece 75.00
Cambridge, Berry Spoon, Gorham 65.00
Cambridge, Fork, 6 7/8 In. 24.00
Cambridge, Teaspoon 13.00
Canterbury, Bonbon, Pierced, Dominick & Haff 30.00
Canterbury, Luncheon Fork, Towle 26.00
Carnation, Teaspoon 15.00
Cattail, Seaford, Durgin 45.00
Celeste, Teaspoon 11.00
Chantilly, Fork, Gorham 29.00
Chantilly, Knife, 9 1/8 N. 18.00
Chantilly, Teaspoon 11.00
Chateau, Oyster Ladle, Lunt 125.00
Chippendale, Cold Meat Fork, Towle 45.00
Chippendale, Sugar Tongs, Towle 18.00
Chrysanthemum, Asparagus Fork, Gold Wash, Durgin 475.00
Chrysanthemum, Beef Fork, 4 Prong, Durgin 95.00
Chrysanthemum, Beef Fork, 6 In., Durgin 45.00
Chrysanthemum, Berry Spoon, Gorham, Gold Wash 85.00
Chrysanthemum, Bonbon, Gold Wash 50.00
Chrysanthemum, Fish Server, Durgin 325.00
Chrysanthemum, Soup Ladle, Durgin 575.00
Chrysanthemum, Vegetable Fork, Durgin, 10 In. 275.00
Classic Rose, Reed & Barton, Service For 8 .... 795.00
Colonial Shell, Salad Set, International, 2 Pc. 80.00
Cottage, Sugar Sifter, 7 3/4 In. 90.00
Douvaine, Sugar Shell, Unger 50.00
Dover, Lettuce Fork, Towle 45.00
DuBarry, Grapefruit Spoon, Durgin, Set of 8 .... 180.00
Duke of York, Tablespoon, Whiting 65.00
Empire, Berry Spoon, Barton 75.00

Empire, Cucumber Server, Whiting 45.00
English Gadroon, Spreader, Gorham 19.00
English Shell, Lunt, Service For 8 .... 875.00
English, Reed & Barton, Service For 8 .... 725.00
Etruscan, Bonbon, Pierced, Dominick & Haff 30.00
Etruscan, Knife, 9 3/4 In. 16.00
Evangeline, Berry Fork, Alvin 23.00
Federal, Reed & Barton, Service For 8 .... 765.00
Fontainebleau, Egg Spoon, Gorham, Set of 8 .... 360.00
Francis I, Dessert Spoon, Reed & Barton 39.00
Francis I, Grapefruit Spoon, Reed & Barton 45.00
French Provincial, Gravy Ladle, Towle 35.00
French Provincial, Pickle Fork, Towle 18.00
French Scroll, Alvin, Service For 8 .... 650.00
Gadroon, Cold Meat Fork, Towle 45.00
Gadroon, Salad Serving Spoon, Towle 45.00
George & Martha, Master Butter, Westmoreland 25.00
Grande Baroque, Tomato Server, Wallace 125.00
Grape, Bonbon, Dominick & Haff 70.00
Grecian, Tablespoon, Whiting, Pair 90.00
Heiress, Heirloom, Service For 8 .... 625.00
Henry II, Fish Knife, Gorham, Pair 90.00
Honeysuckle, Ladle, Whiting, 16 1/2 In. 250.00
Horizon, Easterling, Service For 8 .... 725.00
Hyperion, Cocktail Fork, Whiting 31.50
Hyperion, Gravy Ladle, Whiting 65.00
Ice Tongs, Domestic, Gorham 175.00
Imperial Queen, Lettuce Fork, Whiting 65.00
Imperial Queen, Pusher 55.00
Imperial Queen, Strawberry Fork, Whiting, 6 Pc. 195.00
Iris, Luncheon Fork, Durgin 40.00
Jefferson, Bouillon Spoon 15.00
Joan of Arc, International, Service For 8 .... 725.00
King Richard, Towle, 6 Piece Place Setting 125.00
Kings, Service For 12, English, 145 Pieces 5750.00
Lady Diana, Bonbon, Towle 18.00
Laurette, 6 Piece Place Setting, Towle, 48 Piece 675.00
Les Cinq Fleurs, Ice Cream Fork, Barton, 6 .... 240.00
Les Cinq Fleurs, Salad Server, Mermod & Jaccard 250.00
Lily of The Valley, Demitasse Spoon, Wallace, 6 .... 75.00
Lily of The Valley, Soup, Cream, Gorham 20.00
Lily of The Valley, Tablespoon, Whiting 65.00
Lily, Asparagus Server, Whiting, 10 1/2 In. 625.00
Lily, Bouillon Spoon, Whiting 45.00
Lily, Ladle, Fluted Bowl, Gorham, 15 In. 250.00
Lily, Luncheon Fork, Whiting 40.00
Louis XV, Cold Meat Fork, Dominick & Haff 50.00
Louis XV, Pea Spoon, Whiting, Gold Wash 200.00
Louis XV, Pie Knife, Whiting 135.00
Louis XV, Salad Fork, Whiting 45.00
Louis XV, Salad Set, Whiting 150.00
Louis XV, Set, Whiting, Velvet Lined Oak Box 1200.00
Luxembourg, Beef Fork, Gorham 45.00
Lyric, Knife, 8 3/4 In. 15.00
Martha Washington, Teaspoon, F.Smith 8.00
Mazarin, Bread Fork, 8 In. 100.00
Mazarin, Bread Fork, Dominick & Haff 100.00
Mazarin, Ice Cream Knife, Dominick & Haff, 12 .... 225.00
Mazarin, Ice Cream Slice, Dominick & Haff 210.00
Medici, Spoon, Gorham, Demitasse, Set of 8 .... 160.00
Medici, Sugar Tongs, Gorham 40.00
Medici, Vegetable Spoon, Large 90.00
Monte Cristo, Luncheon Fork, Towle .... 26.00 To 38.00
Mothers, Mustard Ladle 25.00

Mothers, Sugar Spoon	15.00
Newport Shell, Master Salt Spoon, Frank Smith	25.00
Norfolk, Olive Spoon, Dominick & Haff	40.00
Old Baronial, Preserve Spoon, Gorham, 9 1/8 In.	90.00
Old Brocade, Lemon Fork, Towle	18.00
Old Colonial, Cream Soup Spoon, Towle	36.00
Old Colonial, Luncheon Fork, Towle	32.00
Old English, Tablespoon, Towle	30.00
Old French, Iced Tea Spoon	30.00
Old French, Pickle Knife, Gorham	40.00
Old Maryland, Cream Soup, Kirk	28.00
Old Newburg, Jelly Server, Towle	36.00
Orange Blossom, Sardine Fork, Alvin	135.00
Orient, Oyster Server, Alvin	125.00
Paul Revere, Salad Fork, Dominick & Haff, 12	360.00
Pomona, Berry Spoon, Gold Wash, Towle	75.00
Pompadour, Spreader, Whiting	28.80
Prelude, Salt & Pepper, International	22.00
Puritan, Sugar Spoon, Stieff	20.00
Raphael, Master Butter, Alvin	135.00
Renaissance, Ice Cream Knife, Dominick & Haff	300.00
Repousse, Berry Spoon, Kirk	150.00
Repousse, Pie Server, Dominick & Haff	150.00
Rococo, Bonbon, Dominick & Haff	25.00
Rondo, Gorham, Service For 8	725.00
Rose Ballet, International, Service For 8	765.00
Rosette, Sugar Sifter, Carrie, Gorham	100.00
Shell, Fruit Spoon, Towle	16.00
Sorrento, Crumber, Monogram, Alvin	140.00
Strasbourg, Fish Fork, Gorham	65.00
Strasbourg, Food Pusher, Name Ruth	45.00
Strasbourg, Fork, Youth, Name Ruth	25.00
Strasbourg, Lemon Fork, Gorham	22.50
Strasbourg, Stuffing Spoon, Gorham	300.00
Sugar Nip, Towle	18.00
Talisman Rose, Pickle Fork, Whiting	22.50
Versailles, Asparagus Fork, Monogram, Gorham	325.00
Versailles, Ice Cream Spoon, Gorham, Set of 8	400.00
Victoria, Dessert Spoon, Domick & Haff, 10	65.00
Vintage, Soup Ladle, Rogers Bros.	68.00
Vintage, Stuffing Spoon, Durgin	200.00
Violet, Berry Spoon, Wallace	135.00
Violet, Teaspoon, Wallace, Set of 12	150.00
William & Mary, Service For 6, Lunt, 29 Piece	450.00
Winslow, Cold Meat Fork, Kirk	75.00

Clean silver with any acceptable commercial polish. Don't use household scouring powder on silver no matter how stubborn the spot may be. Use a tarnish-retarding silver polish to keep your silver clean. It will not harm old solid or plated wares. Do not use "instant" silver polishes.

Ⓔ Ⓟ Ⓝ Ⓢ Silver plate is not solid silver. It is a ware made of a metal, such as nickel or copper, that is covered with a thin coating of silver. The letters "EPNS" are often found on American and English silver plated wares. Sheffield silver is a type of silver plate.

SILVER PLATE, Argyle, Long Narrow Spout, Wooden Handle, C.1875, 17 In.	100.00
Bank, Duck	25.00
Biscuit Warmer, Handle, Fan Shape When Opened	375.00
Bowl, Nut, Figural Squirrel On Branch, Sheffield, 6 X 6 In.	45.00
Box, Enameled Pastoral Scene, Sheffield, TSE, C.1755, 3 In.	80.00
Butter, Covered, Liner, Roll Top, Poole, 3 1/2 X 7 In.	45.00
Caddy, Decanter, 3 Crystal Bottles, English	225.00
Cake Basket, Swing Handle, Tufts	55.00
Candelabra, 5–Light, Detachable Arms, England, 18 In., Pair	110.00
Candlestick, 3–Light, Sheffield, C.1790, 19 In., Pair	550.00
Candlestick, 8 Panels, Wallace, 9 1/4 In., Pair	35.00
Candlestick, Corinthian Column Form, 17 3/8 In., Pair	1540.00
Candlestick, Louis XV, Shell & Leaf Standard, 12 In., Pair	500.00
Carving Set, Fish, Staghorn Handles, Etched Floral, English	175.00
Case, Cigar, Pocket, Holds 3 Cigars	21.00
Casserole, Open, Pyrex Insert, 2 Ivory Handles, Footed, Pair	90.00
Castor, Pickle, Handles, Medallion Sprig Insert	275.00
Chatelaine, Mirror, Perfume, Ivory Notebook, Repousse, 9 In.	225.00
Cocktail Shaker, Meriden	26.00
Coffee & Tea Set, Repousse Handles, Fruit Finial, 6 Piece	650.00
Coffee Set, Pear Form, Wooden Finial, England, 3 Piece	160.00
Coffee Urn, Egyptian Head, Ring Handles, England, 15 1/4 In.	200.00
Cooler, Wine, Pail Form, Handles, Sheffield, C.1800, 8 In., Pair	2640.00
Cup, Child's, Embossed Kitty, Holding Umbrella, E.Dragsted	30.00
Cup, Child's, Nursery Rhyme, Little Tommy Tucker	45.00
Desk Set, Art Nouveau, Tendrils, German, C.1900, 6 Piece	1200.00
Dish, Covered, Reed & Barton, 10 1/2 X 7 In.	45.00
Dish, Vegetable, Covered, Remembrance, 1847 Rogers	55.00
Eggcup Holder, Spoon, Set of 6	135.00
Epergne, 4 Paw Supports, Detachable Arms, Sheffield, 12 In.	1000.00
Ewer, Wine, Hinged Top, Repousse Body, H.C.& Co.	135.00
Fish Set, Ivory Handles, Engraved, English, 12 Piece	40.00
Flask, Tape Measure, I Made Kentucky Famous In A Measure	75.00
Fork, Oyster, Mayflower, Rogers, Set of 12	50.00
Goblet, Roger & Smith Co., 6 3/4 X 3 1/4 In.	25.00
Holder, Basket, Dogwood Pattern, Green Bowl, Acorns, 12 In.	110.00
Holder, Basketweave, Crackle Glass, Reed & Barton, 10 In.	95.00
Holder, Cigar, Scroll Engraving, Gold Wash Interior, Holds 3	38.00
Humidor, Green Glass, Golfer, Plated Lid, 9 1/2 In.	140.00
Humidor, Vertical Fluting, Figural Pipe Finial, 6 1/4 In.	50.00
Inkstand, Paw Feet, Gadroon Rim, 2 Bottles, Sheffield, C.1830	385.00
Knife Rest, Figural, Cock Pheasant	19.00
Knife, Cake, Sheffield, England, 1900	160.00
Ladle, Engraved Handle & Bowl, Kensington, 1912, 11 1/2 In.	35.00
Ladle, Oyster, Mystic, Rogers, 10 3/4 In.	35.00
Ladle, Oyster, New Century, Rogers, 10 3/4 In.	38.00
Ladle, Oyster, Windsor, Plain	18.00
Ladle, Punch, Heritage, 1847 Rogers	60.00
Lamp, Frosted Rubina Shade, Floral Design, 11 3/4 In.	225.00
Mirror, Hand, Cherubs, Waves, Fish, Beveled	65.00
Mirror, Plateau, Beveled, 10 In.	65.00
SILVER PLATE, NAPKIN RING, see Napkin Ring	
Nut Bowl, Squirrel Perched On Rim	250.00
Pitcher, Hinged Lid, Ball Shape, Repousse Floral, 9 3/4 In.	95.00
Pitcher, Tilting, Barbour, Heavy Repousse	325.00
Pitcher, Water, Camille, Ice Lip, International	78.00
Pitcher, Water, Ice Lip, Grape & Leaf Design, Wilcox	75.00
Platter, Turkey, Oval, Acorn Rims, Smith, Sissons & Co., 1848	2300.00
Punch Set, Pedestal, Ladle, Tray, F.B.Rogers, 12 Piece	375.00

Pusher, Food	24.00
Salver, Armorials, Scrollwork, 1840–50, 27 In.	550.00
Salver, Bird Crest Engraving, Beaded, Sheffield, 9 In.	100.00
Salver, Declaration of Independence, 19th Century, 28 In.	880.00
Salver, George II, Rococo Cartouche, Sheffield, 1830, 21 In.	715.00
Server, Leaf Shape, Footed	45.00
Shaving Mug, Art Nouveau Repousse, Lady, Long Hair, Derby	95.00
Spoon Holder, Statue of Liberty, Holds 12 Spoons	195.00
SILVER PLATE, SPOON, SOUVENIR, see Souvenir, Spoon, Silver Plate	
Spurs, Engraved, Tooled Leather Straps, Conchos, German, Pair	40.00
Sugar & Creamer, Ribbed, Scalloped, Shell Feet	17.50
Tea & Coffee Set, Art Nouveau, German, C.1900, 4 Piece	2970.00
Tea Caddy, Bulbous, Reed & Barton, 4 1/4 X 5 In.	75.00
Tea Caddy, Repousse Floral On Body & Lid, Reed & Barton	65.00
Tea Set, Each Piece On 4 Splayed Feet, Meridan, 4 Piece	90.00
Tea Set, Remembrance, 1847 Rogers, 6 Piece	275.00
Teapot, Rose & Scroll Engraved, Ivory Resistor Handles	70.00
Toothpick, Figural, Boy	60.00
Toothpick, Figural, Porcupine .... 45.00 To	48.00
Toothpick, Figural, Porcupine, 8–Sided Base, Wilcox	42.00
Toothpick, Heart–Shaped Base, Chick By Open Egg	30.00
Tray, Fort Wayne Pattern, Oneida, 5 In.	15.00
Tray, Gallery, 3 Ball & Claw Feet, Wood Interior, Sheffield	28.00
Tray, Handles, Gadroon, Shell & Leaf Corners, 24 In.	105.00
Tray, Meat & Vegetable, Victorian Rose, Rogers, 16 X 22 In.	40.00
Tray, Openwork Gallery, William Rogers, 15 In.	12.00
Tray, Tea, Flat Chased, Rococo Ornament, Sheffield, 27 In.	577.00
Tray, Tea, Heritage, 1847 Rogers	95.00
Trivet, Oval, 8 X 4 In.	18.00
Tureen, On Stand, Covered, Bombe, Sheffield, C.1830, 23 In.	4675.00
Tureen, Queen Anne Fluting, C.1810, Sheffield, 15 In.	1300.00
Tureen, Sauce, Covered, Paw Feet, Sheffield, 7 3/4 In., Pair	1045.00
Wine Cooler, Campana Shape, Motto, Sheffield, 11 In.	990.00
Wine Wagon, 2 Coasters, Vine Design Handle, 21 In.	425.00
SILVER, SHEFFIELD, see Silver Plate; Silver–English	

The silver listed in this book is subdivided by country. Silver–American is the first listing, followed by Silver–Austrian, Silver–Canadian, etc. There are also other pieces of silver and silver plate listed under special categories, such as Napkin Ring or Tiffany, and under Silver Flatware.

SILVER–AMERICAN, see also Tiffany Silver; Silver–Sterling	
SILVER–AMERICAN, Basket, Bread, Towle, 12 1/2 In.	140.00
Basket, Oval, Handle, Chased Leafage & Flowers, Coin	605.00
Beaker, Cylindrical, Henry Hudson, C.1850, 3 In.	385.00
Birth Pendant, Love Birds, Miss Ruth Phelps, Nov.6th, 1780	550.00
Bottle Label, Whiskey & Bourbon, Pair	75.00
Bowl, Art Nouveau, Slipper Feet, Martele, 1905, 12 1/4 In.	3850.00
Bowl, Hand Chased, Frank Whiting	165.00
Bread Tray, Rectangular, Baltimore Silver Co., C.1903	770.00
Butter, Covered, Jones, Shreve, Brown & Co., 1855, 5 In.	660.00
Buttonhook, Lily of The Valley, Whiting	45.00
Calendar, Perpetual, Repousse, Celluloid Inserts, Kirk	165.00
Candelabra, 3–Light, Fluted Vase Shape, 18 In., Pair	935.00
Candlestick, John Roberts, Sheffield, 11 1/2 In., Pair	2200.00
Cann, Baluster, Scroll Handle, J.Brevoort, C.1760, 5 In.	2750.00
Carving Set, Poppy, Fork Stopper, Gorham, 3 Piece	75.00
Case, Card, A.Coles, N.Y.C., C.1860	225.00
Case, Card, Embossed Moose Lodge Insignia	45.00
Case, Cigarette, Nude With Harp, Unger Bros.	170.00
Case, Hinged Cover, Cylindrical, Durgin, 1 3/4 X 2 In.	75.00
Castor, Sugar, William Gale, N.Y., C.1851	192.00
Centerpiece, Pierced, Chased Scroll, Beaded, 14 In.	1430.00
Chafing Dish, Ivory Handles, C.1893, 10 3/4 In. .... *Illus*	1650.00

Chamberstick, Bailey, Bates & Biddle 165.00
Coffee & Tea Set, Repousse Floral, Whiting, 5 Piece 900.00
Coffeepot, Domed Cover, Acorn Finial, 1820, 10 In. 632.00
Coffeepot, Fish Knob, W.Thomson .... *Cover* 850.00
Coffeepot, J.Jr.& N.Richardson, Vase Form, Beading, C.1785 .... 8800.00
Coffeepot, Wooden Churn Shape, Shreve, Stanwood, 6 1/4 In. 450.00
Compote, Open, Floral, Pedestal, S.Kirk, 11 3/8 In., Pair 880.00
Compote, Repousse Rose & Mum, Stieff, Initial P, 5 1/2 In. 80.00
Console Set, Brocaded Poppies, Glass, Mid–1950s, 3 Piece 55.00
Creamer & Sugar Basket, Ball, Black & Co., 1860 .... 675.00
Creamer, Initials M.W., C.1770, E.W.Mark, 4 1/2 In. 550.00
Cup, Beaker Form, 2 S Handles, Monogram, Moulton, 4 In. 467.00
Cup, Drinking, Jacob Hurd, Boston, C.1750, 5 In. 1210.00
Cup, Drinking, R.Humphreys, Philadelphia, C.1775, 5 1/8 In. 6100.00
Cup, Multi–Scroll Handle, Inscription, 1795, 3 In. 660.00
Dish, Clam, Footed, Marked Wallace, 6 X 4 In. 60.00
Dish, Serving, Lady Diana, Towle, 12 1/2 In. 200.00
Dish, Shell Form, Gorham, 9 3/4 In., Pair 350.00
Dresser Set, Floral, R.Wallace & Son, 7 Piece 250.00
Dressing Table Set, Schmitz, Moore & Co., C.1910, 14 Piece 522.00
Fish Slice, Fiddle, John & Peter Mood, C.1835, 12 1/8 In. 770.00
Flask, Cartier, 1 Pt. 275.00
Fork, Olive, E.B.Booth, Rochester, N.Y., C.1860, 8 In. 55.00
Fork, Pie, Bailey & Co., Applied Cow's Head, C.1860 .... 135.00
Fork, Sardine, Lincoln & Foss, Beaded, C.1850 .... 65.00
Fork, Serving, Farringtron & Hunnewell, Boston, C.1860 .... 185.00
Fork, Twist Handle, Bailey & Co., Phil., C.1860, Set of 6 .... 225.00
Fork, Winged Horse, Durgin 50.00
Fork, Youth, Olive Pattern, Wriggins & Wardin, C.1850 .... 30.00
Fruit Basket, Open Weave, Marked Wm.Gale & Son, N.Y. 1100.00
Funnel, Wine Taster, Corkscrew, Leather Case, R.Blackinton 250.00
Hash Dish, Covered, Lampstand, Wm.F.Ladd, C.1840, 11 In. 1540.00
Holder, Toothbrush, Pierced, Unger 105.00
Julep Cup, W.Gale, N.Y., Molded Border, Beaded Rim, Pair 935.00
Kettle, On Stand, Bombe Pear Form, S.Kirk & Son, 18 In. 1870.00
Knife, Folding, Grape Pattern, C.1860 .... 45.00
Knife, Ice Cream Slicer, Gorham, 10 1/2 In. 18.00
Ladle, Fiddle, Monogram S.M.B.Dupuy, C.1830, 12 1/2 In. 770.00
Ladle, Floral Engraved Handle, A.E.Warner, 13 1/2 In. 255.00
Ladle, Gravy, Dewdrop Pattern, A.& W.Wood 75.00
Ladle, Gravy, Lincoln & Foss, Boston 85.00
Ladle, Mustard, A.Coles, N.Y.C., Palace Pattern, C.1860 .... 35.00
Ladle, Mustard, Blackman & Co., C.1835 .... 30.00
Ladle, Mustard, L.Boutier, Coffin Fiddle, C.1810 .... 58.00
Ladle, Punch, Spatula End, Hutton, Eagles On Beak, 14 In. 500.00
Ladle, Punch, Versailles Pattern, Gold Washed Bowl, Gorham 295.00
Ladle, Sauce, H.L. & E.J.Zahm, Bright Cut, C.1860 .... 65.00
Ladle, Sauce, I.Munroe 25.00
Ladle, Sauce, T.K.Emery, Boston, Coin, C.1810 .... 75.00
Match Safe, Unger Bros., Art Nouveau 75.00
Mirror, Dresser, Kissing Scene, Unger Bros. 225.00
Muddler, Chocolate, Renaissance, Dominick & Haff, 15 In. 115.00
Nut Pick, Medallion Pattern, Ball, Black & Co., 11 Piece 35.00
Pastry Server, Bigelow Bros., Coin 225.00
Pepper Box, Pierced Cover, Cylindrical, 1740–50, 3 In. 990.00
Pitcher, Chased Flower & Leaf Design, Whiting, 4 3/4 In. 650.00
Pitcher, Milk, Ovoid, Raised Floral Design, Gorham, 8 In. 275.00
Pitcher, Obadiah Rich, Boston, Engraved, C.1850, 8 1/4 In. 650.00
Pitcher, Presentation, Shreve, Brown & Co., 10 1/2 In. 770.00
Pitcher, R & W Wilson, Philadelphia, 1824–46, 7 3/4 In. 525.00
Pitcher, Water, Paneled, Pedestal, Gorham, 5 Pt., 10 In. 200.00
Platter, Art Nouveau, Oval Cartouche, C.1900, 17 In. 1540.00
Platter, Oval & Circular, Gorham, 1899, 15 1/2 In., Pair 2090.00
Porringer, Keyhole Handle, C.1740, S.Gray, 5 1/4 In. 1650.00

Porringer, Samuel Burt, Boston, C.1740	1400.00
Ramekin, Covered, Caudle Cup Shape, 4 In., Set of 12	2090.00
Salt & Pepper, Chicken, Red Glass Eyes	175.00
Salt, Master, B.Marsh, Coin, Pair	605.00
Salt, Open, Leaf Shaped Boat, Gorham, 1871, 5 1/4 In.	250.00
Salt, Rococo, Glass Liner, J.Heath, C.1765, 4 In., Pair	8800.00
Sauceboat, Baldwin Gardiner, Leaf Tip Rim, C.1830	1870.00
Scissors, Figures On Handles, Sheath	395.00
Scoop, Chrysanthemum Pattern, Durgin	95.00
Scoop, Narcissus Pattern, Unger	80.00
Spoon, Albany, N.Y., Bright Cut Handle, Oval Bowl, C.1795	56.50
Spoon, Baby Feeding, Curved Handle, Watrous	15.00
Spoon, C.C.Garret, Monogrammed, Coin, 7 1/4 In., Set of 6	60.00
Spoon, Dessert, Jones, Lows & Ball, Boston, Fiddle Thread	38.00
Spoon, Dessert, Van Voorhis & Schanck, N.Y.C., C.1790	125.00
Spoon, Egg, Saxon Stag, Gorham	75.00
Spoon, Rice, Gregg Hayden & Co., Charleston, C.1845, 12 In.	475.00
Spoon, Salt, J.Musgrave, Philadelphia, C.1790	75.00
Spoon, Serving, Pear & Bacall, Boston, Mass., 1840s	35.00
Spoon, Serving, T.Steele & Son, Hartford, Conn., 1840s	35.00
Spoon, Serving, Theophilus Bradbury, Mass., 1815	48.00
Spoon, Wm.M.Savage, Monogrammed, Coin, 8 1/2 In., Set of 5	75.00
Stamp Dispenser, Star & Gorham, Black	65.00
Strainer, Lemon, Flower Pierced, Handles, I.M.Mark, 7 In.	330.00
String Holder, Footed, Floral, Ball Shape, Gorham, 3 1/4 In.	225.00
Sugar & Creamer, N.Bogert, N.Y., Floral Finial, C.1830	575.00
Sugar & Creamer, Repousse, Twig Handles, Bigelow, Kennard	400.00
Sugar Basin, Covered, Thibault & Bros., C.1825, 9 1/2 In.	850.00
Sugar Basket, Kidney, Cann & Johnson, N.Y.C., C.1850	385.00
Sugar Scoop, Pedestal, Signed Cartier	35.00
Sugar Shaker, Bailey & Kitchen, Fiddle, C.1840	95.00
Sugar Urn, Richards & Williamson, C.1800, 10 In.	3500.00
Sugar, Bird Finial On Cover, 12 Spoons, Rogers	245.00
Sugar, Covered, Pear Shape, Handles, S.Kirk, 9 In.	825.00
Sugar, Joseph Loring, Covered, 1785–96	650.00
Sugar, Monogram, Inverted Pear Shape, J.Edwards, Jr., 4 In.	450.00
Tablespoon, Bright Cut, B.Wenman, N.Y.C., C.1815	55.00
Tablespoon, C.Babbitt Taunton, Fiddle Coffin	80.00
Tablespoon, E.Chittenden, C.1750	425.00
Tablespoon, E.Chittenden, E.Guilford & New Haven, C.1750	425.00
Tablespoon, Fiddleback, S.Robb, C.1840, Set of 6	195.00
Tablespoon, G.Walker, Phila., Pa., Bird Back, C.1790	175.00
Tablespoon, Initials H.P.In Oval, Revere, C.1780	2200.00
Tablespoon, J.Cluett, Kingston & Albany, N.Y., C.1750	175.00
Tablespoon, J.Lownes, Philadelphia, C.1780	175.00
Tablespoon, J.Vernon, N.Y.C., C.1790	100.00
Tablespoon, P.Lupp, New Brunswick, N.J., Midrib, C.1760	375.00
Tablespoon, P.Syng, Jr., Front Midrib, C.1760	350.00
Tablespoon, Upturned Handle, Rattail Bowl, C.1720	357.00
Tablespoon, William Mitcher, Jr., Richmond, Va., 1818–45	50.00
Tag, Luggage, Hat Box Shape, Monogram	40.00
Tankard, Covered, William Elliot, C.1806	935.00
Tankard, Curved Sides, Benjamin Burt, Boston	2500.00
Tankard, Cylindrical, Flat Domed Cover, Schaats, 6 3/4 In.	6050.00
Tazze, Art Nouveau, Pomegranates, Martele, 1906, 10 In., Pr.	4300.00
Tea & Coffee Set, Dunkirk, 5 Piece	600.00
Tea & Coffee Set, Lincoln & Foss, C.1855, 5 Piece	2100.00
Tea & Coffee Set, Plymouth, Monogram, Gorham, 5 Piece	1500.00
Tea & Coffee Set, Scroll Handles, J.E.Caldwell, 6 Piece	2850.00
Tea & Coffee Set, Tray, Inscription, S.Kirk & Son, 5 Piece	5700.00
Tea & Coffee Set, Tray, Kirk & Son, 6 Piece	3575.00
Tea & Coffee Set, Waterman & Van Ness, C.1830, 4 Piece	2000.00
Tea Caddy Spoon, Coin Silver, Scoop Shape	85.00
Tea Set, Bombe Shape, Wm.Thomson, C.1810, 3 Piece	495.00

Tea Set, Federal, C.1795, Teapot 6 3/4 In., 3 Piece 1800.00
Tea Set, Graff, Washburn & Dunn, Shell Feet, Demitasse 795.00
Tea Set, Jumel Pattern, Whiting Mfg.Co., C.1915, 6 Piece 1500.00
Tea Set, Monogram S, Chester Billings & Son, 3 Piece 250.00
Tea Set, S.Kirk, Landscapes, Floral Finials, C.1840, 3 Pc. 1750.00
Tea Set, W.Thomson, Urn Form, Fruit Finials, C.1815, 4 Pc. 1100.00
Tea Strainer, Spout, Frank Whiting 45.00
Teapot, Acorn Finial, Pear Shape, Boston, Coin, 10 In. 400.00
Teapot, Bombe, Pedestal, Chinoiserie Buildings, Kirk, 1830 .... 1540.00
Teapot, Domed Cover, Bombe Form, S.Kirk, C.1840, 7 In. 605.00
Teapot, J.Richardson, Jr., Swan Neck Spout, C.1800 .... 2640.00
Teapot, Obadiah Rich, Roman Lamp Form, C.1830 .... 7150.00
Teapot, Stand, Frank Whiting, C.1920 .... 485.00
Teapot, Urn Finial, Domed Cover, Jones & Ward, 8 1/4 In. 375.00
Teaspoon, A.Reeder, Trenton, N.J., C.1790 .... 65.00
Teaspoon, B.Cleveland, Newark, N.J., C.1805, Set of 6 .... 250.00
Teaspoon, B.H.Tisdale, Coin, 4 Piece 80.00
Teaspoon, Birdback Pointed End, G.Hendel, Pa., C.1795 .... 135.00
Teaspoon, Bright Cut, R.& W.Wilson, Philadelphia 12.00
Teaspoon, Browne & Seal, Philadelphia, C.1810 .... 18.00
Teaspoon, C.Carpenter, Norwich, Ct., C.1790 .... 65.00
Teaspoon, Coffin Fiddle, B.Wenman, N.Y.C., C.1810 .... 75.00
Teaspoon, Coffin Fiddle, T.Van Riper, N.Y.C., C.1813 .... 40.00
Teaspoon, D.Dupuy, Philadelphia, Coin, 1790 .... 65.00
Teaspoon, D.Rogers, Ipswich, Ma., C.1795, 12 Piece 660.00
Teaspoon, Dexter & Haskins, Coin, 8 Piece 48.00
Teaspoon, E.P.Lescure & Son, Philadelphia, C.1820 .... 18.00
Teaspoon, Eoff & Howell, Coffin-End, C.1805, 4 Piece 140.00
Teaspoon, G.J.Wolf, Del., Bird Back, C.1790 .... 75.00
Teaspoon, J.David, Jr., Philadelphia, Coin, 1790 .... 65.00
Teaspoon, J.Elfreth, Jr., Philadelphia, Midrib, C.1760 .... 375.00
Teaspoon, J.Loring, Boston, C.1790 .... 65.00
Teaspoon, N.Coleman, Burlington, N.J., C.1815 .... 85.00
Teaspoon, S.Emery, Boston, Scroll Back, Coin, C.1790 .... 75.00
Teaspoon, Shell Back, Edward Davis, Newburyport, C.1780 .... 125.00
Teaspoon, T.Bradbury II, Newburyport, Fiddle 35.00
Teaspoon, T.Bradbury, Maine, Fiddle Coffin, C.1810 .... 32.00
Teaspoon, T.T.Wilmot, C.1840 .... 35.00
Teaspoon, W.Hookey, R.I., C.1780 .... 75.00
Teaspoon, W.Kendrick, Louisville, Coin 16.00
Teether, Mother-of-Pearl Handle, Unger Bros., 4 In. 185.00
Tongs, Christopher Hughes, Baltimore, 1744–1824 .... 90.00
Tongs, H.Lewis, Philadelphia, C.1820 .... 75.00
Tongs, I.David, Philadelphia, 1737–94 .... 95.00
Tongs, Sugar, Signed Bailyer, 7 1/4 In. 50.00
Tray, Black, Starr & Frost, 12 1/2 In.Diam. 300.00
Tray, Knife, William Adams, Elongated Oval, C.1830 .... 5500.00
Tray, Monogram, Theo B.Starr, 14 In., Diam. 400.00
Tray, Plain, Kirk, 1925–32, 10 In.Diam. 395.00
Tray, Wavy Rim, Floral Medallions, Wallace, 17 1/2 In. 170.00
Tureen, Soup, Covered, Bombe, Gadrooned, Wm.B.Durgin, 14 In. 1050.00
Vase, Bud, Saxon Stag, Gorham, C.1860 .... 185.00
Vase, Turned Down Openwork Rim, Gorham, 25 3/4 In., Pair 3300.00
Wine, Rooster Stem, Shreve, 6 Piece 750.00
SILVER–AUSTRIAN, Box, Enamel & Rock Crystal Hinged Cover, 3 3/8 In. 1450.00
Candelabra, 5–Light, Secessionist, 21 3/8 In., Pair 3850.00
SILVER–CANADIAN, Mug, Child's, Paul Morin, 1775–1805, Half Pint 950.00
SILVER–CHINESE, Bowl, Pierced With Dragons, Wang Hing, C.1900, 10 1/2 In. 467.00
Cigar Box, Hinged Cover, Dragons, Wood Liner, 1900, 8 In. 1450.00
Mug, Cylindrical, Bands of Lobing, 1820, 3 3/4 In. 1430.00
Salver, Shell Feet, Engraved, Cutshing, 11 7/8 In. 465.00
Tea & Coffee Set, Marke Dshanghai & Luenwo, 7 Piece 1450.00
Teapot, George IV, Domed Cover, Baluster, C.1840, 6 In. 775.00
SILVER–CONTINENTAL, Beaker, Cylindrical, 3–Footed, Gilt, C.1691, 3 7/8 In. 550.00

Casket, Hinged Cover, Enameled, Gilt, 1 7/8 In.	440.00
Mustard Pot, Baluster Ewer, Scroll Handle, 1720, 6 In.	1430.00
SILVER–DANISH, Bottle Opener, Acorn Pattern, Georg Jensen, 4 3/8 In.	68.00
Bowl, Domed Cover, Blossom Finial, Georg Jensen, 7 5/8 In.	935.00
Bowl, Hammered, 8 Foliate Supports, Georg Jensen, 6 1/2 In.	1100.00
Bowl, Ring Foot, Tab Handles, Georg Jensen, 15 3/4 In.	1325.00
Brooch, Earrings, Art Deco, Graduated Circles, Georg Jensen	95.00
Candelabra, 2–Light, Ball Stems, Georg Jensen, 8 1/4 In., Pr.	6600.00
Candlestick, Empire Style, VH Mark, 9 1/8 In., Pair	990.00
Casket, Jewel, Stand, Bombe, Rococo Borders, Michelsen, 10 In.	2200.00
Compote, Vine Stem, Georg Jensen, C.1949, 12 In. ....*Illus*	6600.00
Creamer, Hans Hanson, 6 Oz.	65.00
Flatware, Service For 12, Cactus, Georg Jensen, 108 Piece	6600.00
Fork, Sardine, Cactus, Georg Jensen	35.00
Plate, Beaded, Georg Jensen, 10 3/8 In., 24 Piece	1650.00
Server, Acanthus, Engraved, Jensen, Round	165.00
Server, Fish, Applied Flowers, 1919, 12 3/8 In., Pair	412.00
Spoon, Gold Wash, Blue Enamel, Demitasse, 6 Piece	125.00
Sugar Tongs, Acorn & Scroll Design, Georg Jensen	55.00
Teapot, Reeded & Beaded Borders, Copenhagen, 1814, 6 In.	825.00
Tureen, Grape Handles, Domed Cover, Georg Jensen, 10 1/2 In.	3025.00
Tureen, Soup, Oval, Foliate & Shell Handles, 1923, 16 In.	5060.00
SILVER–DUTCH, Beaker, Crest, Engraved Birds, Mid–17th Century, 4 1/2 In.	1760.00
Compote, Scene, Musicians, Marked	175.00
Mustard, Covered, Cobalt Liner, Cutout Figures	85.00
Spoon, Serving, 9 1/2 In.	75.00
Sugar Urn, Covered, Monogram, Ribbonwork, Marked, 8 In.	1200.00
Wine Cooler, Rams' Heads Handles	8500.00

English silver is marked with a series of four or five small hallmarks. The standing lion mark is the most commonly seen sterling quality mark. The other marks indicate the city of origin, the maker, and the year of manufacture. These dates can be verified in many good books on silver.

SILVER–ENGLISH, Argyle, Ball Finial, Wooden Handle, Sheffield, 6 In.	325.00
Beaker, Double, Engraved, Marked B.M., George IV, 5 7/8 In.	935.00
Bowl, Crown & Shield, Lion & Blackbirds, 1924, 4 1/4 In.	16.00
Box, Covered, Royal Arms, J.Holloway, George III, 3 3/8 In.	880.00
Cake Basket, Handle, R.& S.Hennell, George III, 14 In.	825.00
Cake Basket, Oval, Beaded Flutes, C.Aldrige, H.Green, 1770	1300.00
Cake Basket, Pierced, Wm.Plummer, George III, 13 1/8 In.	1550.00
Candelabra, 5–Light, Collingwood & Co., 19 In., Pair	3075.00
Candlestick, Crest, J.Margas, George I, 6 3/8 In., Pair	3950.00
Candlestick, Fluted Column, Sheffield, 1910, 5 1/4 In., Pair	125.00
Candlestick, Fordham & Faulkner, 1901, 5 3/4 In., Pair	357.00
Candlestick, Matthew Cooper, 1719, 7 1/4 In., Pair	7700.00
Candlestick, R.Jones & J.Schofield, 1776, 12 In., Pair	1400.00
Candlestick, Wm.Cafe, Banded Sconce, 1761, 10 5/8 In., Pair	4180.00
Caster, Swirl Pattern Around Lower Section, 1930	350.00
Centerpiece, Classic Ladies, B.Smith III, George IV, 17 In.	4675.00
Chamberstick, Snuffer, Crest, C.1815, 7 In.	2000.00
Chocolate Pot, Pedestal, 1793, 14 In.	1600.00
Coaster, Wine, John Watson, Sheffield, George III, 6 In., Pr.	935.00
Coffee Set, S.Blackensee, Wood Handles & Finials, 4 Piece	1100.00
Coffeepot, Baluster Form, H.Bateman, George III, 12 1/4 In.	3575.00
Coffeepot, Individual, Sugar Bowl Top, Sheffield, 8 In.	70.00
Creamer, Chased Rococo Design, Rebecca Emes & E.Barnard	185.00
Creamer, Chased Rococo Design, Sheffield, C.1857, 3 5/8 In.	55.00
Cruet Stand, George III, 19th Century, 8 In. ....*Illus*	275.00
Cup, Hester Bateman, Scroll Handles, 1787, 6 1/8 In.	770.00
Cup, Stand, Campana Form, Pedestal, Handles, Barnards, 20 In.	3575.00
Dish, Sweetmeat, Shell Shape, Handles, George II, Pair	825.00
Dresser Set, Satin & Velvet Lining, Sheffield, 6 Piece	385.00
Ewer, Thomas Heming, Oviform, 1772, 10 5/8 In.	4400.00

Flagon, Ribbed Handle, Ribbed Bands At Rim 700.00
Fork, Bread, Pearl Handle, C.1870 .... 65.00
Fork, Pickle, Pearl Handle, England, 1899, Pair 115.00
Frame, Birmingham, Oval, 1913 .... 275.00
Frame, Birmingham, Rectangular, 1910 .... 250.00
Jug, Champagne, C.1920 .... 165.00
Kettle Stand, Triangular, P.Archambo, George II, 9 7/8 In. 1650.00
Kettle, On Stand, Crichton Bros., 1926, 12 1/2 In. 525.00
Knife, Paper, Pearl Handle, 1869 .... 150.00
Ladle, Gravy, Hester Bateman, 1781, Pair 250.00
Ladle, Soup, Shell Shaped Bowl, E.Farrell, 1831 .... 1870.00
Lemon Strainer, Flowerhead Pattern, Handles, 1718, 6 In. 412.00
Muffin Basket, Handles, P.Storr, 1819, 11 In. 4750.00
Mug, Chased Rococo Design, Monogrammed E.A., 1870, 3 In. 70.00
Mug, Christening, Art Nouveau 85.00
Mug, Plain, B.B.Mark, C.1883 .... 125.00
Perfume Cylinder, C.1885, 2 X 3/4 In. 132.00
Plate, Shaped Gadroon Rim, London, 1911, 10 In. 200.00
Platter, Meat, Paul Storr, Acanthus Shells, 1820, 22 3/8 In. 9350.00
Punch Bowl, Victorian, Handles, Pedestal, R.Hennell, 15 In. 1980.00
Punch Bowl, Victorian, Pedestal, Gilt, C.S.Harris, 9 3/8 In. 550.00
Rattle & Teething Ring, Whistle At End 200.00
Rattle, Bells, Pearl Teether & Handle 95.00
Rattle, Cat With Goldfish Bowl, Birmingham, 1937 .... 260.00
Rattle, Cowbell, Birmingham, 1907 .... 135.00
Rattle, Jester, Birmingham, 1937 .... 275.00
Rattle, Teddy Bear, Birmingham, 1938 .... 240.00
Rattle, Whistle, Birmingham, 1888 .... 325.00
Salt, Shell Shape, Ed.Wood, 1740, 3 5/8 In., Pair 467.00
Salver, Armorials, John Carter, 1774, 15 In. 1980.00
Salver, Crichton Bros., George I, 9 & 10 1/2 In., Pair 525.00
Salver, Gabriel Sleath, Male & Female Masks, 1745, 25 In. 4950.00
Scoop & Spoon, Marrow, Marked T.T., 1696, 7 1/8 In. 1100.00
Scoop, Marrow, Alexander Barnet, 1766–67 .... 250.00
Spoon, Buck Crest, Hester Bateman, 1786 .... 110.00
Spoon, Rattail, London, 2 Piece 45.00
Spoon, Sifter, Ann & William Bateman, 1800 .... 225.00
Spoon, Sifter, Sheffield, 1901 .... 130.00
Spoon, Sifter, W.R.Sobey, 1839 .... 135.00
Spoon, Stuffing, Starling Wilford, C.1738 .... 200.00
Spoon, Stuffing, W.Hutton & Sons, C.1900 .... 95.00
Spoon, Tea Caddy, G.Unite, Birmingham, 1852 .... 85.00
Spurs, Georgian, C.1784 .... 302.00
Stand, Dessert, Man, Hunting Suit, Hancock, 9 3/4 In., Pair 3000.00
Stirrups, Spur Back, Button, Buckle, Dated 1750, 3 In., Pair 200.00
Sugar & Creamer, Covered, William Elliott, 1824 .... 467.00
Sugar Bowl, Covered 495.00
Sugar Nips, 1750 .... 125.00
Sugar Shaker, Birmingham, 1914 .... 300.00
Sugar Tongs, Engraved, Marked I.L. 40.00
Tablespoon, Hanoverian Pattern, J.Barbout, 1735 .... 715.00
Tankard, Cylindrical, Domed Cover, Robins, George III, 8 In. 1760.00
Tea & Coffee Set, Britannia Standard, 1912, 5 Piece 1650.00
Tea & Coffee Set, Tray, Barnards, 6 Piece 3400.00
Tea Caddy, George III, Cover, C.1782, 6 In. ....*Illus* 2420.00
Tea Set, Phillip Rundell, C.1820, 4 Piece 6000.00
Teapot, Stand, Straight Sides, R.Hennell, George III, 6 In. 1210.00
Toast Rack, 6 Slice, Birmingham, 1907 .... 85.00
Toast Rack, Chester, 1923, 2 5/8 X 3 In. 75.00
Toast Rack, William Barrett II, William IV, 7 3/4 In. 385.00
Tongs, Pierced, Scrolled, 1770, 6 In. 150.00
Tongs, Sugar, Bright Cut, Peter, Ann, Wm.Bateman, 1803–04 .... 110.00
Tray, Paul Storr, Engraved Armorials, 1827, 7 3/4 In., Pair 6000.00
Tray, Tea, 2 Handles, Wm.Bennett, George III, 21 1/2 In. 2200.00

Tray, Tea, Armorial, Handles, W.Bateman, George III, 30 In. 4675.00
Tray, Tea, Handles, Walker & Hall, C.1905, 31 In. 2750.00
Tureen, Sauce, Paul Storr, Rising From Lion Masks, 1815 .... 1325.00
Urn, Tea, Beaded Borders, C.Wright, C.1770, 20 1/2 In. 1600.00
Urn, Tea, Flame Finial, F.Butty & N.Dumee, 1768, 22 In. 2800.00
Vinaigrette, Grape, 7 Leaf Design, J.Willmore 235.00
Waiter, 3 Hoof Feet, R.Abercromby, George II, 6 In., Pair 522.00
SILVER–FRENCH, Asparagus Tongs, Fiddle Thread, Pierced, 1819–38, 11 In. 715.00
Box, Flat Cover, Half–Rod Ivory Handle, J.E.Puiforcat, 8 In. 4675.00
Buttons, Animal Heads, Bagriot, 1 1/8 & 3/4 In., 18 Piece 1980.00
Coffeepot, Armorial, Pear Shape, Hoof Feet, 1819–38, 8 In. 825.00
Coffeepot, Pear Form, Cardeilhac, 20th Century, 8 3/4 In. 660.00
Dish, Vegetable, G.Falkenberg, 20th Century, 10 In., Pair 550.00
Sucrier, Goblet Shape, Lid, Glass Lining, 12 Spoons, Bibron 1250.00
Sundial & Compass, Butterfield Type, P.Lemaire, 2 5/8 In. 990.00
Tureen, Soup, Covered, Handles, Pedestal, C.1840, 12 In. 1650.00
SILVER–GERMAN, Beaker, Bud Finial, Domed Cover, Saler, 1745, 5 3/4 In. 1450.00
Bowl, Swan Form, Import Marks, 20th Century, 5 3/4 In., Pair 990.00
Box, Sugar, Covered, Octagonal, Paw Feet, 1825, 6 In. 522.00
Candelabra, 3–Light, Rococo, Putti, C.1900, 18 1/2 In., Pair 1980.00
Candlestick, Baluster Stems, Rococo, Dresden, 1900, 9 In., Pr. 1100.00
Cup, Wedding Bell, Nuremberg 150.00
Decanter, Glass, Stirrup Shape Mounted, 1900, 10 3/4 In., Pr. 1650.00
Ewer, Baroque, Satyr's Head On Lid, Nuremberg, 14 1/2 In. 880.00
Figurine, Fighting Cocks, B.Muller, 1922, 9 X 10 In., Pair 1980.00
Match Safe, Art Nouveau 45.00
Plate, Gadroon, Armorial, J.A.Seethaler, 1819, 10 In., 12 Pc. 5060.00
Spice Container, Figural, Pheasant, C.1900, 22 In., Pair 1980.00
Tea & Coffee Set, Animal Head Spouts, 20th Century, 5 Piece 2100.00
Tea & Coffee Set, Art Deco, Louis Werner, C.1925, 4 Piece 2475.00
Tray, Pierced & Engraved, Leipzig, C.1800, 15 5/8 In. 550.00
SILVER–IRISH, Chocolate Pot, Cylindrical, Swan Neck, George II, 10 1/2 In. 1200.00
Coffeepot, Inverted Pear Shape, C.Terry, George III, 14 In. 4200.00
Creamer, J.Nicolson, Cork, C.1795 .... 360.00
Jug, Beer, Pear Shape, Handle, Hamilton, George II, 8 In. 2640.00
Ladle, Gravy, Unicorn Crest, Round Tips, Monogram, 1796, Pair 110.00
Salver, Richard Williams, 1772, 15 3/8 In. 935.00
Sauceboat, Matthew West, Beaded Rim, C.1775, 9 In., Pair 1100.00
Spoon, Platter, Wave & Stipple, Isaac D'Olier, C.1767 .... 125.00
Sugar Tongs, Georgian, Engraved, Marked JP Dublin 50.00
Tureen, Soup, Covered, James Fray, Beading, 1826, 16 5/8 In. 4125.00
SILVER–ITALIAN, Plate, Dinner, Plain Molded Rim, C.1900, 9 In., Set of 6 .... 715.00
Sugar, Covered, Inverted Pear Shape, Catania, 6 3/8 In. 330.00
Tea & Coffee Set, Empire, M.Buccellati, Rome, C.1965, 4 Pc. 4400.00
Vase, Flared, Winged Putti, Milan, 20th Century, 14 1/8 In. 467.00
SILVER–JAPANESE, Shaker & Tray, Cocktail, Hammered, 20th Century, 12 In. 440.00
Tea & Coffee Set, Tray, Dragons, Arthur & Bond, 1900, 6 Pc. 8800.00
SILVER–MEXICAN, Case, Cigarette, Art Deco, 5 1/2 X 3 1/4 In. 75.00
Coffee Set, Ovoid, Plain Surface, Scroll Handles, 4 Piece 600.00
Dish, Vegetable, Covered, Divided, Sanborns 95.00
Tea & Coffee Set, Kettle Stand, Baluster Finial, 7 Piece 2420.00
Tea Set, Scroll Handles, Button Finials, Sanborns, 5 Piece 605.00
Tray, Shaped Rim, Sanborns, 20th Century, 22 7/8 In. 660.00
SILVER–NORWEGIAN, Candelabra, 4–Light, Viking, Andersen, 17 7/8 In., Pair 7975.00
Spoon, Gold Wash, Enamel, Box, Demitasse, 6 Piece 125.00
SILVER–PERUVIAN, Candelabra, 7–Light, Louis XV, 18 In., Pair 1650.00
SILVER–POLISH, Box, Sugar, Covered, Bombe Form, Beaded Rim, 6 1/2 In. 715.00
SILVER–PORTUGUESE, Candlestick, Panel Feet, AR Mark, 7 7/8 In., Pair 600.00
Porringer, Dome Cover, Bombe Form, Marked, 4 3/8 In. 770.00

Russian silver is marked with the cyrillic, or Russian, alphabet. The numbers 84, 88, or 91 indicate the silver content. Russian silver may be higher or lower than sterling standard. Other marks indicate maker, assayer, or city of manufacture. Many pieces of silver made in Russia are decorated with enamel.

SILVER–RUSSIAN, Basket, Cake, Overlaid Napkin, C.1889, 11 3/8 In. ....*Illus*	2860.00
Bell, Table, Imperial Eagle, C.Tegelston, 1839, 4 1/2 In.	1100.00
Box, Cigar, Partly Gilded, Dates 1871–1896, 7 3/4 In.	2300.00
Box, Cigarette, Hinged Cover, Enameled Foliage, 1910, Large	6600.00
Box, Jewelry, Enamel & Plique–A–Jour, C.1910, 5 1/2 In.	3575.00
Cake Basket, Chased Basketweave, Folded Napkin, 1884	2100.00
Cake Basket, Simulated Napkin, Wirework Feet, 1886	4675.00
Case, Cigar, 2 Cartouches, Cossack Driving Cart, 4 5/8 In.	330.00
Compact, Scent Flask & Parasol Handle, Faberge, C.1910	5500.00
Cup & Saucer, Peasant Man, Bear, Faberge, 1894, 4 3/4 In.	2425.00
Cup, Horn Shape, Enameled, O.Kurlyukov, C.1910, 2 5/8 In.	1540.00
Easter Egg, Enameled Flowers, Fitted For Eggcup, C.1900	2310.00
Handle, Cane, St.George, Dragon, Faberge, C.1890, 1 13/16 In.	4675.00
Inkwell, Bogaryr Holding Sword, Marked, C.1900, 10 1/4 In.	3850.00
Mug, Child's, Engraved Scene, C.1891 .... 135.00 To 155.00	
Samovar, Imperial Eagle, Ivory Fittings, C.1900, 15 1/2 In.	3575.00
Sherbet, Plique–A–Jour Enamel, Kuzmichev, C.1900, 6 3/4 In.	1650.00
Snuff Box, Black Enamel Lid, Dated 1873	175.00
Sugar, Pedestal, 2 Handles, 4 In.	135.00
Tea Set, Silver & Niello, Troika Scenes, C.1894, 5 Piece	3300.00
SILVER–SCOTCH, Box, Sugar, Pocket, George Christie, C.1797	900.00
Coffee Pot, Cylindrical, Ed.Lothian, George II, 9 3/4 In.	935.00
Sauce Boat, Lothian & Robertson, George II, 7 1/2 In.	605.00
Tablespoon, J.Heron, Greenock, C.1800	75.00
Tray, Adam Style Pierced, Hamilton & Inches, 22 In.	2750.00

Sterling silver is made with 925 parts silver out of 1,000 parts of metal. The word "sterling" is a quality guarantee used in the United States after about 1860. The word was used much earlier in England and Ireland. Pieces listed here are not identified by country. Other pieces of sterling quality silver are listed under Silver–American, Silver–English, etc.

SILVER–STERLING, Bag, Evening, Mesh, Embossed Handle, Blue Stone In Clasp	195.00
Bonbon, Pierced Design, Billings & Son, 12 Troy Oz.	90.00
Bowl & Underplate, Randahl, 4 In.	30.00
Bowl, Blown–Out Art Nouveau Women's Heads, 5 In.	130.00
Bowl, Center, Footed, Ribbed, Ornamental Rim, 9 1/4 In.	100.00
Brush, Crumb, Art Nouveau, 6 1/4 In.	23.00
Butter, 6 Individual Dishes, Repousse Lily Design	80.00
Button, Art Nouveau Woman, 3/4 In.	24.00
Buttonhook, Matching Shoehorn, Repousse, Mums	40.00

Silver–American, Chafing Dish,
Ivory Handles,
C.1893, 10 3/4 In.

Silver–English, Tea Caddy,
George III, Cover,
C.1782, 6 In.

Silver–Russian, Basket,
Cake, Overlaid Napkin,
C.1889, 11 3/8 In.

Candleholder, Duchin Creations, 3 In., Pair	20.00
Case, Card, Chased Floral On Cover, Flowers, Leaves, Marked	125.00
Case, Card, Engraved Overall, Winged Bird & Branch, Chain	155.00
Case, Card, Gold Bands, 3 1/2 X 2 1/2 In.	75.00
Case, Cigarette, Amethyst Stone In Clasp	50.00
Case, Cigarette, Mailed Letter, Stamp, Dated 1939	110.00
Case, Cigarette, Oriental Design, Monogram, 5 X 3 1/4 In.	35.00
Case, Engraved Floral Lid, Dated May 1st, 1851, 3 5/8 In.	285.00
Case, Hinged Lid, Gadroon Borders, Hand Hammered	55.00
Compote, Marked Preisner, 3 1/4 X 5 In.	30.00
Creamer, Cow, Insect In Lid, 6 X 3 1/2 In.	275.00
Cutter, Cigar, Fits Watch Fob	45.00
Dresser Set, Brush & Comb, 5 Piece	65.00
Flask, Grapes & Leaves, Removable Cup, 3 X 5 In.	155.00
Funnel, Perfume	38.00
Funnel, Wine, Dublin, Wm.Johnson	275.00
Hook, Glove, Holding, Scrolled Edges	14.00
Lipstick Holder, With Hinged Mirror	32.00
Loving Cup, 1904 Presentation, 7 1/2 In., Pair	250.00
Needle Holder, Mechanical, Engraved, 2 In.	150.00
Pitcher, Collar Dated 1929, 10 In.	215.00
Rattle, Baby, Dumbbell Shape, Lullaby	40.00
Shaving Set, Traveling, Art Deco, Hand Blown	55.00
Shears, Grape, Repousse Grape Design	70.00
Shears, Grapes & Leaves In Relief, Marked	85.00
Shoehorn, Engraved Handle, 6 3/4 In.	48.00
Shoehorn, Ornate, 7 In.	35.00
Spoon, Child's, Little Boy Blue	25.00
Spoon, Demitasse, Salem Witch	68.00
Spoon, Nut, Marshall Field & Co.	28.00
SILVER–STERLING, SPOON, SOUVENIR, see Souvenir, Spoon, Sterling Silver	
Spoon, Teddy Bear	75.00
Strainer, Tea, Lily–of–The–Valley Handle	45.00
Sugar & Creamer, Anchor Sign, Large	70.00
Tea Ball, Bucket Shape, With Bail, Chain & Ring, 1 1/4 In.	40.00
Tea Caddy, Engraved Floral Bud Design, Marked, 4 1/2 In.	225.00
Tea Set, Tray, Marked H.H., Miniature, 8 Piece	20.00
Tea Strainer, Wooden Handle, Heart Shape	30.00
Teapot, Victorian, Bright Cut Pewter Overlay, C.1880	295.00
Teething Ring & Rattle, Baby's, Boot Shape	35.00
Tray, Gadrooned Rim, Stylized Florals, Oval, C.1842, 13 In.	350.00
SILVER–SWEDISH, Salt, Viking Boat Form, Cobalt Liner, Powder Horn Pepper	55.00
Spoon, Twist Stem, Ball Finial, Monogram, Bergen, 6 In.	412.00
SILVER–TURKISH, Tray, Scalloped, Cartouche Handles, Strapwork, 26 In.	1100.00

Sinclaire cut glass was made by H.P. Sinclaire and Company of Corning, New York, between 1905 and 1929. He cut glass made at other factories until 1920. Pieces were made of crystal as well as amber, blue, green, or ruby glass. Only a small percentage of Sinclaire glass is marked with the S in a wreath.

SINCLAIRE, Compote, Green, Signed, 6 1/2 X 2 In.	45.00
Cordial, Engraved, Signed, Set of 8	175.00
Decanter, Cranberry To Vaseline, Cane, Fan & Crosshatch, 16 In.	4200.00
Plate, Canvasback	550.00
Plate, Woodcock	650.00
Tray, Silver Thread, 8 Sides	1600.00
Vase, Diamonds & Silver Threads, 12 In.	525.00
Vase, Floral Engraving, 12 In.	165.00
Water Set, Etched Grapes & Vines, Amber Handle, Green, 9 3/4 In.	400.00

Slag glass resembles a marble cake. It can be streaked with different
colors. There were many types made from about 1880. Pink slag
was an American Victorian product of unknown origin. Purple and
blue slag were made in American and English factories. Red slag is
a very late–Victorian and twentieth–century glass. Other colors are
known but are of less importance to the collector.

SLAG, Blue, Creamer, Seaweed Design, English	50.00
Blue, Vase, Open Lattice, 4 1/2 In., Pair	50.00
SLAG, CARAMEL, see Chocolate Glass	
Green, Jar, Covered, Beehive	45.00
Green, Pitcher, Windmill	55.00
Pink, Cruet, Inverted Fan & Feather, Original Stopper	950.00 To 1500.00
Pink, Punch Cup, Inverted Fan & Feather, 2 1/2 In.	235.00
Pink, Spooner, Inverted Fan & Feather, Molded–In, Greentown, Ind.	265.00
Pink, Tumbler, Feather & Fan, St.Clair	35.00
Pink, Tumbler, Inverted Fan & Feather	385.00
Purple, Basket, 4 In.	38.00
Purple, Bowl, Covered, Cherry & Leaf, 3 Sections, 5 1/2 X 7 1/2 In.	80.00
Purple, Butter, Cactus, Covered	275.00
Purple, Butter, Covered, Block & Star, Paneled	60.00
Purple, Cake Plate, Pedestal	60.00
Purple, Creamer, Sunflower	68.00
Purple, Dish, Fox Cover, Iridescent	110.00
Purple, Dish, Hen On Nest Cover, Heisey, 6 In.	425.00
Purple, Dish, Lion, Covered, Westmoreland	85.00
Purple, Dish, Mother Eagle Cover, Iridescent	110.00
Purple, Dish, Ocean Shell, Northwood, 1901	40.00
Purple, Dish, Rabbit Cover, Iridescent	110.00
Purple, Figurine, Billy Cat	45.00
Purple, Goblet	40.00
Purple, Plate, Open Edge, 10 In.	40.00
Purple, Rooster, On Lacy Base, Imperial	85.00
Purple, Spooner, Crossbar & Flute	75.00
Purple, Spooner, Flower Panel	65.00 To 80.00
Purple, Spooner, Oval Medallion	80.00
Purple, Spooner, Scroll With Acanthus	35.00
Purple, Sugar & Creamer, Scalloped Tops, Footed, Creamer, 4 1/2 In.	95.00
Purple, Toothpick, Ring Handle	25.00
Purple, Tray, Shield, Fan & Leaf, Handles	85.00
Red, Butter, Round	38.00
Red, Compote, 4 X 4 In.	50.00
Red, Console Set, Mandarin, 3 Piece	65.00
Red, Fox, Westmoreland	29.50
Red, Pitcher, Windmill	50.00 To 55.00
Red, Vase, Thin Ribbed, 8 In.	30.00
Red, Vase, Thin Ribbed, 12 In.	55.00

Sleepy Eye pottery was made to be given away with the flour
products of the Sleepy Eye Milling Co., Sleepy Eye, Minnesota,
from about 1893 to 1952. It is a heavy stoneware with blue
decorations, usually decorated with the famous profile of the Indian.
Reproductions of the pitchers are being made today. The original
pitchers came in only five sizes: 4 in., 5 1/4 in., 6 1/2 in., 8 in., and
9 in. Sleepy Eye collectors also search for other advertising material
related to the flour mill.

SLEEPY EYE, Barrel, Commemorative, 1982	22.50 To 30.00
Butter Crock, Blue On Gray	210.00 To 365.00
Button, Pinback	90.00
Canister, Coffee, Blue & White	145.00
Cookbook, Loaf of Bread	35.00
Fan, Indian Chief Picture, 1900	175.00
Fan, Mill, Lady	90.00
Label, Barrel, Colored, Sleepy Eye Mills, Sleepy Eye, Minn.	230.00

Label, Cigar Box, 2 1/2 X 6 In.	90.00
Letter Opener, Sleepy Eye Mill	575.00
Light Pull, Sack of Flour	105.00
Match Holder, Wall, Painted Plaster of Paris	298.00 To 400.00
Mirror, Pocket, Reproduction	7.00 To 10.00
Mug, Blue & White, 4 1/4 In.	130.00 To 135.00
Mug, Blue & White, 4 3/4 In.	175.00 To 195.00
Mug, Brown, 1952	34.00
Mug, Commemorative, 1977	80.00
Mug, White, 4 In.	600.00 To 850.00
Paperweight, Bronze	290.00
Pin, 1872–1972 Centennial	3.00
Pin, Club Membership, Blue & White	30.00
Pitcher, No.1, Blue & White, 4 1/2 In.	85.00
Pitcher, No.2, Blue & Gray, 5 1/4 In.	205.00 To 225.00
Pitcher, No.2, Blue & White, 5 1/4 In.	70.00 To 175.00
Pitcher, No.3, Blue & White, 6 1/2 In.	125.00
Pitcher, No.4, Blue & White, Peoria Wine Advertising, 8 In.	290.00
Pitcher, No.5, Blue & Gray, 9 In.	340.00 To 385.00
Pitcher, No.5, Blue & White, 9 In.	175.00
Pitcher, Sesquicentennial, 1981	155.00 To 185.00
Pitcher, Signed Western Stoneware, 4 In.	175.00
Plaque, 75th Anniversary, 1947	12.50
Plate, 1872–1972 Centennial	20.00
Postcard, Complete, Set of 9	350.00 To 500.00
Ruler, 15 In.	600.00
Scraper, Breadboard	320.00
Sign, Indian Chief, Cardboard Fan, 1900	150.00
Spoon, Indian Handle, Silver Plate	82.50
Spoon, Roses, Demitasse	95.00
Stein, Blue & White, 7 3/4 In.	425.00 To 450.00
Stein, Brown & White, 7 3/4 In.	750.00 To 900.00
Stein, Brown, 1952, 5 1/2 In.	260.00
Stein, Brown, 1952, 7 3/4 In.	375.00
Stein, Director's, 1968	175.00
Stein, Flemish Blue On Gray, 7 3/4 In.	405.00
Stein, Solid Cobalt Blue, 7 3/4 In.	495.00
Sugar & Creamer, Stamped Western Stoneware, Co., Blue On White	450.00
Sugar, Signed Monmouth	225.00 To 385.00
Thimble, Aluminum	200.00
Vase, Allover Cobalt Blue, 8 1/2 In.	225.00
Vase, Brown & White, 8 1/2 In.	450.00 To 700.00
Vase, Cattail, Cobalt Blue & White, 8 1/2 In.	250.00
Vase, Frog & Bulrushes, Dragonfly, Blue & Gray, 9 In.	210.00 To 250.00

Slip is a thin mixture of clay and water, about the consistency of sour cream, that is applied to pottery for decoration. It is a very old method of making pottery and is still in use.

SLIPWARE, Figurine, Pig, White Clay, Spots, Albany, 1 3/4 In.	135.00
Jug, Harvest, White, Embossed Clay Screwheads At Handle, 4 In.	150.00

SLOT MACHINE, see Coin–Operated Machine

Smith Bros. Co. Smith Brothers glass was made after 1878. Alfred and Harry Smith had worked for the Mt. Washington Glass Company in New Bedford, Massachusetts, for seven years before going into their own shop. They made many pieces with enamel decoration.

SMITH BROTHERS, Bowl, Melon Ribbed, Yellow Daisies, White Ground, 4 1/4 In.	235.00
Bowl, White Flowers, Green Leaves, Gold Tracing, 9 In.	350.00
Cookie Jar, Pansies, Buds, Glass Lid, 7 1/4 In.	585.00
Mustard, Columned Ribs, Flowers, Blue Dots At Rim, 3 In.	155.00
Powder Box, Roses, Outlined In Gold, 5 In.	450.00
Rose Bowl, Ribbed Panels, Flowers, Signed	250.00
Toothpick, Columned Ribs, Pansies, Blue Dots At Rim	115.00
Vase, Allover Shasta Daisy Design, Dotted Top, 5 In.	225.00

Vase, Clematis Blossoms, Pillow Shape, Borders, 8 3/4 In.	385.00
Vase, Heron In Rushes, Signed, 4 1/2 In.	65.00
Vase, Kate Greenaway Figures, Light Green, 5 3/4 In.	90.00

> Snow Babies, made from bisque and spattered with glitter sand, were first manufactured in 1864 by Hertwig and Company of Thuringia. Other German and Japanese companies copied the Hertwig designs. Originally, Snow Babies were made of candy and used as Christmas decorations. There are also Snow Babies tablewares made by Royal Bayreuth. Copies of the small Snow Babies figurines are being made today and can easily confuse the collector.

SNOW BABIES, Chocolate Pot, Royal Bayreuth, Blue Mark	135.00
Doll, Bisque, Socket Head, Fur Parka, Glass Eyes, 12 In.	250.00
Doll, On Sled, 2 In.	55.00
Doll, Sitting, Arms Down, 1 1/2 In.	25.00
Figurine, Front of Small Old House, Marked Chest, 1 1/2 In.	65.00
Figurine, Lying On Top of Igloo, Polar Bear, Marked, 2 1/2 In.	75.00
Figurine, Santa In Chimney	85.00
Paperweight	50.00
Plate, Playing Flute, Germany	85.00
Playing Musical Instrument, 6 1/2 In.	165.00
Tea Set, Sledding, Child's, Royal Bayreuth, 6 Piece	295.00
SNUFF BOTTLE, see Bottle, Snuff	

> Taking snuff was popular long before cigarettes became available. The snuff was kept in a small box. The gentleman or lady would take a small pinch of the ground tobacco or snuff in the fingers, then sniff it and sneeze. Snuffboxes were made of many materials, including gold, silver, enameled metal, and wood. Most snuffboxes date from the late eighteenth or early nineteenth century.

SNUFFBOX, 2 Sections, Engraved, Armorial Design, Rampant Lions, 1765	125.00
Birch Bark, Deer Scene	40.00
Brass, Engraved G.A.D., Star of David, 1940, Oval, 3 1/2 In.	125.00
Cameo of Dog On Cover, 2–Color Gold, French, Round, 1777	4675.00
Carved Horn Swan, Silver Mounts, C.1780	285.00
Enameled, Jewels Form Basket On Cover, Swiss, 3 5/8 In.	7700.00
Floral Pattern On Cover, Oval, England, C.1840	85.00
Gold & Diamond Set, Rectangular, Swiss, C.1815, 3 3/8 In.	8525.00
Gold & Enamel, G.Reymond & Co., Psyche, Cupid, C.1810, 3 5/8 In.	5775.00
Gold, Circular, G.Reymond & Co., Slip–On Cover, Swiss, 2 3/8 In.	2640.00
Hand Painted, Naughty Connotations, Papier–Mache, C.1820	550.00
La Bretagne, Walnut, Silver Trim	350.00
Louis XV, Gold Mounted, Lacquer, Paris, 1766, 3 3/8 In.	3960.00
Oval Agate Panel On Hinged Cover, Paris, C.1825, 3 3/8 In.	7700.00
Scottish Horn, Stone Mount, C.1780	395.00
Shoe, Wooden, C.1885, 3 3/4 X 3/4 In.	96.00
Tortoise & Horn	55.00
Wall of China Design, Cloisonne, Oval, 2 In. .... 35.00 To	40.00

> Soapstone is a mineral that was used for foot warmers or griddles because of its heat–retaining properties. Soapstone was carved into figurines and bowls in many countries in the nineteenth and twentieth centuries. Most of the soapstone seen today is from China or Japan. It is still being carved in the old styles.

SOAPSTONE, Bookends, Marbled Beige, Maroon	60.00
Box, Jewel, Black Matte, Carved Soapstone Birds	75.00
Figure, Fisherman, Carved Base, Bearded Man, Fish, Basket, 21 In.	300.00
Figurine, Foo Dog, 1850s, 7 1/2 In.	140.00
Figurine, Greyhound, Reclining, 6 In.	75.00
Figurine, Mother & Child, Eskimo, Inuit, Registered	1200.00
Goblet, 5 In.	20.00
Incense Burner, 10 In.	75.00
Incense Burner, Art Deco, 12 In.	125.00

Jar, Covered, 5 Sections, Mottled, Tan, Foo Dog, China, 12 In. 500.00
Toothpick, 3 Monkeys 24.00
Urn, People, Scenes, Plants, Elephant Handles, Mounted, 10 1/4 In. 150.00
Vase, Carved Floral Design, China, 7 In. 85.00
Vase, Double, Monkeys, Birds, Tree Trunk, 8 1/4 X 3 1/2 In. 75.00
Whistle, Double Fish 25.00

> Soft paste is a name for a type of pottery. Although it looks very
> much like porcelain, it is a chemically different material. Most of
> the soft–paste wares were made in the early nineteenth century.
> Other pieces may be listed under Gaudy Dutch or Leeds.

SOFT PASTE, Bowl, Blue Oriental Design, 8 3/4 X 3 5/8 In. 175.00
Bowl, Gothic Building, Light Blue, 9 X 3 7/8 In. 35.00
Creamer, King's Rose .... 135.00 To 165.00
Creamer, Red Masonic Transfer, Floral Enameling, 4 In. 150.00
Cup & Saucer, Handleless, Blue Transfer, Staffordshire 30.00
Cup, King's Rose 50.00
Dish, Classical Building, Quatrefoil Shape, 7 7/8 X 8 In., Pair 70.00
Figurine, Man & Dog, Woman & Goat, English, 5 1/2 In., Pair 60.00
Mug, Mother, Child In Lap, Black Transfer 38.00
Plaque, Thou God Seest Me, Black & Yellow, 6 3/4 In. 125.00
Plate, King's Rose, Luster Trim, English, 9 In. 90.00
Plate, King's Rose, Vining Border, 8 To 8 3/8 In., Set of 5 .... 225.00
Sugar, Covered, Rose & Leaf, C.1840 .... 150.00
Tea Set, Blue Oriental Transfer, Purple Luster Trim, 3 Piece 100.00
Teapot, Medium Blue Transfer, Cows, 5 1/2 In. 90.00

> What could be more fun than to bring home a souvenir of a trip?
> Our ancestors enjoyed the same thing and souvenirs were made for
> almost every location. Most of the souvenir pottery and porcelain
> pieces of the nineteenth century were made in England or Germany,
> even if the picture showed a North American scene. In the
> twentieth century, the souvenir china business seems to have gone to
> the Japanese, Taiwanese, English, and American makers. Another
> popular souvenir item is the souvenir spoon, made of sterling or
> silver plate. These are usually made in the country pictured on the
> spoon.

SOUVENIR, Ashtray, California & Pacific International Expo, Bronze, 1935 .... 20.00
Ashtray, Pan American, Embossed Buffalo 17.00
Ashtray, PGA Championship, July, 1964, Columbus Country Club 85.00
Bag, Canvas, 13 Winter Olympic Games, Lake Placid, N.Y., 1980 .... 45.00
Banner, Ringling Bros.& Barnum & Bailey Circus 10.00
Baseball Bat, Cincinnati Reds, Black, 1970 .... 150.00
Bat, World Series, Cardinals Vs.Athletics, 1931, Miniature 100.00
Beer & Pretzel Set, Century of Progress, 1933, Custard Glass 250.00
Bowl, Panama–Pacific Int.Expo.1915, Redwood Burl, 3 X 2 In. 12.00
Butter, Covered, Custard Glass, Edmore, S.D. 60.00
Card, Pan American, Colored 3.00
Cover, Pillow, Coney Island, Silk 15.00
Cup & Saucer, First Centennial American Independence, 1776–1876 .... 85.00
Frying Pan, Pan American, 1901 .... 12.00
Goblet, Red Flashed, Clear Fluted Bottom, Ohio Centennial, 1912 .... 45.00
Mug, 23 Olympiad, Los Angeles, Budweiser Beer, Polychromed, 1984 .... 75.00
Mug, Beer, Burley & Co., Pan American Exposition, 1901 .... 125.00
Mug, Beer, Glass, Protruding Stars, Paneled Sides, 1776–1876, 5 In. 80.00
Mug, Columbian Exposition, Columbus & Washington Busts, 1893 .... 55.00
Nappy, Glens Falls, Scene, Yellow Ground 45.00
Paperweight, With Ticket For Chicago Day, Dated Oct.9, 1893 .... 35.00
Picture, Reverse Painting On Glass, Cascades, 1904 Expo, Framed 36.00
Plate, Arizona, State Seal, Jerome, Navajo, 1912, 10 In. 18.00
Plate, Bottineau, N.Dakota 17.00
Plate, Cantilever Bridge, Spokane, Washington 20.00
Plate, George Washington & John Adams, 1932 .... 35.00
Plate, Independence Hall, Philadelphia, Openwork Rim, 8 1/4 In. 18.00

Plate, Jamestown Expo., Blue & White, 1907, 9 In.	40.00
Plate, Mindenmines, Missouri	15.00
Plate, Niagara Falls, Gold Rim, Blue, 8 In.	24.50
Plate, Sharon, Kansas	15.00
Plate, St.Louis, Re–Dedication of Santa Maria, Crystal, 1969	11.00
Plate, Vandalie, Missouri	12.00
Platter, Battleship Maine, Sea Shells, Sebring, 1898, 11 In.	12.00
Shoe, Public Library, Des Moines, Wheelock, Cobalt Blue	22.00
Shot Glass, American Exposition, Case, 1901	35.00
Shot Glass, Ruby Saloon, Palestine, Texas, Etched	16.50
Slipper, Gillinder Glass, Embossed Name, 1886 Centennial Exhibit	35.00
Spoon, Chicago Exposition, Sterling Silver, 1893	28.00
Spoon, Moon Landing, 1969, Holland, 4 1/2 In.	10.00
Spoon, Pan American, Embossed Indian Head, Niagara Falls	20.00
Spoon, San Gabriel Mission, Ca., Sterling Silver	35.00
Spoon, Silver Plate, Columbian Expo.Transportation Building	27.00
Spoon, Silver Plate, Heinz Pickles, View of Home Office	7.00
Spoon, Silver Plate, Kansas, Sunflower	10.00
Spoon, Silver Plate, Lincoln Monument, Springfield, Figural, 1904	35.00
Spoon, Silver Plate, McKinley Handle, Eagle Bowl, Temple of Music	50.00
Spoon, Silver Plate, Missouri, Missouri Mule, Cutout	25.00
Spoon, Silver Plate, Norma Talmadge Bust, 6 In.	6.00
Spoon, Silver Plate, Pan Am, Indian, 1901	15.00
Spoon, Silver Plate, Puerto Rico, Shield, Flag, 4 1/2 In.	2.00
Spoon, Silver Plate, Queen Elizabeth Silver Jubilee	7.50
Spoon, Silver Plate, States, Rogers, 1915	9.00
Spoon, Silver Plate, Statue of Liberty, Cutout	20.00
Spoon, Silver Plate, University of Illinois, Dated 1921	12.50
Spoon, Silver Plate, Washington, D.C., Jefferson Memorial, Enamel	18.00
Spoon, Sterling Silver, Alabama, Demitasse	22.00
Spoon, Sterling Silver, Alaska Totem Pole	16.00
Spoon, Sterling Silver, Andrew Jackson On Bowl	28.00
Spoon, Sterling Silver, Anniston, Alabama	29.00
Spoon, Sterling Silver, Atlanta, Ga., Figural, Black Boy, 3 5/8 In.	85.00
Spoon, Sterling Silver, Atlantic City, Cutout Fish Handle	25.00
Spoon, Sterling Silver, Atlantic City, N.J., Lighthouse	30.00
Spoon, Sterling Silver, Auditorium, Milwaukee, 5 1/4 In.	18.00
Spoon, Sterling Silver, Baltimore, Washington Monument, Bowl	22.00
Spoon, Sterling Silver, Bridal Altar, Mammoth Cave, Ky., 5 1/4 In.	23.00
Spoon, Sterling Silver, Butter, Montana, Miner Handle, Anaconda	45.00
Spoon, Sterling Silver, Cairo, Sphinx, Camels In Bowl	30.00
Spoon, Sterling Silver, Calgary, Flowers On Handle, Calgary, Cup	25.00
Spoon, Sterling Silver, Capricorn, Goat, Cherub & Holly Handle	25.00
Spoon, Sterling Silver, Carlsbad Cavern, Totem Poles	25.00
Spoon, Sterling Silver, Catalina Island, Tuna Handle, 5 1/8 In.	45.00
Spoon, Sterling Silver, Chicago Art Institute, 1918	25.00
Spoon, Sterling Silver, Chicago Century of Progress, 1933	30.00
Spoon, Sterling Silver, Chicago, Art Institute, 1918	30.00
Spoon, Sterling Silver, Colorado Skyline	24.00
Spoon, Sterling Silver, Colorado, Buffalo Bill, Lookout Mt.	38.00
Spoon, Sterling Silver, Columbus, Handle, Women's Building, 1893	50.00
Spoon, Sterling Silver, Court House, Fort Worth, Texas, 5 1/2 In.	28.00
Spoon, Sterling Silver, Court House, Fredonia, Kansas, 5 1/4 In.	28.00
Spoon, Sterling Silver, Court House, Peoria, Illinois, 5 In.	26.00
Spoon, Sterling Silver, Court House, Ravenna, Ohio, 5 1/2 In.	18.00
Spoon, Sterling Silver, Cripple Creek, Embossed Burro, 3 1/2 In.	15.00
Spoon, Sterling Silver, D.A.R., Spinning Wheel On Handle	48.00
Spoon, Sterling Silver, Drew University, N.J., Building, 4 1/4 In.	25.00
Spoon, Sterling Silver, Duluth Skyline	23.00
Spoon, Sterling Silver, Easter, Cherubs On Handle, Crown Bowl	45.00
Spoon, Sterling Silver, Edgar Thompson Steel Co., Braddock, Pa.	65.00
Spoon, Sterling Silver, Florida, Alligator Handle, Clown In Bowl	40.00
Spoon, Sterling Silver, Florida, Openwork Handle, Palm Tree	10.00
Spoon, Sterling Silver, Fort Dearborn, 1830	30.00

Spoon, Sterling Silver, Ft.Smith, Arkansas 22.50
Spoon, Sterling Silver, Gettysburg, General Meade Handle, 5 In. 29.00
Spoon, Sterling Silver, Gold Miner, Figure Handle, Dated 65.00
Spoon, Sterling Silver, Government Building Bowl, 1893, 4 In. 50.00
Spoon, Sterling Silver, Grand Canyon, Hopi House 30.00
Spoon, Sterling Silver, Greek Letters On Handle, White Enamel 25.00
Spoon, Sterling Silver, Harvard College 18.00
Spoon, Sterling Silver, Hawaiian Hibiscus, Bonbon, 5 1/2 In. 95.00
Spoon, Sterling Silver, Head of Columbus, Dated 1893 .... 25.00
Spoon, Sterling Silver, Hermitage, Ogden Canyon, Utah 19.00
Spoon, Sterling Silver, High School, Hartford, Michigan ....25.00 To 35.00
Spoon, Sterling Silver, Horseshoe Bend, 5 13/16 In. 65.00
Spoon, Sterling Silver, Hot Springs, Indian Headdress Handle 30.00
Spoon, Sterling Silver, Hudson River, Hudson Ship, Robert Fulton 35.00
Spoon, Sterling Silver, Ill.State Prison, Ear of Corn Handle 95.00
Spoon, Sterling Silver, Illinois, Embossed 17.00
Spoon, Sterling Silver, Indian Figure Handle, Mfgrs.Bldg., 1909 .... 65.00
Spoon, Sterling Silver, Indian In Canoe, 5 1/4 In. 55.00
Spoon, Sterling Silver, LaJolla, Beach Scene, Enameled, Crest 25.00
Spoon, Sterling Silver, Las Vegas, Cowboy, Horse 18.00
Spoon, Sterling Silver, Leif Ericson, 5 15/16 In. 95.00
Spoon, Sterling Silver, Lewis & Clark, Exposition, 1905 .... 50.00
Spoon, Sterling Silver, Lighthouse, Atlantic City, N.J., 4 In. 22.00
Spoon, Sterling Silver, Maccabee Temple, Port Huron, Mi. 15.00
Spoon, Sterling Silver, Manchester, Vt., Bright Cut Flowers 15.00
Spoon, Sterling Silver, Masonic Temple, Chicago 15.00
Spoon, Sterling Silver, Matador 20.00
Spoon, Sterling Silver, Mermaid, Holding Shell, Kansas City, Mo. 12.00
Spoon, Sterling Silver, Methodist Church, Stewartville, Mn. 20.00
Spoon, Sterling Silver, Miami, Seminoles In Everglades, 5 1/2 In. 12.00
Spoon, Sterling Silver, Miner, Portland Gold Mine, Cripple Creek 65.00
Spoon, Sterling Silver, Mining, Man On Handle, Lowering Bucket 45.00
Spoon, Sterling Silver, Missouri, Great Seal On Handle 35.00
Spoon, Sterling Silver, Mt.Washington, N.H., New Summit House 125.00
Spoon, Sterling Silver, New Orleans, 1891 Engraved In Bowl 13.00
Spoon, Sterling Silver, New Orleans, Pelican On Nest, 5 3/4 In. 25.00
Spoon, Sterling Silver, New Orleans, St.Louis Cathedral 32.00
Spoon, Sterling Silver, New York, Statue of Liberty, Cathedral 55.00
Spoon, Sterling Silver, New York, Tower Falls, Rochester 16.00
Spoon, Sterling Silver, Newport, R.I., Fort, Waterfront, 5 3/4 In. 29.00
Spoon, Sterling Silver, Niagara Falls, Indian Maiden Figural 150.00
Spoon, Sterling Silver, Niagara Falls, Indian Maiden, Canoe 25.00
Spoon, Sterling Silver, North Carolina, Demitasse 22.00
Spoon, Sterling Silver, Ogden, Utah 42.00
Spoon, Sterling Silver, Old Faithful & Inn, 5 5/8 In. 12.00
Spoon, Sterling Silver, Ponce De Leon, Figural 52.00
Spoon, Sterling Silver, Portland, Oregon, Mt.Hood On Handle Top 55.00
Spoon, Sterling Silver, Princess Victoria Steamer, Logging Scene 75.00
Spoon, Sterling Silver, Princeton, View of Nassau Hall, 4 7/8 In. 55.00
Spoon, Sterling Silver, Public School, Waycross, Georgia 18.00
Spoon, Sterling Silver, Richmond, Va. 35.00
Spoon, Sterling Silver, Rock Island 18.50
Spoon, Sterling Silver, Salem Witch, Marked Beatrice 1889 .... 24.00
Spoon, Sterling Silver, San Gabriel Mission, Calif. 35.00
Spoon, Sterling Silver, Santa Claus, Merry Christmas, Demitasse 45.00
Spoon, Sterling Silver, Santa Rosa, Ca., Court House 18.00
Spoon, Sterling Silver, Seattle, Totem Pole, Olympic Range View 25.00
Spoon, Sterling Silver, Seattle, Washington, Waterfall In Bowl 45.00
Spoon, Sterling Silver, Sir Francis Drake, Figural, Engraved Bowl 55.00
Spoon, Sterling Silver, Soldier's & Sailor's Monument, Newton 25.00
Spoon, Sterling Silver, Spokane Falls ....18.50 To 30.00
Spoon, Sterling Silver, St.Augustine, Plain Bowl, 5 3/8 In. 12.00
Spoon, Sterling Silver, St.Paul, Minnesota, Capitol 25.00
Spoon, Sterling Silver, State Prison, Joliet, Ill., Enameled Bowl 95.00

Spoon, Sterling Silver, Statue of Liberty Handle, New York	35.00
Spoon, Sterling Silver, Statue of Liberty, Cathedral In Bowl	55.00
Spoon, Sterling Silver, Statue of Liberty, Pierced, New York	28.00
Spoon, Sterling Silver, Summit, Pike's Peak, Columbine Handle	50.00
Spoon, Sterling Silver, Taylor Library, Milford, Ct. .... 25.00 To	30.00
Spoon, Sterling Silver, Tennessee, Demitasse	22.00
Spoon, Sterling Silver, Toledo, Ohio, 1902 On Handle, Armory, Cup	28.00
Spoon, Sterling Silver, Valparaiso, Indiana, Court House	35.00
Spoon, Sterling Silver, Washington Monument Handle, Capitol	28.00
Spoon, Sterling Silver, Westerly, R.I., Man's Head At Handle End	15.00
Spoon, Sterling Silver, White Canoe, Wyoming	65.00
Spoon, Sterling Silver, Wisconsin, State Seal, 5 1/4 In.	18.00
Spoon, Sterling Silver, Wyoming, Bucking Horse & Rider In Bowl	50.00
Spoon, Sterling Silver, Yellow Boat House, Oar-Shaped Handle	15.00
Spoon, Sterling Silver, Yellowstone National Park	28.00
Spoon, Sterling Silver, Yellowstone Park, Bear Handle	32.00
Spoon, Sterling, Alaska Steamship	45.00
Spoon, Sterling, Albright Art Gallery, Buffalo, N.Y.	30.00
Spoon, Sterling, Boy Eating Watermelon On Enameled Handle	135.00
Spoon, Sterling, Confederate Monument, Shreveport, La.	30.00
Spoon, Sterling, Henry W.Grady Monument, Atlanta, Ga.	30.00
Spoon, Sterling, High School & Stadium, Tacoma, Wash.	22.50
Spoon, Sterling, Hotel Oakland, Oakland, Cal.	25.00
Spoon, Sterling, New Park Hotel, Park City, Utah	28.00
Spoon, Sterling, Observation Peak, Ogden, Utah	25.00
Spoon, Sterling, Santa Barbara Mission, California	28.00
Spoon, Sterling, Summit, Pike's Peak, Columbine	50.00
Spoon, Sterling, Umbrella Rock, Tenn.	25.00
Spooner, 3 Dragons, St.Louis, Oct.3, 1899	125.00
Sugar & Creamer, Winston Churchill Portrait, White, Sutherland	15.00
Sugar, Open, Cobalt Porcelain, Barberton High School, 1906	38.00
Toothpick, Deer Park, Wis., Ruby	38.00
Tumbler, Kindred, S.D, Ruby	25.00
Tumbler, Remember Pearl Harbor	9.00

> Spangle glass is multicolored glass made from odds and ends of
> colored glass rods. It includes metallic flakes of mica covered with
> gold, silver, nickel, or copper. Spangle glass is usually cased with a
> thin layer of clear glass over the multicolored layer.

SPANGLE GLASS, see also Vasa Murrhina

SPANGLE GLASS, Basket, Blue, Applied Handle, 8 In.	20.00
Basket, Gold, Pleated Edge, Twisted Clear Handle, 10 In.	80.00
Basket, Twisted Handle, Blue, 7 X 6 3/4 In.	195.00
Ewer, Thorn Handle, Blue, Silver Mica	125.00
Finger Bowl, Underplate, Cobalt Blue, Gold, Aventurine	65.00
Pitcher, Amber, Bulbous, Blown, Cape Cod Glass Co., 5 7/8 In.	125.00
Syrup, Pink & White, Silver	135.00
Vase, Emerald Green, Melon Ribbed, Silver Mica, 6 In.	45.00

> Spanish lace is a type of Victorian glass that has a white lace
> design. Blue, yellow, cranberry, or clear glass was made with this
> distinctive white pattern. It was made in England and the United
> States after 1885. Copies are being made.

SPANISH LACE, Bowl, Cranberry, 4 X 3 In.	75.00
Carafe, Water, Blue	125.00
Celery, Ruffled, White, Bulbous	95.00
Finger Bowl, Vaseline, 4 5/8 X 2 5/8 In.	40.00
Lamp, Banquet, Kerosene Font, Duplex Burner	650.00
Pitcher, Blue, 5 1/2 In. .... 32.00 To	35.00
Pitcher, Water, White Opalescent .... 95.00 To	110.00
Salt & Pepper	175.00
Sugar Shaker, White	110.00
Syrup, Vaseline	145.00
Vase, Folded Over Crimped Top, Blue Opalescent, 6 1/4 In.	50.00

Water Set, Blue, 7 Piece 345.00

> Spatter glass is a multicolored glass made from many small pieces of different colored glass. It is sometimes called "End–Of–Day" glass. It is still being made.

SPATTER GLASS, Basket, 4 Petal Top, Melon Sectioned, Twist Handle, 6 In. 118.00
Basket, Inverted Thumbprint, Ruffled, Thorn Handle, 7 In. 135.00
Basket, Thorn Handle, Maroon, Yellow & Green, 7 1/2 In. 165.00
Bottle, Perfume, Atomizer, Jade Foot, No Bulb, France 54.00
Bowl, Stick, Gaudy Floral, Staffordshire, 14 5/8 X 3 In. 70.00
Cruet, Inverted Thumbprint, Amber, Blue Handle 60.00
Cruet, Red & White, Faceted Stopper, 19th Century, 5 1/2 In. 88.00
Cup & Saucer, Handless, 19th Century 47.50
Darner, Sock, White, Blue, Pink, 19th Century, 5 1/2 In. 140.00
Figurine, Road Runner, Clear Crest, Bill, Tripod Base, 15 In. 100.00
Flask, Opaque Glass Interior, Clear Outer Layer, 7 1/4 In. 350.00
Lamp, Fairy, Embossed Swirl Pattern, Clarke Base, 4 7/8 In. 145.00
Lamp, Fairy, Pyramid, Clarke Base, White Lining, 3 3/4 In. 100.00
Pitcher, Cranberry, White, Maroon, Clear Handle, 8 In. 110.00
Pitcher, Pink & Maroon Spatter, Clear Handle, 7 1/2 In. 80.00
Pitcher, Pink & White Swirl, Clear Handle, 8 In. 225.00
Pitcher, Ruffled Top, Clear Handle, White & Pink, 8 1/2 In. 90.00
Pitcher, Water, Fluted Rim, Yellow Base, Allover Ruby 365.00
Pitcher, Water, White, Pink & Maroon, Clear Applied Handle 85.00
Pitcher, White & Yellow, Orange Trim, 2 3/4 In. 48.00
Vase, Jack–In–The–Pulpit, 5 Point Top, Maroon, White, 11 In. 95.00
Vase, Maroon, Blue, 12 1/4 In. 65.00
Vase, Red, Gray, Green, Pink, Clear Glass, Pear Shape, 9 In. 80.00

> The creamware or soft–paste dinnerware decorated with spatter designs in color is called, of course, spatterware. The earliest pieces were made in the late eighteenth century, but most of the spatterware found today was made from about 1800 to 1850 or is a late nineteenth– and twentieth–century form of kitchen crockery that has added spatter designs. The early spatterware was made in the Staffordshire district of England for sale in America. The kitchen type is an American product.

SPATTERWARE, Bowl, Blue, 11 In. 68.00
Bowl, Cream, Blue, Rust, Whitemore, Iowa, 7 In. 60.00
Bowl, Rockwell City, Iowa, Blue, Rust & Cream, 6 In. 60.00
Bowl, Scrolled Edge, 8 In. 55.00
Cup & Saucer, Apple Tree 2200.00
Cup & Saucer, Bull's–Eye Red Rose Center, Rainbow 55.00
Cup & Saucer, Handless, Blue Stick, Eagle & Shield 100.00
Cup & Saucer, Handless, Brown & Black Rainbow, Rose Center 175.00
Cup & Saucer, Peafowl, Green 150.00
Cup & Saucer, Vine & Berry, Miniature 231.00
Cup Plate, Peafowl 220.00
Cup, School House, Blue, Handless 245.00
Pitcher, Swirl Ribbed Body, Brown, Blue & White Pattern, 9 In. 65.00
Plate, Dahlia, Rainbow, 8 5/8 In. 85.00
Plate, Peafowl, Red, 7 5/8 In. 300.00
Plate, Rainbow, Red & Yellow, 8 1/2 In. 275.00
Plate, Tulip, Blue, 8 5/8 In. 225.00
Platter, Blue, 13 1/2 In. 45.00
Platter, Peafowl, Red, 15 3/4 In. 135.00
Saucer, School House, Blue, 5 3/4 In. 75.00
Sugar, Black, Purple, Rainbow, 5 1/2 In. 25.00
Sugar, Peafowl In Red, Purple, Black, & Green, Lid, 4 1/4 In. 85.00
Sugar, Rose, Blue, 3 5/8 In. 25.00
Teapot, Peafowl, Red, Orange, Black, Green, Blue, 8 7/8 In. 225.00

Spelter is a synonym for a zinc alloy. Figurines, candlesticks, and other pieces were made of spelter and given a bronze or painted finish. The metal has been used since about the 1860s to make statues, tablewares, and lamps that resemble bronze. Spelter is soft and breaks easily. To test for spelter, scratch the base of the piece. Bronze is solid; spelter will show a silvery scratch.

SPELTER, Bust, Thomas Jefferson, Bronzed, Alva Studios, 1954, 10 In.	65.00
Bust, Woman, 11 1/2 In.	125.00
Container, Figural, German Shepherd, For Cigarette Butts	24.00
Figurine, Dachshund, Black & Brown, 4 In.	22.00
Figurine, Horse, Standing, Marbleized Onyx Base, 9 1/2 X 3 In.	165.00
Figurine, Rearing Hose, Signed Colstoll, C.1900, 21 X 21 1/2 In.	250.00
Figurine, Roman Soldiers, Bronzed, 12 In., Pair	175.00
Figurine, Scotty, Begging By Dish, Marked & Dated, 6 In.	35.00
Figurine, Standing Horse, Marbled Onyx Base, 10 3/4 In.	135.00
Inkwell, Stamp Box, White, Dated 1924, 2 Piece	45.00
Urn, Mantel, Empire, Allegorical Figures, 14 In., Pr.	85.00

 The old spinning wheel in the corner has been the symbol of earlier times for the past 100 years. Although spinning wheels date back to medieval times, the ones found today are rarely more than 200 years old. Because the style of the spinning wheel changed very little, it is often impossible to place an exact date on a wheel.

SPINNING WHEEL, Black Paint, Signed & Dated 1857, Norwegian	650.00
Chip Carved, Turned Legs, 45 1/2 In.	235.00
Ivory Trim, 49 3/4 In.	300.00
Upright, Original Blue Paint	225.00

 Spode pottery, porcelain, and bone china were made by the Stoke-on-Trent factory of England founded by Josiah Spode about 1770. The firm became Copeland and Garrett from 1833 to 1847, then W.T. Copeland or W.T. Copeland and Sons until 1976. It then became Royal Worcester Spode Ltd. The word "Spode" appears on many pieces made by the factories. Most collectors include all the wares under the more familiar name of Spode. Porcelains are listed in this book by the name that appears on the piece.

SPODE, see also Copeland; Copeland Spode

SPODE, Butter Chip, Maritime Rose, Blue	12.00
Casserole, Covered, Gainsborough	75.00
Compote, Net Pattern, C.1810	350.00
Cup & Saucer, Florals, C.1815	160.00
Cup & Saucer, Italian	35.00
Cup, Gainsborough	10.00
Invalid Feeder	295.00
Pitcher, Queen's Bird, 5 1/2 In.	35.00
Plate, Christmas Partridge, 1970	40.00
Plate, Flowers & Birds, Gold Design, 6 In.	105.00
Platter, Fairy Dell, 15 In.	50.00
Ring Tree, Pink Roses	30.00
Teapot, Old Salem	65.00
Tureen, Sauce, Wild Rose, C.1830	165.00
Tureen, Soup, Top, Blue	135.00

Spongeware is very similar to spatterware in appearance. The designs were applied to the ceramics by daubing the color on with a sponge or cloth. Many collectors do not differentiate between spongeware and spatterware and use the names interchangeably. Modern pottery is being made to resemble the old spongeware, but careful examination will show it is new.

SPONGEWARE, Bank, Pig, Green-Gray Sponging On Cream, 4 3/4 X 2 1/4 In.	75.00
Bowl, Advertising, Mix With Us, Save Dough, Blue, Rust, 7 In.	65.00
Bowl, Blue & Rust, Gray Paneled, 8 1/4 X 4 3/4 In.	42.00
Bowl, Blue & White, 5 In.	80.00

Bowl, Blue, Rust & Cream, 6 In. 50.00
Bowl, Boone Dairy Products, 4th Anniversary, 6 1/2 In. 50.00
Bowl, Brown & Green On Cream, 3 X 6 3/4 In. 37.50
Bowl, Brown, Blue & Red, Cream Ground, 9 1/2 X 4 7/8 In. 65.00
Bowl, Cream & Green, 10 1/2 In. 130.00
Bowl, Embossed Looped Design, Rim Band, C.1830, 10 3/4 In. 210.00
Bowl, Fluted, 7 In. 38.00
Bowl, Mixing, Blue, Brown, Cream, Wents & Sons of Galva, Iowa 45.00
Bowl, Roseville, Ohio, 15 1/2 In. 165.00
Box, Dovetailed Hump Top, Iron Swing Handles, 24 X 12 X 11 In. 325.00
Butter Tub, Daisy On Lattice, Green & Cream 145.00
Case, Blue & White, 10 3/4 In. 225.00
Chamber Pot, Blue & Gray 120.00
Cooler, Ice Water, Western, Blue & White, 4 Gal. 435.00
Creamer, Cow, With Milkmaid 2200.00
Crock, White Hall, Ill., 1 Qt. 80.00
Jardiniere, Brown & White Sponge Border, Blue, 9 1/2 X 11 In. 140.00
Jug, Maple Leaf, 1 Gal. 45.00
Mug, Brown On Yellow, 4 1/2 In. 65.00
Pitcher, Bulbous Base, Inverted V Design, 9 In. 125.00
Pitcher, Green & Brown, Cream Ground, 7 In. .... 85.00 To 90.00
Planter, Log, Green & Brown, 7 In. 20.00
Platter, Deep Blue, White Ground, 9 X 10 In. 175.00
Soup, Blue & White, Design, 7 1/2 X 2 1/2 In. 125.00
Spittoon, Blue ....80.00 To 145.00
Spittoon, Green & Cream 145.00
Spittoon, Rust Brown Markings, Cream 60.00
Tankard, Green & Rust On Yellow 95.00
Teapot, Brown & Green, Yellow Ground 65.00
Water Cooler, Bust Dots, Blue, Ohio, 2 Part 470.00
Water Filter, Spigot, Blue, White, Glued Lid, 25 In. 225.00

Pottery and porcelain have been made in the Staffordshire district in England since the 1700s. Hundreds of kilns are still working in the area. Thousands of types of pottery and porcelain have been made in the many factories that worked and still work in the area. Some of the most famous factories have been listed separately, such as Adams, Davenport, Ridgway, Rowland & Marsellus, Royal Doulton, Royal Worcester, Spode, Wedgwood, and others. Some Staffordshire pieces are listed under sections like Fairing, Flow Blue, Shaving Mug, etc.

STAFFORDSHIRE, see also Flow Blue; Mulberry
STAFFORDSHIRE, Beaker, Toby, With Hat, C.1850, 4 In. 125.00
Bowl, Vegetable, Covered, Grecian Scenes, Blue 145.00
Bowl, Vegetable, Open, Acropolis, C.1835, 10 1/4 In. 68.00
Bowl, Vegetable, Schenectady On The Mohawk Transfer, Pink 100.00
Box, Pin, Fairing Lady, 3 In. 35.00
Burner, Pastille, House, 1850, 5 In. 135.00
Butter Chip, Longfellow's Home, Meakin 10.00
Butter, Covered, Peasant Gathering Food 40.00
Chocolate Pot, Covered, Franklin, Cobalt Blue, 10 1/2 In. 550.00

The blue Staffordshire patterns were the earliest, with both black and blue transfer designs used during the eighteenth century. Pink, green, or brown transfer designs were used about 1820 and the combination of several colors began about 1820.

Coffeepot, Canova, Blue, Mayer, 12 In. 225.00
Coffeepot, Domed Cover, Dark Blue, Floral, 1825, 11 In. 200.00
Compote, Scalloped Rim, Inside Animal Panels, C.1830, 11 In. 650.00
Creamer, Cow, Black Spots, 1860 .... 115.00
Creamer, Cow, Brown Spots, 1875 .... 85.00
Creamer, Tulip Design, Black Striping, Gaudy, 4 1/2 In. 65.00
Cup & Saucer, Farmers, With Poem, Adams 40.00
Cup & Saucer, Garden Sports, Children 20.00
Cup & Saucer, Milkmaid, Black Transfer, Handleless 20.00
Cup & Saucer, Railroad Scene, Men On Saucer, Handleless 275.00
Cup & Saucer, Strawberry Pattern 195.00
Cup & Saucer, Wadsworth Tower, Wood & Sons, Handleless 180.00
Cup Plate, Italian Buildings Transfer, Brown 45.00
Cup Plate, Red Transfer, An Only Son, Floral, 4 In. 65.00
Cup Plate, Seaweed & Seashell, Green, Alcock 30.00
Cup Plate, Stone Bridge, French Views, Woods, Dark Blue 125.00
Dish, Covered, R.Hall's Select Views, Dark Blue, 12 1/4 In. 250.00
Dish, Hen & Chicks, Polychrome, 8 In. 205.00
Dish, Hen On Nest Cover, Bisque Turned Head, 9 In. 350.00
Dish, Hen On Nest Cover, Polychrome, 6 1/2 In. 200.00
Dish, Hen On Nest Cover, White & Red, Tan Base, 11 In. 595.00
Dish, Vegetable, View of Dublin, Covered, 12 1/2 In. 500.00
Eggcup, Blue, Walmer 55.00
Figurine, Abraham & Isaac, 1850, 14 In. 175.00
Figurine, Andromache Mourning Hector's Ashes, 1800, 9 In. 210.00
Figurine, Black Jazz Clarinetist, Top Hat, Tails, 7 In. 44.00
Figurine, Castle, Dated 1847, 6 X 6 In. .... *Cover* 495.00
Figurine, Charles II Spaniel, Seated, C.1860, 13 In., Pair 150.00
Figurine, Chelsea Cat On Pillow, 2 1/2 In. 125.00
Figurine, Clock, 2 Men In Blue Outfits 95.00
Figurine, Cottage, With Bird, 1840, 2 In. 145.00
Figurine, Couple Courting, Under Umbrella, C.1830, 8 In. 50.00
Figurine, Couple In Arbor, 14 X 9 In. 145.00
Figurine, Cow, Milkmaid, Red Splotches, Girl On Stool, 6 In. 200.00
Figurine, Dalmatian, Blue Base, 1850, 5 In. 105.00
Figurine, Dog, Copper Luster Ears, Facing Pair, 9 1/4 In. 275.00
Figurine, Dog, Seated, Gilt Trim, Enameled Face, 10 In., Pair 170.00
Figurine, Dog, White, Holding Blue Basket, 3 1/2 In. 55.00
Figurine, Dogs, Cream, C.1890, 14 In. 295.00
Figurine, Elijah, Ribbon Mark, C.1925, 10 In. 225.00
Figurine, Elijah, Widow of Zarephath, C.1800, 9 In., Pair 110.00
Figurine, Ewe, Textured Body, 7 1/2 In. 125.00
Figurine, Fireman, With Horn, 9 1/4 In., Pair 270.00
Figurine, Flora, Pratt, 1790, 8 In. 225.00
Figurine, Gallant, With Guitar, C.1850, 10 In. 125.00
Figurine, Hen & Chicks, Polychrome Enamel, 7 3/4 In. 355.00
Figurine, Hunting Dogs, Seated, Red, 8 3/4 In., Pair 300.00
Figurine, Lion, Recumbent, Glass Bead Eyes, 12 In., Pair 200.00
Figurine, Lion, Standing, 3 X 3 1/2 In. 110.00
Figurine, Little Red Riding Hood, Enameled, 7 3/4 In. 80.00
Figurine, Milton, C.1875, 10 1/2 In. 175.00
Figurine, Romeo & Juliet, Under Arbor, 1850, 8 In. 200.00
Figurine, Scotsman & Lady, Clock Below, 14 X 8 1/2 In. 145.00
Figurine, Sheep, Porcelain, 1850, 2 In. 85.00
Figurine, Spaniel, Copper Luster Spots, 10 In., Pair 265.00
Figurine, Spaniel, Cream Glazed, 13 In., Pair 180.00
Figurine, Spaniel, Seated, Gilt Collar, 13 In., Pair 385.00
Figurine, Spaniel, Seated, Gold Collars, 11 1/4 In., Pair 175.00
Figurine, Uncle Tom's Cabin, White Girl On Lap, 1840, 9 In. 125.00
Figurine, Venus, Dolphin Under Hand, Child, C.1800, 8 3/4 In. 150.00
Figurine, Wedding Couple, On Horse Back, 5 1/2 In., Pair 300.00
Figurine, Whippet, Rabbit At Feet, 7 1/2 In. 100.00
Figurine, Whippet, Reclining, Blue Base, 5 In., Pair 110.00
Figurine, Whippet, Seated On Pillow, 3 1/2 In. 60.00

Tiffany, Candlestick,
Bronze, Iridescent
Gold Glass Shade, 17 In.

Staffordshire, Tureen, Jenny Lind,
Polychromed, Covered, Tray

Staffordshire, Group,
2 Men With Bottle
& Lantern, 9 In.

Figurine, White Poodle, 2 Puppies, C.1840, 8 In.	200.00
Figurine, Widow, Ribbon Mark, C.1925, 10 In.	225.00
Figurine, Woman, Sitting, Drinking, Pickwick, C.1850, 5 1/2 In.	150.00
Figurine, Woman, With Guitar, C.1850, 10 In.	125.00
Fruit Basket, Castle View, Clews, C.1830, 12 X 9 In., Pair	850.00
Fruit Basket, Underliner, Harewood House, Dark Blue, 5 In.	250.00
Group, 2 Men With Bottle & Lantern, 9 In. ....*Illus*	200.00
Group, Prince & Princess, Polychrome Enamel, 7 3/8 In.	65.00
Group, Tithe, 1835, 6 In.	190.00
Group, Uncle Tom With Little Eva, Enameled, 10 1/2 In.	195.00
Humidor, Stately Lady, 11 In.	110.00
Inkstand, 2 Birds, C.1850, 3 In.	65.00
Inkwell, Bird's Nest, Snake, C.1840	45.00
Jug, Pearlware, Brown Eagle, Crackling, 1810–15, 5 5/8 In.	1540.00
Jug, Pearlware, Eagle, Olive Branches, C.1815, 6 5/8 In., Pair	825.00
Jug, Satyr's Mask, Knobby Body, Multicolored, 1815, 5 In.	60.00
Leech Jar, Burgundy, C.1850	2475.00
Match Holder, Figural, Elephant	55.00
Match Striker, Boy Carrying Boot	65.00
Mug, Children Fishing, Blue Transfer	55.00
Napkin Ring, Cherubs On Sides	65.00
Pitcher & Bowl, Blue Dragons, White, Mason's, 16 In.Bowl	225.00
Pitcher, Boston State House, City Hall, Stubbs, 6 3/4 In.	200.00
Pitcher, Burma, Oriental Scene, Ford & Sons, 7 1/2 In.	195.00
Pitcher, Dr.Syntax Setting Out, Adams, 4 1/2 In.	110.00
Pitcher, Red Transfer, People Playing Games, 10 In.	50.00
Plate, 3 Terriers After Armfield, Fernyhough, 1895, 9 In.	200.00
Plate, Alphabet, Franklin Maxim, 6 In.	110.00
Plate, American & Independence, Dark Blue, Clews, 7 7/8 In.	185.00
Plate, American & Independence, Dark Blue, Clews, 10 5/8 In.	190.00
Plate, American Sports Baseball Pitcher, Alphabet, 8 In.	110.00
Plate, American Villas, Fruit & Foliage, Blue, 7 1/2 In.	75.00
Plate, Baltimore & Ohio Railroad, Dark Blue, Wood, 9 In.	475.00
Plate, British Views, Medium Dark Blue, 8 1/4 In.	85.00
Plate, Caledonia, Adams, Black & Purple, 10 1/2 In.	75.00
Plate, Child's, Hey Diddle–Diddle, Brown, 5 In.	15.00
Plate, Chinese Marine, Sepia, 10 1/2 In.	240.00
Plate, Christ Church Oxford, Medium Blue, Ridgway, 9 3/4 In.	32.00
Plate, City Hall, N.Y., Ridgway, 10 In.	175.00
Plate, City of Albany, State of New York, Wood, 10 In.	260.00
Plate, Columbian Star, Transfer, 10 In.	75.00
Plate, Commodore MacDonnough's Victory, Wood, 10 In.	215.00
Plate, Deer & Cottages, Medium Blue, Marked Rogers, 10 In.	30.00
Plate, Dr.Syntax, Drawing After Nature, 10 1/2 In.	85.00
Plate, English Fishing Scene, Dark Blue, Clews, 10 In.	60.00
Plate, Erie Canal At Buffalo, Lace Border, Purple, 9 1/2 In.	35.00

Plate, Fairmount Near Philadelphia, Blue, Stubbs, 10 1/4 In. 245.00
Plate, Fall of Montmorenci, Near Quebec, Woods, 8 1/2 In. 150.00
Plate, Hoboken, N.J., Stubbs, 8 In. 175.00
Plate, Hudson River, Purple, Clews, 9 In. 40.00
Plate, Landing of General Lafayette, Clews, 6 3/4 In. 185.00
Plate, Landing of The Fathers At Plymouth Rock, Enoch Wood 125.00
Plate, Monmouthshire Hall, 10 In. 75.00
Plate, Motto & Alphabet, Child In Bed, Angels Above, 5 In. 110.00
Plate, Mycene, Blue, 10 1/2 In. 55.00
Plate, Nahant Hotel Near Boston, Stubbs & Kent, 8 1/2 In. 275.00
Plate, Near Fishkill, Dark Blue, 7 3/4 In. 25.00
Plate, Oriental, Magenta, Ridgway, 10 1/2 In. 22.00
Plate, Pagodas, Dark Blue Transfer, Clews, 8 5/8 In. 35.00
Plate, Park Theatre, New York, Medium Blue, 10 In. 150.00
Plate, Playing At Draughts, Wilkie's Design, 7 7/8 In. 75.00
Plate, Railway, Brown & Red, Wood, 9 1/4 In. 27.00
Plate, Rustic Scene, Floral & Leaf Edge, 1830s, 7 In., Pair 50.00
Plate, Sancho Panza At The Boar Hunt, Dark Blue, 9 5/8 In. 65.00
Plate, Select Scenery, Dark Blue, Clews, 6 3/4 In. 30.00
Plate, Shelter'd Peasants, Medium Dark Blue, 10 In. 45.00
Plate, St.Catharine's Near Guildford, Adams, 9 In., 6 Piece 180.00
Plate, Strawberry Pattern, 7 In. 150.00
Plate, U.S.Capitol, Blue, Floral Border, Adams, 10 In. 65.00
Plate, William Penn's Treaty, Indians, 11 In. 45.00
Platter, Asiatic Palaces, Ridgway, 13 In. 85.00
Platter, Canova, T.Mayer, Light Blue, 17 3/4 In. 45.00
Platter, Cape Coast Castle, Africa, C.1820, 16 In. 400.00
Platter, Chinese Landscape, Clews, 17 3/4 In. 85.00
Platter, Covered, Windsor Castle Scene, C.1825, 14 1/2 In. 300.00
Platter, Doctor Syntax, Dark Blue, Clews, C.1825, 9 X 12 In. 525.00
Platter, English Country Church, Medium Blue, 20 3/4 In. 135.00
Platter, Hermitage En Dauphine, Dark Blue, Wood, 14 3/4 In. 210.00
Platter, Jedburgh Abbey, Roxburghshire, Adams, 17 In. 120.00
Platter, Knight of The Wood Conquered, Clews, 16 1/2 In. 475.00
Platter, Moral Maxims, Brown Transfer, 17 3/4 In. 65.00
Platter, Oriental, Red Transfer, 16 3/4 In. 30.00
Platter, Penitentiary In Allegheny Views, Brown, 15 5/8 In. 200.00
Platter, R.Hall's Select Views, Dark Blue, 17 1/4 In. 335.00
Platter, View of Albany, Green Transfer, Well & Tree, 22 In. 300.00
Platter, View of Dublin, Dark Blue, Wood, 14 7/8 In. 350.00
Platter, Wild Rose, 9 1/2 In. 70.00
Platter, Windsor Castle, Scene, Dark Blue, Clews, 15 In. 225.00
Pot, Marie & Julian, Black On Black, 2 1/2 X 3 In. 295.00
Powder Box, Figural, Woman, With Dog, Marked, 9 In. 190.00
Punch Bowl, Brown Transfer, Floral, 17 X 9 1/2 In. 95.00
Punch Bowl, Medallions of Hunt Scenes, Pink Luster, C.1810 .... 450.00
Soup, Dish, Dam, Waterworks, Philadelphia, Dark Blue, 10 In. 65.00
Soup, Dish, Shepherd & Maiden, Medium Blue, 8 3/4 In. 55.00
Soup, Dish, Vue De Chateau De Coucy, Enoch Wood, 10 1/8 In. 60.00
Spill, Boy, Girl & Sheep Dog, 1850, 9 In. 145.00
Spill, Turret Castle, Clock Tower, 1850, 6 In. 125.00
Stirrup Cup, Fox Head, Yellowware, C.1840, 6 1/4 In. 880.00
Stopper, Toby Jug, Hat, Judy, 10 In. 165.00
Sugar, Mother, Child & Dog, Medium Dark Blue, Adams, 7 In. 50.00
Tankard Set, Indian Transfer, Rust To White, 6 Piece 195.00
Tankard, Drinking Scene, Frog Inside 60.00
Tea Set, Child's, Green Castle Scene, 1830, 18 Piece 110.00
Tea Set, Child's, House That Jack Built, 19 Piece 195.00
Tea Set, Child's, Punch & Judy, Setting For 4 .... 285.00
Teapot, Palestine, Purple 95.00
STAFFORDSHIRE, TOBY JUG, see Toby Jug
Tureen, Jenny Lind, Polychromed, Covered, Tray .... *Illus* 110.00
Tureen, Sauce, Underplate, Cover, Ladle, Bologna, Red & Green 285.00
Tureen, Sauce, Underplate, Hudson Views, Clews 235.00

Tureen, Sauce, Underplate, St.Catherine's Hill, Clews	75.00
Tureen, Sauce, Villa In Regents Park, Dark Blue, 6 In.	115.00
Tureen, Scenery, Medium Blue, 9 1/2 In.	200.00
Tureen, Soup, Underplate, Woodbine, Sepia	425.00
Vase, Boy, Girl & Goat, Polychrome Enamel, 7 1/2 In.	65.00
Vase, Figural, Sheep, Standing, White Polychrome, 6 X 7 In.	250.00
Vase, Mantel, Tree Stump, Leaping Stag Base, 11 In., Pair	250.00

The Fulper Pottery had a long history that entwined with the Stangl Pottery in 1910 when Johann Martin Stangl started work. He bought into the firm in 1913, became president in 1926, and in 1929 changed the company name to Stangl Pottery. The pottery made dinnerwares and a line of limited-edition bird figurines. The company went out of business in 1972.

STANGL, Ashtray, Fisherman, Square, 9 In.	25.00
Ashtray, Gold Ball, Large	15.00
Ashtray, Pheasant, 8 1/4 In.	25.00
Ashtray, Pheasant, 11 In.	25.00
Ashtray, Sailfish, Square, 9 In.	25.00
Basket, Rope Handle, Terra-Cotta	30.00
Bird, Allen Hummingbird, No.3634	35.00
Bird, Bird of Paradise, No.3408	60.00
Bird, Blackbird, No.3402	35.00
Bird, Bluebird, No.3276S	75.00
Bird, Broadbill Hummingbird, No.3629	90.00
Bird, Broadtailed Hummingbird, No.3626	80.00 To 95.00
Bird, Cardinal, No.3444	60.00
Bird, Cardinal, No.3596, Gray	45.00
Bird, Cerulean Warbler, No.3456	35.00 To 45.00
Bird, Chat, No.3590	42.00
Bird, Chestnut-Sided Warbler, No.3812	65.00
Bird, Chickadees, No.3581, Group	130.00 To 145.00
Bird, Cockatoo, No.3580	90.00 To 120.00
Bird, Cockatoo, No.3584	150.00 To 225.00
Bird, Goldfinch, No.3849	75.00
Bird, Goldfinches, No.3635, Group	175.00 To 185.00
Bird, Hummingbirds, No.3599D	175.00 To 185.00
Bird, Indigo Bunting, No.3589	40.00 To 72.00
Bird, Kentucky Warbler, No.3598	40.00
Bird, Key West Quail Dove, No.3454	165.00 To 250.00
Bird, Kingfisher, No.3406S	30.00 To 40.00
Bird, Orioles, No.3402D	100.00
Bird, Painted Bunting, No.3452	125.00
Bird, Penguin, No.3274	250.00
Bird, Red-Faced Warbler, No.3594	30.00
Bird, Red-Headed Woodpeckers, No.3752D	350.00
Bird, Redstarts, No.3490D	115.00 To 165.00
Bird, Rieffers Hummingbird, No.3628	95.00
Bird, Rivoli Hummingbird, No.3627	95.00
Bird, Rooster, No.3445, Yellow	95.00
Bird, Rufous Hummingbird, No.3585	35.00
Bird, Scarlet Tanagers, No.3750D	285.00
Bird, Turkey, No.3275	200.00 To 250.00
Bird, White-Headed Pigeons, No.3518D	450.00
Bird, Wilson Warbler, No.3597	40.00 To 72.00
Bird, Wrens, No.3401D	60.00
Bird, Yellow Warbler, No.3447	45.00 To 80.00
Bowl, Golden Harvest, 5 In.	4.00
Bowl, Salad, Underplate, Terra Rose, 12 1/2 In.	20.00
Bowl, Salad, Underplate, Terra Rose, 14 In.	20.00
Box, Cigarette, Covered, Terra Rose, Tulip Pattern	8.00
Box, Covered, Apple Tree Design	22.00
Butter, Covered, Thistle, 1/4 Lb.	18.00
Candleholder, Terra Rose, 3 In.	20.00

Casserole, Covered, Thistle 25.00
Coffeepot, Bittersweet 8.50
Coffeepot, Golden Harvest, 9 In. 30.00
Creamer, Thistle 6.00
Cup & Saucer, Thistle 8.50
Cup, Magnolia 5.00
Eggcup, Thistle 8.00
Pitcher, Golden Harvest 6.00
Pitcher, Pink Interior, Aqua Outside, Pair 42.00
Pitcher, Tilt, Melon Shape, Red 21.00
Plate, Quail, 11 In. 25.00
Plate, Terra Rose, Yellow Tulip, 12 In. 10.00
Plate, Thistle, Indented Center, 11 In. 15.00
Salt & Pepper, Thistle 10.00
Sugar, Amber Glow 4.00
Sugar, Covered, Thistle 8.00
Teapot, Starflower, Green, 9 In. 25.00
Vase, Horsehead 170.00
Vase, Pillow, Sunflower, Blue, Terra Rose, 12 In. 30.00
Vase, Pillow, Turquoise Blue, Gold Brushed, 7 1/2 In. 20.00
Wall Pocket, Aqua 28.00

Steins have been used by beer and ale drinkers for over 500 years. They have been made of ivory, porcelain, stoneware, faience, silver, pewter, wood, or glass in sizes up to nine gallons. Although some were made by Meissen, Capo-di-Monte, and other famous factories, most were made in Germany. The words "Geschutz" or "Musterschutz" on a stein are the German words for patented or registered design, not company names. Steins are still being made in the old styles.

STEIN, Animals In Jungle Scene, Monkey Handle, Stoneware, 14 In. 330.00
Apostles, Stoneware, 1 Liter 198.00
Barmaid Holding Many Steins, Pottery, Pewter Rim, 1/2 Liter 278.00
Billy Beer, It's The Best, 2 Piece 45.00
Blue Shield, With Lion, Maes-Dort, 8 In. 22.50
Chicago Real Estate Board, Annual Banquet, No.649, 1/2 Liter, 1902 .... 65.00
Child, Top of Barrel, Bavaria, Porcelain, Schierholz, 1/2 Liter 885.00
Couple With Puppies, Pottery, 1 Liter 57.00
Dark Brown Glaze, Stoneware, 8 In. 193.00
Dwarfs & Verse, Pottery, 1 Liter 48.00
Embossed Mountain Scene, Joliet Citizens Brewery, 1/2 Liter 175.00
Embossed Scene, Brown, Green, Figural Pewter Lid, German, 22 In. 195.00
Etched, Indoor Drinking Scene, Pottery, 15 In. 144.00
Figural, Gentleman Rabbit, Musterschutz 1750.00
Floral Design, Pewter Lid, R.M.In Star Mark, German, 15 In. 175.00
Fluted Design, Blown Glass, Green, 15 In. 88.00
Gentleman & Fox, Porcelain, Schierholz, 1/2 Liter 760.00
Glass, Enameled Man, German 40.00
Head of Bismark, Porcelain, Schierholz, 1/2 Liter 363.00
Hunter With Dogs, Hunter As Lid, Pottery, 2 1/2 Liter 209.00
Husaren Rider, Thuringen Faience, C.1780 .... 2145.00
Jackson Square, New Orleans Scene, Stoneware, Pewter Lid, 3 1/4 In. 62.50
Lithophane Bottom, Pewter Cover, German 85.00
Louisiana Purchase Monument, Germany, Porcelain, 3 In. 75.00
Man Dances For Women, Pottery, 1 Liter 44.00
Man, Barbell, Crossed Swords & Shield, Hand Painted, 1/2 Liter 60.00
   STEIN, METTLACH, see Mettlach, Stein
Monk & Maiden, Pottery, 2 Liter 77.00
Monks Scene, Wood, 23 In. 150.00
Naval, Boiler & Drinking Scenes, Pottery, 1 Liter 585.00
Nazi Luftwaffe, Pilot, Knight's Cross 500.00
Outdoor Gathering, Pottery, 1/2 Liter 57.00
People & Dogs In Relief, Baroque Silver On Copper, German, 12 In. 250.00
Pewter, Barrel Shape, C.1840, 1 Liter 150.00

Pewter, Knight, Archway, 3 Ball Feet, Dolphin Finial, Flagon, 12 In. 440.00
Pewter, Stag Embossed On Side, Deer Head On Handle, J.B.Mark 85.00
Pewter, Weaver Occupational Scene, Flagon, 13 In. 385.00
Princeton, Football, Character, 6 1/2 In. 450.00
Regimental, Lithophane, Nude Lady, 1952 .... 125.00
Regimental, Naval Character, S.M.S. Preussen, 1910–12 .... 4180.00
Remy, Soccer Player, 2 Liter 176.00
Saxon Pioneer, Bridge–Building Scene, Porcelain, Dresden, 1/2 Liter 553.00
Scenes of Wagner's Ring Operas, Castle Mark, 8 In. 250.00
Shriner's, New Orleans, Hand Painted, Limoges, 1910 .... 67.50
Stag, Marked Musterschutz 3850.00
Tavern Scene, Pottery, 17 In. 175.00
Viking Figure, Dragon Thumblift, Blown Glass, Light Amber, 17 In. 529.00
Well–Dressed Fox, Pottery, 1/2 Liter 207.00

Stereo cards that were made for stereopticon viewers became popular after 1840. Two almost identical pictures were mounted on a stiff cardboard backing so that, when viewed through a stereoscope, a three-dimensional picture could be seen. Value is determined by maker and by the subject. These cards were made in quantity through the 1930s.

STEREO CARD, Blacks, 4 Piece 20.00
Fishing Scene, Colored 2.00
George Custer, 1860s 150.00
Indian Scene, Colored, 5 In. 5.00
Indian, Big Dog 70.00
Indian, Rattling Runner 55.00
Indian, Sioux Dandy, Tinted 45.00
Sears, Roebuck, Chicago, Mail Order, 40 Different Cards 85.00
Studies of Chiropody, Keystone, 7 X 10 In., 38 Piece 10.00

The stereoscope, or stereopticon, was used for viewing stereo cards. The hand viewer was invented by Oliver Wendell Holmes, although more complicated table models were used before his was produced in 1859.

STEREOSCOPE, Copper, Ivory & Mother–of–Pearl, C.1860, 4 Ft. 1 In. 990.00
Keystone, Cased In Book Shape, 100 Cards 125.00
Perfectscope 12.50
With 20 World War I & 4 Boer War Slides 50.00
STERLING SILVER, see Silver–Sterling

Steuben glass was made at the Steuben Glass Works of Corning, New York. The factory, founded by Frederick Carder and T. C. Hawkes, Sr., was purchased by the Corning Glass Company. They continued to make glass called "Steuben." Many types of art glass were made at Steuben. The firm is still making exceptional quality glass but it is clear, modern–style glass.

STEUBEN, see also Aurene
STEUBEN, Ashtray, Pomona Green, Rounded Triangle Shape, Circular Handle 110.00
Bowl, Aurene, Marked, 6 X 10 In. 950.00
Bowl, Blue Jade Design, Crystal, Signed, 5 In. 90.00
Bowl, Calcite, Aurene Lining, 11 In. 325.00
Bowl, Centerpiece, Fleur–De–Lis, Topaz 325.00
Bowl, Centerpiece, Selenium Red, Signed, 12 In. 195.00
Bowl, Copper Wheel Engraved, Green Foot, Signed, 4 1/2 In. 110.00
Bowl, Grotesque, Clear, Signed, 9 X 5 1/2 In. 120.00
Bowl, Grotesque, Pedestal, Spinach Color Crystal, 6 In. 160.00
Bowl, Grotesque, Pedestal, Spinach Color Crystal, 8 1/2 In. 185.00
Bowl, Iridescent, Footed Base, Signed, 12 In. 425.00
Bowl, Jade, On Alabaster Base, 12 In. 100.00
Bowl, Light Blue Jade Applied Design, On Clear Crystal, 5 X 2 In. 95.00
Bowl, Oriental Poppy, Green Foot, Signed, 4 3/4 In. 650.00
Bowl, Underplate, Rosaline & Alabaster, Footed, Signed 125.00
Bowl, Van Dyke Pattern, Green Foot, 4 1/2 In. 110.00

Box, Dresser, Clear, Black Jade Reeding, Cover, 3 X 4 3/4 In. 125.00
Candleholder, Gold Aurene, Twisted Stem, Signed, 8 In., Pair 495.00
Candlestick, Amber & Green, 12 In., Pair 145.00
Candlestick, Amethyst & Topaz, 10 In. 165.00
Candlestick, Black Stem, 8 Hanging Prisms, Pair 350.00
Candlestick, Blue Aurene, 10 In. 325.00
Candlestick, Celeste Blue, Foot, Candle Cup, Amber Stem, 12 In. 175.00
Candlestick, Green, Twisted Stem, 10 In., Pair 98.00
Candlestick, Hollow Bulbous Stem, Signed, 15 1/2 In., Pair 250.00
Candlestick, Optic Swirl, Green, 10 In., Pair 200.00
Candlestick, Random Bubbled Crystal, Green Threading, Signed, Pair 135.00
Candlestick, Ribbed, Celeste Blue, 10 In., Pair 175.00
Candlestick, Topaz, 8 In., Pair 95.00
Candlestick, Twisted Stem, Blue Aurene, Signed, 10 In., Pair 800.00
Candlestick, White Calcite Base, Gold Aurene Rim, 6 In., Pair 495.00
Champagne, Aurene, Marked Aurene 2061, Paper Label 225.00
Champagne, Oriental Poppy, Green Stem, Signed, 6 1/4 In. 350.00
Champagne, Van Dyke Pattern, Green Swirled Stem, 6 1/2 In. 135.00
Compote, Amber Ribbed Stem, Ruby Bowl, Scalloped Rim, Signed 450.00
Compote, Ball & Wafer Stem, Amber, Signed, 6 X 8 In. 125.00
Compote, Berry & Leaf Pattern, Marked, 3 In. 95.00
Compote, Black Base, Ivory, Signed, 7 In. 250.00
Compote, Rosaline, Alabaster Foot & Stem, 6 X 2 3/4 In. 165.00
Compote, Rosaline, Alabaster, Signed, 8 1/4 In. 175.00
Compote, Rosaline, Black Top Border & Ring On Stand, 4 X 8 In. 475.00
Compote, Underplate, Gold Aurene, Calcite, 14 In. Plate, 4 In. 475.00
Console Set, Selenium Red, Domed Foot, Signed, 3 Piece 225.00
Figurine, Beaver, Large, Pair 595.00
Finger Bowl, Cranberry & Amber, Threaded, Triple Flare 36.00
Finger Bowl, Underplate, Calcite, Gold Aurene 375.00
Flower Frog, Nude Woman 550.00
Goblet, Aurene, Twisted Stem, Signed, 6 In. 275.00
Goblet, Toasting, Crystal, 18 In., Pair 950.00
Goblet, Verre De Soie, Pink Trim On Foot & Rim, 5 1/2 In. 175.00
Goblet, Wine, French Blue, Flared Cup, Signed, 7 1/4 In., Set of 6 .... 210.00
Lamp, Black Dragon, Bristol Yellow, Cloth Shade, Oriental Feet 3500.00
Lamp, Cintra, Acid Cut Back, Fittings 1950.00
Lamp, Pierced Brass Base, Blue Aurene, 27 In. 1575.00
Lamp, Table, Blue Aurene, 27 1/2 In. 475.00
Lamp, Torchere, Moss Agate, 68 In. 2150.00
Mug, Cerise Ruby, 5 3/4 In. 65.00
Nut Set, Ruffled, Gold Aurene, 7 Piece 1200.00
Paperweight, Cat, Green Eyes, Marked, 5 1/2 In. 225.00
Perfume Bottle, Atomizer, Aurene, Engraved Flowers, 9 In. 450.00
Perfume Bottle, Rosaline & Alabaster, Stopper, 4 X 5 3/4 In. 550.00
Pitcher, Water, Aqua, Hawkes Etched 150.00
Plate, Serving, Marina Blue, Copper Wheel Engraved, 8 In. 65.00
Rose Bowl, Rosaline To Alabaster, Fir Cone Pattern, Acid Cut Back 595.00
Salt, Pedestal, Gold Aurene, 1 1/2 In. 225.00
Salt, Sterling Silver Pedestal Foot, Verre De Soie 85.00
Shade, Brown Aurene, Applied Platinum Design Border, Signed 425.00
Shade, Calcite, Gold Trumpets 75.00
Shade, Drape, Green 145.00
Shade, Gold Leaf & Vine, Platinum Border, Dome, 10 In. 2000.00
Shade, Gold Tortoiseshell, Gold Lining, Bell Shape 145.00
Shade, Green Feather, Signed, Large 135.00
Shade, Oak Leaf & Acorn 65.00
Shade, Tortoiseshell, 6 1/4 In. 175.00
Shade, Tulip Shape, Gold Aurene, Signed, 4 1/2 In. 175.00
Sherbet, Calcite 46.00
Sherbet, Engraved, Amber 25.00
Sherbet, Gold Aurene, Underplate, Marked 195.00
Sherbet, Underplate, Amethyst 45.00
Sherbet, Underplate, Gold Calcite 185.00

Sherbet, Underplate, Verre De Soie 65.00
Stemware Set, Trumpet Shaped Bowls, Signed, 43 Piece 900.00
Toothpick, Pinched, Aurene, 2 1/2 In. 175.00
Tumbler, Amber, Flemish Blue Rim, Signed, 5 In. 45.00
Tumbler, Juice, Swirl, Green 85.00
Tumbler, Teardrop In Bottom 100.00
Underplate, Gold Aurene On Calcite, 7 In. 40.00
Urn, Calcite Teardop, Silver Plated Frame, Lion's Head, Claw Feet 145.00
Urn, Ribbed, Classical Shape, Signed, 4 1/2 In. 750.00
Vase, 3–Prong, Amber, Signed 135.00
Vase, Acid Cut Back, Jade Green To Alabaster, Floral, 8 In. 800.00
Vase, Amber, Flower Reserve, Dotted Bands, Marked, 11 In. 500.00
Vase, Aurene, Butterfly, Blue, Signed, 5 1/8 In. 565.00
Vase, Aurene, Gold Luster, Mounted In Tiffany Base, 19 In. 1650.00
Vase, Basket, Gold Aurene Over Calcite, No Handle, 8 1/2 In. 475.00
Vase, Blue Aurene, Ribbed, Signed, 5 In. 650.00
Vase, Blue, Paper Label, 12 In. 950.00
Vase, Butterfly, Blue Iridescent, Signed, 5 1/8 In. 565.00
Vase, Calcite & Gold Aurene, Paper Label, 7 In. 245.00
Vase, Cased, Emerald Green To White, Gold Aurene Interior, 10 In. 600.00
Vase, Diagonal Ribbed, Flared Top, Amber, Signed, 8 In. 125.00
Vase, Diamond–Quilted, Rose Reeded, Signed, 8 In. 175.00
Vase, Diamond–Quilted, Upper Green Reeding, Signed, 12 In. 125.00
Vase, Diving Girl, Stand, 14 In. 2250.00
Vase, Fan Shape, Ribbed Body, Pomona Green Ball Stem, Foot, 8 In. 75.00
Vase, Fan Shape, Ribbed, Ball Stem, Amber, Signed, 6 1/4 In. 60.00
Vase, Fan, Gold Birds, Vines, Gold Base, Signed, 8 3/4 In. 395.00
Vase, Fan, Pomona, Green & Amber Wisteria, 8 In. 85.00
Vase, Fish Among Seaweed, Jade Green, 10 In. 1750.00
Vase, Gold Aurene, Calcite, 8 1/2 In. 430.00
Vase, Gold Aurene, Floriform, Pedestal, Signed, 5 In. 825.00
Vase, Gold Aurene, Trumpet Shape, Pedestal Foot, Signed, 6 In. 210.00
Vase, Gold Aurene, Waisted, Flared Ruffled Top, 4 1/4 In. 165.00
Vase, Grotesque, Clear To Green, Marked, 9 1/4 In. 175.00
Vase, Grotesque, Clear To Red, Signed, 11 In. 225.00
Vase, Grotesque, Cranberry To Clear, 11 1/2 In. 295.00
Vase, Grotesque, Crystal, Signed, 7 X 6 1/2 In. 145.00
Vase, Grotesque, Pedestal, Spinach Green, Signed, 6 1/2 In. 160.00
Vase, Grotesque, Random Bubbles, Green, 4 Ribs, 6 1/4 In. 160.00
Vase, Jack–In–The–Pulpit, Ivorene Iridescent, Signed, 6 1/2 In. 425.00
Vase, Jade, Dark Blue, Signed, 4 1/2 X 7 In. 1150.00
Vase, Lotus, 10 In. 150.00
Vase, Marguerite Engraved, Marked, 10 In. 65.00
Vase, Oriental Poppy, Green Stem & Foot, 4 1/2 In. 750.00
Vase, Oriental Poppy, Mounted In Bronze Tiffany Base, 19 In. 1650.00
Vase, Oriental Poppy, Mounted In Tiffany Cherub Base, 19 In. 1950.00
Vase, Ribbed Lily Shape, Rainbow, Gold Aurene, Signed, 5 1/2 In. 345.00
Vase, Ribbed, Topaz Crystal, Flared Base, Signed, 12 In. 110.00
Vase, Rosaline, Alabaster Pedestal Foot, Signed, 6 In. 150.00
Vase, Ruffled Top, Signed F.Carder, Gold Aurene, 2 1/4 In. 650.00
Vase, Selenium, Etched, Signed Hawkes, 11 In. 525.00
Vase, Trumpet, Pinched Center Forms 2 Lobes, Gold, Signed, 6 In. 210.00
Vase, Tyrian, Baluster, Gray Blue Iridescent, Leafage, 6 3/4 In. 3575.00
Vase, White Iridescent, Flared, Signed, 7 3/4 X 9 1/2 In. 375.00
Wine, Green Jade, Alabaster Twisted Stem, Signed, 7 1/4 In. 110.00
Wine, Green Twisted Stem, Signed, 6 1/2 In. 135.00
Wine, Twisted Alabaster Stem, Jade, Signed, 7 1/4 In. 95.00
Wine, Van Dyke Pattern, Green Twisted Stem, 6 1/2 In. 135.00

Stevengraphs are woven pictures made like fancy ribbons. They were manufactured by Thomas Stevens of Coventry, England, and became popular in 1862. Most are marked "Woven in silk by Thomas Stevens" or were mounted on a cardboard that tells the story of the Stevengraph. Other similar ribbon pictures have been made in England and Germany.

STEVENGRAPH, Bookmark, A Wish	35.00
Bookmark, George Washington, Father of His Country	100.00
Bookmark, Mail Coach	170.00
Call To The Rescue	140.00
Columbus Leaving Spain, Columbian Exposition, 1893, 8 In.	200.00
Good Old Days	140.00
Peeping Tom	195.00
Picture, Heroism At Sea, Original Frame	125.00
Present Time, Coaches, Bridge, Framed	425.00
Signing of Declaration of Independence, Mat, Framed	350.00
The Start	120.00 To 150.00

Stevens & Williams of Stourbridge, England, made many types of glass, including layered, etched, cameo, and art glass, between the 1830s and 1930s. Some pieces are signed "S & W." Many pieces are decorated with flowers, leaves, and other designs based on nature.

STEVENS & WILLIAMS, Basket, Pink, Applied Floral, 3–Footed, Thorn Handle	200.00
Basket, Scissor Cut Top, Stems Form Feet, 8 1/4 In.	595.00
Bottle, Cologne, Swirl Pattern, Red & Green, 5 3/4 In.	650.00
Bowl, Marmalade, Rigaree Band, Plated Basket, 6 In.	135.00
Bride's Basket, Scalloped Rim, Opaque White, 9 In.	190.00
Creamer, Ruffled Tricorner Top, Flowers, Vine Handle	525.00
Cruet, Amber & White, Flattened Stopper, 9 1/2 In.	150.00
Cruet, Amber, Arboresque, Applied Handle, 9 1/2 In.	145.00
Decanter, Intaglio Green To Crystal, Stopper, 16 In.	325.00
Dish, Seashell, Ruffled Rim, Brass Frame, 13 In.	165.00
Finger Bowl, Cranberry On White	40.00
Finger Bowl, Rose To Amber, Citron Threaded, Quilted	65.00
Finger Bowl, Vaseline On White	40.00
Goblet, Birds, Stippled Flower Ground, 8 1/4 In.	495.00
Jar, Sweetmeat, Arboresque, Cranberry & White, 5 In.	165.00
Jar, Sweetmeat, Dolce Relievo, Plated Lid	450.00
Pitcher, Cranberry Overlay, Green Handle, 10 1/2 In.	595.00
Pitcher, Cream, Pink, Ruffled, Vine Handle, 7 1/2 In.	525.00
Pitcher, Pink Satin, Ribbed, Swirled, Handle, 4 3/4 In.	175.00
Pitcher, Ribbed & Swirled, Frosted Handle, 4 3/4 In.	175.00
Pitcher, Ruffled Tricornered Top, Draped, 9 1/2 In.	310.00
Plate, Ruffled Shell, Pink To Green, 4 3/4 In.	175.00
Rose Bowl, Applied Flowers, Leaves, Signed, 6 1/2 In.	175.00
Rose Bowl, Basketweave Pattern, Pink, 4 1/2 X 6 In.	395.00
Rose Bowl, Citron Threaded, Tricornered, 6 In.	80.00
Rose Bowl, Pleated Top, Gold Prunus, Branches, 5 In.	495.00
Rose Bowl, Striped, Swirled, 8 Crimp Top, 3 In.	175.00
Rose Bowl, Zipper Pattern, Amber, Marked, 2 3/8 In.	58.00
Toothpick, Green Intaglio Cut, Sterling Silver Rim	225.00
Vase, 3 Panels, Flowers, Leaves, Green To Clear, 10 In.	815.00
Vase, 8 Crimp Top, Cranberry Centered Leaf, 6 1/2 In.	145.00
Vase, Amber Leaves & Branches, Rose, Ruffled, 14 In.	275.00
Vase, Amber, Fold Top, Signed, 7 In.	225.00
Vase, Applied Lily Pads, Etched, Clear, 10 In.	425.00
Vase, Cream, Tomato Red, Ruffled, Applied Foot, 10 In.	310.00
Vase, Crystal Ruffled Leaves, Cream, Pink Lining, 7 In.	345.00
Vase, Flared, 8 Cherries, Golden Leaves, 21 1/2 In.	850.00
Vase, Fluted Top, Gold, Green Flowers, Signed, 6 In.	210.00
Vase, Fluted, Gold, Applied Flowers, Leaves, 6 1/4 In.	210.00
Vase, Fruit Applique, Amber Handle, Square Top, 8 In.	100.00
Vase, Fuchsia Inside, Scalloped, Amber Leaves, 10 In.	210.00

Vase, Green & Red Pulled Feather, Egg Shape, 7 3/4 In.	875.00
Vase, Jack-In-The-Pulpit, Striped, Ruffled, 9 3/8 In.	110.00
Vase, Lily Pads, Blossoms, Scalloped, Marked, 9 3/4 In.	1650.00
Vase, Maroon, Enameled Design, Signed, 11 In.	290.00
Vase, Peacock's Eye, Ruffled Top, C.1900, 7 In.	215.00
Vase, Raised Floral, Bee, Maroon, 11 In.	185.00
Vase, Ribbed, Pink, Blue & Cream, Signed, 11 In.	485.00
Vase, Ruffled Appliqued Leaf, 8 Crimp Top, 6 1/2 In.	145.00
Vase, Ruffled Leaf Applique, Pink Lining, 5 1/2 In.	145.00
Vase, Ruffled, Wishbone Feet, Blue Swirl, 5 5/8 In.	145.00
Vase, Scalloped, Flowers, Leaves, Signed, 6 1/2 In.	195.00
Vase, Scalloped, Gold & Green Florals, Signed, 7 In.	210.00
Vase, Swirl, 4 Petal Cased Top, Floral Enameling	120.00
Vase, Swirl, Mother-of-Pearl, Lavender & Pink, 12 In.	300.00
Vase, Swirled Air Trap Pattern, 5 In.	85.00

Henry William Stiegel, a colorful immigrant to the colonies, started his first factory in Pennsylvania in 1763. He remained in business until 1774. Glassware was made in a style popular in Europe at that time and was similar to the glass of many other makers. It was made of clear or colored glass and was decorated with enamel colors, mold blown designs, or etching. It is almost impossible to be sure a piece was made by Stiegel, so the knowing collector now refers to this glass as Stiegel type.

STIEGEL TYPE, Bottle, Bride's, Allover Floral, Pewter Collar, 5 1/2 In.	500.00
Bottle, Bride's, Amethyst To Blue Top, Lovebirds, 1797, 6 In.	900.00
Bottle, Polychrome, Flowers, Deer, Dated 1744, 5 1/8 In.	374.00
Flask, Diamond Daisy Wisteria	5500.00
Flip Glass, Sunburst, Phoenix Bird Center, 8 1/4 In.	550.00
Light Bulb, Christmas, Expanded Diamond, 4 Colors, Set of 4	225.00
Mug, Free-Blown, Tulip, Strap Handle, Late 18th Century, 7 In.	425.00
Perfume Bottle, Twist, Cobalt Blue	120.00
Sugar, Cobalt Blue, Applied Foot, 18 Vertical Ribs, Lid, 5 In.	250.00
Tumbler, Blown Enameled Flowers & Band, Molded Panels, Aqua	200.00
Tumbler, Enameled Polychrome Flowers & Band, Amethyst	200.00
Tumbler, Enameled, 5 1/2 In.	825.00

Stoneware is a coarse, glazed, and fired potter's ceramic that is used to make crocks, jugs, bowls, etc. It is often decorated with cobalt blue decorations. Stoneware is still being made.

STONEWARE, Bank, Applied Leaves & Stars Around Slot, Polka Dots, 3 1/4 In.	2950.00
Bank, Red Clay, Dark Brown Floral Design, New Geneva, 6 7/8 In.	275.00
Batter Bowl, Albany Glaze, 1/2 Gal.	60.00
Batter Jar, Blue, White, Bail Handle, Wooden Grip, Flower	195.00
Batter Jug, Bail Handle, Brown	60.00
Batter Pail, Original Tin Caps	900.00
Bean Pot, Taylor's Grocery, Sioux Rapids, Iowa, Brown, White, 6 In.	115.00
Beater Jar, 1/2 Inch Blue Stripe	40.00
Beater Jar, Long's Grocery	40.00
Bird Feeder, 3 In.	125.00
Bottle, Beer, Cincinnati Beer, Embossed In Blue, Cherubs	58.00
Bottle, Blue & White, Western Stoneware	225.00
Bottle, Brushed Cobalt Blue Leaf, 8 /14 In.	225.00
Bottle, Cattail, Blue	175.00
Bottle, Grayish Tan, 3 1/2 X 9 1/2 In.	20.00
Bottle, Medicine, Habits of Drink, Fulham, Label, 1800, 6 In.	70.00
Bowl, Egyptian Ware, Western Stoneware, 8 In.	34.00
Bowl, Geo.W.Miller, Strasburg, Va., Brushed Blue Rim, 10 In.	235.00
Bowl, Grafton, Iowa, Blue Band, 7 In.	45.00
Bowl, Milk, Picket & Diamond Design, Blue & White, 11 In.	75.00
Bowl, Mixing, Cobalt Blue Advertising, Blue & Orange	80.00
Bowl, Mixing, No.2, Eared, Wide Mouth, Pouring Lip, Blue Design	350.00
Bowl, No.3, John B.Carrie & Co., Po'Keepsie, 10 In.	350.00
Bowl, Wedding Ring, Blue & White, 7 In.	62.50

Bowl, Wedding Ring, Blue & White, 8 1/2 In. 75.00
Bowl, Wm.Seebode, General Merchandise, Harris, Iowa, 7 1/2 In. 40.00
Butter Churn, Maple Leaf, 3 Gal. 65.00
Canteen, Bardwell's Root Beer, Deer On Other Side, 11 1/2 In. 575.00
Canteen, Utica Commandery No.3, Rochester, 1900, Whites, 3 In. 200.00
Chamber Pot, Gray, Ft.Dodge 125.00
Chicken Waterer, Cream, Brown, Whitehall 46.00
Chicken Waterer, Foliage Design 1800.00
Chicken Waterer, Illinois Map Front, Marked 60.00
Chicken Waterer, Splash-Proof, Western Stoneware, 2 Piece 29.00
Churn, 3 Blossoms, Brushwork & Slip, Geddes, N.Y., C.1870, 3 Gal. 325.00
Churn, Blue Slip Design, Gray, 5 Gal. 125.00
Churn, Comical, Turkey Type Bird, N.A.White & Co., C.1865, 5 Gal. 850.00
Churn, E.& L.P.Norton, Floral Design, 5 Gal. 300.00
Churn, Stenciled Design, Williams & Reppert, No.5, 17 3/4 In. 175.00
Churn, Wreath In Blue, 5 Gal. 120.00
Cider Set, Grape Cluster & Trellis, Blue, 5 Piece 190.00
Cookie Jar, Blue Flowers 125.00
Cookie Jar, Spongeware Band, Covered 125.00
Cooler, Barrel Shape, J.Bower, No. 3, 13 3/4 In. 140.00
Cooler, Blue Bands 145.00
Cooler, Blue Bands, Water Must Be Put In Before Ice, 3 Gal. 135.00
Cooler, Blue Gray, Embossed, Blue Flowers, Cover, Spigot, 12 In. 295.00
Cooler, Blue Map, Words Ice Water, 8 Gal. 100.00
Cooler, Brown Gray Glaze, Double Ear Handles, 20 1/4 In. 65.00
Cooler, Covered, Blue Bands, 6 3/4 In. 35.00
Cooler, Covered, Blue Bands, 8 In. 40.00
Cooler, Cupid, Blue, 5 Gal. .... 500.00 To 545.00
Cooler, Ice Water, Fort Dodge Stoneware Co., 4 Gal. 250.00
Cooler, Keg Shape, Embossed Stoves, E.& L.P.Norton, 13 3/4 In. 275.00
Cooler, N.Clark, Athens, Bird, Branch In Talons, Ovoid, 15 In. 2000.00
Cooler, Scrolled Flowers, Bands, Dated 1864 .... 900.00
Cooler, Table, Brushed Cobalt Blue Flowers, Gray, C.1870, 3 Gal. 300.00
Cooler, Water, Cupid, Blue, 5 Gal. 525.00
Creamer, Brushed Cobalt Blue Floral Design, 3 1/2 In. 1275.00
Crock, 3 Petaled Tulip, Burger & Lang, N.Y., C., 1875, 2 Gal. 95.00
Crock, Banner, 1893 In Center, 4 Gal. 950.00
Crock, Bird On Hollyhock Stalk, White & Wood, C.1882, 3 Gal. 440.00
Crock, Bird, Cobalt Blue, 2 Gal. 275.00
Crock, Bird, Utica, White, 4 Gal. 225.00
Crock, Blue Flower Leaf, New York, Wide Mouth, 2 Gal. 125.00
Crock, Blue Stenciled Eagle, Gray, Hamilton & Jones, 4 Gal. 465.00
Crock, Blue Vertical Leaf, J.Sheppard, Jr., Geddes, N.Y., 2 Gal. 150.00
Crock, Brushed Cobalt Blue Design, No.4, 11 1/2 In. 65.00
Crock, Brushed Cobalt Blue Flower, No.3, 10 3/4 In. 120.00
Crock, Butter, Blue & Gray, Dentel's, Ackley, Iowa 50.00
Crock, Butter, Blue Gray, Apricots & Honeycomb, Covered, Bail 225.00
Crock, Butter, Buckeye, Blue Advertising 65.00
Crock, Butter, Colonial Pattern, Blue & White, 3 Lb. 110.00
Crock, Butter, Covered, Apricot, Word Butter, Blue & White 125.00
Crock, Butter, Covered, Butterfly, Blue & White 100.00
Crock, Butter, Covered, Daisy & Waffle, Blue & White 100.00
Crock, Butter, Covered, Draped Window Pattern, Blue & White 100.00
Crock, Butter, Covered, Farm Scene, Blue & White 160.00
Crock, Butter, Covered, Panels With Dots & Swags, Blue & White 100.00
Crock, Butter, Covered, Picket Fence, Blue & White 65.00
Crock, Butter, Covered, Swastika, Blue 125.00
Crock, Butter, Daisy & Trellis, Covered 125.00
Crock, Butter, Fair Store, Rockwell City, Iowa, Blue & Gray, 3 Lb. 65.00
Crock, Butter, Fern Leaf, 1 1/2G On Reverse, C.1865, 1 1/2 Gal. 235.00
Crock, Butter, Good Luck, Covered, Blue & White 95.00
Crock, Butter, Indian Sign, Covered, Blue & White 95.00
Crock, Butter, Lambrecht, 1 Lb. 25.00
Crock, Butter, Salt Glaze, Minnesota Stoneware Co., 1 Gal. 55.00

Crock, Butter, Sets of Cucumbers, Peter Herman, C.1870, 1 Gal. 300.00
Crock, Butter, Word Butter In Cobalt Blue, Covered 98.00
Crock, Cat's Face, Cortland, 1/2 Gal. 1825.00
Crock, Chicken, Handles, 6 Gal. 1300.00
Crock, Cobalt Blue Brushed Floral Design, No.3, 10 In. 130.00
Crock, Cobalt Blue Calla Lily One Side, Leaf Other Side, 2 Gal. 45.00
Crock, Cobalt Blue Polka Dot Horse, C.1860, 13 3/4 In. 1800.00
Crock, Cobalt Blue Stylized Leaf, 2 Gal. 125.00
Crock, Cobalt Blue, Leaf & Scrolled Foliage Both Sides, 12 In. 115.00
Crock, Comic Picture, Willie & Minnie, Fulper Bros., 2 Gal. 5000.00
Crock, Dodson & Braun Fine Pickles, 12 X 9 In. 125.00
Crock, Dog, Grass & Fence, Handles, W.Troy, N.Y., 5 Gal. 2200.00
Crock, Donagho, Parkersburg, Gray, Blue, 2 Gal. 100.00
Crock, Double Blossomed Hollyhock, White, C.1886, 10 In. 150.00
Crock, Drink 3 Star Coffee, C.Shenkberg Co., 3 1/2 Gal. 90.00
Crock, E.& L.P.Norton, Bennington, Vt., Leaf Design, 7 1/4 In. 175.00
Crock, Fence Design, Handles, Whites, Utica, 3 Gal. 800.00
Crock, Flourish, Blue Quill Work, Repeated Twice, No.2, 9 5/8 In. 40.00
Crock, Fort Edward Stoneware Co., Cobalt Blue Bird, 11 1/4 In. 145.00
Crock, Frank B.Norton, Wide Mouth, Stylized Floral Spray, 2 Gal. 120.00
Crock, Gray, Blue Bird On Branch, 1 Gal. 225.00
Crock, Hamilton & Jones, Greensboro, Pa., Blue Design, 1 Gal. 95.00
Crock, Hamilton & Jones, Handles, Blue, 3 Gal. 245.00
Crock, Impressed 2, Polka Dot Pecking Chicken, 9 3/8 In. 350.00
Crock, Impressed 4, Blue 1853, L.H., 14 In. 155.00
Crock, Impressed 6, Bird On Branch, Cobalt Slip, 7 3/4 In. 175.00
Crock, Incised Design, Small Upside Down Figure Trim, 9 In. 40.00
Crock, J.Norton & Co., Bennington, Cobalt Bird, 4 Gal. 1700.00
Crock, Looping Flower, A.O.Whittemore, C.1875, 3 Gal. 110.00
Crock, Marshall Pottery, Marshall, Texas, 2 Gal. 25.00
Crock, McCormick Deering, Cylinder, Directions For Lye, 2 Gal. 225.00
Crock, Milton, Greensboro, Pa., Gray, Blue, 1 Gal. 135.00
Crock, Ottman Bros., Fort Edward, N.Y., No.3, Flora 185.00
Crock, Pickle, Blue Band, 5 Gal. 125.00
Crock, Polka Dot Bird On Flowering Branch, 10 3/4 In. 185.00
Crock, Prancing Stag, T.Harrington, Lyons, 4 Gal. 1900.00
Crock, Rupert, Greensboro, Pa., 2 Gal. 200.00
Crock, S.L.Pewtress, New Haven, Ct., 1 1/2, Bird On Branch, 8 In. 275.00
Crock, Salt Glaze, Handles, Design, 4 Gal. 265.00
Crock, Stenciled Blue Label, John Welty, Grocer, No.3, 11 1/2 In. 65.00
Crock, Stenciled Label, D.L.Ratcliff & Co., 5 3/4 In. 120.00
Crock, Stenciled With 8 Blue Stars, Ear Handles, No.3, 3 Gal. 90.00
Crock, Stylized Floral & 4 In Cobalt Blue, 11 1/2 In. 85.00
Crock, Swirled Leaf Design, 1888, 1 Gal. 425.00
Crock, W.Hart, Ogdensburgh 5, Cobalt Blue Fish, 12 3/4 In. 700.00
Crock, West Troy, N.Y., No.3 .... 225.00
Crock, White's, Utica, N.Y., Blue Design, 6 Gal. 425.00
Crock, Wm.Rowley, Middlebury, Ohio, Blue Floral, No.5, 13 In. 200.00
Cuspidor, Albany Slip Interior, F.H.Cowden, 6 In. 95.00
Custard Cup, Blue & White 75.00
Flask, Pig, Salt Glazed, Fine Old Bourbon, St.Louis, C.1860, 7 In. 1300.00
Flask, Pumpkin Seed, Gray, 18th Century, 2 X 4 X 5 1/2 In. 150.00
Flask, Spirit, A.Chamberlain, Hat Shaped Silver Stopper, C.1890 .... 950.00
Flowerpot, Attached Saucer Base, Brushed Cobalt Blue, 10 In. 275.00
Flowerpot, Attached Saucer, Blue Floral, White Glaze, 4 1/4 In. 22.50
Flowerpot, Attached Saucer, Cobalt Blue, Flowers, 9 In. 1825.00
Flowerpot, Attached Saucer, Tan Albany Slip Glaze, 7 3/4 In. 25.00
Hot Water Bottle, Blue & White, Marked 225.00
Hot Water Bottle, Western Stoneware, Marked, Blue & White 155.00
Humidor, Blue & Gray 175.00
Jar, 8 Leaved Fuchsia, Jordan, C.1845, 1 Gal. 150.00
Jar, Apothecary, Royal Arms, 18th Century, London, 7 In. 125.00
Jar, Apple Butter, Brushed Blue, Handle, 6 7/8 In. 65.00
Jar, Bird On Branch, Dark Blue, 12 In. 200.00

Jar, Blossoms, Swirling Stems, Woodruff–Cortland, 2 Gal. 225.00
Jar, Blue Brushed Floral Design, Scalloped Rim, Ovoid, 12 In. 95.00
Jar, Blue Flowers, Tom Suttle, Impressed 5, 15 5/8 In. 300.00
Jar, Blue Jay On Branch, Narrow Mouth, Signed West Troy, 2 Gal. 350.00
Jar, Blue Quill Work, 2 One Side, Flower On Reverse, 11 1/2 In. 50.00
Jar, Blue Vining Foliage, Handles, 7 3/4 In. 105.00
Jar, Blue Woman Walking, Trees, 6 Gal. 1900.00
Jar, Canning, 3 Brushed White Flowers, Narrow Mouth, 8 In. 100.00
Jar, Canning, Blue Label, Fruit & Foliage, Greensboro, 8 In. 250.00
Jar, Canning, Blue Pears, Wavy & Straight Lines, 10 In. 850.00
Jar, Canning, Blue Shoulder Design, 8 1/4 In. 75.00
Jar, Canning, Brushed Blue Design, 6 1/4 In. 150.00
Jar, Canning, Cobalt Blue Bird In Flight, T.F.Reppert, C.1880 .... 395.00
Jar, Canning, Cobalt Blue Lines, Foliage, 9 1/2 In. 550.00
Jar, Canning, Cobalt Blue Scene, Shepherdess Under Tree 2525.00
Jar, Canning, Cobalt Blue Stripes, 7 In. 89.00
Jar, Canning, Collared, Primitive Tulip, C.1850, 1/2 Gal. 160.00
Jar, Canning, Feather Design, Tan, White, 5 5/8 In. 50.00
Jar, Canning, Flower, Brushed Cobalt Blue, 8 In. 175.00
Jar, Canning, Greenish Glaze, White Slip Swags, 8 1/4 In. 1150.00
Jar, Canning, Incised Outline of Bear, 7 3/4 In. 215.00
Jar, Canning, Label With Cherries, Hamilton & Jones, 7 7/8 In. 550.00
Jar, Canning, Red Dog, Gray Glaze, Foliage, S.H.Sooner, 9 In. 85.00
Jar, Canning, Scene of 3 Figures, Tooled Lines, 9 1/2 In. 1300.00
Jar, Canning, Stenciled A.Conrad, New Geneva, Pa., 9 3/4 In. 195.00
Jar, Canning, Stenciled Floral Wreath Design, 9 1/4 In. 100.00
Jar, Canning, Stenciled Label, Jas.Hamilton & Co., 9 3/4 In. 85.00
Jar, Canning, Weir, 1 Gal. 29.00
Jar, Cobalt Blue Design, Double Ear Handles, 17 In. 280.00
Jar, Cobalt Blue Double Flower, Handles, 20 In. 225.00
Jar, Cobalt Blue Floral Design Both Sides, 15 1/2 In. 220.00
Jar, Cobalt Blue Floral, 10 3/4 In. 85.00
Jar, Cobalt Blue Slip Design, No.3, 13 3/4 In. 130.00
Jar, Cobalt Blue Stencil, Hamilton & Jones, 10 In. 100.00
Jar, Cobalt Blue Stencil, I.McCurry, Newcastle, Ohio, 12 1/4 In. 295.00
Jar, Cobalt Blue Stencil, Miller & Hanshumaker, 5 In. 475.00
Jar, Cowden & Wilcox, Harrisburg, Pa., Blue Flower, 9 In. 125.00
Jar, E.J.Brown, Dark Brown, 3 Gal. 65.00
Jar, Ear Handles, Incised Flower Both Sides, Ovoid, 8 7/8 In. 1075.00
Jar, From E.Fowler, Beaver, Pa., Ovoid, 13 1/2 In. 225.00
Jar, Gray, Western Stoneware, Monmouth, Cam Lever Seal, 1/2 Gal. 30.00
Jar, H.& G.Nash, Utica, Cobalt Blue Flower, Ovoid, 10 1/4 In. 75.00
Jar, Hamilton & Jones, Greensboro, Pa., Cobalt Blue Label, 14 In. 200.00
Jar, Hamilton & Jones, Greensboro, Pa., No.2, Label, 12 1/4 In. 150.00
Jar, Hubbell & Ceseboro, Geddes, N.Y., Floral, No.3, 12 3/4 In. 200.00
Jar, Impressed 2, Dangling Cucumber Design, C.1845, 2 Gal. 245.00
Jar, Impressed 2, Flower–Like Design, 11 In. 95.00
Jar, Impressed 3, Cobalt Blue Tulips, Foliage, Ovoid, 14 In. 325.00
Jar, Impressed Hamilton & Co., No.4, Blue Floral, Ovoid, 14 In. 500.00
Jar, Impressed Label, W.J.& E.O.Schror, Covered, Handle, 7 In. 450.00
Jar, Impressed Reeding To Simulate Handles, Tulips, 13 3/4 In. 725.00
Jar, J.Fisher & Co., Lyons, N.Y., Ovoid, Blue Plume, 12 In. 80.00
Jar, John Burger, Rochester, No.4, Stylized Flower, 14 3/4 In. 185.00
Jar, Lines, Cobalt Blue Floral Design, No.3, C.1854, 13 5/8 In. 975.00
Jar, Marshall, Texas, 2 Gal. 35.00
Jar, No.2, Cobalt Blue Foliage Around Shoulder, Ovoid, 12 In. 125.00
Jar, Open Ear Handles, Blue Floral, European, 11 1/2 In. 50.00
Jar, Open Handles, Swags, Foliage Tassels, 11 1/2 In. 2000.00
Jar, R.T.Williams, New Geneva, Pa., Freehand Blue Label, 9 In. 170.00
Jar, R.W.Williams, New Geneva, Pa., No.4, 14 3/4 In. 90.00
Jar, Rooster On A Tree, Cobalt Blue, Edmands & Co., 12 In. 2090.00
Jar, S.Purdy, Ohio, Cobalt Blue, Handles, Ovoid, 13 1/2 In. 175.00
Jar, S.S.Perry, Troy, Brushed Design, 10 1/2 In. 95.00
Jar, S.T.Brewer, Havana 2, Brushed Blue Floral, 10 1/4 In. 205.00

Silver–English, Cruet Stand, George III,
19th Century, 8 In.

Stoneware, Jug, S.Hart, Fulton, N.Y.,
Cobalt Blue, Doves, 3 Gal.

Jar, Satterlee & Mary, Fort Edward, Bird On Branch, Ovoid, 11 In.	200.00
Jar, Single Flower, C.Crolius Mfg., New York, Ovoid, 7 1/2 In.	1100.00
Jar, Slop, White, Dark Blue Bands, Wire Bail, 9 1/2 In.	170.00
Jar, Stenciled & Freehand Label, T.F.Reppert, 16 1/2 In.	95.00
Jar, Stenciled Label With Eagle, Hamilton & Jones, 4, 15 In.	325.00
Jar, Stenciled Label, Hamilton & Jones, Greensboro, Pa., 10 Gal.	475.00
Jar, Stenciled Label, Jas.Hamilton & Co., Ovoid, 8 In.	275.00
Jar, Stripes & 2 In Cobalt Blue, Ovoid, 11 5/8 In.	115.00
Jar, Stripes, Foliage, No.2, 11 1/2 In.	125.00
Jar, T.Reed, 2 Handles, 4 Gal.	325.00
Jar, W.H.Lehew & Co., Strasburg, Va., Foliage Design, 11 In.	85.00
Jar, Weyman's Snuff, Brown Interior, Cream, 9 In.	35.00
Jar, White's, Binghamton, Flower, Ovoid, 7 In.	95.00
Jar, Williams & Reppert, Dark Gray, Blue Stencil, Handles, 24 In.	350.00
Jug, 2 Cobalt Blue Circles, Ovoid, 5 1/4 In.	375.00
Jug, 6 Blossomed Flowers, F.A.Plaisted & Co., 2 Gal.	255.00
Jug, Albany Slip, Sgraffito Design, K.Soper In Wreath, 9 In.	390.00
Jug, Beehive, 2 Flower Blossoms, Leaves, Cortland, C.1870, 2 Gal.	125.00
Jug, Bird, Scrolled Leaf, Tulip Front, W.H.Farrar, C.1860, 2 Gal.	950.00
Jug, Blue Drawing of Man's Head, Ovoid, 11 1/4 In.	525.00
Jug, Blue Peacock On Branch, Gray, 2 Gal.	350.00
Jug, Blue Slip Flowers & Leaves, Gray, 1 Gal.	190.00
Jug, C.Crolius, Manufacturer, N.Y., Blue Brush Work, Ovoid, 15 In.	1100.00
Jug, C.W.Braun, Buffalo, N.Y., Label, 11 1/4 In.	85.00
Jug, Cobalt Blue 3–Petal Flowers, T.Harrington, N.Y., 2 Gal.	185.00
Jug, Cobalt Blue Design, E.Purdy 2, 13 1/2 In.	80.00
Jug, Cobalt Blue Feather Plumes, John Berger, Rochester, 14 In.	115.00
Jug, Cobalt Blue Tulip Plant, 2 Gal.	125.00
Jug, Cobalt Blue Tulip, Ovoid, Chollar, Darby & Co., 2 Gal.	300.00
Jug, Cobalt Stenciling, E.S.& B., 3 Gal.	110.00
Jug, Double Ear Handles, Cobalt Blue Lines, Ovoid, 19 In.	175.00
Jug, Double Spouts, Cobalt Blue Design, Ovoid, 14 In.	125.00
Jug, Embossed Flower, New York Stoneware, 1 Gal.	165.00
Jug, Farrar & Stearns, Fairfax, Vt., 2 Gal.	60.00
Jug, Floral & Leaf Design, Haxtun Ottman, Fort Edward, 1 Gal.	190.00
Jug, Floral Trio, Cobalt Blue, C.Hart, C.1860, 3 Gal.	235.00
Jug, Floral, No.3 In Cobalt Blue, 15 In.	90.00
Jug, Fuchsias, Ovoid, J.F.Brayton & Co., C.1833, 3 Gal.	375.00
Jug, Hart, Sherburne, Blue Floral, 3 Gal.	240.00
Jug, Hittemillers, Dyersville, Ia., Blue & Gray, 1 Gal.	150.00
Jug, Horseshoe, Macomb, 5 Gal.	45.00

Jug, I.M.Mead, Brushed Cobalt Blue At Handles & Label, 11 In.	85.00
Jug, Impressed Charlestown, 2 Tone Brown Glaze, Ovoid, 11 In.	110.00
Jug, Impressed J.Norton & Co., Bennington, Bird, Branch, 14 In.	300.00
Jug, Impressed Label, J.& F.Norton, Cobalt Blue, 16 In.	5100.00
Jug, Impressed White's, Binghamton, Cobalt Blue Flower, 11 In.	265.00
Jug, Incised Eagle, E.Wentworth, Norwich, 1 Gal.	400.00
Jug, J.Seymour, Troy Factory 2, Blue Flower, 14 In.	135.00
Jug, John Burger, Light & Dark Cobalt Blue Floral, 15 In.	400.00
Jug, Joshua Durgin, Portland, 1 Gal.	100.00
Jug, Julius Norton, Bennington, Vt., 1 Gal.	165.00
Jug, L.& B.G.Chace, Somerset, Blue Foliage, 16 In.	250.00
Jug, Leaf & Flower Design, Stetzenmeyer, 2 Gal.	725.00
Jug, Lithia Spring Water, Londonberry, N.H., Cobalt Slip, 3 Gal.	355.00
Jug, M.R.Kennedy, Dover, N.H., No.7, 1 Gal.	85.00
Jug, Molded Handles, Floral Design, 1 Gal.	30.00
Jug, Molded Handles, Floral Design, Word One On Back, 10 3/4 In.	400.00
Jug, Mottled Body, Bunch of Grapes, Troy Pottery, 2 Gal.	295.00
Jug, New York, Flowers & Leaves, Blue, Gray, 1 Gal.	190.00
Jug, Nicholas Baldes, Wilkes Barre, Pa., Bird, Branch, 13 5/8 In.	270.00
Jug, Nicholas Baldes, Wilkes Barre, Pa., Cobalt Blue, 14 In.	175.00
Jug, Reddish Buff Clay, Brown Floral, New Geneva, 7 In.	1000.00
Jug, Rieger & Lindley, Whiskey Merchants, Salt Lake City, 1 Gal.	95.00
Jug, S.Hart, Fulton, N.Y., Cobalt Blue, Doves, 3 Gal. ....*Illus*	425.00
Jug, Seymour, Tray 3, Single Cobalt Blue Flower, 16 In.	90.00
Jug, T.S.Angel & Son, Groceries & Provisions, Watertown, 1 Gal.	75.00
Jug, Taft, Keene, N.H., Blue, 1 Gal.	100.00
Jug, Twin Flower Design, White's, Utica, C.1867, 2 Gal.	125.00
Jug, W.H.Farrar & Co., Geddes, N.Y., Cobalt Blue Bird, 11 In.	4600.00
Jug, W.H.Jones Co., Boston, 1852–1902, 1 Gal.	85.00
Jug, Webster & Berge, Brushed 2, Stenciled Griffins, 13 1/4 In.	135.00
Jug, White's, Utica, Blue Fantail Peacock, Turned Head, 15 In.	1760.00
Jug, White's, Utica, Cobalt Blue Long Legged Bird, 11 1/4 In.	250.00
Jug, White's, Utica, Cobalt Quill Leaf Design, 11 In.	80.00
Keg, Bardwell's Root Beer, Bail, Blue & White	575.00
Keg, Embossed Cobalt Blue Bands, 6 3/8 In.	850.00
Keg, Spirit, Salt Glazed, Brandy, Gin & Rum, 11 In., 3 Piece	605.00
Milk Pan, C.1810, 4 X 16 In.	165.00
Milk Pan, Swirl, Blue & White	15.00
Mold, Jelly, Grape & Leaf, Oval	50.00
Mortar & Pestle, Advertising, John F.Jelke Co., 7 X 1 1/2 In.	275.00
Mug, Barrel Shape, Cobalt Blue Bands, 7 3/8 In.	130.00
Mug, Basketweave, Brown	40.00
Mug, Bird, Brown	40.00
Mug, Blue Brushed Flower, White Glaze, 4 1/2 In.	40.00
Mug, Brushed Cobalt Blue Flower, 4 1/4 In.	325.00
Mug, Cobalt Blue Bands, F.Heyde No.648 4th St., N.Y., 4 1/8 In.	400.00
Mug, Cobalt Blue Bands, Leaf Designs, 5 1/4 In.	450.00
Mug, Flying Bird, Blue & White	175.00
Mug, Golfer, Blue & White, Marked	195.00
Mug, Grape Lattice, Brown	25.00
Mug, Grapes In Medallion, Green Glaze	35.00
Mug, Monk, Blue & Gray, 4 1/2 X 3 1/2 In.	95.00
Mug, Monk, Blue & White	85.00
Mug, Old Man, Brown	45.00
Mug, Spartan, Blue	70.00
Mug, Windmill, Brown	45.00
Mug, Windy City, Blue & White	125.00
Pail, Butter, Ring At Spout, Ears, Evan R.Jones, C.1875, 4 Qt.	395.00
Pie Plate, Blue Pie Crust Rim, Cotton Stamp	120.00
Pie Plate, Coggled Edge, White	85.00
Pitcher, Acorn	140.00
Pitcher, Apricots, Blue & White, 8 In.	95.00
Pitcher, Avenue of Trees, Blue & White, 10 In.	125.00
Pitcher, Bacchus, Nudes In Relief, Meigh, 1844, 12 In.	200.00

Pitcher, Basketweave & Morning Glory, Blue & White 135.00
Pitcher, Batter, Brown Glaze, 2 Qt. 68.00
Pitcher, Blue Bands, Albany Slip Interior, 8 1/2 In. 150.00
Pitcher, Bluebird, Blue & White 215.00
Pitcher, Bowknot & Bluebird, Blue & White, Large 125.00
Pitcher, Boy & Girl Kissing, Blue & White, 10 In. 145.00
Pitcher, Brown Albany Glaze, Bulbous, 1 1/2 Qt. 75.00
Pitcher, Brown Floral Design, Buff Clay, New Geneva, 6 1/2 In. 500.00
Pitcher, Brown Floral Design, Buff Clay, New Geneva, 8 1/8 In. 600.00
Pitcher, Brown Floral, Gray Clay, New Geneva, 4 1/2 In. 625.00
Pitcher, Brown Floral, Gray Clay, New Geneva, 5 3/8 In. 325.00
Pitcher, Butterfly, Blue, White, 8 In. 125.00
Pitcher, Cattail, Blue & White, 7 1/2 In. 130.00
Pitcher, Cattail, Blue & White, 9 In. 100.00
Pitcher, Cherry Band, Blue & White, 8 1/2 In. 125.00
Pitcher, Cobalt Blue Flower, Tooled Ribs On Neck, 5 1/8 In. 100.00
Pitcher, Cobalt Blue Leaf Design, 1 Gal., 8 3/4 In. 600.00
Pitcher, Cow, Blue & White, 8 In. 85.00
Pitcher, Cow, Brown To Green, 6 1/2 In. 75.00
Pitcher, Cowden & Wilcox, Large Flower, Handle, 10 1/4 In. 800.00
Pitcher, Deer & Fawn, Blue & White, 8 In. 165.00
Pitcher, Dutch Windmill, Blue & White, 8 In. 185.00
Pitcher, E.& L.P.Norton, 1 1/2, Floral, 12 1/2 In. 360.00
Pitcher, Eagle Grove, Iowa, Blue Bands 250.00
Pitcher, Embossed Blue Flowers, Whites, Utica, N.Y., 6 1/2 In. 120.00
Pitcher, Floral Design, Cobalt Blue, 10 1/4 In. 375.00
Pitcher, Good Luck, Blue & White, 8 1/2 In. 100.00
Pitcher, Grape Cluster, Brown, 7 X6 In. 95.00
Pitcher, Grape Trellis, Blue, 5 1/2 In. 100.00
Pitcher, Grapes, Blue & White, 9 In. 130.00
Pitcher, Ice Water, Baffle In Top, Blue Floral, 9 In. 2400.00
Pitcher, Incised Floral, Cobalt Blue, 12 1/4 In. 50.00
Pitcher, Indian Chief, Blue & White, 8 In. 175.00
Pitcher, Iowa Chick Hatchery, Iowa City, White, 5 In. 12.00
Pitcher, Lincoln Head, Blue, 5 1/2 In. .... 145.00 To 275.00
Pitcher, Man, Smoking Pipe, Windmill, Dark Brown, 8 1/2 In. 65.00
Pitcher, Molasses, Pinched Spout, Buckeye Pottery, 1 Gal. 30.00
Pitcher, Pine Cone, Brown To Green, 7 1/2 In. 95.00
Pitcher, Poinsettia, Blue & White, 10 In. 225.00
Pitcher, Stag, Blue & White, 8 In. 250.00
Pitcher, Swastikas, Blue Green, 8 In. 60.00
Pitcher, Three Flying Birds, Blue & White, 12 In. 300.00
Pitcher, Water, Embossed, Blue & Gray, 6 Qt. 75.00
Pitcher, Windmill & Bush, Tulips 97.00
Pitcher, Windy City, Blue Gray 100.00
Plate, Gray Salt Glaze, Blue Rim, 8 3/8 In. 275.00
Rolling Pin, 6 Blue Stripes 185.00
Rolling Pin, Blue & White, Wildflower 225.00
Rolling Pin, Wildflower, Gold Advertising, Blue & White 195.00
Salt, Apple Blossom, Blue & White, Hanging 120.00
Salt, Apricot 120.00
Salt, Butterfly, Blue & White, Hanging 125.00
Salt, Daisy & Lattice, Blue, Hanging 95.00
Salt, Daisy, Lid 135.00
Salt, Flemish 465.00
Salt, Floral Design, Blue & White, Hanging 135.00
Salt, Greek Key, Maple Leaf, Blue & White 75.00
Salt, Love Birds, Blue & White, Hanging 325.00
Salt, Peacock, Hanging 300.00
Salt, White Hall Carnation, Lid 82.50
Soap Dish, Blue & White, Rose Beading In Relief, 4 3/4 In. 110.00
Soap Dish, Carnation, Flat Dished Center, Round 135.00
Soap Dish, Triple Roses, Blue & White 95.00
Spittoon, Blue & White .... 125.00 To 175.00

Spittoon, Blue & White Spongeware 125.00
Spittoon, Cobalt Blue 68.00
Spittoon, Lilies & Plumes, Blue & White 90.00
Tankard, Flemish Figures, Blue Gray 170.00
Tankard, Rose & Fan 50.00
Teapot, Strainer Insert, Blue Swirls, Oriental Leaf Design 85.00
Tenderizer, Meat, Blue Design 725.00
Toothbrush Holder, Rose Fish Scale, Blue & White 70.00
Umbrella Stand, Brown Glaze, Butterflies, Western Stoneware 46.00
Vase, Basket of Flowers, Leaves, Diffused Blue, 11 In. 375.00
Vase, Egyptian, Western Stoneware, 9 In. 36.00
Wall Pocket, Blue Design, 5 3/4 In. 900.00
Water Set, Embossed Vintage Design, Green Glaze, 5 Piece 45.00

Stoves have been used in America for heating since the eighteenth century and for cooking since the nineteenth century. Most types of wood, coal, gas, kerosene, and even some electric stoves are collected.

STOVE, Bennett, Wood, Restored 1200.00
Bridge–Beech, Barrel 695.00
Buck Jr.No.2, Cook, Working Condition 650.00
Camp, Charcoal, Lift-Up Top Grate, Wooden Handle, 18th Century 450.00
Camp, Soldier's, Cylindrical, Iron, Door, 18th Century, 5 X 6 1/2 In. 495.00
Charm, Cook, 6 Utensils & Burner Lifter, Salesman's Sample 295.00
Crescent, Cast Iron, Miniature 65.00
Crescent, Cast Iron, Tin Stove Pipe, Miniature 95.00
Evening Star No.20, Parlor 800.00
Franklin, Wood Burning, Gas Log Burner 445.00
Gas, Black, White & Gray Porcelain, Chrome, 3 Ovens, 6 Eyes, 1920s 750.00
Gray Bucks, Wood Burning, 4 Burner Gas 450.00
Grayson, Gas, Cream & Black 395.00
Gurney Mfg.Co., Kitchen Range, Wood Burning, Porcelain, Chrome, 1891 .... 600.00
Home Comfort, Gray Granite 1800.00
Kalamazoo, Range, Coal & Wood, Tan Enamel 250.00
Magic Chef, 4 Burner Gas, Pale Yellow, Black & Gray Marble, 1920s 500.00
Majestic, Cook, Grate, Recast, With Gears, Pair 125.00
Oak, Doe-Wah-Jack, Indian Top, Round 525.00
Prize No.8, White Enameled, Laundry Or Cook 90.00
Roper, Gas, Gray 650.00
Royal, Iron, Sample 70.00
STRAWBERRY, see Soft Paste

Stretch glass is named for the strange stretch marks in the glass. It was made by many glass companies in the United States from about 1900 to the 1920s. It is iridescent. Most American stretch glass is molded; most European pieces are blown and may have a pontil mark.

STRETCH GLASS, Compote, Vaseline, 10 In. 90.00
Console, Blue, Gold Trim, 13 In. 85.00
Salt, Footed 30.00
Vase, Fan, Ice Green, 10 In. 45.00

Sumida, or Sumida Gawa, is a Japanese pottery. The pieces collected by that name today were made about 1895 to 1970. There has been much confusion about the name of this ware, and it is often called "Korean Pottery" or "Poo ware." Most pieces have a very heavy orange–red, blue, or green glaze, with raised three–dimensional figures as decorations.

SUMIDA, Bowl, Oriental People Around Edges, Symbols, 8 1/2 In. 225.00
Brush Pot, 2 Monkeys, Seal Signature, 4 In. 100.00
Mug, Applied Man, With Bowl, Seal Signed, 5 In. 135.00
Pitcher & Mugs, 12 1/2 In., 3 Piece 315.00
Pot, Spout Is Face With Outstretched Hands, Covered 275.00
Tankard, 2 Children Applied, Seal Signature, 12 1/2 In. 495.00

Vase, Boy, With Ball, 8 In.	150.00
Vase, Double Gourd, Birds, Gold, Orange, 1875, 10 In.	140.00
Vase, Man, Sitting On Chair, Gray, Orange-Red, 8 1/4 X 3 In.	95.00
Vase, Oriental Children Protruding, Symbols On Back, 11 1/2 In.	245.00
Vase, Raised Figure of Man Carrying Lantern, Seal Mark, 5 In.	75.00
Vase, Tea House Scene, Waterfall, Bridge, Mezzo-Relievo, 12 1/2 In.	225.00

Sunbonnet Babies were first introduced in 1902 in the "Sunbonnet Babies Primer." The stories were by Eulalie Osgood Grover, illustrated by Bertha Corbett. The children's faces were completely hidden by the sunbonnets. The children had been pictured in black and white before this time, but the color pictures in the book were immediately successful. The Royal Bayreuth China Company made a full line of children's dishes decorated with the Sunbonnet Babies. Some Sunbonnet Babies plates have been reproduced but are clearly marked.

SUNBONNET BABIES, Ashtray, Musicians, Diamond Shape, 5 1/4 In.	98.00
Bell, Washing	85.00
Bonbon, Sewing, 3-Footed	125.00
Book, ABC, 1929	25.00 To 35.00
Book, Sunbonnet Babies In Mother Goose Land, 1927	45.00
Booklet, At Work, At Play, 1904	25.00
Box, Fishing, Covered, Oval, Blue Mark, 4 1/2 X 2 1/2 In.	245.00
Box, Puffy Heart, Covered, Sewing, Blue Mark	195.00
Cake Plate, Ironing, Blue Mark, 10 In.	275.00
Cake Plate, Washing, Open Handles, Blue Mark, 10 1/2 In.	195.00
Candleholder, Handle & Shield, Blue Mark	495.00
Candlestick, Cleaning, Blue Mark, 4 1/4 In.	225.00
Creamer, Washing & Hanging, Royal Bayreuth, 4 In.	125.00
Dish, Feeding, Doing Laundry	65.00
Dish, Pickle, Royal Bayreuth	175.00
Plate, Boy In Overalls, Advertising	60.00
Plate, Washing & Ironing, Royal Bayreuth, 7 1/2 In.	115.00
Plate, Washing, 7 In.	120.00
Platter, No.40 of 1000, Royal Bayreuth, 12 1/2 In.	198.00
Postcard, 7 Days of The Week, Set of 7	45.00 To 75.00
Relish, Washing, Royal Bayreuth, Handle, 8 In.	100.00
Sugar	69.00
Tile, Cleaning, Blue Mark, Round, 6 In.	225.00
Toothpick, Coal Scuttle Shape, Gold Handle, Marked	395.00
Valentine, Two's Company	8.00
Vase, Green Ground, Teplitz Stellmacher, 4 3/4 In.	125.00

Sunderland luster is a name given to a special type of pink luster made by Leeds, Newcastle, and other English firms during the nineteenth century. The luster glaze is metallic and glossy and appears to have bubbles in it.

SUNDERLAND, Creamer, Copper, Roses, Rib Bulb Bottom, 1830s, 5 1/2 In.	48.00
Creamer, Sprig Design, 8 Panel, Baroque, Reg.Mark, 4 1/2 In.	30.00
Humidor, Transfer, Parliament Buildings, Pewter Lock	195.00
Pitcher, Black Masonic Transfer, 6 3/4 In.	100.00
Pitcher, Captain Jones On One Side, Captain Hall On Other	3250.00
Pitcher, Luster, 6 In.	125.00
Plaque, Copper & Pink Luster, Ship Scene, Vase, 1810, 8 X 10 In.	125.00
Punch Bowl, Pearlware, Sailing Vessel, Bridge, 16 In.	1100.00
Shaving Mug, Frog	200.00

Superman was created by two seventeen-year-olds in 1938. The first issue of "Action" comics had the strip. Superman remains popular and became the hero of a radio show in 1940, cartoons in the 1940s, a television series, and several major movies.

SUPERMAN, Bank, Dime Register	85.00 To 100.00
Book, Coloring, Dated 1957, Saalfield	37.00
Bottle, Avon, Plastic, DC Comics Inc.	18.00

Buckle, Belt, Child's 10.00
Button, Superman of America, 1939 .... 15.00
Card, Valentine, 1940 .... 20.00
Decoder 17.00
Display, Pizza Hut, Folds Up, 6 Ft. 35.00
Game, Board, Figure, Cards, Transogram Co., 1954 .... 20.00 To 75.00
Game, Quoit Set, Box 140.00
Game, Speed, Milton Bradley, Large Version 100.00
Lunch Box 25.00
Pin, Holding American Flag, Enameled Brass 35.00
Pin, Pep 10.00
Play Suit, Medium, Ben Cooper, Box, 1974, Medium 25.00
Premium Certificate, Comic, Superman of America, 1940s, Framed 55.00
Ring, Crusader 150.00
Ring, Silver Jet Airplane, Plane Flies Off 48.00
Scissors, Kiddy, Clark Opening Shirt, On Card, 1973 .... 5.00
Siren, Empire, Box, 1978 .... 13.00
Socks, Box, 1949, 8 Pair 450.00
Toy, Krypton Rocket & Launcher, Mailer, 2 Piece .... 60.00 To 85.00
Toy, Tank, Rollover, Linemar 175.00
Tumbler, Batman, Super Hero, Pepsi–Cola 4.00
Tumbler, DC Comics Inc. 8.50
Valentine, Signed Ed & Dave, 1940 .... 12.50
Valentine, Stand Up Type, Copyright 1940 Superman Inc. 10.00

In 1933, the Kraft Food Company began to market cheese spreads in decorated, reusable glass tumblers. These were called "Swankyswigs." They were discontinued from 1941 to 1946, then made again from 1947 to 1958. Then plain glasses were used for most of the cheese, although a few special decorated Swankyswigs have been made since that time. A complete list of prices can be found in "The Kovels' Illustrated Price Guide to Depression Glass and American Dinnerware."

SWANKYSWIG, Antique, Blue, 3 1/2 In. 1.50
Antique, Brown, 3 1/2 In. 1.50
Bicentennial 10.00
Corn, No.1, Italian Blue, 3 1/2 In. 1.25
Daisy, Red, 3 1/2 In. 1.25
Jonquil, 3 1/2 In. 2.00
Kiddie, Blue, 3 1/2 In. 1.50
Posey, Violet, 3 1/2 In. 1.75
Sailboat, Blue, 4 1/2 In. 8.00
Star, Red, 3 1/2 In. 3.25
Tulip No.1, Red, 3 1/2 In. 2.50
Tulip No.3, Yellow, 3 1/2 In. 2.50

All types of swords are of interest to collectors. The military dress sword with elaborate handle is probably the most wanted. Be sure to display swords in a safe way, out of reach of children.

SWORD, Ames, Cavalry Saber, Brass Hilt, Steel Scabbard 800.00
Artillery, 1833 Model, Scabbard 200.00
Bayonet, European, Scabbard, Iron Mounts, C.1880 .... 55.00
Bayonet, French Army, Inscription, Dated 1875 .... 35.00
Bayonet, French, Saber, Scabbard, C.1885 .... 135.00
Bayonet, Navy, Brown, Tetley, Brass Grip, Locking Groove, 1850, 26 In. 200.00
Bayonet, World War I, Mauser, German, Scabbard 25.00
British, Infantry Officer's, Etched Blade, Wilkinson 135.00
Broad, Dutch Military, Curved Blade, C.1830, 23 In. 115.00
Broad, Horseman's, Basket Hilt, Scottish, Mid–18th, 38 1/2 In. 1075.00
Broadsword, Spanish Horseman's, Toledo Blade, Brass Guard, C.1695 ..... 425.00
Bronze Mounts With Figures, Bronze Tsuba 125.00
Cane, Bamboo, Cuban Sheath, Spanish Blade, C.1913 .... 155.00
Cane, Japanese, 19th Century 195.00
Cavalry Trooper's, Leather Grip, Scabbard, Napoleonic Period, 34 In. ... 110.00

Chopper, American, 2 Handles, Iron, Wooden Sheath, Dated 1828	60.00
Cutlass, American Naval, Tapered Knuckle Bow, Revolutionary War	225.00
Cutlass, European Naval Officer's, Lion Head Pommel, 29 In.	130.00
Dagger, Indo–Persian War, German Silver Sheath & Handle, 1925	95.00
Dirk, Piper's, Carved Grip, Stone Top, Scabbard, Scottish	97.50
Dress, European, French, Pearl Grips, Brass Hilt	165.00
Hounslow Hanger, Curved, Staghorn Grip, English, C.1640, 25 In.	385.00
Hunting, Bone Grip, Dog Head Finger Guard, Gilt Design, 23 In.	125.00
Hunting, Brass Hilt, American Revolutionary, 22 In.	185.00
Imperial Russian Pioneer, Scabbard, Crimean War, 19 1/4 In.	165.00
Katana, Fighting, Iron Shipping Design, Lacquer Sheath, 28 3/4 In.	2200.00
Knife, U.S.Trench, Brass Knuckle Type, C.1918	125.00
Knife, U.S.Trench, Triangular Blade, C.1917	45.00
Kris, Carved Duck Head On Handle, Scabbard, 21 In.	150.00
Officer's, German Infantry, Brass Hilt, Scabbard, 33 3/4 In.	117.50
Officer's, Navy, Ivory Grip, Scabbard, English, C.1790, 28 In.	165.00
Officer's, U.S.Militia, Dress, Leather Grip, 1820–30, 32 In.	152.00
Prussian, Artillery, World War I, Parade, Scabbard	125.00
Saber, Cavalry Officer's, Gilt Brass Hilt, Scottish, 31 1/2 In.	310.00
Saber, Spanish Artillery, Spanish–American War	95.00
Samurai, Japanese Army, World War II	200.00
Samurai, Steel Tsuba, Arrow Design, Cord Wrapped Handle, 39 In.	175.00
Short Handle, Lion Head Pommel, Leather Sheath	105.00
Short, Hunting Knife, Hoof & Leg Deer Handle, 1750s, Scottish, 12 In.	325.00
Town, Gilt Brass Hilt, Ebony Grip, Colonial, C.1750, 26 1/2 In.	165.00
Turkish Cavalry Trooper's, Iron Hilt, Pierced Design, Crimean War	135.00
U.S. Army, Surrendered To, Tokyo 1944, Blade By Kanenori	185.00

SYRACUSE China 1871 Syracuse is a trademark used by the Onondaga Pottery of Syracuse, New York. The company was established in 1871. It is still working. The name became the Syracuse China Company in 1966. It is known for fine dinnerware and restaurant china.

SYRACUSE, Cup & Saucer, Maxwell House Coffee, Demitasse	5.00
Cup & Saucer, Old Ivory, Demitasse	20.00
Fish Set, 11 1/2 X 15 1/2 In., 13 Piece	100.00
Paperweight	14.00
Plate, Dinner, Selma	36.00
Plate, Governor Clinton, Gold Trim, 10 In., Set of 7	100.00
Platter, Black Waiter's Head, Coon Chicken Inn, White, 12 In.	130.00

TANKARD, see Stein
TAPESTRY, PORCELAIN, see Rose Tapestry

A tea caddy is a small box made to hold tea leaves. In the eighteenth century, tea was very expensive and it was stored under lock and key. The first tea caddies were made with locks. By the nineteenth century, tea was more plentiful and the tea caddy was larger. Often there were two sections, one for green tea, one for black tea.

TEA CADDY, Bird's–Eye Maple, Lacquer, Twig Handle, Pewter Interior, 7 In.	675.00
Brass, Interior Tin Lid, Engraved Design, Monogrammed Lid, 6 In.	50.00
Brass, Mahogany, Walnut Burl, Inlaid, France, 6 X 11 5 5/8 In.	475.00

Bright Cut Design, Oval, Engraved Crest, Silver, R.Hennell, 1866 .... 935.00
Chippendale, Mahogany, Lock & Key, 1780 .... 475.00
Crichton Bros., Detachable Finial, 1914, 5 7/8 In. 880.00
Cut Glass Bowl, Mahogany Sarcophagus, 1820, 11 In. 200.00
Diamond Escutcheon, Mahogany Veneer, 2 Sections, 10 In. 85.00
Drape & Oval Inlay, Various Woods, England, 18th Century, 5 In. 375.00
Enameled Flowers, Hinged Domed Cover, Russian, C.1900, 3 1/2 In. 2200.00
English Regency, Mahogany, C.1825 .... 475.00
English, Mahogany Veneer, 3 Section Interior, 9 1/4 In. 65.00
Fruitwood, Apple Form, Cover, Stem Handle, England, 4 1/2 In. 450.00
Hand Painted Portrait of Ruth, Vienna, Signed 280.00
Ivory & Shell Covered, British, Early 19th Century, 7 1/2 In. 475.00
Ivory Banding, Tortiseshell, Gold Seal, 18th Century 1175.00
Mahogany Veneer, Inlay, Hinged Cover, Handle, 1790, 7 X 5 X 4 In. 500.00
Molded Design On Lid, Wafer Feet, Mahogany Veneer, 8 In. 95.00
Oriental Figures, Red Lacquer, Raised Gilt Design, 14 In. 990.00
Pear Shape, Hinged Top, C.1825, 5 In. 500.00
Pear Shape, Lock & Hinged Lid, Fruitwood 350.00
Repousse Silver Plate, Reed & Barton, Bulbous, 4 1/4 X 5 In. 55.00
Rosewood, Hinged Cover, Glass Bowl, England, 14 X 7 X 5 In. 75.00
Satinwood & Walnut Inlay, Walnut Foot, 5 1/2 In. 165.00
Satinwood, Velvet Lined, 2 Compartments, George III, 10 In. 200.00
Silver Gilt & Enamel, Russian, N.Alexeev, C.1910, 4 In. 1980.00
Silver, Inlay of Wood, Rosewood, 6 In. 75.00
Soft Paste, Comic Men & Women, No Lid, 4 5/8 In. 130.00
Sterling Silver, Ball & Black Co., C.1855 .... 550.00
Tambour Front, 2 Compartments, Rosewood, Victorian, 8 In. 550.00
Tole, Polychrome Design, Brown Japanning, 6 1/2 In. 145.00
Tole, Smoke Grained, Hinged Cover, Claw Feet, 4 3/4 In. 400.00
Tortoiseshell Veneer, Ivory Handles, Silver Inset 1826, 4 In. 425.00
Tortoiseshell, 2 Sections, Bun Feet, English, 6 In. 375.00
Wood Inlay & Bandings, Design On Cartouches, C.1790 .... 1050.00

There was a superstition that it was lucky if a whole tea leaf unfolded at the bottom of your cup. This idea was translated into the pattern of dishes known as "tea leaf." By 1850, at least twelve English factories were making this pattern; and by the 1870s, it was a popular pattern in many countries. The tea leaf was always a luster glaze on early wares, although now some pieces are made with a brown tea leaf.

TEA LEAF IRONSTONE, Bowl, Square, 7 1/2 In. 35.00
Bowl, Square, Meakin, 7 In. 40.00
Bowl, Square, Meakin, 8 In. 50.00
Bowl, Vegetable, Burgess, Rectangular, 8 In. 25.00
Bowl, Vegetable, Covered, Burgess, Rectangular, 9 In. 50.00
Bowl, Vegetable, Covered, Meakin .... 40.00 To 60.00
Bowl, Vegetable, Pepper Leaf, Covered 85.00
Butter Chip, Shaw, Square 4.00
Butter, Covered, Wedgwood 75.00
Cake Plate, Mellor Taylor, Oval 65.00
Chamberpot, Design On Cover 150.00
Coffeepot, Bamboo, Meakin 120.00
Coffeepot, Davenport 125.00
Coffeepot, Morning Glory, Elsmore & Forster 225.00
Creamer, Shaw, Rectangular, 5 In. 125.00
Cup & Saucer, Adams 30.00
Cup & Saucer, Davenport 50.00
Cup & Saucer, Handleless, Elsinore 55.00
Cup & Saucer, Meakin 60.00
Cup, Clementson 35.00
Gravy Boat, Peerless 60.00
Mug, Wilkinson 60.00
Pitcher & Bowl 450.00
Pitcher & Bowl, Bamboo, Meakin 350.00

Pitcher & Bowl, Ribbed, Burgess 350.00
Pitcher, Milk, Bulbous, Alcock 125.00
Pitcher, Milk, Fish Hook, 8 1/2 In. 85.00
Plate, 6 1/2 In. 12.00
Plate, 9 1/2 In., Set of 4 .... 40.00
Plate, Adams, 7 1/2 In. 10.00
Plate, Adams, 10 In. 15.00
Plate, Clementson, 8 1/2 In. 18.00
Plate, Dessert, Pink Luster, Davenport, Set of 10 .... 200.00
Plate, Meakin, 9 In. .... 11.00 To 12.00
Plate, Wedgwood, 8 1/2 In. 12.00
Plate, Wedgwood, 10 In. 12.00
Platter, Meakin, 11 In. 20.00
Platter, Meakin, 16 X 11 1/2 In. 45.00
Platter, Mellor, Taylor & Co., 11 1/2 In. 50.00
Platter, Rectangular, 15 X 18 In. 35.00
Shaving Mug, Grape Embossed, 12–Sided 110.00
Soap Dish, Covered 115.00
Soup, Dish, Covered, Rectangular Finial 130.00
Sugar, Covered, Bamboo, Meakin 55.00
Tea Set, Child's, Gold Trim, Mellor, Taylor Co., 12 Pc. 300.00
Teapot, Cable Pattern 175.00
Toothbrush Holder 135.00
Tureen, Soup, Covered 450.00

Teco is the mark used on the art pottery line made by the American Terra Cotta and Ceramic Company of Terra Cotta and Chicago, Illinois. The company was an offshoot of the firm founded by William D. Gates in 1881. The Teco line was first made in 1885 but was not sold commercially until 1902. It continued in production until 1922. Over 500 designs were made in a variety of colors, shapes, and glazes. The company closed in 1930.

TECO, Ashtray 70.00
Bookends, Rebecca At The Well, 2 Colors 450.00
Bowl, 5 1/2 X 1 In. 85.00
Bowl, Indented Upper Ridge, Green, 7 In. 95.00
Cup, 4 In. 50.00
Mustard, 4 1/2 In. 75.00
Pitcher, Double Handle, Gray Green, 8 1/2 In. 250.00
Pitcher, Organic Double Handle, Gray Green, 8 1/2 In. 250.00
Tile, 4 1/4 X 4 1/4 In. 165.00
Tray, Dresser, 14 X 10 In. 75.00
Vase, 4–In.Body Handles, 12 Reticulations At 2–Level Opening, 6 In. ... 4620.00
Vase, Bulbous Bottom, Flares To Rim, Medium Green, 5 1/4 In. 100.00
Vase, Bulbous, Undulating Neck, Flared Opening, 4 Handles, 13 In. 1650.00
Vase, Classic Shape, 8 In. 250.00
Vase, Cylindrical Neck, 2 Angular Handles, Porous Matte Green, 7 In. ... 880.00
Vase, Green, Ovoid, 4 3/4 In. 85.00
Vase, Molded Jack–In–The–Pulpit, Tapered Cylinder, Green, 13 In. 400.00
Vase, Ovoid Cylinder, Italian Green, 8 1/2 In. 165.00
Vase, Plum, Brown Speckled Glaze, 4 X 8 In. 325.00
Vase, Ribbed Outside, Green, 4 In. 120.00
Vase, Triangular Crimped Top, Marked, 4 1/2 In. 155.00

The first teddy bear was a cuddly toy said to be inspired by a hunting trip made by Teddy Roosevelt in 1902. Morris and Rose Michtom started selling their stuffed bears as "Teddy bears" and the name stayed. The Michtoms founded the Ideal Novelty and Toy Company. The German version of the teddy bear was made about the same time by the Steiff Company. There are many types of teddy bears, all collected, and the old ones are being reproduced.

TEDDY BEAR, Amber, Straw Stuffed, Swivel Neck, Jointed, Sweater, 1920, 16 In. 350.00
Articulated Head, Limbs, Gold, Glass Eyes, Voice Box, 24 1/2 In. 35.00
Articulated Legs, Gold Plush, Embroidered Face, 23 In. 210.00

Articulated Limbs, Beige, Glass Eyes, Hand Knit Sweater, 21 In. 275.00
Beige Mohair, Straw Stuffed, Jointed, 1930s, 21 In. 245.00
Beige Mohair, Straw Stuffed, Jointed, Growls, 1940s, 28 In. 240.00
Black, Straw Filled, Wooden Bead Eyes, Harness, C.1900, 16 In. 2100.00
Cinnamon Mohair, Fully Jointed, 1930s, 18 In. 225.00
Cinnamon Mohair, Jointed, Hump, Curved Paws, Jointed, 10 In. 150.00
Cinnamon, Straw Stuffed, Metal Frame, Wheels, 19 X 10 In. 150.00
Clements, Embroidered Claws & Nose, 24 In. 425.00
Dark Brown Mohair, Jointed, 1920s, 19 In. 195.00
English Mohair, Fully Jointed, Snakeskin Pads, 5 In. 95.00
Gold Haircloth, Articulated Limbs, Glass Eyes, 22 In. 110.00
Gold Haircloth, Glass Eyes, 19 In. 85.00
Gold Mohair, Jointed, Glass Eyes, 15 In. 95.00
Gold Mohair, Velvet Paw Pads, Stickpin Eyes, 1930s, 22 In. 275.00
Gold, Uniform, 24 In. 160.00
Hermann, Mohair, Jointed, Straw Stuffed, 10 In. 165.00
Ideal, 75th Anniversary, Box, 1978 .... 50.00
Knickerbocker, Beige & White, 15 In. 15.00
Knickerbocker, Brown Mohair, Jointed, Stickpin Eyes, 15 In. 350.00
Margaret Strong, Bride & Groom, 13 1/2 & 14 In., Pair 190.00
Margaret Strong, Growler, Jointed, 20 In. 159.00
Misha Bear, Mascot 1980 Summer Olympic Games, Tag, 12 In. 25.00
Mohair, Straw Stuffed, Pin Jointed, 1920–30, 4 1/2 In. 75.00
P.M.Paris, Jointed, Straw Stuffed, Rust Velour, Labeled, 12 In. 225.00
Paddington, Felt, 2 1/2 In. 10.00
Pink Mohair, Straw Stuffed, Glass Eyes, Jointed, French, 6 In. 75.00
Poland, No.118, Jointed, Glass Eyes, 7 In. 35.00
Reagan Jr., Applause, Gray Plus, Seated, 1979, 11 In. 25.00
Schuco, Growler, Jointed, 1930s, 13 In. 695.00
Shoebutton Eyes, Jointed, 1920s, 12 In. 245.00
Shoebutton Eyes, Smoking Jacket, Black, White Shoes, 22 In. 175.00
Steiff, 1915, Red Mohair, 14 In. 425.00
Steiff, Amber Plush, Straw Filled, Jointed, Ear Button, 13 In. 1400.00
Steiff, Baby, Red Collar, Bell, Tagged, U.S.Zone Label, 16 1/2 In. 750.00
Steiff, Blank Button, 10 In. 425.00
Steiff, Blond Mohair, Shoebutton Eyes, C.1910, 18 In. 1540.00
Steiff, Blond, Button On Ear, 1906, 13 In. 750.00
Steiff, Buff, 1913, 10 In. 200.00
Steiff, C.1905, 16 In. 1100.00
Steiff, Chocolate Brown Mohair, Jointed, Growler, 20 In. 100.00
Steiff, Cream Color, Button & Tag, C.1930, 8 In. 650.00
Steiff, Gold Mohair, Jointed, 14 In. 495.00
Steiff, Gold Plush, Straw Filled, Ear Button, C.1900, 17 In. 1400.00
Steiff, Gold, Jointed, Box, 9 In. 45.00
Steiff, Mohair, Motty, Jointed, 8 1/2 In. 125.00
Steiff, On Wheels, Rocker, 25 X 15 In. 750.00
Steiff, Open Mouth, Button, 14 In. 100.00
Steiff, Original, Straw Stuffed, Mohair, Jointed, Growler, 17 In. 495.00
Steiff, Straw Stuffed, Swivel Head, Mohair, 7 In. 145.00
Steiff, Tagged, 1960s, 9 1/2 In. 95.00
White Mohair, Jointed, Black Glass Eyes, Hump, Growler, 19 In. 350.00
White Plush Haircloth, Glass Eyes, Articulated Limbs, 9 In. 105.00
Yellow Silky Mohair, Straw Filled, Jointed, 20 In. 225.00
Yellow, White Mohair, Pointed Nose, Straw Stuffed, 19 In. 175.00
Yellow–Persimmon Plush, Vinyl Nose, Blue Eyes, 12 In. 58.00
Yogi Bear, Hanna Barbera Tag, 1980, 15 In. 12.00

The first telephone may have been made in Havana, Cuba, in 1849, but it was not patented. The first publicly demonstrated phone was used in Frankfurt, Germany, in 1860. The phone made by Alexander Graham Bell was shown at the Centennial Exhibition in Philadelphia in 1876, but it was not until 1877 that the first private phones were installed. Collectors today want all types of old phones, phone parts, and advertising.

TELEPHONE, Ashtray, AT & T Logo 10.00
 Black Metal Base, Black Bakelite Handset, C.1922 .... 230.00
 Booth, Western Electric, Wooden 375.00
 Booth, With Fan, Oak 150.00
 Brass Transmitter Assembly, Brass Hook, Dial & Receiver, C.1919 .... 280.00
 Candlestick, American Tel.& Tel., Brass, Pat.1915 & 1920 .... 148.00
 Candlestick, Connecticut, 1904 .... 115.00
 Candlestick, French, 1914 .... 275.00
 Candlestick, Utica Fire Alarm Co., Nickel Over Brass 185.00
 Candlestick, Western Electric, 1904 .... 175.00
 Child's, Black Metal, 1930s 50.00
 Chrome Plated Over Solid Brass, Dial, Black Handset, 1930s 170.00
 Danish, French Horn, Desk Model, Green Silk Cord ....55.00 To 135.00
 Dial, Candlestick, Western Electric 165.00
 Erickson, Fiddleback, Wall, Iron Cased 125.00
 Farr Tandem, Oak 900.00
 Flashlight, Bell System, Angle Head, Black Plastic, Letters 5.00
 Kellogg, Dated 1908 .... 95.00
 Kellogg, Wall, Cathedral Type, Oak 175.00
 Leich Electric Co., Wall, Oak 165.00
 Megaphone, Operator, Brass, Hard Rubber, Attached Strap, Pat.1912 .... 40.00
 Mirror, Pocket, Advertising 65.00
 Monarch, Chicago, Oak 175.00
 Paperweight, Bell Telephone, Blue Glass 55.00
 Sign, AT&T, New England Telephone, Porcelain, 1921 Bell, 17 In. 95.00
 Sign, AT&T, New York Telephone, Porcelain, 1921 Bell, 11 X 11 In. 95.00
 Sign, Porcelain, Says Office, With Arrow, 2 Sides, 16 X 20 In. 85.00
 Solid Brass Base, Brass Dial, Black Handset, C.1930 .... 140.00
 Switchboard, 1944 .... 640.00
 Wall, Crank, Wooden, 1913, 26 In. 135.00
 Wall, Intercom, 5 Button, Original, Oak 120.00
 Western Electric, Candlestick, Ringer Box, Call Directory 250.00
 Western Electric, Cranker, Oak, Wall 175.00
 Western Electric, Fiddleback, No.301-A, Walnut 300.00
 Western Electric, Magneto, Brass Bells, Oak Case 38.00
 Western Electric, Wall, For Alexander Graham Bell, 1882 .... 450.00
 White Base, Molded Bakelite, Cloth Cord, Brass Dial, C.1925 .... 260.00

Teplitz refers to art pottery manufactured by a number of companies in the Teplitz–Turn area of Bohemia during the late nineteenth and early twentieth centuries. The Amphora Porcelain Works and the Alexandra Works were two of these companies.

TEPLITZ, Basket, Enameled Leaves, Cobalt Handle, Rim, Czechoslovakia, 7 In. 58.00
 Basket, Owl, Nude Child, Green Drapery On Goose, Molded Base 425.00
 Bowl, Chubby Nude Child, On Back Of Goose, Marked, 13 X 12 In. 425.00
 Bust, Amphora, Art Nouveau, Flowers Form Bodice & In Hair, 16 In. 1100.00
 Bust, Girl, Marked, 12 In. 500.00
 Candlestick, Amphora, C.1895, 12 In. 115.00
 Centerpiece, Girl, Pond, White, Turquoise, 13 In. 975.00
 Compote, Applied Plums & Cherries, Signed, 6 1/4 In. 145.00
 Compote, Art Nouveau, Women & Flowers, High Relief, Amphora, 6 In. ... 400.00
 Creamer, Cobalt Blue, Gold, Ivory, Stellmacher, 4 In. 30.00
 Ewer, Poppies, Bulbs, Gold, Cream Ground, Frond–Like Handles, 9 In. .. 135.00
 Ewer, Purple Poppies, Bulbs, Gold Detail, Cream, RS & K Mark, 9 In. .. 135.00
 Ewer, Purple Poppies, Gold Trim, Molded Florals, Marked, 9 In. 135.00
 Figurine, Greek Youth, With Mandolin, 15 In. 190.00
 Figurine, Lion, Stalking, Rocky Cliff Formation, 10 X 15 In. 275.00
 Humidor, Portrait, Stellmacher 110.00
 Vase, Amphora, 4 Ibis, Mushroom Shape, Turquoise, Orange, Tan, 18 In. . 750.00
 Vase, Applied Gold Grapes, Vines, Green & Pink, 10 In. 125.00
 Vase, Applied Grapes, Vines, Marked, 10 In. 135.00
 Vase, Bird's Head, Jewels, Handles, 5 1/4 In. 48.00
 Vase, Daisies, Gold, 2 Handles, Red Mark, 8 In. 95.00
 Vase, Farm Girl, Pulls Rooster's Tail, Handles, 3 1/2 In. 75.00

Vase, Flowers & Enameling, Speckled Gold, Handles, 12 In. 225.00
Vase, Flowers, Cream Ground, Gold Trim, 6 1/2 In. 70.00
Vase, Flying Birds, Amphora, Enameled, C.1900, 12 1/2 X 7 In., Pair 110.00
Vase, Flying Birds, Multicolored Enameled, C.1900, 7 X 4 In. 39.00
Vase, Girl Pulling Rooster's Tail, Double Handle, Squat, 3 1/2 In. 110.00
Vase, Hercules Fighting Lion, Enameled, 7 1/2 X 5 In. 95.00
Vase, Jeweled Design, Signed, 5 In. 135.00
Vase, Molded Squirrel, Marked, 8 In. 275.00
Vase, Mums, Gold, 2 Handles, Red Mark, 13 In. 195.00
Vase, Orchids, Gold Outlined, Handles, Alexander Mark, 13 1/2 In. 155.00
Vase, Purple & Red Gooseberries, Signed, 7 In. 115.00

Terra–cotta is a special type of pottery. It ranges from pale orange to dark reddish–brown in color. The color comes from the clay, which is fired but not always glazed in the finished piece.

TERRA–COTTA, Birdbath, Shallow Fluted Urn, Pedestal, 19th Century, 26 In. 750.00
Biscuit Jar, Money Bag, Burlap Texture, $100, 000 Front, Europe 65.00
Bust, Woman Playing Mandolin, Artist Signed, Greece, 1870 .... 350.00
Chamberstick, Black Transfer, Small 25.00
Figurine, Girl, Playing Mandolin, C.1870, 15 In. 275.00
Figurine, N.African Woman, Seated, Painted, 1800s, 31 In. 1540.00
Figurine, Owl, Perched On Stump, Silvered, 19th Century, 25 In. 250.00
Jug, Full Dragon Around In Relief, 2 X 3 1/2 In. 45.00
Pitcher, Tooled Surface, Mask Spout, 7 1/4 In. 100.00
Plaque, Putti With Goat, French, 18th Century, 13 X 23 In. 350.00
Ushabti, Crossed Arms, Long Bear, Brown, 3 3/4 In. 145.00
Ushabti, Green Glazed, Raised Back Pillar, 3 1/2 In. 175.00
Vase, Dragons In Relief, 6 In. 25.00

Textile includes many types of printed textiles, table and household linens, and clothing. Some other textiles will be found under Clothing, Coverlet, Rug, Quilt, etc.

TEXTILE, Bag, Flour, Wood Block Print, Mt.Holly Mills, Ohio, 16 X 20 1/2 In. 125.00
Bedspread, Battenburg, 115 X 88 In. 700.00
Bedspread, Battenburg, Ecru, Italian, 1900–10, 72 X 90 In., Pair 395.00
Bedspread, Candlewick, Stylized Floral, M.M.1858, 80 X 82 In. 15.00
Bedspread, Chenille, Child's, White, Blue Scotty Dog, Floral, 1940s 65.00
Bedspread, Counterpane, White, 81 X 88 In. 55.00
Bedspread, Crib, Floral Design, Outlined In White, 32 X 38 In. 60.00
Bedspread, Crocheted, Ecru, 102 X 66 In. 135.00
Bedspread, Crocheted, Filet Design, 1 Piece, 103 X 117 In. 150.00
Bedspread, Crocheted, Irish Pattern, Fringed, Double Size 250.00
Bedspread, Crocheted, Star & Popcorn, Double Bed 165.00
Bedspread, Ecru Net, Cutwork Florals, 84 X 112 In. 65.00
Bedspread, Embroidered, White, White Floral, Eagle, 76 X 88 In. 65.00
Bedspread, Natural Linen, Brown Candlewick Dots, 96 X 112 In. 55.00
Bedspread, Needlework, Sophie Weston Parkinson, 1830, 76 X 84 In. 425.00
Bedspread, Red & Blue Blocked Design, Cotton, 1937, 90 X 108 In. 138.00
Blanket, Embroidered, Esther Williams Aged 69, 72 X 98 In. 6750.00
Blanket, Germantown, Stepped Design, C.1885, 31 X 36 In. 425.00
Blanket, Hand Woven, Embroidered, Ivory, Geometric, 7 X 6 Ft. 800.00
Blanket, Homespun, Crewel, Initials, 19th Century, 74 X 89 In. 795.00
Blanket, Mexican, Blue, Black, Red, Natural, Fringed, 49 X 80 In. 75.00
Blanket, Pendleton Style, Cotton, Indian Designs, 64 X 69 In. 25.00
Blanket, Wool Homespun, Red, Brown, 19th Century, 72 X 72 In. 225.00
Chaps, Cowboy, 3 Batwings, Fringed Shotguns, Marked Batwings 375.00
Crib Cover, Popcorn Stitch Squares, White, Ruffled, 44 In. 145.00
Doily, Battenburg, Linen Center, 21 In. 38.50
Doily, Pineapple, 33 In. 13.00
Doily, Roses, Ecru & White, Round, 25 In. 45.00
Draperies, Victorian, Flowered Damask, 48 X 86 In.Panel, Pr. 125.00
Fabric, Cigarette Print, Silky, 1930s, 6 Yards 35.00
Flag, Jolly Roger, White Canvas, Black Felt, 18 3/4 X 31 3/4 In. 100.00
Luncheon Cloth, White, Crocheted Corners, 33 X 35 In. 15.00

Mattress, Feather Tick, 83 X 63 In. 45.00
Memorial, Embroidered, Painted, Whitney Family, C.1820, 12 X 14 In. 400.00
Needlework, Silver Metallic Edging, Floral, English, 9 X 11 In. 105.00
Needlework, Woman In Garden, Pen & Ink Detail, 11 X 13 3/8 In. 175.00
Piano Bench Cover, Needlepoint, Floral, Deep Blue Ground 35.00
Picture, Embroidered, Autumn, Sally Phelps, 1787, 23 X 19 1/4 In. 9900.00
Picture, Needlework, Girl Under Tree, English, 27 X 23 In. 600.00
Picture, Silk, Young Couple, Eueline Darby, 1807, 15 X 16 1/2 In. 850.00
Picture, Stumpwork, Charles II, Court, 17th Century, 21 X 27 In. 2850.00
Pillow Case, Blue & White Homespun, 19 1/2 X 30 In., Pair 140.00
Pillow Case, Calico Star Design, 1844, 20 X 35 In., Pr. 430.00
Pillow Cover, Wool, Berlin–Work, 19th Century, 15 X 17 In. 165.00
Robe, Buggy, Brown, Gold, Red, Green Floral, Wool 225.00
Runner, Battenburg Lace, 15 X 48 In. 115.00
Runner, Cherubs, Crocheted, 13 X 28 In. 45.00
Runner, Cluny Lace, Cluny Border, Wide Corners, 17 X 42 In. 85.00
Sheet, Homespun Linen, Hand Hemmed, Red Dye Stain, 66 X 76 In. 95.00
Table Cover, Battenburg Lace, Round, 52 In. 65.00
Tablecloth, Battenburg Lace, Border, 26 In. 80.00
Tablecloth, Battenburg Lace, Grape & Leaf Border, Round, 33 In. 150.00
Tablecloth, Battenburg Lace, Grape Pattern, Round, 72 In. .... 150.00 To 195.00
Tablecloth, Battenburg Lace, Grape Pattern, Square, 40 In. 75.00
Tablecloth, Battenburg Lace, Round, 51 In. 75.00
Tablecloth, Battenburg Lace, Yellow, Round, 54 In. 65.00
Tablecloth, Cluny Lace Border, Scalloped Center, Round, 23 In. 38.00
Tablecloth, Cluny Lace, Butterflies, Heavy, 52 X 74 In. 135.00
Tablecloth, Crocheted, 289 Medallions, Square, 54 In. 45.00
Tablecloth, Crocheted, Ecru, Square, 52 In. 65.00
Tablecloth, Crocheted, Pink, 46 X 46 In. 75.00
Tablecloth, Drawn Work, 8 Napkins, Italian Stitching, 72 X 98 In. 350.00
Tablecloth, Embroidered Animals, Flowers, Dated 1907, 52 X 82 In. 55.00
Tablecloth, Printed Watermelon, Children, 1950s, 52 X 48 In. 60.00
Tapestry, Dog & Pheasant In Woods, French Verdure, 108 X 16 In. 7000.00
Tapestry, Family Farm Scene, Italy, C.1920, 19 X 34 In. 32.50
Tapestry, French Drawing Room Scene, Frame, C.1920, 57 X 39 In. 65.00
Tapestry, Garden, Birds, Flemish Verdure, 7 Ft.X 5 Ft.7 In. 4000.00
Tapestry, Jacob & Rachel, Brussels, 10 Ft. X 8 Ft. 4500.00
Tapestry, Knight On Horseback, Aubusson, 9 Ft. 6 In. X 6 Ft. 1200.00
Tapestry, Shepherds & Sheperdesses, Aubusson, 8 Ft.7 In.X 13 Ft. 9000.00
Tapestry, Soldiers, Flemish, 9 Ft. 3 In. X 2 Ft. 3 In. 650.00
Tapestry, Victorian Ladies, Belgium, 26 X 39 In. 68.50
Tapestry, Wisconsin Seal, On Brass Rod, 40 X 53 In. 575.00
Tea Cozy, Mohair Wig, Character Face, Russian, 19th Century 80.00
Tea Cozy, Silk, Gold Embroidered, Victorian 23.00
Towel, Stylized Design, Fringed, Initialed & Dated 1832 .... 250.00
Valance, Bed, Beadwork, English, 18th Century, 7 Ft. 3 In. 3600.00
Valance, Victorian, Fringe, 42 In., 52 In., 56 In., 114 In., 4 Piece 46.50

The thermometer was invented in 1731. It measures temperature of either water or air. All kinds of thermometers are collected, but those with advertising messages are the most popular.

THERMOMETER, 5 Roses Flour, Porcelain, French, English, 1920s, 38 X 8 In. 60.00
Arbuckles Coffee 35.00
Azton–Fisher Tobacco Co., Clown 225.00
B.Q.R.Ointment, Shows Product, Tin 35.00
Biltrite Heels & Soles, Picture of Shoe, Tin 85.00
Black Boy, Wooden 22.50
Brinkley Lumber Co., Del Rio. Texas, Glass 30.00
Camel Cigarettes, Tin, Thermometer In Cigarette 27.00
Caterpillar Bulldozer, Yellow 85.00
Cloverleaf Ginger Ale, 1940s 23.00
Colburn's Mustard, Old Yellow & Blue Paint, Wooden 125.00
Curran Joyce Ginger Ale, With Mirror, 10 X 4 In. 20.00
Dad's Root Beer 25.00

Dandy Dan, Black 12.00
Dr Pepper, 12 In. 25.00
Dr Pepper, Glass Front, Round Dial 35.00
Dr Pepper, Turn of The Century, 17 In. 25.00
Dr.J.H.McClean's Volcanic Oil Liniment, 1888, Round, 10 In. 125.00
Ex–Lax, Keep Regular, Round Dial 135.00
Fire Chief Gasoline, Muskogee, Okla. 22.00
Hickory Bourbon, Metal, Blue Ground, 8 3/4 In. 24.50
Hills Bros.Coffee, Porcelain, Arab, 1915, 9 X 21 In. .... 128.00 To 175.00
Hires Root Beer, Bottle Shape, 27 In. 75.00
Ice Cream, Wooden 75.00
Kendall Motor Oil 60.00
Kentucky Club 65.00
Lowney's Chocolates, Porcelain 75.00
Major Anti–Freeze, Wooden, Drum Majorette, 7 X 36 In. 150.00
Mobil Oil, Gold Can, Flying Red Horse 100.00
Nash Gin Co., Nash, Texas, Pictures Indian, Wagon Train, 1939 .... 20.00
Nature's Remedy, Porcelain ....85.00 To 125.00
Nesbitt's Orange 35.00
Perry Clothes, Rome, N.Y., Wooden 40.00
Ramon's Brownie Pills, Little Dr.Brings Happy Days, Metal 90.00
Red Devil Lighter Fluid, Tin, Fluid With A Thousand Lights 25.00
Red Goose Shoes 210.00
Salem Cigarettes 10.00
Squirt, Embossed Sheet Metal, Litho, Dated 1963, 13 X 6 In. 8.00
Sylvania Radios 65.00
Universal Batteries, 1899 .... 50.00 To 65.00
Veedol Motor Oil 65.00
Ward's Bread, Porcelain, Graphic 225.00

Tiffany glass was made by Louis Comfort Tiffany, the American glass designer who worked from about 1879 to 1933. His work included iridescent glass, Art Nouveau styles of design, and original contemporary styles. He was also noted for his stained glass windows, his unusual lamps, bronze work, pottery, and silver. Other types of Tiffany are listed under Tiffany Pottery, Tiffany Silver, or at the end of this section under Tiffany. The famous Tiffany lamps are under Tiffany, Lamp. Reproductions of some types of Tiffany are being made.

TIFFANY GLASS, Bonbon, Lavender, 8 X 1 1/2 In. 385.00
Bowl, Blown–Out Design, Pedestal, Signed, 10 1/2 In. 400.00
Bowl, Blue Iridescent, Green, Silver Tones, 2 1/2 In. 500.00
Bowl, Blue Iridescent, Ribbed, Flared, Squat, 2 1/2 X 6 In. 500.00
Bowl, Centerpiece, Gold Iridescent, Signed, 4 1/2 X 10 In. 450.00
Bowl, Flared Rim, Ribbed, Platinum Highlights, Signed, 10 In. 950.00
Bowl, Flower, Iridescent Gold, Lily Pads, 5 In. ....Illus 900.00
Bowl, Flower, Peacock Blue, Leaf, Flower Holder, 10 X 2 In. 1600.00
Bowl, Gold Aurene, Scalloped, L.C.T.Favrile, 5 4/8 In. 250.00
Bowl, Gold Iridescent, Signed, 5 1/4 In. 225.00
Bowl, Gold Ruffled Edge, Signed, 7 X 3 In. 590.00
Bowl, Gold Ruffled, Purple Center, Signed, 9 In. 550.00
Bowl, Green Iridescent, Bulbous, Shoulder Lappets, 4 5/8 In. 2100.00
Bowl, Herringbone Pattern, Iridized Green, Signed, 8 1/4 In. 575.00
Bowl, Iridescent Blue, Signed, 2 1/2 X 7 1/4 In. 1200.00
Bowl, Iridescent Gold, Blue Green, Swirl, Signed, 13 1/2 In. 725.00
Bowl, Iridescent Gold, Signed, Paper Label, 10 1/4 In. 750.00
Bowl, Iridescent Pink & Gold, Ribbed, Signed, 4 3/4 In. 150.00
Bowl, Leaf & Berry, Iridescent Gold, 2 1/2 In. ....Illus 750.00
Bowl, Opalescent Herringbone & Snowflake, Green, 8 1/4 In. 575.00
Bowl, Pastel Green, Signed, 12 In. 625.00
Bowl, Pastel, Signed, 6 In. 250.00
Bowl, Ruffled, Blue, 5 In. 450.00
Bowl, Ruffled, Flower Interior, Signed, Label, 5 3/4 In. 850.00
Cake Plate, Opalescent Glass, Scalloped, Signed, 10 In. 575.00

Candlestick, Blue, Swirl, Open Bottom, Signed LCT, 8 1/2 In.	550.00
Centerpiece, Iridescent, Signed, 10 X 4 In.	425.00
Compote, Floriform, Flared Ruffled Rim, Gold, 4 1/2 In.	500.00
Compote, Gold Aurene, Shallow, Signed, 8 1/2 X 4 In.	600.00
Compote, Intaglio Cut Grapevine Band, Signed, 4 X 3 1/2 In.	300.00
Cordial Set, Favrile, Gold	1875.00
Cup & Saucer, Shells & Zigzag On Gold Iridescent, Signed	525.00
Decanter, Gold Iridescent, Red, Blue Highlights, 10 1/2 In.	695.00
Dish, Ruffled, Signed, 2 3/4 X 3/4 In.	150.00
Dish, Sweetmeat, Domed Circular Foot, Marked, C.1900, 10 In.	200.00
Finger Bowl, Ascot, Gold	150.00
Flower Arranger, Gold Lily Pads & Trailings, Signed, 11 In.	1400.00
Flower Frog, Double, Signed, 3 3/4 In.	325.00
Glass, Juice, Morovingian Pattern, Signed, 3 1/4 In.	230.00
Goblet, Reeded Stem, Scalloped, Turquoise, Opalescent Pastel	350.00
Goblet, Stemmed, Gold Vintage Pattern, Signed, 7 In.	350.00
Nut Cup, Amber Iridescent, Signed, 2 7/8 In.	183.00
Ornament, Dragonfly, Blue Ground, Jewels, Chain, 10 X 6 In.	1500.00
Panel, Mosaic, Parrots, Leafage, Framed, 14 1/8 X 16 1/2 In.	6325.00
Paperweight, Green Leaf & Vine In Clear Crystal, 4 In.	200.00
Paperweight, Plaque, Gold Iridescent, Center Swirl, 13 In.	1500.00
Parfait, Opalescent, Signed	255.00
Perfume Bottle, Bulbous, Gold, Leaves, Vines, Stopper, Signed	1800.00
Pitcher, Favrile, Peacock Blue, Signed, 4 In.	550.00
Plate, Lavender, Signed, 9 In.	275.00
Plate, Pink, Signed, 9 In.	275.00
Plate, White Opalescent Rays From Center, Signed, 11 In.	250.00
Punch Cup, Applied Lily Pads, Stems, Pedestal, Signed	185.00
Punch Cup, Gold, Spreading Hollow Stem, Signed, 3 1/2 In.	150.00
Punch Cup, Opalescent Design Middle, Scroll Handle, 3 In.	325.00
Punch Cup, Opalescent Swirl, Reeded Scroll Handle, 3 In.	325.00
Punch Cup, Spreading Hollow Stem, Signed, 3 1/2 In.	150.00
Rose Bowl, Diamond Quilting In Body, Gold, Signed, 5 In.	2800.00
Salt, Gold Iridescent, Open, Squat, 1920, 2 1/2 In., Pair	200.00
Salt, Iridized Gold Glass, Pulled & Twisted Pattern, Signed	185.00
Salt, Ruffled, White Outside, Gold Interior, Signed	185.00
Salt, Urn Shape, 4 Short Feet, Signed, 1 3/8 In.	225.00
Salt, Witch's Pot Shape, Handles, Signed	195.00
Shade, Gold, 6–Sided, Signed, Set of 6	1500.00
Shade, Lotus, Signed, 18 In.	1800.00
Shade, Tulip Shape, Green Feather Design, Signed	500.00

Tiffany Glass, Bowl, Flower, Iridescent Gold,
Lily Pads, 5 In.

Tiffany Glass, Bowl, Leaf & Berry,
Iridescent Gold, 2 1/2 In.

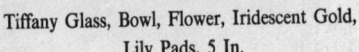

To be sure you have a Tiffany lamp, you must find the words "Tiffany and Co." printed on the metal base. The glass shades were also marked "L. C. Tiffany" or just with the letters "L. C. T." According to the records of the Tiffany Company, all these lamps were marked.

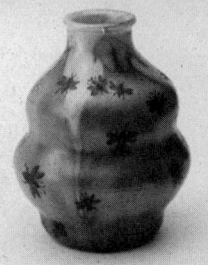  

Tiffany Glass, Vase, Conical, Green Iridescent, 6 In.

Tiffany Glass, Vase, Egg Form, Amber Iridescent, Holder, 13 In.

Tiffany Glass, Vase, Paperweight, Silvery–Violet Vertebrae, 8 In.

Sherbet, Hollow Stem, Copper Wheel Engraved Grapes, Leaves 150.00
Sherbet, Pedestal, Clear Base, Cranberry, 4 1/4 In. 85.00
Vase, Applied Lily Pads, Signed, 6 In. 1150.00
Vase, Blossoms, Silver Trailing, Baluster Form, Marked, 6 In. 1750.00
Vase, Bud, Blue Iridescent, Cylindrical, Signed, 10 In. 450.00
Vase, Bud, Iridescent Gold & Green, Leaf Base, Signed, 10 In. 325.00
Vase, Conical, Green Iridescent, 6 In. ....*Illus* 1300.00
Vase, Cypriote, Blue, 5 In. 750.00
Vase, Cypriote, Rough Texture, Blue, Purple, Signed, 5 1/4 In. 750.00
Vase, Double Gourd, Ribbed Body, Silver Blue, Signed, 2 In. 395.00
Vase, Egg Form, Amber Iridescent, Holder, 13 In. ....*Illus* 3200.00
Vase, Egyptian, Collared, Gold Body, Chain Design, Signed 2350.00
Vase, Floriform, Pulled Feather Design, Signed, 9 3/4 In. 1450.00
Vase, Flower–Form, Bud, Gold Iridescent, Signed, 6 In. 475.00
Vase, Footed, Pastel Pink, Signed, 4 3/4 In. 475.00
Vase, Free–Form Allover Line Design, Blue, Signed, 4 X 6 In. 1400.00
Vase, Free–Form, Iridescent Gold Interior, Marked, 6 In. 350.00
Vase, Gold Iridescent, Blue, Signed, 8 1/2 In. 465.00
Vase, Gold Iridescent, Dimpled, Scalloped, Signed, 3 In. 400.00
Vase, Gold Ribbed, 3–Tier Shape, Pink Highlights, 2 1/2 In. 285.00
Vase, Gold, Flower Form, Ribbed, Cupped Top, Signed, 8 In., Pr. 1400.00
Vase, Green Leaves Top To Bottom, Fat Body, Signed, 6 In. 775.00
Vase, Leaves & Vines, Green Iridescent, Signed, 3 In. 625.00
Vase, Leaves, Gold Iridescent Ground, Signed, 6 1/2 In. 1100.00
Vase, Millefiori, Amber, Shoulder Green Hearts, 5 3/4 In. 1320.00
Vase, Opalescent Green, Floriform, Favrile, Signed, 20 In. 1800.00
Vase, Paperweight, Silvery–Violet Vertebrae, 8 In. ....*Illus* 1700.00
Vase, Phantom Luster Outside, Pulls & Pinches, Signed, 6 In. 350.00
Vase, Red, Green Zigzags, Exaggerated Baluster, 7 In. 9350.00
Vase, Silver 5–Pointed Leaves, Vines, Signed, 5 X 7 In. 3500.00
Vase, Squat, Amber Ground, Swirl Design, Signed, 3 3/4 In. 550.00
Vase, Stand Up Collar, Gold, Red Highlights, Signed, 3 In. 325.00
Vase, Tel–El–Amarna, Bulbous, White Interior, Signed, 7 In. 1850.00
Vase, Trumpet, Gold Iridescent, Domed Foot, Signed, 10 In. 675.00
Vase, Trumpet, Gold To Moss Enamel Base, Marked, 12 In. 915.00
Vase, Twisted Body, Iridized Yellow, Signed, Label, 3 3/4 In. 275.00
Vase, Vitreous Enamel, Sterling Base, Top Rim, Signed, 7 In. 1200.00
Vase, Wafer Pontil, Paper Label, Signed, 11 In. 975.00
Vial, Perfume, Blue, Ovoid, Knopped Protrusions, 3 3/4 In. 2310.00
TIFFANY POTTERY, Bowl, Plums, Ivory Ground, Signed, 8 X 5 In. 595.00
   Bowl, Ruffled Leaves, 6 In. 300.00
   Vase, Deep Green Glaze, Poinsettia Blossoms, 8 In. 600.00
   Vase, Inverted Mushroom, Brown Glaze, 7 In. 500.00
   Vase, Unglazed, Top Opening, 13 1/4 In. 900.00
TIFFANY SILVER, Bowl, 6 Reticulated Sides, 9 In. 355.00
   Bowl, Danish Style, Stylized Handles, 1943–45, 11 1/4 In. 357.00

Bowl, Floral Border, Bombe Form, Monogram, 8 In., Pair	825.00
Brush, Child's, Sterling	49.00
Candlestick, George III Style, Vermeil, 4 In., Pair	425.00
Compote, Pierced Top, Strapwork, C.1920, 9 In., Pair	935.00
Dish, Covered, Entree, Foliat Rim, C.1895, 11 3/8 In., Pair	1650.00
Dish, Covered, Entree, George II Style, C.1925, 10 1/8 In.	550.00
Dish, Leaf Shape, Footed, 2 X 3 1/2 In.	65.00
Dish, Mint, Footed, Scalloped Shape, 2 1/2 X 3 In.	45.00
Dresser Set, Man's, 6 Piece	385.00
Fork, Cocktail, Wave Edge Pattern, C.1885, 18 Piece	605.00
Fork, Ice Cream, Renaissance, Set of 12	70.00
Fork, Luncheon, Wave Edge	48.00
Goblet, Flared Cup, Knopped Stem, C.1907, 4 3/4 In., 6 Piece	357.00
Inkwell, Zodiac, Bronze	225.00
Kettle, Hot Water, Oriental Style, Burner, 12 In.	4675.00
Knife & Bottle Opener, 3 Piece	150.00
Knife, Beekman, 8 In.	60.00
Knife, Dessert, Saratoga Pattern, Pat.1870, 11 Piece	175.00
Knife, Master Butter, Broomcorn	50.00
Ladle, Gravy, Bamboo	125.00
Ladle, Gravy, Persian Pattern, Dated 1872	125.00
Muddler, Twisted Handle, 8 1/4 In.	90.00
Mustard, Ailanthus	75.00
Pin, Leaf Shape, Tiffany Co., 1 3/4 X 1 1/2 In.	18.00
Pitcher, Oriental Style, Pomegranates, Vines, 10 1/8 In.	2375.00
Plate, Dessert, Silver–Gilt, Monogram, 10 In., Set of 24	5225.00
Plate, Engraved Child, Squirrel Border, Marked, 7 In.	185.00
Salad Set, Serving, Faneuil	265.00
Salt, Bright Cut, C.1880, Pair	125.00
Salver, Footed, Engraved, John C.Moore, 1860, 9 1/2 X 12 In.	1100.00
Salver, Ribbon Chased, 3 Shell Feet, C.1860, 10 In.	825.00
Sauce Boat, Wave Pattern, Bombe, Monogram, 7 3/8 In., Pair	1325.00
Scissors, Sheath, Engraved	95.00
Server, Fish, Vintage Pattern, Curved Blade, 5 Oz.	400.00
Server, Pie, St.Dunstan, 1900	325.00
Soup Tureen, Covered, Scroll Handles, C.1870, 16 In.	1325.00
Spoon, Berry, Conch, Wave Edge	250.00
Spoon, Horseradish, Holly Berry	165.00
Spoon, Ice Cream, Oval Bowl, Applied Gold Bird	1000.00
Spoon, Salad Serving, Shell & Thread	225.00
Straws, Drinking, Marked, 7 1/2 In., Pair	28.00
Tamper, Pipe	45.00
Tea & Coffee Set, Octagonal Shape, Tray, C.1860, 4 Piece	1090.00
Tea & Coffee Set, Tray, Acanthus Shaped, 8 Piece	7950.00
Tongs, Sugar, Flemish	60.00
Youth Set, Ailanthus, 3 Piece	150.00

Tiffany objects made from a mixture of materials, such as bronze and glass boxes, are listed here. Tiffany lamps are included in this section.

TIFFANY, Ashtray & Match Holder, Bronze, Venetian, Mink Border, 5 X 4 In.	195.00
Ashtray & Match Safe, Bronze, Spanish, Octagon, Signed, 1 X 7 In.	195.00
Ashtray, Bronze, Gold Dore Finish, 4 X 3 In.	135.00
Ashtray, Bronze, Gold Dore, Scalloped, Ribbed, Signed, Nest of 4	350.00
Ashtray, Pine Needle, Bronze, Amber Glass, Ball Feet, Signed, 4 In.	195.00
Basket, Bronze Holder, Favrile Glass Insert, Signed, 7 In.	450.00
Basket, Glass & Bronze, Bronze Holder, Glass Insert, 7 In., 2 Pc.	450.00
Basket, Medallion Design, 12 X 8 In.	60.00
Blotter Ends, Pine Needle, Corner, Signed, 6 X 2 X 8 In., 4 Piece	200.00
Blotter, Bronze, Bookmark, Knob Handle, Signed, 5 1/2 X 2 1/4 In.	150.00
Blotter, Hand, Adam Pattern, Signed	95.00
Blotter, Pine Needle, Amber Glass, Bronze Knob Handle, 5 3/4 In.	195.00
Book Rack, Bronze & Glass, Adjustable, Grapevine, 14 X 6 1/2 In.	650.00
Bookends, Bronze & Enamel, Gold Dore Finish, 4 3/4 X 6 In.	350.00

Bookends, Bronze, Curved & Linear Raised Design, Signed 275.00
Bookends, Pink Enamel, Bronze, Signed, 4 3/4 X 6 In. 350.00
Bookends, Zodiac, Symbols, Circle & Line Design, Signed, 6 X 5 In. 400.00
Bowl, Centerpiece, Short Stem, Marine Design, Signed, Bronze, 8 In. 225.00
Bowl, Gold Dore Finish, Marine Design, Bronze, Signed, 8 X 4 In. 225.00
Box, Adam, Oval Shape, Pale Blue Enamel, Covered 225.00
Box, Azalea, Bronze & Glass, Signed, Square, 7 In. 750.00
Box, Bookmark, Enameling, Bronze, Signed, 6 X 5 1/2 In. 850.00
Box, Desk, Green Slag, Bronze, Spider Web, Marked, 5 5/8 In. 120.00
Box, Grapevine, Bronze & Glass, Gold Finish, 7 X 4 X 2 In. 400.00
Box, Grapevine, Green Slag Glass, Bronze, Signed, 4 1/2 X 3 1/4 In. 295.00
Box, Grapevine, Green Slag, Bronze, 9 1/2 X 7 In. 950.00
Box, Hinged, Pinecone Needle, Caramel Slag, 4 1/2 X 3 In. 200.00
Box, Indian, Mask & Scroll Hinged Cover, Signed 295.00
Box, Medallion, Bronze, Gold Dore, Signed 350.00
Box, Pine Needle, Amber Slag, Bronze, Signed, 6 X 4 In. 350.00
Box, Pine Needle, Bronze, Amber Slag Glass, Signed, 5 1/2 X 3 In. 350.00
Box, Pine Needle, Bronze, Glass, Signed, 6 X 4 In. 350.00
Box, Stamp, American Indian, Green & Brown Patina, Signed 175.00
Box, Stamp, Grapevine, Green Glass, Bronze, Signed 175.00
Box, Venetian, Bronze, 14K Gold Plate, Signed, 4 X 5 1/2 X 2 In. 450.00
Box, Zodiac, Bronze, Enameled, Cedar Lined, 4 1/2 X 3 In. 350.00
Candelabrum, 2–Arm, Bronze, Gold Favrile Glass Jewels Base, 16 In. 750.00
Candelabrum, 8–Branch, Bronze, Four Arms, Dark Finish, 15 1/2 In. 2500.00
Candle Lamp, Gold Iridescent Base, 2 Piece Metal & Glass Shade 1200.00
Candlestick, 3 Curved Feet, Bobeche, Bronze & Glass, 10 In. 950.00
Candlestick, Blown Glass Through Openings, Bronze, 8 1/2 In. 550.00
Candlestick, Bronze, Glass, 3 Ball Feet, 8 1/2 In. 550.00
Candlestick, Bronze, Iridescent Gold Glass Shade, 17 In. ....*Illus* 1150.00
Candlestick, Cobra, Bronze .... 500.00 To 575.00
Candlestick, Favrile Scallop Enamel Design Shade, Signed, 10 In. 450.00
Candlestick, Green Glass, Bronze, Openings, 3 Ball Feet, 8 In. 550.00
Chamberstick, 2–Arm, Bronze, Green Glass, Fleur–De–Lis, 9 In. 900.00
Chamberstick, Bronze, Curved Arm, Single Candleholder, 5 In. 275.00
Chest, Cigar, Hammered Silver, Stones In Lid, Cedar Lined, 7 X 5 In. 380.00
Clock, Bronze, Zodiac, Bronze Key, Signed, 5 X 4 1/4 In. 750.00
Clock, Carriage, Cloisonne 950.00
Clock, Desk, Bronze, Round Face, Gold Dore Finish, 4 X 4 X 3 In. 450.00
Clock, Mantel, Tortoiseshell, Female Bust Shape, Ormolu, 21 1/2 In. 1100.00
Clock, Regulator, Crystal, Porcelain Dial, Mercury Pendulum 285.00
Compote, Bronze, Favrile Glass, Gold Iridescent Center, 6 1/4 In. 550.00
Compote, Bronze, Footed, 3 Curved Legs, Gold Dore Finish, 4 1/2 In. 195.00
Compote, Geometric Rim Design, Curved Legs, Bronze, Signed, 4 In. 195.00
Compote, Geometric, Bronze, Enamel, Peacock Blue, 2 1/2 In. 525.00
Compote, Indian Pattern, Brass, Signed, 10 In. 275.00
Desk Set, Abalone Shell, Signed, 5 Piece 550.00
Desk Set, Louis XVI, Signed, 4 Piece 200.00
Desk Set, Pine Needle, Amber Glass Insert, Bronze, 5 Piece 485.00
Desk Set, Zodiac, Marked, 8 Piece 2500.00
Frame, Bookmark, Bronze, Signed, 6 1/4 X 6 In. 200.00
Frame, Bronze & Glass, Gold Dore Finish, 12 X 14 1/2 In. 1200.00
Frame, Calendar, Venetian, Bronze, Easel, Signed, 6 1/2 X 6 In. 225.00
Frame, Chinese, Bronze, Signed, 7 1/2 X 6 In. 200.00
Frame, Geometric, Dark Finish, 9 1/4 X 11 1/4 In. 650.00
Frame, Grapevine, Bronze & Glass, Signed, 9 1/2 X 8 In. 550.00
Frame, Grapevine, Easel, Bronze & Slag, 8 3/4 X 7 1/4 In. 475.00
Frame, Indian, Easel, Bronze, Gold Dore, Signed, 7 1/2 X 6 In. 225.00
Frame, Perpetual Calendar, Bronze, Bookmark, Signed, 5 1/2 X 6 In. 250.00
Frame, Pine Needle, Bronze, Glass, Gold Dore Finish, 12 X 15 In. 1200.00
Frame, Zodiac, Easel, Bronze, Signed, 7 X 8 In. 275.00
Humidor, Grapevine, Bronze, Glass, Amber Slag Glass, Double Cover 1500.00
Inkwell, Adam, Bronze, Gold Dore Finish, Oval Shape, 4 X 3 In. 250.00
Inkwell, Adam, Oval, Sunburst Design On Hinged Lid, Bronze 250.00
Inkwell, Aztec Design, Bronze, Tiffany Studio, 5 X 4 In. 130.00

Inkwell, Byzantine, Bronze, Jewel, Round, Signed, 4 1/2 In.	1500.00
Inkwell, Chinese, Bronze, Top Hinged Cover, 6 1/4 X 4 X 4 1/2 In.	450.00
Inkwell, Grapevine, Bronze, Glass, Amber Slag Glass, 3 X 3 3/4 In.	350.00
Inkwell, Indian, Allover Masks, Hinged Cover, Bronze	300.00
Inkwell, Pine Needle, Bronze, Amber Slag, Square, 3 1/4 X 3 In.	250.00
Inkwell, Pine Needle, Bronze, Glass, Green Slag Glass, 7 In.Diam.	600.00
Inkwell, Simulated Nail Heads, Wine Color Enameled, Crab On Top	300.00
Inkwell, Spanish, Bronze, Gold Dore, Hinged Knob Cover, 4 X 6 In.	650.00
Inkwell, Venetian, Double, 14K Gold Plate, Bronze, Signed	550.00
Inkwell, Zodiac, Hexagonal, Hinged Cover, Signed, 6 1/2 In.	350.00
Jar, Geometric Pattern All Around, Bronze, Signed, 2 1/4 In.	95.00
Lamp, 3-Branch, Gold Dore Finish, Red Lily Shades	4500.00
Lamp, Boudoir, Swirled Ribbed, Gilded Shade, Favrile, 13 In.	250.00
Lamp, Bronze, Apple Blossom Border Domical Shade, 18 In.	9900.00
Lamp, Bronze, Stick, 3 Arms Hold Favrile Damascene Shade, 16 In.	3500.00
Lamp, Bronze, Woodbine Leaves, On Glass Domed Shade, Signed, 23 In.	9350.00
Lamp, Candle, Gold Iridescent Candlestick Base, Flange Top, 16 In.	1000.00
Lamp, Candle, Gold Shade, Twisted Base, Feathered Glass, Signed	1200.00
Lamp, Candle, Gold Swirl, Green Feather, Gold Shade, 15 In.	1250.00
Lamp, Candlestick, Bronze, Bamboo, Favrile Cone Shade, 15 In.	950.00
Lamp, Candlestick, Spreading Root Bronze Base, Ribbed Shade	3800.00
Lamp, Desk, 2-Arm, Bronze, Favrile Green Feather Shade, 21 In.	1500.00
Lamp, Desk, Bronze Base, Favrile Glass Shade, 12 1/2 In.	975.00
Lamp, Desk, Counterweight, Bronze Base, 2 Curved Arms	2800.00
Lamp, Desk, Double-Arm, Favrile Shades, Bronze Base, 21 In.	1500.00
Lamp, Desk, Liberty Bell, Bronze Base, Blue Shade, Signed, 15 In.	3500.00
Lamp, Desk, Octagonal Chinese Shade, Bronze Base, 17 In.	3000.00
Lamp, Desk, Ribbed Bronze Base, Bell Shaped Shade, Signed, 18 In.	975.00
Lamp, Dore Gold, Bronze Harp Base, Shade, Signed	1850.00
Lamp, Floor, Aladdin's, Bronze Base, Green & Opal Ground	4500.00
Lamp, Floor, Favrile Shade, Bronze	2500.00
Lamp, Floor, Greek Key, Leaded Shade, Bronze Base, Orange, Green	7650.00
Lamp, Gilt Bronze, 10-Light, Lily Shade, Lotus Pads Base, 21 In.	9900.00
Lamp, Gold Iridescent Shade, Brass Base, Signed, 14 1/2 In.	1185.00
Lamp, Gold Shade, Swirl Base, Pulled Feather, Signed, 15 In.	1250.00
Lamp, Mosque, Gold & Green Shade, Bronze Base, Signed, 8 1/2 In.	1800.00
Lamp, Stalactite, Deep Gold, Feather, Signed, 16 In.	1650.00
Lamp, Student, Bronze Base, Damascene Shade, Signed, 19 1/2 In.	2500.00
Lamp, Table, Fabrique Shade, Bronze Stem & Base, Signed, 21 In.	3500.00
Lamp, Table, Fabrique, Green Shade, Bronze Base, Signed, 24 In.	5500.00
Lamp, Table, Geometric, Green & White Glass, 24 In.	6500.00
Lamp, Table, Parasol, Leaded Shade, Blue Green, 31 In.	8500.00
Lamp, Table, Petals Body, 3-Arm, Bronze Shade, Signed, 10 1/2 In.	850.00
Letter Holder, Indian, 2 Sections, Bronze, Signed, 6 1/2 In.	350.00
Letter Holder, Ninth Century Pattern, Bronze & Jeweled, Signed	450.00
Letter Holder, Pine Needle, Bronze, Glass, 6 X 6 X 2 3/4 In.	450.00
Letter Opener, Adam, Bronze, Curved Handle, Signed, 10 In.	165.00
Letter Opener, Chinese, Bronze, Signed, 10 1/2 In.	150.00
Letter Opener, Graduate, Bronze, Gold Dore, Signed, 9 In.	95.00
Letter Opener, Indian, Bronze, Signed, 10 1/2 In.	150.00
Letter Opener, Venetian, Bronze, Gold Dore, Signed, 10 1/4 In.	165.00
Letter Opener, Zodiac, Bronze, Signed, 10 1/2 In.	150.00
Letter Rack, 19th Century, Bronze & Jeweled, 10 X 6 X 2 1/2 In.	550.00
Letter Rack, Bookmark, Bronze, Signed, 9 X 5 In.	300.00
Letter Rack, Grapevine, 2 Compartments, Signed, 6 1/2 X 10 In.	450.00
Letter Rack, Grapevine, 3 Compartments, Metal, Glass, Signed	650.00
Letter Rack, Grapevine, Bronze, Green Slag, 7 X 8 X 3 In.	500.00
Letter Rack, Indian, 2 Compartments, 11 X 5 3/4 In.	300.00
Letter Rack, Spanish, Bronze, Gold Dore, Border Design, 10 In.	650.00
Letter Rack, Venetian, 2 Compartments, Bronze, 10 X 6 In.	400.00
Letter Rack, Zodiac Symbols Front & Back, Bronze, Signed, 12 In.	400.00
Letter Scale, Pine Needle, Green Slag Glass, Bronze, Glass	225.00
Magnifying Glass, Abalone, Iridescent Discs, Bronze, Signed, 9 In.	395.00
Magnifying Glass, Graduate, Gold Dore	285.00

Match Safe, Geometric, Bronze, Signed, 2 1/4 X 1 3/4 In.	65.00
Match Safe, Pine Needle, Gold Dore, Amber Slag, Signed, 2 X 1 In.	150.00
Match Safe, Venetian, Bronze, Signed, 1 3/4 X 2 1/4 In.	125.00
Note Holder, Venetian, Chain Link & Mink Design, Signed	250.00
Paper Clip, Adam Pattern Across Top, Signed, 4 X 2 1/2 In.	150.00
Paperweight, Beetle	90.00
Paperweight, Bronze & Abalone, Octagon Shape, 3 1/2 X 3 1/2 In.	325.00
Paperweight, Bulldog, Sitting, Dark Patina, 2 1/4 X 1 1/2 In.	425.00
Paperweight, Lion, Brass, Signed	275.00
Paperweight, Owl, Bronze, Dark Patina, 3 X 1 1/4 In.	525.00
Paperweight, Pine Needle, Amber Slag Glass, 3 3/4 In.	225.00
Pen Brush, Pine Needle, Bronze, Glass, Signed, Round, 2 1/4 X 2 In.	150.00
Pen Tray, Chinese, Bronze, Raised Sides, Signed, 12 In.	150.00
Pen Tray, Mosaic, Bronze, Gold Iridescent, 7 3/4 In.	2200.00
Pen Tray, Spanish, Bronze, Gold Dore, Border, 9 3/4 X 3 3/4 In.	250.00
Planter, Bronze & Mosaic Tiles, Insert, Signed, Round, 12 In.	7500.00
Planter, Bronze, Geometric, Gold Dore, 8 1/2 X 2 1/2 In.	350.00
Planter, Turtleback Tiles, Purple & Blue, Insert, Signed, 9 In.	3500.00
Plaque, Stork Against Cattail Ground, Bronze, Signed, 7 X 11 In.	475.00
Plate, Dore, Medallion In Square Panels At Rim, Signed, 10 In.	200.00
Platter, Bronze, Gold Finish, Etched Design Border, 8 1/2 X 2 In.	225.00
Platter, Gold Dore Finish, Deep Well, Bronze, Signed, 9 In.	95.00
Scale, Grapevine, Bronze & Glass, Dark Patina Finish	450.00
Scoop, Cheese, Olympian	225.00
Seal, 3 Scarab, M Monogram On Base	350.00
Seal, Grapevine, Bronze & Glass, 3 X 1 1/2 In.	400.00
Shade, Hanging, Pears, Apples, Grapes, Cherries & Birds, 24 X 13 In.	1200.00
Thermometer, Grapevine, Bronze & Glass, 8 1/2 X 4 In.	550.00
Tray, Abalone, Signed, Round, 9 In.	185.00
Tray, Bookmark, Bronze, Signed, 8 1/2 X 2 3/4 In.	125.00
Tray, Bronze, Gold Dore, Peacock Blue Enameled, Round, 8 1/2 In.	225.00
Tray, Bronze, Gold Dore, Short Pedestal Base, 10 In.	225.00
Tray, Indian, 2 Sections, Masks, Bronze, Signed, 11 X 4 In.	125.00
Tray, Pen, Adam, Center Design, Signed, 9 3/4 X 3 In.	125.00
Tray, Pen, Pine Needle, Bronze	135.00
Tray, Pen, Zodiac Each End, Signed, 9 1/2 X 3 In.	150.00
Tray, Raised Border, Red Jewels, Signed, 12 In.	250.00
Tray, Raised Geometric Design On Rim, Red Jewels, Signed, 9 In.	200.00
Tray, Venetian, 2 Sections, Bronze, Signed, 10 X 3 In.	150.00
Vase, Bud, Glass & Bronze, Signed, 11 In.	450.00
Vase, Jeweled, Bronze, Blue, Signed, 16 In.	2300.00

The Tiffin Glass Company of Tiffin, Ohio, was a subsidiary of the United States Glass Co. of Pittsburgh, Pennsylvania, in 1892. The U.S. Glass Co. went bankrupt in 1963, and the Tiffin plant employees purchased the building and the inventory. They continued running it from 1963 to 1966, when it was sold to Continental Can Company. In 1969, it was sold to Interpace; and in 1980, it was closed. The black satin glass, made from 1923 to 1926, and the stemware of the last twenty years are the best–known products.

TIFFIN, Bell, Table, Cherokee Rose, Box	38.00
Box, Covered, Coralene Flowers, Black Satin, Round	65.00
Candleholder, Double, Cherokee Rose, Pair	40.00
Champagne, Cherokee Rose, 5 1/2 Oz.	12.50
Goblet, Adam, 10 Oz., 5 Piece	75.00
Goblet, Cherokee Rose, 9 Oz.	20.00
Goblet, Persian Pheasant	13.00
Jug, Flanders, Pink, Covered	275.00
Lamp, Parrot, Orange	260.00
Oyster Cocktail, Flanders, Pink	38.00
Parfait, Byzantine	18.50
Parfait, LaFleure, Yellow	20.00
Plate, Cherokee Rose, 6 In.	4.50
Plate, Cherokee Rose, 8 In.	9.50

Plate, Elinor, 8 In.	10.00
Plate, Flanders, Pink, 8 In.	15.00
Plate, LaFleure, Yellow, 6 In.	6.00
Rose Bowl, Black Satin, Relief Poppies	25.00
Sherbet, Flanders, Pink, Low	35.00
Sherry, Princess, 2 Oz.	18.00
Tumbler, Iced Tea, Cherokee Rose, 10 1/2 Oz.	17.50
Tumbler, Iced Tea, June Night, 10 1/2 Oz.	16.50
Tumbler, Princess, 5 Oz.	8.00
Tumbler, Princess, 13 Oz.	15.00
Vase, Black, Floral Design, Bulbous, 9 In.	40.00
Wine, Colonial, Set of 6	30.00
Wine, Elinor	10.00

Tiles have been used in most countries of the world as a sturdy building material for floors, roofs, fireplace surrounds, and surface toppings. Many of the American tiles are listed in this book under the factory name.

TILE, 3–Color, Square, U.S.E.Tile Co., 4 In.	5.00
6–Color, Abstract Flowers, Butterflies, Wheeling	20.00
Allegorical Figures, Dated 1883, Framed, 40 In.X 7 Ft.4 In.	3850.00
Bearded Man, Trent	250.00
Blue Floral, Rushmore Pottery, 5 In.	24.00
Calendar, 1900, Reed, McDufee & Stratten Co., Hancock House	50.00
December, Boy With Mistletoe, Girl, Brown, Wedgwood, 6 In.	55.00
Dog, Square, Hadley	17.50
Duck, Square, Hadley	17.50
Fleur–De–Lis Design, Cambridge, 6 X 9 In.	45.00
German Shepherd, Mosaic Tile Co., Cream Matte, 9 1/2 In.	69.00
Good Luck, Wheatley, 2 Colors, 4 1/8 In.	90.00
Hand Painted, Sardegna, Italy, Signed, 1930s, Pair	60.00
Interstate Industrial Expo., Chicago, Tan, Brown, Minton, C.1880, 6 In.	110.00
Portrait, Pardee, Baby's Face, Signed	95.00
Stoke–On–Trent, Minton, 6 X 6 In.	30.00
Viking Ship Design, Gold, Brown & Blue, Square, 5 3/8 In.	270.00
Viking Ship In Stormy Ocean, 3 Shades of Blue, California	300.00
Wheatley, Good Luck Symbol, 2 Colors, 4 In.	90.00

Tin has been used to make household containers in America since the seventeenth century. The first tin utensils were brought from Europe; but by 1798, tin plate was imported and local tinsmiths made the wares. Painted tin is called "tole" and is listed separately. Some tin kitchen items may be found listed under Kitchen. The lithographed tin containers used to hold food and tobacco are listed under Advertising, Tin.

TINWARE, Basket, Picnic, Educator	85.00
Box, Comb, Embossed Eagle	30.00
Can, Kerosene, Wooden Barrel Frame, Wire Bail, 11 1/2 In.	22.00
Candlestick, Saucer, Lift Tab, 4 In.	35.00
Churn, Syllabub	85.00
Coffeepot, Bird Beak Spout, Brass Lid Finial, 10 In.	175.00
Condiment Caddy, 3–Bottle, Blown Glass, Brass Tops	25.00
Dipper, Hanging, 12 In.	12.50
Foot Warmer, Wooden Posts, Frame	130.00
Lamp, Ufford Patent, Original Brass Labels, 6 In., Pair	175.00
Lantern, Candle, 13 In.	80.00
Lantern, Sliding Door, Pyramidal Top, Ring Handle, 10 1/4 In.	85.00
Match Holder, Hanging, Fitted By Slots	14.00
Matchbox, Lift Lid, Hanging, Germany	22.50
Mold, 8 Sections, Swirl Design, Hole, Dark & Light Gray, 13 X 6 In.	18.00
Mold, Candle, 2 Tube	30.00
Mold, Candle, 3 Tube	30.00
Mold, Candle, 6 Tube, Tapered, 10 X 3/4 In.	75.00
Mold, Candle, 8 Tube	85.00

Mold, Candle, 10 Tube, Top Handles, 10 In. .... ·45.00
Mold, Candle, 12 Tube, 11 1/4 In. 170.00
Mold, Candle, 12 Tube, 6 Each Side, Strap Handle 85.00
Mold, Candle, 12 Tube, Cherry Frame, 10 1/4 In. 900.00
Mold, Candle, 12 Tube, Top Handles 55.00
Mold, Candle, 24 Tube, 2 Handles, 11 X 13 In. 150.00
Mold, Candle, 24 Tube, Cast Pewter Tubes, Wooden Frame, 19 1/2 In. 450.00
Mold, Candle, 24 Tube, Ear Handles, 9 1/2 In. 150.00
Mold, Candle, 25 Tube, Wooden Frame, America, 14 X 21 In. 600.00
Mold, Candle, 55 Tube, Pine Frame 675.00
Mold, Cheese, Heart Shape, Pierced 45.00
Mold, Curved Fish Shape, Fluted, 11 In. 30.00
Mold, Food, Covered, Fluted, Dome Top, Wire Handle, 7 In. 20.00
Mold, Food, Tube, 6 Cone Swirled Sections, Ring 18.50
Mold, Heart Shape, Pierced, Handle, 4 X 5 X 3 In. 55.00
Mold, Maple Sugar, Heart Shape, 3 In. 5.00
Oven, Steamer, Handles, Square 15.00
Pan, Angel Food, Late 1800s, 2 Gal., 12 1/4 In. X 6 In. 50.00
Panel, Punched, Modern Frame, 5 3/4 X 14 3/4 In. 45.00
Pitcher, Milk, Cream City Milwaukee, Label 50.00
Pourer, Candle Wax, Signed Thomas Mills, Philadelphia 175.00
Scoop, Cranberry, Brass Tines 52.50
Scoop, Round Handle, 12 1/2 X 6 1/4 In. 12.00
Skimmer, Handle, Hole, Round Triangle Shape, 7 1/2 X 7 1/4 In. 15.00
Teakettle, Straight Spout, Strap Handle, 8 X 4 In. 95.00
Teapot, Double Cone Skirted, Pennsylvania, 10 In. 285.00

Because tobacco needs special conditions of humidity and air, it has been stored in special containers since the eighteenth century. The tobacco jar is often made in fanciful shapes.

TOBACCO JAR, Black Man's Head, Gold Collar, Smoking Pipe, 5 In. 118.00
Blackamoor Girl, Glazed & Matte 110.00
Chinese Man's Head, Gold Skin, Lavender Hat, 5 In. 95.00
Devil With Beard, Horns, Humidor, 8 In. ....*Illus* 88.00
Egyptian Queen, Majolica, 1880s 100.00
Frog Playing Mandolin, Humidor, 7 In. ....*Illus* 193.00
Grinning Gnome On Barrel, Marked JMI 95.00
Lady's Head, Olive Skin, Lavender Combs, 4 3/4 In. 88.00
Lady's Head, Wearing Fez, Cigar In Mouth 125.00
Lady, Pink Turban, Intaglio Eyes, Majolica, 4 X 5 In. 75.00
Man With Cap, Smoking Pipe 65.00
Man, In Tobacco Pouch 65.00
Monkey Head, Cap, Eye Glasses, Bowtie, Bisque, 6 In. 175.00
Moravian Monk 62.00
Race Car Driver, Humidor, 8 1/2 In. ....*Illus* 303.00
Skull, Black Eyes & Nose, Cream Ground, 5 In. 145.00
South American Indian, Majolica 50.00
Turkish Man's Head, Multicolored 175.00

The toby jug is a very special form of pitcher. It is shaped like the full figure of a man or woman. A pitcher that shows just the top half of a person is not correctly called a toby. More examples of toby jugs can be found under Royal Doulton and other factory names.

TOBY JUG, Abraham & Isaac, 1850, Staffordshire, 14 In. 200.00
Boy, Girl, Bridge, Swan, 1850, Staffordshire, 7 In. 125.00
Captain, Burlington 48.50
Collier, Foaming Ale, C.1775, 10 In. 1100.00
Highlander, Tree, 1850, Staffordshire, 15 In. 135.00
Indian Boy, Green Feather Headdress, Tortoiseshell, C.1860 .... 125.00
King John, Runnymede, 1850, Staffordshire, 13 In. 220.00
Lady Musician, Couch, 1900, Staffordshire, 9 In. 85.00
Man, Tricornered Hat, Erotica, C.1840 .... 495.00
Napoleon, Standing, Evans, Philadelphia, 5 1/2 In. 230.00

Pinocchio Face, Angry, 1830, Staffordshire, 4 In.	150.00
Prince & Princess of Wales, Staffordshire, 8 In.	115.00
Punch, M. Wain & Sons, 6 In.	85.00
Winker, Burlington	48.50

Tole is painted tin. It is sometimes called "japanned ware," "pontypool," or "toleware." Most nineteenth–century tole is painted with an orange–red or black background and multicolored decorations. Many recent versions of toleware are made and sold.

TOLE, see also Tinware

TOLE, Bin, Bread & Cake, Roll Dome Front, Kreamer, 11 X 12 X 13 In.	95.00
Box, Cake, Oak Grain Painted, Inside Shelf, Stenciled Cake, C.1890	32.00
Box, Deed, Dome Top, Brown Japanning, Floral Design, 6 3/8 In.	135.00
Box, Gutter Collection, Black Paint, Silver Date 1854, 17 In., Pair	550.00
Box, Pantry, Old Red Paint, Gold Stencil	28.00
Box, Ring Handle, Black & Yellow Stencil, 4 X 2 3/4 In.	25.00
Box, Sewing, Black Paint, Gilt Striping, Decoupage, Tray, 11 3/4 In.	85.00
Breadbox, Red, 1940s	37.50
Candle Sconce, Embossed Crest, Mirror Panels, 2 Arms, 7 X 12 In., Pair	1656.00
Candleholder, Domed Lid, Black Paint, Yellow, Gold Striping, 4 In.	40.00
Candlestick, Regency Style, Fitted With Hurricane Shade, 21 In., Pair	600.00
Canister Set, Dutch Scenes, White, With Blue, Germany, 11 Piece	85.00
Canister Set, Red, White, Flowers, 1950s, 4 Piece	27.50
Canister, Tea, Japanned, Converted To Table Lamp, 17 1/2 In.	225.00
Canister, Tea, Oriental Figures, Domed Lid, Yellow, 15 In., Pair	1045.00
Canister, Tea, Oriental Seated Lady, Mountain Landscape, 19 In.	275.00
Canister, Tea, Painted Oxblood, Gilt Design, 17 1/2 In., Pair	1325.00
Canister, Yellow, Gold Stars, Names, Red Lid, Miniature, 4 Piece	35.00
Case, Map, Hinged Lid, Handle, Black Paint	17.50
Coffeepot, Gooseneck, Brown Japanning, Floral, 20 5/8 In.	3700.00
Coffeepot, Painted, Oliver Filley, Conn., C.1810	625.00
Coffeepot, Straight Spout, Floral, Dark Ground, 8 5/8 In.	2050.00
Cup, Orange–Red Paint, Gold Stencil Design, 2 1/8 In.	45.00
Flask, Painted, 4 1/2 In.	75.00
Humidor, Fox Hunt Scenes, Teak Lining, 4 1/2 In.	35.00
Lamp, Oil, Baluster, Chinoiserie Floral & Bird, Electric, 14 In., Pair	1000.00
Lamp, Table, Columnar, Faux Tortoiseshell Finish, 15 In., Pair	1000.00
Lantern, Electric Candle, Mustard Yellow, Black Design, Pair	90.00
Mold, Candle, 24 Tube, Handles, 11 1/4 In.	75.00
Mold, Fish, Curved, Hook, 7 X 9 1/2 In.	34.00
Mug, Child's, Blue Panel, Gilt Word Daisy, Flower & Scroll, 2 In.	48.00
Mush Set, Child's, Dressed Bears Riding Lions, Germany, 3 Piece	65.00

Tobacco Jar, Devil
With Beard, Horns,
Humidor, 8 In.

Tobacco Jar, Frog
Playing Mandolin,
Humidor, 7 In.

Tobacco Jar,
Race Car Driver, Humidor,
8 1/2 In.

Screen, Black Ground, Hand Painted Cranes, Tree, 27 1/2 In.	175.00
Strainer, Double Cone, Curved Handle, 13 In.	55.00
Strainer, Teardrop Shape, Blue Paint	38.00
Syrup, Red Apple Front, Leaves, 19th Century, 4 1/4 & 4 In., Pair	300.00
Tea Caddy, Hinged Cover, 4 Claw Feet, Stylized Bouquet Front, 5 In.	400.00
Tray, Bread, Red Paint, Foliage Design, 8 X 12 3/4 In.	1375.00
Tray, Central Oval Reserve, Children Swimming, Victorian, 24 In.	200.00
Tray, Faux Bois, Simulated Dark Wood Marquetry, French, 22 X 28 In.	825.00
Tray, Flower Design, Austrian, 17th Century	2200.00
Tray, House, Tree, Fence, Monkey, Dog, Signed, 30 X 24 In.	2400.00
Tray, Oriental Gentlemen, Pagoda, 19th Century, 26 In.	550.00
Tray, Stand, Fox Hunt Scene, 29 X 21 X 18 1/2 In.	650.00
Tray, Stenciled Border, Fort Independence At Castle Island, 30 In.	475.00
Urn, Oval Reserve, Figures By Lake, Amber Ground, 9 1/2 In., Pair	425.00

Tom Mix was born in 1880 and died in 1940. He was the hero of over 100 silent movies from 1910 to 1929, and 25 sound films from 1929 to 1935. There was a Ralston Tom Mix radio show from 1933 to 1950, but the original Tom Mix was not in the show. Tom Mix comics were published from 1942 to 1953.

TOM MIX, Badge, Decoder	35.00
Badge, Siren, Sheriff of Dobie County, Ralston, 1946	30.00
Bandana, Ralston Straight Shooters, C.1933	75.00
Book, Coloring, Dentist & Doctor Giveaway	25.00
Book, Comic, No.4, Ralston Straight Shooters Giveaway	95.00
Boots, Cowboy, Worn, Original Box	70.00
Bracelet, I.D., Initial R On Front, 1940s	38.00
Compass & Magnifier, Glow In Dark	28.00
Cuffs, Straight Shooters, Leather, 1935, Set of 2	125.00
Decoder, Six–Gun	45.00
Emblem, Cloth	32.00
Knife, Folding	35.00
Label, Cigar Box	22.00
Make–Up Kit, Complete, First Version, Box, Mailer	80.00
Manual, 1941	60.00
Parachute, In Original Mailer	85.00
Periscope	40.00
Poster, Movie, Chasing The Moon, 11 X 14 In.	50.00
Puzzle, Jigsaw, Rexall, Complete, Package	35.00
Ring, Slide Whistle, Aluminum	40.00
Signal Set, Postal Telegraph	45.00
Spurs, Glow In Dark, Aluminum, Ralston Premium, 1940s, Pair	110.00
Telegraph Kit, Battery Operated, Red	75.00
Wristband, Lucky	25.00

Tools of all sorts are listed here, but most are related to industry. Other tools will be found listed under Iron; Kitchen; Tinware; and Wooden.

TOOL, Adze Hammer, Cheney, No.777, Blade, With Nail Slot, Handle	45.00
Adze, Bowl, 6 X 3 In.	45.00
Adze, Connecticut Type, D Handle, Iberian	125.00
Adze, Cooper's, D.R.Barton & Co., Original Handle	18.00
Adze, Shipwright's, Radius Blade, New Handle, 3 In.	9.00
Alcohol Torch, Jeweler's, Box	30.00
Anvil, Detroit Iron Works, 2 1/4 In.	25.00
Auger Bit, Winchester	15.00
Auger, Gunhole, 13 1/4 In.	30.00
Auger, Spiral, Wooden Handle	12.00
Ax, Butchering, Head, 9 1/2 In.	20.00
Ax, Cooper's, Chaffee & Sons, Cincinnati, OH	70.00
Ax, Goosewing, Etched, Original Handle	250.00
Ax, Plum Scout, Case	25.00
Barrel Bung Cutter	12.00
Bellows, Insect Powder, Stenciled, Woodason	35.00

Bevel, Rosewood & Brass, Steel Arm, 9 In. 12.00
Bitstock, Coachmaker's, Metal, Thumblatch, No.5, H.O.White Bros., 1850 .... 85.00
Bitstock, Wood, Winchester, No.1208 .... 15.00
Blowtorch, Brass, Rochester, N.Y. 18.00
Blowtorch, Turner, Double Jet, Brass 28.00
Body Massager, Electric, Bakelite Handle, Dated Jan.12, 1932 .... 50.00
Bootjack, Naughty Nellie, Original Paint 275.00
Box, Keen Kutter, Oak 18.00
Brace, Auger, Hollow, Rosewood Handles, Millers Falls 45.00
Brace, Barn Beam 100.00
Brace, Carpenter's, H.Hawke, Sheffield, Brass & Wood 125.00
Brace, Darling, Pat.20, 1868, Unique Bit–Holding Piece 450.00
Brace, Sheffield, Brass Baluster, Ebony Head, H.Brown & Sons 95.00
Branding Iron, Sheep Marking 55.00
Bucket, Maple Sugar, Red, 2 Metal Hoops, Hook For Tree, 9 1/2 X 12 In. 36.00
Buggy Whip, Carved Ivory Handle, Engraved UI Hotel Boston 125.00
Bullet Mold, Winchester Arms Co., Wooden Handle Grips, 9 1/4 In. 45.00
Bung Pounder, Potasi Brewery, Chicago, Cast Brass 75.00
Buttress, Farrier's, Wooden Rest, 16 In. 13.00
Calculator, Fuller's, Wooden Case, 19th Century, 18 In. 115.00
Calf Weaner, Can't Suck 8.00
Calipers, Double, Wrought, T.F.L.Initials, 10 In. 72.00
Calipers, Lumber, G.T.Younglove, Fitchburg, Mass., 21 X 44 In. 75.00
Calipers, New Hampshire, Set 425.00
Can, Oil, Copper, Hinged Lid, Curved Spout, Pennsylvania, 6 In. 125.00
Capon Castration Kit, Original Box 15.00
Carrier, Carpenter's, 4 Compartments, Square 50.00
Centrifugal Instrument, Circle Flattens, Gains Speed, C.1850 .... 475.00
Chain Cutter & Splicer, Weed, Michigan Chain Co., Pat.1913–1926 .... 15.00
Chest, Carpenter's, Carved, Wood Planes, Sheffield Brace, Tools, 1890 .... 900.00
Chest, Joseph Borow, Lancaster, Pa., 1830–40 .... 950.00
Chisel Set, Patternmaker's, Buck Bros., Set of 7 .... 125.00
Chisel, Barn, Wooden Handle, Marked S.& W.Co., 25 In. 34.00
Chisel, Socket Mortise, Underhill & Brown, 11 1/2 In. 22.50
Chisel, Wood, Winchester, No.4842 .... 32.50
Clippers, Dehorning, Cattle, Cast Iron, Patent 1895 .... 75.00
Clippers, Hand, Haircutting, Browne & Sharpe, Pat.1926 .... 4.25
Cobbler's Bench, Shaker, Old Red & Green Paint 350.00
Compass & Divider, Eagle, Original Box, 1894 .... 12.00
Compass, Engineer's, L.E.Gurley, Troy, N.Y., Dated 1888 .... 95.00
Compass, Portable Dip, Brass Frame, Jos.W.Queen & Co., Case, 1860–93 .... 250.00
Compass, Surveyor's, Brass, Silvered Dial, Samuel Greenleaf, 5 In. 450.00
Corn Grader, Wooden 7.00
Corn Husker, 1 Prong 2.50
Corn Planter, Acme 30.00
Cranberry Scoop, Hand Carved Wood, 15 X 15 In. 145.00
Cranberry Scoop, Handmade, New England, C.1920 .... 15.00
Cresset, Cooper's, 3 Bands Through 3 Vertical Posts 90.00
Crochet Hook, Sailor's, Repairing Nets, Tin Handle, Brass, 8 3/4 In. 39.00
Croze, Cooper's, Sawtooth, Ash, Half Round Style, 4 X 13 In. 30.00
Cutter, Betel Nut, Hand Forged Steel, Inlaid Brass Fish, 18th Century 195.00
Cutter, Garment, National, Book, 1881 .... 18.00
Cutter, Glass, Karelsen Diamond 20.00
Drawing Instruments, Brass, Ivory, Ebony, Mahogany Case, 1900, 7 In. 75.00
Drawing Instruments, Stanley, Ivory, Presentation Leather Case, 1920 .... 120.00
Drawshave, Hudson, 12 In. 18.00
Drill, Bow, Brass Barrel, Steel 3 Jar Chuck, Walnut, 6 1/2 In. 55.00
Drill, Breast, 2 Speed, Mohawk Shelborne, 17 In. 22.00
Drill, Breast, Iron Chick, Beech Handles, Brass, 16 In. 80.00
Drill, Breast, Patent, Keen Kutter, 1896 .... 50.00
Drill, Breast, Winchester, No.8733 .... 60.00
Drill, Electric, A.C.Gilbert, Small 45.00
Drill, Hand, Brass, Steel Gears, Ebony Handles, 11 In. 110.00
Drill, Yankee No.1545, North Bros., Pat.April 15, 1913 .... 35.00

Engine, Weeden No.2, Upright, Pat.1885	35.00
Fence Stretcher, Dated July 13, 1880	20.00
Flash Point Tester, Brass, Copper, Tubing, 4 Ivory Thermometers, Case	185.00
Flashlight, Winchester, Brass, Black Paint, M.E.Co., 9 In.	6.50
Flax Comb, Hanging, Norwegian	30.00
Fork, Laundry, Pine, Long Handle	10.00
Gauge, Axle, Wheelwright's, Wooden Beam, Adjustable Hardware	65.00
Gauge, Butt & Rabbet, Stanley, Wood & Brass, 1892	40.00
Gauge, Clapboard, Stepped Graduations, 5 X 8 1/2 In.	49.00
Gauge, Mahogany Panel, Brass Plates & Wedge, 23 In.	55.00
Gauge, Marking, A.H.Blaisedel, Newton Corner, Mass., June 23, 1869	225.00
Goad, Ox, Carved Tapered Hickory, Sharp Point, 50 In.	30.00
Grain Grader, Seeder & Separator, Mechanical, Wooden, 1900s	295.00
Grain Shovel, Wooden, 11 X 35 In.	225.00
Grain Tester, Brass	200.00
Gun Cleaning Kit, Pat.1881, Box	18.50
Hacksaw, Winchester, No.8020	40.00
Hammer, Ball Peen, Keen Kutter	20.00
Hammer, Chipping, Welder's, With Stamped Buffalo	10.00
Hammer, Marking, Logger's, Square Head, Marked H 8, 3 X 4 X 2 In.	50.00
Hammer, Tie Marking, Railroad, C.T.& I.	45.00
Hatchet, Keen Kutter, 5 In.	30.00
Hatchet, Keen Kutter, Simmons, 3 1/4 In.	45.00
Hatchet, Oval Poll, Triangular Blade, Marked, C.1685	90.00
Hay Knife, Americana, Ratchet Adjustment, Pat.Sept.5, 1898	30.00
Hod Carrier, Tin Lid, Wooden Handle	28.00
Hoof Cleaner, Pioneer, Wooden Handle	17.50
Hook, Cotton Bale, Steel, 14 In.	40.00
Horse Tie, Iron, To Drive Into Tree Or Post, 9 In.	22.00
Ice Hook, Wooden Handle	9.00
Ice Pick, Meat Tenderizer, Food Chopper, Wooden Handle, Iron	15.00
Ice Pick, Winchester, No.9502	22.00
Ice Tongs, Forged Cast Iron, 15 In.	15.00
Insect Destroyer, O'Neil, Manning & Co., Wooden, Wire, 1902	30.00
Jack, Buggy, Wooden, Red Finish, 3 Stepped Lift Handle	30.00
Jack, Cogwheel, Model T	15.00
Jamb Hook, Brass, Soldered Repair, 4 In.	45.00
Jig, Copper's, Barrel, Foot Treadle, 16 X 30 In.	110.00
Jointer, E.W.Carpenter's, Double Wedge, Pat.March 27, 1849, 20 In.	79.00
Keeler, Wooden, New England	675.00
L–Plumb Level, Oak, Iron Plumb Bob, 16 1/2 X 19 In.	150.00
Ladder, Weathered Oak, 4 Rungs	45.00
Ladder, Wooden, Green Paint, 72 1/2 In.	70.00
Lawnmower, C.1900	75.00
Leg Irons, Shackle, Hartford Lock Co.	55.00
Level, Davis, Iron, Fancy, 12 In.	115.00
Level, Hand, Keuffel & Esser	17.00
Level, L.L.Davis, Spirit, Dated 1876	85.00
Level, Machinist's, Brass Vials, Rabone & Sons, Japanned, Iron, 12 In.	35.00
Level, Machinist's, Davis No.1, Inclinometer, Gilt Finish, 6 In.	225.00
Level, Machinist's, Davis No.2, Inclinometer, Pat.Sept.17, 1867, 12 In.	225.00
Level, Marked Case Tractor, Wooden, 6 In.	110.00
Level, Peerless, Vertical & Horizontal Bubble, Wooden	25.00
Level, Rosewood & Mahogany, 2 Nickel Plated Vials & Ends, 18 In.	85.00
Level, Sargent, No.193	28.00
Level, Stanley, No. 3, Dated 1906	20.00
Level, Stanley, No.1890, Carpenter's, Brass Plates, Ends & Top, 26 In.	18.50
Level, Stanley, No.36	15.00
Level, Transit, Buff–Buff, Dated 1917, Box	350.00
Level, Transit, Surveyor's, Brass, Engraved Face, L.Michael, 15 In.	270.00
Level, Winchester, Paper Decal, 16 In.	45.00
Lock, Champion, Brass, 6 Lever, With Keys	15.00
Lock, Skull & Crossbones	210.00
Lock, Slaymaker Ward, Key	7.00

Loom, Barn, Primitive, Hand Hewed 275.00
Loom, Tape, Board, Reed & Crank Handle, 18th Century 430.00
Machine, Ring Sizer, Jewelry Store 95.00
Machine, Trimmer, Wallpaper, 1901 .... 85.00
Mallet, Carpenter's, Burl, 13 3/4 In. 20.00
Maul, Raft, Lumberman's, Iron Ring, Around 24 In.Wooden Handle 50.00
Meat Saw, Winchester, 16 In.Blade 45.00
Mechanical Drawing Ruler, Pinup Girl, Corbin Lock Co., Envelope 22.00
Mechanical Drawing Set, English, Rosewood Case, 19th Century 400.00
Miter Box, Langdon, No.41, Folding 25.00
Miter Box, Stanley No.115, Maple, Birch, Oak, Graduated Quadrant 25.00
Monkey Wrench, Adjustable, Roxbury 125.00
Morse Telegraph Key, Brass, Mahogany, No.20 .... 50.00
Niddy–Noddy, Wooden, Turned, 18 In. .... 45.00 To 85.00
Oven, Drying, For Lab, Copper 28.00
Ovolo, Handle, Smith & Co., 13 1/2 In. 95.00
Padlock, Harvard, 6 Levers 40.00
Padlock, Internal Revenue 100.00
Padlock, Keen Kutter, Brass 80.00
Padlock, U.S.B.I.A.Sealed Lock 100.00
Pan, Gold Panner's, Copper Bottom, 16 In.Diam. 150.00
Panel Gauge, Ebony, Wooden Locking Thumbscrew 125.00
Pelvimeter, Collins, 1800s 25.00
Pig Snouter, Dr.Miller, C.1888 .... 20.00
Plane, Bailey, No. 5 .... 10.00 To 20.00
Plane, Bailey, No.27 .... 22.00
Plane, Block, Keen Kutter, No.120 .... 27.00
Plane, Boxwood Plow, Screw Arm, Brass Adjustment, Slide Lock 195.00
Plane, Cabinet Maker's, Sargent, No.106 .... 45.00
Plane, Cabinet Scraper, Stanley, No.81 .... 42.00
Plane, Chaplin No.1210 .... 60.00
Plane, Coachmaker's Squirrel Tail, Compass Bottom, Cherry, 6 1/2 In. 95.00
Plane, Combination, Stanley No.45, 21 Cutters, Metal Box 179.00
Plane, Combination, Stanley No.55, 55 Cutters, 4 Section Box 465.00
Plane, Corebox, William Bayley, 6 Cutters, Copy of Patent Papers 425.00
Plane, Crewell, Capewell Mfg.Co., 7 1/2 In. 10.00
Plane, Floor, Stanley, No.74, No Handle 250.00
Plane, Hand, P.G.Pearson, Wood & Brass, 3 Sections, Cast Steel Blade 95.00
Plane, Jack, Knowle, Front Knob 225.00
Plane, Jointer, Stanley, No.7 .... 50.00
Plane, Lowell Plane & Tool Co., Pat.1856 & 1857 .... 160.00
Plane, Lynch Skate, Pat.July 17, 1894, 3 1/2 In. 45.00
Plane, Match, Stanley, No.148, 7/8 In. 45.00
Plane, Mold, Stanley No.45, With Blades 140.00
Plane, Molding, Multiform, Dated Aug.1854, Ohio Tool Co., 10 Piece 195.00
Plane, N.Chapin & Co., C.1849 .... 35.00
Plane, Ogee, Ohio Tool Co., 1 1/4 In. 25.00
Plane, Panel Raiding, P.Chapin, Baltimore 210.00
Plane, Plow, Skate Front, Boxwood Arms, Nuts, Brass Trim, Varvill & Co. 165.00
Plane, Plow, Wedge Arms, Brass Tips, Beech, Moseley & Son 55.00
Plane, Rabbet, Handle, Beech, 12 1/2 In. 30.00

To restore old tools, wash wood with Murphy's oil soap, dry, sand with steel wool, apply two coats of Minwax or other oil, then use paste wax and buff. Clean metal parts, then coat with clear lacquer.

Plane, Rabbet, Side, T.Mackenzie, No.3, Loveday St., Pair	65.00
Plane, Rabbet, Stanley, No.90, Steel Cased, Side Spur	95.00
Plane, Round, Andruss, No.18, Newark, N.J., 1 In.	35.00
Plane, Router, Door Trim, Stanley, No.171	190.00
Plane, Sargent No.45, With 24 Blades	150.00
Plane, Sash, Adjustable, J.T.Brown	65.00
Plane, Scotia, Gleave, Oldham St., Manchester, Est.1833, 1 1/8 In.	24.00
Plane, Scrub, Keen Kutter, No.240	80.00
Plane, Shelton No.5	30.00
Plane, Simmons No.4	40.00
Plane, Smooth, Stanley, No.2, Label On Handle	165.00
Plane, Smooth, Stanley, No.4, Type 8	25.00
Plane, Stanley, No. 45, With 22 Blades	160.00
Plane, Stanley, No. 55, With 48 Blades	260.00
Plane, Stanley, No.102 Block	15.00
Plane, Stanley, No.113, Combination	80.00
Plane, Stanley, No.129	35.00
Plane, Stanley, No.192, Scroll Design Handle, Pre–1909	37.50
Plane, Sterling No.45, 18 Blades	85.00
Plane, Sun, Cooper's, No.2122, Beech, 15 1/4 In.	80.00
Plane, Thumb, Boxwood, Straight Bottom, 1/2 X 3 1/2 In.	110.00
Plane, Winchester, No.3205, Corrugated Sole, Iron Bench	70.00
Pleater, Wire Slats, Wooden Frame, Anderson & Rorke, 13 X 9 1/2 In.	150.00
Pliers, Keen Kutter, 5 1/2 In.	20.00
Pliers, Nail Starter, & Hammer, Cobbler's, Combination	17.00
Plumb Bob, Brass, 3 3/4 In.	45.00
Plumb Bob, Turnip Shape, Wire Hook At Top, Homemade, Brass, 4 In.	15.00
Posthole Digger, Red Paint	21.00
Protractor, Carpenter's, Wooden, Quarter Arc, 15 X 15 In.	40.00
Puller, Wagon Wheel, Wooden Handle, Iron Hook, 33 In.	20.00
Rack, Drying, Wood, Wire Mesh, Single	33.00
Rake, Scythe, Hay, 48 1/2 In.	45.00
Ratchet Screwdriver, Yankee 31, Box	15.00
Reamer, Bung, Cooper's, Auger Point, 3 X 15 In.	12.00
Reel, Wooden, Shoe Feet & Hand Crank, Primitive, 24 In.	55.00
Reel, Yarn Winding, Mahogany, 2 Adjustable Bobbins, 47 1/2 In.	170.00
Reel, Yarn, Dovetailed Pine Base, 4 Parts, 36 In.	125.00
Reel, Yarn, Mortised Joints, 30 In.	75.00
Router, Old Woman's Tooth, Beech, Robert Kelly & Sons, 6 In.	33.00
Rule, Folding, Geo.Bermaster 61990	5.00
Rule, Folding, Lufkin 651, 2 Ft.	10.00
Rule, Folding, Stanley, No. 40, Ivory, Caliper, German Silver Binding	195.00
Rule, Folding, Stanley, No. 61	9.00
Rule, Folding, Stanley, No. 68A	12.00
Rule, Folding, Stanley, No.856, 6 Ft.	5.00
Rule, Folding, Upson	15.00
Rule, Hatter's, Boxwood, Brass Caliper, 5 In.	49.00
Rule, Interlox, No.106	20.00
Rule, Parallel, K & E, German Silver & Ebony	24.00
Rule, Rolling, Brass Coated, J.Halden & Co., London & Manchester	85.00
Rule, Stanley, No.40, With Caliper, Ivory, German Silver Trim	145.00
Safe, Used By Wells Fargo, Harrigan Safe Works, Kansas, 6 Ft.	2000.00
Saw, Cane, Holtzapffel & Co., London, Blade Detaches & Folds, 36 In.	220.00
Saw, Crosscut	10.00
Saw, Dovetail, Brass Back, Beech Handle, 5 In.Blade	33.00
Saw, Hand, Winchester, No.10	67.50
Saw, Keen Kutter, Simmons, Hand	32.50
Saw, Posthole, Wooden Frame, Narrow Blade, 20 X 23 In.	30.00
Saw, Salt, Zinc Blade, Wooden Handle, 20 In	35.00
Saw, Scroll, Delta Specialty Co., Pat.1923	155.00
Saw, Wooden Fret, Maple, 6 X 15 In.	45.00
Scissors, Mustache, Celluloid Handles	15.00
Scissors, Winchester, No.9014	20.00
Scorp, Cabinet Maker's, Cherry, Half Round, Curved Handle, 1800, 7 In.	140.00

Scraper, Brass, 12 X 3 In.	55.00
Scraper, Cabinet, Keen Kutter, No.90	20.00
Scraper, Cabinet, Keen Kutter, No.K–79	35.00
Scraper, Stanley, No.80	12.00
Screwbox, Tap, 1 1/2 In.	95.00
Screwdriver, Cabinet Maker's, Tiger Maple	100.00
Screwdriver, Triple Lever, Smith	15.00
Screwdriver, Winchester, No.7122, 3 In.	30.00
Scribe, Timber, 8 X 3 In.	30.00
Scythe Stone, Pike's Indian Pond, Paper Label, Wrapper	16.00
Shave, Stair Rail, Stocky Beech, 2 1/2 X 11 In.	135.00
Shave, Stanley, No.80, Cast Iron, Double Handled	18.00
Shears, Sheep, Wilkinson, England	18.00
Shears, Tailor's, J.Wiss & Sons, Newark, N.J., 14 In.	45.00
Shovel, Coal Saver, 1916	35.00
Shovel, Keen Kutter	15.00
Sickle, Wooden Handle	58.00
Sizer, Ring, Jeweler's, F.E.Allens, 11 In.	20.00
Skutch, Brick Maker's, Brass	50.00
Slick, Carpenter's, Douglass, 3 1/2 In.	35.00
Slick, Iron Forged, J.Urie, 4 1/4 In.	125.00
Slide Rule, Keugeleiser, Instructions, Box	12.00
Speculum, Veterinarian's, For Cattle, Lyre Shape, Iron, 4 X 12 In.	45.00
Square, Adjustable, Brass, Rosewood, 1895	20.00
Square, Cabinet Maker's, Mahogany, Curved Style, 8 1/2 X 14 In.	40.00
Square, Carpenter's, Steel Blade, Walnut Handle, 6 In.	7.00
Stair Saw, Oak, Varnished	50.00
Stair Trammel, Oak	95.00
Stake, Tinner's, 27 X 10 1/2 In.	85.00
Stapler, Acme No.2, Cast Iron	45.00
Stretcher, Hat, Wooden Handle, Sizes Marked, Brass	52.50
Stretcher, Rug, Cast Iron	6.00
Stretcher, Shoe, To Relieve Bunion Discomfort	32.50
Surveying Instrument, Brass, Label, English	550.00
Sweat Scraper, Horse, 2 Handles, Hickory, 1880s	50.00
Tape, Surveyor's, K & E.Leather Cased	13.00
Telegraph Sounder, Western Electric, Mahogany Resonator	55.00
Tester, Battery Cell, King	14.00
Tester, Light Bulb, General Electric	150.00
Tin Snips, Brass, Large	29.50
Tongs, Blacksmith's, Hand Forged, 12 1/2 In.	12.00
Tongs, Blacksmith, 18th–Century	60.00
Tongs, Pipe, Accordion, Iron, Extends To 10 1/2 In.	260.00
Trammel, Lighting, Wood, Dark Finish, Tin Repair, Adjusts From 40 In.	100.00
Trammel, Sawtooth, Iron, 33 In.	25.00
Transit & Level, Surveyor's, Brass, St.Louis, Mo., Wooden Case, C.1845	400.00
Transit, Surveying, Brass Telescope, Tripod, C.1920	225.00
Traveler Wheel, For Measuring Distance	40.00
Trencher, Hand Hewn, Birch, Oblong, 18th Century, 10 1/2 X 19 In.	150.00
Twibil, Wooden Handle, European, Blade, 46 In.	150.00
Vacuum, Hand, 1911	55.00
Vise, Cabinet Maker's, Wooden	95.00
Vise, Saw, Lead Jaws, Wentworths, No.8	17.00
Voltmeter, GE, Wooden Case	30.00
Wagon Brake Shoe, Iron, 20 In.	25.00
Wagon Jack, Wooden, Dated 1805, Mennonite	225.00
Watchmaker's Bench, Roll Top, Oak, 43 X 26 1/2 X 51 In.	650.00
Wedge, Iron Splitting, Wooden Handle, Iron Ring, Tree Design, Iron	15.00
Wetzhahn, Wooden, With Sharpening Stone	65.00
Whetstone, Cattaraugus, Embossed Indian Head, 2 X 5 1/2 In.	17.00
Whetstone, Sears, Roebuck, 2 3/4 X 1 3/4 In.	24.00
Winder, Yarn, Chip Carving On Base, Click Counter, 42 1/2 In.	120.00
Wire Splicers, Fogle, Box	8.50

Wrench Kit, Home Garage, Chicago Mfg.Dist.Co., Wooden Box, 20 Piece 89.00
Wrench, Bemis & Call No.4, 16 In. 28.00
Wrench, Bicycle Spoke, Dudley Mfg., Patent 1894 .... 35.00
Wrench, Buggy, Adjustable, A.P.Joy, Rockingham, N.H., Pat.Feb.L, 1898 .... 55.00
Wrench, Buggy, Adjustable, Wooden Base, Iron Handles, Pat.Applied 75.00
Wrench, Bullard, No.0, Pat.Oct.27, 1903 .... 40.00
Wrench, H.D.Smith Co., Oct.30, 1900 & Feb.23, 6 1/2 In. 20.00
Wrench, Hex, Fordson 10.00
Wrench, J.Casper's Patent, May 6, '13, Lanc.Wis., 11 In. 12.00
Wrench, Keen Kutter, Pat.Jan, 14, 1886, 6 1/2 In. 39.00
Wrench, Lake Superior Wrench Co., Michigan, 16 In. 14.00
Wrench, Pipe, Keen Kutter 35.00
Wrench, Pipe, Quikset 25.00
Wrench, Pipe, Winchester, 14 In. 35.00
Wrench, Shaw, Pat.April 26, 1910, 10 In. 22.00
Wrench, Stillson, Salesman's Sample, 6 In. 22.50
Wrench, Trimo, Adjustable, 18 In. 15.00
Wrench, Wakefield Wizard No.120, Wooster, Mass., 8 In. 30.00
Wringer & Tub Stand, Original Stencil 75.00
Y–Level, K & E, Brass, Case 195.00
Yarn Holder, Pine, 12 X 11 In. 75.00
Yarn Swift, Wooden, Table Clamp, Brown, Red Paint, Folding Arm, 23 In. 23.00
Yarn Winder, Variety of Wood, Curly Maple, 27 X 35 1/2 In. 120.00
Yoke, Child's, Wooden, Red Paint, Black Hand Stenciling, Hand Carved 98.00
Yoke, Shoulder, Wooden, 2 Bucket, Chain 21.00
Yoke, Shoulder, Wooden, Hand Carved, Bucket On Each Side, 35 In. 48.00

Toothpick holders are sometimes called "toothpicks" by collectors. The variously shaped containers made to hold the small wooden toothpicks are of glass, china, or metal. Most of the toothpick holders are Victorian.

TOOTHPICK, see also other categories such as Slag, etc.
TOOTHPICK, Acanthus, Scroll, Purple Slag 90.00
Azalea, Noritake 95.00
Bird & Basket, Amber 29.00
Blue Hand, Holding Torch, Glass 68.00
Brownie, Full Figure, Standing, Pairpoint 145.00
Bubble Lattice, White 80.00
Burmese Glass, Ruffled Top, 2 In. 165.00
Cactus, With Face, Germany 30.00
Champion 25.00
Chick & Wishbone, Silver Plate, Victor Co. 22.00
Clambroth, Souvenir, Peever, S.D. 10.00
Colonial Man, Occupied Japan 14.00
Crane With Fishes Base, Clear, Footed 18.50
Cut Glass, Fleur–De–Lis 15.00
Daisy & Button, Pitcher Shape, Pale Amber 15.00
Delaware, Green, Pressed Glass 80.00
Dog By Top Hat, Blue Glass 75.00
Eureka 28.00
Feather Swirl 15.50
Floral, Pink, White Overlay, 1000 Thumbprints 125.00
Frightened Cat, Figural, Silver Plate 40.00
Guttate, Green 60.00
Guttate, Turquoise Blue Satin Glass 110.00
Hat, Pink Overlay 39.00
Heart Shape, Blue, Milk Glass 14.50
Hobnail, Vaseline Opalescent 65.00
Iris With Meander, Green Opalescent 35.00
Kentucky, Green, Gold 110.00
Leaf Umbrella, Cranberry 110.00
Maiden's Blush 40.00
Milk Glass, Basketweave, 2 Blue Handles, Rosebuds On Rim 18.00
Nestor, Apple Green, Gold & Enamel Design 85.00

Nursery Rhymes, Glass	50.00
Portland, Pink, Banded	60.00
Roosevelt Bears, Carrying Basket Between Them, Bisque	85.00
Scalloped Swirl Etch, Ruby	45.00
Swag & Bracket, Amethyst	35.00
Swan, Blue, Gray, Stoneware	45.00
Urn Shape, Sterling Silver, Gadroon Rim	50.00
Woman's Head, With Dust Cap, Metal, 3 In.	32.50
X–Ray, Green	25.00
York Herringbone, Ruby Stained	30.00

TORQUAY

Torquay is the name given to ceramics by several potteries working near Torquay, England, from 1870 until 1962. Until about 1900, the potteries used local clay to make art pottery vases and figurines in the classical style. Then they began making souvenir wares decorated with painted slip and sgraffito designs. They often had mottos or proverbs, and scenes of cottages, ships, birds, or flowers. Potteries included Watcombe Pottery (1870–1962); Torquay Terra–Cotta Company (1875–1905); Aller Vale (1881–1924); Torquay Pottery (1908–1940); and Longpark (1883–1957).

TORQUAY, Ashtray, Figural, Rabbit, Brown, Blue Ground, Saying, Marked, 5 In.	55.00
Candleholder, Motto Ware	45.00
Cheese Dish, Covered, Motto Ware	70.00
Coffeepot, Scandy, Covered, Marked Watcombe, 5 3/4 In.	60.00
Cracker Jar, Ruby	150.00
Creamer, Motto Ware	30.00 To 35.00
Creamer, Scandy	20.00
Cup & Saucer, Motto Ware, Cottage, Cider Size	75.00
Cup & Saucer, Motto Ware, Du'ee Take An Try It, You'll Love It	22.00
Cup & Saucer, Seagulls, Blue, Oversize	30.00
Dish, Cheese, Motto Ware, Cottage	45.00
Eggcup, Pedestal, Motto Ware	40.00
Inkpot, Scandy, Motto Ware	35.00
Jam Jar, Motto Ware	40.00
Jam Jar, Scandy	26.00
Jar, Tobacco, Black Rooster, Cream Ground, Saying, Marked, 5 In.	75.00
Jug, Puzzle, Motto Ware	55.00
Loving Cup, Motto Ware	60.00
Match Holder, Motto Ware	60.00
Match Holder, Scandy	40.00
Mug, Cider, Motto Ware	35.00
Mug, Motto Ware, Cottage	45.00
Pitcher, Boat Scene	20.00
Pitcher, Cottage	23.00
Pitcher, Cottage Shape, Marked Watcomb, 5 1/2 In.	60.00
Plate, Motto Ware, Cottage, 5 In.	22.00
Plate, Motto Ware, Cottage, 6 1/2 In.	25.00
Plate, Motto Ware, Cottage, 8 In.	45.00
Plate, Peasant Village, Set of 4	55.00
Salt & Pepper	35.00
Spooner, Pigeon Blood	110.00
Sugar & Creamer, Motto Ware, Cottage	55.00
Sugar & Creamer, Watcomb, Motto Ware, Cottage	27.50
Sugar, Open, Fluted Edge, Cockerel Front, Marked Longpark, 4 In.	42.00
Syrup, Pigeon Blood	450.00
Syrup, Ruby	350.00 To 425.00
Tea Set, Motto Ware, 5 Piece	70.00
Teapot, Motto Ware	65.00
Teapot, Sailing Ships	45.00 To 65.00
Tile, Thistle	24.00
Toast Rack, Motto Ware	55.00
Vase, Novelty, Bamboo Tree Stump, Brown Bench, Marked, 5 In.	85.00

Tortoiseshell glass was made during the 1800s and after by the Sandwich Glass Works of Massachusetts and some firms in Germany. Tortoiseshell glass is, of course, named for its resemblance to real shell from a tortoise. It has been reproduced.

TORTOISESHELL GLASS, Celery, Rib & Thumbprint, 6 In.	65.00
Decanter, Ship, Ground Pontil, 11 In.	175.00
Pitcher	185.00
Toothpick, Bulbous Base	28.00
Vase, Ruffled Top, 9 In.	100.00

The shell of the tortoise has been used as inlay and to make small decorative objects since the seventeenth century. Some species of tortoise are now on the endangered species list, and objects made from these shells cannot be sold legally.

TORTOISESHELL, Box, Cathedral Top, Ivory	125.00
Box, Woman Under Glass Lid, Bronze Trim, 3 In.Diam.	325.00
Comb, Hair, 3 1/2 In., Pair	22.00
Patch Box, Silver Design, Cabochon Studs, C.1780, 1 X 2 In.	110.00

Toys are designed to entice children; and today, they have attracted new interest among adults who are still children at heart. All types of toys are collected. Tin toys, iron toys, battery operated toys, and many others are collected by specialists. Dolls, Games, Teddy Bears, and Bicycles are listed under their own categories. Other toys may be found under company or celebrity names.

TOY, Accordion, Emenee Musical Toys	15.00
Acrobat, Boy Over Parallel Bar, Celluloid, Keywind, 10 X 7 In.	25.00
Acrobat, Clown, Animated, Wood & Papier-Mache, Cloth Costume, 6 1/2 In.	95.00
Acrobat, Lady, Circus, Schoenhut	150.00
Acrobat, Mechanical, Windup, Celluloid, 1920s, Japan	150.00
Acrobat, Sand Toy	135.00
Acrobat, Yellow Tights, Suspended Between 2 Sticks, Wooden, 7 In.	35.00
Acrobatic Marvel, Windup, Marx, Box	200.00
Airplane, Aero, Windup, Germany	55.00
Airplane, Army, Windup, Tin, Marx, 18 In.	140.00
Airplane, Barbie's	145.00
Airplane, Circles Tower, Does Tricks, Electric Stick, Lionel, 1938, Box	450.00
Airplane, Defense Bomber, Tin, Wyandotte	40.00
Airplane, Fighter Bomber, Hubley, Box	35.00
Airplane, Jet, Boeing 707, Battery Operated	50.00
Airplane, MX 119, Tin, Wyandotte	40.00
Airplane, National Airlines, DC-8, Friction, Linemar, Box	62.00
Airplane, P-38, Camouflage, Hubley	58.00
Airplane, Pan-Am, Tin, Marx, Large	48.00
Airplane, Police Patrol, Friction, Japan, 1950s	35.00
Airplane, Pressed Board Wings, 4 Props, Wooden, 21 In.Wing Span, C.1940	145.00
Airplane, Scout, Steelcraft, 2 In.Wingspan, 1930s	165.00
Airplane, Seagull, Cast Iron, Orange & Pale Blue Paint, 8 In.	210.00
Airplane, Sky Hawk, Tower, Box	190.00
Airplane, U.S.Marine Air-Sea Rescue, Ideal, Box	30.00
Airplane, Windup, Automatic Toy Co., 1930s	115.00
Airplane, Windup, Tin, Marx, 1930s	65.00
Airplane, Wings & Wheels Fold Up, Hubley	18.00
Airplane, Wyandotte, China Clipper	40.00
Airplane, Wyandotte, Pressed Steel, 2 Wind Engines	20.00
Alabama Coon Jigger, Strauss, 1920s	185.00
Alabama Coon Jigger, Windup, Tin, Lehmann, 1920s	200.00
Alligator, Black Man Riding, Tin	200.00
Alligator, Circus, Schoenhut	225.00
Ambulance, Hillclimber, Unique Art	295.00
Ambulance, Wyandotte, Pressed Steel, 1930	40.00
Anxious Bride, Cycle, Uniformed Rider, Mechanical, Lehmann, 9 In.	2250.00
Aquaplane, Chein	65.00

Aquaplane, Ohio Art 38.00
Arab, On Horse, Burnoose Over White Robe, Scimitar, Jezail, 4 Piece 75.00
Archie's Riverside High Convertible, With 4 Dolls, 1950s 250.00
Armchair, Doll's, Black Striping, 7 3/4 In. 65.00
Armchair, Doll's, Mission Style, 7 1/2 X 12 1/2 In. 40.00
Armchair, Doll's, Slat Back, Splint Seat, Bittersweet Paint, 15 In. 225.00
Armoire, Doll's, Bamboo, Glass Doors 100.00
Army Duck, With Revolving Cannons, Friction, Tin, Japan, 8 1/2 In. 95.00
Army Set, Tonka, 4 Piece 150.00
Army Wagon, Metal Driver, Dinky No.623 .... 30.00
Astronaut, Tin, Battery Operated, Rotate-O-Matic 75.00
Atomic Robot Man, Key Wind, Tin, Japan, 5 In. 225.00
Autobahn, Cars, Buses, 2 Rotating Platforms, Windup, U.S.S.R., Box, 1960s 50.00
Autobus, Lehmann 975.00
Baby, Crawling, Celluloid, 5 In. 16.00
Balking Mule, Jenny, Tin, Windup, Strauss .... 75.00 To 150.00
Ballerina, Mechanical, Marx 53.00
Band Set, Charbens, No.527 .... 175.00
Bandwagon, Circus, Gray Dappled Horses, Red & Yellow Wagon 400.00
Barney Bear Drummer, Battery Operated 55.00
Barney Google, Schoenhut 325.00
Bartender, Charlie Weaver 75.00
Bat-O-Ball, Harold Teen, 1938 .... 40.00
Bathtub, Doll's, Tin, On Legs 14.00
Batmobile, Bat Boat & Trailer, Box, Corgi 40.00
Battleship, Friction, Pressed Steel, Wooden Life Boats, 19 In. 135.00
Battleship, Tin Litho & Wood, Converse, C.1900, 18 1/2 In. 435.00
Battleship, USS Washington, Tin, Windup, Marx 40.00
Battleship, Valiant, Plexiglass Display Case, Surliffe, Box, 1960s 95.00
Battleship, Wooden, Keystone 50.00
Bazooka, Bob Burns, 13 1/2 In. 14.75
    TOY, BEAR, see also Teddy Bear
Bear, Alps, Chicago Cubs, Keywind, Head Bobs, Tail Rotates, Celluloid 75.00
Bear, Ball Playing, Battery Operated, Box 350.00
Bear, Celluloid, Cragstan, Box 32.00
Bear, Dances, Windup, Tin Feet, 1930s 300.00
Bear, Drinking Coffee, Battery Operated 40.00
Bear, Drumming, Battery Operated 65.00
Bear, Knitting, Windup, Japan 17.50
Bear, Mechanical Golfer, Windup 85.00
Bear, On Bicycle, Rides On String, Tin 175.00
Bear, On Wheels, Glass Eyes, Muzzle, Pull Chain Growler, 1930 .... 375.00
Bear, On Wooden Wheels, Steiff, 1904 .... 525.00
Bear, Peanut Vendor, Battery Operated, 5 Actions, Cragstan 150.00
Bear, Rides Bicycle On High Wire, Balance Toy, Tin, 6 3/4 In. 105.00
Bear, Shoemaker, Battery Operated, Box 115.00
Bear, Shoeshine, Battery Operated, Box 110.00
Bear, Teddy The Artist, Battery Operated 75.00
Bear, Thirsty, Windup, Japan, Box 65.00
Bear, Tumbles In Swing, Windup, 1930s 125.00
Bear, Wheels, Original Petz, Brown Plush, U.S.Zone Germany, 7 1/2 In. 100.00
Bear, Yes-No, Schuco, 5 In. 450.00
Bed, Doll's, Brass, Gorham 65.00
Bed, Doll's, Canopy, Embroidered French Linen Covers, 18th Century 650.00
Bed, Doll's, Cast Iron, Headboard With Cherubs, 19 1/2 In. 90.00
Bed, Doll's, Folding, With Mattress & Pillow, 20th Century 45.00
Bed, Doll's, Iron, Mesh Springs 75.00
Bed, Doll's, Metal Flowered Canopy, Gold, Heart At Base 30.00
Bed, Doll's, Metal, 13 1/2 X 7 In. 28.00
Bed, Doll's, Ornate Metal, 7 X 13 1/2 In. 32.00
Bed, Doll's, Rope, Oak, Cherry, Turned Posts, Husk Mattress, 19 In. 75.00
Bed, Doll's, Wooden, C.1910, 19 In. 45.00
Beebop Jigger, Marx, Box 100.00
Beetle, Lehmann, Windup .... 100.00 To 125.00

Beetle, Mechanical, Tin, German, 4 In. 65.00
Bell Cycle, Celluloid Tin, C.1930 .... *Cover* 25.00
Bell Toy, Animated Black Boy, Cloth Costume, Papier–Mache Head, 6 In. 475.00
Bell Toy, Horses, Iron, Silver Paint, Heart In Wheels, 6 1/4 In. 150.00
Bell Toy, Pull, 8 In.Diam.Wheels, 1924 .... 35.00
Bell Toy, Tramp No.47, Cast Iron, 6 In. 325.00
Bell Toy, Trick Pony Bell Ringer No.39, Cast Iron, 7 3/4 In. 400.00
    TOY, BICYCLE, see Bicycle
Big John Chimpee Chief, Battery Operated 25.00
Big Parade, Windup, Tin, Marx 72.50
Billboard, American Flyer, Ringling Bros., Metal, 4 X 7 In. 45.00
Billiard Table, With 2 Players, Tin, Windup, 14 In. 235.00
Biplane, U.S.Navy, Tootsietoy 30.00
Bird Cage, Whistling, Tin 105.00
Bird Whistle, Celluloid, 1 X 2 X 3 In. 12.50
Bird, Canary, Singing, Windup, W.Germany 65.00
Bird, German, Tin, Windup, Sings, Flaps Wings & Tail 65.00
Bird, In Cage, Tin, Windup, Squeak Box, Germany, 3 1/2 In. 95.00
Bison, Steiff, 11 In. 150.00
Black Man, Dancing, Andy's Novelty Co., Milan, Ohio, 12 In. 85.00
Black, Riding Alligator, Tin Litho, Windup, 14 In. 160.00
Blimp, Goodyear, Buddy L, Decals, 4 1/2 In. 30.00
Blockhouse & Fort, Log Type Fence, Elastolin, 6 X 6 X 7 In.House 75.00
Blocks, ABC's, Picture Puzzle Opposite Side, Crandall 225.00
Blocks, Animal, Makes 4 Pictures, 2 1/2 In., 12 Piece 110.00
Blocks, Blondie & Dagwood, Interchangeable, Gaston, Box, 1951 .... 28.00
Blocks, Building, Artoy, Dated 1913 .... 75.00
Blocks, Cardboard, Tuck, Original Box 125.00
Blocks, Chromolith, Wooden, 1877 .... 550.00
Blocks, Flags, Letters On Reverse Side, Box, 7 1/2 X 12 1/2 In., Set 285.00
Blocks, Paper & Wood, Red Riding Hood Cover, 11 X 15 In.Wooden Box 155.00
Blocks, Paper Covered, Bible Verses, J.S.Wesby, Worcester, Mass., 23 Pc. 75.00
Blocks, Puzzle, Santa Claus, Child With Teddy Bear, German, Box 585.00
Blocks, Stacking, Victorian Holiday Scenes, Lithograph 100.00
Blocks, Storyland, McLoughlin, Box, Large Size 175.00
Blocks, Wild Animal Picture, Wooden, McLoughlin 150.00
Blocks, Wooden, Litho Paper Covered, Form Animal Puzzles, 12 Piece 90.00
Board, Alphabet, Foxey Toys, Tin 30.00
Boat, Gun, Friction, Marked Pa.Mar 27, '02, Tin, 15 1/4 In. 55.00
Boat, Polychrome Paint, Tin, Windup, Marked Bavaria, 7 In. 115.00
Boat, Queen Mary, Cunard White Star Liner, Brass Rollers, Dinky 80.00
Boat, Racing, Steam Powered, Bowman, 1930–40, Box, 22 In. 725.00
Boba Fett, Empire Strikes Back, Box 55.00
Bobsled, L.C.McCarthy Stencil, Used For Winter Deliveries With Horse 325.00
Borden Milk Wagon, Pull Toy, Tin, Bottle Lithos, Wooden Horse, 1920s 200.00
Bottle, Nursing, Dolle–Nursette, Accessories, Amsco, Box, Set of 4 .... 18.00
Boxers, 2 Women, Animated, Wood, Papier–Mache, Cloth Costumes, 9 1/4 In. 210.00
Boxers, Rap & Tap In A Friendly Scrap, Windup, Tin, Unique Art, 5 In. 225.00
Boy, Bubble Blowing, Windup, Japan 65.00
Boy, Bubble, Tin, Windup, Marsun Toys 60.00
Boys Favorite Tool Chest, With Tools, Paper Label 50.00
Bucket & Pump, Ohio Art, 1940s 20.00
Buick Ambulance, Black, Tekno 50.00
Building Blocks, Chautauqua Architectural, Paper Label 65.00
Bulldog, On Wheels, Cast Iron, Original Paint 175.00
Bulldozer, Piston Action, Tin, Japan 20.00
Bulldozer, With Robot, Marvelous Mike, Electric Powered, Metal, 13 In. 85.00
Bunny & Cart, Pull Toy, Wooden, Fisher–Price 12.00
Bunny, Holds Cotton Batting Carrot, Papier–Mache, Germany, 3 1/2 In. 58.00
Bunny, Pushing Wheelbarrow, Chein, 6 In. 30.00
Bus, Double Decker, Cast Iron, Rubber Tires, Arcade, 8 In. 90.00
Bus, Double Decker, Cream, Red, Post–War Issue, Dinky 25.00
Bus, Double Decker, Triangle, Metal, 20 In. 375.00
Bus, Greyhound, Kingsbury 350.00

Bus, Greyhound, N.Y.World's Fair, Cast Iron, Arcade 275.00
Bus, Greyhound, Tin, Cragstan, Box 25.00
Bus, Greyhound, Windup, Buddy L, 1939, Large 94.00
Bus, London Double–Decker, Mechanical, Tin, Japan, Box, 10 In. 185.00
Bus, London Trolley, Matchbox, Red, 1st Issue 35.00
Bus, Touring, Dinky, No.953, Large 45.00
Butcher Shop, Wooden, Papier–Mache Meats, German, C.1890, 13 X 7 In. 175.00
Butterfly, Push Toy, Tin 155.00
Cabin Cruiser, Tin, Red, Yellow, Black, White, Ohio Art, 15 In. 20.00
Cable Car, San Francisco, Friction, Passengers 40.00
Cable Car, San Francisco, Wood, 1946 .... 25.00
Cackling Hen, Pull Toy, Fisher–Price 45.00
Cackling Hen, Pull Toy, Wooden, Wyandotte 45.00
Cage, Polar Bear, Overland Circus, 2 Horses, Iron, C.1950, 7 X 14 In. 185.00
Camel, Glass Eyes, Schoenhut 275.00
Camel, Walking, Windup, Tin 150.00
Cannon Kit, Civil War, Marx, Assembly Instructions, Box 50.00
Cannon, Brass Barrel, 14 Spokes In Wheels, Cast Iron, U.S.A., 8 In. 68.00
Cannon, Cast Iron, Bronze Barrel, C.W.Type, 5 In. 40.00
Cannon, Firecracker, 8 In. 80.00
Cannon, Shoots Marbles, Cast Iron, Kilgore Boy Ranger, Pat.1913, 19 In. 125.00
Cannon, Steel Carriage Painted Red & Black, Bronze, 7 1/2 In. 95.00
Cannon, Steel, Tin Turret Base, Turning Adjustments, 12 In. 35.00
Cap Bomb, Head of Black Man Wearing Hat, Cast Iron, 2 In. 200.00
Cap Bomb, Yellow Kid 95.00
Cap Gun, Atomic Disintegrator, Hubley 65.00
Cap Gun, Buc–A–Roo, Cast Iron, Box 35.00
Cap Gun, Cannon 275.00
Cap Gun, Cast Iron, Chrome Finish, Strato, Late 1930s 115.00
Cap Gun, Dragnet, 38 Special, 1950s 10.00
Cap Gun, Dueling, Midget, Flintlock, Hubley, Pair 28.00
Cap Gun, Dynamite Derringer, Box 8.00
Cap Gun, Flintlock, Hubley, Box 20.00
Cap Gun, Hawk 10.00
Cap Gun, Hub, Cast Iron, Mammoth Cap Type, 1940 .... 15.00
Cap Gun, Liberty, Patent 1873 .... 75.00
Cap Gun, Mountie, Kilgore 15.00
Cap Gun, Musket, Boy's Brigade 35.00
Cap Gun, Paper Poppers Super NuMatic 15.00
Cap Gun, Ranger, Cast Iron 35.00
Cap Gun, Remington Arms, Percusssion 15.00
Cap Gun, Rickoshay No.248 .... 35.00
Cap Gun, Rifle, Roy Rogers, Box, 2 Ft. 25.00
Cap Gun, Riot Gun, Removable Crank, Cast Iron 40.00
Cap Gun, Rodeo, Hubley, Box 12.00
Cap Gun, Scout, Tin & Cast Iron, Patent Dec.18, 1917 .... 35.00
Cap Gun, Sheriff, Box 30.00
Cap Gun, Stallion 22, 1950s 16.50
Cap Gun, Stevens, 1878 .... 85.00
Cap Gun, Texan Jr., Hubley, Box 30.00
Cap Gun, Victor 65.00
Cap Gun, Western Boy, Cast Iron 8.00
Cap Gun, Wild Bill Hickock 25.00
Cap Popper, Wooden, Feathers, 1930s 7.50
Capitol Hill Racer, Windup, Tin, Unique Art, Box, 1930s 125.00
Car, '65 Mustang, Friction, Cragstan 15.00
Car, 1928 Ford, Coupe, Arcade, 6 3/4 In. 500.00
Car, Air Flow, Kingsbury 295.00
Car, Alfa Romeo, White, Tekno 45.00
Car, Antique, Shaking, Battery Operated, Cragstan, Box 60.00
Car, Army Staff, Battery Operated, 48 Star Flag, Tin, Marx, Box, 11 In. 145.00
Car, Austin, White Rubber Tires, Cast Iron 25.00
Car, Batmobile, Black, Corgi 25.00
Car, Brink's Armored, Windup 50.00

Toy, Car, Buick, Coupe, Gray–Green, Iron,
C.1927, 8 1/2 In.

Toy, Car, Packard, Sedan, Iron,
2 Working Doors, C.1927, 11 In.

Car, Buick, Coupe, Gray–Green, Iron, C.1927, 8 1/2 In. ....*Illus* 3700.00
Car, Buick, Rubber Tires, Driver, Cast Iron, Arcade, 1929, 8 In. 1150.00
Car, Bullion Transport, Ft.Knox Gold, Lionel 33.00
Car, Cadillac Ambulance, Matchbox 10.00
Car, Capitol Hill Racer, Windup, Unique Art, Box 110.00
Car, Charlie McCarthy, Marx 335.00
Car, Chevy Taxi, Yellow, Matchbox, Box 10.00
Car, Chevy Wagon, Fawn, White, Hubley, 1955, 4 In. 25.00
Car, Chrysler, Royal Sedan, Yellow, Dinky 40.00
Car, Citroen Winter Sports Safari, Decals, Corgi 30.00
Car, Convertible, 1920s Style, Tin Litho, Friction, 1950, Japan, 4 In. 42.50
Car, Convertible, Cast Metal, Hubley 25.00
Car, Convertible, Friction, Linemar 6.00
Car, Convertible, Woody, Wyandotte, 5 X 12 In. 30.00
Car, Cor–Cor Air Flow 495.00
Car, Corvette Stingray, Customized, Corgi 20.00
Car, Dick Tracy, Tin, Marx, 11 In. 75.00
Car, Dipsy, Milton Berle, What The Hey, Marx, 1950 .... 145.00
Car, Ford Cortina GXL, Corgi 40.00
Car, Ford Delivery Roadster, Model 210, Original Paint, Buddy L 675.00
Car, Ford Model T, Top Down, Yellow, Corgi, 1915, Box 45.00
Car, Ford Roadster, Silver, Tootsietoy, 1935, 3 In. 35.00
Car, Ford Sedan Micro Racer, 1957, Windup, Red Roof, Cream Body, Schuco 75.00
Car, Ford Thunderbird, Red, Yellow Interior, Corgi 30.00
Car, Ford, Steering, Tin, Driver, Arms Turn Wheel, Box, Japan, 7 1/2 In. 115.00
Car, Ford, Windup, Guntermann, Box, 1951, 11 In. 350.00
Car, G–Man, Windup, Marx, 14 In. 350.00
Car, Graham Coupe, Build–A–Car, Light & Dark Green, Tootsietoy 65.00
Car, Graham Sedan, 4 Wheel, Tootsietoy 45.00
Car, Green Hornet, Corgi, Box 125.00
Car, Hot Rod, Barbie 50.00
Car, Jaguar E Type Micro Racer, Red, Box, Schuco, 5 In. 100.00
Car, Jaguar Mark XM, Metallic Blue, Dinky 30.00
Car, Jaguar, E Type, Red, Dinky Toys, Box 35.00
Car, James Bond's Aston Martin D.B.5, Scale Model 261, Corgi, 1965 .... 65.00
Car, Kojak's Buick Regal, Box, Corgi 20.00
Car, LaSalle Convertible Sedan, Light Blue, Tan Top, Tootsietoy 185.00
Car, Le Sabre, Friction, Marx, Box 85.00
Car, Leaping Lena, Windup, Tin 100.00
Car, Limo, White Rubber Tires, Dual Side Mounts, A.C.Williams 125.00
Car, Lincoln, Pressed Steel, Wyandotte, 1938 .... 40.00

Car, M.G.Roadster, Doepke, 16 In.	145.00
Car, Man From U.N.C.L.E., Ring, Cream, Corgi	50.00
Car, Mercedes–Benz, 3 Forward Speeds, 1 Reverse, 1 Neutral, Box, 1940s	275.00
Car, Mercury Station Wagon, Metallic Lime Green, Matchbox	4.00
Car, Model A, Sedan, Cast Iron, Arcade	65.00
Car, Model T Ford, 1908, Yellow Wheels, Brown Seat, Dinky	65.00
Car, Model T Ford, Tootsietoy	12.00
Car, Model T Ford, Top Down, Yellow, Corgi, Box, 15 In.	45.00
Car, Mr.Magoo's, Battery Operated, Hubley	135.00
Car, Mustang Mach I, Windup	50.00
Car, Old Timer, Tin, Battery Operated, Japan	30.00
Car, Oldsmobile Toronado, Metallic Blue, Corgi	40.00
Car, Oldsmobile, Rubber, Bullet Shape, Rainbow Rubber Co., 1949, 3 In.	55.00
Car, Packard Convertible, Die Cast, 1930s, 6 In.	45.00
Car, Packard, Sedan, Iron, 2 Working Doors, C.1927, 11 In. ....*Illus*	7000.00
Car, Phantom V, Light & Dark Gray, Dinky Toy	35.00
Car, Plymouth Station Wagon, Fawn & Cream, Corgi, Box	15.00
Car, Police Patrol, Schuco	40.00
Car, Police Squad, Lupor, No.80, Friction	50.00
Car, Police, Battery Operated, 1950s	30.00
Car, Police, Gang Busters, Windup, Marx, 15 In.	225.00
Car, Police, Linemar, Remote Control, Tin, Box	58.00
Car, Police, Turn–O–Matic, Battery Operated, Box	35.00
Car, Porsche Carrera, Windup	50.00
Car, Porsche No.917, Schuco	125.00
Car, Porsche, Targa 911S, Corgi	25.00
Car, Race, Super Sonic, 3–D Head In Cockpit, Litho Wings, Japan, 36 In.	95.00
Car, Racer, Blue, Hubley, 4 In.	12.00
Car, Racer, Mercedes, Windup	295.00
Car, Racer, Schuco, Box, 3 1/4 In.	75.00
Car, Racing, Irish Mail, Hand Powered Steered, Feet, Mail Standard Co.	200.00
Car, Racing, Micro, Schuco, Box, 1950s	35.00
Car, Racing, No.76, Friction, Futuristic, Japan, 1950s	45.00
Car, Racing, Pressed Steel, Windup, Schieble, 7 In.	125.00
Car, Racing, Red, Silver, White Wheels, Auburn, 10 1/2 In.	16.00
Car, Racing, Thimble Drone, Gas Power	175.00
Car, Renault Floride, Blue, Box, Corgi	45.00
Car, Roadster, MG, Doepke	85.00
Car, Roadster, Rumble Seat, Little Jim, J.C.Penney, Sheet Metal, 17 In.	85.00
Car, Roadster, Schieble, Tin, 1920s, 19 X 7 In.	75.00
Car, Rocket Racer, Car of The Future, Marx, Box, 16 1/2 In.	110.00
Car, Rocket Racer, Friction, 1950s, 7 In.	125.00
Car, Roi–Tan Cigar, Advertising Premium, Tin, Wooden, Box, 1939	350.00
Car, Rolls–Royce, Silver Cloud, Friction, Japan, 1950s	300.00
Car, Rolls–Royce, Silver Cloud, Tin, Plates, Box, Japan, 8 1/2 In.	225.00
Car, Saab, Tin, Bandi	22.50
Car, Scarab, Buddy L ....40.00 To	110.00
Car, Sedan, Cast Iron, Arcade, 4 1/2 In.	65.00
Car, Sedan, Windup, Key, Brown, Schuco	65.00
Car, Space Patrol, Friction, Robot Driver, 8 In.	275.00
Car, Sparkling Armored, Friction, Linemar, Box, 1950, 5 In.	25.00
Car, Squad, Dick Tracy, No.1, Marx, 1950s	60.00
Car, Studebaker Lark, Convertible, Tootsietoy, 3 In.	8.00
Car, Sunbeam Talbot, Yellow, White, Dinky Toy	15.00
Car, Thunderbird Convertible, 13 In.	165.00
Car, Thunderbird, Retractable Top, Windup	125.00
Car, Touring, Friction, Tin, Cast Iron Wheels & Driver, 7 3/4 In.	400.00
Car, Volkswagen, Bump & Go, Battery Operated, White, Race Stripes, Taito	53.00
Car, Volkswagen, Dinky	20.00
Car, Volkswagen, Micro Racer, Windup, Original Key, Schuco	60.00
Car, Volkswagen, Taxi, Tekno, Red	55.00
Car, White Rubber Tires, Wyandotte, 1930s	30.00
Car, With Lady Driver, Windup, Tin, Hand Painted, Occupied Japan	125.00
Carnival Shooting Gallery, Ducks, Windup, Plastic Gun, Ohio Art, 1960s	50.00

Carousel, German, Clockwork, Painted Tin, 9 Figures, C.1905, 17 In. 660.00
Carpenter's Set, 6 Tools, Germany, Box 48.00
Carpet Sweeper, Little Daisy, Wooden, Bissell 35.00
Carpet Sweeper, Little Gem, Girl With Bonnet, Bissell 38.00
Carriage, Baby, Celluloid 65.00
Carriage, Doll's, Cobalt Blue, Blue, White Leather Lining, Fringed Top 275.00
Carriage, Doll's, Green Paint, Double Front Wheels, Yellow Stencil 325.00
Carriage, Doll's, White Wicker, 26 X 27 In. 85.00
Carriage, Doll's, Wicker, Shirley Temple 350.00
Carriage, Doll's, Wicker, With Parasol 275.00
Carriage, Doll's, Wooden, Green, 3 1/2 In. 22.00
Carriage, Doll's, Wooden, Red Calico Lining, Wooden Wheels, Whitney 350.00
Carriage, Horse–Drawn, Lipton Tea 25.00
Cart, 2 People, Windup, Tin, Polychrome Paint, Lehmann, 5 1/2 In. 300.00
Cart, Chester Gump, Cast Iron, Arcade 400.00
Cart, Chicken, Windup, Polychrome Design, Tin, 7 In. 30.00
Cart, Donkey, Marx, Windup, Tin, 8 In. 40.00
Cart, Farm Tumbrel, Farm Hand & Horse, British 22.00
Cart, Ice Cream Vendor, Tin, Windup, Celluloid Boy, Box 55.00
Cart, Jenny Mule, With Driver, Strauss 195.00
Cash Register, Little Folks 65.00
Cash Register, Tom Thumb .... 11.00 To 35.00
Cat & Ball, Lever Activated, Felt Ears, Wooden Ball, Tin, 8 In. 30.00
Cat, Blond Mohair, Yellow Green Glass Eyes, Ear Button, 17 In. 330.00
Cat, Cloth Stuffed, Litho, Weighted Base, Pat.July 5, 1892, 13 In. 50.00
Cat, Halloween, Black, Steiff Tagged, Ear Button, 9 In. 85.00
Cat, Masquerade, Hanna Barbera, Mask 10.00
Cat, Milk Drinking, Battery Operated 75.00
Cat, Mohair, 8 1/2 In. 65.00
Cat, Rabbit Fur, Pull Cord, It Meows, 10 In. 350.00
Cement Mixer, Doepke 150.00
Chair, Doll's, Heavy Wicker, 8 In. 35.00
Chair, Doll's, Wicker, 5 In. 12.00
Champion Weight Lifter, Battery Operated 65.00
Chaps, Child's, Gene Autry, Pictures 45.00
Charleston Trio, Windup 350.00
Charlie Chaplin, With Cane, Windup, Tin 385.00
Charlie Clown, Battery Operated, Box 45.00
Charlie Weaver, Bartender, Battery Operated .... 38.50 To 60.00
Charlie Weaver, Bartender, Battery Operated, Tin, Rosko, Box, 13 In. 95.00
Chemistry Set, Dovetailed Box, Complete, 1934 .... 23.00
Chemistry Set, Gilbert, Tin Box 40.00
Chest, Doll's, 2 Drawers, Oak, 6 In. 60.00
Chick Inside Egg, Tin, Windup 30.00
Chicken, Hopping, Flapping Wings, Mechanical, Tin, Box 20.00
Chicken, Mechanical, Push Head Down, Lays Eggs, Tin, 7 In. 122.00
Chicken, Pecking, Animated, Cedar, 12 In. 30.00
Chickmobile, Peter Rabbit, Lionel 525.00
Chimp, Jocko, Brown Mohair, Straw Stuffed, Squeaker, Steiff, 1950 .... 45.00
Chimpanzee, Brown, Jointed, Steiff 35.00
Choo–Choo, Tin, Windup, Linemar 25.00
Circus Wagon, 8 Paper Covered Animals, Fisher–Price, 1932, 15 In. 200.00
Circus, Cast White Metal, Marked Germany, Box, 21 Piece 350.00
Cleaning Set, Dust Mop & Pan, Tin Litho Sweeper, Box 25.00
Clicker, Children At Carnival, Tin Litho, 1920 .... 20.00
Clock, Hickory Dickory, Musical, Mattel 30.00
Clothespins, In Wooden Keg, Doll's, 12 Pins, 2 In. 10.00
Clown Plays Tune On Zilotone, 3 Records, Tin 150.00
Clown, Balloon Vendor, Battery Operated 75.00
Clown, Big Top Champ Circus Clown, Battery Operated 95.00
Clown, Circus, Schoenhut 75.00
Clown, Drummer, Windup, Wooden Feet, Tin Body, Plastic Head, Black 25.00
Clown, In Barrel, Stock, Germany, Tin, 1908 .... 265.00
Clown, Magic Man, Puffs Smoke From Head, Battery Operated 145.00

Clown, On Wheels, Original Polychrome Paint, Papier–Mache, 5 3/4 In. 170.00
Clown, Performing Acrobat, Penny Toy 185.00
Clown, Playing Drums, Box, Battery Operated 45.00
Clown, Playing Trombone, Keywind, Cloth Over Tin 300.00
Clown, Roller Skates, Japan, Box, 6 In. 250.00
Clown, Spring Seat, Shoots Man Into Trapeze, 3 Clowns, 24 In. 75.00
Clown, Tumbler, Celluloid, Wire, Cloth, Japan 38.00
Clown, Windup, Chein 85.00
Clown, With Mule, Lehmann, Cob 285.00
Clucking Hen, Push Toy, Wooden Handle, Tin, 7 1/2 In. 30.00
Cocker Spaniel, Ride–On, Voice, Steiff, 1950s 425.00
Coffee Server, Dollhouse, Brass, 2 Part, 1 1/2 In. 8.75
Colonial Warrior, Battlestar Galactica, Large, 1978 .... 35.00
Colorforms, Star Trek, 1975 .... 15.00
Colorforms, Wonder Woman, 1976 .... 5.00
Comb Set, Doll's, Swan, 4 Piece 25.00
Combat Tank, Sparkling, Windup, Marx, Box, Large 65.00
Combat Team, Set, 12 G.I.'s, Comet, Box 30.00
Combine, Wooden Front Paddle, Massey Harris Self–Propelled, Driver 75.00
Comic Scope Projector, Remington–Morse 12.00
Commando Joe, Ohio Art, Box .... 100.00 To 115.00
Concrete Mixer, Buddy L 120.00
Construction Kit, No.343, Motor, Hundreds of Pieces, Wooden Box 125.00
Convoy Set, 13 Warships, Tootsietoy, Box, 1940s 75.00
Cookie Cutters & Baking Accessories, Betty Crocker, Box, 1960s 55.00
Cookstove, Queen, Cast Iron, With Lids & Utensils 53.00
Coon Jigger, Somestepa, Marx 175.00
Coon Jigger, Strauss .... 275.00 To 350.00
Couch, Doll's, Bliss 35.00
Couch, Fainting, Doll's, Gold Velvet Cover, 30 1/2 X 13 In. 200.00
Country Camper, Barbie, Box, 1970 .... 17.00
Covered Wagon, 2 Horses & Driver, Polychrome Paint, Tin, 22 In. 1650.00
Cowboy, Celluloid, Japan, Miniature, 1940s 12.00
Cowboy, On Rocking Horse, Mechanical, Tin, Cragstan, Box, 6 In. 95.00
Cowboy, Standing, Shooting Rifle, Composition, Painted, Elastolin 15.00
Cowboy, With Pistol, Plastic, Barclay 8.00
Crabby Lobster, Steiff, 4 1/2 In. 125.00
Cradle, Doll's, Blue–Green Paint, Primitive, Half Moon Rockers, 22 In. ... 75.00
Cradle, Doll's, Cutout Heart Top Crest, Pine & Poplar, 26 In. 175.00
Cradle, Doll's, Folding, Label, Patent 1873 .... 135.00
Cradle, Doll's, Heart Cutouts, Original Red Paint 150.00
Cradle, Doll's, Oak, Blue, Red & Black Piping 195.00
Cradle, Doll's, Oak, Eastlake 185.00
Cradle, Doll's, Orange Red Paint, Black & Yellow Striping, 11 In. 40.00
Cradle, Doll's, Painted Flower On Sides, Pine, 9 X 16 X 9 In. 67.50
Cradle, Doll's, Paneled Head & Foot Boards, Walnut, 22 1/4 In. 135.00
Cradle, Doll's, Wicker .... 52.00 To 65.00
Cradle, Doll's, William & Mary, Grain Painted, Over Gray, 17 X 12 In. 475.00
Cradle, Doll's, Wooden, Burgundy Paint, Gray Wash Interior 45.00
Crapshooter, Battery Operated, Cragstan, Box 65.00
Crawling Baby, Celluloid, 1950s 25.00
Crawling Indian, Tin, Windup, Litho, Ohio Art Co., 8 In. 45.00
Crocodile, Windup, Tin, Kellerman, C.1925 .... 75.00
Cupboard, Doll's, Corner, 3 Shelves, 2 Doors, Tynietoy, 7 3/4 In. 175.00
Cupboard, Doll's, Kitchen, Cream & Red, Metal, Wolverine, 15 X 11 In. 12.00
Cupboard, Doll's, Step Back, Salmon & Blue Paint, N.Y., C.1850, 30 In. ... 475.00
Cupboard, Open, Scalloped Crest, Original Paint, 24 In. 245.00
Dancer, Articulated, Polychrome Paint, Rod, Wooden, 12 In. 55.00
Dancing Black Man, Tin, Windup, W & E, Japan, Early 1950s 95.00
Dancing Black, Double, Clockwork, Windup, Ives, C.1880, 10 In. 605.00
Dancing Dog, Stick In Mouth, Windup 18.00
Dancing Sam, Mechanical, Lithography, Box, 1950s, 9 In. 140.00
Dandy Digger, Yellow & Green, Buddy L, No.33, 1936 .... 85.00
Dapper Dan, Jigging Porter, Plays Drums, Cymbals, Windup, Marx, 1924 ..... 750.00

Daredevil Motorcycle Cop, Unique Art, Box 145.00
Deer, Pulling French Wicker Cart, Bisque Doll, Tin, 8 1/2 In. 275.00
Dining Set, Doll's, German, 1920s, 6 Piece 55.00
Dinner Set, Doll's, 4 Napkins, Germany, C.1890, 6 X 7 In.Box, 10 Piece 125.00
Dinner Set, Little Hostess, Hazel Atlas 45.00
Dirigible, Cast Iron, 1930s 50.00
Dirt Spreader, Doepke, 2 Piece 70.00
Dish Set, Little Miss Muffet, Tin Carrying Case 20.00
Dish Set, Opaque Blue, Green, Yellow, Akro Agate, 15 Piece 49.00
Dishwasher, Tin, Box, Structo 35.00
Dog, Black & White Mohair, Iron Wheels, 1900s 137.50
Dog, Clockwork, Jumping From Hind Legs, Wagging Tail, G.Decamps, C.1900 .... 440.00
Dog, Counting, Tin, Windup 18.00
Dog, Nodding Head, Keywind, Celluloid, Occupied Japan 35.00
Dog, On Cast Wheels, Pull, Pine, Varnished, 3 1/4 In. 155.00
Dog, On Wooden Wheels, Red Ribbon, Bell, Stuffed, Cloth, 5 3/4 In. 20.00
Dog, Pianist, Battery Operated 75.00
Dog, Poodle, Button Eyes, Woolly Ears & Tail, 9 In. 30.00
Dog, Poodle, Circus, Mane, Schoenhut 210.00
Dog, Poodle, Steiff, 14 In. 55.00
Dog, Pull Toy, On Tin Wheels, Plush Cloth Covered Body, 5 In. 85.00
Dog, Stuffed, Velvet, Button Eyes, 10 In. 10.00
Dog, Terrier With Ball, Plush, Windup, Box 25.00
Dog, Terrier, Walking, Hat In Mouth, Occupied Japan, Box, 4 In. 45.00
Dog, Wee Scottie, Tin, Windup, Marx 35.00
Dog, With Shoe, Windup, Schuco 195.00
Dog, With Shoe, Windup, Tin, Japan, 3 3/4 In. 65.00
Dog, With Slipper, Windup, Celluloid, Occupied Japan 40.00
Dog, Zaza The Poodle, Madame Alexander 225.00
Dogpatch Band, Unique Art, Windup, Tin .... 300.00 To 500.00
  TOY, DOLL, see Doll
Dollhouse, 2–Story, Victorian, Porch, Cream & Deep Green, 22 X 18 In. 225.00
Dollhouse, 7 Rooms, Metal, 1940 .... 30.00
Dollhouse, Barbie's 1st Dream House, Cardboard 45.00
Dollhouse, Bliss Type, Fireplace, German Litho, 1900s 495.00
Dollhouse, Bliss Type, Lace Curtains, Turn of Century 550.00
Dollhouse, Bliss, Litho Paper On Wood, 2 Story, 3 Porches, 20 In. 1450.00
Dollhouse, Bliss, Metal Rails On 3 Floors, Box, 19 In. 785.00
Dollhouse, Cardboard, Complete, 1930s 10.00
Dollhouse, Coconut, Wallpaper, Dunham, 19 X 12 X 7 In. 175.00
Dollhouse, Colonial, Wooden, Porch, Electrified, 1960s, 36 X 21 X 26 In. 1150.00
Dollhouse, Dolls, Renwall, Set of 6 .... 65.00
Dollhouse, Dolly's Cottage, Cardboard, To Assemble, Paper Dolls, 1920 .... 110.00
Dollhouse, Dutch, Gabled, Lift–Roof, 1930s 225.00
Dollhouse, Folding, Bedroom, Cast Iron Furniture, Arcade, C.1927 .... 395.00
Dollhouse, Furniture, Bathroom, Folding, Cast Iron, Arcade 365.00
Dollhouse, Furniture, Bathroom, Metal, Tootsietoy, 4 Piece 25.00
Dollhouse, Furniture, Cabinet, Corner, Bird's–Eye Maple 12.00
Dollhouse, Furniture, Cardboard, 1930s, 10 Piece 38.00
Dollhouse, Furniture, Chair, Floral On White, Dresden, 3 In. 30.00
Dollhouse, Furniture, Dining Room Set, Walnut, Strombecker, 9 Piece 49.50
Dollhouse, Furniture, French Apartment, Gilded Woods, C.1890 .... 1850.00
Dollhouse, Furniture, Icebox, Ivory 16.00
Dollhouse, Furniture, Lamp, Tootsietoy, Blue 10.00
Dollhouse, Furniture, Living Room Set, Tootsietoy, Box 85.00
Dollhouse, Furniture, Parlor Set, Table, Germany, C.1890, Box, 5 Piece 50.00
Dollhouse, Furniture, Settee, Cast Iron, Arcade, 1800s 25.00
Dollhouse, Furniture, Toilet 14.00
Dollhouse, Furniture, Victorian, Wooden, 20 Piece 115.00
Dollhouse, Furniture, Victrola, Tootsietoy 18.00
Dollhouse, Furniture, Wicker, 1915, 4 Piece 235.00
Dollhouse, Gray Ranch, Stamped WPA 125.00
Dollhouse, Isinglass Windows, Litho Over Wood Roof, 4 Sides, Victorian 360.00
Dollhouse, Lift–Off Top, Schoenhut, Signed 325.00

Dollhouse, National Guard Building, Litho On Wood, 4 Rooms, C.1910 .... 1650.00
Dollhouse, Roof & Side Opens, Schoenhut, Labels, 18 1/2 X 20 1/2 In. 135.00
Dollhouse, Rug, Tobacco Flannel, Japanese Flag Print, 1890s, 5 X 8 In. 3.00
Dollhouse, Sirns & Lyons, Original Box, 1881 .... 325.00
Dollhouse, Tudor, 2 Story, 9 Rooms, Painted, Canadian, 61 X 39 In. 2300.00
Dollhouse, Tudor, 8 Rooms, Hallways, Attic, C.1920, 22 X 41 In. 400.00
Dollhouse, Victorian, 2 Floors, Paper, Curtains, 24 In. 295.00
Dollhouse, Victorian, Cardboard, Folding, McLoughlin, Box, 20 X 18 In. 700.00
Dominoes, Musical, Theo.Presser Co., Philadelphia, Box, C.1894 .... 85.00
Donald The Drummer, Linemar 225.00
Donkey, Bobbing Head, Celluloid, Occupied Japan 14.00
Dottie The Driver, Mechanical, Tin, Plastic Girl, Marx, Box, 7 In. 55.00
Dozer, Diesel, Windup, Marx, Box 80.00
Drawing Set, Barbie, Electric 26.00
Drawing Set, James Bond, Electric, Box 45.00
Drawing Set, Winky Dink, Box 45.00
Dresser, Chest, Doll's, Mirror, Mary Lu, Cream, Green Paint, J.C.Penney 100.00
Dresser, Doll's, Handmade, Mirror, Pressed Panels, 1903 .... 135.00
Drum Major, Pluto, Windup, Linemar 200.00
Drum Major, Windup, Tin, Wolverine, 1930s, 14 In.Square Base 75.00
Drum, Design On Tin, Wooden Bands, Uncle Wiggly's Parade, 1924 .... 55.00
Drum, Peanuts, Chein, 1969, 9 X 11 In. 15.00
Drum, Tin, Ohio Art 40.00
Drummer Boy, Let Boy Play, While You Swing & Sway, Windup, Marx, Box 365.00
Drummer, Tiger, Windup, Linemar 35.00
Drummer, Windup, Elastolin 12.00
Drunkard, Windup, Top Hat, Martin 500.00
Duck, 3 Ducklings, Pull Toy, Plastic Wings, Wooden, Fisher–Price, 1960s 15.00
Duck, Dairy, Lazy Dazy, Marx 50.00
Duck, Friction, Tin, Gely, Germany, 1912 .... 20.00
Duck, Red Top Hat, Tuxedo, Watch Chain, Celluloid, 1 1/2 X 2 X 4 In. 25.00
Duck, Wooden, Wooden Wheels, Pull Toy, 1935 .... 23.00
Duck, Yellow, Glass Eyes, Steiff, 1950s, 6 1/2 X 5 In. 25.00
Ducks, Mama & Ducklings, Walking, Celluloid 15.00
Dumbo, Windup, Marx 250.00
Dump Cart, Buddy L 900.00
Dune Buggy, Yellow, Tonka 18.00
Egg Beater, 1923 .... 14.00
Egg Beater, Betty Taplin, Tin, 5 1/2 In. 8.00
Electronic Laser Rifle, Empire Strikes Back, Box 90.00
Elephant, Circus, Windup, Celluloid, Occupied Japan, Box 65.00
Elephant, Dancing, Balanced On Rear Legs, Raised Trunk & Forelegs 40.00
Elephant, Glass Eyes, Schoenhut 95.00
Elephant, On Wheels, Painted, Republic, 9 In. 125.00
Elephant, On Wheels, Pull String Growler, Glass Eyes, Steiff, 15 In. 250.00
Elephant, On Wooden Wheels, Stuffed Gray Felt, Button Eyes, 9 1/2 In. 235.00
Elephant, Pull Toy, Movable Trunk, Bell, 9–Spoked Wheels, 6 1/2 In. 425.00
Elephant, Tricycle Spinner, U.S.Zone, Box 129.00
Elephant, Walking, Cloth Over Tin, Battery Operated 65.00
Elephant, Windup, Celluloid, Occupied Japan, Box, 5 In. 40.00
Elf, Advertising, Keebler, 20 In. 58.00
Elf, Push Toy, Animated, Paddles Wheel, Wooden, 32 In. 115.00
Elmer Fudd, Fire Chief, Pull Toy 55.00
Engine, Locomotive, Polychrome Paint, Tin, 12 In. 150.00
Engine, Steam, Weeden .... 65.00 To 75.00
Erector Set, Blue Metal Box, 1935 .... 40.00
Erector Set, Gilbert Mysto, Wooden Box, Instructions, 1915 .... 100.00
Erector Set, Gilbert, Book, Engine, Cone, 7 1/2 In. 85.00
Erector Set, Gilbert, No.1 1/2, Unused, Complete, Box, 1935 .... 25.00
Erector Set, Gilbert, No.3, Manuals, Wooden Box, 22 1/2 In. 265.00
Erector Set, Gilbert, No.4, With Motor No.4 .... 52.00
Erector Set, Gilbert, No.10072, Instruction Book, Motor, Metal Box 60.00
Erector Set, Gilbert, Rocket Launcher 70.00
Erector Set, Mecanno, Instruction Booklet, 1914 .... 100.00

Erector Set, Morecraft, Wood & Cardboard Box, 1946	42.00
Express Wagon, Tin, Iron Spoke Wheels, Small	125.00
Farmer In The Dell, Tin, Hand Crank, Mattel, Box, 1953	25.00
Felix The Cat, Fisher–Price, Pop–Up, Dated 1926	30.00
Felix, On Scooter, Windup, Tin, Nifty	750.00
Ferdinand The Bull, Ideal, Papier–Mache	45.00
Ferdinand The Bull, Jointed Composition, No Tail, 9 In.	45.00
Ferdinand The Bull, Windup, Tin, Marx	100.00
Ferris Wheel, 6 Gondolas, Chein, 1930s	100.00
Ferris Wheel, Mickey & Hercules, Chein	245.00
Ferris Wheel, Tin, 4 Riding Children, Tin, Gibbs	295.00
Fiddle Player, Windup, Painted Face, Felt Costume, Schuco, 5 In.	175.00
Fighters, Knockout Champs, Marx, 1930s	325.00
Figure, Captain Maddox, Marx, Box	65.00
Fire Engine Set, Tootsietoy, Box, 8 Piece	120.00
Fire Engine, Elevating Snorkel Pumper, Tin, Box, Japan, 13 In.	55.00
Fire Engine, Friction, Tin, 5 Firemen, Extension Ladder, Box, Japan	50.00
Fire Engine, Tin, Battery Operated, Amico, Box	50.00
Fire Pumper, Cast Iron, Kenton	68.00
Fire Pumper, Windup, Wood, Tin & Cast Iron, 9 1/2 In.	300.00
Fire Truck, Doepke	110.00
Fire Truck, Extension Ladder, Buddy L	165.00
Fire Truck, Midgetoy	12.00
Fire Truck, Pumper, Cast Iron, Williams, 1920s	150.00
Fire Truck, Texaco Promotional, Tin, Marx, 1950s	85.00
Fire Truck, Windup Siren, Extension Ladder, Doepke, 29 In.	138.00
Fire Truck, Windup, Germany, 1930s	215.00
Fire Truck, Windup, Keystone	135.00
Fire Truck, Winky–Blinky, Fisher–Price, 1940–50	25.00
Firefighting Set, Tonka	30.00
Fireman Joe, Climbs 24 In.Ladder, Metal, Windup, Marx	185.00
Fireman, With Hose, Barclay	25.00
Fish, Windup, Tin, Chein	45.00
Flashlight, Captain Ray–O–Vac, Rocket Ship Box	28.00
Flashlight, Wrist Ray, Mickey Mouse Club	15.00
Flying Saucer, Battery Operated, Tin, Box	60.00 To 78.00
Flying Saucer, Best Saucer Ever Made, Battery Operated, Cragstan, Box	225.00
Flying Saucer, Dome Lights Up, Man Appears In Hatch, Battery, Japan	280.00
Fordson Tractor, Cast Iron, W & K On Wheels, Removable Driver, 6 In.	125.00
Fox, Begging, Mohair, Straw Stuffed, Jointed Head, Steiff, 25 In.	625.00
Frankenstein, Mechanical, Air Power, Universal Studios, Box	60.00
Fred Flintstone, Riding Dino, Battery Operated	145.00
Freedom Train, Mechanical, Tin Litho, Elenee, Box, 18 In.	65.00
G.I.Joe & His K–9 Pups, Windup, Unique, Box, 1941	135.00
G.I.Joe & Jeep, Windup, Unique Art, Box	185.00
TOY, GAME, see Game	
Gander, Long Neck, Rattle Inside, Celluloid, 2 X 3 X 5 In.	25.00
Gas Station, Buddy L, Box	40.00
Gay Caballero, On Donkey, Mechanical, Occupied Japan, Box, 5 1/2 In.	225.00
Gay Goblins, Schoenhut	125.00
General Alarm Fire House, Windup, Car & Truck Shoot Out, Box, Marx	285.00
General Grant Smoking, Windup, Bellows Blow Smoke, Lifts Arm To Lips	4500.00
Gilbert Lab Technician Set, For Girls, Tin Cabinet	20.00
Girl Skater, Metal, Barclay No.177	8.00
Girl, In Sleigh, Tin, Penny Toy	80.00
Goat, Bleating, Mechanical, Fur Covered, Schoenhut	325.00
Golden Glockenspiel, Case, Instructions, 1953	20.00
Good Time Charlie, Box, Battery Operated	80.00
Goose, Lays Eggs, Celluloid, 4 In.	15.00
Goose, Tulla, Standing, White, Wire Covered Feet, Steiff, 5 3/4 In.	50.00
Goose, Windup, Tin, Unique U.S.A.	60.00
Gorilla Shooting Gallery, Battery Operated, Box	95.00
Gorilla, Glass Eyes, Original Label In Ear, Steiff, 61 In.	500.00
Grader, Adams Diesel Road, Doepke, No.2006, 26 In.	165.00

Graf Zeppelin, Pressed Metal, Orginal Paint & Decals, 32 In. 500.00
Gumball Machine, Rocket Ship, 1950s, Box 185.00
Gun & Holster Set, I Spy, Box, 1964 .... 25.00
Gun & Holster Set, Wyatt Earp, Guns, 2 Holsters, Box, 1959 .... 50.00
Gun, Cosmic Ray, Captain Meteor, Holster 23.00
Gun, Derringer, Hubley, 3 In., Pair 18.00
Gun, G–Man, Windup, Long, Marx, 1950s 25.00
Gun, Pom–Pom, Marx, Box 45.00
Gun, Sparkling Action Automatic Pistol, Space Gun 15.00
Gyroscope, Wonder Clown, Wood & Tin, Windup 20.00
Ham & Sam, Kobe 475.00
Ham & Sam, Piano Players, Windup, Tin 350.00
Hamper, Doll's, Pink Wicker, Wooden Lid 17.50
Handcar, Moon Mullins & Kayo, Windup, Tin 285.00
Handcar, Moon Mullins, Tin, Windup, Marx 350.00
Handcar, Railroad, Girard 75.00
Happy Kitty, With Butterfly, Windup, Fur Covered, Box, Japan, 1950s 20.00
Happy Santa, Mechanical, Tin, Vinyl Face, Japan, Box, 9 In. 250.00
Haunted House, Battery Operated, Marx 375.00
Helicopter, G.I.Joe 45.00
Helicopter, Marx, Box 25.00
Hessian Soldiers, Scissors Toy, Pennsylvania, 12 Soldiers 742.50
Highchair, Doll's, Blue & Cream, 1952 .... 22.00
Highchair, Doll's, Tin, Blue, Yellow Trim, Amsco 15.00
Hippopotamus, Circus, Schoenhut .... 225.00 To 245.00
Hippopotamus, Glass Eyes, Schoenhut 350.00
Hobbyhorse, Carved Body & Head, Dapple Gray Paint, Glider, 50 In. 550.00
Hobbyhorse, Dapple Gray Paint, Oilcloth Harness, Stick, 36 In. 550.00
Hobbyhorse, Walking Type Runners, Glass Eyes, Wooden, 28 In. 500.00
Holster, Red Ryder, Leather 7.00
Honeymoon Express, Windup, Tin, Marx, 1927 .... 85.00
Horse & Cart, Pull Toy, Gebbs 75.00
Horse & Cart, Pull Toy, Tin, 11 In. 100.00
Horse & Wagon, Pull Toy, Fisher–Price, Wooden, 16 In. 40.00
Horse Cart & Open Carriage, Cast Iron, Red & Black Paint, 11 1/2 In. 170.00
Horse, Action Clown Playing Cymbals & Drum, Pull Toy, Tin Litho 350.00
Horse, Black Hair, Leather Trim, Saddle, Stirrups, Wood Base, 11 1/4 In. 275.00
Horse, Black Paint & Leather, Wood Legs, Papier–Mache, C.1850, 7 In. 185.00
Horse, Circus, Wooden, Leather Saddle, Dapple Gray, Schoenhut, 7 In. 275.00
Horse, Laminated Wood, Worn Dapple Gray Paint, Steel Base, 47 In. 325.00
Horse, Oilcloth, C.1920, 9 In. 45.00
Horse, On Cast Wheels, Pine, Varnish, Black Harness, 3 1/2 In. 155.00
Horse, On Iron Wheels, Hide Covered, Horsehair Mane, Tail, 21 In. 170.00
Horse, On Tin Wheels, Mohair, Head Down, Pull Voice, Steiff, 20 In. 395.00
Horse, On Wheeled Platform, Straw Stuffed, Red Metal 175.00
Horse, On Wheels, Felt Cover, Wooden, 1930s, 8 In. 95.00
Horse, On Wheels, Papier–Mache, 11 In. 225.00
Horse, On Wheels, Papier–Mache, Painted Black, C.1890, 5 1/2 In. 115.00
Horse, On Wheels, Papier–Mache, Wool Hair & Tail, Victorian, 5 X 5 In. 85.00
Horse, On Wheels, Straw Filled, 1890s, 11 In. 75.00
Horse, On Wheels, Stuffed, 1930s 70.00
Horse, Papier–Mache, Germany, 8 In. 140.00
Horse, Platform, Steiff, C.1910 .... 285.00
Horse, Pull Toy, Dapple Gray Paint, Horsehair Mane & Tail, 15 X 14 In. 425.00
Horse, Pull Toy, Hide Covered, Glass Eyes, Red, White Striping, 34 In. 300.00
Horse, Pull Toy, Mohair, Rockers 1100.00
Horse, Pull Toy, Original Dapple Gray, Yellow Base, 4 1/2 In. 120.00
Horse, Pull Toy, Papier–Mache Body, Wooden Legs, Germany, 11 X 12 In. 165.00
Horse, Pull Toy, Wooden Cart, Tin, Germany, 1923, 9 1/2 In. 45.00
Horse, Removable Rocker, Red Striping, Cloth Covered, 50 3/4 In. 225.00
Horse, Riding, Tin, Named Mobo 150.00
Horse, Rocking, Dapple Gray, Horsehair Forelock, Tail, 1880, 38 X 45 In. 575.00
Horse, Rocking, Double, New England, C.1850 .... 2600.00
Horse, Rocking, Double, Victorian, Red & Blue Paint, Straw Filled Seat 175.00

Horse, Rocking, Hide Covered, 6 Ft.Rocker 600.00
Horse, Rocking, Leather Saddle, Bridle & Stirrups, 52 In. 935.00
Horse, Spark Plug, Cloth, Straw Stuffed, 1920s 75.00
Horse, White Dappled, Platform, Cloth Covered, Germany 350.00
Horse, White, Red Buckboard Wagon, Wheels, Platform, C.1890, 10 X 27 In. 625.00
Horse, Wonder, Mobo, Metal, 1930s 175.00
Horseless Carriage, Fringe On Top, Clockwork Mechanism, 1900 .... 750.00
Horses & Wagon, Sand & Gravel, Cast Iron, 10 In. 130.00
Howitzer, Olive Green, British, 5 In. 16.00
Hula Dancer, Aloha Hawaii 38.00
Hungry Baby Bear, Mechanical, Mama & Baby, Tin, Plush, Japan, Box, 10 In. 225.00
Ice Skates, Long Wooden Pad, Leather Straps, 17 In. 120.00
Ice Skates, Streamline Glider Skates, Chicago, Box 18.00
Ice Skates, The Brownie, Webster City, Iowa 18.50
Ice Skates, Union Hardware Co., Clamp-On, Pat.1899 .... 22.50
Ice Skates, Williams & Co., Wood Pad, Short Curled Blades, 1835 .... 130.00
Ice Skates, Winchester, No.10, Key 30.00
Indian Joe, With War Drum, Battery Operated, Box 65.00
Indian, Crawling, Windup, Tin, Tomahawk In Hand, Ohio Art 38.00
Indian, Sitting, Beating Drum, Composition, Painted, Elastolin, 2 In. 18.00
Indian, Warpath, Battery Operated 35.00
Iron & Ironing Board Set, Child's, Battery Operated, Box 8.00
Iron, Child's, Lady Dover, Electric 20.00
Iron, Child's, Sunny Suzy, Electric 10.00
Iron, Wolverine, Electric 8.00
Ironing Board, Folding, Pine, C.1918, 18 In. 17.00
Ironing Board, Folding, Tin, Bopeep 12.00
Ironing Board, Snow White & Dwarfs, Tin 20.00
Ironing Board, Wolverine, Little Bopeep Litho 12.50
Jack-In-The Box, Pinocchio, Turn Knob In Back, Nose Grows, Poem Around 75.00
Jack-In-The-Box, Bisque Shoulder, 6 1/4 In. 175.00
Jack-In-The-Box, Clown, 20th Century, Square, 4 In. 110.00
Jack-In-The-Box, Papier-Mache Clown, Crepe Paper Costume, 6 1/2 In. 85.00
Jack-In-The-Box, Papier-Mache Dog Head, Woolly Ruff, Paper Top, 5 In. 65.00
Jack-In-The-Box, Papier-Mache Face, Striped Fabric Covered, 7 In. 270.00
Jack-In-The-Box, Papier-Mache, Yellow Hat, Crepe Paper Costume, 5 In. 65.00
Japanese Boy, On Cycle, Pre-World War II 175.00
Jazzbo Jim, Tin, Windup, Unique Art, 1921 .... 185.00 To 375.00
Jeep, Army, With Trailer, Marx, Box 50.00
Jeep, Commando, No.612, Dinky, Box 9.50
Jeep, Friction, Rubber Tires, Tin, Japan, Box, 10 In. 28.00
Jeep, Spotlight, Marx, Box 115.00
Jeep, U.S.Army Amphibian, Wooden, Redycut, Box 12.00
Jeep, Willys, Blue, Battery Operated Headlights, 1950s, 11 In. 40.00
Jet Mouse, Litho Tin Body, Vinyl Head, 8 1/4 In. 110.00
Jet Roller Coaster, Wolverine, 21 In. 70.00
Jigger, Bee Bop, Windup, Marx 135.00
Jigger, Black Dancer, White Hat, Red Jacket, Jointed, Wooden, 12 In. 95.00
Jigger, Tombo, Box 525.00
Jocko Chimpanzee, Steiff, 13 1/2 In. 75.00
Joe Penner & Duck, Windup, Tin, Marx 290.00
Jolly Bambino, Box 225.00
Jolly Jigger, Dutch Boy, Schoenhut 850.00
Jolly Jigger, Schoenhut 650.00
Jolly Popcorn Vendor, Battery Operated 35.00
Jolly Santa, Battery Operated, Alps, Japan, 12 1/2 In. 65.00
Jr.Aircraft Spotter Kit 10.00
Jr.Spelling & Number Board, 1940s 29.00
Jukebox, Electronic, 15 X 17 In. 125.00
Jumbo The Elephant, Playing Xylophone, Fisher-Price 25.00
Jump Rope, Wooden Soldier Handles, Marked Germany 12.00
Jumping Robot, Rocket Ship, Mechanical, Tin, Japan, Box, 6 In. 295.00
Kaleidoscope, Handmade, Wallpaper Covered, 19th Century, 7 In. 195.00
Kangaroo, Boxing, Stands On Hind Legs & Tail, With Boxing Gloves 25.00

Kit, Dick Tracy Crime Stopper 35.00
Kitchen Set, Utensil Rack, 4 Utensils, Pots & Pans, Box 25.00
Kitchen, Doll's, Wooden, 1940s, Box 13.00
Kriss Kricket No.678, Fisher–Price 30.00
Lamb, Glass Eyes, Metal Button In Ear, Steiff, 8 1/2 In. 35.00
Lamb, Pull, Tin Wheels, Wood & Composition, 4 In. 75.00
Li'l Abner Dogpatch Band, Windup, Tin, Unique Art 675.00
Lift Loader, Marx, Box 55.00
Lion, Bubble Blowing, Battery Operated, Box 80.00
Lion, Bubble Blowing, Tin, Windup 18.00
Lion, Circus, Schoenhut 200.00
Lion, Sitting, Glass Eyes, Steiff, 4 1/2 In. 45.00
Lion, Standing, Button, Steiff, 7 In. 60.00
Lion, Steiff, 14 X 12 In. 145.00
Lion, Taylor & Barratt, British, 4 1/8 In. 3.50
Lion, Windup, Linemar 45.00
Little Bopeep, Tommy Toy 75.00
Locomotive, Spirit of 1776 Bicentennial, Battery Operated 30.00
Loom, Hand Weaving, Picture of Children Making Potholder, Box, 1949 .... 10.00
Lorry, Army, Caterpillar Type, British 20.00
Lotus Racers, Corgi 65.00
Louis Armstrong, Windup, Box 250.00
Loveseat & 2 Armchairs, Doll's, Rattan & Leather, C.1875 .... 605.00
Ma & Pa Grocery Store, Living Quarters Upstairs, Handmade 45.00
Machine Gun, Marx 35.00
Mamma's Boy, Windup, Marx 400.00
Mammy, Gravity Walker, Wood, Red Dress & Bandanna, 1938, 4 In. 65.00
Man & Woman, Dancing, Polychrome, Tin, Windup, Made In Bavaria, 8 In. 550.00
Man On Flying Trapeze, Windup, Tin, Wyandotte, Box, 9 In. 85.00
Man With Pipe, Pushing Wheelbarrow, Penny Toy 42.50
Man, Drunkard, French, Windup, Martin Co., Box, 1890s 750.00
Man, Playing Violin, Windup 90.00
Man, With Top Hat, Articulated, Polychrome Paint, Tin, 11 In. 100.00
Mercury Explorer, Battery Operated, Marked T.P.S., Japan, Box, 8 In. 125.00
Merry Makers Mouse Band, Windup, Marx 615.00
Merry–Go–Round, Bisque Head Riders, Schoenhut 1600.00
Merry–Go–Round, Mattel, 1951 .... 65.00
Merry–Go–Round, Musical, Marx, Box, Small 70.00
Merry–Go–Round, Planes & Horses, Wolverine 145.00
Merry–Go–Round, Wolverine, Horses, Airplanes, Box, 1930s, 11 X 12 In. 195.00
Microphone, Philmore Junior, Box, 1930s 20.00
Microscope Set, 125 Power, Geo.Borgfeldt Corp.Dist., Box, 8 X 12 In. 25.00
Microscope, Gilbert, Box 16.00
Milk Truck, Town, Metal Wheels, 12 In. 65.00
Milk Wagon, Chinese Man Driver, Key Wind, Signed Hee–Haw, Tin 125.00
Milky The Cow, Kenner, Box 35.00
Mischievous Monkey, Battery Operated 145.00
Monkey, Acrobat, Windup, 4 1/2 In. 45.00
Monkey, Bubble Blowing, Battery Operated .... 45.00 To 95.00
Monkey, Carousel, Ringing Bell, Mechanical 125.00
Monkey, Circus, Schoenhut 295.00
Monkey, Climbing, Lehmann, Original Tag, Box 425.00
Monkey, Climbing, Polychrome Paint, Tin, 8 In. 35.00
Monkey, Climbing, Zippo, Marx 100.00
Monkey, Consul, The Educated Monkey, Tin, Box, 5 1/2 X 6 In. 35.00
Monkey, Crap Shooting, Cragstan, Battery Operated .... 40.00 To 65.00
Monkey, Cyclist, Windup, Box, 1930s 95.00
Monkey, Cymbals & Drum, Advertising Lone Star Roofing, Windup, Box 65.00
Monkey, Drummer, Plush Covered, Felt Trim, Glass Eyes, Tin, Windup, 8 In. 12.50
Monkey, Guitar Sam, Battery Operated 85.00
Monkey, Marvelous, Tin, Windup, Marx 95.00
Monkey, Mohair, Jointed, Tin Face, 3 In. 65.00
Monkey, On Ferris Wheel, Tin 295.00
Monkey, On Wheels, Steiff, C.1915 .... 275.00

Monkey, Playing Fiddle, Tin, Windup, Germany ....95.00 To 175.00
Monkey, Rock 'N' Roll, Battery Operated, Box 150.00
Monkey, Trumpet, Battery Operated 75.00
Monkey, Tumbling, Marx, Tin, Box, 1930s 100.00
Monkey, Walking, Windup, Fur Covered, Japan, 5 1/2 In. 32.50
Monkey, With Cymbals, Windup, German, Large, 1930s 125.00
Monkey, With Guitar, Windup, Occupied Japan 18.00
Monkey, Yes–No, Schuco, 13 In. .... 210.00 To 295.00
Monoplane, Empire Express, Propeller Turns & Makes Noise, 1920s 200.00
Moon Mullins, Handcar, Marx 400.00
Moon Rocket, Battery Operated 55.00
Mopsy, Steiff, Tag, Button, 8 1/2 In. 60.00
Mortimer Snerd Band, Box 675.00
Motorboat, Sea Queen, Man Steering Wheel, Friction, Tin, Japan, 10 In. 75.00
Motorcycle, 2 Cops, Sidecar, Hubley, 8 1/2 In. 485.00
Motorcycle, Champion, Cast Iron 100.00
Motorcycle, Cop, Camouflage Shield, Windup, Marx, 8 1/2 X 6 In. 85.00
Motorcycle, Driver, Army Uniform, Nazi Wehrmach License, Keywind 400.00
Motorcycle, Driver, Marked Patrol, Cast Iron, 6 1/2 In. 35.00
Motorcycle, Hubley, Cast Iron 25.00
Motorcycle, Man, Driving Monkey On Back, Jumps On & Off, Tin, Japan 90.00
Motorcycle, Mystic, Windup, Tin, Marx .... 55.00 To 65.00
Motorcycle, Police, Side Car, Siren, Windup, Tin, Marx, 1939 .... 98.00
Motorcycle, Policeman, White Rubber Wheels, Champion, 5 In. 50.00
Motorcycle, Rider, Battery Operated 25.00
Motorcycle, Rider, Cast Iron, Rubber Tires, 1930 .... 47.50
Motorcycle, Rider, Sidecar, Cast Iron, Hubley 60.00
Motorcycle, Schuco, U.S.Zone, Germany 135.00
Motorcycle, Sidecar, Harley Davidson, Tekno 50.00
Motorcycle, Sidecar, Indian, Hubley, 1929 .... 225.00
Motorcycle, Sidecar, Windup, Tin, Marx .... 130.00 To 400.00
Mountain Cable Car, Lehmann 35.00
Mouse, Tumbling, Windup, Schuco 185.00
Mouse, With Ladder, Mechanical, Tin, Felt, Schuco, Box, 4 1/2 In. 145.00
Moving Picture Theater, Black Sambo, Playette, Box, 1942 .... 45.00
Moving Van, Courtland, Windup, Tin 20.00
Moving Van, Original Paint, Decal, Tailgate, Son–Ny, 26 In. 395.00
Moving Van, Ralston, Mayflower 18.00
Moving Van, Wooden, Buddy L 175.00
Mr.MacPooch, Box, Battery Operated 65.00
Mr.Mercury, Robot, Marx, Box 400.00
Mr.Robot, Battery Operated, Red Body, Cragstan, 10 1/2 In. 475.00
Mule & Moonshine, Activated By Marbles, Wooden, Japan, 7 In. 30.00
Mule, Balky, Lehmann, 1903 .... 195.00 To 495.00
Mule, Balky, Windup, Marx .... 65.00 To 75.00
Mule, Painted Eyes, Schoenhut 150.00
Music Box, Bird In Cage, Tin, Wire, Wooden, Worn Original Paint, 6 In. 60.00
Music Box, Snoopy, Mattel 35.00
Musician, Saxophone Player, Black, Windup, Tin 365.00
Musicians, Black, Double, Hand Painted, Guntherman 725.00
My Dolly's Nursing Set, Doll, Glass Nurser, Tin Tub, Box, 6 Piece 12.50
New Pretty Village, Boat House Set, No.545, C.1897 .... 95.00
Noah's Ark, 8 Animals, 1 Figure, Cloth Hinge On Lid, Miniature 210.00
Noah's Ark, 18 Animals, White, Red Roof, 14 In.Ark, 19th Century 275.00
Noah's Ark, 32 Carved Animals, Pine, Applied Veneer Trim, 22 In. 1500.00
Noah's Ark, 86 Carved Animals, Wooden, Polychrome Paint, 19 1/2 In. 2900.00
Noah's Ark, 97 Carved Figures, 4 People, Animals, Pine, Painted 7400.00
Noah's Ark, Wooden Animals & People, Pine, 22 In. 1500.00
Noah's Ark, Wooden, Painted, 54 Animals, C.1880, 23 X 12 In. 2500.00
Nurse's Kit, Transogram, 1953 .... 10.00
Nutty Mad Indian, Mechanical, Tin, Vinyl Head, Drum, Marx, Box, 10 In. 110.00
Oceanliner, Arnold, Windup, 10 Lifeboats, Key, 18 In. 175.00
Ocelot, Steiff, 15 In. 100.00
Overland Stage, Linemar 110.00

Ox, On Iron Wheels, Steiff, Button, C.1913 .... 245.00
Pail, Sand, Shovel, Tin, Ohio Art 6.00
Pail, Sand, Treasure Island, Tin, U.S.Metal Toy Co. 20.00
Paint Set, Alice In Wonderland Litho On Lid, Tin, 8 X 22 In. 25.00
Panda, Picnic Bear, Battery Operated, Box 95.00
Panda, Shoe Shining, Battery Operated, Box 115.00
Papa Bear, Walks, Smokes Pipe, Battery Operated, Tin, Clothes, Japan 25.00
Parrot, Windup, Tin, 9 In. 165.00
Pastry Set, Tin Bowl, Grater, Eggbeater, Rolling Pin, DeLuxe Game Corp. 50.00
Peacock, Strutting, Windup, Tin 60.00
Peanut Vendor, Battery Operated, Cragstan, Box 150.00
Pecking Chickens, Polychrome Paint, All Wooden, 10 In. 65.00
Pedal Car, 1935 Ford 450.00
Pedal Car, Airplane 295.00
Pedal Car, Batman 115.00
Pedal Car, Dodge 1250.00
Pedal Car, Fire Truck, Smith Miller 350.00
Pedal Car, Horse & Sulky, English, C.1950 .... 165.00
Pedal Car, Mac 950.00
Pedal Car, Mustang, Yellow, 1965 .... 245.00
Pedal Car, Yard Bird 1000.00
Penguin, On Skis, Poles, Wings Flap, Windup, Japan, 5 In. 42.00
Penguin, Windup, Plush On Tin, Key & Box, 5 In. 85.00
Penguin, Yes–No, Windup, Mohair, Schuco, 8 In. 275.00
Peter Rabbit, Pulling Cart, Little Rabbit Driving, Tin 85.00
Phonograph, Bingola, Windup, Tin Litho, Winged Cherubs, Germany 120.00
Phonograph, Busy Bee, Disc Model 35.00
Phonograph, Kiddyphone, With Horn, Side Lithos, Windup, Germany 108.00
Phonograph, R.C.A., Alice In Wonderland, Characters All Around 145.00
Phonograph, Tin, Windup, Silent Night Record, Zilotone 150.00
Piano, Baby Grand, American Mfg.Co., 13 X 10 X 10 In. 45.00
Piano, Bliss, Red Paint, 20 1/2 X 10 1/2 X 19 1/2 In. 240.00
Piano, Jaymar 25.00
Piano, Original Dark Finish, Schoenhut Paper Label, 19 1/2 In. 45.00
Piano, Player, Tin, Chein, 28 In. 165.00
Piano, Schoenhut, 14 White Keys 95.00
Pianolodeon, Piano, Electric, Chein, 2 Rolls 150.00
Pig, Glass Eyes, Schoenhut .... 225.00 To 375.00
Pig, Pink Felt, Ribbons & Felt Flowers Around Neck, Lenci, 4 1/2 In. 150.00
Pig, Playing Horn, Battery 18.00
Pigeon, Voice Box, Windup, Tin, Wheels Marked Made In Bavaria, 8 In. 175.00
Piggy Cook, Battery Operated 75.00
Pilot, R.A.F., Standing, Arm Akimbo On Left, Black Gloves 20.00
Pinball Machine, Gottlieb Bank–A–Ball 125.00
Pinball Machine, Wolverine, Disney 40.00
Pinocchio, Acrobat, Windup, Tin, Marx, 1930s 150.00
Pip–Squeak, Lion, Papier–Mache, Wooden Cage, Wheels, 7 In. 32.50
Pip–Squeak, Rooster, Pull Toy, Wooden Cage, Germany, 5 1/4 In. 65.00
Pistol, Click, Wyandotte, 1920s 10.00
Pistol, Daisy, No.72, Double Barreled 50.00
Pistol, Flintlock Jr., Hubley, 7 In. 18.00

If you have a battery-operated 1940s toy like "smoking grandpa," you might want to replenish the smoke-maker when it wears out. Just put a few drops of sewing machine oil into the smoking tube. An electric spark in the toy causes the oil to smoke and allows the toy to puff on a cigarette, pipe, or cigar.

Pistol, Paper Shooting, Super-Numatic 12.00
Pistol, Water, Daisy, 1930s, Box 20.00
Plane, Sky Circus Biplane, Battery Operated 45.00
Play-Doh, Star Wars, Kenner, Box, 1977 .... 24.00
Playasax, Mechanical, 20 Music Rolls, In Original Boxes, Q.R.S. 200.00
Playland Whip, 4 Bumper Cars, Kid's Heads Bobbing About, 1930s 150.00
Pluto, On Unicycle, Linemar, Box 400.00
Pluto, Pop-Up, Fisher-Price 40.00
Pluto, Whirling Tail, Marx, Box 75.00
Polar Bear, 2 Cubs, On Wheels, Plush Covered, Glass Eyes, 7 1/4 In. 70.00
Polar Bear, Circus, Schoenhut 350.00
Polar Bear, Fishing, Plush, Tin Base, Mechanical, Cragstan, Box, 10 In. 235.00
Polar Bear, Growling Mechanism, Steiff Tag, 16 In. 600.00
Policeman, Railroad Station, Bobby Uniform, Red & White Armband 25.00
Policeman, Traffic, Arm Outstretched, Bobby Uniform 14.00
Pony, Rocking & Pull, Customized Leather Saddle, Life Size 2750.00
Pool Player, Mechanical, Tin Litho, Hand Painted, Germany, 7 1/2 In. 875.00
Pool Table, Cues & Balls, C.1920, 10 X 19 In. 20.00
Poosh-M-Up Jr.Pinball 33.00
Pop Gun, Metal, Wooden Handle, 17 In. 27.50
Pop Gun, Weasel, General Specialty Mfg., 2 X 2 X 12 In. 12.00
Popeye, Carrying Birdcage, Windup, Marx 165.00
Popeye, Express, Parrot, Windup 175.00
Popeye, Jitterbug Band, Box, 1930s 125.00
Popeye, Olive Spins In Chair Above Popeye, Windup, Linemar 845.00
Porky Pig, Holding Umbrella, Tin, Windup, Marx, Box 170.00
Porter, Red Cap, Tin, Windup, Marx, 8 1/2 In. 75.00
Printing Press, Marx 22.00
Projector, Give A Show, Kenner, Box, 1972 .... 12.00
Pumper, Fire, Hubley, 2 Horses, 20 In. 325.00
Punch & Judy, Stage Base, Black Mammy Watches, Bell Rings, Germany 750.00
Puppet, Dogpatch, Li'l Abner, Vinyl Head, Cloth, Allied, Set of 4 .... 58.00
Puppet, Ferdinand The Bull, Cloth, Composition Head, Painted, Crown Toy 30.00
Puppet, Flub-A-Dub, Push 25.00
Puppet, Lucifer, Effanbee, Black 125.00
Puppet, Mutt & Jeff, Wooden Stick, 11 In., Pair 50.00
Puppet, Ricky Ricardo, Jr. 25.00
Puppy, Happy, Original Box, Key Wind 15.00
Rabbit, Automaton, Irons At Ironing Board, Head Moves, 1900, 14 In. 650.00
Rabbit, Blue Pants, Holding Basket, German 250.00
Rabbit, Corn Eating, Battery Operated 60.00
Rabbit, Drinking Milk, Windup 45.00
Rabbit, Drumming, Battery Operated, Box 95.00
Rabbit, Girl, Basket On Back, Painted Wood, Pull Toy, German 200.00
Rabbit, Glass Eyes, Head Revolves, Carries Carrot, Papier-Mache, 1909 .... 115.00
Rabbit, Playing Cymbals, Windup 30.00
Rabbit, Playing Xylophone, Windup 65.00
Rabbit, Pulling Egg On Wheels, Chein 20.00
Rabbit, Pulling Wagon, Chein, Tin, 11 In. 45.00
Rabbit, Pushing Chick, Eggshell Shaped Carriage, Celluloid, 2 1/2 In. 15.00
Rabbit, Reclining, Steiff, 9 In. 55.00
Rabbit, Sitting, Light Tan & Brown, Steiff, Button, 6 In. 45.00
Racetrack, Tin Track, Bridge, 3 Tin Windup Cars, Marx 50.00
Rad-Cycle, 3 Wheel Cart, Uniformed Driver, Tin, Lehmann, Box, 5 In. 1750.00
Radio Rex, Battery, Wooden Dog House, Celluloid Bulldog Pops Out, 1922 .... 125.00
Ram, Pull Toy, Wooden, Composition Head, Woolly Coat, Tin Wheels, 7 In. 210.00
Rap-N-Tap, In A Friendly Scrap, 1921 Edition, Box 475.00
Rattle, For A Good Child, Embossed Eagle, Tin, 5 3/4 In. 30.00
Refrigerator, White Enameled, Litho On Inside Door, Wolverine, 14 In. 22.00
Rickshaw, Doll's, Wicker 60.00
Rickshaw, Metal, Rubber Spoked Wheels 75.00
Ride 'Em Cowboy, Celluloid, With Gun, Marx, 1950s, 6 1/2 In. 100.00
Rifle, Benjamin Franklin, B.B., Pump-Up 35.00
Ring-A-Ling Circus, Windup, Marx 685.00

Ringmaster, Circus, Schoenhut 150.00
Robot Set, Zeroid 40.00
Robot, Astronaut, Cragstan 950.00
Robot, Atom, Tin, 1950s 195.00
Robot, Attacking Martian ....70.00 To 130.00
Robot, Battery Operated, Opening Head To Reveal Camera, Box, 12 In. 895.00
Robot, Capsule Robo G, Vinyl, Fires Missiles From Chest, 3 Figures 75.00
Robot, Chief Man, Battery Operated, Silver Body, 12 In. 695.00
Robot, Dino, Battery Operated, Head Opens To Reveal Dinosaur Head 725.00
Robot, Dynamic Fighter, Battery, Box 52.00
Robot, Fighting, Battery Operated, Shoulder Antenna, Action, 11 In. 275.00
Robot, Gemini Astronaut, Battery Operated 95.00
Robot, Mars King, Tin .... 150.00 To 175.00
Robot, Marvelous Mike, 1954 .... 145.00
Robot, Moon Explorer, Crank Windup, Red Plastic Hands, 7 In. 175.00
Robot, Mr.Machine, Plastic, Windup, Large 28.00
Robot, Mr.Mercury, Battery Operated, Tin, No Light, 12 In. 1275.00
Robot, Planet, Mechanical, Sparking Action From Chest, Tin Body, Japan 255.00
Robot, R2–D2, Star Wars, Radio Control, Kenner, Box, 1978 .... 125.00
Robot, Robbie, Remote Control, Red Shoes & Hands, Tin Hands, 9 In. 575.00
Robot, Robert, Box, 1950s 275.00
Robot, Smoking Spaceman 650.00
Robot, Space Dog, Tin 185.00
Robot, Space Explorer, Battery Operated, Reveals TV Screen, 7 1/2 In. 500.00
Robot, Sparking, Windup, Argentina, 6 In. 150.00
Robot, Sparking, Windup, Japan, 6 In. 195.00
Robot, Sparky, Original Tag 85.00
Robot, Super Space Capsule, Battery 95.00
Robot, Television Spaceman, Battery Operated, Tin & Plastic, 14 In. 295.00
Robot, Thunder, Battery Operated, Box, 11 In. 1350.00
Robot, UFO Super Hero, Box, Tin 175.00
Robot, Variant of Apollo 2000, Battery Operated, Japan, 12 In. 175.00
Robot, Walks, Windup, Linemar, 6 In. 275.00
Robot, With Spark, All Tin, Windup Key, Sy Toys, Japan 185.00
Robot, Zoomer, 1950s 175.00
Rocket Launcher Set, Gilbert 50.00
Rocket Ship, N.A.S.A.Apollo, Tin, Celluloid Pilot, Spaceman On Tether 240.00
Rocket Ship, Tom Corbett, Tin, Sparks, Marx, 12 In. 675.00
Rocket, Apollo, Battery Operated 73.00
Rodeo Joe, Cowboy & His Crazy Car, Windup, Tin, Unique Art 110.00
Roller Coaster, 2 Cars, Windup, Tin, Chein, Box, 1938 .... 150.00 To 190.00
Roller Skates, Clamp–On, Winchester 27.50
Roller Skates, Remington 18.00
Roller Skates, Winchester 18.00
Roller Skates, Wooden Wheels & Frames, Patent 1884 .... 70.00
Roller Skates, Wooden Wheels, Metal Frame, Patent 1914 .... 20.00
Rolmonica, Harmonica That Plays Rolls of Tunes, Bakelite, 8 Rolls 120.00
Roly Poly, Black Man, Papier–Mache, 4 1/8 In. 120.00
Roly Poly, Clown, Papier–Mache, 7 1/2 In. 105.00
Roly Poly, Happy Hooligan, Schoenhut 225.00
Roly Poly, Pancho, Schoenhut 85.00
Rookie Pilot, Crazy Car Action, Tin, Marx, Box, 6 1/2 In. 275.00
Rooster, Pulling Wagon, With Eggs & Hen, Celluloid, 1 1/4 X 2 1/4 In. 15.00
Rube Rabbit, Rhythm, Turn Handle, Rabbit Dances To Dixie, Mattel 32.00
Sailboat, Windup, Germany, 1940s 65.00
Sailor, Walking, Lehmann 275.00
Sand Sifter, 3 Little Pigs, Chein 35.00
Sandcrawler, Star Wars 235.00
Sandy Andy, Fullback, Tin, Mechanical, Dated 1919 .... 175.00 To 200.00
Sandy Andy, No.60, Box 30.00
Santa Claus, Celluloid Head, Rings Bell, Tin, Box, Windup 35.00
Santa Claus, Mechanical, Celluloid Head, Tin, Box, Japan, 4 1/2 In. 55.00
Santa Claus, Mechanical, Tin, Velvet, Japan, Box, 13 In. 125.00
Santa Claus, On Sled, Tin, Celluloid, Windup, Japan, 8 In. 55.00

Santa, Riding Polar Bear, Papier–Mache, 10 In. 120.00
Saxaphone, Tin .... 16.00 To 25.00
Scale, Tin Scoop, Cast Iron 20.00
Scale, Weights, Ex–Act 40.00
Schmoo, Vinyl, Rattle Inside, 10 In. 45.00
School Slate, Framed, Double Hinged, National School, 11 X 8 In. 29.00
Scooter, Felix 300.00
Scooter, Metal, 3 Skate–Type Wheels 35.00
Scotty, Black Curly, Straw Stuffed, Glass Stick Eyes, 13 In. 50.00
Scotty, Running, Friction, Tin, Box, 12 In. 125.00
Seal, Fins & Tail Move, Tin, Windup, Germany, 7 1/2 In. 85.00
Seal, Revolving Ball, Lehmann, Tin 38.00
Searchlight Tower, For Train, Metal, Box, 13 1/2 In. 85.00
Searchlight Truck, Dodge, Red, Vilmer, Box, 5 In. 20.00
Seesaw Swing, Linemar 50.00
Sewing Machine, American Girl, Instructions, Box 35.00
Sewing Machine, Berlin 40.00
Sewing Machine, Betsy Ross, Portable, Electric 15.00
Sewing Machine, Black Enamel, Bird & Berries, Germany 65.00
Sewing Machine, California Stitch Mistress 48.00
Sewing Machine, Casige, Turquoise, Small Flat Head 30.00
Sewing Machine, Electromatic, Metal, West Germany 30.00
Sewing Machine, Gateway 15.00
Sewing Machine, Hansel & Gretel 45.00
Sewing Machine, Jet Sew–A–Matic 35.00
Sewing Machine, Junior Miss 12.00
Sewing Machine, Kayanee Sewmaster, Berlin 35.00
Sewing Machine, Little Beauty, Germany, 4 1/2 X 4 1/2 In. 26.00
Sewing Machine, Little Betty 15.00
Sewing Machine, Little Lady, Hand Operated, Metal 25.00
Sewing Machine, Little Modiste, Cream, Metal, 6 1/4 X 4 X 5 In. 10.00
Sewing Machine, Little Red Riding Hood 1 Side, Wolf Other Side 15.00
Sewing Machine, Little Sissy, Lindstrom 35.00
Sewing Machine, Sewmate, Red, Plaid Box 30.00
Sewing Machine, Singer, Beige .... 60.00 To 75.00
Sewing Machine, Singer, Dated 1925, Original Box 85.00
Sewing Machine, Singer, Little Touch & Sew, 1966 .... 25.00
Sewing Machine, Stitch Mistress, Blue, Box 50.00
Sewing Machine, Stitchwell 45.00
Sewing Machine, Straco, England, Red Metal Base, Plastic Top 32.00
Sheep, Wooden Feet & Head, Wool Body, 5 1/2 In. 85.00
Ship, Battle Cruiser, Tootsietoy 15.00
Shooting Gallery Target, Duck, Cast Iron 45.00
Shooting Gallery, Mechanical, Pistol & Shotgun, Wyandotte, Box 85.00
Shooting Gallery, Posse, Windup, Wyandotte, Late 1940s 50.00
Skeeter Bug, Windup, Lindstrom, Box 200.00
Ski Ride, 2 Skiers Race On Coaster, Tin, Chein, Box, 19 1/2 In. 250.00
Skier, Windup, Tin, Schoenhut, Box 350.00
Sky Rangers, Windup, Unique Art, Box 265.00
Sled, Flexible Flyer, 3 Seater 100.00
Sled, Iron Runners, Wooden Top, Red Striping, Yellow Stenciling, 29 In. 125.00
Sled, Round Iron Runners, Red, Blue Paint, C.1890, 23 X 9 In. 145.00
Sled, Victorian, Signed Paris, Maine 250.00
Sled, Yankee Clipper, Oak, Graphics 45.00
Smoky Sam, Wild Fireman, Windup, Marx 140.00
Snake, Rattler, Steiff 125.00
Snapping Alligator, Windup, Japan, Box 55.00
Snoopy, Squeak, Rubber 8.00
Snowman, Battery Operated, Modern Toys 45.00
Solax–X Space Rocket, Battery Operated 45.00
Soldier Drummer, Windup, Tin, Red Litho, Chein, 1930, 9 In. 75.00
Soldier, Advancing, Tommy Gun, Plastic, Barclay 4.50
Soldier, Arab, On Foot, Red Cloak, White Burnoose, Jezail 14.00
Soldier, At Attention, Manoil 14.00

Soldier, Behind Big Gun, Red Spoked Wheels, Cast Iron 25.00
Soldier, Bicycle Dispatch Rider, Painted, Cast Metal, Manoil 7.00
Soldier, Black Watch Piper, Box .... .50
Soldier, Bugler, British, In Khaki, Johillco 3.00
Soldier, Bugler, Pod Foot, White Helmet, Barclay 30.00
Soldier, Charging, Barclay 10.00
Soldier, Crawling, Windup, Tin, Key, Marx, 7 1/2 In. 80.00
Soldier, Drum Major, Brown Sash, Long Baton, Britain 36.00
Soldier, Drummer, British, In Khaki, Johillco 1.00
Soldier, Grenade Thrower, Beton 3.00
Soldier, Gunner, Machine Gun, Lying, Britain 2.50
Soldier, Infantry Private, Marching, Tin, Marx 5.00
Soldier, Kneeling, Firing, Tin, Marx 10.00
Soldier, Machine Gunner, Kneeling, Barclay 10.00
Soldier, Machine Gunner, Prone, Manoil 16.00
Soldier, Medical Officer, Standing, Long White Jacket, Britain 6.00
Soldier, Mounted Honor Guard, Banner, Walking Palamino, Wehrmacht 165.00
Soldier, Seated Machine Gunner, Tin Helmet, Barclay 6.00
Soldier, Stretcher Bearer, Manoil 10.00
Soldier, Studying Full Color Map, Officer, Lineol 85.00
Soldier, Tommy Gunner, Cast Metal, Painted, Tin Helmet, Barclay 9.00
Soldier, Union Flag Bearer, Movable Arm, Britain 5.00
Soldier, World War I Officer, With Sword, Elastolin 20.00
Soldier, Wounded, Walking, Cast Metal, Painted, Manoil 6.00
Soldiers, On Horseback, Horses Rear As Knob Is Turned, Wooden, 9 In. 350.00
Somstepa Coon–Jigger, Unique Art, Tin, Windup, 9 1/4 In. 170.00
Space Capsule, Friendship 7, Rotating Astronaut, Sparks, Japan 75.00
Space Patrol 2019, Battery Operated 30.00
Space Patrol, Battery Operated, Astronaut Driver, Lights, Noise, 12 In. 395.00
Space Ship, Litho Whale Shape, Windup, Opens Mouth As It Moves, 9 In. 425.00
Space Ship, Steel, Wyandotte, 1930s 75.00
Space Ship, USA NASA Gemini, Revolving Astronaut, Battery Operated 80.00
Space Tank, Friction, Japan, Box, 6 In. 125.00
Spaceman, Flying Saucer, Sky Patrol, Box, 1960s 70.00
Spaceship, Z–101, Friction, Tin, Sparking Mechanism, Japan, 6 3/4 In. 65.00
Speed Boy Delivery, Windup, Marx 190.00
Speedboat, Baby L, Red & Yellow Litho, Figure & Flag, 1920s 100.00
Squirrel, Windup, Tin, Plush Coat, Fur Tail, Glass Eyes, 5 1/2 In. 10.00
Stable, With Horses, Wagon, Cast Iron, C.1900 .... 495.00
Stagecoach Diligence, Elastolin, 16 In. 50.00
Stagecoach, Frontier Express, Windup, Tin, Box, 8 1/4 In. 60.00
Stagecoach, Overland, Battery Operated, Cragstan 125.00
Starship Enterprise Flying Model Rocket, Star Trek, Estes, 1975 .... 16.00
Station Wagon, Cadillac, Box, 21 In. 150.00
Station Wagon, Tin, Friction, Brown, Cortland, 1940s, 7 In. 20.00
Steam Engine, Tender, Marked LVRR, Black Paint, Red & Gold Trim, Iron 105.00
Steam Engine, Weeden, Horizontal, Brass Boiler, Cast Iron Base 100.00
Steam Engine, Wilesco Model D–10, West Germany 95.00
Steam Roller, Army, Metal, Hubley, 10 3/4 In. 20.00
Steam Roller, Huber, 9 In. 425.00
Steam Shovel, Friction, Linemar, Box 23.00
Steam Shovel, Iron Body & Wheels, Keystone, 20 In. 175.00
Steam Shovel, Marx–Lumar 145.00
Steam Shovel, Pressed Steel, Structo, 16 In. 65.00
Steam Shovel, Tonka No.50 .... 125.00
Steamship, On Wheels, Tin, Germany, 7 1/2 In. 24.00
Store, Parker Toytown, No Stock 175.00
Stove, Daisy, Cast Iron 35.00
Stove, Electric, Green, Cream, Little Lady, On Legs 26.00
Stove, Electric, Heating Coils, Green, Red, 9 In. 20.00
Stove, Little Chef, Electric 48.00
Stove, Marx, 1940s 15.00
Stove, Potbellied, Spark Cap, Lifter, Gray Iron Casting Co., 13 In. 225.00
Stove, Red & White, Tin, Wolverine 25.00

Stove, Snow White, Tin	20.00
Stove, Sparking, Tin, Windup, Ohio Art, 7 1/2 In.	22.00
Stove, Tin, Wolverine	35.00
Stroller, Doll's, Cast Iron, Blue, Arcade	30.00
Stroller, Doll's, Chein, 2–Wheeler, Wooden Handle	30.00
Stroller, Doll's, Ohio Art, Metal, 20 X 12 In.	35.00
Stroller, Doll, Collapsible, Metal Wheels, Metal Frame, Oilcloth	35.00
Stubborn Donkey, Clown, Lehmann, C.1910	150.00 To 195.00
Submarine, 2 Brass Deck Guns, Wolverine, Tin	85.00
Submarine, Power, Kenner, 1965	12.00
Submarine, Seawolf, G.I.Joe, Box	35.00
Surrey, 2 Horses, Driver, Passenger, Cloth Top, Cast Iron, 13 In.	150.00
Swan, Walking, Crying, Wears Top Hat, Tin, Japan, Box, 8 In.	110.00
Swimmer, Girl, Windup, Celluloid	30.00
Table, Nursery Rhyme Figures, Porcelain Top	65.00
Table, Sewing, Folding, Impressed Measurements	45.00
Table, With Drawer, Teddy & Elephant Decals	60.00
Tank, Army, Pop–Up, Marx	100.00
Tank, Cap Shooting, Friction, Frankonia, Japan	65.00
Tank, Premier, Box, Late 1940s	40.00
Tank, Rollover, Tin, Windup, Wooden Wheels, Marx	38.00
Tank, Space, Battery Operated, Astronaut Driver, 8 In.	110.00
Tank, Space, Battery Operated, Tin Half Figure of Robie Driving, 6 In.	395.00
Tank, U.S.Zone, Sparking, Gama, Box	225.00
Tank, World War I, Doughboy Pops To Shoot, Side Blue Gears, Marx, 1936	60.00
Tank–98–Gama, Sparking Machine Guns, West Germany, Box, 1950s	145.00
Tanker, Semi, Texaco, Buddy L	55.00
Target Hunter, With Rifle, Mechanical, Wyandotte, 1940	85.00
Taxi, 1949 Ford, Tin, Meter Box, Battery Operated, 1950s, Box, 12 In.	265.00
Taxi, Skyview, Buddy L, Wooden	150.00
Taxi, Tricky, Marx	45.00
Taxi, Yellow, Cast Iron, Arcade, 9 In.	475.00
Taxi, Yellow, Plymouth, No.278, Dinky, Box	12.00
Tea Set, Berries Pattern, Ornate, Service For 4, 15 Piece	95.00
Tea Set, Doll's, Jasperware Type, Pink, White, Dancing Children, 13 Pc.	78.00
Tea Set, Little American Maid, Mixed Colors, Box	60.00
Tea Set, Little Hostess, Japan, Box, 17 Piece	47.50
Tea Set, Mirror, Aluminum, Cutouts Fit Dishes, 1920, 7 Piece	26.00
Tea Set, Mother Goose, Tin, Chein, 7 Piece	30.00
Tea Set, Porcelain, Victorian Children Scenes, Germany, 1890, 21 Piece	200.00
Tea Set, Wedding Theme, Pelicans, Tin, Ohio Art, 14 Piece	75.00
TOY, TEDDY BEAR, see also Teddy Bear	
Teddy Bear, Bakelite, For Crib	45.00
Teddy Bear, Pull Toy, Gold Haircloth, Cast Iron Wheels, 12 1/2 In.	450.00
Teddy Bear, Pull Toy, Russet Plush, Straw Filled, Wheels, C.1910, 11 In.	425.00
Teeter–Totter, Mechanical, Tin, Gibbs, C.1910, 14 1/2 In.	95.00
Telephone, Candlestick, Dial, Red Tin	12.00
Telephone, Child's, Connect Cord, Battery Operated, Metal	18.00
Telescope, Extends 3 Ft., Picture of Boy Gazing Through Box, 1930s	20.00
Tent, Circus, Schoenhut	850.00
Theater, Black Sambo, Playette Moving Picture, Box, 1942	45.00
Thresher, McCormick Deering, Cast Iron, Arcade	220.00 To 475.00
Tiger, Glass Eyes, Stuffed, Steiff, 18 In.	60.00
Tinker Target, Milton Bradley	215.00
Tippy Canoe, Strauss	125.00
Toe Joe Acrobatic Clown, Ohio Art	45.00
Tom Corbett Molding Set, Box	95.00
Tom Sawyer & Huck Finn, Standing Together, Metal, Embossed, 4 In.	15.00
Tom, Tom, The Piper's Son, Tommy Toy	60.00
Tony The Tiger, Walks Upright, Growls, Marx	80.00
Tool Chest, Dovetailed, Plane, Signed Bliss, U.Union	85.00
Tool Set, Little Gem, Wooden Case, Filled	48.00
Toonerville Trolley, Polychrome, Cast White Metal, F.Fox, 3 1/2 In.	275.00
Toonerville Trolley, Windup, Tin, Fontaine Fox, 1922	600.00

Toonervision, Captain Kangaroo, 1967 .... 10.00
Top, Rainbow, Marx, Box 10.00
Top, Spinning, Colorful Litho, Chein, 1940s 10.00
Top, Whistling, Tin, Ohio Art, 1930s 15.00
Top, Wooden, Metal Point, Red, Green, Yellow Stripe, Dated 1899 .... 75.00
Tractor Trailer, Highway Express, Marx 55.00
Tractor Trailer, Hook'N Ladder, Buddy L 95.00
Tractor Trailer, Trans Continental Express, Structo 45.00
Tractor, 10–Wheel, Mack 165.00
Tractor, Allis–Chalmers, Cast Iron, Arcade 65.00
Tractor, Army, Marx 45.00
Tractor, Cast Iron, Arcade, 4 1/2 In. 45.00
Tractor, Caterpillar, Cast Iron, Arcade 625.00
Tractor, Climbing, Midget, Marx, Original Box 75.00
Tractor, Cockshutt, Red, Rubber Wheels, Cast Iron, 7 3/4 In. 375.00
Tractor, Euclid Caterpillar, Corgi, Box 100.00
Tractor, Farm, Massey Harris, Red, Rubber Wheels, Cast Metal, 7 1/4 In. 395.00
Tractor, Farm, Windup, Tin, German, 7 In. 40.00
Tractor, International, Plow, No.806 .... 325.00
Tractor, Massey Harris, Rubber Wheels, Driver, Cast Metal, 7 1/2 In. 250.00
Tractor, Massey–Ferguson 65, Corgi 35.00
Tractor, Rubber Treads, Electric, Forward & Reverse, Box, Japan, 7 In. 65.00
Tractor, Rubber Wheels, Driver, Cast Metal, Oliver, 8 1/2 In. 250.00
Tractor, Windup, Bing Werke 245.00
Tractor, Windup, Marx, Box 40.00
Tractor, Windup, Structo, 1920 .... 75.00
Train Scenery Set, Lionel Toy Corp, Cardboard, 6 Piece 30.00
Train Set, Electric, Gilbert, American Flyer, Box 65.00
Train Set, Wooden, 5 Cars, 4 Ft. 60.00
Train, Bunny, Pink, Windup, Litho, Chicks, Circular Track, 1920s, Marx 800.00
Train, Car, Coal, Lionel, No.3659 .... 25.00
Train, Car, Lionel, Heinz Pickle 15.00
Train, Cragstan Shuttle Freight, Box 65.00
Train, Eagle, Friction, 1950s 25.00
Train, Engine, Black Paint, Yellow & Gold Trim, Cast Iron, 7 In. 50.00
Train, Engine, Lionel, No.252 .... 75.00
Train, Flintstone Bedrock Express, Box 325.00
Train, Freight Set, Lionel, No.258, 1938 .... 75.00
Train, Hafner, Mechanical, 4 Cars, 12 Sections of Track 85.00
Train, Honeymoon Express, Windup, Marx 75.00
Train, Joy Line Coach, Windup, Tin 130.00
Train, Locomotive, Coal Fired, Miniature, Works 3500.00
Train, Locomotive, Lionel, No.2338, Milwaukee, Diesel 550.00
Train, Locomotive, The Western, Battery Operated, 4 Actions, Tin, Japan 20.00
Train, Log Car, Lionel, No.3461 .... 25.00
Train, Marx, Electric, Tin, 1940s 35.00
Train, Marx, New York Central, 3 Cars, 1940s 85.00
Train, Marx, Tin, Track & Transformer, Box, 1930s 45.00
Train, Marx, Track, Station, 1930–40 .... 150.00
Train, Mechanic, HO Scale, Barclay 5.00
Train, Riding, Original Paint, English, 1920s 600.00
Train, Silver Mountain Express, Battery Operated, Box 25.00
Train, Strombecker, Freight, Wooden, World War II 45.00
Train, Tin Board, Town, Track, 2 Tunnels, 13 X 22 In. 100.00
Train, Twin, Sheet Metal, Battery, Woodhaven Metal Stamping, Box, 28 In. 95.00
Tricky Fireman, Litho Base, Marx, Box 145.00
Tricky Taxi, Marx, Box 26.00
Tricyclist, Clockwork, Bisque Head, Iron Bike, American, C.1890, 11 In. 2850.00
Troll, Dam, Tagged Clothes, 12 In. 65.00
Troll, Gorilla 20.00
Trolley Car, Suburban, Heavy Gauge, Ives 125.00
Trolley, O Gauge, Mini–Toy 85.00
Truck, Aerial Ladder, Original Paint & Decals, Buddy L 475.00
Truck, Andy Gump, Graham 95.00

Truck, Army, Buddy L, 1940s	55.00
Truck, Army, World War I, Tin, Pea–Shooter Cannon, Chein	50.00
Truck, Auto Haul, 4 Vehicles, Structo, 22 In.	40.00
Truck, Bell Telephone, Dolly, Pole, Windlass, 3 Tools, Hubley, Box	150.00
Truck, Buckeye Auto Transit, Ohio Art Co.	42.50
Truck, Buddy L Express Line, No.35, Red Cab, Green Van, Original Paint	225.00
Truck, Cement Mixer, Buddy L	2275.00
Truck, Cement Mixer, Matchbox, 3–A2	30.00
Truck, CF, Tandum, Friction, Box	175.00
Truck, Chevrolet Wrecker, Box, 15 In.	85.00
Truck, Chevy Wrecker, Japan, Rubber Tires, Tin, Box	17.00
Truck, Coca–Cola, Plastic, Marx, 5 In.	65.00
Truck, Coca–Cola, Steel & Plastic, Buddy L, Box	50.00
Truck, Deluxe Delivery, Tin Litho, Marx, Box, 1950s, 11 In.	83.00
Truck, Dirt Spreader, Doepke	50.00
Truck, Dodge Flat Bed, Green & Yellow, Vilmer	10.00
Truck, Domaco Gas & Oil, Tootsietoy	70.00 To 75.00
Truck, Dump & Scoop, Double Hydraulic, Marx, 26 In.	65.00
Truck, Dump, 1951 Ford, Hubley	35.00
Truck, Dump, A.C.Mack, 12 In.	695.00
Truck, Dump, Arcade, C.1920, 10 1/2 In.	300.00
Truck, Dump, Battery Operated Headlights, Red, Rubber Tires, Girard	95.00
Truck, Dump, Ford, 6 Tires, Hubley, 1946, 9 In.	35.00
Truck, Dump, Front Crank, Original Paint, Keystone, 26 In.	225.00
Truck, Dump, Hydraulic, Buddy L, 1920s	200.00
Truck, Dump, K–5, International, 1940	20.00
Truck, Dump, Keystone Ride 'Em, Red & Green, 25 In.	125.00
Truck, Dump, Kingsbury, Clockwork, 11 In.	200.00
Truck, Dump, Mack, Cast Iron, 12 In.	495.00
Truck, Dump, Model T, 1929, 24 In.	65.00
Truck, Dump, Packard, Balloon Tires, Keystone, 26 In.	265.00
Truck, Dump, Painted, Decals, Sturditoy Construction, 27 In.	575.00
Truck, Dump, Steel, Wooden Wheels, Wyandotte, 1930s	30.00
Truck, Dump, Wooden Wheels, Buddy L, 17 In.	95.00
Truck, Esso Gasoline, Friction, 1950s	30.00
Truck, Euclid Earth Hauler, Doepke, No.2009, 27 In.	245.00
Truck, Fanny Farmer Delivery, Friction, Tin, Japan, 8 In.	115.00
Truck, Fire Ambulance, Tin, Blue, Tekno, 7 In.	155.00
Truck, Fire Engine Ladder Wagon, Arcade Decal, Paint, 7 1/4 In.	45.00
Truck, Fire Hose, Mack, Gold Firemen Front & Rear, Tootsietoy	40.00
Truck, Fire, Aerial Ladder, Buddy L, 1920s	400.00
Truck, Fire, Ladder On Top, Red, Moko Lesney, Box	32.00
Truck, Fire, Pumper, Arcade, Pontiac, 4 1/2 In.	150.00
Truck, Fire, Water Tower, Keystone, 1920s	350.00 To 375.00
Truck, Ford, Friction, Mobilgas	20.00
Truck, Ford, Stake Body, A.C.Williams, 7 In.	275.00
Truck, Gas, Cast Iron, Arcade, 5 In.	110.00
Truck, Gerber Baby Food, 50th Anniversary, 24 Made, Winross, 1978	100.00
Truck, GMC, Silver, Tootsietoy, Box, 1939	10.00
Truck, GMC, Triton Oil, Model Toys	125.00
Truck, Heinz Pickle, Metalcraft	98.00
Truck, Hook & Ladder, LaFrance, 1926	75.00
Truck, Horse–Drawn, Ladder Cast Iron, 19th Century	150.00
Truck, Horse–Drawn, Ladder, Cast Iron, 19th–Century	150.00
Truck, Ice Cream, Arctic, Kilgore, 8 In.	350.00
Truck, Ice, Cast Iron, Hubley, 8 In.	195.00
Truck, International Army, Corgi	65.00
Truck, K.O.Ice Wagon, Graham	95.00
Truck, Krogers, Friction, 1950s	35.00
Truck, Ladder, Friction, Sheet Metal, Driver, D.P.Clark, 1905, 22 In.	275.00
Truck, Military, Pulling Cannon, Buddy L	95.00
Truck, Mobil Gas, Tootsietoy	20.00
Truck, Mobil Oil, Friction, 1950s	30.00
Truck, Moon Mullins Police Van, Graham	90.00

Truck, Motor Market Delivery, Marx, 1940s, 14 In.	14.00
Truck, Pay Hauler, International Dump Truck, 18 In.	150.00
Truck, Pennsylvania Railroad, Friction, Sheet Metal, Japan, 6 1/2 In.	12.00
Truck, Pepsi Delivery, Buddy L, Box, 1960s	48.00
Truck, Pickup, 1920s Style, Tin Litho, Friction, Japan, 1950, 6 1/2 In.	42.50
Truck, Quarry Dump, International Pay Hauler, C.1959, 18 1/2 In.	150.00
Truck, Red, Buddy L Line, No.27, 1933, 30 In.	375.00
Truck, Removable Post Hole Digger, Bell Telephone, Cast Iron, 10 In.	355.00
Truck, Sand & Gravel, Marx, 1940	75.00
Truck, Sand & Gravel, Pressed Steel, Buddy L, 13 In.	22.00
Truck, Semi, Tonka, Our Own Hardware	95.00
Truck, Shell Oil, Embossed Lettering, Rubber Tires, Tootsietoy	50.00
Truck, Soft Drink, Hubley, Yellow & Red, Box	35.00
Truck, Stakebed, Hubley, Cast Iron, 5 In.	45.00
Truck, Star Kist Tuna, Tonka, 14 In.	125.00
Truck, Structo, Windup, 1950s	25.00
Truck, Supermarket Delivery, Buddy L, Tin, 13 In.	35.00
Truck, Texaco, Buddy L, 24 In.	35.00
Truck, Tow, Driver, Old Red & Yellow, Cast Iron, 16 1/2 In.	395.00
Truck, Tow, Toyland Garage, Windup, Structo	30.00
Truck, Tow, White Rubber Tires, Cast Iron, Hubley, 3 3/4 In.	20.00
Truck, Trailer, Tootsietoy, Box	235.00
Truck, Transport Trailer, Mack, 7 1/2 In.	295.00
Truck, Turbine, Hook & Ladder, Structo, 30 In.	15.00
Truck, U.S.A.Army, Canvas Over Bed, Structo, Box	50.00
Truck, U.S.Guided Mobile Missle, Marx	98.00
Truck, Wrecker, Cast Iron, Hubley, 6 1/2 In.	75.00
Trunk, Doll's, Divided Insert Tray, Original Paper, 14 X 9 In.	125.00
Trunk, Doll's, Domed, Wooden, Leather Cover, Clothes, C.1900, 22 X 10 In.	450.00
Trunk, Doll's, Domed, Wooden, Paper Lining, Tray, Mirror, C.1880, 13 In.	425.00
Trunk, Doll's, Paper Lined, Lift Out Tray, Brass Hardware, 11 X 20 In.	80.00
Trunk, Doll's, Wooden, Paper Covered, 39 Garments, 1880, 13 X 19 In.	500.00
Trunk, Doll, Black Metal, Blue Trim, 24 In.	45.00
Trunk, Doll, Red Simulated Alligator, Stickers, 1950s, 10 X 20 In.	35.00
Tugboat, Neptune, Battery Operated, Japan	47.00
Turkey, Composition, Metal Feet, Germany, 5 In.	25.00
Turkey, Strutting Tom, Windup, Tin, Blomer & Schuler, 1940s	125.00
Turtle, On Wheels, Riding, Steiff	225.00
Turtle, Steiff, Green, Brown & Tan, Button & Tag, 14 In.	55.00
Turtle, Windup, Tin ... Cover	25.00
Typewriter, American Flyer, Original Box	25.00
Typewriter, Berwin, Tin, 1940s	25.00
Typewriter, Bing, Jr., No.3, Case	50.00
Typewriter, Buddy L	10.00
Typewriter, Deluxe Dial, Marx	15.00
Typewriter, Dial, Berwin Superior	12.00
Typewriter, Dial, Louis Marx, Box	17.50
Typewriter, Simplex ... 25.00 To 35.00	
Typewriter, Tom Thumb ... 17.50 To 25.00	
Typewriter, Unique Art	20.00
Umbrella, Doll's, 11 In.	15.00
Uncle Sam, Tin Drum, Silk Top, Eagles, Flag, Noble Co., 1940s	25.00
Union Station, Terminal, Train Guard, Caution Sign, Tin, Marx	35.00
Vacuum Cleaner, Sandy Andy, Cast Metal	40.00
Vacuum Sweeper, Little Gem, Bissell	55.00
Viewer & Compass, Rin Tin Tin	75.00
Viewmaster Junior Projector, 8 Reels, Original Box	20.00
Viewmaster Junior Projector, With 50 Film Reels, Box	70.00
Village, Hotel, Houses, McLoughlin Bros., Box, 1897	120.00
Village, Keystone, Wooden, Box	90.00
Violin, Box, Czechoslovakia, C.1920	60.00
Waffle Iron, Child's, Cast Iron, Stover Jr.	75.00
Waffle Iron, Wagner	10.00
Wagon, American Beauty	30.00

Wagon, Champion Express, White Rubber Tires, Cast Iron	55.00
Wagon, Driver, Pulled By 2 Horses, Rich, Labels, 28 In.	365.00
Wagon, Evening Bulletin Express, Wooden, 36 In.	595.00
Wagon, Express, Pulled By Goat, Cast Iron	120.00
Wagon, Express, Wooden Bed, Cast Iron Wheels, 9 In.	115.00
Wagon, Hay, Driver, Cast Iron, C.1900	165.00
Wagon, Ladder, 2 Horses, Cast Iron, 27 1/2 In.	375.00
Wagon, New Milk Wagon & Horse, Windup, Tin, Marx, Box, 10 3/4 In.	125.00
Wagon, Overland, Extra Red Runners For Snow	450.00
Wagon, Radio Flyer, Metal, White Tires, 4 In.	30.00
Walrus, Paddy, Steiff, Button, Script, 9 1/2 In.	70.00
Warship, Spanish, Designed To Break When Hit, C.1900, Metal, 15 In.	160.00
Wash Set, Doll's, Celluloid, Box, 5 Piece	35.00
Wash Set, Tub, Washboard, Wooden Clothes Pins	30.00
Washboard, Little Pet, With Sack of Clothespins	12.00
Washboard, Marked Sanitary, 6 1/2 In.	15.00
Washboard, The Midget	32.00
Washing Machine, Sunny Suzy, Wolverine, 1930s	49.00
Washing Machine, The Princess, Battery Operated	85.00
Washing Machine, Wash–A–Matic, T.N.Brand, Box	30.00
Washtub, Doll, Brass, 13 In.	65.00
Water Can, Raggedy Andy, Tin, Chein	12.00
Water Pistol, Repeater, No.71, Metal	12.50
Water Pistol, Sheet Metal, Red Paint, Wyandotte, 7 In.	12.00
Water Tower, No.9, Sturditoy, Original Decals, 33 In.	295.00
Watercolor Set, Wooden Case, German, 1914	6.00
Watering Can, Ohio Art, Indian & Duck Design	25.00
Wheelbarrow, Horse Stenciled On Side Panels, Original Paint	95.00
Windmill, Tin, Litho, Linemar	30.00
Winebarrel Truck, Dodge, Red, Vilmer, Box, 4 In.	15.00
Wonder Cyclist, Boy Pedals, Steers, Bell, Tin, Marx, 1920s, 9 1/2 In.	385.00
Wringer, White Rollers	45.00
Xylophone, Cragstan, Box, 1950s	30.00
Xylophone, Schoenhut, 8 Key	55.00
Yakety–Yak Talking Teeth, Windup, Box, 1949	15.00
Yo–Yo, Duncan, Whistling, Metal	27.00
Zebra, Steiff, 11 In.	75.00
Zeppelin, Aluminum, Tootsietoy	125.00
Zeppelin, Hindenburg, Tin, Germany, 11 1/2 In.	700.00
Zeppelin, Windup, Lehmann	275.00
Zigzag, Black & White Men, Tin, Mechanical, Lehmann, 5 In.	1250.00
Zilotone, Clown With 4 Records	350.00

> Tramp art is a form of folk art made since the Civil War. It is usually made from chip–carved cigar boxes. Examples range from small boxes and picture frames to full–sized pieces of furniture.

TRAMP ART, Box, Canada, Applied Maple Leaves, Horseshoe, Heart, 8 X 18 In.	250.00
Box, Comb, Hanging, Drawer	55.00
Box, Hinged Lid, Mirror Inside	45.00
Box, Jewelry, Geometric Design, Made of Matchsticks	25.00
Box, Jewelry, Velvet, Signed, 11 X 6 In.	175.00
Box, Lift Top, Eagles & Stars, 1901, 12 X 9 X 9 In. ....*Illus*	70.00
Box, Sawtooth Allover, Velvet Lined, Pedestal, 12 X 11 In.	70.00
Box, Sewing, 1 Drawer, Pincushion Top	50.00
Chest, Mirror, Glove Drawers, 2 Lower Drawers, Miniature	165.00
Comb Holder, Wall, Shelf, Mirror	30.00
Desk, Child's, Slant Top, Drawer, Porcelain Hardware, 1890s	265.00
Dollhouse, 2 Story, Hinged Doors, Porch, 4 Rooms, 21 X 28 In.	3525.00
Frame, Chip Carved, 9 X 11 1/2 In.	20.00
Frame, Color, 16 X 20 In.	140.00
Frame, Shadow Box, 19 X 10 In.	50.00
Humidor, Cigar, Inverted Double Pyramid, C.1885, 10 X 11 In.	125.00
Matchbox, Comb Case, 2 Carved Birds Plaques, Silver, Gold, Wall	175.00
Plant Stand, 3–Legged, 27 1/2 In.	30.00

Tramp Art, Stand, 2 Drawers,
Lift Top Compartment, 28 X 17 In.

Tramp Art, Box, Lift Top, Eagles & Stars,
1901, 12 X 9 X 9 In.

Stand, 2 Drawers, Lift Top Compartment, 28 X 17 In. ....*Illus* 300.00
Stand, Lift Top, 2 Drawers, Black Paint, Gallery, 1820–40, 28 In. 300.00

Animal traps may be handmade. One of the most unusual is the mouse trap made so that when the mouse entered the trap, it was hit on the head with a mallet. Other traps were commercially manufactured and often are marked with the name of the manufacturer. Many traps were designed to be as humane as possible, and they would trap the live animal so it could be released in the woods.

TRAP, Ant, Calpro, Ceramic, 1920s 18.00
 Bear, Cast Iron Jaws & Teeth, Tempered Steel Springs, 36 In. 145.00
 Eel, Woven Splint, 34 In. 15.00
 Fish & Eel, Steel Mesh, Walton 55.00
 Fly Killer, Daisy, Flat Oblong Tin, Pat.Feb.28, 1888 .... 20.00
 Fly, Domed, Wire, C.1880, 10 In. 48.00
 Fly, Mechanical, Clock Round 550.00
 Fly, Wire 12.00
 Fox, Herter's 10.00
 Minnow, Glass 40.00
 Mouse Exterminator, N.J.Wigginton, Pat.July 30, 1918, Glass, Embossed 18.00
 Mouse, Bear Trap Shape 15.00
 Mouse, Catch–Em–Alive, Tin & Wood 46.50
 Mouse, Dead Fall, Wooden, 18th Century 440.00
 Mouse, Electric, Directions, Box 25.00
 Mouse, Sure Catch, Wooden 10.00
 Newhouse, No.14, Chain 30.00
  TREEN, see Wooden

Trivets are now used to hold hot dishes. Most trivets of the late nineteenth and early twentieth centuries were made to hold hot irons. Iron or brass reproductions are being made of many of the old styles.

TRIVET, 12 Hearts, Cast Iron, Wilton, 12 In. 50.00
 Bust of George Washington, Cast Iron 45.00
 C.D.Kenny Co., Lettering In Script Forms Trivet 60.00
 Crescent Stoves 110.00
 Cross & Crown, Colebrookdale Iron Co., Pottstown, Pa., Cast Iron 32.00
 Double Heart, 3 Legs, Ornate, Iron 35.00
 Doves, Brooms, Interlocking Hearts, Iron, Wilton 10.00
 Eagle, Heart, Wreath, Iron, Wilton, 3 & 5 1/4 In., 2 Piece 6.00

Engraved Reticulated Top, Wooden Handle, Brass, 15 X 12 In.	425.00
Enterprise E, Cast Iron	17.00
Fork Rest, Elongated Triangle Shape, Iron, 18 1/2 In.	20.00
George Washington, Cast Iron	35.00
Good Luck To All Who Use, Horseshoe, Cast Iron	30.00
Good Luck, Wilton, Brass	20.00
Griswold, No.207, Iron	18.00
Griswold, No.297, Iron	18.00
Heart Shape, Penny Feet, Iron, 6 In. ....95.00 To	155.00
Horse Center, 3 Legs, Brass, 3 1/2 In.	85.00
Horseshoe, God Bless Our Home, Gold Letters, Green Anchor, 1887	58.00
Horseshoe, Masonic Emblem Inside, Cast Iron	15.00
Howell H Rails, Cast Iron	17.00
I Want U Comfort, Iron Stand	24.00
I Want U, Strause Gas Iron Co., Philadelphia, Pa., Cast Iron	30.00
Laclede S, Cast Iron	17.00
Man of War, Iron	15.00
O.M.Co., Cast Iron	20.00
Ober Square, Cast Iron, No.2	20.00
Openwork, Cabriole Legs, Brass, 5 3/4 X 8 1/4 X 4 In.	25.00
Oval, Brass, 5 3/4 X 9 3/4 In.	10.00
Owl, Brass	14.00
Reticulated Top, Brass, 10 3/4 In.	65.00
Reticulated Top, Brass, Round, 7 5/8 X 4 1/4 In.	30.00
Star & Sunburst, Cast Iron	23.00
Tree Shape, Marked Family Tree, Cast Iron	10.00
Turtle, Cast Iron, 9 1/2 In.	40.00
W.H.Howell Co., Cast Iron	25.00
Wire, For Pressing Iron, Triangular, Footed, Handle	30.00

Trunks of many types were made. The nineteenth–century sea chest was often handmade of unpainted wood. Brass–fitted camphorwood chests were brought back from the Orient. Leather–covered trunks were popular from the late eighteenth to mid–nineteenth centuries. By 1895, trunks were covered with canvas or decorated sheet metal. Embossed metal coverings were used from 1870 to 1910. By 1925, trunks were covered with vulcanized fiber or undecorated metal.

TRUNK, Blue Finish & Lettering	522.00
Curved Sides & Lid, Polychrome Tole Design, Paper Lined, 13 In.	130.00
Dome Top, Bunches of Grapes Fittings, Brass Lock, Lid Compartments	375.00
Dome Top, Design On Top, Flame Graining, Iron Lock, 26 3/4 In.	385.00
Dome Top, Pine, Handles, Swags & Arcs, Black, C.1825, 11 X 14 X 28 In.	500.00
Dome Top, Red & Cream Sponge, Boston, 1803 Dated Newspaper Lining	650.00
Dome Top, Red Graining, Yellow Striping, E.D.Initials, 29 1/2 In.	200.00
Dome Top, Stylized Floral Design, Black, L.L.Cover, 1800, 12 X 23 In.	1400.00
Jenny Lind, Leather, Dated 1840–60	350.00
Leather Trim, Brass Tacks, Wallpaper Lined, Pine, 17 1/2 X 8 1/2 In.	95.00
Leather, Original Shipping Tags, Dated 1750–80, Small	225.00
Leather, Paper Label, John Clement's Trunk Maker, Sample, 8 In.	65.00
Norwegian, Old Red, Ola Rogne, Small	125.00
Norwegian, Original Black Paint	195.00
Red Leather, Black Trim, Brass Studs, Iron Lock, R.Burr, Boston, 8 In.	215.00
Spanish, Oak, Sculptured Front, Late 18th Century, 32 X 77 X 27 In.	2000.00

The Tuthill Cut Glass Company of Middletown, New York, worked from 1902 to 1923. Of special interest are the finely cut pieces of stemware and tableware.

TUTHILL, Bishop's Hat, Rolled Rim, Intaglio Vintage Pattern, Signed	500.00
Bowl, Diamond Point Sides, Intaglio Flower Base, 13 In.	600.00
Bowl, Intaglio Cut Edge, Geometric Cut Center, Signed, 6 In.	200.00
Bowl, Mayonnaise, Flashed Hobstars	90.00
Decanter, Green To Pink To Clear, Gorham Sterling Silver Collar	800.00
Jug, Whiskey, Intaglio Thistles, Signed	350.00
Pitcher, Intaglio Pansy	295.00

Plate, Vintage, Signed	300.00
Tray, Ice Cream, Vintage & Brilliant, Rectangular	1500.00

The first successful typewriter was made by Sholes and Glidden in 1874. Collectors divide typewriters into two main classifications: the index machine, which has a pointer and a dial for letter selection, and the keyboard machine, most commonly seen today.

TYPEWRITER, American Typewriter Co., Indicator Type	125.00
Blickensderfer No.5, Wooden Case	150.00
Hammond, Oak Case, 1921	100.00
Merritt Index, Wooden Cover, Interior Cover, Instructions	375.00
Practical, No.4, On Oak Base	110.00
Simplex, No.1, Wooden Base	32.50
Underwood, New York World's Fair, 1939	35.00
Underwood, Standard, Portable, Case, 1920, 10 X 8 X 4 In.	65.00
Yost, No.4, Double Keyboard	250.00

Uhl pottery was made in Evansville, Indiana, in 1854. The pottery moved to Huntingburg, Indiana, in 1908. Stoneware and glazed pottery were made until the mid–1940s.

UHL, Beanpot, Brown Lid, Cream, Qt.	32.50
Casserole, Covered, Rose, 6 In.	35.00
Churn, 4 Gal. ....85.00 To	95.00
Container, Cottage Cheese, Tin Top, Marked Kreem–Rich Brand	42.50
Cookie Jar, Rose	45.00
Crock, 1/2 Gal.	20.00
Crock, 2 Gal.	8.00
Jug, Water, Rose	35.00
Pitcher, Covered, Blue Grape	165.00
Pitcher, Lincoln, 6 In.	250.00
Shoe, Baby's, Yellow, 5 In.	40.00
Spittoon, Blue	95.00
Teapot	35.00
Vase, Blue Green, 3 In.	20.00
Wall Pocket, Cone Shape	50.00

The first known umbrella was owned by King Louis XIII of France in 1637. The earliest umbrellas were sunshades, not designed to be used in the rain. The umbrella was embellished and redesigned many times. In 1852, the fluted steel rib style was developed and that has remained the most useful style.

UMBRELLA, Child's, Carved Teddy Bear Handle	95.00
Dog's Head Handle, Carved Ivory	185.00
Food, White Net, Victorian, 53 In.	25.00
G.Washington Portrait On Horn Handle, Steel Ribs, Ivory Tips	225.00
Gold & Pearl Handle, Black	30.00
Paper, Texas Centennial Expo., 1936	30.00
Parasol, Amber Handle, Floral Black Cloth	190.00
Parasol, Black Lace	58.00
Parasol, Black Silk	38.00
Parasol, Carved Wooden Handle	50.00
Parasol, Hand Painted Scene, Japan, 1930s	45.00
Parasol, Paper, Bamboo, Occupied Japan, Full Size	22.00
Parasol, Tea, Hand Painted Floral, Butterfly, Oriental, C.1930	35.00
Parasol, Victorian, Black Taffeta, Lined, Small	45.00
Pearl & Brass Handle	37.50

The Union Porcelain Works was established at Greenpoint, New York, in 1848 by Charles Cartlidge. The company went through a series of ownership changes and finally closed in the early 1900s. The company made a fine quality white porcelain that was often decorated in clear, bright colors.

UNION PORCELAIN WORKS, Oyster Plate, 9 1/2 In.	95.00
Pitcher, Red, Green, Gold Flowers, 12 In.	250.00

UNIVERSITY OF NORTH DAKOTA, see North Dakota School of Mines

Val St Lambert

Val St. Lambert Cristalleries of Belgium was founded by Messieurs Kemlin and Lelievre in 1825. The company is still in operation. All types of table glassware and decorative glassware were made. Pieces were often decorated with cut designs.

VAL ST.LAMBERT, Ashtray, Frosted Fruit, Scalloped Rim, Marked, 4 Piece	50.00
Bone Dish, Star Ray Base, Set of 4	50.00
Box, Covered, Scenic, Frosted, Signed, 2 3/8 X 4 3/8 In.	550.00
Candlestick, Embossed, Name, Paper Label, 12 In., Pair	110.00
Candy Dish, Covered, Cobalt Blue Cut To Clear, Gold Grapes	325.00
Coaster, Frosted Intaglio Archer Bottom	24.00
Compote, Crystal, Script Signature, 8 1/2 In.	40.00
Compote, Sterling Silver Base, Signed, 7 1/2 X 3 In.	75.00
Decanter, Cordial, Cranberry Cut To Clear, Label, 12 In.	165.00
Decanter, Whiskey, Crisscross Cutting, Square	85.00
Dresser Set, Lemon Yellow & Crystal, Signed, 6 Piece	350.00
Figurine, Pistol, Signed, 10 1/2 In.	60.00
Liqueur Set, Diamond Pattern, Green To Clear, 13 Piece	795.00
Paperweight, Rock, Blank, Engraved PHD	20.00
Plate, Pilgrim Family, 1969	425.00
Plate, Rembrandt, 1970	20.00 To 40.00
Plate, Reubens & Rembrandt, 1969, 8 In., Pair	120.00
Plate, Van Gogh & Van Dyck, 1969, Pair	85.00
Rose Bowl, Cameo, Frosted White, Floral, Signed, 6 X 8 In.	285.00
Sugar & Creamer	35.00
Toothpick, Cranberry To Frosted Webbed Pattern	225.00
Tumbler, Blue Over Clear, Cameo Figures, 6 In., Set of 6	350.00
Vase, Baluster, Clear, Thistle, 16 In. *Illus*	900.00
Vase, Cameo Glass, Wisteria Blossoms, 11 1/2 In.	2850.00
Vase, Cameo, Green Foliate Design, 10 In.	995.00
Vase, Craquelle, Brass Art Nouveau Applique, Signed, 8 In.	55.00
Vase, Diamond Shaped Design, Blue, Signed, 5 In.	145.00

Vallerysthal Glassworks was founded in 1836 in Lorraine, France. In 1854 the firm became Klenglin et Cie. It made table and decorative glass, opaline, cameo, and art glass. A line of covered, pressed glass animal dishes was made in the nineteenth century. The firm is still working.

VALLERYSTHAL, Butter, Carrot Finial, Covered, Milk Glass, Signed	75.00
Dish, Cat Cover, On Drum, Blue, Portieux	65.00
Dish, Dog Cover, On Flower Base, Blue Milk Glass	80.00
Dish, Fish Cover, Signed	85.00
Dish, Fox Cover, Basketweave Base, Label	55.00
Dish, Hen On Nest Cover, Cobalt Blue, 2 In.	45.00
Dish, Hen On Nest Cover, Milk Glass, Marked, 2 1/4 In.	25.00
Dish, Hen On Nest Cover, Red Comb	25.00
Dish, Patterned Quilt Cover, With Dog, Milk Glass, Signed	350.00
Dish, Pumpkin Cover, Milk Glass, Looped Stem Finial, Signed	75.00
Dish, Sardine Cover	95.00
Figurine, Squirrel On Acorn, Milk Glass, Signed	90.00
Salt, Hen On Nest Cover	35.00

Van Briggle Pottery was made by Artus Van Briggle in Colorado Springs, Colorado, after 1901. Van Briggle had been a decorator at the Rookwood Pottery of Cincinnati, Ohio. He died in 1904. His wares usually had modeled relief decorations and a soft, dull glaze. The pottery is still working and still making some of the original designs.

VAN BRIGGLE, Ashtray, Indian Maiden, Corn, Turquoise, Aqua, 6 In.	65.00 To 100.00
Bookends, Dog, Blue, A Mark	145.00
Bookends, Owl, Spread Out Wings, Green Matte, C.1910	135.00
Bookends, Puppies, Rust & Green	95.00
Bookends, Squirrel, Maroon & Blue, 7 In.	85.00 To 100.00

Bowl & Flower Frog, Dated 1915 .... 125.00
Bowl, AA Marks, Turquoise, 5 1/2 X 4 1/2 In. 30.00
Bowl, Dragonfly, Dark Plume, Marked, 6 X 3 1/2 In. 65.00
Bowl, Siren of The Sea, Seashell Frog, Blue 295.00
Candleholder, Turquoise, 3 In. 20.00
Chamberstick, Dark Blue, 7 In. 100.00
Creamer, Turquoise Blue, 3 In. 25.00
Dish, Lilypad, Orchid 72.00
Ewer, Turquoise Matte, Marked, 7 1/4 In. 75.00
Figurine, Cat, Brown Glaze, 15 In. 65.00
Figurine, Donkey, Black, 5 In. 25.00
Figurine, Donkey, Blue, 5 In. 30.00
Figurine, Donkey, Rose, 5 In. 45.00
Figurine, Elephant, Blue, 5 In. 45.00
Figurine, Elephant, Jade Green, 5 In. 45.00
Figurine, Indian Girl, Pounding Maize, Turquoise, Marked 85.00
Flower Frog, 3 Frogs, Rose Glaze 30.00
Flower Frog, Honey Brown & Green, 1915 .... 85.00
Lamp, Leopard, Shade, Signed 225.00
Lamp, Night, Owl, Maroon 85.00
Lamp, Nude, Turquoise, 18 In. 225.00
Lamp, Owl, Red, 6 In. 195.00
Lamp, Persian Rose, Shade, Signed 225.00
Lamp, Swan, Maroon Matte 125.00
Paperweight, Rabbit, Blue, Marked 50.00
Planter, Conch Shell, Aqua 55.00
Plaque, Indian, Blue, 4 1/2 In. 55.00
Rose Bowl, Persian, Initialed, 6 X 2 In. 35.00
Shade, Butterflies, Cylindrical, 18 In. 15.00
Sugar & Creamer, Child's, Persian Rose, Hexagonal, 2 In. 50.00
Tile, Stylized Flower, Green & Yellow Glaze 65.00
Vase, 3 Indian Heads, Plum & Blue, 11 1/4 In. 165.00
Vase, Blue & Maroon, Circling Leaves, Bowl Shape, 1920s, 6 In. 45.00
Vase, Blue, Brown Bottom, 3 1/2 X 6 In. 90.00
Vase, Blue–Green Matte, Flower Stem Design, 2 1/2 In. 20.00
Vase, Blue–Green, 4 1/2 In. 28.00
Vase, Brown Matte Glaze, Bulbous, Thick Neck, 1903, 4 In. 475.00
Vase, Bud, Black, Anna Van Briggle 15.00
Vase, Bud, Midnight Glaze, Blue, 7 In. 50.00
Vase, Conch Shell, 9 In. 25.00
Vase, Conch Shell, Persian Rose, 12 1/2 In. 45.00
Vase, Cylindrical, Blue Flowers, Signed, 12 1/2 In. 70.00
Vase, Floral Handle, Turquoise Ming, Early 1920s, 9 1/2 In. 140.00
Vase, Incised Floral & Leaves, Ming Blue, 5 X 3 In. 40.00
Vase, Leaves, Fleur–De–Lis, Signed, 1908–11, 2 1/8 In. 40.00
Vase, Lorelei, Green Figure, Brown Ground, Logo, 9 1/2 In. 375.00
Vase, Molded Leaf Design, Burgundy, Blue, Marked, 3 X 6 In. 40.00
Vase, Molded Moths, Burgundy Red, Blue On Moths, 1920s, 4 In. 40.00
Vase, Mottled Green, Maroon, 1905, 4 X 6 In. 450.00
Vase, Overlapping Leaves, Blue & Maroon, 8 In. 45.00
Vase, Plum Matte, 6 In. 90.00
Vase, Raised Leaves, Stems, Blue, 12 1/2 In. 85.00
Vase, Squatty, Turquoise, Ming, Signed, 3 In. 20.00
Vase, Symmetrical Flower Design, 1908–11, 2 1/2 X 3 1/2 In. 35.00
Vase, Yucca Leaves, Dark Blue, 2 Handles, 1909, 13 1/2 In. 100.00
Wall Pocket, Blue 45.00

Vasa Murrhina is the name of a glassware made by the Vasa Murrhina Art Glass Company of Sandwich, Massachusetts, about 1884. The glassware was transparent and was embedded with small pieces of colored glass and metallic flakes. Some of the pieces were cased. The same type of glass was made in England. Collectors often confuse Vasa Murrhina glass with aventurine, spatter, or spangle glass. There is much confusion about what actually was made by the Vasa Murrhina factory.

VASA MURRHINA, see also Spangle Glass

VASA MURRHINA, Basket, Blue Mist, 7 In.	115.00
Basket, Rose Bowl Shape, Mica Flakes, 8. Crimp, Rose, 8 In.	175.00
Basket, Twisted Thorn Handle, Mica Flakes, 5 3/4 In.	100.00
Bride's Bowl, Ruffled Rim, Silver Mica, 11 1/2 In.	135.00
Pitcher, Gold Flecks, Salmon Interior, Amber Handle, 9 In.	98.00
Rose Bowl, 8 Crimp Top, Mica Flakes In Swirl Pattern	95.00
Spooner, Silver Flakes	30.00
Tumbler, Cranberry Spatter	60.00
Tumbler, Pink Satin	385.00
Tumbler, Pink Spatter, Cased	50.00
Vase, Autumn, Orange, 4 In.	22.00
Vase, Aventurine, Green & Blue, 4 In.	38.00
Vase, Blue Mist, 8 In.	58.00
Vase, Handles, Electric Blue, 7 In., Pair	95.00
Vase, Jack–In–The–Pulpit, Blue Inside, White, 5 5/8 In.	95.00
Vase, Jack–In–The–Pulpit, Fluted, Spatter, Mica, 5 1/2 In.	55.00
Vase, Jack–In–The–Pulpit, Pink, Mica Flakes, 5 3/4 In.	118.00
Vase, Rose Mist, Paper Label, 8 In.	68.00
Vase, Thorny Handle, White Lining, Mica Flakes, 8 In.	110.00

Vaseline glass is a greenish–yellow glassware resembling petroleum jelly. Some vaseline glass is still being made in old and new styles. Pressed glass of the 1870s was often made of vaseline–colored glass. Some pieces of vaseline glass may also be listed under Pressed Glass in this book.

VASELINE GLASS, Aquarium, Seahorse, Bronze Wash Over Iron Legs, 13 In.	325.00
Berry Set, Diamond Spearhead, 7 Piece	250.00
Bottle, Perfume, Molded Pattern, Knob Stopper, 7 In.	195.00
Bowl, Diamond, Button & Baby Thumbprint, Pedestal, 8 In.	48.00
Bowl, Pink Scalloped Rim, Footed, 8 In.	45.00
Butter, Jackson, Enameled, Opalescent, Covered	145.00
Candlestick, Art Deco, Enameled Flowers, 7 In., Pair	125.00
Candlestick, Loop Base, Petal Socket, 7 In.	40.00
Candlestick, Stretch, 8 1/2 In., Pair	68.00
Candy Jar, Footed, 12 Panel Design, 9 1/2 In.	50.00
Centerpiece, Scalloped Panels, 11 1/2 X 5 In.	110.00
Compote, Cactus, 6 In.	25.00
Compote, Inverted Fan & Feather, Northwood, 4 3/4 In.	150.00
Compote, Jelly, Iris Meander, Opalescent	24.00
Console Set, Black & Gold, Enameled Flowers, 9 In.	175.00
Creamer, Jackson, Enameled, Opalescent, 5 1/4 In.	110.00
Creamer, Oaken Bucket	25.00
Creamer, Panels of Cherries & Leaves, Wreath, 4 1/2 In.	50.00
Cruet, Daisy & Cube	78.00
Cruet, Dewey, Original Stopper	125.00
Cruet, Optic, Original Stopper	110.00
Cruet, Swag With Brackets, Original Stopper	155.00
Cruet, Thumbprint	43.00
Goblet, Starred Loop, Goblet	26.00
Hat, Daisy & Button, Reverse Brim, 2 3/4 In.	23.00
Inkwell, Embossed Advertising On Glass Lid	95.00
Marmalade, Canary Yellow, Diamond & Button, 5 X 5 In.	150.00
Pitcher, Milk, Daisy & Button With Crossbar	42.00
Salt, Triangle Pattern, 3 Sides, 2 In.	15.00

Webb, Vase, Flowering Bough,
Aqua Ground,
Cameo, Marked, 7 3/4 In.

Val St.Lambert, Vase,
Baluster, Clear, Thistle,
16 In.

Venetian Glass, Figurine, Priest,
Red & Black Robe, 14 In., Pair

Sauce, Three Panel, Footed	12.00
Slipper, Daisy & Button, Cat At Buckle	85.00
Spooner, Diamond Spearhead	110.00
Spooner, Stork Pattern	45.00
Sugar Shaker, Reverse Swirl, Speckled	115.00
Sugar, Reverse Swirl, Covered	175.00
Syrup, Daisy & Button, Thumbprint Panels	145.00
Syrup, Double Thumbprint Band, Pewter Lid	80.00
Syrup, Reverse Swirl, Speckled	160.00
Syrup, Rope & Thumbprint, 1884	125.00
Table Set, Petticoat, 4 Piece	157.50
Toothpick, Hobnail	22.00
Toothpick, Reverse Swirl	65.00
Tray, Daisy & Button With Crossbar, 10 1/2 X 8 3/4 In.	60.00
Tumbler, Diamond Spearhead	75.00
Tumbler, Sunburst On Shield	85.00
Tumbler, Two Panel	28.00
Vase, Bud, Etched, Ruffled Top, 9 In.	30.00
Vase, Fan Shape, Opalescent Hobnail, Scalloped, 6 In.	65.00

Venetian glass has been made near Venice, Italy, from the thirteenth to the twentieth century. Thin, colored glass with applied decoration is favored, although many other types have been made.

VENETIAN GLASS, Bottle, Clown, 17 In.	150.00
Bowl, Hand Blown, Applied Design, 3 1/4 X 5 1/2 In.	35.00
Box, Gold Embedded, Pink, Blue Fruit Finial, 5 X 6 In.	70.00
Candlestick, Dolphin, Diamond–Quilted, Aqua, Clear, Pair	125.00
Candlestick, Green, C.1890, 13 In., Pair	500.00
Ewer, Dolphin, 1900, 11 In.	75.00
Figurine, Priest, Red & Black Robe, 14 In., Pair ....Illus	400.00
Swan, Blue Bowl, Clear Wings, 3 1/2 In.	15.00
Vase, Pulled Design, Lion Head Prunts, 18th Century	485.00

Verlys glass was made in France after 1931. It was made in the United States from 1935 to 1951. The glass is either blown or molded. The American glass is signed with a diamond–point–scratched name, but the French pieces are marked with a molded signature. The designs resemble those used by Lalique.

VERLYS, Ashtray, Rearing Horse	50.00
Bowl, Fish, Clear, Signed, 19 1/2 In.	250.00
Bowl, Mary & Her Lamb, Signed Schmidt, Dated 1940	220.00
Bowl, Molded Waterlilies, Leaves, Script Signed, 13 3/4 In.	140.00

Bowl, Pinecone, 6 In. .... 60.00 To 97.50
Bowl, Tassel, Directoire Blue, 12 In. 125.00
Candleholder, Frosted Leaves, American, Pair 55.00
Candy Dish, Embossed Flowers On Lid, Marked, 7 In. 375.00
Tray, Figural Duck, Frosted 30.00
Vase, Alpine Thistle, Clear & Frosted 195.00
Vase, Frosted Lovebirds On Base, 4 1/2 X 6 1/2 In. .... 55.00 To 75.00
Vase, Grasshopper, Frosted, Signed, 5 1/4 In. 95.00
Vase, Lovebirds, Signed, 6 1/2 X 4 In. .... 50.00 To 125.00
Vase, Mandarin, Signed, 10 In. 160.00
Vase, Thistle, Signed, 10 In. 250.00

Vernon Potteries, Ltd., started in Vernon, California, in 1931. It became Vernon Kilns by 1948. The company made dinnerware and figurines until it closed in 1958. Collectors search for the brightly colored dinnerware and the pieces designed by Rockwell Kent, Walt Disney, and Don Blanding.

VERNON KILNS, Bowl, Cereal, Hawaiian Flowers 4.00
Bowl, Fantasia, 1940 .... 150.00
Bowl, Fruit, California, 9 In. 10.00
Bowl, Monterey, 5 1/2 In. 4.00
Bowl, Mushroom, Fantasia, Pink, Not Decorated 95.00
Bowl, Organdie, 8 3/4 In. 5.00
Bowl, Vegetable, Organdie, Divided, 10 In. 20.00
Bowl, Winged Nymph, Turquoise 45.00
Casserole, Cattail, Covered 25.00
Casserole, Gingham, Covered, 8 In. 30.00
Charger, Salamina, Rockwell Kent, 16 1/2 In. 230.00
Chicken Pie Server, Covered, Gingham, Stick Handle 15.00
Chop Plate, Medicine Man, 8 1/2 In. 30.00
Chop Plate, Old West, The Fleecing, 8 1/2 In. 30.00
Chop Plate, Organdie, 12 In. 12.00
Chop Plate, Pueblo, Old Southwest 50.00
Cookie Jar, Little Red Riding Hood 65.00
Creamer, Homespun 10.00
Cup & Saucer, Cattail 7.00
Cup & Saucer, Modern California, Blue, Demitasse 10.00
Cup & Saucer, Organdie 8.00
Cup & Saucer, Raffia, Large 50.00
Cup & Saucer, Yosemite, Demitasse 20.00
Cup, Hawaiian Flowers 10.00
Dish, Soup, Tam-O'-Shanter, 8 1/2 In. 10.00
Dish, Tidbit, Brown-Eyed Susan, 3 Tiers 17.00
Eggcup, California, Blue 8.00
Gravy Boat, Gingham 7.50
Mug, Homespun, Straight Side, 3 1/2 In. 12.00
Plate, California, Yellow, 10 1/2 In. 5.00
Plate, Dinner, Hawaiian Flowers, Ultra Shape, 8 1/2 In. 30.00
Plate, Floral, Hand Painted, 5 Color, 12 1/4 In. 60.00
Plate, Franz Liszt 15.00
Plate, General MacArthur .... 14.00 To 20.00
Plate, Grand Canyon Park, 10 In. 6.50
Plate, Hawaiian Flowers, 10 1/2 In. .... 5.00 To 12.00
Plate, Hawaiian Flowers, Don Blanding, Blue, White, 12 In. 15.00
Plate, Homespun, 6 1/4 In. 1.25
Plate, Lei Lani, 10 1/2 In. 30.00
Plate, Los Angeles, City of Angels, Blue 20.00
Plate, Louisiana 7.00
Plate, Minnesota, Blue & White, 1948 .... 6.50
Plate, Mission, Santa Barbara 12.00
Plate, Organdie, 7 In. 4.25
Plate, Republican Convention, 1956, 13 In. 35.00
Plate, Salamina, 8 1/2 In. 45.00
Plate, Salamina, Rockwell Kent, 10 1/2 In. 18.00

Plate, Scene, Miami, 10 1/2 In.	20.00
Platter, Gingham, Round, 12 In.	10.00
Platter, Organdie, 11 1/2 In.	25.00
Platter, Salamina, 14 In.	115.00
Salt & Pepper, Organdie	5.00
Server, Tidbit, Organdie, 2 Tier	18.00
Sugar & Creamer, Gingham	10.00
Syrup, Drip Cut Top, Organdie	45.00
Tea Set, Hawaiian Flowers, Blue, 3 Piece	45.00
Teapot, Little Red Riding Hood	125.00
Teapot, Yellow	20.00
Tray, Canape, Hawaiian Coral, Divided	20.00

Verre de soie glass was first made by Frederick Carder at the Steuben Glass Works from about 1905 to 1930. It is an iridescent glass of soft white or very, very pale green. The name means glass of silk, and it does resemble silk. Other factories have made verre de soie, and some of the English examples were made of different colors. Verre de soie is an art glass and is not related to the iridescent, pressed, white Carnival glass mistakenly called by its name.

VERRE DE SOIE, see also Steuben

VERRE DE SOIE, Bowl & Saucer, Cut Floral Design, Steuben, 4 3/4 In. Bowl	75.00
Candlestick, No.5194, 12 In.	95.00
Goblet, Pink Trim On Foot & Rim, Steuben, 5 1/2 In.	175.00
Perfume Bottle, Pastel Blue Stopper, Marked, 10 3/4 In.	365.00
Perfume Bottle, Pink, Dabber Stopper, Steuben	185.00
Perfume Bottle, Rose, Jade Stopper, Steuben, 2 1/2 In.	150.00
Salt, Frosted, Flaring Bowl On Pedestal, 1 1/2 In.	65.00
Sherbet, Underplate, Steuben, 4 Sets	800.00
Tumble–Up, Steuben, 7 In.	185.00
Vase, Flared Ruffled Top, Steuben, Signed, 3 In.	125.00

Vienna Art plates are round metal serving trays produced at the turn of the century. The designs, copied from Royal Vienna porcelain plates, usually featured a portrait of a woman encircled by a wide, ornate border. Many were used as advertising or promotional items and were produced in Coshocton, Ohio, by J.F. Meeks Tuscarora Advertising Co. and H.D. Beach's Standard Advertising Co.

VIENNA ART, Plate, Jamestown, 1907	95.00
Plate, Madonna Della Sedia, Anheuser–Busch, 10 In.	65.00
Plate, Mythological Scene, Tin	55.00

VIENNA, see Royal Vienna

The Villeroy & Boch Pottery of Mettlach was founded in 1841. The firm made many types of pottery, including the famous Mettlach steins. It is confusing for the collector because although Villeroy and Boch made most of its pieces in the city of Mettlach, Germany, they also had factories in other locations. There is a dating code impressed on the bottom of most pieces that makes it possible to determine the age of the piece.

VILLEROY & BOCH, see also Mettlach

VILLEROY & BOCH, Chamberstick, Black, 13 In.	50.00
Cigar Holder, Ashtray, Art Deco, Paper Label, 1930s, 6 In.	50.00
Hot Plate, Gold Greek Key Rim, Green, 4 Feet, 7 In.	27.50
Mug, Hires Root Beer, Join Health & Cheer	130.00 To 160.00
Plate, Gaudy Stick Spatter, Floral, Marked, 9 In.	55.00
Plate, Holy Family, Gemalde Von Rembrandt, 1977	198.00
Server, Asparagus, Lid Forms Handle, Silver Plated Holder	40.00
Vase, Art Deco Design, Signed, 12 In.	85.00
Vase, Cherubs, Applied Flowers, Gray Ground, Marked, 12 In.	295.00

VOLKMAR
Corona N.Y.

Volkmar pottery was made by Charles Volkmar of New York from 1879 to about 1911. He was associated with several firms, including the Volkmar Ceramic Company, Volkmar and Cory, and Charles Volkmar and Son. Volkmar had been a painter, and his designs often look like oil paintings drawn on pottery.

VOLKMAR, Lamp, Blended Colors, Arts & Crafts 225.00
   Vase, Green, 5 1/2 In. 150.00

Volkstadt was a soft–paste porcelain manufactory started in 1760 by Georg Heinrich Macheleid at Volkstadt, Thuringia. Volkstadt–Rudolstadt was a porcelain factory started at Volkstadt–Rudolstadt by Beyer and Bock in 1890. Most pieces seen in shops today are from the later factory.

VOLKSTADT, Figurine, Man Proposing To Lady, Cupid & Putto, 7 In. 225.00
   **WALLACE NUTTING photographs are listed under Print, Nutting. His
reproduction furniture is listed under Furniture.**

Frederich Walrath was a potter who worked in New York City, Rochester, New York, and at the Newcomb Pottery in New Orleans, Louisiana. He died in 1920. Pieces listed here are from his Rochester period.

WALRATH, Bowl, Figural Nude On Pedestal, 8 In. 500.00
   Flower Frog, Figural, Nude 300.00
   Vase, Green Matte Glaze, 6 1/4 In. 90.00
   WALT DISNEY, see Disneyana
   WALTER, see A. Walter

IOGA

Warwick china was made in Wheeling, West Virginia, in a pottery working from 1887 to 1951. Many pieces were made with hand painted or decal decorations. The most familiar Warwick has a shaded brown background. The name "Warwick" is part of the mark and sometimes the word "IOGA" is also included.

WARWICK, Chocolate Pot, Brown Glaze 75.00
   Cup & Plate, Oswald Rabbit, 1946 .... 35.00
   Flower Frog, In Water Lily 65.00
   Humidor, Covered, Monk, IOGA 95.00
   Humidor, Down East Fisherman, Smoking Pipe, Gold, IOGA, 6 1/2 In. 215.00
   Mug, Bulldog, IOGA 85.00
   Pitcher, Monk, Dark Brown, IOGA, Large 125.00
   Plate, Catfish, 9 1/2 In. .... 55.00 To 95.00
   Plate, Monk, Reading, IOGA, 9 1/2 In. 50.00
   Spittoon, Floral, IOGA 105.00
   Tankard, Mug, IOGA, 3 In. 245.00
   Tobacco Jar, Metal Lid, Champion Rodney Stone On Side, Bulldog 150.00
   Vase, Blonde, IOGA, 11 In. 300.00
   Vase, Brown Floral, IOGA, 12 1/2 In. 65.00
   Vase, Charcoal, Girl, Portrait In Full Color, Twig Handle, 11 In. 165.00
   Vase, Gypsy Decal, Twig Handles, Red, 10 1/2 In. 50.00
   Vase, Lady, Rose In Teeth, Peacock Feather In Hat, IOGA, 8 In. 95.00
   Vase, Monk, IOGA, 11 In. 195.00
   Vase, Poinsettia, Twist Handles, IOGA, 11 3/4 In. 98.00
   Vase, Ring Handles, Stork Design, IOGA, Signed, 11 1/2 In. 195.00

Watch fobs were worn on watch chains. They were popular during Victorian times and after. Many styles, especially advertising designs, are still made today.

WATCH FOB, 1893 World's Fair 20.00
   1st Vermont National Guard Encampment, 1910 .... 32.00
   3 Little Pigs 12.00
   Abraham Fur, Green Ground 75.00
   Adamant Suits 15.00
   Admiral Dewey, Welcome Home Hero, Flagship Olympic, Brass 20.00
   Advance Dairy Mfg., Commercial Ice Cream Machine 50.00

Advance Rumely	75.00
Altman Taylor Rooster	75.00
American Legion, 11th Annual Convention, 1929	16.00
Anaconda Co., Butte, Mt.	60.00
Anheuser–Busch, Sterling, With Chain	65.00
Atlantic City, Billiken Front, R.O.J.31st Meeting, 1948	24.00
Atlas Life Insurance	20.00
Avery Tractor ....45.00 To 50.00	
Babe Ruth, Score Keeper On Back	100.00
BPOE, Elk's Tooth, 18K Gold	135.00
Braided Human Hair, Watch Chain, Victorian	75.00
Bucyrus Erie Machinery	45.00
Buffalo Bill–Pawnee Bill	75.00
Buffalo Steam Roller Co.	135.00
Buick, Celluloid, Blue & White	75.00
Bull Durham, Figural Bull, 14K Gold Plate	30.00
Bulldog, Cigar Cutter, Sign of The Bulldog, John W.Merriam Co.	95.00
Case Eagle, Oval	40.00
Cherry Smash, Celluloid Insert	115.00
Chicago Technical College, Leather Strap, 1930	15.00
Cleveland Tractor Co.	15.00
Dairymen Convention, Cow & Milk Bucket, 1912	50.00
Dead Shot Powder, Celluloid Center ....175.00 To 250.00	
Dixie Kid Cut Plug, Embossed, Kid, 1 7/8 X 1 1/2 In.	125.00
Doctor's Bag, Figural, Sterling Silver	55.00
Dutch Cleanser	20.00
East Buffalo Brewery Lager Beer	38.00
Elephant, Green Glass, Blue Nixon Name Each Side, 1 1/4 In.	35.00
Elk's Tooth, Gold Filled Setting, 1910	45.00
Excelsior Henderson Motorcycle	100.00
Flying Bird, Heintz	85.00
Ford, Tractor With Frontloader, Backhoe, Nickel Plate On Brass	60.00
Fordson Tractor ....50.00 To 85.00	
Franklin Fire Insurance, Obverse, Fire Pumper, Brass	30.00
Gardner–Denver, Jackhammer Shape	14.00
Goodrich Steamship Lines	45.00
Goodyear, Tire Encircling Globe, Enamel	65.00
GOP Elephant, Brass, Raised Trunk & Foot, 1 3/4 In.	18.00
Green River Whiskey, Embossed, Black Man, Horse, 1907	95.00
Grit, Authorized Salesman, Clover & Horseshoe Back, Brass	20.00
Halcomb Steel	15.00
Hamilton–Brown Shoes	45.00
Heider Tractor	90.00
Heinz Pure Food Products	35.00
Human Hair, Braided	195.00
Hupmobile, Porcelain	200.00
Indian Head, Brass	32.00
Indian Motorcycle, C.1920	50.00
Interlocking Stove Silo Co., Cows, Silo, Wichita, Kans.	50.00
International Harvester, Red, White & Blue Enamel On Brass	55.00
Jersey Cream Whiskey	20.00

Go outside and try to read your house numbers from the street. If you can't read them, get new, larger ones. Police, responding to an emergency, must be able to see the numbers in your address.

Jess Willard, World Champion, Stamped Metal, Painted, 1 1/2 In. 25.00
John Deere, Brass 50.00
John Deere, Embossed Deer Bust 30.00
Kellogg's Toasted Corn Flakes, Box Shape, Brass .... 50.00 To 75.00
Keystone Overalls 18.00
Lady's, P.H.Hadley, Bellows Falls, Vt., Sterling Silver 15.00
Lava Soap, Celluloid 25.00
Lehigh Portland Cement 25.00
LeTourneau 150.00
Lewis & Clark Exposition, 1905 .... 90.00
Lovell & Covel Chocolates 15.00
Marion Power Shovel Co. 40.00
McCormick Line, Globe Shape, Brass, 1 In. 12.00
Military Order of Serpent, Bucyrus, O., Leather Strap, 1927 .... 5.00
Monarch Paint, Metal, Celluloid Center 16.00
Napoleon In Relief, Napoleon Flour, Brass 45.00
Nash Hardware Co., Panther Cutlery, Ft.Worth, Texas 50.00
Old Dutch Cleanser, Blue, White Lady, Embossed Yellow Porcelain 40.00
Old Reliable Coffee, Brass 35.00
P & H Steamshovel 20.00
Panama Pacific Exposition, San Francisco, 1915 .... 37.50
Phoenix Brewery .... 35.00 To 40.00
Port Huron Steam Tractor 165.00
Primrose Separator 60.00
Red Diamond Overalls, Celluloid 20.00
Remington Ilion, N.Y., 1916 .... 175.00
Russell Grader 15.00
Savage Arms, Indian With Rifle 70.00
Sharples Separator 50.00
Shell Oil Co. 120.00
Sherburne R.R.Supplies 50.00
Spanish War Veterans, Bronze, Leather Strap, 1902, 1 1/2 In. 6.00
Taft & Sherman, Celluloid Button, Manmade Fob, 1908, 2 In. 25.00
Trojan Yale Mover, Brass, Embossed Farm Machinery 10.00
True Tagg Paint, Painter Kissing Lady, Painting Man's Nose 75.00
U.S.Naval Fleet, 1908, Leather Strap, Marked, 1 1/2 In. 12.00
U.S.Steel, Sterling Silver 22.00
Velvet Tobacco, Enameled Brass, 1900s 58.00
Wallis Tractor, Strap Type 90.00
William J.Bryan 79.00
Wisconsin Butter Maker's Assoc., 1911 .... 12.00
Wizard Shoes, Celluloid 25.00
Wrestlers, Brass 27.50

The pocket watch was important in Victorian times because it was not until World War I that the wristwatch was used. All types of watches are collected: silver, gold, or plated. Watches are listed by company name or by style.

WATCH, Acutron, Wristwatch, Date Display, 18K Gold, 1970s 500.00
  Acutron, Wristwatch, M–7, Stainless, Spaceview, Pigskin Strap 200.00
  Appleton, Pocket, Original Case 295.00
  Auburndale, Wristwatch, Porcelain Dial, 10–Min.Timer, Pat.1879 .... 249.00
  Aurora, Pocket, 15 Jewel 150.00
  B.W.Raymond, Pocket, Indicator, 23 Jewel 450.00
  Barbie, Wristwatch 15.00
  Bartlett, Pocket, Coin Silver, Keywind 70.00
  Barwise Watch Co., Pocket, Open Face, Silver, 18 Size, 1875 .... 410.00
  Bovet, Pocket, Open Face, Jump Second, Pearl Face, 1850 .... 1210.00
  Bradley, Wristwatch, Star Wars, 3CPO & R2D2, Box, 1977 .... 45.00
  Breitling, 18K Gold, Premier Chromo 225.00
  Bullingford, English Verge Chain Drive, Pair Case, C.1780 .... 135.00
  Bulova, Wristwatch, Lady's, 10K Gold, 4 Diamonds, 23 Jewel 200.00
  Bulova, Wristwatch, Lady's, 14K Gold Case, Gold Filled Stretch Band 175.00
  Bunn Illinois, Pocket, 21 Jewel, Porcelain Dial, 60–Hour Movement 349.00

Burlington, Pocket, Gold Case, 21 Jewel	130.00
Calame Robert, Pocket, Hunting, Enamel & Pearl	3120.00
Cartier, Wristwatch, Lady's, 18K Gold, 18 Jewel, Platinum, 1930	5225.00
Columbus, Pocket, 15 Jewel	60.00
Cressarow, Wristwatch, White Gold, Diamonds ....*Illus*	100.00
Cyma, Wristwatch, Man's, 14K Gold, 1950	100.00
Diadem, Hunting, Deuber Special, Anchor, C.1889	150.00
Dick Tracy, Wristwatch	69.00
Elgin, Pin On, Lady's, Art Deco, 14k Gold	100.00
Elgin, Pocket, Hunting, 14K Gold, Enamel Dial, Floral Engraved	250.00
Elgin, Pocket, Hunting, 14K Gold, Nickel Movement	110.00
Elgin, Pocket, Hunting, Lever Set, 14K Gold, 15 Jewel, 12 Size	250.00
Elgin, Pocket, Hunting, Railway Timer, Birds, 17 Jewel	725.00
Elgin, Pocket, Hunting, Roman Numerals, Porcelain Dial, 14K Gold	250.00
Elgin, Pocket, Hunting, Silver, Keywind, Used On Ocean Liner	625.00
Elgin, Pocket, Lady's, Monogram, 14K Gold, 1918	125.00
Elgin, Pocket, National, H.H.Taylor, Roman Numerls, Second Hand	225.00
Elgin, Pocket, Open Face, Sterling, Engraved Design	48.00
Elgin, Pocket, Porcelain Face, Silverine Case, 2 1/4 In.	55.00
Elgin, Wristwatch, Aviators, U.S.Army Air Corps, Silver, 8 Sides, 1917	299.00
Elgin, Wristwatch, Open Face, GM Wheeler, 14K Gold, 17 Jewel	625.00
Elgin, Wristwatch, Presentation, Firestone, 14K Gold, 17 Jewel, 1938	250.00
Fellows U.S.Watch Co., Pocket, Butterfly Cutout, Nickel Plate	429.00
Frank Buck, Sunwatch, Ecplorer	20.00
Glycine Watch Co., Wristwatch, Gold, Square Cut Rubies, Ruby Clasp	1300.00
Gruen, Wristwatch, Lady's, Gold Filled Band, 14K White Gold	90.00
Gruen, Wristwatch, Man's, Gold Filled Stetch Band, 14K Gold, 1940s	250.00
Hamilton, Bracelet, 14K White Gold, 17 Jewel	475.00
Hamilton, Pin On, Lady's, Art Deco, Chatelaine Pin, 14K Gold	125.00
Hamilton, Pocket, Buster Brown Shoes	150.00
Hamilton, Pocket, Case Metal, 21 Jewel, 18 Size	90.00
Hamilton, Pocket, Model 950B, Yellow Gold Filled, 23 Jewel	335.00
Hamilton, Pocket, Model 974, No.16, Open Face, Gold Filled	150.00
Hamilton, Pocket, Model 990, 21 Jewel	145.00
Hamilton, Pocket, Model 990, Open Face, 21 Jewel	175.00
Hamilton, Pocket, No. 925, Open Face, 17 Jewel	110.00
Hamilton, Pocket, No.524431, Swing Out Movement, 21 Jewel	135.00
Hamilton, Pocket, Railroad, 10K Gold Filled, 21 Jewel	100.00
Hamilton, Pocket, Railroad, Open Face, Gold Filled, Lever Set, 17 Jewel	85.00
Hamilton, Pocket, Up–Down Winding Indicator, Mahogany Case	465.00
Hamilton, Pocket, Yellow Gold Filled, Elinvar, 21 Jewel	130.00
Hamilton, Wristwatch, Man's, Flexible Mesh Band, 14K Gold, 19 Jewel	675.00
Hampden, Pocket, Champion, 18 Size	100.00
Hampden, Pocket, Hunting, Engraved, 15 Jewel, 30–In.Chain	125.00
Hampden, Pocket, Hunting, Keywind, Silver, Porcelain Dial	60.00
Hampden, Pocket, Hunting, Lady's, Diadem Movement, 15 Jewel	80.00
Hampden, Pocket, Open Face, Gold, Perry Model, 17 Jewel	50.00
Howard, Pocket, Enamel Dial, Signed, 14K Gold Case, 23 Jewel	790.00
Howard, Pocket, Railroad Chronometer, 21 Jewel, Series 11, 5 Positions	325.00
Huguenin, Pocket, Hunting, Porcelain Dial, 18K Gold Case	225.00
Illinois, Pocket, Bunn Special, 60–Hour, 10K Gold, 21 Jewel	210.00
Illinois, Pocket, Gold Filled, 15 Jewel, C.1895	295.00
Illinois, Pocket, Hand Painted Dial With Eagle, Horse & Flag	145.00
Illinois, Pocket, Open Face, Keywind Keyset, Coin Silver Case	90.00
Ingersoll, Pocket, Boy Scout, Logo, National Council, New York	75.00
Ingraham, Pocket, Admiral Byrd, Explorer, Silverode, Pat.1907, 18 Size	85.00
Lady's, Wristwatch, Art Deco, 14K White Gold, C.1919	80.00
Lady's, Wristwatch, Art Nouveau, Blue Enamel Bezel Dial, C.1885	300.00
Leroy, Pocket, Open Face, Musical, Repeater, 18K Gold, C.1815	3950.00
Leroy, Pocket, Repeater, Cylinder, Champleve Dial, 18K Gold, C.1799	1295.00
Leverette, Pocket, Open Face, Germany, 14K Gold Case	155.00
Longines, Pocket, Open, Sterling Silver, Daisies Back, 15 Jewel	45.00
Longines, Wristwatch, Diamond Porcelain Face, 14K Gold Mesh Bracelet	600.00
Longines, Wristwatch, Man's, 4K Gold Case	290.00

Longines, Wristwatch, Square Face, 18K Gold	285.00
Lonville Watch Co., Wristwatch, Swiss, 14K Gold, 17 Jewel	275.00
Lucerne, Wristwatch, Bracelet, Snap Closure, Allover Rhinestone, Box	65.00
M.J.Tobias, Pocket, Open Face, Double Time, 18K Gold, C.1850	625.00
Manhattan, Pocket, Duplex Escapement, Case, Art Nouveau Florals	149.00
Mappin & Webb, Pocket, 6 Subsidiary Dials, Keyless, C.1900	250.00
Marconi, Pendant, Skeleton, 14K Gold	300.00
Mighty Mouse, Wristwatch, Swiss, Red & Blue Cloth Band, 1950s	20.00
Movado, Wristwatch, Black Dial, Gold Hands, 18K Gold	400.00
Movado, Wristwatch, Chronograph, Black Dial, 18K Gold, 1945, 1 1/4 In.	1540.00
Movado, Wristwatch, Spaulding–Gorham, Sterling, Gold Stripes, C.1939	350.00
Nabisco, Wristwatch, Cracker Design Around Face	75.00
Omega, Wristwatch, Black Dial, Automatic, Round, C.1940	99.00
Omega, Wristwatch, Man's, Leather Band, 18K Gold, 17 Jewel	300.00
Omega, Wristwatch, Seamaster, Automatic, 14K Gold	160.00
Paillet, Lapel, White Gold, Diamond, Pearl, Enameled Cupid, 1 1/8 In.	3300.00
Patek Philippe, Pocket, Hunting, 18K Gold, 1900, 1 In.	110.00
Patek Philippe, Wristwatch, Stainless Steel, Self–Winding, 18K Gold	1760.00
Paul Ditisheim, Wristwatch, Swiss, Platinum, 15 Jewel	300.00
Pendant, Sunburst Center, Keywind, C.1839	250.00
Pocket, Hunting, Automated Erotic Scene, 18K Gold, 1 7/8 In.	1325.00
Pocket, Lady's, Open Face, Red Roses, Scene of Maiden, Gold Numerals	365.00
Pocket, Packard Motor Car Co., Presentation, Logo, 14K Gold	500.00
Pocket, Swiss, Musical, Enameled, Woman With Book, Key, 1825	4675.00
Porter & Dyson Co., Pocket, Open Face, Swiss, 14K Gold, 17 Jewel	100.00
Rockford, Pocket, Demaskeen, 17 Jewel, 18 Size	172.00
Rockford, Pocket, Hunting, Gold, Exposed Escapement, C.1894	275.00
Rockford, Pocket, Hunting, Pink, Gold Multicolored Dial, 18 Size	110.00
Rockford, Pocket, Hunting, Porcelain Dial, Gold Hinged	72.00
Rolex, Wristwatch, Military, Bubble Back, 24–Hour Dial, Black	340.00
Rolex, Wristwatch, Pink Gold, Stainless Steel, 15 Jewel, 1940, 1 In.	665.00
Rolex, Wristwatch, Silver Dial, Raised Markers, Fluted Bezel	425.00
Rolex, Wristwatch, Tonneau, Pink Gold, Stainless Steel, 17 Jewel, 1930	1760.00
Russian, Hunting, Czar Nicholes Award, Silver, Portrait, Swords	350.00
Sandoz, Pocket, Calendar, 8–Day, Baby Blue Multicolored Dial	144.00
South Bend, Pocket, Hunting, 15 Jewel	175.00
South Bend, Pocket, Open Face, Engraved Silver Case, 17 Jewel	48.00
Space Cadet, Wristwatch	75.00
Spiro Agnew, Wristwatch, Red, White & Blue Strap	49.00
Tavannes, Wristwatch, Arabic Numbers, 14K Gold, 15 Jewel, C.1925	350.00
Tiffany, Pocket, Open Face, 8–Day, Signed Porcelain Dial, 20 Size	200.00
Tobias, Pocket, Rose In Hunting Case, Keywind	42.00
Tony The Tiger, Wristwatch	25.00
Touchon, Pocket, Open Face, Wolf Tooth Wind, 18K Gold	1500.00
Vacheron & Constantin, Chronograph, Silver, C.1917	249.00
Vacheron & Constantin, Chronometre Royal, 18K Gold, 19 Jewel, 1960	1210.00
Vacheron & Constantin, Purse Form, 2 Tone Gold, Deco, 1925, 1 3/4 In.	1210.00
Vacheron & Constantin, Semi–Skeletonized, 18K Gold, 17 Jewel	5500.00
Waltham, Model 16S, Crescent, 21 Jewel	350.00
Waltham, Pocket, Coin Silver Lever Set, 15 Jewel, 18 Size	65.00
Waltham, Pocket, Crescent, Porcelain Dial, 17 Jewel	40.00
Waltham, Pocket, Demi–Hunter, Gold Filled, 15 Jewel, 30–In. Chain	145.00
Waltham, Pocket, Face of Man, 14K Gold	140.00
Waltham, Pocket, Hunting, Lady's, 14K Gold, 1891	285.00
Waltham, Pocket, Hunting, Repeating, 14K Gold, C.1888, 2 In.	2970.00
Waltham, Pocket, Hunting, Yellow Gold Filled, Chain, 17 Jewel	140.00
Waltham, Pocket, Jeweled Gilt Keywind Movement, 14K Gold	225.00
Waltham, Pocket, Model 1899, Silveroid Case, 17 Jewel	70.00
Waltham, Pocket, Open Face, Gold, Sante Fe Route, 17 Jewel, 1896	180.00
Waltham, Pocket, Open Face, Nickel Movement, 14K Gold, 17 Jewel	160.00
Waltham, Pocket, Open Face, Vanguard, 10K Gold, 23 Jewel	295.00
Waltham, Pocket, Porcelain Dial, Sterling Silver, 18 Size	35.00
Waltham, Pocket, Vanguard, Adjustable Positions, 10K Gold, 23 Jewel	295.00
Waltham, Pocket, Vanguard, Railroad, Up–Down Indicator, 23 Jewel	400.00

Waltham, Pocket, Vanguard, Up–Down 36–Hour Indicator, 23 Jewel	1215.00
Waltham, Railroad, Presentation, Lever Set, 14K Gold, 21 Jewel	500.00
Waltham, Wristwatch, Chevalier, Enameled Bezel, Velvet Strap	150.00

Waterford–type glass resembles the famous glass made from 1783 to 1851 in the Waterford Glass Works in Ireland. It is a clear glass that was often decorated by cutting. Modern glass is being made again in Waterford, Ireland, and is marketed under the name "Waterford."

WATERFORD, Decanter, 13 1/2 In.	100.00
Salt Set, 3 Piece	70.00
Vase, Trumpet Shape, Crisscross Cutting, Star Rayed Base, 8 In.	105.00

WAVE CREST WARE

Wave Crest glass is a white glassware manufactured by the Pairpoint Manufacturing Company of New Bedford, Massachusetts, and some French factories. It was decorated by the C. F. Monroe Company of Meriden, Connecticut. The glass was painted in pastel colors and decorated with flowers. The name "Wave Crest" was used after 1898.

WAVE CREST, Biscuit Jar, Baroqued Scrolls, Florals, Ovoid, 8 In.	235.00
Biscuit Jar, Floral Design On 4 Sides, 10 1/2 In.	295.00
Biscuit Jar, Metal Handle, Rococo, Pink, Enameled, 5 1/2 In.	185.00
Biscuit Jar, Orange Rose, Leaves, Tongs, Signed, 13 1/2 In.	285.00
Bowl, Brass Cherub, Rococo, Pink Enameling, Signed, 5 1/2 In.	310.00
Bowl, Pink Flowers, Open Brass Rim, 1 3/4 X 4 In.	60.00
Box, Baroque Shell Design, Hinged Cover, 3 1/4 X 3 In.	235.00
Box, Blue Glossy Finish, Blown–Out Zinnia On Lid, Signed	375.00
Box, Brass Collar, Scrolls, Blossoms, 7 In.	75.00
Box, Brown Crown, Shell, Blue, White, Flowers, Hinged, 4 X 5 In.	225.00
Box, Cherub Design, Original Lining, Oval, Green Ground, 5 In.	295.00
Box, Collar & Cuff, Hinged Lid, Puffy, 6 1/2 X 5 3/4 In.	750.00
Box, Collar & Cuff, Puffy Mold, Egg Crate, 6 1/2 X 5 3/4 In.	695.00
Box, Collar & Cuff, Robin On Cover	1550.00
Box, Covered, Swirl, Raised Enamel, Pink, Signed, 5 1/2 In.	285.00
Box, Crystal, Pink Frosted, White Beaded, Gold, Mark, 5 In.	975.00
Box, Dresser, Floral Swirl, Blue, 4 In.	195.00
Box, Dresser, Hinged Cover, Baroque Shell Design, 3 1/4 X 3 In.	215.00
Box, Dresser, Hinged Cover, Helmschmied Swirl, Enameled Flowers	158.00
Box, Dresser, Pink, Blue Enamel Flowers, Hinged	150.00
Box, Egg Crate, 4 Brass Feet, 6 X 6 In.	560.00
Box, Enameled Holly, Swirl, Brass, Helmschmied, 4 X 7 In.	595.00
Box, Floral Enameling, Signed Helmschmied, 5 1/2 In.	375.00
Box, Floral Scrolls, Covered, Blue, Signed, 5 1/4 X 3 1/2 In.	285.00
Box, Frosted Glass, Hinged, Lavender & White Flowers, 4 X 5 In.	165.00
Box, Glove, Embossed Rococo, Blue Base, Marked, 9 1/2 In.	1150.00
Box, Glove, Pale Pink, Lavender Floral, Oval, Marked, 8 1/2 In.	440.00
Box, Glove, Roses, Hinged Cover, Ormolu Feet, 6 X 9 1/2 X 5 In.	995.00
Box, Gold Tracery Blossoms, Foliage, Clear, 5 1/2 X 3 3/4 In.	745.00
Box, Hinged Cover, House, Pond Scene, Lined, Pink, 3 3/4 X 3 In.	145.00
Box, Hinged Cover, Shell Design, Blue Flowers, Marked, 3 1/4 In.	230.00
Box, Hinged Cover, Shells & Flowers, Signed, 3 1/4 X 2 3/4 In.	180.00
Box, Hinged, Square Helmschmied Swirl, Square, 3 X 2 3/4 In.	165.00
Box, Jewelry, Horizontal Ribbed Collar, Puffy Swirl Base, 7 In.	395.00
Box, Jewelry, Tree Scene On Hinged Lid, Marked, 9 1/2 In.	1200.00
Box, Lid, Forget-Me-Nots, Scrolls, Green Lining, Banner, 3 In.	188.00
Box, Pink Frosted, White Beading, Gold Design, 5 In.	975.00
Box, Pink Swirl, Enameled Floral Lid, Hinged Lid, 4 1/2 In.	195.00
Box, Pink, Blown–Out Design, Floral, Red Banner Mark, 7 1/4 In.	385.00
Box, Pink, White Scroll & Flowers, Red Banner Mark, 5 1/2 In.	375.00
Box, Puffy, Bronze Mounts, Red Banner Marked, 7 In.	450.00
Box, Scrolls, Design On Top & All Sides, Signed, 7 X 5 1/2 In.	675.00
Box, Shell Cover, Brass Collar, Daisies, 4 In.	75.00
Box, Swirl Mold, Allover Pink Blossoms, Round, 5 3/4 In.	240.00
Box, Swirl Mold, Hand Painted Scene, Storks, 6 1/2 In.	1200.00

Card Holder, Pale Blue, Red Banner Mark, 6 X 3 1/2 X 4 In. 245.00
Dish, Flowers, Swirled, Square, 3 1/4 In. 70.00
Dish, Pin, Engraved Ormolu Rim, White Enameling, 4 1/4 In. 115.00
Dish, Ring, Kittens Playing In Grass, Ormolu Handles, 3 In. 150.00
Dish, Swirl Ribbing, Forget–Me–Nots Allover, 4 1/4 In. 115.00
Ewer, Eggshell, Signed, 13 1/2 In. 125.00
Ewer, Pale To Deep Green, Floral, Signed, 19 In. 125.00
Fernery, Egg Crate, Raised Enameling, Signed, 7 In. 190.00
Fernery, French Enameling, Footed, Pale Blue, Signed, 7 In. 325.00
Fernery, Hand Painted Daisies, Fern, Brass Collar, Signed, 8 In. 225.00
Frame, Picture, Scrolled, Mums, Beaded Rim, 6 1/4 X 4 1/4 In. 335.00
Frame, Scrolling, Variegated Florals, 6 1/4 X 4 1/4 In. 355.00
Hair Receiver, Brass Cover, Enameled Daisies, Signed, 6 In. 275.00
Hair Receiver, Embossed Floral, Black Mark, 5 1/2 In. 325.00
Humidor, Embossed Rococo 625.00
Jar, Blue & Pink Floral, Enameled, Black Banner Mark, 2 1/4 In. 65.00
Jardiniere, Chrysanthemums, Enameled Dots, 8 1/2 In. 165.00
Jardiniere, Yellow & Pink Flowers, Cupid Feet, 8 1/2 In. 700.00
Paperweight, Ormolu Top, 8 Sides, Enameled 350.00
Planter, Beaded Collar & Base, Scrolls, Florals, Red Banner 150.00
Planter, Beaded Collar, Baroque Scrolls, Enameled, Marked 315.00
Planter, Puffy Egg Crate Mold, Forget–Me–Nots, Round, 6 1/2 In. 255.00
Powder Jar, Embossed & Enameled Flowers, Covered, Signed 210.00
Salt & Pepper, Allover Baroque, Pink Asters, Pewter Lids 165.00
Salt & Pepper, Alternating Swirls, Asters, 2 3/4 In. 235.00
Salt & Pepper, Pink & Blue Forget–Me–Nots, Pewter Tops 90.00
Salt & Pepper, Raised Petals, Bulbous, White Dotting, Signed 135.00
Salt & Pepper, Ribbed Base, Enameled Flowers, 3 1/8 In. 135.00
Salt & Pepper, Swirl, Blue Floral, Shaded Pink 78.00
Salt & Pepper, White & Beige Swirls, Enameled, 2 3/4 In. 235.00
Saltshaker, 6 Sides, Baroqued Scrolls, Florals, 3 1/2 In. 65.00
Saltshaker, Swirl Mold, Flowers, Yellow Ground, 2 1/4 In. 80.00
Saltshaker, Tulip 40.00
Spooner, Tall Swirled Handle, Metal Top 158.00
Sugar & Creamer, Metal Covers, Floral, White, Pink 125.00
Sweetmeat, Paneled Sides, Floral, Signed, 8 In. 325.00
Sweetmeat, Rococo, Metal Top, Pastel Florals, Signed, 7 1/2 In. 290.00
Syrup, Enameled Spray of Wild Roses, Silver Plated Top, Handle 435.00
Tobacco Jar, Flower Medallions, Hinged Lid, Red Banner, 5 In. 475.00
Toothbrush Holder, Covered, Pink Flowers, Embossed, Blue Mark 450.00
Tray, Pin, Shell Design, Flowers, Brass Handles, Red Banner Mark 160.00
Tray, Pin, Swirled Enameled Flowers, 4 1/2 In. 90.00
Vase, 4 Dolphin Feet, Embossed Rococo, Blue, Marked, 10 1/4 In. 385.00
Vase, Baroque Design, Enameled Flowers, Beading, 10 1/2 In. 395.00
Vase, Baroque Design, Pink, Burgundy Flowers, Marked, 10 1/2 In. 475.00
Vase, Blue, White, Mauve, Brass Feet & Handles, 12 In. 950.00
Vase, Bronzed Base, Embossed Blank, Enameled Florals, 7 In. 160.00
Vase, Dolphin Feet, Embossed, Red Banner Mark, 10 1/4 In. 375.00
Vase, Embossed Enameled Flowers, Bronzed Base, 6 1/2 In. 160.00
Vase, Hand Painted, Delicate Flowers, Ormolu Feet, 5 In. 150.00
Vase, Ornate Bronzed Base, Enamel Florals, 6 1/2 In. 160.00
Vase, Scrolls, Jeweled Ormolu, Beaded Rim, Marked, 10 1/2 In. 475.00
     WEAPON, see also Gun; Rifle; Sword; etc.
WEAPON, Cannon, Brass, Strong Firearms Co., New Haven, 10 Gauge 1000.00
Cannon, Mounted On Wooden Frame, Wood Wheels, Coat–of–Arms, 1671 .... 450.00

The earliest American weather vanes were used in seventeenth–century Boston. The direction of the wind was an indication of coming weather, important to the seafaring and farming communities. By the mid–nineteenth century, commercial weather vanes were made of metal. Today's collectors often consider weather vanes to be examples of folk art, even though they may not have been handmade.

WEATHER VANE, Arrow, Copper, 2 Balls On Iron Rod, Directionals, 48 1/2 In. 55.00

Weather Vane, Cow, L.W.Cushing, Copper,
Zinc, 17 1/2 X 27 1/2 In.

Arrow, Copper, 3–Dimensional, Star Finial 700.00
Bluefish, 21 In. 230.00
Buck, Running, Sheet Iron, C.1860, 16 X 24 In. 850.00
Car & Driver, Mounted On Lightning Rod, American, 53 In. 375.00
Circus, Performer On Horse, Wooden, Original Paint 2200.00
Cock, Copper, Orb & Directional, J.W.Fiske & Co. 1760.00
Cock, With Arrow, Copper, Traces of Gilding, 24 X 21 In. 650.00
Codfish, Copper, Directionals, New England, 1880, 9 X 16 In. 5175.00
Codfish, Molded Copper, Scales, Directionals, C.1880, 35 In. 4700.00
Cow, L.W.Cushing, Copper, Zinc, 17 1/2 X 27 1/2 In. ....*Illus* 4180.00
Cow, Silhouette, Sheet Metal, Wooden Base, 31 X 32 1/2 In. 160.00
Deer, Running, Maryland, C.1880 .... 4500.00
Dragon, Cast Iron 1700.00
Eagle, 16 In.Wingspan, On Ball, Directions 1100.00
Eagle, Copper, 33 In.Wingspan, On Ball, 19th Century, 31 In. 1925.00
Eagle, Copper, Gold Gilding Under Yellow Paint, New England 2595.00
Eagle, Full–Bodied, Directional Arrow, Copper 600.00
Ewe, Molded Copper Body, Tail, Metal Head, American, 18 In. 1150.00

Weather Vane, Mayflower, Silhouette,
Sheet Copper, C.1920, 39 In.

Horse, Copper, Directionals, 36 1/2 In. 1300.00
Horse, Full–Bodied, Sheet Metal, 20 3/4 In. 100.00
Horse, Jumping, Hollow Body, Cast Zinc Head, Copper, 32 In. 600.00
Horse, Leaping Through Hoop, Hollow Body, Copper, 30 1/2 In. 1800.00
Horse, Prancing, Silhouette, Iron, 13 1/2 In. 180.00
Horse, Prancing, Silhouette, Sheet Iron, 19 1/4 In. 75.00
Horse, Running, Ears Laid Back, Zinc, 21 X 39 In. 1000.00
Horse, Running, Full–Bodied, Copper, Zinc Head, 29 X 17 In. 575.00
Horse, Running, Full–Bodied, Zinc, Traces of Gold Leaf, 39 In. 1000.00
Horse, Running, Gilt Traces, Copper, Directionals, 31 In. 475.00
Horse, Running, Iron, 25 X 25 In. 250.00
Horse, Running, Molded Copper, Zinc, C.1890 .... 2100.00
Horse, Running, Silhouette, Sheet Iron, Black Paint, 27 In. 95.00
Horse, Running, Silhouette, Sheet Iron, Black Paint, 49 In. 475.00
Horse, Running, Worn Gold Leaf, Harris & Co., C.1878, 26 In. 600.00
Horse, Silhouette, Sheet Iron, Holes, Paint Traces, 23 In. 850.00
Horse, Silhouette, Sheet Iron, Iron Shaft, 27 X 60 In. 500.00
Horse, Standing, Copper, Zinc, J.Howard & Co., 24 1/4 In. 5775.00
Horse, Trotting, Sheet Metal, Copper Ball, 18 X 15 In. 185.00
Long Boat, 2 Hunters, 33 In. 250.00
Mayflower, Silhouette, Sheet Copper, C.1920, 39 In. ....*Illus* 1900.00
Mermaid, Silhouette, Sheet Iron, Blue–Green Paint, 19 In. 400.00
Pig, Copper, Mustard Yellow, 38 In. 1700.00
Pig, Wooden, Tin Applied Ears, Wire Tail, Arrow, 32 X 17 In. 485.00
Plow, Horse Type, Sheet Copper, Zinc, 19th Century, 22 1/2 In. 7425.00
Ram, Copper, Utica, N.Y., C.1890 .... 1300.00
Rooster, Cast Zinc Head & Body, Sheet Metal Tail, 25 In. 1100.00
Rooster, Copper, Feathers, Early 20th Century, 3 Ft.11 In. 1600.00
Rooster, Copper, Wooden Base, 20th Century, 32 In. 250.00
Rooster, Handmade, Tin, 20th Century 70.00
Rooster, Iron, Sheet Iron Tail, 19th Century, 30 1/2 X 34 In. 3025.00
Sailing Ship, Wooden, C.1890 .... 1200.00
Sheep, Copper, 1880s, 24 In. 2420.00
Sheep, Molded Copper, Applied Ears, Gilt, 1880, 20 X 24 In. 2200.00
Stag, Leaping, Copper, Polychrome, J.W.Fiske, 32 X 31 1/2 In. 8800.00
Winged Serpent, Cast Metal, On Stand 1700.00

Webb Webb glass was made by Thomas Webb & Sons of Stourbridge, England. Many types of art and cameo glass were made by them during the Victorian era. The factory is still producing glass. Webb Burmese and Webb Peachblow are special colored glasswares of the Victorian period.

WEBB BURMESE, Basket, With Buttons, 6 1/4 X 6 1/4 In. 225.00
Bowl, Floral Design, Applied Glass At Rim, Marked, 6 1/4 In. 1110.00
Bowl, Fluted Top, 3 3/4 X 2 3/4 In. 185.00
Bowl, Hexagonal Top, Berries, Leaves, 4 X 3 1/4 In. 300.00
Dish, Sweetmeat, Silver Plated Holder, Fluted, 6 5/8 In. 275.00
Lamp, Fairy, Applied Leaf Holds Menu Card, 4 X 5 1/2 In. 495.00
Lamp, Fairy, Fluted Bowl, Yellow Feet, Clarke Insert, 6 1/2 In. 750.00
Lamp, Fairy, Marked Clarke Base, 4 3/4 In. 210.00
Lamp, Fairy, Matching Ruffled Base, Clarke Cup, 5 1/4 In. 495.00
Lamp, Fairy, Pressed Burmese Insert, Fluted Bowl, Dome Shade 750.00
Perfume Bottle, Gold Branches, Gold Wash Cap, 5 In. 750.00
Pitcher, Water, Egyptian Shape, Yellow Handle, 6 7/8 In. 675.00
Plate, Ruffled Edge, Flowers & Leaves, 7 1/2 In. 465.00
Rose Bowl, 6 Crimp, Leaves, Enameled Flowers, 2 1/4 In. 295.00
Rose Bowl, 8 Crimp Top, Acid Finish, 2 3/8 X 2 3/8 In. 165.00
Rose Bowl, 8 Crimp Top, Coral Flower Buds, Leaves, 2 1/2 In. 295.00
Rose Bowl, 8 Folded–In Petals Top, Signed, 2 3/4 X 2 1/8 In. 250.00
Rose Bowl, Flowers, Leaves, Salmon Pink, 3 3/8 X 3 1/4 In. 365.00
Sugar & Creamer, Pine Cones, Brown Buds, Green Needles 925.00
Toothpick, 5 Petal Flower, Leaves, 6–Sided Top, 2 5/8 In. 275.00
Toothpick, Square Top, 2 1/4 X 2 3/4 In. 175.00
Toothpick, White & Blue Enameled Flower, Brown Leaves, 3 In. 275.00

Tumbler, Whiskey, Diamond–Quilted, Yellow, Mt.Washington 185.00
Vase, 5 Petal Flower Design, Ruffled Pedestal Foot, 4 In. 300.00
Vase, 6–Sided Top, Ball Shape, Acid Finish, 3 1/8 In. 165.00
Vase, Bottle Shape, Green Leaves, Signed, 10 In. 995.00
Vase, Bud, Morning Glory Form, Footed Holder, 7 1/2 In., Pair 585.00
Vase, Burnt Orange Pods, Green, Tan Leaves, Crimped, 4 1/2 In. 255.00
Vase, Flared Ruffled Top, Green & Tan Ivy Leaves, 3 1/8 In. 325.00
Vase, Flower Petal Top, Berries, Leaves, 3 3/8 In. 325.00
Vase, Flower Petal Top, Berries, Leaves, Signed, 2 1/2 In. 325.00
Vase, Fluted Top, Striped Effect, 3 1/4 X 3 1/2 In. 188.00
Vase, Fluted, Striped Effect, Acid Finish, 4 X 3 In. 165.00
Vase, Folded Over Star–Shaped Top, Acid, 4 X 3 In. 185.00
Vase, Ivy Leaves, Ribbed Effect, Pedestal Foot, 4 1/2 In. 325.00
Vase, Lavender, Pink & Yellow Blossoms, Pods, 3 1/2 In. 285.00
Vase, Petal Top, Berries, Pink To Yellow, Signed, 2 3/4 In. 425.00
Vase, Ruffled Pedestal Foot, Ruffled Rim, 2 1/2 X 3 5/8 In. 325.00
Vase, Rust Mums, Green Leaves & Branches, Signed, 10 In. 1100.00
Vase, Stick, Salmon Pink, Yellow, Dimpled Base, Floral, 7 In. 475.00
Vase, Trumpet, Crimped, Ormolu Stand, 6 3/4 In. 210.00
Waste Bowl, Crimped, 5 3/4 X 2 3/4 In. 225.00
WEBB PEACHBLOW, Bowl, Cream Lining, Silver Plated Rim, 4 1/4 X 9 In. 395.00
Celery, Raised Floral, Pedestal, 2 Handles, Signed, 8 1/2 In. 220.00
Epergne, Mirror Base, 3 Branches, Crystal Leaves 2295.00
Ice Bucket, Swirl Design, Handle, Signed, 5 1/4 In. 225.00
Perfume Bottle, Silver Top, Pink Amber, 3 7/8 In. 695.00
Perfume Bottle, Sterling Silver Cap, Prunus & Butterfly 495.00
Rose Bowl, Egg Shape, 5 Petal Top, Cream Lining, 6 1/2 In. 350.00
Vase, Birds In Gold & Silver, 10 1/4 In., Pair 1000.00
Vase, Bottle Shape, Ribbed At Narrow Neck, 8 1/4 In. 180.00
Vase, Cameo Flowers & Leaves, White Bands, 4 5/8 In. 1650.00
Vase, Crystal Branch Feet, Cream Lining, Swirls, 5 3/4 In. 550.00
Vase, Crystal Branches & Berries, Loop Feet, 5 3/4 In. 495.00
Vase, Deep Rose To Cream, Coin Gold Daisies, 6 7/8 In. 625.00
Vase, Gold & Silver Design of Flowers, Bird, 9 3/8 In. 695.00
Vase, Gold Branches & Prunus Blossoms, Cream Lining, 7 In. 295.00
Vase, Gold Flowers & Leaves, Butterfly, 5 3/8 In. 295.00
Vase, Gold Flowers & Leaves, Gold Butterfly, 8 1/4 In. 495.00
Vase, Gold Insects, Pine & Cherry Blossoms, 6 1/2 In. 340.00
Vase, Gold Prunus, Bird In Flight, Branches, 8 3/4 In. 595.00
Vase, Opaque White To Pink To Crimson, Signed, 8 In. 195.00
Vase, Pink, Gold Branches, Prunus Blossoms, 11 In., Pair 1250.00
Vase, Protruding Branches In Gold, Bird In Flight, 9 In. 550.00
Vase, Quilted, Bulbous, Signed, 11 1/2 In. 185.00
Vase, Red To Pink, Gold Branches, Floral, 10 In. 495.00
Vase, Red To Pink, Gold Design, 7 1/2 X 4 3/8 In. 850.00
Vase, Rose To Pink, Prunus, With Bee, Cream Lining, 8 In. 650.00
Vase, Spider & Birds, Rose, Pink, Gold Branches, 11 In. 850.00
WEBB, Ashtray, Double, With Match Holder, Intaglio Ship, Signed 150.00
Basket, Red, 29 Air–Trapped Dark Stripes, Gold Thorn Handle, 6 In. 310.00
Biscuit Jar, Marble, Deep Maroon, Enameled, Metal Top, Signed, 7 In. 175.00
Bowl, Gold Prunus Design, Cream Lining, 6 Crimp, Gold Feet, 5 3/4 In. 550.00
Bowl, Gold Rim, White Center To Strawberry, Signed, 8 1/2 In. 175.00
Bowl, Opaque, Cranberry Trim, Ruffled, Amber Feet, 6 3/4 X 7 X 10 In. 495.00
Bowl, Scalloped, Fluted Edge, Pink, White Overlay, Signed, 10 1/2 In. 185.00
Bowl, Scalloped, Robin's–Egg Blue, Signed, 10 In. 165.00
Bride's Basket, Blue Mother–of–Pearl, Scalloped, Metal Base, 10 In. 195.00
Bride's Basket, Raised Enameling, Peacock Blue, Holder, Signed, 11 In. 260.00
Bride's Bowl, Fluted, Scalloped, Pink, Signed, 11 In. 135.00
Bride's Bowl, Folded Sides, Scalloped, Opaque White, Signed, 12 In. 185.00
Bride's Bowl, Gold Enameling, White Exterior, Pairpoint Holder 275.00
Bride's Bowl, Pink To Strawberry Top, Enameled Floral, Signed, 12 In. 210.00
Bride's Bowl, Raised Enameling, Metal Stand, Signed, 12 In. 295.00
Bride's Bowl, White To Apricot, 11 In. 195.00
Compote, Cranberry Center, Opaque White, Metal Stand, Signed, 9 In. 195.00

Goblet, Twisted Amber Stem, Engraved Allover, Marked, 10 In. 32.00
Goblet, Twisted Rope Stem, Allover Tulip & Geometric Design, 10 In. 55.00
Lamp, Double Wick, Azure Blue, Brass Base, Signed, 29 In. 1025.00
Mug, Sterling Silver Mountings, Simulated Ivory, Marked, 4 In. 895.00
Perfume Bottle, Cameo, Lay Down, Cameo, Teardrop Shape, Hinged Cap 625.00
Perfume Bottle, Gold Prunus & Butterfly, 4 3/4 In. 495.00
Perfume Bottle, Gold Prunus, Sterling Silver Dome Lid, 3 1/2 In. 325.00
Perfume Bottle, Ivory Satin Glass, Allover Bamboo Design, 5 1/4 In. 250.00
Pitcher, Honeycomb, Cut Velvet Blue, 8 In. 295.00
Pitcher, Pale To Opaque Blue, Crystal Handle, Birds, Marked, 12 In. 235.00
Pitcher, Peacock Eye Pattern, Applied Handle, Green, 7 In. 275.00
Pitcher, Raised Floral, Birds On Nest, White, Blue, Signed, 12 In. 235.00
Pitcher, Raised Gold, Butterflies, Clear Handles, Signed, 8 In., Pair 295.00
Pitcher, Scalloped, Frosted Handle, White To Gold, Signed, 6 In. 145.00
Rose Bowl, Amberina, Diamond–Quilted, Cream, 9 Crimp Top, 7 1/4 In. 1200.00
Rose Bowl, Clear Applied Rigaree & Feet, Button Mark, 5 1/2 In. 175.00
Rose Bowl, Raised Florals, 3 Feet, Peacock Blue, 8 1/2 In. 245.00
Salt, Berry Prunus, Applied Berries At Sides, Cranberry, 3 X 2 In. 65.00
Spooner, Alexandrite, Expanded Diamond Interior, Crimped, 4 1/4 In. 645.00
Tazza, Amberina, Honeycomb Design, 4 7/8 In. 425.00
Toothpick, Alexandrite, 6–Pointed Top, 2 3/4 In. 495.00
Toothpick, Alexandrite, Bulbous Base, Rose To Citron, 2 7/8 In. 695.00
Toothpick, Enameled Flowers, Yellow Satin Cased 395.00
Toothpick, Raspberry, White Design, Leaves, 2 X 3 In. 435.00
Urn, Gold Enameling, Butterfly, Pedestal, Signed, 12 In. 175.00
Vase, Amethyst Lilies & Leaves, Etched Crystal, 8 1/4 In. 365.00
Vase, Applied Coralene Poppies, Leaves, Handle, Signed, 6 In. 125.00
Vase, Beige, Bulbous, Bright Enameling, Signed, 10 1/2 In., Pair 295.00
Vase, Birds & Butterfly, Yellow Ground, Pink Lined, Marked, 12 In. 325.00
Vase, Blown In, Azure, Blue, Raised Gold, Floral, Signed, 13 1/2 In., Pr. 750.00
Vase, Blue Ribbed, Cut Velvet, Signed, 8 In. 225.00
Vase, Blue Tulips, Leaves, Trumpet Shape, 9 1/4 In. 365.00
Vase, Blue, Diamond–Quilted, Cut Velvet, 8 1/2 In. 190.00
Vase, Bottle Shape, Green Leaves, Signed, 10 In. 995.00
Vase, Bronze, Gold Floral, Bulbous, Signed & Numbered, 10 1/2 In. 175.00
Vase, Brown Shaded, Gold Prunus Design, Cream Lining, 13 3/8 In. 495.00
Vase, Cameo, Citron, White Butterfly, Signed, 9 In. 1400.00
Vase, Cameo, White, Coral, Cut Back, Lemon, Morning Glories, 6 In. 1600.00
Vase, Chubby Birds, Butterfly, Gold Prunus Enameling, Marked, 12 In. 475.00
Vase, Coral Overlay, Applied Opalescent Leaves, Footed, 5 3/4 In. 325.00
Vase, Coralene Flowers, Blue, White, Beige, Signed, 10 1/4 In. 265.00
Vase, Coralene, Applied Orange & Green, Azure Blue, Signed, 7 In. 175.00
Vase, Drape Design, Rainbow, Signed, 7 In. 235.00
Vase, Egg Shaped, Prunus Branches, Squiggle Ground, C.1885, 6 In. 3850.00
Vase, Etched Panels, Enameled Flowers, Leaves & Insects, 9 1/2 In. 595.00
Vase, Fan Top, Pink, Signed, 6 1/2 In. 175.00
Vase, Flowering Bough, Aqua Ground, Cameo, Marked, 7 3/4 In. ....*Illus* 900.00
Vase, Foliage, Pale To Peacock Blue, Clear Overlay Inside, 8 In. 325.00
Vase, Frosted Pink, Ribbed, Footed, Square Indented Top, Signed, 8 In. 165.00
Vase, Gold Floral, Coral Overlay, White Lining, 9 X 4 1/4 In. 350.00
Vase, Gold Prunus Blossoms & Pine Needles, Shaded Brown, 13 3/8 In. 495.00
Vase, Gold To Rose, Cream Lining, Reverse Amberina, 12 1/4 In. 650.00
Vase, Gold, Bluebirds, Flowers, Dragonfly, Marked, 10 1/2 In., Pair 525.00
Vase, Mother–of–Pearl, Blue Satin Finish, Indented, Marked, 6 1/2 In. 215.00
Vase, Mother–of–Pearl, Bulbous, Square Top, Signed, 7 1/4 In. 225.00
Vase, Opaque White To Pale Yellow, Frosted Handles, 9 X 9 In. 170.00
Vase, Opaque, Carved Flowers, Frosted Cranberry, Signed, 10 3/8 In. 2495.00
Vase, Passion Flower Design, Indigo Blue Ground, 8 1/2 In. 1580.00
Vase, Raindrop, Mother–of–Pearl, Coralene Flowers, 11 In. 300.00
Vase, Raindrop, Scalloped, White Inside, Signed, 6 1/2 X 8 In. 195.00
Vase, Raised Gold Floral, Bird & Butterfly, Maroon, Signed, 12 In. 210.00
Vase, Red Palm Fronds, Butterfly On Back, 6 1/4 In. 975.00
Vase, Reverse Amberina Coloring, Gold To Rose, 12 1/4 In. 650.00
Vase, Ruffled, Applied Leaves, Cream Lining, Coral, 11 7/8 In. 395.00

Vase, Snowflake Design, Gold Tracery, Butterflies, Handle, 6 1/4 In.	595.00
Vase, Teal Blue To Salmon, Satin Glass, Square, Dimpled Sides, 11 In.	450.00
Vase, White Floral, Multicolored Leaf Design, Pink Cased, 11 In.	295.00
Vase, White Floral, Pale Green, Signed, 4 1/2 In.	290.00
Water Set, Satin, Robin In Tree, 7 Piece ....*Illus*	1850.00
Wine, Alexandrite Honeycomb, 4 1/2 In.	750.00

WEDGWOOD Josiah Wedgwood, although considered a cripple by his brother and forbidden to work at the family business, founded one of the world's most successful potteries. The pottery was founded in England in 1759. A large variety of wares has been made, including the well-known jasperware, basalt, creamware, and even a limited amount of porcelain. There are two kinds of jasperware. One is made from two colors of clay, the other is made from one color clay with a color dip to create the contrast in design. The firm is still in business.

WEDGWOOD, Ashtray, Etruria, Dartmouth College	15.00
Bank, Peter Rabbit	45.00
Biscuit Barrel, Jasperware, Nickel Silver Top, 6 X 5 In.	250.00
Biscuit Barrel, Light Blue & White, 9 In.	600.00
Biscuit Barrel, Waffle, Pewter Cover & Handles, 6 1/2 In.	990.00
Biscuit Jar, Blue Jasper, Silver Plated Fittings, Ivory Finial	130.00
Biscuit Jar, Dark Blue, Ladies, Floral Border, Silver Plated Lid	155.00
Biscuit Jar, Jasperware, Acorn, Gray, White, Domed Cover, 8 In.	250.00
Biscuit Jar, Jasperware, Yellow & Black	375.00
Bonbon, Leaf Shape, England, 1866	300.00
Bottle, Water, White Lions' Heads, Grape Garlands, Large	55.00
Bowl, Blue Interior, Gold Peacocks, 6 In.	350.00
Bowl, Butterfly Luster, 6 In.	120.00
Bowl, Butterfly Luster, Octagonal, 7 In.	450.00
Bowl, Commemorative, Kentucky Derby, 1947, 9 1/2 X 4 1/2 In.	450.00
Bowl, Dancing Hours, Black, White, 8 In.	375.00
Bowl, Daventry Pattern, Luster, 7 In.	210.00
Bowl, Dragon Luster, Octagonal, Fruit Interior, Marked, 6 1/2 In.	375.00
Bowl, Dragon Luster, Octagonal, Orange Exterior, 9 In.	400.00
Bowl, Fairyland Luster, Dragons, Lavender, Footed, 9 X 5 1/2 In.	500.00
Bowl, Fairyland Luster, Geese & Hummingbirds, Octagonal, 7 In.	750.00
Bowl, Fairyland Luster, Opalescent, Grass & Sky, Wee Folk, 5 In.	485.00
Box, Cigarette, Queensware, Embossed Grapevine, 3 1/2 X 5 In.	30.00
Box, Covered, Dragon Luster, Window Finial, Marked, 5 5/8 In.	450.00
Box, Covered, Queensware, Light Blue, Berries, Vine, 4 X 5 In.	90.00
Box, Jasperware, Classical Figures On Cover, Square, 2 In.	100.00
Bust, Shakespeare, Black Basalt, Marked, 10 In.	115.00

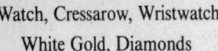

Watch, Cressarow, Wristwatch,
White Gold, Diamonds

Webb, Water Set, Satin, Robin In Tree,
7 Piece

Calendar Plate, 1976 .... 5.00
Candleholder, Sphinx, 1790, Pair 3500.00
Candlestick, Capriware, C.1840, 6 1/2 In. 350.00
Candlestick, Dark Blue & White, Regency Period, 6 In., Pair 750.00
Candlestick, Jasperware, Salmon & White, 5 In., Pair 390.00
Candlestick, Jasperware, White Bands, Blue & White, 6 In., Pair 125.00
Chamberstick, Loop Handle, Sage Green, 4 In. 75.00
Charger, Majolica, Liberte, 14 3/4 In. ....*Illus* 1265.00
Child's Set, Peter Rabbit, 4 Piece 70.00
Clock, Blue & White Relief, Marked, 7 1/2 In. 50.00
Clock, Tricolor, C.1850, 8 In. 1150.00
Compote, Yellow Luster Outside, Copper Luster Trim, C.1920, 4 In. 100.00
Cookie Jar, Jasperware, Sage Green & White 135.00
Cookie Jar, Jasperware, Salmon & White, 4 X 6 1/2 In. 395.00
Cookie Jar, Jasperware, Squirrel Finial, Dark Blue & White 135.00
Creamer, Black Basalt, Lady Medallions, Instruments In Between 165.00
Cup & Saucer, Buxton, Turquoise 18.00
Cup & Saucer, Diceware, 3 Color, C.1900 .... 1150.00
Cup & Saucer, Diceware, Green, Yellow, White, Marked 850.00
Cup & Saucer, Jasperware, Blue & White, Rope Handle 145.00
Cup & Saucer, Jasperware, Tricolor, Medallions, Fruit, Ram's Head 795.00
Cup, Fairyland Luster, Leapfrogging Elves, Flame Luster, 2 In. 495.00
Figurine, Cleopatra, Seated, Rock, Asp On Wrist, Black, 9 1/4 In. 575.00
Figurine, Cupid, Winged, Sitting On Rock, Basalt, 8 In. 550.00
Figurine, Elephant, Ivory Colored Tusks, Black, Marked, 3 1/2 In. 375.00
Figurine, Rooster, Hen, Hand Painted, Pair 135.00
Gravy Boat, Buxton, Turquoise 35.00
Jam Jar, Jasperware, Classical Lady Figures, Dark Blue, 4 1/4 In. 95.00
Jam Jar, Jasperware, Plated Lid, Attached Saucer, 3 1/2 In. 285.00
Jam Jar, Saucer, Jasperware, Tricolor, Plated Lid, 18th Century 225.00
Jar, Sweetmeat, Tricolor, Lavender Bands, Sage Green, 4 1/2 In. 495.00
Jug, Classical Ladies In Panels, Salt Glaze, Pre-1850, 6 1/2 In. 175.00
Jug, Jasperware, Classical Figures, Black & White, 6 1/4 In. 165.00
Jug, Milk, Crimson, 4 1/2 In. 650.00
Matchbox, Jasperware, Green 25.00
Pepper Pot, Raised Grapes & Leaves, White, Bulbous, 3 1/2 In. 95.00
Pepper Pot, White Figures, Dark Blue, Marked, 2 1/2 X 4 1/4 In. 48.00
Pin Tray, Cupid & Cherubs Center, Blue & White, 2 1/2 X 4 In. 40.00
Pin Tray, Jasperware, Grecian Ladies & Children, 6 X 3 3/4 In. 35.00
Pitcher, Basalt, Silver Mounted, Signed, C.1790 .... 2400.00
Pitcher, Classical Figures, Trees, Bird, Cherub, Dark Blue, 6 In. 130.00
Pitcher, Covered, Jasperware, Classical, Grapes, Marked, 8 In. 145.00
Pitcher, Crimson, Rope Handle, 4 3/4 In. 450.00
Pitcher, Jasperware, Classical Figures, Blue & White, 2 3/8 In. 70.00
Pitcher, Jasperware, Classical Scene, Geometric Rim, Green, 4 In. 97.00
Pitcher, Jasperware, White Figures, Dark Blue, 3 3/4 In. 75.00
Pitcher, Union Harp, Shamrock, Basalt, 1790, 5 In. 130.00
Plaque, Diana & Ceres, Green, 5 7/8 In., Pair 300.00
Plaque, Jasperware, Black & White, 1968, 2 X 10 In. ....*Illus* 165.00
Plate, Angel, 6 In. 33.00
Plate, Arkansas Centenial, Blue, 1935 .... 30.00
Plate, Birthplace of Whittier, Haverhill, Ma., Etruria, 9 In. 28.00
Plate, Child's, Peter Rabbit 25.00
Plate, Dog Standing Over Gun & Game, Blue Transfer, 9 In. 40.00
Plate, Harvard Memorial Hall, 10 In. 27.00
Plate, Independence Hall, Cobalt, 9 1/2 In. 30.00
Plate, Ivanhoe, Black Knight, Blue & White, 10 In. 65.00
Plate, Jasperware, Grecian Ladies & Children, 8 1/2 In., Pair 90.00
Plate, Litchfield, 6 In. 15.00
Plate, Memorial Hall, Washington, D.C., Blue, 9 1/4 In. 45.00
Plate, Old State House, Boston, Blue & White, 1888 .... 35.00
Plate, Signing of Declaration of Independence, C.1900, 10 In. 30.00
Plate, Spinning Wheel, Garden Tools, Creamware, 8 In. 150.00
Plate, Sportive Love, Black Basalt, Templeton, 1971 .... 29.00

Wedgwood, Charger,
Majolica, Liberte,
14 3/4 In.

Wedgwood, Plaque, Jasperware,
Black & White, 1968, 2 X 10 In.

Plate, Texas Commemorative, 1836–1936, Blue & White, Marked	30.00
Plate, Washington & Lee University, Campus Walk, 1749–1949	15.00
Plate, Washington's Headquarters, Blue, 9 1/4 In.	65.00
Plate, Wayside Inn, Blue, 9 1/4 In.	50.00
Plate, Wellesley College, Blue, 9 1/4 In.	75.00
Platter, Well & Tree, Blue Willow, Scalloped, 21 In.	250.00
Punch Bowl, Harvard University, Red Transfer, 5 1/2 X 12 In.	275.00
Salt & Pepper, Jasperware, Salmon & White, 4 In.	185.00
Sardine Box, Majolica, Brown, White, 8 X 7 1/2 X 3 In. ....*Illus*	275.00
Soup Cup, Terra–Cotta, Capriware, Enameled, 4 In. ....*Illus*	225.00
Sugar & Creamer, Basalt, Union Emblem, 1850 .... 155.00 To	225.00
Sugar & Creamer, Black Basalt, Shamrock, Thistle & Rose Design	60.00
Sugar & Creamer, Cornflower	45.00
Tea Set, Blue & White, 4 Demitasse Cups & Saucers, 7 In.Teapot	200.00
Tea Set, Jasperware, Lilac, 3 Piece	350.00
Teapot, Basalt, 1830, 9 In.	65.00
Teapot, Black Basalt, Colored Enameled Flowers, 4 1/2 In.	335.00
Teapot, Blue Jasper Dip, 4 3/4 In.	35.00
Teapot, Franklin & Washington, Green, 1890	175.00
Teapot, Jasperware, All Around Grecian Scene, Blue, 7 1/2 In.	325.00
Teapot, Jasperware, Classical Lady Figures, Dark Blue, 3 3/4 In.	145.00
Teapot, Queensware, Painted Bamboo, 1860	100.00
Teapot, White Classical Figures, Royal Blue	130.00
Tile, Girls, Mounted In Footed Metal Frame, Square, 6 In.	58.00
Tile, Old Man of The Mountain	65.00

Wedgwood, Sardine Box, Majolica, Brown,
White, 8 X 7 1/2 X 3 In.

Wedgwood, Soup Cup,
Terra–Cotta,
Capriware, Enameled, 4 In.

Wedgwood, Vase,
Fairland, Luster,
12 In.

Wedgwood, Tureen, Majolica,
Berry Motif,
Covered, 6 X 10 X 7 In.

Wedgwood, Tureen, Majolica, Flowers,
Pheasants, 8 X 13 X 5 In.

Weller, Lamp Base,
Bluebird, Marked,
13 1/2 In.

Tray, Dresser, Jasperware, 8 Sides, Blue & White, 11 X 8 In.	110.00
Tray, Minuteman, White On Blue, 3 1/4 X 6 In.	20.00
Tray, Queensware, Pierced Edge, Oval, 10 In.	75.00
Tureen, Majolica, Berry Motif, Covered, 6 X 10 X 7 In. ....*Illus*	600.00
Tureen, Majolica, Flowers, Pheasants, 8 X 13 X 5 In. ....*Illus*	1265.00
Urn, Basalt, Maidens, 1895, 9 In.	150.00
Urn, Basalt, Wavy Rim, 1870, 8 In.	200.00
Urn, Sphinx Head, Rosso Antico, C.1805, 10 1/2 In. ....*Illus*	4125.00
Vase, Candlemas, Fairyland Luster, 8 1/2 In.	650.00
Vase, Candlemas, Fairyland Luster, 10 1/2 In.	300.00
Vase, Classical Relief, Light Blue & White, 11 In.	350.00
Vase, Daventry, Gilded Fairyland Luster, 8 1/2 In.	1450.00
Vase, Dragon Luster, Bulbous, Gold Dragons & Trim, 11 1/4 In.	375.00
Vase, Dragon Luster, Dark Blue, Gilded, 8 In.	335.00
Vase, Fairland, Luster, 12 In. ....*Illus*	1750.00
Vase, Fairyland Luster, Fairy Lady, Birds, Marked, 9 1/2 In.	1195.00
Vase, Fairyland Luster, Fairy Under The Rainbow Scene, 9 In.	2050.00
Vase, Green, Lilac & White, 5 In.	1550.00
Vase, Jasperware, Allegorical Maidens, Black & White, 12 In., Pair	1300.00
Vase, Jasperware, Classical Figures, Dark Blue, 4 3/4 X 3 1/4 In.	110.00
Vase, Jasperware, Medallions, Dark Blue & White, C.1870, 7 1/4 In.	510.00
Vase, Oriental Figured Luster, Blue, Gilded, & Green, 7 1/4 In.	550.00
Vase, Portland, 1865, 8 In.	450.00
Vase, Portland, Phrygian Head Below, Black & White, 10 1/2 In.	3400.00
Vase, Presentation, Basalt, 1920, 4 In.	100.00
Vase, Rosso Antico, Marked, C.1805, 8 3/8 In. ....*Illus*	990.00
Vase, Satyr Head, Blue Medallion, C.1800, 3 1/2 In.	150.00
Vase, Trumpet, Basalt, Early 19th Century, 11 In.	500.00
Vase, Victoria Ware, Figurine In Ivory, Gold Trim, 8 In.	395.00
Vase, White, Green, & Lilac, 5 In.	1350.00

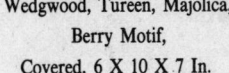

Weller pottery was first made in 1873 in Fultonham, Ohio. The firm moved to Zanesville, Ohio, in 1882. Art wares were first made in 1893. Hundreds of lines of pottery were made, including Louwelsa, Eocean, Dickens, and Sicardo, before the pottery closed in 1948.

WELLER, Ashtray & Matchbox Holder, Bronze Ware, 3 X 5 1/2 In.	50.00
Ashtray, Squirrel, Glazed	38.00
Basket, Forest, 10 In.	45.00
Basket, Hanging, Claywood, Chains	25.00
Basket, Hanging, Forest	125.00
Basket, Hanging, Orris, 6 In.	35.00
Basket, Hanging, Voile, Chains	35.00

Wedgwood, Vase, Rosso Antico, Marked,
C.1805, 8 3/8 In.
Wedgwood, Urn, Sphinx Head, Rosso Antico,
C.1805, 10 1/2 In.

Basket, Oak Leaf	18.00
Basket, Tutone, 1925, 9 X 7 In.	42.50
Basket, Warwick, Rustic	55.00
Basket, Woodcraft, Log, 9 1/2 In.	75.00
Bowl, Ardsley, Kingfisher Centerpiece, 10 X 17 In.	395.00
Bowl, Baldin, C.1920	35.00
Bowl, Dickens Ware, Green Glaze, Pansies, Artist Signed, 8 In.	95.00
Bowl, Flower Frog, Boy Fishing, Lattice, 1920s	175.00
Bowl, Glendale, Flower Frog, Nest of Bird Eggs, Signed, 15 In.	395.00
Bowl, Golden Glow, Flower Frog	135.00
Bowl, Muskota, Fishing Boy	275.00
Bowl, Orris, Leaf, 5 In.	10.00
Bowl, Panella, Footed, Blue, 7 In.	35.00
Bowl, Turada, 4 1/2 X 2 1/4 In.	110.00
Bowl, Woodcraft, Squirrel In Relief, 3 1/2 In.	50.00
Bowl, Woodcraft, Squirrels Sitting In Leaves & Branches, 7 In.	75.00
Candleholder, Ardsley	30.00
Candleholder, Barcelona, Pair	65.00
Candleholder, Lorbeek, Blue, Pair	27.50
Candleholder, Tutone, Green & Rust, 6 3/4 X 7 1/4 In.	40.00
Candleholder, Woodrose, Saucer Base, Finger Ring, Pair	68.00
Candlestick, Arcola, 12 In., Pair	70.00
Candlestick, Bonito, 5 In.	35.00
Candlestick, Eocean, 8 In.	55.00
Candlestick, Eocean, Large, Pair	165.00
Candlestick, Marvo, Pair	20.00
Candlestick, Melrose, 13 In., Pair	150.00
Clock, Louwelsa, 12 In.	750.00
Compote, Zona, 5 1/2 In.	45.00
Console Set, Cornish, Ivory, Bowl, 7 1/2 In., 3 Piece	60.00
Console Set, Glendale, Flower Frog, 4 Piece	240.00
Console Set, Ragenda, Maroon, 3 Piece	95.00
Console Set, Silvertone, Flower Frog, 4 Piece	225.00
Console, Coppertone, Bell Shape, Paper Label, 11 1/2 In.	65.00
Cookie Jar, Mammy	335.00
Cookie Jar, Muskota, Cats On Fence	275.00
Cornucopia, Greora	80.00
Creamer, Mammy	185.00
Crocus Pot, Greora	100.00
Ewer, Art Nouveau, Slender, Light Green, Peach, 9 In.	100.00
Ewer, Cameo, Blue, 10 In.	20.00

Ewer, Dickens Ware, Floral Design, 12 In.	595.00
Ewer, Louwelsa, Leaves	125.00
Ewer, Louwelsa, Yellow Flowers, Signed, 6 In.	145.00
Ewer, Roba, Brown, 6 In.	50.00
Ewer, Wild Rose, Green, 7 In.	18.00
Figurine, Crow, Yard Ornament	400.00
Figurine, Dog, Sitting, Muskota, 5 1/2 X 4 3/4 In.	75.00
Figurine, Frog, Brown, Green, White, Black, 3 5/8 In.	85.00
Figurine, Kneeling Woman, Muskota, 6 In.	55.00
Figurine, Nude, With Duck, Hobart	48.50
Figurine, Parrot, On Perch, Hi–Glaze, Brighton, 7 1/2 In.	75.00
Figurine, Turtle, Coppertone, 1 1/2 X 4 1/4 In.	75.00
Figurine, Turtle, Crawling Out of A Lily, Muskota, 5 In.	55.00
Flower Frog, Brighton, 9 In.	70.00
Flower Frog, Cherub	35.00
Flower Frog, Coppertone, Frog & Lilly, 17 In.	175.00
Flower Frog, Crab, Muskota, 1 1/2 X 5 In.	15.00
Flower Frog, Cream & Black Stripes, 4 1/2 In.	5.00 To 15.00
Flower Frog, Girl, Green, 8 1/2 In.	45.00
Flower Frog, Girl, Matte Turquoise, Hobart, 8 1/2 In.	85.00
Flower Frog, Muskota, 4 1/2 In.	50.00 To 55.00
Flower Frog, Nude Boy With Swan, Aqua, 6 1/2 In.	55.00
Flower Frog, Nude Girl, Sitting On Rock, White	95.00
Flower Frog, Swan, Brighton, 5 1/2 In.	40.00
Flowerpot, California Mission Scenes, Claystone, 8 X 12 In.	590.00
Flowerpot, Roma	45.00
Ginger Jar, Panella, Blue	30.00
Humidor, Dickens Ware III, Scene, Man Smoking	165.00
Humidor, Knifewood	300.00
Humidor, Turada	160.00
Humidor, Woodcraft, Acorn Shape, Squirrel Finial, 9 X 6 In.	300.00
Inkwell, Turtle, Insert, Lid, Signed	300.00
Jar, Baldin, 6 X 7 In.	70.00
Jar, Blue Ware, Footed, 7 In.	105.00
Jardiniere, 2 Woodpeckers, 9 1/2 In.	125.00
Jardiniere, Chrysanthemum, 8 In.	65.00
Jardiniere, Dickens Ware, Floral, Signed, 12 In.	130.00
Jardiniere, Etna	150.00
Jardiniere, Fairfield, 6 1/2 In.	25.00
Jardiniere, Flemish, 6 In.	65.00
Jardiniere, Forest, 4 1/2 In.	90.00 To 100.00
Jardiniere, Frog Crawling Up Side, Pond Plants, Coppertone, 7 In.	135.00
Jardiniere, Grape & Grapevine Design, Pedestal, 40 In.	600.00
Jardiniere, Louwelsa, Floral, Signed, 10 1/2 In.	220.00
Jardiniere, Raised Enameled Bluebirds, Flowers, 6 1/2 X 8 1/2 In.	125.00
Jardiniere, Satyr In Vineyard, Marked, 10 In.	495.00
Jardiniere, Souevo, 8 1/2 X 9 In.	140.00
Jardiniere, Woodcraft, 3 Fox Heads, 6 3/4 X 5 3/4 In.	70.00
Jardiniere, Woodland, 6 X 7 In.	107.50
Jug, Dickens Ware, Blackhawk Indian, Handle, 5 3/4 In.	475.00
Jug, Dickens Ware, Men Playing Checkers, 4 3/4 In.	375.00
Jug, Turada, 6 In.	125.00
Lamp Base, Bluebird, Marked, 13 1/2 In.	*Illus* 250.00
Lamp Base, Louwelsa, Oil, High Glaze, Brown Floral, Signed	350.00
Lamp, Oil, Louwelsa, Chrysanthemums, Standard Glaze	190.00
Lamp, Roma, 12 1/2 In.	145.00
Mug, Creamware, Indian	75.00
Mug, Dickens Ware, Bouquet Floral, Leaves, Cobalt Blue, 7 In.	210.00
Mug, Dickens Ware, Indian, Signed L.J.Burgess, 1901, 6 In.	395.00
Mug, Eocean, Plum Design, 5 In.	75.00
Mug, Etna, Red Flowers, Gray	67.50
Mug, Floretta, Grapes	95.00
Mug, Turada, 6 In.	100.00 To 125.00
Napkin Ring, Figural, Standing Owl	57.50

Pitcher, Art Nouveau, Green, Brown To Peach, Matte Glaze 130.00
Pitcher, Coppertone, Fish Handle 265.00
Pitcher, Dickens Ware, Blue, Green Bisque, Sea Serpents, 12 In. 370.00
Pitcher, Dickens Ware, Floral Design, 12 In. 395.00
Pitcher, Eocean, Gray To Eggshell, Pansies, Signed, 6 1/2 In. 100.00
Pitcher, Etna, Maroon Flowers, 10 1/2 In. 110.00
Pitcher, Louwelsa, 3 Feet, Deep Orange Carnation Design, 5 In. 65.00
Pitcher, Louwelsa, Grape Cluster On Brown Ground, Signed, 17 In. 300.00
Pitcher, Louwelsa, Indian Chief Portrait, Brown High Glaze, 12 In. 795.00
Pitcher, Louwelsa, Squat, Pansy Design, Shaded Brown, Signed, 3 In. 75.00
Pitcher, Marvo, Green, 8 In. 85.00
Pitcher, Tankard, Louwelsa, Monk's Portrait, 12 1/2 In. 2200.00
Pitcher, Wild Rose, Blue, 11 In. 30.00
Pitcher, Zona, Kingfisher, Cobalt Blue, 80 Oz. 75.00
Planter, Creamware, 3 1/2 In. 60.00
Planter, Duck & Rabbit, 8 In. 35.00
Planter, Forest, Ink Stamp, 4 1/2 In. 55.00
Planter, Lido, Triangular 26.00
Planter, Persian Rose, Scalloped, Flower Frog, 6 In. 40.00
Plate, Child's, Zona 30.00
Spittoon, Baldin, Large 95.00
Stein, Dickens Ware, David Copperfield Scene, Verse 395.00
Stein, Jumping Frog, 7 In. 435.00
Stein, Louwelsa, Hummingbird On Side, 6 1/2 In. 250.00
Sugar, Open, Mammy 300.00
Syrup, Mammy 325.00
Tankard, Aurelian, Berries, Signed Herald, 12 In. .... 275.00 To 350.00
Tankard, Dickens Ware, 5 1/2 In. 125.00
Tankard, Floretta, Grapes, 10 1/2 In. 95.00
Tankard, Louwelsa, Bright Mums, 12 1/2 In. 75.00
Teapot, Mammy 450.00
Teapot, Syrup, Sugar & Creamer, Mammy, 4 Piece 500.00
Tray, Coppertone, Frog, Lily Pad, 16 X 10 1/2 In. 160.00
Umbrella Stand, Ardsley, 19 In. 280.00
Umbrella Stand, Flemish 185.00
Umbrella Stand, Marvo 150.00
Umbrella Stand, Woodcraft, 21 In. 750.00
Urn, Copra, Pedestal, 9 1/2 In. 110.00
Urn, Roman Monumental, Applied Fruit, 11 X 13 1/2 In. 150.00
Vase, 2 Parrots On Branch, Glendale, 8 1/2 In. 200.00
Vase, Ardsley, Green Cattails, Water Lilies, 7 1/4 In. 35.00
Vase, Art Nouveau, Floral, 8 In. 65.00
Vase, Athens, Terra–Cotta Matte, Gargoyles In Relief, 9 1/2 In. 225.00
Vase, Aurelian, Blackberry Design, Artist W.T., 12 X 10 In. 345.00
Vase, Aurelian, Squat, Handle, Yellow Flower, 3 1/2 In. 135.00
Vase, Baldin, 6 1/2 In. 28.00
Vase, Baldin, 8 1/2 In., Pair 60.00
Vase, Baldin, Apples, 6 X 6 1/2 In. 95.00
Vase, Barcelona, 8 In. 95.00
Vase, Blue Ware, 9 In. 130.00
Vase, Bonito, Handles, Marked, 5 In. 40.00
Vase, Bronze Ware, 10 In. 65.00
Vase, Bud, Double, Oak Leaf, 7 In. 18.00
Vase, Bud, Glendale, Nesting Bird, Double, 7 In. 140.00
Vase, Bud, Triple, Roma, 2 In. 30.00
Vase, Bud, Warwick, 7 In. 20.00
Vase, Cameo, Blue, 7 In. 25.00
Vase, Chase, Footed, 10 In. 150.00
Vase, Coppertone, 6 In. 32.00
Vase, Cornish, Tan, Slender, 8 1/2 In. 18.50
Vase, Daffodils, Hudson, 10 In. 170.00
Vase, Darsie, Blue, 7 1/2 In. 20.00
Vase, Delta, Deep To Light Blue Matte Glaze, Iris, Marked, 7 In. 175.00
Vase, Dickens Ware II, Deer Leaping Log, Pillow 245.00

Vase, Dickens Ware, High Glaze, Stairway Scene, 2 Men, 14 1/2 In. 140.00
Vase, Dickens Ware, Monk Portrait, Blue On Blue Glaze, 14 In. 375.00
Vase, Dickens Ware, Portrait of Monk Winetaster, Signed, 7 In. 160.00
Vase, Dickens Ware, White Tail, Indian Chief, 9 In. 600.00
Vase, Dogwood, 7 X 3 1/2 In. 22.50
Vase, Eocean, 10 In. 225.00
Vase, Eocean, Beethoven Cameo, 12 In. 285.00
Vase, Eocean, Large Red Flower, 6 3/4 In. 65.00
Vase, Eocean, Pansy Design, 8 In. 135.00
Vase, Etna, 5 In. 95.00
Vase, Etna, 6 In. 55.00
Vase, Etna, 10 1/2 In. 110.00
Vase, Etna, Floral, 10 In., Pair 250.00
Vase, Etna, Floral, Gray, Signed, 6 In. 115.00
Vase, Etna, Gray Shaded, Floral, 8 In. 185.00
Vase, Etna, Gray Shaded, Floral, Hourglass Shape, 4 1/2 In. 80.00
Vase, Etna, Pink Flowers, 6 In. ....90.00 To 100.00
Vase, Fan, Voile, 8 In. 45.00
Vase, Fan, Woodcraft, 5 1/2 In. 35.00
Vase, Fleron, 4 3/4 In. 35.00
Vase, Floral, Green, 7 In. 15.00
Vase, Floretta, 4 3/4 In. 45.00
Vase, Floretta, 6 In. 58.00
Vase, Floretta, Art Nouveau Shaped Vines, Raspberries, 5 X 5 In. 72.00
Vase, Floretta, Cream, Pink Flowers, 10 In. 175.00
Vase, Floretta, Grapes, 9 In. 95.00
Vase, Forest, 8 In. 55.00
Vase, Forest, 12 In. 75.00
Vase, Forest, Fan, 7 In. 60.00
Vase, Glendale, 4 Marsh Birds At Nest, Other Landing, 6 1/2 In. 145.00
Vase, Glendale, Bird & Nest, Bulbous, 11 1/2 In. 170.00
Vase, Glendale, Bird In Nest, 4 In. 60.00
Vase, Glendale, Bird Watching Nest, Earth Colors, 7 In. 150.00
Vase, Gloria, Double, 4 1/2 In. 30.00
Vase, Hudson, 6 In. 140.00
Vase, Hudson, 10 In. 225.00
Vase, Hudson, Blue Shaded, Floral, D.England, 7 In. 195.00
Vase, Hudson, Blue, Bird On Blackberry Branch, 13 In. 200.00
Vase, Hudson, Daisies, 11 In. 350.00
Vase, Hudson, Dogwood, 6 1/4 In. 40.00
Vase, Hudson, Dogwood, Signed Walsh, 6 In. 135.00
Vase, Hudson, Double Handle, Slip Mums, Signed, 5 1/2 In. 155.00
Vase, Hudson, Flowers, Blue, Signed Timberlake, 7 1/2 In. 175.00
Vase, Hudson, Lavender Flowers, 5 1/2 In. 40.00
Vase, Hudson, Leaves & Berries, Blue, 7 In. 195.00
Vase, Hudson, McLaughlin, 9 In. 150.00
Vase, Hudson, Pillsbury Roses, Gray To Pink, 12 In. 375.00
Vase, Hudson, Pink To Pale Green, Pillsbury Artist, 5 1/4 In. 195.00
Vase, Hudson, Vine Design, White, Artist HP, 9 1/2 In. 285.00
Vase, Hudson, Waterlilies, Signed Timberlake, 8 In. 180.00
Vase, Indian, Full Headdress, Green Matte, 5 1/2 In. 425.00
Vase, Iris Design, Orange, Yellow, 11 In. 150.00
Vase, Ivoris, Footed, Applied Flower, 7 In. 35.00
Vase, Kenova Line, Figural Frog, Green Matte, Artist Signed, 7 In. 125.00
Vase, Klyro, 7 In. 15.00
Vase, Klyro, 9 In. 30.00
Vase, Knifewood, Owls, 8 1/4 In. 145.00
Vase, Knifewood, Peacock, 11 In. 135.00
Vase, LaSa, Bulbous, 3 1/2 In. 115.00
Vase, LaSa, Ovoid, 1920s, 8 In. 350.00
Vase, LaSa, Scenic, Iridescent Glaze, 8 3/4 In. 295.00
Vase, LaSa, Trees & Mountains, Gold Outline, 8 In. 90.00
Vase, LaSa, Trumpet Shape, Pine Tree Design, 7 1/4 In. 50.00
Vase, LeMar, Red & Black Palm Landscape, 3 1/2 In. 55.00

Vase, LeMar, Red Glaze, Black Trees & Scenery, 7 X 13 In.	175.00
Vase, LeMar, Trees, Red & Black, Paper Label, 6 In.	125.00
Vase, Lido, Blue To Green, 6 In.	30.00
Vase, Lily Design, Silvertone, 9 In.	80.00
Vase, Lonhuda, Handles, Yellow & Rust, 9 X 6 In.	285.00
Vase, Loru, Burgundy, 8 3/4 In.	30.00
Vase, Louwelsa, 3 Handles, 6 In.	165.00
Vase, Louwelsa, Bulbous, Orange & Green Mums, Brown Ground, 6 In.	125.00
Vase, Louwelsa, Cherries, Handles, Bulb Top, 6 In.	55.00
Vase, Louwelsa, Chrysanthemums On Browns, Olives, 5 X 2 1/2 In.	75.00
Vase, Louwelsa, Earth Tones, Enameled Fruit, McLaughlin, 14 1/2 In.	185.00
Vase, Louwelsa, Floral, Handles, 6 In.	85.00
Vase, Louwelsa, Gold Flowers, Signed LB, 8 1/2 In.	125.00
Vase, Louwelsa, Hand Painted, Jonquil, Foliage, Signed, 6 X 3 In.	150.00
Vase, Louwelsa, King In Robe & Crown, Blue, 12 In.	175.00
Vase, Louwelsa, Leaves & Berries, Mitchell, Handles, 12 In.	195.00
Vase, Louwelsa, Long Stemmed Florals, 11 1/2 In.	125.00
Vase, Louwelsa, Mums, Bulbous, Signed, 6 In.	100.00
Vase, Louwelsa, Poppy Design, Blue, Signed, 8 1/2 In.	400.00
Vase, Louwelsa, Yellow Flowers, Signed, 9 1/2 In.	125.00
Vase, Louwelsa, Yellow Roses, Green, Orange Leaves, 15 1/2 In.	155.00
Vase, Malvern, 6 1/2 In.	40.00
Vase, Manhattan, 7 In.	40.00
Vase, Manhattan, Plum, 6 1/4 In.	50.00
Vase, Marvo, 9 In.	45.00
Vase, Marvo, Bulbous, 8 In.	30.00 To 35.00
Vase, Marvo, Green, 9 In.	40.00
Vase, MiFlo, Handles, 9 1/2 In.	40.00
Vase, Neiska, 11 1/4 In.	70.00
Vase, Oak Leaf, Blue, 9 In.	19.50
Vase, Orange Matte, White Hunt Scene, Chase, 8 1/2 X 7 In.	195.00
Vase, Panella, 9 In.	35.00
Vase, Panella, Blue, 5 1/2 In.	45.00
Vase, Patra, 3 Footed, 7 In.	32.00 To 40.00
Vase, Patra, 5 In.	33.00
Vase, Roma, 4 In.	20.00
Vase, Roma, Grape, 10 In.	60.00
Vase, Roma, Marked, 12 1/2 In.	125.00
Vase, Sicard, Poppy Design, 12 In.	290.00
Vase, Sicard, Signed, 7 In.	185.00
Vase, Sicard, Trefoil Rim, Triangular, Clover Leaves, Dots, 6 1/2 In.	275.00
Vase, Silvertone, 9 In.	70.00
Vase, Silvertone, 16 In.	165.00
Vase, Silvertone, Lily, 10 In.	80.00
Vase, Silvertone, Morning Glories, 11 X 6 In.	95.00
Vase, Silvertone, Sunflower, Twisted Handles, 7 In.	60.00 To 65.00
Vase, Softtone, Blue, Impressed Mark, 12 1/2 In.	45.00
Vase, Souevo, 4 1/2 In.	75.00
Vase, Turada, 2 1/2 X 4 1/2 In.	110.00
Vase, Turkis, 5 In.	25.00
Vase, Velva, 9 1/2 In.	35.00
Vase, Warwick, Pillow, 7 In.	35.00
Vase, Wild Rose, 9 1/2 In.	25.00
Vase, Wild Rose, Footed, Blue, 1928, 7 1/2 In.	25.00
Vase, Wild Rose, Green, 7 In.	22.50
Vase, Wild Rose, Green, 8 In.	20.00
Vase, Wild Rose, Green, Handles, 9 1/2 In.	28.00
Vase, Wild Rose, Hand Painted, Hudson, 13 1/4 In.	475.00
Vase, Wild Rose, Pink, 8 1/2 In.	34.00
Vase, Wild Rose, White Rose, Blue Ground, 10 1/2 In.	28.00
Vase, Woodcraft, 10 In.	40.00
Vase, Woodcraft, Apples On Branch, Winding Around Tree, 9 In.	35.00
Vase, Woodrose, 7 In.	38.00
Vase, Woodrose, 10 In.	40.00

Vase, Zonia, 11 1/2 In.	300.00
Wall Pocket, Floral, Lavender Flowers	30.00
Wall Pocket, Glendale	150.00
Wall Pocket, Muskota	125.00
Wall Pocket, Woodcraft, Full Molded Squirrel	110.00
Wall Pocket, Woodcraft, Owl, 10 In.	60.00
Wall Pocket, Woodrose, Lavender, 7 In.	38.00
Wall Pocket, Woodrose, Pink, 6 1/2 In.	25.00

Thomas J. Wheatley worked with the founders of the art pottery movement in Cincinnati, Ohio, including M. Louise McLaughlin of the Rookwood Pottery. In 1880, he established his own pottery. Wheatley Pottery was purchased by the Cambridge Tile Manufacturing Company in 1927.

WHEATLEY, Vase, Applied Leaves & Flowers, Mottled Ground, Marked, 12 In.	150.00
Vase, Bulbous, Green Matte, Angled Feet, 10 3/4 In.	650.00
Vase, Diamond Shape, Florals, Mottled Yellow Ground, 8 1/2 In.	95.00
Vase, Flattened Oval, Primrose & Buds, Marked, 11 3/4 In.	100.00
Vase, Molded Leaves, Alternating With Buds, C.1905, 10 3/4 In.	650.00

Whieldon was a potter in England who worked alone and with Josiah Wedgwood in eighteenth–century England. Whieldon made many pieces in natural shapes, like cauliflowers or cabbages. The tortoiseshell glazed pieces are known as "clouded ware."

WHIELDON, Dish, Leaf, Green Glaze, Stem Forms Handle, C.1760, 9 3/4 In.	2500.00
Dish, Scrolled Panels, Green Glaze, C.1760, 8 3/8 In.	1600.00
Figurine, Cat, Seated, 6 In.	3200.00
Figurine, Cockerel, Molded Feathering, 4 In., C.1760	950.00
Figurine, Hawk, C.1780, 8 1/4 In.	400.00
Flask, Tortoiseshell Glaze, C.1770	1800.00
Plate, 9 1/2 In.	285.00
Plate, Lobed	1200.00
Tea Caddy, 3–Story House, C.1760, 5 1/8 In.	3400.00
Teabowl, Saucer, Tortoiseshell Glaze, C.1760, Saucer 2 5/8 In.	800.00
Teapot, Concave Shoulder, Globular Shape, Vines, C.1760, 4 In.	3300.00

Willets Manufacturing Company of Trenton, New Jersey, worked from 1879. The company made belleek in the late 1880s and 1890s in shapes similar to those used by the Irish Belleek factory. They stopped working about 1912. Pieces were marked with a variety of marks, all including the name Willets.

WILLETS, Basket, Spaghetti Strands, Applied Lilies-of-The-Valley, 9 In.	875.00
Bowl, Portrait, Black Mark, 7 1/2 In.	275.00
Bowl, Ruffled, Coral Handles, Paste Gold Sprays, Marked, 4 1/4 In.	175.00
Bowl, Wild Roses, Leaves, Gold Handles, Gold Rim, 7 X 4 In.	170.00
Cider Set, Belleek, 1880–90, 7 Piece	395.00
Cup & Saucer, Bouillon, Gold Twig Handle, Molded Design	85.00
Cup & Saucer, Bouillon, Ruffled Rim, Lotus Handles, Pink Mark	100.00
Cup & Saucer, Demitasse, Gold Brush Rim, Small Flowers, Pink Mark	75.00
Cup & Saucer, Embossed, Veining Traced In Gold, Red Mark	85.00
Mug, 2 Dutch Children, Dragon Handle, Hand Painted	95.00
Pitcher, Cider, Cherry Design	105.00
Pitcher, Cider, Hand Painted Dogwood, Beige Ground, 5 In.	195.00
Rose Bowl, Hand Painted Roses, Gold Tracery, Signed	125.00
Sugar & Creamer, Brushed Gold Rims, Yellow Flowers	125.00
Tankard, Lizard Handle, St.Bernard	650.00
Tankard, Monk Filling Wine Bottles, Black Mark, 13 In.	400.00
Tankard, Serpent Handle, St.Bernard, Artist Signed, 15 In.	750.00
Vase, Hand Painted Long Green Leaves Allover, 32 X 15 In.	350.00
Vase, Portait, Art Nouveau Woman, 1900s, Serpent Mark, 12 In.	160.00
Vase, Roses On Green, Hand Painted, 8 In.	100.00
Vase, Tiger Lilies, Red Ground, Ovoid, E.Delsart, 15 1/2 In.	475.00
Vase, White Cranes, Black & Gray, Cream Ground, 16 In.	235.00

WILLOW, see Blue Willow

Stained glass and beveled glass windows were popular additions to houses during the late nineteenth and early twentieth centuries. The old windows became popular with collectors in the 1970s; today, old and new examples are seen.

WINDOW, Banker's, Chestnut & Oak, Pennsylvania, 36 X 46 In. 325.00
Leaded Glass, 1 Side Stylized Feathering, F.L.Wright, 16 X 30 In. 5775.00
Leaded, Stippled Glass, Geometric, Square, 4 Ft. 100.00
Leaded, Woman, Flowing Hair, Wooden Frame, 1880–1910, 42 X 32 In. 2500.00
Trumeaux, Louis XVI, Parcel Gilt, Green Paint, Mirror, 72 In., Pair 4125.00

Wood carvings and wooden pieces are listed separately in this book. There are also wooden pieces found in other sections, such as Kitchen.

WOOD CARVING, 3 Cherubs, Reclining, Mahogany, 19 1/2 In. 65.00
3–Masted Schooner, Full Sail, American Flag, 11 1/2 X 20 In. 650.00
Box, Black Lacquer, Figural Scene Lid, Zu Spat, 3 In. 40.00
Breadboard, Knife, Carved Bread, Round, 2 Piece 65.00
Christ, Oak, Parcel Gilt, Salvatore Mundi, 30 1/2 In. 300.00
Deer, Composition Antlers, Brown & White Paint, 6 1/4 In. 27.50
Dragon, Mouth Open, Leg Moves, Japan, 19th Century, 27 1/2 In. 700.00
Eagle & Shield, Crossed Flags, Polychrome Paint, 42 1/2 In. 2850.00
Eagle, E Pluribus Unum, 24K Gold Leaf, P.Libbey, 40 X 18 In. 950.00
Eagle, Gold Surface, C.1860, 34 In.Wingspan 2700.00
Eagle, Pine, Raised Wings, On Log, Bernier, C.1910, 13 1/4 In. 3850.00
Eagle, Side View, Arrow, Bellamy Type, Dry Finish, Pine, 23 In. 800.00
Eagle, Spread Wings, American, Clutching Furled Flag, 42 In. 575.00
Eagle, Spread Wings, Inscribed Banner, Bellamy, 9 X 25 In. 4950.00
Elephant, Ebony, Jeweled, Ivory & Brass, 7 X 8 In. 495.00
Elephant, Teakwood, 34 X 32 In. 3000.00
Figurehead, Eagle, Wings Back, 19th Century, 19 X 7 In. 2000.00
Fishing Scene, Comical, Early 20th Century, 18 X 24 1/2 In. 1500.00
Floral Arrangement, Fence, Polychrome, 19th Century, 8 In. 150.00
Goblet, Treenware, Laburnum Wood, 18th Century, Pair 425.00
Hunter & His Dog, Friendship, Maine, G.R.Huey, C.1920, 14 In. 550.00
Lizard, Glass Eyes, Old Green Paint, 20th Century, 41 In. 295.00
Mask, Festival, Man With Golden Beard, Glass Eyes, 10 In. 65.00
Mask, Ivory Teeth & Eyes, Bearded, Chinese 75.00
Old Man & Child, Man Holding Creatures, Teak, Chinese, 27 In. 95.00
Rooster, Stands On Ball, Mounted On Stepped Block, 10 In. 275.00
Shelf, Wall, Chip Carved 200.00
State Seal, Banner Says Dirigo, Sailors, Anchor, 45 In. 1045.00
Totem, Indian, Polychrome, 1 Piece, Pencil Inscription, 9 In. 105.00
Unicorn Head, Continental, Open Mouth, 46 1/2 In. 1400.00
Wood Hawk, Outstretched Wings, Brown, 20th Century, 16 In. 1980.00

Wood was used for many containers and tools used in the early home. Small wooden pieces are called "treenware" in England, but the term "woodenware" is more common in the United States.

WOODEN, see also Kitchen; Advertising; Tool
WOODEN, Barrel, Pork, Staved, Lock–Lapped Hoops, Stave Handles, 17 In. 350.00
Basket, Covered, Marquetry, Herringbone, Mermaid Figures, 10 In. 100.00

Wooden items should be kept off windowsills. Direct sunlight will harm the wood finishes.

Don't store wooden bowls and other pieces on their sides. This can cause them to warp.

Bin, 4 Sections, 31 1/2 X 9 X 18 1/2 In. 165.00
Bootjack, Tiger Maple, Folding 30.00
Bowl, 17 X 26 1/2 X 4 1/2 In. 85.00
Bowl, Ash Burl, Dark Finish, 10 1/2 X 4 In. 240.00
Bowl, Ash Burl, Handles, Oval, 14 1/2 X 10 1/2 In. 825.00
Bowl, Burl, Flared Sides, Irregular Oblong Shape, 17 X 21 In. 700.00
Bowl, Burl, Irregular Shape, 1 5/8 X 3 7/8 In. 95.00
Bowl, Burl, Protruding Lip, Tooled Rings At Bottom, 14 1/2 X 5 In. 500.00
Bowl, Burl, Rimmed & Footed, Late 18th Century, 11 X 4 1/2 In. 475.00
Bowl, Carved Edge Flange Forms Handles, Old Red, 17 X 24 1/4 In. 85.00
Bowl, Child's, Turned, 18th Century, 4 3/4 X 5 5/8 In. 95.00
Bowl, Chopping, Burl, Dry Finish, Molded Edge, 19 1/2 In. 1050.00
Bowl, Hand Hewn, Red & Blue Paint, 12 1/2 X 36 1/2 X 4 1/2 In. 115.00
Bowl, Mill Scene, Mounted On Octagonal Frame, 17 1/2 In. 40.00
Bowl, Oblong, Patina, 9 3/4 X 17 1/4 In. 60.00
Bowl, Old Red Paint, American, Bird's-Eye Maple, 32 3/8 X 9 In. 150.00
Bowl, Turned, Dark Finish, 18 3/4 X 19 1/2 X 6 In. 85.00
Bowl, Turned, From 1 Piece of Poplar, 22 X 7 1/2 In. 145.00
Bowl, Turned, Original Putty Paint, 18th Century, 6 1/4 X 6 In. 225.00
Bowl, Turned, Original Red In & Out, Early 19th Century, 6 X 19 In. 355.00
Bowl, Turned, Salmon Paint, Foot, American, 19th Century, 6 In. 175.00
Bowl, Yellow Paint, 26 In. 245.00
Bowl, Zigzag Design Rim, European, 11 X 4 In. 60.00
Box, 6 Drawers, Blue Over Green, Mid-19th Century, 8 X 16 In. 395.00
Box, Apple, Pine, Scalloped Edges, 9 X 13 3/4 In. 177.00
Box, Dough, Covered, Blue-Green Paint, Dovetailed, 34 In. 240.00
Box, Dough, Walnut, Square Nail Construction, 34 1/2 In. 115.00
Box, Lid, Wooden Spring Fastener, Blue Paint, Floral, 6 X 4 In. 27.00
Box, Original Red Sponging, Yellow Ground, Bird On Side, 5 3/4 In. 1000.00
Box, Shoeshine, Hinged Top With Foot Rest 20.00
Box, Tole Design, Black Ground, Dome Top, Brass Bail Handle, 12 In. 900.00
Box, Walnut, Hinged Lid, Dovetailed, 37 3/4 X 7 X 3 1/4 In. 35.00
Breadboard, Mustard Yellow Over Gray, 19th Century, 18 X 24 In. 250.00
Bucket, Brown Flame Graining On Yellow, Wire Bail Handle, 7 In. 165.00
Bucket, Pine, Yellow, Says Clear Vinegar, Bail Handle 48.00
Bucket, Red Paint, 12 X 9 1/2 In. 45.00
Bucket, Red, Buttonhole Lapped Hoops, New England, Handle, 9 In. 350.00
Bucket, Stave Constructed, Iron Bands, Wire Bail, Handle, 3 1/2 In. 45.00
Bucket, Storage, Covered, Painted Green, Name Nutmegs, 11 1/2 In. 300.00
Bucket, Sugar, Copper Nails, Bail Handle, 6 1/2 X 7 In. 72.00
Bucket, Sugar, Covered, Turned, Wire & Wooden Bail Handle, 10 In. 225.00
Bucket, Sugar, Interlocking Hoops, Old Medium Green, Lid, 10 1/2 In. 195.00
Bucket, Sugar, Stave, Blue Paint, Wooden Handle, Wire Bail, 7 In. 325.00
Bucket, Sugar, Wire Bail Handle, Small 55.00
Bucket, Wire Bands, Gray Paint, Staved, Bail Handle, 8 In. 60.00
Bucket, Wooden Ears, Bentwood Handle, Old Red Paint, 11 In. 225.00
Bust, Duke of Wellington, Boxwood, Signed & Dated, 9 In. 525.00
Canteen, Militia, Painted, Red, Blue, Initials D.P.U., 19th Century 500.00
Canteen, Staved, Carved B.& H.Both Sides, 19th Century, 10 In. 50.00
Cup & Saucer, Painted Floral, Lehnware 575.00
Curtain Rod, Victorian Style, Wooden Loops, 4 Ft. 8.00
Egg Rack, Hard Boiled, Birch, Salt Dip Pockets, 1800s, 12 Holes 220.00
Figurine, Horse, Black Paint, Laminated & Carved, 26 1/4 In. 1000.00
Firkin, Old Mustard Paint, Lid, American, Late 19th Century, 9 In. 240.00
Firkin, Sugar, Original Blue-Green Paint, 14 1/4 In. 125.00
Firkin, Wooden Lap Bands, Primitive 55.00
Goblet, Painted Floral, Pedestal, Lehnware 1200.00
Grain Measure, Metal Bands, Cross Stretcher Bottom, Fry, N.H., 9 In. 23.00
Hand Mirror, Pine, Worn Green Paint, 2 1/2 X 4 3/4 In. 150.00
Hat Stand, Pedestal, Original Paint, 10 In. 8.50
Humidor, Doghouse Shape, Dog, Glass Eyes, Lid, Cigar Rack, 9 In. 75.00
Jar, Original Dark Red Sponging, Covered, Poplar, 7 3/8 In. 525.00
Jar, Pease, Flared Top, Varnish Finish, 3 3/4 In. 12.50
Jar, Poplar, Dark Red Sponging, Yellow Ground, 13 1/4 In. 370.00

Worcester, Mug, Dragon, Marked, C.1760,
3 3/8 In.
Worcester, Coffeepot, Dragon, Marked,
1760–65, 8 In.

Jar, Poplar, Red Sponging, 4 3/8 In.	150.00
Jar, Turned, Wooden Handle, Wire Bail, Natural Refinished, 11 In.	45.00
Keg, Oak, Brassbound, Victorian, Oval Tapered Form, 25 1/2 In.	247.00
Key, Bed, Handmade, For Tightening Rope Beds, 16 1/2 X 16 In.	37.50
Ladle, Hand Carved, 13 3/4 In.	30.00
Mortar & Pestle, Burl, 6 3/8 In.	150.00
Mortar & Pestle, Mortar Hollowed From Tree Trunk, 20 In.	35.00
Mortar & Pestle, Turned, 18 1/2 In.	100.00
Mortar & Pestle, Worn Blue Paint Over Yellow, 7 In.	100.00
Paddle, Burl, Hook Finial For Edge Of Bowl, New Jersey, 13 In.	900.00
Peel, Pie, Hanging Hole, Oblong Edge Blade, 20 In.	42.00
Picture, Marquetry, Figure Riding Horse, 20th Century, 14 X 17 In.	50.00
Plate, Treenware, Beaded, Natural Patina, 19th Century, 7 1/2 In.	150.00
Pot, Pounce, Lignum Vitae, Dark, England	275.00
Pounce Sander, To Dry Ink, Dark Blue Banded Paint, 18th Century	85.00
Rack, Spoon, Brown & Gray Paint, Hand Carved, Square Nails, Pre–1850	385.00
Rack, Spoon, Wall, 2 Tiers, Red Paint, Open Compartment, 17 1/2 In.	600.00
Rack, Towel, Maple, 2 Bars, T Shape Ends, Red Paint, 28 X 28 In.	125.00
Rattle, Baby, Interlocking Key Design, Half Moons, Hearts, C.1830	85.00
Rolling Pin, Treenware, Grooved Rectangular Base, 6 1/2 In.	110.00
Saffron Box, Dome Covered, Painted Floral, Footed, Lehnware	160.00
Salt, Master, Turned Cherry, Pedestal, Early 1800s, 3 X 3 In.	28.00
Scoop, Burl, Checkered Design, American, Late 18th Century	250.00
Scoop, Cranberry, F.L.Buckingham Mfg., Mass., Fitted As Rack	150.00
Scoop, Cranberry, Original Paint & Canvas, 1906	170.00
Scoop, Grain, Hawkeye Feed, Muscatine, Iowa	40.00
Shovel, Grain, Signed Lewis Ackes 1840, 35 In.	55.00
Spice Chest, Footed, Joseph Lehn	7500.00
Spoon, Large Bowl, Hook Handle, Norwegian	45.00
Stamp, Embroidery, Columns, Half Round Shape, 18th Century, 4 In.	140.00
Tray, Apple, Dovetailed Construction, 16 1/2 X 26 In.	95.00
Tray, Bread, Hitchcock Chair Co., Green Paint, Stenciling, C.1860	55.00
Trencher, Original Blue, American, 19th Century, 20 In.	500.00
Tub, Wooden Bands, Double Handles, Green Brown Paint, 13 1/2 In.	245.00
Vase, Spill, Yew, Dark, England, Pair	325.00
Vase, Turned Bird's–Eye Maple, 5 In.	20.00
Watch Hutch, Primitive, Gray Paint, Hanging Crest, 8 In.	295.00
Weather House, Husband & Wife Come Out & Forecast Weather, German	35.00

Worcester porcelains were made in Worcester, England, from 1751. The firm went through many name changes and eventually, in 1862, became The Royal Worcester Porcelain Company Ltd. Collectors often refer to Dr. Wall, Barr, Flight, and other names that indicate time periods and artists at the factory. It became part of Royal Worcester Spode Ltd. in 1976.

WORCESTER, see also Royal Worcester

WORCESTER, Basket, Center Rose Florettes, Twig Handles, C.1765, 8 1/2 In.	1450.00
Basket, Dessert, Twisted Handles, C.1765, 6 3/4 In.	1200.00
Beaker, Floral Sprays, Roundel, Flight & Barr, C.1807, 4 In., Pair	200.00
Bowl, Bengal Tiger, Scalloped, C.1773, 11 1/2 In., Pair	2000.00
Bowl, Covered, Dr.Wall, Fluted, Floral Finial, 18th Century	40.00
Coffeepot, Dragon, Marked, 1760–65, 8 In. ....*Illus*	3190.00
Creamer, Flower Garland, Turquoise Bands, 4 In.	225.00
Cup & Saucer, Handleless, Dr.Wall, Courting Scene, C.1770, Pair	600.00
Cup, Blue & White Floral, Chamberlain, C.1794	115.00
Mug, Dragon, Marked, C.1760, 3 3/8 In. ....*Illus*	1980.00
Plate, Dr.Wall, Cobalt Fishscale Ground, C.1775, 9 3/4 In.	1100.00
Sauce Boat, Dr.Wall, Swan's Neck Handle, C.1751, 7 In.	350.00
Sauce Boat, Leaf Form, Branch Handles, C.1751, 8 In., Pair	700.00
Spice Jar, Covered, Cobalt Fishscale, Medallions, 6 1/2 In.	450.00
Tea Service, Swirl Body, Blossoms, C.1815, 41 Piece	1200.00
Teabowl, Tulip Sprays, Wave Form Body, 18th Century, Marked	60.00
Teapot, Gold, Blue, Red, Chamberlain, 1790s	325.00

Souvenirs of World War I and World War II are collected today. Be careful not to store anything that includes live ammunition. Your local police station will tell you how to dispose of the explosives.

WORLD WAR I, Cartridge Belt	9.00
Compass, Engineer's, Gurley	55.00
Dog Tag	6.50
Dress Shirt & Trousers, Alpaca	15.00
Flag, U.S.Infantry	75.00
Flight Cover, Eddie Rickenbacker, Autographed	125.00
Frame, Iron, Crossed Flags, Swords, Cannon, Eagle On Top	38.00
Handkerchief, Greetings From Camp Dix, N.J.	9.50
Helmet, Dress, German	30.00
Holster, Leather, U.S.Army	25.00
Knife, Bolo, Bowie, Hardwood Grip, U.S., 9 5/8 In.	45.00
Knife, Trench, Knuckle Duster, U.S., Scabbard	80.00
Map, Western Battlefields, Pocket	15.00
Periscope, Trench, Wooden	40.00
Poster, Help The Red Cross, Nurse, Soldier, 1918, 19 X 28 In.	95.00
Poster, Journee Du Poilu, French, 48 X 32 In. ....*Illus*	50.00
Poster, Marine Recruiting, J.M.Flagg, 28 X 40 In.	250.00
Poster, Pour La France, French, 1915, 45 X 31 In. ....*Illus*	100.00
Poster, U.S.Army Builds Men, Doughboy, Flag, 19 X 30 In.	200.00
Poster, Victory Loan, Said We Couldn'T Fight, 41 X 30 In.	150.00
Salt & Pepper, Bullet Shape, Camp Lewis	10.00
Uniform, Overseas, Cap, Leggings, Wool	65.00
WORLD WAR II, Album, Cigarette Cards, German, Complete	45.00
Ammunition Pouch, German	10.00
Ammunition Pouch, Russian	8.00
Armband, Nazi, Black, White & Red	22.50
Bag, Bread, German	20.00
Bank, Wooden Tank, Save For Victory, 1940s, 2 X 6 X 3 In.	12.00
Bayonet, Leather Belt, German	35.00
Belt & Buckle, Nazi	35.00
Belt & Buckle, Tropical, Web	50.00
Belt, Cartridge, England	15.00
Binoculars, Submarine, Nazi, 7 X 50 In.	125.00
Binoculars, U.S.Army	45.00
Bomb, Navy, Dummy, Post World War II	45.00

World War I, Poster, Journee Du Poilu,   World War I, Poster, Pour La France, French,
French, 48 X 32 In.   1915, 45 X 31 In.

Book, Mein Kampf, Presentation Copy	60.00
Box, Ammunition, Metal	20.00
Buckle, Navy, Nazi	38.00
Buckle, Navy, Ornate Anchor & Flower Center, Japanese	80.00
Button, Anti–Hitler, 2 1/2 In.	35.00
Button, Remember Pearl Harbor, Wooden, Liberty Bell, 1 In.	20.00
Canteen & Cup, Engraved Assignments of GI Who Carried It	35.00
Cap, AAF Overseas, Khaki	6.00
Clock, Aircraft, Waltham, 8–Day	25.00
Currency, Nazi Concentration Camp, Theresienstadt	30.00
Dagger, German Storm Trooper	125.00
Dagger, Luftwaffe, Amber Handle, Silver Plated Mounts, 1937	150.00
Dagger, Navy, German, Engraved Blade, Dress Knot	285.00
Dagger, Nazi S.A., Kuno Ritter Sheath, Strap	130.00
Dagger, Nazi, Rad.Sr.Exc.H.T.On Crossguard, No Scabbard	375.00
Dagger, Officer's, Luftwaffe, Silver Bullion Strap	220.00
Flag, Battle, Nazi, 3 X 5 Ft.	20.00
Flag, Japanese Naval Squadron, With Standard	600.00
Flag, Red Cross, American Motor Corp.	25.00
Gas Mask, German	25.00
Hat, Fur, German	75.00
Helmet, Cloth, U.S.Print, Army Air Force	18.00
Helmet, Luftschutz, Insignia, Wings, Swastika	95.00
Helmet, Nazi, Goggles, Military Badges	75.00
Iron Cross, Nazi, Ribbon, 1 Side 1813, Reverse 1939, Swastika	65.00
Jacket, Flight, Size 38	68.00
Knife, Commando, Aluminum Grip, 12 In.Sheath	40.00
Knife, Trench, Oval Brass Guard, Antler Grip, 6 3/4 In.	42.50
Knife, Utility, Nazi Paratrooper, Sliding Handle	150.00
Letter Opener, Sword, Swastika, Name, Ivory Handle, 8 In.	60.00
Mug, Trench Art, Made From Shell Casing	40.00
Overcoat, Woman's, Army Green Wool, Canadian	45.00
Overcoat, Woman's, Green Wool, U.S.A., Unused	40.00
Periscope, Sniper, Case, Japanese	225.00
Pin, Wings, Glider Pilot, Sterling Silver, 3 In.	100.00
Playing Cards, American Red Cross, Box, Dated 1943	10.00
Poster, Buy A Bond Before Sunset, Stars, Stripes, 20 X 30 In.	125.00
Poster, Every Canadian Must Fight, 1943, 21 X 30 In.	45.00
Poster, Gee, Wish I Were A Man, Girl In Sailor's Outfit, 1918	600.00
Poster, Plant A Victory Garden, 1943, 22 X 28 In.	45.00
Poster, Sullivan Brothers Missing In Action, 22 X 28 In.	30.00

Poster, U.S.Dept.of Navy Aeronautics, 18 X 24 In. 150.00
Poster, We Shall Not Fail, King George, Churchill, 15 X 18 In. 35.00
Punch Cartoon, Hitler & Nazis, Full Page, 1924–36 .... 5.00
Radio, Telephone, Zeppelin Terminal, Nazi 200.00
Raincoat, Man's, Naval, Black Rubberized 40.00
Range Finder, Cloth Case, Japanese 200.00
Ration Book, M.Powell, Wellsburg, W.Va., Stamps, 1944–45 .... 8.00
Ring, Swastika, Good Luck, Grass, 4 Leaf Clover, Small Size 25.00
Sextant, Air Force, Wood Base 35.00
Sextant, Lifeboat, Case, Instructions 95.00
Soap Saver, Uncle Sam, War 12.00
Spoon, Trench Art, Aluminum, Doughboy Bowls, Pair 20.00
Spyglass, U.S.Navy, Case 195.00
Stationery Packet, Navy, Comic Design, Package, 1942 .... 25.00
Stopwatch, Wood Case, Japanese 140.00
Sword, Officer's, Nazi Army, Marked 150.00
Telegraph, Marine, Double Face, Handles, German 685.00
Telephone, Field, German 110.00
Telephone, Signal Corps, Leather Case 35.00
Telescope, Ship, Japanese, Large 250.00
Telescope, U.S.N., Quartermaster's, 16X 195.00
Tunic, Medical Officer's, Nazi 195.00
Wallet, SS Insignia, Leather 15.00

Souvenirs of all world's fairs are collected. The first fair was the
Great Exhibition of 1851 in London. Memorabilia of fairs include
directories, pictures, fabrics, ceramics, etc.

WORLD'S FAIR, Apron, 1965, Color 15.00
Ashtray, 1904, St.Louis, Mo. 20.00
Ashtray, 1933, Century of Progress, Brass 25.00
Ashtray, 1933, Lucky Penny 35.00
Ashtray, 1935, California & Pacific Exposition, Bronze 20.00
Ashtray, 1939, San Francisco, White Metal 15.00
Ashtray, 1964, New York 10.00
Badge, 1893, Beale Style 65.00
Badge, 1933, Security Guard 45.00
Badge, Employee's, Century of Progress, Red 25.00
Bank, 1939, Round, Glass, New York 35.00
Bank, N.Y., Unisphere, Children On Reverse 30.00
Beanie, 1939, N.Y., Blue & Orange, Symbols 10.00
Bedspread, 1893, Needlepoint, 12 Buildings 350.00
Bell, 1926, Walnut Base 95.00
Book, 1893, Atlas 50.00
Book, 1893, Photographs, 9 1/2 X 9 In. 95.00
Book, 1904, Grandeur of The Universal Exposition, St.Louis 35.00
Book, 1933, Century of Progress 17.50
Book, 1933, Official View, Kaufmann & Fabry Photos, 24 Pages 15.00
Book, 1939, Palestine Pavilion, New York 7.00
Book, 1940, Official Guide, New York 15.00
Bookmark, 1933 .... 4.50
Bottle Opener, 1933 .... 5.00
Bowl, 1933, White Metal, Silver Finish, Japan, 6 1/2 In. 7.00
Box, 1900, Jewelry, Color Print, Lid, Palais D'Electricite 50.00
Box, 1908, Jewelry, Scottish National Expo, 2 3/4 In. 40.00
Brochure, 1939, Heinz Dome, Folds Out, 14 X 20 In. 20.00
Button, 1900, Blanke's World's Fair Coffee, 1 In. 6.00
Button, 1904, World's Fair Souvenir Beer, St.Louis, 7/8 In. 5.00
Button, 1933, I Was There, Logo, Red, White & Blue, 3/4 In. 12.50
Catalog, 1939, Lullaby Furniture, New York 12.00
Cigarette Case, 1933, Chicago 35.00
Coin Purse, 1904, St.Louis 12.00
Cup & Creamer, 1893, Ruby Glass 85.00
Cup, 1904, Porcelain Over Metal, Napoleon, Thomas Jefferson 50.00
Cup, 1904, St.Louis, Palace of Electricity 20.00

Dispenser, Cigarette, 1904, St.Louis	25.00
Fan, 1904, Gold Dust Twins, Paper, Repaired	38.00
Faucet, 1893, Columbian, Decal, Wooden	20.00
Filmstrip, 1939, Box, 2 Piece	15.00
Flue Cover, 1904	22.00
Game, Pinball, 1933, Glass Cover, Wooden, 10 Balls, 11 X 17 In.	75.00
Globe, 1893-1933, Tin, Iron Stand, With Seal, 4 1/2 In.	38.00
Handkerchief, 1893, Embroidered Flowers	20.00
Handkerchief, 1893, Embroidered World's Fair, Rosie	35.00
Handkerchief, 1904, St.Louis	20.00
Hat, 1933, Al Smith, Metal	50.00
Hatchet, 1893, George Washington On Blade, Glass, Libbey	55.00
Horseshoe, 1939, Metal	35.00
Inkwell, 1904, Crab	40.00
Inkwell, 1939, Sphere	15.00
Juice Squeezer, 1893	65.00
Ladle, 1939, New York	12.00
Lard Pail, 1876, Naphey's, Miniature	14.00
Letter Opener, 1904, Bronze, Eagle, Indian, St.Louis, 7 In.	40.00
Letter Opener, 1933, 3-D Building On Handle	12.00
Luggage Tag, 1893, Columbian, Metal	40.00
Match Holder, 1893, Souvenir Shoe, Chicago	22.00
Match Safe, 1904, Ringen Quick Meal Stove	75.00
Match Safe, 1904, Silver Metal, Black Paint, St.Louis	32.00
Mirror, Hand, 1904, Beveled, Small	35.00
Mug, 1933, Hall of Science, Travel & Transportation Palace	40.00
Napkin Ring, 1904	10.00
Paperweight, 1893, Administration Building	45.00
Paperweight, 1904, Festival Hall & Cascades, 4 X 3 In.	8.00
Pen, 1933, Oversized, 10 In.	9.00
Pencil, 1933, Oversized, 10 In.	9.00
Pennant, 1933, Felt, 28 In.	16.00
Photograph, 1893, Cramer's Isochromatic, Dry Plate	100.00
Picture, 1893, Cloth, Red, White & Green, 18 X 19 In.	65.00
Picture, 1893, Lewis & Clark, 1905, Guards, Framed, 14 X 18 In.	95.00
Pill Box, 1904, Painted Porcelain Top	40.00
Pillow Cover, 1939, Silk	12.00
Plaque, 1939, Woman, Wooden	35.00
Plate, 1893, Scenes Around Edge, Columbus, Bronze, 18 In.	350.00
Plate, 1893, U.S.Govt.Building, Dark Blue, Wedgwood, 8 1/4 In.	40.00
Plate, 1904, Festival Hall & Cascade Gardens, 7 In.	17.00
Plate, 1933, 30 Scenes, Century of Progress, Chicago	15.00
Plate, 1933, Science Hall, Pickard	10.00
Plate, Salad, 1893, Crescent Shape, Lagoon Picture, Pair	28.00
Portfolio, 1893, Columbian Exposition	50.00
Postcard Set, 1933, Chicago	6.00
Postcard, 1939, New York, 12 Different Photos	20.00
Puzzle, Jigsaw, Bird's-Eye View, 1933, 17 1/2 X 11 1/2 In.	28.00
Record, 1964, New York, Triumph of Man, Original Jacket	7.50
Ring, 1933, Chicago, Travel & Transport	20.00
Rubber Hotdog, 1933, American Hairless Dog, Mail Box, 6 In.	15.00
Salt & Pepper, 1893, Egg Shape, Columbian Exposition On Front	25.00
Salt & Pepper, 1933, Trylon & Perisphere, Celluloid, Chicago	18.00
Salt & Pepper, 1939, Trylon & Perisphere, Pink, Lenox	85.00
Saucer, 1904, St.Louis, U.S.Government Building	20.00
Scarf, 1964, New York City Scenes	12.00
Scarf, Table, 1904, Washington & Jefferson, 18 X 18 In.	100.00
Scoop, 1893, Oak, Round	55.00
Shoe, 1893, Libbey, Frosted	45.00
Shot Cup, 1934, Metal, Silver Finish, Emblem, 4 1/2 In.	9.00
Spoon, 1893, Columbus Head Handle, Ornate Bowl, Silver	10.00
Spoon, 1898, Transportation Building Bowl, Leonard Mfg., 6 In.	15.00
Spoon, 1939, New York, Silver Plate	15.00
Stein, 1904, St.Louis, Bronze, 3 In.	65.00

Stock Certificate, 1893, Columbian, 2 Shares 275.00
Stock Certificate, 1901, Pan American Expo., 1 Share 150.00
Stool, 1939, Kan–O–Seat, Wooden, Cane, Foldup, 9 X 28 In. 20.00
Sugar, 1893, Ruby Glass 40.00
Tablecloth, 1939, 50 X 100 In. 85.00
Tapestry, 1933, Airplane & Blimp Scene 65.00
Tea Set, Doll's, 1933, Metal, Box 20.00
Teapot, 1940, Gold Sphere & Obelisk, Hall China, 6 In. 125.00
Thermometer, 1933, Metal, Avenue of Flags Picture, 5 X 7 In. 6.00
Thermometer, 1939, Inside Large Key 50.00
Thimble, 1892, Chicago, Sterling Silver 150.00
Tie Clip, 1934, Emblem 8.00
Tip Tray, 1904, Red Raven Splits 65.00
Toothpick, 1893, Chicago, Thumbprint, Ruby 30.00
Toy, Bus, 1933, Greyhound Line, Iron, Blue–White, 10 1/2 In. 250.00
Tray, 1893, Scene of Fair, Tin 35.00
Tray, 1939, Reverse Painted On Glass, Chicago, 11 X 17 In. 48.00
Tray, 1939, San Francisco, White Metal 15.00
Tray, Serving, 1939, New York, 18 X 12 In. 20.00
Tumbler, 1893, Columbian Exposition, Ruby, 2 1/2 In. 25.00
Tumbler, 1904, St.Louis, Metal 14.00
Tumbler, 1939, Different Fair Scenes, N.Y., 4 In., Set of 6 .... 45.00
Tumbler, 1939, Enameled Federal Pavilion 15.00
Umbrella, 1933 .... 25.00
Vase, 1893, Vaseline, Cattails, Rabbits, Sawtooth, 4 1/4 In. 125.00
Vase, 1904, Scene of Electricity Bldg., St.Louis, 6 In. 150.00
Vase, 1933, Tin, Brown Marbelized 125.00
Walking Stick, 1939, Dog's Head 24.00
Watch Fob, 1904, Jefferson & Napoleon, Aluminum 20.00
Watch Fob, 1933, Century of Progress 25.00
Wine, 1903, Ruby Glass 40.00
Woven Silk, 1893, Phoenix, Machinery Hall, 10 1/2 In. 150.00
Woven Silk, 1901, George Washington, B.B.Tilt, 7 1/2 In. 110.00

> Yellowware is a heavy earthenware made of a yellowish clay. It
> varies in color from light yellow to orange–yellow. Many
> nineteenth– and twentieth–century kitchen bowls and jugs were
> made of yellowware. It was made in England and in the United
> States. Another form of pottery that is sometimes classed as
> yellowware is listed in this book under Mocha.

YELLOWWARE, Bank, Pig, Brown Rockingham Glaze, 3 3/4 In. 20.00
Bean Pot, Marked Watt, 8 1/2 X 6 1/2 In. 30.00
Beater Jar, Riverside Dairy 48.00
Bedpan, Flying Turkey 47.50
Bowl, Blue & Pink Bands, 10 In. 18.00
Bowl, Blue Bands, 7 In. 22.00
Bowl, Brown & White Bands, 6 1/2 In. 9.00
Bowl, Brown & White Bands, 8 In. 20.00
Bowl, Brown & White Stripes, 12 In. 50.00
Bowl, Brown Stripes, 6 In. 12.00
Bowl, Brown Stripes, 8 In. 37.00
Bowl, Brown Stripes, 10 In. 20.00
Bowl, Brown Stripes, 12 In. 30.00
Bowl, Cottage Pattern, Girl Watering Flowers, 10 In. 115.00
Bowl, Mixing, Brown & White Bands, 8 In. 20.00
Bowl, Mixing, Brown & White Stripes, 10 X 4 1/2 In. 25.00
Bowl, Mixing, Brown & White Stripes, 2–Tone Glaze, 13 In. 45.00
Bowl, Mixing, Rockingham Sponging, 12 3/8 X 5 3/4 In. 55.00
Bowl, Mixing, Wide Blue Band, 8 1/2 In. 22.50
Bowl, Raised Panel Design, 8 In. 35.00
Bowl, Roseville, 9 In. 45.00
Bowl, White Bands, 3 In. 65.00
Bowl, White Stripes, 10 In. 32.00
Bowl, White Stripes, 11 3/4 X 5 5/8 In. 32.00

Butter, Butterfly Blue, Bail, Covered	155.00
Butter, Peacock At Fountain With Palms	60.00
Canister, Tea, Penn.Dutch Flower	100.00
Chamber Pot, Black Stripes, White Band, Seaweed Design, 10 In.	65.00
Crock, Cheese, Covered, Kraft Krock, Tavern Scene	42.50
Crock, State Fair Peanut Butter, Red Letters	65.00
Crock, Sugar, Pantry	75.00
Cup, Custard, 2 Blue & 1 Pink Bands, 6 Piece	180.00
Decanter, Applied Masonic Designs, Impressed Perry, 8 In.	95.00
Dish, Covered, Rockingham Sponging, 2 Sections, 9 In.	55.00
Jar, Grease	100.00
Jar, Spice, Covered	50.00
Jug, Brown, 7 In.	15.00
Jug, Green Circles, Brown Daubs, 4 7/8 In.	195.00
Jug, Puzzle, 2 Tone Clear & Green Glaze, Europe, 8 In.	30.00
Jug, Vinegar, Advertising, 4 1/2 In.	40.00
Mold, Corn	58.00
Mold, Pinwheel Design	38.50
Mold, Wheat Sheaf, 6 In.	45.00
Mug, Barrel, White Interior, 16 Oz.	35.00
Mug, Blue Mocha Design	245.00
Mug, Compliments of Retail Grocer's Assoc., Davenport, IA	38.00
Mug, F.D.R.New Deal	24.00
Pie Plate	10.00
Pitcher, Acanthus Leaves, Brown & Green Sponging, 6 7/8 In.	65.00
Pitcher, Brown & Green Sponge Spatter, 4 5/8 In.	50.00
Pitcher, Green Cows, 8 In.	95.00
Pitcher, Rooster, 6 In.	49.00
Plate, Beaded, 8 In.	40.00
Rolling Pin, Original Handles	265.00
Salt & Pepper	76.00
Salt, Hanging, Wooden Lid	45.00
Salt, Open	75.00 To 90.00
Spittoon, Rockingham Glaze	48.00
Sugar, Covered, Small	75.00
Sugar, Open, Small	65.00
Teapot, Brown & Green Sponging, 5 1/2 In.	225.00

ZANE WARE

Zane Pottery was founded in 1921 by Adam Reed and Harry McClelland in South Zanesville, Ohio, at the old Peters and Reed Building. Zane pottery is very similar to Peters and Reed pottery, but it is usually marked. The factory was sold in 1941 to Lawton Gonder.

ZANE, Bowl, Glossy, Flared, 3 1/2 X 10 In.	20.00
Vase, Landsun, 6 In.	30.00

LA MORO

The Zanesville Art Pottery was founded in 1900 by David Schmidt in Zanesville, Ohio. The firm made faience umbrella stands, jardinieres, and pedestals. The company closed in 1962. Many pieces are marked with just the words "La Moro."

ZANESVILLE, Vase, Bulbous, Floral, La Moro, Signed M.Gillie, 7 1/2 In.	250.00

ZSOLNAY PÉCS

Zsolnay pottery was made in Hungary after 1862 and was characterized by Persian, Art Nouveau, or Hungarian motifs. A series of new Zsolnay figurines with green–gold luster finish is available in many shops today. Early Zsolnay was not marked; but by 1878, the tower trademark was used.

ZSOLNAY, Bowl, Gold, Green Iridescent Luster, 7 In.	290.00
Ewer, Green, 11 1/2 In.	135.00
Figurine, Bedlington Terrier	75.00
Figurine, Nude, Resting	250.00
Figurine, Russian Brown Bears, Plinth, Max & Beba, 1911, 8 X 11 In.	175.00
Jug, Enameled Large Flowers, Cream Ground, Luster, Handle, 9 In.	195.00
Jug, Puzzle, 3 Looped Protrusions, Flowers, Marked, 6 3/4 In.	175.00

Jug, Puzzle, Multicolored Florals, Gold Outlined, Signed 155.00
Jug, Puzzle, Persian Pattern, Marked, 7 1/2 In. .... 105.00 To 165.00
Jug, Wedding, Peacocks, Rose Ground, Handle, Bulbous, Marked, 11 In. 650.00
Plate, Art Nouveau, 8 1/2 In. 90.00
Urn, Flowers, 2 Handles, 11 In. .... 200.00 To 250.00
Vase, Bud, Reticulated Outer Layer In Brown & Green, 3 3/4 In. 155.00
Vase, Iridescent Green, Signed, 6 In. 60.00
Vase, Melon Ribbed, Green, 6 In. 60.00
Vase, Reticulated, Double Wall, Steeple Mark, 6 1/2 In. 325.00
Watering Can, Floral, 5 In. 80.00